A CLIMBER'S GUIDE

to the

TETON RANGE

4TH EDITION

A CLIMBER'S GUIDE TO THE TETON RANGE

4TH EDITION

RENNY JACKSON & LEIGH N. ORTENBURGER

PHOTOGRAPHY BY GREG WINSTON

MOUNTAINEERS
BOOKS

MOUNTAINEERS BOOKS is dedicated to the exploration, preservation, and enjoyment of outdoor and wilderness areas.

1001 SW Klickitat Way, Suite 201, Seattle, WA 98134
800-553-4453, mountaineersbooks. org

Printed in China
Distributed in the United Kingdom by Cordee, www.cordee.co.uk

Fourth edition, 2023
Copyeditor: Laura Case Larson
Design and layout: Kate Basart/Union Pageworks
Topographic illustrations: John McMullen
Cartographer: Pease Press Cartography
All photographs by Greg Winston unless credited otherwise
Cover photograph: *Early morning winter light on the Teton Range and the imposing North Face of the Grand Teton*
Back cover photograph: *Jane Jackson sends the superlative second pitch of the O-Mega Crack.* (Photo by Eric Bissell)
Photos: page 2, *Willi Unsoeld on the traverse into the "V," Grand Teton North Face* (Leigh Ortenburger); pages 6–7, *Winter winds buffet the high peaks of the Tetons.* (Derek Craighead); page 8, *Looking past the Crooked Thumb at a heavily rimed Grand Teton North Face* (Greg Winston); pages 16–17, *Conrad Anker, Grand Teton* (Jimmy Chin); pages 66–67, *Doug Workman, Grand Teton* (Jimmy Chin); pages 500–501, *Mark Synnott, Grand Teton* (Jimmy Chin)
Illustrations on pages 68, 80, 138 178, 273, 313, 361, 413, and 491 by Eldon N. Dye; page 265 by Rhiannon Klee Williams; and page 474 by Jim Springer

Library of Congress Cataloging-in-Publication data is on file at https://lccn.loc.gov/2022030991. The ebook record is available at https://lccn.loc.gov/2022030992.

Mountaineers Books titles may be purchased for corporate, educational, or other promotional sales, and our authors are available for a wide range of events. For information on special discounts or booking an author, contact our customer service at 800-553-4453 or mbooks@mountaineersbooks.org.

PRINTED ON FSC®-CERTIFIED MATERIALS

MIX
Paper | Supporting responsible forestry
FSC
www.fsc.org
FSC® C008047

ISBN (paperback): 978-1-68051-197-0
ISBN (ebook): 978-1-68051-198-7

An independent nonprofit publisher since 1960

For my friend

LEIGH

To other Teton climbers who are not forgotten

Pete Armington
Walt Bailey
Allan Bard
Fred Beckey
Barry Bishop
Merrill Bitter
Tim Bond
Orrin and Lorraine Bonney
Bean Bowers
Jake Breitenbach
Jim Bridwell
William "Bill" Buckingham
Nick Clinch
Doug Coombs
John & Margaret Smith Craighead
Julie Culberson
Don Decker
Dan Doody
Charles Dotter
Paul Driscoll
Gary Falk
John Fonda
Fred Ford
Charlie Fowler
Jack Fralick
Catherine Freer
Howard Friedman
Harry Frishman
George Gardner
Susan Garlow
Art Gilkey
Bill Givens
Mark Givens
Don Goodrich
Harold Goodro
John Gottman
Hal Gribble
John Harlin
Gary Hemming
William "Bill" Hooker
Tom Hornbein
John Hudson
James "Jim" Huidekoper
Don Hultz
John Jackson
Bert Jensen
Jim Kanzler
Hayden Kennedy & Inge Perkins
Peter Koedt
Layton Kor
Hans Kraus
Juris Krisjansons
Wray Landon
Fritz Lippmann
Alex Lowe
David Lowe
Jeff Lowe
W. V. Graham Matthews
Travis McAlpine
Doug McClaren
John Mendenhall
Craig Merrihue
Kathryn Miller
Tom Milligan
Glenn Milner
Tim Mutch
Chris Onufer
Heather Paul
Bob Perkins
Patrick Petersen
Karl Pfiffner
Richard "Dick" Pittman
Chuck Pratt
Jim Ratz
Tom Raymer
Rick Reese
Royal Robbins
Steve Romeo
Hans Saari
Patti Saurman
Kim Schmitz
Pete Sinclair
David Sowles
Jared Spackman
Allen Steck
Joseph Stettner
Paul Stettner
Terrence "Mugs" Stump
Larry Swanson
David Swift
Guy Toombes
Jolene Unsoeld
Susan Walker
Ray Warburton
Fritz Wiessner
Jay Wilson
Gary Wise
Mark "Big Wally" Wolling
Elizabeth D. "Betty" Woolsey

And to the great pioneers

Fred and Irene Ayres
Barry Corbet
Henry "Hank" Coulter
Betsy Cowles Partridge
Eleanor Davis (Ehrman)
Jack Durrance
Albert R. Ellingwood
Richard "Dick" Emerson
Glenn Exum
Fritiof Fryxell
Kenneth Henderson
Eldon Petzoldt
Paul Petzoldt
Richard Pownall
Phil Smith
Robert Underhill
Willi Unsoeld

Contents

Overview Map of Climbing Section Locations 13
Forewords 14

PART 1: OVERVIEW 17

Introduction 18
History 20
A Climber's Perspective on Teton Geology, *Joe Stern, PhD* 41
Climbing in the Tetons 50
How to Use This Book 60

PART 2: ROUTES ON THE PEAKS 67

SECTION 1
SOUTH OF DEATH CANYON 68

Granite Canyon 68
Open Canyon 69
Peak 9,815 69
Peak 10,450 (Rendezvous Mountain) 69
Rock Springs Buttress 70
Peak 10,753 (Cody Peak) 70
Peak 10,706 (No Name Peak) 70
Rendezvous Peak 70
Granite Canyon, South Side Rock Climbs 71
 Goat Rocks 71
 Sharkshead Pinnacle 71
 Granite Central Buttresses 72
 Phil's Pickle 73
 Buchwald's Blister 73
Peak 10,277 73
Peak 9,925 73
Peak 10,308 73
Peak 9,814 73
Housetop Mountain 73
Peak 10,116 74
Spearhead Peak 74
Mount Hunt 74
Two Elk Peak 74
Murphy Peak 75
Tukuarika Peak 75
Prospectors Mountain 75
Fossil Mountain 78
Peak 10,612 78
Mount Bannon 79
Mount Jedediah Smith 79
Mount Meek 79
Peak 10,300 79
Peak 11,094 79

SECTION 2
DEATH CANYON TO AVALANCHE CANYON 80

Death Canyon 80
Avalanche Canyon 81
Death Canyon, South Side Rock Climbs 82
Point 9,840+ 89
Moxie Tower 89
Death Canyon, North Side Rock Climbs 89
 Ticky-Tacky Pinnacles 89
 Omega Buttresses 90
 Eastern Omega Buttresses, East of Ship's Prow 91
 Omega Buttresses, Eastern Section/Ship's Prow 91
 Omega Buttresses, Central Section 94
 Omega Buttresses, Western Section 97
 Found Arrow Spire 98
 Harrington Spire 98
 Sentinel Turret 98
 Snaz Buttress 102
Albright Peak 114
Static Peak 115
Peak 10,696 116
 Stewart Draw 116
Stewart Draw, South Side Rock Climbs 116
Buck Mountain 117
Buck Mountain, West Peak 125
Veiled Peak 125
Avalanche Canyon (South Fork), North Side Rock Climbs 126
Mount Wister 126
Peak 10,960+ (Wanda Pinnacle) 132
Nessmuk Spire 132
Broken Arrow Spire 132
Avalanche Canyon (North Fork), North Side Rock Climbs 133
Matternought Peak 134

SECTION 3
GARNET CANYON PEAKS 138

Garnet Canyon 138
Shadow Peak 139
Nez Perce 141
Garnet Canyon, South Side Rock Climbs 150
Cloudveil Dome 151
Spalding Peak 155
Gilkey Tower 157
Icecream Cone 157
South Teton 158
Middle Teton 159
  Lower North Face Routes 170
  Upper North Face Routes 172
  West Side Routes 176
Bonney's Pinnacle 177
Pinocchio Pinnacle 177

SECTION 4
THE GRAND TETON AND THE ENCLOSURE 178

Structure of the Peak 178
History 179
General Information 179
Speed Records and Other Notable Events 179
Grand Teton 180
  Exum Ridge West Face 186
  Southern Ridges 191
  East Face Routes 205
  East Ridge and North Face Routes 214
  West Face Climbs 236
  Valhalla Canyon 246
The Enclosure 248

SECTION 5
THE GRAND TRAVERSE 265

History 265
Strategy 267
Approach 267
  Teewinot Mountain to Mount Owen 268
  Mount Owen to the Grandstand 269
  Grand Teton: Italian Cracks to Owen-Spalding 270
  Middle Teton: North Ridge to Southwest Couloir 270
  South Teton to Nez Perce 270
Descent 272

SECTION 6
GARNET CANYON TO GLACIER GULCH 273

Glencoe Spire 273
Teepe Pillar 276
Second Tower 279
Molar Tooth 281
Okie's Thorn 282
Pemmican Pillar 283
Fairshare Tower 283
Fairshare Tower, Watchtower 283
Red Sentinel 287
Garnet Canyon, North Side Rock Climbs 290
Disappointment Peak 291
  East Face Routes 292
  Northern Routes 294
  Southern Arêtes, Couloirs, and Ridges 298
  West Face Routes 309
Peak 10,080+ 312
Surprise Lake Pinnacle 312

SECTION 7
GLACIER GULCH TO CASCADE CANYON 313

Glacier Gulch 313
  South Side Rock Climbs 314
  North Side Rock Climbs 315
Worshipper 316
Idol 316
Crooked Thumb 317
Teewinot Mountain 319
Peak 11,840+ 327
East Prong 327
Mount Owen 328
Rabbit Ears 348
  North Ear 348
  South Ear 348
Peak 10,640+ 348
Peak 10,405 348
Art-and-Brent Pinnacle 348
McCain's Pillar 348
Faultline 349
The Wall 349
Peak 10,635 350
Table Mountain 350
Yosemite Peak 354
Peak 10,650 358
South Wigwam 358
North Wigwam 358
Peak 10,720+ 359
Littles Peak 359
Peak 10,245 359
Peak 10,880+ 360

Mount Fryxell (Peak 11,270) 360
McClintock Peak 360
Buckingham Palace 360

SECTION 8
CASCADE CANYON TO LEIGH CANYON 361

Cascade Canyon 361
Hanging Canyon 363
Paintbrush Canyon 363
Fourteen-Hour Pinnacle 363
Cascade Canyon, North Side Rock Climbs 365
  Yellow-Bellied Buttress 365
  Banded Buttress 365
  Ayres' Crag 5 365
  Symmetry Crag 4 366
  Storm Point Cliffs 367
  East Cascade Buttresses 374
Storm Point 374
Ice Point 379
Hangover Pinnacle 380
Baxter's Pinnacle 380
Cube Point 384
Symmetry Spire 387
Symmetry Crags 397
Symmetry Crag 4 397
Symmetry Crag 5 398
Rock of Ages 398
Ayres' Crags 401
  The Schoolhouse (Ayres' Crag 1) 401
  Ayres' Crag 2 402
  Ayres' Crag 3 402
  The Blockhouse (Ayres' Crag 4) 402
  Ayres' Crag 5 402
Jaw Crags 403
The Jaw 403
Camels Head 403
Needles Eye Spire 404
Needles Eye Spike 404
Minga Spire 404
Mount St. John 404
Hanging Canyon, North Side Rock Climbs 406
Rockchuck Peak 408
Ice Man Pinnacle 410
The Outlier 410
Peak 10,919 410
Mount Woodring 411
Mount Kimburger 412

SECTION 9
LEIGH CANYON TO MORAN CANYON 413

Leigh Canyon 413
Leigh Canyon, North Side Rock Climbs 414
Mount Moran 422
Structure of the Peak 424
History 424
Approaches 425
  Mount Moran, South Buttress (South Aspect) 426
  Mount Moran, South Buttress (West Aspect) 446
East Horn 450
West Horn 452
Unsoeld's Needle 452
  Mount Moran, Southeast and East Aspects 453
  Mount Moran, Northeast and North Aspects 458
Mount Moran, North Summit 463
Peak 11,795 463
Peak 9,940 464
Peak 12,000+ 464
The Zebra 465
Rotten Thumb 465
Peak 11,840+ 466
Thor Peak 466
Pinetop and Point 10,000+ 469
  Pinetop 469
  Point 10,000+ 469
Peak 11,126 469
Peak 10,952 470
Peak 10,880+ 470
Maidenform Peak 470
Cleaver Peak 471
Dragon Peak 473

SECTION 10
MORAN CANYON TO WEBB CANYON 474

Moran Canyon 474
Snowshoe Canyon 475
Waterfalls Canyon 476
Quartzite Canyon 476
Colter Canyon 477
Peak 10,345 477
Peak 10,484 477
Peak 10,300 477
Window Peak 477
Green Lakes Mountain 477
Dry Ridge Mountain 478
Peak 10,160+ 478
Peak 10,474 478
Doubtful Peak 478
Raynolds Peak 479
Image 479

Counterimage 479
Traverse Peak 480
Primrose Peak 480
Bivouac Peak 481
Moran Canyon, North Side Rock Climbs:
Bivouac Peak, South Shoulder 485
Peak 10,625 485
Rolling Thunder Mountain 485
Peak 10,880+ 486
Blackwelder Peak 487
Eagles Rest Peak, East Peak 487
Eagles Rest Peak 487
Anniversary Peak 488
Peak 10,720+ 488
Doane Peak 488
Peak 11,200+ 489
Peak 11,238 489
Marmot Point 489
Ranger Peak 489
Peak 10,716 490
Peak 10,686 490
Peak 10,732 490
Mount Robie 490

SECTION 11
NORTH OF WEBB CANYON 491

Webb Canyon 491
Owl Canyon 492
Berry Creek 492
Glacier Peak 493
Peak 10,010 493
Peak 9,970 493
Moose Mountain 493
Peak 10,360 494
Peak 10,422 494
Peak 10,270 494
Peak 10,333 494
Peak 9,924 494
Elk Mountain 494
Owl Peak 495
Peak 8,602 496
Webb Canyon, North Side Rock Climbs 496
Peak 7,185 496
Elk Ridge 496
Forellen Peak 497
Red Mountain 497
Peak 8,688T 497
Survey Peak 498
Peak 8,803T 498
Peak 8,582T 498
Mount Berry 498
Dave Adams Hill 499
Harem Hill 499

PART 3: WINTER CLIMBING IN THE TETON RANGE 501

SECTION 12
WINTER CLIMBING OVERVIEW AND ROUTES 502

Overview 502
Winter Waterfall Ice and Mixed Routes 510
Jackson Hole Mountain Resort Area 510
Peak 10,450 Ice and Mixed Climbs 510
Peak 10,753 (Cody Peak) 510
Death Canyon 511
South Side Ice Climbs 512
North Side Ice Climbs 512
Avalanche Canyon 514
Garnet Canyon 514
Disappointment Peak 515
Teewinot Mountain 515
Cascade Canyon 515
Leigh Canyon 516
Waterfalls Canyon 516
Teton Canyon 517
South Side Ice Climbs 517
East Side Ice Climbs 518
Darby Canyon 518

Acknowledgments 519
Appendix A: Staying Alive in the Tetons 521
Appendix B: The Best Climbs in the Tetons 529
Appendix C: General References 533
Index of Peaks and Routes 534

Overview of Climbing Section Locations

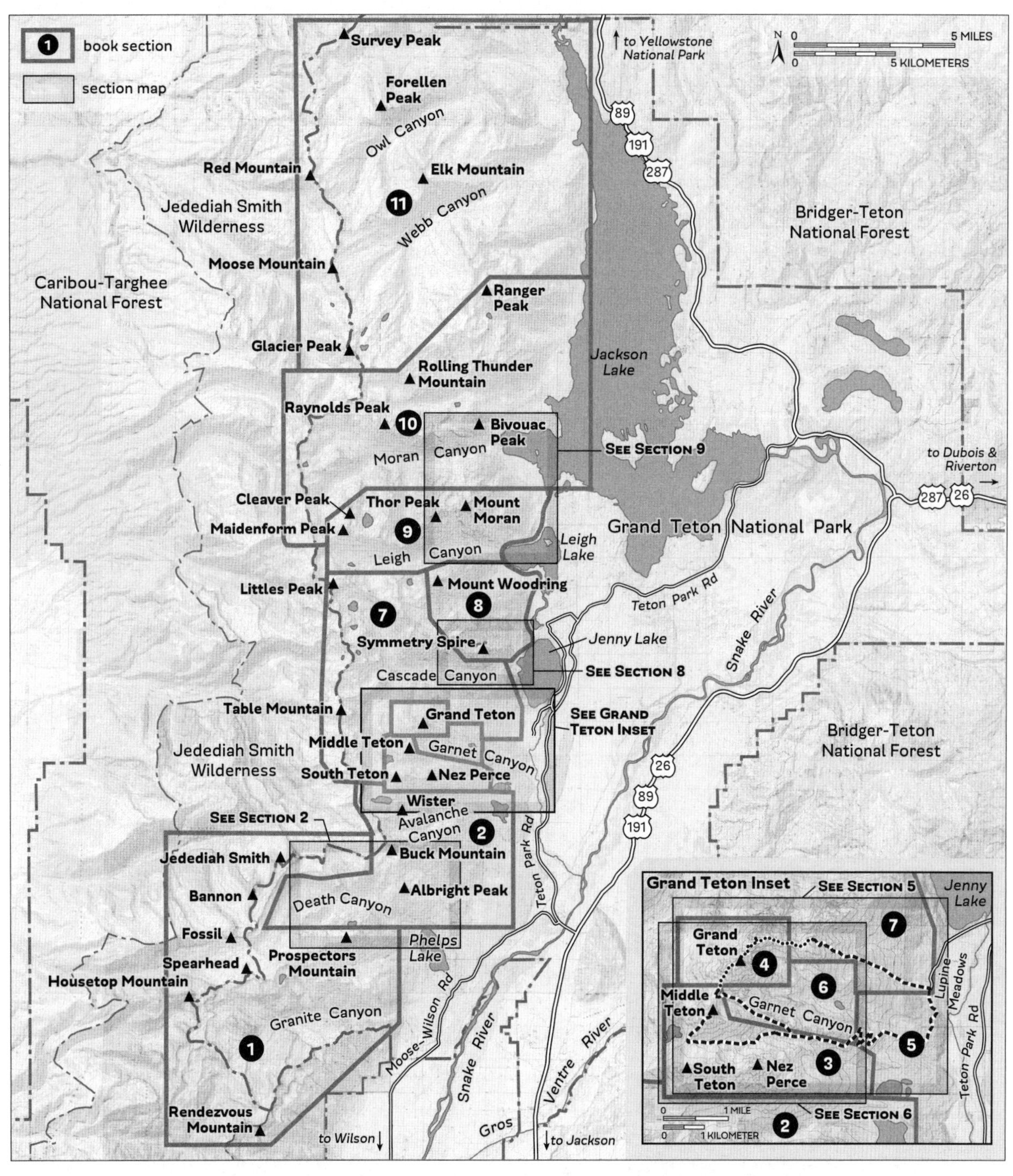

Forewords

In the early 1970s Renny and I did a lot of climbing together in the Wasatch Mountains, near our homes in Salt Lake City. Back then we never would have guessed how much the Tetons would influence our lives, or the impact Leigh Ortenburger's *A Climber's Guide to the Teton Range* would have on Renny. We certainly went to the Tetons when we could, and we practically memorized the guidebook, but we never imagined we would still be climbing Teton routes together in 50 years' time, or that the guidebook would become as much Renny's as Leigh's. The Tetons have done pretty well by us, despite some hard times, and the publication of this fourth edition of the famous guidebook is a marker of our good fortune.

We were using the 1965 second edition in those days. It was fairly up to date, but new routes were going up constantly, many by Leigh himself, and it seemed like a new edition would come out soon. As it was, the third edition didn't appear for 31 years. The story of the interlude, and their partnership, is now a familiar part of the Teton saga: a story of how Leigh apparently would never wrap up his painstaking research, and of him recruiting Renny to help in 1985. Of the publication of reprint, interim, and stop-gap versions, and then the almost-there 1990 preliminary edition. Of how all seemed lost when Leigh died in the 1991 Oakland Hills Fire, and then how Renny, supported by Leigh's family, regrouped and brought the book home in 1996.

Leigh spent summers in Jackson Hole in the 1970s, when we got to know him. He paid attention to anyone busy in the Tetons, and Renny, who had become a Jenny Lake climbing ranger, was soon his good friend and regular climbing partner. I didn't know Leigh as well, but we shared a fascination with Teton history and trivia, and we had a great time doing the first ascent of a Teton peak together, even with the rain and too much steep snow. When he needed help with his guidebook and recruited Renny, whose meticulous attention to detail nearly equaled his own, it seemed an obvious match. And so it was; their collaboration has mattered as much to the Tetons as the storied partnerships of Fritiof Fryxell with Phil Smith, and Paul Petzoldt with Glenn Exum.

An approaching climber is dwarfed by the North Face of the Grand Teton. (Photo by Vic Zeilman)

Now, another episode in the story of their collaboration has been wrapped up with this new edition. Renny has filled it with fresh route information and illustrations, and he has overhauled the descriptions from earlier editions. I'm particularly impressed with his newly refined photo diagrams, based on Greg Winston's terrific photographs. Renny has updated the general subject contents and has scattered in fascinating vignettes written by some of the pioneers. It's also nice to see the traditional elements he's carried over from earlier editions, especially the Eldon Dye artwork, which has graced the guidebook since the first printing in 1956.

The guide has always been attentive to the past, and I value it as a history book as much as a source of climbing information. As I thumb through the routes, mostly what I see are the names of my heroes, and my friends. For me, it turns out the best thing about climbing in the Tetons is knowing Teton climbers, either in person or vicariously through their accomplishments. Leigh and Renny consulted, befriended, or climbed with most of the people whose names appear, and they chased down other long-departed pioneers in the vast Teton archives. The history of Teton climbing, and climbers, is known to an extent unique in this country, thanks to their efforts.

An awful lot of climbing has been done in these remarkable mountains over the past hundred-plus years. There are great classics of American climbing, modern extremes, casual walk-ups, wilderness obscurities, and everything in between. Some routes are incredibly good, others pretty bad, but they all share a magnificent natural setting, and nearly all are in this guidebook. Although over a thousand routes are here, pioneering in the range hasn't ended. I see possibilities that need to be checked out, and fresh eyes will see more. And, as always, young climbers will forever come up with new adventures of a type and magnitude inconceivable to previous generations. I have no idea what future guidebooks will be like, but whatever form they might take, I don't doubt *A Climber's Guide to the Teton Range*, with its beginnings 70 years in the past, will continue as a work in progress for some time to come.

—Paul Horton
January 2023

Greg Winston on the crest above the North Fork of Teton Creek

There is a place on the divide where I can stand at a confluence of time and space and memory, where I can look down to the west and see and hear my father working his way up the talus to the ridge, and, if I turn to look east, the Teton peaks and canyons spread out like a map of possibilities. The late-summer sun glints off the boulders here and there, and the even-then-anachronistic clank of his ice-axe-used-as-walking-stick against the rocks rises to me. When he is close enough, I see that he is grinning under his battered black hat.

Thirty-six years ago, when Renny and my father began their collaboration on a revised edition of this guidebook, they must have shared a similar sense of excitement about the routes and trails they had each traversed in the range as well as their path forward together. Their shared love of and deep knowledge and curiosity about the Teton Range made them the perfect team for the researching and writing that lay ahead of them. Renny has carried this work forward to the present moment with intellect, wit, and grace as well as a level of perseverance that my father would have said boggles the mind and continually inspires me. My father was lucky to have Renny as his partner on this project, and as a friend in life.

I was carried through these mountains before I could walk. My mother and father told my sister and me stories and pointed to passes and summits when we followed in their footsteps. I learned to read the three-dimensional map, repeating names: *Symmetry Spire, Timberline Lake, Irene's Arête, Rolling Thunder Mountain*. Repeating phrases: *just around the corner, let's just look around and see what we can see, the last unclimbed peak!* The history of those who came before us—Doc Fryxell, Phil Smith, so many others—was as integral to the stories I was told as the topography. My family and these mountains interlock in space and time.

Able to see and understand the history of the exploration of the Teton Range, share his encyclopedic knowledge of its mountains and routes, and lay out a map for all of us to continue exploring, Renny stands up on a high ridge, with the mountains in front of him, and their history behind. From my current vantage point, Renny is not just placed at the exact point in space and time to bring this work into the world; Renny is that exact point. We are lucky to have this guidebook he has made so that we may stand beside him.

—Carolyn Ortenburger
February 2023

PART 1
Overview

Introduction

Tucked away in the northwest corner of Wyoming is a small gem of a mountain range that erupts from the sagebrush plain of Jackson Hole a mile and a half into the sky. Though the Tetons are a range in miniature, measuring roughly 40 miles long and 10 to 15 miles wide, they are an arena in which a lifetime of adventure can be found. "This defiant topography," Utah professor Bob Smith explains, "was born of seismic disaster, as the Teton fault repeatedly and violently broke the earth." Over 10 million years of large quakes, the valley sank and the mountains rose—an estimated total movement of 23,000 feet. Steady uplift countered the forces of erosion, preserving sharp crests and precipitous faces. There are no other high peaks close by, only the downsloping flatlands of Jackson Hole and the fields of southern Idaho. As climber Rolando Garibotti has observed, "the plains are what make this range remarkable." Nothing diminishes its monolithic effect. And at 13,770 feet, the Grand Teton towers more than 800 feet above the rest. Its crystalline shape forms the epitome of the range, the emblem of what an alpine realm *should* look like.

Sooner or later, virtually everyone who has done any mountain climbing in the United States visits the Tetons and ascends one or more of the high peaks. There is perhaps no climbing area in the country that can match the Tetons for general mountaineering of an alpine nature with excellent rock, moderate snow climbing, *and* accessibility. Highways and secondary roads lead nearly to the foot of the peaks. The summit of the Grand Teton is little more than three horizontal miles from the nearest approach road. Every peak between Death Canyon on the south and Moran Canyon on the north can be climbed in one day from a campsite in the valley, although most of the higher and more distant peaks are seldom climbed in less than two days. And the climbing is enjoyable!

This combination of characteristics provides an excellent training ground for the novice climber as well as for the vast majority of climbers who simply seek enjoyable and challenging routes. There are also extremely difficult mixed alpine testpieces for those who aspire to travel to the other great ranges of the world. From the large Himalayan expeditions of the past to the modern alpine-style ascents of today, Teton climbers have played a key role in pioneering new routes throughout the world. Today the Tetons enjoy a reputation as perhaps *the* ski-mountaineering mecca of the United States. Garnet Canyon, once a haven for those solitary parties attempting a rare winter ascent of the Grand Teton, now sees throngs of skiers and riders enjoying its many chutes, couloirs, and faces.

The Tetons have been intensively climbed in and explored, perhaps more so than any other range of equal size on the continent. As a result, almost every peak has multiple routes on it, and the Grand Teton and its satellite peak, the Enclosure, now have a total of 136 distinct routes and variations to their summits. It should not be thought that the relatively small number of peaks allows one to "climb out" the range in a few weeks or even years. New routes remain to be explored, first winter ascents await the intrepid, and the winter months open the range to easy travel on skis. For those whose goals do not include climbing, there is an unlimited opportunity for hiking, on or off the 242-mile trail system. The weather is usually pleasant, and during most of August one will find clear climbing days.

Not least among the attractions of the Tetons is the abundance of wildlife. Under the protection of the National Park Service (NPS), moose, elk, deer, bear, marmots, and pikas, as well as 17 different species of carnivores, have flourished and are sometimes encountered by mountaineers and skiers. The birds, the flora, and the geology of the range are other features attractive to those interested in the natural scene. Because the pursuit of climbing is so intimately connected to geology, a special chapter—A Climber's Perspective on Teton Geology, included later in Part 1—is devoted to this subject. To gain a broad and deep understanding of and appreciation for the Tetons, climbers are also urged to study the references at the end of that chapter.

As a point of historical interest, the Grand Teton was well known to travelers in the early 19th century as an important landmark located near the headwaters of the Snake River, which originates just to the north in the Teton Wilderness outside of Yellowstone National Park. The Tetons were also central to the fur-trapping business that prospered in the beaver-rich rivers and streams surrounding the range. Much of the first (nonindigenous) exploration of the wild areas of western North America was carried out by fur trappers, whose stories and exploits have become legendary. Those who wish to learn more about this fascinating era of American history will find a list of excellent historical accounts in General References at the back of this book. References to literature covering the flora, fauna, and geology of the Teton area are also provided there.

There is intentional emphasis in this guide on the area between Death Canyon to the south and Moran Canyon to the north. It is this area of crystalline rock—with the exception of a few crystalline peaks north of Moran Canyon—that has attracted the most attention from mountaineers. The easy sedimentary peaks that lie in the southern part of the range, along the divide between Jackson Hole and Teton Basin to the west, and those in the northern part of the range receive very little climbing traffic. However, they remain worthwhile objectives for those with more moderate aspirations.

To minimize repeated geographical explanations throughout the route descriptions in Part 2, this guidebook assumes that the reader will also have in hand the US Geological Survey (USGS) topographic map of Grand Teton National Park. This map is essential to understanding both the nomenclature and the directions to the routes and is remarkably accurate considering the extremely rugged terrain. Sixteen elevations absent from the published map appear in this book; these figures were obtained from study of the manuscript of this map in the National Archives in Washington, DC. Nowadays it is possible to simply hop online or pull out a smartphone and check an elevation using one of many interactive mapping websites, programs, and apps. In particular, TopoZone.com and CalTopo.com are excellent free online resources for USGS-based topographic maps, including those covering Grand Teton National Park. Google Earth and Google Earth Pro, also free and available online, are invaluable for exploration and trip planning. These tools were used extensively in the creation of this edition.

There are three primary categories of names that appear in this book. First are those that have the official approval of the US Board on Geographic Names; perhaps these should have been accorded a distinguishing mark, but readers in doubt concerning the status of a name can refer to the USGS map. If the name appears on the map, it has been officially approved; if it does not, then it is almost certainly unofficial (there are very few names that have been approved but do not appear on the map). There is a second, smaller category of names that appear on US Forest Service (USFS) maps, in publications of various geologists who have studied the area, or on maps used by NPS rangers. Finally, there are a good many unofficial names that have been in more or less common usage among Teton climbers for years.

The authors have not seen fit to engage in any wholesale naming of peaks in the belief that this is a prerogative reserved for those who made the first ascent. Certainly there is nothing to be gained but confusion through efforts to change names that have already appeared in print, no matter how lofty the intention. In the absence of any overpowering reason to attach identifying names, perhaps our generation should leave to the next at least some peaks to name. The authors have also followed the practice of the Sierra Club in identifying unnamed peaks by their elevations (such as Peak 11,117). However, the following names have been attached by the authors: Murphy Peak, Two Elk Peak, Tukuarika Peak, Spalding Peak, Gilkey Tower, Bonney's Pinnacle, Pemmican Pillar, Fairshare Tower, Symmetry Crags, Ayres' Crags, Blockhouse, Unsoeld's Needle, Blackwelder Peak, and Anniversary Peak. A fascinating history of the place names of Jackson Hole and Grand Teton National Park will be available soon: look for *Names on the Range* by Paul Horton.

Climbers on the uppermost portion of the Exum Ridge, nearing the summit of the Grand Teton (Photo by Eric Bissell)

History

During the years following his 1872 expedition to survey the remote and wild Yellowstone region of Wyoming, Dr. Ferdinand Vandeveer Hayden presented a series of lectures to both organized groups and the public at large. These lectures were illustrated with stunning images by the photographer William Henry Jackson and the artist William Henry Holmes. Prominent among the dazzling array of pictures were the first views of the Teton mountain range, now one of the most recognizable and well-known national park regions in the United States. The American public was amazed by the dramatic scenery and the fact that such landforms existed within the country. Imaginations were stirred by visions of needlelike pinnacles and snow-covered, sharply defined summits. Images of the Teton Range are now so prevalent that the rugged peaks have almost become the symbolic representation of what mountains should look like.

The Tetons played a pivotal role in the historical development of climbing and mountaineering in the US. Phrases such as "the home of American mountaineering" and "the center of United States alpinism"[1] have long been used to describe the region and its relative importance in the evolution of American climbing. Initially, the primary draw was the opportunity to explore and map a previously unknown area of the country, even if this meant enduring the hardships involved in traveling to the isolated Tetons. Once this irresistible range became easily accessible, with highways leading almost to the foot of the peaks, mountaineers from all over began to arrive. Today, the summit of the Grand Teton is little more than three horizontal miles from the nearest approach road. Additionally, every peak between Death Canyon on the south and Moran Canyon on the north can be climbed in one day from the valley. And the climbing challenges are tremendous!

The Grand Teton has become one of the most popular peaks in the US, ranking as one of the finest mountaineering objectives in the country. This reputation is certainly deserved. A complex mountain, it offers a wide variety of challenging routes on its many faces and ridges. Today one has a choice of some 136 routes and variations on the Grand Teton and the Enclosure—a collection of outstanding alpine climbs that sets the Grand apart from and above the lesser peaks of the range. Enjoyable ridge scrambling, high-angle rock walls, moderate snowfields, glaciers, and steep ice chutes are all to be found on this varied mountain. And from its summit almost every other peak in the range can be seen, with Teewinot Mountain being the most prominent, its sharp pinnacles silhouetted against the flat plains of Jackson Hole. The Wind River Range forms the eastern horizon, where one can easily pick out flat-topped Gannett Peak, the highest in Wyoming. To the north one can see well into Yellowstone National Park and beyond—to Pilot, Index, and Granite Peaks. The rolling hills and cultivated fields of Idaho complete the vista to the west.

The climbing history of the Teton Range is lengthy and convoluted, extending from the middle of the 19th century to the present day; only a summary can be offered here. In a broader sense, this rich history is woven intricately into the more complex evolution of climbing in the United States. Many of the climbers who passed through the Tetons in the 19th and 20th centuries helped shape not only Teton climbing history but also the trajectory of mountaineering in this country and throughout the world.

Trappers, Explorers, Surveyors

British, American, and French Canadian fur trappers and traders were the among the first nonindigenous people to explore the wilderness of western North America. In the early 19th century, before beaver hats became passé in Europe, the beaver-rich rivers and streams surrounding the Teton Range were a focal point for a booming trapping industry. The Grand, Middle, and South Tetons—the famous "Trois Tetons" (roughly translated, "three breasts")—were familiar landmarks to those crisscrossing this rugged part of the United States. Most of the hardy mountain men who lingered in the area were more interested in the abundant game in the valleys than in mountain climbing and exploration. But some looked up toward the high peaks with curiosity.

One such individual was an expatriate Brit by the name of Richard "Beaver Dick" Leigh, who came to the Rockies in 1849 and made his home in Teton Basin from 1863 to 1899. Leigh spent most of his time trapping in the canyons on the west side of the range, but there is some indication that his explorations penetrated the very heart of the mountains. Toward the end of the century, he wrote a letter to the editor of the *Rocky Mountain News* that included the following note:

> ***As I know no liveng man as ever crossed from the East to the west side of the range althow I believe it can be done in one plas only without going to the conant trale north of the Trale creek pass south and that it over the sadle betwene grand teton and the one on the south of it altho myself and John Lunphara of Bitterroad vally tryet in 58 but it was too much for us.***[2]

This passage places Leigh and his companion in Garnet Canyon, later regarded as the hub of Teton climbing, sometime during 1858.

Beaver Dick Leigh guided many expeditions to both sides of the Tetons during the latter half of the 19th century. This included the 1872 Hayden Survey Expedition, during which the first recorded attempt to ascend the Grand Teton occurred. Leigh was apparently Nathaniel

Beaver Dick Leigh (Photo courtesy of the Jackson Hole Historical Society & Museum)

Pitt Langford's source for a sentence in his 1873 article in *Scribner's Monthly*:

The great theme of talk about our campfire was the proposed ascent of the Tetons. Beaver Dick said our design was not new. The ascent had been often tried, and always without success. An old trapper by the name of Michaud, as long ago as 1843, provided himself with ropes, rope-ladders, and other aids, and spent days in the effort, but met with so many obstructions he finally gave it up in despair. "You can try," said Dick, significantly; "but you'll wind up in the same way."[3]

Who was this intrepid individual who had attempted an ascent of the Grand Teton 29 years earlier? He may have been Michaud LeClaire, who served as a messenger for the Hudson's Bay Company, carrying dispatches from Fort Hall (near present-day Pocatello, Idaho) to Montreal, Canada. The ledger books of the Columbia River Fishing and Trading Company for 1837 also include a page for a Mitchael LaClair.[4] And in a book he wrote some years later about this period of western exploration and expansion, Langford identified a Michaud Le Clair as operating a toll bridge across the Smith Fork of Bear River in 1862.[5]

Beginning in 1867, Dr. Ferdinand Vandeveer Hayden began a series of expeditions into relatively unknown areas of the American West to survey their natural resources. Hayden was successful in obtaining appropriations from the US Congress for these explorations, and his parties were made up of naturalists, scientists, and their assistants. His annual survey reports were usually met with great popular approval, so much so that the congressional appropriations steadily grew. The 1872 Hayden Survey Expedition, formally known as the US Geological Survey of the Territories, marked the beginning of recorded exploration of the Teton Range. This was the second of the famous Hayden Surveys to travel through the Yellowstone region, and Congress had allotted $75,000 for the expedition.

Hayden had a distinct knack for convincing extremely talented individuals to join him on these daring, exploratory ventures. One such individual was William Henry Jackson, who was just beginning his career as a photographer when he first linked up with Hayden in 1870. Through the relatively new medium of photography, Hayden wished to convince others in Washington, DC, that certain choice areas of the West should be established as natural preserves, protected from exploitation, and safeguarded for future generations. Jackson's images, paired with paintings by landscape artist and fellow 1871 survey member Thomas Moran, helped fuel the push to create Yellowstone National Park, the world's first such protected area, in March 1872. While the idea for Yellowstone did not originate with Hayden, he is recognized by some as having been the first to promote the concept in public.[6]

1872 Hayden Survey Expedition, Snake River Division encampment, Teton Canyon (Photo by W. H. Jackson, courtesy of Grand Teton National Park archive)

A segment of the 1872 Hayden Survey known as the Snake River Division fell under the capable leadership of James Stevenson, Hayden's right-hand man and longtime friend. The main objectives of the Snake River Division were to explore, map, and report on the Teton Range and the country to both the east and the west. One of the party's guests was Yellowstone's first superintendent, Nathaniel P. Langford, who had lectured, written articles, and lobbied tirelessly to have the park established. The Snake River Division traveled north from Ogden, Utah, by horseback along the old stagecoach route to Fort Hall. Converting to a pack train at this point, they then ventured east and established a base camp at the mouth of Teton Creek on the west side of the range on July 23, 1872. They occupied this base camp for nine days until August 2.

On July 27, a party of six, including Jackson, Charles Campbell, Philo J. Beveridge, Alexander Sibley, and perhaps John M. Coulter explored the north fork of Teton Canyon for the first time. They also made the first ascent of Table Mountain, where just below the summit Jackson exposed his now-famous negatives that would give the world its first glimpse of these mighty peaks.

Meanwhile, 14 other members of the expedition attempted an ascent of the Grand Teton, leaving camp on July 28 and establishing a high camp in the south fork of Teton Canyon. Two of the 14, Langford and Stevenson, claimed to have reached the summit of the Grand on July 29, 1872. The key to the climb, as described by Langford, was a 70°, precariously attached ice sheet that began about 300 feet below the summit and extended upward for some 175 perilous feet. Three other members of the expedition reached the Lower Saddle: Frank Bradley, a geologist, stopped and explored the area while waiting (in vain) for his assistant to arrive with the mercurial barometer. Two 17-year-old boys, Sidford Hamp and Charles Spencer, continued above the Lower Saddle with Langford and Stevenson. At some point below the ice sheet, Hamp slipped and fell roughly 50 feet before stopping. Shaken,

1872 Hayden Survey Expedition Camp, Snake River Division; from left to right: Sidford F. Hamp, Frank H. Bradley, James Stevenson, Nathaniel P. Langford, Robert Adams, Jr. (Photo by W. H. Jackson, courtesy of Grand Teton National Park archive)

"Photographing in High Places," taken in 1872 just east of the summit of Table Mountain (Photo by W. H. Jackson, from the Leigh Ortenburger papers)

he continued up to the start of the ice but chose not to attempt this final obstacle. Spencer waited with him as Langford and Stevenson pushed on for the top.

The two divisions of the survey reunited on August 13 in the Lower Geyser Basin of Yellowstone National Park. Four days later, on August 16, 1872, the entire expedition assembled, listened to remarks by their intrepid leader Hayden, and were immortalized in several photographs taken by Jackson. Langford then came forward with the surprising proposal that the great peak that he and Stevenson had climbed be known as Mount Hayden. This was met with cheers, and Hayden not only accepted but stated that he considered it the highest honor of his life. (However, the name never took hold, and the toponym reverted to the trappers' somewhat crude "Grand Teton.")

Had Langford and Stevenson really set foot upon the true summit of the Grand? This question remains the crux of a long-standing controversy. In 1898, when William O. Owen's party reached the summit, they found no evidence of prior human passage. No cairn had been erected, and nothing had been left behind. Also, no photographic evidence exists from the 1872 climb. It is possible that Langford and Stevenson may not have had enough time to do much of anything except find their way safely down off the peak, but there is good reason to be dubious of their claim of a successful ascent.

The two men clearly reached the apex of the western spur of the peak—the Enclosure—as they were the first to describe the archaeological structure located at that lofty site. (The name for the structure was later applied to the entire western bulk of the Grand.) The day after the expedition ended, Langford gave an account of his and Stevenson's climb to a reporter from the *Helena Daily Herald*. The resulting news item detailed the man-made enclosure but erroneously placed it on the summit of the Grand Teton:

The top of the Teton, and for 300 feet below, is composed entirely of blocks of granite, piled up promiscuously, and weighing from 20 to 500 pounds. On the apex these granite slabs have been placed on end, forming a breastwork about three feet high, enclosing a space six or seven feet in diameter; and while on the surrounding rocks there is not a particle of

dust or sand, the bottom of the enclosure is covered with a bed of minute particles of granite not larger than the grains of common sand, that the elements have worn off from these vertical blocks until it is nearly a foot in depth. This attrition must have been going on for hundreds and, perhaps, thousands of years, and it is the opinion of Mr. Langford that centuries have elapsed since the granite slabs were placed in the position in which they were found.[7]

This was not the only published account of Langford and Stevenson's ascent to misreport the enclosure as being on the summit of the peak. However, by the time Hayden's official survey report came out in 1873, Langford had shifted the location of the enclosure to a buttress below the true summit:

We found on one of the buttresses, a little lower than the extreme top of the mountain, evidence that at some former period it had been visited by human beings. There was a circular inclosure about seven feet in diameter, formed by vertical slabs of rough granite, and about three feet in height, the interior of which was half filled with the detritus that long exposure to the elements had worn from these walls. It could not have been constructed less than half a century ago, when Indians only inhabited this region.[8]

A similar passage made it into "The Ascent of Mount Hayden," Langford's 1873 article for *Scribner's Monthly*. Immediately after describing the "bald, denuded head" of the "main summit," as well as the ibex tracks and flowers he and Stevenson had found there, Langford segued to their discovery of the enclosure. "On the top of an adjacent pinnacle, but little lower than the one we occupied, we found a circular enclosure," he wrote. "It was evidently intended, by whomsoever built, as a protection against the wind, and we were only too glad to avail ourselves of it while we finished our luncheon." After taking in the views, the pair renegotiated the intimidating 70° ice sheet back down to where they had left their young companions, Hamp and Spencer. "Great caution was necessary while passing down the ice belt lest it should become detached," Langford wrote, "but it was our only passage-way to the bottom, and we were greatly relieved when we reached in safety the cranny occupied by Hamp and Spencer."[9]

On its own, Langford's article is riddled with logical holes. Most notably, how did he and Stevenson make their way from the summit of the Grand (13,770) to the Enclosure (13,280+) without first descending to Hamp and Spencer? A near-vertical section of rock guards the Enclosure immediately above the Upper Saddle (13,160+). Presuming Langford and Stevenson started their ascent from the vicinity of the Upper Saddle, they would have needed to retrace their route back down the west aspect of the Grand, then descend to a point about 100 feet below the Upper Saddle, and then scramble up the easy southeast side of the Enclosure to its summit. It is not as straightforward as simply traversing a low-angle ridge from one high point to the next. The absence of any description of his and Stevenson's route from the "main summit" to the top of this "adjacent pinnacle" is suspicious—and conspicuous. After all, every other stretch of the climb is conveyed in breathless detail. Even more curious is that they somehow avoided the crux ice sheet along their jaunt from the summit to the Enclosure, yet they still had to go back down it to return to Hamp and Spencer. It follows that the ice sheet was probably located just below the Enclosure, not at some point higher above.

Two manuscripts that preceded the published article further undermine Langford's storytelling, hinting at an evolution in his account. While the second of these drafts does not vary too much from the Scribner's piece, the first more than complicates the narrative of a successful ascent. It was handwritten on yellow, legal-size paper, with each page numbered at the top.[10] (As recently as 1992 this manuscript was erroneously cited as Langford's actual journal from 1872 because "it is more spontaneous, less dramatized, less embellished, and sometimes more specific than the Scribner's article.")[11]

On page 35 of this initial draft, after detailing how he and Stevenson navigated the 70° ice sheet, Langford recalled their final steps to the summit:

From this point the surface was more broken, and not more difficult to ascend than below the ice, and, clambering over the granite fragments, at 3. P.M., tired and hungry, after 9 hours of hard effort, we reached the summit, the first white men who ever accomplished this oft attempted feat. (Size of summit in feet)

Archaeological curiosities ~~on~~ near top. ~~Granite~~[12]

Roughly two-thirds into the page, the bottom is torn off. A note in the margin reads, "See page 35½ of ms." That page describes the summit of the Grand in general terms, seemingly disconnected from the final line of the torn page referencing "archaeological curiosities ~~on~~ near top." Why did Langford correct the location of the enclosure, crossing out the word "on" and penciling in "near" above it? Why did he refer to himself and Stevenson as "the first white men" to reach the top (an assertion that made it into the final article)? And what was on the missing bottom third of that page? Together, these editorial choices suggest that perhaps the pair never set foot on the true summit. Perhaps they instead reached a separate

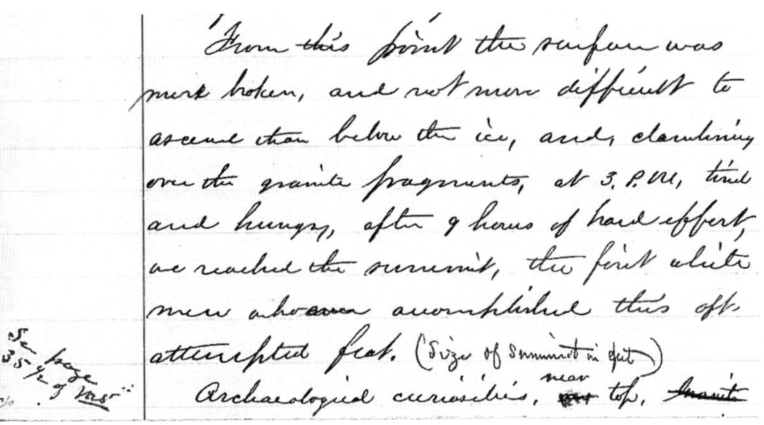
From this point the surface was more broken, and not more difficult to ascend than below the ice, and, clambering over the granite fragments, at 3. P.M., tired and hungry, after 9 hours of hard effort, we reached the summit, the first white men who ever accomplished this oft-attempted feat. (Size of Summit in feet)
Archaeological curiosities, ~~on~~ near top, ~~Granite~~

Page 35 of the Langford manuscript (Courtesy of the Yellowstone Heritage and Research Center, Gardiner, MT)

"Looking off from the summit of Mount Hayden," by Thomas Moran. Drawing taken from *Scribner's Monthly*, Volume VI, No. 2, June 1873, pg. 146, "The Ascent of Mount Hayden," by N. P. Langford.

The W. H. Jackson sketch that provided the basis for the Moran drawing for *Scribner's Monthly*

high point that had clearly been visited before. The replacement of "on" is particularly damning, as it aligns with those first reports that described the enclosure as being on top of the Grand. Moreover, their climbing time from the upper reaches of Teton Canyon to the summit of the Grand of nine hours (increased to 10 hours in the published article) is nothing short of incredible, even if the Enclosure marked the apex of their ascent.

A selection of illustrations by different artists accompanied the *Scribner's* article. Some of these stylized renderings depict dramatic climbing scenes: Stevenson hanging on by the barest of handholds, his legs dangling over a significant void; the men descending a steep, icy passage using a rope; Hamp clambering up an ice-encrusted cliff. One illustration—Looking Off from the Summit of Mount Hayden, bearing the particular monograph of Thomas Moran—shows two figures on the "summit." Behind them rises what very well could be the higher, true apex of the Grand Teton. Langford was apparently dissatisfied with the artwork's lack of realism. In a letter to Franklin Spalding in 1898, he wrote, "Scribner and Co.'s artist desired me to give him some idea of the top of the mountain, and of the place where young Hamp slipped. I could not convey to a man who had never seen the mountain any correct idea of our surroundings at these two points and did not attempt to do it. His imagination supplied what I could not furnish. . . . The views on pages 145 (Narrow Escape of Mr. Hamp) and 146 (Looking Off from the Summit of Mount Hayden) are imaginary and represent nothing real."[13]

Moran reportedly based his summit scene on one of William Henry Jackson's sketches.[14] In the sketch in question, two men gaze out at the views from the top of what is clearly the Enclosure, a pennant planted next to the distinctive slabs of granite. It bears the note "top of Mt Hayden."

It may never be known definitively whether Langford and Stevenson looked off from the true summit of "Mount Hayden." Some insist that they did, but it strikes this author (R. Jackson) that a concise, objective presentation of the facts concerning the 1872 attempt has yet to be made. The available evidence seems to point toward a successful ascent of the Enclosure, not a climb of the Grand.

Another enduring mystery is the question of who built the enclosure. It is possible that this was done by the mysterious Michaud during his attempt. It is far more likely, however, that indigenous people constructed it long before 1843, possibly as a vision quest site. It is also conceivable that these same people scrambled past the Upper Saddle and then on to the top of the Grand Teton in some long-forgotten era.

Five years after Langford and Stevenson's ascent, four members of the 1877 Hayden Survey party made another attempt on the Grand. In July of that year, Thomas Cooper, Stephen Kubel, Peter Pollack, and Louis McKean reached the Lower Saddle from the west and continued toward the Upper Saddle for several hundred feet. At this point Pollack and McKean apparently stopped while Cooper and Kubel continued a considerable distance farther. The various accounts of this climb differ, and it is not certain whether they reached the Upper Saddle or the Enclosure.

In 1878, sheer chance prevented a successful ascent of the Grand Teton by a third Hayden Survey party. James Eccles, a member of the London-based Alpine Club, together with his Chamonix guide Michel Payot, accompanied the Hayden expedition to the Teton-Yellowstone region; they were slated to attempt the peak with triangulator A. D. Wilson and his assistant Harry Yount (and perhaps also A. C. Ladd) on August 20. However, Eccles and Payot were detained at the last minute by a necessary search for two mules that had strayed from their camp in the Hoback, and they were unable to join Wilson. If they had, it seems probable that they would have reached the summit since Payot was a professional guide and Eccles, an experienced mountaineer. The previous summer, on July 31, 1877, Eccles and Payot had climbed a technically difficult route on the south face of Mont Blanc in the Alps. That they were now in the Tetons was significant in that a guide and client were for the first time planning an ascent of the Grand Teton—a precursor to the thousands of guided parties who now climb the peak each summer. As it was, Wilson's party got as far as the Enclosure, where he took a series of readings with his heavy surveying instruments. Ninety-seven years later, in 1975, Leigh Ortenburger discovered a metal matchbox inscribed with "A. D. Wilson," in Wilson's own handwriting, in a crack at the summit of the Enclosure. Not only was Wilson the most experienced climber in the Hayden Survey at that time, but he may well have been the best climber in the United States in the 1870s. He had climbed many of America's higher peaks, including Mount Rainier, and was very disappointed and quite chagrined at having failed to reach the summit of the Grand.

In 1880, while passing through Jackson Hole during a hunting expedition, a well-to-do itinerant Englishman and member of the Alpine Club, William A. Baillie-Grohman, explored the environs of the Grand Teton and reached the Lower Saddle in a haphazard attempt from a low camp. Based on his journal entries, it seems reasonable to assume that Garnet Canyon had been explored for the second time in recorded history.[15]

The Grand Controversy

The second unsubstantiated ascent of the Grand Teton was by Captain Charles Kieffer, Private Logan Newell, and a third man, probably Private John Rhyan, on about September 10, 1893. The only evidence for this ascent is an April 3, 1899, letter from Kieffer to William O. Owen in which Kieffer described his climb.[16] A check of Kieffer's military records shows that he was stationed at Fort Yellowstone during the summer of 1893 and hence presumably had the opportunity to make the ascent. If Kieffer's drawing accompanying his letter is to be taken literally, it shows his route to have been the Exum Ridge! This technically difficult route was not climbed until Glenn Exum's remarkable solo ascent in 1931. Kieffer's letter also indicated that he returned in 1895 but failed because "the gradual snow field . . . had fallen and left a steep jump off that we could not climb."

In 1891, two years before Kieffer's possible summit, William O. Owen made his first unsuccessful attempt to climb the Grand Teton. Accompanied by his wife, Emma Matilda, Mathew B. Dawson, and Dawson's wife, Jennie Dawson, he apparently reached a point somewhere between the Lower and Upper Saddles via the couloir from Dartmouth Basin.

Owen returned in 1897 with Frank Petersen and made several more attempts from different directions, including one in the couloir that descends to the Teepe Glacier from above the Second Tower. He was nearly killed during a glissade on the glacier below, a foreshadowing of one of the most common types of climbing accidents today. Finally, on August 11, 1898, a party of six sponsored by the Rocky Mountain Club (formerly the Rocky Mountain Climbers Club, or RMCC, established in 1896 in Denver, Colorado) started toward the Grand Teton from a camp in the cirque north of Shadow Peak. At the Lower Saddle Thomas Cooper, a veteran of the 1877 attempt, decided not to continue, and Hugh McDerment elected to go no farther at the Upper Saddle. The remaining four—Owen, Petersen, Rev. Franklin Spalding, and John Shive—continued to the summit, with Spalding largely responsible for leading and finding the route.

The Rocky Mountain Club climb was the first documented ascent of the Grand Teton. Two days later Spalding, Petersen, and Shive returned to the summit and constructed an enormous cairn "that should be visible to the settlers in Jackson Hole."[17] They wedged the short staff of their metal Rocky Mountain Club pennant, which contained a summit register, into the top of the cairn and finished chiseling their names into the summit block. As they made their mark, Owen obtained photographs from the Enclosure. He wished to leave no doubt as to who had first ascended the Grand Teton.

Over 70 years later, in August 1969, Leigh Ortenburger discovered the site of Owen's camp in the cirque between Shadow Peak and Nez Perce. He also found a cache of 27 very heavy eyebolt "pitons" that had been discarded in 1898. One of these pitons, quite solidly placed in a drilled hole, can be found today in a boulder at the 1898 campsite. The only piton placed by Owen on the Grand Teton (presumably on one of his earlier attempts) was found by Rich Perch and Dan Burgette in a crack in the lower end of

Camp Owen in Shadow Peak cirque, August 12, 1898; from left to right: Frank Peterson, Thomas Cooper, William O. Owen, Hugh McDerment, John Shive (Photo from the Leigh Ortenburger papers)

John Shive, Franklin Spalding, and Frank Petersen on the summit of the Grand Teton on the first certain ascent, August 11, 1898. (Photo by William O. Owen, from the Leigh Ortenburger papers)

the Stettner Couloir on July 6, 1984. Other pitons had previously been found abandoned on the rocks: in 1934 on the upper Owen-Spalding route and in 1948 at the start of the Pownall-Gilkey route.

The now-famous controversy between Owen and Nathaniel Langford broke out shortly after the 1898 climb, when Owen published a full-page article in the *New York Herald* in which he claimed to have been part of the first group to ascend the Grand Teton. The outdoor magazine *Forest and Stream* then became the primary forum in which their acrimonious dispute played out before a national audience. In a series of letters to the editor and in various statements and affidavits, the antagonist Owen waged verbal war with the protagonist Langford. The debate, which continues to the present day, may be the greatest and most enduring American mountaineering controversy. Since historical "proof" is extremely unlikely to be forthcoming for either side of the argument, it may be best simply to say that in 1872 Langford and Stevenson may have climbed the Grand Teton; in 1893 Kieffer, Newell, and Rhyan may have climbed it; and in 1898 Spalding, Owen, Petersen, and Shive definitely succeeded in reaching the summit.

Ten days after the ascent of the Grand Teton in 1898, the T. M. Bannon topographic party ascended Buck Mountain and saw the banner the Owen party had left on the summit of the Grand Teton. This topographic party also climbed several of the easy peaks along the divide during their work, which culminated in the USGS Grand Teton quadrangle. Although the 1898 ascent of the Grand Teton received considerable publicity, it did little to attract other mountaineering visits. During the summer of 1912, while studying the geology of sedimentary strata, primarily on the west slope of the Tetons, Professor Eliot Blackwelder made a few ascents of peaks on and west of the divide.

The ascent of the north summit of Mount Moran in 1919 by LeRoy Jeffers drew more publicity than perhaps any other single Teton ascent. His climb was due, in part, to an article that had appeared in a 1918 issue of *Scientific American*[18] containing this challenging statement: "The summit has never been attained and probably never will, as the last 3,000 feet of the mountain are sheer perpendicular walls of rock."

The Jeffers climb provided the competitive motivation for a party of three—Dr. LeGrand Haven Hardy, Ben C. Rich, and Bennet McNulty—to make the first ascent of the higher south, or main, summit in 1922. Jeffers showed up 10 days later to complete what he disappointingly discovered to be the second ascent.

Gentleman Climbers and Lady Alpinists

The summit of the Grand Teton was not visited again for 25 years. This lack of attention is truly astonishing since wide notice was given to the 1898 ascent and there was much climbing activity in the United States and Canada during the intervening quarter century. The Teton Range was still relatively isolated from any major population center, however, and therefore remained largely unexplored. The next phase of activity began on August 25, 1923, when three graduate students from Montana State College (MSC) made the third documented ascent and descent of the Grand Teton (the Owen party had climbed the peak twice). Quin Blackburn, the leader (who would later serve in the Antarctic with Richard Byrd), David DeLap, and Andy DePirro climbed the Owen-Spalding route in a single day—without ropes or any technical climbing equipment.

On the evening of August 24, the three MSC students stumbled into a campsite of the only other climbers in the entire Teton Range at the time, asking how to find "the routes of Langford or Owen. . . . We've got to be back in Missoula soon and we just have tomorrow." The group—eight mountaineers with the Colorado Mountain Club (CMC)—laughed at the idea of a one-day ascent. But they told the Montanans that it was possible to approach by Bradley Creek and then on up Bradley Canyon (Garnet Canyon was called Bradley Canyon at that time, named for Frank Bradley, geologist of the 1872 Hayden Survey Expedition)."[19]

With that scrap of information, the "Montana boys" left the valley at 7 AM. Eight and a half hours later, they arrived at the Upper Saddle. Both a written description of the climb by DeLap and a letter from DeLap to Owen indicate that the trio had little or no knowledge of the Owen-Spalding route itself. While Blackburn and DePirro attempted a steep corner under a curtain of icicles in the vicinity of today's rappel route, DeLap wandered out on a ledge leading north. He negotiated the "Crawl" on his belly and then, 40 feet later, reached the abrupt end of the ledge. "From this point a break in the wall extended vertically upward," he later wrote in an appendix for Leigh Ortenburger's *Tetoniana*. "A huge rectangular-shaped rock of dimensions

10 × 8 × 6 feet was lodged in the chimney [known today as the "Double Chimney"] in such a way that its upper edge nearest me stood about eight feet directly overhead. . . . I returned to report my findings." DeLap led his friends back to the chimney, which they surmounted creatively, having no rope. DeLap recounted:

As Blackie was the heaviest man, Andy and I boosted him up so that when he stood on our shoulders he could climb in the V-shaped and rather steeply inclined opening between the wall and huge rectangular rock eight feet above where we stood. Fortunately, it was just wide enough so that Blackie could wedge his body into it tightly. . . . I boosted Andy up till he could get hold of Blackie's legs. . . . How was I to reach Blackie's legs, which were over a foot above my reach? . . . Andy [took] off one pair of trousers. Blackburn [let] the legs down to me while Andy held him securely in the V-shaped niche. By twisting the legs of the trousers and pulling myself upward aided by placing my caulked shoes against the wall, I had little difficulty.[20]

For the second chimney, they made a human ladder. At 5:55 PM they scrawled a succinct note—"Colder than hell."—in the summit register that the 1898 party had left. The first one-day ascent was in the finest of traditions: a small, light expedition that shunned all notoriety.

VICTORY! The Montana party on the summit of the Grand Teton on August 25, 1923; Quin Blackburn (left) and Andy DePirro (right). The metal banner with the words THE ROCKY MOUNTAIN CLUB had been left of the summit by the Owen-Spalding party twenty-five years earlier. The 1898 summit register can be seen between Blackburn's boots. (Photo from the Leigh Ortenburger papers)

Hermann Buhl (left) and Albert R. Ellingwood in the Enclosure during their successful ascent of the Grand Teton, August 17, 1924 (Photo by Carl A. Blaurock, from the Leigh Ortenburger papers)

The Colorado Mountain Club mountaineers who had given the Montanans their information were there at the invitation of Horace M. Albright, then the superintendent of Yellowstone National Park. Albright had contacted several climbing clubs with the express purpose of attracting the attention of mountaineers to the unlimited climbing potential of the region. This, he hoped, would generate publicity about the Teton Range—an area that Albright passionately felt should be protected and preserved as a national park. The CMC group included Albert Russell Ellingwood and Eleanor Davis (Ehrman). Ellingwood, a professor of political and social science, had learned to rock climb in the English Lake District while attending Oxford University. He was easily one of the strongest climbers of the day and had made the first ascent in 1920 of Lizard Head in Colorado, the most technically difficult climb in the United States at the time. Davis, a physical education instructor at Colorado College, where Ellingwood also taught, was a strong climber and a vice president of the CMC.

Of the eight who started out from the group's camp in Bradley (Garnet) Canyon, just five reached the Enclosure. From that point only Davis and Ellingwood continued to the top, climbing as equal partners and swapping leads. They reached the summit of the Grand on August 27, 1923, two days after the trio from Montana.[21] "The day was wonderfully clear and the view from the top," Davis wrote, was "all that one's heart could desire."[22] At the time, strong female climbers were rarely seen in the predominantly male-dominated sport of mountaineering, yet in the Tetons Davis ushered in a tradition that has continued to the present day, namely noteworthy alpine achievements by women who can hold their own in the sport.

On August 29, Ellingwood, accompanied once again by Davis and E. W. Harnden (one of the three who had stopped and waited at the Enclosure while Davis and Ellingwood summited the Grand), approached the Middle Teton by way of the previously unexplored south fork of Bradley (Garnet) Canyon. Intent upon making the mountain's first ascent, Ellingwood did so via the steep couloir that now bears his name. His companions waited a short distance below the summit while a brief storm slammed into the peak. After the storm cleared, and after they had descended to the high saddle between the Middle and South Tetons, Ellingwood and the indomitable Davis went on to make the first ascent of the Northwest Couloir route of the South Teton. All in all, this was an incredibly productive trip by the visiting Colorado mountaineers.

Ellingwood returned the following year with fellow CMC member Carl Blaurock, climbed the Grand Teton once again, and then pioneered the Northeast Ridge route to the top of Mount Moran. Davis returned three years later and led two other members of the CMC up Moran, making the first female ascent of the peak and repeating the Northeast Ridge route. For the first time, mountaineers were traveling to the Tetons from their home ranges, pursuing climbing in their leisure time as a recreational activity and a component of adventure travel.

Mountain Guiding Arrives in the Tetons

Guided climbing in the Teton Range traces its origins to Paul Petzoldt and the year 1924. Petzoldt began his lengthy career as a world-class climber and professional mountain guide with four ascents of the Grand Teton in 1924. On one of these climbs, Petzoldt guided some Jackson Hole locals up the Grand: the group included 59-year-old Geraldine Lucas, a retired schoolteacher and Jackson Hole homesteader, who became the second woman to reach the summit. On another climb, William O. Owen, a day shy of his 65th birthday, got to the summit a second time thanks to Petzoldt's quickly developing expertise. On August 4, 1925, after the first successful ascent of the Grand Teton that year, the first known mountaineering fatality in the range occurred when Theodore Teepe slid to his death while descending the remnant glacier on the upper eastern face of the peak. This feature has been referred to as the Teepe Glacier ever since. Petzoldt was instrumental in the recovery of Teepe's body.

The summers of 1925 and 1926 saw the first climbs by Phil Smith and Fritiof Fryxell, who over the next decade would shape much of the climbing history of the range. Fryxell's excellent account of Teton climbing history up to 1931 appears in his book *The Teton Peaks and Their Ascents*. Smith made the first ascents of Disappointment Peak and Mount Wister in 1925 and 1928, respectively. Horace Albright's dream of a Grand Teton National Park became reality on February 26, 1929, and Fryxell and Smith became the first members of the ranger staff. Fryxell wrote this about the park's establishment: "The peaks—these are the climax and, after all, the raison d'être of this park. For the Grand Teton National Park is preeminently the national park of mountain peaks—the Park of Matterhorns."[23]

The Golden Age

Fritiof Fryxell and Phil Smith seized the moment and began systematically exploring the range, making many first ascents and placing summit registers on the prominent peaks. A complete record of the climbing history of the range is available, beginning in 1898, due largely to Fryxell's painstaking transcription of these summit registers to a card file. Fryxell and Smith also initiated the practice, in force up through 1993, of requiring climbers to check in with park authorities as a safety measure and to report all new routes and unusual climbs. In 1929 and 1930 they made the first ascents of Teewinot Mountain[24], Nez Perce, Mount St. John, and Symmetry Spire. Fryxell, climbing solo, made the first ascents of Rockchuck Peak and Mount Hunt. With others he climbed Mount Woodring (Peak 11,590) and Bivouac Peak for the first time.

Many of the climbers who had made important first ascents and who were key players in the development of Teton climbing up to this point were members of the various mountaineering and outing clubs scattered throughout the country. The Rocky Mountain Climbers Club (1896), the American Alpine Club (1902), and the Alpine Club of Canada (1906) were among the first of these organizations. Universities such as Harvard, Yale, Dartmouth, and others all had mountaineering clubs that were formed in the 1920s. These clubs produced many strong climbers and provided a framework for the organization of climbs and expeditions. A healthy spirit of competition existed between groups, and year after year they came to the fabled Teton Range.

By 1929 the Grand Teton had become, as the great New England climber Robert Underhill noted, the "foremost mountaineering peak in the United States." Nonetheless, as Underhill also observed, this worthy pyramidal summit had only one route, the Owen-Spalding."[25] For "any respectable mountain," his partner Kenneth Henderson added, this was a "serious lack."[26]

When a Jackson local heard that the two Appalachian Mountain Club members intended to resolve the east ridge of the Grand, he laughed, "Well, I'll tell you just how far they'll get—to the foot of that first big tower. Then they'll come back!" Underhill and Henderson, however, had the necessary technical skills, acquired

Phil Smith, Robert L. M. Underhill, and Fritiof M. Fryxell on the summit of Mount Owen on the first ascent, July 16, 1930. (Photo by Kenneth A. Henderson, from the Leigh Ortenburger papers)

Fritiof M. Fryxell and Phil Smith unveil the plaque that they placed on the summit of the Grand Teton commemorating the Owen ascent, July 30, 1929. (Photo from the Leigh Ortenburger papers)

at well-known New England rock-climbing areas like New Hampshire's Cannon Mountain and during trips to the Alps (where Underhill had climbed both the Brenva Spur on Mont Blanc and the Peuterey Ridge). Albert R. Ellingwood and others had attempted the formidable east ridge, but in 1929 Underhill and Henderson found the key to getting around the Molar Tooth, a needlelike gendarme partway up. The pair made a short rappel to a thin ledge, which led past icy clefts and rotten chimneys back onto the ridge.

The Second Tower proved to be the psychological crux. Underhill wrote: "What—whether anything—lay above and beyond the overhang we could not see. Should no further traverse here be possible our chances of passing the great tower were very feeble. A redescent over the [protectionless] slabs . . . was not to be thought of with equanimity." Underhill committed, pulling himself up to the rim. "I . . . called out to Henderson that the day was ours." The men declared their East Ridge route to be equal to some of the more technical climbs in the Alps, such as those on the Weisshorn and Matterhorn. Underhill was also a philosophy instructor, and of the view from the summit he remarked, "Unlike that from an aeroplane it possesses a solid basis and continuous foreground which maintain the relationship between the observer and the object observed at the same time that they remove the one from the other; the observer has the curious sensation of being both of the world he contemplates and yet not of it."

In 1930, with Fryxell and Phil Smith, Underhill and Henderson climbed the summit knob of Mount Owen, which had balked three attempts in 1927 and one in 1928. The two men also climbed the spectacular Teepe Pillar in 1930. Underhill's travels took him across the United States, and he may well have been the person most responsible for the development of roped climbing in the country at that time. At the request of Francis Farquhar, editor of the *Sierra Club Bulletin*, Underhill submitted his famous article "On the Use and Management of the Rope in Rock Work," which earned him an invitation to the Sierra in 1931 to share his revolutionary techniques and provide instructional training. He joined some of the strongest climbers in California at the time on a landmark climb: the East Face of Mount Whitney. The select group included Norman Clyde, sometimes referred to as the dean of the Sierra Club climbers," Glen Dawson, and Jules Eichorn.

The summer of 1931 was very important in the history of Teton mountaineering. On July 15, 1931, Glenn Exum, while working as Paul Petzoldt's assistant guide and at his boss's suggestion, made his famous solo ascent of the ridge on the Grand Teton that now bears his name. Petzoldt pointed out a large ledge cutting across the west side of a major southern ridge. "Ex," he said, "why don't you go over there, take a look at that ledge, and if you think it will go, why go, and we'll meet you on top."

Exum, clad in a pair of Petzoldt's football cleats (two sizes too big), followed the ramp (Wall Street) until a gap opened above hundreds of feet of air:

That day the wind was blowing from the southwest and I got up there to the end of that ledge and it scared me, but when I called out to Paul, he couldn't hear me and didn't answer. I walked away from that ledge seven times, until I finally got up there and saw those little handholds and the boulder on the ridge. When you got to the eastern extremity of Wall Street, why, there isn't any place to jump from. So I climbed as high as I could until I was sorta secure, and I jumped from a standing start.

Once on the other side of what is now known as the "Step Across," he realized he couldn't go back. Suddenly lonely, he looked around: far away, two figures appeared on another unclimbed crest. Underhill and Smith were at work on the easternmost southern ridge (now known as the Underhill Ridge). Exum tried shouting, but the wind blew the sound away. He said to himself, "'Well, I'm just going to climb and quit talking.' The fear left me and I just started floating along."[28]

Paul Petzoldt and Glenn Exum, August 1930 (Photo from the Leigh Ortenburger papers)

That same month, Underhill teamed up with Petzoldt for the first ascent of the East Ridge route on Mount Moran. This came after a whirlwind week during which Underhill and Fryxell, in quick succession, established the East Ridge of Nez Perce, the North Ridge of the Middle Teton, and the North Ridge of the Grand Teton.

That final climb has become a touchstone for generations of Teton climbers. At the time of its first ascent, the North Ridge of the Grand Teton was regarded as the most difficult alpine climb in the United States. Even today it has a reputation as the classic climb in the range. Although it had previously been dismissed as unclimbable by all who examined it, Underhill and Fryxell secretly believed it was worth a try, especially after Underhill's solo reconnaissance of the route in 1930. Leaving their campsite at Amphitheater Lake at 5:30 AM, the two climbers proceeded up and across the Teton Glacier and arrived at the top of the Grandstand at 9:55 AM. The serious climbing then began, and they soon found themselves beneath the infamous Chockstone Chimney. Describing the crux of the climb, Fryxell later wrote:

> ***Five feet out on the sheer west wall of the chimney we both found toe-room, and I climbed to Underhill's shoulders, then to his head. I could touch the chockstone but nowhere find the slightest hold. When exhausted by futile efforts I lowered myself to Underhill's side and we resorted to pitons. Underhill drove a first piton at the limit of his reach, and, from my shoulders, a second one three feet higher. A ring was snapped into each. After we were both roped securely to these, Underhill mounted to my shoulders and, using the upper ring, launched an offensive. But because of the absence of holds he likewise failed and dropped back to my shoulders. When rested he tried a second time, with the same result. At the third attempt he found a foothold well out to the right and, somehow, pushed himself over onto the chockstone—a magnificent exhibition of rock climbing.***[29]

Not mentioned in his narrative (but confessed in Underhill's) was Fryxell's final, desperate admonition: "Stand on the piton!" The older generation of American climbers disapproved of pitons. Some felt that intermediate protection diminished the opportunity to test the leader's commitment and bravery. In the June 1930 issue of *Appalachia,* Underhill described the use of direct aid as being in the same "ambiguous" ethical position as fixed ropes and oxygen: "Though they may be accepted by certain mountaineers on certain occasions, they have no inherent justification and we see attempts constantly made to do without them." Although Underhill preferred to keep climbing "natural," he helped introduce a form of the "artificial assistance" he'd decried. The result opened up new possibilities.

Also in the summer of 1931, Fryxell made the first climbs of Cloudveil Dome, East Horn, Storm Point, and Ice Point. Hans Wittich climbed the Dike route on Mount Moran and the Wittich Crack on the Grand Teton. During the next four years the following major first ascents were completed, chiefly due to the efforts of Fryxell and Phil Smith: Rolling Thunder Mountain, Eagles Rest Peak, Ranger Peak, Veiled Peak, and Prospectors Mountain. Fred and Irene Ayres made their first visit to the park in 1932 and subsequently accomplished many first ascents, notably Rock of Ages and other pinnacles around Hanging Canyon, the West Horn, and Traverse Peak. Irene also accumulated an impressive list of first female ascents. These included Disappointment Peak, Storm Point, and Symmetry Spire—all in 1932. In 1934 she continued her streak with Mount Owen, Rockchuck Peak, Bivouac Peak, and Mount Moran's Skillet Glacier.

Ayres was just one of a number of notable female climbers who were active during the 1930s, following Eleanor Davis's early lead. Elizabeth Cowles (Partridge), who was later linked with the climbing history of Mount Everest, emerged as a strong climber with the first female ascent of the East Ridge of the Grand Teton in 1935, climbing with Glenn Exum and Paul Petzoldt. The following year, Fred and Irene Ayres teamed up with the adventurous Margaret Smith (Craighead) to establish a new route on Mount Wister.

As interest shifted mid-decade to the making of new routes, Petzoldt continued to be a force. He guided during the summers and did many important new climbs, such as the first ascents of Thor Peak; the North Face, West Couloir route on Buck Mountain; the West Ridge of Mount Moran; and the Koven, West Ledges, and Northeast Snowfields routes on Mount Owen. He also made the pioneering first winter ascent of the Grand Teton, with his brother Eldon and Fred Brown, on December 19, 1935. They skied to the Caves in Garnet Canyon on the first day and then spent two days ferrying loads to the Lower Saddle. From there they proceeded to the summit via the Owen-Spalding route. The group experienced a pleasant temperature inversion that allowed them to be in shirtsleeves on the summit while the valley below was locked in a -20°F deep freeze.

In the same decade T. F. Murphy, the chief of the party assigned by the US Geological Survey (USGS) to map Grand Teton National Park, ascended a great number of vantage points to determine elevations and sketch the topography. During the summers of 1934 and 1935, he climbed most of the peaks south of Buck Mountain, almost all the peaks of the divide, a few of the peaks west of Mount Moran, and many of the peaks bordering Webb Canyon. A climber visiting one of these lonesome peaks may find a cairn that was probably built by Murphy and his assistants, Mike Yokel Jr. and Robert E. Brislawn.

Jack Durrance, Alpinist and Rock Climber, and the Prewar Period

On August 25, 1936, during his first summer in the Tetons, Jack Durrance teamed with Paul and Eldon Petzoldt to make the first climb on the north face of the Grand

Jack Durrance (Photo by Henry Coulter, from the Leigh Ortenburger papers)

Teton—the most famous north face in the United States. Durrance had come to the Tetons to work for Petzoldt's burgeoning guiding business. Previously, he had spent eight years in Germany, attending high school in Garmisch and working in Munich. There, he had come in touch with climbers who were pushing the standards in the Alps, including the Schmid brothers, who had made the stunning first ascent of the north face of the Matterhorn.

For their ascent of the North Face route on the Grand, the trio left the valley very early in the morning to sneak by a party camped at Amphitheater Lake. This strong group included Fritz Wiessner, William "Bill" House, and Elizabeth "Betty" Woolsey, and rumor had it they were in the Tetons to attempt the same climb. Earlier that same summer, Wiessner and House had made the impressive first ascent of the South Face route on Mount Waddington in British Columbia, which at the time was the most difficult climb in North America. Woolsey had rock climbed back East and was captain of the US Women's Olympic Ski Team from 1937 to 1940. After being scooped on the Grand's North Face, Wiessner satisfied himself by completing the first free ascent of Robert Underhill's North Ridge route accompanied by House a few days later. This was a magnificent achievement, quite possibly the country's first climb at the 5.8+ level of difficulty. Wiessner, an expatriate from Germany, was an outstanding rock technician and alpinist. Both Durrance and Wiessner were brilliant climbers who greatly influenced the American climbing scene; their paths would cross again in the Himalaya on the legendary K2 expedition of 1938.

Henry Coulter (Photo by Jack Durrance, from the Leigh Ortenburger papers)

Durrance was a passionate rock climber whose favorite routes were the ridges. With Henry Coulter and other Dartmouth climbers he made many first ascents: the East Ridge of Disappointment Peak, the Durrance Ridge of Symmetry Spire, the North Face of Nez Perce, the Southwest Ridge and Northwest Ridge of Mount Owen, the Southwest Ridge of the Enclosure, and the Northwest Ridge, Durrance Direct (Lower Exum Ridge), and West Face routes on the Grand Teton. Robert Underhill and Fritiof Fryxell had considered the West Face to be the last remaining problem on the Grand. It required the skill and experience of the next generation, however, to make the first successful ascent.

From left to right: Margaret Bedell, Margaret Smith Craighead, and Mary Whittemore on the summit of the Grand Teton, August 3, 1939 after the first "manless" ascent (Photo taken by Anne Sharples, courtesy of the Craighead family)

On August 13, 1940, Durrance and Coulter hiked into the pristine cirque on the northwest side of the Grand that they named Valhalla Canyon. Five companions helped carry loads so they could establish a camp in the majestic cirque. In Durrance's words, they had taken "everything we owned" including two light sleeping bags; rain capes; a pair of nailed boots; a camera; a large, rubberized-cloth bivouac sack; and a Primus stove and pot. Their technical arsenal included "a short ice axe, ten rock pitons imported from Europe and a 120-foot, linen climbing rope from the Plymouth Cordage Company."[30] The pair set off for their objective early the next morning. Expecting to encounter difficult rockwork, they climbed in high-top, smooth-soled sneakers, but in case the rock was wet they also carried Durrance's felt-soled klettershoes and Coulter's rope-soled sandals. Legend has it that as Durrance was beginning the crux final pitch of the climb, he turned to Coulter, wondering if the belay was on, and was met with a loud snore. Durrance unleashed an abusive tirade and Coulter, by now wide awake, assured his friend that he could indeed safely proceed. This was a landmark climb and, even today, the West Face of the Grand Teton, a route that is seldom done, has a well-deserved reputation for being one of the most classic and difficult alpine climbs in the range.

Many of Durrance's routes are now considered classics, and at the time they were pioneered, they represented the highest caliber of American rock climbing. A pivotal figure in the national climbing scene, Durrance epitomized the transition from the "gentleman climber" to the totally committed climber and alpinist.

In a final spurt of activity in the years before the United States entered World War II, Paul Petzoldt led the now-popular North Ridge and CMC routes on Mount Moran. And Margaret Smith (Craighead), who counted Durrance among the strong male partners she climbed with during the 1930s, teamed up with Ann Sharples, Mary Whittemore, and Margaret Bedell for the first "manless" ascent of the Grand Teton on August 3, 1939. At the time, Smith downplayed their achievement, writing, "This may have been of importance to the record of events, but to us it was just another climb." Understated as it was by Smith it nevertheless made the regional news: "Another successful invasion of the field of sport by the weaker sex," reported the *Salt Lake Tribune.*[31] At the end of the decade Elizabeth Cowles added to her groundbreaking climbs: she made the first female ascents of the North Ridge routes on Mount Moran and the Grand Teton in 1940, and she participated in the first ascent of the Petzoldt Ridge on the Grand with Paul Petzoldt, Mary Merrick, and Frederick Wulsin Jr. in 1941.

These achievements capped a period of imaginative and daring route development, spearheaded by dedicated climbers. The scene was about to change again, but it would have to wait until the world was no longer preoccupied with war.

World War II

Climbing in the Tetons ground to a halt during the war years. Many of the climbers were in the service, some enlisting in the 10th Mountain Division, which was established in July 1943. The precursor to the division—the First Battalion of the 87th Mountain Infantry Regiment—was formed toward the end of 1941 at Fort Lewis, Washington, and the soldiers trained on the slopes of Mount Rainier. Camp Hale, Colorado, later became the primary training center. A number of climbers and mountaineers who would go on to make significant contributions to American climbing served with this famous group. Men such as Paul Petzoldt and David Brower acted as instructors, imparting their knowledge and expertise to the troops. A significant wartime advancement was the development and later availability of specialized equipment such as nylon climbing ropes, ring angle and wafer pitons, and aluminum carabiners. The war also brought climbers from different areas together for the first time, which allowed for much information sharing.[32]

Grand Teton, North Wall

Between 1936 and 1940, 200 to 400 climbers successfully ascended Teton peaks each year. Those numbers ballooned in the years following World War II, which saw an enormous increase in climbers visiting Grand Teton National Park, with a corresponding rise in the investigation of new routes and ascents of old routes that had been climbed only once. New walls, ridges, and couloirs, purposely avoided by the prewar climber as being too difficult, were now sought out and explored for the first time with a competence rarely matched by earlier climbers. The most important new routes and first ascents of this period, some now considered classics, include the North-Northwest Ridge of Buck Mountain; the North Face, West Chimney of Mount Wister; the Direct South Ridge of Nez Perce; the North Face of Cloudveil Dome; the Southeast Ridge of the Middle Teton; the West Face of the Exum Ridge; the Red Sentinel; the Southwest Ridge of Disappointment Peak; the North Face and Northwest Ridge of Teewinot Mountain; the North Face and North Ridge of Mount Owen; the Southwest Ridge of Storm Point; the Direct Jensen Ridge of Symmetry Spire; the East Face of Thor Peak; the South Face I of Bivouac Peak; and the Direct Finish to the North Face of the Grand Teton. Nearly all of these were pioneered by a small group of active mountaineers including William Buckingham, Don Decker, Richard Emerson, Art Gilkey, Paul Kenworthy, Robert Merriam, Leigh Ortenburger, Richard Pownall, and Willi Unsoeld. Many of these men served prestigiously as either climbing guides or seasonal climbing rangers.

The direct North Face route on the Grand was the major achievement of this period. Climbers have a peculiar fascination for cold, icy, and foreboding north faces. The great north faces of the Alps, best represented by the Eiger Nordwand, were long considered the ultimate alpine objective, fraught with danger from falling rock and ice. Since its first ascent by the Petzoldt brothers and Jack Durrance, the North Face of the Grand had taken on this mystique, becoming the stuff of legend. It was the challenge of the uppermost headwall, the *direttissima* north face, that now beckoned to the next generation. In August 1949, climbing guides Pownall and Gilkey teamed up with Ray Garner to attempt the climb. Pownall brilliantly led the now-famous Pendulum Pitch, tensioning across a blank section and gaining access to the highest of the four upward-sweeping ledges that are found on the face. After 17 hours the best climbers of the day found themselves on the summit.

In 1953 climbing guides Leigh Ortenburger and Willi Unsoeld and climbing ranger Richard Emerson unlocked the final portion of the Direct Finish. Because of the face's daunting reputation, prospective climbers had to overcome an enormous amount of inner fear to even attempt the route. During their ascent, Emerson, a master rock technician who had learned his craft in the 10th Mountain Division, led the Pendulum Pitch free as well as the delicate friction traverse into the "V." A new classic had been climbed.

Both Emerson and Unsoeld participated in the 1963 American Mount Everest Expedition. During that trip Unsoeld teamed up with Thomas F. Hornbein to make the first ascent of the West Ridge route, one of the classic mountaineering feats in the history of the sport. Ortenburger, besides being the primary climbing historian of the Teton Range, became America's foremost Andean mountaineer. Durrance's West Face route received its second ascent during the summer of 1953 by Ortenburger and Michael Brewer. Ortenburger and Emerson, as well as Don Decker, also pioneered the Direct South Buttress of Mount Moran. Durrance's climbs had been equaled and surpassed; a new generation was making its mark.

The second postwar decade, from 1955 to 1964, saw a rapid advance in climbing ambition, courage, competence, and equipment. In step with rock-climbing progress throughout the United States, new routes were pioneered that required a high level of technical skill in free climbing and pitoncraft. The use of expansion bolts to ascend blank faces debuted during this period, although, surprisingly, rock-drilling equipment had been taken—but not used—on the 1898 ascent of the Grand. The first bolts used in the United States were placed in 1939 by David Brower and his team on their successful climb of Shiprock in New Mexico. There is a great proliferation of bolts in some areas of the country today, especially since the advent of portable, motorized drills. Fortunately there are, even now, few bolts in Teton rock. Direct aid (or artificial) climbing, which was a rarity in the Tetons prior to 1958, became an accepted practice and was required on many of the most difficult new routes.

Rock Climbing in the 1960s: The Yosemite Influence

By 1960 the number of climbers visiting the Tetons each year had grown to 2,300. The most significant climbs of this era were made by Fred Beckey, William Buckingham, Yvon Chouinard, Barry Corbet, William Cropper, John Dietschy, David Dingman, David Dornan, John Gill, James Langford, Peter Lev, Rick Medrick, Leigh Ortenburger, Irene Beardsley (Ortenburger), Richard Pownall, Al Read, Royal Robbins, Pete Sinclair, Herb Swedlund, Willi Unsoeld, and Ken Weeks. In many instances the new climbs, often variations rather than routes, were made on smaller faces and ridges. With a new emphasis on rock climbing rather than general mountaineering, three important areas—the south ridges of Mount Moran, the south ridges of Disappointment Peak, and the buttresses in Death Canyon—were extensively developed, although the routes in general do not lead to any summits. The easier sedimentary peaks at the north and south ends of the range, untouched by previous climbers, were explored by Arthur J. Reyman, John C. Reed Jr., Howard R. Stagner Jr., Leigh Ortenburger, and Irene Beardsley (Ortenburger).

A partial list of the more important climbs of this era includes the Raven Crack, the Snaz, the Pillar of Death in Death Canyon, the Wedge on Buck Mountain, the Direct North Face of Mount Wister, Big Bluff on the south side of Garnet Canyon, the Robbins-Fitschen and Taylor routes on the Middle Teton, the Northwest Chimney and the Medrick-Ortenburger on the north face of the Grand Teton, the Black Ice Couloir on the Enclosure, the North Face and Northeast Face of Teepe Pillar, the North Face of the Red Sentinel, the several north face and south ridge routes of Disappointment Peak, the Northwest Face of Teewinot Mountain, the Serendipity Arête and Crescent Arête of Mount Owen, the three east face routes on Table Mountain, the Chouinard route on the east face of Yosemite Peak, the South Face of Ayres' Crag 5, the Direct South Face of Symmetry Spire, and the several ridge and buttress routes and North Face of Mount Moran.

The deliberate search for difficult rock climbs, new in the Tetons, became the goal of many climbers. Through and into the 1950s, the range had been regarded as primarily a mecca for alpinists. Now the climbers who passed through the Tetons may have just been to Yosemite, the Bugaboos, or the Shawangunks. Climbers who had learned their craft at one of these areas brought with them to this, the most accessible of alpine ranges, a level of rock-climbing skill not seen in preceding generations. Home for many of the climbers of this era was the abandoned Civilian Conservation Corps (CCC) camp at the south end of Jenny Lake, originally known as Camp NP-4." This camp was built in 1934, and was occupied through 1942, as part of President Franklin D. Roosevelt's New Deal; the CCC was one of many programs designed to lift the nation out of the Great Depression—the worst economic downturn in its history. By some estimates, up to 500 workers built trails and backcountry cabins and removed inundated trees from around the shore of Jackson Lake, whose surface area had increased by 50 percent after the construction of a dam in 1916. The National Park Service (NPS) eventually established a more official climbers' campground at the site of the old CCC camp, with a camping limit of 30 days as opposed to the then usual 10. The C-Camp, as it was called, became home and general hangout for the numerous climbers passing through the Tetons on their way to and from other climbing destinations across the country.

Among the C-Camp's occupants in 1957 were Southern Californians Yvon Chouinard and Ken Weeks, who had started climbing during nest-raiding excursions as falconers. Chouinard is now looked upon as one of the most influential figures in modern American and international mountaineering. His talent and expertise encompassed every climbing discipline—from rock- and icecraft to bouldering and aid climbing. Chouinard's ice tools and pitons, products of the Great Pacific Iron Works company, revolutionized rock- and ice-climbing techniques everywhere. Among his many first ascents in the Tetons, he is perhaps most remembered for opening up several routes in Death Canyon, including the Snaz and the Raven Crack. He also coauthored the tongue-in-cheek *Guide to the Jenny Lake Boulders* with America's most notable bouldering specialist, mathematician John Gill.

Also during the summer of 1957, the first ascent of the classic Irene's Arête was accomplished by John Dietschy and Irene Beardsley. Beardsley continued to knock off cutting-edge alpine climbs, including the first all-female ascent of the North Face of the Grand Teton with Sue

Irene Beardsley (Photo by Renny Jackson)

George Lowe leading the Slab Pitch on the first winter ascent of the North Ridge of the Grand Teton (Photo by Dave Carman)

Swedlund in 1965. Later, while raising children and pursuing a career as a physicist, this remarkable individual became the first woman to climb the fearsome Annapurna I, an 8,000m peak in Nepal.

Royal Robbins and Joe Fitschen were active in the Tetons during this period. Robbins was one of the strongest rock climbers in the world at the time, as evidenced by such legendary climbs as the first continuous ascent of the Nose and the first ascents of the Salathé and North America Wall routes on El Capitan in Yosemite. Since the Tetons were the crossroads of American mountaineering at the time, individuals passing through the climbers' camp brought new ideas, expertise, and an era of intense competition. A few days after the first ascent of the awesome Northwest Chimney route on the Grand by Teton regulars Ortenburger, Beardsley, and David Dornan, the route saw its second ascent by Robbins, Chouinard, and Fitschen. The three Californians upped the ante—and stirred up the regulars—by finishing with the crux pitches of Durrance's West Face route.

Another Yosemite climber who traveled to the fabled Teton Range during this era was Herb Swedlund, who began as an Exum guide in 1961. Swedlund had a strong background in rock climbing, exemplified by his success with Warren Harding and Glen Denny on the Southwest Face of Mount Conness in the High Sierra a few years before. On July 29, 1961, Swedlund partnered with Ray Jacquot to make the first ascent of the Black Ice Couloir on the Grand Teton, perhaps *the* classic ice route in the United States. Generations of climbers had peered into the depths of the couloir from the Upper Saddle and had simply shaken their heads, dismissing the gully as too dangerous to be considered as a climbing route. It had repulsed several attempts by the leading ice specialists of the day including Chouinard. After the first successful ascent by Swedlund and Jacquot, it joined the ranks of other legendary climbs—those that were often discussed but seldom repeated. Swedlund had climbed the elegant South Buttress Right on Mount Moran four days earlier with Dornan; with the Black Ice Couloir, he had completed first ascents of the finest rock and ice routes in the entire range in a weeklong tour de force.

From 1964 to 1975, the search for new routes continued, with the emphasis once again centered on rock climbing. Bivouac Peak's huge south face was climbed in 1969 by George Lowe and Juris Krisjansons. Krisjansons returned with Yvon Chouinard in 1970 for a more difficult line that center-punched the face. Other new face routes were found (the South Face of Spalding Peak; the Briggs-Higbee Pillar on the north face of the Middle Teton; the West Face of the Enclosure; the Northwest Face of Mount Owen; the Direct North Face of the Crooked Thumb; the Western Buttress and North Buttress of Mount Moran), and untrodden ridge routes were climbed (the Upper North Ridge of Prospectors Mountain; the Northwest Arête of Mount Wister; the South Ridge, Brimstone Chimney of the Second Tower). The small pinnacle of the Red Sentinel yielded two new and difficult routes. A new pinnacle—McCain's Pillar—provided a difficult ascent. Some of the better climbs were but variations on previous routes: the Garnet Traverse on the Direct South Ridge of Nez Perce, the Direct Buttress on the Northwest Ridge of Teewinot Mountain, and the Italian Cracks on the North Ridge of the Grand Teton. Other innovative climbs included the South Buttress Central of Mount Moran and the Southeast Chimney and Simpleton's Pillar on the Grand Teton. A significant technical advance was made with the first free ascent of the South Buttress Right on Mount Moran in 1973 by Steve Wunsch and Art Higbee, using a bypass of the main aid pitch.

The major contributors of these climbs were Irene Beardsley (Ortenburger); Roger Briggs; Yvon Chouinard; Peter Cleveland; Jim Erickson; Art Higbee; John Hudson; Dave Ingalls; Ray Jacquot; Peter Koedt; Juris Krisjansons; George H. Lowe III; David Lowe; Mike, Greg, and Jeff Lowe; Leigh Ortenburger; Rick Reese; Royal Robbins; Don Storjohann; Ken Weeks; Ted Wilson; and Steve Wunsch.

Summer-season snow routes, ice climbs, and mixed climbs also proliferated. New routes on Cloudveil Dome (Zorro Snowfield), Mount Moran (Sickle Couloir), and the South Teton (Southeast Couloir) proved notable. Ice climbing was sought and found in the infamous Run-Don't-Walk Couloir on Mount Owen and the Hidden Couloir of Thor Peak. New mixed rock-and-ice climbs of major proportions were discovered or pieced together on the northwest flank of the Grand Teton, such as the combined Black Ice Couloir–West Face and the Lowe Route on the formidable northwest face of the Enclosure. Following the only weakness in that huge wall, George Lowe and Mike Lowe tackled difficult aid and free climbing in an immense chimney system.

Winter Alpinism

Starting in 1965 with the first winter ascent of Mount Owen, a small group of committed and talented climbers from the Salt Lake area began a systematic series of pioneering winter climbs in the Teton Range. From February 28 to March 2, 1968, about a year before the ice-climbing revolution, Maurice Horn, George Lowe, and Greg and Mike Lowe climbed the North Face of the Grand Teton in one alpine-style push. As historian Andy Selters writes, "Wearing [crampons] to climb steep icy rock like that on the Grand Teton in winter seemed only somewhat more reasonable than flapping your arms to fly."[34] Mike Lowe remembered people warning that there would be no rescue. "This, of course, provided us with more incentive."

Since they expected to climb cold rock with fingerless gloves, the Lowes prepared by skiing barehanded at Utah's resorts. On February 27, with Horn they dug a cave into the bergschrund below the north face. For the next four days, they alternated leading and hauling. Greg remembered the "sloughy snow on slabs. . . . You'd run the rope out with no protection, looking for the islands of rock that jutted above the verglas and snow." Having lost a crampon, he climbed without them, brushing snow off with his fingers and frictioning on sections of stone with the soles of his shoes.

Apart from hoarfrost, the Pendulum Pitch was mostly dry. Although Horn was unaccustomed to the "scraping and grinding" of metal on rock, he discovered that crampons worked better than boots on the small holds. Recalling the impending fourth nightfall, Mike said:

> ***George was about sixty feet out on very shaky protection. He had left his light in his pack on the ledge. For two hours, he yelled down to us describing his difficulty in finding a piton placement to rappel back to the ledge. I was belaying him from my sleeping bag, and it was very cold. I knew he was feeling for cracks with gloveless fingers and he was getting desperate. Finally, he yelled that he had an anchor but was not sure that it would hold. [He said] he would down climb as I gave him some tension. He arrived safely at the ledge in starlit darkness. I broke out laughing. . . . He had been climbing so intensely that he had forgotten to remove his dark-lensed glacier goggles.***[35]

They survived a frigid open bivouac and summited in the morning. "Afterward," Greg said, "we thought we could probably figure out how to do most climbs." This extraordinary ascent shattered the psychological barriers for winter climbing and encouraged similar challenges over the next few years. The first winter ascent of the West Face route of the Grand Teton by George Lowe and Jeff Lowe in 1972 is perhaps the finest example of the extreme winter alpinism that gained momentum in this period. In 1978 on the North Ridge of 23,442-foot Latok I in Pakistan, George encountered terrain—"thin ice over angled rock that you have to deal with gently, so you don't break it off"—that reminded him of the West Face of the Grand in winter. Both men went on to make other cutting-edge climbs throughout the world, with George participating in the first ascent of the East Face of Mount Everest and Jeff becoming America's foremost ice specialist.

Mike Munger in Death Canyon (Photo by Rich Perch)

The Climbers' Ranch

After the closing of the C-Camp in 1966, the Jenny Lake campground became the main gathering place for climbers for the next few years. However, a degree of conflict arose between vacationing park visitors and the more raucous climbers, who often stayed in the Tetons for extended periods of time and for whom climbing had become a way of life. This tension was the source of considerable consternation for the Jenny Lake Rangers, who were tasked with keeping law and order in their small region of authority within the park.[36] This changed in 1970 with the opening of the Grand Teton Climbers' Ranch under a permit granted by the Park Service to the American Alpine Club. Originally known as the Double Diamond Dude Ranch, which opened in 1924, it exists these days as a kind of sanctuary, insulating climbers from the hustle and bustle of the millions of other park visitors who, fortunately, know nothing of its existence.

In the late 1970s, one inhabitant of the Climbers' Ranch was Mike Munger, a rock climber and alpinist from Boulder, Colorado, who had emerged as one of the most powerful climbers there. In the summer of 1977, he began a systematic exploration of the range, opening up many new and difficult routes as well as free climbing several of the older aid lines. From Rock Springs Buttress to Mount Moran, he logged an impressive number of ascents during an intensive three-year period. In 1977 he spent a fair amount of time on Mount Moran's No Escape Buttress, putting a direct finish on the original Direct South Face route as well as establishing No Survivors and Gin and Tonic, both technically difficult and runout rock climbs. That year he also made the first free ascent of the Open Book and the difficult Satisfaction Buttress on Disappointment Peak. In 1978 Munger turned his attention to the Snaz Buttress in Death Canyon, establishing Lot's Slot, Cottonmouth, and Fallen Angel. During that same summer he discovered the climbing potential of the high-alpine south face of Cloudveil Dome, putting up the now-classic Armed Robbery, with Silver Lining following in 1979. Also in 1979, Munger rediscovered Broken Arrow Spire on the south side of Avalanche Canyon, where he put up two new lines and then freed the intimidating Pownall-Unsoeld route on the huge north face of Disappointment Peak, establishing Pin Time.

Many other talented climbers accompanied Munger on these adventures throughout the range. These included Yvon Chouinard, Jim Donini, Bill Feiges, Charlie Fowler, Rick Liu (manager of the Climbers' Ranch for several years), Bill Nicholson, Rich Perch, Buck Tilley, and Steve Wunsch.

Charlie Fowler was another talented climber from Colorado and early denizen of the Climbers' Ranch; he explored the alpine realm of the Grand Teton, establishing the High Route on the remote northwest face of the Enclosure in 1977 with Steve Glenn and Route Canal on the north face with Jeff Lowe in 1979. Jim Donini, climbing with Rick Black, eliminated the aid on the intimidating Lowe Route, a rarely repeated and extremely strenuous alpine climb on the Enclosure, in 1977. During this frantic period of climbing activity and route development, Caveat Emptor on the Snaz Buttress was finally completed. Many outstanding rock climbers had worked on this route over the years, but the first complete ascent fell to Climbers' Ranch residents Jim Beyer and Buck Tilley in July 1979. Of all the climbs done in Death Canyon during this period, Caveat alone stands as the often repeated classic. Beyer also managed the impressive and isolated West Dihedrals on Mount Moran that same year. The previous summer, Tilley had freed the original line on the super-classic South Buttress Right with Jim Mullin, and in 1979 a young mountain guide named Stan Mish managed to free the aid crack on the Direct South Buttress, bringing the 5.12 grade into the range for the first time.

To the Millennium

The 1980s and 1990s saw important developments in novel directions. The existing extremes of the Teton climbing spectrum, both mixed alpine climbing and pure rock climbing, were explored and extended. On the north side of Death Canyon two classic climbs were discovered: Aerial Boundaries was put up by Jackson locals in 1985, and Charlie Fowler returned to the area in 1987 to establish Sunshine Daydream with Alison Sheets. The proximity to Jenny Lake of the southwest ridge of Storm Point resulted in several new variations on generally good rock in the vicinity of Guides' Wall.

Beginning in 1977, the Grand Teton yielded five more routes or variations on its broad eastern expanse: the Horton East Face, the Beyer East Face I and II, the Otterbody Chimneys, and the Keith-Eddy East Face. Jim Beyer continued to emerge as one of the primary new route developers of the period, with an eye toward unexplored areas and quality rock climbs. Beyer's continued search for long routes of first-class climbing led him to the huge diagonal west face of the south ridge of Mount Moran. To complement his West Dihedrals route, he added the Revolutionary Crest (1982) and the Sandinista Couloir. Taking advantage of scheduled mountain patrols near the generally sunny south side of the Grand, Jenny Lake Rangers climbed the prominent offwidth crack on the west face of the Exum Ridge, the Gold Face, the Burgette Arête, and Jim's Big Day. The first winter ascents of the South Buttress Right and Staircase Arête on Mount Moran, as well as the second winter ascent of the North Ridge route on the Grand, were accomplished by the strong alpine team of Alex Lowe and Jack Tackle in 1985.

Perhaps the major accomplishment of this period was the development of new, high-level mixed routes on the north and west sides of the Grand Teton. Prolific alpinist Steve Shea established two very difficult ice lines on the north face of the Grand in 1980, and in 1981 Michael Stern contributed two additional important climbs, Loki's Tower (with Mark Whiton) and the Visionquest Couloir (with Steve Quinlan). Alberich's Alley was added in 1982 (by Renny Jackson and Peter Hollis) to the other classic ice lines on the west sides of the Grand and the Enclosure. Jackson also took part in the first ascent of Emotional Rescue, a route he and Steve Rickert put up on the golden rock of the Enclosure buttress during the summer of 1985. The set was extended in 1991 with Beyer's impressive and improbable Lookin' for Trouble on the north face of the Enclosure. These alpine climbs, when added to the existing routes—the North Ridge, the West Face, the Black Ice Couloir, the Northwest Chimney, the Lowe Route, and the High Route—enhanced an alpine arena already unmatched in the United States. Fittingly, on the first day of winter toward the end of 1991, Jackson and Alex Lowe did the first winter ascent of the dark and foreboding Northwest Chimney route.

The return of truly alpine conditions to the Tetons during the summer of 1993, brought on by generally poor weather, directed climbers' attention toward untraveled, ephemeral ice lines and major mixed climbs. The north chimney of Cloudveil Dome (Nimbus) was finally climbed, and the south-facing chute on the Second Tower was linked with the upper East Ridge route of the Grand. The High Route on the Enclosure was done largely as a thin ice climb, and the Goodro-Shane route on the north face of the Grand was repeated in difficult late-fall conditions.

Perhaps as a prelude for things to come, in February 1996 Jackson locals Hans Johnstone and Mark Newcomb made the first winter ascent of the Hossack-MacGowan Couloir on the north face of the Grand Teton—and then turned around and skied the line, thus setting a high bar for future ski mountaineering in the US.

Many climbers contributed to these advances in Teton mountaineering and rock climbing, notably Jim Beyer, Dan Burgette, David Carman, Yvon Chouinard, Jim Donini, Mike Fischer, Charlie Fowler, Paul Gagner, Keith Hadley, Paul Horton, Renny Jackson, Ron Johnson, Hans Johnstone, Jason Keith, Tom Kimbrough, Stephen Koch, Norm Larson, Alex Lowe, Jeff Lowe, Ron Matous, Greg Miles, Mark Newcomb, Leigh Ortenburger, Steve Quinlan, Steve Rickert, Steve Shea, Alison Sheets, Jim Springer, Michael Stern, Jack Tackle, Buck Tilley, Tom Turiano, Mark Whiton, Jim Woodmencey, and Steve Wunsch.

The Modern Era

Over the last few decades, the Teton Range has once again assumed a prominent place in the United States as an alpine mecca. It is not for the climbing that mountaineers travel in huge numbers to this little range now but for the chance to ride the various couloirs and faces when the peaks are locked in winter's embrace. Alpine touring and ski and snowboard mountaineering have exploded in popularity in recent years. Accessibility, improvements in equipment, the proliferation of route information and the ability to convey it rapidly via social media, and the relative ease of winter travel have all contributed to this dramatic increase in use. Still, now two decades into the 21st century, new climbing routes and significant first winter ascents continue to be established.

Interestingly, this new route development has been carried out by a relatively small number of local Teton climbers, with a few notable exceptions. With the Grand as one of the focal points, Jim Beyer continued to develop great routes, adding the Golden Arête (1999) and the Crystal Tower (1999) to his other climbs on the east face. Crystal Right, put up by locals Aaron Gams, Toby Stegman, and Brian Mulvihill in 2010, is another beautiful route on exquisite rock that joins the Crystal Tower for the final pitch. On the west side of the Exum Ridge, Beyer added Captain Stupid (1999) and the Beyer-Hartman (2002). Difficult mixed lines on the north face of the Grand were opened by local powerhouses Hans Johnstone, Stephen Koch, and Mark Newcomb. Most recently, once again on the Grand's north face, new territory was discovered with the onsight of the North Buttress Direct by Mark Jenkins and Justin Bowen in 2020. The futuristic classics Golden Pillar (2003) and Bean's Shining Wall of Storms (2012), developed by Johnstone and Greg Collins, stand alongside the Crystal Tower routes as some of the best climbs of this modern era.

A number of new high-quality climbs have been established in Death Canyon by a cadre of local Teton climbers. Breaking Barriers, a long and difficult route on the south side, was established by Brendan O'Neill and Zack Martin in 1999. On the same side of the canyon, guides Mark Givens and Joel Kauffman put up the Alien Wall in 2009. Also in 2009, the Raven Crack was climbed as a winter mixed climb by Koch and Sam Magro. On the Snaz Buttress, the Fountainhead (2003) and Freedom Fighter (2004) were opened by Collins, O'Neill, Doug Workman, Evan Howe, Bob Goodwin, and Sue Miller. Both Collins and Johnstone freed the classic O-Mega Crack in 2007. The Omega Triangle (Gams and Mulvihill) joined the Guardian of Death (Collins and Nate Opp) on the lower north side of the canyon in 2009.

Local climber and historian Paul Horton continued to explore and find new routes. Along with Charlie Thomas, he put up the Sunset Face on Nez Perce, the South Face Right on Spalding Peak, and the Forgotten

Hans Johnstone on the first ski descent of the Hossack-McGowan on the Grand Teton, February 16, 1996 (Photo by Mark Newcomb)

A climber negotiates the huge overhang (5.12-) of the fourth pitch of Bean's Wall on the Grand Teton. (Photo by Eric Bissell)

Arête on Mount Moran, all in 2003. Rediscovering excellent-quality rock on the lower north face of the Middle Teton, Johnstone free climbed the Taylor route with David Gonzales and established the North Wall with Collins. Inge's and the Middle Finger, two extremely difficult routes on this north face, continue to be worked out by Collins and Johnstone. Across the glacier to the north, two difficult routes on the south face of Teepe Pillar were put up by guides, one in 1999 by Jim Howe and Jason Keith and another by Opp and Sam Hennessey in 2015. Mike Abbey and Sam Macke opened new routes on the Second Tower and the west face of Disappointment Peak in 2017.

The massive south buttress of Mount Moran enticed climbers once again: in 2000, Beyer returned with visiting Alaskan alpinist John Kelley to establish a very difficult and runout 10-pitch route that goes directly up the immense slab of the 1967 South Buttress Central climb and then finishes with the Direct South Buttress to the summit. Prior to this Beyer had established the South Buttress Drifter and the Whirl of Hate, both of which he put up solo. In a remarkable one-day effort in 2006, Johnstone, Collins, and fellow Teton strongman Bean Bowers onsighted the South Buttress Prow on the leading edge of the buttress. Collins and Johnstone returned in 2007 and redpointed the South Buttress Houdini, crossing the classic South Buttress Right at its midpoint and continuing up a left-trending weakness that had been explored earlier by locals Nate Fuller and Patrick Wright.

Although it seems interest in winter first ascents has given way to ski mountaineering, a number of prize climbs have been done in the last few decades. In January 1997, longtime local winter alpinist Norm Larson put up a route on the north face of Mount Wister with Callum Mackay; four years later, in February 2001, he and Johnstone established a new route in winter on the south face of Cloudveil Dome. After numerous attempts, Johnstone, Newcomb, and Renny Jackson nabbed the first winter ascent of the Direct South Buttress on Mount Moran in March 2001. These three teamed up with Koch for the first successful wintertime Grand Traverse in January 2004. Three years later, in March 2007, Collins and Johnstone climbed the North Ridge route of Mount Owen in winter.

Mixed routes have been explored and established high on the peaks and as one-day cragging adventures. Kelley was active in 2002, putting up Three Shots in the Dizzy Wind and Prospect of an End on the northwest face of the Enclosure, and the Minor Fourth Couloir on Mount Moran. Taking advantage of early-season ice in 2010, Nate Brown and Macke climbed a hard mixed route on the north face of the Middle Teton. This same pair also completed a mixed route across the canyon, navigating the couloir leading to the Teepe Col in February 2015. On Peak 10,450 (Rendezvous Mountain) Brown, Macke, and Mulvihill have established a few multipitch mixed climbs, all as one-day cragging ascents.

Winter ski descents of the Grand Teton, both guided and unguided, are commonplace these days. Johnstone and Rick Hunt descended major portions of the East Ridge route on skis in 2006. Then in March 2013, Collins and O'Neill made one of the most astonishing and technical ski descents in the range when they descended the famous North Face of the Grand. Interspersed with 10 single-rope rappels, the pair found acceptable snow conditions on the four famous ledges of that route. After nearly reaching the top of the Guano Chimney, they climbed back up to the western edge of the First Ledge, rappelled to the Grandstand, and skied that to the Teton Glacier. They then skied Glacier Gulch to the valley floor, thus completing a traverse of the peak and a 7,000-foot ascent and descent!

Traverses and mountain endurance triathlons have also become popular among the Jackson Hole climbing community. For details on a few of these grueling events and challenges, see Traverses, Enchainments, Picnics, and Other Sufferfests in the Climbing in the Tetons chapter. The FKTs (fastest known times) on the Grand Teton and the Grand Traverse have been broken and set again and again over the past few years.

The Teton Range occupies a special place in the history of American climbing. It is marked with the stories—inspiring, tragic, terrifying, amusing—of the many climbers and alpinists who tested themselves on these peaks in the 19th and 20th centuries. And it remains open to new lines, new possibilities, new stories, even as pressures related to overuse strain NPS resources. In recent decades, climbing has exploded as a recreational activity, both in the Tetons and elsewhere around the world. Park rangers here struggle with the management and preservation of extremely crowded high-altitude regions such as the Lower Saddle, through which thousands of climbers pass each year on their way up the Grand Teton. As we are now well into the 21st century, what the future may have in store with regard to climbing is anyone's guess. Undoubtedly, mountaineers will forever be drawn to the Teton Range and the long, classic alpine routes leading to the summits of its peaks.

REFERENCES

Bonney, Orrin H., and Lorraine G. Bonney. *The Grand Controversy*. New York: AAC Press, 1992.

Chelton, Dudley, and Bob Godfrey. *Climb! Rock Climbing in Colorado*. Boulder, CO: Published for the American Alpine Club by Alpine House Publishing, 1977.

Jones, Chris. *Climbing in North America*. Berkeley, Los Angeles, London: Published for the American Alpine Club by the University of California Press, 1976.

Ortenburger, Leigh N., and Reynold G. Jackson. *A Climber's Guide to the Teton Range*. 3rd ed. Seattle: Mountaineers Books, 1996.

Runte, Alfred. *National Parks: The American Experience*. Lincoln, NE: University of Nebraska Press, 1979.

ENDNOTES

1. Chris Jones, *Climbing in North America* (Berkeley, Los Angeles, London: Published for the American Alpine Club by the University of California Press, 1976).
2. Richard [Beaver Dick] Leigh, letter to the editor, *Rocky Mountain News*, probably late December 1894.*
3. Nathaniel P. Langford, "The Ascent of Mount Hayden," *Scribner's Monthly*, June 1873 (vol. 6, no. 2), p. 135 (full article pp. 129–57).
4. Fort Hall Ledger Book, 1837, Columbia River Fishing and Trading Company, MS 938, p. 136, Oregon Historical Society, Portland, OR.*
5. Nathaniel Pitt Langford, *Vigilante Days and Ways* (Chicago: A. C. McClurg, 1912; copyright 1890 by Langford), pp. 116–19.
6. Mike Foster, *Strange Genius: The Life of Ferdinand Vandeveer Hayden* (Niwot, CO: Roberts Rinehart Publishers, 1994), p. 235.
7. "Dr. Hayden's Geological Survey," *Helena Daily Herald*, September 9, 1872 (vol. 11, no. 33), p. 1, c. 2.*
8. Nathaniel P. Langford, "Report of N. P. Langford on the resources of Snake River Valley," in *Sixth Annual Report of the United States Geological Survey of the Territories, 1872* (Washington, DC: Government Printing Office, 1873), pp. 89–90.
9. Langford, "The Ascent of Mount Hayden," pp. 145–46.
10. Handwritten copy of "N. P. Langford's Second Trip to Yellowstone and the Tetons with the Hayden Survey," 1872, Original Manuscripts of Nathaniel P. Langford, SHELF J(LANGFORD), Yellowstone Heritage and Research Library, Gardiner, MT.* From Leigh Ortenburger: This manuscript "is arranged chronologically with dates in the margin, suggesting that it was the first draft of the published article in the form of notes from a diary or other material. The language is much more reportorial than the frequently flowery prose of the finished article; it also contains notes for subjects to be included later. It appears, after careful study, to be more reliable than the published version since there is always the tendency to embellish a story when it is presented to an eager audience. The first draft was intended by Langford for no one but himself. . . . The [*Scribner's*] article was central to many of the criticisms of the Stevenson-Langford climb and its details and its editing are therefore worthy of careful analysis."
11. Orrin H. Bonney and Lorraine G. Bonney, *The Grand Controversy* (New York: AAC Press, 1992), p. 17.
12. This author (R. Jackson) enlisted Emily J. Will, D-BFDE, a board-certified document examiner, to discern the word that had been crossed out in Langford's handwritten manuscript between "Archaelogical curiosities" and "top." In a letter dated October 30, 2021, she identified it as *on*.
13. Bonney and Bonney, *The Grand Controversy*, pp. 52–53.
14. Bonney and Bonney, *The Grand Controversy*, p. 53.
15. William A. Baillie-Grohman, *Camps in the Rockies* (New York: Charles Scribner's Sons, 1882).
16. The Kieffer letter was first uncovered in the William O. Owen papers at the Western History Research Center [now the American Heritage Center], University of Wyoming, Laramie, by Leigh N. Ortenburger in the spring of 1959.*
17. W. O. Owen, "The Ascent of the Grand Teton," *Alpine Journal* 19, no. 145 (August 1899): pp. 536–43.
18. "The Jackson Hole Country of Wyoming," *Scientific American*, March 30, 1918, p. 272.
19. At a meeting held June 3, 1931, the US Board on Geographic Names gave official status to 61 place names in Grand Teton National Park that had previously been approved by the National Park Service. Garnet Canyon was originally named for Frank Bradley, the 1872 Hayden Survey geologist who was one of the members of the expedition that made it to the Lower Saddle.
20. Leigh N. Ortenburger, *The Grand Teton 1923*, vol. 1, *Tetoniana: History of the Exploration of Grand Teton National Park* (self-pub., 1968).
21. Albert Russell Ellingwood, "Our American Matterhorn," *Outdoor Life*, September 1924 (vol. 44, no. 3), p. 183.
22. Eleanor Davis, "The Tetons," *Trail and Timberline*, August 1924 (no. 71), pp. 9–10.
23. Fritiof M. Fryxell, "The Grand Tetons: Our National Park of Matterhorns," *American Forests and Forest Life* 35 (August 1929): p. 455.
24. Fritiof M. Fryxell. *The Teton Peaks and Their Ascents* (Grand Teton National Park, WY; The Crandall Studios, 1932), pp. 74–75. Fryxell states: "In *Outing* for December, 1915, appears an account by J. D. Reardan ("Up Grand Teton," pages 267–278) describing the adventures experienced by a party of three soldiers who set out to climb the Grand Teton and eventually reached the top only to find they had scaled the wrong mountain. Though Reardan's descriptions are not sufficiently exact to point to any known peak, for some time the writer was inclined to regard Teewinot as the mountain referred to in this account. Recently, the writer made contact with Major Reardan himself and learned that his ascent was made on "about October 5, 1910." To the information available in the published account, Major Reardan added additional details (letters of February 3 and 22, 1931) which make the identification of his peak even more puzzling. He states that "We climbed to the very top of the peak we were on and . . . the last thousand feet of it was bare rock and the side was quite precipitous." This might well refer to Teewinot, though the estimated extent of the peak above timberline would have to be doubled to agree with this peak. Continuing, the Major says, "The top of the peak we were on was not more than ten by twenty feet, roughly, in size and not so very flat at that. There was nothing available to build a cairn or other marker. Each of us left an article of our equipment with our initials scratched on with the point of a knife. We wedged them into the crevices of the rock as near the topmost point as possible. I left an aluminum Army canteen with 'J. D. R.' scratched on it. I have forgotten what the others left." This description scarcely fits the summit of Teewinot, which is a long ridge yielding an abundance of loose boulders. Furthermore, the summit of Teewinot was carefully scrutinized by Smith and the writer at the time of our ascent, and on the two subsequent visits to the top by the writer, and no records found. After examining the topographic map and a number of photographs of Teewinot, Major Reardan expressed himself as being "certain that it was not this peak," being confident instead that it was Mt. Owen. But this conclusion must be in error as the several accounts of his climb make no reference to the large snowfields which must be crossed in this ascent, nor do the details of the description (except for the reference to scarcity of summit boulders) at all point to Mount Owen. When Owen was climbed in 1930, no records were found on its summit."

    Leigh Ortenburger also corresponded with Reardan while conducting research for earlier editions of this book. In a series of letters during the early 1960s, Ortenburger supplied Reardan with a number of good aerial photographs of the central peaks in the range as well as a number of detailed questions regarding the approach to the climb, the climb itself, and the view from the top. Reardan did his best to recall these details nearly fifty years after the fact and in a letter dated November 22, 1961, stated, "A study of the photos that you sent leads me to believe that we climbed Mt. Teewinot." This writer (R. Jackson) believes that the evidence for an ascent of Teewinot by Reardan is inconclusive. Perhaps at some future date an old Army canteen with the initials "J. D. R." scratched into its surface will be found in a crack somewhere and settle this old Teton mystery. (Source: Ortenburger, Leigh N., Teton History, M1503/Box 5; Reardan Correspondence re: 1910 ascent; Stanford University Libraries, Department of Special Collections).
25. Robert L. M. Underhill, "The Grand Teton by the East Ridge," *Alpine Journal* 42, no. 241 (November 1930): pp. 267–77.
26. *Canadian Alpine Journal* 18 (1929): pp. 96–97.
27. Jones, *Climbing in North America*, p. 127.
28. Glenn Exum, *Never a Bad Word or a Twisted Rope: A Collection of Climbing Stories*, ed. Charles Craighead (Moose, WY: Grand Teton Natural History Association, 1998).
29. Fritiof M. Fryxell, *The Teton Peaks and Their Ascents* (Grand Teton National Park, WY: The Crandall Studios, 1932), pp. 56–57.
30. Jack Durrance and Henry Coulter, interview by Reynold Jackson, September 23, 1988.
31. Molly Loomis, "Women on the Tetons," *Jackson Hole Magazine*, October 14, 2015. https://jacksonholemagazine.com/women-on-the-tetons.
32. Gerald B. Cullinane (member of 87th Mountain Infantry Regiment, F Company, 10th Mountain Division), interview by Reynold Jackson, December 6, 1997.
33. John Daugherty, *A Place Called Jackson Hole: A Historic Resource Study of Grand Teton National Park* (Moose, WY: Grand Teton National Park, National Park Service, 1999).
34. Andy Selters, *Ways to the Sky: A Historical Guide to North American Mountaineering* (Golden, CO: AAC Press, 2004).
35. Renny Jackson, "Mountain Profile: The Grand Teton," *Alpinist* 33 (Winter 2010–11), p. 50, based on interviews by the author.
36. Pete Sinclair, *We Aspired: The Last Innocent Americans* (Logan, UT: Utah State University Press, 1993).

Notes marked with an asterisk (*) were taken from an as yet unpublished manuscript by Leigh N. Ortenburger on the history of the Teton Range in the 19th century and are based on his research. Ortenburger is considered by many to be *the* climbing historian of the range.

A Climber's Perspective on Teton Geology

Joe Stern, PhD

The steep, rocky peaks of the Teton Range rise so abruptly from the contrastingly flat valley of Jackson Hole that even the most casual observer has some intuition that powerful geologic forces created this stunning landscape. Part of the appeal of climbing in the Tetons is that it brings you up close with this incredible geology, and this proximity often inspires a natural interest in the subject among climbers. The main reason for providing this overview of Teton geology is to add depth to the experience of climbing in the range for those who are interested (and to give climbers something to read on those occasional bad weather days).

Climbers should also want to know about the geology of the Tetons for practical reasons. The distribution of various rock types and patterns in faulting, uplift, erosion, and weathering all combine to influence where the best climbing is located. Understanding the dominant orientations of fractures, drainages, and glacial features can help with routefinding, which is often one of the biggest challenges in Teton climbing. Knowing some geology can also help climbers better assess rockfall and other objective hazards in the dynamic alpine environment. Anyone traveling on or near the range's active glaciers would do well to receive a primer on glaciology. Regardless of your perspective, the Tetons are even more impressive and intriguing when you learn more about how they formed.

Overview: The Big Picture

The spectacular but compact Teton Range in northwest Wyoming runs roughly north–south for about 40 miles and is 10–15 miles wide. The western slope of the range dips gently toward Teton Valley in Idaho and is covered with younger sedimentary rocks. The steep eastern front of the range rises dramatically from Jackson Hole with up to 7,000 feet of relief exposed between the valley floor and summit elevations. The crystalline rocks exposed at the core of the range are gneisses and granites that are between 2.5 and 2.9 billion years old—some of the oldest rocks on the continent. Despite the exceptional antiquity of the rocks that make up the Teton peaks, the mountains themselves are some of the youngest on Earth, with most of the uplift of the Teton Range occurring along the Teton fault in just the last 2 to 10 million years. Repeated glaciations over the past 2 million years carved out spectacular horns, arêtes, and U-shaped valleys and left behind moraines, lakes, and erratic boulders. Many aspects of Teton geology are considered active today including several glaciers, the Teton fault, and the Yellowstone Hot Spot.

The following discussion reviews the almost 3-billion-year geologic history of the Teton Range, more or less chronologically.

Layered Gneiss: The Most Common Rocks

Most of the exposed rock in the Teton Range is 2.5- to 2.9-billion-year-old heterogeneous layered gneiss. Gneiss is a type of metamorphic rock with alternating bands of light and dark minerals that is formed when previously existing sedimentary or igneous rocks are subjected to intense heat and pressure. The light minerals are mostly quartz and feldspar,

This page: The central part of the Teton Range from Jackson Hole. The mountains are composed of 2.5- to 2.9-billion-year-old gneiss and granite. Most of the uplift of the range occurred in the last 2 to 10 million years along the Teton fault, which cuts across the middle of the picture along the base of the range. The peaks and canyons of the Teton Range and the flat valley of Jackson Hole were carved during repeated glaciations over the past 2 million years.
Opposite: A truly wild winter aerial of the western aspect of the Grand Teton (Photo by Lanny Johnson)

while the dark minerals are mainly biotite and hornblende. Conspicuous layering occurs on centimeter-to-meter scales and reflects the combined effects of inherited layers from the preexisting rocks and the realignment of minerals as they were recrystallized, compressed, and sheared during metamorphism. Layers in the gneiss can be relatively flat and planar or bent and twisted by up to three generations of folding that occurred during metamorphism.

Most of the layers in the gneiss are tilted 30°–60° to the east. Climbs that follow this plane of dominant layering tend to be lower angle and easier, such as the East Face routes on Buck and Teewinot Mountains. North and south faces cut across this dominant layering and thus tend to harbor steeper and more difficult climbs like those found in Death Canyon.

The layered gneiss includes minor occurrences of many different metamorphic rock types including amphibolite, migmatite, and schist. Amphibolite is a dark, coarse-grained metamorphic rock composed mainly of hornblende, plagioclase feldspar, and quartz. Migmatite refers to rocks that have undergone partial melting under extreme heat and pressure, but have not quite totally melted to become igneous rocks. The quartz and feldspar bands in migmatite are often wildly contorted because these light-colored minerals melt at lower temperatures than the darker minerals. Schist is a shiny, mica-rich rock that has undergone less intense metamorphism than gneiss.

A peculiar feature called bright-eyed gneiss occurs in some of the layered gneiss along the trail in Death Canyon, where conspicuous white feldspar halos surround dark, millimeter-scale magnetite grains. These formed during metamorphism as the central magnetite took in all the iron normally used to make biotite and hornblende, leaving the surrounding area void of these minerals and dominated by white feldspar.

Another rock type in the Tetons featuring "eyes" is the 2.8-billion-year-old augen gneiss. *Augen* is the German word for eyes, but unlike the bright-eyed gneiss, this gneiss lacks pupils. Augen gneiss contains distinct oblong, centimeter-scale white feldspar crystals that stand out against a darker-gray, fine-grained matrix. This rock type is not exposed over a very large area, but most of the excellent climbing on Mount Moran is composed primarily of augen gneiss. Augen gneiss typically forms from metamorphism of an igneous rock that already had large feldspars, such as granite.

Mount Owen Granite: The Best Rock for Climbing

Most of the best Teton climbs are found on the 2.55-billion-year-old Mount Owen granite. This golden, knobby-textured igneous rock with large crystals and intermittent fractures feels like it was made for climbing and scrambling. The central part of the range and the highest peaks are composed of Mount Owen granite, including Mount Owen, most of the Grand and Middle Tetons, all of Disappointment Peak and Nez Perce, the south side of Cloudveil Dome, and parts of Teewinot Mountain and the Snaz Buttress in Death Canyon. The great cragging in Teton Canyon is also mostly on Mount Owen granite.

Granite is a silica-rich intrusive igneous rock that forms when previously existing rocks completely melt to form new minerals that crystallize below Earth's surface. The Mount Owen granite is composed primarily of quartz, feldspar, plagioclase, biotite, and muscovite. This unit has traditionally been classified as a quartz monzonite (which contains more feldspar and less quartz than granite), but recent geochemical analyses place it in the granite category. The Mount Owen granite contains abundant pegmatite veins where individual crystals of quartz and feldspar can be up to several centimeters across.

Garnet is a minor constituent of the Mount Owen granite, but this mineral is familiar to Teton climbers because the eponymous canyon is used to approach so many classic routes in the central part of the range. Twelve-sided red-brown crystals of garnet occur in both the Mount Owen granite and its associated pegmatite. Garnets the size of softballs have been found in Garnet Canyon and on surrounding peaks. While it is certainly nice to look at, none of the garnet in the Tetons is gemstone quality because it has all been partially altered to other minerals during metamorphism.

The larger dark specks are garnet crystals in Mount Owen granite found along the trail in Garnet Canyon. The white band containing the garnets is mostly quartz and feldspar; some of the smaller dark minerals are biotite and hornblende. Many of the best climbs in the range are found on Mount Owen granite, a knobby-textured, silica-rich intrusive igneous rock.

Rendezvous Metagabbro: Rock Springs Buttress

The 2.69-billion-year-old Rendezvous Metagabbro is exposed around Jackson Hole Mountain Resort and the somewhat inappropriately named Granite Canyon. The excellent climbing at Rock Springs Buttress occurs on this unit. Gabbro is a coarse-grained igneous rock with dark, iron-rich minerals. The Rendezvous Metagabbro is a weakly metamorphosed gabbro that has retained its coarse-grained igneous texture with centimeter-scale hornblende and plagioclase grains.

Wyoming Province: Ancient Continents and Collisions

The 2.5- to 2.9-billion-year-old gneiss, granite, and metagabbro found in the Tetons are part of a broader region that geologists refer to as the Wyoming Province. The Wyoming Province encompasses mountain ranges where igneous and metamorphic rocks older than 2.5 billion years are exposed. This geologic province is centered on the state of Wyoming and includes the Teton Range, the Wind River Range, and the Beartooth, Bighorn, Laramie, and Granite Mountains. The Teton Range represents the western margin of the Wyoming Province, and the ancient rocks of this region are some of the oldest in North America.

When Earth formed 4.5 billion years ago, it was too hot for continents to exist. The oldest rocks in the world show us that the planet had cooled enough for continents to form by 4 billion years ago. The oldest rocks in the Wyoming Province are over 3 billion years old and are remnants of one of Earth's earliest continents. At that time in Earth's history, continents probably covered less than half the surface area they cover today. Oceans existed and so did life, but only in the form of single-celled bacteria and archaea.

From 2.9 to 2.5 billion years ago, the western margin of the Wyoming Province was an active plate boundary where a series of convergent tectonic events formed the gneiss, granite, and metagabbro that we climb on. This included smaller-scale collisions with island arcs and microcontinents, a larger-scale continent-to-continent collision, and ocean plate subduction. The layered gneiss in the Tetons formed when sedimentary and volcanic layers that had been deposited on the Wyoming Province continental margin were compressed and metamorphosed at depth during these collisions. The mineral composition of the Rendezvous Metagabbro suggests that it formed from subducted ocean plate material that partially melted and intruded into the overlying continental crust. The Mount Owen granite formed from the melting of metasedimentary rocks during a collision near the end of this period.

It is difficult to comprehend these incredibly old ages and easy to get lost in the onslaught of apparently slight differences in the ages of these most ancient events. However, the Mount Owen granite is 150 million years younger than the older metamorphic rocks found in the Tetons. As it was cooling and rising, the Mount Owen granite intruded into all the older gneisses; irregular boundaries and complex relationships can be seen throughout the range between these two units. In some places, large inclusions of layered gneiss became entrained in the rising melt of granite and now appear to be floating in the granite. This can be seen on the south side of the Grand Teton, where darker sections of gneiss (e.g., the Black Face pitch of the Durrance Direct [Lower Exum Ridge]) stand out against the surrounding lighter-colored granite. In other places, dikes of Mount Owen granite and its associated pegmatite intruded into fractures in the layered gneiss. For example, climbers hiking up Garnet Canyon will notice dramatic crisscrossing white stripes of granite pegmatite cutting across darker gneiss on the north face of Cloudveil Dome.

In addition to the eastward tilt of the layered gneiss, both the gneiss and granite tend to fracture and fault along two dominant planes: a steeply tilted north–south and east–west conjugate pair that intersect at roughly right angles. The orientations of these dominant weaknesses resulted from tectonic events as these rocks were forming over 2.5 billion years ago. The intermittent cracks that we climb in the Tetons tend to follow these vertical, perpendicular sets of fractures. Individual cracks tend to be short in the Tetons because the rocks are generally too uniform and strong (Mount Owen granite) or too heterogeneous (layered gneiss) for large fractures to propagate. These dominant planes of weakness in the oldest Teton rocks have persisted through geologic time, so younger tectonic events have tended to reactivate these ancient faults and fractures.

Diabase Dikes: Stripes through the Mountains

Perhaps the most visually striking rocks in the Tetons are the vertical black diabase dikes that cut straight through the older, lighter-colored gneiss and granite but not through the younger sedimentary rocks. The largest of these dikes splits the east face of Mount Moran and runs seven miles through the range with a width of 100 to 150 feet. Dikes that are 20 to 60 feet wide cut roughly east–west through the Middle Teton and the south side of the Grand Teton. There are numerous smaller black dikes throughout the Tetons and, as it turns out, the western US in general.

These black dikes are made of diabase, an intrusive igneous rock containing dark, coarse-grained, basalt-type minerals such as pyroxene, feldspar, hornblende, and biotite. The dikes tend to be nearly vertical and trend west-northwest, often following preexisting weaknesses in the granite and gneiss. They formed when hot molten material from Earth's mantle rose to fill cracks in the continental crust as the penultimate supercontinent Rodinia began to pull apart and break up around 770 million years ago.

In areas where the diabase dikes are more resistant to erosion than the surrounding rocks, the dikes protrude, as on the east face of Mount Moran adjacent to the CMC route. In many areas in the Tetons, the dikes are less resistant to erosion than the surrounding rocks so they erode away into deep gullies, couloirs, and clefts, as on the Middle and Grand Tetons. Old climbing routes ascend the obvious straight lines of the most prominent diabase dikes, but the rock is blocky, fractured, and loose, providing poor protection opportunities. Granites and gneisses near the dikes are often stained red due to alteration of minerals in the presence of iron-rich hydrothermal fluids as the dikes were emplaced. A prominent example of this red staining next to a black dike can be seen from the Lower Saddle along the base of the Exum, Petzoldt, and Underhill Ridges of the Grand Teton.

Younger Sedimentary Rocks: Flat Summits and Sport Climbs

In the core of the Teton Range, all the younger sedimentary rocks have been completely eroded away to expose the very old gneiss and granite. But the northern and southern parts of the range and the western slope remain blanketed by sedimentary deposits of various thicknesses. Seismic studies show that the valley of Jackson Hole is filled with up to 20,000 feet of sedimentary rock.

The oldest sedimentary rock in the Tetons is the 520-million-year-old Flathead Sandstone, which is a red-brown-white, quartz-rich beach deposit. Prominent exposures of this layer occur on the broad, flat-topped summits of Mount Moran, Bivouac Peak, Traverse Peak, and Rolling Thunder Mountain. These northern summits are broader and flatter than the sharp, crystalline peaks of the central part of the range because they have a horizontal layer of Flathead Sandstone on top.

The single-pitch sport climbing at Blacktail Butte is on 360-million-year-old Madison Limestone that has been tilted to near vertical. Although typically associated with the Tetons, Blacktail Butte is probably an anomalous fault block that slid down from the Gros Ventre Mountains. The Madison Limestone is mostly calcium carbonate from marine deposits and contains fossil corals, crinoids, and brachiopods. The climbs here can feel pretty polished, which is partly due to the high traffic that this convenient and scenic area gets; Blacktail Butte has also been glaciated, and limestone is a bit softer than the dolomite that makes up other nearby crags.

Climbing is also found on the 450-million-year-old Bighorn Dolomite, another fossiliferous marine deposit. Dolomite is similar to limestone, but some of the calcium carbonate has been altered by the addition of magnesium. The Bighorn Dolomite forms sharp, crimpy climbs and occasional cracks. It can be found at Corbet's and S&S Couloirs near the top of the aerial tram at Jackson Hole Mountain Resort (Peak 10,450) and at a few crags in Teton Canyon.

Laramide Orogeny: Initial Uplift of the Region

The area where the Tetons stand so loftily today was submerged by an ocean as recently as 80 million years ago. Uplift of the Teton region began around 70 million years ago with the Laramide orogeny. An orogeny is a mountain-building event, usually caused by the collision of two tectonic plates. This particular orogeny caused the uplift of its namesake Laramie Mountains along with the Wind River Range and Rocky Mountains.

Uplift in the Teton region during the Laramide orogeny occurred along three major faults. The Buck Mountain fault is a compressional or reverse fault that trends north–south just west of the range crest from Buck Mountain to Mount Moran. Older granite and gneiss have been thrust westward on top of younger sediments with up to 3,000 feet of offset along this fault. Part of the reason for the locations of the highest peaks in the Tetons is this extra boost provided by the Buck Mountain fault. Other major Laramide faults include the steeply dipping Forellen Peak fault in the northern Tetons and the Cache Creek fault, which cuts through Teton Pass and forms the southern boundary of the range.

Mountain ranges are usually uplifted along plate boundaries, but Laramide uplifts are located at least several hundred miles east of the western margin of the North American Plate. The usual explanation for this is that shallow subduction of the Farallon Plate under the North American continent transferred compressional forces far inland. Additionally, the western US has been stretched out since the Laramide orogeny by Basin and Range extensional faulting, so Laramide uplifts were originally only about half as far from the plate boundary as they are today. This transition from compression to extension was caused by the sinking of the Farallon Plate, which allowed for the influx of less dense material under North America and the growth of the strike-slip San Andreas fault, which pushed the zone of compressional tectonics farther north along the western margin of the continent. The Tetons are located at the northeastern edge of the Basin and Range Province.

By the end of the Laramide orogeny around 50 million years ago, northwest Wyoming would have had some elevated topography, but nothing like the modern Teton Range existed yet. The dramatic relief of the Tetons is primarily the result of uplift along the Teton fault and glacial carving.

The Grand Teton from the Lower Saddle. Large inclusions of darker-layered gneiss can be seen in the lighter-colored Mount Owen granite. A prominent black diabase dike cuts across the bottom of the steeper part of the mountain. Granite and gneiss next to the dike are stained red from the addition of iron when the dike was emplaced.

The Teton Fault and Yellowstone Hot Spot: Rapid Uplift

Most of the uplift of the Teton Range (and subsidence, or sinking, of Jackson Hole) has occurred along the Teton fault, which runs for 40 miles north-northeast along the entire eastern front of the range. The Teton fault is an extensional or normal fault that dips 45°–75° to the east, with the Teton block moving up to the west and the Jackson Hole block moving down to the east. The Teton Range is tilted westward with a steeper east side and gentler west side because of the orientation of the Teton fault. And despite the apparent flatness of Jackson Hole, the valley is also slightly tilted to the west because of this fault. Some recent studies have proposed that the Teton fault (and Teton Range) used to extend much farther north, possibly all the way to the Gallatin Range in Montana, but the encroachment of the Yellowstone Hot Spot obliterated the northern two-thirds of the range.

The Yellowstone Hot Spot began as a mantle plume around 16 million years ago under southwest Idaho and has since migrated to its current position under the national park, or so it would seem when looking at a map view of the hot spot's track through time. In fact, the entire North American Plate has been moving westward at a few centimeters per year over this interval, which has brought northwest Wyoming to the hot spot rather than vice versa. The Yellowstone Hot Spot got close enough to the Teton fault around 5 million years ago that the increased heat flow associated with the hot spot led to enhanced motion along the fault. Geologists are still untangling the details of the relationships between the Teton fault, the Yellowstone Hot Spot, Basin and Range extension, and loading and unloading from glaciers.

One of the great debates of Teton geology concerns the age of the Teton

Fault scarp along the Teton fault at the base of Rockchuck Peak from the Cathedral Group turnout. The Teton fault is a normal fault that dips 45°–75° to the east, with the Teton block moving up to the west and the Jackson Hole block moving down to the east. The offset between the two white lines is about 60 feet.

fault. Some researchers argue that significant motion on the Teton fault initiated around 15 million years ago due to Basin and Range extension. Others argue that virtually all the offset along the Teton fault occurred after the arrival of the Yellowstone Hot Spot around 5 million years ago. Recent work suggests that the Teton fault may have initiated at different times along its length, and these questions continue to be a field of active research. There is general agreement that most of the uplift of the Teton Range occurred along the Teton fault in the last 2 to 10 million years.

Regardless of exactly when it started, a lot of motion has occurred along the Teton fault in a geologically short period of time. West of the fault, the Flathead Sandstone sits 6,000 feet above the valley floor on the flat-topped summit of Mount Moran. This same layer has been found east of the fault 20,000 feet below the surface in Jackson Hole using seismic imaging techniques. An offset of 26,000 feet over 5 to 15 million years requires average offset rates of a few inches per century. This amount of offset is typical for the central part of the Teton fault from about Death Canyon to Mount Moran, but the northern and southern segments of the fault have experienced only about half that. The central Tetons have thus received a double boost from faulting: first from the Laramide-age Buck Mountain fault and later from increased uplift along this portion of the Teton fault.

The easiest place to see an obvious offset along the Teton fault is from the Cathedral Group turnout, where a 60-foot-tall scarp is visible to the west along the lower reaches of Rockchuck Peak. Conspicuous small landslide scars off the northwest shores of Jenny and Leigh Lakes are also present right on the Teton fault. In some places the Teton fault can be traced as a single line, but like most other faults, along most of its length the Teton fault is more of a zone of faulting with multiple closely spaced parallel segments. For example, from the trail junction 1.7 miles in from the Lupine Meadows trailhead, the Valley Trail splits off down a minor valley that follows one segment of the Teton fault while the Garnet Canyon trail goes uphill along a separate segment of the fault that exposes a natural spring.

Motion along the Teton fault has occurred during discrete major earthquakes. Many thousands or tens of thousands of large earthquakes have been responsible for the overall uplift of the Teton Range and subsidence of Jackson Hole along various segments of the Teton fault over time. The Teton fault is considered an active fault, and direct evidence exists for multiple magnitude 7 or greater earthquakes in the last 15,000 years. But the fault has been conspicuously quiescent over the last 5,000 years, leading some to speculate that it is overdue for a large rupture. Some studies suggest that the Teton fault is still capable of producing up to a magnitude 7 or 7.5 earthquake. Others have pointed out that glacial unloading following the end of the last ice age probably caused increased rates of fault motion starting around 15,000 years ago that then slowed down for the last few millennia.

Part of the reason the Tetons are so steep and dramatic is that they were uplifted rapidly along a young fault. The other major influences on the topography and landforms of the Teton Range are the erosion and deposition by repeated glaciations over the last 2 to 3 million years.

Glaciations: Carving the Landscape

Northern Hemisphere continental glaciation began around 3 million years ago and intensified around 1.8 million years ago. A continental ice sheet has persisted in northern polar regions over this time, with glaciers growing and shrinking over regular 40,000- and 100,000-year cycles controlled by changes in Earth's orbit. The biggest northern continental ice sheet never quite reached the Tetons, but large ice sheets formed around Yellowstone and flowed south. Mountain glaciers in the Tetons likely formed during each of these repeated glaciations. In the Tetons, the last two glacial events wiped out the evidence for all the preceding ones, so we turn our attention to the most recent Pinedale and penultimate Bull Lake glacial events.

During the Bull Lake glaciation, which lasted from about 160,000 to 130,000 years ago, a large continental ice sheet formed over the highlands around Yellowstone. The migration of the hot spot carved out a broad east–west lowland track that continues to allow winter Pacific storms to penetrate far inland, bringing abundant snowfall to the region. The Yellowstone ice sheet flowed south through

Jackson Hole and extended almost to Hoback Junction. It carved out the valley and scoured Blacktail Butte and the Gros Ventre Buttes. Glacial ice was around 2,000 feet thick in the town of Jackson during the Bull Lake glaciation, covering Snow King Mountain. Mountain glaciers formed in the Tetons during this event, but most erosional and depositional landforms from the Bull Lake glaciation have been overprinted by younger Pinedale events.

The Pinedale glaciation was the most recent major ice age in the Tetons, lasting from about 35,000 to 15,000 years ago. Pinedale glaciers were less extensive than their Bull Lake counterparts but still substantial. The Yellowstone ice sheet reached just south of Jackson Lake during the Pinedale glaciation. The hefty mass of this glacier was sufficient to depress Earth's surface, and when the ice sheet melted it deposited a barrier of debris called a moraine along its southern margin. Glacial meltwater filled the depression enclosed by this moraine to form Jackson Lake. Jenny, Bradley, Taggart, and Phelps Lakes were formed in a similar fashion but by mountain glaciers coming out of the major canyons of the Teton Range. Almost all the modern lakes in the Tetons were formed at the end of the Pinedale glaciation when these glaciers began to melt. The lakes at the mouths of the canyons formed around 14,000 to 15,000 years ago, while higher-elevation lakes such as Lake Solitude formed after the glaciers had receded farther up the canyons around 11,000 years ago. The floor of Garnet Canyon was exposed around 11,000 to 12,000 years ago.

Pinedale glaciers were up to 1,000 or 2,000 feet thick in the major canyons of the Tetons. They carved U-shaped valleys such as Cascade, Garnet, and Death Canyons. Climbers will notice the difference between the smooth, glacier-polished walls lower in these canyons and the more textured, knobby rocks of the unglaciated higher elevations. The steep, pointy peaks of the central Tetons are classic examples of horns, where glaciers have eroded valleys on all sides, leaving prominent isolated summits. Climbers often think of an arête as a feature like Irene's Arête, but to geologists this term refers to a narrow, rocky ridgeline formed when two parallel mountain glaciers carve neighboring valleys, such as the sharp ridge between the South Teton and Nez Perce.

Most of the carving of the Teton Range occurred during glacial periods because glaciers are much more effective at breaking down hard rocks and transporting eroded material than water or wind. During an ice age, glaciers accumulate at the higher-elevation heads of canyons in cirques and then flow downhill when they reach sufficient mass. Individual ice ages lasted tens of thousands of years, and glaciers would have ebbed and flowed substantially even within those periods. These glaciers picked up everything from microscopic mineral grains to massive boulders as they plowed through the Teton canyons. They also ground and scoured bedrock on the canyon floors and walls, removing material and sometimes leaving behind linear striations that indicate the direction of glacier travel on more resistant bedrock. Some of the most convenient climbing in the Tetons occurs where glaciers brought erratic boulders to the base of the mountains, such as the those found at Bouldertown, on Boulder Island, and near the Jenny Lake campground.

Modern Glaciers: Little Ice Age and New Insights

Eleven active glaciers are officially listed on the Grand Teton National Park handout *Glaciers and Glacial Features*. Ten glaciers have been previously named on US Geological Survey maps: Teton, Middle Teton, Teepe, Schoolroom, Petersen, Falling Ice, Skillet, and East, Middle, and West Triple glaciers. In addition, there is another unnamed glacier near Glacier Peak. At least three of these (Teepe, Peterson, and the one beneath Glacier Peak) may have lost enough ice volume that they are no longer flowing and are therefore considered to be inactive. There are also several unnamed ice/snowfields and rock glaciers scattered throughout the park.

The traditional understanding has been that the larger glaciers from the Pinedale glaciation melted away completely by around 11,000 years ago and the modern glaciers in the Tetons are remnants from a minor cold interval called the Little Ice Age, which lasted from about 1250 to 1900 CE. However, a recent study of sediment cores from Delta and Surprise Lakes shows that the Teton Glacier has existed in some form for at least the past 10,000 years. The Teton Glacier was probably

Crossing a crevasse on the Teton Glacier cowboy-style. The Teton Glacier is the largest of the 10 modern glaciers in the Tetons. Recent research shows that the Teton Glacier has existed in some form for at least the last 10,000 years, reaching its maximum extent over this time period during the Little Ice Age (1250–1900 CE).

a rock glacier or small debris-covered glacier from 10,000 to 6,300 years ago; since 6,300 years ago, the Teton Glacier has been a glacier, reaching its maximum extent during the Little Ice Age and generally shrinking since then. The extensive moraines at the Moraine campsites in upper Garnet Canyon and between Teton Glacier and Delta Lake are deposits from the Little Ice Age. Climbers will notice that these moraines are much less consolidated and more unstable to travel on than the older Pinedale moraines, such as the tree-covered ridges leading up to the Phelps Lake Overlook or the 1.7-mile trail junction on the Garnet Canyon Trail.

Glaciers start to form when enough snow accumulates in an area that it gets compressed under its own weight and recrystallizes into denser ice. This icefield then becomes a glacier when it grows big enough to flow downhill. This flow occurs because the mass of overlying ice provides enough pressure to melt a thin layer at the bottom of the glacier, which lubricates the boundary between the ground and the glacier. Variations in friction between different parts of the glacier also cause ice to flow at different rates within the glacier. Bergschrunds are large cracks that mark the boundary between non-moving steeper ice and the flowing glacier. These can be formidable barriers to travel even on the smaller glaciers of the Tetons. Crevasses tend to form along the margins of a glacier and at convexities where the upper parts of a glacier are moving at different speeds. Crevasses form in the upper brittle part of glaciers and can be up to 150 feet deep. Dangerous moats can also be present where glaciers, snowfields, or icefields meet rock. Climbers should be aware of the hazards of bergschrunds, crevasses, moats, icefall, and rockfall when traveling on or near glaciers in the Tetons.

Glacier flow tends to be sporadic rather than continuous, characterized by surges and standstills. A glacier is considered active if there is evidence for modern flow. A few of the largest remaining glaciers in the Tetons are still active, with ice at the center of the Teton Glacier moving at around 30 feet per year during surges. Some of the smaller glaciers in the Tetons are probably not still moving and thus are not true glaciers anymore. Glaciers in the Tetons have generally been losing mass since the end of the Little Ice Age, with increased rates of loss in the past few decades. An average 25 percent surface area loss for the Teton, Middle Teton, and Teepe Glaciers from 1967 to 2006 has been primarily attributed to warmer summers (rather than less snowy winters). Smaller glaciers seem to be melting faster than larger ones. It is likely that this trend will continue, but it is also possible that mini versions of the biggest Teton glaciers will persist in the coldest nooks of the range. Glaciers in the Tetons are being actively monitored and studied. The combination of increased summer temperatures and the destabilization of glaciers, icefields, and snowfields has been shown to increase objective hazards due to rockfall in other ranges of the world; climbers in the Tetons would be wise to continue to exercise caution in this continually changing alpine environment.

Erosion: Rockfalls and Landslides

During warmer periods between or after ice ages such as today, weathering in the Tetons tends to be dominated by freeze-thaw frost wedging, so most erosion occurs during rockfalls and landslides. Mountain streams can transport fine-grained sediment, but larger material like boulders will remain in the canyons until it can be removed by glaciers. The pattern of rockfalls and landslides is stochastic, meaning that predicting any one event is impossible, but some general trends have been observed. Exposure ages of talus deposits show that the highest rockfall rates seem to occur right after glaciation. The highest rockfall rates today tend to occur at mid-elevations, around 10,000 to 11,000 feet, near the heads of cirques and along faults. The fixed rope through the headwall in upper Garnet Canyon just below the Lower Saddle is a high-traffic example of such an area. North faces have higher erosion rates and more lichen than south faces, so most classic climbs tend to be on southerly aspects. Very little erosion occurs on resistant ridge crests.

A massive landslide occurred on June 23, 1925, on Sheep Mountain (Sleeping Indian) in the Gros Ventre Range. The scar from this event is visible from many places in the Tetons. A combination of factors contributed to this slide, but it occurred after rapid snowmelt and a series of large storms saturated the ground. Debris from this slope failure dammed the Gros Ventre River at Lower Slide Lake. This landslide is a good reminder of the weakening effects of water on soil and rock. Climbers should be extra careful about rockfall and landslide hazards in the days during and after large storms and when snow is melting quickly. It is prudent to wait a day after a significant rain before climbing many of the routes in the Tetons.

In most mountain ranges, the drainage divide follows the crest of the range, like how the Continental Divide runs along the crest of the Wind River Range. In the Tetons, the drainage divide is located west of the range crest near the park boundary. This peculiar pattern results from the rapid uplift along the Teton fault on the eastern front of the range. Compared with the gentler west side of the range, this rapid uplift has allowed steeper streams and glaciers to cut deeper canyons that now extend east through the range crest.

Are the Tetons Still Rising?

Long-term offset rates along the Teton fault are on the order of a few inches per century, with the Jackson Hole block subsiding more than the Teton Range has been uplifted. Geologists expected to find similar motion occurring when they started measuring modern fault offset. GPS measurements in the last couple of decades have shown that the Teton block is rising at a rate of around 10 inches per century while the Jackson Hole block is also rising, although at a much slower rate. This surprising result is probably caused by heating and inflation due to the Yellowstone Hot Spot. So, yes, the Tetons are still rising. The Grand Teton is probably around a foot taller today than when the Owen-Spalding party climbed the peak in 1898.

Another apparent uplift of the Teton Range has resulted from updating the vertical datum that references sea level in the area. This guidebook makes the practical choice to follow USGS topographic maps and use the 1927 vertical datum as the basis for reporting elevations. For example, the Grand Teton has an elevation of 13,770 feet with the 1927 vertical datum. In some other resources, climbers will notice that peak elevations have been updated to the 1988 vertical datum, which gives an elevation of 13,775 feet for the Grand Teton.

Conclusion: Geology of the Best Teton Climbs

Many of the best routes in the Tetons share one major geologic similarity: they are made of Mount Owen granite. This includes the Exum Ridge, Petzoldt Ridge, Golden Pillar, North Ridge, and Bean's Shining Wall of Storms of the Grand Teton; Irene's Arête and the East Ridge of Disappointment Peak; Mount Owen's Serendipity and Intrepidity Arêtes; Emotional Rescue and the other routes on the northwest face of the Enclosure; and the Snaz and Caveat Emptor in Death Canyon. The Mount Owen granite exists only in the Tetons, and the presence of this rock unit and its associated pegmatite with large crystals is part of what makes climbing in the range so fun and unique.

The Grand Teton stands as the highest peak in the range partly because it is composed of the most homogeneous portion of the Mount Owen granite. The central portion of this very strong rock is particularly resistant to weathering and erosion. The Grand Teton is also in the central part of the range that has been uplifted the most along both the Buck Mountain and Teton faults. This combination of a strong homogeneous rock type and enhanced uplift along faults also explains why Mount Moran is so much taller than its neighbors. However, Mount Moran and its classic south buttress routes consist mostly of augen gneiss. This augen gneiss is particularly uniform and fine-grained because Mount Moran was the center of a recently identified zone of deformation, where stress accumulated during a collision 2.62 billion years ago that joined the northern and southern Tetons.

East faces and ridges tend to have lower-angle scrambles and easier climbs because they follow the layering in the gneiss and the tilt of the range from the Teton fault. North and south faces are often steeper because they cut across this dominant layering. South faces and ridges generally have the most classic moderate-to-difficult climbs in the Tetons because they are steep and have less weathering and lichen than northern aspects.

The best Teton climbs tend to be on the highest central peaks, on southern or eastern aspects, and on Mount Owen granite. But, of course, there are exceptions to all these criteria. Great routes exist in the southern Tetons and in the remote northern part of the range, on northern and even western aspects, and on gneiss, metagabbro, limestone, and dolomite. Wherever you climb in the Teton Range, you are bound to come across some amazing examples of the 3-billion-year series of geologic events that produced these incredible mountains.

REFERENCES

Brown, S. J., J. R. Thigpen, J. A. Spotila, W. C. Krugh, L. M. Tranel, and D. A. Orme. "Onset Timing and Slip History of the Teton Fault, Wyoming: A Multidisciplinary Reevaluation." *Tectonics* 36, no. 11 (November 2017): 2669–92.

Byrd, J. O. D., R. B. Smith, and J. W. Geissman. "The Teton Fault, Wyoming: Topographic Signature, Neotectonics, and Mechanisms of Deformation." *Journal of Geophysical Research* 99, no. B10 (1994): 20095–122.

Chamberlain, K. R., C. D. Frost, and B. R. Frost. "Early Archean to Mesoproterozoic Evolution of the Wyoming Province: Archean Origins to Modern Lithospheric Architecture." *Canadian Journal of Earth Sciences* 40, no. 10 (October 2003): 1357–74.

Edmunds, J., G. Tootle, G. Kerr, R. Sivanpillai, and L. Pochop. "Glacier Variability (1967–2006) in the Teton Range, Wyoming, United States." *Journal of the American Water Resources Association* 48, no. 1 (2011): 187–96.

Foster, D., S. H. Brocklehurst, and R. L. Gawthorpe. "Glacial-Topographic Interactions in the Teton Range, Wyoming." *Journal of Geophysical Research* 115, no. F1 (2010). https://doi.org/10.1029/2008JF001135.

Frost, B. R., C. D. Frost, M. Cornia, K. R. Chamberlain, and R. Kirkwood. "The Teton – Wind River Domain: A 2.68–2.67 Ga Active Margin in the Western Wyoming Province." *Canadian Journal of Earth Sciences* 43, no. 10 (2006): 1489–510.

Frost, B. R., S. M. Swapp, C. D. Frost, D. A. Bagdonas, and K. R. Chamberlain. "Neoarchean Tectonic History of the Teton Range: Record of Accretion against the Present-Day Western Margin of the Wyoming Province." *Geosphere* 14, no. 3 (2018): 1008–30.

Hampel, A., R. Hetzel, and A. L. Densmore. "Postglacial Slip-Rate Increase on the Teton Normal Fault, Northern Basin and Range Province, Caused by Melting of the Yellowstone Ice Cap and Deglaciation of the Teton Range?" *Geology* 35, no. 12 (2007): 1107–110.

Larsen, D. J., S. E. Crump, and A. Blumm. "Alpine Glacier Resilience and Neoglacial Fluctuations Linked to Holocene Snowfall Trends in the Western United States." *Science Advances* 6 (2020): eabc7661.

Larsen, D. J., M. S. Finkenbinder, M. B. Abbott, and A. R. Ofstun. "Deglaciation and Postglacial Environmental Changes in the Teton Mountain Range Recorded at Jenny Lake, Grand Teton National Park, WY." *Quaternary Science Reviews* 138 (2016): 62–75.

Love, J. D., J. C. Reed Jr., and A. C. Christiansen. *Geologic Map of Grand Teton National Park, Wyoming.* Miscellaneous Investigations Series Map I-2031, 1:62,500 scale. US Geological Survey, 1992.

Love, J. D., J. C. Reed Jr., and K. L. Pierce. *Creation of the Teton Landscape.* Moose, WY: Grand Teton Natural History Association, 2003.

Pierce, K. L., J. M. Licciardi, J. M. Good, and C. Jaworowski. *Pleistocene Glaciation of the Jackson Hole Area, Wyoming.* Professional Paper 1835. Reston, VA: US Geological Survey, 2018.

Puskas, C. M., R. B. Smith, C. M. Meertens, and W. L. Chang. "Crustal Deformation of the Yellowstone–Snake River Plain Volcano-Tectonic System: Campaign and Continuous GPS Observations, 1987–2004." *Journal of Geophysical Research* 112 (2007): B03401.

Conrad Anker on the Horse, just below the summit of the Grand Teton (Photo by Jimmy Chin)

Climbing in the Tetons

This chapter is designed to assist climbers with trip planning. It opens with an overview of the general weather patterns found in the Teton Range and then details some of the rules that the National Park Service (NPS) has set in place for Grand Teton National Park, generally having to do with backcountry overnight use. Mountain rescue, guiding services, climbing equipment, and bouldering and sport-climbing opportunities are also covered. Because this range is so accessible, any number of traverses, enchainments, and linkups are possible, limited only by a climber's imagination; one section is dedicated to some of these many adventures that await.

Teton Climatology

Jim Woodmencey, Meteorologist

Every climb has its season. This is true in the Teton Range, as it is in most of the other great mountain ranges of the world. The seasonal fluctuations in the weather in the Tetons, or more comprehensively, the climate of this place, will have relevance to the choice, and perhaps ultimately the success, of one's chosen climb. For instance, mid-July—when temperatures in the valley are hitting 90°F—is not the season to attempt to climb Run-Don't-Walk Couloir on Mount Owen. And attempting to climb the Owen-Spalding on the Grand Teton in January in a T-shirt and tennis shoes might be considered somewhat dim-witted. That's not to say that these two feats have not been tried, nor should you rule out the possibility of an anomalous record-breaking weather situation that could allow these ascents to be accomplished, in the aforementioned seasons, quite successfully.

Some knowledge of the climate of this area may assist you in planning for certain routes in certain seasons. More specifically, an understanding of the seasonal weather patterns and the potential extremes of weather in these mountains will not only increase one's chances for success but also decrease one's chances of getting into a dangerous and life-threatening situation. If nothing else, it should impart a greater respect for the power of these mountains and the weather that occurs here.

It should be noted that the weather has played a role in many of the search and rescue missions launched by the Jenny Lake Rangers over the years. People get stuck in these mountains in bad weather, and often they can't get out on their own.

The Tetons lie in a climate zone classified as "alpine tundra," flanked by "alpine" valleys; therefore, one would expect an alpine environment to exist. That would necessarily denote some rather harsh weather, a good portion of the time, to produce such a climate. A region just doesn't qualify as "alpine" in the climate world with pleasant weather all the time. Alpine regions, by definition, are characterized by ample precipitation, which sustains the forests they contain and makes for cool summers. Alpine tundra regions—the peaks themselves—are classified as very cold and windy.

Regular visitors to the higher Tetons have experienced the strong winds of the Lower Saddle, they have descended through raging storms with the snow blowing sideways and the visibility near zero, and they have had to worry about hypothermia and frostbite as they made their way, as fast as possible, to the relative safety of the valley—not in the middle of winter, but right in the middle of July, supposedly the hottest and driest month of the year in the Tetons. Although not the rule for that time of year, these exceptional conditions can present themselves, at some point, almost every summer.

For the winter enthusiast, the Tetons have proven themselves time and again to have some of the harshest weather on the face of the earth, with -20°F to -30°F temperatures at 12,000 feet, steady winds exceeding 120 miles per hour, and

Climbing ranger and meteorologist Jim Woodmencey in the Black Ice Couloir during a winter ascent (Photo by Renny Jackson)

overnight snowstorms that raise the avalanche danger so high that retreat from some locations in the range would be ill-advised. On the other hand, there are those handful of days in the middle of winter when it is so calm that it would be possible to light a match at the Lower Saddle or wear a light shirt in 30°F temperatures under cobalt-blue skies.

The timing of the weather is key to the success of any climb in this range, at any time of the year. To plan a trip here in July to climb the Grand Teton by one of its classic routes is usually a good choice, as July is the warmest and driest month of the year. Knowing whether the preceding winter or spring was wetter or drier than normal, and whether it has been snowing up high in the previous two weeks, might be additional pertinent, timely information to have. The climate here, as in any location, is a collection of averages from 30 or more years of weather data. What's happening any given week can easily be way above or below what is considered normal for that time of year.

With that caveat, it is still recommended that you do some planning from a "monthly average" perspective. Also, the longer your stay, the better your chances are of hitting a particular season's ideal conditions.

NORMALS

The climate station for Moose, Wyoming, is located behind Park Headquarters, where it has been since 1959. It is the closest daily climatological station to the Teton mountains. The data presented for temperature and precipitation throughout this section comes from the Moose station. The averages and records are from the long-term record, between 1959 and 2016. This station's normals are quite a bit different from the normals seen in the town of Jackson, which is less than 15 miles farther south and 200 feet lower in elevation. There is no climate station in the mountains; however, Jackson Hole Mountain Resort and the Bridger-Teton Avalanche Center (BTAC) lab there have collected over 20 years of winter weather data from the 9,000-to-9,500-foot elevation.

Wind data are more difficult to summarize because they contain both speed and direction and are very sensitive to the exact location where the measurement is taken. The best information on the mountain winds has been obtained at the Upper Rendezvous Station (10,300 feet) at Jackson Hole Mountain Resort near the south end of the range. These data show that summertime wind directions are predominately from the southwest and west, with a speed of over 20 miles per hour about 10 percent of the time, and an average speed of about 10 miles per hour.

On any given day there will be radical differences in the weather both linearly, from the south end of the range to the north end, and vertically, from the valley floor to the ridgetops. In general, changes in the atmosphere will occur more rapidly in the vertical. Temperature, wind speed, and precipitation amounts and intensity can be significantly different, at the same time, between the valley floor and 11,000 feet. This is a consideration often disregarded by or not inherently obvious to the uninitiated, as can be observed on any summer day as people leave the trailhead in 70°F weather in a T-shirt and shorts for a climb of a peak, with temperatures at 11,000 feet in the mid-30s and windchill temperatures on top hovering at around 5°F in a 30-mile-per-hour wind. Carrying the proper clothing to accommodate changing conditions is imperative most of the year.

THE SEASONS

Characterizing the seasons around Jackson Hole and the surrounding mountains is best put with the old adage: "There are nine months of winter and three months of bad skiing." Some years there are only a couple of weeks of bad skiing; others, we have up to four months where the skiing isn't very good! Still, there are a few observations to be made regarding each season, both from personal experience and from the climate data.

One can infer several things by perusing the climate data. First, it is a good assumption that the months with the most precipitation also have the greatest abundance of cloudy days, and conversely. (See *Figure 1*.) Second, temperatures on a daily basis will fluctuate greatly, depending heavily on the amount of cloud cover each day. (See *Figure 2*.) A clear night will produce much colder temperatures in the valley overnight than a cloudy one, even as a cloudy day will keep daytime high temperatures cooler than the averages shown.

Average Monthly Precipitation (inches) Moose, WY

(Average annual precipitation 21.34")

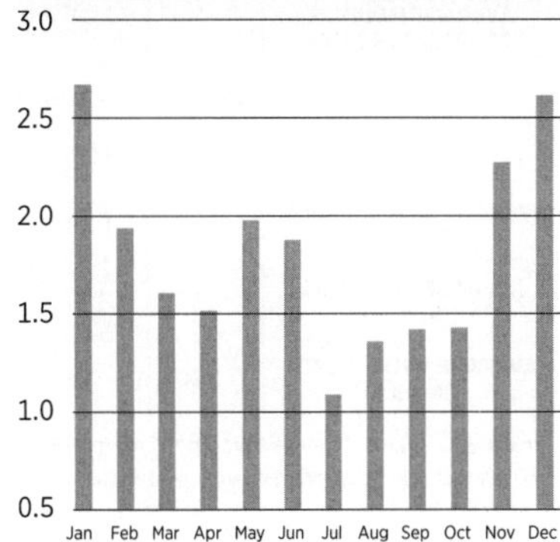

FIGURE 1. Source: MountainWeather™ meteorologist Jim Woodmencey (mountainweather.com)

Average Monthly Max/Min Temperatures (°F) Moose, WY

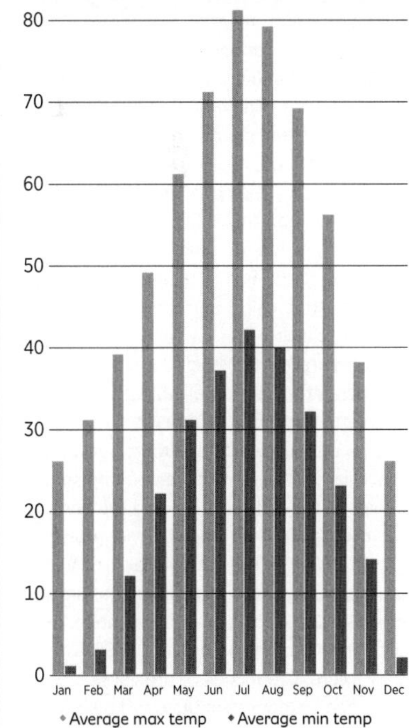

FIGURE 2. Source: MountainWeather™ meteorologist Jim Woodmencey (mountainweather.com)

Monthly Climate Summary for Moose, WY

	JAN	FEB	MAR	APR	MAY	JUN	JUL	AUG	SEP	OCT	NOV	DEC	ANNUAL
AVERAGE MAXIMUM TEMPERATURE (°F)	26	31	39	49	61	71	81	79	69	56	38	26	52
AVERAGE MINIMUM TEMPERATURE (°F)	1	3	12	22	31	37	42	40	32	23	14	2	22

ALL-TIME RECORD HIGH TEMPERATURE = 97°F ON AUGUST 15, 2003 ALL-TIME RECORD LOW TEMPERATURE = -46°F ON JANUARY 1, 1979

	JAN	FEB	MAR	APR	MAY	JUN	JUL	AUG	SEP	OCT	NOV	DEC	ANNUAL
AVERAGE PRECIPITATION (INCHES)	2.62	1.89	1.61	1.52	1.95	1.74	1.15	1.33	1.40	1.44	2.14	2.55	21.34
AVERAGE SNOWFALL (INCHES)	43	29	20	10	2	0.1	0	0	0.4	5	23	39.5	172
AVERAGE SNOW DEPTH (INCHES)	27	33	30	12	0	0	0	0	0	0	4	16	10

FIGURE 3. Source: MountainWeather™ meteorologist Jim Woodmencey (mountainweather.com)
NOTE: Includes all verified data available from 1959–2016 from the Moose, WY, climate station.

It would be reasonable in a given month to expect daytime temperatures to be plus or minus 10°F from the monthly averages. (See *Figure 3*.)

Spring: By the end of March winter is waning, and daytime high temperatures in the valley are well above freezing, up into the 40s. On a sunny day, the season's first climbers can be found on the south face of the Blacktail Butte practice rock at midday. In the mountains the snowpack is at its maximum; with a good freeze overnight, the spring skiing and climbing is at its best, and many of the peaks are skied into the middle of May. By then the valley is getting muddy, and climbers and skiers must endure a mile or so of quagmire to get to the receding snow line. New snowstorms on the valley floor are still a possibility in the month of May. May is also the wettest spring month, and afternoon cloud buildup over the mountains is more commonplace.

Summer: By the first of June, the snow line has retreated to well above the valley floor and afternoon thunderstorms over the mountains are beginning to show up more regularly. The chances of long spells of wet weather dwindle toward the end of the month. Of the three summer months (June, July, and August), June is the wettest. July is normally the hottest and the driest month of the year in the range. An exception was the summer of 1993, when there were 3.29 inches of precipitation recorded at Moose for July, and over 6 feet of snow fell that month at the Lower Saddle. This went on to become the coldest and wettest summer in Jackson Hole history. Thunderstorms and the danger of lightning, most often in the afternoon hours, are prevalent through the month of August. Even so, July and August are the months most popular with climbers: the weather is usually the most pleasant, average precipitation is lowest, and the hours of daylight are significantly longer than the rest of the year—an important consideration at this latitude. (See *Figure 4*.)

Fall: The days become significantly shorter into and through September. The weather can still remain quite nice, even up high in the mountains, though with slightly cooler temperatures. However, climbers should be aware that September usually brings with it the first good snowstorm in the high mountains, and this can ice over even the south-facing routes on the major peaks. Typically, there are some nice stretches of fall, or even summerlike, weather into October, but the frequency and reliability of these days from year to year are hit and miss. By November, winter has settled into at least the mountains, sometimes without enough snow to ski but with too much snow for casual walking.

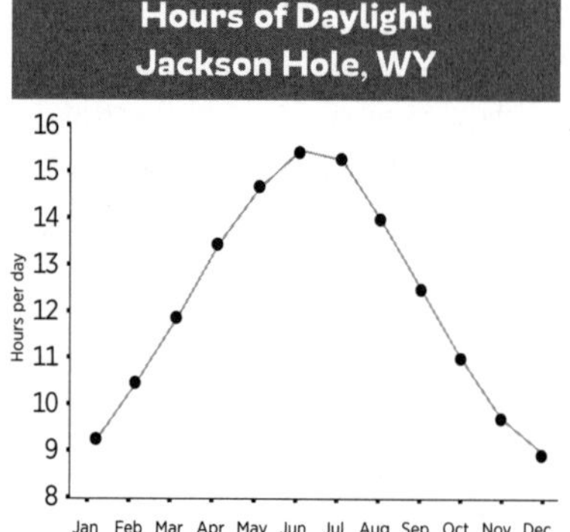

FIGURE 4. Latitude = 43°22'N, Longitude = 110°26'W

Winter: The Tetons can have wintry conditions almost any month of the year, but December and January are typified by a lot of snowfall and very few clear days. There are periods when high pressure builds over the northern Rockies and the Tetons experience a two-week drought, but more often than not it is hard to find a stretch of more than four or five days in a row from December to February without measurable precipitation in the valley. Keep in mind, also, that there are days when it is snowing in the mountains and not snowing on the valley floor. There are also many days, throughout the year, when it will be cloudy in the mountains and, at the same time, sunny over the valley.

A comparison of the amount of snowfall in the mountains versus the valley shows that December and January are the snowiest months of the year and that during each of the four winter months, December through March, the snowfall at around 9,500 feet at Jackson Hole Mountain Resort is almost consistently twice that recorded at the valley floor station in Moose. (See *Figure 5*.) Again, it should be stressed that it is possible in any winter month to experience more than twice the normal snowfall amount, or in dry years to receive half the normal amount of snow.

Another wintertime weather phenomenon worth mentioning is the inversion. In the winter months, especially December

Average Monthly Snowfall (in.)

MONTH	MOOSE, WY (6,450)	MOUNTAINS (9.500)
December	39.5	79
January	29	85
February	29	72
March	20	66

FIGURE 5. Data taken from Moose, Wyoming, climate data, 1959–2016, and from Jackson Hole Mountain Resort, 1974–2018. These are the monthly averages for both locations. The extremes for both locations vary widely, and it is possible for a given month to receive more than double the average snowfall shown or to have an entire month go by in the winter with less than half the average monthly snowfall.

through early February, temperature inversions will set up during periods of high pressure or clear skies. An inversion, by definition, is when the air temperature rises with height; normally temperatures get colder as elevation increases. During an inversion the mountains are warmer as the cold air drains to the valley floor. This is also, in general, the best time for winter ascents of the higher peaks. It can be brutally cold in the valley (-10°F to -30°F) and, at the same time, a relatively pleasant 10°F to 20°F up in the mountains.

For the sake of trivia, the official records for maximum and minimum temperatures for Moose, Wyoming, are 97°F from August 2003 and -46°F from January 1979. Those are the extremes of temperature, which are certainly not approached on a regular basis.

WEATHER RESOURCES

To the mountaineer, the weather forecast is a requisite item. Without one, climbers would be negligent in their approach to the Teton Range. It is important to gather as much information about the weather as possible *before* going into the mountains and to pay attention to the warning signs; not only will this increase your chances for success, but it will also ensure your safety. To echo David Brower, these are big mountains and they can create their own weather.

A variety of sources provide weather forecasts for any location in the Tetons, with the National Weather Service (NWS) being probably the best option for this type of forecast. General weather pattern information is also pertinent; this can be obtained through NWS Discussions, from both the Riverton and Pocatello NWS offices. A wide variety of additional forecast information and weather maps can be found online. For Teton-specific weather and climate information, as well as weather maps, visit www.mountainweather.com, maintained by Jim Woodmencey, the author of this climatology section of the guidebook.

The Jenny Lake Ranger Station usually has the most current weather information for the mountains and also the most current conditions reports for specific climbing routes.

In the winter, the Bridger-Teton Avalanche Center (BTAC) can be called (307-733-2664) for the latest avalanche hazard and mountain weather forecast; this is an invaluable resource in the Teton Range in the winter, from the first of December through early April. To view the forecast online, visit www.jhavalanche.org.

Once you are in the mountains, an indispensable tool for updated weather information is a National Oceanic and Atmospheric Administration (NOAA) weather radio. This is a lightweight and simple means by which to hear what is going on in the atmosphere while out on an extended trip. This is a 24/7 service provided nationwide by the NWS and can be received with a special radio or with any receiver with the proper frequency programmed in. (Many models are available from electronics stores and other retailers for as low as $30.) The closest broadcast station to the Tetons is in Pocatello, Idaho—frequency 162.55 MHz—and can be received from many locations around the range, especially up at the ridge crests.

National Park Service Policy

Since the Teton Range lies almost entirely within the boundaries of Grand Teton National Park, climbing and camping in the Tetons are subject to regulations designed to protect the natural resources and promote safety. Park administrators are charged with the dual and difficult responsibility of overseeing valid recreational use by climbers and maintaining the protection of park resources. The National Park Service (NPS) rangers directly in charge of the administration of the Teton backcountry, the Jenny Lake Rangers, are for the most part climbers themselves and understand that "the freedom of the hills" is an integral part of being a mountaineer. But they also understand that reasonable backcountry regulations are essential to protect the park for future generations. Certain limitations are both unavoidable and understandable considering the hordes of visitors who come to this outstandingly beautiful but compact mountain range each year. Individually we may hike, camp, and climb without leaving apparent evidence of our passage, but collectively we can have a massive impact.

RESOURCE PROTECTION AND LEAVE NO TRACE

Climbing in the Teton Range is now more popular than ever, and the number of climbers visiting the range annually has grown at an astonishing rate over the last few decades. As the main user group of the mountainous region of Grand Teton National Park, and especially as a group that primarily travels off-trail, climbers have a particular responsibility to keep impacts on the environment to an absolute minimum.

The western slope of the Teton Range borders the Jedediah Smith Wilderness (part of the Caribou-Targhee National Forest), which contains 123,451 acres of land that was designated as such by Congress in 1984. The portion of the mountain range that lies within Grand Teton National Park has been recommended to Congress by the NPS to be included in the National Wilderness Preservation System. Following NPS policy, the recommended wilderness is managed as if it were designated wilderness. Rules and regulations, many of which are common throughout the NPS system, have been enacted to try to ensure that the wilderness character of the range is maintained for future generations. In addition to these, the **seven principles of Leave No Trace** have evolved over time to help users minimize the effects that recreational activities may have on this wonderful place. They are listed below with the permission of the Leave No Trace Center for Outdoor Ethics. These principles can be applied anywhere, at any time, while taking part in recreational activities.

1. **Plan ahead and prepare.**
   - Know the regulations and special concerns for the area you'll visit.
   - Prepare for extreme weather, hazards, and emergencies.

- Schedule your trip to avoid times of high use.
- Visit in small groups when possible. Consider splitting larger groups into smaller groups.
- Repackage food to minimize waste.
- Use a map and compass or GPS to eliminate the use of marking paint, rock cairns, or flagging.

2. Travel and camp on durable surfaces.

- Durable surfaces include maintained trails and designated campsites, rock, gravel, sand, dry grasses, and snow.
- Protect riparian areas by camping at least 200 feet from lakes and streams.
- Good campsites are found, not made. Altering a site is not necessary.

In popular areas:

- Concentrate use on existing trails and campsites.
- Walk single file in the middle of the trail, even when it is wet or muddy, and avoid creating new descent routes or approaches. Do not shortcut across switchbacks.
- Keep campsites small. Focus activity in areas where vegetation is absent.

In pristine areas:

- Disperse use to prevent the creation of campsites and trails. Whenever possible, walk on rock or gravel, not on plants or soil.
- Avoid places where impacts are just beginning. Camp on durable sites such as sand or gravel, thick duff, and dry soils covered with grass or sedge.

3. Dispose of waste properly.

- Pack it in, pack it out. Inspect your campsite, food preparation areas, and rest areas for trash or spilled foods. Pack out all trash, leftover food, and litter.
- Utilize toilet facilities whenever possible. Otherwise, deposit solid human waste in catholes dug 6 to 8 inches deep, at least 200 feet from water, camps, and trails. Cover and disguise the cathole when finished. Note that in some high-use areas of the Tetons (for example, Garnet Canyon and Leigh and Jackson Lake campsites), there is a requirement to pack out your solid human waste using products designed for that purpose.
- Make every attempt to pack out toilet paper rather than burning it. Hygiene products must be packed out.
- To wash yourself or your dishes, carry water 200 feet away from streams or lakes and use small amounts of biodegradable soap. Scatter strained dishwater.

4. Leave what you find.

- Preserve the past: examine and photograph, but do not touch or take, cultural or historical structures and artifacts.
- Leave rocks, plants, and other natural objects as you find them.
- Avoid introducing or transporting nonnative species.
- Do not build structures or furniture, and do not dig trenches.

5. Minimize campfire impacts.

- Campfires can cause lasting impacts to the environment. Use a lightweight stove for cooking.
- Campfires are allowed, only during times of low fire danger, at the designated campsites on Leigh and Jackson Lakes, using established fire rings.
- Keep fires small. If wood gathering is allowed, only use down and dead wood from the ground that can be broken by hand.
- Burn all wood and coals to ash and put out campfires completely.

6. Respect wildlife.

- Observe wildlife from a distance. Do not follow or approach them.
- Never feed animals. Feeding wildlife damages their health, alters natural behaviors, habituates them to humans and human food and trash, and exposes them to predators and other dangers.
- Store your food and trash securely in the bear-proof storage boxes provided at many of the designated backcountry campsites. If you plan to camp at a dispersed camping zone without a box, when you obtain your backcountry camping permit, you may also need to pick up a bear-proof storage container.
- As in most national parks, pets are not allowed on the trails.
- Avoid wildlife interactions during sensitive times, such as in winter and when animals are mating, nesting, or raising young.

7. Be considerate of other visitors.

- Respect other visitors and protect the quality of their experience.
- Be courteous. Yield to other users on the trail, especially if they are going uphill.
- Step to the downhill side of the trail when encountering pack stock.
- Take breaks and camp away from trails and other visitors.
- Let nature's sounds prevail. Avoid loud voices and noises.

To reiterate principle number six, respect the native wildlife of the mountains. While it is fascinating to watch the bears, moose, deer, elk, and bighorn sheep from a distance, remember that these animals are trying to make a living in a sometimes harsh environment, so do not disturb them unnecessarily. Most of the animals are more interesting than troublesome or dangerous. Those in the troublesome category include small varmints such as the ubiquitous marmots, who are more than willing to chew through the wall of an expensive tent to reach food carelessly left inside. Avoid this form of minor disaster by cooking outside the tent and securing your food supply: either hang it from a tree (12 feet high and 6 feet from the trunk or nearest branch) or large boulder or store it in a bear-proof locker or container.

In the potentially dangerous category are moose and bears. For both, beware of surprising a female with young, whom she will earnestly protect. Black bears constitute the main problem, and Teton climbers should obtain a copy of the NPS pamphlet describing strategies for avoiding trouble in bear country. Follow the same rules regarding food and cooking as for smaller critters. Many bear incidents can be chalked up to foolish behavior on the part of the hiker or climber. Grizzly bears are potentially a more serious problem, and their range seems to be spreading south from the northern canyons. Carrying bear spray, and keeping it easily accessible, is *highly* recommended!

Another less obvious form of danger lurks in the apparently clear water of the mountain lakes and streams. Harmful organisms such as *Giardia* and *Campylobacter* may be transmitted through untreated water, causing intestinal disorders, including severe diarrhea. To avoid getting sick, do one or more of the following: pack in your water supply from approved sources in the valley (spigots and drinking fountains), apply some type of treatment to mountain water in your water bottle or bladder, boil the mountain water for at least five minutes, or use one of many commercially available water filters designed for backpacking.

CAMPING AND CLIMBING REGULATIONS

In 1994 regulations that required registration for climbing, off-trail hiking, and over-snow travel away from plowed roads were deleted from the Code of Federal Regulations. It was the hope at that time that this regulation change would be accompanied by a renewed commitment by climbers to take responsibility for their actions and the actions of their party while in the mountains. Climbers should always make sure that someone (a friend or family member) has detailed knowledge of their party's plans and timetable. If for some reason that is not possible, a voluntary registration system is available. Parties going out overnight *must* obtain a backcountry permit in advance. These are available at the visitor centers at Moose or Colter Bay and at the Jenny Lake Ranger Station. The ranger station is open every day from Memorial Day until the end of September and is staffed by knowledgeable climbing rangers whose responsibilities include patrolling the backcountry and the routes on the peaks, providing information on current climbing conditions, and performing the sometimes highly technical mountain rescues. These rangers can provide sound advice based on many years of experience in the range. For current conditions during the summer months, call the Jenny Lake Ranger Station at 307-739-3343 or visit tetonclimbing.blogspot.com.

The following climbing rules and regulations, similar to those that have been imposed elsewhere in the United States by climbers, are included here as a reminder:

1. **Do not disturb historical or archaeologically or environmentally sensitive areas.**
2. **Do not scar, chisel, glue holds onto, or otherwise deface the rock.**
3. **Leave fixed protection and anchors with great discretion.**
4. **Accept responsibility even for the impact of other climbers in the mountain environment by removing rotten slings and garbage from climbs, bivouac sites, and descent routes.**
5. **Motorized equipment (including power drills) is prohibited in the backcountry of the Grand Teton.**

Maximum camping occupancy limits, defined either by designated campsites or by camping zones, have been specified for the most heavily used canyons in the range to limit use to a level that the natural resources of soil, vegetation, and wildlife can sustain. Because of these quotas, camping permits for specific times and locations may not always be available during the peak summer months because they are issued on a first-come, first-served basis. For general permit information, consult www.nps.gov/grte/planyourvisit/permitsandreservations.htm.

For specific backcountry campsite reservation information, visit www.nps.gov/grte/planyourvisit/bcres.htm. Make sure to download the park's excellent *Backcountry Camping* brochure and watch their informative "Backcountry Travel" video.

For specific climbing regulations in Grand Teton National Park, visit www.nps.gov/grte/planyourvisit/climb.htm. Current NPS policy regarding climbing is codified in Director's Order (DO) #41. This important NPS directive "recognizes that climbing is a legitimate and appropriate use of wilderness" and then goes on to outline certain restrictions and prohibitions placed on the practice of climbing as a legitimate use. It is worth reading and can be found at www.nps.gov/policy/DOrders/DO_41.pdf.

Regarding the important topic of fixed anchors, DO #41 has the following to say:

Fixed anchors or fixed equipment should be rare in wilderness. Authorization will be required for the placement of new fixed anchors or fixed equipment. Authorization may be required for the replacement or removal of existing fixed anchors or fixed equipment. The authorization process to be followed will be established at the park level and will be based on a consideration of resource issues (including the wilderness resource) and recreation opportunities. Authorization may be issued programmatically within the Wilderness Stewardship Plan or other activity-level plan, or specifically on a case-by-case basis, such as through a permit system. Prior to the completion of the park's Wilderness Stewardship Plan or other activity-level plan, the park superintendent may approve new fixed anchors or fixed equipment on a case-by-case basis.

As it currently stands, permission can be granted in Grand Teton National Park for new route development that involves the placement of fixed anchors, but it is *strongly* suggested to obtain such permission before going ahead with any plans. Recently, fixed anchors have gone in without permission on sections of the Grand Traverse and the Italian Cracks climbing routes. This is extremely unfortunate as it allows no input from the collective climbing community and, equally importantly, park administrators who are charged with climbing and resource management.

Accidents and Mountain Rescue

The skilled, dedicated NPS Jenny Lake Rangers are willing to do everything possible to rescue someone in need. However, climbers have a primary responsibility to do their best to extricate themselves from their own predicament. In the event of an accident, climbers should depend first on themselves and their party members: Practice self-rescue to the extent that it is possible. Do not depend solely on the NPS rescue team, because factors such as weather, darkness, and perceived objective hazards to the rescue team itself may considerably delay or even prevent a rescue effort. In the high mountains, hypothermia is particularly dangerous following an accident; if symptoms appear, the victim should be helped immediately with dry clothing, a sleeping bag, and warm drinks, if these are available.

In the event of a life-threatening injury, however, efforts should be made to obtain assistance as rapidly as possible. This is now most commonly done via cell phone, although coverage in some parts of the range can be spotty. Getting a text out may sometimes be possible even if a call cannot be made. In lieu of direct communication with 911, try notifying an adjacent party on the mountain. They may have a working phone and/or emergency medical skill that will be crucial for a patient's survival. Do not leave the victim alone unless it is absolutely necessary. When notified, the Jenny Lake Rangers will make every reasonable effort to take rapid and effective rescue action. Information needed by the rescue team includes the time of the accident, the exact location of the victim, the nature of the injuries, the equipment at the accident scene, the number of persons there, and their plan of action (if any).

Of primary importance is an attitude that it is a personal responsibility to do your best to rescue yourself—and that you *will* survive no matter what. For more information on common accident scenarios and how to avoid them, see Appendix A.

Mountain Guides

For nearly a century professional mountain climbing guides, officially approved by the NPS, have been operating in Grand Teton National Park. In recent years the proportion of Teton climbers who use the guiding services has increased significantly, attesting to the current acceptability of this form of mountaineering. Climbing with guides provides inexperienced climbers, or those with no mountain experience at all, a mechanism to reach the high peaks and begin mastering all the various mountain skills. Climbers not sufficiently experienced to be confident in accepting responsibility for the safety of their climbing party may well wish to utilize the guiding services.

Grand Teton National Park provides two mountain guide and climbing concessions for those desiring professional instruction in mountaineering or rock climbing or for those who wish to climb the Teton peaks. The two concessions are Exum Mountain Guides, with an office at Jenny Lake, and Jackson Hole Mountain Guides, with an office in Jackson. Both concessions are operated by guides with extensive experience and good safety records. The rates, which can be obtained either directly from the guides or from Grand Teton National Park Headquarters in Moose, Wyoming, are reasonable and have been approved by the government. The guides maintain two established high camps in the range and can supply most of the special equipment required for an ascent. Although the months of July and August are the peak months, guiding continues throughout the year, with winter ski guiding becoming more and more popular.

Climbing Equipment

In the Teton Range there is a tradeoff between having all the gear you might wish to have and being able or willing to carry all the weight. The approaches can often be several miles with 2,000 to 4,000 vertical feet of gain, from the valley to the base of what may be a relatively short rock climb.

An ice axe—and the knowledge of and practiced skill in its use for safety—is an essential item on many of the routes for much of the summer, even on rock routes when the approach or descent involves a snow or ice slope. Skill with an ice axe is perhaps the single most important thing besides common sense that climbers can carry into the mountains. Snow and ice conditions change considerably from year to year, and there is the usual decrease in snow as the summer progresses from spring to autumn. Current information will be available at the Jenny Lake Ranger Station.

For the rock routes, a "standard Teton rack," if there is such a thing, would probably be similar to one used elsewhere in the mountainous regions of the country. The exact selection comes down to personal preference and no dogma will be given here. A suggestion might be as follows: camming devices, in a size range from 0.3" to 3.5"; a complete set of stoppers from small to medium size; a number of regular-length runners or alpine draws; a number of regular quickdraws; and free carabiners.

If anything specific in the way of protection is known to be essential for a route, it will be mentioned in the text. This will usually be a reference to the largest size of protection that is needed or to items of special emphasis. Pitons are rarely necessary on the popular routes, but they can be useful on the major alpine routes. If the rock on such a route is iced or becomes iced while the climb is under way, a small selection (5 to 10) of pitons of various sizes can provide an extra margin of safety.

Climbing helmets are *strongly* recommended for Teton climbing routes. Many contain loose rock, fully capable of being unleashed by natural causes or by other climbers. On any climb where there may be another party higher on the route, a thinking, rational human being will wear a helmet. Friends of both authors of this book would not be alive today had they not been wearing a helmet when a rock came down. Indeed, I (R. Jackson) owe my life to the critical protection that a good climbing helmet provided. Wear one.

Smartphone Applications

Most climbers carry smartphones into the mountains these days, and there are many ways that they can be useful. Consider downloading mobile applications (apps) to assist with navigation and specific route information. The Gaia GPS app is an excellent tool for navigation, particularly in the trailless canyons and during the winter months. The Mountain Project app contains a wealth of information about climbs throughout the US and the world, including the Tetons. This author (R. Jackson) has found the comments sections following the climbing route descriptions to be both entertaining and informative.

Weather apps are also helpful. This author uses wX, which displays current conditions, forecasts, alerts, and radar for locations across the US based on data from the National Weather Service. It is easy to bookmark and set up weather maps for different areas for quick reference. Other indispensable conditions-related websites include MountainWeather (www.mountainweather.com), a Teton-specific weather site administered by meteorologist and climber Jim Woodmencey, and www.jhavalanche.org, the Bridger-Teton Avalanche Center (BTAC) website.

Traverses, Enchainments, Picnics, and Other Sufferfests

In a small mountain range such as the Tetons, where the peaks are not immense and roads can deliver climbers directly to the base, a traverse of one or two or more of the high peaks offers a great day—or even several days—of pleasant mountaineering.

An accessible, nontechnical option is to traverse the range on one of the various maintained trails, from west to east or vice versa; this is an enjoyable way to cover a lot of ground in the Teton backcountry. One of the best routes is the Teton Canyon–Cascade Canyon traverse through the beautiful and scenic Alaska Basin.

In the south end of the range several days can be spent on a series of traverses along the park boundary (Reyman, 1960), starting with the peaks on the northeast ridge of Rendezvous Peak and continuing west and north to the pass southwest of Buck Mountain where the Alaska Basin Trail crosses the divide. Another interesting sedimentary traverse, which can be done in one long day, crosses the five peaks circling Open Canyon (Ortenburger, Melton, Monahan, and Dornan, 1960). Although a climb of Buck Mountain has been combined with that of Veiled Peak in one day (Irvin and Lowry, 1957), this latter small peak is more easily and naturally combined with Mount Wister (Unsoeld, Ortenburger, and Vogel, 1952). This combination is especially appropriate if a high camp is established for the climb of Wister, because in this case there will usually be adequate time for the extra ascent of Veiled Peak.

The principal area for high traverses, however, is the Garnet Canyon area. The most obvious combination is that of the South and Middle Tetons (Ellingwood, 1923). This traverse is easily accomplished using the regular routes on each, if the start is made from a camp in Garnet Canyon. The ridge from Cloudveil Dome to Gilkey Tower is a portion of the encircling ridge that provides worthwhile mountain scrambling (F. Fryxell and Hilding, 1931). If one is interested in major summits, one can climb Nez Perce, descend to the floor of the south fork of the canyon, climb the South Teton (Fryxell and Smith, 1930), and even include the Middle Teton (Goldthwaite, 1931); or, more thoroughly, one can traverse the entire ridge from the Middle Teton to Nez Perce (Ayres, 1932). The first traverse in the other direction as far as the South Teton was done a year later (P. Petzoldt and Hendricks, 1933). The traverse of the three Tetons is also a good day's climbing, making use of the North Ridge route of the Middle Teton either for descent (south to north, Durrance and Butterworth, 1938) or for ascent (north to south, Merrill McLane and Jack Snobble, 1946). The combination of the entire ridge from Nez Perce to the Grand Teton is a long and exhausting effort (Pownall and Brewer, 1950). It is also possible to combine the various pinnacles and towers in the Grand Teton area, or to do them in combination with major routes on the larger peaks; in this category are the Enclosure, Pinocchio Pinnacle, Bonney's Pinnacle, Glencoe Spire, Teepe Pillar, Pemmican Pillar, Fairshare Tower, the Red Sentinel, Okie's Thorn, the Molar Tooth, and the Second Tower.

The classic ridge connecting Teewinot Mountain to Mount Owen provides an excellent day with continually impressive views (east to west, T. Edwards and McNeill, 1940); in the other direction, this traverse is more difficult and was first accomplished in 1963 (west to east, A. Steck, D. Long, and J. Evans). If the traverse is made from Teewinot to the Grand Teton, one is confronted with the Grand's difficult north side. This is usually climbed now using the Italian Cracks variation, however when it was first done the more classic North Ridge route was used (Unsoeld, Pownall, and Schoening, 1959). This is now referred to as the Cathedral Traverse and is a fantastic day in the

Steve Rickert on the first couple of moves during the first ascent of Emotional Rescue, Enclosure Buttress, July 26, 1985 (Photo by Renny Jackson)

mountains. The Grand Traverse, from Teewinot to Nez Perce, is *the* ultraclassic traverse in the Teton Range (see Section 5 for Grand Traverse information). On Teewinot, as on the Grand, some interest can be added to the climb by including some or all of its main pinnacles—the Crooked Thumb, the Idol, the Worshipper—during the ascent, although the inclusion of the Crooked Thumb implies ascent (or possibly descent) of a north face route (Ortenburger and Buckingham, 1953). To the west of the Cathedral Group, the Wigwam divide, a line of easy peaks, forms the western boundary of Cascade Canyon and extends from the Wall to Littles Peak. A traverse of these peaks should not prove difficult but perhaps rather long for a single day.

The Mount St. John area offers many opportunities to make a full day's climb of several of the relatively small peaks of that group. It is customary to include Ice Point with the ascent of Storm Point rather than to climb either one by itself (F. Fryxell and Hilding, 1931). Symmetry Spire can be easily combined with Storm Point (E. Petzoldt, 1935). Storm Point and Ice Point, climbed by their regular routes, can be combined either with the regular route of Symmetry Spire (A. Sharples, M. Bedell, and Comey [all-female ascent], 1939) or with its Southwest Ridge route (Maxwell and Fix, 1948). Following an ascent of Symmetry Spire, one can also head west and climb as many of the Symmetry Crags as time and energy permit (Ayres, 1934). The five Ayres' Crags make a fine day of pinnacle climbing (Ortenburger and R. Fryxell, 1953); the smaller pinnacles at the head of Hanging Canyon, from the Canine Tooth to the Jaw, require less energy (P. Robinson, B. Briggs, P. Crosby, and B. Brett, 1952). Although clearly any section of the ridge surrounding Hanging Canyon can be selected and traversed, the longest yet completed is that from Mount St. John to the Canine Tooth (Ortenburger and Hemming, 1954). Because the ascent of Rockchuck Peak can be made in such short order, one may consider traversing the ridge to Mount St. John in the same day (M. Ladd, J. Ladd, A. Pratt, H. Pratt, and M. Bartlett, 1946). The peaks between the Jaw and the crossing of the Teton Crest Trail over the Cascade-Paintbrush divide make an unusual and long day (W. Buckingham and Bierer, 1954; W. Buckingham and West, 1958).

On the climb of Mount Moran, one or both of the horns can be included (West Horn, Ayres, Creswell, and Ortenburger, 1951; East Horn, Robinson, Briggs, and Brett, 1951); they provide outstanding views of the east face of the mountain. The entire west ridge of Mount Moran from Thor Peak is a very long traverse along a high ridge that is very rotten in places and not recommended (P. Petzoldt and Hartline, 1935). West of Mount Moran a pleasant day's traverse comprises all the peaks surrounding Cirque Lake (Ortenburger and Buckingham, 1953).

An almost unlimited number of traverses are possible in the wilder north end of the Teton Range. Here as in the south end, extensive traverses are ideal for those who enjoy moving through the mountains in ways that do not involve the surmounting of technical difficulties (Ortenburger, Beardsley [Ortenburger], Peterson, and Wilson, 1963). The complete Bivouac Peak–Raynolds Peak ridge involves many towers and much interesting scrambling, but the return from Raynolds Peak is a long proposition no matter how it is done (Fonda and Buckingham, 1955). The ridge linking Mount Robie (10,881) with Eagles Rest Peak is fully as long but is neither as high nor as rugged as the Nez Perce–Teewinot Mountain ridge; it yields more than one high-level traverse—for example, Mount Robie to Ranger Peak, and Doane Peak to Eagles Rest Peak (Ortenburger and Beardsley [Ortenburger], 1957).

In the 21st century, ultra-endurance athletes from Jackson Hole and beyond have taken the idea of traversing several peaks or climbing multiple routes in a day, or even combining different activities with the Teton Range as the venue, in previously unimaginable directions. One unique innovation has been the mountain endurance triathlon. On July 29, 2012, local climber, writer, photographer, and environmental activist David Gonzales established the Picnic, an endurance challenge that involves biking from the town square in Jackson to the Jenny Lake east side overlook, swimming across the lake, hiking to the Lupine Meadows trailhead, climbing the Grand Teton, and then reversing the whole process. Taking things one level further is the Moranic, established July 27, 2014, and centered on the more remote Mount Moran. This similar challenge starts at Jackson's town square with a bike ride to String Lake, where participants then run to Leigh Lake, swim across to the Falling Ice Glacier drainage, and hike to the start of the CMC route; after climbing to the summit of Moran, they reverse the entire route back to the town square for full value. The so-called Triple Buck, established July 3–4, 2015, combines a two-way bike, a two-way swim of Phelps Lake, and a traverse of Albright Peak, Static Peak, and Buck Mountain. The possibilities are endless!

Picnics are now used to train for new and even bolder projects. From August 27 to 30, 2015, local Jackson climber Ryan Burke created what he calls the Perception Traverse, a tour of the central Teton peaks over four days that takes in 25 different summits and covers 65 miles with 78,000 feet of elevation gain and loss. Burke expanded the Grand Traverse by beginning his adventure with an ascent of Mount Moran and then tagging six peaks to the north of the Traverse and another five peaks to the south of it. The following year, Burke supersized the Perception and completed what he called the Fight or Flight Traverse, a seven-day, 50-peak tour through the range (August 20–26, 2016). Burke tallied 102 miles of travel and 122,000 feet of elevation gain and loss, again using the Grand Traverse as the centerpiece of this astonishing endeavor. (Details for both routes are available on Mountain Project.)

Yet another sufferfest was accomplished in 2019 by endurance athletes Kelly Halpin and Fred Casey Most. From September 5 to 6, 2019—over the course of 1 day, 19 hours, 29 minutes, and 34 seconds—the pair followed the hydrographic divide of the Teton Range from north to south, beginning at Glade Creek/Berry Creek and finishing up at Teton Pass. Their serious undertaking, dubbed the Teton Center Punch Traverse, involved scrambling on technical terrain, a shortage of available drinking water, adverse weather conditions, and sleep deprivation. They logged 70 miles of travel and 22,000 feet of elevation gain on the trip. Paul Petzoldt had done a similar traverse decades before, a trip he referred to as the High Adventure Trail, although he traveled from south to north and stayed west of the hydrographic divide.

As a rookie climbing ranger in the 1970s, I (R. Jackson) spent some of my workdays in the Jenny Lake Ranger Station signing climbers out for climbs. At that time, Grand Teton National Park had a climbing registration system. On one of these days a young Charlie Fowler walked in around midmorning in cutoffs and a ratty-looking T-shirt and signed out for Guides' Wall and the Southwest Ridge route of Symmetry Spire. I said, "Charlie, those are in two different locations, Cascade Canyon and the Symmetry Couloir." Charlie said that he knew that, of course, and that he was soloing. He would first climb Guides', continue up to the top of Storm Point, traverse over to the base of Symmetry, and then climb the Southwest Ridge route. I said something like, "Oh, okay, that sounds good." Charlie came back a few hours later and said that he had had a fun day. That was my introduction to the concept of enchainment—the linking of two or more routes in a day (or a single outing).

Climbing in the Teton Range is very conducive to such linkups, and many great ones have been done. In Death Canyon, the Snaz Buttress stands out. The Snaz–Caveat Emptor–Aerial Boundaries or the Snaz–Caveat Emptor–Sunshine Daydream come to mind, both facilitated by the rappel route on the Snaz. A linkup of southern ridges—such as that of the Direct South Ridge of Nez Perce, the Buckingham (Southeast) Ridge on the Middle Teton, and the complete Exum Ridge on the Grand Teton—provides an excellent multiday tour, or a big single-day ascent for those who are super fit. Paul Gagner, a climbing ranger in the 1980s, linked the Grand's three southern ridges (Exum, Petzoldt, Underhill) in a day. In 1996, on the other side of the Grand, Alex Lowe climbed a new, difficult first-ascent variation on the Serendipity Arête of Mount Owen and then traversed over and went up the Italian Cracks on the Grand Teton, also as a day climb. A year later, local Teton hardmen Hans Johnstone and Mark Newcomb linked the three north faces of the Cathedral Group (Teewinot, Mount Owen, Grand Teton) in a day. Many such combinations exist, limited only by one's imagination.

Bouldering and Sport Climbing

In the past, bouldering in the Teton Range was limited to a small number of glacial erratics scattered on the valley floor along the margin of the mountains. This has changed with the rising popularity of the sport, and new areas of interest have been discovered and developed; information abounds online, including on blogs and popular sites like Mountain Project. One of the new bouldering hot spots is Delta Lake in Glacier Gulch. Social media has fueled an explosion of use in this formerly pristine region of the park, which is now also a popular hiking destination. An obvious social trail takes off from the north end of the first switchback corner along the trail to Surprise and Amphitheater Lakes (above where the trail splits at the second junction from the Lupine Meadows trailhead, with the left branch heading into Garnet Canyon); this unofficial trail cuts up into Glacier Gulch to reach Delta Lake. Please be respectful and adhere to the principles of Leave No Trace (see *Resource Protection* earlier in this chapter) when accessing this and all areas within Grand Teton National Park.

In addition to the bouldering areas, several excellent, bolt-protected sport-climbing areas are also available in the Teton region. For a much more thorough discussion of these, refer to *Rock Climbing Jackson Hole and Pinedale, Wyoming: A Day Climber's Guide*, an excellent guidebook by Wesley Gooch. The main areas are listed here from south to north. Information can also be obtained at the Jenny Lake Ranger Station, the American Alpine Club's Grand Teton Climbers' Ranch, or mountaineering stores in Jackson and Moose.

Rock Springs Buttress and the Tram: Rock Springs Buttress, located in the drainage south of Peak 10,450, contains the highest concentration of high-quality sport climbs in the Jackson Hole area. In addition, several bolt-protected sport climbs are located high on Peak 10,450 (the one with the tram to its summit). After getting off on top, walk down to the vicinity of tower #5, where two famous couloirs (ski runs) take off toward the north. The first of these is known as Corbet's Couloir (named for Barry Corbet), and several climbs are located on both the eastern and western walls of the couloir. The second of the couloirs, S&S Couloir (named for Simms and Sands), is located immediately down to the east. There are a number of sport climbs on the eastern wall of this couloir. A newly developed crag in Tensleep Bowl, the Happy Hour Wall, contains a collection of moderate sport-climbing routes. Information for this and other sport-climbing venues in the Jackson Hole area can be found on Mountain Project and elsewhere online.

Blacktail Butte: This is the central of several steep-sided hills or buttes that rise out of the flat floor of Jackson Hole; it is located immediately east of the village of Moose. Many bolt-protected sport routes are located on the south-facing limestone cliffs at the northwest corner of the butte. They vary in difficulty from 5.10 to 5.13. A small parking area is located about 0.75 mile north of Moose Junction on US Highway 26/89, on the east side of the road. The main cliff (25m high) and a smaller one to the west can be seen a short distance above the parking area. Use the switchback trail to access the main lower cliff. Please stay on the trail. It is also useful to remember that, because of its proximity to the road, Blacktail Butte attracts novice climbers, hikers, and "rappellers." *Beware* of loose rock and *do not* knock anything down. A more moderate collection of sport routes is found on a few small cliffs located south of the main lower wall. Follow a trail that crosses a small creek before heading up the drainage where these cliffs are located. Information regarding the climbs here can be found in the Gooch guide.

Taggart: Park at the Taggart Lake trailhead and follow the trail north for about 0.25 mile. This boulder is due west of the trail behind the horse corrals.

Climbers' Ranch: This large boulder is located on a morainal ridge just west of the ranch.

Lupine Meadows: This collection of three boulders is about 0.5 mile up the trail from the Lupine Meadows trailhead. Look for them on the west side of the trail just after crossing the bridge over the Glacier Gulch stream.

Jenny Lake: These four famous boulders, located near the Jenny Lake Ranger Station, were chronicled in the humorous *Guide to the Jenny Lake Boulders*, written by John Gill and Yvon Chouinard in 1958. From the south end of the Jenny Lake campground, walk north along the bike path that runs along the west side of the campsites. After almost 0.2 mile you will notice the steep, south-facing wall of Cut-Finger Rock. Falling Ant Slab is located just to the west overlooking Jenny Lake. Red Cross Rock is located to the northeast of Cut-Finger and sports the famous Gill Problem (B2, or V9 in the modern difficulty rating system) on its overhanging east side. Mount Fonda rounds out the group and is practically on the road just north of Red Cross. It is interesting to note that these boulders may have the distinction of being the first place in the country where gymnastic chalk was used. Richard Emerson, who was the first to climb on the boulders, was in the habit of using forest duff on his hands to improve his grip. John Gill, a former college gymnast, began using chalk on these boulders sometime during the 1950s.

String Lake and Leigh Lake: Although a number of smaller boulders are located on the moraines that surround these lakes, two large top-roping boulders are of primary interest. From the String Lake picnic area, walk north for 1.1 miles to the bridge over the outlet stream from Leigh Lake. The short portage from String Lake to Leigh Lake takes off to the north from here. The largest and perhaps most interesting boulder is located on Boulder Island in the south end of Leigh Lake. Some manner of conveyance across the water of the lake will be needed to reach the island. Once on the island, scrambling leads to the top from the east side. There are two bolt stations on top for top-roping the north and west sides. For the second boulder, cross the bridge to the west across the Leigh Lake outlet stream and walk about 0.1 mile northwest toward Paintbrush Canyon. Look for a large boulder to the south that is somewhat hidden in the trees. Scrambling up the east side leads to the top.

Bouldertown: For this area park at the Cathedral Group turnout on the Jenny Lake scenic loop road. The boulders are on the moraine about 0.2 mile north of the parking area. There are six major glacial erratics located in close proximity to one another with several top-rope and boulder problems at a wide range of difficulty levels.

Darby Canyon: This canyon on the west side of the Tetons, accessed from between Victor and Driggs in Idaho, features a small, south-facing limestone crag with about 20 short routes. Most of these climbs are in the 5.8–5.10 range.

Teton Canyon: This area contains a high concentration of developed climbs on limestone as well as granite. Refer to the Gooch guide for detailed route descriptions.

Badger Creek: This area is located on the west side of the range, about 3 miles north of Tetonia, Idaho. A dirt road takes off to the north just past town and intersects the Badger Creek drainage after about 3 miles. Turn east and drive about 0.5 mile. The small outcrops of igneous rock can be seen rising above the road a short distance to the south.

How to Use This Book

For the climber who is new to the Teton Range, navigating your way through this guidebook in order to find a specific peak or route can be a daunting task. The featured peaks are listed in the Contents. If you know the name of the route, look in the Index; you'll also find peaks listed here. If you know only the general area in which you would like to climb, look at the overview map on page 13, which shows the areas described in each of the eleven sections of this book. Additionally, there are five other area maps located within the sections that show locations and approaches for some of the most popular climbs. You might also find some inspiration in Appendix B: The Best Climbs in the Tetons, which were selected based on the author's (R. Jackson) personal opinion and experience. Once you find your way to your objective, the following information is standardized throughout this guidebook and will hopefully prove to be both accurate and helpful. Enjoy the climbing in the Tetons!

Route Descriptions

The route descriptions in this text have been placed into 11 sections that are arranged geographically from south to north. They have been compiled from several different sources: the authors' own experiences; interviews with and accounts provided by other climbers; accounts published in mountaineering journals; and mountaineering records maintained by the National Park Service (NPS). Leigh Ortenburger corresponded with climbers across the US for nearly 40 years while gathering information. Considerable effort has been expended to chronicle every route that has been done in the Teton Range, with the notable exceptions of Rock Springs Buttress and the other rock climbs on Peak 10,450, as well as the sport-climbing areas on the west side of the range including Teton and Darby Canyons. The descriptions of how to get to the bases of the climbs have also been carefully researched. In some of the descriptions, information is meager due primarily to a lack of reliable data. Keep in mind that in many cases the first ascent has been the only ascent and that quite often it was done many years ago. Climbing terminology has changed over the years and a significant attempt has been made to update and standardize much of this terminology. Remember that the fine points of routefinding are left to the individual climber and that there is no substitute for this very necessary skill.

For many of the peaks, a **chronology** precedes the route descriptions to provide the reader with a concise climbing history of the area or formation. Following the chronology, all the known climbing routes on the peak have been assigned a number and listed in the order in which they appear—in a counterclockwise or clockwise fashion—around the peak (or an aspect of the peak). The starting point for this geographic ordering of routes is often (but not always) the "regular route," the most commonly used route of ascent or descent on the peak. To further assist the reader, a ▲ symbol is used to denote each "regular route." The Grand Teton was used as the model for the rest of the peaks, with the Owen-Spalding route listed first as one of two "regular routes" (the other being the Exum Ridge route); in this case the Owen-Spalding was chosen for its historical importance as well as for being a standard route of ascent and descent on the mountain.

There are some notable departures from this ordering scheme. One example is Disappointment Peak, a complex mountain with many climbs. Its routes are presented in four sections: East Face Routes; Northern Routes; Southern Arêtes, Couloirs, and Ridges; and West Face Routes. Beginning with the Southeast Ridge (one of the peak's two "regular routes"), the first two sections list the climbs in counterclockwise fashion, from south to north. The third section then switches to a clockwise arrangement—beginning with the first routes on the south side of the peak and ending with those on its west face—to reflect how climbers would encounter them while walking up Garnet Canyon. This is also the case for the route listings for the north side of Death Canyon and for the south and west side of Mount Moran in Leigh Canyon.

The **naming** of a particular route has been left up to the first-ascent party; however, names have not been suggested in every case. If a name was not given, one was assigned based on either the physical location of the route or, more simply, the names of the first-ascent party.

The **difficulty classification** and **first-ascent information** then follow. The first-ascent data are based on extensive personal study and correspondence relating to the climbing history of the Teton peaks. This is a subject of some interest to climbers and deserves publication with accuracy, so any information regarding errors will be appreciated. In some cases, notably in the northern and southern ends of the range (where the peaks are easy but relatively remote), the party listed as having made the first ascent was very likely preceded by climbers currently unknown and unlisted in the records. (Careful readers may note that some climbers are identified by two or more names. This is unintentional, as much of this first-ascent information is based on how climbers signed a summit register on a given day. A casual Bill or Julie may have been feeling more like a formal William or Julia while taking in the views from the top, or perhaps a storm was approaching and there wasn't enough time to append the usual "Jr." At this point it is difficult to ascertain whether slightly divergent names constitute one person or several people. See tetonclimbinghistory.com for a meticulous record of summit registers from the late 1920s into the 1980s, thanks to Paul Horton.)

The main body of each route description comprises four categories of information: (1) **access to the route** or, in some cases, group of routes, including where to park and the proper canyon for the approach; (2) **approach considerations** such as what trail to take, where to leave the trail, and how to recognize the start of the climb, including landmarks at the base and landmarks up above on the route; (3) **route and/or pitch details**, including special route considerations such as the seriousness of the climb or a particular pitch (protection and rockfall), the recommended method for making the climb (one day versus bivouac on route), special equipment recommendations, and escape possibilities, when known; and (4) the **route of descent** from the top of the climb or from the summit of the peak and the extent of rappelling (if any). At the end of the body of the description, additional

gear information, **time** information, and **bibliographical references** are given, if these are known. Only those bibliographical references that contain information significant for a prospective climber have been included. If a route has been climbed only once, these references are highly recommended reading in addition to the description given in this book.

This guidebook has been revised several times over the decades, updated to reflect new information and new ways of presenting it. Climbers have continued to put up new routes, of course, and will continue to do so. Specific to this fourth edition is an entirely new set of **photographs and "phototopos"**: Over about a five-year period, considerable effort was invested in getting images both from the air and on foot in many remote locations, with the goal of capturing the peaks at the best time of day and in the best possible light so as to show as much detail as possible. Route diagrams were then applied to many of the photographs using Adobe Illustrator. The goal was not to clutter the photographs with too many extra graphics, and therefore the route line is simply that—a dotted line with an associated description of the type of climbing on a particular pitch and its difficulty.

For some routes, a conventional **topo diagram** is included in addition to the phototopo. See the Topo Diagram Key, ***Figure 6***, for information about the numerous symbols used on the topos. These are by now well standardized and should be familiar to climbers from across the United States. The overall goal is to

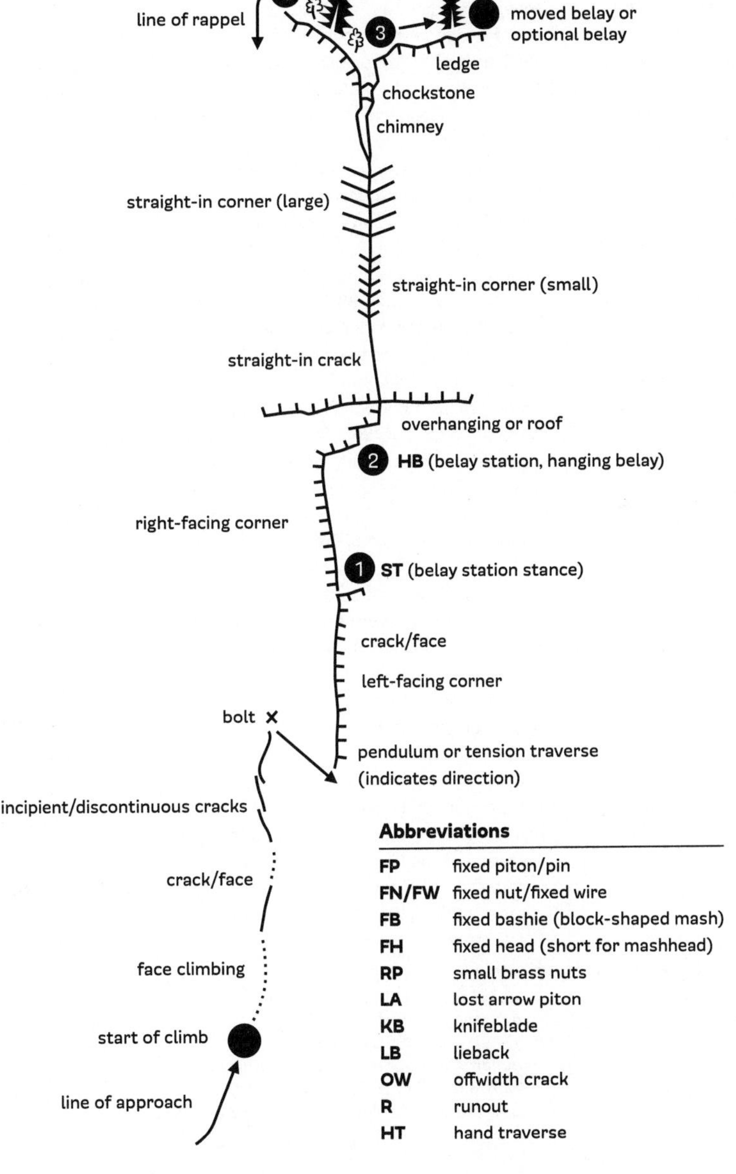

FIGURE 6. Topo Diagram Key

present as much information as possible by a range of methods including, of course, the written description of the climb.

The term early season refers to the summer climbing period beginning about June 15 and lasting to about July 10. During this period the climbing in most of the couloirs and some of the canyons will be entirely on snow; glissading will be at its best, making fast descents possible on some peaks. Almost every route will require an ice axe and the knowledge of its use for safety. The term late season refers to the period from about August 1 to September 15. By this time the snow is mostly gone, the glaciers will show bare ice, and during the daytime it will be hot in the sun. Most of the peaks will be accessible by at least one snow-free route.

The directions given in the route descriptions are in terms of the climber facing the summit of the peak. A peak has been arbitrarily defined within this text, with very few exceptions, as having three closed 80-foot contour lines (using the 1968 USGS maps). A systematic attempt has been made to use the following two sets of terms in order of decreasing size: saddle, col, and notch; and canyon, gully, couloir, chute, chimney, and crack. The terms used to describe other parts of a mountain are standard in mountaineering literature: arête, bench, chockstone, crag, face, ledge, moraine, needle, overhang, pinnacle, pitch, scree, shelf, slab, spire, and talus.

A NOTE ON ROPELENGTHS

Readers will notice that the lengths of pitches do not necessarily coincide with today's longer ropes. Standard ropes have gone from being 120 feet (37m) to 150 feet (46m) to 165 feet (50m) to the familiar lengths of 60m and 70m in use today—and who knows what's next? Each of these ropelengths is aligned with a particular climbing era, which is something to keep in mind when navigating a route description from an earlier decade.

Maps and Elevations

In addition to a smartphone with a GPS/map application, having a good old-fashioned map in hand, as well as skill with a compass, can be extremely valuable—especially if one's phone battery dies during an extended trip. An extensive and detailed set of topographic maps in the 7.5-minute series covers Grand Teton National Park. Published by the US Geological Survey (USGS) at a scale of 1:24,000 (2.64 inches per mile), 16 of these quadrangle sheets encompass the entire Teton Range and its approaches. The quadrangle sheet on which a peak appears is listed alongside its entry in this book.

The history of the mapping of the Teton and Yellowstone region begins with the 1872 Hayden Survey Expedition (see the History chapter). Through the efforts of chief topographer Gustavus R. Bechler and his assistants, the first detailed map—***Sources of the Snake River***—emerged. Dr. Ferdinand Vandeveer Hayden's expeditions continued in 1878 and 1879, with further mapping and triangulation work conducted in the area by A. D. Wilson, Bechler, Fred A. Clark, and artist William Henry Holmes. This resulted in the map entitled ***Parts of Western Wyoming and Southeastern Idaho***. The Teton Range really came into focus in 1901 when the USGS published the Grand Teton quadrangle, surveyed by T. M. Bannon and Arthur Stiles in 1898–99. From that point on the USGS has continued to produce and update maps of the range. The most well-known of these is the set of topographic maps mentioned above bearing a publication date of 1968. These can also be accessed online on a number of websites, including TopoZone.com and CalTopo.com. The single large USGS sheet showing the entire park at a scale of 1:62,500 (about 1 inch per mile) remains available; it is possible to purchase updated versions of this map (privately printed) on water-resistant paper. In some cases the elevation of a peak is followed by the letter T. This indicates that a spot elevation was determined by photogrammetric methods (see the peaks in Section 11).

The majority of elevations provided throughout this guidebook were obtained using the 1968 maps. This includes the elevation of the Grand Teton, which is given as 13,770 feet. That figure has climbed steadily over time, much more quickly than the measured rise of the Teton fault:[1]

- **13,747 feet** (USGS Grand Teton quadrangle, surveyed in 1899)
- **13,750 feet** (USGS Grand Teton quadrangle, reprinted 1931 and 1946)
- **13,766 feet** (USGS Topographic Map of the Grand Teton National Park, 1948)
- **13,770 feet** (USGS Grand Teton National Park, 1968)
- **13,771.65 feet** (US Army Corps of Engineers GPS observation, October 1991)[2]
- **13,775 feet** (National Geodetic Survey Datasheet PID OX0838)

(**Note:** According to the topoView interface on the USGS website, the elevation of the Grand Teton is 4,199m or 13,776.2 feet—a gain of 6.2 feet since 1968. Meanwhile, to the north, the elevation for Mount Moran is given as 3,835m or 12,582 feet, representing a net loss of 23 feet since 1968!)

With Google Earth and Google Earth Pro, it is now possible to pinpoint the exact elevations of peaks, subpeaks, and other features throughout the range—and those figures may not match the elevations provided here. Google Earth is an indispensable tool for researching routes. Also valuable for backcountry mapping and trip-planning purposes is CalTopo.com, which offers a range of map layers, even in its free version.

This edition of the guidebook also includes a few rudimentary maps—an area overview plus details of the major canyons (Death Canyon, Garnet Canyon, Cascade Canyon, and Leigh Canyon)—to help orient the reader. These are not intended to replace a GPS smartphone app or a detailed topographic map.

LEGEND

- NPS maintained or "improved" trail
- approach route
- 0.1 mileage between points
- peak
- climb or landmark
- camp
- lake
- stream
- waterfall

Difficulty Ratings

The determination of the difficulty rating of a particular climb has always been a subject of considerable discussion among climbers. Many attempts have been made to devise a logical, easy-to-understand difficulty rating system that would be both universally accepted and then consistently used. Such a system has not yet appeared. Ultimately, any system by which climbs are categorized by difficulty relies on consensus. The rating system described here is used in some form or another throughout this country and therefore should be familiar to most climbers using this text. Generally, the classifications given in the text have been made on the basis of good summer-time conditions; one should expect the difficulty to be much greater if the rock is wet, covered with snow, or icy. For routes about which little is known, the estimation of difficulty errs on the high side to avoid misleading the inexperienced.

GRADE

The first part of the rating system used in this book is a roman numeral from I to VI, in ascending order of ***overall difficulty***. It is applied only to an entire climb and never to individual moves or pitches within the climb. This overall difficulty is estimated by the consideration of many factors, including the following: the length of the route, measured by both time and distance; the average difficulty of all of the individual pitches; the difficulty of the hardest pitch; the ease of escape or retreat, if required; the extent to which adverse weather conditions may create problems; the various objective dangers of the route such as rockfall; and, somewhat more vaguely, the challenge or degree of commitment implied by the route. Most of the Teton routes are either Grade I or Grade II. It should be noted that some one-pitch climbs are listed herein as Grade I even though the single pitch may be very difficult.

I: These routes require little or no commitment in the sense of either time or difficulty. After leaving the approach trail, only a few hours are required for the climb, and retreat or escape is trivial. Little or no mountain experience is needed to undertake these routes. Single-pitch rock climbs, of whatever difficulty, are put into this category.

II: These are routes of moderate magnitude, usually requiring much of a day. They may involve some significant climbing, but escape or retreat routes are available. Some mountain experience may be needed to climb these routes safely.

III: For most climbers these routes require a full day, involve serious climbing difficulty, consist of several pitches, and require some commitment in the sense that escape or retreat will involve technical difficulties. Considerable mountaineering or rock-climbing skills and experience are needed for safe passage on these routes.

IV: All of these routes are long, requiring a full day of difficult climbing after a significant approach, have many difficult pitches, are committing in the sense that retreat is usually nearly as difficult and time-consuming as completing the route, and may be hazardous in bad weather conditions.

V: These routes will generally require more than a single day on the technical portion of the climb, have numerous very difficult pitches, and require considerable physical strength and stamina. Technical proficiency on both rock and ice may also be required, and these routes are roughly equivalent to two Grade IVs.

VI: In this book only three routes—the Grand Traverse (see Section 5) and Whirl of Hate and the Kelley-Beyer route on the south side of Mount Moran—are given this rating. Elsewhere, Grade VI climbs usually require two or more days of hard climbing.

CLASS

The second part of the system is represented by a series of numbers, in ascending order of difficulty, that attempt to describe the most technically difficult climbing move, series of moves, or section of climbing that one is likely to encounter during the climb.

1.0: Mountain hiking, on- or off-trail. (No use of hands.)

2.0: Easy scrambling with little exposure. Ice axe may be important for safety. (Occasional use of hands; some steepness of the terrain is implied; almost no one would feel that a rope is needed for safety.)

3.0: Scrambling with some exposure. Inexperienced climbers may want to be roped. Ice axe and knowledge of its use are important for safety. (Considerable use of hands; some may want to be roped; average attentive person can climb this level without fear of falling.) Also described as 3rd class.

4.0: Exposed climbing. Ice axe and knowledge of its use are essential for safe passage. (Many will want to be roped; an unsecured fall could result in serious injury or death.) Also described as 4th class.

5.0: Exposed, serious climbing requiring application of technical rock-climbing skills. (Most will want to be roped; pitches of sufficient length to warrant some manner of intermediate protection during belayed climbing.)

At this point, because the range of difficulty becomes quite large, additional number(s) are placed after the decimal point to further describe the most difficult technical moves of a particular climb. The Yosemite Decimal System (YDS), as this scale of rating difficulty is known, is the widely accepted standard in this country and is therefore used throughout this guide. Currently in the United States the YDS scale extends from 5.0 to 5.15. Established through the joint efforts of Royal Robbins, Don Wilson, and Chuck Wilts in the early 1950s, the YDS was originally known as the Sierra-Wilts System and then somewhat later as the Southern California System. It was first suggested by Royal Robbins as a means of classifying practice routes on Tahquitz Rock.

Steve Rickert on the dark side of the Grand Teton, approaching Loki's Tower (Photo by Renny Jackson)

In many climbing areas further subdivisions, especially within the upper difficulty levels, add precision in the form of lowercase letters (***a*** to ***d***) or symbols (**+** and **-**) appended to the decimal ratings. For example: 5.10b, 5.11+, 5.12-, 5.13c. Both conventions are used in this guidebook. Generally speaking, letter grades are applied when there is a fairly solid consensus as to the difficulty. When there is no consensus or when the climb has not had many ascents, a + or - symbol may be applied, indicating a range in the letter grade (e.g., 5.12- = 5.12a/b, 5.12 = 5.12b/c, and 5.12+ = 5.12c/d).

5.0–5.3: This is often referred to as "easy 5th class" in the figures (the topos and phototopos). This general class spans the point where most parties will want to rope up, construct sound anchors, and begin to belay and place protection.

5.4–5.5: The climbing is still easy, but the handholds and footholds tend to be smaller, requiring skill and strength to climb, and greater attention must be paid to placing protection along belayed pitches.

5.6–5.13: Most of the technical rock climbs described in this guide fall into this range of difficulty ratings.

Note: Trad ratings in the mountains are very subjective. The Owen-Spalding route on the Grand Teton, for example, has an overall rating of 5.4, with a few moves of 5.5 in the Double Chimney. This assumes that the climb is as dry as it can be and that the climber is on what is considered by most to be the well-established route. A bit of water seepage here and there, a spot or two of verglas, or an accidental traverse slightly off-route can all contribute to a perceived increase in difficulty. Add the heightened sense of awareness that comes with considerable exposure or the threat of an approaching storm, and an "easy" climb can feel far more serious than its rating.

Speaking of seriousness, some climbs also include a "Seriousness Rating." The few that are used in this book have been used sparingly, which is surprising given the amount of loose rock that is found in these mountains. Besides referring to loose rock, these modifiers can refer to areas where protection is difficult or nonexistent. In general terms, the following definitions apply:

PG-13: Difficult or insecure protection or loose rock, with some injury potential; in one instance this is used to point out seasonal snowfields on the east face of Teewinot where numerous accidents have occurred.

R: Poor protection with high potential for injury.

X: A fall would likely result in serious injury or death.

The American Alpine Club's "International Grade Comparison Chart" is presented with permission herein for climbers who are used to other grading systems. (See *Figure 7*.)

THE AMERICAN ALPINE JOURNAL 2019

AAJ

INTERNATIONAL GRADE COMPARISON CHART

SERIOUSNESS RATINGS

These often modify technical grades when protection is difficult

PG-13: Difficult or insecure protection or loose rock, with some injury potential

R: Poor protection with high potential for injury

X: A fall would likely result in serious injury or death

YDS=Yosemite Decimal System
UIAA=Union Internationale des Associations D'Alpinisme
FR=France/Sport
AUS=Australia
SAX=Saxony
CIS=Commonwealth of Independent States/Russia
SCA=Scandinavia
BRA=Brazil
UK=United Kingdom

Note: *All conversions are approximate. Search "International Grade Comparison Chart" at the AAJ website for further explanation of commitment grades and waterfall Ice/mixed grades.*

YDS	UIAA	FR	AUS	SAX	CIS	SCA	BRA	UK	
5.2	II	1	10	II	III	3			D
5.3	III	2	11	III	III+	3+			
5.4	IV-	3	12		IV-	4			VD
5.5	IV IV+		13		IV	4+			S
5.6	V-	4	14		IV+	5-		4a	HS
5.7	V V+		15	VIIa		5		4b	VS
5.8	VI-	5a	16	VIIb	V-	5+	4 4+	4c	HVS
5.9	VI	5b	17	VIIc		6-	5 5+	5a	E1
5.10a	VI+	5c	18	VIIIa	V	6	6a	5b	
5.10b		6a		VIIIb					
5.10c	VII-	6a+	19			6+	6b		E2
5.10d	VII	6b	20	VIIIc	V+		6c		E3
5.11a	VII+	6b+		IXa		7-	7a	5c	
5.11b		6c	21	IXb		7	7b		
5.11c	VIII-	6c+	22		VI-	7+			E4
5.11d	VIII	7a	23	IXc			7c	6a	
5.12a	VIII+	7a+	24				8a		E5
5.12b		7b	25	Xa	VI	8-	8b		
5.12c	IX-	7b+	26	Xb		8 8+	8c		
5.12d	IX	7c	27				9a	6b	E6
5.13a	IX+	7c+	28	Xc			9b		
5.13b		8a	29			9-	9c		
5.13c	X-	8a+	30			9	10a		E7
5.13d	X	8b	31	XIa	VI+		10b		
5.14a	X+	8b+	32	XIb			10c	7a	E8
5.14b	XI-	8c	33			9+	11a		
5.14c	XI	8c+	34	XIc			11b	7b	E9
5.14d	XI+	9a	35				11c		E10
5.15a	XII-	9a+	36	XIIa		10	12a		
5.15b	XII	9b	37		VII		12b		
5.15c		9b+	38	XIIb			12c		E11
5.15d	XII+	9c	39						

FIGURE 7. Source: *American Alpine Journal*

AID

A number of climbs in this text are given an artificial-climbing difficulty rating. This is represented by the letter A followed by a number from 0 to 5, in ascending order of difficulty. This number indicates the difficulty of the hardest artificial or direct aid pitch of the route. Because few of the routes in the Tetons involve artificial climbing, this part of the rating will be absent for most of the routes. While the lower levels of artificial climbing, such as A0, A1, and A2, can ordinarily be done using standard equipment, certain specialized equipment or techniques often will be required for the higher levels. This includes items such as hooks, copperheads, RURPs, knifeblades (KBs), tie-off loops, and so forth. Because some of the route descriptions contained herein are quite ancient and, in many cases, represent the first ascent, the prospective climber should be aware that some ratings are going to be wrong.

Equipment has improved, techniques have progressed, and there have not been that many "new" aid climbs put up in the Tetons.

Note: A "C" rating refers to aid placements made without the use of a hammer.

A0: This lowest of aid ratings indicates occasional aid moves, often done without aiders (etriers), such as pulling up on a piece of protection. This is also known as "French free" in some areas.
A1: Placements are solid and easy—the best type, often referred to as "bombproof" or "capable of holding a truck."
A2: Protection is slightly harder to place and capable of holding less.
A3: More inventive techniques are required for placing protection; placements can hold only a short fall.
A4: Involves several placements in a row that can hold only body weight.
A5: Expect many A4 placements in a row with big falls possible.

ICE

Because it is impossible to accurately describe the difficulty of a particular stretch of ice using the same system that describes rock, a fourth designation is applied to routes that are primarily ice climbs. A WI or AI is placed at the front of this portion of the rating. The **WI** (water ice) refers to ice climbs that are primarily seasonal in nature, such as frozen waterfalls that usually melt out completely by summer and reemerge in winter. **AI** (alpine ice) refers to ice climbs that are usually present year-round, even during the summer months—a category that includes the classic alpine gullies and couloirs. A series of numbers from 1 to 5 then denote an ascending order of difficulty. The Scottish grading system, in which roman numerals were used to indicate overall ice difficulty, has in many areas evolved to this method of numeration. Additionally, the + symbol is used to further describe climbs that are at the uppermost end of a particular numerical ice grade.

1: Glacier walking requiring the use of crampons and an ice axe.
2: Mountain routes for which basic knowledge of the use of ice tools and crampons is suggested. Most of these routes in the Tetons are on glaciers or moderately angled snow couloirs.
3: Most climbers would prefer to have two ice tools and place intermediate protection during the climb; reasonable rests and good stances for placing protection are present.
4: The climbing is long and strenuous, and vertical ice is likely to be encountered at the crux of the route.
5: Also long and strenuous, but with significant sections of vertical ice offering few rests.
6: Expect a full ropelength of vertical ice climbing with no rests.

MIXED

These routes require dry-tooling techniques (modern ice tools used on rock) and are climbed in crampons; actual ice is sometimes present.

M1–M3: Easy, low-angle terrain; usually no tools required.
M4: Slabby to vertical with some technical dry tooling.
M5: Some sustained vertical dry tooling.
M6: Vertical to overhanging with difficult dry tooling.
M7: Overhanging; powerful and technical dry tooling; less than 10m of hard climbing.
M8–M12: Increasingly difficult overhanging terrain; at the upper end of the scale, this usually involves gymnastic climbing on the undersides of roofs.

Time Information

Time information is given at the end of the descriptive material for some of the routes. This information was acquired through statistical study of past climbing ascent times (excluding the descent time), recorded on the cards that were filed with Grand Teton National Park after each climb. (Note that the climbing registration system was discontinued in Grand Teton National Park in the early 1990s; the figures accurately reflect the number of hours required by those who made the ascent prior to that time.) In those cases where a range of times is given—for example, 4½ to 6 hours—the meaning is that one-third of those past climbers took less than 4½ hours, one-third took between 4½ and 6 hours, and one-third took more than 6 hours. Hence, to use this information properly, prospective climbers must estimate their own speed as being either fast (will require less than 4½ hours), medium (will require somewhere between 4½ and 6 hours), or slow (will require more than 6 hours). Where no range is indicated, the single median value of the time distribution is listed. The reason for omitting the time range information in some instances is that there were not enough recorded climbs of the route in question to provide a statistically valid estimate of this range. A single number—for example, 7¾ hours—means that half of the past climbers took less than 7¾ hours and half required more than 7¾ hours. In all cases the climbing times are given with reference to the camping location.

This time information has not been updated to any great degree since the previous edition and therefore provides only an estimate. Climbing styles have changed, and innovations in equipment and clothing have shaved significant weight off gear, while also making it safer. The Teton peaks are being climbed in a much lighter and faster manner than ever before.

ENDNOTES

1. Todd Cedarholm, a professional land surveyor (PLS) based in Jackson, Wyoming, provided these figures.
2. As reported by the Associated Press on October 26, 1991. The survey was performed by Rich Greenwood, Ray Warburton, and Jeff Scully, all of Jackson, Wyoming. The measurement was not accepted for publication by the National Geodetic Survey (NGS).

A Note about Safety

Safety is an important concern in all outdoor activities. No guidebook can alert you to every hazard or anticipate the limitations of every reader. Therefore, the descriptions of roads, trails, routes, and natural features in this book are not representations that a particular place or excursion will be safe for your party. When you follow any of the routes described in this book, you assume responsibility for your own safety. Under normal conditions, such excursions require the usual attention to traffic, road and trail conditions, weather, terrain, the capabilities of your party, and other factors. Keeping informed on current conditions and exercising common sense are the keys to a safe, enjoyable outing.

—Mountaineers Books

PART 2

Routes on the Peaks

SECTION 1

South of Death Canyon

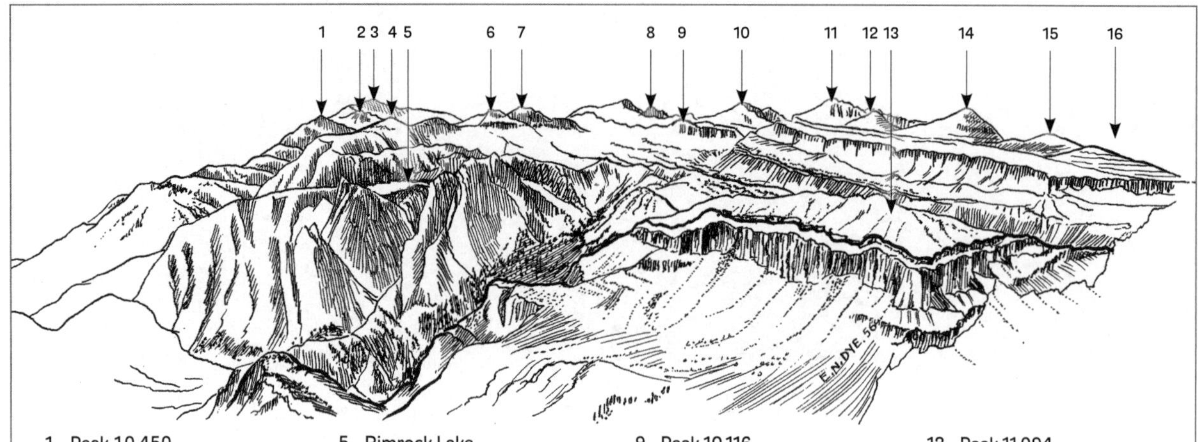

1. Peak 10,450
2. Peak 10,753
3. Rendezvous Peak
4. Prospectors Mountain
5. Rimrock Lake
6. Tukuarika Peak
7. Two Elk Peak
8. Peak 10,308
9. Peak 10,116
10. Housetop Mountain
11. Fossil Mountain
12. Peak 10,612
13. Peak 11,094
14. Mount Bannon
15. Mount Jedediah Smith
16. Mount Meek

Southern Teton Peaks from the Summit of Buck Mountain

Granite Canyon

Prior to the completion of the aerial tram to the summit of Peak 10,450 (commonly referred to as Rendezvous Mountain) at Jackson Hole Mountain Resort in 1966, Granite Canyon was the domain of the horse packer, frequently from the west side of the divide, and was seldom entered by climbers. The sedimentary peaks surrounding the canyon were not then, and are not now, high on the priority list of Teton climbers. Since 1966, however, the ease of access provided by the tram both to the heights (10,450) and to the upper canyon have enormously increased the foot traffic in Granite Canyon. Peak 10,450 is one of the standard starting points for multiday trail hikes on the Teton Crest Trail connecting to Cascade or Paintbrush Canyon. A favorite hike (12 miles) is now the trip from the top of the tram down the back side on the Rendezvous Mountain trail, then back out Granite Canyon to the Granite Canyon trailhead.

The mouth of the canyon is reached directly from the Granite Canyon trailhead, which is located on the Moose-Wilson Road about 2 miles north of its junction with the northern access road to Teton Village. The trail stays on the north side of Granite Creek from the mouth of the canyon past the Granite Canyon patrol cabin, until finally crossing the stream in the north fork just below Marion Lake, one of the primary destinations in the canyon. The generally accurate 7.5-minute USGS quadrangle maps (Teton Village and Rendezvous Peak) for some reason fail to show the eight switchbacks on this trail. The drainage of the small side canyon immediately west of Peak 10,450 provides a speedy method of ascent to or descent from Peak 10,450, but crossing Granite Creek and the gigantic sedimentary boulders therein causes some difficulties. At the first junction on the trail the left fork is the Rendezvous Mountain trail, which leads south, up the upper south fork of the canyon, to the summit of the mountain. To reach the head of the south fork at the pass (9,960+) just northwest of Rendezvous Peak (10,927) involves nothing more than cross-country hiking.

The upper middle fork of the canyon is best reached via a cutoff trail connecting the Rendezvous Mountain trail with the Teton Crest Trail and leading to Marion Lake at the head of the north fork. Another approach used by both hikers and horse parties is via the Teton Crest Trail and Moose Creek Divide (9,085). This trail originates at Highway 22/33, goes up Phillips Canyon and over Phillips Pass (8,932) into upper Moose Canyon, and enters Granite Canyon at Moose Creek Divide.

The main trail in the north fork leads to beautiful Marion Lake, a splendid camping area nestled just below the cliffs of the shelf below Housetop Mountain. Leading up to the lake the trail passes to the right of a curious natural bridge, located on the south side of the creek at 8,700 feet, just west of the junction with the Open Canyon trail. This is known as the Arch, and it is a common ski destination during the winter season. From Marion Lake the Teton Crest Trail leads over a pass (9,560+) on its way north to Fox Creek Pass (9,540+) at the head of Death Canyon. To reach Mount Hunt Divide (9,710), which provides the link with Open Canyon, take the right fork at the junction of the main north fork of the Granite Canyon trail with the Open Canyon trail. Secluded Indian Lake (9,805) lies high above the canyon at its north rim. It can be reached from the Open Canyon trail by hiking up the side canyon containing its outlet stream. Starting up this drainage from the floor of Granite Canyon is not recommended. The lake is perhaps most easily reached via the separate drainage immediately above and north of the upper Granite Canyon patrol cabin. Hike up to the head of this side stream, either from its intersection with the Open Canyon trail or directly from the cabin, and contour on a bench around to the right (east) to the lake.

The nature of the sedimentary rock in the southern and northern ends of the Teton Range is conducive to the formation of sinkholes and caves. Exercise some caution in cross-country hiking in such limestone terrain because some of these caves are simply and suddenly holes in the flat ground. A number of these are to be found on the slopes of Rendezvous Mountain and in Granite, Open, and Death Canyons. Two well-known caves, Wind Cave and Ice Cave, are found on the west slope of the range in Darby Canyon, as shown on the USGS Mount Bannon quadrangle. Some of these caves are very deep and entry and exit are difficult. Indeed, elsewhere in the range is one of the deepest caves in the United States. While these natural features may be of intriguing interest to climbers, details regarding the location of such formations are better presented in speleological journals and books since, to some extent, specialized equipment beyond that used in normal mountaineering is required to explore these formations safely.

Open Canyon

Open Canyon provides access to a half dozen of the highest peaks in the south end of the range. Although the peaks are sedimentary, an enjoyable day of ridge running is available to those who do not require vertical difficulty. The usual approach is from the Death Canyon trailhead (see *Death Canyon* in Section 2 for directions to this trailhead) via the Valley Trail, over the Phelps Lake Overlook, and down to the junction with the Death Canyon trail near the west shore of Phelps Lake. Follow the left fork and cross the bridge over the creek coming out of Death Canyon. Continue south as the trail climbs along the lowest slopes of Prospectors Mountain. Up on the lateral moraine take the right fork at the first of two junctions and hike into the canyon. At the point where the trail crosses the main Open Canyon stream, an important side stream, shown as intermittent on the map, comes down from the north, draining the major cirque lying below the upper northeast face of Prospectors Mountain. This drainage can be easily ascended or descended, and if the final ridge on the right (north) is gained and climbed to the high point (10,560+), a route to or from Rimrock Lake can be put together.

Open Canyon can also be accessed from the Laurance S. Rockefeller Preserve trail network (see *Death Canyon* in Section 2 for directions). There are good trails on the north and south sides of Phelps Lake, all of which eventually lead to the west/southwest side of the lake, where they join the trails mentioned above.

The trail continues to the vicinity of the forks, where it starts a steep uphill section to pass over the south rim of the canyon at Mount Hunt Divide (9,710) and then drops into the upper portions of Granite Canyon. From the point (8,700) where the trail leaves the canyon floor to go up to the Mount Hunt ridge, it is easy to continue up the canyon in any direction. In early season the north-facing slope leading to Mount Hunt Divide will be covered with snow and an ice axe will be useful, perhaps essential. The beautiful alpine Coyote Lake (10,201) lies high at the head of the south fork. Even Indian Lake in Granite Canyon can be reached by crossing over the saddle (10,080+) west of Mount Hunt and contouring around the slopes to the lake.

PEAK 9,815

(1.6 mi WSW of Apres Vous Peak)
Map: Teton Village

Easily reached from almost any direction, this small, rounded peak lies on the boundary of Jackson Hole Mountain Resort just northeast of Peak 10,450, where the aerial tram terminates. A high point on the same ridge about 1.6 miles farther to the northeast is Apres Vous Peak (8,426), which is reached by a chairlift from the ski area.

ROUTE 1. SOUTHWEST RIDGE. I, 1.0. Various ski resort trails lead to the cirque southwest of the peak; the summit is easily attained from there.

ROUTE 2. NORTHEAST RIDGE. I, 3.0. Probable first ascent in May or June 1934, by T. F. Murphy and Robert E. Brislawn. From the Teton Village parking area take the road to Apres Vous Peak and follow the ridge to Peak 9,815. A short section of exposed scrambling will be encountered near the top.

PEAK 10,450 (RENDEZVOUS MOUNTAIN)

(2.7 mi NE of Rendezvous Peak)
Map: Teton Village

Innumerable visitors in both winter and summer reach this peak using the effortless Jackson Hole Mountain Resort aerial tram that terminates on the summit. Peak 10,450 provides a good viewpoint for the high peaks to the north and serves as a conveniently high starting point for hikes in Granite Canyon and climbs of other peaks in the southern portion of the Teton Range. There has been some confusion of names concerning this peak, which has no official name. The ski area refers to this single peak as Rendezvous Mountain or Rendezvous Peak. The name Rendezvous Mountain, according to the US Geological Survey (USGS), is the entire massif extending from the mouth of Granite Canyon on the northeast to Phillips Pass on the southwest, but that usage is rarely encountered. Peak 10,450 lies about midway along this ridge that makes up Rendezvous Mountain. Rendezvous Peak (10,927) is a specific summit, the highest point of Rendezvous Mountain.

The eastern slope of Rendezvous Mountain was largely unexplored before the early 1960s, when snow studies were done preceding the construction of Jackson Hole Mountain Resort. The winter of 1965–66 was the ski area's first commercial season, with three lifts operating. The aerial tram was completed on July 31, 1966, after 26 months of construction.

The cliffs immediately below the tram's tower #5 contain bolt-protected sport climbs, with the only drawback being that the location necessitates the expense of a tram ticket. The setting is spectacular, and the climbing is on steep dolomite featuring pockets and edges. From the summit of Peak 10,450, walk down to the east a short distance to either of the two famous couloirs on the north side of the mountain. The first (and larger of the two) is Corbet's Couloir, one of the most infamous ski runs in the country. The second, which is much narrower, is called S&S Couloir and is just a short distance

farther east. The climbs are located on the upper, east-facing walls of each couloir. There are also a few difficult routes on the north-facing side of Corbet's Couloir. Development of these high-altitude crags included the following individuals: Richard and Kathryn Collins, Greg Miles, Sam Lightner Jr., James Burwick, Brents Hawks, Jim Kanzler, and Mike Fischer.

Chronology

NORTHEAST RIDGE: [probable] May or June 1934, T. F. Murphy, Robert E. Brislawn
SOUTHWEST RIDGE: July 24, 1960, Arthur J. Reyman

ROUTE 1. SOUTHWEST RIDGE. I, 1.0. First known ascent July 24, 1960, by Arthur J. Reyman, by a traverse from Peak 10,750. On the summit Reyman found a cairn but no record. The trail from Granite Canyon now ascends this ridge, although it is more often used for descent than for ascent. In early season considerable snow will be encountered along this trail.

ROUTE 2. NORTHEAST RIDGE. I, 1.0. Probable first ascent in May or June 1934, by T. F. Murphy and Robert E. Brislawn. The saddle (9,520+; known as Tensleep Saddle) at the base of this broad ridge can be reached either from the northwest by bushwhacking up from the Granite Canyon trail or by hiking in from the southeast using a network of trails that the ski area has constructed in recent years. If approaching from Granite Canyon, the main stream must be crossed.

ROCK SPRINGS BUTTRESS (ca. 9,200)

(0.8 mi S of Peak 10,450)
Map: Teton Village

This fine crag is rather conspicuous as one approaches Teton Village along the road from the south. The buttress is located high on the southeast side of Rendezvous Mountain (on which the aerial tram is located), forming the north wall of Rock Springs Canyon. The first examination of these fine cliffs of crystalline rock was apparently carried out sometime before March 1967, when Maurice Horn made a sequence of pioneering climbs with Steve Smith and Rod Dornan. The central rock feature here is now known as Rock Springs Buttress, and it contains the highest concentration of good climbs (sport, trad, and mixed) in the entire Jackson Hole area. As of 2020 there were some 60+ routes on the main buttress as well as the smaller crags to the east and west. Most are multipitch, high-quality climbs on outstanding rock. For route descriptions of the entire area, see the excellent guidebook *Rock Climbing Jackson Hole and Pinedale, Wyoming*, by Wesley Gooch.

PEAK 10,753 (CODY PEAK)

(1.5 mi NNE of Rendezvous Peak)
Map: Rendezvous Peak

This sedimentary peak is the first major summit along the ridge extending south from the top of the aerial tram on Peak 10,450 to Rendezvous Peak. A fine day of ridge running can be enjoyed by making the double traverse from the tram to Rendezvous Peak and back. An unofficial name, Cody Peak, has been applied by the nearby ski area. During the winter the Grand National Powder 8's competition has been held on its north slope, in which skiers pair up to create their best figure eights in Cody Bowl just outside the ski area boundary. Three couloirs on this mountain have also become legendary among skiers: the Once Is Enough and Twice Is Nice Couloirs are located on the southeast side of the mountain, while the formidable Central Couloir is on the north side.

ROUTE 1. SOUTHWEST RIDGE. I, 2.0. First ascent July 24, 1960, by Arthur J. Reyman. The break in the west wall of this peak can be found by traversing north from the saddle between this peak and Peak 10,706. Once above the wall, follow the southwest ridge to the summit.

ROUTE 2. ▲ NORTH RIDGE. I, 2.0. First descent July 24, 1960, by Arthur J. Reyman; first known ascent in August 1968, by Leigh Ortenburger. Easily climbed, this route is part of the Rendezvous Mountain ridge traverse.

PEAK 10,706 (NO NAME PEAK)

(1.0 mi NNE of Rendezvous Peak)
Map: Rendezvous Peak

The normal approach to this peak is along the north ridge from Peak 10,753, but it can be easily reached from the extreme southern portion of Granite Canyon or directly from the east. The eastern approach, using Fish Creek Road north from the town of Wilson, has the complication of requiring permission to park a car because the land along the road is in private ownership.

Chronology

EAST RIDGE: October 14, 1937, Arthur Rust, Nick Dietrich
SOUTHWEST RIDGE: July 28, 1955, Gene Balaz, Redwood Fryxell (descent); July 24, 1960, Arthur J. Reyman (ascent)
NORTH RIDGE: July 24, 1960, Arthur J. Reyman (descent); August 1968, Leigh Ortenburger (ascent)

ROUTE 1. SOUTHWEST RIDGE. I, 1.0. First descent July 28, 1955, by Gene Balaz and Redwood Fryxell; first ascent July 24, 1960, by Arthur J. Reyman. This easy route is used for traversing to or from Rendezvous Peak.

ROUTE 2. EAST RIDGE. I, 1.0. First ascent October 14, 1937, by Arthur Rust and Nick Dietrich. Two hours of bushwhacking up the lower ridge takes one to the final steeper east ridge leading directly to the summit. This ridge lies immediately south of Pinedale Canyon, an unofficial name given by local skiers.

ROUTE 3. ▲ NORTH RIDGE. I, 1.0. First descent July 24, 1960, by Arthur J. Reyman; first known ascent in August 1968, by Leigh Ortenburger. This ridge is used for the standard traverse from Peak 10,450, the top of the ski area tram, to Rendezvous Peak. It involves no difficulties.

RENDEZVOUS PEAK (10,927)

Map: Rendezvous Peak

Although this peak is neither inside nor on the boundary of Grand Teton National Park, it affords an excellent vantage point for most of the southwestern portion of the park. In addition, the terrain surrounding it offers features that contrast markedly with the usual climbing areas.

The complex structure of Rendezvous Peak requires some description. The upper portion consists of a northeast–southwest wedge, 0.3 mile long, with the summit near the southwest end. Four ridges support this wedge: the east ridge, which rises directly from Jackson Hole to the northeast end of the wedge; the south ridge, which is divided into three subridges south of the 10,332-foot southern subsummit; the west ridge, which splits into the broad west slope and the southwest ridge that descends to Phillips Pass after crossing Peak 10,053; and the north ridge, which splits into the northwest ridge (which passes over Peak 10,277 before reaching Moose Creek Divide) and the northeast ridge that continues over Peak 10,706. Some difficulty may be experienced in identifying the peaks and streams in this area. During most summers the long, horizontal snow crescent that lies just beneath the saddle between Peak 10,706 and the northeast end of the summit wedge of Rendezvous Peak serves as one identification point from the east.

In addition to the aerial tram, several approaches are possible, depending on the route to be used to reach the summit. From the west, the side road up Moose Creek from Highway 33 south of Victor, Idaho, leads to the trailhead (Highway 33 becomes Highway 22 across the Idaho-Wyoming border). The Moose Creek trail then heads up the canyon past Moose Creek Meadows to Moose Creek Divide (9,085), which divides Moose and Granite Canyons. The upper portion of this trail can also be reached via Coal Creek, which holds the first main trail leaving Highway 22 on the west side of Teton Pass. From the divide (9,197) at the head of Coal Creek, drop down Mesquite Creek to Moose Creek Meadows.

From the southeast, the road north from Wilson offers access to the direct east approach to Rendezvous Peak. This same road also leads to the mouth of Phillips Canyon. The Phillips Canyon trail begins here, crosses Phillips Pass southwest of Rendezvous Peak, and joins the Moose Creek trail about 2 miles south of Moose Creek Divide. Another approach to Phillips Pass starts from the gravel road that extends out to Phillips Ridge from the north hairpin curve on Highway 22 over Teton Pass.

Chronology

WEST RIDGE: August 20, 1898, T. M. Bannon, George A. Buck
SOUTHWEST RIDGE: August 4, 1933, Fritiof Fryxell, Leland Horberg
SOUTH RIDGE: August 4, 1933, Fritiof Fryxell, Leland Horberg (descent)
NORTHWEST RIDGE: [probable] May or June 1934, T. F. Murphy, Robert E. Brislawn; July 28, 1955, Gene Balaz, Redwood Fryxell (descent)
EAST RIDGE: June 23, 1941, Henry Coulter, Merrill McLane, Stewart Mockford
NORTHEAST RIDGE: July 28, 1955, Gene Balaz, Redwood Fryxell

ROUTE 1. WEST RIDGE. I, 1.0. First ascent August 20, 1898, by topographer T. M. Bannon and his assistant George A. Buck. Rendezvous Peak was ascended by Bannon and Buck from the head of Moose Creek to establish a triangulation station, known in the records of the US Geological Survey (USGS) as "Phillips Station." It is uncertain that this easy ridge was the route used, but it is the most likely.

ROUTE 2. SOUTHWEST RIDGE. I, 1.0. First ascent August 4, 1933, by Fritiof Fryxell and Leland Horberg. From Phillips Pass, climb easily to the summit over the 10,053-foot southwest peak. **Time:** 7½ hours from the mouth of Phillips Canyon.

ROUTE 3. SOUTH RIDGE. I, 1.0. First descent August 4, 1933, by Fritiof Fryxell and Leland Horberg. From the high saddle (10,160+) at the head of Jensen Canyon this ridge can be easily climbed. From the east one could hike all the way up Jensen Canyon to this saddle or approach from the west via the north fork of Phillips Canyon.

ROUTE 4. EAST RIDGE. I, 2.0. First ascent June 23, 1941, by Henry Coulter, Merrill McLane, and Stewart Mockford. No difficulties will be encountered on this long ridge. **Time:** 8 hours from the base of the peak.

ROUTE 5. ▲ NORTHEAST RIDGE. I, 2.0. First ascent July 28, 1955, by Gene Balaz and Redwood Fryxell. The long, bare saddle connecting Peak 10,706 to the northeastern summit of Rendezvous Peak is gained either directly from the east or from Peak 10,706, as was done by the first-ascent party. The southwestern, reddish summit is easily reached. **Time:** 5½ hours from the base of the ridge.

ROUTE 6. ▲ NORTHWEST RIDGE. I, 3.0. Probable first ascent in May or June 1934, by T. F. Murphy and Robert E. Brislawn; first descent July 28, 1955, by Gene Balaz and Redwood Fryxell. To reach this ridge take the Rendezvous Mountain trail, either from the valley starting at the Granite Canyon trailhead or from the top of the aerial tram on Peak 10,450. Leave this trail where it crosses the south fork of Granite Creek, and head due south to the saddle separating Rendezvous Mountain from Peak 10,277. The upper portions of the canyon and the final ridge require some scrambling.

GRANITE CANYON, SOUTH SIDE ROCK CLIMBS

Map: Teton Village

At intervals along the south side of Granite Canyon are buttresses and small towers featuring rock-climbing routes. These are listed here from east to west.

Goat Rocks (ca. 7,600)

(0.6 mi NE of Apres Vous Peak)

This cliff is located on the map between 7,200 and 7,600 feet at the north end of the park boundary on the northeast ridge of Apres Vous Peak. Goat Rocks forms the eastern end of the north face of this peak.

ROUTE 1. NORTH SIDE. I, 3.0. First ascent August 2, 1980, by Randy and Jan Harrington. Approach from the vicinity of Point 7,062 in lower Granite Canyon, as shown on the map. Three pitches were climbed on this route. While the rock is licheny and sometimes loose, the views from the route are good.

Sharkshead Pinnacle (ca. 9,200)

(0.8 mi W of Apres Vous Peak)

This 150m buttress or pinnacle is a noticeable feature of Granite Canyon, the first prominent buttress protruding from the canyon's south wall. It can be located on the map as the sharp arête extending north from Point 9,503, 0.8 mile west of Apres Vous Peak. The name is derived from the notch, which looks like a shark's head pointing upward when seen from the east. This shark's head is the identifying feature as one proceeds up the Granite Canyon trail. The couloirs that are located on either side of this buttress—Mile Long Couloir (east) and Endless Couloir (west)—figure prominently in local skiers' lore and legend.

ROUTE 1. EAST COULOIR AND WEST FACE. I, 3.0. First known ascent August 24, 1969, by T. Keith Liggett and Philip S. Peterson, who found a tin can on the summit. Scramble up the east couloir (Mile Long Couloir) to the notch separating the pinnacle from the mountain, and then climb around on the west face to the summit. An easier approach is to use the trails of the ski resort to reach the south ridge of Granite Canyon and then drop down to the notch.

FIGURE 1-1. Sharkshead Pinnacle. (A) Givler's Arête *(Route 2)*, III, 5.9; (B) Open Heart Surgery *(Route 3)*, III, 5.11a

ROUTE 2. GIVLER'S ARÊTE. III, 5.9. First ascent August 25, 1979, by Keith Hadley and George Montopoli. (See *Figure 1-1.*) This six-pitch route follows the crest of the north arête of this pinnacle fairly closely. From a ledge about 30m to the west of the lowest point of the arête, climb up an easy chimney and belay on the east side of a block. The first pitch goes up a right-facing corner or large flake (4 to 5 inches to begin with, then 3 to 4 inches) and is the most difficult pitch on the route. The next pitch of 5.5 rock is followed by a more demanding 46m lead of 5.8 difficulty. Move the belay to the east approximately 9m to a tree, where the fourth lead (30m) continues up and slightly left on 5.7 rock to a belay point very close to the crest of the arête on a slab. The next lead continues upward past a flake, followed by a stretch of unprotected 5.7 face climbing. Two sections of 5.8 are then encountered, the first being a thin left-facing corner and the second an exciting lieback. The final 20m pitch is 5.6, and the climb finishes with a scramble up and across the summit ridge. This arête can be approached in a downhill fashion from the top of the tram by following the ridge down to Point 9,503 and then descending the east couloir (Mile Long Couloir; see *Route 1*) to the base of the arête. Alternatively, the Bridger Gondola at Jackson Hole Mountain Resort, followed by a short walk up to the ridge crest, can be used to access these climbs. **Gear:** Large devices are needed on the first pitch.

ROUTE 3. OPEN HEART SURGERY. III, 5.11a. First ascent in June 2000, by David Bywater and Chris Harder. (See *Figure 1-1.*) **Pitch 1:** At the toe of the north-facing arête running the length of the pinnacle, begin climbing right of the arête following the path of least resistance. Trend up and right toward the prominent dihedral with a beautiful hand crack visible high on the face above. Belay at a good stance as the rock begins to steepen (5.7, 24m). **Pitch 2:** Climb steeper rock through a 5.9 roof to a good ledge at the base of the dihedral (5.9, 15m). **Pitch 3:** Climb the hand crack (protection 0.5" to 2") in the dihedral until it ends at an obvious belay ledge (5.11a, 12m). **Note:** It is possible to combine the second and third pitches. **Pitch 4:** Climb left to a trough-like feature that leads to a notch on the crest (5.6, 30m). **Pitches 5–6:** The route joins the last two pitches of Givler's Arête *(Route 2)* to the summit.

Granite Central Buttresses (ca. 9,000)

(1.0 mi NW of Apres Vous Peak)

At 7,400 feet, about halfway to the upper patrol cabin in Granite Canyon, the trail reaches an open willow meadow directly across the stream from large buttresses on the south side of the canyon. This section of willows is shortly beyond the sixth switchback corner in the trail. There are two climbs on the lower portion of the good rock of these buttresses, between 7,600 and 8,000 feet.

Chronology

THE HELL YOU SAY: August 8, 1980, Randy Harrington, Leo Larson

LIGHTNING CRACK: June 28, 1981, Rich Perch, John Carr

ROUTE 1. LIGHTNING CRACK. II, 5.10. First ascent June 28, 1981, by Rich Perch and John Carr. From the far (west) end of the aforementioned willows, one can look across to the south side of the canyon and back to the east and see on the more easterly (and northerly) of the two lower buttresses this easily recognized crack, which resembles a jagged lightning bolt, on a large west-facing slab. This crack leads directly to the crest of the buttress. After an initial pitch to reach the beginning of the crack, climb 12m up the 5.10 offwidth crack, which is to the left of a large left-facing corner.

ROUTE 2. THE HELL YOU SAY. II, 5.9. First ascent August 8, 1980, by Randy Harrington and Leo Larson. On the west face of the more westerly (and southerly) of the two lower buttresses, two large, vertical cracks extend upward for some 46m. This route of three pitches ascends the right crack for two pitches to gain the beginning of a well-defined ramp leading up and right. The third lead goes up this ramp to its end where a short climb back left ends the route. Descent involves first ascending a prominent couloir to gain a complicated system of couloirs down to the northeast. **Gear:** For protection take a normal rack with a couple of large nuts as well as camming devices.

Phil's Pickle (ca. 8,400)

(1.35 mi WNW of Apres Vous Peak)

This, the smaller and more easterly of the two pinnacles seen from just past the eighth switchback corner on the Granite Canyon trail, has the appearance of a pickle.

ROUTE 1. SOUTHEAST CORNER. I, 5.1. First ascent August 23, 1969, by T. Keith Liggett and Philip S. Peterson. This route ascends a small open book on the southeast corner of the 20m pinnacle.

Buchwald's Blister (ca. 8,400)

(1.35 mi WNW of Apres Vous Peak)

From the Granite Canyon trailhead take the trail upcanyon to a point about 150 feet past the eighth switchback corner on the trail. If the light is right, two pinnacles can be seen on the south side of the canyon above a long talus slope. The larger, Buchwald's Blister, can be recognized by a vertical yellow west face and smooth, downsloping slabs on the north face. It appears on the map as a small 8,400-foot contour line circle about 0.2 mile east of Point 8,545.

ROUTE 1. EAST COULOIR. I, 1.0. First descent August 23, 1969, by T. Keith Liggett, Caryl E. Buchwald, and Philip S. Peterson. This easy couloir descends to the east from the notch between the wall and the pinnacle.

ROUTE 2. NORTH FACE. I, 5.4. First ascent August 23, 1969, by T. Keith Liggett, Caryl E. Buchwald, and Philip S. Peterson. This route, consisting of one 40m lead, starts near the middle of the north face of the pinnacle and makes a traverse left to the small chimney, which is climbed to easier rock leading to the summit.

ROUTE 3. WEST COULOIR. I, 3.0. First ascent August 23, 1969, by T. Keith Liggett, Caryl E. Buchwald, and Philip S. Peterson. This west couloir is mostly a scramble to the notch between the wall and the summit of the pinnacle.

PEAK 10,277

(0.7 mi N of Rendezvous Peak)

Map: Rendezvous Peak

This grassy, round-topped peak with a broad, flower-covered northwest ridge is easily climbed from almost any direction.

ROUTE 1. NORTHWEST SLOPE. I, 1.0. First ascent July 24, 1960, by Arthur J. Reyman. Walk up from Moose Creek Divide, the 9,085-foot pass crossed by the trail from Moose Creek into the middle fork of Granite Canyon.

ROUTE 2. SOUTHEAST SLOPE. I, 1.0. First descent July 24, 1960, by Arthur J. Reyman. Walk up from the saddle that connects with the Rendezvous Mountain ridge.

PEAK 9,925

(1.8 mi SE of Housetop Mountain)

Map: Rendezvous Peak

ROUTE 1. WEST SLOPE. I, 1.0. The T. M. Bannon topographic party placed a benchmark here in 1899. On July 22, 1960, Arthur J. Reyman climbed this tree-covered slope and found a 6-foot cairn on the summit.

ROUTE 2. SOUTHEAST SLOPE. I, 1.0. Probable first ascent July 26, 1931, by Leslie Shaw Henrie. Walk up to the northwest from Moose Creek Divide (9,085).

PEAK 10,308

(1.0 mi S of Housetop Mountain)

Map: Rendezvous Peak

The northeast ridge of this sedimentary peak appears unsuitable for climbing, while the west slope probably provides the easiest access to the summit. The most convenient approach, however, is from Granite Canyon on the east.

ROUTE 1. SOUTH RIDGE. I, 2.0. First ascent July 22, 1960, by Arthur J. Reyman. On the same day Reyman also reached Peak 10,315 (0.6 mile south-southwest) via the northeast slope and Point 10,240+ (0.4 mile southwest) via the east slope. From Point 10,240+ on the park boundary, a knife-edge ridge must be traversed to reach Peak 10,308.

ROUTE 2. NORTHEAST RIDGE. I, 4.0. First ascent August 16, 1998, by Paul Horton. This ascent confirmed the decomposing ridge's unsuitability for climbing; the line of least resistance on or near the crest is insecure and exposed.

PEAK 9,814

(1.8 mi ESE of Housetop Mountain)

Map: Rendezvous Peak

Also known as Pandora's Box or Pandora's Mountain, this small peak separating the middle and north forks of Granite Canyon is a popular winter destination, offering a number of beautiful couloirs on its northern side. There is a remarkable natural bridge—the Arch—on the lower sedimentary cliff band on the northwest flank of the peak at about 8,700 feet. Skiing the couloir through the Arch is a highly sought-after winter objective. The formation is perhaps the largest of its kind in the park, with an opening that measures about 18m high by 9m wide. In the summer look for it on the south side of the north fork of Granite Creek, just past (west of) the junction of the Granite Canyon and Open Canyon trails. It is apparently most easily seen in midafternoon when the sun shines behind it.

ROUTE 1. WEST SLOPE. I, 1.0. Probable first ascent in May or June 1934, by T. F. Murphy and Robert E. Brislawn; first known ascent July 23, 1960, by Arthur J. Reyman. Proceed from the Teton Crest Trail where it crosses the 9,280+-foot pass just west of the peak and south of Marion Lake.

HOUSETOP MOUNTAIN (10,537)

Map: Rendezvous Peak

Housetop Mountain is located just outside (west of) the Grand Teton National Park boundary between the Game and Fox

Creek drainages. Before 1931 this name was applied to the 10,916-foot peak that is 2.5 miles to the northeast, which is now officially named Fossil Mountain.

ROUTE 1. SOUTHEAST RIDGE. I, 1.0. Probable first ascent in May or June 1934, by T. F. Murphy and Robert E. Brislawn. On July 22, 1960, Arthur J. Reyman climbed this route from the Game Creek trail and followed the divide to the summit, where an empty cairn was found. The ridge can also be reached from the high bench in Granite Canyon just east of the divide, using the Teton Crest Trail.

PEAK 10,116

(0.8 mi ENE of Housetop Mountain)
Map: Mount Bannon

Overlooking Marion Lake, this peak is protected on the north and the east by a serious sedimentary cliff band, which must be passed on the south. In late season the small lake on the high bench south of the peak becomes a mudflat without a water supply for camping.

ROUTE 1. SOUTHWEST SLOPE. I, 1.0. First known ascent July 23, 1960, by Arthur J. Reyman, who found an empty cairn on the summit. Leave the trail about 0.25 mile south of Marion Lake. Go south and west around the base of the cliffs at the west side of the lake. Easy flower-covered benches lead to the plateau above the cliffs; from there the remainder of the climb is easy.

SPEARHEAD PEAK (10,131)

Map: Mount Bannon

The northern aspect of this peak is quite imposing and resembles Devils Tower in miniature. A walk completely around the base of the peak requires only 30 minutes and shows that the most interesting climbing lies on the northern half of the west face and on the north face proper. The best approach to Spearhead Peak is by the Death Canyon trail to Fox Creek Pass at the park boundary. Walk 0.5 mile south along the trail toward Marion Lake to the area west of Spearhead Peak. Considerable caution should be used in the cracks and chimneys on this peak because of the nature of the rock, which in the lower sections is Bighorn Dolomite and at the summit is Gallatin Limestone.

Of the high points to the east, Point 10,440+ (1 mile southeast of Spearhead Peak) has been reached by horseback, and Point 10,495 (1.3 miles east of Spearhead Peak) was first reached on July 12, 1960, by Arthur J. Reyman from the northwest. These two points enclose Indian Lake on the west and north.

ROUTE 1. ▲ SOUTH RIDGE. I, 4.0. Probable first ascent in May or June 1934, by T. F. Murphy and Robert E. Brislawn; first known ascent either in 1941, by Allan Cameron and Judy Cameron, or on July 17, 1941, by Arthur J. Reyman. From the trail to the west, scramble up loose limestone blocks to the south side of the final tower. One 9m pitch on the southeast side of the ridge leads onto the summit area; a rope may be useful for protection on this final pitch. The holds are large, but many are loose.

ROUTE 2. NORTH FACE, EAST CHIMNEY. I, 5.1. First ascent August 18, 1955, by Gene Balaz and Beatrice Burford. This is a short and delicate 46m climb on which gear is needed for protection.

ROUTE 3. IN SEARCH OF . . . . I, 5.8. First ascent July 15, 1991, by Paul Horton and Bill Alexander. This one-pitch climb is on the southwest side of the peak and is 50m in length. The pitch begins with a 5.8 corner followed by a loose and blocky section of 5.4. After climbing a 5.4 chimney (no protection), traverse into a larger, easier chimney. At the top of this chimney step out to the left onto 5.6 face climbing that leads to the summit of the peak. **Gear:** Medium-size protection is suggested for this climb.

MOUNT HUNT (10,783)

Map: Grand Teton

This sedimentary peak shares a characteristic with a few other technically easy Teton peaks: a cairn of unknown origin was found on its summit during the early systematic exploration of the range. An excellent view of the seldom-visited Coyote and Indian Lakes can be had from the summit. The peak was named for Wilson Price Hunt, leader of the overland Astorian expedition, which in the fall of 1811 entered Jackson Hole via Hoback Canyon and left via Teton Pass. A triangulation station, "Picture Point No. 6," was established on September 3, 1946, by A. K. Andrews and J. Clark on the 9,877-foot high point along Mount Hunt's broad lower east ridge. Now known as Olive Oil, this point is a popular ski destination during the winter months.

Chronology

EAST RIDGE: August 24, 1929, Fritiof Fryxell
WEST RIDGE: [probable] June 27, 1934, T. F. Murphy, Robert E. Brislawn, Arthur Boles, Mike Yokel Jr.; July 31, 1936, Leland Horberg, LeRoy Brissman (descent)

ROUTE 1. WEST RIDGE. I, 1.0. Probable first ascent June 27, 1934, by T. F. Murphy, Robert E. Brislawn, Arthur Boles, and Mike Yokel Jr.; first descent July 31, 1936, by Leland Horberg and LeRoy Brissman. From the Death Canyon trailhead, follow the Valley Trail and cross the bridge over Death Canyon Creek. Continue around the west side of Phelps Lake to the cutoff to the Open Canyon trail. Take this trail up the canyon to the point at about 8,960+ feet where it turns left (south) toward Mount Hunt Divide, away from the creek. Leave the trail here and continue up the canyon to the broad saddle between Mount Hunt and Two Elk Peak (the Open Canyon fault goes through this saddle). From here follow the easy ridge over the 10,560+-foot subpeak toward Mount Hunt. It would also be possible to skirt this subpeak around the north side to visit the small 10,000+-foot lake and then ascend the talus and scree to rejoin the west ridge of Mount Hunt. See *American Alpine Journal* 12, no. 2 (1961): p. 374.

ROUTE 2. ▲ EAST RIDGE. I, 2.0. First known ascent August 24, 1929, by Fritiof Fryxell, who found an empty cairn on the summit. From the Death Canyon trailhead (see *Death Canyon* in Section 2) take the Open Canyon trail to Mount Hunt Divide (9,710) between Open Canyon and Granite Canyon, just east of Mount Hunt. The cliff above this point can be avoided by continuing a short distance south along the trail before scrambling up to the summit. If one continues very far south, the route might more correctly be called the southeast slope. **Time:** 6½ hours from the Death Canyon trailhead. See *Appalachia* 18, no. 3 (June 1931): pp. 209–32, illus.

TWO ELK PEAK (10,905)

(0.9 mi NW of Mount Hunt)
Map: Grand Teton

This flat-topped summit, the south member of a double peak, lies at the head of Open Canyon and shows prominently

from certain positions in Jackson Hole. The Open Canyon fault runs through the saddle between this peak and Mount Hunt; the throw, or amount of displacement of the fault, is about 2,800 feet. The name was given for the members of the first known ascent party, as seen from a distance.

Chronology

NORTHWEST WALL: July 12, 1960, David Dornan, Mark Melton, Mona Monahan, Leigh Ortenburger
SOUTHEAST RIDGE: July 12, 1960, David Dornan, Mark Melton, Mona Monahan, Leigh Ortenburger (descent); June 9, 1967, R. Erickson, K. Eggart, M. Wischmayer (ascent)
NORTH CHIMNEY: June 14, 1974, Richard Day, John Kevin Fox (descent)
WEST RIDGE: August 20, 1995, Jim Springer

ROUTE 1. WEST RIDGE. II, 5.4. First ascent August 20, 1995, by Jim Springer. The crumbling gendarmes are generally passed on the south, but some must be climbed over their tops. This route is not recommended.

ROUTE 2. ▲ SOUTHEAST RIDGE. I, 1.0. First descent July 12, 1960, by David Dornan, Mark Melton, Mona Monahan, and Leigh Ortenburger; first ascent June 9, 1967, by R. Erickson, K. Eggart, and M. Wischmayer. Gain the saddle between this peak and Mount Hunt either from Open Canyon or from Granite Canyon; the broad ridge above leads to the summit. This is the only easy route on this peak, which is otherwise surrounded by sedimentary cliffs. See *American Alpine Journal* 12, no. 2 (1961): pp. 373–79.

ROUTE 3. NORTH CHIMNEY. I, 4.0. First descent June 14, 1974, by Richard Day and John Kevin Fox. From the col between this peak and Murphy Peak, traverse 60m around to the right (west) side of Two Elk Peak, passing one chimney blocked by chockstones, to reach a recess in the cliffs. Climb a 12m chimney at the left (north) corner of this recess to the top of the first cliff band. The second band above is climbed via an easier 6m chimney to the north end of the summit plateau. Both chimneys are solid, but there is much loose rock on the bench between the first and second cliff bands.

ROUTE 4. NORTHWEST WALL. I, 5.1. First ascent July 12, 1960, by David Dornan, Mark Melton, Mona Monahan, and Leigh Ortenburger. A 22m pitch on the rotten dolomite west-northwest wall is necessary to pass the cliff band.

MURPHY PEAK (10,800+)

(1.0 mi NW of Mount Hunt)
Map: Grand Teton

This peak is the more northerly of the pair of flat-topped summits at the head of Open Canyon. It is named in honor of the US Geological Survey (USGS) topographer T. F. Murphy, who produced the first Grand Teton National Park map (with 50-foot contour intervals) in 1938, without the now-standard use of aerial photogrammetry methods.

ROUTE 1. WEST WALL. I, 3.0. First ascent in May or June 1934, by T. F. Murphy and Robert E. Brislawn. Similar to Two Elk Peak, Murphy Peak is ringed by cliffs, but a single break in the western cliffs offers probably the only easy route. At the extreme south end of the flat summit, a cairn containing a nail but no note was found by a party in 1960; this cairn was very likely built by the Murphy party while surveying the southern part of the Teton Range. See *American Alpine Journal* 12, no. 2 (1961): pp. 373–79.

ROUTE 2. WEST CHIMNEY. I, 5.1. First ascent June 14, 1974, by Richard Day and John Kevin Fox. About 60m south of the main break in the western wall of this peak (see *Route 1*) is a broad chimney that also leads up through the wall. Scramble up the chimney until it forks, then climb the left fork to the bench above, from which one can continue easily left (north) to the summit.

TUKUARIKA PEAK (10,988)

(0.9 mi NNW of Mount Hunt)
Map: Grand Teton

The second highest of the sedimentary peaks in the southern Teton Range, this peak is seldom climbed. While it holds little technical interest, its summit provides a viewpoint from which one can appreciate the structure of Prospectors Mountain, and both peaks can be climbed in the same day from Open Canyon. Tukuarika is a Shoshone name for the Sheepeater Indians, who commonly visited the Teton region before Euro-American expansion.

Chronology

NORTHEAST RIDGE: July 12, 1960, David Dornan, Mark Melton, Mona Monahan, Leigh Ortenburger
WEST RIDGE: July 12, 1960, David Dornan, Mark Melton, Mona Monahan, Leigh Ortenburger (descent)
SOUTH SIDE: August 24, 1969, Lyle Olson, Craig Olson, Kirsten Olson, Kim Olson

ROUTE 1. WEST RIDGE. I, 2.0. First descent July 12, 1960, by David Dornan, Mark Melton, Mona Monahan, and Leigh Ortenburger. There is a step on the lower portion of this ridge that can be avoided by traversing left (north) to a couloir. This couloir leads back onto the ridge, which is then followed to the summit.

ROUTE 2. SOUTH SIDE. I, 2.0. First ascent August 24, 1969, by Lyle Olson, Craig Olson, Kirsten Olson, and Kim Olson. From Coyote Lake keep right (east) to avoid the cliff bands that ring the southwestern end of the peak.

ROUTE 3. NORTHEAST RIDGE. I, 1.0. First ascent July 12, 1960, by David Dornan, Mark Melton, Mona Monahan, and Leigh Ortenburger. From the Open Canyon trail climb easily up to the saddle between Prospectors Mountain and Tukuarika Peak. Then follow the northeast ridge to the summit. See *American Alpine Journal* 12, no. 2 (1961): pp. 373–79.

PROSPECTORS MOUNTAIN (11,241)

Map: Grand Teton

The sedimentary capping on this large and bulky mountain, the highest south of Death Canyon, has apparently prevented the development of the same level of interest that climbers have shown for the crystalline peaks in the center of the range. Yet Prospectors Mountain is an impressive Teton peak, both for the view that its summit affords of the range to the north, south, and west, and for the excellent exposures of crystalline rock on its north and northeast sides. These cliffs rise over 900m from the floor of Death Canyon and provide excellent climbing routes. The name commemorates the efforts of the early prospectors at the head of Death Canyon about 2.5 miles to the west.

Rimrock Lake, which hangs in a small cirque on the upper northern slope of this mountain, is a place of remarkable but fragile alpine beauty, worthy of the effort required to reach it. Point 9,829, 1.4 miles to the west-northwest, was first reached via the southwest slope on July 20, 1960, by Arthur J. Reyman.

Chronology

SOUTHEAST SLOPE: June 23, 1932, Phil Smith, Ray Cutter

EAST RIDGE COULOIR (BANANA COULOIR): [probable] June 23, 1932, Phil Smith, Ray Cutter (descent); [probable] June 22, 1934, Fritiof Fryxell (ascent)

SOUTHWEST RIDGE: October 18, 1940, Allyn Hanks, Bennett Gale

NORTHWEST RIDGE: July 23, 1955, John Fonda, Gene Balaz, Robert Sellars

var—**NORTH COULOIR:** June 14, 1974, Richard Day, John Kevin Fox

EAST RIDGE, NORTH BASTION: August 1, 1961, Dennis Wik, Stuart During

UPPER NORTHEAST FACE I: August 28, 1963, Ted Vaill, John A. Thomas

APOCALYPSE ARÊTE: July 14, 1964, William Buckingham, Ted Vaill

var—July 7, 1989, Janet Wilts, Tom Vercolen

UPPER NORTH RIDGE: July 12, 1966, Peter Cleveland, Ted Vaill

APOCALYPSE COULOIR: June 18, 1978, Greg Lawley, Owen Anderson (main couloir to the Four Horsemen portion of the ridge); April 17, 1994, Mark Newcomb, Stephen Koch (main couloir to northwest-facing upper couloir, ascent and descent)

UPPER NORTHEAST FACE II: August 1984, Yvon Chouinard, Rick Ridgeway

ROUTE 1. ▲ SOUTHWEST RIDGE. I, 1.0. First ascent October 18, 1940, by Allyn Hanks and Bennett Gale. See *Death Canyon* in Section 2 for directions to the Death Canyon trailhead. From there take the Valley Trail, then the Open Canyon trail, to a point at about 8,960+ feet where the trail turns left (south), away from the main creek in Open Canyon. Continue up the northwest fork of the canyon to the saddle between Prospectors Mountain and Tukuarika Peak. From this saddle, which in mid-July is covered with beautiful alpine flowers, there is no difficulty in following the broad ridge directly to the summit of Prospectors Mountain. Little more than hiking is involved unless the season is so early that an ice axe is required for safety on the snow slope. See *American Alpine Journal* 12, no. 2 (1961): pp. 373–79.

ROUTE 2. SOUTHEAST SLOPE. I, 1.0. First ascent June 23, 1932, by Phil Smith and Ray Cutter. After turning off the Open Canyon trail, at the same point as in *Route 1*, cross to the north side of the stream and scramble north up a broad ridge or a series of easy scree-filled couloirs, past grassy benches, to the center of three summit knolls. Before the construction of the trail up Open Canyon, earlier ascents attacked the mountain from this more southeasterly direction. **Time:** 6 hours from the Death Canyon trailhead.

ROUTE 3. ▲ EAST RIDGE COULOIR (BANANA COULOIR). II, 3.0. Probable first descent June 23, 1932, by Phil Smith and Ray Cutter; probable first ascent June 22, 1934, by Fritiof Fryxell. This route can easily be used for ascent, but it serves as the fastest and best route, by far, of descent from the summit of Prospectors Mountain. On the 7.5-minute USGS quadrangle map, a couloir or drainage is shown due east of the summit, with semipermanent snow in the upper section and a permanent stream in the lower section that joins the main Open Canyon creek at the 8,000-foot contour line. The Banana Couloir is the broad couloir or drainage to the northeast. It is shown on the map as having an intermittent stream that joins the Open Canyon creek near the 7,760-foot contour line. From the summit descend about 0.25 mile along the plateau to the broad saddle connecting to the northeast summit before turning east down into the couloir. For those experienced with the use of an ice axe, this couloir in early season can be glissaded on unbroken snow all the way to the creek in Open Canyon. The popularity of this route increases substantially during the winter months, when it is done as a ski descent of nearly 3,000 feet.

ROUTE 4. EAST RIDGE, NORTH BASTION. II, 4.0. First ascent August 1, 1961, by Dennis Wik and Stuart During. This climb appears to have been along the broad ridge that separates the East Ridge Couloir *(Route 3)* from the main upper northeast face. No further information is available.

ROUTE 5. UPPER NORTHEAST FACE I. II, 5.6. First ascent August 28, 1963, by Ted Vaill and John A. Thomas. Due east of the summit of Prospectors Mountain is one of the major features of the mountain—a large, wide couloir starting about 1 mile up the Open Canyon trail and leading northwest to a major cirque bounded on the west by the ridge above and east of Rimrock Lake. Northeast of this cirque is the ridge crest at the top of the main 900m northeast face, rising almost directly from the floor of Death Canyon. Above and southwest of the floor of the cirque is the 250m upper northeast face, where this route is located. The last 0.5 mile before the summit is a plateau of sedimentary rubble; the face itself, however, is of good crystalline rock.

From the top of the moraine on the west side and above Phelps Lake, continue on the Open Canyon trail about 1 mile up the canyon, and then turn northwest up the wide couloir described above. Nearing the face, one can see a steep, snow-filled secondary couloir bisecting the upper northeast face into two sections. This is now referred to as the V Couloir by the ski-mountaineering community. The route begins at the top of an inverted V some 60m to the left (southeast) of this couloir and goes nearly directly up the face to its highest point. After scrambling to the top of the inverted V, continue up to the left on slabs beneath an impressive overhanging wall (the Yellow Garden Wall). Now work to the right and climb steep, slabby rock with good holds, past a smooth slab with small holds, and around an overhang (5.4) to the ledge above. A 5.1 open book, followed by three more leads of similar difficulty up and left, brings one to a small belay cave beneath a great overhang on the upper section of the Yellow Garden Wall. From the cave, ease around a corner to the right onto a ledge that leads diagonally up to a short, grassy slope.

The face above this slope is bounded on the left by a large, vertical chockstone chimney and on the right by a rock chute leading to a window overlooking the bisecting couloir mentioned above. Climb the center of the face (5.6) to an open book, above which is a good belay stance under a small overhanging tower. The next lead goes around the tower on the left, up a smooth slab, and onto the top of the tower. After climbing another steep slab with beautiful holds, scramble up the last pitch on easy rock to the sedimentary summit plateau. Walk the final 0.5 mile to the summit cairn. See *American Alpine Journal* 14, no. 1 (1964): p. 188.

ROUTE 6. UPPER NORTHEAST FACE II. II, 5.8. First ascent in August 1984, by Yvon Chouinard and Rick Ridgeway. This route apparently lies to the right of *Route 5* and ascends the buttress to the left of the snow couloir that cuts through this upper northeast face. Five pitches of good rock are involved.

ROUTE 7. APOCALYPSE COULOIR. II, 4.0, steep snow. First ascent June 18, 1978, by Greg Lawley and Owen Anderson via the main couloir to the Four Horsemen portion of the ridge; first ascent and descent April 17, 1994, by Mark Newcomb (skis) and Stephen Koch (snowboard) via the lower main couloir and steeper upper section. When Prospectors Mountain is viewed from the northeast, a distinct couloir—steep and snow-filled, in early summer—will be seen rising from a point just south of the switchbacks in Death Canyon (across from the Snaz Buttress area) and leading toward the Four Horsemen, the pinnacles between the top of Apocalypse Arête (Point 9,996) and the upper north ridge. With binoculars, one might notice a significant amount of ice originating on the steep wall forming the south side of the lower couloir. This is the Apocalypse Couloir, one of the most sought-after ski-mountaineering descents in the entire range. From the northeast vantage point, however, it is not possible to see the upper half of this now-famous ski descent, as it disappears into the upper rock wall for nearly 300m after a 90° turn (see *Figure 2-1*). Three 30m rappels permit access into this steep upper section from the ridge and shelf above. The first-ascent party (Lawley and Anderson) climbed straight up the main couloir toward the Horsemen and skipped the hard left that leads to the upper couloir, which almost every party uses these days for the ski descent. It fell to the strong pair of Mark Newcomb and Stephen Koch to discover the steeper upper section, first ascending it and then leading the way in its descent. Most parties now enter the couloir by rappelling in from the top.

ROUTE 8. APOCALYPSE ARÊTE. II, 5.7. First ascent July 14, 1964, by William Buckingham and Ted Vaill. This long and sharp ridge forms the top of some of the facets of the north face of Prospectors Mountain and is bounded on the left (southeast) by the impressive Apocalypse Couloir (see *Figure 2-1*). From the 8,000-foot contour to the 9,996-foot tower that forms the summit of the ridge, the primary orientation of this ridge is east–west; at this point the ridge turns abruptly southwest, past Point 10,560+ above and east of Rimrock Lake, to the summit of the mountain. The climb is started by leaving the Death Canyon trail (see *Death Canyon* in Section 2) at about the 7,600-foot level, crossing the stream, and scrambling up talus blocks to the base of the ridge. One could also reach the ridge by continuing on the trail to the Death Canyon patrol cabin and then contouring and bushwhacking southeast back to the base of the ridge.

The first third of the arête offers no difficulties and consists of 3.0 scrambling until a vertical-to-overhanging 60m step is reached. A direct attack on this step

A climber on Purple Reign (5.12b), Rock Springs Buttress (Photo by Kent McBride)

will probably require artificial climbing, so descend slightly to the left and traverse under the face of the step on ledges; then zigzag back about halfway up the step to a 4.0 pitch that leads to the top of the step. After another 3.0 interlude, a wall about 20m high will be met. Slightly to the right of the crest is a small dihedral with a loose flake above. Use a variety of techniques, including liebacking and stemming, to climb this pitch (5.7); take great care with the flake, which is almost completely detached. Another section (2.0) leads to a third prominent steep step about two-thirds of the way up the ridge. Most of this step is not difficult (4.0), but the slightly overhanging top section is climbed via a 5.4 jam crack on small holds. Two towers are passed by 3.0 scrambling before the top of the arête is reached at 9,996 feet. The four pinnacles named the Four Horsemen, which suggested the name for this arête and which extend southwest toward the summit of Prospectors Mountain, begin at this point and can be seen on the map. The summit of the arête is the first of the Horsemen. The second is ascended easily by its northwest side, whereas the third involves a 5.1 pitch on its south side. To descend from this third pinnacle, rappel from the large boulder on its summit. The fourth Horseman possesses a narrow summit flake, which is climbed, appropriately, à cheval. The first-ascent party descended to Death Canyon from this point in a couloir to the northwest.

Variation: II, 5.6. First ascent July 7, 1989, by Janet Wilts and Tom Vercolen. Instead of starting the route at the base of the ridge, begin around to the right on the north wall of the lower ridge by scrambling 30m up easy rock. The first short pitch starts from a block and goes up through trees and bushes to a ledge, where a 6m traverse left and up leads to a belay ledge. The second lead (46m) works up and left to an obvious crack (5.6), above which one angles left on a face, avoiding a right-facing open book. The next full pitch goes up the face above to the belay ledge, from which 120m of scrambling up and left leads to the main ridge route.

ROUTE 9. UPPER NORTH RIDGE. II, 5.1. First ascent July 12, 1966, by Peter Cleveland and Ted Vaill. Apocalypse Arête *(Route 8)* leads to the most northerly point of Prospectors Mountain, Point 9,996, before traversing the Four Horsemen to end along the next flat section of the north ridge. The upper north ridge lies immediately above the far (south) end of this flat section; hence, one could climb Apocalypse Arête to approach this route. The first-ascent party, however, ascended the second couloir west of Apocalypse Arête to reach this point, the base of the next steep step of the ridge; the couloir lies well to the east of the outlet stream from Rimrock Lake. To reach the top of this steep step, climb slabs on the right (west) side of the face of the step. The top of this step is Point 10,560+, which can also be easily reached via its west ridge from Rimrock Lake (see *Death Canyon* in Section 2) or from the cirque to the east. The final section of the north ridge above, leading to the sedimentary cap, is a long knife-edge containing many towers. Stay on the crest, where interesting and exposed 5.1 climbing will be found traversing these towers, which are frequently rotten and loose. The first two climbs of this route used different methods to pass the final tower. The first-ascent party bypassed it on the left (east) side by traversing into a couloir, whereas the second-ascent party reached the same couloir by climbing out to the right (west) from the sharp notch preceding the tower to gain a saddle on the far side and then the couloir. If this route is combined with Apocalypse Arête, it will be a two-day climb or a very long one-day climb; this was first done by Leigh Ortenburger and Jenny Davidson on July 25 and 26, 1974.

ROUTE 10. NORTHWEST RIDGE. I, 2.0. First ascent July 23, 1955, by John Fonda, Gene Balaz, and Robert Sellars. For directions to Rimrock Lake, see *Death Canyon* in Section 2. Walk around the right (west) shore to the south end of the lake. Follow the talus slope and ledges up to the skyline saddle. Climb left (southeast) from this saddle to the summit knoll.

Variation: **NORTH COULOIR.** I, 3.0. First ascent June 14, 1974, by Richard Day and John Kevin Fox. From the south side of Rimrock Lake, instead of heading to looker's right up the talus slope and ledges to the northwest ridge, bear more left and climb a steep, narrow snow couloir between two rock buttresses. From the top of the couloir, join the upper northwest ridge and follow it to the summit knoll. In early season this is a good and rapid descent route, providing that one has ice axe skills for safety.

FOSSIL MOUNTAIN (10,916)

Map: Mount Bannon

This mountain presents the boldest outline of all the rounded peaks on the southern divide. It received its name in 1930 from Fritiof Fryxell, who had found specimens of coral and brachiopods on the peak; previously it was known as Housetop Mountain, a name descriptive of its appearance. In 1931, when the US Board on Geographic Names approved 61 place names in Grand Teton National Park (including Fossil Mountain), "Housetop" migrated to a peak a few miles to the south.

ROUTE 1. SOUTHWEST RIDGE. I, 2.0. First ascent July 9, 1933, by Leland Horberg and Frank Swenson. In May or June 1934, T. F. Murphy and Robert E. Brislawn also probably climbed this peak from the south.

ROUTE 2. ▲ SOUTHEAST SIDE. I, 2.0. First ascent July 17, 1941, by Arthur J. Reyman. From Fox Creek Pass ascend the south cliff band to the upper bench; a small bit of routefinding may be required. From here, the talus of the east slope leads to the south ridge, which is followed to the summit.

PEAK 10,612

(0.7 mi S of Mount Bannon)

Map: Mount Bannon

This unremarkable summit lies on the sedimentary divide above the Death Canyon Shelf between Fossil Mountain and Mount Bannon.

ROUTE 1. SOUTH SLOPE. I, 1.0. First ascent August 27, 1957, by William Edwards, Don Moser, and Robert Page, from the end of the road in Darby Canyon (see *Mount Jedediah Smith*).

ROUTE 2. NORTH SLOPE. I, 1.0. First descent July 17, 1960, and first ascent July 18, 1960, by Arthur J. Reyman. Proceed from the upper bench above the Death Canyon Shelf.

ROUTE 3. EAST SLOPE. I, 1.0. First ascent July 21, 1960, by Arthur J. Reyman and two others.

MOUNT BANNON (10,966)

Map: Mount Bannon

The highest of the string of sedimentary peaks rising above the Death Canyon Shelf, this peak was named to honor the pioneer US Geological Survey (USGS) topographer T. M. Bannon, who in 1898 undertook the intimidating task of preparing the first Grand Teton quadrangle using traditional field methods of horse and plane table; the map, now out of print, was surveyed in 1899 and published in 1901.

Chronology

EAST SLOPE: [probable] May or June 1934, T. F. Murphy, Robert E. Brislawn
SOUTH SLOPE: July 17, 1960, Arthur J. Reyman

ROUTE 1. SOUTH SLOPE. I, 1.0. First known ascent July 17, 1960, by Arthur J. Reyman, by a traverse from Peak 10,612. From the Teton Crest Trail on the Death Canyon Shelf, pass the sedimentary wall above via a talus slope to a ledge sloping for about 120m up and right (north) onto the upper bench. From there the route is easy.
ROUTE 2. EAST SLOPE. I, 2.0. Probable first ascent in May or June 1934, by T. F. Murphy and Robert E. Brislawn. On August 9, 1955, Hervey Voge, Harriet Parsons, William Hail, Nancy Slusser, Jerry Klein, Ed Nauer, Ralph Starr, William Moser, Roger Kuhn, Virginia Romain, Ben Cummings, Jean Atchinson, and John Gerstle climbed this route from the trail on the Death Canyon Shelf (ca. 9,500) via a notch in the cliff wall, which is seen on the map due east of the peak. They found an empty 4-foot cairn on the summit. **Time:** 3 hours from the Death Canyon Shelf.

MOUNT JEDEDIAH SMITH (10,610)

Map: Mount Bannon

This unimpressive peak on the divide scarcely does justice to this extraordinary man, who was one of the greatest of the trapper-explorers of the American West. After the passage of the Astorians in 1811 and 1812, Jedediah Smith rediscovered Jackson Hole in 1824, entering via the Hoback River and exiting through Conant Pass.

ROUTE 1. SOUTHWEST SLOPE. I, 1.0. First known ascent August 27, 1957, by William Edwards, Don Moser, and Robert Page. This party found a cairn on the summit containing a penny but no record. Start from the end of the road in Darby Canyon (8.3 miles from the entrance at Highway 33 in Idaho, 3 miles south of Driggs). The south ridge (I, 1.0), starting from the pass at 10,050 feet, can be approached in the same manner or by traversing from Mount Bannon.
ROUTE 2. EAST SLOPE. I, 1.0. First descent July 17, 1960, by Arthur J. Reyman. First ascent September 20, 1960, by Al Read and Ann MacFarlane. Use the same approach as for *Mount Meek, Route 1.*
ROUTE 3. ELBOW BUTTRESS, MICHELLE'S ROUTE. I, 5.8. First ascent July 22, 2000, by Michelle Montopoli, George Montopoli, and Leo Larson. This climb is located approximately 7 miles into Death Canyon from the Death Canyon trailhead. Elbow Buttress is a prominent buttress located at the "elbow" of Death Canyon, where the canyon makes a sharp bend to the south. The buttress, which faces east, is on the hillside below the Death Canyon Shelf on the west side of the trail, roughly below Mount Jedediah Smith. The climb begins with scrambling up a low-angle slab to the base of a large, left-facing 60m dihedral that cuts the east face of the buttress in half. About 40m up the dihedral is a large roof that runs horizontally to the south. **Pitch 1:** Ascend the corner to a belay (5.7, 25m). **Pitch 2:** Traverse south below the roof until it ends at another left-facing corner and belay (5.8, 46m). **Pitch 3:** Climb directly up cracks and broken ground to the top of the buttress.

MOUNT MEEK (10,681)

Map: Mount Bannon

Towering above the popular Mount Meek Pass between the Death Canyon Shelf and Alaska Basin, this sedimentary peak was named for renowned mountain man Joe Meek, who visited Jackson Hole in 1835, 1839, and 1840, the final year of the colorful fur trappers' era.

ROUTE 1. SOUTHWEST SLOPE. I, 2.0. Probable first ascent in May or June 1934, by T. F. Murphy and Robert E. Brislawn. On July 17, 1960, Arthur J. Reyman climbed this route and found an empty cairn on the summit. From the Death Canyon trail at 8,400 feet (see *Death Canyon* in Section 2) scramble up to the Death Canyon Shelf, taking a route just left (south) of the stream southeast of Mount Meek. From the Death Canyon Shelf south of Mount Meek Pass, a steep chute provides a break in the Mount Meek cliff band and allows access to the upper bench. The ascent is easy from this upper bench. When used for descent, this route requires some routefinding skills. This slope, the west face, and the northwest ridge are also easily approached and climbed from Darby Canyon.
ROUTE 2. NORTHEAST COULOIR. I, 4.0. First ascent July 21, 1995, by Jim Springer. From Mount Meek Pass traverse 180m to the northwest along the base of the cliffs. Then ascend the 180m, 40°–50° snow couloir. This route is suggested as an early-season climb.

PEAK 10,300

(0.8 mi E of Mount Meek)
Map: Grand Teton

Of little mountaineering importance, this small peak forms the east boundary of Mount Meek Pass on the divide.

ROUTE 1. SOUTHEAST CORNER. I, 1.0. First known ascent July 19, 1960, by Arthur J. Reyman, who found an empty cairn on the summit. The approach to the summit mass is easy from all sides, but the final buttress is most easily climbed from the southeast.

PEAK 11,094

(1.0 mi WSW of Buck Mountain)
Map: Grand Teton

This conspicuous sedimentary peak, the highest on the divide south of Buck Mountain, has received remarkably little attention considering its proximity to the Teton Crest Trail. The uppermost section of the peak is comprised of Bighorn Dolomite.

ROUTE 1. WEST RIDGE. I, 2.0. First ascent August 30, 1958, by Howard R. Stagner Jr., who found an empty cairn on the summit. This ridge can be attained at several places, even though it is guarded on the north by a cliff band. The peak can be approached via the Teton Crest Trail or the Alaska Basin Trail to Alaska Basin or, from the west, via the trail up the south fork of Teton Canyon to Alaska Basin.
ROUTE 2. NORTHEAST COULOIR. I, 3.0. First ascent September 15, 1963, by Chuck Satterfield and Bruce Morley. From the Buck Mountain divide on the Alaska Basin Trail, climb the first couloir, which is rotten, left (east) of the nose of the northeast ridge cliff.

Death Canyon to Avalanche Canyon

Buck Mountain from the Northeast

Death Canyon

Death Canyon is a very long canyon with one of the oldest trails in the Teton Range running through it. Built in 1920–21, it is one of the few trails that passes over the divide. To reach the Death Canyon trailhead from Park Headquarters in the village of Moose, drive south on the narrow and winding Moose–Wilson Road for 3.1 miles and take the signed, paved turnoff road to the trailhead. In less than a mile, this road changes to a pretty rough dirt road that leads another mile to the parking area at the old Whitegrass Ranger Station (now a residence). From the parking area take the Death Canyon trail past the Phelps Lake Overlook at the top of the moraine that impounds the lake and, after two long switchbacks, drop down to the mouth of the canyon. An alternate approach is available, one that was made possible by the generous donation of the JY Ranch to Grand Teton National Park by Laurance S. Rockefeller in 2001. Parking is available on the east side of the Moose–Wilson Road at the Laurance S. Rockefeller Center, and trails up to and around both the north and south sides of Phelps Lake link up with the main Death Canyon trail at the mouth of the canyon. This approach is probably a mile longer but involves a pleasant walk around either side of the lake without the elevation gain and loss of the standard approach.

Once in the spectacular canyon, the climber is soon flanked on both north and south by remarkable rock walls. A total of eight switchback corners will be encountered on the trail in the canyon itself, just before the Death Canyon patrol cabin is reached in the level region near the forks of the trail. The Omega Buttresses on the north wall of the canyon are approached from the vicinity of the second switchback corner. The main group of rock-climbing routes on the Snaz Buttress is reached from the start of the first level section of the canyon before reaching the patrol cabin; leave the trail at the eighth switchback corner after entering the canyon.

The north fork trail rises in near-endless switchbacks, first to the Static Peak divide (10,790) and then through No-Wood Basin to the Buck Mountain divide (10,480+). This north fork trail is heavily used by hikers going to or coming from the Teton Crest Trail in Alaska Basin on the west slope of the range. An alternative cross-country route to the Static Peak divide, directly from the east, is available. From the trail about halfway between the Death Canyon trailhead and the Phelps Lake Overlook, a small climbers' trail will be found leading off to the right, heading north toward Stewart Draw. For those who are familiar with this area during the winter months, the trail in Stewart Draw follows the drainage between Maverick on the north and Wimpy's Knob to the south. After about 2 miles and near the 8,600 foot contour line, a small drainage will be seen angling up and south, and this leads up into the cirque immediately east of Static Peak. A second alternative, which provides a long glissade in early season, is the next large drainage to the south on the southern slopes of Albright Peak (10,552). This can be accessed by contouring around the west side of Albright Peak from the Static Peak divide.

The longer south fork trail continues at Fox Creek Pass (9,540+) via the Teton Crest Trail to Marion Lake at the head of Granite Canyon. From Fox Creek Pass the Teton Crest Trail can also be taken north along the Death Canyon Shelf to Mount Meek Pass (9,726), which provides a second method of entering or leaving Alaska Basin. A major southerly side canyon, commonly harboring mountain sheep, leads from the south fork to the remote Forget-me-not Lakes, high on the slopes of Prospectors Mountain. Another attractive side canyon, Connors Basin, leads north from the south fork and provides access to the divide between the seldom-climbed Peaks 10,300 and 11,086.

In a small cirque high on the south walls of Death Canyon is the isolated and beautiful Rimrock Lake. If one plans to visit this lake, be prepared to treat the fragile alpine environment surrounding the lake with the respect it deserves and requires. Great care must be taken with the tundra plants near the lake. To reach this lake from the Death Canyon trail, proceed past the patrol cabin (7,840) and across the bridge where the trail moves over to the south side of the main creek for the first time. The main drainage stream from the lake will be seen above, and to the right (west) is a smaller talus gully narrowing at the top and ending in a small cliff band. The left side of the main drainage stream can be followed to reach the lake, but roped climbing (5.4) will be required on the exposed and frequently wet slabs. A much better route ascends a slope with trees after crossing the bridge, heading toward the talus gully on the right, until near the top. It is then possible to turn left (east) with a brief section of rock scrambling onto a small ridge leading easily to the lake. In early season and midseason the upper portion of this gully will contain moderate snow, requiring an ice axe for safety.

Avalanche Canyon

One of the major Teton canyons, Avalanche Canyon serves as an important and attractive route of approach to Buck Mountain, Mount Wister, Veiled Peak, the South Teton, and, less commonly, Cloudveil Dome and Nez Perce. Adding to its appeal, this canyon seems to be the summer home of a good percentage of the moose in the park. Seldom does one enter the canyon without seeing one or more moose in the area around the forks. Outstanding high-country campsites are found in the north fork of the canyon.

The preferred route into the canyon is around the north side of Taggart Lake on an unmaintained trail developed by the numerous climbers and hikers entering the canyon. (Note that if one attempts to gain the mouth of the canyon by hiking around the south side of Taggart Lake, an unpleasant swamp—clearly shown on the map—must be negotiated on the west shore of the lake, just south of the stream from Avalanche Canyon.) From the Taggart Lake trailhead, which is nearly 0.2 mile south of the Taggart Creek bridge on Teton Park Road, start up the trail and take the first right fork that soon crosses to the north side of the creek. Do not try the service road here because it dead-ends at a water tank. At the junction 1.1 miles from the trailhead, take the Bradley Lake trail, the right fork. After 0.25 mile, turn left (west) off the trail and cut cross-country down toward Taggart Lake, then hike north on the trail near the shore of the lake toward the moraine separating Taggart and Bradley Lakes. (One can also stay on the Taggart Lake trail, the left fork, down to the lake and then turn right on the lakeshore trail to gain this same point, but this is longer.) On the open slope before reaching the top of the moraine (at the point where the trail crosses the 6,960-foot contour line and before reaching the first switchback corner), leave the main trail where a small but distinct trail heads west toward the canyon. This narrow trail stays on the north side of the creek through some boggy areas and passes a very large, isolated boulder (featuring several interesting top-rope or highball boulder problems) near the forks of the canyon. The trail can be followed fairly easily all the way to this point, about 2 miles west of Taggart Lake, where one can turn into either the north or south fork of the upper canyon, depending on the destination. Avalanche debris in the form of downed trees causes this trail to shift and become more difficult to discern from one year to the next.

South Fork: From the fork in Taggart Creek, climb up toward the south fork of Avalanche Canyon on either side of the stream. Several campsites can be found along the shore of the shallow lake that lies just above the first headwall. Farther up the canyon there is considerable talus; feasible campsites are not numerous here but, with effort, can be found, even with water. At the west end of the canyon and under the southeast slopes of Veiled Peak are several high, grassy benches that will provide adequate, though windy, campsites with running water. The col (10,800+) between Veiled Peak and Mount Wister is easy to cross if one wishes to descend the north fork of the canyon. Another alternative exit is to ascend the slopes, covered with snow in early season, to the divide and the Teton Crest Trail in upper Alaska Basin.

North Fork: The climb up to the elegant Lake Taminah can be made either to the right or to the left of the splendid Shoshoko Falls. The initial headwall above the forks is, however, usually passed via the main talus slope descending from the north. The right (east) side of this slope is bounded by a small stream originating on the south slopes of Nez Perce. By following this streambed up a few hundred feet, one can avoid many of the bushes and contour easily over toward the falls. The upper end of the talus provides access to Lake Taminah by a nearly horizontal traverse. There are excellent campsites near the mouth of this lake. Do not attempt to pass the lake along its south shore. Use the north shore even though it appears to be somewhat longer. West of Lake Taminah and below the second headwall that leads to Snowdrift Lake is a meadow with deep grass. An enormous boulder will be found at the northwest corner of this meadow. Under it there is some space for a bivouac, but in early season the meadow and boulder may be wet and partially covered with snow.

Pass this second headwall on the right (north) up to one of the highest lakes in the park, Snowdrift Lake (10,006); it will have snow or ice on its shores until late in the season. In early season the snow on this headwall is steep enough to require the use of an ice axe for safety. The campsites among the krummholz near Snowdrift Lake are some of the finest in the park and care should be taken to leave this fragile alpine environment exactly as it is found. Try to stay on the rock slabs as much as possible while traveling through this pristine area. The saddle between Mount Wister and Veiled Peak can be easily gained directly from the east end of Snowdrift Lake. The base of the Wall at the west end of the canyon can readily be approached, and an easy hike to the north from the lake takes one to small Kit Lake (10,320+), an above-timberline camping option. Exit from the canyon can be made by continuing easily to the north over the saddle (10,560+) between the Wall and the South Teton and then joining the trail in the south fork of Cascade Canyon. This route can be reversed by hiking up the south fork of Cascade Canyon trail, taking the left fork to the Cascade-Avalanche divide, and descending into the uppermost portion of the north fork of Avalanche Canyon.

To descend the north fork from Lake Taminah, follow the climbers' trail down toward the forks, edging east to meet the end of the main Avalanche Canyon trail. The extensive avalanches of the winter of 1985–86 uprooted or knocked over many trees in this and almost every other canyon in the range, so debris will be encountered, hindering progress.

DEATH CANYON, SOUTH SIDE ROCK CLIMBS

Map: Grand Teton

The remarkable exposure of crystalline rock on the south wall of Death Canyon, which constitutes the north face of Prospectors Mountain, offers several difficult climbs on steep, dark-colored rock. Moss and lichen are present, sometimes in large quantities, and perhaps this has kept exploration to a minimum over the years. Late summer to early fall is the recommended season for climbs on this side of the canyon because crossing the creek can be nearly impossible during periods of high runoff. (See *Figures 2-1* and *2-2* for an overview.) Three couloirs cut through the lower northeast face: The upper two are, from west to east, the Apocalypse Couloir (*Prospectors Mountain, Route 7*) and Son of Apocalypse Couloir—major ski-mountaineering objectives during the winter months. Another unnamed couloir (it has been referred to as Ice Box) is located farther east toward the mouth of Death Canyon. This unnamed couloir (see *Figure 2-2*) and its neighbor to the west (Son of Apocalypse Couloir) lie on either side of Point 8,996, as shown on the USGS Grand Teton 7.5-minute quadrangle. This region sees much more traffic now in winter, both from those climbing Prospectors Falls and from skiers descending the challenging Apocalypse Couloir or one of its neighbors.

The south wall of Death Canyon, seen before the trail reaches the level section of the canyon, rises from about the 7,300-foot level and ends as the north edge of a major cirque (see *Prospectors Mountain, Route 5*) that drains southeast into Open Canyon. The distinct Apocalypse Arête (*Prospectors Mountain, Route 8*) rises toward the southwest from the top of the large, triangular talus cone at the base of this face. The upper portion of this talus, and more especially the couloir behind (south of) Apocalypse Arête (the Apocalypse Couloir), will harbor snow well into midseason. About one-third of the way up the wall, a large, tree-covered ledge or bench cuts across the entire face, diagonaling from lower left to upper right. It crosses the Prospectors Falls drainage and ends in the Apocalypse Couloir.

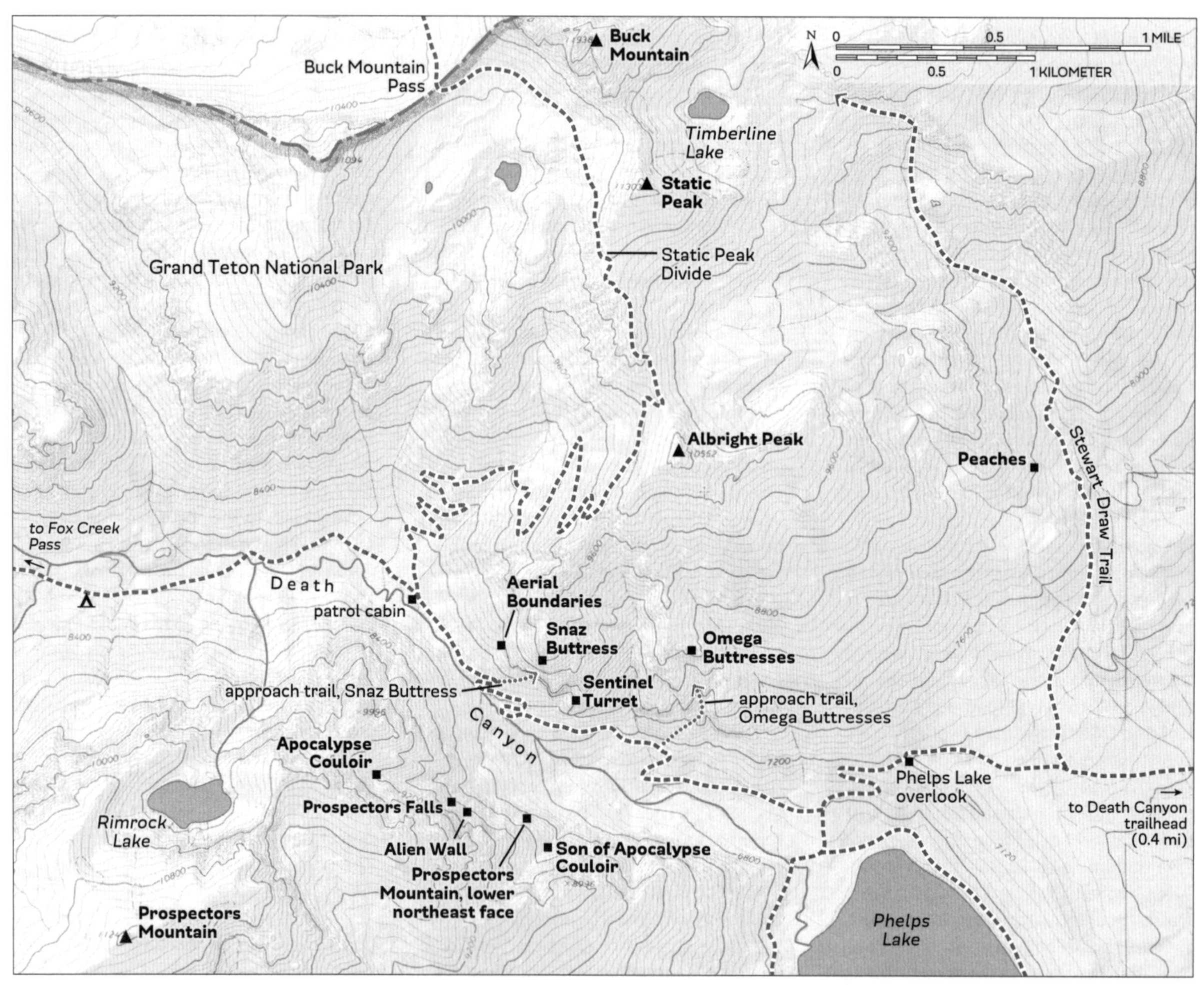

FIGURE 2-1. Prospectors Mountain, lower northeast aspect overview

Routes 1–7 can be reached either by crossing the Death Canyon creek on the Valley Trail and then bushwhacking up on the south side of the canyon or by locating a suitable log to cross before the switchbacks along the Death Canyon trail. The suggested point of access for *Routes 8–12* is one of the upper switchback corners nearest to the creek and just opposite the scree/talus cone of the Apocalypse Couloir. After negotiating the creek crossing (assuming it is late season and the creek is way down), wander over toward the base of Prospectors Falls. The climbs are listed from east to west.

Chronology

POOP-OUT PINNACLE: Summer 1963, Rick Medrick, Peter Lev
RAVEN CRACK: August 3, 1964, Yvon Chouinard, Mort Hempel
NORTHEAST FACE: June 25, 1973, Eric Bjornstad, Robert Degles
YELLOW JAUNTICE: June 30, 1977, Mike Munger, Kent Lugbill
PREDATOR: July 1987, Jack Tackle, Jim Donini
BLACK DIAMOND: August 13, 1987, Yvon Chouinard, Lynn Hill, Russ Raffa, Sandy Stewart
CARSON-WHITON: August 17, 1990, Andy Carson, Mark Whiton
WELCOME MAT: August 1999, David Bywater, Bill Culbreath
BREAKING BARRIERS: September 1999, Brendan O'Neill, Zack Martin; FFA August 29, 2017, Michael Gardner, Brian Smith
DESTINED TO BECOME A CLASSIC: September 2007, Renny Jackson, David Bywater
ALIEN WALL: September 2, 2009, Mark Givens, Joel Kauffman
NORTHEAST FACE III: August 2, 2014, Brian Smith, Joe Stern
BEE'S KNEES: July 11, 2020, Aaron Diamond, Zach Little
var—**TECHNICOLOR ODYSSEY:** July 10, 2021, Noah McCorkel, Kaylee Pickett, Clark Henarie

ROUTE 1. BLACK DIAMOND. II, 5.10. First ascent August 13, 1987, by Yvon Chouinard, Lynn Hill, Russ Raffa, and Sandy Stewart. This route ascends the first major formation on the left (south) side as one enters Death Canyon. "The Diamond Buttress" has been suggested as a name for this particular crag. A fairly smooth face will be seen up and left, containing a left-leaning yellow dihedral that is the landmark for the route. From the talus below the face, scramble right, up an ascending ramp to its end, which is still a bit left of the dihedral. From this point climb a moderate (5.6) pitch to a large pine tree. Scramble another 60m to the base of the upper wall, where the route stops wandering and becomes a good rock climb. The first lead is a 5.7 runout. The next lead, also a runout (5.10), goes under and just left of the yellow dihedral. The third long (50m) pitch goes up the dihedral (5.10). Now continue straight up for another ropelength (5.8). The fifth pitch, the final one, wanders right, up through overhangs (5.7); finish by following a ramp and ledges out to the right and top out. Descent is made to the east.

ROUTE 2. BEE'S KNEES. II, 5.10-. First ascent July 11, 2020, by Aaron Diamond and Zach Little. (See *Figures 2-2* and *2-2a*.) This climb is located on the lowest, most easterly rock formation on the south side of Death Canyon just to the west of *Route 1*. **Pitch 1:** From a large ledge, follow a vague weakness up past a dead tree, then head left (east) to a ledge. Climb up from the ledge, clip a fixed pin, and continue up and east in a short left-facing corner to another fixed pin (5.8). Above this the corner becomes a ramp and leads west to a belay with fixed pins. **Pitch 2:** Climb a short off-fingers crack (5.8) to a roof and continue up into the right-facing corner above (5.7 fingers). At the top of the corner continue up through blocky terrain to a traverse right via a 5.6 crack that leads to a belay near a tree on a good ledge. **Pitch 3:** Climb easier terrain up and left in a weakness to a fixed anchor below an acute dihedral (5.6). **Pitch 4:** Stem up the steep corner over an overlap (5.8) to an incipient right-curving crack and climb up and west (5.10-) past a small stump. Above here steep face climbing leads around a small roof (5.8) and then to easier terrain. Belay at a fixed anchor on a large, grassy ledge beneath a steep, smooth wall. (**Note:** Watch out for rope drag if linking pitches 3 and 4.) The descent has been done with four rappels using a 70m rope. **Gear:** The first ascensionists used one #3 Camalot C4; a double set of #0.3–#2 Camalot C4s; one set of #00–#2 Camalot C3s; one set of stoppers (offsets useful); many runners; and a 70m rope.

***Variation:* TECHNICOLOR ODYSSEY.** II, 5.11-. First ascent July 10, 2021, by Noah McCorkel, Kaylee Pickett, and Clark Henarie. (See *Figures 2-2* and *2-2a*.) This excellent variation has already had several ascents and is reported to be high quality. Vibrant, multicolored lichen that is found on this wall suggested the route's name. It diverges at the top of the second pitch of *Route 2* where a belay can be found on the west side of the large tree ledge. **Pitch 3:** Move right on the ramp beneath a bulge for about 6m until it is possible to step back left above the bulge (5.8). Make sure gear is available before committing to this move. Then climb up and left using edges and flakes (strenuous and reachy with poor feet) to an obvious undercling. Climb past the undercling (5.10) and traverse right for a meter or so and then up to another undercling/flake. Move directly right, staying low in order to gain the base of a beautiful orange corner. Ascend the corner (5.9) and exit left at the top on good holds. Belay at a good stance directly below the steep headwall and roof above at the top of this 35m quality and somewhat complex pitch. **Pitch 4:** From the belay, move up and right to the base of the headwall and climb a steep face past a small fixed nut on jugs, slopers, and crimps (5.10+). Continue up to and over the roof via some "wild and burly" moves (5.11-). A steep finger crack (5.9) then leads to perfect hands (5.8) and an exit left onto the huge right-leaning ramp and a belay (30–35m). **Pitch 5:** Climb up and west along the ramp until it is possible to get onto an upper ramp that leads to a tree. At this point turn up to the left and follow cracks up and left (5.8). Traverse left around a black block and pull up to the summit on jugs. This pitch is short and a bit dirty, but the climbing is still fun and the moves to the summit are memorable. **Descent:** From the top of pitch 5 scramble left (east) over some boulders and a juniper bush. Spot the slung block and rap back down the steep face to the huge ramp. From here, scramble down the ramp (4th class) to the top of Bee's Knees and utilize that route for the remainder of the descent. **Note:** Take extra rappel sling material as it has been reported that critters have been chewing on slings that have been left on the block at the top of the climb. **Gear:** Lots of small/tiny stuff; offsets are useful; (.3-1) × (2); 2-3 × (1); many runners; 70m rope.

FIGURE 2-2. Lower Death Canyon, south side rock climbs

ROUTE 3. WELCOME MAT. II, 5.10. First ascent in August 1999, by David Bywater and Bill Culbreath. This climb is located on one of the lowest rock outcrops on the south side of Death Canyon. The climb is immediately west of a smooth wall and begins in a right-facing feature from a ledge with a flake on it. Climb up just to the right of the smooth wall in this feature on a moss-covered slab. Break out right (west) to a short chimney section (5.8). Step out of the chimney and climb via a lieback on a smooth edge to the belay. The second pitch climbs another right-facing feature (5.10) up to a few trees and is the better of the two pitches.

ROUTE 4. DESTINED TO BECOME A CLASSIC. III, 5.11-. First ascent in September 2007, by

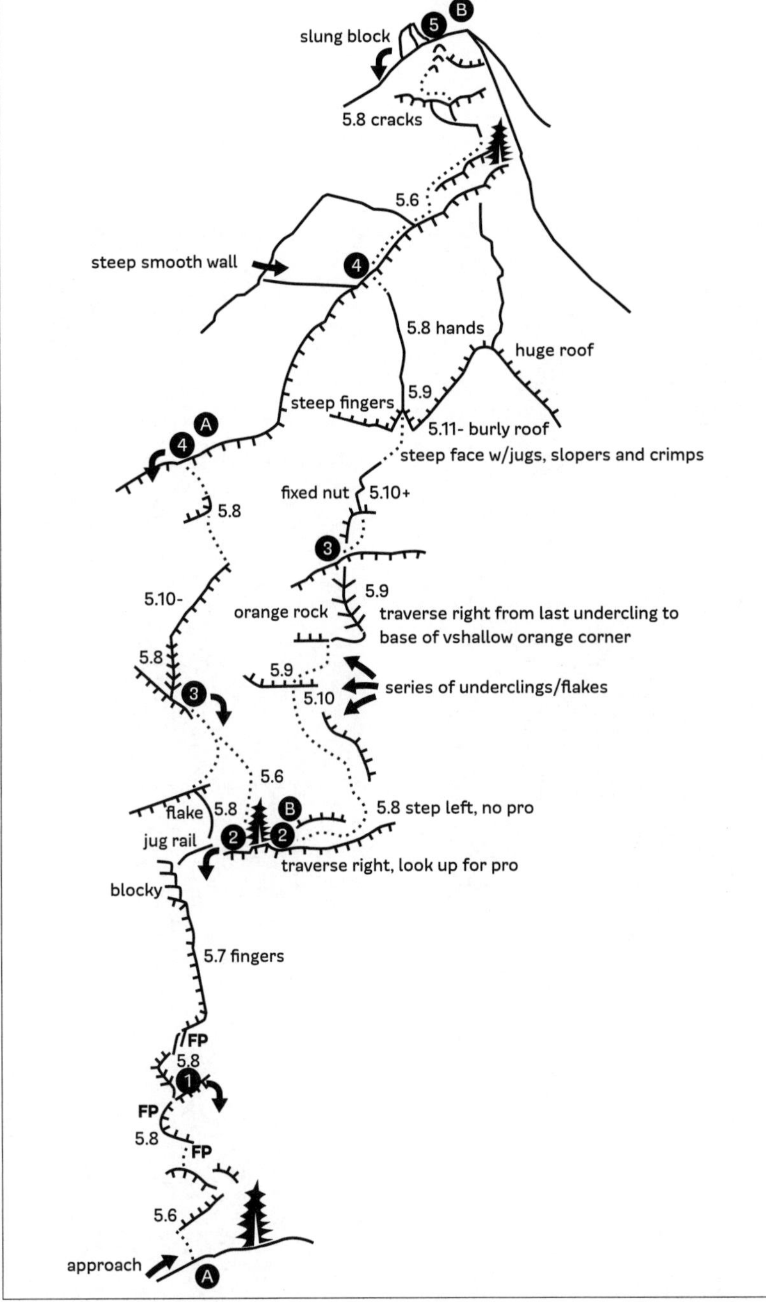

FIGURE 2-2A. Death Canyon, south side rock climbs. (A) Bee's Knees *(Route 2)*, II, 5.10-; (B) Bee's Knees variation, Technicolor Odyssey, II, 5.11-

Renny Jackson and David Bywater. (See *Figure 2-2*.) Many would argue that Teton guidebook descriptions could be generalized to "one hell of an approach for a few good pitches of climbing!" This route fits that description perfectly. Once across the Death Canyon creek, bushwhack up toward the lowest and most easterly of the couloirs mentioned in the introduction to these climbs (unnamed couloir) and pass the initial steep step on the right. Then climb several pitches on the west side of the couloir (some vegetated and licheny sections will be encountered) to reach two final pitches that ascend a single crack system through two roofs. These two pitches are located on an arrowhead-shaped feature at the uppermost end of the couloir on its west side. The upper of the two roofs is the crux (5.11-), and it leads to easier crack climbing above. Descend to the Valley Trail on the south side. **Gear:** For protection take a set of stoppers and a double set of cams from 0.3" to 3".

ROUTE 5. NORTHEAST FACE. IV, 5.7. First ascent June 25, 1973, by Eric Bjornstad and Robert Degles. This long climb was made from a bivouac on the south side of the creek in Death Canyon after the usual approach via the Death Canyon trail. While the line more or less leads up toward a large, yellow, triangular wall (clearly discernible from the Death Canyon trail below), the lower portion of the climb is characterized by bushes, trees, and mossy chimneys. After exiting from this vertical jungle, high-angle, clean, but often fractured and loose rock is found, containing blank areas that are passed by traversing 1m right or left. The first-ascent party encountered a variety of climbing on this face and, in line with the era, used pitons, including large ones, to protect the route. The climb ends on the ridge leading east from Point 10,560+, which forms the north edge of the subsidiary canyon just below the upper northeast face of Prospectors Mountain. Descent is easily made down this subcanyon to the mouth of Open Canyon at 7,600 feet. **Time:** 12 hours.

ROUTE 6. BREAKING BARRIERS. IV, 5.11-, A1, or IV, 5.12-. First ascent in September 1999, by Brendan O'Neill and Zack Martin; first free ascent August 29, 2017, by Michael Gardner and Brian Smith. The route derives its name from the Zack Martin Breaking Barriers Grant offered by the American Alpine Club in Zack's memory (Zack Martin died just before his 25th birthday on Thanksgiving Day 2002). This route was established over a two-day period with only two bolts placed (on lead) on the entire climb. Reported to be "challenging and extremely fun, with a wide variety of climbing on very high-quality rock," it generally follows the path of least resistance up the west side of the first major buttress on the lower northeast section of Prospectors Mountain. See *Figures 2-3* and *2-4* for route details.

The first six pitches ascend just to the right (west) of a steep, mossy drainage. The aim is to gain the large, tree-covered ledge at the base of the upper yellow/orange face. Once on this ledge, a right-facing corner and large roof on the west side of the upper face will be visible above. The seventh and eighth pitches lead up via cracks and an arête to a belay below the corner. The ninth pitch ascends out right via hand and fist jams, passing a small roof (5.10-), to a hanging belay just under the huge roof. At this point the route changes character from crack climbing to face climbing. A short pitch leads out left from the belay to a stance out to the east. The 11th pitch is the crux (5.11-, A1 or 5.11+/5.12-), leading past two bolts and a fixed head to the next belay. Move the belay to the base of a left-facing corner, then climb out to the right-hand skyline and up for the final three pitches, which begin with a 4-inch crack and then continue up a series of "boulders, small

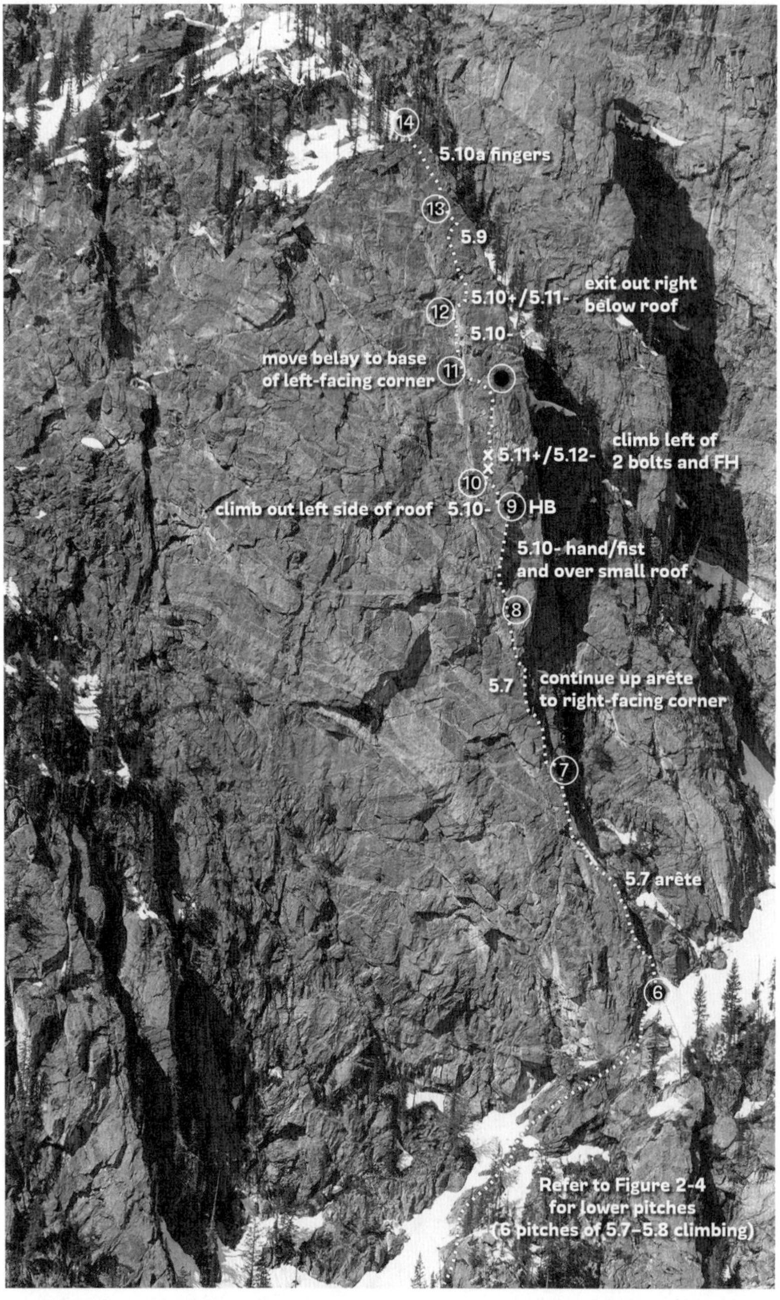

FIGURE 2-3. Prospectors Mountain, lower northeast face, Breaking Barriers *(Route 6)*, IV, 5.12-

FIGURE 2-4. Prospectors Mountain, lower northeast face overview. Breaking Barriers *(Route 6)*, IV, 5.12-

towers, and a perfect 5.10a finger crack up a sheer wall." The 14th pitch is short and leads to the top of the climb. The first-ascent party descended the gully to the east "without headlamps, and the descent, complete with multiple dark rappels and stuck ropes, was treacherous!" It is suggested that teams start early and move fast. **Gear:** For protection bring a standard rack with a double set of cams to 4", a set of stoppers, and slings and draws.

ROUTE 7. NORTHEAST FACE III. IV, 5.9. First ascent August 2, 2014, by Brian Smith and Joe Stern. (See *Figure 2-5.*) This route ascends the buttress between *Routes* 6 and *8* and is not recommended by the first-ascent party, who were looking for an adventure and were nevertheless rewarded. In a way similar to the start of *Route 6*, reach the large, tree-covered ledge by following the path of least resistance on the west side of a steep, mossy drainage beneath the lower northeast face of Prospectors Mountain. Smith and Stern encountered scrambling and pitches up to 5.8 or 5.9 in difficulty in this lower section. Once on the ledge, traverse to the west and begin climbing up a tree-covered ridge, following it for several pitches (5.7) until it intersects the steep upper face. At this point, traverse west for half a ropelength, then ascend cracks on the right side of the face, immediately left of the western, prominent prow of the upper buttress. The climb finishes with three pitches on the steep face and is the crux of the route, with "some heady sections, but also the most fun climbing on the route." To descend, downclimb the gully immediately to the east until you arrive at the traverse pitch. Then continue down the tree-covered ridge to the main ledge. Once on the main ledge, head to the west until beneath the Alien Wall *(Route 8)*, where a series of rappels from trees (several single- and double-rope rappels) leads back to the base of the wall.

ROUTE 8. ALIEN WALL. IV, 5.10. First ascent September 2, 2009, by Mark Givens and Joel Kauffman. (This author, R. Jackson, made the second ascent of this route with Gary Falk and Mark's father, Bill Givens. Good-quality climbing was found on a long, adventure-filled day!) From the base of Prospectors Falls, climb and scramble (some 5th class involved) a few hundred meters up on the west side of the falls to a point where it is possible to cross the falls drainage and follow a forested bench to the east below the main wall. (See *Figure 2-5.*)

Pitch 1: Begin the climb from this bench and proceed up a broken ridge left of the Raven Crack (5.6, 55m). **Pitch 2:** Climb up and slightly left, pulling a small bulge/overhang with good finger locks. Continue up to a small, obvious fir tree, belaying above it on a small ledge (5.10-, 30m). **Pitch 3:** Traverse left for 20m past a steep wall, using both good face holds and small cracks for gear. After rounding the distinct edge of this portion of the wall, the angle decreases slightly. Head up excellent climbing on solid rock to a grassy ledge (5.9, 50m). **Pitch 4:** Continue up and slightly right on this highly featured wall

FIGURE 2-5. Prospectors Mountain, lower northeast face. (A) Breaking Barriers *(Route 6)*, IV, 5.12-; (B) Northeast Face III *(Route 7)*, IV, 5.9; (C) Alien Wall *(Route 8)*, IV, 5.10; (D) Predator *(Route 9)*, IV, 5.11, A2; (E) Raven Crack *(Route 10)*, IV, 5.9

via wild face holds, then move back left. Good protection and many belay options on small ledges exist (5.8, 60m). **Pitch 5:** Continue up a tight left-facing corner with excellent protection, then move left onto a thin, exposed flake, climbed via finger locks. Move back into the corner and belay on a block (5.9, 55m). **Pitch 6:** Continue up a crack system to a short offwidth, then follow excellent hand and finger cracks to another left-facing corner. Loose blocks that mark the entry into this corner are easily avoided, and the belay is on a block/ledge (5.9, 55m). **Pitch 7:** This last pitch continues up a shallow crack on the steepening headwall to a small bulge/overhang. At this point, traverse left for 3m, then move up and back right. Follow a crack system up and slightly right, using solid face holds and cracks (5.9, 55m). Descend by way of a long series of double-rope rappels from trees, more or less down the route. Once back at the tree-covered bench, traverse east to where another three or four double-rope rappels lead to the ground. This is a good climb. **Gear:** For protection take a double set of cams from 0.4" to 3.5", one 4" piece, and a set of stoppers.

ROUTE 9. PREDATOR. IV, 5.11, A2. First ascent in July 1987, by Jack Tackle and Jim Donini. (See *Figure 2-5*.) This route takes a line very close to the crest that forms the left (east) edge of the Raven Crack or couloir. Proceed up the main large talus cone at the base of the north cliffs of Prospectors Mountain. The initial task is to reach the major horizontal bench or ledge system that extends across the face, about one-third of the way up from the talus. Head up the Apocalypse Couloir (west) to a point where one lead of horizontal 3rd-class scrambling permits exit back to the left (east) onto the broken wall below the bench. Two leads of steep rock (5.8 and 5.7), continuing back to the east, take one to the easier rock at the upper end of Prospectors Falls, allowing easy access to the bench. Scramble up the beginning of the Raven Crack (*Route 10*) past a chockstone to the first of the upper nine pitches of the route. After one lead of 5.6, exit left onto the difficult rock of this route, which is just left (east) of the Raven Crack. One lead (5.10) is then followed by a severe left-facing corner (5.11). The next lead (5.10) continues in this corner, but some aid (A2) is needed to pass a dirt-filled crack. A jog to the right at the end of this lead brings one to the start of the fifth pitch, again in a steep corner (5.9), to and past a ledge. Move left and up past a tree to the belay point. The next lead goes up a face (5.8) and cuts back right to a crack, which is then climbed. The final three leads of similar difficulty continue upward on this same line, exiting onto the top of the wall. The first-ascent party descended by means of 10 rappels down the face to the east of the route, to and past the bench to the talus cone. An alternate descent is to hike down the drainage on the back (south) side of the top of the climb. This drainage is easily followed using game trails to hit the Open Canyon trail at 7,600 feet.

ROUTE 10. RAVEN CRACK. IV, 5.9. First ascent August 3, 1964, by Yvon Chouinard and Mort Hempel; first winter ascent in January 2009, by Stephen Koch and Sam Magro. The Raven Crack is in the long black crack or chimney in the middle of the dark south wall of Death Canyon across from the Snaz Buttress. (See *Figure 2-5*.) Magro described his and Koch's winter climb as "1,200' of spectacular, sustained, mixed climbing at the WI5, M7 level." The description that follows is from the first-ascent party of Chouinard and Hempel.

Start by passing Prospectors Falls on the right (west) side via exposed 4.0 climbing. At the top of the waterfall, traverse left onto ledges (3.0), then diagonal up and right to a chimney (3.0), which leads to a grassy slope marking the beginning of the climb. The first pitch is 43m (4.0) to a belay ledge. Next ascend a crack for 4.5m; then traverse right to another crack and follow it for 30m to a ledge at the end of the lead. Ascend the chimney above the ledge and climb, with small 5.6 face holds, to the right of the overhang at the top. From here a jam crack leads to a belay ledge. The fourth pitch goes up and then right for 3m to another crack, which takes one to a ledge at the base of a large overhang. The next pitch is the crux of the route (5.9): Traverse left, then back diagonally to the right. Where possible, climb the overhang onto a face with small holds. Climb the detached flake above, carefully using downward pressure. From the top of the flake climb through the "funnel," a squeeze chimney, to a ledge; bypass an overhang on the right (5.7) and make a belay in the chimney above.

Now climb right out of the chimney and follow a ledge that traverses right; after the ledge peters out, continue via face climbing diagonally right to the Waldorf-Raven, an enormous, grassy ledge. The next lead starts at the extreme left end of this ledge on 4.0 rock, then a slanting chimney is climbed, using face holds (5.7) on the right wall, up to a grassy belay ledge. The pitch above follows a jam crack to the next belay ledge at the base of a chimney. The final lead ascends this chimney, which narrows to a lieback crack, to an enormous, tree-covered ledge that traverses the entire wall. If one does not wish to continue to the summit of the mountain, walk left (east) along this ledge to an open area where a large couloir, the one farthest south, descends to the talus slope below.

ROUTE 11. CARSON-WHITON. III, 5.9. First ascent August 17, 1990, by Andy Carson and Mark Whiton. Very little information is available about this climb, which begins in the Apocalypse Couloir immediately west of Prospectors Falls in an area of white rock. After the first three leads, cut back to the east toward the Raven Crack (*Route 10*) to a chimney that is followed to a bench. Follow the bench back to the west and climb a very steep face for three pitches (5.9, 5.7, and 5.7). Protection is poor in this section. Traverse west for two pitches across an easy ledge to a point where 5.9 climbing leads around a corner. Another 5.9 pitch finishes the climb.

ROUTE 12. YELLOW JAUNDICE. III, 5.10. First ascent June 30, 1977, by Mike Munger and Kent Lugbill. Approach the large, triangular talus cone at the base of Prospectors Falls and the Apocalypse Couloir. The face above the talus, to the south and somewhat east of Apocalypse Arête (*Prospectors Mountain, Route 8*), contains three main chimneys or large corners separating sections of dark-colored, nearly vertical rock. Yellow Jaundice ascends a yellow or white crack system on the easternmost of these dark walls; this relatively small crack system diagonals upward slightly from right to left.

Starting from the talus, or snow, climb up broken and somewhat rotten rock and ledges to reach the large, tree-covered bench about one-third of the way up the face; the climbing is more difficult in the upper part before reaching the bench. The first pitch above the bench is steep and like a jungle with rotten rock until some ledges are reached. Next, a moderate right-facing dihedral, past some trees, brings one to the crux pitch with an overhanging section. The first half of the third lead goes up a chimney and then up an easier right-facing dihedral to the right of the overhanging section. Now climb down and left under the roof and then up and right via a crack above to a sloping belay stance (5.10). Rope drag on this pitch suggests dividing it into two short leads. The next two pitches proceed up and right out of the crack system, switching from one dihedral to another and ending left at a belay on a large ledge. The sixth lead goes up and left in a crack and along a down-pointing flake to its top, then left and up onto the left edge of a large platform (difficult). The next pitch traverses right and then up a fist crack past a ledge. The final lead involves diagonal climbing via finger cracks to the summit block, where a cairn will be found. This is a hard climb to a distinct summit, which can be discerned as such from the highway. Unfortunately, the protection for the difficult climbing is relatively poor.

ROUTE 13. POOP-OUT PINNACLE. II, 5.1. First ascent in summer 1963, by Rick Medrick and Peter Lev. This small pinnacle is located halfway up the north face of Point 9,996, the culmination of Apocalypse Arête. One pitch was climbed on the north ridge.

POINT 9,840+

(2.1 mi SW of Buck Mountain)
Map: Grand Teton

Point 9,840+ is an obvious, plateau-like formation located on the north side of Death Canyon, slightly more than 1 mile west of the patrol cabin. Its south face is split by a large dihedral/chimney system that is prominent when viewed from the trail below.

ROUTE 1. THE LOST WORLD PLATEAU. II, 5.8. First ascent August 28, 1992, by Paul Horton and Brent Bishop. This route ascends the dihedral/chimney system in six pitches. Boulder fields and gullies lead to the base of the dihedral, which is then scrambled for a hundred or so meters. A broad ledge marks the start of the technical climbing on the steeper cliff above. The route follows the obvious system with occasional wanderings onto the right-hand face. It consists of generally easy 5th-class climbing with a few 5.7 or 5.8 sections. A standard rack will suffice, but the face-and-chimney pitch near the top is difficult to protect. The summit area is a wooded, granitic prominence at the end of a grassy limestone spur. It is an unusual place that is cut by deep chimneys and couloirs. To descend, downclimb into gullies lying due west and follow them down through cliff bands to the grassy slopes above the trail.

MOXIE TOWER (9,360+)

(1.35 mi SW of Buck Mountain)
Map: Grand Teton

This considerable tower is the largest of three that lie on the prominent buttress that separates the central and westerly of the three streams descending from the north into Death Canyon near the patrol cabin. Overlooked for decades because it is usually not easily seen, Moxie Tower is readily visible from the valley given correct lighting conditions. Even the map neglects this tower, as no closed contour is depicted on the USGS Grand Teton quadrangle sheet.

ROUTE 1. SOUTHEAST CORNER. II, 5.8. First ascent September 25, 1987, by Andy Carson and Paul Horton. Approach via Death Canyon and take the Alaska Basin Trail up from the Death Canyon patrol cabin to the fifth switchback corner. Leave the trail here and head left into the drainage of the central of the three streams. Cross the stream and climb toward the largest of the towers. The first ropelength goes up the east side of the south face (5.8) and provides access to the next section, about 60m of 3rd-class scrambling along the crest of the south ridge. The second pitch (5.8, 30m) follows the east side of the crest to the belay. The final full ropelength is on moderate rock (5.6) and ends only 9m short of the summit. Descent involves two rappels down the northwest side of the tower into the next drainage to the west, which is easily descended to the Death Canyon trail just west of the patrol cabin.

ROUTE 2. NORTHEAST RIDGE. II, 5.6. First ascent August 1, 1994, by Jim Dorward and Randy Benham. Approach in a similar fashion as for *Route 1*, then scramble to the prominent northeast corner. Climb along the crest for two and a half ropelengths over easy, lichen-covered rock. Two overhanging sections are bypassed on the right. The descent involves downclimbing to a point 15m above the col separating the tower from the next buttress to the north, where a short rappel is necessary.

DEATH CANYON, NORTH SIDE ROCK CLIMBS

Map: Grand Teton

This group of climbs located on the northern walls of lower Death Canyon, along with those on the south buttress of Mount Moran, constitutes the most concentrated collection of difficult, multipitch rock climbs in the Teton Range. Many of these climbs share both a common approach—relatively short, via the Death Canyon trail from the Death Canyon trailhead—and a common descent route, simplifying the descriptions. While some loose rock will be encountered, especially on the less heavily climbed routes, in general the rock is excellent and steep. The routes are listed from east to west.

Ticky-Tacky Pinnacles (ca. 8,160+)

(2.1 mi S of Buck Mountain)

These two small pinnacles lie on the eastern fringe of the various cliffs on the north side of Death Canyon and are separated from Ship's Prow by a broad col with a tree. A good view of the pinnacles can be obtained by traversing left (west) out from this col. The name was applied after ticks were unexpectedly found on the higher pinnacle by the first-ascent party. The second pinnacle (Tacky) has a prominent 2m S-shaped crack on its west face.

ROUTE 1. THAT'S RIDICULOUS. I, 5.9. First ascent July 29, 1993, by Janet Wilts and Robert Irvine. This climb is located on the south face of a small pinnacle southeast of Ship's Prow—almost surely Ticky-Tacky Pinnacles. Approach as for the Ship's Prow routes (see *Omega Buttresses, Eastern Section/Ship's Prow*) and, at the same elevation where one would walk the short distance west over to the base of those routes, go east to the base of this climb. Begin by climbing the right crack on the south face just left of an overhang. The crack widens to offwidth size; climb past a ledge and a bulge to the belay (44m). The next pitch ascends the sharp hand crack to the left and then moves around to the west side of the arête. Face climbing takes one back to the east side and the top of the climb.

ROUTE 2. WEST SIDE. I, 5.6. First ascent July 4, 1964, by Bill and Julie Briggs. From the second switchback corner on the trail in Death Canyon, continue on the trail 120 feet to a talus slope. Ascend this talus slope 46m to a buttress that blocks access to a large couloir. Pass this buttress on the left up to a large chockstone and cave. Gain the couloir by passing the chockstone on the right. Directly above on the left side of the couloir is Ship's Prow. Continue up the couloir for about 90m to the col separating Ticky-Tacky Pinnacles from the pillar. Take ledges out onto the west face of the first pinnacle (Ticky). At the end of the ledges a 3m hand traverse takes one to easier ground below the notch between the two pinnacles.

Omega Buttresses (ca. 9,120+)

(2.1 mi S of Buck Mountain)

Immediately to the east of Sentinel Turret is a large drainage, Sentinel Gully, shown on the map as an intermittent stream that enters the main creek in Death Canyon from the north just below the 6,800-foot level. Farther east another (the only other) larger, open gully descends toward the southeast to the mouth of the canyon where its seasonal stream ends just above the Valley Trail bridge across the Death Canyon creek. The name, Omega Buttresses, has been applied to the entire wild collection of cliffs, walls, and towers that lies between these two major gullies. To specify route locations, it is useful to divide these buttresses into three sections: western; central; and eastern, as defined in *Figure 2-6*.)

Over the years since 1964, numerous rock climbs have been made in this general area and many of these routes remain little known. Some of the routes described here still have unresolved locations, but because their descriptions are available, they have been included in the hope of motivating research into their whereabouts. The enterprising climber of today may well encounter old iron and other paraphernalia in unlikely places. One cause of the confusion regarding these routes is the omission of a major switchback on the Death Canyon trail from the USGS Grand Teton quadrangle. It is to be found between the 6,800-foot contour line on the east and the intermittent stream from Sentinel Gully on the west. It extends from about 6,800 to 7,000 feet. To the extent possible, the routes below are listed from east to west.

Chronology

OMEGA TOWER: August 11, 1964, Barry Corbet, Rick Medrick

DIHEDRAL OF HORRORS: August 18, 1967, John Behrens, Peter Avenali; FFA September 1981, Beverly Boynton, Bob Graham

var—May 19, 2002, Paul Horton, Heather Paul

var—**THE EDGE OF HORROR:** August 10, 2011, Ian Eastman, Andy Tyson

CHIMNEY OF DEATH: July 22, 1968, Andy Cox, Mike Yokell

FIGURE 2-6. Albright Peak, Omega Buttresses overview

SHIP'S PROW PILLAR, MAN-O-WAR: July 12, 1970, Thomas Dunwiddie, Roger Zimmerman
SWIZZLE STICK: August 7, 1971, Dave Erickson, David Smith, Joseph Bowman
TRAPEZOID CHIMNEY: June 5, 1975, Mike Yager, Tom Huckin
SPLOOGE: June 28, 1976, Kelly Elder, Matthew Childs
SOUTH BUTTRESS: July 3, 1976, Gordon Brooks, Charlie Gunn, Jim Schubert
CARDIAC ARÊTES: August 9, 1981, Rich Perch, Randy Harrington
var—**DCD (DEATH CANYON DIRECT):** August 1977, Charlie Fowler, Dennis Grabnegger, Kent Lugbill
WHITON'S CORNER: September 4, 1983, Mark and Diane Whiton
ANNALS OF TIME: August 19, 1984, Keith Cattabriga, Dale Dawson
var—**LYCRA:** August 1987, Jay Pistono, Keith Cattabriga, Bob Stevenson
var—**NO QUESTION:** June 25, 1993, Steve Sullivan, Mark Berry
CATHY'S CORNER: August 19, 1986, Cathy Pollack, Rhys Harriman
RIGHT PARALLEL CRACK: July 1987, Rhys Harriman, Tim Quinlan
THAT'S RIDICULOUS: July 29, 1993, Janet Wilts, Robert Irvine
MANUFACTURED CRISIS: July 1999, Aaron Gams, Pono Faulkner
BRAEBURN'S CORNER: August 1999, Jim Beyer, Zack Martin
O-MEGA CRACK: FFA, May 2007, Greg Collins, Hans Johnstone
OMEGA TRIANGLE: July 30, 2009, Aaron Gams, Brian Mulvihill
GUARDIAN OF DEATH: October 2009, Greg Collins, Nate Opp

Eastern Omega Buttresses, East of Ship's Prow

This large area lies to the east of Ship's Prow and is separated from it by a substantial steep couloir.

ROUTE 1. CRACK OF DAWN. III, 5.10. First ascent August 20, 1987, by Yvon Chouinard and Sandy Stewart. This climb is on the first major rock formation on the north side of Death Canyon. Take the trail into Death Canyon to the point where the first stream crosses the trail. Hike up the streambed to the base of the buttress. The first pitch is an obvious 1.5-to-2-inch perfect jam crack (5.8) on a vertical wall. The next lead, directly above on an indistinct prow, goes up to and over a short overhang, where one moves left back onto the prow (5.9); this is a runout lead on crumbly rock. The third pitch is difficult (5.9) and continues up a red-rock wall, followed by another lead over a 5.9 overhang. After a fifth pitch on enjoyable 5.7 rock, the final short lead on the last wall goes straight up cracks (5.8), finishing off to the right on 5.10 moves. The descent from this route is via scrambling off to the right.

ROUTE 2. SHERM'S CRACK. I, 5.9. First ascent June 19, 1976, by Sherm Wilson, Don Hultz, and Mo Donohue. Sherm's Crack is on the buttress to the east of Ship's Prow. From the right place on the Death Canyon trail, one can see a steep orange slab with a crack up the middle. Approach from the second switchback corner on the trail in the canyon proper and scramble up to the base of the crack. The route consists of one pitch up the difficult crack.

ROUTE 3. DONINI'S CRACK. II, 5.10. First complete ascent July 26, 1976, by Rich Perch and Jay Wilson; an incomplete attempt had been made in June or early July 1976, by Jim Donini. Approach as for Sherm's Crack *(Route 2)*. Climb the one pitch up Sherm's Crack and then wander on ledges up to a right-leaning crack. The next lead goes up through an overhang, a 5.10 roof. The route ends with a mixture of climbing, scrambling, and roofs, including some 5.9 rock. From the top the descent is over to the left (west) and down the gully just east of Ship's Prow.

Omega Buttresses, Eastern Section/Ship's Prow

This eastern section consists of a flatiron-like tower, named Omega Tower in 1964, and the climbs on either side. The name was given during the first climb on these buttresses in response to the inadvertent destruction of an expensive wristwatch, a token of Barry Corbet's membership in the 1963 American Mount Everest Expedition. In more recent years this tower has become known as Ship's Prow Pillar (now shortened further to Ship's Prow). This section is isolated on both sides by very steep couloirs containing loose rock and trees; these angle up to the northwest and can be found on the USGS quadrangle map. To assist in identification of Ship's Prow: From the middle of the long switchback after the second switchback corner in Death Canyon, one can observe on the right (east) edge of the cliffs above a pointed pillar resembling a flatiron or the prow of a ship and bounded on the left (west) by a conspicuous, sharp-edged left-facing corner. The corner—the Dihedral of Horrors route *(Route 7)*—is capped by a large black roof with a white vein of rock in it. The south face of the pillar to the right of this dihedral is steep to overhanging, with another black roof, lower than the one capping Dihedral of Horrors, on its right (east) side.

Approach: The approach for these climbs has been established over time by a good climbers' trail that leaves the main Death Canyon trail about 0.2 mile up from the second switchback corner in a group of trees. After a few steep switchbacks that lead up to a wall, traverse east into a gully. Proceed up this gully (some scrambling) to the base of Ship's Prow and a flat area that is good for staging and hanging packs.

Descent: A 46m rappel from anchor slings around the large tree on the east side of the top of Ship's Prow will deposit climbers in the gully on the east side. Descend on a trail for 30m or so until it goes into some trees. Look for another anchor on a large branch of a tree. This second rappel leads to a small saddle, from which a short downclimb puts one in a gully. A trail in the gully leads back to the base of the climbs and any stashed packs. As always, check the anchor slings before committing to them.

ROUTE 4. OMEGA TOWER. II, 5.8, A1. First ascent August 11, 1964, by Barry Corbet and Rick Medrick. This was the original climb in the area east of Sentinel Turret, made on an Exum Guides' Day outing. It is not clear that Omega Tower, named at the time, is the same as Ship's Prow, and the exact location of this 1964 route is uncertain. It is thought to be located immediately to the west of the descent gully from the routes on Ship's Prow. From the trail at the entrance to Death Canyon (below the 7,000-foot level), a flatiron-like tower, the second of three, can be seen up to the right (north) on the eastern fringe of the rock. This route ascends the short, steep face of the "small flatiron-like" tower. Scramble to the highest point of 3.0 rock at the base of the face. The belayer can be anchored about 3m out to the right on a diagonal ledge. Now traverse 4.5m up and left along a narrow ledge to a vertical lieback crack that can be climbed with good holds to a large ledge on the right corner of the face. Next traverse left around a corner onto the center of the face where 6m of delicate 5.8 face climbing with excellent protection brings one to a good belay ledge. The second lead of this short route requires great care in passing around and up a very loose flake to a short wall leading to the bottom of an overhang. A good crack in the middle of the overhang can be climbed with aid to the easy rock above, which leads to the top of the tower.

ROUTE 5. SHIP'S PROW PILLAR, MAN-O-WAR. II, 5.8. First ascent July 12, 1970, by Thomas Dunwiddie and Roger Zimmerman. This climb goes up the east face of what is, in all likelihood, Ship's Prow, and portions of it may have become what is now Cardiac Arêtes *(Route 6)*. The first pitch is recognizable as a nice moderate-angle slab. The first lead goes up and along the sharp right edge of the slab to a large chockstone capping the break between the slab and the right wall. Now face climb (5.7) on the left to a small, grassy spot above. The next pitch starts from the meadow in a lieback (5.7) up flakes on the right side. Follow the corner/crack directly up past a few bulges to reach another grassy ledge for the belay. The third lead takes a 6-inch crack in the inside corner above the belay ledge to a large, prominent flake. Pass the flake to the right to an easy trough leading up and right; climb through a narrow and steep bulge in the trough to reach a low-angle slab that faces southeast. Climb to the top of the slab to the base of a steep, east-facing wall, below the black roof on the east side of the south face (mentioned in the Ship's Prow introduction).

On the next pitch, the crux of the route (5.8), pass the overhang using the rightmost of two cracks to the right of the overhang; this crack is better described as a tight dihedral with only a thin crack in the back. Use face holds on the right in this dihedral until a good horizontal hold in a crack on the left permits passing the difficult bulge at the top of the dihedral. The final long lead (5.7) follows the crack above to the top, passing three bulges or overhangs on the left, right, and left, in that order. The pitch ends with easier rock. All leads are a full 46m, except for the crux, and are well protected on excellent rock.

ROUTE 6. CARDIAC ARÊTES. II, 5.9. First ascent August 9, 1981, by Rich Perch and Randy Harrington. (See *Figure 2-7.*) Cardiac Arêtes, a two-lead variation on Man-o-War *(Route 5)*, takes a line out on the south face of the buttress before it traverses to the east side of the formation, finishing on steep, predominantly good rock with adequate protection. **Pitch 1:** Begin climbing as for the first pitch of Dihedral of Horror *(Route 7)*. After climbing the initial slab (5.7), find a belay where convenient. **Pitch 2:** Continue up and right in an easy, blocky corner (5.6) to a belay at the base of a big flake. **Pitch 3:** Climb up and past the flake and then around to the east side of the formation in an easy trough (a traverse to or from the gully to the east is possible here). Cut back left on a ledge and belay off a broad, sloping ledge near the base of two cracks. **Pitch 4:** Climb the right-hand crack (5.9), the one climbed on the first ascent. The left-hand crack is better but slightly harder at 5.10- (thin hands to hands); it was likely used in the DCD variation below. Continue up and belay where convenient. **Pitch 5:** Climb to the top of the formation via a crack system on terrain that begins to become lower angle, passing a 5.8 bulge along the way.

FIGURE 2-7. Albright Peak, Omega Buttresses, eastern section/Ship's Prow. (A) Annals of Time *(Route 10)*, II, 5.9; (B) Right Parallel Crack *(Route 9)*, II, 5.9; (C) Dihedral of Horrors *(Route 7)*, II, 5.9; (D) Dihedral of Horrors, variation: The Edge of Horror, II, 5.11+R; (E) Cardiac Arêtes, variation: DCD overhang, II, 5.10; (F) Cardiac Arêtes *(Route 6)*, II, 5.9

***Variation:* DCD (DEATH CANYON DIRECT).** II, 5.10. First ascent in August 1977, by Charlie Fowler, Dennis Grabnegger, and Kent Lugbill. This two-pitch variation is known only through a rudimentary topo. Although the location is uncertain, the 5.10 overhang is tentatively identified in *Figure 2-7*. The original description indicates that the first lead is a 15m perfect hand-jam crack (5.10-), which starts as right-facing, continues with the midsection left-facing, and ends as a right-facing crack or corner (this is likely the left-hand crack option of the fourth pitch of Cardiac Arêtes); then a small overhang is passed to a sloping ledge for the belay. At this point Fowler et al. probably traversed out left on the south face to the 5.10 overhang and then continued to the top of Ship's Prow via easier climbing.

ROUTE 7. DIHEDRAL OF HORRORS. II, 5.8, A3, or II, 5.9. First ascent August 18, 1967, by John Behrens and Peter Avenali; first free ascent in September 1981, by Beverly Boynton and Bob Graham. This dihedral, the next one to the east of *Route 8*, is located at the west edge of the south face of Ship's Prow. It is capped by a huge, flat, black-rock roof, the Diamond Roof, which is cut by a vein of white rock. *Figure 2-7* shows the free version of what originally was an aid route. Follow the standard Ship's Prow approach to a large bench directly beneath the south side of the formation. This bench has a large, living tree on it and is also the bench from which one can begin Annals of Time *(Route 10)*. Dihedral of Horrors starts just to the east of the tree.

Pitch 1 (three alternatives): (1) Climb the 2002 variation (5.10b, see below), located behind the big tree. (2) Climb the middle of the slab above the bench, trending slightly right (5.7). This is a long pitch, but the climbing eases up and leads to a belay in ledgy terrain. (3) Climb up the right side of the slab in a trough/weakness on easier terrain (5.6). Whichever option is used, move the belay up to a large, flat ledge. **Pitch 2:** Climb up directly behind the tree from the right side of the ledge (awkward 5.9 stem), or climb up from farther west along the ledge (5.8). Locate a belay where convenient in ledgy terrain above. **Pitch 3:** Climb up and right into the main dihedral on steepening terrain (difficult moves; 5.9 immediately below the belay) and belay at a small stance. **Pitch 4:** Climb directly above the belay in the corner (5.9 move) and continue up to the roof, where a great hand traverse (5.6) takes one out and right to an exposed belay on the south face. The next pitch is very short, but belaying here prevents rope drag and aids in communication. **Pitch 5:** Continue up the crack and belay where convenient on top.

Variation: II, 5.10b. First ascent May 19, 2002, by Paul Horton and Heather Paul. This is a difficult one-pitch start to Dihedral of Horrors or Annals of Time *(Route 10)*. From the bench beneath the south side of Ship's Prow, traverse out to the west on a ledge for approximately 30m to the base of a crack system that leads in from the left up to the initial slab pitch of Dihedral of Horrors. This variation begins behind the big tree. (See *Figure 2-7*.) Climb up a shallow right-facing feature to a finger crack through a small overhang, which is the crux of this pitch (5.10b). Join the Dihedral of Horrors route at the top of its first pitch.

***Variation:* THE EDGE OF HORROR.** II, 5.11+R. First ascent August 10, 2011, by Ian Eastman and Andy Tyson. The initial reconnaissance and cleaning of this route was done by Kent McBride and Greg Collins. This variation climbs the wall and the arête to the east from the ledgy terrain at the top of the second pitch of Dihedral of Horrors. (See *Figure 2-7*.) To quote from Mountain Project: "The climb is defined by exposed climbing off the deck, small fussy gear and aesthetic climbing up a gorgeous arete. It can be done as one long rope-stretching pitch or broken into two pitches." **Pitch 1:** From the belay at the top of the second pitch of Dihedral of Horrors, either climb an easier hand crack (5.9) on the left side of the wall or tackle a 5.10+ start on the right. Head up to a small ledge where a #3 Camalot placement is crucial to prevent a ground fall. Move slightly right and then up a small corner system; look for small (0.25"–0.5") placements through here. Climb the corner system to a piton, clip it, and move right around the arête and then up onto a small ledge. There is a bolt here if one chooses to set up a belay. **Pitch 2:** Climb left off the ledge up a small seam to insecure holds on the arête, clipping a bolt that is approximately 4.5m above the optional belay. Continue up the arête, working small holds for another 6m to easier ground above. Reach a ledge for the next belay.

ROUTE 8. WHITON'S CORNER. II, 5.8. First ascent September 4, 1983, by Mark and Diane Whiton. Immediately to the right of the two parallel cracks (see *Routes 9* and *10*) is a corner that is approached in the same manner as the cracks. From the base of the Right Parallel Crack, make a short traverse to the right and down a bit to get access to this corner. One long lead up the corner reaches the same shallow col.

ROUTE 9. RIGHT PARALLEL CRACK. II, 5.9. First ascent in July 1987, by Rhys Harriman and Tim Quinlan. (See *Figure 2-7*.) This crack is approached in the same manner as the left parallel crack (see *Route 10*), but unfortunately it is an unpleasant climb, both rotten and hard.

ROUTE 10. ANNALS OF TIME. II, 5.9. First ascent August 19, 1984, by Keith Cattabriga and Dale Dawson. (See *Figure 2-7*.) On the face to the left (northwest) of the conspicuous left-facing corners, one of which is the Dihedral of Horrors route *(Route 7)*, are two parallel cracks in an otherwise unbroken wall. This route ascends the left-hand crack, and today this upper crack pitch (the original route's crux) is usually done in conjunction with a climb of Dihedral of Horrors. Together they make a fine day of climbing with a relatively short approach (by Teton standards!). However, Annals of Time was originally done as a separate three-pitch route: It began with a left-facing corner (5.7), then the next pitch continued up and right through some blocky terrain (5.8) to the base of the crack that can be seen from far below. The last pitch—the main event—is quality crack climbing, passing through two 5.9 roofs in its 37m length. The route ends on the shallow col that separates Ship's Prow from the upper mountain.

***Variation:* NO QUESTION.** II, 5.9+. First ascent June 25, 1993, by Steve Sullivan and Mark Berry. This 27m left-facing corner adds one pitch of climbing to Annals of Time. At the point where the approach gully narrows, move out and right and undercling around a block to get to the base of the corner.

***Variation:* LYCRA.** II, 5.10-. First ascent in August 1987, by Jay Pistono, Keith Cattabriga, and Bob Stevenson. On the second lead, instead of moving right and up on 5.8 rock, go straight up a crack on thin holds. Many small wires and RPs protect this pitch.

Omega Buttresses, Central Section

This central section is easily recognized by a conspicuous diagonal crack or narrow chimney that cuts up steeply to the east from near the base of the O-Mega Crack *(Route 16)*. This has been referred to as the Trapezoid Chimney. On the eastern end of this buttress is a deep, white-colored indentation with a prominent right-facing corner leading to its west side. This is Manufactured Crisis *(Route 13)*. The white indentation is capped by a large overhang in darker-colored rock. Guardian of Death *(Route 12)* ascends this extremely difficult overhang. The routes located in this central section were, for the most part, established fairly recently and therefore the information about them is more reliable.

ROUTE 11. BRAEBURN'S CORNER. III, 5.11a. First ascent in August 1999, by Jim Beyer and Zack Martin. This climb is known only by a topo from the first-ascent party, so the details shown in *Figure 2-8* should be taken with a large bag of salt. Begin the route by going up near the start of Manufactured Crisis *(Route 13)* with a section of 3rd class to a ledge. Belay out right on the ledge near the base of a crack. The first pitch climbs the crack through a roof (5.9) and then continues up the crack to a section of face climbing past an old ¼" bolt. Trend up and left to a ledge and the belay. The second pitch goes out right via 5.5 face climbing to a belay at the base of a hand crack. Then climb via 5.9 hands up to a 5.10+ stem section past a bolt and continue with face climbing (5.10) past a fixed nut to a hanging belay at the bottom of a rounded flake feature. The fourth pitch ascends the right side of the flake (5.10-) to a roof, which is exited via its right side (5.11a), and then goes up discontinuous cracks (5.6–5.7) to a belay on a ledge. Fourth-class climbing leads to the top of the climb. The descent is via the gully to the east down to a double-rope rappel, which leads to the base of Ship's Prow. Adventure awaits!

ROUTE 12. GUARDIAN OF DEATH. III, 5.12+/5.13a, A0. First ascent in October 2009, by Greg Collins and Nate Opp. (See *Figure 2-8*.) Follow the approach for Manufactured Crisis *(Route 13)*. This five-pitch route climbs up to and over the huge overhang just to the right of that climb. Start up a right-trending crack (5.7 fists) with a small overhang and then a slab to a ledge and a belay at a bolt. The second pitch goes up and left from the belay onto the arête past a fixed pin, then continues up via heady 5.9 face climbing to a two-bolt anchor. The third pitch goes up a hand crack to a slab with three bolts (5.10c between second and third bolts) and then to a hanging belay at two bolts. The huge roof is next! Collins has free climbed all but a half meter of it at 5.12+/5.13a. The final pitch climbs the face just east of the arête (5.5). The descent is via the gully to the east down to a double-rope rappel; it is also possible to rappel the route with two ropes. **Gear:** For protection take quickdraws and aiders; a set of stoppers; and a set of cams to hand size.

FIGURE 2-8. Albright Peak, Omega Buttresses, central section. (A) Manufactured Crisis *(Route 13)*, II, 5.11bR; (B) Guardian of Death *(Route 12)*, III, 5.12+/5.13a, A0; (C) Braeburn's Corner *(Route 11)*, III, 5.11a

ROUTE 13. MANUFACTURED CRISIS. II, 5.11bR. First ascent in July 1999, by Aaron Gams and Pono Faulkner. (See *Figure 2-8.*) This route ascends the major right-facing corner system on the eastern facet of the central section of the Omega Buttresses. It consists of three pitches, and the approach is via the regular approach for Ship's Prow (see *Omega Buttresses, Eastern Section/Ship's Prow*); from the base of Ship's Prow, scramble west into a gully and traverse west another 60m to the base of the corner system. Begin by scrambling up easy 5th-class terrain to a ledge with blocks on it. The first pitch starts in the corner itself, but step right where it steepens and then back left where obvious, and head up through blocky terrain to a ledge. Proceed up the main corner via a 5.8 lieback and belay at a slung block. The second pitch begins with a minimally protected 5.8+ section to the first of two bolts that are passed via 5.11b climbing. A runout stretch above (5.10-R) leads up to a hanging belay beneath a small roof. The third pitch continues up the corner (5.9 lieback) and exits out right via an upward-slanting crack to the east to a belay at a tree. Two double-rope rappels return one to the base of the climb. **Gear:** For protection take a set of stoppers and a double set of cams to 3.5"; a few micro cams and a set of small offsets could also be useful.

ROUTE 14. TRAPEZOID CHIMNEY. II, 5.7. First ascent June 5, 1975, by Mike Yager and Tom Huckin. The exact location of this route, originally called Trapezoid Tower, is a mystery—and it may remain that way since the first-ascent party stated that they could not recommend the route because of the loose rock they encountered. Although the identification is not certain, it appears to this author (R. Jackson) that the first ascensionists followed the main chimney system on the south face of the central buttress. Their description of the summit of the tower—"an anvil-like formation having a large indentation and roof halfway up its southeast ridge"—matches the central of the Omega Buttresses. Continuing, they noted that the formation had "a reddish south face, bounded by two nearly vertical, but slightly diverging, cracks or chimneys that give the face a trapezoid shape."

From the highest point directly below the tower, proceed upward via 4.0 scrambling to a broad ledge where a solitary spruce (the largest tree in the vicinity) will be found. The first ropelength goes directly up a narrow crack system (5.4) containing one 5.7 mantel. An easy scramble then takes one to the base of the chimney, the rightmost of the two defining the trapezoid; this chimney is followed for the remainder of the route. The next ropelength ascends a short wall to the right, connecting with the chimney 6m up and ending at a belay alcove. The following lead passes a large, loose chockstone flake (5.6); use caution here. A ropelength of scrambling ends at a cul-de-sac caused by a narrowing of the chimney. The route ascends the short, vertical 5.7 wall to the left before angling back to the top of the overhang. The top is then reached by easy scrambling.

FIGURE 2-9. Albright Peak, Omega Buttresses, central section, Omega Triangle *(Route 15)*, III, 5.11

ROUTE 15. OMEGA TRIANGLE. III, 5.11. First ascent July 30, 2009, by Aaron Gams and Brian Mulvilhill. (See *Figure 2-9.*) This route is on the triangular-shaped wall to the west of the Trapezoid Chimney and consists of five quality pitches on excellent rock. Use the regular approach for Ship's Prow (see *Omega Buttresses, Eastern Section/Ship's Prow*) and traverse over to the base of the chimney. Begin climbing approximately 6m to the east of the chimney system, heading toward a hand crack that narrows to fingers through a bulge and then ends on a ledge. Either go left into the chimney or climb up to the right via stemming (loose) to a ledge leading left into the chimney, then ascend the chimney (5.7) to a belay on a chockstone. The second pitch goes left out of the chimney to a small right-facing feature, then up to a ledge from which face climbing (5.10-) leads to a crack through a roof and up to another ledge for the belay at the base of a wide, deep, flaring crack. An alternative hand traverse avoids the apparently committing face climbing above the first ledge on this short pitch. The third pitch begins with a bolt-protected 5.11 boulder problem up and right that permits access to a thin 5.10 crack that gradually widens to fingers just before a ledge. Above the ledge, step left to another finger crack (5.10-), which widens to thin hands just below the belay ledge. The so-called Zanzibar Finish (climbed on the original ascent) climbs the deep, blocky dihedral (5.8) above the belay in one long pitch (60m). After exiting the roof at the top of the corner, 5.6 wandering takes one to a ramp and the top of the climb.

A two-pitch variation was completed at a later date to the west of the Zanzibar Finish. Climb out left to a bolt-protected face (5.10, two bolts) to a ledge, above which is a right-facing corner (5.11- stemming) and a belay ledge. The final pitch of this variation begins with a short right-facing corner that leads to a right-facing flake (5.10- lieback). Above this, easy 5th-class climbing leads to the ramp and the top of the climb. The descent consists of a 4th-class traverse to a gully that is downclimbed to a big tree. Continue traversing east from the tree into a larger gully that leads down to a double-rope rappel anchor (difficult to see), which deposits one near the base of Ship's Prow. **Gear:** For protection take a set of stoppers and a double set of cams from 0.4" to 3". (Source: Written description from Aaron Gams)

ROUTE 16. O-MEGA CRACK. II, 5.12b. First free ascent in May 2007, by Greg Collins and Hans Johnstone. (See *Figure 2-10.*) A number of people worked on this route over the years, including Greg Collins, Hans Johnstone, Bean Bowers, and Sam Lightner Jr. The first redpoint ascent was by Collins, who spent at least 10 days on the route over time, equipping it and replacing/installing bolts, cleaning it, and rehearsing the moves. It is difficult to understand just how much effort is involved in establishing a route of this caliber with the best materials. Johnstone free climbed the route afterward with David Gonzales. The route may overhang by as much as 20°, but it is reported to be excellent and is highly recommended. The first pitch involves 5.12b crimping past six bolts and a fixed pin to a small stance. A 5.10+ hand crack finishes the pitch at a two-bolt anchor. The second pitch begins with a welcome bolt, just above the anchor, and then a handrail on a flake leads right and then up to a second bolt. Difficult climbing (5.12b) then leads up and left to an overhanging hand crack (5.11), which is said to have pods. The pitch finishes with a difficult, fingery overhang, above which the angle lessens to the belay anchor. Both pitches are 28m–30m. **Gear:** Recommended protection includes quickdraws, a set of stoppers, and two sets of cams from finger to hand size.

Jane Jackson on the superlative O-Mega Crack, central Omega Buttress, Death Canyon (Photo by Eric Bissell)

FIGURE 2-10. Albright Peak, Omega Buttresses, central section, O-Mega Crack *(Route 16)*, II, 5.12b

Omega Buttresses, Western Section

This western section extends from Sentinel Gully on the west to a deep, V-shaped indentation on the east. This indentation is bounded by very steep, smooth walls composed of alternating layers of light- and dark-colored rock on either side. This section is also recognized by the large chimney system cutting through the center of the south face that *may* be the Chimney of Death *(Route 20)*. The following routes represent my (R. Jackson's) best guess as to their relative position from east to west on this section of the Omega Buttresses.

ROUTE 17. CATHY'S CORNER. II, 5.7. First ascent August 19, 1986, by Cathy Pollack and Rhys Harriman. This four-pitch climb enters the central V-shaped indentation between the western and central sections of the Omega Buttresses and ascends the chimney to its left (west) edge. Approach from the Death Canyon trail and head toward the base of the V. Considerable scrambling among the trees and slabs is required to reach the area below the V. The initial lead (5.4) goes up into the V and gains the beginning of the left chimney. The next two leads (5.6 and 5.7) follow straight up this chimney. The final face, if continued directly, would be much more difficult, so an exit traverse is made up and to the right (5.6). A couloir was used to descend, although it is not known which one, and "some rappelling was required."

ROUTE 18. SOUTH BUTTRESS. II, 5.7. First ascent July 3, 1976, by Gordon Brooks, Charlie Gunn, and Jim Schubert. This climb on the south face of the western section of the Omega Buttresses ascends the conspicuous diagonal, narrow chimney on the right (east) facet of the face. This chimney is the first break in the layered wall to the right of the central indentation of the face. From the trail, scramble about 120m up ledges from the northeast side of Sentinel Gully. The base of the large chimney with trees at the bottom will be approached from the left. From a belay alcove above two trees near the base of this chimney, traverse up and to the right, heading toward a prominent horn (5.7). Move 12m above the horn to the belay ledge, which is in the diagonal chimney that is followed for the next two leads. The second pitch continues up this chimney through a V-shaped notch in a roof to a thin ledge for the second belay stance. Here, a second chimney with several chockstones parallels and joins the main diagonal chimney. A smaller vertical chimney with a chockstone about even with this ledge is now on the left. The next lead moves up—partly on the face to the right of this chimney, partly in the chimney—until access is gained onto the smooth face to the right. Now make a long traverse (5.7) out to the right on the clean face under a prominent arch (a series of roofs), then go through a break in the arch and up past a 5.7 ceiling on loose blocks to reach the easy ground at the end of this third lead; a fixed piton was found on the traverse by the first-ascent party. The route ends at the top of the right shoulder of the face, a crest with trees. Descent is via ledges leading north to a gully and then a scramble down to the main Death Canyon trail.

ROUTE 19. SPLOOGE. I, 5.7. First ascent June 28, 1976, by Kelly Elder and Matthew Childs. This very short climb is on the lowest slabs just above the main trail below the western section of the Omega Buttresses. The route starts in a left-facing corner and moves right out onto the face from the top of the corner. The second short lead moves up the slabby face. Descent was off to the west.

ROUTE 20. CHIMNEY OF DEATH. II, 5.8. First ascent July 22, 1968, by Andy Cox and Mike Yokell. Although the exact location remains uncertain, this climb was originally stated to be on the first major buttress east of Sentinel Turret. Approach from the first large boulder field past the second switchback corner on the trail in Death Canyon proper; go straight up the boulder field to the base of the rock. Scramble one ropelength up and then left until under a prominent left-facing open book. The first lead (5.4) proceeds 9m up the book past a corner and then makes a 15m traverse left to a piton belay at a corner. The next pitch of 24m goes straight up the face above, past a ceiling and the wall above to two solid trees. Scramble up and right 9m to a dead tree stump for a belay under an obvious wall. The long third lead (5.7) goes straight up the wall to the right of the stump for 30m to a left-facing open book. Climb the book for 6m, then go 3m up a chimney to a 3m traverse to another belay tree. The next pitch of 43m goes more easily up and left to a solid belay tree in a chimney under a left-facing wall. Now climb 9m up the wall to a bench, where one turns left up a difficult wall with a vertical 6m jam crack; a boulder for belay will be found after another 6m. The sixth pitch starts with a 9m lieback in a left-facing open book toward the prominent chimney or open book (Chimney of Death), which leads for the next four leads all the way to the crest. The next 90m up the chimney involves moderate climbing past bulges and chockstones to reach a large roof in the chimney. The ninth lead (5.8) passes this roof by a 2+m traverse to the right and then involves a hand traverse back left into the chimney, which is followed to the crest. The final pitch goes up the crest to the summit of the buttress.

ROUTE 21. SWIZZLE STICK. II, 5.6. First ascent August 7, 1971, by Dave Erickson, Dave Smith, and Joseph Bowman. Little is known about this route, originally stated to be on the first buttress to the right (east) of Sentinel Turret. From the base of the face about 120m of scrambling (3.0) and climbing leads to a ledge below the steep part of the face. From this ledge the route follows a prominent crack leading up and angling slightly right. Apparently four pitches are involved, with the most difficult moves (5.6) on the first and fourth leads.

Found Arrow Spire (ca. 7,500)

(2.1 mi S of Buck Mountain)

This pinnacle is located on the east flank of Sentinel Turret about 90m below the summit. A prominent horizontal band of white rock cuts across both the pinnacle and the Turret.

ROUTE 1. SOUTH AND EAST FACES. I, 5.1. First ascent August 26, 1964, by Ted Vaill and Brad Merry. From the Death Canyon trail, ascend Sentinel Gully, the talus couloir just east of Sentinel Turret, to a point where it is possible to traverse back to Found Arrow Spire on wide ledges. The spire overhangs on all sides, but a moderate route was found from the notch to the west, between the spire and the face of the Turret. This single-pitch climb begins on the overhanging face above the notch in a wide crack; after 4.5m move out to the right to the corner of the exposed south face and head up and right to a small platform. The 1-square-meter summit is then easily reached from the east. Descent is made by rappel from a piton into the notch.

Harrington Spire (8,240+)

(2.1 mi S of Buck Mountain)

In the notch separating Sentinel Turret from the upper ridge that eventually leads to Albright Peak is a distinct pinnacle, which apparently remained unclimbed during the first 30 years of climbing on Sentinel Turret.

ROUTE 1. THE PILGRIMAGE. II, 5.9R. First ascent by Trevor and Eddie Bowman (date unknown). This accidental two-pitch climb is located on the wall to the right of Harrington Spire. The approach is by way of Sentinel Gully and the climb is 6m–9m right of the 23m crack system mentioned in *Route 2*. The first pitch begins with easy 5th-class climbing up a vegetated crack and leads to a tree at the halfway point. Climb past the tree and up a chimney to its top, where a 5.7 exit to the right is made to a belay ledge. Move the belay 15m to the right to the base of a fist crack. The second pitch goes up the crack to a right-facing corner; climb the corner for a short distance, then exit left on the face (5.9R) for 9m–12m to a belay under small roofs. One double-rope rappel reaches the first ledge, and then a single-rope rappel reaches the base of the climb.

ROUTE 2. EAST FACE. II, 5.7. First ascent August 20, 1988, by Randy Harrington and Evan Kaplan. Follow the approach up Sentinel Gully described in *Sentinel Turret, Route 1*, and take the large ledges out to the left (south) to reach the base of the 23m crack system that is used in that route. Instead of climbing directly up to the notch, start 3m to the right and climb a crack for about 18m. At the point where the crack ends, make a traverse to the right (5.7) for 3m to a point where one can scramble up and right to the spire, whose summit is attained by a mantel move.

Sentinel Turret (8,240+)

(2.1 mi S of Buck Mountain)

As one enters Death Canyon on the trail, and even from various places in the valley, a steep, conspicuous buttress that culminates in a separate flat summit block is seen about halfway up the wall on the north side of the canyon. On the map Sentinel Turret is easily identified as the only place where the 7,600- and 8,000-foot contour lines overlap. This appropriately named buttress or tower was the first rock climb explored in Death Canyon. It is separated from the Snaz Buttress, the larger formation to the west, by a steep couloir guarded by a cliff band at its base. The broad Sentinel Gully is shown on the map as the westerly of the two streams descending from the north into the Death Canyon creek near the mouth of the canyon. This major drainage defines the east face of Sentinel Turret and separates it from the Omega Buttresses, which lie immediately to the east.

Sentinel Turret suffers from inadequate information regarding the exact location of its various routes and variations; only the East Ledges *(Route 1)* and the Southwest Ridge *(Route 3)* are well identified. However, because considerable detail on these routes is available, the descriptions are included below even though the locations of the climbs remain uncertain. Perhaps these descriptions will motivate research leading to their rediscovery.

Chronology

SOUTH FACE: August 3, 1959, Yvon Chouinard, Bob Kamps
var—August 16, 1967, Jim Erickson, Sheldon Smith
var—July 20, 1969, Mike and Jane Yokell
var—**DOOMSDAY DIHEDRAL:** July 11, 1970, Jim Erickson, Dave Erickson
var—**BLACK CHIMNEY:** August 1975, David Lowe, Leigh Ortenburger
var—**BEELINE:** September 3, 1975, Jim Beyer, Jerry Cantor; FFA July 1979, Jim Beyer, Misa Geisey
var—**THAT SUSHI THING:** Summer 1986, Jason Keith, Greg Marin

EAST LEDGES: August 3, 1959, Yvon Chouinard, Bob Kamps (descent); August 26, 1964, Ted Vaill, Brad Merry (ascent)

SOUTHWEST RIDGE: June 21, 1964, Jeff Foott, Chuck Satterfield, Peter Koedt, Steve Miller
var—June 27, 1964, Chuck Satterfield, Barry Corbet

ROUTE 1. EAST LEDGES. II, 5.5. First descent August 3, 1959, by Yvon Chouinard and Bob Kamps; first ascent August 26, 1964, by Ted Vaill and Brad Merry, and also apparently the route of September 7, 1964, by Chuck Satterfield, David Allen, Ron Weber, and Kathy Fauerbach. The eastern aspect of Sentinel Turret is approached out of the major drainage to the east, Sentinel Gully, which separates the Turret from the Omega Buttresses. This large gully is recognized as the second stream crossing as one proceeds west along the trail after entering Death Canyon. Scramble up this gully, at places somewhat unpleasant, until one can cut back left (south) on horizontal ledges to a point about 23m below the notch separating Sentinel Turret from the rest of the mountain above (Albright Peak). This notch also separates the small, sharp pinnacle of Harrington Spire. One pitch of roped climbing is required to gain the notch, from which the summit of the Turret is easily reached.

ROUTE 2. SOUTH FACE. III, 5.8. First ascent August 3, 1959, by Yvon Chouinard and Bob Kamps. This high-angle rock climb on the lower south ridge or face is in principle the primary route on this tower. Experience over the past 60 years shows, however, that it is uncommonly difficult to find; few parties claim to have located the original line. *Figure 2-11* shows a 5.9+ variation that leads to the finish of the 1959 Chouinard-Kamps route. What follows is a description closer to the original 1959 route. From the Death Canyon trailhead, hike up the Death Canyon trail toward the prominent tower on the north side of the canyon entrance. Leave the trail at the first talus slope past Sentinel Turret, after passing a section of slabs just off the trail, then walk back east to the upper cliff band. Continue to the apex of a small, grassy slope and look for a triangular alcove with a wide, left-leaning crack rising from its top. About 30m above that is a perfect vertical 15m dihedral.

Climb the crack to the large horizontal ledge below the dihedral. Move right on the ledge about 15m and climb a prominent broken crack system (5.7) for a ropelength. Do *not* go right after this pitch even though there is a ledge that permits such a lead. Continue up one more pitch in this crack system to easier ground. From this point an easy two-pitch variation is possible by continuing up a right-facing corner to big ledges, where a long traverse

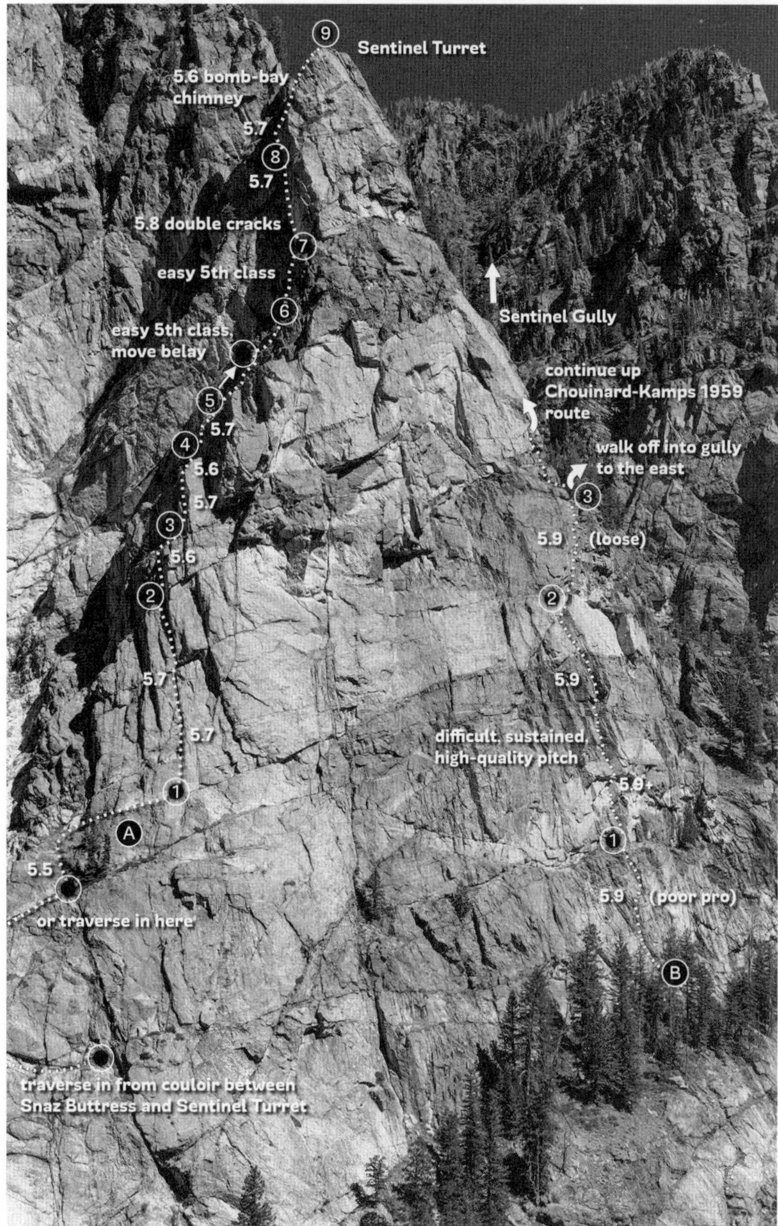

FIGURE 2-11. Sentinel Turret. (A) Southwest Ridge *(Route 3)*, III, 5.8; (B) South Face variation with 1959 Chouinard-Kamps finish *(Route 2)*, III, 5.9+

A skier descending the lower portion of the Apocalypse Couloir, Prospectors Mountain (Photo by Adam Fabrikant)

leads right (east) to the top of the slab pitch described below. The proper and more difficult route, however, makes a non-obvious traverse right all the way to the right skyline. The slabs above, which form the crux pitch (5.8) on the right skyline, are now climbed for 30m to a ledge with trees. The final two leads (5.7) continue up thin cracks and a knobby face to the summit. The easy descent route is into Sentinel Gully, the drainage to the east that leads down to the Death Canyon trail (see *Route 1*). Make a 30m rappel onto ledges that can be contoured to the north into the bottom of the gully; a second rappel may be desired. Some climbs of Sentinel Turret have been made using this gully as the approach to the middle of this route, coming in from the east around to the main crack system.

Variation: **THAT SUSHI THING.** III, 5.10-. First ascent in summer 1986, by Jason Keith and Greg Marin. This variation was named by Alan Hunt on a failed attempt during the summer of 1985. The climb starts near the base of the 1959 Chouinard-Kamps route, if one is able to decipher that particular mystery. A full ropelength of crack and face climbing (5.8) leads to the large ledge just below and west of the clean dihedral visible from the trail below. The next pitch ascends a good, clean crack (5.7 to 5.8) and the clean dihedral to a belay from which the Chouinard-Kamps route leads up and to the right. Climb up and left toward a short arête and then back to a 5.8 corner. Continue through a 5.8 overhang followed by a traverse left to a 5.10- roof and right-facing corner to the belay. Face climbing then leads past a large block (5.7) to a large ramp. Rejoin the 1959 route and continue to the top.

Variation: II, 5.9, A2. First ascent August 16, 1967, by Jim Erickson and Sheldon Smith. This variation leads rather directly from the base to the upper part of the 1959 Chouinard-Kamps route on Sentinel Tukret and lies to the right (east) of the Doomsday Dihedral variation (described below); however, the actual starting point is not clearly defined. Climb two or three pitches up toward a prominent open book, described as a clean, square-cut, right-facing 37m dihedral. A short, blank wall (5.9) then leads to the start of the dihedral, which was nailed using a thin A2 crack in the back. Nine more meters up the left wall completes this crux pitch. Four additional pitches along the same general line connect the top of the dihedral to the upper end of the traverse ramp on the 1959 route; at this point the original route is joined for the final three or four leads to the summit.

Variation: III, 5.8. First ascent July 20, 1969, by Mike and Jane Yokell. This incomplete variation of uncertain location apparently followed, or at least crossed, a previous climb or two, as evidenced by old iron that was encountered in two places. Proceed along the Death Canyon trail to a section of low-angle slabs and scramble up past trees to an inside corner with bushes, ending on a large, grassy ledge at the base of a 70° face. The first lead (5.6) goes up this face, just left of a chimney or inside corner, for 40m to a large, treed ledge (6m wide). The next ropelength ascends the face above (5.7) to a left-leaning ramp, ending in a difficult unprotected corner (5.8) for a belay on a 4-inch ledge. Six meters of 5.4 from the left end of this small ledge permits moving the belay to a more substantial ledge above. The next long pitch moves 2.5m left to an overhang (5.7), which is passed to gain access to a vertical crack and chimney system. Climb this system and belay from the top of a 3m flake. Continue up the chimney, passing an overhang (5.7), into the inside corner above. Nine meters of easier climbing (5.2) on the same line gains a large, grassy bench for the next belay. Similar climbing for 37m leads to the crest of the southwest ridge at another large, grassy ledge where an old ring piton may be found. The final lead starts up a short face to a left-slanting crack that is passed on the left into an overhanging corner. Climb this corner onto a face and traverse back to the right to an inside corner with a crack. Climb the crack on the left side of the corner (5.9), past an old 1" angle piton, to exit left onto a belay ledge (1m wide, 1.2m long). This placed the 1969 party at the base of a short but very difficult face about 21m below the summit; time did not permit completing the route to the summit.

Variation: **DOOMSDAY DIHEDRAL.** IV, 5.9. First ascent July 11, 1970, by Jim Erickson and Dave Erickson. The major feature of this relatively long but uncertain route is a large white dihedral near the left (west) edge of the south face of Sentinel Turret. This Doomsday Dihedral is located about 120m above the base of the face, and a crack system can be seen leading up to the dihedral. Unfortunately, directions to reach the start of this climb are unavailable. The first pitch (5.4) goes up a 46m chimney to a ledge near a tree. The next lead (5.7) aims right of the dihedral on face climbing to a ledge just below two parallel left-angling cracks, which are easily seen from below. Climb the left-hand crack (5.7) past a bulge to a ledge just right of a large slab. The fourth short pitch (5.9) goes upward for 15m in a jam crack to a poor belay stance from a piton. Now traverse left (5.6) on rotten rock for 9m around a corner to a belay point. The sixth lead, after an additional 9m traverse left, reaches the dihedral, which is climbed on difficult, rotten rock (5.9) with poor protection for 15m. The final lead of this variation, again on poor rock, goes up the right-hand crack above, surmounts a roof (5.9), and ends on a ledge, roughly on the southwest ridge of Sentinel Turret. Four more leads of lesser difficulty on the ridge, where old iron from a previous party was found, are required to reach the summit. This climb is dangerous due to the rotten and sometimes poorly protected rock and contains only two enjoyable pitches; it is not recommended.

Variation: **BEELINE.** III, 5.8, A1, or III, 5.9. First ascent September 3, 1975, by Jim Beyer and Jerry Cantor; first free ascent in July 1979, by Jim Beyer and Misa Geisey. This eight-pitch variation starts to the left (west) of the 1959 Chouinard-Kamps route but the location of its beginning is uncertain. After an initial ropelength of moderate rock (5.5) to a ledge, the second pitch moves up a face and past a crack (5.6) to a belay. The third lead goes up a groove of similar difficulty, then slightly to the right to the base of a prominent white open book or right-facing corner. This open book, the main feature of this variation, is climbed for one lead but is abandoned out to the left on the fifth pitch. Move left past a small right-facing corner to a second such corner and up past an overhang on the left using hand-and-fist technique (5.9) to somewhat easier face climbing and a belay. The sixth lead moves right and up past a large flake to the base

Buck Tilley on the first ascent of Caveat Emptor (Photo by Renny Jackson)

of an easy ramp that is followed left out to its end. Now climb back right over loose rock (5.6) to the belay for the final lead, a 4th-class pitch to a tree at the top of the climb.

Variation: **BLACK CHIMNEY.** III, 5.9. First ascent in August 1975, by David Lowe and Leigh Ortenburger. This variation ignores the admonition given in the main description and goes right at the end of the second pitch. Move right for 43m along a diagonal crack and ledge to large, loose, black boulders at the beginning of a vertical open chimney. The lead up this black chimney is difficult (5.9) and ends on a ledge with trees on the ridge crest. The final leads of the standard route lie somewhere above.

ROUTE 3. SOUTHWEST RIDGE. III, 5.8. First ascent June 21, 1964, by Jeff Foott, Chuck Satterfield, Peter Koedt, and Steve Miller. This route lies to the left (west) of the standard South Face route *(Route 2)*. *Figure 2-11* depicts a total of nine pitches of climbing to reach—from the west—the notch that separates Sentinel Turret from Harrington Spire and the upper mountain.

Variation: II, 5.6. First ascent June 27, 1964, by Chuck Satterfield and Barry Corbet. This line, similar to the one climbed six days earlier, also leads to the notch between Sentinel Turret and Harrington Spire but ascends an open book, containing rotten rock, to the right (south) of the regular line but still to the left of the South Face route.

Snaz Buttress (9,440+)

(2.0 mi S of Buck Mountain)

The Snaz Buttress is the major large buttress on the north side of Death Canyon that forms the lower portion of the southwest ridge of Albright Peak. This buttress was listed under the hackneyed and seldom-used "Cathedral Rock" in previous editions. Its eastern edge is the steep couloir that bounds Sentinel Turret on the west. The Snaz Buttress is the last formation on the north before the canyon opens out into the flat area near the patrol cabin; it lies directly across the canyon from Apocalypse Arête *(Prospectors Mountain, Route 8)*.

Approach: To approach the climbs on this buttress, take the Death Canyon trail to the last switchback before entering the first level section of the canyon where the patrol cabin is located. At the eastern end of this switchback (the eighth switchback corner after entering the canyon), a short scramble up off the main trail leads to a well-defined climbers' trail that takes one to the base of the climbs. Just below and a few meters to the east of the start of the first pitch of the Snaz is a small, conveniently located alcove/cave where climbers can stash or hang gear not needed on the climb.

The three most popular climbs are the Snaz *(Route 7)*, Sunshine Daydream *(Route 6)* to the east, and Caveat Emptor *(Route 8)* to the west. Each one starts with the first pitch of the Snaz.

Rappel descent: The descent for *Routes 6–8* nowadays is usually done by rappelling the Snaz. The belays are fixed points, and in some cases expansion bolts have been added, but it is always recommended that one inspect the anchors very carefully before committing to them. Two ropes are necessary for these rappels; many use a 60m rope and a tag line of equal length.

Standard Snaz walk-off descent: Before the Snaz rappel route became an established method of descent, this was the primary means of getting off the buttress. From the top of the final pitch of the Snaz, continue up slabs for approximately 90m (4th class and easy 5th class) to a broad, tree-covered bench. If this walk-off route is chosen, use extreme caution on these slabs because they are very slippery when wet! Contour around to the west past the southwest corner of the buttress, then downclimb easy chimneys on the west side to the scree gully that leads down to the main Death Canyon trail. Some may want to do a rappel from a large tree right before the main scree gully. A lower bench descent option for Aerial Boundaries *(Route 16)* and Escape from Death *(Route 15)* also leads off to the west without continuing up the slabs (see *Figure 2-23*); if this lower option is taken, two 30m rappels will be necessary to access the main descent gully.

Chronology

PILLAR OF DEATH: July 19, 1964, Rick Medrick, David Dornan
var—August 17, 1976, Eric Engberg, Stephen Angelini
THE SNAZ: August 4, 1964, Yvon Chouinard, Mort Hempel
var—**SNAZETTE:** [probable] 1974, John Bragg
var—**COUSIN LEROY:** August 31, 1987, Dave Insley, Dan Barto
var—**COUSIN LEROY'S UNCLE:** June 10, 1994, Tom Kimbrough, Beverly Boynton
ESCAPE FROM DEATH: July 5, 1967, Rick Reese, Ted Wilson, Mike Ermarth
THE WIDOWMAKER: August 18, 1969, Kevin Donald, Jim Erickson
LOT'S SLOT: July 16, 1978, Mike Munger, Buck Tilley
VAS DEFERENS: July 18, 1978, Jim Beyer, Buck Tilley
var—**AUGUST 11TH START:** August 11, 1978, Buck Tilley, Bill Danford
FALLEN ANGEL: July 18, 1978, Yvon Chouinard, Mike Munger
COTTONMOUTH: July 25, 1978, Mike Munger, Buck Tilley
SCHMITZ-KANZLER DIHEDRAL: [probable] 1979, Kim Schmitz, Jim Kanzler
SHATTERED: July 4, 1979, Jim Beyer, Buck Tilley
CAVEAT EMPTOR: July 9, 1979, Jim Beyer, Buck Tilley
var—July 24, 1979, George Montopoli, Mike Munger
ALPINE COW: Late 1970s (unfinished), Mike Munger et al.
AERIAL BOUNDARIES: September 1985, Greg Miles, Mike Fischer, Jeff Bjornsen, Tom Vajda
var—**FNG:** July 16, 1995, Eric Gabriel, Bill Culbreath
SUNSHINE DAYDREAM: September 2, 1987, Charlie Fowler, Alison Sheets
WALKER: July 10, 1994, Pike Howard, Eric Busch
THE FOUNTAINHEAD: September 2003, Evan Howe, Doug Workman, Greg Collins, Bob Goodwin
FREEDOM FIGHTER: 2004, Greg Collins, Sue Miller, Brendan O'Neill

ROUTE 1. WALKER. II, 5.10-. First ascent July 10, 1994, by Pike Howard and Eric Busch. This climb is the first known route on the uppermost cliff of the Snaz Buttress. It starts from the huge upper ledge that most of the preceding routes finish on. For the first pitch look for a left-facing corner (5.8+) with a loose block situated slightly to the east. Ascend this, proceed up past two ledges with trees on them to the base of a shallow corner with a finger crack in it, and belay. Climb the corner (5.8) and continue up past three more ledges to an obvious, splitter-type hand crack located just to the right of a rock pillar and some loose blocks. From the top of the crack, face climb (5.7) to the belay. Another shallow corner requiring thin protection (5.9) is then encountered, followed by a 5.7 chimney. This third pitch ends with a 3m hand crack (5.9+). Many variations are possible for the finish of the climb. (**Note:** The first-ascent party used a 60m rope on their climb.)

ROUTE 2. PILLAR OF DEATH. III, 5.8, A2. First ascent July 19, 1964, by Rick Medrick and David Dornan. (See *Figure 2-12*.) The Pillar of Death is the prominent buttress or pillar of rock on the right (east) side of the Snaz Buttress; this side is bounded on the right by the steep couloir that separates Sentinel Turret from the Snaz Buttress. To reach the base of the climb, follow the regular approach to the Snaz Buttress

FIGURE 2-12. Albright Peak, Snaz Buttress. (A) Fallen Angel *(Route 3)*, IV, 5.10+; (B) Pillar of Death *(Route 2)*, III, 5.8, A2

and traverse out to the east until the gravelly ramp of *Route 3* is located. The route itself, the first climb done on the impressive Snaz Buttress, starts on the left (west) of the crest just past a small pine tree in the broken rock of a 5.6 chimney system. When possible, diagonal up to the right and end the first lead beneath a short overhang. The next pitch goes over the overhang and proceeds diagonally to the right on a moderate, but rotten, ledge to a somewhat insecure belay beneath an apparently blank wall. The third lead, difficult (5.8) and exposed, is the crux of the climb. Traverse 24m farther to the right with poor protection, then diagonal upward over rock of doubtful quality. At the end of this lead make a series of delicate steps up and to the right to reach the good ledge 6m above. Now climb off the belay ledge to the right; with a piton or two for aid, pass several small overhangs to reach a large open-book chimney for a good belay stance.

The fifth lead (5.6) ascends the wide chimney above, via the crack on the right, to an exit at a difficult step; from here climb onto a broad, sloping ledge. Walk around the corner to the left and up to the far (west) end of the ledge, where the next lead ascends easy rock to a good belay in a short chimney beneath a large overhanging chockstone. The seventh pitch leads out of this chimney, passing the chockstone on the right, then crossing over to the left and up an easy overhang onto a wide ledge at the base of a gully. The final two easy leads ascend to the top of this gully and then traverse right to the top of the pillar. To descend, scramble to the top of the rock below the upper face and traverse high around to the left (west) on a ledge system that eventually leads to the standard Snaz walk-off descent. Except for the third pitch, this route is on generally good rock with good protection, but nearly every pitch has a difficult section.

Variation: III, 5.9. First ascent August 17, 1976, by Eric Engberg and Stephen Angelini. While this climb was believed by the first-ascent party to be in the vicinity of the Pillar of Death, it may have been on the southwest side of Sentinel Turret; the exact location is not known. Evidence of previous ascent was found during the first three and a half pitches in the form of rappel slings and two pitons at the end of the second pitch. The main clue regarding the location of the route is the profile of rock on the north skyline. After entering Death Canyon, a profile in the form of a triangular nose protruding from a vertical wall is seen. This profile forms the left wall of a dihedral. The route follows a system of cracks that leads to and through this dihedral.

The first pitch (5.4, 46m) goes up a system of small ledges to a grass-covered ledge for a belay at a pine tree. The next lead avoids the grungy corner above the tree by climbing the face (5.6) to the right to a ledge. The third ropelength moves left to a left-leaning, right-facing corner. Climb this (5.7) to its top, exiting left and then moving back right to a belay on sloping rock. The fourth pitch (27m) goes up and slightly right to an awkward, narrow, rounded chimney. A difficult (5.8) offwidth jam crack above leads to a flake system in a slot that extends to an insecure belay below an overhanging, V-shaped slot. The next lead traverses out 6m on the left wall on loose rock around the corner. Continue this rising traverse 12m to the left (5.6) to a jam crack formed by the inside corner of the rock profile mentioned at the beginning. After 18m up this jam crack (5.8), a good belay stance will be found. The final pitch (21m) goes up the rightmost of two cracks for 12m to an overhanging finish (5.9), where one exits slightly left. The last 9m is face climbing to a large, sloping ledge that was believed to be the southwest shoulder of Sentinel Turret. From this high point it appeared that there were two additional easy pitches to a prominent triangular point, followed by more-difficult climbing. Thus, it appears that this was an incomplete route. Engberg and Angelini desceded by walking down and left, where two rappels, with slings in place, took them to a gully. Several more slings were found in place in the gully. This might have been the standard Snaz walk-off descent couloir or the couloir separating the Snaz Buttress from Sentinel Turret.

ROUTE 3. FALLEN ANGEL. IV, 5.10+. First ascent July 18, 1978, by Yvon Chouinard and Mike Munger. See *Figures 2-12* and *2-13* for some limited detail of this complicated route. Expect a committing climb with routefinding difficulties. The beginning of the climb is on a gravelly 3rd-class ramp about 90m to the right (east) of the Snaz *(Route 7)*. The descent is via the standard Snaz walk-off, except that from the top of this climb one must first scramble about 120m up and to the west to a point above the top of the Snaz. **Gear:** For protection take a standard rack to 4" with many small nuts.

ROUTE 4. SCHMITZ-KANZLER DIHEDRAL. IV, 5.10. Probable first ascent in June 1979, by Kim Schmitz and Jim Kanzler. This route goes up an extensive corner system to the left (west) of Fallen Angel *(Route 3)* and comes out on the left (west) side of a small tower. The first lead is up a rotten squeeze chimney. The route above comprises about nine pitches of corners, faces, and a chimney or two. Descent is via the standard Snaz walk-off. **Gear:** For protection take a standard rack and a good supply of camming devices.

ROUTE 5. SHATTERED. IV, 5.10. First ascent July 4, 1979, by Jim Beyer and Buck Tilley. The exact location of this route is not known; hence, it is not marked on photographs within this text. This difficult route, located somewhere between Fallen Angel *(Route 3)* and the Snaz *(Route 7)*, starts in a crack system about 10m to the right (east) of the Snaz. (An unfinished line, Judgment Day, also by Tilley and Beyer, lies slightly farther to the right.) This route unfortunately contains sufficient loose rock as to not be recommended by the first-ascent party. From the grass-covered ledge at the base of the second pitch of the Snaz, move 9m to the right onto a small buttress. The first lead (46m) involves face climbing straight up across small ledges to a belay on a sloping ledge. The next pitch starts up and left on a short ramp, then moves up the face above past a small black roof (5.9), and finishes by moving back right and up onto a sloping belay ledge that

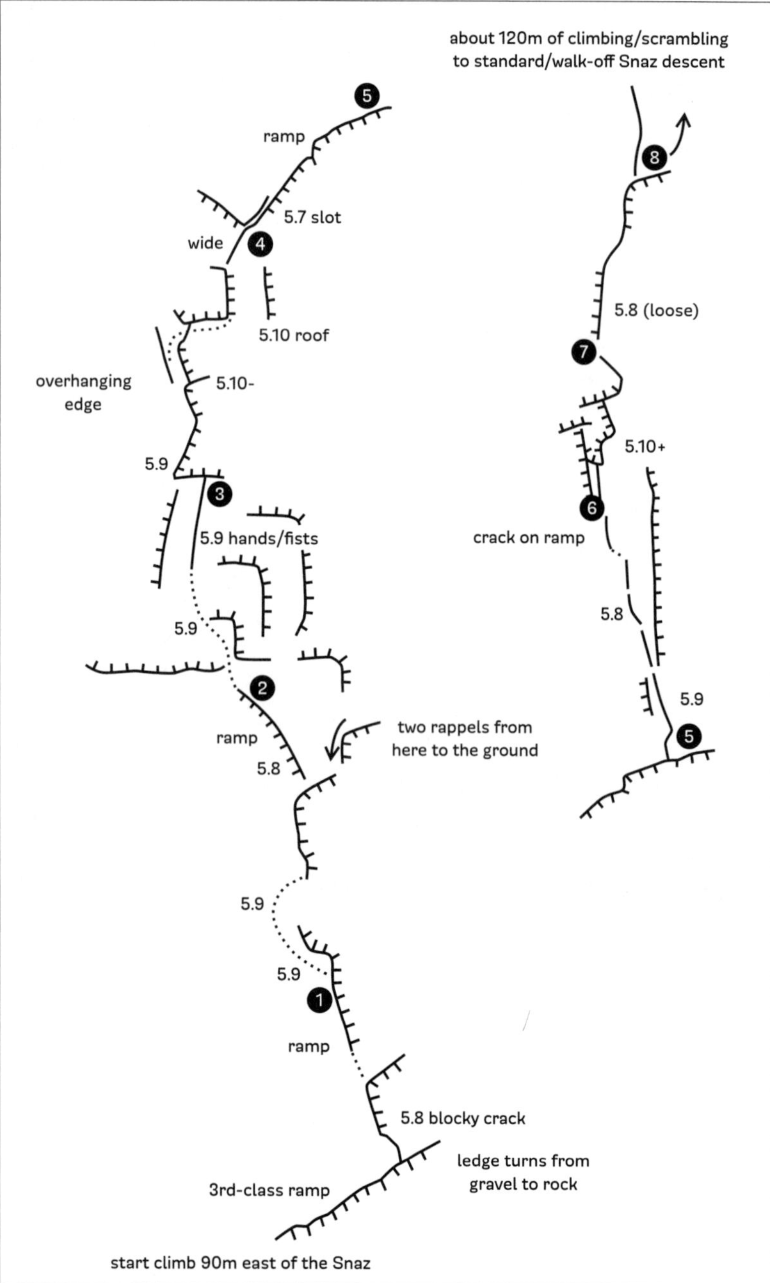

FIGURE 2-13. Albright Peak, Snaz Buttress, Fallen Angel *(Route 3)*, IV, 5.10+

diagonals up and left. Now climb up the left-diagonaling hand crack (5.10) and belay from above a small pedestal that lies at the beginning of a rotten chimney. The fourth lead moves up and left on the face to gain a face crack that leads up and slightly right past a block (5.10-) to the next belay ledge. Move right on this ledge and then climb a chimney, dihedrals, and a face for a long ropelength; from the base of this chimney a ramp will be seen leading diagonally left over to the Snaz. The sixth pitch goes up an inside corner and then up and right along a left-facing corner. The next lead goes up a shallow gully to a chimney and, after passing a chockstone, exits onto a belay at the beginning of another gully. The final pitch goes up and left in this gully to a point from which the standard Snaz walk-off descent can be made. The last four pitches contain very loose rock, hence the name of the route.

ROUTE 6. SUNSHINE DAYDREAM. IV, 5.11-. First ascent September 2, 1987, by Charlie Fowler and Alison Sheets; first winter ascent January 24, 2001, by Hans Johnstone and Stephen Koch. (See *Figure 2-14.*) This difficult route on the "golden face" to the right of the Snaz *(Route 7)* is a recommended climb. Climb the first three pitches of the Snaz. **Pitch 4:** From the bolted anchor belay at the top of third pitch of the Snaz, climb out and to the right (5.8) through intimidating terrain beneath a small overhang and around the corner to a 5.8 crack that leads up and left to a belay stance (2.5"–3.5" protection needed for the anchor). **Pitch 5:** From the belay climb up to a bolt (the original ¼" bolt has been replaced/upgraded) and then face climb (5.10-) past it for 3m to a horizontal band that is then traversed to the east to a steep, thin crack. Climb the crack until it ends (5.10+), and then go left to another crack that leads to a big ledge. (**Note:** An easier variation via 5.10- crack climbing leads up from an alternate belay located just a few meters to the east of the top of the fourth pitch.) **Pitch 6:** Easy climbing leads up and left to a belay under a thin finger crack. **Pitch 7:** Climb the finger crack (5.11-) and proceed up wide cracks to a belay that is just below a large, partially detached flake (the "coffin flake"). **Pitch 8:** Begin this long and varied pitch by following a crack system immediately left of the flake. At its top, exit left (5.10) to a small ledge. Proceed past a small overhang and an easier wide section above to the base of an offwidth. Climb the offwidth (5.8)—or the face to the right—to the belay. The final pitch reaches the same large ledge that the Snaz tops out on, and most parties rappel the Snaz for the descent (two ropes necessary). **Gear:** For protection take a regular rack with a set of stoppers, a double set of camming devices from finger to hand size, and at least one 4" piece.

FIGURE 2-14. Albright Peak, Snaz Buttress, Sunshine Daydream *(Route 6)*, IV, 5.11-

FIGURE 2-15. Albright Peak, Snaz Buttress. (A) The Snaz *(Route 7)*, IV, 5.9; (B) Variation: Snazette, IV, 5.10c; (C) Variation: Cousin Leroy, IV, 5.9; (D) Variation: Cousin Leroy's Uncle, IV, 5.10

ROUTE 7. THE SNAZ. IV, 5.9. First ascent August 4, 1964, by Yvon Chouinard and Mort Hempel. (See *Figures 2-15* and *2-16*.) In correspondence between Leigh Ortenburger and Chouinard, Chouinard revealed the origins of the route's intriguing name: "The Snaz is a name formed by taking S from Snazzy and *Naz* from Lord Buckley, the hipster who calls J. Christ The Nazz, meaning from Nazareth." Lord Richard Buckley (1906–60) was a stand-up comedian and recording artist who anticipated the Beat generation and influenced many contemporary figures. Buckley's recording of "The Nazz" (available on YouTube) is well worth listening to. A few months after establishing the Snaz, Chouinard was ensconced in his hammock on El Capitan's North America Wall with his partners Royal Robbins, Chuck Pratt, and Tom Frost. It was their seventh night on the Yosemite big wall and the group had reached the Cyclops Eye just ahead of deteriorating weather. Hempel serenaded the group from far below with an array of folk songs via two-way radio.

The Snaz is the corner system located in the heart of its namesake buttress, and this classic and popular Teton climb contains beautiful rock that can be well protected. In general, it follows the obvious dihedral that cuts up the center of the face but occasionally goes slightly right or left to avoid overhangs. The nine pitches of the Snaz are delineated in *Figures 2-15* and *2-16*. At the end of the ninth lead, the angle eases considerably and the character of the climb changes abruptly. These days most parties begin rappelling from the top of the ninth pitch, or even lower. The Snaz rappels (two ropes necessary) are used for descent from neighboring routes as well. (For the walk-off alternative, see the introduction to these climbs.) **Gear:** For protection take a standard rack with doubles in the hand-size to 4" range.

Variation: **SNAZETTE.** IV, 5.10c. It is likely that this pitch was first led by John Bragg in or around 1974. (See *Figure 2-15*.) This is the crack that is immediately left (west) of the standard fourth pitch (wide crack) of the Snaz route. From the bolted belay at the top of the third pitch, move down and left a few meters to work up the very steep start of the crux 5.10c crack. Once over the initial bulge, the difficulty eases and the crack widens gradually to enjoyable hands, going from 5.10a to 5.8 at the top. Either belay here or continue up to the right to the fourth pitch of the Snaz and the belay alcove.

Variation: **COUSIN LEROY.** IV, 5.9. First ascent August 31, 1987, by Dave Insley and Dan Barto. (See *Figures 2-15* and *2-16*.) This variation provides a three-pitch alternative ending to the Snaz. Climb the Snaz past the roof of the seventh pitch to the

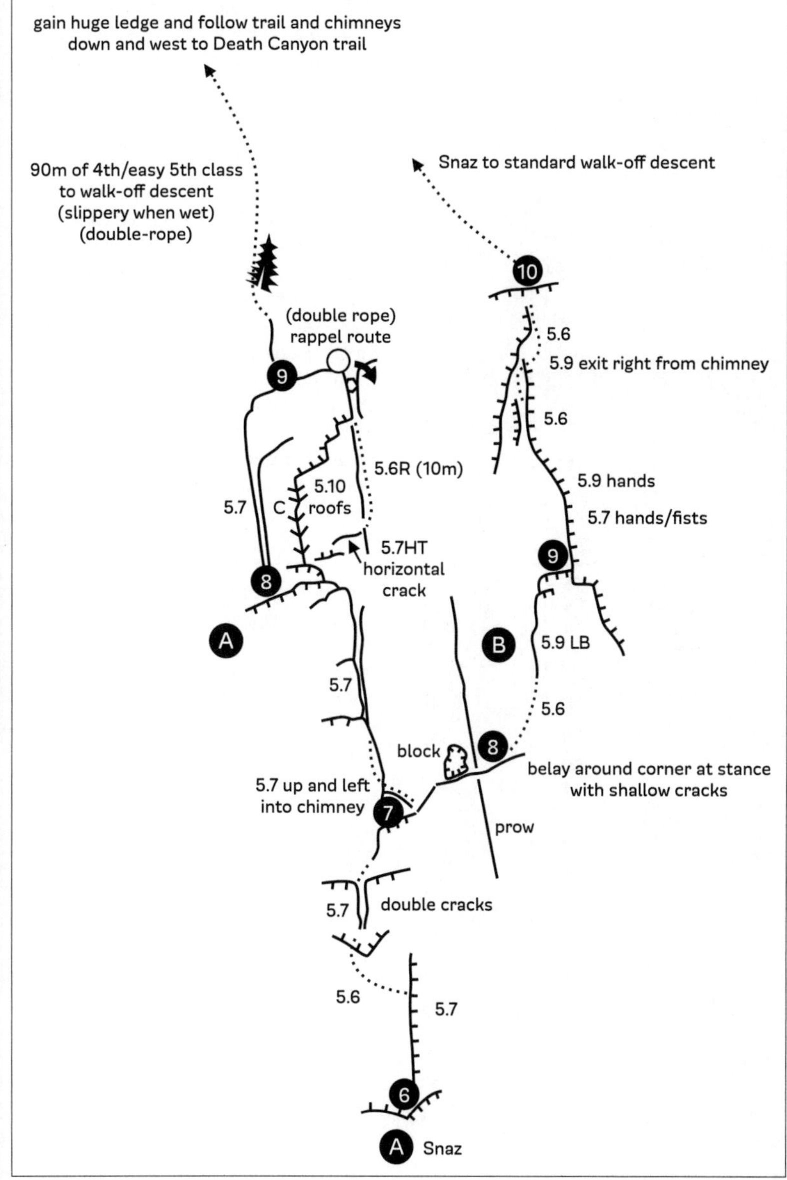

FIGURE 2-16. Albright Peak, Snaz Buttress. (A) The Snaz *(Route 7)*, IV, 5.9; (B) Variation: Cousin Leroy, IV, 5.9; (C) Variation: Cousin Leroy's Uncle, IV, 5.10

belay ledge. Instead of continuing upward for the eighth lead, move right on the ledge 23m, past a large block, and set up a belay just around a prow at a stance with shallow cracks. Face climbing (5.6) then leads up to a brown flake. A 5.9 lieback takes one to the top of the flake and a belay stance. From there, a hand/fist crack (5.7 to 5.9) leads to the base of a chimney. Climb the 5.6 chimney to its top (wide protection), where a 5.9 move out and right provides an escape to a 5.6 crack. This 43m final pitch leads to a tree at the top of the climb. The Snaz rappel route begins a short distance to the west (two ropes necessary). Alternatively, the walk-off descent can be reached via 90m of 4th- and easy 5th-class climbing. **Gear:** TCUs are very helpful for protection, as well as other devices to 4".

***Variation:* COUSIN LEROY'S UNCLE.** IV, 5.10. First ascent June 10, 1994, by Tom Kimbrough and Beverly Boynton. (See *Figures 2-15* and *2-16*.) This one-pitch variation provides an alternate finish for the Snaz. From the ledge at the base of the final pitch of the Snaz, climb a corner that leads up to a series of stepped roofs (5.10). The pitch finishes in a chimney that has a chockstone in it.

ROUTE 8. CAVEAT EMPTOR. IV, 5.10c. First complete ascent July 9, 1979, by Jim Beyer and Buck Tilley. (See *Figure 2-17*.) Caveat Emptor is an outstanding, highly recommended rock climb—one of the finest routes in Death Canyon. It involves five pitches at the 5.10- to 5.10+ level.

History: The section of the Snaz Buttress between the Snaz *(Route 7)* and Cottonmouth *(Route 11)* has an extensive history of attempts, partial climbs, and unfinished routes. On July 5, 1974, Jim Donini, John Bragg, and Steve Wunsch climbed the first four pitches of the current Caveat Emptor route but then joined the Snaz at the top of its third pitch. An unfinished line, Alpine Cow *(Route 9)*, which has the same start as the current Caveat but heads straight up to a left-curving arch instead of angling right, was first attempted on July 1, 1977, by Mike Munger and Ron Matous. On June 12, 1977, Matous and Keith Hadley climbed two additional pitches in the general vicinity of Caveat. In 1979 Jim Beyer and Buck Tilley added the current beginning (the first pitch of Alpine Cow) and ending pitches of Caveat, making the first ascent of the entire route and giving it the name High Tension Eliminate. The second ascent apparently was made on July 24, 1979, by Munger and George Montopoli, who provided a more direct variation on the first pitch, to separate the Cow from Caveat. The following year, on June 24, 1980, Rich Perch and Sandy Stewart made the third ascent of the complete route and applied the current name: Caveat Emptor, Latin for "let the buyer beware." A second attempt on Alpine Cow by Munger and Jim Donini on July 27, 1980, left that line still unfinished. Munger returned on August 17, 1980, with Gordon Brooks and Charlie Gunn to attempt yet another (unfinished) line between the Cow and Cottonmouth.

Route Description: Caveat Emptor and the Snaz share the same first pitch. From the large ledge at the top of this pitch scramble up and west to the base of a left-leaning chimney, where the difficult climbing begins. The third pitch starts up the chimney to a fixed pin, traverses right (5.10-), then continues straight up (5.9) to a right-facing corner; climb this corner and diagonal right to the belay at the base of a large pillar. The next excellent pitch ascends by means of finger locks, liebacks, and hand jams (5.9) to an overhang that is passed on the right (5.10-), then continues up the crack above to a comfortable belay ledge in dark rock (50m). *Figure 2-17* shows the two options for the next pitch: 5.10-, with thin protection, or awkward/wide 5.7; both end up at the same place after a short distance. The sixth pitch climbs an overhanging hand-and-fist crack (5.10c), followed by a left-leaning ramp or corner, then goes through a small overhang (5.10-) and up to a small belay ledge. A variation leads up and right from the top of the ramp up a right-facing feature to the same belay (5.10b/c). The seventh lead (the crux) begins with face climbing up and left to a fixed pin not more than 3m above the belay. Continue up on steep rock past a series of small holes (one of which used to hold a bashie for protection on this formidable pitch), move left, and then head back right to gain a small ledge (alternative belay). Proceed up and left via 5.8R face climbing to a good belay ledge at the base of a ramp. Protection on this pitch can be tricky, but it can be obtained—look around and be inventive. The final easier lead finishes past a large flake and up the left-leaning ramp to the first rappel station.

Two ropes are necessary for the Snaz fixed-anchor rappel route. If not rappelling, follow 4th- and easy 5th-class terrain for 90m to the standard Snaz walk-off descent. **Gear:** For protection take a standard rack of nuts, including small offset nuts, and camming devices with extra pieces in the 2"–3.5" range.

Variation: IV, 5.10. First ascent July 24, 1979, by Mike Munger and George Montopoli. This variation starts from the base of the cliff to the right (east) of the ramp of the regular start to the route. Climb directly upward on difficult and poorly protected rock to join the upper end of the normal first lead of Caveat Emptor.

ROUTE 9. ALPINE COW. IV, 5.11+ (unfinished). This difficult and as-yet-unfinished climb was accomplished primarily by Mike Munger during a series of attempts during the 1970s. It was pushed to its current high point by Sandy Stewart in 1987 with Eric Reynolds. (See *Figure 2-18*.) Approach as for the Snaz *(Route 7)* and Caveat Emptor *(Route 8)*, and begin with the initial pitch

FIGURE 2-17. Albright Peak, Snaz Buttress, Caveat Emptor *(Route 8)*, IV, 5.10c

A climber on the sixth pitch of the Snaz (Photo by Adam Fabrikant)

of those routes. After the first three pitches of Alpine Cow, one can traverse over to Caveat Emptor and finish via the upper pitches of that climb. This is a good alternative start. The fourth pitch has been climbed two different ways. Munger led the intimidating roof at the large chimney/offwidth to the left of the belay shown on the topo. Very awkward moves left under the roof and then steep liebacking lead to the belay for the fifth pitch (5.11+). Stewart climbed the overhang to the right: Start under a small, square hold over the lip. From that hold reach left and stand up (5.11). Two shallow KBs are clipped, then move left to a thin seam (5.9). After clipping another KB ascend the seam up to the double-bolt belay stance (5.11). The route has been pushed only 9m–12m farther out under a gray roof (5.10). The current high point ends in a rotten quartz wall.

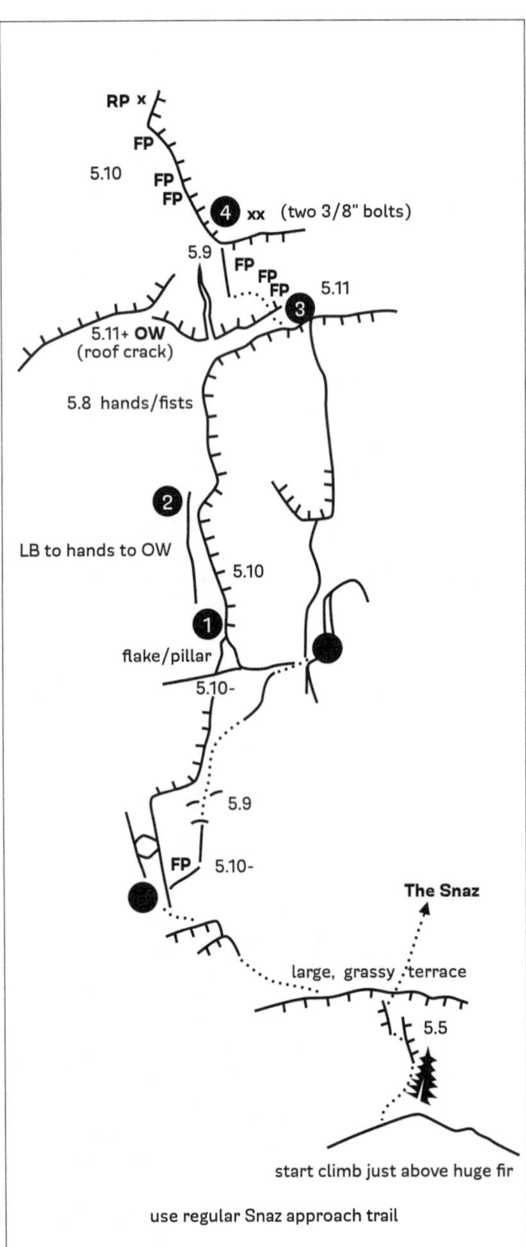

FIGURE 2-18. Albright Peak, Snaz Buttress, Alpine Cow *(Route 9)*, IV, 5.11+ (unfinished)

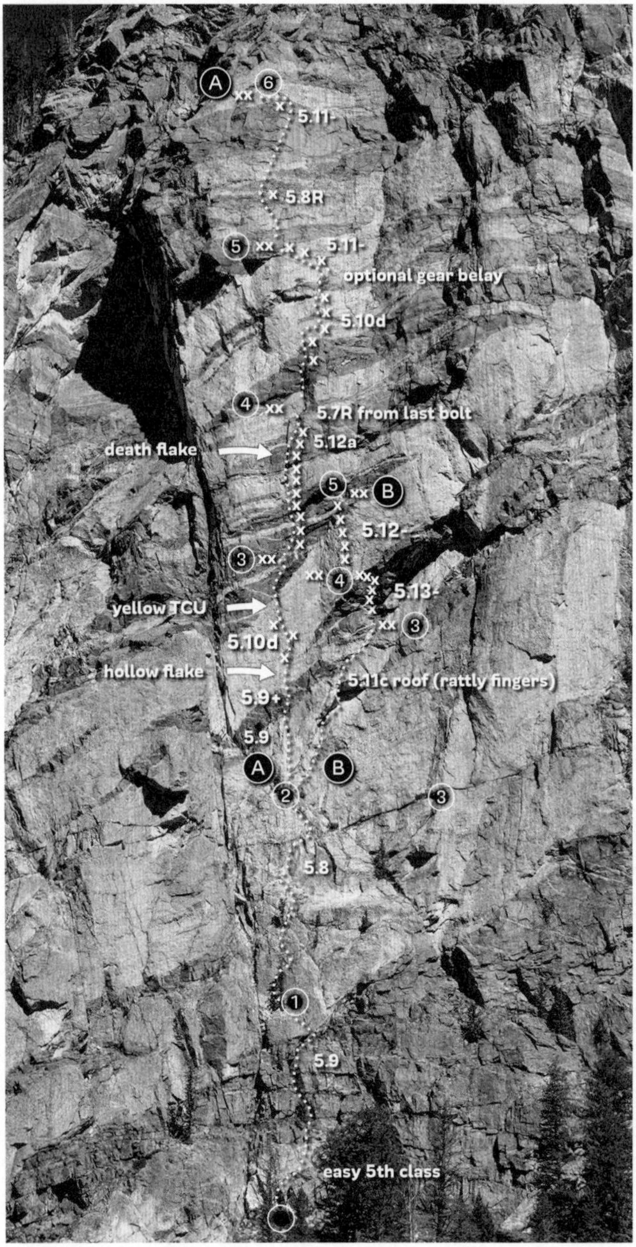

FIGURE 2-19. Albright Peak, Snaz Buttress. (A) The Fountainhead *(Route 12)*, IV, 5.12aR; (B) Freedom Fighter *(Route 10)*, IV, 5.13-

ROUTE 10. FREEDOM FIGHTER. IV, 5.13-. First ascent in May 2004, by Greg Collins, Sue Miller, and Brendan O'Neill; first free ascent by Greg Collins. Collins, who went so far as to create a mock-up of the crux in his local rock gym, managed the redpoint after six days of climbing on the route, at times solo. A testament to Collins's persistence and resilience, the name Freedom Fighter perhaps echoes with a bit of Rastafarian ethos. (See *Figure 2-19.*) This route was put up in good style—ground up and with all of the bolts hand-drilled on lead. It is another classic testpiece on this very proud section of the Snaz Buttress.

Begin by climbing the initial two pitches of the Fountainhead *(Route 12)*. The third pitch trends up and slightly east in a right-facing feature to a roof that is climbed via a rattly finger crack (5.11c) and onto the face above, where a crack leads east to a two-bolt belay. Pitch four is the crux: a 5.13- ceiling passing six protection bolts, leading to another two-bolt anchor on the face above. The fifth pitch continues up the white face, passing five protection bolts (5.12-) to the belay for the crux fifth pitch of Cottonmouth *(Route 11)*. This is the apex of Freedom Fighter, and descent can be made from here via rappel with a 70m rope. **Gear:** For protection bring 10 quickdraws, a set of stoppers, and a set of cams with extras in the "rattly finger" size (which apparently depends on the size of the climber's fingers!).

ROUTE 11. COTTONMOUTH. IV, 5.10+R. First ascent July 25, 1978, by Mike Munger and Buck Tilley. See *Figure 2-20* for the details of this seven-pitch route. It shares the same two start options as Vas Deferens *(Route 14)* and Lot's Slot *(Route 13)*. Before reaching the belay below the corner at the top of the second pitch of those climbs, trend right on easy terrain to a lower belay on a ledge with a tree. The climbing increases significantly in difficulty from here. This is a committing route, with marginal protection on the crux pitch. Use the standard Snaz walk-off descent. **Gear:** In addition to a standard rack, take many small nuts, offsets, and micro cams.

ROUTE 12. THE FOUNTAINHEAD. IV, 5.12aR. First ascent in September 2003, by Evan Howe, Doug Workman, Greg Collins, and Bob Goodwin. (See *Figure 2-19.*) Primarily the vision of Howe and Workman, this difficult route was put up in good style over a yearlong period—with nearly a dozen days spent on its installation and with bolts placed on lead, by hand, and ground up. A classic testpiece, it ascends what could be considered the proudest portion of the Snaz Buttress. The approach utilizes the usual climbers' trail to the Snaz, and descent is made via rappel from the top of the sixth pitch, now considered to be the apex of the climb.

The route begins immediately to the east of the Lot's Slot chimney system. After an easy 5th-class scramble up a ramp leading right (optional belay), the first pitch continues up to a large tree

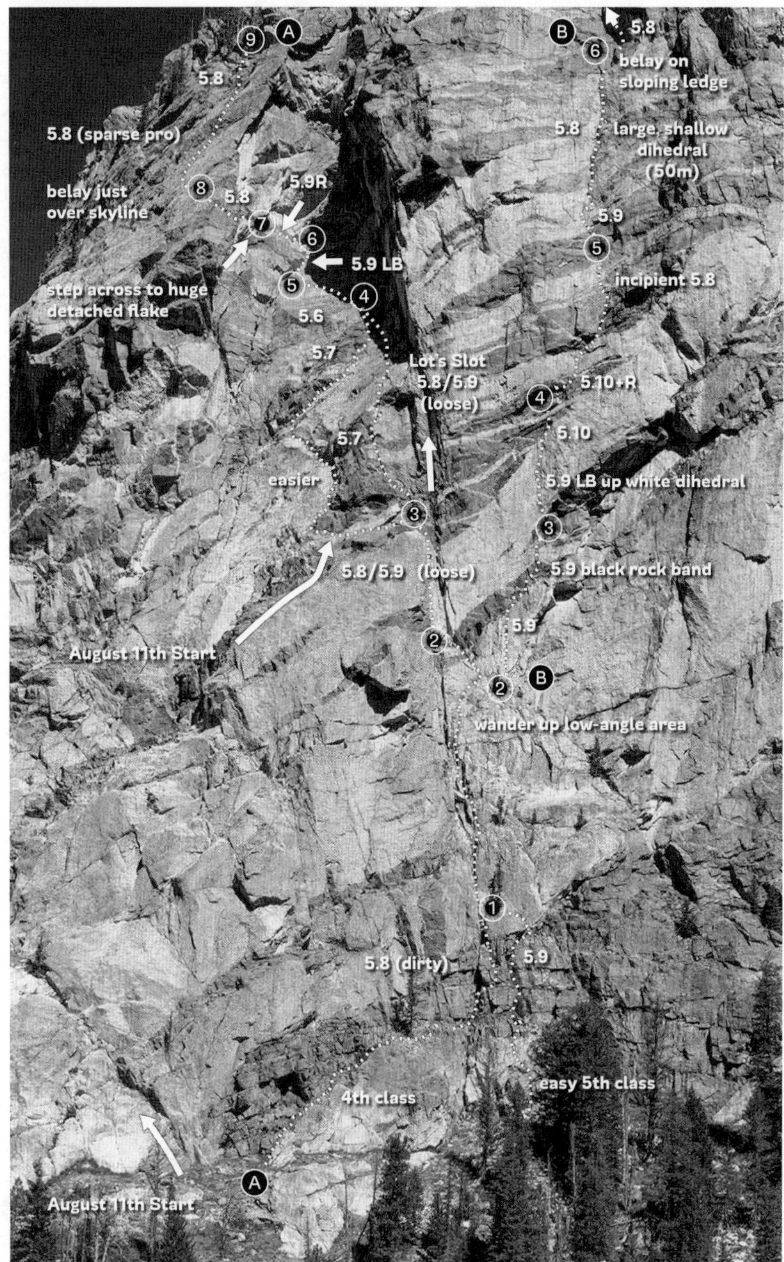

FIGURE 2-20. Albright Peak, Snaz Buttress. (A) Vas Deferens *(Route 14)*, IV, 5.9R; (B) Cottonmouth *(Route 11)*, IV, 5.10+R

through a small overhang and then to a crack (5.9). The second pitch continues up past a tree to a right-trending crack (5.8) and then to a section of face climbing that leads to a belay. Cottonmouth *(Route 11)* and Freedom Fighter *(Route 10)* both diverge to the east at this point. The third pitch begins in a 5.9 crack system and leads to the top of a pillar with some loose rock near the top. Then climb 5.9+ face moves to a hollow flake in the white rock just west of Cottonmouth's white dihedral. Beyond the flake, face climb past three bolts to a left-facing feature, at the top of which one can place a small cam (yellow TCU). Continue up to a ledge that slants up and right to a belay with two bolts. The fourth pitch is the crux and is equipped with 10 bolts (5.12a). Around the seventh or eighth bolt, look out for a "death flake." Climb out right past three more bolts to a runout section of 5.7 climbing and a two-bolt belay. The fifth pitch goes straight up from the belay in dark rock to a small roof that leads to 5.10d face climbing past five bolts. The pitch ends at an optional gear belay, or continue west past three bolts (5.11-) to a bolted anchor that is used for rappel. The last pitch goes up a right-facing feature (5.8R) and then finishes with a 5.11- section of stemming on excellent rock. Descent can be made by rappelling the route; this requires a 70m rope. **Gear:** The caveat from the first-ascent team is "lots of tricky gear." Their suggested rack list includes 10 draws; eight slings; one #6 RP; one set of HB offset brass nuts (especially #7–#10); two sets of #00–#3 TCUs; one set of cams 0.75"–3"; and one set of stoppers.

ROUTE 13. LOT'S SLOT. IV, 5.10. First ascent July 16, 1978, by Mike Munger and Buck Tilley. (See *Figures 2-20* and *2-21*.) This route was the first of the lines established on the buttress to the left of the Snaz *(Route 7)*. Located about 50m west of that route, Lot's Slot and Vas Deferens *(Route 14)* follow the same initial three pitches up a prominent chimney system, the Slot, with two options for the start (shown in *Figure 2-20*). The upper section of this chimney system is marked by a very large left-facing corner that forms the right (east) edge of a large amphitheater. The route continues for eight leads directly up the system, passing to the right of a set of overhanging arches. Climbers should be aware that the pitch out of the alcove is *very* serious, loose, and runout 5.9! Use the standard Snaz walk-off descent.

ROUTE 14. VAS DEFERENS. IV, 5.9R. First ascent July 18, 1978, by Jim Beyer and Buck Tilley. (See *Figures 2-20* and *2-21*.) This route and Lot's Slot *(Route 13)* are both identified in their upper section by a very large left-facing corner that forms the right (east) edge of a large amphitheater. Both start in the very broken rock of

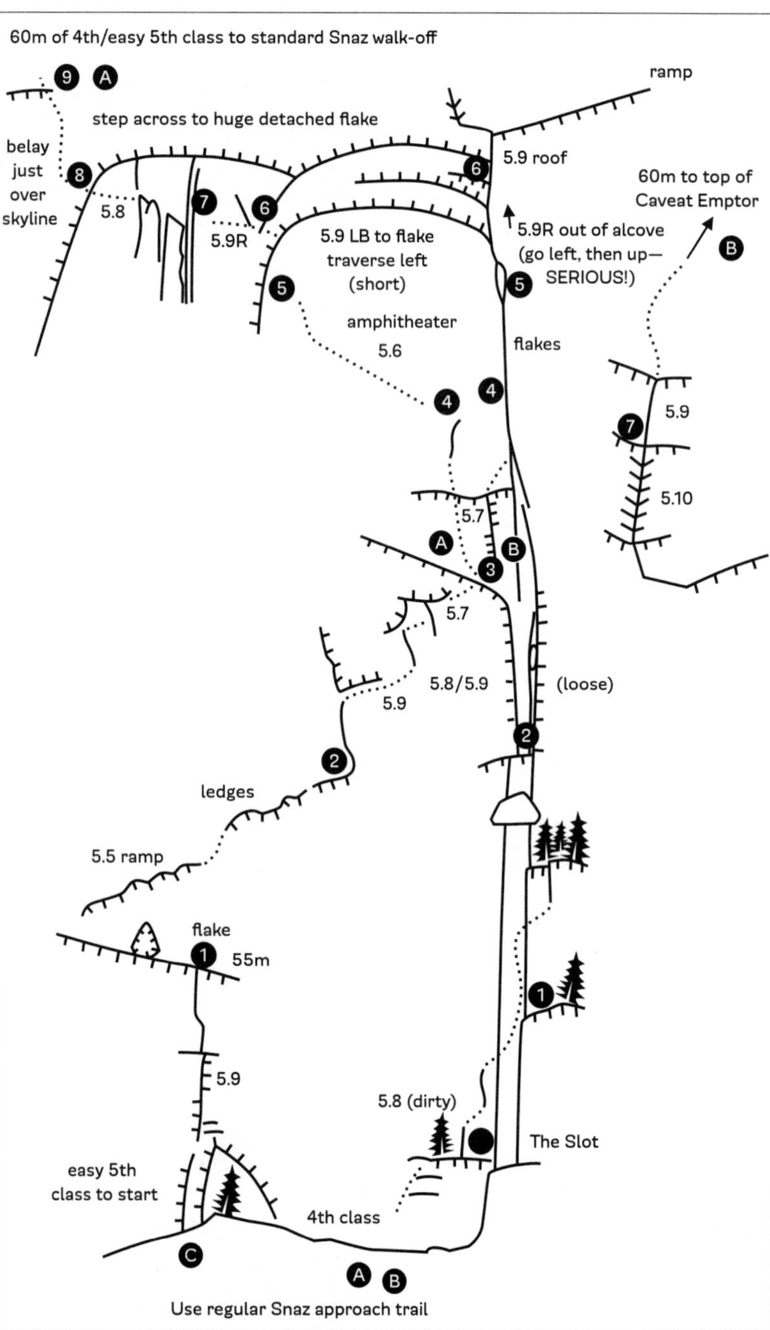

FIGURE 2-21. Albright Peak, Snaz Buttress. (A) Vas Deferens *(Route 14)*, IV, 5.9R; (B) Lot's Slot *(Route 13)*, IV, 5.10; (C) Vas Deferens, variation: August 11th Start, IV, 5.9

a prominent chimney system, the Slot. The approach is the same as for the Snaz *(Route 7)*, but Vas Deferens starts about 50m to the west. (**Note:** The initial portion of this route, as it was originally climbed, can be replaced by the August 11th Start variation, which consists of three pitches and is recommended; this starts 30m west [left] of the Slot.) **Pitch 1:** See *Figure 2-20* for two possible ways—dirty 5.8 to the left or 5.9 to the right—to gain the ledge with a tree (to the right of the Slot) that marks the top of this initial pitch. **Pitch 2:** Continue up the Slot before wandering up a low-angle area to a belay in the Slot beneath a left-facing corner. **Pitch 3:** Climb the corner (5.8/5.9, loose) and belay on a ledge at the top. **Pitch 4:** Three alternatives, shown in *Figure 2-20*, provide access to the slab beneath the main amphitheater. (1) The easiest of these traverses west along the top of the August 11th Start before heading up (5.7) toward the slab. (2) Another 5.7 line stays just left of the Slot. (3) It is also possible to continue directly up Lot's Slot, which involves more loose 5.8/5.9 climbing. **Pitch 5:** Move up and left across the slab below the huge overhanging arches (5.6). **Pitch 6:** Lieback (5.9) to a flake, then traverse left a short distance and belay. **Pitch 7:** A short, unprotected face pitch leads left again to a belay next to a huge detached flake (5.9R). **Pitch 8:** Step across to the flake and continue left to a belay just over the skyline (5.8). **Pitch 9:** Climb up through runout terrain to the top of the climb (5.8, 60m). Use the standard Snaz walk-off descent. **Gear:** A standard rack to 3.5" with additional small offsets and micro cams suffices for protection.

Variation: **AUGUST 11TH START.** IV, 5.9. First ascent August 11, 1978, by Buck Tilley and Bill Danford. (See *Figures 2-20* and *2-21*.) This worthwhile variation of three good pitches leads into Vas Deferens at the top of that route's third pitch. It starts about 30m to the left (west) of the Slot.

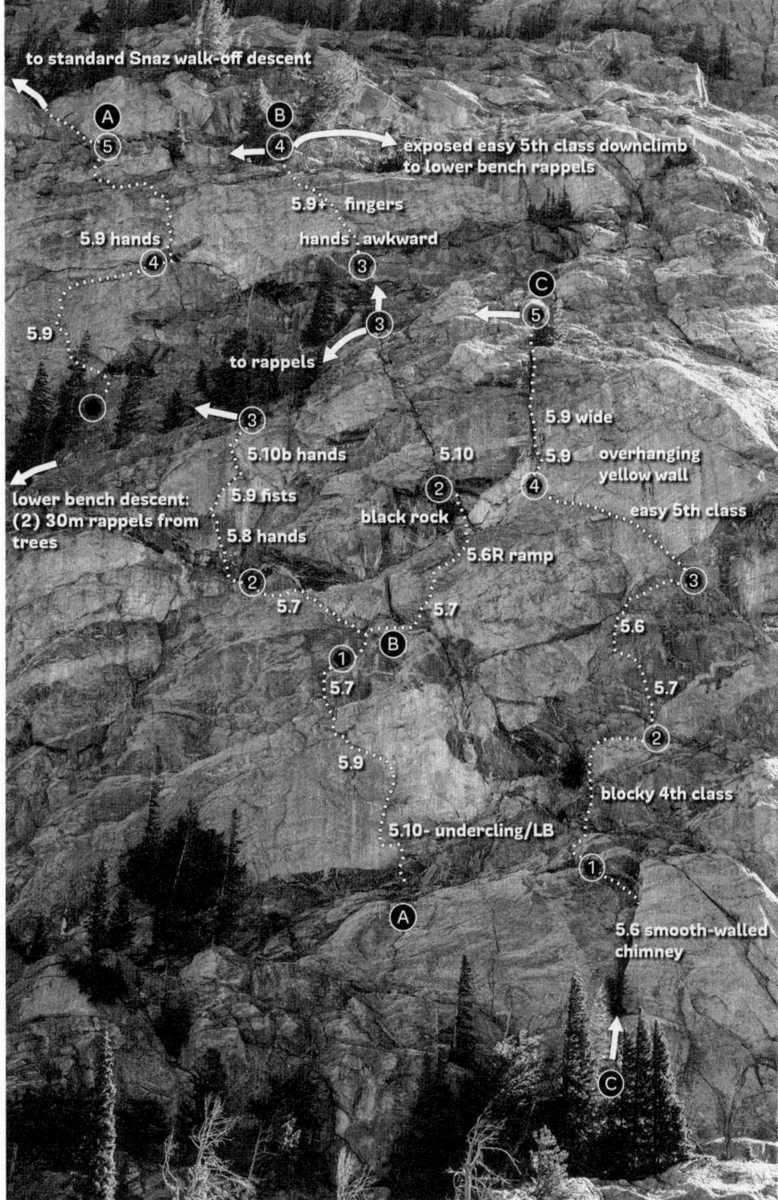

FIGURE 2-22. Albright Peak, Snaz Buttress, west end. (A) Aerial Boundaries *(Route 16)*, II, 5.10b; (B) Aerial Boundaries, variation: FNG, II, 5.10; (C) Escape from Death *(Route 15)*, II, 5.9

ROUTE 15. ESCAPE FROM DEATH. II, 5.9. First ascent July 5, 1967, by Rick Reese, Ted Wilson, and Mike Ermarth. (See *Figure 2-22*.) As viewed to the east a few hundred feet downcanyon from the Death Canyon patrol cabin, the southwest ridge of the Snaz Buttress can be seen in profile. This route, an enjoyable one-day climb on good rock with good protection, begins at the base of that ridge in a large, prominent chimney in light gray rock. For the approach, take the Death Canyon trail beyond the southwest ridge of the main buttress until the steep, polished chimney at the beginning of the climb is visible. The base of this chimney is located just below and to the east of the base of the first pitch of Aerial Boundaries *(Route 16)*. The first lead goes directly up this chimney to a belay ledge. From the top of the chimney, continue up through blocky 4th-class terrain to the base of a wall. The third pitch goes up and left on the wall above (5.7) to a ledge and then out and right on the ledge to the start of an easy ramp leading left (west). The fourth lead continues up and passes left under an overhanging wall to the belay at the base of a prominent wide crack. The final pitch goes up this difficult crack (5.9) onto the ledge above. Follow the second descent option for Aerial Boundaries: take the lower bench down and left (west), then do two 30m rappels from trees to reach the scree leading back to the trail.

ROUTE 16. AERIAL BOUNDARIES. II, 5.10b. First ascent in September 1985, by Greg Miles, Mike Fisher, Jeff Bjornsen, and Tom Vajda. (See *Figures 2-22* and *2-23*.) This is a recommended route characterized by difficult climbing right off the ground. For the approach take the Death Canyon trail to the level part of the upper canyon. Scramble up the talus slope and then up and east to the southwest corner of the Snaz Buttress. The flakes of the first pitch can be seen on the yellow wall above. The complexity of this fine route is best presented in the phototopo, *Figure 2-22*. While none of the five leads are easy, the first and third are the most difficult. *Figure 2-23* illustrates two alternatives for the descent: (1) From the top of the fifth pitch, scramble and walk about 120m up to the standard Snaz walk-off descent. (2) Traverse down and west along the large, tree-covered bench at the top of the third pitch (some scrambling toward the end) to where one can do two 30m rappels from trees to get to the Snaz descent gully. It is also possible to gain this lower bench from the top of the fifth pitch by carefully downclimbing (easy 5th class) to the south; once on the bench, cut back west to reach the rappels. **Gear:** For protection take a standard rack to 4".

Variation: **FNG.** II, 5.10. First ascent July 16, 1995, by Eric Gabriel and Bill Culbreath. These guys were lost but nevertheless found a good climb! See *Figure 2-22* for the details of this variation. At the top of the third pitch, one can either continue straight up a 5.9+ finger crack or traverse down and left (west) to finish with the two upper leads of Aerial Boundaries.

ROUTE 17. THE WIDOWMAKER. III, 5.8. First ascent August 18, 1969, by Kevin Donald and Jim Erickson. (See *Figure 2-24*.) This route starts in the prominent dihedral on the west face of the Snaz Buttress and follows it to the top. For the approach, take the Death Canyon trail to the point where the level part of the upper canyon is entered. Scramble up the talus slope of the Snaz walk-off descent route, which is immediately west of the Snaz Buttress, and continue up the gully to the point where the easy Snaz descent chimneys are visible. The route is in the prominent west-facing dihedral that starts above the top of the descent gully. The first two pitches go nearly straight up, first in a squeeze chimney and then in a right-facing corner (both 5.7), to end on a belay ledge. Move the belay about 15m up and left to a large block and the beginning of the next lead, which is a 5.7 lieback up a long right-facing corner to a sloping belay ledge. Now continue up over a white chockstone (5.8) in a right-facing corner. The fifth lead passes some large, loose blocks between right- and left-facing corners and ends with a small 5.8 crack. The route ends with a final easier lead up and slightly left. Some loose rock requiring caution will be found on these last pitches. To descend, scramble over to the standard Snaz walk-off descent.

FIGURE 2-23. Albright Peak, Snaz Buttress, standard Snaz walk-off descent and lower bench descent for Aerial Boundaries *(Route 16—shown)* and Escape from Death *(Route 15)*

ALBRIGHT PEAK (10,552)

(0.9 mi S of Static Peak)

Map: Grand Teton

This peak, along with its neighbor to the north, Static Peak, forms a high and elongated extension of the southeast ridge of Buck Mountain, adding to its apparent bulk. The upper 300m of the peak is easy from all directions, but on the south the Pleistocene glacial action formed Death Canyon, leaving the lower 600m carved into steep walls of predominantly good

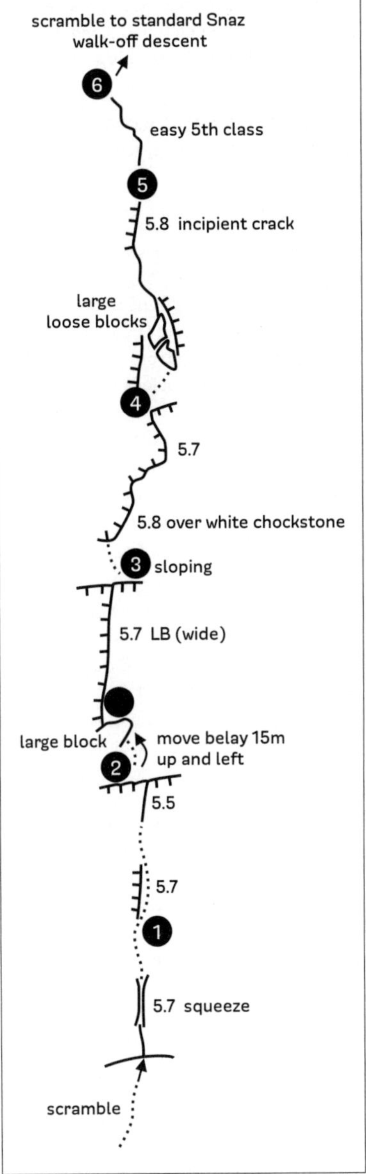

FIGURE 2-24. Albright Peak, Snaz Buttress, The Widowmaker *(Route 17)*, III, 5.8

crystalline rock, yielding the excellent routes that are described under *Death Canyon, North Side Rock Climbs*. The Alaska Basin Trail provides easy access to the summit of this peak, as does its eastern slope. The peak was officially recognized as Albright Peak in 1991 during planning for the 50th-anniversary celebration of the creation of the Jackson Hole National Monument by Franklin D. Roosevelt. This act of preservation culminated the work and dedication of such visionaries as Horace M. Albright and John D. Rockefeller Jr.

Chronology

NORTH RIDGE: [probable] June 1934, T. F. Murphy, Robert E. Brislawn
EAST SLOPE: July 6, 1960, William and Harriette Wallace
SOUTHWEST RIDGE: August 18, 1975, Leigh Ortenburger, John Whitesel

ROUTE 1. SOUTHWEST RIDGE. II, 5.6. First ascent August 18, 1975, by Leigh Ortenburger and John Whitesel. The summit pyramid of Albright Peak (10,552) extends in a modest ridge to the southwest for about 0.75 mile, where it ends as the top of the Snaz Buttress, before it drops precipitously, forming the north wall of Death Canyon. None of the rock climbs on the Snaz Buttress (see *Death Canyon, North Side Rock Climbs, Snaz Buttress*) were established to continue along the upper southwest ridge to the summit of Albright Peak. This route attains the upper ridge at its extreme southwest point (9,440+) from the east. Take the Death Canyon trail to the second stream crossing—the one from the large drainage, Sentinel Gully, that separates Sentinel Turret from the Omega Buttresses. Follow the East Ledges route on Sentinel Turret *(Sentinel Turret, Route 3)* to the notch separating the Turret from the ridge above. Pass the pinnacle in the notch (likely Harrington Spire) and climb one or two pitches up to the north out of the notch. The next portion of the route involves scrambling, with occasional roped climbing depending on the exact route chosen, to reach the extreme southwest point described above. From this point to the summit of Albright Peak there are no serious difficulties, although some scrambling requiring care is involved in passing a rocky portion of the ridge crest.
ROUTE 2. EAST SLOPE. I, 1.0. First ascent July 6, 1960, by William and Harriette Wallace. The open eastern slope of Albright Peak offers no difficulty to the experienced cross-country hiker. This slope is most directly approached via a bushwhack up from the Phelps Lake Overlook, the initial high point on the Death Canyon trail. It can also be reached from the drainage east of Albright Peak and south of Stewart Draw.
ROUTE 3. ▲ NORTH RIDGE. I, 1.0. Probable first ascent in June 1934, by T. F. Murphy and Robert E. Brislawn; first known ascent in June 1957, by Howard R. Stagner Jr., Tom Haggart, David Chaterfield, and Fred Fish. The obvious approach to this peak is via the Alaska Basin Trail in Death Canyon, which leads to the saddle between this peak and Static Peak. The short ridge above, leading south directly to the summit, is not difficult.

STATIC PEAK (11,303)
Map: Grand Teton

This high but minor summit is frequently and easily climbed from the Static Peak divide (10,790) and is an excellent objective for hikers of the Alaska Basin Trail. A small icefield lies at the base of the steep and crumbly north face of this peak, immediately south of Timberline Lake. A triangulation station was established on the summit of Static Peak in 1946 by Curtis LeFever of the US Coast and Geodetic Survey.

Chronology

SOUTHWEST RIDGE: [probable] June 1934, T. F. Murphy, Robert E. Brislawn
NORTH RIDGE: August 10, 1953, Paul Burgess, Alan Williamson (descent)
EAST RIDGE: June 6, 1961, Michael Petrilak, Scott Arighi, Joan Oosterwyk, Irma Ireland, D. Jan Black
NORTH FACE: June 19, 1971, Jeb Schenck, Bob Stevenson

ROUTE 1. ▲ SOUTHWEST RIDGE. I, 1.0. Probable first ascent in June 1934, by T. F. Murphy and Robert E. Brislawn. Almost all the ascents of this peak have been made from the Alaska Basin Trail, which mounts the southwest ridge of Static Peak to within 150m of the summit. **Time:** 40 minutes from the Alaska Basin Trail; 6½ hours from the Death Canyon trailhead.
ROUTE 2. EAST RIDGE. I, 1.0. First recorded ascent June 6, 1961, by Michael Petrilak, Scott Arighi, Joan Oosterwyk, Irma Ireland, and D. Jan Black. Approach from upper Stewart Draw. There is some loose rock on this ridge, but no difficulties.
ROUTE 3. NORTH FACE. II, 5.4. First ascent June 19, 1971, by Jeb Schenck and Bob Stevenson. Approach via Stewart Draw and Timberline Lake and take the steep snow leading to the base of the north face. This face is generally loose and rotten except for the dihedral used for this ascent. The route goes up this dihedral, where the rock is reasonably sound for a meter or so on either side.

ROUTE 4. NORTH RIDGE. II, 5.1. First descent August 10, 1953, by Paul Burgess and Alan Williamson. No information is available, but the rock on this ridge is likely to be unsound.

PEAK 10,696

(0.8 mi E of Buck Mountain)
Map: Grand Teton

This rounded forepeak of Buck Mountain provides the northern counterpart to Static Peak on the south. Although Buck Mountain is the primary objective of climbers in this part of the range, Peak 10,696 is now frequented by skiers in winter. This peak and its northeast extension over Point 9,975 have the same effect as Static and Albright Peaks in making Buck Mountain appear from the valley to be more massive than it really is. When one looks up at this area from the valley floor, a very large avalanche path will be seen immediately south of Point 9,975. Flanking the slide path on the south is a triangular face just in front of Peak 10,696. The name 25-Short (referring to the number of feet that Point 9,975 is shy of 10,000) has been applied to the slopes north and east of Point 9,975. Its neighbor to the south, the large triangular face already mentioned, is widely known as Maverick Ridge. The skiing potential of 25-Short was first noticed by residents of Beaver Creek in the early 1950s and then later again by Barry Corbet in the early 1960s. Accessed today from either the Taggart Lake trailhead or the vicinity of the old White Grass Ranch, these two areas are the most popular winter destinations in the range for skiers and riders.

ROUTE 1. WEST RIDGE. I, 4.0. Probable first ascent in June 1934, by T. F. Murphy and Robert E. Brislawn; first recorded ascent June 6, 1961, by David Grant, Lucille Grant, Tom Wepfer, David Murray, and Paul Weinstein, who found an empty cairn on the summit. From Timberline Lake (see *Buck Mountain, Route 8*) proceed to the saddle separating this peak from Buck Mountain. The first portion of the ridge is steep and contains some loose rock; this can be climbed directly or bypassed on the north. Bypass the small gendarmes above and to the right (south); then climb the summit block via a short 4.0 pitch.

ROUTE 2. EAST RIDGE. I, 1.0. First ascent July 10, 1966, by Thomas Gagnon, Douglas Curr, Gene Eckman, and Robert Andrews. Approach can be made directly from the east up from the Valley Trail or from the vicinity of Taggart Lake, using game trails to timberline, and then along the northeast ridge over Point 9,975 to the summit.

Stewart Draw

On the massive eastern expanse of Buck Mountain is Stewart Draw, which is more of a large stream drainage than a genuine canyon. It is given separate treatment here because it is an important access route, primarily to Buck Mountain, and its description requires some details. In the upper draw the trail is obvious, but the entire region around the base of Buck Mountain is confounded by obscure remnants of old horse trails dating from the days of the White Grass Ranch.

Start from the Death Canyon trailhead, following the Valley Trail west toward the Phelps Lake Overlook for about 0.5 mile until, just before the third footbridge on the trail, a small subsidiary trail leads off to the north. Take this old trail into a large meadow, but do not continue all the way around the western edge of the meadow because the trail is easily lost. Instead, hike into the meadow for 100 yards along the trail and then angle across the meadow, aiming for the western edge of trees that extend into the meadow from the east; erratic boulders will be found here. Now follow due north along the edge of these trees, passing small fragments of old trails, and cross two small creeks, the second of which is marked by a large cairn on its south side. Continue north along the edge of the trees until two horse trails that join are encountered. Take this trail, now well defined, over a small ridge and into Stewart Draw, crossing the drainage stream near a huge boulder. At this point a buttress featuring several rock climbs rises above on the south side of the draw (see *Stewart Draw, South Side Rock Climbs*, below). Continue up into the canyon on the substantial trail, past the old horse camp, staying mostly on the right (north) side of the creek, to the large cirque below Timberline Lake. One way to reach the lake is to take the large couloir that leads southwest from this cirque up the south flank of Static Peak and then traverse back to the right (north) onto the moraine that borders the lake on the east. If a two-day trip is desired, a camping spot can be found along the lakeshore or in the cirque below.

STEWART DRAW, SOUTH SIDE ROCK CLIMBS (ca. 9,000)

Map: Grand Teton

The standard approach for the regular route on Buck Mountain is from the Death Canyon trailhead up through Stewart Draw, the small, steep canyon on the east slope (see *Stewart Draw*, above). A rock buttress rising from the south side of this canyon provides a relatively attractive area for rock climbing, because the approach is conveniently short. The routes are listed from west to east; see *Figure 2-25* for an overview.

ROUTE 1. PEACHES. II, 5.8. First ascent June 28, 1980, by Yvon Chouinard and Kathryn Collins. Approach via the trail into Stewart Draw (see *Buck Mountain*). About halfway up this small canyon, a prominent wall will be seen on the south side of the drainage, where this climb is located. This route starts just left of an overhang at the base of the buttress. The technical details of this route are presented in *Figure 2-26*. In some places on this route the rock is loose and protection is at times scarce. Descent is easily made to the northwest to the base of the climb.

***Variation:* CASH FOR LESS.** II, 5.10. First ascent in July 1987, by Paul Gagner and Jim Woodmencey. (See *Figure 2-26*.) This difficult one-pitch variation, on the golden rock face to the left of Peaches, features two bolts for protection in addition to two fixed pitons.

ROUTE 2. SPIGOLO NERO. II, 5.7. First ascent in July 1980, by Yvon Chouinard and Kathryn Collins. This route is to the left (east) of the more popular Peaches *(Route 1)*. The first lead passes an overhang (5.7) on the left. Two more pitches lead to the final section, consisting of cracks.

ROUTE 3. LARSON RIDGE. II, 5.8. First ascent July 18, 1980, by Leo Larson and Randy Harrington. (See *Figure 2-25*.) The approach and descent for this route are the same as for Peaches *(Route 1)*. This five-pitch route follows the left (east) ridge of the steep wall of the Peaches buttress and contains similar interesting climbing, although there is some loose rock and lichen. The climbing begins immediately to the right of the left (east) ridge at the base of the buttress, on gray rock to the left of a group of large boulders. Parallel the ridge up past a 5.8 overhang, then trend right on a fractured wall, past a large roof, until one can turn upward in an overhanging lieback (5.8) to gain the ridge to the left. The second lead (46m) proceeds up the ridge on slabs, past a 5.8 overhang and a second smaller overhang to reach the belay. Two pitches of easier climbing on the ridge crest lead to the final short 5.7 pitch on poor rock on the summit pinnacle.

BUCK MOUNTAIN (11,938)

Map: Grand Teton

The first ascent of this major peak was made by the topographer T. M. Bannon and his recorder, George A. Buck, 10 days after the Owen-Spalding party climbed the Grand Teton in 1898. On the main (east) summit they built a large cairn for use as a triangulation point, known as "Buck Station," doubtlessly named after Bannon's recorder. A weathered US Geological Survey (USGS) marker can be found on the summit to this day, although the letters are hard to read. (The mountain also has a west summit, slightly shorter at about 11,800 feet, as well as a subpeak, known as the West Peak, with an elevation of 11,600+ feet.) "Alpenglow" was once suggested for the name of the peak, after the appearance of its north face in the evening from the vicinity of Jenny Lake; but "Buck" retains the official sanction of the US Board on Geographic Names. The southernmost of

FIGURE 2-25. Stewart Draw. (A) Larson Ridge *(Route 3)*, II, 5.8; (B) Peaches, variation: Cash for Less, II, 5.10; (C) Peaches *(Route 1)*, II, 5.8

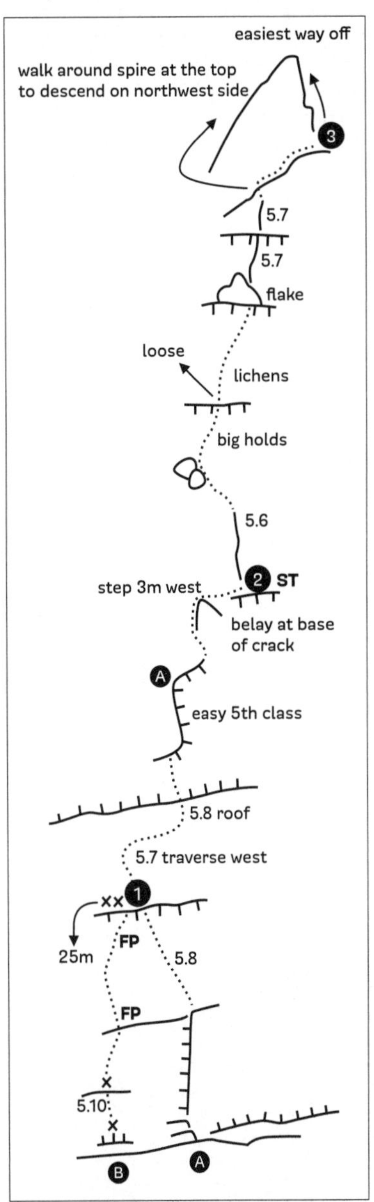

FIGURE 2-26. Stewart Draw. (A) Peaches *(Route 1)*, II, 5.8; (B) Peaches, variation: Cash for Less, II, 5.10

the crystalline peaks, Buck Mountain is also the highest peak south of the Garnet Canyon group, and therefore its summit offers an excellent and unusual view of the rest of the range. It is a fine objective for the mountaineer. In the early part of the 20th century, Buck Mountain may have been climbed by local ranchers, but no records were left. From the east, which is the usual route, the ascent is not hard, but from any other direction varying degrees of difficulty will be met. Several fine climbs have been worked out on the north side, while much of the south side remains unexplored. The high basin just below the south cliffs of Buck Mountain is traversed by the Alaska Basin Trail and has come to be known as No-Wood Basin.

For the approach to the eastern routes on the peak, see *Stewart Draw*, above. The approach for the southern routes, which also starts from the Death Canyon trailhead, takes the Death Canyon trail and Alaska Basin Trail to No-Wood Basin. For the north face routes, approach via the south fork of Avalanche Canyon.

Chronology

EAST FACE: August 21, 1898, T. M. Bannon, George A. Buck
EAST RIDGE: August 15, 1931, Fritiof Fryxell
var—**EAST FACE APPROACH:** August 23, 1934, Ernest Scheeff, Heinz Recker
var—August 17, 1949, Edmond Lowe, William Primak, Reinhold Mankau
var—**SOWLES:** August 12, 1962, David Sowles, Robert Brooke, Sherman Lehman
SOUTH COULOIR: September 17, 1934, Floyd Wilson, Felix Bloch
var—August 17, 1956, John Fonda, Marilyn Domer, Frank Pitman

Topographer T. M. Bannon and his recorder, George A. Buck, established "Buck Station" on the summit of Buck Mountain on August 21, 1898. This weathered USGS mark was chiseled at that time. (Photo courtesy of Todd Cedarholm)

SOUTHEAST RIDGE: October 6, 1935, Phil Smith, Malcolm Smith
var—August 1, 1953, Rainer, Beth, Peter, and David Schickele
var—August 3, 1962, Donald Monk, Les Wilson, George Wallerstein, John Post
var—September 15, 1963, Chuck Satterfield, Bruce Morley
NORTHEAST COULOIR: July 2, 1937, Donald Grant, Robert Grant
NORTH FACE, WEST COULOIR: July 16, 1940, Paul Petzoldt, Elizabeth Cowles (Partridge) (ascent); June 14, 1946, Dick Pownall, Albert Boursault (descent)
SOUTHEAST COULOIR: August 29, 1940, John and Elizabeth Buck
NORTH FACE, EAST COULOIR: July 17, 1941, Fred Ayres, Allan Cameron, Judy Cameron
WEST RIDGE: August 27, 1935, Phil Smith, Herman Petzoldt, Walcott Watson (attempt); August 11, 1953, Leigh Ortenburger, Steve Jervis, Mary Sylvander (descent); July 16, 1957, John Dietschy, David Dingman, James Langford, Karl Pfiffner (ascent)
NORTH-NORTHWEST RIDGE: July 23, 1954, Richard Emerson, Don Decker, William Clayton
var—**THE WEDGE:** August 2, 1961, Herb Swedlund, David Dornan, Peter Lev
var—**THE FREE WEDGE:** August 14, 1993 (unfinished), Greg Miles, Mark Limage
NORTH CENTRAL RIDGE: August 23, 1959, Barry Corbet, Rick Medrick, Sterling Neale
WEST SUMMIT, SOUTH FACE: July 28, 1964, Rick Medrick, Dean Moore
SOUTHWEST COULOIR: July 26, 1980, Randy Harrington
WEST SUMMIT, SOUTH RIDGE: June 28, 1981, Yvon Chouinard, Juris Krisjansons
NORTH FACE, THE BUCK SANCTION: August 6, 1992, Tom Turiano, Stephen Koch

ROUTE 1. WEST RIDGE. II, 5.7. First descent August 11, 1953, by Leigh Ortenburger, Steve Jervis, and Mary Sylvander; first ascent July 16, 1957, by John Dietschy, David Dingman, James Langford, and Karl Pfiffner; attempted on August 27, 1935, by Phil Smith, Herman Petzoldt, and Walcott Watson. This is the ridge that forms the southwest boundary of the south fork of Avalanche Canyon. The best approach is probably via the Alaska Basin Trail, although the ridge can be reached more directly via the south fork of Avalanche Canyon. In addition to its west summit, Buck Mountain has another lower subsidiary West Peak. The beginning of this ridge involves little more than uphill walking, but one rotten overhanging corner pitch is required to reach the easy scramble to the top of the West Peak. Between the West Peak and the west summit is a large gendarme with a smooth south face. Two pitches up a steep shelf on the west face of this obstacle lead to a third rather difficult pitch up and right (south) around the top of the gendarme. From the notch behind this tower, moderate climbing brings one to the west summit. The only remaining difficulty now is a short, overhanging pitch (5.7) just past the notch between the west summit and the main (east) summit. The rotten rock encountered makes this route somewhat hazardous. **Time:** 6½ hours from the Alaska Basin Trail. See *American Alpine Journal* 9, no. 29 (1955): pp. 147–49; 11, no. 32 (1958): pp. 83–88.

ROUTE 2. SOUTHWEST COULOIR. II, 5.7. First ascent July 26, 1980, by Randy Harrington. (See *Figure 2-27*.) From the extensive talus slope lying at the base of the West Peak, this southwest couloir slants up to the right toward the col that separates the West Peak of Buck Mountain from the upper west ridge. Scramble up this couloir until directly beneath the gendarme on the west ridge (see *Route 1*), where a secondary open couloir is taken easily to the right (east). Ascend this couloir until its right fork steepens, then turn directly up, or slightly left (west), to the ridge just behind (east of) the gendarme. From this point join the upper West Ridge route, staying slightly on the north side of the ridge, and follow it to the summit. The most difficult pitch on this route is the short, overhanging lead at the notch between the west summit and the main summit.

ROUTE 3. WEST SUMMIT, SOUTH FACE. II, 5.8. First ascent July 28, 1964, by Rick Medrick and Dean Moore. (See *Figure 2-27*.) This face, or buttress, which is approached from Death Canyon via the Alaska Basin Trail, leads to the west summit of Buck Mountain. The beginning of the climb, amid loose rock, is in the gully in the lower right edge of the face. Climb about 37m up a diagonal ledge to the left until the ledge ends at the beginning of a sloping chimney. After ascending this easy chimney for 4.5m, the second lead passes the steep wall above via a 4.5m overhanging jam crack (5.8); this crack seems to be the only break in the wall. Above this crack, traverse to the left until it is possible to climb around and over a number of blocks to a ledge that leads back to the right to the belay point. The third lead ascends easy overhangs on the right, reaching, via 4.0 rock, a good belay at the start of the upper half of the face. From this position, the face appears formidable. The next pitch is well protected and easier than it appears. First traverse left for 12m, then around some blocks for 9m, and finish by climbing up and to the right past blocks

FIGURE 2-27. Buck Mountain, south aspect. (A) West Peak, South Couloir, II, 3.0; (B) Southwest Couloir *(Route 2)*, II, 5.7; (C) West Summit, South Face *(Route 3)*, II, 5.8; (D) West Summit, South Ridge *(Route 4)*, II, 5.8; (E) South Couloir *(Route 5)*, II, 5.7; (F) Southeast Ridge, variation: 1962, II, 5.4; (G) Southeast Ridge *(Route 6)*, II, 4.0; (H) Southeast Ridge, variation: 1963, II, 5.7

and flakes to a good ledge. The fifth lead traverses up and around a corner to the right before continuing for 30m to a good belay below an overhang. The last pitch goes over this overhang onto a ledge and then proceeds to the right to the bottom of a corner. This corner is readily climbed via small holds on the left face and the crack in the corner. This section can be well protected, and one exits easily to the right over the overhang at the top of the crack. Scrambling then leads to the west summit; the main summit can be reached as in *Route 1*. This climb is an interesting problem in routefinding, and care should be taken with the considerable quantity of loose rock on the ledges. The first-ascent party felt that the route was comparable to Symmetry Spire's Southwest Ridge *(Symmetry Spire, Route 4)*.

ROUTE 4. WEST SUMMIT, SOUTH RIDGE. II, 5.8. First ascent June 28, 1981, by Yvon Chouinard and Juris Krisjansons. (See *Figure 2-27*.) This route lies to the right (south) of *Route 3* but still avoids the initial section of this well-defined ridge. Climb the right-hand portion of the south (or southwest) face of the west summit to gain the crest of the south ridge at the lowest convenient point. The ridge is then followed all the way to the west summit, from which one takes the upper West Ridge route *(Route 1)* to the main summit of the mountain.

ROUTE 5. SOUTH COULOIR. II, 5.7. First ascent September 17, 1934, by Floyd Wilson and Felix Bloch. (See *Figure 2-27*.) The south couloir runs diagonally up the south face to the notch that separates the sharp west summit from the higher main (east) summit. From the Alaska Basin Trail south of Buck Mountain, climb the shallow couloir. Pass to the right (east) of a short cliff near the bottom of the couloir to reach the notch in the summit ridge (the same notch is reached from the north by *Route 13*). The west summit can now be reached very easily; but to attain the main summit on the right (east), one must surmount a short, overhanging pitch (5.7) on the ridge crest. The 1934 party found a cairn of unknown origin on the west summit. **Time:** 8½ hours from the Death Canyon trailhead.

Variation: II, 5.4. First ascent August 17, 1956, by John Fonda, Marilyn Domer, and Frank Pitman. This party apparently avoided the 5.7 pitch out of the notch on the ridge crest by turning straight up the wall shortly before reaching the notch at the upper end of the couloir. This took them directly to the summit.

ROUTE 6. SOUTHEAST RIDGE. II, 4.0. First ascent October 6, 1935, by Phil Smith and Malcolm Smith. (See *Figures 2-27* and *2-28*.) The southeast ridge of Buck Mountain rises from the saddle connecting Static Peak with Buck Mountain. Although the original climb was done in 1935, the standard route on this pleasant ridge is the 1963 variation. The lower portion of the southeast ridge of Buck Mountain contains a large, distinct tower, separated from the upper portion of the ridge by a small notch. There are couloirs on both sides, north and south, leading to this notch. The original Southeast Ridge route easily ascends the couloir on the north side from the vicinity of Timberline Lake, usually approached via Stewart Draw. One could also approach over the Buck-Static saddle from the Alaska Basin Trail and No-Wood Basin on the south. After reaching the notch, the only difficulty on the upper ridge is a row of overhangs about two-thirds of the way up the ridge. Pass these on the left (south and west), and then scramble to the main summit. The 1935 party may well have used, in part, the ridge to the left (south) of the main southeast ridge; this ridge begins below the notch and blends into the main ridge about 90m above the notch.

Variation: II, 5.1. First ascent August 1, 1953, by Rainer, Beth, Peter, and David Schickele. The southeast ridge can also be reached by the easy couloir on the south side of the ridge. This couloir leads to the notch behind the initial tower on the ridge. The ridge can probably be reached at several places near or above this notch. The approach for this variation is from the Alaska Basin Trail in Death Canyon.

Variation: II, 5.4. First ascent August 3, 1962, by Donald Monk, Les Wilson, George Wallerstein, and John Post. (See *Figure 2-27*.) The couloir leading from the south to the notch on the southeast ridge is bounded on the left (west) by a ridge subsidiary to the main southeast ridge. This variation ascends the subsidiary ridge, or face, staying well left of the couloir. After meeting the main southeast ridge about 90m above the notch, the climbing becomes easier.

Variation: II, 5.7. First ascent September 15, 1963, by Chuck Satterfield and Bruce Morley. (See *Figures 2-27* and *2-28*.) From Timberline Lake, scramble up to the saddle between Static Peak and Buck Mountain, where this ridge route begins; in early season an ice axe will be needed to reach this saddle. The Alaska Basin Trail from the Static Peak divide can also be used for the approach to this ridge. The first section forms a large tower with a distinct, separate summit. The initial portion of this variation uses the south ridge of this tower, the first arête left (south) of the Buck-Static saddle. The first two pitches are not difficult—5.6, with some loose rock. The crux third pitch (5.7) continues up a slightly overhanging corner from a sloping belay ledge and leads to the summit of the tower. Descend about 9m to the east and contour around to reach the notch where the upper ridge begins. This upper section is not difficult, bypassing some overhangs on the left (south and west) before the final scramble to the summit. This is a pleasant but short climb with some loose rock, offering an alternative to the standard East Face *(Route 8)* or East Ridge *(Route 9)*.

ROUTE 7. SOUTHEAST COULOIR. II, 5.1. First ascent August 29, 1940, by John and Elizabeth Buck. (See *Figure 2-28*.) West-southwest of Timberline Lake is the saddle separating Static Peak from Buck Mountain. Rising from this saddle is the southeast ridge of Buck Mountain, which includes a large, distinct tower. This

FIGURE 2-28. Buck Mountain, east aspect. (A) Southeast Ridge, variation: 1963, II, 5.7; (B) Southeast Ridge *(Route 6)*, II, 4.0; (C) Southeast Couloir *(Route 7)*, II, 5.1; (D) East Face *(Route 8)*, II, 3.0; (E) East Ridge, East Face approach variation; (F) East Ridge *(Route 9)*, II, 4.0

southeast ridge effectively separates the east and south faces of Buck Mountain, so that a different approach is usually used for these two faces. The main cliff band, below the upper east face of Buck Mountain, rises directly above and west of Timberline Lake and is separated from the southeast ridge by the steep and narrow southeast couloir. Because the beginning of the couloir is almost at the same level as the Buck-Static saddle, one can approach this route from No-Wood Basin on the south side of Buck Mountain and traverse from the saddle over to the bottom of the couloir, as was done by the first-ascent party. This apparently was the first time the east side of the mountain had been reached in this way. More directly, one can ascend the talus slope above Timberline Lake and then climb the couloir. The top opens out onto the upper east face, where *Route 8* can then be easily followed to the summit. In early season steep snow will be encountered on this route, requiring knowledge of the use of an ice axe.

ROUTE 8. ▲ EAST FACE. II, 3.0. First ascent August 21, 1898, by T. M. Bannon and George A. Buck; on May 29, 1961, Barry Corbet, Eliot Goss, and Anne LaFarge ascended and descended this route on skis. (See *Figure 2-28.*) This pleasant climb is the popular and standard route to reach the summit of this major Teton peak. Both the approach and the summit view are scenic, and the time required for the ascent is not excessive, all combining to make for an enjoyable day in the mountains. From the Timberline Lake cirque pass to the right (north) of the steep cliffs rising above the lake, then make a long upward traverse to the left over moderate snow (early season) back to the center of the face. More slabs and grassy ledges with some snow patches (depending on the season) then lead to the summit. As cliff bands lurk below their lower edges, use great caution in traversing any snow patches. In early season the climbing will be almost entirely on snow from the cirque to the summit. **Time:** 6¼ to 7 hours from the Death Canyon trailhead. See *Appalachia* 18, no. 3 (June 1931): pp. 209–32, illus.

ROUTE 9. EAST RIDGE. II, 4.0. First ascent August 15, 1931, by Fritiof Fryxell. (See *Figures 2-28* and *2-29.*) This enjoyable ridge climb is the recommended route on this side of the peak. Only the uppermost portion of the ridge that extends down into the south fork of Avalanche Canyon is utilized today, using the same approach to Timberline Lake as *Route 8* and then the 1949 variation to intersect the ridgecrest. This ridge actually faces more north than east and it forms the left or eastern margin of the north face. A more accurate geographic label for this feature would be the northeast ridge, and it has been referred to as such over the years, beginning with Fryxell. From the Timberline Lake cirque, pass to the right (north) of the steep cliffs rising above the lake, then climb up along the right-hand margin of the east face to gain the ridge crest, which is then followed to the summit. In places the ridge is sharp and exposed, providing excellent views down the north face.

Like many other routes in the range, the history of this route is complicated and has evolved over the years since 1931. Fryxell approached this route via Avalanche Canyon and climbed up from the vicinity of the shallow lake just above the first headwall in the south fork, avoiding the lower portion of the ridge by ascending the prominent talus cone to the east. He exited from the top of the cone to a steep couloir that led into the bowl-like snowfield just below and north of the upper east ridge. Following a weakness up and to the west, Fryxell climbed a wide, 90m chimney that led finally to the crest of what is now known as the upper East Ridge route and followed that to the summit. His diary entry from that day describes

FIGURE 2-29. Buck Mountain, northeast aspect. (A) East Ridge, Avalanche Canyon approach *(Route 9)*, II, 4.0; (B) East Ridge, variation: East Face approach; (C) East Ridge, variation, Avalanche Canyon approach: Lowe-Primak-Mankau; (D) East Ridge variation: Sowles, II, 5.7; (E) North Face, East Couloir (Bubble Fun Couloir; *Route 13*), II, 5.4; (F) North Face, West Couloir (Newc Couloir; *Route 15*), II, 5.7

the final portion of the climb from the snowfield: "Up about 300' of slabs to the base of the black cliff. Scaled latter by a steep, narrow chimney, somewhat to the right . . . About 300' long & containing several chockstones; not particularly hard but lots of fun. This brought me out on the crest of the NE ridge perhaps 800' from the summit. The east lake is full of ice-bergs. Climbed the east ridge along its crest or left side, and at 1:10 stood by the big cairn last seen in 1928."

Previous editions of this book have credited the first ascent of this route to the 1934 party; however, after studying its history, it is this author's belief that Fryxell deserves the credit as he was the one who first climbed its classic upper section. (**Note:** If climbing the route as Fryxell did in early season or even midseason, this enjoyable climb will be largely on snow. But in late season the lower snow chute reportedly develops crevasses with overhanging upper lips, forcing one onto the rock, which is steep, very wet, and downsloping. The upper chimney will be bare, with some ice and chockstones exposed.) See *Appalachia* 18, no. 3 (June 1931): pp. 209–32, illus. and *Appalachia* 19, no. 1 (June 1932): pp. 86–96. Thanks to Paul Horton and Tom Turiano for discussions regarding the naming of this route and to Tom for pointing to Fryxell as the first ascentionist.

***Variation:* EAST FACE APPROACH.** August 23, 1934, Ernest Scheeff, Heinz Recker. (See *Figure 2-28.*) This variation utilizes the initial part of *Route 8*, and instead of traversing up and south across the east face, climbs straight up and intersects the crest of the east ridge which is followed to the summit. This has become what is the usual East Ridge route.

Variation: II, 4.0. First ascent August 17, 1949, by Edmund Lowe, William Primak, and Reinhold Mankau. See *Figure 2-29*. Instead of climbing directly up the couloir from the top of the talus cone, cut over to the right (west) and attain the crest of the ridge, which juts out at right angles to the north face. Follow this ridge to the bowl-like snowfield to rejoin the main route. See *Chicago Mountaineering Club Newsletter* 3, no. 6 (August 1949): pp. 25–26.

***Variation:* SOWLES.** II, 5.7. First ascent August 12, 1962, by David Sowles, Robert Brooke, and Sherman Lehman. (See *Figure 2-29.*) This moderately difficult climb also reaches the bowl-like snowfield via the subridge used by the 1949 party; but the crest of this subridge is gained from the west, not the east. Use the same approach as in *Route 13* to the bench below the north face. Instead of following this bench (covered with snow in early season) out to the right (west), climb the 120m wall above and immediately east of the east end of this bench. The top of this wall is the subridge referred to above. Because of the loose rock encountered on the climb, this variation is not recommended.

ROUTE 10. NORTHEAST COULOIR. II, 3.0. First ascent July 2, 1937, by Donald Grant and Robert Grant. This is the easiest route from Avalanche Canyon. Climb directly up from the small, shallow lake just above the first headwall in the lower south fork of Avalanche Canyon toward the very broad talus bench that lies below the north face of Peak 10,696. Follow this bench up and right (west) over huge talus boulders to the saddle between Peak 10,696 and Buck Mountain. From this point one can either stay on the crest and climb the upper East Ridge route *(Route 9)* or make an upward traverse to the left (south) and complete the ascent via the regular East Face route *(Route 8)*. **Time:** 6 hours from the south fork of Avalanche Canyon.

ROUTE 11. NORTH FACE, CHABOT-JOHNSTONE. IV, 5.10+, A2. First ascent fall, 1996, by Doug Chabot and Hans Johnstone. (See *Figure 2-30.*) Little is known, or should I say *remembered*, about this big route on the north face. Nevertheless, an approximate line of ascent is shown on the figure. Two pitches out of a total of six are difficult (5.10+), with the last one having a short section of A1/A2 on it. The approach to the climb is made via the south fork of Avalanche Canyon.

ROUTE 12. NORTH FACE, THE BUCK SANCTION. III, 5.8+. First ascent August 6, 1992, by Tom Turiano and Stephen Koch. (See *Figure 2-30.*) This climb of nine pitches ascends the uncharted wall that is located on the eastern sector of the north face. From the scree slope below the face, begin the first of two pitches (4th class) that slant upward to the west to get to the bottom of *Route 13*. The second pitch consists of some loose 5.5 to 5.6 climbing (chimneys). Next, climb (3rd class) east over to the large ledge that cuts across the face for two ropelengths (spectacular), passing beneath some black dihedrals. The objective for the finish of the route is to intersect the large, curving chimney that cuts across this upper section of the face at its top. The fifth pitch consists of 5.7 face climbing to a belay on a sloping ledge. The next pitch ascends a nice 5.8 crack to a belay near a block. Face climb (5.7) left over to a left-facing corner and then back right on knobs to a belay ledge. Then traverse over to a scary flake and then up to a short left-facing corner. From the top of the corner, 5.6 face climbing leads to a ledge near the large chimney system mentioned earlier. The final pitch ascends the last portion of this chimney and joins the upper East Ridge route *(Route 9)*.

ROUTE 13. NORTH FACE, EAST COULOIR (BUBBLE FUN COULOIR). II, 5.4. First ascent July 17, 1941, by Fred Ayres, Allan Cameron, and Judy Cameron. (See *Figures 2-29* and *2-30.*) This is the more easterly of the two large couloirs that cut the north face of Buck Mountain, and in the ski-mountaineering world it has become known as the Bubble Fun Couloir. The problem of this route is to get into the couloir, which at its lower end dwindles down to a crack in a nearly vertical face. Lying below the entire north face of Buck Mountain is a broad, usually snow-covered bench, which is where this route starts. Approach via the south fork of Avalanche Canyon, then head up the snow slope to the left (east) end of the bench. Cross the bench (usually covered with snow) to a point about 60m west of the crack, which is the lower continuation of the east couloir. A delicate, 30m horizontal traverse back to the left (east) leads to a flake that brings one to a wide ledge. Then make an upward traverse to the right (west); a ropelength leaves one among downsloping slabs. Climb another 15m of interesting rock, up and back to the left, to the easy ground of the couloir itself. Once in the couloir, climb either on its right (west) side or cross over to the right and proceed directly up the more difficult North Central Ridge route *(Route 14)* to the summit. **Time:** 10½ hours from the south fork of Avalanche Canyon. See *American Alpine Journal* 5, no. 2 (1944): pp. 220–32, illus.; *Appalachia* 24, no. 2 (December 1942): pp. 199–208, illus.

ROUTE 14. NORTH CENTRAL RIDGE. III, 5.7, A1, or III, 5.8. First ascent August 23, 1959, by Barry Corbet, Rick Medrick, and Sterling

FIGURE 2-30. Buck Mountain, north aspect. (A) North Face, Chabot-Johnstone *(Route 11)*, IV, 5.10+, A2; (B) North Face, The Buck Sanction *(Route 12)*, III, 5.8+; (C) North Face, East Couloir (Bubble Fun Couloir; *Route 13*), II, 5.4; (D) North Central Ridge *(Route 14)*, III, 5.8; (E) North Face, West Couloir (Newc Couloir; *Route 15*), II, 5.7; (F) North-Northwest Ridge *(Route 16)*, III, 5.7; (G) North-Northwest Ridge, variation: The Wedge, IV, 5.6, A4; (H) West Peak, North Couloir, II, 5.1

Neale. (See *Figure 2-30*.) The north face of Buck Mountain is cut by two steep and very large couloirs; the summit lies at the apex of the distinct ridge that separates these couloirs. This route ascends this central ridge, which rises from the broad bench (commonly covered with snow) at the base of the north face. Approach this bench as in *Route 13*. Climb the snow on the bench to near its highest point. The ascent of the wall immediately above, which truncates the lower end of the ridge, provides the principal difficulty of the route. Immediately after leaving the snow, traverse approximately 46m to the right (west) past two right-facing corners; two face-climbing pitches (5.7) then take one to an area of ledge systems and easier ground. Then climb 60m of 3rd-class ground up and east to the point where the ridge becomes well defined. From here to the summit the route along the ridge crest is straightforward 3.0 climbing, with the exception of one 3m section, which required aid on the first ascent but goes free at 5.8. This north face route is perhaps the best route on this peak from an aesthetic standpoint. **Time:** 10 hours from the south fork of Avalanche Canyon.

ROUTE 15. NORTH FACE, WEST COULOIR (NEWC COULOIR). II, 5.7. First ascent July 16, 1940, by Paul Petzoldt and Elizabeth Cowles (Partridge); first descent June 14, 1946, by Dick Pownall and Albert Boursault. (See *Figures 2-29* and *2-30*.) The north face of Buck Mountain is cut by two steep, prominent couloirs; this route ascends the westerly of these broad couloirs. Since its first ski descent in 1995 by local climber and ski mountaineer Mark Newcomb, it has become known as the Newc Couloir. To reach the beginning of this couloir, one can approach the broad bench lying below the main north face from the east (see *Route 13*) and then continue west across the bench to the couloir. Or more directly, one can angle left up easy rock to the right (west) end of the bench and gain access to the couloir. Ascend the open couloir above, avoiding the loose rock, mainly on the left (east) side of the couloir, by climbing up the right wall of the couloir. Ice is likely to be encountered on this route, except in late season. Almost immediately after one reaches the summit ridge, there is a short, overhanging pitch (5.7); once past this pitch, the ridge can be easily followed eastward to the summit. **Time:** 5 hours from the south fork of Avalanche Canyon. See *Trail and Timberline*, no. 353 (May 1948): pp. 67–70, illus.

ROUTE 16. NORTH-NORTHWEST RIDGE. III, 5.7. First ascent July 23, 1954, by Richard Emerson, Don Decker, and William Clayton. (See *Figure 2-30*.) This ridge leads to the west summit of Buck Mountain; hence, it is the first ridge west of the central north ridge, which leads to the main summit (see *Route 14*). It forms the west boundary to the couloir of *Route 15*. From the south fork of Avalanche Canyon two approaches are possible: (1) one can climb onto the snow bench at its eastern end (as in *Route 13*) and traverse all the way over to the base of this north-northwest ridge, or (2) one can scramble up the easy rock angling toward the west end of the bench, which is the beginning of the ridge—the better option. The route now progresses for three ropelengths up the extreme east corner of the triangular face, the Wedge, which forms the lower portion of the north-northwest ridge. Climb a chimney that opens out onto an exposed platform at the top of a detached flake. The next pitch is the key to the climb. On the first ascent a rope was thrown over a small flake about 3m up, which gave the leader an upper belay for the difficult face lead diagonally left up to the flake. Walk out to the right on the small flake, then traverse left back around the corner of the face on a downsloping ledge about a meter above. On the corner above, climb the steep and exposed rock for 12m before making a delicate and difficult 9m traverse left into a large chimney. It is recommended that this be made in two leads; otherwise, there will be considerable rope drag. Now climb upward, edging right (north) to the 2.5-square-meter platform at the very top of the triangular face.

The way is now clear, up the sharp arête leading toward the west summit. A cockscomb formation higher up on the arête is bypassed on the left (east) by descending about 1m. Unless one particularly wants to visit the west summit, it is better—at a point level with the sharp notch separating the west summit from the higher east summit—to traverse left off the ridge into this notch. Then climb the 5.7 overhanging pitch up out of the notch and proceed easily over to the summit of Buck Mountain. This is a long route and an early start is recommended. *Route 8* is probably the most suitable route for descent, in which case one would finish at the Death Canyon trailhead (by way of the trail down Stewart Draw); plan a car shuttle accordingly. **Time:** 10¾ hours from the south fork of Avalanche Canyon.

***Variation:* THE WEDGE.** IV, 5.6, A4. First ascent August 2, 1961, by Herb Swedlund, David Dornan, and Peter Lev. (See *Figure 2-30*.) This climb was a significant achievement in the Tetons at the time because it involved extensive aid climbing at a very difficult standard on a high, alpine wall. Swedlund compared the climb to that of Mount Conness in the Sierra, whose elegant west face he had climbed in 1959 with Warren Harding and Glen Denny. The lower 90m, wedge-shaped section of the north-northwest ridge is essentially vertical. There have been few repeats of this route since the first ascent. Take the large, slanting ledge that

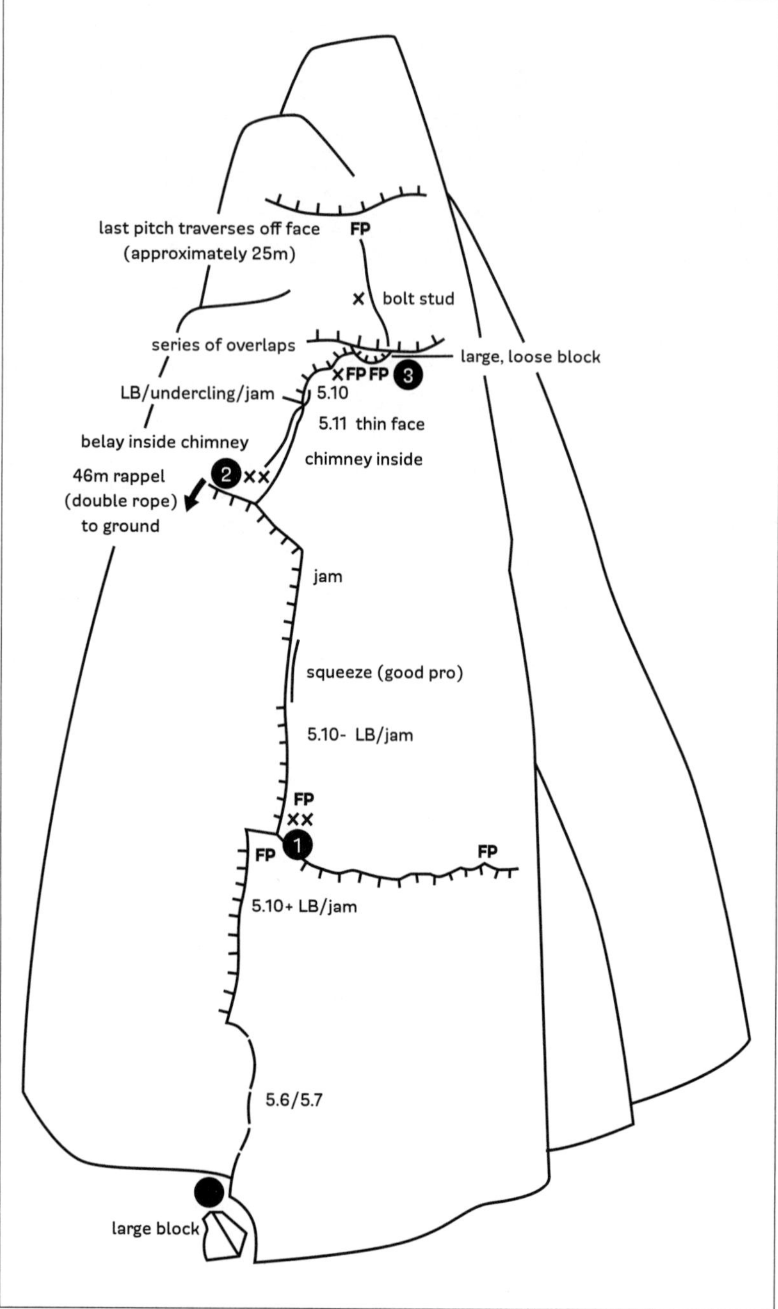

FIGURE 2-31. Buck Mountain, North-Northwest Ridge *(Route 16)*, variation: The Free Wedge, IV, 5.11 (unfinished)

ends under the Wedge to the base of a corner on the left side of the face. Climb a pitch up this corner to an aid lead that starts by nailing up under a roof. Then drop down to a slab until it is possible to pendulum around the corner to the right (west). Less difficult climbing then leads to a belay stance just right of the center of the face. The next lead of about 24m involves some difficulty in the placing of pitons for aid up discontinuous crack patterns, which lead slightly to the left on vertical or overhanging rock. From a bolt, belay the next 18m lead, which works up and slightly right, and then from another bolt traverse left (east) off the face using poor pitons, including at least one knifeblade. The original climb of this severe route required two days and the placement of about 50 pitons; all of the belays on the face were from slings. See *American Alpine Journal* 13, no. 1 (1962): pp. 216–20.

***Variation:* THE FREE WEDGE.** IV, 5.11 (unfinished). First ascent August 14, 1993, by Greg Miles and Mark Limage. (See *Figure 2-31.*) This variation marks the first real attempt to free climb this alpine wall and it may, in fact, differ slightly from the 1961 ascent described above. Although this climb was pushed free just beyond the top of the third pitch and remains unfinished, it stands as a significant achievement and is therefore listed here. Begin with easy face climbing (5.6 to 5.7) up and into a right-facing corner system on the left side of the face. The climbing increases in difficulty in the corner (5.10+) to a fixed piton under a small roof. Traverse down and right on small holds (5.10+) to the only real ledge on the face and belay at the base of another right-facing corner. For the second pitch, steep liebacking and jamming (5.10-) lead to a belay stance inside a chimney. The third pitch goes up and right on small face holds (5.11) to a very steep, gently arching crack system (5.10) that ends at a small roof where a bolt was found. Two pitons now back up the bolt. Another bolt (stud) and fixed piton were visible in a crack system that angles up and left off the face. Miles and Limage's attempt ended at this point, however, because of a large, loose block over which one must climb to finish the route. **Gear:** Take protection to 3.5" with extras in the 2"–3" category. Small wired nuts are also suggested.

BUCK MOUNTAIN, WEST PEAK (11,600+)

Map: Grand Teton

This subpeak, seldom climbed for its own sake, must be traversed in order to climb the complete west ridge of Buck Mountain, starting from the divide.

Chronology

NORTHWEST RIDGE: August 21, 1921, Roland W. Brown Sr., Roland W. Brown Jr., Melba Brown, Carvel Brown, Hattie Robinson, Phebe Robinson
NORTH COULOIR: June 26, 1977, Paul Horton, James Alto
SOUTH COULOIR: June 26, 1977, Paul Horton, James Alto (descent)

ROUTE 1. SOUTH COULOIR. II, 3.0. First descent June 26, 1977, by Paul Horton and James Alto. (See *Figure 2-27.*) This talus-filled gully leads from the bench south of the West Peak to the notch just east of its summit; it contains one 5m cliff band. It is but a scramble from the notch to the top.

ROUTE 2. NORTH COULOIR. II, 5.1. First ascent June 26, 1977, by Paul Horton and James Alto. (See *Figure 2-30.*) From the south fork of Avalanche Canyon scramble for 150m up the lower portion of this couloir. In early season moderate-angle snow climbing for six ropelengths takes one to the notch east of the West Peak, from which the summit is easily attained. The angle of the snow is not as steep as it appears from below. Rock on the sides of the couloir is poor and, because the sun hits this slope early in the day, the snow may be unpleasantly soft. This couloir was first descended on skis by Brendan O'Neill, at which time it was named Uncle Buck.

ROUTE 3. NORTHWEST RIDGE. I, 4.0. First ascent August 21, 1921, by Roland W. Brown Sr., Roland W. Brown Jr., Melba Brown, Carvel Brown, Hattie Robinson, and Phebe Robinson. This very early Teton ascent made by local citizens from Teton Basin is unusual in that the record of the climb was found intact in 1957, and so has not been lost to history as were other similar climbs of the period. There are few difficulties on this ridge, but the rock is loose.

VEILED PEAK (11,330)

Map: Grand Teton

The outstanding characteristic of this small peak is the spectacular view of Mount Wister from the summit. Veiled Peak does have a prominent feature, however, in its sharp but rotten north ridge, which rises 1,300 feet from the shores of Snowdrift Lake. The cirque immediately northwest of the peak harbors a significant but seldom-visited glacier. The summit of the peak, situated nearly but not exactly on the hydrographic divide between Avalanche Canyon and Alaska Basin, is easily approached from the Teton Crest Trail. In addition, both forks of Avalanche Canyon and the south fork of Cascade Canyon provide suitable approaches. The first ascent was the result of Avalanche Canyon being used as a shortcut from the Cascade Canyon trail workers' camp to Park Headquarters at Beaver Creek. The easily distinguished Buck Mountain fault crosses the foot of the west ridge.

Chronology

NORTHEAST LEDGES: September 18, 1932, Phil Smith, Walcott Watson
WEST RIDGE: July 17, 1940, Paul Petzoldt, Elizabeth Cowles (Partridge)
EAST RIDGE: July 13, 1940, William and Harold Plumley, Jack and William Fralick (partial); August 27, 1952, Willi Unsoeld, Leigh Ortenburger, Beatrice Vogel (complete)
SOUTHEAST FLANK: August 3, 1954, Martin Benham, Jeanne Price
NORTH RIDGE: June 18, 1960, Bill Echo, Dean Millsap
var—**THE DUCK:** June 18, 1960, Bill Echo, Dean Millsap
SOUTH RIDGE: August 17, 1963, William Buckingham, Margaret Pevear
var—**DIRECT BUTTRESS:** September 24, 1971, John Bousman, Dave Reed

ROUTE 1. WEST RIDGE. I, 5.1. First ascent July 17, 1940, by Paul Petzoldt and Elizabeth Cowles (Partridge). Because this party reported the climb as being less difficult than others have reported, it is likely that the ridge was not followed directly. There is a couloir south of the true ridge that has been used as a route of ascent. It is also possible to traverse out to the north when confronted by the difficulties of the crest of the ridge.

ROUTE 2. SOUTH RIDGE. II, 5.6. First ascent August 17, 1963, by William Buckingham and Margaret Pevear. This distinct ridge of excellent rock can be approached either via the south fork of Avalanche Canyon or from the Teton Crest Trail via Death Canyon. The ridge is reached from the left (west) via a couloir of loose rock. Follow the couloir to a notch formed by a rotten dike. (The steep, rotten section of the ridge, culminating in the gendarme that forms the south side of the notch, is thus avoided.) The first pitch is an easy 23m corner just left (west) of the crest. Scramble up to an overhanging tower, which can be passed by descending slightly to the left and then climbing the west face of this tower. To avoid use of aid on the 30m tower above, traverse right on a shelf for 21m, past two prominent chimneys (these will probably go), to the high-angle face just right of the second chimney. The lead up this face brings one to the crest of the ridge just beyond the top of the tower. Climb a pitch just 3m to the right (east) of the crest to the beginning of the sixth pitch. Work up about 20m, then cross the crest back to the left. After about a meter exit left onto a ledge, then move up to the belay stance on the crest. The final pitch passes over two easy towers to the summit. See *American Alpine Journal* 14, no. 1 (1964): p. 188.

Variation: **DIRECT BUTTRESS.** II, 5.6. First ascent September 24, 1971, by John Bousman and Dave Reed. This variation adds four pitches by starting at the base of the initial buttress that the normal South Ridge route avoids.

ROUTE 3. SOUTHEAST FLANK. II, 4.0. First ascent August 3, 1954, by Martin Benham and Jeanne Price. From Alaska Basin one can cross along the base of the south ridge to gain access to the southeast flank of Veiled Peak. Once past the south ridge, relatively straightforward scrambling, staying clear of both adjacent ridges, then leads to the summit.

ROUTE 4. EAST RIDGE. II, 5.7. First complete ascent August 27, 1952, by Willi Unsoeld, Leigh Ortenburger, and Beatrice Vogel; on July 13, 1940, William and Harold Plumley and Jack and William Fralick, all of the Chicago Mountaineering Club, climbed the southeast slope to the small notch in this ridge and then continued up most of the ridge above before traversing right across the north ledges to gain the summit by the uppermost west ridge. The complete East Ridge route is a straightforward climb up a well-defined crest. If one stays precisely on the ridge, one 5.7 friction pitch will be encountered about three-quarters of the way up. However, at several points one can leave the crest of the ridge to the right (north) and find easier climbing. **Time:** 1½ hours from the summit of Mount Wister. See *American Alpine Journal* 8, no. 3 (1953): pp. 542–45.

ROUTE 5. ▲ NORTHEAST LEDGES. I, 3.0. First ascent September 18, 1932, by Phil Smith and Walcott Watson. From Snowdrift Lake either work directly up the northeast slope or first gain the saddle (10,800+) between Veiled Peak and Mount Wister and then cut out onto the northeast face at almost any point west of the saddle. The summit can be reached by scrambling up ledges.

ROUTE 6. NORTH RIDGE. II, 5.1. First ascent June 18, 1960, by Bill Echo and Dean Millsap. From Snowdrift Lake this ridge can be climbed directly to the summit past several pinnacles of dubious quality.

Variation: **THE DUCK.** II, 5.7. First ascent June 18, 1960, by Bill Echo and Dean Millsap. This is the first pinnacle (10,960+) north of the summit of Veiled Peak. The party who made the third ascent of the Duck—Mark Chapman and Andy Kegley, on July 10, 1976—reported the climb to be four pitches, starting on the east face slabs: two easy 5th-class leads to a steep 5.7 pitch on a south-facing wall just left of an alcove, then one exposed 4th-class lead to the summit.

AVALANCHE CANYON (SOUTH FORK), NORTH SIDE ROCK CLIMBS

Map: Grand Teton

Located partway up the south fork of Avalanche Canyon, on the southeast side of Mount Wister, is a steep buttress of excellent rock that is approximately 90m high. The name Fracture Line Buttress was applied to this formation by its discoverers. This buttress is situated directly across from the north face of Buck Mountain and slightly upcanyon from the small lake in the south fork.

ROUTE 1. I, 5.10. First ascent August 13, 1993, by Greg Miles and Mark Limage. There is a large, downsloping ledge from which these climbs begin at the base of the buttress. Scramble up onto this ledge. When looking at the buttress this two-pitch route is located just right of a prominent wide crack that curves up and slightly right. Climb a corner to a roof that is surmounted by a traverse to the right via jugs and a pocket. Traverse back to the left on the lip of the roof and then climb up and over a bulge to a horizontal crack that leads left to a belay. Continue up one more pitch to the top or walk left and downclimb to the base.

ROUTE 2. I, 5.11. First ascent August 13, 1993, by Greg Miles and Mark Limage. This climb is located near the right edge of the buttress and to the right (east) of the first route. Begin by climbing up to the large ledge from the east, heading for the large overhang at the eastern edge of the buttress (5.10-). Above the overhang is an obvious thin, clean-looking crack leading out from the apex of the roof. Lieback and undercling out and over the roof (5.11), straight up to where the crack splits. The right crack is finger to hand size while the left involves liebacking up flakes. A 46m rappel from the top of the pitch leads back to the large ledge at the base.

MOUNT WISTER (11,490)

Map: Grand Teton

This peak was named after Owen Wister, the famous author of *The Virginian*, who visited Jackson Hole several times before 1900 and later had a summer home there. As viewed from the valley, Mount Wister is not a prominent peak. This fact, combined with the lack of a maintained trail up Avalanche Canyon, perhaps explains why it has been somewhat neglected by mountaineers. Nonetheless, this important Teton peak provides interesting climbing, especially on the north face where there are now five distinct routes. From the summit impressive views can be obtained of the northern aspect of Buck Mountain and the southern walls of the Garnet Canyon peaks. Wister has three distinct summits, of which the easternmost is the highest. The central summit is usually bypassed by most parties, but the west summit must be traversed by climbers of *Routes 1, 9, 10,* and *11*.

Chronology

NORTHEAST COULOIR: September 23, 1928, Phil Smith, Oliver Zierlein
var—September 23, 1928, Phil Smith, Oliver Zierlein (descent); August 4, 1950, Gerald and Ted Brandon, Don Zastrow, Finn Brunevold (ascent)
WEST RIDGE: August 23, 1929, Fritiof Fryxell
SOUTHEAST COULOIR: June 27, 1931, Phil Smith
var—July 6, 1935, Malcolm Smith
SOUTHWEST RIDGE: August 16, 1931, Fritiof Fryxell
NORTHWEST FACE: August 16, 1931, Fritiof Fryxell (descent); July 19, 1960, Charles and Cora Sanders (ascent)
SOUTH COULOIR: July 5, 1936, Fred Ayres, William and Harold Plumley (descent); July 19, 1936, Fred and Irene Ayres, Margaret Smith (Craighead) (ascent)
NORTH FACE, WEST CHIMNEY: August 27, 1952, Willi Unsoeld, Leigh Ortenburger, Beatrice Vogel
var—July 20, 1961, Ray Jacquot, J. Orren Church

NORTH FACE, EAST CHIMNEY: August 22, 1956, James T. Smith, Bill Hoy (partial); September 9, 1957, Bill Pope, Mary Kay Pottinger (complete)
DIRECT NORTH FACE: July 20, 1961, Layton Kor, Gary Cole
NORTHWEST ARÊTE: August 30, 1966, John Hudson, Frank Sarnquist
NORTHWEST COULOIR: August 26, 1968, William Chadwick, Wallace Hunter
NORTH FACE, SAVED BY THE SHEEP: January 19, 1997, Norm Larson, Callum Mackay

ROUTE 1. WEST RIDGE. II, 5.4. First ascent August 23, 1929, by Fritiof Fryxell. The saddle between Mount Wister and Veiled Peak, which is the starting point for this climb, can be approached in four different ways. The two most direct ways are via the south fork or the north fork (shorter) of Avalanche Canyon, as the saddle is attained quite easily from either direction. Another possibility is via the south fork of Cascade Canyon, which joins the north fork of Avalanche Canyon at the saddle (10,560+) between the South Teton and the Wall. A fourth possibility is via the Teton Crest Trail to Alaska Basin, then over the divide into the south fork of Avalanche Canyon. The route above the saddle is fairly obvious. The ridge can be followed either slightly to the right (south) or slightly to the left (north) of the crest. The west summit of Wister will be reached first and must be traversed to get to the higher main (east) summit. The central summit is usually bypassed via ledges on its north side but can also be passed on the south. **Time:** 4 hours from Snowdrift Lake. See *Appalachia* 18, no. 3 (June 1931): pp. 209–32, illus.

ROUTE 2. SOUTHWEST RIDGE. I, 4.0. First ascent August 16, 1931, by Fritiof Fryxell. The upper south side of Mount Wister contains three ridges, each leading to one of the three summits; two well-defined couloirs separate these ridges. A broken cliff band supporting scattered trees guards the approach to these couloirs and ridges. Take the talus-filled south fork of Avalanche Canyon up to near its west end, past the 10,000-foot level, veering right above the single krummholz and grass area, as if heading toward the saddle west of Mount Wister. Gain the western of the three ridges from the west, and climb the ridge along the right (east) side of its crest. The climbing becomes increasingly interesting toward the summit. About 90m below the summit, the first-ascent route crossed over into the next couloir or chimney to the right (east). Before reaching the notch, and about 15m below the summit, climb a narrow, vertical chimney with chockstones, using stemming to gain the summit. This route differs from *Route 3* in that one ascends farther west to the uppermost section of the canyon before turning up the mountain. **Time:** 4½ hours from the south fork of Avalanche Canyon. See *Appalachia* 19, no. 1 (June 1932): pp. 86–96.

ROUTE 3. SOUTH COULOIR. II, 4.0. First descent July 5, 1936, by Fred Ayres and William and Harold Plumley; first ascent July 19, 1936, by Fred and Irene Ayres and Margaret Smith (Craighead). This route ascends the large couloir leading from the south fork of Avalanche Canyon to the notch immediately west of the summit. The beginning of this route can be recognized from below as a bare talus cone leading to a steep watercourse break in the initial cliff band. This is the last (farthest west) talus before reaching the krummholz and grass area, which begins at about 10,000 feet. Some scrambling to pass the initial cliff band is required. Three leads of 4.0 climbing will be found.

ROUTE 4. SOUTHEAST COULOIR. I, 3.0. First ascent June 27, 1931, by Phil Smith. The southeast side of Mount Wister is composed of a complex series of broken cliff bands and shallow couloirs; several routes are possible. Take the south fork of Avalanche Canyon to about 9,600 feet; do not start up the mountain too soon. The correct couloir leads to the main col, east of the summit, that separates Peak 10,960+ from Mount Wister. The lower part of this couloir appears as an indentation in the talus slope, just at the left (west) edge of the section containing trees. Once past the initial cliff band, where the couloir narrows, no difficulty will be encountered until the east ridge col is reached. Follow the delightful east ridge to the summit. **Time:** 4½ hours from the south fork of Avalanche Canyon. See *Appalachia* 19, no. 1 (June 1932): pp. 86–96.

Variation: II, 4.0. First ascent July 6, 1935, by Malcolm Smith. Instead of taking the main southeast couloir that ends at the east ridge col, start as in *Route 3* to gain the open upper talus slope past the initial cliff band. Then, instead of entering the upper south couloir, climb up and slightly right (east) to the base of the broken face above. Ascend this face, using one of the shallow couloirs that leads upward, to join the east ridge just short of the summit.

ROUTE 5. NORTHEAST COULOIR. II, 4.0. First ascent September 23, 1928, by Phil Smith and Oliver Zierlein. A conspicuous couloir rises from the north fork of Avalanche Canyon just below the headwall leading to Lake Taminah. Climb this couloir to the east ridge, which is followed to the summit. Near the ridge crest the couloir narrows to a wide chimney and the climbing becomes more difficult. This route has perhaps not been used since the first ascent because the easier 1928 variation (described next) was discovered on the descent.

▲ ***Variation:*** II, 4.0. First descent September 23, 1928, by Phil Smith and Oliver Zierlein; first ascent August 4, 1950, by Gerald and Ted Brandon, Don Zastrow, and Finn Brunevold. (See *Figure 2-32*; only the upper portion of the route is visible.) This variation, a northeast approach to the upper east ridge, is the most straightforward method of reaching the summit of Mount Wister; it has the advantage of leading directly to the summit, without having to climb over or around either of the other two lower summits. From Lake Taminah cross the outlet stream and turn left (south) up into a small, snow-filled cirque that contains the apparent remnant of what was a small glacier at the northwest foot of Peak 10,960+. Ascend the loose talus and scree slope that leads to the broad col in the east ridge, between the summit and Peak 10,960+. In early season and midseason this entire slope will be covered with snow, an advantage over the loose rubble encountered later in the season; however, an ice axe will be essential. Once the crest is reached, turn right (west) and scramble up along the left (south) edge of the fine east ridge to the summit. See *Appalachia* 18, no. 3 (June 1931): pp. 209–32, illus.

ROUTE 6. NORTH FACE, EAST CHIMNEY. III, 5.6. First partial ascent August 22, 1956, by James T. Smith and Bill Hoy; first complete ascent September 9, 1957, by Bill Pope and Mary Kay Pottinger. (See *Figure 2-32.*) This prominent chimney marks the left (east) edge of the steep and slabby north face of Mount Wister. See *Avalanche Canyon, North Fork* for the approach to Lake Taminah. Ascend the talus that leads to the base of the north face, then gain the beginning of the chimney either

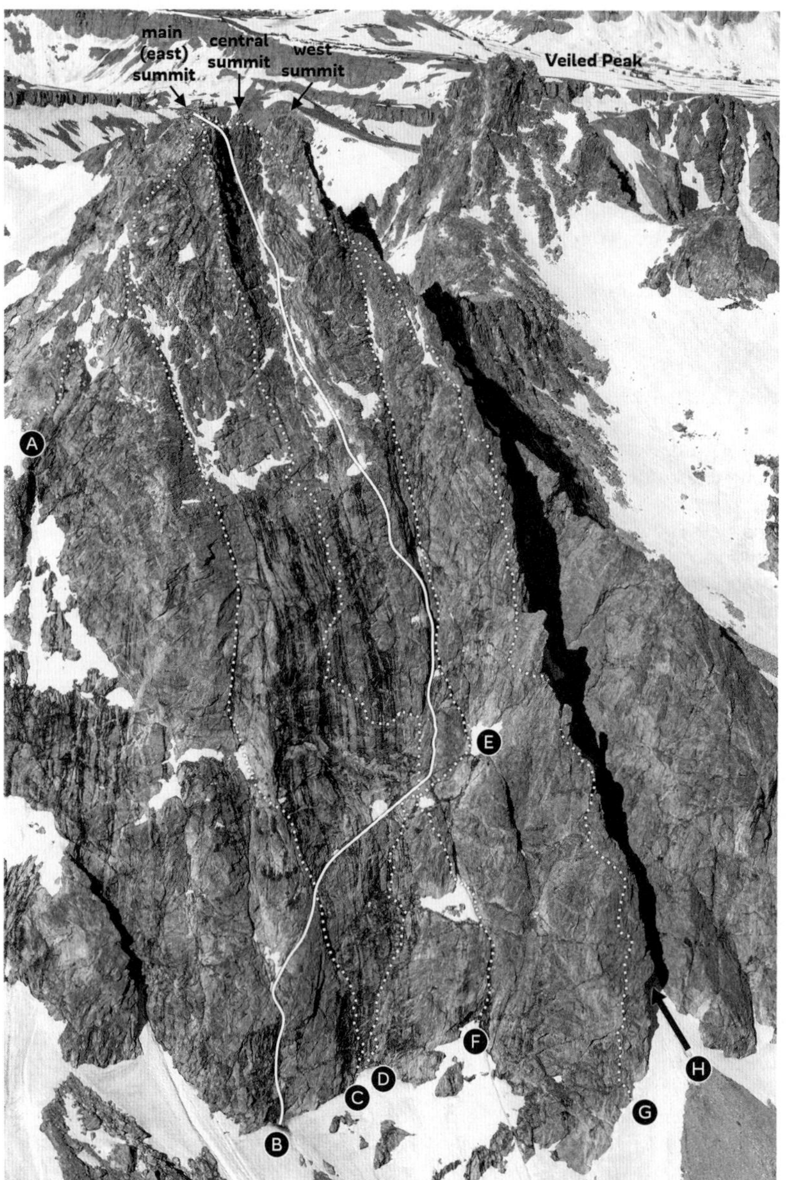

FIGURE 2-32. Mount Wister, northeast aspect. (A) Northeast Couloir *(Route 5)*, variation: 1928, II, 4.0; (B) North Face, Saved by the Sheep (winter, approximate; *Route 8*), IV, 5.7R, M4; (C) North Face, East Chimney *(Route 6)*, III, 5.6; (D) Direct North Face *(Route 7)*, original 1961 start (Kor-Cole), III, 5.10-; (E) North Face, West Chimney *(Route 9)*, II, 5.6; (F) Direct North Face *(Route 7)*, alternate start, shown on Figures 2-32, 2-33, and 2-34; (G) Northwest Arête *(Route 10)*, IV, 5.9; (H) Northwest Couloir *(Route 11)*, II, 5.7, A1

directly or (easier) from the east via a fairly obvious ledge. Two or three pitches, which include some scrambling up the lower section of the chimney, bring one to the steeper, upper section. Since the chimney is often wet, climb the first pitch on either the right or left wall. Both have apparently been used, but the right is perhaps preferable. Pass a small bulge; then go into and up the chimney. On the next pitch (37m) pass a large chockstone by climbing in behind it. On the third pitch (24m) one encounters a chockstone that can be surmounted by stemming over it on the outside. Next is a lead up loose rock to a roof, which can be passed by careful climbing on the right wall up and out of the chimney. At this point the angle eases considerably, enabling one to scramble up the slabs to a point on the east ridge about 60m short of the summit. Although the rock is somewhat loose, this is an enjoyable, well-protected climb.

ROUTE 7. DIRECT NORTH FACE. III, 5.7, A2, or III, 5.10-. First ascent July 20, 1961, by Layton Kor and Gary Cole; first known free ascent August 26, 2002, by Renny Jackson and Jack McConnell. (See *Figures 2-32, 2-33,* and *2-34.*) McConnell and this author (R. Jackson) attempted to follow Layton Kor's route description, provided below, though we started to the right of where the Kor route begins. The line in *Figures 2-32* and *2-33* should *not* be taken for the exact Kor route—it is a best guess. *Figure 2-34* represents what McConnell and I climbed; while it does not necessarily match up with Kor's description, the route that is detailed is highly recommended: every pitch is of high quality and on excellent rock. Of all the routes on the north side of Mount Wister, this is the one to do. However, one must wait until later in the summer when the face is as dry as it gets.

Layton Kor's Description: This climb starts on the north face between the two great chimney systems and ascends to the upper part of the slabby north face. The first pitch diagonals up and right where a jam crack leads up to the second grassy terrace of *Route 9*. Starting at the corner of the chimney, climb a difficult jam and ledge system over a small roof to bypass the more obvious chimney. One easy ropelength leads to an obvious traverse left (10m) on a 3m ledge. After the disappearance of the ledge, climb down a 2m crack and continue the traverse diagonally left. The next lead (40m) ends at a belay on a 2.5m ledge. Again traverse diagonally left (east), past a flake (a piton should be found here), to the base of a small roof. A good belay stance will be found behind the huge boulder at the top of this roof. The next pitch of 18m above the boulder required aid to pass another small roof. Now traverse right (west) on a wide, grassy ramp for 3m before angling left up a smooth slab to the base of a third small roof, which is at the edge of the left (east) corner of the face. Two ropelengths bring one to the easy climbing at the base of the final north summit arête. Most of this arête can be climbed directly on the crest. The difficult section of the arête is near the top in a chimney on the right side of the crest. From

FIGURE 2-33. Mount Wister, Direct North Face *(Route 7)*, III, 5.10-

midway up this chimney, traverse right to a 4-inch jam crack up the face to an obvious hole. Climb straight up out of this hole, past a small overhang; then scramble up boulders to the summit, only 15m away. The northeast couloir (see *Route 5*) is used for the descent. **Gear:** A set of stoppers and a double rack of cams to 3" should suffice for protection. See *American Alpine Journal* 13, no. 1 (1962): pp. 216–20.

ROUTE 8. NORTH FACE, SAVED BY THE SHEEP. IV, 5.7R, M4. First ascent January 19, 1997, by Norm Larson and Callum Mackay. (See *Figure 2-32*.) For decades, Teton winter-climbing aficionados longed for this face to become encased in ice. In some years huge, hanging sheets of ice, not quite touching down, would form, but the climb refused to materialize. Many came to believe it might happen during some rare fall or spring, when exactly the right combination of water and temperature would coincide to create a magnificent icy north wall. Larson—an experienced Teton alpinist—had watched this phenomenon over the years, and he had enough motivation and experience to get the first winter ascent. Given the difficult mixed conditions he found on the face, it seems appropriate that he was accompanied by colorful local Scotsman Mackay.

In terms of a route description, it's best to refer to Larson's recollection:

"I do remember we thought we did 17 pitches. Pitches, though, were determined by where we could get anchors. Wister on that side has quite compact rock, and solid anchors were quite hard to find. I remember we started near the east chimney [see Route 6] on an ice- and snow-covered ramp, trending right. The start was really hard and Callum fell off repeatedly [while following] until there wasn't any snow or ice left. . . . There also was no pro for the first 30 meters or so. After that we trended right a bit, but mostly up to another break in a rock band. That had some mixed ice and rock and a bit of pro. Mostly I remember just climbing, looking for any sort of pro. It was mostly . . . good sticky snow with a bit of ice here and there and occasionally some rock. I seem to remember that it felt like there was really only one way to go most of the time, which kept me going forward. Eventually after another rock band there was kind of a wide-open snow gully we followed. The last pitch went up a slabby snow section to a little step, which led to the summit. It was the crowning achievement of my Teton climbing. I felt that I had to use everything I had learned alpine climbing on that route."

For the descent the pair used the northeast couloir (see *Route 5*), which contributed to the naming of the route. "When we got to the top it was getting late," Larson explained. "I wanted to go off the northeast side and drop back to our skis in the north fork [of Avalanche Canyon]. I wasn't sure which gully to go down. Looked over [the] edge and I spooked two bighorn sheep that were just below the summit. They jumped into the correct gully and we followed their tracks down, which was a total time-save for us. Still skied out in the dark. Again."

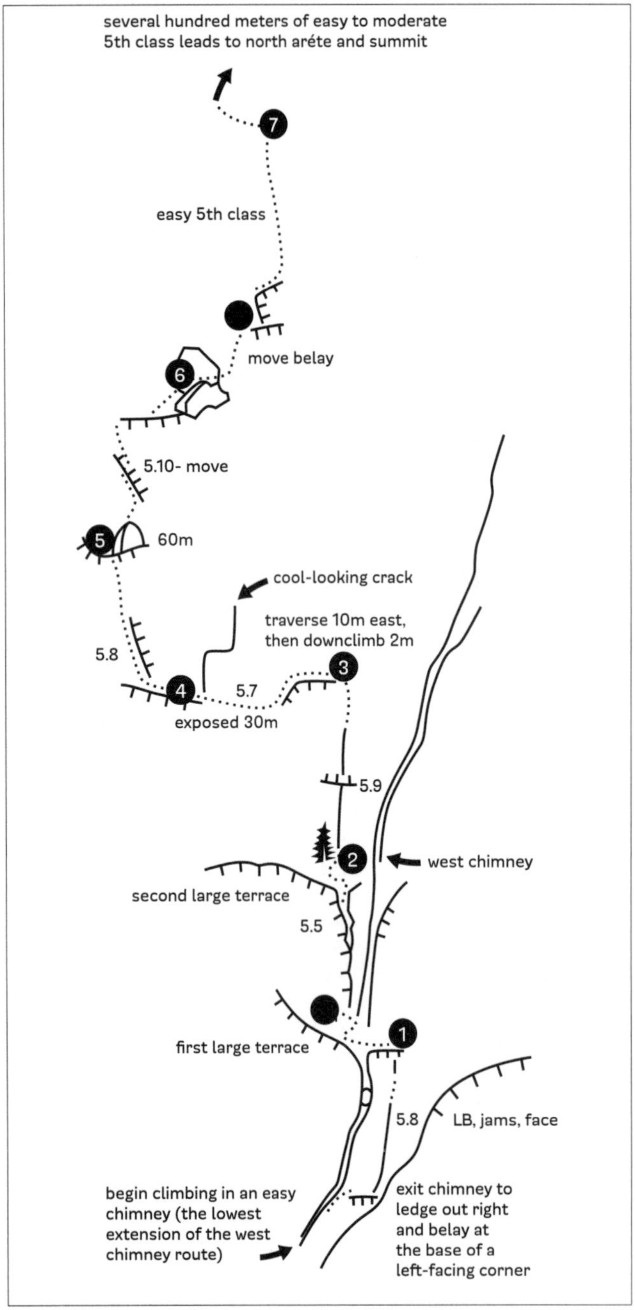

FIGURE 2-34. Mount Wister, Direct North Face (with alternate start; *Route 7*), III, 5.10-

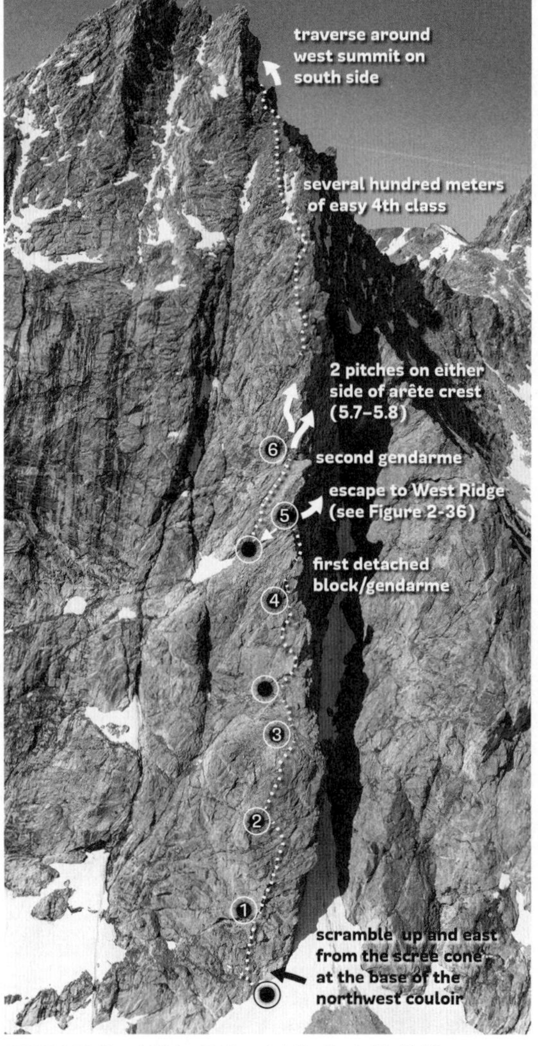

FIGURE 2-35. Mount Wister, Northwest Arête *(Route 10)*, IV, 5.9

ROUTE 9. NORTH FACE, WEST CHIMNEY. II, 5.6. First ascent August 27, 1952, by Willi Unsoeld, Leigh Ortenburger, and Beatrice Vogel; a previous attempt, stopped by a storm, was made on August 27, 1946, by Ray Van Aken, Wallace Degen, John Montgomery, Eugene Paul, and Don Woods. (See *Figure 2-32*.) The problem of this interesting route is to get into the great chimney at the right (west) edge of the smooth north face. There are two grassy terraces on the lower part of the main north face, and from the higher terrace one can easily get into the chimney itself. A small chimney, roughly in the middle of the face, gives access to the first of these grassy terraces. The first pitch is the hardest of the route. Climb out of the small chimney to the right (west) past an awkward overhang to a good belay spot. Continue upward for two pitches to the first grassy terrace. From here, two more pitches lead up and to the right (west) to the second terrace. Climb easily into the great chimney and scramble a hundred or so meters up to the crest of the west ridge, which will be attained just west of the west summit. Then follow *Route 1* to the main (east) summit. **Time:** 5½ hours from Lake Taminah. See *American Alpine Journal* 8, no. 3 (1953): pp. 542–45.

Variation: II, 5.6. First ascent July 20, 1961, by Ray Jacquot and J. Orren Church. Instead of continuing upward to intersect the west ridge, a more direct route to the summit cuts left (east) near the top of the chimney onto the upper portion of the north face; the summit is then reached from the north.

ROUTE 10. NORTHWEST ARÊTE. IV, 5.9. First ascent August 30, 1966, by John Hudson and Frank Sarnquist. (See *Figures 2-35* and *2-36.*) This route is on the well-defined ridge between the west chimney on the north face (see *Route 9*) and the prominent northwest snow couloir (see *Route 11*) at the extreme west side of the face. It forms the right (west) edge of the north face proper. This long ridge, about 550m, contains 10 or more pitches of fairly sustained climbing with some sections of poor rock, but with generally good protection. This route was high on this author's (R. Jackson's) Teton list for a long time, and I finally did it in the summer of 2016. My partner and I were on-route for the initial five pitches until we began traversing out toward the northwest couloir. Having done this route as well as the Direct North Face *(Route 7)*, I would recommend the latter, hands down. *Figure 2-36* illustrates an escape to the West Ridge route *(Route 1)*, which can then be followed to the summit. There are many variations possible on this arête, however, and the few parties who have done it have likely taken several different routes. Given the poor condition of the trail (as of 2016), parties should expect a long, adventurous day.

The climb begins from a small, grassy ledge at the base of the ridge below a prominent right-facing corner located just to the east of the northwest couloir. From the belay, step up to and climb a flake (5.8) and continue into the corner. When protection becomes difficult to find, step out left, climb around this short section, and move back into the corner. At the beginning of the corner, a 4" piece is nice to have. Continue up to the top of this corner (5.9) and belay in an alcove of shattered rock. The second pitch begins with an awkward step up into the chimney above (5.8), which is followed to its top and another ledge for the belay. The third pitch continues up past a flake and a 5.7 crack, followed by face climbing to the left and up to a belay. Move the belay up along the base of the wall to an obvious-looking crack, and for the fourth pitch climb the

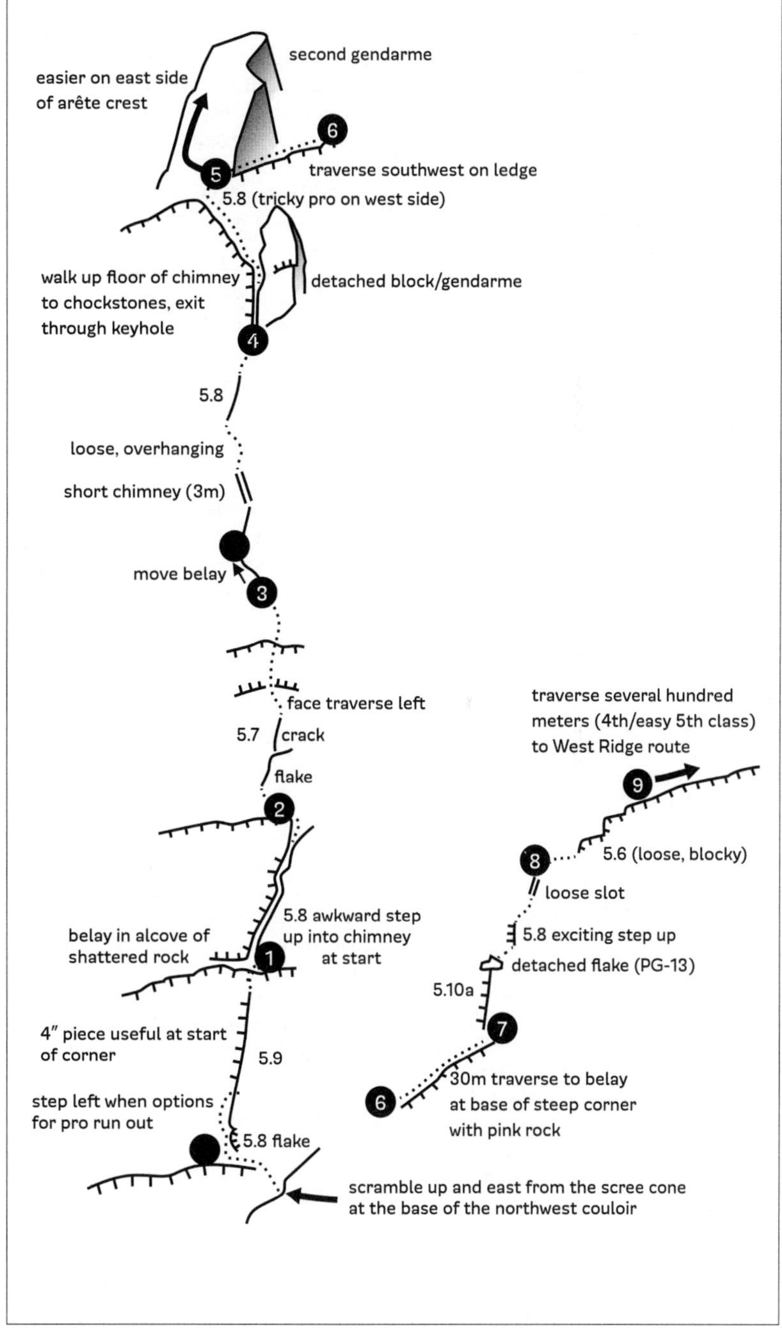

FIGURE 2-36. Mount Wister, Northwest Arête *(Route 10)*, IV, 5.9

crack, followed by a short chimney. The pitch continues up steep and loose terrain to a 5.8 crack that is climbed to the base of a large chimney. The chimney is formed by the huge detached block or gendarme on the ridge crest. For the fifth pitch, walk up the floor of the chimney to some chockstones and exit through a "keyhole." Once through this feature, climb up through steep terrain on the west side of the ridge (5.8, tricky to protect) to a belay at the base of the second gendarme (this one is prominent when viewed from Lake Taminah).

A large ledge (loose rock on it) leads out to the southwest toward the West Ridge route, which is where this author went. Instead of taking the ledge, it is possible at this point to pass the gendarme in two leads, either by climbing up and right and then regaining the crest at the first possible crack or by staying on its eastern side (recommended); this would likely involve 5.7–5.8 climbing and then several hundred meters of 4th- and easy 5th-class climbing to where the arête joins the west ridge. One can then scramble around to the south side of the west summit and up to the main summit of the peak. At least one party has reported a steep 5.9+ finger crack on the next-to-last pitch and then a steep corner followed by a few A1 moves to yet another finger crack on the final lead. This depends on where one goes, of course, but difficult, loose climbing is prevalent on the west side of the arête. Descend via the northeast couloir (see *Route 5*). **Gear:** For protection take a set of stoppers, a double rack of cams, and one 4" piece. A few micro cams are useful as well.

ROUTE 11. NORTHWEST COULOIR. II, 5.7, A1. First ascent August 26, 1968, by William Chadwick and Wallace Hunter. (See *Figure 2-32.*) This is the large snow couloir that bounds the west edge of the north face of Mount Wister. At its base is one of the finest talus cones in the range. From the meadow in Avalanche Canyon west of Lake Taminah, ascend the talus (or snow) cone leading to the entrance of the couloir. Conditions in the couloir will depend on the season. Apparently, there is quite a bit of loose rock in the couloir when the snow is gone, which is fairly typical throughout the range. In early season two snow pitches bring one to a prominent overhang that is passed on the left (5.7, A1). The next 200m–250m of snow climbing may contain ice patches in late season. Beyond where the couloir splits, continue straight up as it narrows and then traverse right off to the west ridge and follow *Route 1* to the summit.

ROUTE 12. NORTHWEST FACE. II, 5.1 to 5.7. First descent August 16, 1931, by Fritiof Fryxell; first ascent July 19, 1960, by Charles and Cora Sanders. There are several lines of varying difficulty on the northwest face of Mount Wister, which lies between the west ridge and the ridge that forms the western edge of the northwest couloir (see *Route 11*); sooner or later all these lines join the upper west ridge. A portion of this face contains smooth, sound rock. From Snowdrift Lake, scramble more or less directly up toward the west summit until reaching a break in the ridge west of the northwest couloir. The first-ascent party traversed south onto the upper west ridge after ascending a narrow chimney. In early season, the small gully or chimney that forms the upper continuation of the northwest couloir can be followed, mostly on snow, to gain the upper west ridge. Or one can cross this gully and ascend five pitches of crack and face climbing to gain the uppermost west ridge at the top of the northwest arête (see *Route 10*). In early season the lower portion of this face is a moderate-angle snowfield.

PEAK 10,960+ (WANDA PINNACLE)

(0.3 mi E of Mount Wister)
Map: Grand Teton

Rarely climbed, this peak consists of a group of three pinnacles on the east ridge of Mount Wister. The USGS quadrangle map shows that the highest pinnacle is sufficiently separated from Mount Wister to deserve "peak" status. The unofficial name, Wanda Pinnacle, was given by the second-ascent party in 1955. The most westerly of the three pinnacles is the most difficult.

ROUTE 1. WEST RIDGE. I, 5.1. First recorded ascent August 4, 1954, by Richard Long, Tim Bond, and Mike Schoeman. This tower probably had been ascended at an earlier date—a piton that was not placed by the 1954 party was found in 1955. The climb begins at the broad col that separates this pinnacle from the main (east) summit of Mount Wister. The rock is somewhat loose.

ROUTE 2. SOUTH RIDGE. II, 5.6. First ascent July 10, 1994, by Paul Horton and Ryan Hokanson. This route ascends the south ridge of the central and highest of the group of pinnacles on the east ridge of Mount Wister. From the south fork of Avalanche Canyon, work up to the emergence of this ridge from the broken slopes. An initial roped pitch is followed by about 120m of scrambling. Three pitches of cracks and slabs on excellent rock that stay generally right of the ridge crest bring one to 3.0 climbing that leads to the summit. The peculiarly shaped western pinnacle was also climbed via a 5.6 pitch of good rock on the east face.

NESSMUK SPIRE (9,600+)

(1.1 mi ENE of Buck Mountain)
Map: Grand Teton

This minor summit, or buttress, is located 0.3 mile north-northeast of Peak 10,696 and is shown on the map as an isolated contour of 9,600 feet.

ROUTE 1. EAST FACE. I, 5.4. First ascent August 31, 1971, by Robert Weinreb and Barry Voight. Ascend the south fork of Avalanche Canyon past the small lake (sometimes a swamp or even dry), following the stream up toward the bench below the north face of Peak 10,696. On the right (west), just before reaching this bench, is the east face of Nessmuk Spire.

BROKEN ARROW SPIRE (8,640+)

(1.6 mi E of Mount Wister)
Map: Grand Teton

This distinct pinnacle lies on the south side of Avalanche Canyon, about 0.3 mile east of the forks of the canyon. It is separated from the remainder of the mountain above by large gullies on both the east and west sides but has only a small notch. It can be seen from the valley if the light is just right. In 1979, the name Abandoned Pinnacle was also applied to this tower.

ROUTE 1. WEST RIDGE. I, 5.4. First ascent August 7, 1968, by Paul Myhre and Eric Stern. This moderate route was climbed using four nuts.

ROUTE 2. ALONE. II, 5.9. First ascent July 7, 1979, by Mike Munger. This route starts in a right-facing corner (5.4) between two dead trees at the base of the north face of the spire, leading past a thornbush patch to another dead tree. Traverse left toward a grassy crack that angles up and right. Climb a finger crack (5.9) to the right of the grassy crack, until one can traverse into the main crack at a bush, then proceed up this 4-inch crack to a belay stance at its top. The next lead is difficult straight up (5.9) but can be climbed on easier rock (5.5) slightly to the left to a stance below an overhang. Climb this overhang (5.9) and then a finger crack (5.8) above, just right of a second overhang, to a ledge. The next pitch goes left, past a 5.9 overhang, and up a right-facing corner to a tree at a belay ledge. The final lead is 4th class, past trees, ending at a tree left of and near the summit.

ROUTE 3. LOST. II, 5.10. First ascent July 13, 1979, by Mike Munger and Buck Tilley. This route lies to the right of *Route 2*. Take the same start, through the thornbush patch to the dead tree. Instead of traversing left here, climb the 5.8 right-facing corner that slants up and right from the tree for a full ropelength to a belay ledge. The final section below the ledge is a difficult headwall (5.10). The second lead moves left up over an overhang (5.9) and up a left-facing corner (5.7) to a belay just above a detached flake. The next pitch (5.8) goes up and left into a corner left of a roof to the same ledge that was reached on *Route 2* after the second overhang. From this ledge, instead of traversing left, one can climb a 5.6 broken corner to the next belay ledge and then take easier rock (5.4) straight up toward the summit.

AVALANCHE CANYON (NORTH FORK), NORTH SIDE ROCK CLIMBS (10,480+)

Map: Grand Teton

Rising directly above and north of the east end of Lake Taminah in Avalanche Canyon is a set of buttresses containing excellent rock. These buttresses have the advantage of a relatively short approach and can be seen from the valley in morning or evening light. The routes are presented here from west to east. (Note: The route lines are approximate in *Figure 2-37*.)

ROUTE 1. FLYING BUTTRESS, GOOD FOR THE SOUL. II, 5.7. First ascent June 18, 1993, by Tom Lohuis and Bill Stanley. (See *Figure 2-37*.) Separated from and west of the main central buttress (see *Route 2*) is a flying buttress upon which this climb is located. The main feature of the route, a prominent right-facing corner, is obvious from below. The route begins 9m to the west of several pine trees, and the first pitch goes up the blocky face, heading for a ledge below three left-facing flakes. Climb any one of the flakes to a shallow left-facing corner and continue for 9m until the main right-facing corner is in sight. The second pitch works up the leftmost crack in the main corner until one can step right into a crack that skirts a small overhanging block (below a large roof). Climb left to the slot in the roof and jam on up (5.7), belaying 8m higher in a shallow corner. Ascend this corner to a small left-facing ramp that ends in a short, overhanging corner (5.7). After passing this obstacle, take the straightest line up to the flat ridge crest and belay. The fourth lead ascends a short headwall containing a jammed block. Work to the right around this block and run the rope out to a belay. From here the summit is easily reached. Descend the gully to the west back down to the base of the climb.

ROUTE 2. BLIND MAN'S BLUFF. III, 5.9. First ascent August 26, 1978, by Rich Perch, Yvon Chouinard, and Kent Lugbill. (See *Figure 2-37*.) Anyone familiar with Rich Perch, master of puns and wordplay, knows how this route got its name. Blind Man's Bluff ascends the central buttress, which is over 200m in height. The climb starts on the left part of the face of the buttress, but right (east) of the obvious gully that separates the flying buttress on the left from the main central section of the buttress. Scramble up about 100m of 3rd- and 4th-class rock and scree to

FIGURE 2-37. Avalanche Canyon, north side rock climbs, south aspect. (A) Flying Buttress, Good for the Soul *(Route 1)*, II, 5.7; (B) Blind Man's Bluff *(Route 2)*, III, 5.9; (C) County 5 *(Route 3)*, III, 5.8; (D) Yukon Jack Arête *(Route 5)*, II. 5.7

reach the steep section. After an initial 5.7 pitch, the next lead involves a short traverse left, followed by 5.9 climbing up a left-facing corner. The third lead passes over a small overhang to reach a ramp that diagonals down, from left to right, across the face of the buttress. Another 5.7 pitch above this ramp leads to a pedestal/ledge. The final lead (5.8) from the left end of this ledge goes up a beautiful straight-in crack, from the top of which the summit is easily reached. This is a good crack-and-overhang climb on golden Teton rock and is probably the best of these five routes.

ROUTE 3. COUNTY 5. III, 5.8. First ascent August 7, 2010, by Zac Harlow and Oliver Deshle. (See *Figure 2-37.*) This climb is located just to the east of Blind Man's Bluff *(Route 2)* on the central buttress. Much of this route could also be part of *Route 4*. Look for a small roof with a hand crack in the middle of it. **Pitch 1:** Start just to the right of the hand crack through the roof, following a ledge/crack system that leans from right to left and avoids the crack (5.8, 46m). **Pitch 2:** Climb up and right into a small left-facing corner that is climbed to its top, then continue up and left via face climbing that gets easier and leads to a belay (5.8, 70m). **Pitch 3:** Continue straight up via face and crack climbing for another long pitch (5.7, 70m). **Pitch 4:** Continue up, passing two trees. After passing the second tree, climb to the left to reach a left-facing corner and a belay at its top (5.6, 46m). Fourth-class climbing then leads to the top of the climb. To descend, follow the summit ridge back to the north and proceed down the west-facing couloir that takes one back to Lake Taminah.

ROUTE 4. LUGBILL-WHITE. III, 5.9. First ascent in late August 1978, by Kent Lugbill and Wendy White. This route follows the right (east) edge of the same central buttress as *Route 2*. While this route also contains about the same amount of climbing, including two good pitches (5.8 and 5.9), it is not as continuous because the steep rock is broken by low-angle sections.

ROUTE 5. YUKON JACK ARÊTE. II, 5.7. First ascent July 29, 1979, by George Montopoli and Bob Howard. (See *Figure 2-37.*) From the talus slope below Lake Taminah, this sharp arête will be seen 300m above and to the west of a gully that is identifiable by a huge block that obstructs passage (this gully, known as the Nugget, is a sought-after ski and snowboard descent during the winter months). A dihedral can be seen on the right side of this arête from low in the talus slope. Proceed to Lake Taminah and climb up to the trees near the base of three buttresses located just east of the big talus slope beneath the south face of Cloudveil Dome. This climb is located on the left side of the third buttress to the east. Traverse in the trees back to the east to the west end of the easternmost buttress and look for a corner containing white rock. Start up the climb for 18m on the left side of this corner. The next pitch (5.7) goes up this fine dihedral through white quartz rock. The final lead goes up to a ramp leading left into an open book containing the crux overhang (5.7).

MATTERNOUGHT PEAK (11,360+)

(0.3 mi SE of the South Teton)
Map: Grand Teton

This peak is the prominent point above and northwest of Lake Taminah and about 0.3 mile southeast of the South Teton. It is surprising that the peak was overlooked for so many years, but the first-recorded-ascent party did find a Band-Aid can with no note on the summit. A well-defined col separates Matternought Peak from Gilkey Tower on the South Teton–Cloudveil Dome ridge.

Chronology

EAST COULOIR AND EAST RIDGE: July 25, 1960, George Hurley, Jean Tuomi
WEST COULOIR, NORTH RIDGE: July 25, 1960, George Hurley, Jean Tuomi (descent); August 16, 1972, Leigh Ortenburger, Irene Beardsley (Ortenburger) (ascent)
TAMINAH ARÊTE: August 29, 1976, Kent Lugbill, Jim Tate
var—July 12, 1979, Norm Larson, Dick Olmstead
DEM BONES: July 1994, Bill Alexander, Mason Reid
THE Z RIDGE: Summer 1996, Richard DuMais, Zaidee Huidekoper Fuller
LOS HUESOS: July 1, 2007, Aaron Gams, Brian Mulvihill
LAZY BONES: September 2, 2007, Trevor Bowman, Bryan Schmitz

ROUTE 1. WEST COULOIR, NORTH RIDGE. II, 4.0. First descent July 25, 1960, by George Hurley and Jean Tuomi; first ascent August 16, 1972, by Leigh Ortenburger and Irene Beardsley (Ortenburger). The cirque between Matternought Peak and the South Teton harbors an interesting small glacier and can be reached by contouring into the cirque from the east end of Snowdrift Lake or by climbing directly up from the meadow west of Lake Taminah. In either case the north col separating Matternought Peak from the South Teton–Cloudveil Dome ridge is easily attained via the western couloir. A short climb, bearing slightly left, is then required to reach the summit. For descent this route can be a tricky downclimb; it is much easier to rappel.

ROUTE 2. THE Z RIDGE. II, 5.7. First ascent in summer 1996, by Richard DuMais and Zaidee Huidekoper Fuller. This route could be used as a start for Taminah Arête *(Route 3)* and is located on the ridge directly below the beginning of that route. The climb begins in a chimney/gully system and follows this for a couple of pitches, eventually working up and east via corners and face climbing (5.6). Cross the prow of the ridge and follow it up over several steps in the ridge for another couple of pitches. Climb a final short, clean step followed by an airy traverse along the crest to the top for a total of six to seven pitches of climbing. For a much longer day continue up *Route 3*; otherwise, descend the slopes to the west back down to Lake Taminah.

ROUTE 3. TAMINAH ARÊTE. III, 5.9. First ascent August 29, 1976, by Kent Lugbill and Jim Tate. (See *Figure 2-38.*) From the west end of Lake Taminah one can see the top of this long and spectacular ridge, and the climbing matches the appearance. The rock is solid and enjoyable, and the pitch featuring quartz knobs is exceptional. Ascend the talus slope diagonally to the northwest and angle up through a break in the first rock step. Traverse west beneath huge overhanging arches in the next rock step, which eventually leads to the toe of the arête. A more straightforward approach can be made from Snowdrift Lake, where a simple traverse on tree-covered ledges provides access to the base of the arête. There are at least two options for getting started on this ridge, but the route basically stays very close to the ridge crest, providing considerable exposure down the sheer west face at times. Scramble up over easy, blocky rock on the east side of the arête to the base of the first pitch, which goes up the orange rock wall above via a 5.9 crack that leads to the top of the first tower. For the

FIGURE 2-38. Matternought Peak, Taminah Arête *(Route 3)*, III, 5.9

second pitch, climb along the ridge crest over blocks for 30m (5.5).

The next lead, the Quartz Crystal Pitch, is quite spectacular if one stays on or near the edge of the arête. This face contains numerous huge quartz crystals that provide steep and exciting climbing, easier than might be expected (5.6), for nearly 50m. From the belay, climb up to the Golden Ladder—a short (6m) 5.7 section without protection that features great climbing on golden knobs. This fourth pitch ends at a sharp notch, at which point 60m of 4th-class climbing leads to the final pitches. The sixth pitch climbs either the right side of a pedestal feature (5.6) or a chimney (5.9) nearer the crest of the ridge to the west. From the top of the sixth pitch, 120m of scrambling leads to the summit of Matternought Peak.

Descent from the summit can be made by going down *Route 7*, which leads back to Avalanche Canyon. This descent route is treacherous, especially when wet, because it involves downclimbing slabs and some rotten rock—take care! **Gear:** Protection consists of a regular rack with a set of stoppers and cams to 3". **Note:** This route has been done in conjunction with Sunrise Ridge on Gilkey Tower *(Gilkey Tower, Route 2)*—a combination that provides a great day in the mountains.

Variation: III, 5.8. First ascent July 12, 1979, by Norm Larson and Dick Olmstead. From Lake Taminah, take the gully leading toward the west side of the main south buttress of Matternought Peak; as one approaches this buttress, it is seen to have a triangular south face. Climb the west side of the buttress, which is steep in the bottom section. This variation contains a total of five pitches, two of which were 5.8 in difficulty. The rock on this variation is solid.

ROUTE 4. LAZY BONES. III, 5.10b. First ascent September 2, 2007, by Trevor Bowman and Bryan Schmitz. (See *Figure 2-39.*) This is reported to be an excellent climb on good rock, comparable to Dem Bones *(Route 6)*; see that route for approach details. Begin the climb approximately 30m left of the rosy alcove mentioned in *Route 6*, on a beautiful face split by a thin crack. **Pitch 1:** Go up the thin crack to the point where the difficulty increases significantly (after about 15m), then traverse left (described as "cruxy and rather spicy") to a blunt arête that is climbed to a small ledge. Belay here or continue up cracks to a stembox that is climbed via a finger crack to a large belay ledge (5.10b, 70m). **Pitch 2:** Face climb up a slab to the right of a vegetated crack to a right-facing corner, then continue up to the large ledge that runs across the face and belay (5.8, 30m). **Pitch 3:** Ascend an obvious right-facing corner via a hand/fist crack to a belay on small ledges (5.6, 70m). **Pitch 4:** Go up via easy 5th-class climbing through a section of white rock to a belay ledge below the final headwall (5.4, 30m). **Pitch 5:** This route finishes to the left of Dem Bones on the splintered arête of the brown headwall above. Discontinuous cracks lead to a difficult bulge (some loose blocks) and then the top of the climb (5.10a, 24m). See *Route 6* for descent information. **Gear:** For protection take a set of stoppers

FIGURE 2-39. Matternought Peak, Lazy Bones *(Route 4)*, III, 5.10b

FIGURE 2-40. Matternought Peak, Los Huesos *(Route 5)*, III, 5.10+

with an emphasis on the medium size; a double set of cams to 2"; and singles from 2.5" to 3.5". The first-ascent party used a 70m rope. (Sources: First-ascent party; Mountain Project)

ROUTE 5. LOS HUESOS. III, 5.10+. First ascent July 1, 2007, by Aaron Gams and Brian Mulvilhill. (See *Figure 2-40.*) Los Huesos ("the Bones") is located between the other two routes on this face; see Dem Bones *(Route 6)* for approach details. Begin by scrambling up to the base of the leftmost of three right-leaning, left-facing dihedrals. Continue up easy 5th class to a blocky belay alcove. The second pitch begins with a step up on a black knob (5.10-) and then climbs left to a left-facing corner (offwidth/stem, 3.5" piece useful) that is ascended to a flake (5.8 hand traverse left), followed by 5.6 wandering to a belay on the big ledge that cuts across the face (some loose rock here). For the third pitch, start by climbing a short left-facing corner to its top and exit right (5.8, awkward). Continue up and right to a 5.9 roof, followed by 5.10- moves to a crack that is climbed to its exit onto easier terrain; the exit involves a big reach to a horn (5.10+, protected with small nuts). Continue up this easy 5th-class terrain to a belay at the base of a flaring crack. The fourth pitch goes up this crack (5.8 flared hands) to join Dem Bones at the base of the awkward ramp below the final head-wall. This route finishes with a 5.9+ crack (fingers to hands) located just right of the final straight-in crack of Dem Bones. The Dem Bones finish is reported to be better, however. See *Route 6* for descent information. **Gear:** For protection take a set of stoppers, two sets of cams to 2", and one 3.5" piece for the second pitch. (Source: first-ascent party)

ROUTE 6. DEM BONES. III, 5.10. First ascent in July 1994, by Bill Alexander and Mason Reid. (See *Figures 2-41* and *2-42.*) This was the first of the three routes that are now established on the buttress located on the southeast side of Matternought Peak. The same approach is used for all of these excellent climbs: Proceed up Avalanche Canyon to Lake Taminah and then continue up the grassy slope past Blind Man's Bluff *(Avalanche Canyon [North Fork], North Side Rock Climbs, Route 2)*. Look for a gully that leads up to the large ledge at the base of the obvious triangular face above. A small "rosy alcove," composed

FIGURE 2-41. Matternought Peak, Dem Bones *(Route 6)*, III, 5.10

scramble around corner and then across slabs to descent gully
7
5.10 hands
6 belay behind block
5.6 awkward ramp/ledge
5
flake/slot
flake
5.9 flared hands
4 pod
big roof
5.9+
5.7 hands
bigger roof
21m 3
pedestal
5.8 **LB**
2 64m
easy 5th class
5.9
slab
easy 5th class
ST 1
5.8
flake
biggest roof
stem
rosy alcove
3rd-class gully

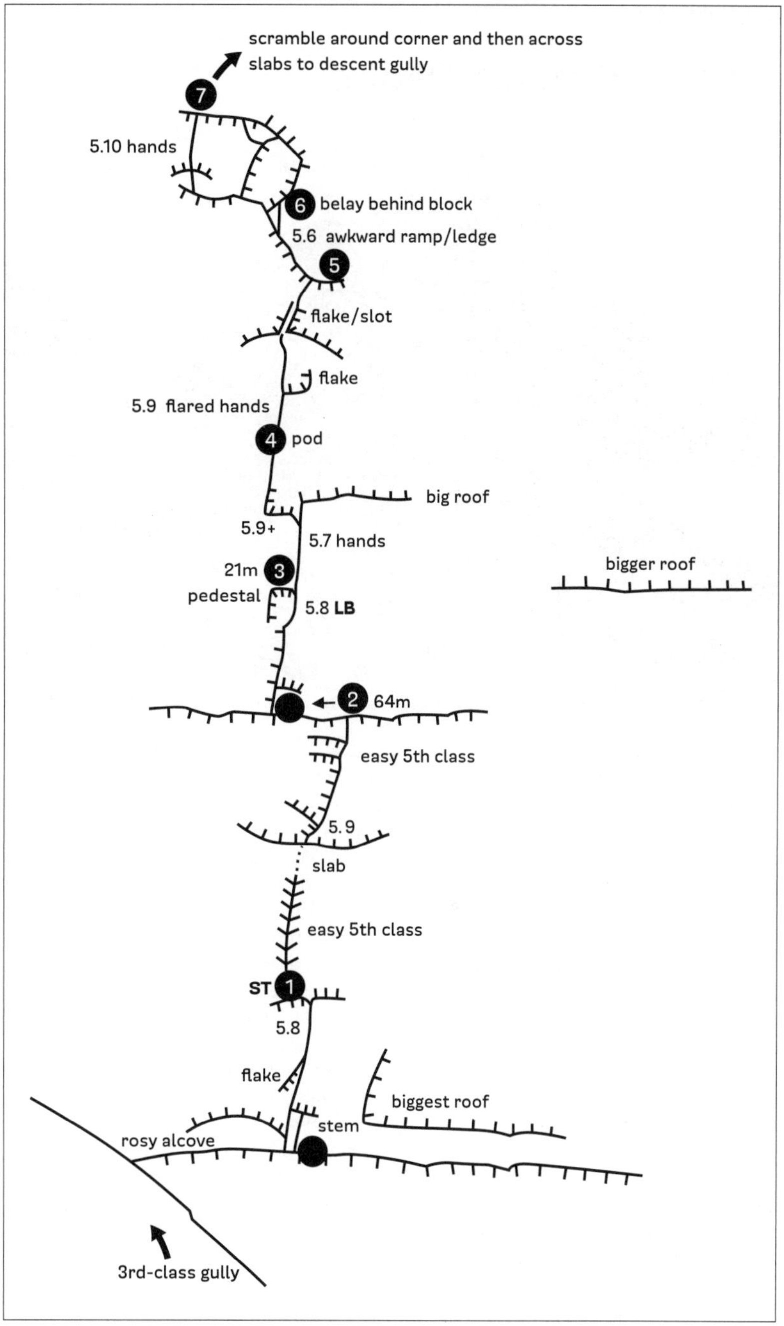

FIGURE 2-42. Matternought Peak, Dem Bones *(Route 6)*, III, 5.10

of shattered pink rock and situated just to the left of the largest roof near the bottom of the face, is the reference point for the start of the climb. Allow approximately four hours for this approach. *Figure 2-42* delineates the details of the climb. To descend, scramble around the corner at the top, then continue across slabs to a descent gully. One could also continue up the ridge crest to the summit of Matternought Peak. This is a recommended climb in an outstanding setting.

ROUTE 7. EAST COULOIR AND EAST RIDGE. II, 5.1. First recorded ascent July 25, 1960, by George Hurley and Jean Tuomi. From the north fork of Avalanche Canyon along the north shore of Lake Taminah, proceed up the considerable talus slope toward the cirque under the south side of Spalding Peak and Cloudveil Dome. Matternought Peak lies just west of this cirque. Take the east couloir to its intersection with the moderate east ridge. Some wet slabs, which may hold snow, will be met before reaching the col in the east ridge. Use care in this section. Once on the ridge two roped pitches will be found, followed by scrambling to the summit. The first-ascent party descended the north ridge and utilized a 30m rappel for descent to the col. See *American Alpine Journal* 12, no. 2 (1961): pp. 373–77.

SECTION 3

Garnet Canyon Peaks

Middle Teton from the Southeast

Garnet Canyon

Located in the center of the range, Garnet Canyon is the epicenter from which most of the Teton mountaineering activity radiates. It forms the principal approach to the three Tetons—the South Teton, Middle Teton, Grand Teton—as well as many other central peaks, pinnacles, and rock climbs. Every summer a few thousand climbers camp at one of several sites in the canyon. Because of the impact of this volume, the National Park Service (NPS) has placed limitations on the numbers of campers at these sites, and permits must be obtained. The Lower Saddle (11,600+) between the Middle Teton and the Grand Teton is considered by many to be the best camping area for climbs of the Grand Teton by standard routes. The advantages are a short summit day (2,200 feet/670m) and commonly a colorful sunset; the disadvantages are a paucity of good campsites, little protection from the elements, and an almost continuous cold wind from the southwest. Other camping areas are discussed below. The Garnet Canyon approach to the Lower Saddle is standard, but a completely different (and more difficult) route via Dartmouth Basin (see *Cascade Canyon, South Fork* in Section 8) can be used for either ascent or descent.

Access to Garnet Canyon begins at the Lupine Meadows trailhead: turn west off Teton Park Road at the Lupine Meadows junction (about 0.7 mile south of South Jenny Lake Junction), cross the bridge over Cottonwood Creek, and continue 1.5 miles (west and then south) on the dirt road that leads across Lupine Meadows to the parking area (6,732) at the beginning of the trail.

Approach to the Platforms and the Meadows: Follow signs to the end of the maintained trail at the creek in Garnet Canyon. The overall water quality in Garnet Canyon has experienced an unfortunate decline during the past few years, which corresponds directly to increased use. It is advisable to drink selectively here, and throughout the Teton Range for that matter. If starting from the American Alpine Club Climbers' Ranch, a small trail up Burned Wagon Gulch is used to join the Garnet Canyon trail in the vicinity of the first junction. This climbers' trail begins immediately west of the bridge across Cottonwood Creek on the access road to the ranch, heads north and passes the Lucas-Fabian Homestead on the west, and then turns due west up Burned Wagon Gulch. Proceed up this open valley, staying mostly on the right (north) side, and join the Garnet Canyon trail at or just below the first junction.

The flat area with trees just across the stream from the end of the trail is known as the Platforms (8,960) and it provides an excellent campsite; in the early years of the park there were tent platforms here used by trail crews. In early season this camping area will be covered with snow. The Platforms is a useful camping site for climbs of Nez Perce, Cloudveil Dome, the South Teton, and the Middle Teton, and for rock climbs on Disappointment Peak. However, other sites higher in the canyon are equally suitable and are somewhat closer to the peaks. In an effort to minimize the erosion caused by random climbers' trails, the NPS has improved a climbers' trail (unmaintained) from the end of the maintained trail at the Platforms to the Lower Saddle. This trail starts some 30 feet north of Garnet Creek among large boulders, stays north of the creek, and can be easily followed through the next section, a boulder field, to the Meadows (9,200). Much of the area immediately east of the Middle Teton where the canyon forks was covered by morainal material from a landslide in 1951; over the decades it has recovered only some of the original features that led to the name, the Meadows, for this area. The vegetation here is fragile, so use care not to disturb the plants and flowers. Recovery is very slow at these altitudes.

North Fork (to the Caves and the Lower Saddle): See *Figure 6-1* in Section 6 for a visual of this part of the approach. The main features of the north fork of Garnet Canyon are the initial headwall (above the Meadows) containing Spalding Falls; the Petzoldt Caves (10,100); the Middle Teton Glacier moraine; the final headwall; and the Lower Saddle at the head of the canyon. (**Note:** Described here is the standard route to the Lower Saddle as used in midseason or later; in early season a different route, described below, is strongly advised because of the danger inherent in crossing the snow slopes above the Caves.)

Follow the NPS climbers' trail up from the Meadows, taking the steep switchbacks leading to the north up the talus to the right (east) of Spalding Falls, then through the trees, and finally back west to the Caves. At the Caves there is an important campsite just above the highest trees above Spalding Falls. Adequate protection from the weather is available for about six persons. In very early season considerable snow will be found here. The Caves is one of the three principal camping areas for Grand Teton ascents, and those who wish to trade the rigors of Lower Saddle camping for a noticeably longer summit day (3,700 feet/1,130m) will find the Caves a good compromise.

From the Caves take the NPS trail as it zigzags almost straight up the long slope above the Caves toward some scrub pines. When very near the base of Fairshare Tower, which looms above, turn left (south) to stay on the NPS trail and make a nearly horizontal traverse to reach the lower end of the conspicuous Middle Teton Glacier moraine that runs down the center of the upper canyon floor from the Lower Saddle. Do not take the diagonal trails that will be seen traversing out to the left (south) from above the Caves. While slightly shorter than the NPS trail, these will involve, during much of the year, one or more traverses across steep snow slopes, some of which have poor runouts and moats. These can and should be avoided by taking the trail straight above the Caves, as already described. On the moraine itself several campsites will be found; this Moraines camping zone is another suitable alternative to the Lower Saddle. Although the sites are not as attractive as those at the Caves, they do provide a shorter summit day.

The narrow crest of the moraine is then followed to the upper headwall beneath the saddle. A fixed rope (the only one in the range) will be seen off to the right (north) leading up the usually wet slabs and cliff, providing assistance on this headwall. From the top of the fixed rope the trail traverses left (south) and up along the top of the headwall to reach the lowest portion of the saddle. *Use great caution* with the loose rubble in this area, as rocks kicked off here will go over the headwall and the chances are very good that other climbers will be just below. On the saddle itself, where small high-altitude tundra plants are found, use care to stay on the designated trail and step on gravel or rocks to preserve these fragile and beautiful flowering plants.

Early in the season the fixed rope may be covered by snow and ice; in this case, climb directly up the moderately steep snow couloir in the center of the headwall. This will require the careful use of an ice axe. For those experienced in the art of glissading, this couloir makes a fast route of descent from the Lower Saddle, but it is not recommended after the middle of the season when crevasses open up and boulders appear in the runout slope at the bottom of the couloir. As an alternative to following the crest of the moraine to the final headwall, walk along the flat glacier to the south of the moraine. This will not be as fast as the moraine crest except in early season when the glacier is covered with snow.

For early-season ascents, when the entire canyon is covered with snow down to the vicinity of the Platforms, the usual route up to the Caves and across the slope above to the lower end of the moraine is *not* recommended. Much or all of this long slope will be covered with snow and, in taking the shortest line, many climbers erroneously make an upward, diagonal, and dangerous traverse on moderately steep snow to reach the moraine. Most of this snow slope has no runout and ends in a substantial cliff band—the lower headwall that contains Spalding Falls. Numerous serious, even fatal, accidents have occurred here. Experience with ice-axe self-arrest or with snow belaying is strongly recommended before attempting this section of the approach to the Lower Saddle. When these dangerous conditions are present, the preferred route is to climb from the west end of the Meadows directly up the moderately steep snow slopes next to the east cliffs of the Middle Teton to get past the first headwall and gain the Middle Teton Glacier moraine. This, too, will require the knowledge of how to use an ice axe, but it has the advantage of being nearly straight up rather than diagonal. If one is ascending or descending this portion of the route early in the day before the sun has softened the surface, crampons will make the climbing easier and safer, but they are not essential on this approach to the Lower Saddle. Kicking or cutting steps in the snow will suffice, if done with care. When the snow is gone, this alternative near the Middle Teton is not recommended because the morainal material here is very loose.

Bear-proof food storage boxes have been installed at nearly all of the camping spots in Garnet Canyon, and there are a few metal poles for hanging food and packs at the Lower Saddle. This may change, however. In many other areas of the backcountry of the park, boxes have been removed and a switch to bear-proof cannisters (issued by NPS) or Ursacks has taken place. In any case, take food storage seriously! Not only will this prevent bears from getting a food reward but it will deter the voracious marmots and other creatures that will chew right into a tent for tasty morsels left behind.

South Fork: Little description is required for the route from the Meadows to the saddle (11,360+) between the Middle and South Tetons. Much of this section is an extended boulder and talus field. There are few routefinding problems, and the difficulty of the snow slopes is moderate; however, an ice axe is recommended, especially in early season. For those experienced in glissading, there are two steep snow couloirs near the Middle Teton. In late season a minimal climbers' trail beginning at the Meadows leads up toward the saddle at the head of the south fork. There are very few usable campsites in this fork of the canyon, but there are two or three grassy benches providing flat spaces as well as a small site at the saddle itself. See *Figure 3-1* for an overview of the peaks in this region.

SHADOW PEAK (10,725)

Map: Grand Teton

This attractive small peak, while infrequently climbed, is a common sight for those who traverse into Garnet Canyon along the trail. Shadow Peak lies on the eastern margin of the Teton Range, protruding from the southeastern base of Nez Perce. Fritiof Fryxell, who named the peak, described it this way in his 1930 report to the park superintendent concerning place names in Grand Teton National Park: "A prominent spur which, in the afternoon, lies in the shadow of the large adjacent mountain, Nez Perce Peak." The high cirque just north of the peak is a beautiful and relatively wild

FIGURE 3-1. South Teton to Nez Perce, southeast aspect overview

place, compared to the heavily traveled Garnet Canyon. Shadow Peak consists of a long ridge with many points of nearly equal elevation, and the true summit is not easily found by the casual climber. The only certain way of reaching the summit is to climb them all, and this has seldom been done.

Chronology

EAST RIDGE: June 26, 1927, Phil Smith, Dorothea Marston
var—**DAY-OF-REST PINNACLE:** August 17, 1949, Ray Van Aken, George B. Harr, Christine Cole
NORTHWEST COULOIR: September 1, 1941, Judy Cameron (descent); June 21, 1955, John and Jean Fonda (ascent)
NORTH FACE: July 24, 1950, Robert and Doris Merriam, Leigh Ortenburger
WEST RIDGE: July 20, 1955, John Lowry, George Ewing
SOUTHEAST FACE: September 3, 1963, Ted Vaill, Hank Janes
REESE-WILSON: July 12, 1967, Rick Reese, Ted Wilson
var—September 23, 1979, Rich Troy, Tom Newman

ROUTE 1. WEST RIDGE. II, 5.1. First ascent July 20, 1955, by John Lowry and George Ewing; first descent August 27, 1960, by Ronald Gibbs and Thomas Smyth. From the Platforms in Garnet Canyon ascend the right (west) talus cone leading up to the bench above the south walls of the canyon. From this bench enter the cirque between Shadow Peak and the east ridge of Nez Perce. Contour around in a southwesterly direction to the col separating the two peaks. Start climbing eastward along the summit ridge. The first large tower, the most difficult one, is climbed via a 25m lead up jam cracks on its southwest face. The highest point is either the third tower east of the col or the second, depending on how the count is made. After gaining the summit, one can continue the west-to-east traverse, but steep western faces of more towers will be encountered. The Knight, a spectacular monolith about 4.5m high, is reached during the eastward scramble along the ridge crest. It was climbed for the first time by Lowry and Ewing, who used small holds on its west face.

ROUTE 2. SOUTHEAST FACE. II, 5.6. First ascent September 3, 1963, by Ted Vaill and Hank Janes. From a point about 1.3 miles up Avalanche Canyon (see *Avalanche Canyon* in Section 2), ascend the large couloir with an intermittent stream on the southeast slope of Shadow Peak. About three-quarters of the way up the couloir, cut diagonally up and left (northwest) to the base of the southeast face. This face guards the direct southeast approach to the eastern portion of the Shadow Peak ridge; the couloir below the right (east) edge of this face leads to the main col in the east ridge, described in *Route 3*. Near the center of the face, scramble 60m up a couloir (filled with loose rock) to a shallow cave, where water will usually be found. Climb directly up the 5.1 face above the cave. The second pitch goes around to the right and up a vertical 8m wall (5.4) to a 1m-wide ledge. From this ledge ascend a 5.6 open book formed by the face itself and a smooth, square pillar on the right. Once above this pitch scramble some 90m up and west to the summit ridge; work west along this ridge to the summit or, if short on time or perseverance, to the highest convenient point. The Day-of-Rest Pinnacle (see *Route 3*) will be east of the point at which the summit ridge is reached. See *American Alpine Journal* 14, no. 1 (1964): p. 188.

ROUTE 3. ▲ EAST RIDGE. I, 4.0. First ascent June 26, 1927, by Phil Smith and Dorothea Marston. The long, tree-covered ridge leading toward Shadow Peak from Bradley Lake is easily ascended to the high point (10,160+) east-northeast of the main summit ridge. This point overlooks the cirque that is north of Shadow Peak and east of Nez Perce. Descend to the col in the east ridge, where the significant climbing begins. Above the col climb the ridge for a couple of ropelengths, generally staying left (south) of the crest. To reach the true summit of Shadow Peak most easily, contour around the south side of the walls guarding the first high point, the Day-of-Rest Pinnacle (see the following variation), and then continue west to the summit. Two or three rappels down the steep west faces of the intervening towers may be desired by parties making the complete traverse to the highest point.

Variation: **DAY-OF-REST PINNACLE.** II, 4.0. First ascent August 17, 1949, by Ray Van Aken, George B. Harr, and Christine Cole. This party reached the main col in the east ridge of Shadow Peak from the cirque to the north (see *Route 1*). To gain this col, ascend the snow couloir leading east out of the cirque; an ice axe is recommended. Follow the ridge to a rotten gendarme; make a small detour off the ridge to the left (south) and continue along the south side of the ridge crest to the summit of the first tower, the Day-of-Rest Pinnacle. The highest point of Shadow Peak, which lies well to the west, was not reached by the party who pioneered this variation. It is possible to descend either north or south (easier) off the ridge crest, thus bypassing the steep west face of this pinnacle, before continuing west toward the true summit. **Time:** 6 hours from Jenny Lake; 4⅔ hours from the Platforms.

ROUTE 4. NORTH FACE. II, 5.6, A1. First ascent July 24, 1950, by Robert and Doris Merriam and Leigh Ortenburger. To reach this route, take the same approach as for *Route 1* to the cirque just below this face. A short snow tongue leads up to the face almost directly below the summit of the Day-of-Rest Pinnacle (see *Route 3*). From the east end of this snow tongue, scramble about 50m up and slightly left to the base of the first pitch. Climb 9m up to the right (west) to an overhanging flake and then back to the left another 9m to a belay position on a 1m-wide downsloping ledge. A crack leads up from the east end of this ledge, which required aid on the first ascent. About 9m up this crack a large, loose slab will be encountered. The next pitch is a tricky horizontal traverse back to the right (west) for about 12m. A series of chimneys then leads left (east) up to the notch between the rotten gendarme on the east ridge and the summit.

Instead of climbing out on the east side of the peak (which one can do easily), traverse right (west) along a wide, horizontal ledge back onto the north face. Climb directly up to the summit from this ledge. Some loose rock will be found on this last section. The final pitch comes out on the Day-of-Rest Pinnacle, which is the culmination of the north face. The highest point of Shadow Peak lies to the west. **Time:** 10 hours from Jenny Lake. See *American Alpine Journal* 9, no. 2 (1955): pp. 147–49.

ROUTE 5. REESE-WILSON. III, 5.7. First ascent July 12, 1967, by Rick Reese and Ted Wilson. This distinct north face route starts from the same point as *Route 4*—the eastern end of the snow tongue below the main north face. Instead of climbing up and left, this route goes directly up the nose of the face for about 1m and then cuts to the right on an upward traverse for about 60m to a very large flake that forms a chimney. Just left of this flake climb straight up the short and very steep wall (5.7), then continue on easier rock, which is steep and has no cracks, for 52m (5.4) to a poor belay spot that offers no means of anchoring. (**Note:** With a 70m rope, it may be possible to bypass this stance.) The next pitch is up a large depression in the face for about 35m to the base of an overhanging wall. Cut right (west) here up along a ledge (5.5) to complete the route onto the summit ridge. A total of six leads are involved in this route. The rock on the north face of Shadow Peak cannot be recommended due to poor protection and an abundance of loose rocks and flakes.

Variation: III, 5.7. First ascent September 23, 1979, by Rich Troy and Tom Newman. This variation, while similar to the original 1967 route, starts from the western of the two snow tongues or ramps below the north face. Take the ramp out (east) for about 30m and then turn directly upward until the summit ridge is reached. Five pitches of consistent difficulty are climbed, with much rotten rock being the main problem. The ridge crest is reached immediately to the right of the Knight, mentioned in *Route 1*.

ROUTE 6. ▲ NORTHWEST COULOIR. II, 5.1. First descent September 1, 1941, by Judy Cameron; first ascent June 21, 1955, by John and Jean Fonda. Ascend the cirque between Shadow Peak and Nez Perce toward the col separating the two peaks, as in *Route 1*, until this northwest couloir can be seen in its entirety. It is easily recognized as the large snow tongue (in early season or midseason) or distinct rotten couloir (late season) that leads to the summit ridge, just west of the main north face (see *Route 4*). Ascend this couloir to a point short of the vertical wall at its head, where ledges lead right (west) onto the summit ridge crest. The ridge is reached east of the true summit, so scramble west to the highest point.

NEZ PERCE (11,901)

Map: Grand Teton

This peak, with the exception of Shadow Peak, marks the end of what is actually the long east ridge of the South Teton and what has officially become the end of the Grand Traverse. Nez Perce is a prominent sight from Jenny Lake, where its outline in the early years of the park suggested to some the name "Howling Dog." Beyond its silhouette one may notice the appearance of a preacher or an alien, depending upon the way the snow patches on the northeast face melt out during the spring months. The official name comes directly from the Nez Perce (pronounced "nay pur-say") tribe of Native Americans who hunted in the region near the Teton Range.

Nez Perce consists of five peaks: the East Peak, the East Summit, the main summit, the West Summit, and the West Peak. Deep notches detach the East Peak and the East Summit, but only a shallow col distinguishes the West Summit from the main summit. The West Peak is separated by a conspicuous squarish notch. The two intersecting couloirs that bound the north face are distinctive features of this peak. These are called the Hourglass Couloirs, and they see much traffic from skiers during the winter months. The same is true for the couloir on the south side of the peak, the Sliver Couloir. The northwest side of the peak is the only side that offers easy access to the summit. The sharp west ridge has several small pinnacles, the highest of which apparently was not climbed (5.1) until August 15, 1952, when Richard Irvin claimed the first ascent. The view from the summit is one of the better ones in the park, showcasing not only the Garnet Canyon group but also the peaks to the south. Nez Perce is not an exceptionally long climb from the valley; with an early start, even the more difficult routes can be done in a day.

Chronology

NORTHWEST COULOIRS: July 5, 1930, Fritiof Fryxell, Phil Smith
var—**SOUTH COULOIR APPROACH:** June 30, 1934, Hans Fuhrer, Alfred Roovers
var—July 19, 1951, Whitney Borland, John Spradley, Robert Ellingwood, Alfred Bush, Charles Pavlick, Barbara Weber, Sayre Rodman, Erwin Jaggi
var—August 14, 1952, Willi Unsoeld, Don Kirkpatrick

EAST RIDGE: July 12, 1931, Robert Underhill, Fritiof Fryxell (ascent); August 9, 1940, Jack Durrance, Henry Coulter (descent)
var—**EAST HOURGLASS COULOIR:** July 3, 1933, Paul Petzoldt, Sterling Hendricks
var—**SLIVER COULOIR:** August 19, 1936, Fred and Irene Ayres, Allan Cameron
var—**EAST SUMMIT BYPASS:** September 9, 1938, Dr. John Buck, Raymond Creekmore, Donald Grant, O. O. Heard, William Kemper
var—**EAST SUMMIT, SOUTH FACE:** August 24, 1945, Joseph Stettner, John Speck
var—**EAST SUMMIT, SOUTHEAST FACE:** July 15, 1949, Jim Harrang, Robert Brooke, Pete Brown
var—**EAST PEAK, NORTH FACE:** September 4, 1951, Tony Soler, Art Lembeck, Ray Moore
var—**HERNANDO'S HIDEAWAY:** July 4, 1954, F. Keith Spencer, Richard Becker
var—**UPPER SOUTHEAST CHIMNEY:** August 9, 1959, William Glosser, Pat Purdy, Jay Edwards, Peg Fowler
var—**EAST PEAK, EAST HOURGLASS RIDGE:** July 9, 1962, Steven Derenzo, Peter Gardiner, Richard Goldstone, Frank Knight

SOUTHEAST FACE: July 21, 1935, Malcolm Smith

NORTH FACE: July 27, 1940, Jack Durrance, Fred Ayres, Henry Coulter (attempt); August 9, 1940, Jack Durrance, Henry Coulter
var—August 14, 1940, Edward McNeill, John A. McCown, Thomas L. Johnston, Thomson Edwards, Charles J. Webb
var—**WEST HOURGLASS COULOIR:** August 11, 1942, Orrin Bonney, Ernest Guild (ascent); August 16, 1951, Ed Keller, Bill Sloan, Bob Borbridge (descent)

DIRECT SOUTH RIDGE: July 3, 1954, Robert Merriam, William Buckingham, W. Edward Clark
var—Early July 1966, Paul Ledoux Jr., William Schipel
var—**GARNET TRAVERSE:** August 10, 1967, Jack Weicker, Leigh Ortenburger
var—**LOWER RIDGE:** July 18, 1969, Peter and Rosanne Cleveland
var—June 29, 1989, Keith Schultz, Jack Tcholske

SOUTH FACE: August 1, 1955, W. V. Graham Matthews, Mary Ann Matthews

SOUTHEAST COULOIR: September 3, 1960, Lloyd Arnesen, Victor Wylie
var—July 3, 1987, Bob Graham, Jack Bellorado

SOUTH-SOUTHWEST RIDGE: August 13, 1970, Leigh Ortenburger, Irene Beardsley (Ortenburger), David Coward

CHIEF JOSEPH BUTTRESS: July 31, 1988, Tom Turiano, Dan Powers

NORTH FACE, GUIDES' DISCOUNT: September 1999, Keith Cattabriga, Martin Vidak, Ray Warburton

WEST PEAK, SOUTH RIDGE: September 14, 2002, Paul Horton, Heather Paul

SUNSET FACE: July 5, 2003, Paul Horton, Charlie Thomas

CHIEF JOSEPH BUTTRESS, BULLOCK-PAGE: Date unknown (but pre-2021), Steve Bullock, Sam Page

CHIEF JOSEPH LEFT: 2021, Cody Evans, Casey Heerdt

ROUTE 1. ▲ NORTHWEST COULOIRS. II, 4.0. First ascent July 5, 1930, by Fritiof Fryxell and Phil Smith. (See *Figure 3-2*.) From the Lupine Meadows trailhead, take the Garnet Canyon trail to the Platforms. Continue upcanyon to the Meadows, the relatively flat bouldery area just east of the Middle Teton. From here climb talus or snow, depending on the season, toward the col between Nez Perce and Cloudveil Dome. The route lies on the flank of the west ridge, well north of the crest, so do not continue all the way to the col. Beyond the lower cliffs of Nez Perce, there are several shallow couloirs leading southeast. All of them can be climbed, but one of the central ones is easier although a bit difficult to find. There is much loose and unpleasant rock in this part of the climb. Scramble up broken ledges, traversing left (north) toward the slabs that lead out northward from the squarish notch between the West Summit and the small West Peak. This notch will now be about 100m off to the right. The usual route crosses these slabs and then traverses left (north) before turning up a series of cracks and chimneys that lead back toward the ridge west of the summit. Continue east along the narrow arête that connects this ridge with the true summit. If there is a choice, this route on Nez Perce is recommended for early season, because much of the loose rubble will be covered by snow.

To descend from the summit, follow the arête leading west and downclimb the north side of the ridge past the West Summit (this section is sometimes rappelled) to the main rappel point, where many old slings will be found. An 18m rappel (partly free) can be made from this point down to the squarish notch mentioned earlier; however, it is also a simple matter to downclimb carefully back around above the slabs. In early season the lower descent is facilitated by the long snow slope, which is excellent for those experienced in glissading. **Time:** 4¼ to 6 hours from Garnet Canyon; 6⅛ to 7½ hours from Jenny Lake. See *Appalachia* 18, no. 4 (December 1931): pp. 388–408, illus.;

FIGURE 3-2. Nez Perce, northwest aspect. (A) East Ridge (upper section; *Route 9*), II, 5.4; (B) Northwest Couloirs *(Route 1)*, II, 4.0

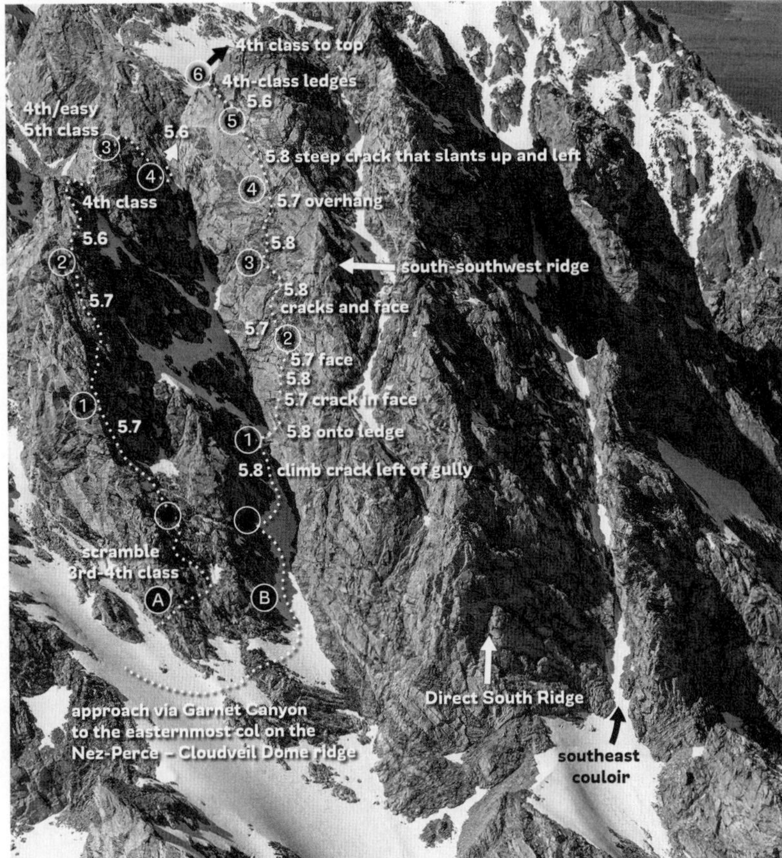

FIGURE 3-3. Nez Perce, south aspect. (A) West Peak, South Ridge *(Route 2)*, II, 5.7; (B) Sunset Face *(Route 3)*, III, 5.8

Chicago Mountaineering Club Newsletter 2, no. 6 (July–December 1948): pp. 2–3; *Chicago Mountaineering Club Newsletter* 5, no. 1 (January 1951): p. 5.

***Variation:* SOUTH COULOIR APPROACH.** II, 4.0. First ascent June 30, 1934, by Hans Fuhrer and Alfred Roovers. Although it has rarely been done, it is possible to reach the ridge between Cloudveil Dome and Nez Perce from the south by hiking up Avalanche Canyon and turning north up the large talus cone just below Shoshoko Falls. This party reached the west ridge of Nez Perce at a point east of the main col that lies close to Cloudveil Dome. By adroit selection of the proper southern couloir, one can attain the ridge at a secondary col about 0.2 mile west of the summit. From the ridge cut left (north) onto the northwest ledges and join the regular *Route 1* just below the slabs.

Variation: II, 4.0. First ascent July 19, 1951, by Whitney Borland, John Spradley, Robert Ellingwood, Alfred Bush, Charles Pavlick, Barbara Weber, Sayre Rodman, and Erwin Jaggi. From the squarish notch between the West Summit and the West Peak, it is possible to traverse left (first north, then east) all the way over to the east ridge above the East Summit and then finish the climb on the upper easy portions of that ridge (see *Route 9*).

Variation: II, 5.6. First ascent August 14, 1952, by Willi Unsoeld and Don Kirkpatrick. It is possible to climb a difficult crack directly up out of the squarish notch on the west ridge of Nez Perce. After a single lead, the rappel slings are passed, and one can then climb on the north side to the West Summit and follow the arête to the top.

ROUTE 2. WEST PEAK, SOUTH RIDGE. II, 5.7. First ascent September 14, 2002, by Paul Horton and Heather Paul. (See *Figure 3-3.*) This ridge is the one farthest west on the south aspect of Nez Perce. The route follows the ridge to the West Peak and continues to the prominent squarish notch, where it meets the 1952 Unsoeld-Kirkpatrick variation to *Route 1* and takes its crack to the summit. It's a pleasant climb on good rock.

Approach from the Meadows in Garnet Canyon, as in *Route 1*, but leave that route and scramble to the easternmost col on the ridge between Nez Perce and Cloudveil Dome. The col is well to the east of the sharp pinnacle on the ridge. From the col drop down scree and/or snow to the base of the route. Scramble up ledges for about 60m to the start of steeper rock. From there the first two very long leads ascend the steep part of the ridge, utilizing cracks a short way to the right of the crest. Belay options are plentiful. Then climb over or around the towers on the horizontal section of the ridge for three easier pitches, eventually descending a short distance to the squarish notch. Climb the nice pitch of the 1952 Northwest Couloirs variation and follow easy terrain to the summit.

ROUTE 3. SUNSET FACE. III, 5.8. First ascent July 5, 2003, Paul Horton and Charlie Thomas. (See *Figure 3-3.*) This steep southwest face lies beneath the West Summit, about 30m west of the main summit. In the evening the face catches sunlight long after most of the range has fallen into shadow, thus its name. A large, prominent dihedral slices up from left to right, dividing the wall into upper and lower sections. This route is more serious than its rating might indicate: the climbing is steep and continuous, and some of the rock on the lower section requires care.

Approach from Garnet Canyon, as in *Routes 1* and *2*. From the col drop down scree and/or snow to the gully at the base of the southwest face. Scramble up the gully and belay where it steepens. The first pitch goes up the gully's dirty rock to overhanging blocks, moves left to cleaner cracks in a face, and then becomes easy as the gully opens up again. The next lead initiates the climbing on the steep southwest face. Cross the gully and, after some tricky moves, go right on a ledge to attain a nice crack. Climb the crack and continue up faces and fractures to a belay. About 100m above, a band of overhangs cuts across the face. The next two pitches head for a weakness at the left end of the overhangs, surmounted rather easily, to reach a nice ledge on the outside corner formed by the major dihedral.

From the belay ledge on the outside corner, beautiful cracks can be seen slanting leftward across the headwall above. Cross the dihedral, go up a short chimney, and ascend the diagonal cracks to a belay, all in a very long pitch of fine, continuous climbing on excellent rock. The last pitch goes up a short face leading to 4th-class ledges heading up and left to join the west ridge and easy ground. The summit is a few minutes away. **Gear:** A 60m rope and extra medium pieces are recommended.

ROUTE 4. SOUTH-SOUTHWEST RIDGE. III, 5.6. First ascent August 13, 1970, by Leigh Ortenburger, Irene Beardsley (Ortenburger), and David Coward. (See *Figure 3-3.*) This ridge lies immediately west of the Direct South Ridge *(Route 5)* and leads to the West Summit about 30m west of the main summit. Use the same approach as for *Route 5*—from the Platforms in Garnet Canyon up into the cirque between Shadow Peak and Nez Perce. Traverse westward past the base of the Direct South Ridge and turn up the first gully leading north. Avoid the vertical beginning of this south-southwest ridge by climbing the large, obvious chimney on the west flank of the ridge. After three straightforward pitches, the chimney culminates in an overhang, which is passed by an awkward 6m pitch (5.6) on the left (west) side. The fifth lead, up a narrow chimney and out on the exposed face to the right, leads to the crest of the ridge. From this point it appears it would be possible to attack the remainder of the ridge directly on the ridge crest to the West Summit. This party, however, continued on 4th- and easy 5th-class rock for about 100m on the right (east) side of the crest to the shallow col between the West Summit and the main summit. This is an enjoyable climb on good rock.

ROUTE 5. DIRECT SOUTH RIDGE. III, 5.7+. First ascent July 3, 1954, by Robert Merriam, William Buckingham, and W. Edward Clark. (See *Figure 3-4.*) This route is generally considered to be the finest available on this peak, although *Route 3* may now compete for that title. Of the various ridges on the south side of Nez Perce, this is the one that leads directly to the summit. To approach this ridge, take the Garnet Canyon trail from the Lupine Meadows trailhead to the Platforms. Suitable camping areas for this route are the Platforms or the Meadows areas.

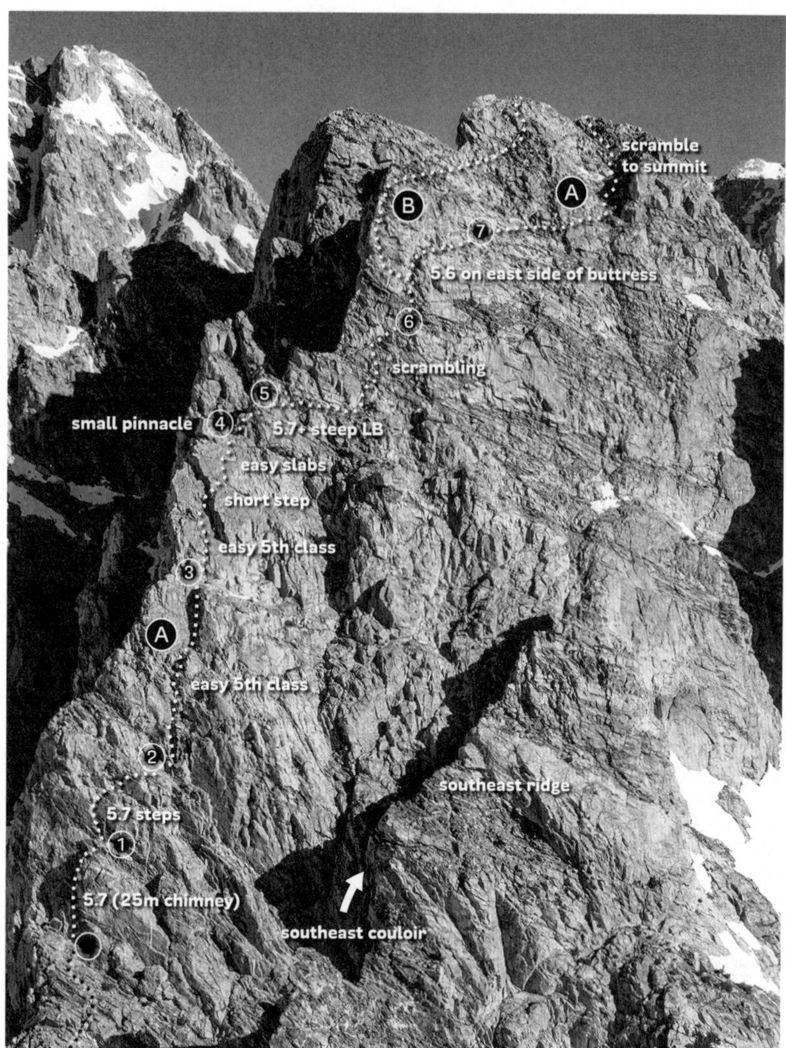

FIGURE 3-4. Nez Perce, south aspect. (A) Direct South Ridge *(Route 5)*, III, 5.7+; (B) Variation: Garnet Traverse, III, 5.8

Two major couloirs (either snow slopes or talus slopes, depending on the season) will be seen leading to gaps in the cliffs above the Platforms. Either of these can be used (the easterly is perhaps the easier option) to access the cirque between Shadow Peak and Nez Perce. From the col at the head of either couloir, contour to the south along the bench that leads to the upper cirque, which is bounded by the north face of Shadow Peak and the southeast face of Nez Perce. From the upper end of the cirque, two cols—the main one and a smaller one up and to the north—will be seen. Scramble up the gully to the upper col, where a traverse 60m farther to the west and up leads to the start of the route. (If additional climbing is desired, it is also possible to pass through the lower col to the base of the ridge, which leads to the higher col. Two or three pitches, the first of which is 5.6, take one to the top of the tower, which is separated from Nez Perce by the higher col. A short rappel is then required to descend to the col and proceed as already described.)

The first pitch is up a 25m chimney (5.7) on the right side of the crest. Another 150m of climbing near the crest brings one to a point just below a small pinnacle, which is easily passed on the right (east) side. After the short, steep lieback crux pitch (5.7+) out of the notch behind the pinnacle, there is a 60m section of scrambling and contouring right (north) up to a steep, massive buttress. A short section of 5.6 climbing leads to another rightward traverse and then a bit of scrambling to the summit. This is an excellent and enjoyable climb on predominantly good rock (a rarity for Nez Perce). For descent use the regular Northwest Couloirs route *(Route 1)*. **Time:** 7½ hours from Garnet Canyon. See *American Alpine Journal* 9, no. 2 (1955): pp. 147–49; *Dartmouth Mountaineering Club Journal*, 1957, p. 28, illus.

Variation: III, 5.7+. First ascent in early July 1966, by Paul Ledoux Jr. and William Schipel. This variation starts just left (west) of the initial 25m chimney of the standard route. Climb a short distance up to a ramp system that slants sharply up and left across the face. Follow this ramp system for six ropelengths until it turns around a corner and stops. Just short of this corner are two obvious vertical cracks in the wall above. Climb the right crack for four leads to reach the small pinnacle of the standard route, which is then followed to the summit. This variation, apparently all on the left (west) side of the ridge crest, contains fine climbing on excellent rock and is a good alternative, especially if the 25m chimney is wet.

***Variation:* GARNET TRAVERSE.** III, 5.8. First ascent August 10, 1967, by Jack Weicker and Leigh Ortenburger. (See *Figure 3-4*.) This significant variation goes directly up the "steep, massive buttress" referred to in the description of the original Direct South Ridge route. Climb directly upward to the left corner of the buttress. Make a somewhat tricky traverse across the face to the right and up to a black rock band, where it is possible to climb back left again to a white ramp leading to a narrow ledge below a large flake. Belay from either the base or the top of this flake, which is climbed using lieback technique. Climb the face 3m above the top of the flake and then make a very delicate friction traverse left out to the extreme corner, where holds leading upward will be found. A single garnet crystal provides the crucial foothold on this traverse. This direct and consistently steep variation contains excellent rock.

***Variation:* LOWER RIDGE.** III, 5.7+. First ascent July 18, 1969, by Peter and Rosanne Cleveland. The upper south ridge was reached from Lake Taminah in Avalanche Canyon (see *Avalanche Canyon, North Fork* in Section 2) by climbing the lower stepped section of the ridge. This adds considerably to the length of the climb.

Variation: III, 5.10-. First ascent June 29, 1989, by Keith Schultz and Jack Tcholske. This variation—an alternative to the first pitch—is located just left of a chimney, perhaps the 25m 5.7 chimney of the normal route. It begins with a left-leaning, left-facing 5.9 corner. This is followed by an overhang and a 5.8 right-facing corner. After climbing past another roof, the pitch finishes with a 5.10- crack.

ROUTE 6. SOUTH FACE. III, 5.7. First ascent August 1, 1955, by W. V. Graham Matthews and Mary Ann Matthews. (See *Figure 3-5* for an overview of the southeast aspect of Nez Perce.) This route ascends the

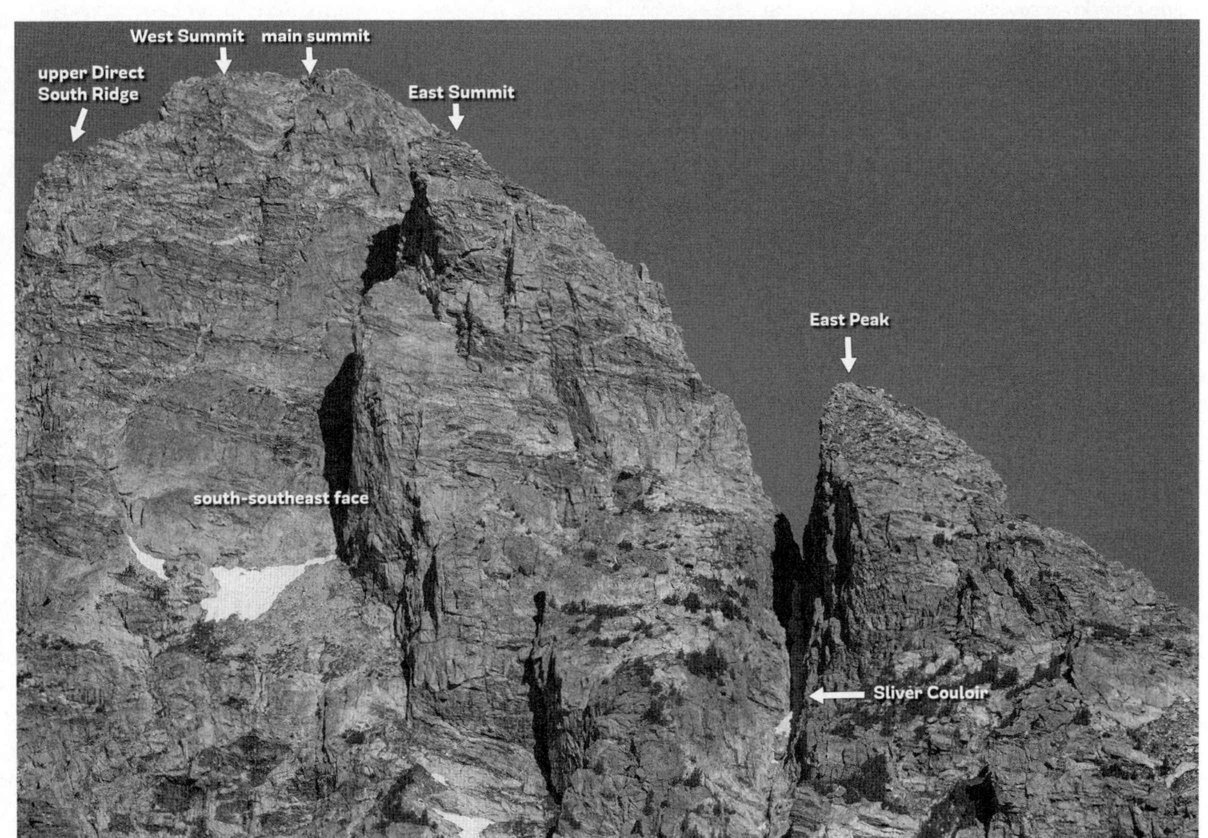

FIGURE 3-5. Nez Perce, detail of the southeast face, East Ridge *(Route 9)*, variation: East Summit, South Face, II, 5.7

face that lies immediately east of the south ridge and west of the southeast ridge that connects with Shadow Peak. The approach is the same as for *Route 5*. The first section consists of straightforward scrambling for about 150m directly up the face to a very large and grassy (or snow-covered) ledge. Ascend some 75m of 4th-class friction slabs to a large ledge covered with loose rock. About 9m above this ledge is a belay spot; from here climb a short distance and then traverse to the right (northeast) for 30m to an obvious belay spot below a nearly vertical wall. The 24m section directly above the belay is difficult because only small holds are available. Two more difficult pitches follow to a point about 30m left (southwest) and 18m above the notch between the East Summit and the main summit. The final three or four leads of this route bring the climber to the crest of the east ridge, about 46m east of the summit. See *American Alpine Journal* 12, no. 1 (1960): pp. 125–27.

ROUTE 7. SOUTHEAST COULOIR. III, 5.6, A1. First ascent September 3, 1960, by Lloyd Arnesen and Victor Wylie. (See *Figure 3-4*.) This route ascends the couloir that separates the Direct South Ridge *(Route 5)* from the southeast ridge that connects Nez Perce with Shadow Peak. Follow the approach for *Route 5* from the trail in Garnet Canyon up to the higher col on the Shadow Peak–Nez Perce ridge. Instead of traversing west from this col for 60m over to the beginning of the Direct South Ridge, descend slightly into the couloir on the far (west) side of the col and scramble north up this first couloir to the large chimney where the climb begins. The first short pitch of about 20m on steep rock and some talus leads to a belay spot at an overhang. This is turned on the left with a short bit of aid, followed by friction climbing to the next belay stance. The next 60m consists of broken talus. A moderate 12m rock section continues up the couloir to a point from which one can traverse left and up over a series of easy ledges to a prominent notch. A good belay will be found 9m above the notch. The next section angles up and left toward the south ridge but stays away from that crest, instead reaching the summit from the southeast. In this upper portion of the climb, there is some intermingling with the South Face route *(Route 6)*.

Variation: II, 5.6. First ascent July 3, 1987, by Bob Graham and Jack Bellorado. This variation begins just below the first (lower) of the two cols mentioned in *Route 5*. Proceed up into a gully for a short distance and find a ledge that traverses out and right onto a slabby, southeast-facing buttress. A few pitches of climbing and then a rappel into the prominent notch mentioned in the main route description put one nearly in the middle of the upper south face. Easy climbing following the path of least resistance leads to the summit.

ROUTE 8. SOUTHEAST FACE. II, 5.1. First ascent July 21, 1935, by Malcolm Smith. (See *Figure 3-5* for an overview.) There are probably several alternative routes on this face, and it is not clear exactly where the parties who have climbed it have gone; the following route description is the one that was given by Smith. From the cirque between the base of the east ridge of Nez Perce and Shadow Peak, ascend into the bowl that is south of the east ridge and east of the southeast face of Nez Perce. The right (north) edge of this face is bounded by the chimney system that descends from the notch between the East Summit and the main summit. The left (south) edge of this face is bounded by the southeast ridge of Nez Perce, which rises from the higher col reached as one traverses over toward the beginning of the Direct South Ridge route *(Route 5)*. The southeast ridge culminates at a small tower, separated by a small notch from the upper southeast face of the mountain. This route begins near the south edge of the face, in a shallow couloir (this start is similar to that of the 1987 southeast couloir variation, above). A short distance above the starting point, traverse right across smooth, steeply sloping rock without losing any altitude to a point in the middle of the southeast face, just above a snow patch that is present most of the summer. It is also possible to reach this point directly from below, and probably even from the right. After reaching this point, a series of ledges and steep, broken cliffs can be followed without great difficulty to the summit. This is an enjoyable climb on good rock.

ROUTE 9. EAST RIDGE. II, 5.4. First ascent July 12, 1931, by Robert Underhill and Fritiof Fryxell; first descent (north traverse of East Summit) August 9, 1940, by Jack Durrance and Henry Coulter. (See *Figure 3-2* for the upper portion of this climb.) This route has achieved some popularity because of its accessibility from the Garnet Canyon trail. From the Platforms, follow a climbers' trail that leads up to a small notch on the bench above the south walls of Garnet Canyon, at the edge of the cirque between Shadow Peak and Nez Perce. From the meadows on the bench, two broad shelves with scattered trees angle up, from right to left, to meet the east ridge. Take the upper shelf all the way to the ridge, where two ropelengths lead to the top of a small pinnacle; behind and to the south is a deep chimney (see the Hernando's Hideaway variation, below). From the small notch behind this pinnacle, climb a jam crack (6m) on the north side and then move back onto the ridge. It is then just a scramble to the top of the East Peak. To reach the notch between the East Peak and the East Summit, which is just below, downclimb about 18m slightly on the north side of the ridge to a rappel point. Now make either one long rappel (46m) or two rappels (30m and 15m) to the notch; it is also possible to downclimb slightly on the north side to reach the second rappel point. This sharp notch is the apex of the East Hourglass Couloir to the north and the Sliver Couloir to the south (see the 1933 and 1936 variations, below).

From the notch there are two possibilities: (1) Climb directly up and out of the notch on the west side. The first short pitch bears left on small holds. This pitch is followed by a traverse up and right for one or two ropelengths to ledges on the north side. At the first convenient point, turn left and up onto the crest of the ridge again. The difficulty will depend on the exact route selected to get past this steep section of the ridge. Then scramble to the East Summit. (2) From the notch, contour right (north) for about 46m to a shallow chimney that leads upward and back toward the ridge. About six ropelengths bring one to the crest of the ridge above the steep section.

From the East Summit, either make a 37m rappel (entirely free) to the notch between the East Summit and the main summit or climb partway down the north side before rappelling 18m to this notch. The downclimb is not easy to find. Old slings will be found at both rappel sites. Another (more difficult) possibility is to downclimb all the way to the notch. From the notch scramble the remainder of the ridge westward to the main summit. **Time:** 6½ to 9 hours from Garnet Canyon; 8 to 11½ hours from Jenny Lake. See *American Alpine Journal* 5, no. 2 (1944): pp. 220–32, illus.; *Appalachia* 18, no. 4 (December 1931): pp. 388–408, illus.; *Chicago Mountaineering Club Newsletter* 2, no. 6 (July–December 1948): pp. 2–3; *Trail and Timberline*, no. 447 (March 1956): pp. 47–48.

***Variation:* EAST HOURGLASS COULOIR.** II, 5.4. First ascent July 3, 1933, by Paul Petzoldt and Sterling Hendricks. (See *Figure 3-2*.) This climb starts from the apex of the talus cone that forms the bottom half of the "hourglass" below the north face. Follow the left (east) couloir, sometimes using the rock on the left (east) edge, straight to the notch between the East Peak and the East Summit. This couloir and its analog on the south side, the Sliver, are sought-after ski- and snowboard-mountaineering objectives during the winter months. The Sliver is commonly ascended from the Shadow Peak cirque side, and then a descent is made of the East Hourglass Couloir. A more demanding trifecta is sometimes done, with this route providing access to the West Hourglass Couloir, which is also climbed and then descended. Once this has been accomplished, the East Hourglass Couloir is reclimbed and the Sliver is descended, thus completing the linkup.

***Variation:* SLIVER COULOIR.** II, 5.4. First ascent August 19, 1936, by Fred and Irene Ayres and Allan Cameron. (See *Figure 3-5*, which shows the upper portion of the couloir.) The Sliver Couloir now enjoys enormous popularity during the winter months as a ski- and snowboard-mountaineering objective. From the Shadow Peak cirque, continue around and south past the base of the east ridge of Nez Perce on grass and scree ledges to this large couloir, which extends from the cirque up to the notch between the East Peak and the East Summit. Ascend the couloir, formed from a line of weakness in the rock formations. Some loose rock should be expected. On the north face this same line continues as the East Hourglass Couloir (see the preceding variation). From the notch continue up the regular East Ridge route.

***Variation:* EAST SUMMIT BYPASS.** II, 5.6. First ascent September 9, 1938, by Dr. John Buck, Raymond Creekmore, Donald Grant, O. O. Heard, and William Kemper. On this variation the East Summit is bypassed completely. From the notch between the East Peak and the East Summit, a series of ledges, chimneys, and flakes takes one completely around the north face of the East Summit to the very steep snow (in early season) leading to the notch between the East Summit and the main summit. This traverse is on poor and loose rock with some danger from falling objects (ice, rocks).

***Variation:* EAST SUMMIT, SOUTH FACE.** II, 5.7. First ascent August 24, 1945, by Joseph Stettner and John Speck. (See *Figure 3-5*.) This difficult and exposed variation on the upper south face of the East Summit can be started either by traversing up and left (south) out of the notch between the East Peak and the East Summit or by climbing partway up the Sliver Couloir (see the 1936 variation, above). In either case, gain the broad, steeply inclined shelf that parallels the ridge crest about halfway up the south face of the East Summit. Some easy roped climbing will be required to reach the upper (west) end of this ledge. From here directly ascend the steep, difficult, and very exposed face above, climbing just to the left (west) of an overhanging nose. See *The Iowa Climber* 2, no. 2 (Summer 1948): p. 70, illus.

***Variation:* EAST SUMMIT, SOUTHEAST FACE.** II, 5.6. First ascent July 15, 1949, by Jim Harrang, Robert Brooke, and Pete Brown. From the Nez Perce–Shadow Peak cirque, traverse south around the base of the East Peak to the Sliver Couloir (see the 1936 variation, above), which leads to the notch between the East Peak and the East Summit. Scramble up this couloir for about 60m until one can easily exit left (west) onto the large, slanting shelf described in the East Summit, South Face variation. Proceed up (west) along this shelf past one buttress to the base of a steep, obvious 12m chimney leading north up toward the ridge crest. To reach the top of the East Summit from the top of this chimney, bear left (diagonally) up a series of cracks and flakes for about four pitches.

***Variation:* EAST PEAK, NORTH FACE.** II, 5.6. First ascent September 4, 1951, by Tony Soler, Art Lembeck, and Ray Moore. This route goes directly up the very steep north face of the East Peak from a broad bench that cuts across the face. For the approach to the broad bench, which is about halfway between the floor of Garnet Canyon and the top of the East Peak, see the East Hourglass Ridge variation, below. Little information is available on this route. It involves some 4th-class climbing with at least three pitches that are 5th class.

***Variation:* HERNANDO'S HIDEAWAY.** II, 5.4. First ascent July 4, 1954, by F. Keith Spencer and Richard Becker. Follow the standard approach past the base of the east ridge to its southeast side. Here, a deep, prominent chimney system, about 120m long, leads to the ridge east of the East Peak and isolates the small pinnacle mentioned in the description of the standard East Ridge route. A short bit of climbing past an overhang leads into the lower portion of this chimney. The first two pitches require stemming before the chimney opens up a bit. Chockstones fill the narrower upper portion. The final pitch brings one out onto the east ridge and is less difficult. This splendid chimney was originally described as "undesirable, narrow, deep, dark, wet, and slimy."

***Variation:* UPPER SOUTHEAST CHIMNEY.** II, 5.4. First ascent August 9, 1959, by William Glosser, Pat Purdy, Jay Edwards, and Peg Fowler. Follow the standard approach past the base of the east ridge to the bowl at the base of the southeast face of Nez Perce. From the northwest corner of the bowl climb directly up the chimney (or small couloir) at the extreme right (north) edge of the southeast face, using mainly the left side of the chimney. This chimney leads to the notch between the main summit and the East Summit. This route cannot be recommended due to the considerable danger of falling rock.

***Variation:* EAST PEAK, EAST HOURGLASS RIDGE.** II, 5.4. First ascent July 9, 1962, by Steven Derenzo, Peter Gardiner, Richard Goldstone, and Frank Knight. The left (east) border of the East Hourglass Couloir is a distinct ridge that begins at the intersection of the Hourglass Couloirs and leads to the top of the East Peak of Nez Perce. This ridge is divided into two sections by the broad bench that cuts across the north face of the East Peak about halfway from the floor of Garnet Canyon to the summit. This variation ascends the upper portion of the ridge. The initial task is to gain the broad bench, which holds a small, permanent snowfield, below the north face of the East Peak. Take the standard approach from the Platforms to the grassy meadow on the initial bench just above the south walls of Garnet Canyon. Proceed southwest to the low-angle slabs that form the east end of the broad bench. Climb these slabs, near the right edge of a small chute, to an obvious ledge leading right (north). From the end of this ledge one can bushwhack west onto the broad, open bench. Continue easily west to the base of the complex of chutes leading up to the crest of the East Hourglass Ridge. Take the middle chute to the sharp notch between a pointed gendarme and the large buttress on the left (south). From the notch angle left (east) on broken rock for about 18m to some steep, shallow chimneys. Climb straight up for 9m to a sloping ledge that angles right toward the very exposed northwest corner of the buttress. Continue beyond the end of the ledge, past an awkward niche, to a groove in the light-colored rock that leads to the top of the buttress. Four ropelengths take one to the top of the East Peak.

ROUTE 10. CHIEF JOSEPH LEFT. III, 5.10+. First ascent in 2021, by Cody Evans and Casey Heerdt. (See *Figure 3-6*.) The start of this climb is located a short distance to the east of the original line on Chief Joseph Buttress *(Route 11)*, and the approach is the same as for that route. **Pitch 1:** Begin in the leftmost of three right-leaning, right-facing corners on the eastern edge of the buttress. Climb a flake inside this corner (5.8), which gradually gets harder until one exits the corner with delicate crack and face moves (5.10+) to a good stance on a slab. Continue up the slab (5.7R), looking for gear and trending right until a great belay seat with grass is found. A perfect hand crack is directly above. **Pitch 2:** Step right and climb enjoyable crack and face moves (5.7) to easier ground. Continue up to a bulge and follow a weakness through it (5.8) to a large ledge above; belay here. **Pitch 3:** Climb up one small step and gain a weakness that is taken as far out to the west as it will allow. Then pull over a bulge through good rock and continue up the dark V slot above to a broad ledge and the belay (5.7). **Pitch 4:** At this point the route joins the original line on the buttress *(Route 11)*. Partway up this pitch, break out left onto the arête until a good jam crack is obtained. Follow this crack (5.8) on good rock to a large ledge, which is also the top of the fifth pitch of *Route 11*. Belay below a daunting-looking wide corner. **Pitch 5:** As in *Route 11*, avoid the corner by traversing right around the arête on a fun handrail. Continue up easier terrain (5.5–5.6) to exit the buttress, either following *Route 11* or staying just left of that line (both options eventually merge). From the top of the climb, scramble up 3rd-class terrain to the crest of the east ridge of Nez Perce to access the walk-off descent, described in *Route 11*.

FIGURE 3-6. Nez Perce, north aspect. (A) Chief Joseph Left *(Route 10)*, III, 5.10+; (B) Chief Joseph Buttress *(Route 11)*, III, 5.10-; (C) Chief Joseph Buttress, Bullock-Page *(Route 12)*, III, 5.9+

Gear: A double set of cams from micro to 3.5" is suggested, with some additional Camalot C3s. An ice tool in early season will also prove useful.

ROUTE 11. CHIEF JOSEPH BUTTRESS. III, 5.10-. First ascent July 31, 1988, by Tom Turiano and Dan Powers. The original name for this route was "Joe's Butt." It ascends the buttress on the north face of the East Peak, rising directly from a small snowfield on the broad bench at the base of the face. To reach this small snowfield from the Platforms camping area, ascend via a climbers' trail that leads up the first couloir to the southeast, which provides access to the Nez Perce–Shadow Peak cirque. Once the ridge crest is gained, follow it up and west past a small meadow. Continue west up ramps that lead up and into the small cirque containing the snowfield. Walk west along the broad bench to the west side of the snowfield. Scramble up talus and scree to the grassy 3rd-class ramp that diagonals up and back to the left (east). Refer to *Figure 3-6* for the technical details of the route. (**Note:** One does not want to do this climb when there is as much snow on it as in the photo.) For the descent, scrambling leads down to the northeast for a few hundred meters. Look for a smaller spur ridge that forms the eastern edge of the cirque containing the snowfield. Follow this spur ridge down to the eastern edge of the small snowfield. **Gear:** For protection take a regular rack to 3".

ROUTE 12. CHIEF JOSEPH BUTTRESS, BULLOCK-PAGE. III, 5.9+. First ascent by Steve Bullock and Sam Page (date unknown). This route is located immediately west of *Route 11* (see *Figure 3-6*) and it ends at the same point on the east ridge of Nez Perce. The approach and descent are the same as for *Route 11*. Details of the route are outlined in *Figure 3-7*. **Gear:** For protection take a selection of stoppers and camming devices to 3".

ROUTE 13. NORTH FACE, GUIDES' DISCOUNT. III, 5.9R. First ascent in September 1999, by Keith Cattabriga, Martin Vidak, and Ray Warburton. (See *Figure 3-2*.) This route, which rises out of the East Hourglass Couloir, is not a recommended climb: "Several of the pitches were dangerously loose," explained Cattabriga. "Perhaps its only redeemable quality is it seems to be an independent line, top to bottom." This route can be seen most easily from the

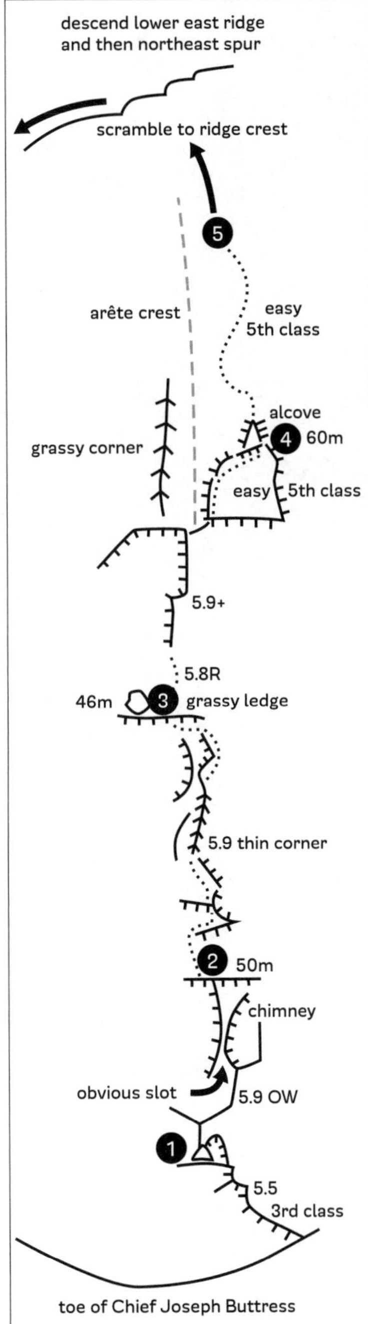

FIGURE 3-7. Nez Perce, Chief Joseph Buttress, Bullock-Page *(Route 12)*, III, 5.9+

north fork of Garnet Canyon, where the stream coming from the Teepe Glacier cirque crosses the main trail. Look for a big right-facing corner rising out of the East Hourglass Couloir, approximately halfway up from where the Hourglass Couloirs split. The first pitch (5.8, ugly) climbs up and left from the couloir, and the belay is on a ledge at the base of the right-facing corner. The first-ascent party found an old rappel sling on this ledge. Start the second pitch by going up the first part of the corner, then climb a crack through a roof (5.9, rotten). The third pitch, which according to Cattabriga "was actually pretty good," goes up a splitter crack (5.8) to the right of the corner and then up the left side of a chimney (no protection) to a rubble-strewn ledge for the belay. For the fourth pitch (5.9), wander up to the base of another right-facing corner, climb to a stance, and belay. One more short pitch takes one to the top of this second corner and a belay. From here one can gain the summit via about 120m of 3rd- and 4th-class climbing.

ROUTE 14. NORTH FACE. III, 5.6. First ascent August 9, 1940, by Jack Durrance and Henry Coulter; a previous attempt by Durrance, Coulter, and Fred Ayres was turned back by a storm. (See *Figure 3-2*.) This is the broken face that rises directly to the summit from the intersection point of the two Hourglass Couloirs. From the Platforms proceed well into the Meadows of Garnet Canyon before turning south up the long talus cone that forms the lower half of the "hourglass." The route starts at the top of the talus where the two Hourglass Couloirs cross. Scramble up about 60m onto a wide ledge. Above this ledge is the first pitch of climbing—an obvious jam crack in the middle of the 9m face above. From the ledge at the top of this pitch, climb 4.5m up the left corner of the face above to a stance on the corner itself; then traverse left on a delicate friction ledge into an easy chimney. From the comfortable ledge at the top of this chimney, continue up in a large chimney leading to the right (west). After two long pitches, the chimney peters out at a point somewhat west of the main summit. Start edging left (east) until beneath a vertical section, which can be climbed on excellent holds. From the top of this section, scramble out on the main summit ridge very near the summit. This description is only one of the many variations that have been climbed on this large face. In general, the more direct the route to the summit, the more difficult it will be. **Time:** 7 to 9½ hours from Garnet Canyon.

Variation: III, 5.6. First ascent August 14, 1940, by Edward McNeill, John A. McCown, Thomas L. Johnston, Thomson Edwards, and Charles J. Webb. (See Figure 3-2.) This party attempted the Durrance and Colter climb but lost the route after about 100 meters. Nevertheless they forged ahead, beginning with a 70m traverse "to the west to an overhang and up a large crack which slants slightly NE for 120m." This was described as "rather difficult climbing" in the summit register. The party then climbed a long couloir and finished by going "directly up the face to the top." Webb was a member of the Dartmouth Mountaineering Club and had presumably spoken to Durrance and/or Colter about the route.

Variation: **WEST HOURGLASS COULOIR.** II, 4.0. First ascent August 11, 1942, by Orrin Bonney and Ernest Guild; first descent August 16, 1951, by Ed Keller, Bill Sloan, and Bob Borbridge. (See *Figure 3-2.*) Starting from the top of the talus cone below the intersection of the two Hourglass Couloirs, this variation follows directly up the right (west) couloir, sometimes using its right wall. During most of the season the couloir will be snow-filled. From the top of the couloir, angle back left toward the main summit, which is now somewhat to the east. As an option, there are at least three places, one-half to three-quarters of the way up the couloir, where one can cut left (east) out onto the north face from the couloir. In early season, this couloir provides a fast descent via glissade for experienced climbers. This couloir is frequented by skiers and riders throughout the winter.

A climber descends from the top of the Subalpinist in Garnet Canyon. (Photo by Kent McBride)

GARNET CANYON, SOUTH SIDE ROCK CLIMBS (ca. 9,600)

Map: Grand Teton

The conspicuous walls on the south and north sides of the lower section of Garnet Canyon contain some excellent rock, and many climbs have been worked out on these cliffs. These routes do not lead to the summit of any peak. The southern routes are described in this section.

ROUTE 1. BIG BLUFF. III, 5.6, A5. First ascent August 12, 1960, by Royal Robbins and Joe Fitschen. The ascent of this impressive overhang, which rises directly above and south of the Platforms, illustrated, at the time, state-of-the-art Yosemite aid techniques. Starting from the gully to the west of the overhang, ascend easy ledges to the broad terrace under the 46m overhang. Begin near the left side of the overhang and climb diagonally to the right, up a steep red flake, to a bolt on a sloping ledge. Now traverse horizontally 9m and then upward to a quartz-like rock formation where a bolt hole should be found (a bolt was placed but fell out after it was used); this pitch is extremely difficult. The route now angles generally up to the left to the top edge of the overhang. Use caution with the large, loose flake that is met during the climb. Most of the climb is artificial; many pitons and three bolts were used on the first ascent. See *American Alpine Journal* 12, no. 2 (1961): pp. 373–77; *Sierra Club Bulletin* 46, no. 8 (October 1961): pp. 53–54.

ROUTE 2. LEMON CRACK. III, 5.9, A3. First ascent August 1, 1969, by Peter Cleveland and Mike Yokell. This overhanging route, on the same cliff as *Route 1*, generally diagonals from left (east) to right (west). Start the climb at a cave with a large roof, beneath a white face characterized by a lemon-shaped block about 6m high (visible from the trail below the Platforms). The first lead of 21m uses aid (A3) over the initial roof and then up the "lemon," ending with 9m free (5.8) to a large ledge with grass. Next drop down to the right, traverse around a corner, and diagonal up and right (5.9) past the tip of a tree (which grows from the ground up to this point) onto a belay ledge at the end of 27m. The third pitch (5.6) is an 18m traverse right on ledges and then up to a large belay ledge just below an open book. The next lead (5.7) avoids this open book by traversing right and up (9m) to a large, sloping ledge for the belay below an overhanging open book that diagonals off to the left. For the fifth pitch (27m), use aid to ascend the open book, then mantel onto a sloping ledge on the left. At this point a very difficult tension traverse to the right permits access to a good ledge, from which one can walk around the corner to the belay position. The sixth lead is long (43m), consists of 5.7 climbing, and bypasses an overhanging band on the left. The final pitch is up easy rock to the top of the cliff. The climb is continuously interesting, containing a surprising amount of free climbing for a face that overhangs slightly from bottom to top.

ROUTE 3. OPP-VAN SCIVER. I, 5.12- PG-13. First ascent in August 2008, by Nate Opp and Lisa Van Sciver. This climb is located on an overhanging buttress of dark-colored rock just east of the West Hourglass Couloir (see *Nez Perce, Route 14*) on the lower north-facing side of Nez Perce. The climb consists of a right-trending crack (tricky gear near the bottom) and a bolted line and is described as "a long pitch of steep rock."

ROUTE 4. SUBALPINIST. II, 5.12a. First ascent in August 2017, by Greg Collins, Brandon Gust, Paul Kimbrough, and Nate Opp. This climb, consisting of three pitches, is located just below *Route 3* on the lower north side of Nez Perce. Hike up talus or seasonal snow to a white ledge and an alcove under the overhang. A short right-facing corner (5.9, 15m) leads to a nice belay ledge in white rock. The second pitch consists of a 5.12a arête that overhangs severely. It has big holds and affords good protection. A short 5.6 pitch then leads to the top. **Gear:** For protection bring two finger-size cams, two "rattly finger-size" cams, and one small cam (five total), plus quickdraws (some longer).

ROUTE 5. MIDDLE TETON CAVE ROUTE. II, 5.12b. First ascent in August 2015, by Greg Collins and Adam Freund. This climb is located in the "cave" that is adjacent to the Cave Couloir, a place that traditionally holds snow long into the summer months and is a popular destination for die-hard skiers and snowboarders. It is above the Meadows and just below the east buttress of the Middle Teton. The climb follows the crack system in the ceiling of the cave, and the first pitch increases rapidly from 5.11 to 5.12b in difficulty.

CLOUDVEIL DOME (12,026)

Map: Grand Teton

On the long east ridge of the South Teton leading down toward Nez Perce, Cloudveil Dome is but one of several high points and pinnacles. Although it is not sufficiently separated from the upper portion of this ridge to be considered a separate peak, Cloudveil Dome was named before the first ascent because of its prominence when viewed from Jackson Hole and has become a standard Teton mountaineering objective. Even though the regular routes offer little difficulty to the experienced climber, the climb of Cloudveil Dome is nevertheless a worthwhile undertaking because its rounded summit provides a fine viewpoint for many of the peaks surrounding Garnet Canyon. All of the routes on the peak can be approached via Garnet Canyon and will require a full day from the valley; however, it is more pleasant to start from a camp at the Platforms or the Meadows. Although the south face routes can be approached via Avalanche Canyon, it is more straightforward to go up from Garnet Canyon to the Cloudveil Dome–Nez Perce col and then down and around from there. The south side of this approach is shown in *Figure 3-8*. Also shown is the most popular route on the south face, Armed Robbery *(Route 5)*; see that route for more-detailed approach and descent information for the south face climbs.

Chronology

EAST RIDGE: July 21, 1931, Fritiof Fryxell, Anderson Hilding
WEST RIDGE: July 21, 1931, Fritiof Fryxell, Anderson Hilding (descent); August 5, 1932, Fred Ayres (ascent)
NORTH FACE: August 22, 1950, Richard Pownall, Paul Kenworthy
var—August 1, 1961, Jim Greig, Fred Wright
SOUTHEAST RIB: August 17, 1951, John Driggs, Gary Driggs
MATTHEWS SOUTH FACE: July 31, 1955, W. V. Graham Matthews, Mary Ann Matthews
var—**MISS DEMEANOR:** July 23, 1986, Paul Duval, Beverly Boynton
CUT LOOSE: August 2, 1977, Yvon Chouinard, Rick Black
ARMED ROBBERY: August 15, 1978, Mike Munger, Rick Liu
CONTEMPORARY COMFORT: September 2, 1978, Charlie Fowler, Bill Feiges
SILVER LINING: July 12, 1979, Mike Munger, Bill Nicholson
WFR: July 11, 1990, Jim Dorward, Steve Rickert
NIMBUS: July 1993, Alex Lowe, Stephen Koch
TEMPORARY DISCOMFORT: February 11, 2001, Hans Johnstone, Norm Larson

ROUTE 1. WEST RIDGE. II, 3.0. First descent July 21, 1931, by Fritiof Fryxell and Anderson Hilding; first ascent August 5, 1932, by Fred Ayres. This route is used exclusively for making the traverse from the South Teton (or from Cloudveil Dome to the South Teton). The ridge itself is but a scramble and offers no difficulties. **Time:** 4 hours from the summit of the South Teton.

FIGURE 3-8. Cloudveil Dome, south face overview. (A) Matthews South Face *(Route 2)*, II, 5.6, A1; (B) Matthews South Face, variation: Miss Demeanor, III, 5.9; (C) Armed Robbery *(Route 5)*, IV, 5.8R; (D) Silver Lining *(Route 6)*, IV, 5.10+; (E) WFR *(Route 7)*, III, 5.8; (F) Cut Loose *(Route 8)*, III, 5.10

ROUTE 2. MATTHEWS SOUTH FACE. II, 5.6, A1. First ascent July 31, 1955, by W. V. Graham Matthews and Mary Ann Matthews. (See *Figures 3-8* and *3-9*.) See *Avalanche Canyon* in Section 2 for the approach to Lake Taminah. From the east end of the lake, ascend the talus gully toward the south face of Cloudveil Dome, which contains a considerable expanse of high-angle rock featuring several worthwhile routes. At the base of the south face is a broad bench formed in a band of crumbly red rock that cuts horizontally across the south ridges of Nez Perce, Cloudveil Dome, and the South Teton. Two parallel cracks or ramps diagonal steeply up and to the left (west) across the south face above the bench. Ascend the lower crack or ramp across the south face, to a point on the west side of the face where the crack peters out. From here, go around the corner and then directly up for about four pitches to a broad ledge that leads right (east) to the higher of the two cracks or ramps. Climb this crack back to the west, arriving at the summit ridge just west of the summit. **Time:** 6¾ hours from Avalanche Canyon. See *American Alpine Journal* 10, no. 1 (1956): pp. 116–19.

Variation: **MISS DEMEANOR.** III, 5.9. First ascent July 23, 1986, by Paul Duval and Beverly Boynton. (See *Figures 3-8*, *3-9*, and *3-10*.) Approach via Avalanche Canyon or Garnet Canyon (see *Route 5* for the latter). This two-pitch climb is reached by continuing up the Matthews South Face ramp, past the point where one begins the fourth pitch of Armed Robbery *(Route 5)*. The route then joins the easier finish of the Matthews South Face.

ROUTE 3. TEMPORARY DISCOMFORT. IV, 5.10. First ascent February 11, 2001, by Hans Johnstone and Norm Larson. (See *Figure 3-10*.) Approach via Garnet Canyon, as in *Route 5*. This is a significant route, especially considering it was a wintertime first ascent by two local hardmen. The pair climbed up to the Matthews South Face *(Route 2)* ramp on the south face, past the start of the fourth pitch of Armed Robbery *(Route 5)*, and then continued up for two pitches of 5.10 climbing before the angle eased off on the upper portion of the mountain. They may have repeated *Route 4*, but since that climb is imperfectly known, Temporary Discomfort is included here as a distinct and separate route.

ROUTE 4. CONTEMPORARY COMFORT. IV, 5.10. First ascent September 2, 1978, by Charlie Fowler and Bill Feiges. This imperfectly known route apparently takes a line similar to that of the lower portion of Armed Robbery *(Route 5)* to reach the Matthews South Face *(Route 2)* ramp and then follows this ramp out farther to the west, arching up and left. When the crack thins out, a 5.10 pitch is climbed to reach a steep dihedral leading upward. Fourth-class climbing back to the right (east) then provides access to the upper diagonal ramp. From here the line leads more or less directly to the summit, perhaps along a line similar to that of the upper portion of Silver Lining *(Route 6)*. This route may differ from *Routes 3* and *5* only in the section between the two ramps.

FIGURE 3-9. Cloudveil Dome, south face detail #1. (A) Matthews South Face *(Route 2)*, II, 5.6, A1; (B) Matthews South Face, variation: Miss Demeanor, III, 5.9; (C) Armed Robbery *(Route 5)*, IV, 5.8R; (D) Silver Lining *(Route 6)*, IV, 5.10+

FIGURE 3-10. Cloudveil Dome, south face detail #2. (A) Matthews South Face *(Route 2)*, variation: Miss Demeanor, III, 5.9; (B) Temporary Discomfort *(Route 3)*, IV, 5.10; (C) Armed Robbery *(Route 5)*, IV, 5.8R; (D) Silver Lining *(Route 6)*, IV, 5.10+; (E) Southeast Rib *(Route 9)*, II, 5.7

ROUTE 5. ARMED ROBBERY. IV, 5.8R. First ascent August 15, 1978, by Mike Munger and Rick Liu. (See *Figures 3-8, 3-9,* and *3-10.*) Armed Robbery and Silver Lining *(Route 6)* climb the corners on either side of the great central column of the upper part of the south face, and both routes are highly recommended. The Garnet Canyon approach is usually used for this climb. Take the Garnet Canyon trail from the Lupine Meadows trailhead. Proceed west past the Meadows in Garnet Canyon and into the south fork, heading to the col just east of Cloudveil Dome. Extra gear can be left here at the col because the descent route returns down the east ridge (see *Route 10*) to this point. From the col drop down to the south and look for a red (dike rock) couloir with much loose rock. Climb down into this couloir until it is possible to scramble westt around and onto the broad bench at the base of the south face of Cloudveil Dome.

This route proceeds roughly directly up the south face toward the summit from the bench. Instead of following the Matthews South Face *(Route 2)* ramp across the face (the easier alternative), the first-ascent party climbed three pitches on the face below and to the left, gaining the ramp about one-third of the way along its extent. The first pitch (43m) from the bench goes up a short left-facing corner (5.6) to a belay ledge. The second lead (5.6) goes up a left-facing corner, passing a horn on the right, and up past a small ledge to another belay ledge. The final pitch (46m) onto the Matthews South Face ramp is easier; set up the belay beneath the large roof that is directly below the central pillar on the upper section of the wall.

The fourth pitch proceeds up and left, which allows a traverse back right above a smaller roof. Then climb blocky terrain (5.7) to the upper right edge of the main large overhang. Traverse left (west)—5.8R; serious, exposed, difficult pro, and be aware of rope drag!—to the lower end of the left-hand crack system. (The right side of the pillar is the Silver Lining route.) The rest of the fourth pitch and the fifth pitch ascend this very enjoyable crack system (5.8 hands). At the top of the fifth pitch, the upper of the two ramps that cut across the face will be intersected. A quick escape can be made on easier ground by generally following this ramp up and to the west. The first-ascent party continued more or less straight up for two more pitches, finishing very close to the summit. **Gear:** A double set of cams from 0.75" to 3.5" with extras in the hand size, plus a set of stoppers, will be useful. Descent is made by way of the east ridge.

ROUTE 6. SILVER LINING. IV, 5.10+. First ascent July 12, 1979, by Mike Munger and Bill Nicholson. (See *Figures 3-8, 3-9,* and *3-10.*) Use the same approach as for Armed Robbery *(Route 5)* and follow the first three pitches of that route to the Matthews South Face *(Route 2)* ramp. Begin the fourth pitch as for Armed Robbery, then move up and right (east) toward the right-facing corner of the central column. Climb past the right edge of a large overhang (5.10) and up the right side of the pillar (two pitches, 5.10 and 5.9). From the top of the pillar, climb up and right to a belay on the upper of the two main parallel ledges or ramps that diagonal steeply up across the south face from lower right (east) to upper left (west). The sixth lead goes up a thin left-facing corner (5.10+) to a belay just below an overhang. Climb a slot (5.8) in the middle of the overhang to pass it and continue in the crack to the end of the lead and a large ledge. This ledge leads off to the right to the east ridge (see *Route 10*) and is straightforward. Instead, one can continue straight up in a right-facing corner system—with one section of 5.8/5.9 climbing past a chockstone (awkward squeeze)—and then proceed a short distance to the summit of the peak. This route is more difficult than Armed Robbery and is a recommended climb on very good rock. For protection bring a wide range, including many small to medium nuts and a double set of cams to 4".

ROUTE 7. WFR. III, 5.8. First ascent July 11, 1990, by Jim Dorward and Steve Rickert. (See *Figure 3-8.*) Use the same approach as for Armed Robbery *(Route 5)*. Immediately right (east) of the ramp that curves up to the left toward the upper section of the face, look for an obvious crack system leading up the middle of a triangular buttress. The first three pitches ascend this crack system. At the top of the crack a delicate traverse right with little protection brings one to a ramp that is followed for 9m to the crest of the buttress. A deep chimney can now be seen leading up and to the right behind the southeast section of the face. Ascend this chimney for two pitches, topping out near the east ridge. Scramble up and left 15m to the ridge, which can be followed to the summit (see *Route 10*). **Gear:** Protection devices to 3.5" are suggested for this route.

ROUTE 8. CUT LOOSE. III, 5.10. First ascent August 2, 1977, by Yvon Chouinard and Rick Black. (See *Figure 3-8.*) As is not uncommon in the Tetons, there are probably several variations available on this face, and the one that was climbed in 1977 is described here. On August 30, 1954, William Buckingham and Roald Fryxell climbed a route on this eastern portion of the face, but their line of ascent is uncertain.

Use the same approach as for Armed Robbery *(Route 5)* to reach the bench at the base of the south face of Cloudveil Dome. The route starts on the broken face about 10m to the right (east) of the chimney that forms the bottom of the upper (right-hand) of the two parallel crack or ramp systems that diagonal across the south face. The first 46m on the face (5.7) leads to a large ledge at the base of a steep white wall containing two cracks. Climb the right-hand crack to the point where it becomes a left-facing dihedral, then traverse out to the left for 6m to a belay ledge. The third pitch ascends a steep face (5.9) to a roof that is passed on the left (5.10). Above the roof, traverse right to a belay stance, beyond which there are two options for the next 43m pitch. (1) One can climb the very difficult corner (5.10) directly above the belay to a point a short distance above its top and then traverse right into a right-facing dihedral (5.8), which is followed to a large ledge. (2) Or, easier, one can traverse directly right from the belay over to the beginning of the right-facing dihedral. The final lead is easier (5.6), staying left on the steep wall, and takes one to a narrow ridge, which is then followed, ending about 90m east of the summit. In places, protection is somewhat difficult to place on this route, but the rock is excellent.

ROUTE 9. SOUTHEAST RIB. II, 5.7. First ascent August 17, 1951, by John Driggs and Gary Driggs. This late entry into the annals of Teton climbing history was discovered by Paul Horton through exceptional sleuthing, as well as a climb of the route in 2003. This climb is one of three distinct lines that have been completed on the eastern portion of the south face of Cloudveil Dome, although it is located just around the edge of the face. (See *Figure 3-10.*) Approach via the Cloudveil Dome–Nez Perce col, as for *Route 5*. The eastern boundary of the precipitous south face is formed by a distinct edge, which appears as a rib in a certain light. Between this edge and the east ridge lies a narrow, less steep face of good rock. The base of this face is in the prominent, curved chimney/gully just west of the main couloir beneath the col. The narrow face becomes more ramp-like partway up; this lower-angle terrain eventually steepens into a short headwall on the flank of the east ridge, high on the peak. The route begins at the base of the face, which is attained by scrambling across the chimney/gully from the main couloir. The first couple of pitches, 5.7 on nice rock near the left side of the face, are the most challenging until the final headwall. The climb continues up easier terrain for a few pitches, following the path of least resistance. At the top of the ramp, where the rock steepens into the headwall, a 5.7 pitch attains the east ridge (see *Route 10*) and the scramble to the summit.

ROUTE 10. ▲ EAST RIDGE. II, 5.0. First ascent July 21, 1931, by Fritiof Fryxell and Anderson Hilding. (See *Figure 3-11.*) From the Garnet Canyon Meadows, ascend a talus and scree slope (better when it is covered with snow in early season) to the col just east of Cloudveil Dome. Turn west at the col and proceed up the ridge. Only one 5th-class pitch will be encountered, located slightly to the right (north) of the ridge crest; the remainder is enjoyable scrambling over good rock. From the col one can also swing left (south) of the ridge crest and follow broad ledges to the edge of the south face. Make an exposed move (easy 5th class) up and left (west), past a sharp detached flake, and then turn back right (east) to regain the crest a few ropelengths east of the summit. **Time:** 4 to 5 hours from Garnet Canyon; 7 to 8 hours from Jenny Lake. See *Appalachia* 18, no. 4 (December 1931): pp. 388–408, illus.; *Trail and Timberline*, no. 408 (December 1952): pp. 179–80.

ROUTE 11. NIMBUS. III, 5.9, A1, WI5. Attempted in February 1986, by Dave Carman and Norm Larson, at which time the name Mare's Tail was applied; first ascent in July 1993, by Alex Lowe and Stephen Koch. This climb was attempted a number of times before its successful ascent. Another fine example of a very temporary route, it is said to be very good when it is "in," which is most likely to occur late in the spring when the nights are cold. (See *Figure 3-11.*) Climb up the snow slopes below the eastern section of the north face until an area of loose, slabby rock is encountered. Proceed up this portion of the climb on easy 5th-class rock toward the start of a snow-and-ice gully. For their second pitch, Lowe and Koch ascended this gully and exited via a steep, icy wall (5.8). Their third pitch started with a 5.8 corner and finished with 18m of vertical ice to a hanging belay on a slab. The fourth pitch was the crux,

FIGURE 3-11. Cloudveil Dome, north aspect overview. (A) East Ridge *(Route 10)*, II, 5.0; (B) Nimbus *(Route 11)*, III, 5.9, A1, WI5; (C) North Face *(Route 12)*, III, 5.6; (D) Spalding Peak, Zorro Snowfield, variation: Sgt. Garcia Couloir, II, 5.1

involving 5.9, A1 climbing to exit to an ice pillar. At this point the chimney system opened up into a snow-and-ice gully for the fifth and final pitch. Easy scrambling on wet rock led to the shoulder of the east ridge, which provided a straightforward descent route (see *Route 10*).

ROUTE 12. NORTH FACE. III, 5.6. First ascent August 22, 1950, by Richard Pownall and Paul Kenworthy. (See *Figure 3-11*.) The lower portion of Cloudveil Dome that faces directly north is vertical, almost overhanging; the upper, narrow portion faces northeast, slanting steeply upward from lower left (east) to upper right (west). This route goes up a section of the lower north face and then ascends the northeast face toward the summit. From the south fork of Garnet Canyon ascend the steep snow leading directly toward the gray slabs at the base of the eastern part of the north face, which can be readily recognized by the branched intrusions of light rock in the face. Cross the bergschrund onto the rock and climb with care about 46m up these downsloping slabs (some loose rock here), then traverse left (east) to the base of a very steep 8m chimney near the left edge of the face. Ascend this difficult chimney, passing an overhang, to a belay. After two or three ropelengths of climbing above this chimney, climb up to the right (west), making an exposed traverse across a steep, platelike slab pitch. Climb to the beginning of the long, narrow northeast face. The first steep part of this section is climbed at the left (south) edge. The upper part is lower angle and leads more easily to the top shoulder of the main north face. From here one can scramble to the summit dome. See *American Alpine Journal* 8, no. 1 (1951): pp. 176–81.

Variation: III, 5.8, A1. First ascent August 1, 1961, by Jim Greig and Fred Wright. This variation provides a more direct route to the base of the upper slanting portion of the northeast face. From the topmost snow below the face, climb the initial slabs as in the preceding route. Instead of traversing left (east) to reach the steep chimney (as in the original 1950 route), climb the prominent gray ramp that angles up to the right to about 8m below its top. A downsloping ledge goes back left (east) from this point across a steep face. Step onto this ledge, climb a 2m loose flake, and from the top of the flake cross the steep face to the left on small holds to an overhanging crack. Ascend this crack using aid and make a short traverse left (east) to the base of a rotten chimney, which is then climbed. The angle of the large chimney above this one is not excessive; from the top of this second chimney the original route is rejoined at the beginning of the upper northeast face. Some of the leads on this variation are long (43m).

SPALDING PEAK (12,240+)

(0.25 mi W of Cloudveil Dome)
Map: Grand Teton

This is the first peak west of Cloudveil Dome on the long Cloudveil Dome–South Teton ridge. Although it is higher than Cloudveil Dome, Spalding Peak is rarely an isolated and deliberate objective. It is just one of the high points that must be crossed during the relatively popular traverse of this fine ridge.

Chronology

EAST RIDGE: July 21, 1931, Fritiof Fryxell, Anderson Hilding (ascent); August 5, 1932, Fred Ayres (descent)
WEST RIDGE: July 21, 1931, Fritiof Fryxell, Anderson Hilding (descent); August 5, 1932, Fred Ayres (ascent)
NORTH SNOWFIELD: June 29, 1934, Herman Eberitzsch, Emil Papplau
ZORRO SNOWFIELD: August 5, 1964, Ray Jacquot, J. Hallein, M. Ihne
var—**SGT. GARCIA COULOIR:** July 13, 1996, Joe Quinn, Neil Gleichman
SOUTH FACE: July 14, 1966, Dick Williams, John Hudson
NORTHEAST RIDGE: October 15, 1976, John Kevin Fox, Roger Mellen
SOUTH FACE RIGHT: September 28, 2003, Paul Horton, Charlie Thomas

ROUTE 1. ▲ WEST RIDGE. II, 4.0. First descent July 21, 1931, by Fritiof Fryxell and Anderson Hilding; first ascent August 5, 1932, by Fred Ayres. This short ridge separating Spalding Peak and Gilkey Tower is exposed 4th class. Ordinarily, the well-defined col between these two peaks is reached only along a traverse from the South Teton to Cloudveil Dome, or vice versa. An ascent of the west ridge of Spalding Peak normally involves first climbing Gilkey Tower and descending its east face to this col. However, along a slightly less-than-pure traverse from the South Teton to Cloudveil Dome, this col can also be reached from the snowfield below the Icecream Cone, by crossing the north face of Gilkey Tower (about halfway up) on a very broad talus ledge. From the col follow the ridge to the summit.

ROUTE 2. SOUTH FACE. III, 5.7, A2. First ascent July 14, 1966, by Dick Williams and John Hudson. The south face of Spalding Peak is well defined, bounded on both sides, east and west, by sharp couloirs or chutes that slant up from right (east) to left (west). Near the center of the face, a third prominent chute cuts upward at the same angle. A direct approach to this face is up the very long talus slope from the east end of Lake Taminah in Avalanche Canyon. The preferable approach is from Garnet Canyon, up and over the Cloudveil Dome–Nez Perce col and down the easy couloir about 90m to a distinctive reddish rock band, which marks the dike that passes from east to west along the south margins of the Nez Perce–South Teton ridge. Follow this reddish rock band west to a ramp sloping downward to the west to reach the top of a talus slope. The route starts at the base of the central chute, climbing generally on the left (west) side on 4.0 or 5.1 rock for about 90m to large scree ledges. Scramble 12m up broken rock until a 5.4 traverse on blocks to the right leads to the base of an obvious dihedral. Climb the dihedral 9m to its top and exit on aid in a diagonal crack leading around a corner. The next pitch continues up to gain the base of a second steep dihedral. Climb this dihedral to an overhanging section where a hand traverse (5.7) leads up to broken ledges slanting up and left. Traverse left for 90m to a ridge crest. Climb the ridge and finish by scrambling up a gully and ridge to the summit.

ROUTE 3. SOUTH FACE RIGHT. III, 5.10c. First ascent September 28, 2003, by Paul Horton and Charlie Thomas. (See *Figure 3-12*.) This route on the right side of the south face follows a series of steep dihedrals that extend from a broad terrace at the base up to the ridge just east of the summit. Approach from Garnet Canyon, cross the col on the main Cloudveil Dome–Nez Perce ridge, and descend to the bench below the south face of Cloudveil Dome. Follow the bench west to the gully between Cloudveil Dome and Spalding Peak. Scramble up the gully and adjacent slabs (some 4th class) to the broad terrace at the base of Spalding Peak's steep south face. The slabs may be wet, and snow will likely be found on the terrace until midseason or late season. A big, obvious dihedral with two overhangs slants up to the right; there is a smaller parallel corner 4m to the left. The first pitch climbs the crack in the big dihedral to an uncomfortable belay near its top; the second overhang is the crux (5.10c). The rock is somewhat dirty but the protection is very good on this long and continuous lead. The following short pitch (5.6) goes up the last bit of the dihedral and traverses left under overhangs to the far side of an easy slab. Another relatively short pitch with some doubtful rock ascends a corner under an overhang to a leftward hand traverse (5.9), then face climbs up to the belay on a ledge. The ledge diagonals all the way across the face. There is a tempting dihedral directly above this belay; however, the route lies to the left, where a much longer dihedral system extends all the way to the summit ridge. Attain these attractive corners via a long (60m) pitch that traverses on the diagonal ledge left for about 15m before turning up a short face and engaging the dihedrals above (5.7). Two more lengthy (60m) pitches on excellent rock (some 5.8, mostly 5.7) ascend the dihedrals to the ridge crest. The summit is a short scramble to the west.

ROUTE 4. ▲ EAST RIDGE. II, 3.0. First ascent July 21, 1931, by Fritiof Fryxell and Anderson Hilding; first descent August 5, 1932, by Fred Ayres. From the summit of Cloudveil Dome descend west a short distance to the broad col separating Cloudveil Dome from Spalding Peak. From the col scramble easily up a long ridge about 100m to the summit. See *Appalachia* 18, no. 4 (December 1931): pp. 388–408, illus.

ROUTE 5. ZORRO SNOWFIELD. II, 4.0. First ascent August 5, 1964, by Ray Jacquot, J. Hallein, and M. Ihne. The Zorro Snowfield on the northeast side of Spalding Peak, seen from the vicinity of the Garnet Canyon Meadows as Z-shaped in early or midseason, is the most conspicuous feature of this mountain. The lower right end of the "Z" is reached by scrambling from the main snowfield above the first headwall in the south fork of Garnet Canyon. The zigzagging snowfield is then followed to reach the col between Spalding Peak and Cloudveil Dome; from the col one can turn either west to Spalding Peak or east to Cloudveil Dome. The snowfield is quite exposed, with numerous cliff bands lurking below it.

***Variation:* SGT. GARCIA COULOIR.** II, 5.1. First ascent July 13, 1996, by Joe Quinn and Neil Gleichman. (See *Figure 3-11*.) This steep couloir, adjacent to the Zorro Snowfield, was used to access *Cloudveil Dome, Route 1*, and the first ascensionists then went on to traverse to the South Teton. The name refers to Zorro's comic foil, the portly Sergeant Garcia. The pair were aiming for the

FIGURE 3-12. Spalding Peak, south aspect, South Face Right *(Route 3)*, III, 5.10c

Zorro route but chose this couloir instead, accessing it via a wide ramp that slants upward from east to west beneath the right side of the north face. Some mixed climbing was encountered at the top of the couloir that involved crawling behind a chockstone.

ROUTE 6. NORTHEAST RIDGE. II, 5.4. First ascent October 15, 1976, by John Kevin Fox and Roger Mellen. This ridge separates the region of the Zorro Snowfield, which leads to the broad col east of Spalding Peak, from the main north snowfield of Spalding Peak. Proceed into the south fork of Garnet Canyon past the initial two small headwalls to the upper talus field (or snowfield in early season) that leads to the Middle Teton–South Teton saddle. Scramble back toward the northeast ridge, staying left (east) of the lower snout of the north snowfield of Spalding Peak. Gain the ridge crest at an obvious bench; this is the upper right corner of the "Z" of the Zorro Snowfield. The serrated ridge above contains several moderate roped pitches, ending on the east ridge of the peak a short distance from the summit. This is a pleasant climb, with the difficulty dependent on how closely the crest is followed.

ROUTE 7. NORTH SNOWFIELD. II, 4.0. First ascent June 29, 1934, by Herman Eberitzsch and Emil Papplau. Use the same approach as for the Northeast Ridge route *(Route 6)*. From the upper portion of the south fork of Garnet Canyon, climb directly to the lower snout of this snowfield, which lies directly below and north of the summit of Spalding Peak. The route is a straightforward but steep snow climb leading to the col just west of the summit.

GILKEY TOWER (12,320+)

(0.3 mi W of Cloudveil Dome)

Map: Grand Teton

This is the sharp peak midway along the long Cloudveil Dome–South Teton ridge and is made up of several high points. Similar to Spalding Peak, Gilkey Tower is normally ascended only when making this ridge traverse. This Teton peak was named in memory of the Teton guide Art Gilkey, who lost his life in the 1953 attempt on K2, the second-highest mountain in the world.

Chronology

EAST FACE: July 21, 1931, Fritiof Fryxell, Anderson Hilding (ascent); August 5, 1932, Fred Ayres (descent)
WEST RIDGE: July 21, 1931, Fritiof Fryxell, Anderson Hilding (descent); August 5, 1932, Fred Ayres (ascent)
NORTH FACE: August 15, 1955, Dick Bonker, Tom McCalla
NORTHEAST SNOWFIELD: September 7, 1964, Howard Wignall, Dennis Wignall
SUNRISE RIDGE: August 16, 1972, Leigh Ortenburger, Irene Beardsley (Ortenburger)

ROUTE 1. ▲ WEST RIDGE. II, 4.0. First descent July 21, 1931, by Fritiof Fryxell and Anderson Hilding; first ascent August 5, 1932, by Fred Ayres. This route, which starts from the col separating Gilkey Tower from the Icecream Cone, is used when making the traverse from the South Teton to Cloudveil Dome. The col can be reached along the ridge by making a genuine traverse of the Icecream Cone, up its west face and down its east face to the col. However, much more commonly, the col is gained from the South Teton by traversing along the top edge of the snowfield (icefield in midseason to late season, crampons useful) around and under the north face of the Icecream Cone. The small towers at the beginning of this ridge near the col are usually bypassed during the Cloudveil Dome–South Teton traverse. A party in 1962 found records on these towers dating from 1932.

ROUTE 2. SUNRISE RIDGE. II, 5.4. First ascent August 16, 1972, by Leigh Ortenburger and Irene Beardsley (Ortenburger). This distinct and pleasant south ridge rises to Gilkey Tower from the col that separates Matternought Peak from the Nez Perce–South Teton ridge. The first portion of the ridge is a tower, whose summit is reached after three leads (5.4), the last of which goes right around an overhanging bulge. From the top of this tower climb an easy chimney onto the crest of the ridge between Gilkey Tower and the Icecream Cone. Follow this to the summit.

ROUTE 3. ▲ EAST FACE. II, 3.0. First ascent July 21, 1931, by Fritiof Fryxell and Anderson Hilding; first descent August 5, 1932, by Fred Ayres. From the col that separates Spalding Peak from Gilkey Tower, enjoyable climbing brings one to the summit of Gilkey Tower, after an encounter with a small pinnacle just short of the summit. See *Spalding Peak, Route 1* for methods of reaching this col; it is usually attained during the traverse from Cloudveil Dome to the South Teton.

ROUTE 4. NORTHEAST SNOWFIELD. II, 4.0. First ascent September 7, 1964, by Howard Wignall and Dennis Wignall. This is the same snowfield as described in *Spalding Peak, Route 7*. Follow that route to the col just east of Gilkey Tower. From the col turn right and follow the East Face route *(Route 3)* to the summit.

ROUTE 5. NORTH FACE. II, 5.4. First ascent August 15, 1955, by Dick Bonker and Tom McCalla. This long, seldom-climbed route starts from the prominent snowfield lying at the base of the face and leads directly up to the center of the main overhang on the north face. The overhang can be passed by climbing the shallow chimney in its center. A large horizontal bench will be passed about halfway up this face.

ICECREAM CONE (12,400+)

(0.1 mi E of the South Teton)

Map: Grand Teton

This distinct, well-named conical peak is the first one east of the South Teton. Even though it is but a small tower, it provides the finest climb of the Cloudveil Dome–South Teton traverse.

Chronology

EAST FACE: August 5, 1932, Fred Ayres
WEST FACE: August 1, 1940, William Shand, Benjamin Ferris

ROUTE 1. WEST FACE. II, 5.6. First ascent August 1, 1940, by William Shand and Benjamin Ferris. This route, which is seldom climbed, ascends one of the chimneys on the steep west face, about 1m north of the actual notch separating the Icecream Cone from the South Teton. To descend by this route most climbers will find a rappel (23m) convenient.

ROUTE 2. ▲ EAST FACE. II, 3.0. First ascent August 5, 1932, by Fred Ayres. This broken face provides the only easy route to the summit. The col separating Gilkey Tower from the Icecream Cone, where this route begins, is usually reached during the east-to-west traverse from Cloudveil Dome to the South Teton. When making this ridge traverse from west to east (as is done on the Grand Traverse; see Section 5), it is customary, but less than pure, to use this route to climb the Icecream Cone. This is done through the expedient of reaching this col from the South Teton by traversing east along the top edge of the snowfield (icefield in midseason to late season, crampons useful) that exists under the north face of the Icecream Cone.

SOUTH TETON (12,514)

Map: Grand Teton

The South Teton, one of the famous "Trois Tetons" of 19th-century history, is but the fifth-highest peak in the range. Although the South Teton is not easily visible from Jackson Hole, it is prominent from Teton Basin to the west. It is one of the easiest of the major summits to reach and in the early days was climbed frequently. The regular route *(Route 7)* is approached from Garnet Canyon and begins at the saddle between the Middle Teton and the South Teton (see *Garnet Canyon, South Fork*). The South Teton can be climbed from the valley in one day, as is true of most of the peaks accessible from Garnet Canyon, but a camp at the Platforms or higher is recommended if one desires a leisurely trip. Other approaches to this high peak are the south fork of Cascade Canyon (see *Cascade Canyon, South Fork* in Section 8) and Avalanche Canyon (see *Avalanche Canyon* in Section 2).

Chronology

NORTHWEST COULOIR: August 29, 1923, Albert R. Ellingwood, Eleanor Davis (Ehrman)
WEST RIDGE: August 21, 1924, Paul Petzoldt
NORTH FACE: July 5, 1930, Fritiof Fryxell, Phil Smith (partial); July 19, 1957, Yvon Chouinard, William Mason (complete)
EAST RIDGE: August 5, 1932, Fred Ayres (descent); July 3, 1933, Paul Petzoldt, Sterling Hendricks (ascent)
var—July 19, 1940, William and Harold Plumley, Jack and William Fralick
var—August 24, 1962, Edward F., John, and Lawrence Little
SOUTH RIDGE: July 2, 1955, W. V. Graham Matthews, Mary Ann Matthews
NORTH CHIMNEY: June 25, 1973, Harvey Gould, Robert Goren
SOUTHEAST COULOIR: August 1, 1973, Jim "Ole" Olson, Tom Watson

ROUTE 1. WEST RIDGE. II, 4.0. First ascent August 21, 1924, by Paul Petzoldt. This route is only slightly more difficult than the regular route, *Route 7*. The best approach is via the south fork of Cascade Canyon to the saddle (10,560+) between the South Teton and the Wall; an unmaintained but good side trail leads from the main Teton Crest Trail below the Schoolroom Glacier to this broad saddle. However, the north fork of Avalanche Canyon can also readily be used to gain this saddle. From the saddle proceed up the broad ridge. The upper part of the west ridge is the most difficult and can be avoided by cutting horizontally left (north), when one is halfway up the ridge, toward the couloir that provides access to the main north slope. Some steep, loose scree will be encountered on this traverse. This couloir is the primary break in the rotten cliffs that protect the Middle Teton–South Teton saddle from the west; it leads to a shoulder on the ridge above the saddle and on the edge of the north slope. Another alternative, which also evades the upper west ridge, crosses to the right (south) about halfway up the ridge and enters a broad couloir that leads up the southwest face. From the top of this couloir scramble among the boulders of the summit ridge to the north slope. Once on the north slope, by either scheme, proceed to the couloir of *Route 7*. This route cannot be recommended because of an abundance of very rotten rock. See *Appalachia* 18, no. 3 (June 1931): pp. 209–32, illus.

ROUTE 2. SOUTH RIDGE. II, 3.0. First ascent July 2, 1955, by W. V. Graham Matthews and Mary Ann Matthews. See *Avalanche Canyon* in Section 2 for the approach and possible campsites. It would also be possible, but less direct, to approach via the south fork of Cascade Canyon and descend 120m into the north fork of Avalanche Canyon to the beginning of the ridge. The lower portion of the south side of the South Teton is composed of two main ridges, separated by a steep, narrow, snow-filled couloir. Both ridges contain several subridges. The two ridges and the couloir converge just above a prominent notch in the mountain (about 240m below the summit). This notch was formed by the weathering out of the major reddish dike that runs east–west along the south side of Nez Perce to the base of the southwest face of the South Teton; the dike disappears when it intersects the main Buck Mountain fault, which is easily distinguished along the lower portion of the southwest and west faces of the South Teton.

From the flat area just east of Snowdrift Lake, scramble up toward the western ridge of the two main ridges. It is easiest to bypass the initial buttresses (and gendarmes) of the ridge and stay slightly to the left (west) side of this ridge as far as the dike notch, which is marked by the uppermost snow in the adjacent couloir. From the notch one can climb directly up, or one can traverse out to the right to gain the uppermost rock of the eastern south ridge and ascend that to the final, unified south ridge. Either way, this section contains the principal problems of the route, partly due to some sections of poor rock. This upper ridge leads directly to the summit without difficulty. **Time:** 4½ hours from Avalanche Canyon.

ROUTE 3. SOUTHEAST COULOIR. II, 5.4. First ascent August 1, 1973, by Jim "Ole" Olson and Tom Watson. This prominent snow couloir, easily seen from the highway southeast of the South Teton, cuts directly up the southeast slope of the South Teton, ending on the south ridge about 60m below the summit. It is yet another example of a snow-climbing route that has become a sought-after ski-mountaineering objective. From Avalanche Canyon in the vicinity of Snowdrift Lake (see *Avalanche Canyon, North Fork* in Section 2), gain the high cirque below the south faces of Gilkey Tower and the Icecream Cone and reach the broad snowfield at the upper end. From this snowfield turn left (west) and upward to the base of the couloir, which consists of about nine leads of snow climbing. About two-thirds of the way up this couloir, a short rock wall capped by a large chockstone presents the principal difficulty on the route; it is passed on the left. The final three snow leads become increasingly steep, ending with a very steep cornice section at the top. Some rockfall may be encountered, but belay positions and protection are good. In some years and seasons a couple of ropelengths of ice may be encountered. This is a good climb; crampons are recommended.

ROUTE 4. EAST RIDGE. II, 4.0. First descent August 5, 1932, by Fred Ayres; first ascent July 3, 1933, by Paul Petzoldt and Sterling Hendricks. The first climbs of this route were made as part of the traverse from the South Teton to Cloudveil Dome, or conversely. In the course of this traverse, descend from the various pinnacles west of Gilkey Tower to the snowfield that lies at the north base of the Icecream Cone. Then contour along the top edge of the snowfield and climb a short couloir to the notch between the Icecream Cone and the South Teton. In late season, and in some years in midseason, this snowfield becomes ice, making crampons necessary. This notch can also be reached by first climbing the Icecream Cone and then rappelling down the west face of the

Icecream Cone directly to the notch. From the notch climb the loose rock of the ridge to the summit, staying for the most part on the right (north) side.

Variation: II, 4.0. First ascent July 19, 1940, by William and Harold Plumley and Jack and William Fralick. A large snowfield extends down into the south fork of Garnet Canyon from beneath the north faces of the Icecream Cone and the South Teton and west of Gilkey Tower. This snowfield provides access to the notch between the Icecream Cone and the South Teton, from which the east ridge can be followed to the summit. This variation is more interesting than *Route 7* for those seeking some experience on snow, but it is essential to know how to use an ice axe. In late season, and in some years even in midseason, the upper portion of this snowfield becomes ice, and crampons are necessary. **Time:** 4½ hours from Garnet Canyon.

Variation: II, 4.0. First ascent August 24, 1962, by Edward F., John, and Lawrence Little. From the summit ridge of the South Teton, a spur of broken rock extends down to the northeast toward Garnet Canyon. This small ridge forms the right (west) boundary of the snowfield that reaches the notch between the Icecream Cone and the South Teton. It provides a climb longer than *Routes 4, 5,* and *7* but is of only modest difficulty. After climbing to a point somewhat above the level of the notch, cross to the left (southeast) and reach the summit via the upper portion of the east ridge.

ROUTE 5. NORTH FACE. II, 5.6. First partial ascent July 5, 1930, by Fritiof Fryxell and Phil Smith; first complete ascent July 19, 1957, by Yvon Chouinard and William Mason. Because of icy conditions, the pioneering 1930 party was forced to contour left (east) to the east ridge and finish the climb to the summit by *Route 4.* From the bottom of the center of the face, climb directly up for about seven ropelengths on good but wet rock (possibly dry in late season). The last pitch is the hardest and it brings one out onto the summit ridge only 30m east of the summit. This is a short but enjoyable climb. **Time:** 5½ hours from Garnet Canyon. See *Appalachia* 18, no. 3 (June 1931): pp. 209–32, illus.

ROUTE 6. NORTH CHIMNEY. II, 5.1. First ascent June 25, 1973, by Harvey Gould and Robert Goren. The main north face of the South Teton is bounded on the right (west) by a very narrow and moderately steep couloir that diagonals up to the right from the top of a snow tongue extending up from the main snowfield below the face. This couloir or chute ends on the summit ridge only a short distance west of the summit boulders. Approach via the south fork of Garnet Canyon, but turn up onto the initial snowfield well before reaching the Middle Teton–South Teton saddle. In early season the couloir is a snow climb, starting at about 30° and steepening to 45° near its top.

ROUTE 7. ▲ NORTHWEST COULOIR. II, 4.0. First ascent August 29, 1923, by Albert R. Ellingwood and Eleanor Davis (Ehrman). (See *Figure 3-13.*) This regular route has become a popular Teton climb to one of the major summits of the range. From the saddle between the Middle Teton and the South Teton, climb the talus slope and the ridge of the South Teton heading toward the snowfield that protects this couloir, which lies on the north flank of the northwest ridge. The shallow couloir is easily seen from the saddle. With luck, something of a climbers' trail will be found in this section of talus. Cross the snowfield near its top edge to gain the short upper couloir, which leads onto the summit ridge only 30m west of the summit. A little scrambling over large boulders brings one to the top. While this is not a difficult climb, an ice axe and rope are recommended for inexperienced climbers for the snowfield crossing; even in late season, at least one stretch of moderately steep snow must usually be crossed to reach the upper couloir. **Time:** 50 to 90 minutes from the saddle; 4 to 5½ hours from Garnet Canyon; 6½ to 9¼ hours from Jenny Lake. See *Appalachia* 18, no. 3 (June 1931): pp. 209–32, illus.

MIDDLE TETON (12,804)

Map: Grand Teton

Many people consider the Middle Teton, third highest of the Teton peaks, to be one of the most interesting mountains of the range. Its structure is complex and harbors numerous routes, although only two—the Southwest Couloir *(Route 1)* and the North Ridge *(Route 32)*—are climbed frequently. With very few exceptions these are also virtually the only routes used

FIGURE 3-13. South Teton, Northwest Couloir *(Route 7)*, II, 4.0

for descent. The complexity of ridges and couloirs, especially on the south side of the mountain, has made the early climbing history very difficult to resolve; the first ascents of some routes as reported in the chronology may in fact have been made in previous years.

The Middle Teton is one of just two peaks in the range that afford genuine glacier routes to the summit. At the southwest base of the mountain is Icefloe Lake (10,652), the highest lake in the Teton Range. A black diabase dike forms a prominent part of the peak. Starting at the base of the east ridge, it follows this long ridge part of the way to the Dike Pinnacle, then veers off to the north to intersect the north ridge in a sharp notch before disappearing down the northwest side of the mountain. The high point on the north side of this dike notch is the North Peak; it was first climbed on July 5, 1940, by Paul Petzoldt and Elizabeth Cowles (Partridge). The Dike Pinnacle is the distinct subpeak (12,200+) on the crest of the east ridge; the col separating this pinnacle from the summit is reached from the north via the upper tongue of the Middle Teton Glacier and from the south by way of the Ellingwood Couloir. In addition, there are two distinct summits of the Middle Teton. The north summit is a few feet higher than the south summit, but from the couloir of the regular route it is impossible to tell which is higher. Both the Dike Pinnacle and the south summit of the Middle Teton were first reached on August 28, 1929, by Fritiof Fryxell and Phil Smith.

From the summit an excellent view is obtained of the entire south side of the Grand Teton; hence, the Middle Teton can be recommended as a warm-up for those planning to ascend one of the south ridges of the Grand. The northern aspect of the mountain, between the Middle Teton Glacier and the Northwest Ice Couloir *(Route 33)*, contains a considerable expanse of some of the finest solid Teton rock. The standard approach for climbing the Middle Teton is via Garnet Canyon; only rarely has the mountain been climbed by another approach. Doubtlessly, any of the routes can be climbed in one long day from the valley, but it is convenient to establish a high camp in Garnet Canyon.

Chronology

ELLINGWOOD COULOIR: August 29, 1923, Albert R. Ellingwood (ascent)

SOUTHWEST COULOIR: July 16, 1927, H. Oswald Christensen, Morris Christensen, and Irven Christensen
var—July 15, 1967, Rod McCally, John Harkness

SOUTHEAST COULOIR: August 28, 1929, Fritiof Fryxell, Phil Smith

SOUTH COULOIR: August 28, 1929, Fritiof Fryxell, Phil Smith (descent)
var—[probable] July 3, 1959, Curt Butler

NORTH RIDGE: July 17, 1931, Robert Underhill, Fritiof Fryxell (ascent); July 4, 1933, Paul Petzoldt, Sterling Hendricks (descent)
var—July 5, 1940, Paul Petzoldt, Elizabeth Cowles (Partridge)

NORTHEAST FACE: August 24, 1936, Fritz Wiessner, William House, Elizabeth Woolsey

NORTHWEST SLOPE: [possible] August 27, 1939, Stanley Grites, Frank Garbocz, Adam Koj; [probable] July 16, 1940, W. Heidholm; [certain] September 6, 1954, William Hooker, Peter Ludwig, Peter Luster, Craig Merrihue

SHAND-FERRIS: August 1, 1940, William Shand, Benjamin Ferris

SOUTHWEST RIDGE: August 8, 1940, Jack Durrance, Henry Coulter (complete); July 17, 1931, Robert Underhill, Fritiof Fryxell (partial descent); [probable] August 24, 1937, H. K. and Elizabeth Hartline (partial ascent)

MIDDLE TETON GLACIER: August 4, 1944, Sterling Hendricks, Paul Bradt

BUCKINGHAM (SOUTHEAST) RIDGE: August 15, 1954, William Buckingham, Virgil Day
var—July 7, 1961, Herb Swedlund, Peter Geiser
var—July 9, 1994, Peter Lenz, Curt Pollock

DIKE: September 14, 1954, Richard Irvin, Floyd Burnette
var—September 15, 1935, Malcolm Smith, Newell Rohrer, Francis Neimann

WEST RIDGE: August 4, 1955, William Buckingham, Mary Lou Nohr

GOODRICH CHIMNEY: September 4, 1955, Don Goodrich, John Reppy

CHOUINARD RIDGE: July 2, 1957, Yvon Chouinard, Ken Weeks

ROBBINS-FITSCHEN: July 30, 1960, Royal Robbins, Joe Fitschen

NORTHWEST ICE COULOIR: June 16, 1961, Peter Lev, Jim Greig
var—Date and party unknown

TAYLOR: August 26, 1961, Royal Robbins, Jane Taylor; FFA summer 2008, Hans Johnstone, David Gonzales

DIKE PINNACLE, SOUTH RIDGE: August 1, 1962, Ants Leemets, Raivo Puusemp
var—**BEYER SOUTH RIDGE:** July 11, 2020, Jim Beyer (solo)

BRIGGS-HIGBEE PILLAR: July 8, 1974, Roger Briggs, Art Higbee

SHEA-BREASHEARS: June 1978, Steve Shea, David Breashears

WHITON-WIGGINS DIHEDRAL: September 20, 1981, Mark Whiton, Earl Wiggins

LINE OF LEES'S RESISTANCE: June 30, 1986, David Koch, Evelyn Lees

JACKSON-WOODMENCEY DIHEDRAL: June 25, 1988, Renny Jackson, Jim Woodmencey

DIRECT EAST BUTTRESS: July 19, 1989, Tom Turiano, Matthew Goewert; FFA July 21, 1992, Renny Jackson, Kevin Moore

BUFFALO GALS: August 1, 1996, Renny Jackson, Ron Johnson

DEW DROP INN: August 10, 1996, Eric Gabriel, Andy Byerly

NO CUMBRE, NO RUTA: July 14, 1997, Alex Lowe, Travis Spitzer

PINNACLE ROUTE: August 2000, Mike Ruth, Brian Piddick

WEST FACE, ELECTRIC CORNER: August 2000, David Bywater, Craig Holm

DIKE PINNACLE, NORTH FACE I: July 23, 2002, David Bywater, Ron Johnson

DIKE PINNACLE, NORTH FACE II: August 2, 2008, Aaron Gams, Brian Mulvihill

BROWN-MACKE: November 2010, Nate Brown, Sam Macke

NORTH WALL: August 2015, Greg Collins, Hans Johnstone

MIDDLE FINGER: July 2019, Greg Collins, Hans Johnstone

INGE'S: (unfinished) Greg Collins et al.

ROUTE 1. ▲ SOUTHWEST COULOIR. II, 3.0. First ascent July 16, 1927, by H. Oswald Christensen, Morris Christensen, and Irven Christensen, after climbing the South Teton earlier the same day. See *Figures 3-14* and *3-15*, in which very early snow climbing on this route is depicted. Expect loose rock and scree later on in the season when the snow is gone. This is the very popular regular route used by most parties and is approached via the south fork of Garnet Canyon. To avoid getting lost in one of the many southern couloirs, climb *all the way* to the saddle between the Middle Teton and the South Teton until Icefloe Lake can be seen below; then, and only then, turn north up the largest and most obvious couloir visible from the saddle. There is no difficulty in the lower sections of the couloir. However, if the climb is made in early season or early in the day, crampons may prove useful in the steeper snow of the upper sections. An ice axe—and more importantly, the knowledge of how to use it—will be needed. Considerations such as these may lead some parties to turn out of the couloir to avoid the snow. One can do this at many different places, but in general it is best not to turn out until relatively high in the couloir. In a dry season or late in the season, something approximating a trail will be found up this couloir, as this is a very popular climb. But because the route is so popular, use *great* caution with the loose rocks—other climbers may be below. On approaching the notch between the north and south summits, keep in mind that the left (north) summit is higher. About 30m below the notch, climb to the left and hit the west ridge a short distance from the summit. Follow the ridge easily to the airy summit. As a variation, use the right (south) side of the couloir to avoid some of the steep upper sections. However, do not follow this too far because the summit

FIGURE 3-14. Middle Teton, southwest aspect. (A) Southwest Couloir *(Route 1)*, II, 3.0; (B) Southwest Ridge *(Route 2)*, III, 5.6, A1

lies on the opposite (north) side of the couloir. On the descent it is advisable to go *all the way* down to the saddle before turning east down the canyon; the snowfield northeast of the saddle is steep in early season and, as shown in *Figure 3-14*, many accidents have occurred along this shortcut. **Time:** 4½ to 6 hours from Garnet Canyon; 6½ to 8 hours from Jenny Lake. See *Appalachia* 18, no. 3 (June 1931): pp. 209–32, illus.; 19, no. 1 (June 1932): pp. 86–96.

Variation: II, 5.1. First recorded ascent July 15, 1967, by Rod McCally and John Harkness. This variation attains the saddle between the South Teton and the Middle Teton directly from the west. In the early years of the park this variation may well have been done by more than one exploring party. From Icefloe Lake, which is infrequently used as a campsite, this variation provides a direct start to the standard Southwest Couloir route on the Middle Teton. However, this climb is explicitly *not* recommended because considerable dangerous and rotten rock will be encountered, even though the absolute difficulty is not severe.

ROUTE 2. SOUTHWEST RIDGE. III, 5.6, A1. First complete ascent August 8, 1940, by Jack Durrance and Henry Coulter. Previous climbs on this ridge include a partial descent on July 17, 1931, by Robert Underhill and Fritiof Fryxell, and a probable partial ascent on August 24, 1937, by H. K. and Elizabeth Hartline. (See *Figures 3-14* and *3-15*.) This ridge, which might also be called a series of indistinct towers, forms the right (east) boundary of the southwest couloir (see *Route 1*). The difficulty of this climb, like some others in the park, depends on how closely the crest of the ridge is followed. Ascend the south fork of Garnet Canyon to the saddle between the South Teton and the Middle Teton. The large, easily identified first tower, which marks the beginning of the ridge, can be bypassed on the west by gaining the crest of the ridge at one of several different points from the regular Southwest Couloir route. On the original ascent, however, this difficult tower was climbed, using pitons for aid, via the overhanging crack on the very steep face, slightly on the west side of the tower.

Climb three 18m pitches from the notch behind this tower; then scramble to a short, overhanging step in the ridge and climb this on its exposed south side. About 90m of moderate climbing then leads past the junction of a subsidiary ridge from the east and to the base of a massive tower. Some steep climbing is then required to get onto the higher of the two wide ledges that slope upward to the left. Follow this ledge back to the left until it crosses the ridge crest. Then either climb the ridge directly or follow the ledge around to the left, where it is a simple matter to regain the crest. Follow the ridge past several indistinct towers to a tower at the end, which is separated from the vertical southwest face of the south summit by a distinct notch. Descend to this notch and cut left (north) and up to the main (north) summit. **Time:** 10 hours from Garnet Canyon. See *American Alpine Journal* 4, no. 2 (1941): pp. 304–6.

ROUTE 3. CHOUINARD RIDGE. II, 5.4. First ascent July 2, 1957, by Yvon Chouinard and Ken Weeks. (See *Figure 3-15*.) This is the somewhat jumbled ridge immediately west of the south couloir (see *Route 4*), and it is approached in the same manner. It contains good rock and is an enjoyable climb. Ascend the south fork of Garnet Canyon until it becomes possible to see the entire Ellingwood Couloir *(Route 6)* leading to the col between the Dike Pinnacle and the main (north) summit of the Middle Teton; then climb (on snow until late season) the bottom section of the Ellingwood Couloir to the point where it is split into two branches by the southeast ridge. The left (west) branch is the broad and open beginning of the south couloir. Cross over to the rock at the beginning of the Chouinard Ridge, which is on the left (west) side of this snow couloir. The first seven ropelengths on this ridge are easy 5th-class climbing, and then an inside corner (difficult when wet) must be passed. A few more easy pitches then lead to a break in the ridge, which in early season is filled with snow. Climb a chimney above the snow patch to a small cave; then leave the cave on the left to reach another cave directly above. Now, traverse to the right to regain the ridge crest; follow it to the point where it joins the southwest ridge (see *Route* 2) near its final tower. From this tower it is but a short distance to the summit. See *American Alpine Journal* 12, no. 1 (1960): pp. 125–27.

ROUTE 4. SOUTH COULOIR. II, 4.0. First descent August 28, 1929, by Fritiof Fryxell and Phil Smith. (See *Figure 3-15.*) The exact history of the climbs on the south side of the Middle Teton between the southeast and southwest ridges is confused because the topography is ill defined and the nomenclature for this region has only recently been clarified. The climbing is not, in general, difficult, and there are many route possibilities. The south couloir is the couloir immediately west of the southeast ridge (see *Route* 5); it leads northwest to the small notch that separates the top of the southwest ridge (see *Route* 2) from the sharp south summit of the Middle Teton. The left (western) boundary of this couloir is the fairly well-defined Chouinard Ridge *(Route 3)*, which parallels the southeast ridge and terminates on the southwest ridge near its final tower. It is not known for certain when (or if) this south couloir was first ascended.

Use the same approach as for the Chouinard Ridge. The southeast ridge always sharply defines the right (east) edge of the south couloir; once the beginning of the couloir is reached, there is little routefinding difficulty. The upper part of the couloir is rather narrow and steep and ultimately leads below and past the vertical southwest and west faces of the south summit of the Middle Teton. Pass the notch between the north and south summits and proceed to the main (north) summit.

Variation: II, 4.0. Probable first ascent July 3, 1959, by Curt Butler. This variation leaves the couloir about halfway up, at the point where there is a break in the Chouinard Ridge on the left (west). In early season the snow in the south couloir extends all the way to the crest of the Chouinard Ridge. Cross this ridge into the next shallow couloir and follow it to the crest of the southwest ridge; then proceed along that ridge to the summit (see *Route* 2).

ROUTE 5. BUCKINGHAM (SOUTHEAST) RIDGE. III, 5.7. First complete ascent August 15, 1954, by William Buckingham and Virgil Day. (See *Figures 3-15* and *3-16.*) This major ridge of excellent rock forms the left (west) edge of the prominent Ellingwood Couloir and leads directly to the south summit of the Middle Teton. It is one of the most enjoyable of the moderate rock routes out of Garnet Canyon. The difficulty depends on exactly which variation is chosen from among the several possible options. Take the Garnet Canyon trail from the Lupine Meadows trailhead to the Platforms. Proceed past the Meadows and up into the south fork of the canyon. The southeast ridge can be seen rising from the junction of the Ellingwood Couloir *(Route 6)* and the south couloir (see *Route* 4), which is on the west side of the southeast ridge. From this point, halfway up the south fork of Garnet Canyon, turn right and climb a talus and scree cone (covered with snow

FIGURE 3-15. Middle Teton, southeast aspect. (A) Southwest Couloir *(Route 1)*, II, 3.0; (B) Southwest Ridge *(Route 2)*, III, 5.6, A1; (C) Chouinard Ridge *(Route 3)*, II, 5.4; (D) South Couloir *(Route 4)*, II, 4.0; (E) Buckingham (Southeast) Ridge *(Route 5)*, III, 5.7; (F) Ellingwood Couloir *(Route 6)*, II, 5.1; (G) Dike Pinnacle, South Ridge (*Route 7*), II, 5.7, A3 and variation: Beyer South Ridge IV, 5.10; (H) Southeast Couloir *(Route 8)*, II, 5.4

in early season or midseason, requiring an ice axe) leading to the bottom of the Ellingwood Couloir and the beginning of the ridge. One can avoid the crest of the ridge entirely by climbing the right (east) side of the ridge, which would be the left (west) side of the couloir, until near the Dike Pinnacle col. Then turn up and left to gain the ridge crest near the base of the south summit.

However, the standard Buckingham Ridge route begins with approximately 200m of 3rd- to easy 5th-class scrambling up the crest to a steep, smooth buttress. From the eastern edge of the buttress climb four ropelengths up and generally left (west). The difficulty ranges from 5.7 to 5.8 depending on the line taken, and the climbing consists mainly of cracks, corners, and slabs. Move the belay into the notch for the climb of the small tower on the ridge (5.7 out of the notch). Once atop the tower, the belay can then be moved onto chockstones located in the chimney behind it to the north. Proceed up 4.0 and 5.1 slabs for two pitches. Walk north on the large ledge below the final headwall to the base of some easy chimneys. Climb these for a ropelength (5.1) to another ledge. Easy broken rock then brings one to the top of the south summit. A single-rope rappel can be done from the north side of the south summit. This provides access to the easy eastern slabs and the true summit of the peak. Because this southeast ridge is broad, many variations are possible, especially in the upper portions and in the lower section leading to the buttress.

Variation: III, 5.7, A1, or III, 5.8. First ascent July 7, 1961, by Herb Swedlund and Peter Geiser; a line of similar difficulty was taken on August 16, 1964, by Peter Cleveland and Peter Crane. Instead of bypassing on the right the "steep, smooth buttress" mentioned in the standard Buckingham Ridge route, there are two ways, originally with the use of aid, to climb the buttress directly. The first pitch begins at the base of the buttress and ascends a series of steep slabs. The wall above is then climbed to a 5.7 jam crack. The third pitch traverses right for 1.5m to a vertical crack in the wall, which is climbed (A1) up and over a small overhang to rejoin the standard route. An alternative direct variation on this buttress lies somewhat to the left (southwest) and, after passing an overhang (A3) at the end of the first long lead, stays near the left edge of the buttress and reaches a gunsight notch after another three or four leads. One pitch beyond this notch places the climber on easier ground.

Variation: III, 5.9. First ascent July 9, 1994, by Peter Lenz and Curt Pollock. This variation apparently ascends the final headwall of the south summit in a more direct fashion than the original Buckingham Ridge route. From the large ledge located below the final headwall, climb a 5.8 dihedral for 37m that then leads into a deep chimney system and belay. Proceed up the chimney past some loose blocks and belay under a chockstone after 23m. After getting around the chockstone (5.9 face), climb the final 23m of the chimney (5.9) to a blocky ledge, from which easy climbing leads to the south summit. **Gear:** Bring protection to 4".

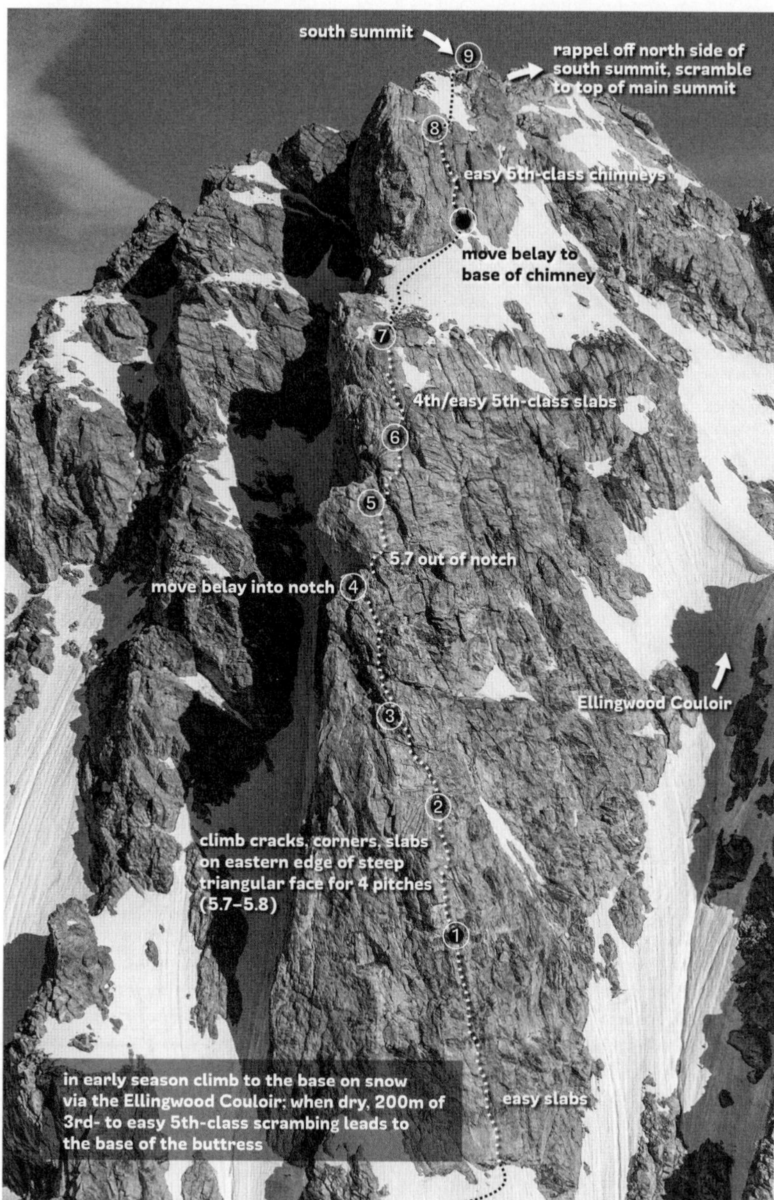

FIGURE 3-16. Middle Teton, south aspect, Buckingham (Southeast) Ridge *(Route 5)*, III, 5.7

ROUTE 6. ELLINGWOOD COULOIR. II, 5.1. First ascent August 29, 1923, by Albert R. Ellingwood; Eleanor Davis (Ehrman) and E. W. Harnden stopped a few minutes below the summit during a brief storm in which Ellingwood went on to the summit alone. Because it is likely that the 1923 party used only the upper portions of this couloir, the first complete ascent may have been made many years later; one probable ascent was on August 5, 1934, by Glenn Exum, James Cooley, and Macauley Smith. (See *Figure 3-15.*) In late season this couloir will be a rock climb up slabs, with isolated patches of ice in a few chimneys. In early season, however, the slabs are covered, and this route becomes a rather steep, pure snow-and-ice climb, requiring careful use of the ice axe. In general, this route is slightly on the left (west) side of the couloir. From the Dike Pinnacle col climb to the summit as described in *Route 8*. See *Appalachia* 18, no. 3 (June 1931): pp. 209–32, illus.

ROUTE 7. DIKE PINNACLE, SOUTH RIDGE. II, 5.7, A3. First ascent August 1, 1962, by Ants Leemets and Raivo Puusemp. The summit register entry by the first-ascent team simply reads, "South Buttress"—not a lot to go on. But because this route is mentioned in Orrin and Lorraine Bonney's guidebook (see below), it is chronicled here. (See *Figure 3-15.*) Use *Route 6* as the approach to the lower portion of the ridge and then climb it to the highest point beneath the uppermost buttress of the Dike Pinnacle. **Pitch 1:** Start diagonally up and left on high-angle rock. Traverse back right where the angle eases off, then climb up to a bulge under a small overhanging corner; lead up and left over the bulge and corner (A2), then traverse out on a face and up to a large ledge (5.7, 43m). **Pitch 2:** Climb up left and then right to a broken, steep ledge leading up left to large flake. Jam or lieback the flake and climb up to a good belay ledge on the south ridge of the buttress (5.6, 37m). **Pitch 3:** Climb on ledges just left of the face proper; belay on a small ledge in a chimney on a corner (5.5, 18m). **Pitch 4:** Climb up a steep ledge to an overhang; climb the right side of the overhang onto a face. Traverse right, then climb up to a large ledge (5.6, 37m). Scramble left and through a short, easy, and yet broken and overhanging section. Follow the ridge, crossing two dikes, and join the Southeast Couloir route (*Route 8*) to the summit of the pinnacle. One can then continue to the summit of the Middle Teton via that route. (Source: Orrin H. Bonney and Lorraine G. Bonney *Field Book, The Teton Range and Gros Ventre Range*, 2nd rev. ed. [1977], pp. 198, 200)

Variation: **BEYER SOUTH RIDGE.** IV, 5.10. First ascent July 11, 2020, by Jim Beyer (solo). This variation is described by Beyer as "always on or near the south face/west face arête. This rock ridge is narrow; a lot of the difficulties of my route could be avoided by simply traversing a ledge left or right to snow or [an] easier route." At any rate this route is straighter and more direct than the original 1962 line, even though Beyer stopped on top of the small spire located just to the west of the Dike Pinnacle. It likely shares some pitches with the 1962 route, especially in the middle section of the ridge.

Pitch 1: Exit the Ellingwood Couloir (*Route 6*) near the base of the first tower and climb up from a ledge, crossing the arête to the west side, and climb overhanging 5.8. Exit the west face, crossing the arête again to gain a small ledge and a belay. **Pitch 2:** From the belay climb an overhanging hand crack up and right (east) and belay where convenient (5.10). **Pitch 3:** Ascend easy 4th-class terrain to the top of the tower and rappel 15m to the notch. **Pitch 4:** From the notch climb a 6m runout section (5.7) and then easier terrain to a ledge and belay. **Pitches 5–6:** Two pitches of climbing just east of the arête lead to a ledge and a belay beneath a smooth, steep face. **Pitch 7:** Climb on the west side of the arête up overhanging, featured terrain (5.8). **Pitch 8:** Continue up the arête via "wild, overhanging jugs" (5.7). The route then eases off and continues upward for approximately 200m of 3rd-class climbing. **Pitch 9:** Rope up again near the arête and beneath an easy slab. Climb the slab and then go up through a slot and belay on a small ledge. **Pitch 10:** Cross over to the west side of the arête via big horns and climb a wet slot to a belay on a small ledge (5.8). **Pitch 11:** Climb "Yosemite-like" cracks, staying on the west side of the arête, and then traverse farther west until a "Belly Roll move" leads to a belay at the base of the small spire mentioned above (5.9). **Pitch 12:** The final pitch ascends this spire on its west side via an easy ramp, finishing with 5.7 moves to the top. A short rappel from the spire (15m) deposited Beyer at the col at the top of the Ellingwood Couloir, from which he descended the lower portion of *Route 13*.

ROUTE 8. SOUTHEAST COULOIR. II, 5.4. First ascent August 28, 1929, by Fritiof Fryxell and Phil Smith. During their climb, Fryxell and Smith also made first ascents of both the Dike Pinnacle and the south summit of the Middle Teton. (See *Figure 3-15.*) Ascend the south fork of Garnet Canyon to where the large Ellingwood Couloir (*Route 6*), which leads to the col between the Dike Pinnacle and the summit of the Middle Teton, is clearly visible. The southeast couloir is the next (rather poorly defined) couloir to the east. After the first 60m in this narrow couloir, which starts from a snow bench, either cut left (west) to gain the left fork, a shallow couloir leading to the ridge crest, or continue in the indistinct right fork of the couloir directly to the east ridge. From the ridge it is a scramble to the summit of the Dike Pinnacle.

Fortunately, the traverse to the summit of the Middle Teton, while a bit complex, is not as terrifying as the view might indicate. From the summit of the Dike Pinnacle, downclimb on loose, steep rock (some may prefer to rappel the last part) to the notch between the Dike Pinnacle and a large gendarme. From this notch it is apparently possible to descend about 60m down the gully to the south in order to pass this gendarme and then climb back up to the snow col on the far side. It is more straightforward, however, to traverse around the south side of the gendarme, remaining at about the same level as the notch, to a point from which an 18m rappel puts one near the snow col that separates the gendarme from the main (north) summit mass of the Middle Teton. The slabby east face of the Middle Teton, which is now directly above this snow col, can be climbed either on the right (north) or left (south) of the snow couloir that descends from the notch between the south and north summits of the mountain. In early season very steep snow must be expected in the couloir itself. The most direct route is probably slightly to the left of this couloir, which is partially blocked by a large chockstone not far below the notch between the two summits. Once above this point, easy rocks on the right (north) of the couloir lead to the main summit, which is gained from the east.

See *Appalachia* 18, no. 3 (June 1931): pp. 209–32, illus.; *Sierra Club Bulletin* 16, no. 1 (February 1931): pp. 47–54, illus. (The marked photograph in this latter article is incorrect with respect to the route of ascent.)

ROUTE 9. DIKE. III, 5.6. The history of this route is perhaps as unusual as any in the park. In 1929 Fritiof Fryxell and Phil Smith (see *Route 8*) attained the east ridge from the south and included the upper two-thirds of this route, including the Dike Pinnacle. On September 15, 1935, Malcolm Smith, Newell Rohrer, and Francis Neimann climbed a major portion of the route but avoided most of the lower dike by attaining the crest from the northeast, via a prominent chimney. On July 20, 1940, Jack Durrance, Joseph Hawkes, and Margaret Smith (Craighead) made the first climb of the lower dike, but a broken ice axe prevented their continuing past the Dike Pinnacle to the main summit. On September 4, 1940, Durrance returned with Henry Coulter, James Huidekoper, and Herbert Weiner to attempt the complete ascent, but a storm intervened after they had climbed the lower dike. In the early 1950s several ascents were made via the dike to the summit of the Dike Pinnacle, but none of these parties persevered to the main (north) summit. On September 10, 1954, Craig Merrihue, William Hooker, Peter Luster, and Peter Ludwig climbed the lower dike, bypassed the Dike Pinnacle, and then continued to the summit. It appears that the first complete ascent that included all three essential features—the lower dike, the Dike Pinnacle, and the main summit—was made on September 14, 1954, by Richard Irvin and Floyd Burnette. This route is the longest and one of the most interesting on the Middle Teton; some parties report as many as 22 roped pitches. This is the only route that ascends the entire east ridge. **Note:** *Figure 3-17* shows the initial portion of this route.

From the Meadows at the forks of Garnet Canyon, climb the talus or snow to the base of the black dike, which provides the means for surmounting the first steep section of the ridge. The first few pitches on the dike itself are relatively high angle, but the rock is fairly solid and generally better than one might expect. Within the first several pitches there is little opportunity to leave the dike, and routefinding is minimal because the dike is less than 12m wide. After several ropelengths there are two alternatives: one can remain on the dike itself and climb perhaps the most difficult portion of the route, or one can avoid this difficult section by climbing the easier rock to the left (south). Either way, the uppermost portion of the east ridge, where the angle eases off, will be reached and only scrambling is necessary to reach the summit of the Dike Pinnacle. The dike itself, however, veers off to the north some distance east of the Dike Pinnacle, passes beneath the upper Middle Teton Glacier, and reemerges to cut through the north ridge, forming a conspicuous sharp notch. Hence, one must leave the dike before attaining the summit of the Dike Pinnacle. From there, follow *Route 8* to the main summit of the Middle Teton.

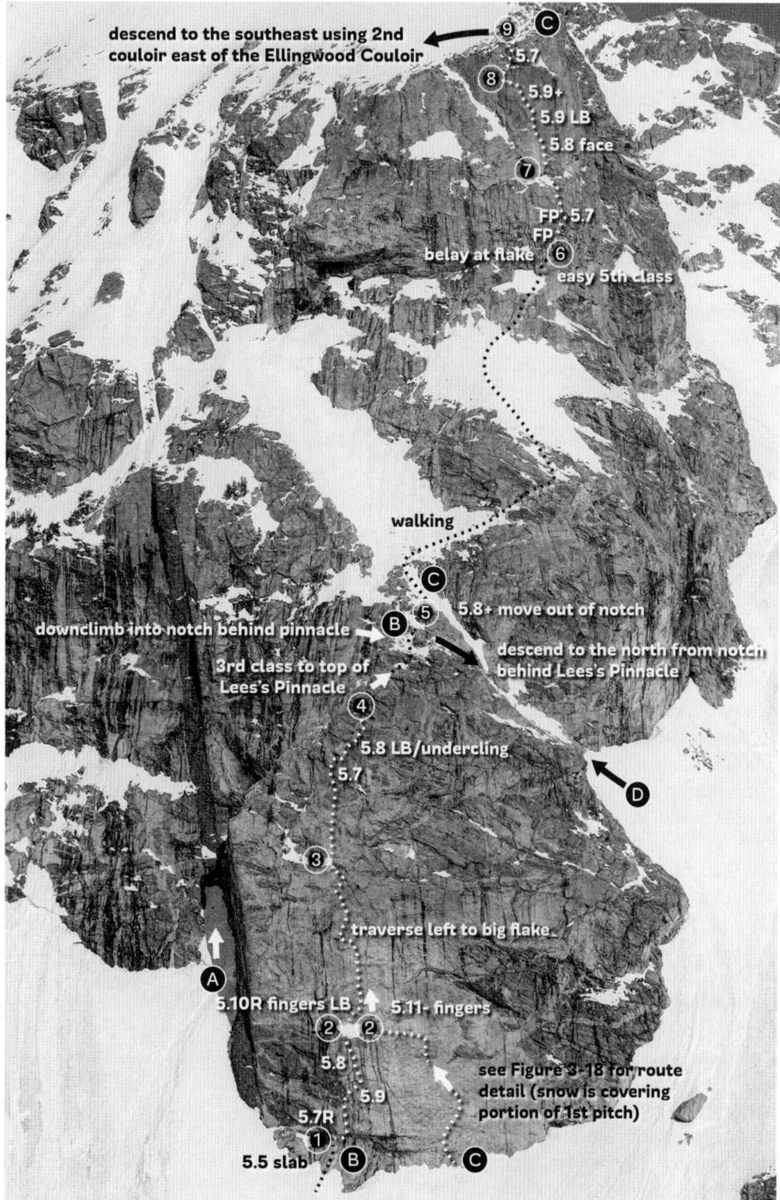

FIGURE 3-17. Middle Teton, east buttress. (A) Dike *(Route 9)*, III, 5.6; (B) Line of Lees's Resistance *(Route 10)*, III, 5.10R; (C) Direct East Buttress *(Route 11)*, IV, 5.11-; (D) Dike, variation: 1935, III, 5.8+

For those who opt to stop at the summit of the Dike Pinnacle, the following descent options are suggested: If ice axes are carried, the eastern tongue of the Middle Teton Glacier on the north can be quickly descended on snow in early season from the point where it reaches the crest of the east ridge; in late season, however, ice will be encountered on this descent route. When that is the case, descend to the south, or slightly southeast, from the same point on the east ridge for some 150m into the distinct couloir east of *Route 8*. Follow this large couloir all the way to a large, grassy bench some 180m above the canyon floor; two short rappels may be required to pass two chockstones. Contour west along this bench for about 300m to a wide gully that leads to the canyon floor. **Time:** 9 hours from Garnet Canyon. See *Harvard Mountaineering* 12 (May 1955): pp. 57–58.

Variation: III, 5.4, A1, or III, 5.8+. First ascent September 15, 1935, by Malcolm Smith, Newell Rohrer, and Francis Neimann. The most easterly buttress of the Middle Teton extends about 100m east of the beginning of the dike. This buttress is almost separated from the remainder of the east ridge of the mountain by two steep chutes—one from the south, very near the base of the dike, and one from the north. After ascending the talus or snow from the floor of Garnet Canyon directly to the easternmost point of this buttress, bear right along the base of the cliffs until naturally directed into the north chute, which begins as an open couloir. The upper end narrows considerably and is blocked by a large chockstone. Pass the chockstone on the right and traverse left to the small notch between the east buttress and the remainder of the ridge. The first 4.5m out of the notch (5.8+) required a shoulder stand on the first ascent. Above this steep, smooth pitch, climb up and left to the dike where the main route is joined.

ROUTE 10. LINE OF LEES'S RESISTANCE. III, 5.10R. First ascent June 30, 1986, by David Koch and Evelyn Lees. (See *Figures 3-17* and *3-18*.) At the extreme lower end of the east ridge of the Middle Teton, just to the right of the black dike, is a major buttress, separated from the remainder of the ridge above by two steep, narrow couloirs, one on the north and the other on the south. The slabby rock of this buttress is exceptionally clean, smooth, and steep, providing tremendous exposure. This climb starts just left of the lowest point of the buttress. The first lead ends at a ledge after a long section (43m) of face climbing (5.5), including fingertip liebacks. (**Note:** In *Figure 3-17* this first pitch is mostly covered with snow.) From the ledge, climb a 5.7R crack and at its top exit right (5.9) to a small overhang. Once past the overhang, climb the 5.8 crack above to a large, sloping ledge and belay at a fixed piton. The third lead, the initial crux at 5.10R, involves fingertip liebacks and

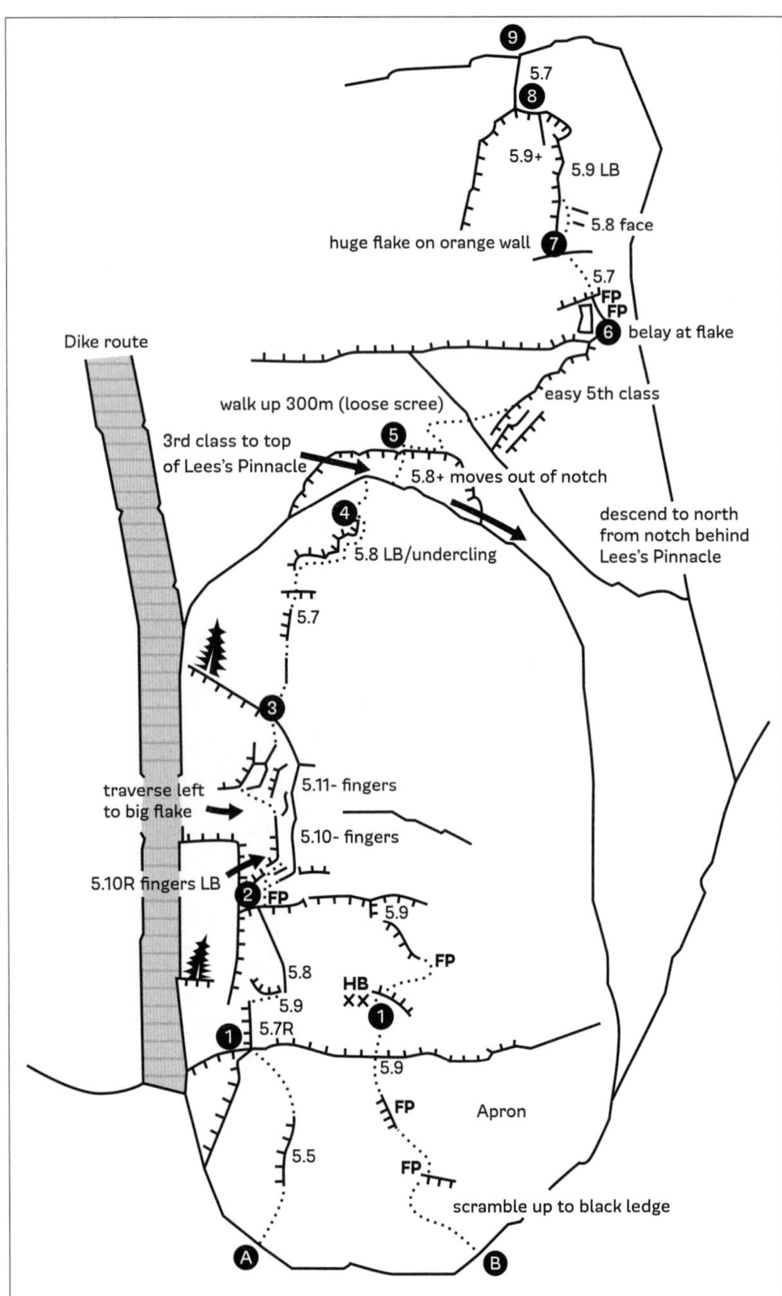

FIGURE 3-18. Middle Teton, east buttress. (A) Line of Lees's Resistance *(Route 10)*, III, 5.10R; (B) Direct East Buttress *(Route 11)*, IV, 5.11-

then a traverse left to a big flake. Belay on a good ledge. For the fourth pitch, climb up to a short right-facing corner (5.7) and then up to an overhang that is climbed via lieback and undercling moves (5.8). Above, 3rd-class climbing leads to the top of Lees's Pinnacle, a high point along the buttress. For descent it is suggested that the couloir to the north be used, as the one to the south requires a 46m rappel. In midseason to late season it is fairly straightforward to downclimb the northern couloir. However, loose and gritty rock will be encountered. **Gear:** A large rack, ranging from brass nuts to #3 camming devices, seems necessary to provide adequate protection on this exposed route.

ROUTE 11. DIRECT EAST BUTTRESS. IV, 5.9, A2, or IV, 5.11-. First ascent July 19, 1989, by Tom Turiano and Matthew Goewert; first free ascent July 21, 1992, by Renny Jackson and Kevin Moore. This route is twice as long as *Route 10*, but both routes share the fourth pitch. Start at the base of the buttress on low-angle slabs from a small black ledge where a fixed piton will be found. The details of the route are best presented in the topos: see *Figures 3-17* and *3-18*. It is probably best to belay at the two bolts after climbing the first 5.9 pitch; this is a hanging belay, however. Climb past a small overhang and then continue out and right to the beginning of a small ramp, where a fixed piton will be found. Continue up the ramp to the left to its end where a tricky step down and left will have to be negotiated. Climb the steep section above via a 5.9 crack and step up onto a large, sloping ledge. A 5.5 traverse to the south on this ledge places one at the belay at the base of the crux pitch. The thin crack above was aided during the first ascent, using tied-off ½" to ¾" pitons for approximately 18m (it protects well with small cams). After reaching the alcove at the top of the crack, continue up to a belay at two fixed pitons. The next pitch is the same as in *Route 10*.

The descent to the notch behind the top of Lees's Pinnacle is easily made, and the exit moves up the short wall to the west are 5.8+ and unprotected. The next section involves walking up some loose scree, which detracts only slightly from the route's overall quality. (**Note:** This area is snow-covered in the photo for *Figure 3-17*, which shows very early season conditions.) From a belay situated next to a large flake, ascend a crack up and over a bulge (5.7). The astonishing old fixed pitons found at the top of the bulge are of unknown provenance. The next lead, behind a huge flake, is continuously difficult and one of the most interesting of the route. Face climb (5.8) into a chimney behind the flake to reach a 5.9 lieback. Where the lieback narrows to a nasty offwidth, move out and left (5.9+) onto the outside face of the giant flake. Finish by climbing up a crack on this face to the belay. The final pitch, a 5.7 crack, emerges on the top of the buttress. For descent, a route can be worked out on the southeast side of the Middle Teton, using the second couloir east of the Ellingwood Couloir *(Route 6)*. Two rappels, one wet, are required. This climb is highly recommended. **Gear:** For protection take a wide selection including RPs and camming devices to 3.5". A double set of small camming devices is useful for the crux finger crack.

Climber at the Dike Pinnacle col, Middle Teton (Photo by Lanny Johnson)

ROUTE 12. SHAND-FERRIS. III, 5.4. First ascent August 1, 1940, by William Shand and Benjamin Ferris; this party ended their climb at the Dike Pinnacle and did not continue to the summit. One of the most prominent features of the Middle Teton, when viewed from the northeast (for example, from Disappointment Peak), is the large buttress that projects northward from the east ridge into the north fork of Garnet Canyon. This route utilizes the sloping east face of this buttress to gain access to the crest of the east ridge. The most direct approach to this route from the Meadows is to ascend the slope just under the east cliffs of the Middle Teton. In this way one is led naturally toward the east face of the buttress. One can also contour in to this same point from the trail above the Caves. The slabby face above, with its abundance of loose rock, can very likely be climbed in several ways. It appears that one could either proceed upward to the crest of the buttress and then follow it south to the point where it intersects the east ridge, or climb in or near the chimney at the extreme left (south) edge of the face. The first alternative on this face is probably easier. The difficulty will undoubtedly depend on the exact route selected. From the crest of the east ridge, which is reached above the difficult climbing of the Dike route (see *Route 9*), proceed as in *Route 8*.

ROUTE 13. MIDDLE TETON GLACIER. III, 5.4, AI2+. First complete ascent August 4, 1944, by Sterling Hendricks and Paul Bradt; on August 13, 1933, W. T. Allemann made a partial ascent via the left branch to the east ridge of the Dike Pinnacle. (See *Figures 3-19* and *3-20*.) On the north side of the Middle Teton the broad Middle Teton Glacier extends all the way up to the Dike Pinnacle, where it splits; the left (east) section leads to the east ridge, and the right section leads to the snow col between the Dike Pinnacle and the true summit. This route is recommended as an early-season climb because crampons can then be worn all the way to the summit. From the Caves follow the usual route to the Middle Teton Glacier (see *Garnet Canyon, North Fork*). The standard climb of this route ascends the glacier to just below the Dike Pinnacle. Then traverse right (west) into the steep snow couloir leading to the snow col between the Dike Pinnacle and the true summit. The bergschrund at the lower end of this couloir is passed on the left. Proceed up to the col, keeping on the left side of the couloir all the way. In late season, and sometimes in the middle of the season, the surface of the upper couloir above the bergschrund will be hard snow or ice. From the col follow *Route 8* to the summit. In late season on the lower glacier several crevasses open up and the snow cover disappears. It is possible to avoid the steep upper snow-and-ice couloir by the simple expedient of following the eastern section of the Middle Teton Glacier onto the east ridge. This minimizes the difficulties of reaching the ridge, but then one must climb over the Dike Pinnacle (not trivial) to the main summit, as in *Route 8*. **Time:** 6 hours from the Caves.

ROUTE 14. DIKE PINNACLE, NORTH FACE I. III, 5.9. First ascent July 23, 2002, by David

FIGURE 3-19. Middle Teton, overview of north face routes. Middle Teton Glacier *(Route 13)*, III, 5.4, AI2+; Dike Pinnacle, North Face I *(Route 14)*, III, 5.9; Dike Pinnacle, North Face II *(Route 15)*, III, 5.10-; Northeast Face *(Route 16)*, II, 5.4, A1; Inge's *(Route 17)*, II, 5.13b (unfinished); Taylor *(Route 18)*, V, 5.11a; North Wall *(Route 19)*, V, 5.10d, A2; Middle Finger *(Route 20)*, V, 5.11+/5.12a; Shea-Breashears *(Route 21)*, IV, WI5+, M[unknown]; Robbins-Fitschen *(Route 22)*, IV, 5.10-, A1; Brown-Macke *(Route 23)*, IV, 5.9+, A2, WI6+; Whiton-Wiggins Dihedral *(Route 24)*, III, 5.9; Briggs-Higbee Pillar *(Route 25)*, III, 5.10; Jackson-Woodmencey Dihedral *(Route 26)*, III, 5.10-; Pinnacle Route *(Route 27)*, III, 5.10+, C1; Goodrich Chimney *(Route 28)*, II, 5.6; No Cumbre, No Ruta *(Route 29)*, IV, WI5, M7, A0; Dew Drop Inn *(Route 30)*, III, 5.10; Buffalo Gals *(Route 31)*, III, 5.10; North Ridge *(Route 32)*, II, 5.6; Northwest Ice Couloir *(Route 33)*, III, 5.6, AI3; Northwest Slope *(Route 34)*, II, 5.1

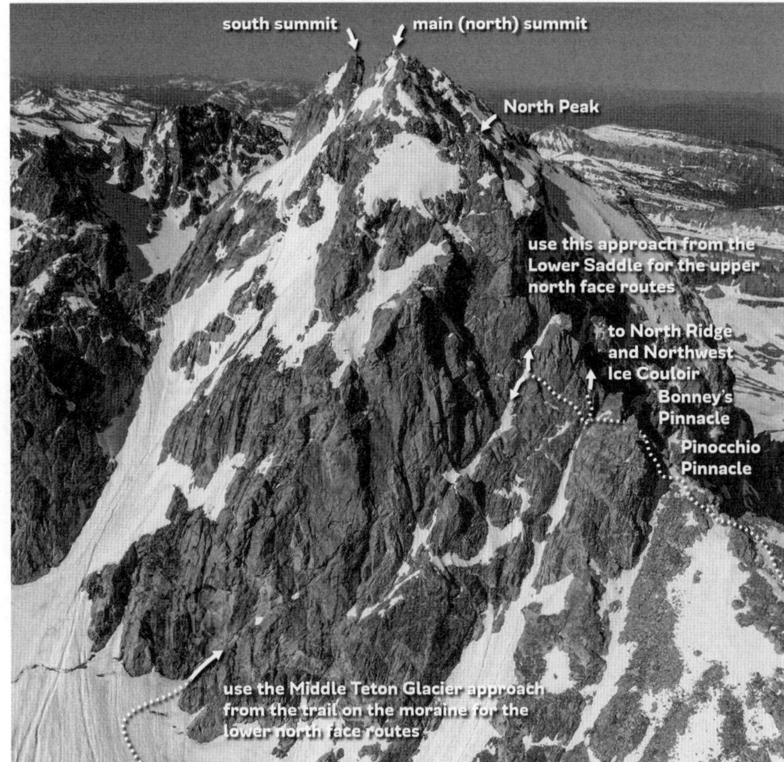

FIGURE 3-20. Middle Teton, detail of approaches for upper and lower north face routes

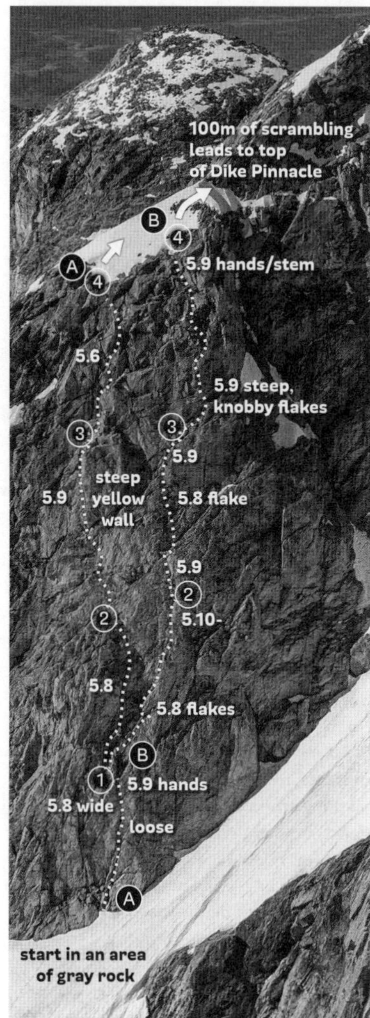

FIGURE 3-21. Middle Teton, Dike Pinnacle. (A) North Face I (Bywater-Johnson; *Route 14*), III, 5.9; (B) North Face II (Gams-Mulvihill; *Route 15*), III, 5.10-

Bywater and Ron Johnson. (See *Figures 3-19* and *3-21*.) This route ascends a fairly direct line up the north face of the Dike Pinnacle and was the first route put up on this wall. The approach is via *Route 13*, which could necessitate carrying ice axes and wearing crampons—and maybe bringing them up the climb for the descent, depending upon which route is chosen. Just before the upper couloir, climb over to the base of the face and look for a large right-facing corner near the center of the wall. Begin by climbing a left-facing corner (somewhat loose), and then step left past a roof and into a crack system (5.9) that leads to a belay ledge. The second pitch ascends the large right-facing corner (5.8), heading for the steep yellow wall above. The third pitch ascends the left-facing corner that forms the left (east) side of this steep wall (5.9). Belay on a good ledge at the top. The final pitch goes up a series of ledges and corners (5.6) to the top of the face. About 100m of scrambling leads to the top of the Dike Pinnacle. For the descent, either downclimb the upper portion of *Route 13* to the base of the climb or continue to the summit via the upper portion of *Route 5* or *Route 8*. Later in the season the upper portions of either route may be fairly dry, allowing access to the southwest couloir (see *Route 1*) for the descent into the south fork of Garnet Canyon.

ROUTE 15. DIKE PINNACLE, NORTH FACE II. III, 5.10-. First ascent August 2, 2008, by Aaron Gams and Brian Mulvilhill. (See *Figures 3-19* and *3-21*.) This climb just to the west of *Route 14* is reportedly on mostly good rock, with a slightly loose beginning; it was the second route on the face. The approach and the descent are the same as for *Route 14*. Begin with the first pitch of that route, but instead of climbing the right-facing corner, climb up and right on a ramp that leads to some large flakes. Undercling these flakes (5.8) up and left to reach a ramp that leads back right (west) to a left-facing corner, which is climbed (5.10-) to a small belay ledge. The third pitch ascends another left-facing corner (5.9) to a ledge, then heads up a steep right-facing flake (5.8), moves up and right to a right-facing corner (5.9), and reaches a belay in an alcove. The fourth pitch begins with scrambling up and right on a ramp for 6m before climbing up to cracks that then lead up through some flakes (5.9). After this, easier terrain leads up and east to a final hand crack/stem in a left-facing corner (5.9) that finishes the climb. **Gear:** For protection take two sets of cams from 0.75" to 2", and one each from 2.5" to 4.5". (Source: Aaron Gams)

ROUTE 16. NORTHEAST FACE. II, 5.4, A1. First ascent August 24, 1936, by Fritz Wiessner, William House, and Elizabeth Woolsey. Ascend the Middle Teton Glacier as in *Route 13* toward the col between the Dike Pinnacle and the summit of the Middle Teton. Just below the mouth of the steep snow-and-ice couloir that leads to this col, ascend a crack in the rocks to the right (west) for about 30m to more difficult ground. A shoulder stand was used to pass this area of smooth rock and loose debris on the first ascent. Easier climbing leads to the broad, grassy ledge (in early season this may be covered with snow) about halfway up the face. From here climb a series of cracks diagonally up and left (south) to a rotten rock couloir, which is the continuation of the dike from the east ridge. Cross the treacherous couloir at about the same altitude as the Dike Pinnacle and continue up and left (south) across smooth slabs to the main narrow couloir descending from the notch between the south and main (north) summits. Ascend this couloir to the easy rocks below and immediately east of the summit. Scramble to the top.

Middle Teton, Lower North Face Routes

All but one of the routes described below are approached by way of the lower portion of the Middle Teton Glacier: see *Route 13*, as well as *Figures 3-19* and *3-20*. From the trail on the Middle Teton moraine, a prominent ledge can be seen slanting steeply upward toward the right (west) across the eastern portion of the lower north face. This ledge meets the glacier below the main bergschrund. *Route 17* begins below this prominent ledge, and *Routes 18–20* utilize it to access the beginning of the climbing. *Routes 22* and *23* start off the glacier at different points west of the ledge.

The following routes were originally done as nonsummit rock climbs, with the exceptions of *Routes 18* and *22*, which joined the North Ridge route *(Route 32)* near the top of the North Peak and followed that route to the summit. This required a short downclimb and/or rappel into the notch near the top and then a short climb to the summit.

ROUTE 17. INGE'S. II, 5.13b (unfinished). This extremely difficult route has not yet been redpointed. The name was given in memory of the talented rock climber and alpinist Inge Perkins, who perished in an avalanche in Montana in 2017. Several climbers have worked on this route including Greg Collins, Hans Johnstone, Brendan O'Neill, and Dana Larkin, as well as Perkins herself before her passing. (See *Figures 3-19* and *3-22*.) The route consists of three pitches and begins off the glacier, just below the ledge that cuts across the lower north face. The first pitch goes up via cracks and face climbing through a bulge (5.11a) and then onto the ledge. The second pitch is the crux, ascending an overhanging, east-trending thin crack (likely 5.13b) to a two-bolt belay. The third pitch, which begins with three protection bolts and then continues up a crack system to the belay (5.11b), represents the current high point of the route.

ROUTE 18. TAYLOR. IV, 5.9, A4, or V, 5.11a. First ascent August 26, 1961, by Royal Robbins and Jane Taylor; first free ascent in summer 2008, by Hans Johnstone and David Gonzales. (See *Figures 3-19* and *3-22*.) This difficult climb is located near the eastern edge of the lower north face of the Middle Teton and is reported to consist of good climbing on excellent rock. Easy 5th-class climbing ascends from the Middle Teton Glacier to the large ledge leading west to the base of the route. Begin climbing in a left-facing

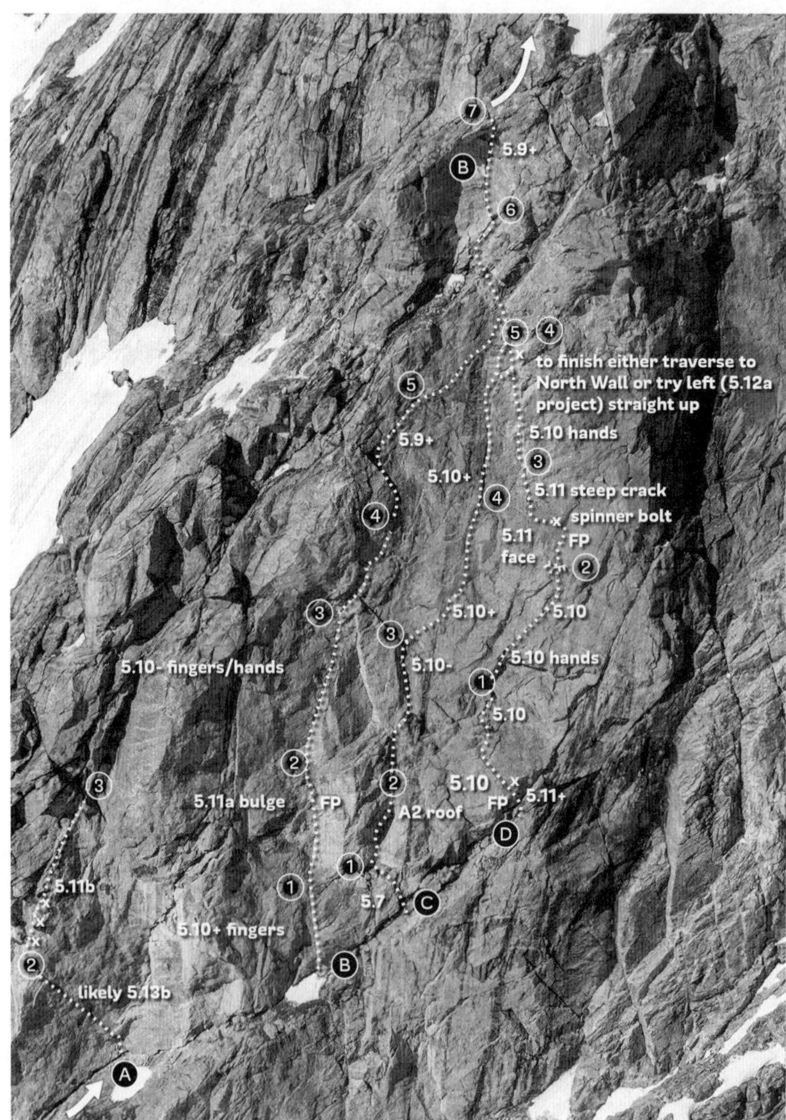

FIGURE 3-22. Middle Teton, lower north face. (A) Inge's *(Route 17)*, II, 5.13b (unfinished); (B) Taylor *(Route 18)*, V, 5.11a; (C) North Wall *(Route 19)*, V, 5.10d, A2; (D) Middle Finger *(Route 20)*, V, 5.11+/5.12a

corner (5.10+ fingers) to a belay below a steep white face. Climb through a difficult bulge past a fixed piton (5.11a) to a belay at the base of a steep left-facing corner. Ascend the corner using finger and hand jams (5.10-) to where the difficulty eases and belay. Climb up and west to the base of a steep, short corner and belay again. After the corner, continue up and west via 5.9+ climbing to a ramp leading up and farther west and belay. Proceed up the ramp to where it steepens, then cut left on slabby terrain and set up a belay for the final pitch, a 5.9+ crack through a roof. This brings one out onto the easy upper portions of the mountain east of the north ridge; scramble to the summit or descend the north ridge (see *Route 32*). For details of the first ascent, see *American Alpine Journal* 13, no. 1 (1962): pp. 216–20; *Sierra Club Bulletin* 46, no. 8 (October 1961): pp. 53–54.

ROUTE 19. NORTH WALL. V, 5.10d, A2. First ascent in August 2015, by Greg Collins and Hans Johnstone. (See *Figures 3-19* and *3-22.*) Located immediately right (west) of the Taylor route *(Route 18)*, this is a good route with just a short section of aid. The first pitch is short, up and left to a good belay. The second pitch climbs the roof above via aid (A2, pins useful). Belay just above the roof. The third pitch goes up a beautiful crack system (5.10-) to a belay out on the face. The fourth pitch, which trends up and right, was described as a "scary onsight" (5.10+) by Collins, who led it with pins, presumably knifeblades and Lost Arrows. The fifth pitch is also 5.10+ in difficulty. This route was descended by the pair, with fixed anchors every 50m. It is also possible to continue up and finish with the final pitch and a half of *Route 18*. **Gear:** For protection take a set of stoppers and many small nuts; a complete complement of cams; and pitons, with an emphasis on knifeblades and Lost Arrows.

ROUTE 20. MIDDLE FINGER. V, 5.11+/5.12a. First ascent in July 2019, by Greg Collins and Hans Johnstone. (See *Figures 3-19* and *3-22.*) Start on the prominent ledge above the Middle Teton Glacier. **Pitch 1:** This climb begins with very difficult climbing right off the ledge, up and over a roof (5.11+) past a fixed pin and a bolt, and then ascends a crack, where the climbing eases off to 5.10, to a perfect belay. **Pitch 2:** Head up and right through a roof (5.10 hands) and then continue to another great belay ledge via 5.10 crack climbing. **Pitch 3:** Climb up to a fixed pin and then to a spinner bolt (5.10). From the bolt, face climb up and left (5.11) to a steep crack. Climb the crack (5.11) to the belay on a good ledge at the base of a left-facing corner. **Pitch 4:** Climb the corner via steep hands (5.10) and either escape left to finish the pitch along *Route 19* or try climbing directly up past a bolt (5.12a project). Either way, the Taylor Route *(Route 18)* can be joined from the top of this pitch, or one could descend as in *Route 19*.

ROUTE 21. SHEA-BREASHEARS. IV, WI5+, M[unknown]. First ascent in June 1978, by Steve Shea and David Breashears. See *Route 23* for some detail, as well as *Figures 3-19* and *3-23*. This climb likely went up a chimney system, also referred to as the Robbins Chimney, on the eastern portion of the Middle Teton's north face. Stained black from water flow, this system becomes a drainage pathway on an annual basis, and large icicles are often seen hanging in it during late spring—but very rarely are they continuous. Shea and Breashears made their ascent during one of those rare years in which it had formed up.

Looking back on the climb, Shea offered the following:

As you may remember that was a particularly heavy and late snow year. And we were all ice and mixed crazed at the time. Old-school mixed, I should say. I believe we first went to the [Lower] Saddle in late May for our long stay at the old Exum hut. We observed lots of ice, but this one on Middle really stood out. Greg Lowe, who was with us [as part of a ski film project], called it [the] Robbins Chimney. I had had little experience in the Tetons before save one trip up the Grand some years prior. So we always referred to it as the Robbins Chimney. At any rate, it was obvious and fat that spring. . . . I remember we traversed into the business and then up. I recall the ice was midwinter brittle on the first part, but not much else. I'm not sure if we went to the summit. We were up there so many times for the skiing and filming that we probably blew it off. I think we got over to the north ridge [see **Route 32*****] and came down. That is all I know or remember; that was forty years ago.***

This difficult climb was way ahead of its time and was put up by two of the country's most accomplished alpinsts. Years later, when the final pitch was climbed again by Nate Brown and Sam Macke (see *Route 23*), they found it to be WI6+ and described it as "difficult and dangerous."

ROUTE 22. ROBBINS-FITSCHEN. IV, 5.10-, A1. First ascent July 30, 1960, by Royal Robbins and Joe Fitschen. (See *Figures 3-19, 3-23*, and *3-24.*) Ascend the Middle Teton Glacier to the bottom of the easternmost of the prominent chimneys on the north face of the Middle Teton. Climb 150m up a series of cracks and blocks on the right side of the lower extension of the chimney to the ledge at the beginning of the 150m wall right of the wet chimney. Using aid, climb the vertical crack about 8m to the right of the chimney. The last pitch on the wall angles steeply upward to the right, passing the final overhangs on the right via difficult free climbing (5.10-). (Both *Route 24* and *Route 26* finish via this final pitch.) From the top of the wall there is no great problem in reaching the main (north) summit from east of the north ridge. See *American Alpine Journal* 12, no. 2 (1961): pp. 373–77; *Sierra Club Bulletin* 46, no. 8 (October 1961): pp. 53–54.

ROUTE 23. BROWN-MACKE. IV, 5.9+, A2, WI6+. First ascent in November 2010, by Sam Macke and Nate Brown. (See *Figures 3-19* and *3-23.*) This wild route was put up in good style by these local Jackson Hole climbers in "full winter conditions." It intersects *Route 22* in the middle section of that route, and it joins *Route 21* for its final pitch. Approach from the Middle Teton Glacier and then head up the Bonney's-Pinocchio couloir. The apex of this couloir is the sharp notch between Bonney's Pinnacle and the north ridge of the Middle Teton. Climb out of the couloir to the south where obvious (5.6) and traverse around a prow to a smaller secondary couloir/chimney system that angles downward and to the east from a point above the notch mentioned above. According to Brown and Macke, the first two pitches above this secondary couloir were "difficult and slabby and large Peckers made them seem sane!" They aided the crack pitch using thin pins to 1.5" pieces. This led to the final WI6+ pitch, which they described as "difficult and dangerous." As with any big, mixed Teton route, the difficulty of this climb is extremely conditions dependent.

FIGURE 3-23. Middle Teton, north face, Brown-Macke *(Route 23)*, IV, 5.9+, A2, WI6+

Middle Teton, Upper North Face Routes

The next 11 routes *(Routes 24–34)* are most easily approached via the regular North Ridge route *(Route 32)* and a couple of ledges/ramps that originate from the notch behind Bonney's Pinnacle: see *Figure 3-20*. These ledges can be snow-covered in early season, which may also indicate that some of the rock climbs are wet; the prospective climber should factor this in when contemplating a route on the upper north face. The rock quality on nearly all of these routes is very good, and both the setting and the relatively short approach from the Lower Saddle make them appealing.

To reach *Routes 24–31*, climb up and left (east) out of the sharp notch behind (south of) Bonney's Pinnacle for 46m–60m to a large ledge on which one can make a downward traverse to the east, not always easily, across the entire north face. In early season a snow couloir leading down to the Middle Teton Glacier will be crossed in the course of this scramble; an ice axe is useful in this section. These same routes culminate on top of the North Peak. From this point a downclimb to the southwest (a few 5th-class moves) into the sharp dike notch places one at the uppermost portion of the North Ridge route *(Route 32)*, one short pitch below the summit.

ROUTE 24. WHITON-WIGGINS DIHEDRAL. III, 5.9. First ascent September 20, 1981, by Mark Whiton and Earl Wiggins. (See *Figures 3-19* and *3-24*.) This fine route on the excellent rock that characterizes the north side of the Middle Teton is steep and of sustained technical difficulty. Belay points are comfortable and protection is good. Apparently, this route follows the same line as the Briggs-Higbee Pillar *(Route 25)* for its second and third pitches, but it starts below and well left of that climb. Approach as for *Route 25* but continue the traverse eastward for an additional 30m or so. The first pitch begins in a left-facing corner and then moves through an overhang (5.9) to gain a belay near, but left of, the bottom of the left dihedral, as described in *Route 25*. Climb the next three pitches of the Briggs-Higbee Pillar. (**Note:** *Figure 3-24* shows this route continuing up the fourth pitch of *Route 25* because it is not known precisely which line the first-ascent party took.) Rather than cutting left under the final overhanging headwall to the sloping belay at the base of *Route 25*'s final lead, bear up and right (west) to a comfortable belay ledge. Finish with the final pitch of the Robbins-Fitschen route *(Route 22)*, which is also how *Route 26* reaches the top of the face. Easier slabs and snow can now be taken to the top of the North Peak by traversing up and west.

ROUTE 25. BRIGGS-HIGBEE PILLAR. III, 5.10. First ascent July 8, 1974, by Roger Briggs and Art Higbee. (See *Figures 3-19* and *3-24*.) This route on the scenic and alpine north face of the Middle Teton lies well left (east) of the North Ridge route *(Route 32)*. From the notch south of Bonney's Pinnacle, access the large ledge that cuts across the north face. Descend and traverse east past two major chimney systems, the second of which is the Goodrich

Chimney (*Route 28*), until it is possible to climb toward the dihedrals that mark the central portion of the north face. Two dihedrals, the left one right-facing and the right one left-facing, are now directly above.

From a large ledge at the base of the right dihedral, the first lead angles left using a lieback and thin crack to a small stance just left of the base of the left dihedral. For the second pitch, climb up and left to the base of an overhang just left of the bottom of the dihedral. Climb an overhanging crack (5.9) for 9m to a ledge, traverse 3m left along this ledge, and continue up to a belay ledge another 6m higher. The third lead (40m) follows the corner above for 9m and then ascends a steep, right-angling crack for 3m (5.9) before traversing right to a ledge; easier rock is then followed up and left to the belay. The next pitch goes up (5.9, 30m) to the base of the final overhanging headwall and then continues up and left under the headwall to a sloping belay stance at the base of an overhanging corner. The fifth and final lead climbs this corner (5.10). Once above this point, easier slabs and snow can be taken to the top of the North Peak by traversing up and west.

ROUTE 26. JACKSON-WOODMENCEY DIHEDRAL. III, 5.10-. First ascent June 25, 1988, by Renny Jackson and Jim Woodmencey. (See *Figures 3-19* and *3-25*.) This route on the excellent rock of the north face of the Middle Teton attacks directly the leftmost (right-facing) of the two dihedrals described in *Route 25*. The first pitch begins in the same way as *Route 25*,

FIGURE 3-24. Middle Teton, north face. (A) Whiton-Wiggins Dihedral *(Route 24)*, III, 5.9; (B) Briggs-Higbee Pillar *(Route 25)*, III, 5.10

FIGURE 3-25. Middle Teton, north face. (A) Jackson-Woodmency Dihedral *(Route 26)*, III, 5.10-; (B) Pinnacle Route *(Route 27)*, III, 5.10+, C1

involving a face climb to a small overhang where a lieback (5.9) is taken around its left edge. Then follow a crack back to the right, up and into the huge corner. The second lead goes directly up the right-facing dihedral above, using crack climbing and stemming techniques (5.8). At the top of this corner, exit out left and face climb into a perfect belay alcove on top of a large block. The next lead on easier rock (5.6) takes one to a comfortable belay ledge. The final lead of this route is the same as the last pitch of the Robbins-Fitschen route *(Route 22)*. Move up and left around a flake (5.8) and then stem up and left to a sloping ledge. Stem past a fixed pin (5.10-) using finger locks and step around the corner, where easier climbing is found leading a short distance to the top of the climb. One can then continue to the top of the North Peak by traversing easier slabs and snow up and to the west.

ROUTE 27. PINNACLE ROUTE. III, 5.10+, C1. First ascent in August 2000, by Mike Ruth and Brian Piddick. This interesting pinnacle was also attempted by Renny Jackson and Ron Johnson earlier in 2000. (See *Figures 3-19* and *3-25*.) Located on the pinnacle to the left (east) of the Goodrich Chimney *(Route 28)*, this worthy free-climbing goal awaits a second ascent. From near the base of the pinnacle, climb up and west to a belay at a fixed pin. The second pitch begins with unprotected face climbing (5.10) up and left to gain a thin crack (5.10+) that is followed up to the next belay. Then climb up and left to a small right-facing corner and proceed from the top of this corner to a roof with double cracks in it. Climb through the roof (5.10, C1) and then up to a hand traverse (5.10) that leads 4.5m left to cracks, where another move of C1 leads to easier climbing and the belay just below the top of the pinnacle. After gaining the top of the pinnacle, climb down into the notch and continue up to finish by *Route 25* or *Route 22*.

ROUTE 28. GOODRICH CHIMNEY. II, 5.6. First ascent September 4, 1955, by Donald Goodrich and John Reppy. (See *Figures 3-19* and *3-24*.) This is the second prominent chimney left (east) of the north ridge of the Middle Teton, as seen from the Lower Saddle. From the notch south of Bonney's Pinnacle, access the large ledge that slants steeply down to the east across the north face. Descend along the ledge to the base of the second chimney system. The route goes directly up this chimney system for about six pitches; the last pitch out of the chimney and onto the slabs of the upper northeast face is difficult because of ice. For this reason, this route is recommended only for late season when wetness and ice will be at a minimum. From the top of the chimney easier slabs and snow can be taken to the top of the North Peak by traversing up and west. **Time:** 6½ hours from the Caves. See *American Alpine Journal* 10, no. 1 (1956): pp. 116–19.

ROUTE 29. NO CUMBRE, NO RUTA. IV, WI5, M7, A0. First ascent July 14, 1997, by Alex Lowe and Travis Spitzer. (See *Figure 3-19*.) This 240m route is located in the obvious chimney system just to the west of the Goodrich Chimney *(Route 28)*. On their ascent, Lowe and Spitzer climbed several mixed pitches that led to a final ice pillar, the technical crux of the route. Spitzer's attempts to free the rock moves leading to the pillar ended with "whippers with tools and crampons." The pair switched leads and Lowe unexpectedly had to pull on gear to get to the ice—very unlike him in those days. "It was a great day in the Tetons!" Spitzer exclaimed.

In his report for the 1998 *American Alpine Journal*, Spitzer wrote, "The route was named in response and protest to bogus debates circling the climbing community that new routes must top out on true summits of a claimed peak or they do not and should not exist. Hence, we did not go to the summit of the Middle. One hell of a good route, though."

ROUTE 30. DEW DROP INN. III, 5.10. First ascent August 10, 1996, by Eric Gabriel and Andy Byerly. (See *Figures 3-19* and *3-26*.) This route and Buffalo Gals *(Route 31)* are both located on the clean section of rock just east of the north ridge. From the notch south of Bonney's Pinnacle, access the large ledge that cuts down and east across the north face. Traverse out on another ledge to the east from a point under the big roof of Buffalo Gals for approximately 30m and belay at the base of one of two cracks, both of which lead up to the same belay and a fixed rappel station. Each of these cracks is 5.10 and about 30m in length. The second pitch goes through a 5.8 roof, then up a ramp to the right, and then back east on a ledge to belay (60m). Next climb up to a right-facing corner and face climb (5.8) above this up and right to join *Route 31* for the end of its last pitch. From there 4th- and easy 5th-class climbing leads to the top of the North Peak.

ROUTE 31. BUFFALO GALS. III, 5.10. First ascent August 1, 1996, by Renny Jackson and Ron Johnson. Sometimes it is impossible to get a particular song or melody out of one's head, and on this day it was the classic American folk tune "Buffalo Gals." (See *Figures 3-19* and *3-26*.) Approach as for *Route 30*; once on the large ledge that slants down and to the east across the north face, set up a belay beneath the intimidating roof through which this route goes. The first pitch offers superb climbing up to and through the roof above (5.10), chimneying between the "buffalo cheeks"—easier than it looks!—and then up a 5.10- crack to a belay ledge. The second pitch begins with a hand crack (5.7), after which easy climbing leads first up and right and then to the left to a belay partway up a ramp. The third pitch continues up the ramp until one can step to the right (west) where a hand traverse leads to a 5.10 hand crack and a belay next to a boulder on a ledge. The fourth pitch consists of 5.7 face climbing straight up to a belay among some boulders. Fourth- and easy 5th-class climbing then leads up and to the right to the top of the North Peak. **Gear:** For protection take a double rack of cams to 4"; stoppers are useful as well.

ROUTE 32. NORTH RIDGE. II, 5.6. First ascent July 17, 1931, by Robert Underhill and Fritiof Fryxell; first descent July 4, 1933, by Paul Petzoldt and Sterling Hendricks. (See *Figures 3-19*, *3-20*, and *3-27*.) From the Lower Saddle between the Middle Teton and the Grand Teton, climb toward the base of the north ridge. Two large pinnacles that provide interesting scrambling will be met. Traverse the first, Pinocchio Pinnacle, on the west and the second (higher) one, Bonney's Pinnacle, on the east. On the far side (south) of the second pinnacle is a notch formed by the erosion of a small diabase dike. (**Note:** On the first ascent of this route, an alternate ramp leading up and left and then back right was taken from this notch; it brought one to the Room, a cavernous indentation in the ridge. What follows is the much easier route taken nowadays.) Downclimb into the notch, then climb up and right for a few meters to a ledge that extends out to the southwest to the left edge of the Northwest Ice Couloir *(Route 33)*. Now head toward the notch formed by the black dike, keeping on the right side of the north ridge, staying in or near the northwest gully, and using a series of small connecting ledges and cracks. When the dike is reached, walk left (east) up its crumbling slope to the sharp notch it forms with the north ridge. Climb directly out of this notch, either using the face directly above or climbing large, somewhat loose blocks slightly to the right (west). This pitch is the most difficult portion of the North Ridge route. **Note:** A few meters below the notch, look for a short right-facing corner that leads up and around to the south. A traverse to the right leads to this corner. This is much easier than climbing up and out of the notch. Either way, easy ledges and slabs then lead up and around (east) to the summit. To descend by this route, it is convenient to rappel into the dike notch. **Time:** 4½ hours from the Lower Saddle; 6¾ to 8½ hours from Garnet Canyon. See *Appalachia* 19, no. 1 (June 1932): pp. 86–96; *Chicago Mountaineering Club Newsletter* 2, no. 6 (July–December 1948): p. 6.

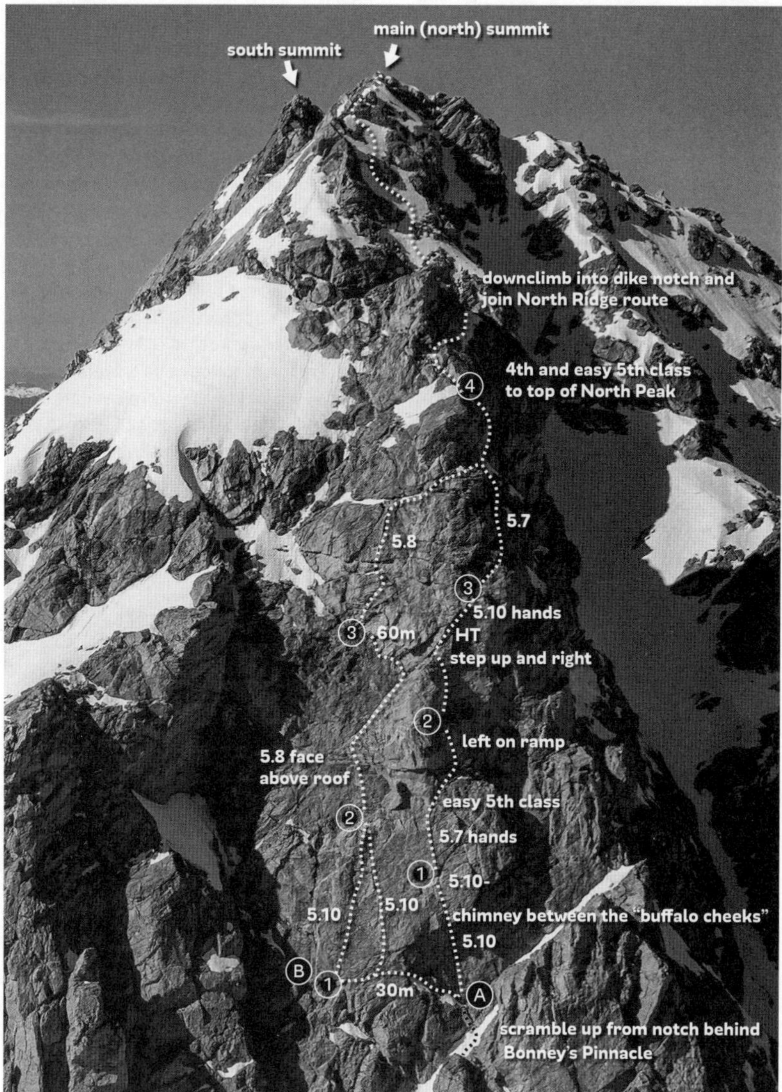

FIGURE 3-26. Middle Teton, north face. (A) Buffalo Gals *(Route 31)*, III, 5.10; (B) Dew Drop Inn *(Route 30)*, III, 5.10

Variation: II, 5.6. First ascent July 5, 1940, by Paul Petzoldt and Elizabeth Cowles (Partridge). The standard North Ridge route described above bypasses the North Peak. This variation includes, one way or another, the summit of the North Peak on the way to the main (north) summit. The difficulty of the climb (5.6 to 5.9) will vary depending on the exact line chosen. Only a short distance after cutting right (west) out of the Room (see above), turn back left toward the ridge crest and a small notch. Cross over to the left (east) side of the ridge and climb a series of ledges on the upper northeast face of the north peak. After 60m–90m the angle eases off, and one can continue easily to the North Peak summit, reaching it from the east. From this point a downclimb to the southwest (a few 5th-class moves) into the sharp dike notch places one at the uppermost portion of the North Ridge route, one short pitch below the summit.

Another possibility after leaving the Room is to stay on the right (west) side of the ridge, keeping very near the crest. On the smooth, downsloping slabs on the west face of the North Peak, traverse back and forth up the horizontal and vertical cracks. A third possibility is to climb ledges and cracks up and left from the notch behind Bonney's Pinnacle, staying east of the Room but near the crest of the north ridge on predominantly excellent rock. Several pitches of enjoyable climbing will be found in this section.

ROUTE 33. NORTHWEST ICE COULOIR. III, 5.6, AI3. First ascent June 16, 1961, by Peter Lev and Jim Greig. (See *Figure 3-19*.) See *Route 32* for the approach from the Lower Saddle to the sharp dike notch behind (south of) Bonney's Pinnacle. Climb the wall on the far side of this notch and traverse right (west) into this northwest couloir. Climb more or less straight up the couloir, which ends on the west ridge a very short distance from the summit. The climb varies from a snow route in early season to perhaps the easiest of the classic Teton ice routes from midseason to late season. The angle of the couloir approaches 50° near the top. See *American Alpine Journal* 13, no. 1 (1962): pp. 216–20.

Variation: III, 5.6, AI4. First ascent unknown. This variation provides a much more difficult start to the original climb. Approach the base of Pinocchio Pinnacle via the trail that wanders upward from

FIGURE 3-27. Middle Teton, North Ridge *(Route 32)*, II, 5.6

the Lower Saddle. One can traverse easily out on a promontory to the southwest to obtain an impressive view of this variation. Careful scrambling (4th class) down a chimney/gully to the southeast provides a reasonable entry into the couloir. This approach can be seen in *Figure 3-28* just below and left of Pinocchio Pinnacle. The serious climbing is 24m–30m in length and is AI4 in difficulty. From the top of this steep ice another 18m–24m of climbing leads to the point where one would normally enter the couloir on *Route 33*.

ROUTE 34. NORTHWEST SLOPE. II, 5.1. Possible first ascent August 27, 1939, by Stanley Grites, Frank Garbocz, and Adam Koj, or September 6, 1954, by William Hooker, Peter Ludwig, Peter Luster, and Craig Merrihue. (See *Figure 3-19.*) Refer to *Route 32* for the approach from the Lower Saddle to the sharp dike notch behind (south of) Bonney's Pinnacle. Surmount the wall on the far side of this notch and traverse right (west) into the prominent northwest couloir of *Route 33*. Now pursue a diagonal course up and right (west) toward the west ridge, which can be reached at various points and then followed directly and easily to the main (north) summit (see *Route 36*). This diagonal course crosses the Northwest Ice Couloir, which until late season is snow- or ice-filled, requiring the use of an ice axe. Once on the far (west) side, the ill-defined ridge that forms the right (west) boundary of the couloir can be crossed in several places.

Middle Teton, West Side Routes

Presently there are only two routes on this seldom-visited facet of the Middle Teton. Both are difficult to get to but perhaps offer a true wilderness experience.

ROUTE 35. WEST FACE, ELECTRIC CORNER. II, 5.9. First ascent in August 2000, by David Bywater and Craig Holm. (See *Figure 3-28.*) This fairly obscure route has the distinction of being the only known climb on this remote face. The name recalls the harrowing day of the first ascent, during which the party finished the final 5.9 pitch in a hair-raising electrical storm. The approach for the climb is made from the south fork of Garnet Canyon to the saddle between the Middle and South Tetons. From a point just above the saddle, traverse to the north and across the uppermost portion of the couloir that descends to Icefloe Lake. At this point look for the most obvious traverse ledge leading around to the north beneath a steep-walled south-facing buttress. After passing around this buttress, continue north, past a prominent gully/weakness, until a second steep buttress is encountered. Continue around to the north end of this buttress to reach a huge left-facing corner. Scramble up to the base of the corner to a good belay stance. **Pitch 1:** Climb past very loose flakes to solid rock left of the main corner. Continue on good rock to a belay stance (5.7, 24m). **Pitch 2:** Follow discontinuous cracks to a small, solid ledge at the base of a beautiful hand crack (5.8, 15m). **Pitch 3:** Climb the hand crack to the base of a large roof. Pass the roof to the right, continuing up and right on steep rock until lower-angle terrain is reached (5.9, 46m). From here continue to the summit via the upper West Ridge route *(Route 36)* or traverse over to the southwest couloir, the route that is used for the descent (see *Route 1*).

ROUTE 36. WEST RIDGE. II, 5.4. First ascent August 4, 1955, by William Buckingham and Mary Lou Nohr. The long west ridge of

FIGURE 3-28. Middle Teton, west aspect, West Face, Electric Corner *(Route 35)*, II, 5.9

the Middle Teton separates Icefloe Lake on the south from the perennial snow/icefield or rock glacier in upper Dartmouth Basin, the neglected canyon on the west side of the popular Lower Saddle. Interestingly, the first known crossing of this ridge occurred on July 29, 1872, during the Langford-Stevenson climb of the Enclosure. The lower section of this ridge turns north-northwest at Point 11,256 and forms the western rim of Dartmouth Basin and the eastern boundary of the south fork of Cascade Canyon. In its entirety it is 2.6 miles long—one of the longer continuous ridges in the range. To access this route, take the trail up the south fork of Cascade Canyon (see *Cascade Canyon, South Fork* in Section 8); at about 1.5 miles past (south of) the forks, cross a stream and bushwhack up a gully to the broad col (9,600+) at the base of the first step of the west ridge of the Middle Teton. Scramble up the ridge to the first tower. Keep directly on the ridge over several black towers and across a flat, brushy area; then climb the ridge to the high point marked by the 10,720-foot contour. Descend to the col to the east and climb steep, rotten rock over several small towers. Climb the next large tower and descend to the east to the beginning of the rotten-red-pinnacles section of the ridge next to the main mass of the Middle Teton. At this point the first-ascent party descended about 60m and bypassed these pinnacles on the south in order to reach the steep cliffs of the main mass of the mountain. These cliffs are climbed in four pitches up a steep and difficult chimney just south of the crest of the west ridge. Another possibility is to climb back to the ridge crest at the notch separating the last pinnacle from the mountain and then climb directly up the ridge. The last portion of the ridge lies back at a lower angle and is easily followed to the main (north) summit. See *American Alpine Journal* 10, no. 1 (1956): pp. 116–19.

BONNEY'S PINNACLE (12,160+)

(0.15 mi N of the Middle Teton)
Map: Grand Teton

This pinnacle is the higher of the two at the base of the north ridge of the Middle Teton. It is passed but not often climbed by those intent upon the North Ridge route of the Middle Teton *(Middle Teton, Route 32)*.

ROUTE 1. EAST FACE AND SOUTH RIDGE. I, 4.0. First known ascent August 11, 1948, by Orrin and Roger Bonney, who found a cairn containing a decomposed and illegible record. From the Lower Saddle traverse Pinocchio Pinnacle on the west, go through the notch between the two pinnacles, and climb easily the east and south sides of this small tower.

PINOCCHIO PINNACLE (12,160+)

(0.15 mi N of the Middle Teton)
Map: Grand Teton

This, the lower of the two pinnacles at the base of the north ridge of the Middle Teton, is named after its profile as seen from the summit of Bonney's Pinnacle. These two pinnacles, which provide interesting climbing and an excellent view of the south side of the Grand Teton, are a worthwhile excursion from the Lower Saddle if one has the energy and an hour to spare.

ROUTE 1. EAST FACE. I, 4.0. First ascent July 17, 1951, by Robert Merriam, William Whitfield, and Bertha Howald. From the Lower Saddle, traverse around the west side of this pinnacle to the notch between it and Bonney's Pinnacle. The face is a short climb.

ROUTE 2. NORTH FACE. I, 5.1. First ascent July 31, 1960, by Kellen Staley and Bill Echo. Approach from the Lower Saddle directly to the base of the north face. Climb about two-thirds of the face before angling left (east) to the northeast ridge. The final pitch to the summit is the most difficult.

SECTION 4

The Grand Teton and the Enclosure

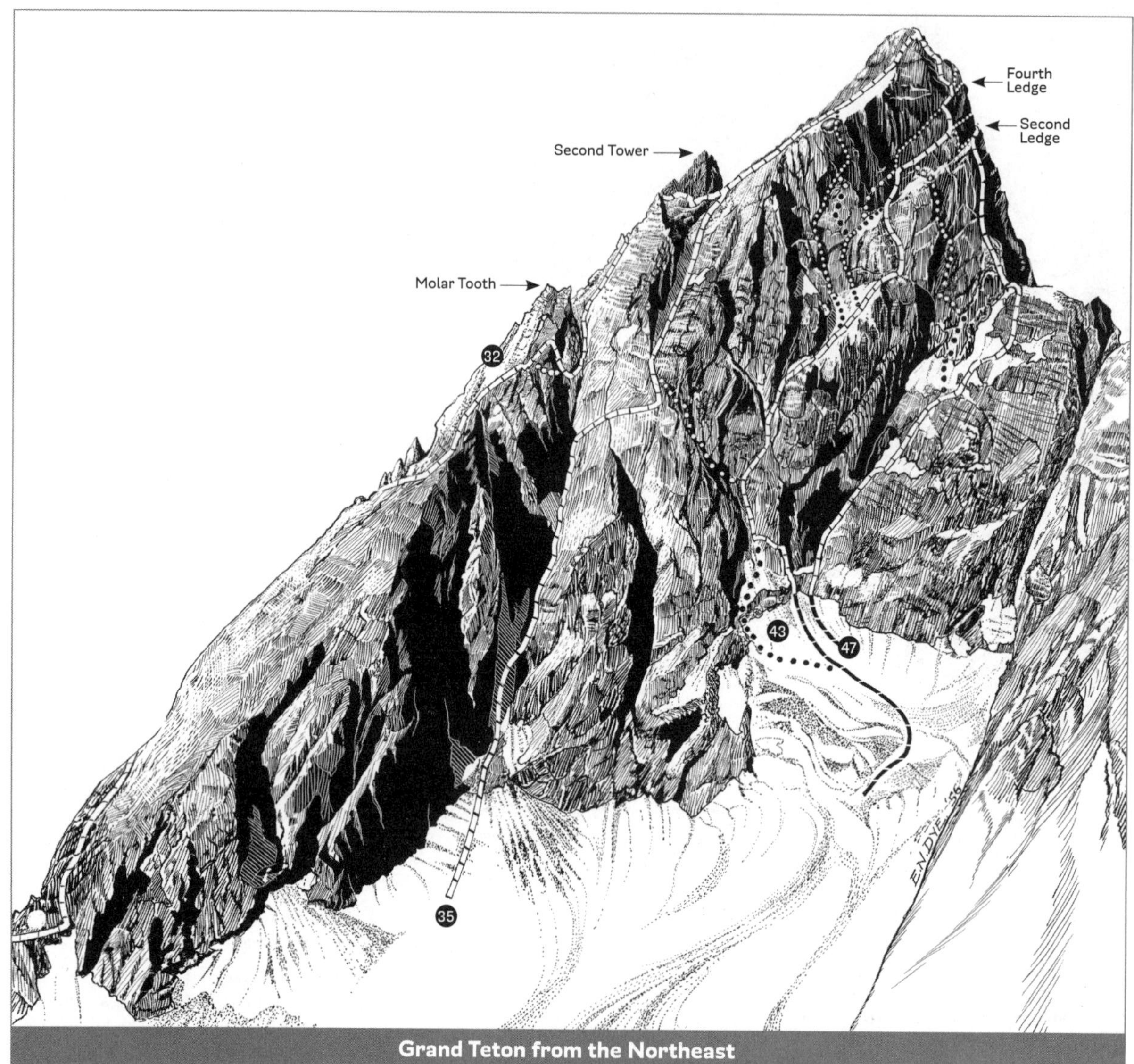

Grand Teton from the Northeast

The Grand Teton is not only the highest peak in the Teton Range but also the focal point of climbing activity. From any approach to the range, the Grand towers above the lesser peaks and beckons the climber almost irresistibly. A wide variety of problems will be encountered on the many faces and ridges of this complex mountain. Today, one has a choice of some 114 routes and variations to the summit, with 22 more available on the adjacent Enclosure. But even the easiest of these are not to be underestimated.

Structure of the Peak

The structure of the Grand Teton is complex. On the south (or slightly west of south), it is bounded by the broad and windy Lower Saddle (11,600+), which separates the Grand from the Middle Teton. The much sharper Gunsight Notch (12,160+) on the north isolates its neighbor, Mount Owen. The Teton Glacier lies at the foot of the steep and renowned north face, with the southern portion of its terminal moraine at the base of the very long and pinnacled east ridge, which descends directly into Glacier Gulch. The slabby upper southeast face of the mountain harbors, through most normal seasons, both the East Ridge Snowfield (higher) and the Otterbody Snowfield (lower), the latter named many decades ago for its remarkable resemblance to the animal. (Originally the name was "Otter's Body," though the contracted form, Otterbody, is now commonly used.) Below the steep rock of the southeast face is the Teepe "Glacier," a prominent snow/icefield in Garnet Canyon, just south of the Grand's east ridge. (The Teepe Glacier has melted almost completely during at least three summers of record—1931, 1988, and 2021—so strictly speaking it is considered to be inactive or a remnant glacier.)

Teepe Pillar and Glencoe Spire, two major pinnacles towering above the north fork of Garnet Canyon, are separated from the upper mountain by the Black Dike, which cuts across the southern portion of the Grand Teton at about 12,000 feet. The three distinct major ridges on the south aspect—the Exum, Petzoldt, and Underhill (see *Grand Teton, Routes 8, 13*, and *16*), named for pioneer Teton mountaineers of the 1930s—all rise from this very conspicuous dike. The first two are separated by the Beckey Couloir (rock; see *Grand Teton, Route 12*) in the lower part and by the Ford Couloir (snow) in the upper part; the narrow Stettner Couloir (see *Grand Teton, Route 15*) separates the latter two. Above the Lower Saddle two large couloirs or gullies extend upward for 1,500 feet to the Upper Saddle (13,160+), which lies at the base of the upper western cliff band and separates the summit of the Grand from that of the Enclosure, a name now applied to the entire western spur (13,280+) of the mountain. Originally this name was used more narrowly to describe only the circular artificial structure on the summit of this subpeak. The Enclosure itself is supported by a southwest ridge, which extends down into Dartmouth Basin, and a very long northwest ridge with origins in Cascade Canyon some 5,600 feet below. A small, rarely visited snow/icefield lurks at the base of the west face of the Enclosure. The impressive northern aspect of the Enclosure rises vertically above the upper south end of Valhalla Canyon and is separated from the Grand Teton by the well-known Black Ice Couloir (see *Grand Teton, Route 51*), which terminates at the Upper Saddle. The west wall of the Grand extends from the Black Ice Couloir north to the north ridge, which reaches from the Grandstand, above Gunsight Notch, up to the summit.

The structure of this remarkable mountain dictates how the climber approaches it, depending upon the route chosen. The most common approach by far is Garnet Canyon for the popular routes on the south aspect of the peak: see *Garnet Canyon* in Section 3. Other approaches that are used less commonly, ordered here based on popularity, include Glacier Gulch (see Section 7), Valhalla Canyon (described later in this section), and Dartmouth Basin (see *Cascade Canyon, South Fork* in Section 8). These days the Grand is also approached regularly via the Grand Traverse (see Section 5). Largely due to climate change, the Valhalla Traverse, used to access some of the most difficult alpine routes on the peak, has fallen in popularity.

History

The Grand Teton has a long and sometimes turbulent history. See the History chapter at the beginning of this guidebook for a survey of everything from the earliest recorded foray up to the Enclosure and the controversy that continues to roil over who first reached the summit of the Grand to modern feats of alpinism. A rich and varied cast of climbers have left their mark on this storied peak.

General Information

The Grand Teton ranks as one of the finest mountaineering objectives in the United States. This reputation is certainly deserved. Enjoyable ridge scrambling, high-angle rock walls featuring very difficult free climbing, moderate snowfields, glaciers, and steep ice chutes are all to be found on this varied peak. From the summit almost every other peak in the Teton Range can be seen, with the notable exception of Mount Owen. (To see Mount Owen one must descend the north ridge a short distance.) The peak that retains the greatest prominence from this viewpoint is Teewinot Mountain, its sharp pinnacles silhouetted against the flat plains of Jackson Hole. The Wind River Range forms the eastern horizon, and one can easily pick out flat-topped Gannett Peak, the highest in Wyoming. To the north one can see well into Yellowstone National Park and beyond, probably to Pilot, Index, and Granite Peaks. To the west, Idaho is beautiful with its cultivated fields and rolling hills, but the western horizon is too distant for positive identification of the peaks.

Note that early-season climbs will usually entail greater—frequently *much* greater—difficulties than are described here. Under such conditions, which may also arise during or after a severe storm in any season, snow and ice can be expected on any route on the Grand Teton. A moderate climb, such as the Owen-Spalding route *(Grand Teton, Route 1)*, can be extremely difficult if severely iced. An ice axe and crampons may become essential for the climb. Because snow and ice coverage varies from year to year, climbers should always inquire at the Jenny Lake Ranger Station for current conditions before setting out on a climb. An ascent of the Grand Teton requires adequate preparation, skill, and equipment.

The usual rule is to allow two full days for the ascent and descent of the Grand Teton; this holds for every route. Depending on the route, a high camp can be established on the Lower Saddle; in Garnet Canyon; near Surprise Lake; on the Teton Glacier; in Valhalla Canyon; or in Dartmouth Basin. However, one-day ascents are increasingly commonplace, sometimes driven simply by the lack of available overnight permits. For those who are very familiar with the mountain, even long routes such as the East Ridge *(Grand Teton, Route 32)* and the North Ridge *(Grand Teton, Route 47)* are quite possible in a day. The only route offering an expeditious means of descent from the summit is the Owen-Spalding route; very few descents have been made by other routes. A worthwhile and recommended 15-minute side trip from the Upper Saddle to the summit of the Enclosure (this is easier than it appears) will yield an excellent view of the entire west face of the Grand Teton.

Speed Records and Other Notable Events

The original speed record of 5 hours, 22 minutes for the round-trip from the Lupine Meadows trailhead to the summit and back was set on August 17, 1939, by John Holyoke and Joseph Hawkes. This record has since been broken: first by Jock Glidden on August 12, 1973, with a time of 4 hours, 11 minutes (with no shortcutting); then by Bryce Thatcher on August 26, 1981, in 3 hours, 47 minutes, 4 seconds (with no rappel); next by Creighton King on August 10, 1983, in 3 hours, 30 minutes, 39 seconds (with no shortcutting); and again by Bryce Thatcher on August 26, 1983, in 3 hours, 6 minutes, 25 seconds (with no rappel). Over the years the actual "trail" in Garnet Canyon has varied, so these times may not be perfectly comparable. The unofficial "trail" past the end of the maintained trail, which terminates at the Platforms, was constructed in the summer of 1977; in 1939 and 1973 there was no trail.

Amazingly, Thatcher's record held for 29 years. It was finally broken by the ace Spanish ski mountaineer and ultrarunner Kilian Jornet in 2 hours, 54 minutes, 1 second on August 12, 2012 (with shortcutting, which cut the linear distance of the run, albeit over much steeper terrain). The day before, on a "recce run" with his partner, Emelie Forsberg, they ran a time of 3 hours, 51 minutes—the FKT (fastest known time) for a woman. Jornet's record stood for only 10 days: on August 22, Rocky Mountain National Park ranger Andy Anderson broke it by less than 1 minute with a time of 2 hours, 53 minutes, 2 seconds—and with no shortcutting. (**Note:** The National Park Service [NPS], asks users not to use shortcuts because of a variety of resource impacts that occur.)

Other events of note on the Grand Teton include the first ski descent on June 16, 1971, by Bill Briggs. As a variation, on June 11, 1982, Rick Wyatt successfully descended on skis using pin bindings and cross-country boots. Although illegal, the speediest descent to date was completed via paragliding on September 19, 1987, by Jim "Jaime" Olson from just below the summit on the top part of the Buckingham Buttress and Underhill Ridge. The escapades continued when Stephen Koch nabbed the first snowboard descent of the Grand on June 9, 1989. Then, during the spring of 1994, Koch (on snowboard) and Mark Newcomb (on skis) descended major portions of the Black Ice Couloir, with both climbers alternating belaying one another. The Enclosure Ice Couloir (see *The Enclosure, Route 7*) was descended in a similar fashion by Alex Lowe and Andrew McLean shortly afterward.

At once aesthetically beautiful and extremely intimidating, the Hossack-McGowan Couloir drops precipitously down the north face of the Grand from the East Ridge Snowfield. Hans Johnstone and Mark Newcomb climbed and skied the route on February 16, 1996, thus making its first winter ascent as well as the first ski descent. Then on March 31, 2013, Brendan O'Neill and Greg Collins raised the bar when they skied portions of the North Face of the Grand (*Grand Teton, Route 43*). The pair down-climbed and rappelled from the summit to the Third Ledge. They then skied the Third Ledge to the Second Ledge, rappelled to the First Ledge, and skied nearly 300m to the Guano Chimney. Here they cramponed back up to the top of the First Ledge and rappelled down to the Grandstand, which they skied before continuing out and down Glacier Gulch to the valley floor.

The Jackson Hole climbing community has long been characterized by a spirit of adventure and a desire to push further into the unknown. In a recent tour-de-force example of this ethos, Ryan Burke tagged the summit of the Grand three times in a 24-hour period on August 4, 2017. The Picnic, or the Grand Teton Triathlon, has also grown increasingly popular as a unique Jackson Hole endurance challenge. It is the brainchild of local writer and photographer David Gonzales, who completed the first Picnic in 2012 after two previous attempts. It involves biking from Jackson's town square to Jenny Lake in Grand Teton National Park, swimming across the lake, climbing the Grand Teton, and then doing the whole thing in reverse for a total of 46 miles of biking, 2.6 miles of open-water swimming, and 20 miles of hiking and climbing.

GRAND TETON (13,770)

Map: Grand Teton

Over the 150-year recorded history of climbing on the Grand Teton, routes to its summit have been established that will satisfy anyone's taste. From the Owen-Spalding route *(Route 1)* to Bean's Shining Wall of Storms *(Route 3)*, almost all degrees of difficulty can be found—but even the easiest routes require a level of mountaineering skill and good judgment. See the introduction to Section 4, above, for information regarding the structure, routes, and history of this iconic peak, the highest in the Teton Range.

For the approach and campsites for *Routes 1* through *31*, see *Garnet Canyon* in Section 3; for *Routes 32* through *47*, see *Glacier Gulch* in Section 7; for *Routes 48* through *51*, see *Valhalla Canyon* later in this section, before *The Enclosure*. Note that these are general approach and camping guidelines. More detailed approach directions as well as alternatives can be found within the individual route descriptions.

Chronology

OWEN-SPALDING: August 11, 1898, William O. Owen, Franklin Spalding, Frank Petersen, John Shive
var—**WITTICH CRACK:** June 27, 1931, Hans Wittich, Walter Becker, Rudolph Weidner
var—**EMERSON CHIMNEY:** August 24, 1948, Richard Emerson, Pat Harison (Emerson)
var—**COLLINS-HUME:** July 16, 1994, Greg Collins, David Hume
var—**PSEUDO EMERSON:** Date and party unknown

EAST RIDGE (WITH NORTHERN TRAVERSE OF THE MOLAR TOOTH): July 22, 1929, Robert Underhill, Kenneth Henderson (ascent); August 2, 1935, Paul Petzoldt, William Loomis (descent)
var—**SOUTHERN TRAVERSE OF THE MOLAR TOOTH:** August 12, 1935, Paul Petzoldt, Glenn Exum, Elizabeth Cowles (Partridge)
var—**SOUTH MOLAR TOOTH COULOIR:** July 28, 1936, Paul Petzoldt, Karl Keuffel, James Monroe
var—July 28, 1936, Paul Petzoldt, Karl Keuffel, James Monroe
var—September 7, 1955, Leigh Ortenburger, Irene Beardsley (Ortenburger)
var—August 11, 1957, James Langford, William Cropper
var—**TRICKY TRAVERSE OF THE MOLAR TOOTH:** July 9, 1972, Robert Irvine, David Lowe, Jim "Ole" Olson
var—July 25, 1977, Jon King, Chuck Fitch
var—**NORTH MOLAR TOOTH COULOIR:** January 31, 1984, Alex Lowe

POWNALL-GILKEY: [probable] June 27, 1931, Hans Wittich, Walter Becker, Rudolph Weidner (descent); August 1948, Richard Pownall, Art Gilkey (ascent)
var—**COLLINS-COOMBS:** September 2, 1993, Greg Collins, Colby Coombs

EXUM RIDGE: July 15, 1931, Glenn Exum (ascent); August 24, 1936, Jack Durrance, Ethel Mae Hill (descent)
var—**FLIPPING TOKENS TO HOBOKEN:** July 3, 2022, Brady Johnston, Greg Collins, Kent McBride

UNDERHILL RIDGE: July 15, 1931, Robert Underhill, Phil Smith, Francis Truslow (ascent); September 5, 1937, Paul Petzoldt, Phil Smith, William House (descent)
var—**DIRECT:** August 30, 1953, William Buckingham, Steve Smale, Ann Blackenburg (Mansfield), Charles Browning, Jack Hilberry
var—**WILSON CRACK:** September 2, 1965, Ted Wilson, Rick Reese

NORTH RIDGE: July 19, 1931, Robert Underhill, Fritiof Fryxell (ascent); FFA August 30, 1936, Fritz Wiessner, William House, Percy Olton, Beckett Howorth; July 6, 1933, Paul Petzoldt, Sterling Hendricks (descent, top half); September 3, 1955, Willi and Jolene Unsoeld (descent, bottom half)
var—**EAST GUNSIGHT APPROACH:** ca. August 22, 1936, Fritz Wiessner, Paul Petzoldt, Brad Gilman, Beckett Howorth, William House, Elizabeth Woolsey
var—**WEST GUNSIGHT APPROACH:** August 6, 1940, Jack Durrance, Henry Coulter, Merrill McLane, Chap Cranmer
var—**VALHALLA APPROACH:** July 31, 1960, Pete Sinclair, Jake Breitenbach, Leigh Ortenburger, Irene Beardsley (Ortenburger)
var—**ITALIAN CRACKS:** August 19, 1971, Howard Friedman, Peter Wollan
var—**CHOCKSTONE BYPASS:** August 10, 1974, Jim McCarthy, Gerald Barnard
var—**ODETTE-SHERNER:** August 7, 1994, Chuck Odette, Jim Sherner

STETTNER COULOIR: [probable] July 30, 1933, Sam Younger, Albert Strube (descent); June 30, 1964, Charles Schaeffer, Bob Schaeffer, Mark Fielding, Curtis Stout (ascent on snow, left fork); August 17, 1969, Leigh Ortenburger, Jennifer Ronsiek (ascent on rock, right fork)

PETZOLDT-LOOMIS OTTERBODY: August 2, 1935, Paul Petzoldt, William Loomis (ascent); September 10, 1936, Paul Stettner, Art Lehnebach (descent)
var—August 6, 1961, J. Gordon Edwards, Kenneth Proctor

NORTH FACE: August 25, 1936, Jack Durrance, Paul and Eldon Petzoldt
var—August 14, 1941, Paul and Bernice Petzoldt, Glenn Exum, Hans Kraus
var—August 13, 1949, Richard Pownall, Ray Garner, Art Gilkey
var—**DIRECT FINISH:** July 24, 1953, Richard Emerson, Willi Unsoeld, Leigh Ortenburger
var—July 9, 1954, William Buckingham, Fred Ford
var—August 24, 1955, Willi Unsoeld, Frank Ewing
var—September 2, 1955, Willi and Jolene Unsoeld
var—**UPPER SADDLE START:** July 31, 1960, Bill Echo, John Waage, Keith Staley, Dean Millsap
var—**NORTH RIDGE START:** August 11, 1976, Jim Donini, Rick Black, Michael Cole (from 1931 North Ridge route); July 20, 1977, George Montopoli, Ralph Baldwin (from Italian Cracks variation)

DURRANCE DIRECT (LOWER EXUM RIDGE): September 1, 1936, Jack Durrance, Kenneth Henderson
var—**THIN MAN:** September 4, 1957, Charles Plummer, Sterling Neale, Samuel Silverstein
var—September 2, 1959, Rick Medrick, Thomas Marshall
var—**DIRECT START:** August 1986, Jim Williams, Robin Moore
var—**GOLD FACE:** June 27, 1988, Renny Jackson, Jim Woodmencey
var—**DIREXUM:** June 25, 1990, Carl Haiss, Joe Miller
var—August 27, 1990, Mark Whiton, John Berry
var—**WOODEN SHIPS:** July 20, 2017, Michael Gardner, Jimmy Voorhis; July 1, 2019, Michael Gardner, Vic Zeilman (completed)

SMITH OTTERBODY: September 5, 1937, Phil Smith, Paul Petzoldt, William House

BECKEY COULOIR: September 10, 1937, Joseph and Paul Stettner (descent); August 31, 1941, Joseph and Paul Stettner (ascent)

HOSSACK-MACGOWAN COULOIR: August 8, 1939, Jack Hossack, George MacGowan
var—August 24, 1962, Pete Sinclair, Leigh Ortenburger
var—June 25–26, 1990, Todd Cozzens, James Earl

WEST FACE: August 14, 1940, Jack Durrance, Henry Coulter
var—**DIRECT WEST CHIMNEY:** August 13, 1960, Tom and William Spencer
var—**BLACK ICE–WEST FACE COMBINATION:** July 23, 1967, George Lowe, Mike Lowe
var—**TRAVERSE TO UPPER SADDLE:** February 2–4, 1971, George and David Lowe, Greg and Jeff Lowe
var—**DIRECT APPROACH:** August 28, 1973, Jim "Ole" Olson, Doyle Nelson
var—**TILLEY-NICHOLSON TRAVERSE:** July 20, 1978, Buck Tilley, Bill Nicholson
var—**NEUTRON BURN:** August 7, 1989, Jon Patterson, Pete Keane

PETZOLDT RIDGE: July 14, 1941, Paul Petzoldt, Elizabeth Cowles (Partridge), Mary Merrick, Fred Wulsin Jr.
var—**DIRECT:** August 30, 1953, Willi Unsoeld, LaRee Munns, James and Rodney Shirley, Austin Flint
var—**PETZOLDT-TO-EXUM TRAVERSE:** August 31, 1954, Robert Brooke, Tom McCormack (ascent); August 9, 1980, Bruce Coulter (descent)
var—**DOUBLE OVERHANG:** June 25, 1986, George Montopoli, Leo Larson

GOODRO-SHANE: August 9, 1953, Harold Goodro, Jim Shane
var—July 2, 1961, Tom Spencer, Ron Perla

WEST FACE OF THE EXUM RIDGE: July 23, 1954, Richard Pownall, Robert Merriam
var—July 14, 1981, Yvon Chouinard, Cullen Frishman, Naoe Sakashita

BUCKINGHAM BUTTRESS: August 19, 1955, William Buckingham, Richard Hill, Ray Secoy
var—**ORTENBURGER ARÊTE:** July 1991, Brent Finley, Susie Harrington, Leigh Ortenburger
var—**WHERE IN THE BUCKINGHAM ARE WE?:** July 30, 2020, Vic Zeilman, Ryan Schuster

LEV: July 12, 1960, Peter Lev, Jim Greig, William Glosser, David Laing; FFA July 30, 1988, Renny Jackson, Rich Perch, Steve Rickert, Leigh Ortenburger
var—**JACKSON-WOODMENCEY:** Summer 1988, Renny Jackson, Jim Woodmencey
var—**EAST FACE LEFT:** October 4, 2001, Aaron Gams, Jeff Burke

NORTHWEST CHIMNEY: July 26, 1960, David Dornan, Leigh Ortenburger, Irene Beardsley (Ortenburger)
var—**WEST FACE FINISH:** August 4, 1960, Royal Robbins, Joe Fitschen, Yvon Chouinard
var—**JACKSON-KIMBROUGH CONTORTION:** August 9, 1980, Renny Jackson, Tom Kimbrough
var—**HUMMINGBIRD WALL:** August 1990, Beverly Boynton, Ted Kerasote

BLACK ICE COULOIR: July 29, 1961, Ray Jacquot, Herb Swedlund
var—**ALBERICH'S ALLEY:** July 22, 1982, Peter Hollis, Renny Jackson

MEDRICK-ORTENBURGER: August 14–15, 1963, Rick Medrick, Leigh Ortenburger

NORTHEAST BUTTRESS: August 24–25, 1970, Paul Myhre, Dale Sommers; FFA ca. July 30, 1978, Jon King, Charles Foster
var—**LITTLE WING:** July 16–17, 1976, Tom Deuchler, Dave Moerman

SIMPLETON'S PILLAR: June 16–17, 1972, Jeff Lowe

SOUTHEAST CHIMNEY: August 5, 1973, David Lowe, Leigh Ortenburger

HORTON EAST FACE: August 14, 1977, W. D. Horton, Paul Horton, Robert Snyder

GRAND NORTH COULOIR (SHEA'S CHUTE): ca. August 1, 1978, Jon King, Charles Foster (mostly rock); June 6, 1980, Steve Shea (mostly ice)

ROUTE CANAL: June 17, 1979, Jeff Lowe, Charlie Fowler

BEYER EAST FACE I: July 14, 1979, Jim Beyer

OTTERBODY CHIMNEYS: September 14, 1979, Kim Schmitz

NO NAME GULLY: 1979 or 1980, Steve Shea

LOKI'S TOWER: August 2, 1981, Mark Whiton, Michael Stern
var—July 17, 1984, Renny Jackson, Steve Rickert

BEYER EAST FACE II: August 15, 1981, Jim Beyer, Dan Grandusky

JACKSON-RICKERT CRACK: June 20, 1986, Renny Jackson, Steve Rickert

AMERICAN CRACKS: July 7, 1988, Mike Colacino, Calvin Hebert (attempt); July 14, 1988, Mike Colacino, Jim Earl (complete, to top of climb)

BURGETTE ARÊTE: July 26, 1988, Dan Burgette, Jim Springer
var—**ANGEL BOY OW:** August 2, 2008, David Bywater, Renny Jackson

IT'S NOT A CHIMNEY: September 6, 1989, Jim Dorward, Dan Burgette
var—**IT IS (TOO) A CHIMNEY:** September 1990, Ralph Cooley, Jerry Johnson, Tony Jones

KEITH-EDDY EAST FACE: August 17, 1991, Jason Keith, David Eddy

EAST FACE, LEFT CENTER: July 1994, Renny Jackson, Ron Johnson (first two pitches); fall 2002, Aaron Gams, John Steinbauer (second two pitches)

GOLDEN ARÊTE: July 1999, Jim Beyer, Zack Martin
var—**OFFSPRING:** August 1999, Jim Beyer, Zack Martin

CRYSTAL TOWER: August 27, 1999, Jim Beyer

CAPTAIN STUPID (GOT TO KILL): September 8, 1999, Jim Beyer (solo)

THE RED AND THE BLACK: August 8, 2001, Keith and Alan Cattabriga

BEYER-HARTMAN: July 8, 2002, Jim Beyer, Dan Hartman

GOLDEN PILLAR: July 11, 2003, Greg Collins, Hans Johnstone

ALEX LOWE MEMORIAL ROUTE: October 5, 2004, Stephen Koch, Mark Newcomb

EAST FACE DIRECT: September 3, 2006, John Steiger, John Fowler

SQUEEZE BOX: February 6, 2007, Hans Johnstone, Stephen Koch

CRYSTAL RIGHT: August 16, 2010, Aaron Gams, Toby Stegman (with Brian Mulvilhill on an earlier attempt)

BEAN'S SHINING WALL OF STORMS: July 22, 2012, Greg Collins, Hans Johnstone

NORTH BUTTRESS DIRECT: August 15, 2020, Mark Jenkins, Justin Bowen

ROUTE 1. ▲ OWEN-SPALDING. II, 5.4. First ascent August 11, 1898, by William O. Owen, Franklin Spalding, Frank Petersen, and John Shive; first winter ascent December 19, 1935, by Paul and Eldon Petzoldt and Fred Brown (accomplished outside the "official" winter season of December 20–March 20); second winter ascent March 3–6, 1949, by Paul Petzoldt, John Lewis, and Ted Lewis. This famous route goes from the Lower Saddle (11,600+) between the Middle Teton and the Grand Teton to the Upper Saddle (13,160+) between the Enclosure and the Grand Teton, then breaks out onto the west face and up to the summit. When conditions are good, this traditional route remains the easiest way to reach the top of the mountain; when iced up, however, this route can be extremely difficult. For the approach to the Lower Saddle, see *Garnet Canyon* in Section 3. The terrain between the Lower Saddle and the Upper Saddle can be negotiated in several ways but the climbing is not difficult; a climbers' trail will be found covering much of it. Nevertheless, some climbing parties may, depending on conditions, wish to use a rope for safety before reaching the Upper Saddle. The major difficulties of the route lie above the Upper Saddle.

History: The early history of this route sparked what is perhaps one of the most enduring first-ascent controversies in mountaineering. Over 120 years have passed since William O. Owen and his party stood on the summit of the Grand Teton, and the debate over whether Nathaniel P. Langford and James Stevenson preceded them 26 years earlier continues to this day. No smoking gun has emerged, no proof beyond a reasonable doubt. There are three different camps, each with its ardent supporters: those who believe that Langford and Stevenson climbed the peak on that day in July 1872; those who believe that the Owen party, who definitely reached the summit on August 11, 1898, was the first to do so; and those who believe that an indigenous person (or persons) reached the summit earlier than either party. After all, whoever built the enclosure—discovered on its lofty aerie by the Langford-Stevenson party—could have continued on to that higher point above, driven to see what was up just a bit farther. And then, to keep things interesting, what about the letter from Captain Charles Kieffer to Owen detailing a possible 1893 ascent? See the History chapter for more on this early era of Teton exploration.

Strategy: Most parties climb this route over two days with a camp somewhere in Garnet Canyon. However, now that it has been done in the incredibly fast roundtrip time of 2 hours, 53 minutes, 2 seconds, many climbers go with the light-and-fast option of skipping the overnight and doing it in just one day. This has become commonplace during the summer when the route is dry.

FIGURE 4-1. Grand Teton, south aspect, Black Dike to Upper Saddle detail

Route Description: See *Figure 4-1* for approach detail. Take the trail leading upward (north) from the Lower Saddle to and past the Black Dike. Avoid trampling the fragile alpine vegetation. Immediately beyond the dike is a large, smooth-faced tower called the Needle. Do not go to the right (east) side of the Needle and try to ascend the large eastern couloir (the Wall Street Couloir) that lies at the base of the walls of the Exum Ridge; it contains steep sections and much loose rock, and there are problems in exiting from the upper end. Instead, proceed up along the left (west) wall of the Needle on ledges and sections of rough climbers' trail. The area west of the Needle and east of the southwest ridge is composed of two separate couloirs. The most westerly of these curves down and west as it drops steeply into Dartmouth Basin. With a bit of dark humor, this couloir has acquired the name Idaho Express, as a number of fatalities have occurred there, primarily during the early season due to slips on snow in its upper reaches. The couloir immediately west of the Needle extends with only minor breaks all the way to the Upper Saddle. The two couloirs are separated by a curious knob or small tower, and in early season both contain nearly continuous snow. During the winter or spring, getting to the Upper Saddle can be a straightforward snow climb weaving up the two couloirs. During the main summer climbing season the best route stays on the left (west) flank of the ridge that extends from the Needle to near the Upper Saddle. The one described here—see *Figure 4-2*—was worked out by Glenn Exum during his years as a guide.

Continue around the west side of the Needle to a large chimney with a chockstone, which is the first break in its west wall. Just past this chimney, climb abruptly up and right across a small face back into the chimney above the chockstone. (**Note:** Continuing straight up and right here will lead to the Briggs Slab, while going left will lead to the Sack-of-Potatoes Chimney.) Continue easily up and right (30m) to a wide outlook ledge. Turn to the north here and find the Eye of the Needle, a tunnel that leads under an enormous boulder. One can squeeze through this tunnel, exiting onto a small ledge (icy in early season) at the far (north) end. If the tunnel is blocked by

FIGURE 4-2. Grand Teton, south aspect, Eye of the Needle detail

Margaret Smith Craighead negotiates the Crawl on the first "manless" ascent of the Grand Teton, August 3, 1939. (Photo courtesy of Derek Craighead)

snow in early season, climb over the top and back down to the ledge.

Follow this small ledge north past an exposed corner, known as the Belly-Roll-Almost, into the gully that is the upper extension of the initial chockstone chimney. (Just around the corner to the north is the Briggs Slab, which offers a slightly more difficult way of getting to this point.) Continue up and left (north) to the edge of this gully. From here to the Upper Saddle one can simply take the path of least resistance along the west side of the main ridge, which will be on the right leading from the Needle to near the Upper Saddle. A better, but also more intricate, scheme involves climbing onto the crest of the main ridge above at a section of black rock (known as the Black Rock Chimneys), staying on the right (east) side of the crest for 60m, and then crossing back (west) into the upper main couloir to reach the Upper Saddle.

An impressive view can be obtained by looking down the north side of the Upper Saddle at the steep Black Ice Couloir *(Route 51)*. A little scrambling is required to reach the relatively flat area just under the west cliffs of the Grand Teton. This area is slightly above and east of the lowest point of the Upper Saddle. The standard descent rappel point is at the top of the cliffs above. Caution should be exercised here because the scree is treacherously loose and a slip could entail serious consequences. If there is a party above the rappel point, beware; they are likely to knock down loose rocks.

Several routes diverge from this point on the west side of the Grand Teton. (See *Figures 4-3* and *4-4*.) The Owen-Spalding route leads left (north), and most parties rope up before starting out on the scree ledge leading out of sight to the north. The first obstacle on this ledge is a very large detached flake known as the Belly Roll, which one can easily pass on the outside by using the excellent handholds along the top edge. Proceed about 6m farther along the ledge to the famous Crawl, or "Cooning Place." This is a very exposed ledge, perhaps 18 inches wide, directly under an overhang. The time-honored method, the one used by the first-ascent party, is to crawl on one's stomach along this ledge, as the overhang prevents standing or even going on hands and knees. However, there are enough footholds 1m down on the face below this ledge for one to use the edge of the ledge for handholds and simply walk along on the outside. Neither method is difficult but the exposure is exhilarating. On the far (north) side of the Crawl, continue easily along the ledge for about 3m. (To avoid becoming enmeshed in the difficulties of the Great West Chimney, do not traverse too far north here.) The Double Chimney, the crux of the route, is about 4.5m up and 4.5m to the left of this point. (This name has been retained, although it is now inappropriate, since the huge flake that divided the chimney into two parts collapsed against the north wall in the summer of 1951.) Climb this chimney (5.5) to a good belay at the large, sloping ledge at the base of the next feature, the Owen Chimney.

To pass the next section there is a choice. The most obvious option is the large Owen Chimney, which starts almost

FIGURE 4-3. Grand Teton, west aspect, above the Upper Saddle. (A) Owen-Spalding *(Route 1)*, II, 5.4; (B) Owen-Spalding, variation: Wittich Crack, II, 5.6; (C) Owen-Spalding, variation: Collins-Hume, II, 5.11-; (D) Owen-Spalding, variation: Pseudo Emerson, II, 5.8, M4-; (E) Owen-Spalding, variation: Emerson Chimney, II, 5.8; (F) Pownall-Gilkey *(Route 2)*, II, 5.8; (G) Pownall-Gilkey, variation: Collins-Coombs, II, 5.10-

directly above and angles slightly up to the right. A jam crack on the right side of this chimney is sometimes ice-free when the main chimney is iced. Another commonly used alternative from the top of the Double Chimney is the Catwalk, an easy but very exposed 46m series of ascending slabs leading due south toward the standard rappel point. (Before continuing the ascent, the climber can observe the descent rappel route from the south end of these Catwalk slabs, where one can see on the opposite side of a 9m-wide, rotten chute the sling rope used for rappelling [30m] to the Upper Saddle. (**Note:** At this elevation on the west side of the Grand Teton, there is a broad, sloping bench that extends from the Exum Ridge *[Route 8]* all the way north to the Great West Chimney.)

From the south end of the Catwalk climb north and east a short distance (18m) up to the huge chimney system that is the obvious break in the wall above. This chimney system—Sargent's Chimney—is climbed on the left (north) side, although the right branch will also go (there is a rappel anchor that is often used to descend this chimney, but one can also downclimb around it a few meters to the north). From the top of the chimney proceed upward and slightly to the left (north) for about 60m until one encounters a 9m, 45° slab. This slab, which can often be wet or have patches of verglas, can be avoided on its south side. Above this slab traverse a short distance to the right (south), then scramble left up to the summit about 23m above.

Descent: For a long time the traditional method of descent was simply to downclimb the route, but today the standard rappel—from slings around block near the south end of the Catwalk—is done far more often than the downclimb. This 30m rappel takes one all the way down to a point where it is possible to walk down to the Upper Saddle, thus eliminating the lower part of the Owen-Spalding route (the Catwalk, the Double Chimney, the Crawl, and the Belly Roll). This rappel was discovered on August 18, 1948, by Richard Pownall, Ralph Johnson, and Jim Harrang. (The first rappel to the Upper Saddle was made earlier, on July 20, 1948, by Richard Emerson and Fred Golomb, who utilized a point somewhat to the south.) It is a spectacular rappel, as the lower portion of it is free.

FIGURE 4-4. Grand Teton, west aspect, Owen-Spalding *(Route 1)*, II, 5.4

An additional rappel point (two bolts with chains) was established about 3m to the north of the standard rappel in 2007; this is a 40m double-rope rappel.

Descent Safety Notes: The standard rappel is a 30m rappel and may therefore be done with a single 60m rope. However, when deploying the rope, make sure to *toss it off to skier's left* (south)—that way it will reach the ground! If thrown off to the north, the rope *will not reach*, and this has caused a number of accidents. This standard rappel is maintained annually, but *always* inspect the slings. And take great care when moving around and over to the rappel anchors, as loose rock is abundant here.

The area around the rappel points has been the scene of accidents and fatalities over the years. A major contributing factor to these accidents is the common presence of multiple parties, including large guided groups, waiting to use the rappel anchors. This can cause confusion, distraction, and at times a great deal of anxiety, especially when a storm is approaching or in progress—an already hazardous and tense situation.

If escape is urgently needed and conditions do not permit downclimbing the Owen-Spalding route, and both the standard and 40m rappel stations are in use, there is another option: Instead of descending all the way to the standard rappel point, cut left (south) when about 6m to 9m above the rappel point and cross the small buttress above the standard rappel point to gain another single-rope rappel point. Slings will be found here. Getting to this point requires traversing above both lower rappel points through an area with much loose rock—be extremely careful! This rappel goes down into the chimney immediately south of the regular 30m rappel. Look for a large chockstone from which another single-rope rappel will take one to just above the Upper Saddle.

Below the Upper Saddle, descend by the same route used for the ascent, but make sure to go right (west) a short distance before turning down into the main couloir to avoid accidentally getting into the Wall Street Couloir. Because of loose rock and steep sections, this large eastern couloir immediately west of the walls of the Exum Ridge is *not* recommended for descent. Also remember that the Eye of the Needle, the key to an easy descent, is found on the right (west) side of the ridge that extends from near the Upper Saddle down to the Needle. After descending about 90m in the main couloir, cross the ridge to the left (east), descend 60m farther, and cross back to the right (west) to the black rock.

From near the ridge crest one should be able to see the Eye of the Needle. If this route is missed, one can continue down the main couloir to the right (west), but some unpleasant cliff bands and steep, hazardous snow will be met before one moves back left toward the Black Dike to gain the Lower Saddle. **Time:** 3¾ to 4¾ hours from the Lower Saddle; 5¾ to 7 hours from the Caves; 6 to 7½ hours from Garnet Canyon; 8½ to 10 hours from Jenny Lake.

See *Alpine Journal* 19, no. 145 (August 1899): pp. 536–43, illus.; *American Alpine Journal* 3, no. 3 (1939): pp. 304–9, illus.; *Appalachia* 18, no. 3 (June 1931): pp. 209–32, illus.; 22, no. 4 (December 1939): pp. 533, 535; *Chicago Mountaineering Club Newsletter* 2, no. 6 (July–December 1948): p. 6; *Die Alpen* 5 (1929): pp. 330–36, illus.; *Mazama* 13, no. 12 (December 1931): pp. 63–71, illus.; 19, no. 12 (December 1937): pp. 12–16, illus.; *Outdoor Life*, September 1924 (vol. 44, no. 3): pp. 181–86, illus.; *Outing*, 1901 (vol. 38, no. 3): pp. 302–7, illus.; *Princeton Alumni Weekly* 28, no. 24 (1928): pp. 711–18, illus.; 920–21; 29, no. 24 (1929): pp. 756–63, illus.; *Scribner's Monthly*, June 1873 (vol. 6, no. 2): pp. 129–57, illus.; *Sierra Club Bulletin* 12, no. 4 (1927): pp. 356–64, illus.; *Summit*, August 1957 (vol. 3, no. 8): pp. 10–11, 21, illus.; June 1960 (vol. 6, no. 6): p. 24; October 1961 (vol. 7, no. 10): pp. 18–21, illus.; *Trail and Timberline*, no. 71 (August 1924): pp. 9–10, illus.; no. 83 (August 1925): pp. 1–8, illus.; no. 179 (September 1933): pp. 123–25, illus.; no. 389 (May 1951): pp. 58–60, illus.

***Variation:* WITTICH CRACK.** II, 5.6. First ascent June 27, 1931, by Hans Wittich, Walter Becker, and Rudolph Weidner. (See *Figures 4-3* and *4-4*.) This remarkable but short (43m) route suffered the misfortune of being lost for 24 years and was then misidentified for another eight years. Thus, the ascent of this route was not repeated until 1963. The Wittich Crack is not as subject to ice as the Double Chimney of the Owen-Spalding route; hence, it is recommended as an alternate when the Owen-Spalding is severely iced. In addition, the excellent rock makes this route worthwhile for its own sake, but it is more difficult than the Owen-Spalding when both are dry. Proceed to the Upper Saddle and continue north toward the Belly Roll. About 3m to 5m south of the large block of the Belly Roll, there is an obvious crack system leading directly upward through the vertical wall. Ascend this crack system to an alcove beneath a large overhang. Pass this overhang on its left (north) side by face holds and hand jams (5.6) and pull out onto the slabs in the middle of the Catwalk. Rejoin the main Owen-Spalding route to reach the summit. See *Appalachia* 19, no. 1 (June 1932): pp. 86–96; *Nature Friend* 25, no. 7 (July 1947): pp. 5–11.

***Variation:* COLLINS-HUME.** II, 5.11-. First ascent July 16, 1994, by Greg Collins and David Hume. (See *Figure 4-3*.) This one-pitch variation to the main Owen-Spalding route is a fine rock climb on excellent rock. From the Upper Saddle just to the north of the big chimney and standard rappel, climb up and left to a right-facing corner. Then traverse south and go up and over a difficult (5.11-) overhang that is hard to protect (while hanging on!). Continue up to the prominent gray corner seen from below and finish the pitch at the south end of the Catwalk.

***Variation:* PSEUDO EMERSON.** II, 5.8, M4-. First ascent unknown. (See *Figure 4-3*.) This route ascends the chimney that is immediately south of the standard rappel. It is usually wet or icy, depending on the time of year and air temperatures. It can be done in one or two pitches.

***Variation:* EMERSON CHIMNEY.** II, 5.8. First ascent August 24, 1948, by Richard Emerson and Pat Harison (Emerson). (See *Figure 4-3*.) From the Upper Saddle the cliff band above and to the east is seen to be broken by three major chimney systems. The one on the north, vertical and usually wet, leads to a cave beneath a huge boulder a few meters north of the standard rappel point. The central deep chimney—the Pseudo Emerson, commonly containing ice—lies immediately to the right (south) of the line of the standard rappel. Fifteen meters farther to the right is the third chimney system, the Emerson Chimney, which cuts up through two bands of black rock to the bench at the top of the cliff band. From the Upper Saddle, climb up and right on broken rock to a flake at the base of the chimney. After passing the initial difficulties of getting into the chimney, a fixed piton (an Army horizontal) will be found halfway up this lead. At the top, where the chimney becomes an overhang, climb left and up (5.8) onto the bench. This bench is isolated from the main large bench, which extends across the southwest and west faces of the Grand Teton from the Exum Ridge to the Great West Chimney. One must climb a narrow, diagonal ledge up and left (north) to join the upper Owen-Spalding route or blocks up and right (south) to join the upper Exum Ridge route (see *Route 8*).

ROUTE 2. POWNALL-GILKEY. II, 5.8. Probable first descent June 27, 1931, by Hans Wittich, Walter Becker, and Rudolph Weidner; first ascent in August 1948, by Richard Pownall and Art Gilkey. (See *Figure 4-3*.) Proceed to the Upper Saddle as in the Owen-Spalding route *(Route 1)*. Traverse right (south) from the Upper Saddle out to the end of a gradually steepening and narrowing ledge system. At the end of this ledge a block will be found with a thin crack on its left edge. Climb this crack to the top of the block and then continue up the crack system (5.8) via hand jams to a large ledge. The second pitch goes up an easier crack (5.6) to the broad bench extending across the southwest face of the Grand Teton. At this point one can traverse directly to the Exum Ridge route *(Route 8)* or to the Owen-Spalding. It is more interesting, however, to continue across the bench and up a fine, large chimney that leads to the uppermost mountain before joining one of the aforementioned routes. Because this route faces southwest on a smooth, high-angle wall, it offers an alternative to the Owen-Spalding in early season or just after a storm. It is significantly more difficult, however, and the crux may be complicated by running water because the route drains a portion of the large bench above. **Time:** 7 hours from the Lower Saddle. See *American Alpine Journal* 8, no. 1 (1951): p. 180.

***Variation:* COLLINS-COOMBS.** II, 5.10-. First ascent September 2, 1993, by Greg Collins and Colby Coombs. (See *Figure 4-3*.) This one-pitch variation of the regular Pownall-Gilkey route ascends the finger crack on the striped wall to the north. The pitch is 46m in length and is said to be of very high quality with excellent protection.

Grand Teton, Exum Ridge West Face

Much of what is seen of the Grand Teton from the Lower Saddle is the west face of the Exum Ridge, which rises above the right-hand couloir (the Wall Street Couloir) that leads to the Upper Saddle. *Routes 3–7* are all located on this face and are accessed by finding a way into the Wall Street Couloir. Where to cross the prominent rib of rock that separates this

couloir from the Owen-Spalding Couloir, the couloir used for the ascent of the Owen-Spalding route *(Route 1)*, is determined by the climbing objective.

For the upper three routes, which begin quite close to each other in the uppermost part of the Wall Street Couloir, a traverse from above the Black Rock Chimneys is probably the best choice: proceed upward from the Lower Saddle as one would for the Owen-Spalding route, take a detour to the east at a point just below the Upper Saddle, and then descend the Wall Street Couloir a short distance to where the climbing starts. For the lower routes to the south, the better option is to traverse toward Wall Street above the Eye of the Needle and then go up the Wall Street Couloir. See *Figures 4-1* and *4-2* for overviews of this area.

All of these routes get sun in the afternoon, but they can be numbingly cold in the morning. Be very aware that they are subject to the full fury of any incoming storms.

ROUTE 3. BEAN'S SHINING WALL OF STORMS. IV, 5.12b. First ascent July 22, 2012, by Greg Collins and Hans Johnstone. (See *Figures 4-5* and *4-6*.) This beautiful route, named for the indomitable Edwin "Bean" Bowers, is a fitting memorial to a man who loved

FIGURE 4-5. Grand Teton, Exum Ridge west face, Bean's Shining Wall of Storms *(Route 3)*, IV, 5.12b

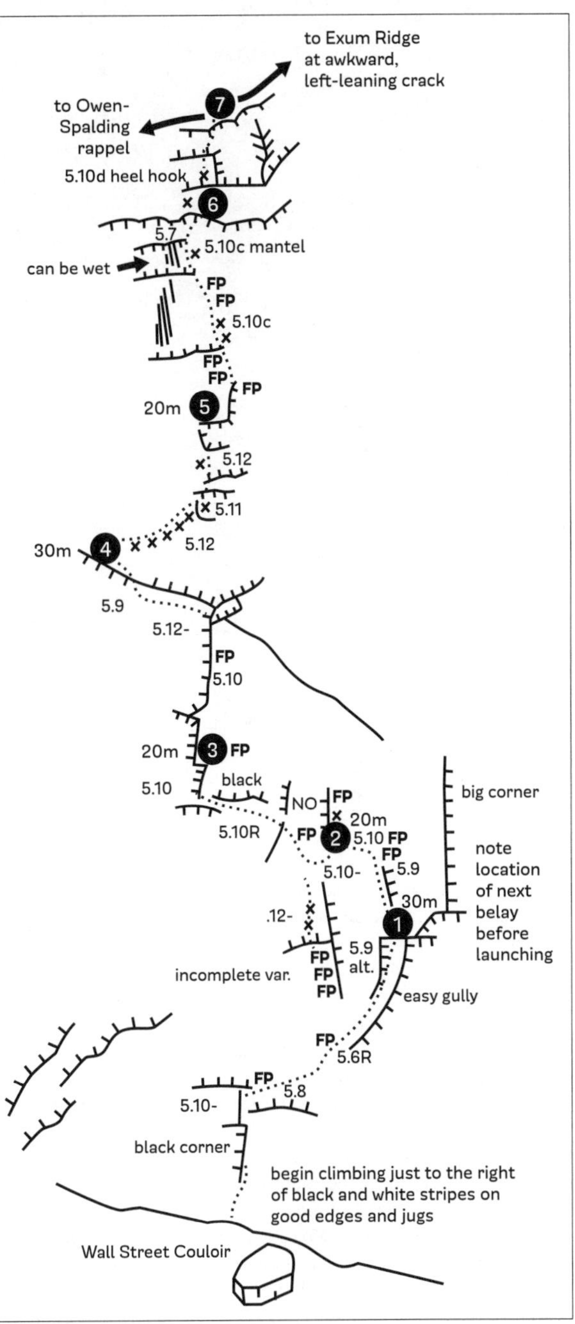

FIGURE 4-6. Grand Teton, Exum Ridge west face, Bean's Shining Wall of Storms *(Route 3)*, IV, 5.12b

Eric Bissell leading the crux fifth pitch of *Bean's Shining Wall of Storms*. (Photo by Jane Jackson)

life and was a superb, world-class alpinist. It is also fitting that it is currently the most difficult route on the Grand Teton, proudly situated facing the prevailing wind and storm direction head-on—another testament to Bean. From near the base one can look up and see a prominent right-facing corner near the middle of the face. The crux pitches are located just left (north) of this corner.

Pitch 1: Begin climbing just to the right of black and white stripes on good edges and jugs. Ascend a broken roof (small cams), then traverse right on good holds (no gear). Step right into an easy gully. Belay from cams on a good ledge (30m). **Pitch 2:** Note the location of the next belay before leaving the anchor. Climb steep rock with big holds, then step left to a belay from a bolt and a fixed piton (20m). **Pitch 3:** Downclimb (5.10-) and then traverse left and up past a fixed piton to tiny cam placements. Continue left on good holds without gear (5.10R) to a short crux in a corner. Belay from a fixed piton and wires; large cams placed high in the corner protect the follower (20m). **Pitch 4:** Climb an awesome corner, protected with finger-size cams and wires (and one fixed piton), then hand jam and heel hook through a big roof (#2 and #3 Camalots). Belay on a large ledge (30m). **Pitch 5:** Climb the bolted face with a fingery crux (optional tiny cam and medium stopper), and belay on a good ledge from small cams and medium wires (5.12b, 20m)—or continue up the next pitch. **Pitch 6:** Climb past fixed pitons and bolts up a beautiful 5.10c face with big holds to a one-bolt belay (30+m). **Pitch 7:** Finish with a super-steep stem and a 5.10d heel hook over a roof (20m, protected with wires, cams, and a bolt). Either exit right (south) to the upper Exum Ridge (see *Route 8*) at the awkward, left-leaning crack or go left (north) to the standard Owen-Spalding rappel (see *Route 1*). This is a classic Teton route with excellent, steep rock and good protection at the hardest sections of climbing. **Gear:** For protection bring two sets of cams, from tiny to wide hands size; one set of stoppers; and many quickdraws.

ROUTE 4. BEYER-HARTMAN. III, 5.10a. First ascent July 8, 2002, by Jim Beyer and Dan Hartman. (See *Figures 4-7* and *4-8*.) This climb has had only a few ascents, but it is recommended based on position and rock quality. Begin just above *Route 5* and climb easier terrain (5.6), passing a fixed pin to a ledge and the belay. Instead of traversing right on the ledge, climb straight up via a 5.9 crack and belay at a stance in an alcove below a small triangular roof. The third pitch climbs through the roof (5.7) and then up to a belay ledge just to the left of a large flake. The fourth pitch—the Mica Nipple Pitch—starts by going out to the north on some thin flakes, which are eventually passed via face climbing past a fixed pin (5.9+), and then continues up to a bolt (5.10a). Face climb from the bolt up and right to a ledge and belay at the base of a right-facing corner. From the belay face climb up and right to a bolt (5.8+) and then back left to the top of the corner (5.9); belay on a ledge. (A 5.10+ variation on the fifth pitch—first ascent by David Bywater and Martin Vidak—climbs to the left, directly up a ¾-inch crack in the corner, and then continues up through an overhang.) The sixth pitch goes straight up to a large ledge and a belay at the base of a large, obvious chimney. Climb the chimney (5.6) and exit to the right (5.9) or the left (5.9+) to the top of the climb. From this ledge, either head right (south) to join the upper Exum Ridge at the awkward, left-leaning crack (see *Route 8*) or escape to the left (north) to the standard Owen-Spalding rappel (see *Route 1*).

ROUTE 5. CAPTAIN STUPID (GOT TO KILL). III, 5.9+. First ascent September 8, 1999, by Jim Beyer (solo). (See *Figures* 4-7 and 4-8.) This route was Beyer's first venture on this facet of the Grand Teton, and he established it solo. The first pitch goes up through two overhangs to a ledge. A 5.6 chimney to the south is then climbed to another ledge. The third lead climbs a series of discontinuous cracks, the first a 5.9 finger crack. The second section is reached via 5.8 face climbing and has a 5.9 stemming section. Another section of face leads to a 5.9 crack that curves to the right and puts the climber

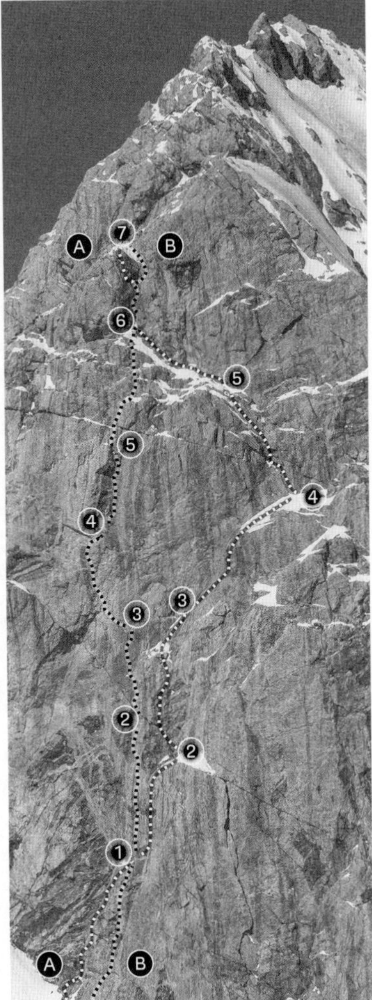

FIGURE 4-7. Grand Teton, Exum Ridge west face. (A) Beyer-Hartman *(Route 4)*, III, 5.10a; (B) Captain Stupid (Got to Kill; *Route 5*), III, 5.9+

to the Boulder Problem in the Sky on upper Exum Ridge
awkward, left-leaning crack
V-pitch
5.9
5.9+
5.6 chimney
to Owen-Spalding rappel
move belay
5.7+
5.5
Bywater/Vidak var. (5.10+) ¾" crack in corner and through roof
5.9
5.8 OW/flare
5.8+
Mica Nipple Pitch (5.10a)
5.7
FP
5.9+
undercling, seems hollow
5.9
5.7
5.9 stem
5.8
5.9 fingers
hands (avoid)
5.6
5.9
5.7/5.8
5.6
FP
Wall Street Couloir

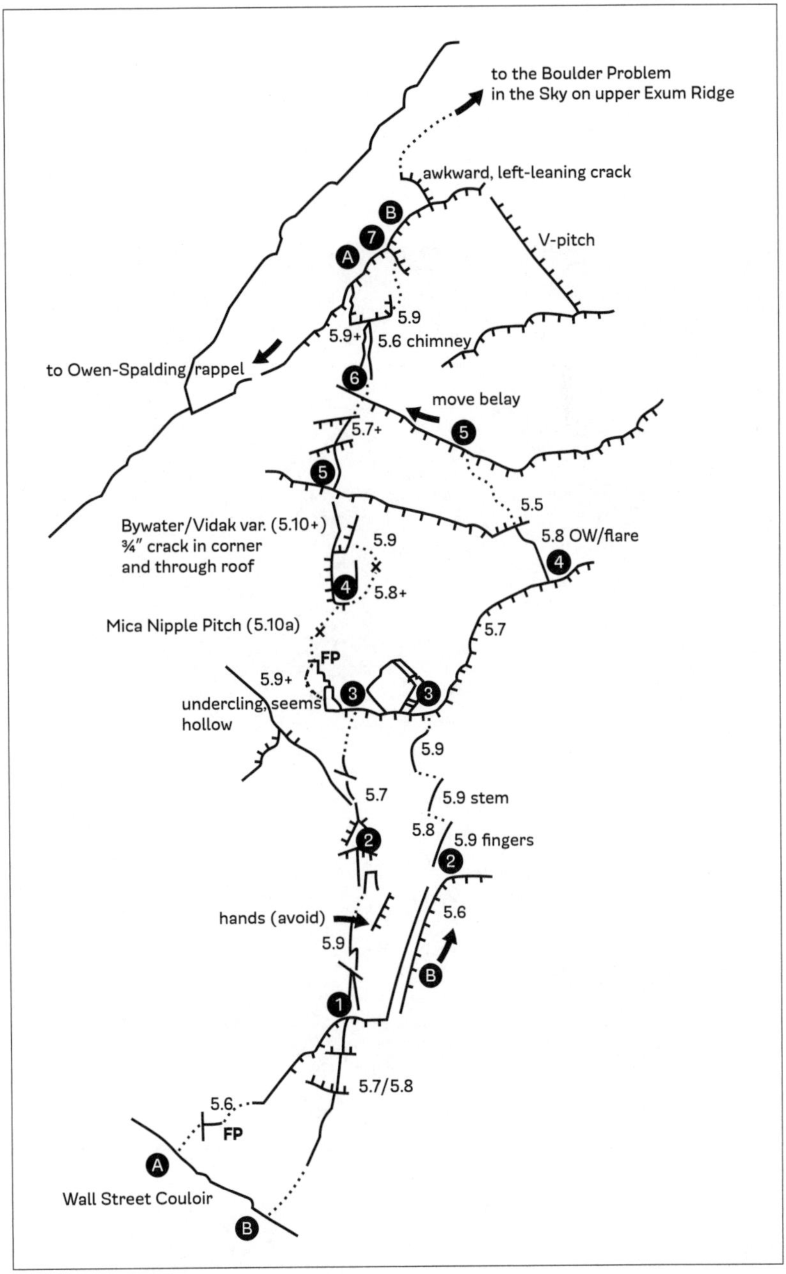

FIGURE 4-8. Grand Teton, Exum Ridge west face. (A) Beyer-Hartman *(Route 4)*, III, 5.10a; (B) Captain Stupid (Got to Kill; *Route 5*), III, 5.9+

on a ledge with a large flake at the base of the fourth pitch. A short section of 5.7 in a left-facing corner puts one on a large ledge. Traverse right (south) to the base of a 5.8 offwidth/flare and belay. Climb up and north via this flare and easier climbing to a large ledge. Move the belay north to the base of the easy chimney at the top of *Route 4*'s sixth pitch. Climb the chimney (5.6) and exit to the right (5.9). From the ledge at the top of the climb, either go right (south) to join the upper Exum Ridge at the awkward, left-leaning crack above the V-pitch (see *Route 8*) or traverse left (north) to the standard Owen-Spalding rappel (see *Route 1*).

ROUTE 6. JACKSON-RICKERT CRACK. III, 5.10R. First ascent June 20, 1986, by Renny Jackson and Steve Rickert. (See *Figures 4-9* and *4-10*.) On the upper west face of the Exum Ridge is a wide, zigzagging crack in an apparently vertical wall. It is perhaps the most prominent feature of the face when viewed from the Lower Saddle. This climb ascends this crack, which starts just above the beginning of the West Face of the Exum Ridge *(Route 7)*. From the Lower Saddle, follow the approach for *Route 7* to the point directly below a large, open dihedral/corner system in the face above. This seven-pitch route shares the same start as *Route 7* but moves left onto much more difficult ground after the first lead. At its top, this route joins the Exum Ridge *(Route 8)* at the beginning of the V-pitch. **Gear:** Protection in the beginning of the offwidth is difficult to obtain, hence the R rating, although a very large cam may work here.

FIGURE 4-9. Grand Teton, Exum Ridge west face, Jackson-Rickert Crack *(Route 6)*, III, 5.10R

ROUTE 7. WEST FACE OF THE EXUM RIDGE. III, 5.8. First ascent July 23, 1954, by Richard Pownall and Robert Merriam. (See *Figure 4-10*.) While much of the west face of the Exum Ridge is sheer, it is broken in a few places. This route ascends the main vertical break in the upper portion of the wall, a very large, open dihedral/corner system. From the Lower Saddle, proceed as in *Route 8*, crossing the ridge of the Needle into the Wall Street Couloir. Instead of continuing out to the Wall Street ledge, scramble north up the couloir some 90m until directly below the dihedral in the face above. Begin by scrambling up and right for 12m–15m to the start of the main corner. **Pitch 1:** Climb a short, wide 5.8 crack and then run the rope out to a belay on a ledge. *Route 6* begins here and heads toward the offwidth crack above. **Pitch 2:** Begin with 4th-class climbing that leads up the steepening main corner (5.7, 46m). **Pitch 3:** Continue up the corner past a fixed pin to the base of a chimney (5.6/5.7, 50m). **Pitch 4:** Ascend a right-facing corner in the chimney to near its top and belay at a fixed pin (5.7, 30m). **Pitch 5:** Face climb (5.7) out and to the left and belay on a ledge above the main dihedral. Then zigzag out to the left and back right and then left again and join *Route 6* at the top of its fifth pitch, as shown in *Figure 4-10*. **Pitch 6:** Gain a large ledge by means of a short 5.8 offwidth/flare. This ledge provides an escape to the north to the standard rappel described in *Route 1*. It is also possible to head right to join the Exum Ridge *(Route 8)* below the V-pitch. (The V-pitch is easily located from the Lower Saddle by looking for what appears to be the highest point on the Grand, which is actually the top of this pitch.) Another alternative is to continue up *Route 6*, chimneying around a chockstone (5.7) before either cutting right along a ledge to the start of the V-pitch or negotiating a 5.8 finger crack that meets the V-pitch partway up. **Time:** 10¼ hours from Garnet Canyon. See *American Alpine Journal* 9, no. 2 (1955): pp. 147–49.

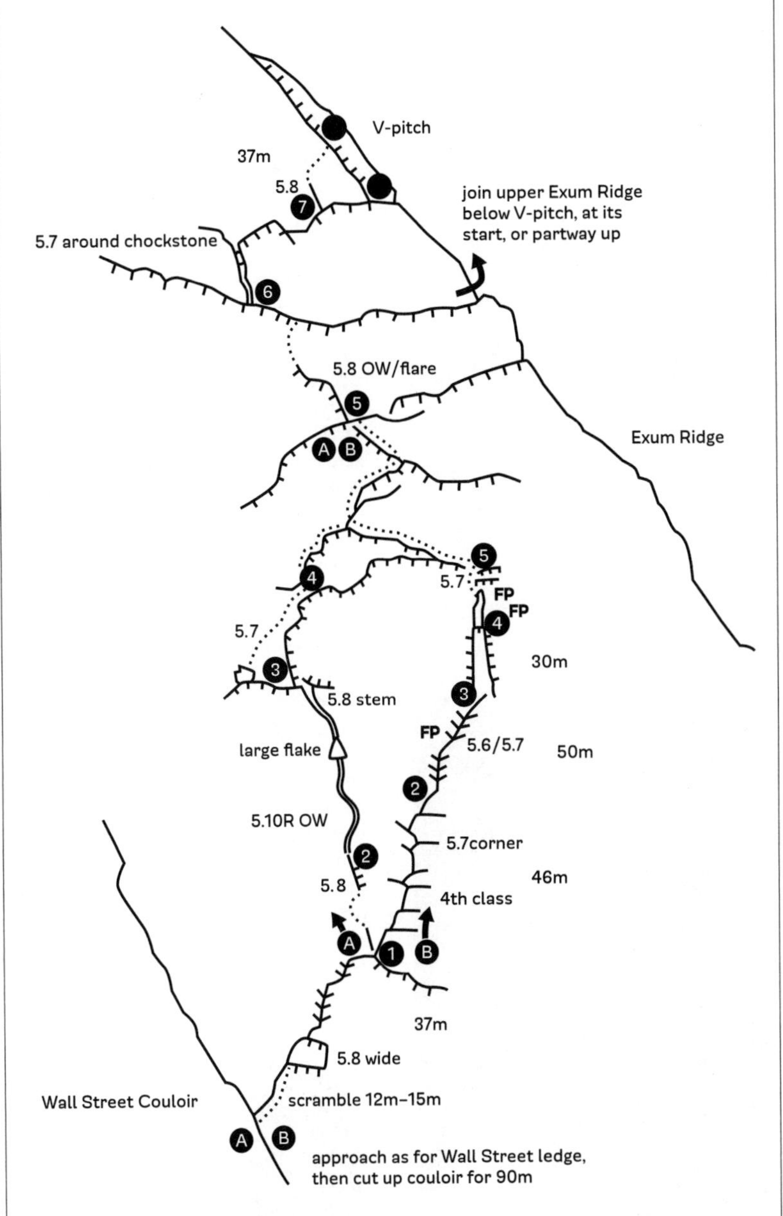

FIGURE 4-10. Grand Teton, Exum Ridge west face. (A) Jackson-Rickert Crack *(Route 6)*, III, 5.10R; (B) West Face of the Exum Ridge *(Route 7)*, III, 5.8

Variation: III, 5.8. First ascent July 14, 1981, by Yvon Chouinard, Cullen Frishman, and Naoe Sakashita. This significant variation is little known and only a general description can be provided. Proceed as in the regular Exum Ridge route *(Route 8)* to the beginning of Wall Street. This variation starts in the huge chimney system that rises directly above the beginning of Wall Street. To avoid the ridge crest the variation repeatedly angles left (north) in a sequence of chimneys, cracks, and ledges. It may cross the very large right-facing corner of the original 1954 route. The Exum Ridge route is not rejoined until rather high up on the ridge, but the exact location is uncertain.

Grand Teton, Southern Ridges

The three great southern ridges of the Grand Teton, named appropriately for three of the pioneering climbers of the range, are best approached from the Lower Saddle. See *Figure 4-11* for an overview. From the crest of the saddle a few trails lead upward (north) to the Black Dike, an intrusive feature that is prominent as it slices its way from Cascade Canyon to Glacier Gulch. Three-quarters of the way up from the saddle to the dike, a trail takes off to the east: this is the first part of the Black Dike Traverse, which can be used to access Glacier Gulch. Expect some hard and frozen snow on this traverse in early season, which may necessitate carrying an ice axe (and possessing a high level of skill in its use) and cutting a few steps—techniques that should be in the toolbox of every mountaineer. Later on, when the snow has melted, a trail takes one across this traverse, all the way over to Teepe Col and beyond.

During the evening of September 2, 2007, a house-size boulder that was wedged near the top of the Stettner Couloir came loose and broke apart on its way down to the lateral moraine area of the Middle Teton Glacier. Pieces of it, as well as other displaced rock, came crashing down into the Park Service's designated Moraines camping zone in the north fork of Garnet Canyon. The accompanying dust cloud was quite spectacular, and fortunately no one was injured. This major rockfall has made crossing the bottom end of the Stettner Couloir during the summer climbing season quite hazardous; the approach to any of the routes on the east face (see *East Face Routes*, below) may be made significantly safer by going up from the Teepe Glacier side.

ROUTE 8. ▲ EXUM RIDGE. II, 5.6. First ascent July 15, 1931, by Glenn Exum; first partial descent July 25, 1933, by Stephen Koelz; first complete descent August 24, 1936, by Jack Durrance and Ethel Mae Hill, the first of three such descents by Durrance that summer; first winter ascent February 19–20, 1972, by David Lowe, Jock Glidden, and David Smith. (See *Figure 4-12*.) For generations this outstanding ridge has been *the* route of choice to the summit of the Grand Teton. The combination of ready access, southern exposure, and moderate but exciting climbing on a line leading directly to the summit ensures its continued popularity. Although the Owen-Spalding route *(Route 1)* is a simpler climb and is recommended for those with less mountaineering experience, the Exum Ridge route features excellent rock and—in good weather—will be in sunshine once Wall Street has been passed. The Exum Ridge route is also not as subject to severe icing as the Owen-Spalding. Two disadvantages, however, are the length of the route and the relative difficulty of descending in bad conditions from partway up the climb; after passing Wall Street it is almost easier to continue to the summit than to descend. Even so, three methods of escape from various points along the ridge are described below.

History: On July 15, 1931, Glenn Exum was assisting Paul Petzoldt with the guiding of two clients on the Owen-Spalding. "Ex, why don't you go over there, take a look at that ledge, and if you think it'll go, why go, and we'll meet you on top," Petzoldt said. Exum traversed over and climbed along the ledge until it ended abruptly at what seemed an impossible gap.

"I walked away from the ledge seven times, until I finally got up there and saw those little handholds and the boulder on the ridge," he later recalled. "So I climbed as high as I could until I was sorta secure, and I jumped from a standing start." It is interesting for the climber of today to contemplate the spectacular leap that Exum made from the end of Wall Street over to the large boulder on the other side and what was perhaps going through his mind as he psyched himself up for this maneuver. After Exum flung himself across, he scrambled up the ridge and met Petzoldt and the clients on the summit. Petzoldt exclaimed, "My God, Ex, do you know what you have done?"

No stranger to impressive feats himself, Petzoldt soloed the Exum Ridge on the same day as Exum for the second ascent—after guiding his clients up the Owen-Spalding (though he used a more traditional means of ascent as he traversed the Wall Street section). On the third ascent of the route—by Petzoldt, Theodore Koven, and Gustav Koven, one week after Exum's daring solo climb—the three men found a haversack containing a can of beans, a can opener, and notepaper (dated 1921) on the Wall Street ledge, signifying a surprising early attempt, probably by Teton Basin residents (see *Buck Mountain, West Peak, Route 3,* in Section 2).

FIGURE 4-11. Grand Teton, south aspect, southern ridges approach detail. (A) Wall Street Couloir; (B) regular approach for Durrance Direct (Lower Exum Ridge); (C) first chimney pitch of Durrance Direct; (D) alternate lower ramp approach for Durrance Direct; (E) upper ramp approach (5.1); (F) alternate approach for Durrance Direct, variation: Gold Face; (G) start of It's Not a Chimney, Burgette Arête, Beckey Couloir; (H) start of Petzoldt Ridge, variation: Petzoldt Direct; (I) Stettner Couloir; (J) Chevy Couloir; (K) Ford Couloir; (L) Glencoe Col; (M) start of regular Underhill Ridge; (N) approach for east face routes; (O) Otterbody Snowfield

Glenn Exum (Photo by Leigh Ortenburger)

Strategy: The Exum Ridge is usually done in two days, with a bivouac on the Lower Saddle or the Middle Teton Glacier moraine; however, one-day ascents are commonplace.

Approach: See *Figures 4-1* and *4-2*. Take the trail leading upward (north) from the Lower Saddle to and past the Black Dike. Avoid trampling the fragile alpine vegetation. Immediately beyond the dike is a large, smooth-faced tower called the Needle. Proceed up along the left (west) wall of the Needle on ledges and sections of rough climbers' trail. A large chimney (with chockstones), the first break in the west wall of the Needle, will be seen rising above to the east. Just past this chimney climb abruptly up and right across a small face back into the chimney above the chockstone. Continue easily up and right (30m) to a wide outlook ledge. Turn to the north here and find the Eye of the Needle, a tunnel that leads under an enormous boulder. One can squeeze through this tunnel, exiting onto a small ledge (icy in early season) at the far (north) end. If the tunnel is blocked by snow in early season, climb over the top and back down to the ledge. Follow this small ledge north past an exposed corner, known as the Belly-Roll-Almost, into the gully that is the upper extension of the initial chockstone chimney. Continue up in this gradually steepening gully for 46m to the small notch on the crest of the ridge that extends from the Needle toward the Upper Saddle. From this notch, the huge Wall Street ledge can be seen across the wide Wall Street Couloir. (This ledge was named by Paul Petzoldt during one of his early guided ascents, for a client who was a Wall Street banker by profession.) A descending traverse along ledges and chimneys leads across the couloir to the lower left end of Wall Street. Take the huge Wall Street ledge out to its right (south) end and rope up and set the belay.

Route Description: The exposed gap to the boulder ledge on the ridge crest—the Step Across—is passed either by balancing around on the narrow extreme end of Wall Street or by using the ledge for handholds. In good weather welcome sunshine should be found here. Two ropelengths now lead to the wall of the first large tower. The initial 18m is the Golden Stair, or Golden Staircase, a section of solid, knobby, golden Teton rock; the remainder involves

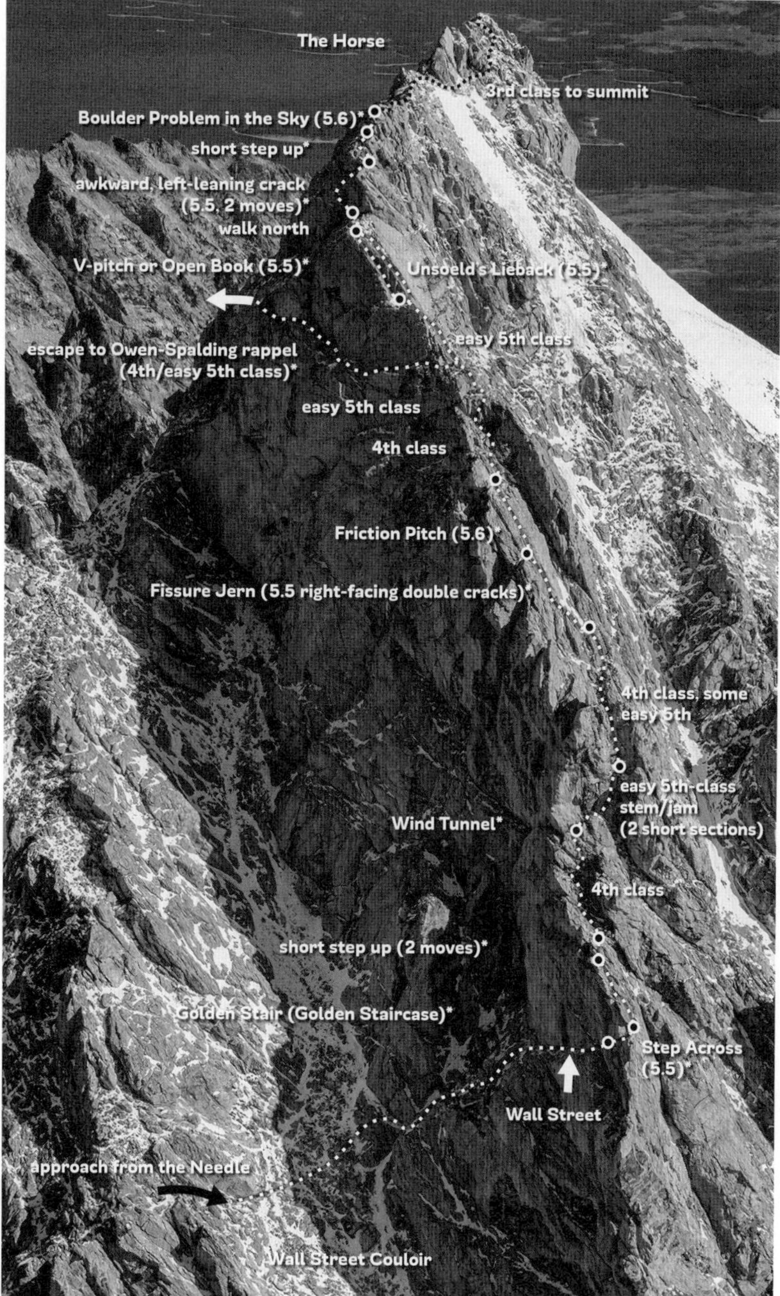

FIGURE 4-12. Grand Teton, south aspect, Exum Ridge *(Route 8)*, II, 5.6. **Note:** Pitches marked with an asterisk (*) are usually belayed.

scrambling along on almost horizontal rock. At the tower turn right (east), enter a chimney (the Wind Tunnel), and climb over blocky terrain until it is possible to turn to the north and climb toward a wide, steep gully. A few stemming/jamming moves (frequently wet or icy) provide access to the gully. Climb either the right or left edge of this gully for the next ropelength (46m). A second ropelength goes slightly right and then back left, ending near the crest. The boulder ledge at the base

A climber on the Friction Pitch, Exum Ridge route, Grand Teton. (Photo by Renny Jackson)

of the Friction Pitch, now out of sight almost directly above, can be reached by going either right or left from this point. The option to the left, the traditional route, involves a slanting chimney on the west side of the crest followed by a short face and crack onto the boulder ledge. (Carman's Pinnacle, a slender spire located farther west on the crest, makes for a delightful side trip at 5.5/5.6.) The alternative to the right, more commonly used in recent years and shown in *Figure 4-12*, uses a right-facing double-crack system—the Fissure Jern—near the right edge of the ridge crest to gain the same ledge in one long lead. The ridge itself here is fairly broad, and the use of the word *crest* refers simply to the high point between the left and right edges of that ridge.

From the boulder ledge climb the Friction Pitch. This lead, the most difficult of the route, goes almost directly up from the boulder ledge on relatively smooth and unbroken rock, reaching a good ledge and anchors after 40m. Begin this crux pitch by climbing directly above the belay for 4.5m, then trend slightly left to two large black knobs before heading up and slightly right (9m) to gain a shallow groove leading to the belay. Little protection is available along this lead; fortunately, the difficult friction move (5.6) is only about 5m above the belay, and one can place a small nut or two at the traverse left. From the top of the Friction Pitch, scramble up and right across the top of a black-rock gully to a very small notch (sometimes filled with snow). Continue scrambling for two pitches near the ridge crest until it is convenient to cross over to the left (west) side of the crest to the base of the V-pitch (also known as the Open Book), a large left-facing corner at the top edge of the west face of the Exum Ridge. Climb the V-pitch (46m) to its finish at a broad bench; walk across this bench to the next tower, just west of the crest in an area of black rock. An awkward, left-leaning crack (two moves, often wet or icy) is then ascended. Now move back right to the crest, where a short step up leads to the next tower, which is climbed near its prow by means of a short jam crack. This is the Boulder Problem in the Sky, and it consists of a couple of 5.6 moves. At the top of the crack follow the horizontal ridge crest to the base of the summit block. From here traverse right (east) along the top edge of the southeast snowfield. The summit is attained by easy blocks from the southeast.

If caught by a storm partway up the ridge, one can descend the route to a point just above the Golden Stair where a rappel (18m) can be made directly down onto the end of Wall Street. A second escape, somewhat difficult and exposed, is available between the Friction Pitch and the V-pitch; a ledge system, beginning with an exposed step-around on loose blocks on the west face of the ridge, starts at a small notch about 46m above the top of the Friction Pitch. Follow this ledge, up and down, for about 100m past more loose blocks to the lower end of the broad bench leading toward the standard descent rappel on the Owen-Spalding route. If higher on the ridge, a third, easy method of escape, from the top of the V-pitch, is to make a horizontal traverse left (northwest) across the broad bench to reach the Owen-Spalding route and the standard descent rappel.

Variations: There are so many small variations available on this ridge that it is possible to make two or three ascents and scarcely touch the same rock twice. These will not be detailed here, but a few major variations must be mentioned. The inexperienced climber should appreciate that this multiplicity of variations implies that, should the exact route described here be lost, there is little cause for concern because almost any upward course will, sooner or later, place one on the summit.

The Friction Pitch can be avoided by two methods. On the pitch below, traverse even farther to the right (east) into a gully parallel to it. There is loose rock and sometimes ice in this gully, so it is not highly recommended. Once in the gully, climb to the black-rock area at the top of the Friction Pitch. Or take the Puff-n-Grunt Chimney, which is actually a difficult (5.6 to 5.7) corner between the Friction Pitch and the gully already mentioned. Some difficulty will be experienced in getting to this corner from the starting ledge. When the V-pitch is iced, one can simply keep on the right (east) side of the ridge and climb a system of cracks in the slabs out to the east. Between these cracks and the arête edge of the V-pitch is Unsoeld's Lieback (5.5), yet another alternative. Finally, at the summit block a very interesting and worthwhile variation can be used. Instead of traversing right (east) underneath the summit block, cut left (west) 15m before climbing up into the cleft between the summit block and a detached rock mass leaning against it. Then scale the west side of the summit block to its knife-edge crest and ride this arête, known as the Horse, to the summit. **Time:** 5 to 6 hours from the Lower Saddle; 6¾ to 7¾ hours from the Caves; 7 to 9 hours from Garnet Canyon; 9¼ to 11 hours from Jenny Lake. See *Appalachia* 19, no. 1 (June 1932): pp. 86–96; *Chicago Mountaineering Club Newsletter* 2, no. 2 (May–November 1946): pp. 17–18; 5, no. 6 (December 1951): p. 16; 10, no. 1 (February 1956): pp. 10–11; 15, no. 1 (February 1961): pp. 4–7; *Trail and Timberline*, no. 447 (March 1956): pp. 47–48; no. 491 (November 1959): pp. 169, 171.

***Variation:* FLIPPING TOKENS TO HOBOKEN.** II, 5.12b/c. First ascent July 3, 2022, by Brady Johnston, Greg Collins, and Kent McBride. (See *Figure 4-14*.) This two-pitch variation provides a very difficult start to *Route 8*, and features perhaps the most difficult free moves yet done on the Grand Teton. It is located on the face above the beginning of Wall Street just to the south of a prominent chimney. Use the normal approach for Wall Street and near the start of the chimney, scramble up and right onto a blocky ledge, belaying on its right side at the base of the wall. **Pitch 1:** Begin by stepping to the right on jugs, passing a few fixed pins. Climb a crack and corner and then reach left and begin a traverse left with heel hooking to an overhanging thin crack (crux). Continue up this crack that eventually eases to 5.11 to a small comfortable belay ledge with a fixed anchor (5.12b/c). **Pitch 2:** Climb up and left via hand jamming to the main ledge just below the start of the Wind Tunnel pitch on *Route 8*. **Gear:** For protection take three sets of tiny to finger-size cams and two sets of cams in the hand size range.

ROUTE 9. DURRANCE DIRECT (LOWER EXUM RIDGE). III, 5.7. First ascent September 1, 1936, by Jack Durrance and Kenneth Henderson (to summit); second ascent in 1938, by Jack Durrance and Andrew McNair (to Wall Street); first winter ascent February 2, 1976, by Tom Ballard, Tom Shreve, Daniel Winner, and Gregory Lee (to summit). (See *Figure 4-13*.) This notable climb, one of the most impressive of the early Durrance routes, goes up the lower segment of the Exum Ridge from the Black Dike to the end of Wall Street. This section is steeper and much more difficult than the rest of the ridge above. Durrance considered it his best route in the Tetons. It is an excellent choice for climbers seeking good difficult rock on the Grand Teton and is especially suitable as an early-season climb because it is south-facing with few ledges to hold snow. An ice axe, however, is recommended for early-season ascents. In addition, the weather, which almost always comes in from the southwest or west, can be easily monitored as the climb progresses.

Approach: See *Figure 4-11* for approach details. Before starting out for this route, it is useful to pick out the major landmarks from the Lower Saddle. The first of these is the initial 40m chimney, which starts at the top of the first step of the ridge; from the saddle, this chimney has the appearance of a large left-facing corner. Note the large ramp diagonaling from the beginning of the chimney down to the right past the apex of the Black Dike at the base of the Exum Ridge. For the easiest approach, gain this ramp near the foot of the Petzoldt Ridge and scramble diagonally left (west)

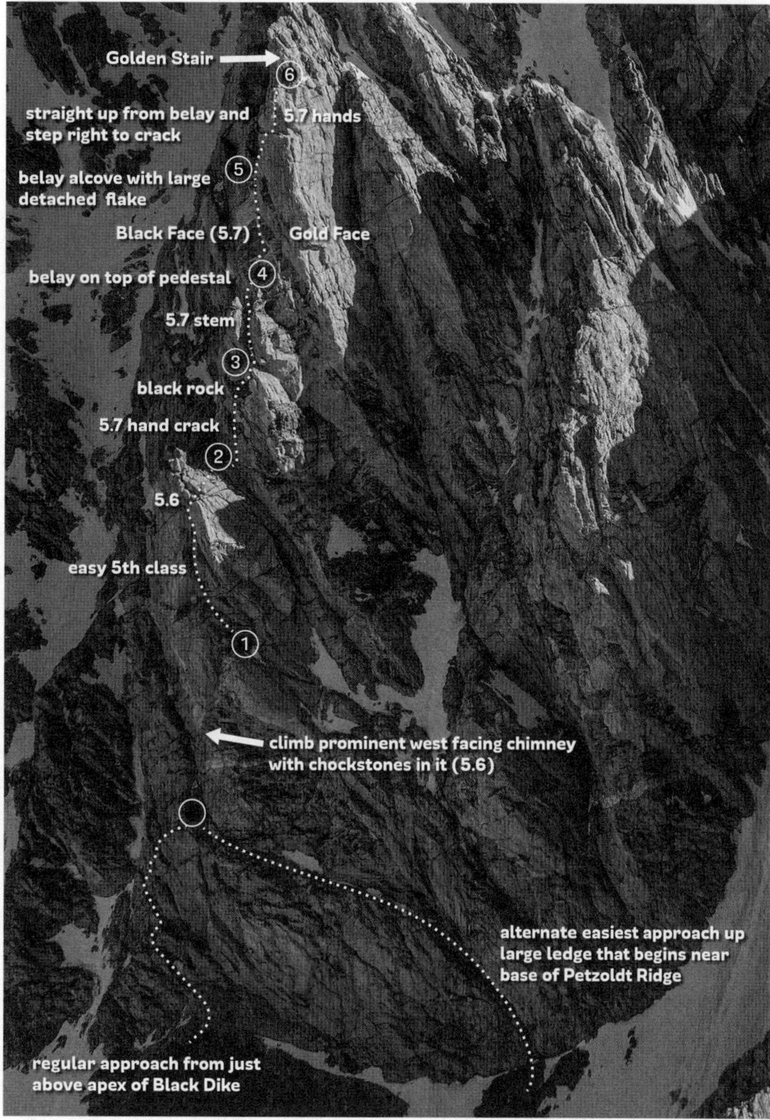

FIGURE 4-13. Grand Teton, south aspect, Durrance Direct (Lower Exum Ridge; *Route 9*), III, 5.7

back to the base of the chimney. The regular approach is more direct: from the apex of the Black Dike, go straight up the lowest section of the ridge below the chimney, through an area of reddish rock, to reach the base of the chimney at the top of the first step in the ridge.

Route Description: Pitch 1: Climb up into the chimney, over the first chockstone, and behind the second; traverse out on the wall to the right (south) for one exposed meter, then move back into the chimney just beneath the large chockstone that blocks the top. The left wall yields a route past this obstacle to the wide ledge (with cairn) at the top of the second step. Belay just a bit farther, at the ridge crest. (This chimney can be avoided by walking right [east] along the ledge at the top of the first step until somewhat right [east] of the crest. The face above can then be climbed to complete this chimney alternative.) **Pitch 2:** Another ropelength (5.6) on the left (west) flank of the ridge brings one to the top of the third step. An easier alternative to this direct method of reaching the third step is to traverse 30m or more around to the right (east) to the obvious slabs that angle left, back up to the ridge crest at the third step. At this point it is possible to escape from the ridge by traversing left (west) along a broken, black-rock ledge into the Wall Street Couloir west of the Exum Ridge, near the lower end of Wall Street. However, it is the steeper section above that leads to the end of Wall Street and provides the best climbing.

Pitch 3: Climb a steep, left-leaning hand crack (5.7) to a section of fun climbing in black rock. Belay at the base of a short chimney. **Pitch 4:** Climb the chimney above to a notch below a chockstone, then go up and over the chockstone to the belay at the base of the Black Face. The 80° Black Face above this notch is the crux of the climb and a beautiful pitch. **Pitch 5:** First climb 3m above the belay, then traverse up and right (east) toward a loose flake in the middle of the face. Next, go almost straight up and slightly left via a 5.6 crack to a belay stance in an alcove at the upper left (west) edge of the face. This face, a beautiful example of high-angle climbing with adequate holds, contains many suitable cracks for protection, but the ledges are narrow and the angle is constant.

Pitch 6: From the alcove at the top of the face, either move left (west) to an easy left-facing corner that leads to the boulder ledge at the end of Wall Street or climb up and right to a 5.7 hand crack. The left alternative leads to an alcove just west of the Step Across at the beginning of the Exum Ridge *(Route 8)*, while the right one reaches the base of the Golden Stair on the east side of the Step Across. **Time:** 9 hours from the Caves. See *Appalachia* 21, no. 2 (December 1936): pp. 268, 271, illus.; *Dartmouth Mountaineering Club Journal*, 1957: pp. 24–25; 1958: pp. 31–34.

***Variation:* THIN MAN.** III, 5.7. First ascent September 4, 1957, by Charles Plummer, Sterling Neale, and Samuel Silverstein. This variation starts from the third step of the lower Exum Ridge. Climb straight up the face to a cave from which the first belay can be made. From here ascend to the right and up the face for about 4.5m; then continue diagonally right around a black overhang to a steep crack, at the top of which is the second belay stance. The 9m jam crack above leads directly to the base of the Black Face.

Variation: III, 5.7. First ascent September 2, 1959, by Rick Medrick and Thomas Marshall. From the alcove at the top of the Black Face it is possible to continue directly up the ridge, reaching the boulder ledge at the end of Wall Street slightly from the east. This involves face climbing and a well-protected 5.7 crack.

***Variation:* WOODEN SHIPS.** III, 5.10-R. First ascent July 20, 2017, by Michael Gardner and Jimmy Voorhis; route completed July 1, 2019, by Michael Gardner and Vic Zeilman. (See *Figure 4-14.*) This route is

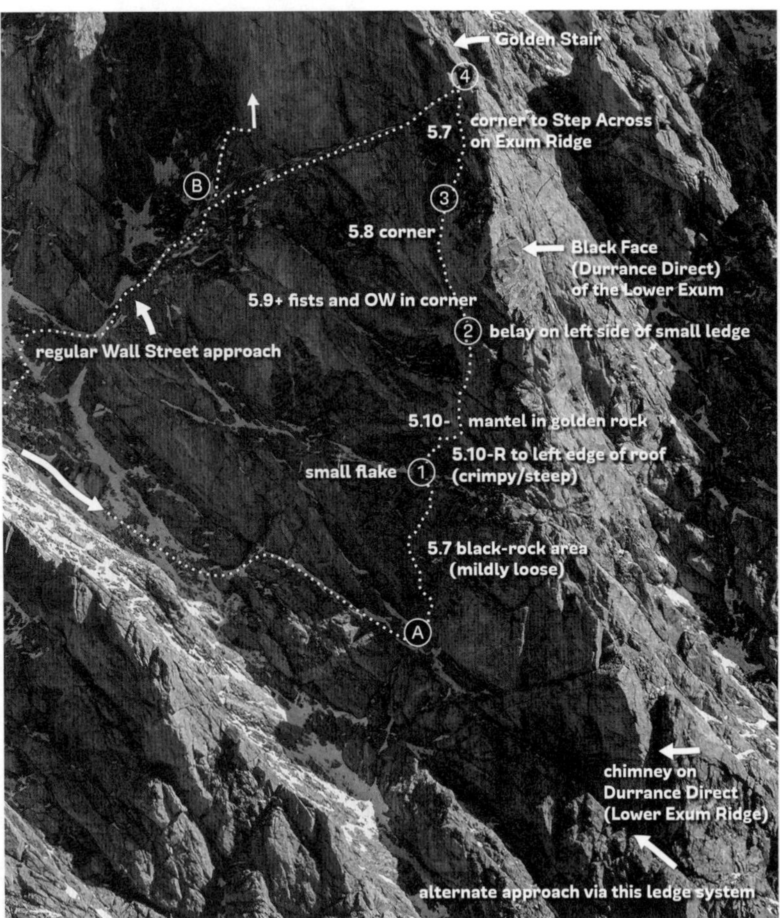

FIGURE 4-14. Grand Teton, south aspect. (A) Durrance Direct (Lower Exum Ridge; *Route 9*), variation: Wooden Ships, III, 5.10-R; (B) Exum Ridge *(Route 8)*, variation: Flipping Tokens to Hoboken, II, 5.12b/c

a tribute to longtime Exum guide George Gardner, a beloved husband and father and all-around fantastic person. The route name is derived from George's favorite song, written and composed by David Crosby, Paul Kantner, and Stephen Stills, with versions eventually recorded both by Crosby, Stills & Nash and by Jefferson Airplane. The final verse conveys the boyish enthusiasm for life and sense of adventure that George embodied.

Follow the approach from the Lower Saddle to the Needle, as in *Figures 4-1* and *4-2*. Once over the Needle, instead of taking the regular approach to Wall Street, locate a big ledge lower down in the Wall Street Couloir and traverse out to the south on this ledge to a point nearly directly below the end of the Wall Street ledge. The first pitch begins here, immediately south of a large memorial cairn. **Pitch 1:** Wander upward through a mildly loose area of black rock to a large ledge (5.7). **Pitch 2:** From a belay near a small flake, climb up through a steep, tricky-to-protect area via crimpy climbing to the left edge of a small roof (5.10-R). Climb up through the roof (5.10-) to an area of golden rock. Traverse directly right with good feet for 3.5m to another section of black rock. Climb up the black rock with good holds to a 5.10- mantel onto the upper golden face. Easier climbing up the golden face leads to multiple belay options at the base of a slightly curving wide crack. **Pitch 3:** Ascend the crack via fist and offwidth jamming (5.9+) to a belay in black rock on a small ledge just below the Step Across at the end of Wall Street. **Pitch 4:** Climb up via a beautiful corner (5.7) that leads directly up to the famous Step Across and a belay at the base of the Golden Stair. **Gear:** For protection take a double set of cams to 3", a set of stoppers, and a few micro cams.

***Variation:* DIRECT START.** III, 5.8. First ascent in August 1986, by Jim Williams and Robin Moore. From the apex of the Black Dike, rather than scrambling up to the start of the route via the regular approach, go downhill to the east to the base of the buttress. Climb from the lowest point up small corners and cracks. Three pitches lead to the large ledge at the top of the second pitch (the top of the chimney) of the standard route. Some loose rock will be found on the second pitch.

***Variation:* DIREXUM.** III, 5.9. First ascent June 25, 1990, by Carl Haiss and Joe Miller. This variation may, in fact, be nearly the same as the preceding one. It is two pitches in length and intersects the regular Durrance Direct at the top of the main chimney at the bottom. Begin just above the Black Dike to the right of a large flake. Face climbing leads up and right to a right-facing corner (5.9) in pink rock. Continue up and left on easy 5th-class ground or climb a crack (5.9, then 5.8 offwidth) to the large ramp by which one can traverse to the chimney on the regular route. The second pitch ascends the south face of the slab that forms this chimney. It consists primarily of 5.7 face climbing with a short 5.9 crack in the middle.

***Variation:* GOLD FACE.** III, 5.10-. First ascent June 27, 1988, by Renny Jackson and Jim Woodmencey. (See *Figure 4-15*.) This variation of four pitches goes up a section

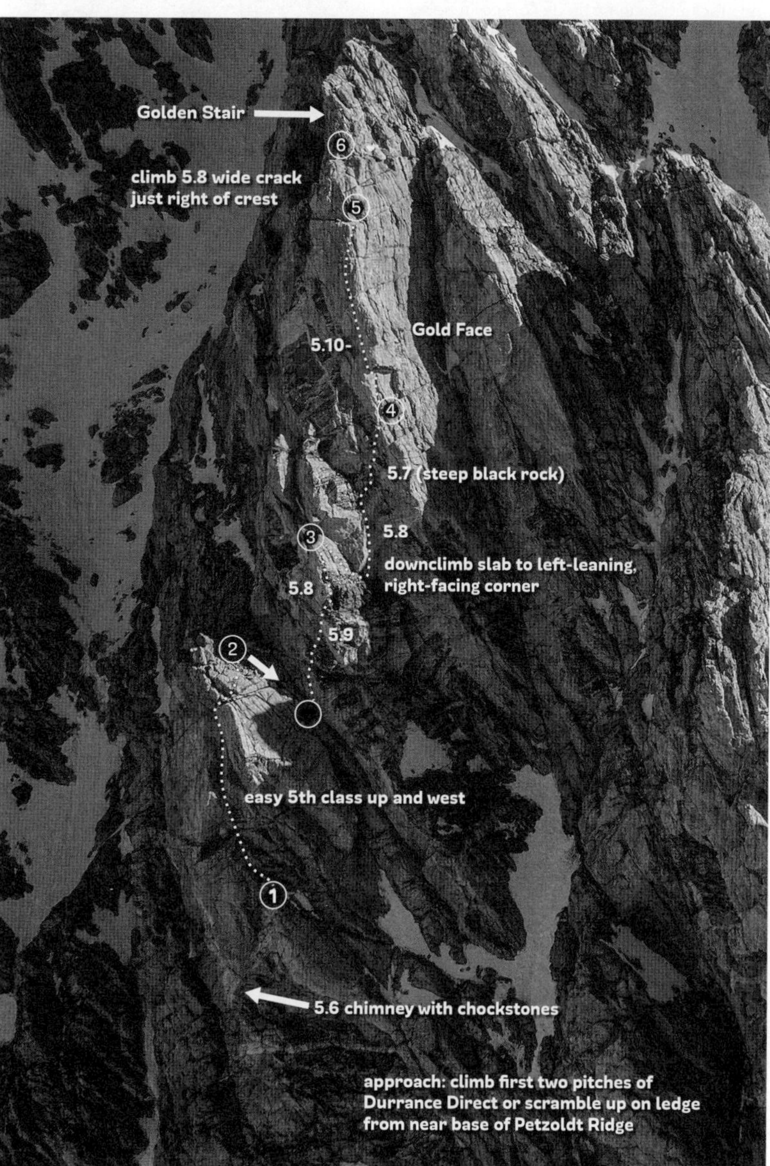

FIGURE 4-15. Grand Teton, south aspect, Durrance Direct (Lower Exum Ridge; *Route 9*), variation: Gold Face, III, 5.10-

of very steep, golden rock out to the right (east) of the Black Face of the standard Durrance Direct. **Pitches 1–2:** Climb the first two pitches of the Durrance Direct and begin this climb down and to the east of the left-leaning hand crack of that route's third pitch. As shown in *Figure 4-15*, move the belay down and to the right approximately 6m. (Alternatively, see *Figure 4-11* for an upper ramp approach to this climb.) **Pitch 3:** Climb up past flakes and cracks through a bulge (5.9) to a belay under an overhang. **Pitch 4:** Downclimb the slab to gain a right-facing corner that is climbed (5.8) past the right end of a roof to and up a steep, black-rock face to a belay ledge. **Pitch 5:** This next long lead is the crux of this variation, going up to and passing the left end of an overhang and then heading straight up the Gold Face via nice crack climbing (5.10-). **Pitch 6:** The final lead ascends a 5.8 crack just to the right of the ridge crest and gains the boulder ledge at the end of Wall Street from the southeast.

Variation: III, 5.10. First ascent August 27, 1990, by Mark Whiton and John Berry. This difficult two-pitch variation ascends cracks just left of *Route 10* on the eastern facet of the Exum Ridge. Presumably one climbs *Route 10* until just below the main chockstone. From this point traverse up and left to the base of an obvious, vertical crack system. This hand-to-finger-size crack passes through two bulges (first 5.10-, second 5.10) and ends at a stance in black rock after a full 50m. The second pitch goes straight up the 5.7 hand crack above for 30m.

ROUTE 10. IT'S NOT A CHIMNEY. III, 5.9. First ascent September 6, 1989, by Jim Dorward and Dan Burgette; attempted on July 26, 1939, by Paul Petzoldt and Jack Fralick. (See *Figure 4-16*.) The main feature of this route is the conspicuous long chimney system that parallels the lower Exum Ridge on the right (east), terminating just above the Golden Stair on the upper Exum Ridge route *(Route 8)*. This Petzoldt-Fralick Chimney lies between the Beckey Couloir *(Route 12)* and the crest of the Exum Ridge. From the Black Dike, at the foot of the buttress that extends between the bases of the lower Exum Ridge and the Petzoldt Ridge, there are two large ramps that slant up to the left (west). The lower left ramp is the

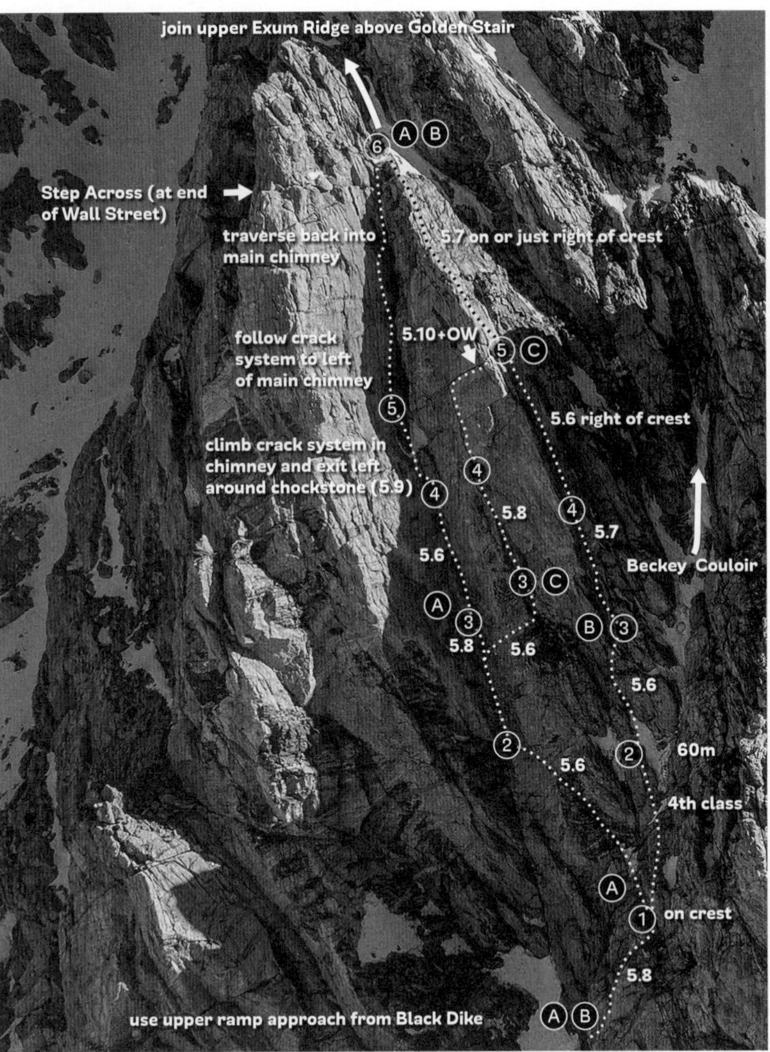

FIGURE 4-16. Grand Teton, south aspect. (A) It's Not a Chimney *(Route 10)*, III, 5.9; (B) Burgette Arête *(Route 11)*, III, 5.8; (C) Burgette Arête, variation: Angel Boy OW, III, 5.10+

easy alternate approach to the Durrance Direct (Lower Exum Ridge; *Route 9*), and the upper right one leads to the start of the Beckey Couloir. This route takes the upper ramp (5.1), angling for 52m up to the southwest corner of the buttress (see *Figure 4-11*).

From a point just beyond and left of a large flake, climb a short crack system over a bulge (5.8) and then directly up a 12m dihedral, finishing back to the left to a belay ledge. A 30m traverse left across the drainage and slabs now takes one into the base of the Beckey Couloir and then over to beginning of the large Petzoldt-Fralick Chimney, which is bounded on the right by the Burgette Arête *(Route 11)* and on the left by the lower Exum Ridge. The first lead up the chimney is over a black-rock section (5.8) to easier ground. The next pitch continues up the chimney for another 37m (5.6) to a belay stance below the chockstone pitch; this probably marked the high point of the 1939 attempt, as a piton and carabiner were found at the base of the chockstone in 1989. Now climb a crack system in the chimney and exit left around the chockstone (5.9). The final difficult lead (5.9) follows a crack system on the face to the left of the chimney proper and traverses right (5.7) back into the chimney near the top of the pitch. This pitch is consistently difficult, but the rock is good and there are good cracks for protection. One can now easily (4.0) traverse left (west) from the top of the chimney onto the Exum Ridge at a point above the Golden Stair. Follow *Route 8* to the summit. **Gear:** A suggested rack should include a full set of wired stoppers and protection to 3.5".

Variation: **IT IS (TOO) A CHIMNEY.** III, 5.9. First ascent in September 1990, by Ralph Cooley, Jerry Johnson, and Tony Jones. Climb It's Not a Chimney to the obvious first chockstone and belay in the alcove above it. From this point on, the chimney is very steep and angles slightly to the east. The width varies from about 1m to 2m for the rest of its length. Proceed up the chimney, beginning on the right-hand wall. The entire distance from the belay to the second chockstone is consistently steep and difficult (5.9) and is the crux. The angle then eases, and a good belay can be found after climbing over the third chockstone (5.6). Fourth-class climbing leads up and west to where the upper Exum Ridge *(Route 8)* is joined just above the Golden Stair. **Gear:** Bring protection to 2" for this climb.

ROUTE 11. BURGETTE ARÊTE. III, 5.8. First ascent July 26, 1988, by Dan Burgette and Jim Springer. (See *Figure 4-16.*) This route ascends the buttress or arête that bounds the Petzoldt-Fralick Chimney on the right (east); this chimney and the arête lie on the right (east) side of the lower Exum Ridge. Follow the upper ramp from the Black Dike toward the beginning of the Petzoldt-Fralick Chimney (see *Route 10* and *Figure 4-11*). This route shares its first pitch with *Route 10.* Instead of climbing over to the chimney, the next pitch angles right and up to the start of the Becky Couloir route (4th class, 60m). The third lead goes up an inside corner (5.6) to the belay. Now cut right across a face into and up another dihedral just right of the crest. The fifth pitch moves back left to just right of the crest, where the protection is thin. The sixth lead continues up just right of the crest (5.7), then a final section of 4th-class scrambling takes one to the upper Exum Ridge *(Route 8)* at a point above the Golden Stair.

Variation: **ANGEL BOY OW.** III, 5.10+. First ascent August 2, 2008, by Dave Bywater and Renny Jackson. (See *Figure 4-16.*) This three-pitch variation ascends the prominent wide crack visible to the east of the Black Face pitch of the Durrance Direct (Lower Exum Ridge; *Route 9*). Use the same approach as for *Route 10*, then take an obvious traverse right (east) out of the Petzoldt-Fralick Chimney to gain the crack system that eventually leads to the crux offwidth. Finish the route via the upper pitch of the main Burgette Arête route. **Gear:** Wide camming protection (7"–12") is useful for this climb.

ROUTE 12. BECKEY COULOIR. II, 5.4, or II, AI3 mixed. First descent September 10, 1937, by Joseph and Paul Stettner, after making the fourth ascent of the North Ridge route *(Route 47)*; first ascent August 31, 1941, by Joseph and Paul Stettner; second ascent June 29, 1948, by Fred Beckey, W. V. Graham Matthews, and Ralph Widrig. (See *Figures 4-16* and *4-19.*) This broad couloir separates the Exum Ridge from the Petzoldt Ridge. A most unusual aspect of the 1941 ascent was that it started from the floor of the north fork of Garnet Canyon and reached the Black Dike directly via the steep, broken face to the right (east) of the small but spectacular waterfall that drains the couloir; this waterfall is just west of Glencoe Spire. From the Black Dike to the left (west) of the base of the Petzoldt Ridge, take the upper ramp approach, as shown in *Figure 4-11.* The first two pitches of *Route 11* lead to the start of this route. Climb the steep but sound rock of the couloir to the notch behind the main tower of the Petzoldt Ridge. The couloir is wide and offers a considerable expanse of rock with many possible variations. For those seeking an enjoyable mixed climb, the recommended time to climb this route is in early season, when the couloir is filled with snow and ice. From the notch, continue up *Route 13.* See *American Alpine Journal* 7, no. 2 (1949): pp. 221–22; *Appalachia* 23, no. 1 (June 1940): pp. 101–3, illus.; 27, no. 2 (December 1948): pp. 227–29.

ROUTE 13. PETZOLDT RIDGE. III, 5.6. First ascent July 14, 1941, by Paul Petzoldt, Elizabeth Cowles (Partridge), Mary Merrick, and Fred Wulsin Jr.; first winter ascent January 30, 1976, by Glenn Milner, Donnie Black, and Joseph Costello. This important ridge, which lies between the Underhill Ridge and the Exum Ridge, contains some of the most enjoyable rock in the park—very steep but with enough knobs to prevent excessive difficulty. More than one line is possible, so the difficulty will depend on the exact route followed. An ice axe is needed for ascents during most of the summer because moderately steep snow will be found in the Ford Couloir, which extends above the final tower on the ridge proper.

Traverse the Black Dike from either the Lower Saddle or the Teepe Glacier to the Stettner Couloir, the snow couloir just west of the Underhill Ridge. Most of the ascents of the Petzoldt Ridge are made by climbing up this couloir for approximately 30m before turning left (west) onto the rock. The following description is one of many possible variations.

Climb one ropelength to a small black-rock area with good holds. From the top of this black-rock area, climb right to a series of slabs leading to a left-facing corner system. A chimney leads out of this corner system and onto the easier climbing above. After two ropelengths, climb left onto an exposed and steeper pitch nearly on the left corner of the ridge. Ascend another ropelength to a high point on the ridge and descend 3m to some broad ledges. From here climb either the ridge itself or a chute to the right to reach a belay beneath a short chimney. Above the chimney a short scramble leads to the top of the main tower of the ridge.

Although a few parties have downclimbed to the notch, a 15m rappel is recommended. From the notch follow the Ford Couloir, the snow couloir leading toward the summit, for about two ropelengths before traversing when convenient to the right (east) onto the upper Buckingham Buttress (see *Route 14*), the next rock ridge to the east. Because the crest of this buttress is attained well above its steep initial section, this rock ridge is easily followed to the summit block. Early in the season this last 150m will be on snow. **Time:** 7½ to 8½ hours from the Lower Saddle. See *Dartmouth Mountaineering Club Journal,* 1956: pp. 34–38; *Trail and Timberline,* no. 354 (June 1948): pp. 79–83, illus.

Variation: **PETZOLDT DIRECT.** III, 5.7+. First ascent August 30, 1953, by Willi

Unsoeld, LaRee Munns, James and Rodney Shirley, and Austin Flint. (See *Figure 4-17*.) This major—and highly recommended—variation starts at the base of the ridge at the Black Dike and then goes directly up the nose of the ridge instead of along its right (east) side. It is longer and more difficult than the preceding standard route and has the advantage of leading past the Window, an interesting and prominent feature of the Petzoldt Ridge. This is *the* route to do on the ridge, and when combined with the classic upper Exum Ridge *(Route 8)*, it rivals the complete Exum as the finest south side route on the Grand Teton.

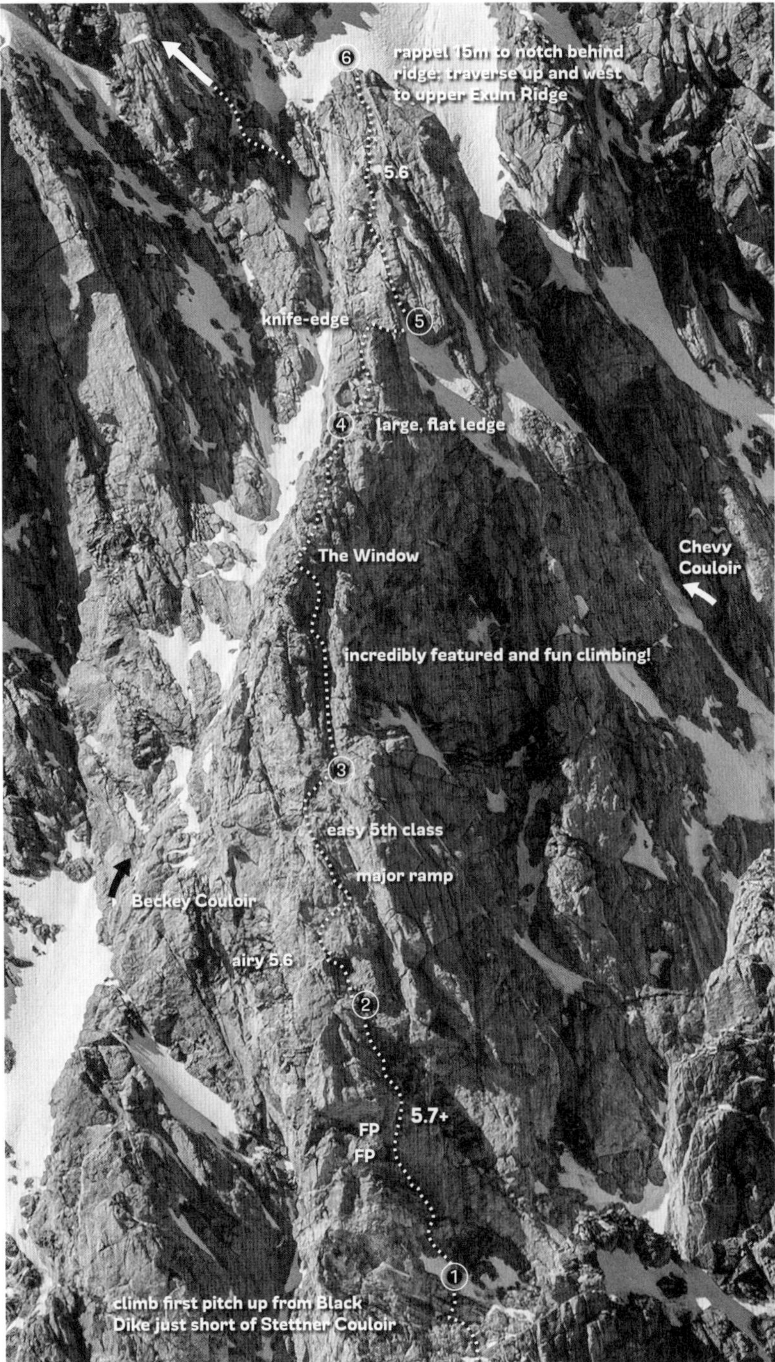

FIGURE 4-17. Grand Teton, south aspect, Petzoldt Ridge *(Route 13)*, variation: Petzoldt Direct, III, 5.7+

Approach from the Lower Saddle as for the standard Petzoldt Ridge, but start upward on the rock just before getting to the Stettner Couloir (see *Figure 4-11*). **Pitch 1:** Climb moderate red rock at the toe of the ridge for about 60m to reach a ledge, where the steeper and more difficult climbing begins. **Pitch 2:** Continue up and left past a few old fixed pins toward a steep slot. Climb up through this slot (5.7+ crux) and belay above on an exposed knob on the crest. **Pitch 3:** A chimney separates the top of the knob from the wall above. Step across onto the wall and climb up and left around an overhang. Work straight up and then back right through steep terrain to a belay near the crest and below the Window (look for nests of garnet crystals at this belay!). **Pitch 4:** Climb up toward the Window on incredibly featured and fun climbing. One can either climb over the Window (5.6) or go through this unique feature (from east to west) onto easy ledges, ending with a short, awkward crack (5.7) that takes one back onto the crest. Belay on a large, flat ledge. **Pitch 5:** A short pitch climbs up to and across a knife-edge to a belay in an alcove. **Pitch 6:** This final pitch takes one to the top of the main tower of the ridge. Rappel anchors are found just down on the north side of the summit, and a 15m rappel takes one to the notch.

***Variation:* PETZOLDT-TO-EXUM TRAVERSE.** III, 5.6. First ascent August 31, 1954, by Robert Brooke and Tom McCormack; first descent August 9, 1980, by Bruce Coulter. For those desiring more climbing on this route, immediately after rappelling into the main notch on the Petzoldt Ridge, cut left (west) up a diagonal ledge to the beginning of the gully that parallels the first large tower of the Exum Ridge on the right (east). Then follow *Route 8* to the summit. This combination gives about twice as much rock climbing as is found on either *Route 8* or *Route 13* by itself, and because none of it is excessively difficult it is recommended for those seeking a long, enjoyable climb. This option also provides an emergency retreat route from the

Petzoldt Ridge off the mountain: once the Exum Ridge route is joined, climb down to the top of the Golden Stair, where an 18m rappel takes one to the end of the Wall Street ledge. **Time:** 10½ hours from the Lower Saddle. See *Stanford Alpine Club Journal*, 1955: pp. 48–50.

***Variation:* DOUBLE OVERHANG.** III, 5.9. First ascent June 25, 1986, by George Montopoli and Leo Larson. From the belay stance at the end of the second pitch of the Petzoldt Direct, instead of moving left (west) past a black overhang and fixed pin, move right 3m to the base of the major dihedral. Climb directly up this dihedral, over two difficult overhangs, to gain its upper section. Rejoin the standard Petzoldt Direct variation at the end of this single lead.

ROUTE 14. BUCKINGHAM BUTTRESS. III, 5.6. First ascent August 19, 1955, by William Buckingham, Richard Hill, and Ray Secoy. (See *Figures 4-18* and *4-19.*) This buttress or ridge begins just above where the Stettner Couloir forks. The Ford Couloir is located on the western side of the buttress, and the expansive east face snowfield rises from the top of the buttress to the edge of the Grand Teton's north face. The Grade III rating reflects the fact that another route must be climbed in order to get to this route or either of its two variations. The first ascent was made after an ascent of the Petzoldt Ridge *(Route 13)*, by way of a descent (to the east) of about 75m from the main notch of that ridge. It is also possible to approach by climbing the Stettner Couloir to where it forks, although this is not recommended because of significant rockfall there. A short vertical pitch must be climbed to get onto the face of the ridge. Ninety meters of very steep cracks and chimneys near the middle of the broad ridge leads to a small notch on the left (west) side of the ridge. At this point traverse a short distance alongside a large flake out onto the west face of the ridge. Now climb a long but easy chimney, then traverse back out onto the south face of the ridge on a good series of ledges that peters out below a large, ceiling-type overhang. Make a delicate step to the opposite wall of the chimney, which ends at the ceiling. Then climb 30m of high-angle, knobby rock to the more nearly horizontal section of this ridge. From here in late season the climb to the summit is an easy scramble; in early season expect an exhilarating snow climb.

FIGURE 4-18. Grand Teton, south aspect, Buckingham Buttress *(Route 14)*, variation: Where in the Buckingham Are We?, III, 5.8

***Variation:* WHERE IN THE BUCKINGHAM ARE WE?** III, 5.8. First known ascent July 30, 2020, by Vic Zeilman and Ryan Schuster. Zeilman and Schuster did this climb after an ascent of the Petzoldt Ridge *(Route 13)* in order to avoid the crowds on the upper Exum Ridge *(Route 8)*. (See *Figure 4-18.*) After completing the rappel off the top of the Petzoldt Ridge, descend 10m–15m to the east, crossing the bottom of the Ford Couloir and the top of the Chevy Couloir, to the toe of the left (west) side of the buttress. **Pitch 1:** Climb an awkward, left-trending ramp (5.7), then zigzag a short way up and right through overlaps and ledges to a face-climbing move straight up (crux) and easier ground above. Belay on a large ledge (5.7/5.8, 40m–46m). **Pitch 2:** Traverse right (east) on the ledge and climb up vertical crack systems for 30m. Make a step-around move to the right and continue up to nice belay ledge on the right (5.6, 60m). **Pitch 3:** Traverse down and right and climb a short step. Continue straight up—fun and easy climbing—to a prominent notch near the top of the buttress (5.5, 53m). **Pitch 4:** Climb a Friction Pitch–like face (a reference to the Friction Pitch of *Route 8*) above the notch for 23m to easier ground leading to the top of the buttress (5.4, 30m). Scramble along the eastern edge of the Ford Couloir to reach the summit of the Grand Teton.

***Variation:* ORTENBURGER ARÊTE.** III, 5.10-. First ascent in July 1991, by Brent Finley, Susie Harrington, and Leigh Ortenburger. Of the nearly 90 first ascents, new routes, and variations that Leigh Ortenburger pioneered in the Tetons, this was his final climb. It is located on the east side of the Buckingham Buttress and directly across from the top of the Underhill Ridge. Begin by climbing in a groove for one ropelength until a roof is encountered. From the belay beneath the roof, move out and left (west) via 5.10- face climbing and then continue up on easier ground to finish the pitch. An additional lead takes one to the top of the buttress, from which one can continue scrambling to the summit.

ROUTE 15. STETTNER COULOIR. II, AI3, steep snow. Probable first descent July 30, 1933, by Sam Younger and Albert Strube; first ascent on snow June 30, 1964, by Charles Schaeffer, Bob Schaeffer, Mark Fielding, and Curtis Stout; first ascent on rock August 17, 1969, by Leigh Ortenburger and Jennifer Ronsiek; first winter ascent January 14, 1981, by Bill Danford and Gene Forsythe.

A Historical Sidenote: Since the 1956 publication of the first edition of this guidebook, a curious problem arose concerning the nomenclature of the couloirs on the south side of the Grand Teton. In 1955, correspondence between Leigh Ortenburger and Joseph Stettner suggested that their (Joseph and Paul Stettner's) 1941 ascent of the Grand Teton had been made via the couloir between the Petzoldt and Underhill Ridges. That couloir was therefore named the Stettner Couloir, and the next one to the west—the Beckey Couloir *(Route 12)*, separating the Exum and Petzoldt Ridges—was named in recognition of the presumed first ascent of that couloir in 1948 by Fred Beckey, W. V. Graham Matthews, and Ralph Widrig. Sometime after 1956, Jack Fralick, a longtime climbing friend of the Stettner brothers, indicated that he believed that the 1941 ascent had been via the Beckey Couloir, based on his examination of a movie made during the climb. A reexamination of this movie in 1989 verified Fralick's belief, with the result that the long-standing names Beckey Couloir and Stettner Couloir are now understood to have been incorrectly applied for the past 60-plus years. While this error is lamentable, it seems that to attempt a change in names at this late date would be unwise and would result in considerable confusion. So, for better or worse, the original names will be retained.

History: The probable first descent of the Stettner Couloir occurred on July 30, 1933, by Sam Younger and Albert Strube—an apparent mistake when the Owen-Spalding route could not be found. The first ascent on snow was on June 30, 1964, by Charles Schaeffer, Bob Schaeffer, Mark Fielding, and Curtis Stout, who exited via the left fork. The first ascent on rock was bravely accomplished on August 17, 1969, by Leigh Ortenburger and Jennifer Ronsiek, who exited via the right fork.

In early season this right fork has primarily been a snow climb, but the exit at the top previously required two pitches of rock climbing to pass a giant chockstone in its upper end. The climber would exit the room beneath the chockstone by means of a tunnel/chimney that permitted access to the upper couloir and the top of the Underhill Ridge. During some seasons one could also climb a 12m vertical pillar of ice over the chockstone near the top of the right fork. This used to provide a difficult (WI4+, first climbed by Steve Shea and David Breashears in 1978) alternative exit to the top of the Underhill Ridge.

This all changed on the evening of September 2, 2007, when the house-size chockstone dislodged and broke apart as it plummeted into the Moraines camping zone of Garnet Canyon. Fortunately, no one was hurt—including parties camped there and climbers on their way either up or down from the Lower Saddle. The right fork of the couloir was permanently altered, erasing the two routes that had been established around the chockstone.

On June 16, 1971, Bill Briggs made his famous ski descent of the Grand Teton, working his way down from the summit and onto the skier's-right side of the east face. "Skiing off the summit on the hard crust, in and around the rocks . . . was one of the finest experiences on skis I've ever had," Briggs later recalled in a 2011 interview for *Powder* magazine. "Then, you go out on the central ridge and it's corn snow. And it's perfect corn, and then you have this narrowing ridge and the skis are performing perfectly and you do it all in rhythm." He went over to the top of the Underhill Ridge, into the upper Stettner Couloir (as it was called prior to the chockstone falling out), rappelled over the chockstone, and then made his way down the lower Stettner. Upon reaching the bottom of the lower couloir, he traversed to the east and skied the Teepe Glacier—an "unreal, surreal scene," as he put it. "First of all, you're all alone and the whole thing is dark. Going into a dark, foreboding situation. You go out into it and it's all frost feathers. You ski through it and it makes a tinkling sound as it breaks. . . . Absolutely surreal, I mean, I've never even come close to something like that ever again."

The Teton Range has become perhaps *the* ski-mountaineering mecca of the US, and the crown jewel is certainly a ski descent of the Grand Teton. The most popular ascent and ski-descent route utilizes three couloirs: the lower Stettner Couloir; the Chevy Couloir, a two-pitch ice route (early season); and the Ford Couloir to the summit. Fred Ford, an Exum guide, was hit by rock- and icefall in this couloir on June 28, 1955, and subsequently lost his life during a dramatic three-day rescue operation conducted by the nascent Jenny Lake Rangers rescue team. Known earlier as Ford's Couloir, this trifecta is now referred to simply as the Stettner-Chevy-Ford; it is the route described below.

Route Description: Approach this climb via either the Black Dike Traverse or the Teepe Glacier. (See *Figures 4-11* and *4-19.*) Enter the Stettner Couloir and proceed upward about 100m to the Chevy Couloir connection. The lower Stettner may be runneled from avalanches and may have one or two steep, narrow sections of ice. The Chevy is snow and ice and leads up and west toward the notch behind the top of the Petzoldt Ridge. It is useful to have two ice tools and a few ice screws for protection for the Chevy Couloir, depending on one's level of expertise. In addition to a few screws, a small rack of rock protection is useful for the climb and for maintenance of the rappel anchors.

Anchors are visible on both sides of the Stettner–Chevy connection and are used for rappels during the descent. Once in the Ford Couloir it is useful to proceed up and to the east to get on the broad rib that rises from the Buckingham Buttress. Avoid the shooting gallery of the Ford Couloir if at all possible and move quickly. One can also use the Stettner's left fork to exit higher up, above the Chevy Couloir, although this may involve some rock climbing up and over slabby terrain in order to enter the bottom of the Ford Couloir.

As an early-season or winter climb, the Stettner Couloir needs to be approached with careful consideration given to snow stability: this area sees early sun, and rapid warm-up is possible. Several close calls have occurred when avalanches and/or rockfall have swept this couloir. With climate change now a factor, this route should be avoided during the main climbing season and at any time when the temperatures are sufficiently warm to dislodge the considerable amount of material that remains after the release of the massive chockstone. Climbers should move very quickly across the bottom of the couloir if going around the corner to the east face rock climbs (see *East Face Routes*, below). Speed is safety. See *American Alpine Journal* 2, no. 2 (1934): pp. 254–55.

FIGURE 4-19. Grand Teton, south aspect, Stettner Couloir *(Route 15)*, II, AI3, steep snow

ROUTE 16. UNDERHILL RIDGE. II, 5.6. First ascent July 15, 1931, by Robert Underhill, Phil Smith, and Francis Truslow; first descent September 5, 1937, by Paul Petzoldt, Phil Smith, and William House (using rappels on the west side). Underhill attempted this ridge on July 18, 1930, with Kenneth Henderson on the same day as their successful first ascent of Teepe Pillar, but they were stopped by a violent thunderstorm. (See *Figure 4-20.*) This route ascends the easternmost and shortest of the three major south ridges of the Grand Teton. The Underhill Ridge forms the right skyline ridge of the Grand Teton as seen from the Lower Saddle, and the route starts from the highest point of the Black Dike, which cuts across the south side of the mountain. This highest point is Glencoe Col, between the Underhill Ridge and Glencoe Spire. Because the route is located on the west side of the ridge crest, it dries out more slowly than the Petzoldt or Exum Ridge routes (see *Routes 13* and *8*); in general, it is a colder climb. An ice axe is recommended for early-season ascents of this ridge.

From the col scramble 15m north up easy red rock, then traverse horizontally to the right of the red slabs until the wall of the first tower is met (see *Figure 4-11*). A series of cracks angles up (west) and left (south) 37m to the top of the slabs (belay where convenient). Continue west for 60m on easier rock to the prominent ledge system that leads around to the left (west) side of the tower. From near the end of this ledge climb a 12m chimney to a broad ledge. A very difficult chimney (probably the one Underhill climbed on the first ascent) leads directly up from this broad ledge. Instead of using this chimney, go around the corner to the left (north) where an easier chimney leads upward. At the top of this chimney an overhang forces the climber out onto the right wall on very small holds. With a handhold on the right edge, swing onto a small ledge, from which the Underhill Chimney is regained for the belay. The next lead brings one back to the ridge crest.

Traverse around to the right (east) and then up to the steep, black face of the

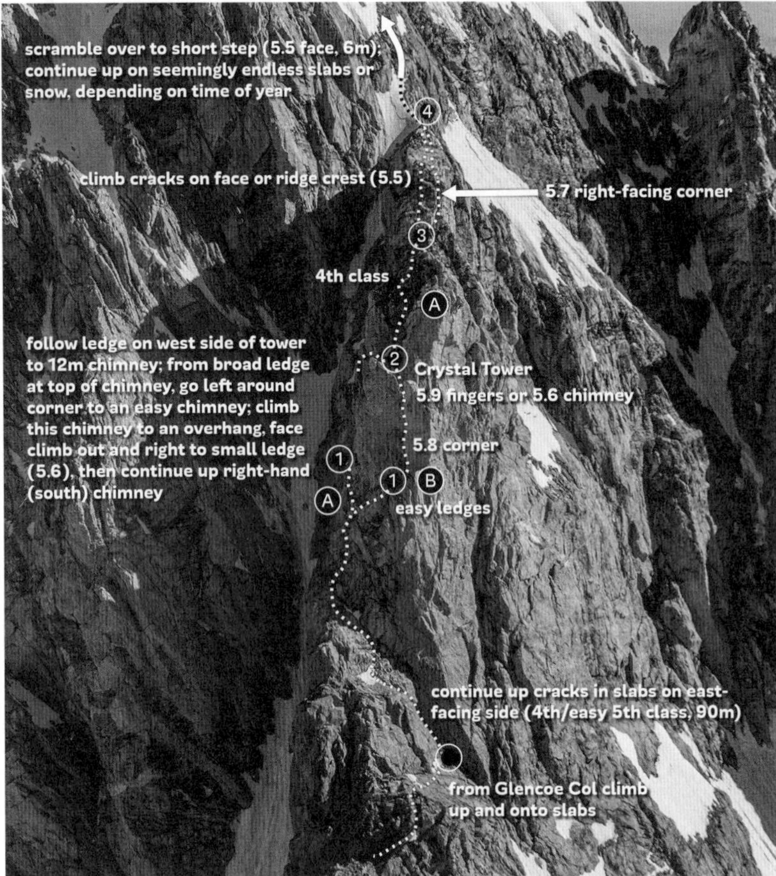

FIGURE 4-20. Grand Teton, southern ridges. (A) Underhill Ridge *(Route 16)*, II, 5.6; (B) Variation: Direct, III, 5.8

main tower. A good crack system in the middle of this face allows enjoyable climbing (5.5) to the ridge crest, which is then followed to the shallow col that is at the top of the upper portion of the Stettner Couloir. As an alternative, a right-facing corner near the right-hand margin of this face can also be climbed (5.7). From this col, which is approximately even with the end of Wall Street on the Exum Ridge route, a short pitch (5.5) is required to pass the steep beginning of the slabs of this upper southeast face. In early season one can then ascend the moderate snow slope toward the summit block; later in the season, scramble up and left across seemingly endless slabs to the rocky upper Buckingham Buttress, which leads to the summit block. Then make a slight traverse to the left (west) and finish the climb by the easy top portion of the Exum Ridge route. **Time:** 5¼ hours from the Lower Saddle. See *American Alpine Journal* 8, no. 3 (1953): pp. 542–45; *Canadian Alpine Journal* 20 (1931): pp. 72–86, illus.; *Sierra Club Bulletin* 42, no. 6 (June 1957): pp. 62–63.

***Variation:* WILSON CRACK.** III, 5.9. First ascent September 2, 1965, by Ted Wilson and Rick Reese. This variation of about three pitches provides a different and much more difficult start for the Underhill Ridge. Instead of proceeding to Glencoe Col, climb the snow of the Stettner Couloir a short distance until a wide crack bending to the right can be seen in the (eastern) wall above. Moderate climbing brings one to this crack, which is climbed with difficulty (5.9) past a bulge in its upper part. The standard route is joined at the main ledge system leading around the west side of the ridge.

***Variation:* DIRECT.** III, 5.8. First ascent August 30, 1953, by William Buckingham, Steve Smale, Ann Blackenburg (Mansfield), Charles Browning, and Jack Hilberry. (See *Figure 4-20.*) From the Lower Saddle a conspicuous, white, angular pinnacle (the Crystal Tower) is seen on the skyline on the lower section of the Underhill Ridge. This variation goes up the spectacular chimney that separates this pinnacle from the remainder of the ridge. Follow the standard route to the south end of the main ledge, which leads around the

Climbing ranger Andy Byerly on patrol on the second pitch of the Crystal Tower (Photo by Renny Jackson)

left (west) side of the ridge. Instead of traversing along this ledge, climb 9m up and to the right on broken black rock to the base of the chimney separating the pinnacle from the ridge. The first portion of this chimney overhangs slightly and is most easily climbed out to the left via a 5.8 finger crack in a left-facing corner. At the top of the corner, either traverse right and into the chimney (5.6) or continue up a nice crack system on the face to the left (5.9). Climb up to the notch and then onto the knife-edge at the left. One can then climb the next step in the ridge to rejoin the standard route at the face of the main tower.

Grand Teton, East Face Routes

The rock climbs on the east face of the Grand Teton—see *Figure 4-21* for an overview—are usually approached via the Black Dike Traverse from the Lower Saddle all the way over to Glencoe Col. At this point one can descend from the col and then make a traverse north to the climbs on the east face, or one can climb directly up from the col (3rd class/4th class) and make a descending traverse north on slabs that lead to the same area (the latter is shown in *Figure 4-11*). However, this approach has become much more hazardous since the rockfall event of 2007 in the Stettner Couloir (see the preceding *Southern Ridges* section). Depending upon the time of day and year, as well as a party's projected speed across the bottom of the Stettner, it may be wise to consider a more direct approach up the Teepe Glacier from the vicinity of Corbet's High Camp (the Jackson Hole Mountain Guides base camp) instead. A set of lightweight crampons can facilitate this approach for early-season climbs.

It was an interesting process unraveling the history of the routes in this area, as there is some misinformation out there.

ROUTE 17. CRYSTAL TOWER. III, 5.10. First ascent August 27, 1999, by Jim Beyer.

FIGURE 4-21. Grand Teton, overview of east face routes. Crystal Tower *(Route 17)*, III, 5.10; Crystal Right *(Route 18)*, III, 5.10, A0; Lev *(Route 19)*, III, 5.8; Lev *(Route 19a)*, variation: Jackson-Woodmency, III, 5.9+; Lev *(Route 19b)*, variation: East Face Left, III, 5.9+; The Red and the Black *(Route 20)*, III, 5.10+, A0; East Face, Left Center *(Route 21)*, III, 5.10-; Southeast Chimney *(Route 22)*, III, 5.9; Beyer East Face I *(Route 23)*, III, 5.9; Keith-Eddy East Face *(Route 24)*, III, 5.10-; East Face Direct *(Route 25)*, III, 5.9+; Beyer East Face II *(Route 26)*, III, 5.8; Horton East Face *(Route 27)*, III, 5.7; Smith Otterbody *(Route 28)*, III, 5.6; Golden Arête *(Route 29)*, IV, 5.11d; Golden Arête *(Route 29a)*, variation: Offspring, III, 5.11, A1

(See *Figure 4-22.*) This beautiful route, established by the avid Teton explorer and new route aficionado Jim Beyer, is located on the lower east face of the Underhill Ridge (see *Route 16*). Beyer has described the climb as having "good pro, excellent rock, great climbing, cool summit," which this author (R. Jackson) can confirm, having done it several times. If approaching via the Black Dike Traverse from the Lower Saddle: scramble up from Glencoe Col, traverse north on the big ledge to the base of the climb, and set a belay for the first pitch.

Pitch 1: Climb a steep crack that leads around the corner onto a ledge from which one can belay the next pitch (5.9, 15m). **Pitch 2:** Climb straight up, passing a few fixed heads, and eventually into a dihedral on the left (south) side of the arête; some meandering is necessary to obtain protection and find the easiest way. Fun 5.8 climbing then leads to a belay on an obvious ledge. Although it is apparently possible to traverse over to the corner on the south side of the arête fairly early, this traverse has been described as "difficult to pinpoint." (**Note:** One can also skip the difficulties of the lower portion of this pitch by traversing in from a bit farther up the regular Underhill Ridge route [see the short start variation in *Figure 4-22*]. Continue up the initial corner above the start of the first 5.9 pitch until another traverse [5.9] across the south face of the tower becomes obvious. Join the regular Crystal Tower climb at the top of the second pitch.) **Pitch 3:** Begin with a steep 5.10- move into a thin crack, which eventually leads up to a left-leaning 5.10 corner. Jam and undercling this corner, moving up and left to the final bulge. Pull through the bulge (5.10) and continue up and left on unprotected 5.6 terrain to a good belay below a left-leaning wide crack. Keep a lookout for the "mica fist," a curious erosional feature composed of biotite mica on the upper portion of the pitch. **Pitch 4:** Climb a 5.6 face to the left of the wide crack and continue around to the northeast side of the tower. An exposed traverse (easy) ends at a ledge for the belay. **Pitch 5:** Climb to the top of the tower using a combination of cracks, flakes, knobs, and chicken heads and locate the two-bolt belay/rappel anchor on the summit.

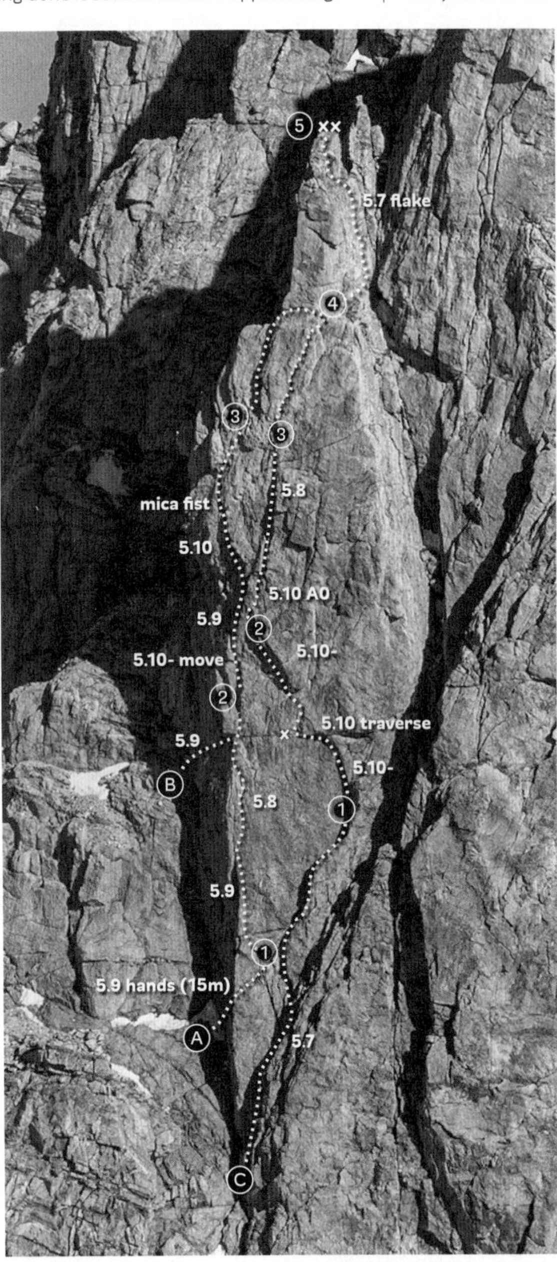

FIGURE 4-22. Grand Teton, east aspect. (A) Crystal Tower *(Route 17)*, III, 5.10; (B) Crystal Tower, high start variation; (C) Crystal Right *(Route 18)*, III, 5.10, A0

To descend, rappel 30m to where it is possible to downclimb and scramble to the west side of the Underhill Ridge, then continue rappelling that route back to the col. Keep in mind that this descent initially trends toward the Stettner Couloir before going back around to the eastern side of the Underhill Ridge. The anchors have moved over the years and some are a bit tricky to find. They will no doubt require maintenance from time to time. Most parties complete five rappels with one 60m rope to get down—caution is advised! **Gear:** For protection take a double set of cams, from 0.5" to 3", and one each at 3.5" and 4". Include two sets of nuts as well—offsets are useful—and possibly a set of offset brass nuts.

ROUTE 18. CRYSTAL RIGHT. III, 5.10, A0. First ascent August 16, 2010, by Aaron Gams and Toby Stegman (with Brian Mulvilhill on an earlier attempt). (See *Figure 4-22.*) This great climb on exquisite orange granite starts up the Lev route *(Route 19)*, but one could begin with the first pitch of the Crystal Tower route *(Route 17)* instead. After about 9m, head up and left (away from the right-trending diagonal Lev ramp) toward the orange face of the Crystal Tower. Follow cracks (5.7) to gain an easy, right-trending trough and belay at its top, below a left-facing dihedral (46m). The Traverse Pitch is next: Follow the left-facing dihedral (5.10-) to a black roof. A finger traverse (5.10-, protected with a green Alien) leads left to a bolt at the break in the roof. Clip the bolt and go up to a 5.9 lieback that leads to a leftward traverse (5.10-, good gear) to a belay stance on top of an obvious flake (30m). (**Note:** On the first attempt, Brian Mulvilhill led this pitch and ran it out above the break in the roof to the regular Crystal Tower route! A few weeks later

Toby Stegman and Aaron Gams came back, installed the bolt, and completed the climb.) The third pitch goes up and left to where the crack becomes a very steep left-facing dihedral (5.10, A0, probably 5.11 free). Continue up the dihedral (5.8) and belay on a small stance out left (30m). The fourth pitch goes up and right on crystals over a couple of small, slanting roofs to gain a right-trending crack (5.8). Belay on a gravel ledge at the base of the final pitch of *Route 17* (27m). Then climb that pitch up the right side of the tower to its top (5.7). Descend as described in *Route 17*. **Gear:** For protection take a double set of cams from 0.5" to 3.5". Nuts are also useful, including one set of offsets.

ROUTE 19. LEV. III, 5.6, A1, or III, 5.8. First ascent July 12, 1960, by Peter Lev, James Greig, William Glosser, and David Laing; first free ascent July 30, 1988, by Renny Jackson, Rich Perch, Steve Rickert, and Leigh Ortenburger. (See *Figure 4-23.*) Immediately to the right (east) of the Crystal Tower on the Underhill Ridge is a huge, extensive chimney system marked by a very prominent branch that leads due west back onto the ridge. This route ascends the excellent rock to the east of this huge chimney. It is best viewed from the vicinity of Teepe Col. If one approaches via the Black Dike Traverse, scramble up the easy section of red rock from Glencoe Col toward the base of the wall of the initial tower on the ridge. Instead of turning left (west) as for the regular Underhill Ridge route *(Route 16)*, descend 30m on the scree shelf to the right to the chimney/crack system on the right of the initial tower. Two pitches up enjoyable rock lead into the section where the chimney splits and widens. The larger branch continues back left (west) toward the ridge crest at the notch behind the final pitch of the Crystal Tower *(Route 17)*.

FIGURE 4-23. Grand Teton, east aspect. (A) Lev *(Route 19)*, III, 5.8; (B) Variation: East Face Left, III, 5.9+

The Lev route ascends the left edge of the right (north and east) portion of the chimney system. The second pitch ends in an alcove (a fixed angle piton will be found here) just above a large and loose chock-stone. Climb out right under a small roof onto the small ridge or face above, which leads to a well-defined 1m-wide ledge. The ledge is at the base of a short, very steep 6m wall that is broken by a vertical crack. Climb this 5.8 crack (originally aided) onto easier ground above, leading to a wide ledge holding a large boulder, just beneath a huge overhanging section of gray rock. From this point an extension of the original chimney system can be seen over to the right (north) leading steeply up toward an overhang; this contains the open-book crux of *Route 23*. Instead, take the easier stepped ramp leading up and out to the left (south). After about 24m on this ramp, turn up and slightly right in a crack leading to a belay ledge. A final short crack in a left-facing corner takes one from this ledge onto easier rock leading onto the crest of the Underhill Ridge at the base of its final tower; that route is joined at this point (5.5). A distinct but more difficult line can be maintained all the way to the top of the ridge by climbing cracks in a corner (5.7) on the extreme right edge of the face past another fixed angle piton. From the top of the Underhill Ridge, proceed to the summit as in *Route 16*. This climb is characterized by good rock and is quite enjoyable.

***Variation:* JACKSON-WOODMENCEY.** III, 5.9+. First ascent in summer 1988, by Renny Jackson and Jim Woodmencey.

(See *Figure 4-24.*) This climb was conceived as an exploratory probe of the prominent wide cracks on the east side of the Underhill Ridge above the Crystal Tower. Begin with the first pitch of the standard Lev route. Continue up, passing a chockstone around its left side, and belay at the base of a very clean left-facing corner. Climb the corner (5.9) and belay. The probe into the wide crack on the left was unsuccessful. Instead, a traverse (5.9+) was made via flakes to the final pitch of the standard Lev route. Continue up the Lev route, which finishes on the regular Underhill Ridge route *(Route 16)*. A more direct start was done by Keith Cattabriga in 1994, in which two more pitches on the initial portion of the east side of the face were climbed (the second pitch was a 5.10 left-facing corner).

***Variation:* EAST FACE LEFT.** III, 5.9+. First ascent October 4, 2001, by Aaron Gams and Jeff Burke. (See *Figure 4-23.*) After three pitches, this variation joins the standard Lev route, which meets the regular Underhill Ridge route *(Route 16)* along the last pitch to the top. Begin to the right (north) of both the Lev route and the left-facing corner of the Red and the Black *(Route 20)*. Start up a small left-facing dihedral and then trend left to the belay (5.6R). Other details of the next two pitches of the climb are shown in *Figure 4-23*. **Gear:** A double set of cams from 0.75" to 3" and a set of nuts should be adequate for protection. (Source: Aaron Gams, *Teton Rock Climbs* [Ground Up Press, 2012])

FIGURE 4-24. Grand Teton, east aspect. (A) Lev *(Route 19)*, variation: Jackson-Woodmencey, III, 5.9+; (B) The Red and the Black *(Route 20)*, III, 5.10+, A0

ROUTE 20. THE RED AND THE BLACK. III, 5.10+, A0. First complete ascent August 8, 2001, by Keith and Alan Cattabriga. (See *Figure 4-24.*) This route derives its name from the two distinct colors of the dike material at Teepe Col and the color scheme of the uniform of the Royal Canadian Mounted Police (RCMP). During their first attempt on the route in the summer of 1994, the Cattabriga brothers were "sent scurrying like insects to the Lev route by the repulsive offwidth, without giving it a good go." In 2001 the pair returned with "courage in their rucksack" and completed the climb. The final two pitches—the fourth and the fifth—are the business of the route. A "torpedo flake" wedged in the crack on the fourth pitch comes with the admonishment "use in moderation only." And the offwidth pitch that caps the climb may well go free at 5.11—or even harder; the Cattabrigas aided it at 5.10+, A0. **Gear:** For protection the Cattabrigas took one set of cams from small C3s to 4"; one #5 Camalot; one #6 Camalot; one 5.5" tube chock; one 6" tube chock; and one #7 Tricam. **Note:** The hanging belay at the start of the last pitch consisted of a #5 Camalot, a #7 Tricam, and a 6" tube chock; no bolts were placed.

ROUTE 21. EAST FACE, LEFT CENTER. III, 5.10-. First ascent of first two pitches in July 1994, by Renny Jackson and Ron Johnson; first ascent of second two pitches in fall 2002, by Aaron Gams and John Steinbauer. (See *Figure 4-25.*) This route was unwittingly put together by two separate parties with an eight-year span in between. To the right (north) of the left-facing corner of the Red and the Black *(Route 20)*, look for a finger crack arcing up and right on the face above. The first pitch begins with good hands behind a flake (5.9) and then joins the finger crack (5.10-) to a belay on the face. After a short

FIGURE 4-25. Grand Teton, east aspect. (A) East Face, Left Center *(Route 21)*, III, 5.10-; (B) Beyer East Face I *(Route 23)*, III, 5.9

stretch through a roof (5.8), the next pitch follows easy 5th-class terrain to a ledge. At this point the first party exited up via the Beyer East Face I route *(Route 23)*. Eight years later, the second party climbed up and left to a steep 5.9 crack and, via a 5.8R mantel, made their way up to the main large ledge that cuts across the face. They then continued up through a 5.9 roof located between the Lev route *(Route 19)* and the Beyer East Face I route to parallel cracks that provided an exit to the regular Underhill Ridge *(Route 16)* or the 5.7 corner variation of that route. The fun climbing on this face is extensive, and several route combinations are possible. **Gear:** Suggested protection includes a double set of cams, with an emphasis on finger size to 3.5", and one set of nuts.

ROUTE 22. SOUTHEAST CHIMNEY. III, 5.9. First ascent August 5, 1973, by David Lowe and Leigh Ortenburger. (See *Figures 4-21* and *4-26.*) The southeast chimney is a significant feature of this side of the mountain. Extending for over 90m, it lies near the center of the east face of the Underhill Ridge and ends near the shallow notch that separates the final tower of the ridge from the main slabs of the upper southeast face. It is characterized by a broad, right-facing wall in the lower half and an equally large left-facing wall in the upper half. This route has the same start as the Lev route *(Route 19)* on the east side of the Underhill Ridge. Climb the first leads of that route on interesting rock to gain the wide ledge beneath the huge, overhanging gray-rock area. This ledge is unique on the Grand Teton, being the common intersection point for many different routes. Go horizontally right for one easy ropelength along the base of the wall, past the base of the right-facing corner of the upper Beyer East Face I route *(Route 23)*, to a belay position among some blocks. Continue this traverse right to reach the southeast chimney itself at the right edge of this wall. Climb the first 15m of the chimney on either the inside or the outside. The strenuous and awkward crux pitch is the narrowing section of the chimney containing two smooth flakes, one of which protrudes from the chimney. This lead is difficult (5.9) because the face to the right of the chimney is smooth and the left wall is vertical. Once past these flakes, continue to a belay point in the same chimney, which now forms the right edge of a slabby face. The third lead of the chimney begins by either climbing directly upward or partially using the slabs to the left. This is followed by 18m of easy climbing on the right side of the chimney to some 5.7 cracks. Finally, by stemming one can reach a belay in a small alcove. The steep section of the narrow chimney above goes at 5.7 as well. The exit from the chimney involves the use of some small holds and a splendid lieback in the crack to which the chimney has now dwindled. Scramble easily up to the shallow col on the main Underhill Ridge (see *Route 16*), where the usual southeast slabs are followed to the summit of the mountain. The rock on this route is excellent.

ROUTE 23. BEYER EAST FACE I. III, 5.9. First ascent July 14, 1979, by Jim Beyer; first winter ascent January 29, 1993, by Renny Jackson and Larry Detrick (to top of climb). (See *Figure 4-25.*) This important climb is an excellent route in the same class as, and perhaps even better than, the Durrance Direct (Lower Exum Ridge; *Route 9*). The steep rock section is not extensive but is of high quality. Access the beginning of this route from Glencoe Col or from the snow at the top of the Teepe Glacier (see the *East Face Routes* introduction for both approaches). Either approach option requires one to locate the huge right-facing dihedral (usually wet and/or icy) in the main wall above. At the bottom of this dihedral is a large ceiling or arch cut back in to the left (south).

The first pitch (46m) leads onto the main steep face out and around to the left on the outside of the dihedral. Begin by climbing up a small right-facing corner. After 6m a few moves of 5.9 permit an exit out and to the left of a roof to a small ledge. Then ascend a 5.8 crack to a belay stance. The second pitch is probably one of the nicest crack pitches in the range. Climb up to the small overhang directly above the belay and undercling and lieback out to a small stance at the base of the crack. The 37m hand-and-fist crack above (5.8) eventually leads to a comfortable belay ledge with some loose flakes on it. Above the belay step around to the right and then up and onto a big ledge. Climb out and right again to a flake and then up to a large, easy ramp (5.4) that leads left (south) to the wide ledge with boulders beneath the huge, overhanging gray-rock area described in *Routes* 19 and 22. This ledge is the common intersection point for several different routes.

Traverse the ramp up and to the south to a steep corner and belay. This spectacular open book is the crux of this Beyer route, starting with cracks (5.6) that turn into a right-facing corner (5.8). Halfway up the corner a few moves of 5.9 out and up the right side of a small overhang lead to the scenic finish of this pitch. The view looking down to the valley floor, framed by the spires of Teepe Pillar and the great towers of the Grand Teton's east ridge, is well worth the climb. The top of this pitch places one at the edge of more downsloping slabs, where the first of the layered black rock of the upper Underhill Ridge is encountered. Climb easily up and left past a small roof and around a corner to gain the crest of the Underhill Ridge, just below its final black-face tower. From this point the regular Underhill Ridge *(Route 16)* is followed to the summit. For protection, take a standard rack with perhaps some 4" pieces for the wide crack.

ROUTE 24. KEITH-EDDY EAST FACE. III, 5.10-. First ascent August 17, 1991, by Jason Keith and David Eddy. The name Ritual de lo Habitual was applied by the first ascensionists. (See *Figure 4-26*.) Use either of the approaches mentioned in the introduction to the east face routes to access the base of the huge right-facing dihedral in the main wall (described in *Route 23*). The first pitch begins up the face of this corner for 30m (5.9). Exit to the left and belay at the base of a finger crack a short distance to the north of the hand-and-fist crack of the preceding route. The second pitch ascends this finger crack for 30m (5.10-). From the top of the crack climb up off the ledge past some flakes and then step right and climb a 5.9 finger crack to a large, sloping ramp. From this point numerous exit options are available because four other routes are in the general vicinity. The distinctly separate finish of this route goes up just left of the finish of the Southeast Chimney route

FIGURE 4-26. Grand Teton, east aspect. (A) Keith-Eddy East Face *(Route 24)*, III, 5.10-; (B) Beyer East Face II *(Route 26)*, III, 5.8

(Route 22). Climb out of a blocky gully using a 5.7 flake/crack, which then leads to a short 5.10- section. The next pitch covers easier terrain. From the ramp at the top of this pitch, the route finishes with a 5.8 right-facing corner that is somewhat loose.

ROUTE 25. EAST FACE DIRECT. III, 5.9+. First ascent September 3, 2006, by John Steiger and John Fowler. (See *Figures 4-21* and *4-27*; but note that the route line depicted in these phototopos is approximate.) This route lies between the Keith-Eddy East Face *(Route 24)* and the Beyer East Face II *(Route 26)*. Approach via either the Black Dike Traverse to Glencoe Col or the Teepe Glacier, as described in the introduction to the east face routes. About 10m left of the parallel cracks marking the start of the Beyer East Face II is a right-facing dihedral choked with large blocks. Third-class terrain leads to a good belay ledge on one of the blocks in the dihedral. **Pitch 1:** The first pitch is intricate. From the ledge, step down and right to a weakness that turns into an easy shallow corner after several moves. A few meters up the corner, step out right to an incipient crack that is used to gain an obvious flake farther to the right. The flake is just below the long, black horizontal break/roof system stretching from the base of the Keith-Eddy East Face dihedral across the face to the initial Beyer East Face II dihedral. Make a few moves right along the top of the flake and turn the bulge above the horizontal break to a small left-facing dihedral. Work right and climb up another small corner to a small roof, which is skirted on the left into a shallow left-facing corner. Continue up the corner until it is possible to traverse right and up into another shallow left-facing corner. Climb this corner and weakness above for about 12m to a small but secure belay alcove (55m). **Pitch 2:** Ascend an obvious finger crack above and left of the belay to its end, then step left (past an obvious protruding rock) to another crack that ends on a ledge. Make a few moves left, surmount a bulge, then continue straight up easy ground to a belay on broken ledges (60m). **Pitch 3:** Climb straight up the slab above, aiming for the left end of a large rectangular roof on top of the slab. Belay from a sloping ledge next to the roof (65m). **Pitch 4:** Ascend the easy left-facing dihedral above, which changes to a steeper right-facing corner. Climb the hand crack in the corner to its end on top of a large flake, then traverse right and up for about 5m to an intermittent crack system. Belay 15m higher at a small stance (52m). **Pitch 5:** Continue up the crack system until it arches right and ends under short headwall. Step right and climb the headwall to easy climbing that ends on top of the initial Underhill Buttress (35m). Join the Underhill Ridge *(Route 16)* or one of its variations to the summit (about 300m). **Gear:** For protection take one set of brass nuts and a set of stoppers; double cams from ⅜" to 3"; one 3.5" cam (useful); and many slings. (Source: Mountain Project)

FIGURE 4-27. Grand Teton, East Face Direct *(Route 25)*, III, 5.9+

ROUTE 26. BEYER EAST FACE II. III, 5.8. First ascent August 15, 1981, by Jim Beyer and Dan Grandusky; attempted August 25, 1969, by Rick Reese, Leigh Ortenburger, Burt Janis, and Sherm Beacham. (See *Figure 4-26*.) This route lies between the East Face Direct *(Route 25)* and the Horton East Face *(Route 27)*. It is important that dry conditions be sought for this climb because melting snow on slabs in the middle of this route will provide, at best, unpleasant conditions. This route follows a completely distinct line from the lower of the two small snow patches above the Teepe Glacier to the shallow col separating the top of the Underhill Ridge from the upper southeast slabs of the Grand Teton. See the introduction to the east face climbs for the two possible approaches to this initial snow patch.

From the upper edge of the snow patch (visible in *Figure 4-26*), start up an initial short, blocky section to a belay stance below a pair of parallel cracks that angle up from left to right. A long, black roof looms above and left of these cracks. Climb the cracks (5.7), which eventually lead to a left-facing corner, and belay on a good ledge after a hand traverse. Climb partway along this ramp and then cut back up a 5.6 face, angling left to reach a right-facing corner. This second pitch goes up this corner and then steps around to the left (5.8) to gain the slabby middle portion of the route. Run out the rope up a shallow gully in these slabs to a large ledge at the base of the final steep section. The fourth pitch is an outstanding

Doug Coombs on the first ski descent of the Otterbody, east face of the Grand Teton (Photo by Mark Newcomb)

5.7 lead with good protection. Start in a left-facing corner and angle right to climb a steep finger crack on the outside edge of a rib. The final lead continues up a right-facing corner, moves easily right across slabs, and proceeds up the final rocks to the col at the top of the Underhill Ridge. Follow the upper Underhill Ridge *(Route 16)* to the summit.

ROUTE 27. HORTON EAST FACE. III, 5.7. First ascent August 14, 1977, by W. D. Horton, Paul Horton, and Robert Snyder. (See *Figure 4-21.*) This route connects the lower end of the Smith Otterbody chimney system (see *Route 28*) with the "front feet" of the Otterbody Snowfield. The rock on this route is generally sound, but it is important to make this climb in dry conditions, either late in the season or in a dry year. See *Route 28* for the approach to the slabs at the beginning of the route. Climb one long pitch up the Smith Otterbody line. From the belay, leave the Smith Otterbody and follow corners up and left for 30m to a comfortable ledge beneath a headwall. To pass this wall the next lead follows the narrowing ledge left (south) to its end, where a few face moves up a slab lead to a belay (5.7, 46m). Third- and 4th-class climbing leads up and right on ledges into the main feature of the route, the huge left-facing corner system below the "head" and "front feet" of the Otterbody Snowfield. One easy pitch up the left face of this corner takes one to a belay below another headwall. The crux pitch (5.7) above goes a short way up the wall, then traverses into a small open book in the right-hand wall with face climbing above to enter the crack at the back of the book; continue up to a belay ledge. A right-leaning chimney in the wall above has a tricky start but becomes easier and leads onto the rubble at the edge of the snowfield, where *Route 28* is rejoined.

ROUTE 28. SMITH OTTERBODY. III, 5.6. First ascent September 5, 1937, by Phil Smith, Paul Petzoldt, and William House. In late July or early August 1930, Phil Smith and Robert Underhill attempted this route but were stopped by ice on the rock. (See *Figure 4-21.*) This route ascends the prominent chimney system that is the only major break in the wall above the Teepe Glacier and below the Otterbody Snowfield. This very large chimney leads toward the "hind feet" of the Otterbody Snowfield and serves as a principal drainage path for the melting snow. Hence, if reasonably pleasant conditions are desired, this route should be attempted only in late season and very early in the day, before the sun's warmth melts the snow above.

The approach to the base of the chimney can be made either directly up the Teepe Glacier from the vicinity of Corbet's High Camp (the Jackson Hole Mountain Guides base camp) or along the Black Dike Traverse from the Lower Saddle. From Glencoe Col one can scramble along a system of ledges above the top edge of the glacier all the way to the slabs below the chimney. These tricky slabs lead to the base of the vertical section of the chimney system; they are exposed to some danger from falling rock. After the initial pitches, a chimney with an overhang must be passed. In early season and midseason, this overhang is an icy waterfall. Above this section, using the rock parallel to and on the right of the original chimney, climb about 60m to the Otterbody Snowfield. The snowfield will be reached somewhat north of the "hind feet."

Climb diagonally back toward the left (south) using ledges on the outside of the snowfield or, if necessary, along the rather steep snowfield itself. The traditional method of exit from the snowfield is to kick steps up the snow to the "shoulder" of the Otterbody, where a break in the wall—a wide chimney—leads to the slabby, partially snow-covered upper southeast face of the Grand Teton. A second method requires proceeding to the "nose" of the Otterbody, from which one can climb to the shallow col separating the top of the Underhill Ridge (see *Route 16*) from the upper southeast face. In late season, when this route is presumably being climbed, great expanses of slabs are exposed on this upper southeast face. Many paths can be threaded upward, but perhaps the easiest heads almost due west toward the ridge that forms the upper extension of the Buckingham Buttress. Slightly more difficult, but more direct, is a route well out on the southeast face, over slabs and snow, all the way to the summit block. Or, by making a substantial detour, one can cross over to the right (north) and join the East Ridge route (see *Route 32*). **Time:** 8½ hours from the Caves. See *Canadian Alpine Journal* 20 (1931): pp. 72–86, illus.

ROUTE 29. GOLDEN ARÊTE. IV, 5.11d. First ascent in July 1999, by Jim Beyer and Zack Martin. (See *Figure 4-28.*) Beyer reported that he led the crux third pitch—the 5.11d "endurance flash"—ground up with a combination of free climbing and aid, and that he hand-drilled the protection bolts. Martin then followed the pitch free. They pulled the ropes and Beyer managed a redpoint the next day. A total of 15 bolts were placed on the climb, with three of those for belay anchors. After five pitches, join *Route 28*: Beyer and Martin proceeded up the upper "shoulder" of the Otterbody Snowfield, continued up and around the Buckingham Buttress, and finally headed up 200+m of snow in the Ford Couloir to the summit of the Grand Teton. **Gear:** In addition to quickdraws, take one set of nuts to 1" and one set of cams to 3".

***Variation:* OFFSPRING.** III, 5.11, A1. First ascent in August 1999, by Jim Beyer and Zack Martin. (See *Figure 4-28.*) This distinct variation to the north of the Golden Arête follows left-facing and left-arching corners. Four bolts were placed on the first ascent; three were at belays. Beyer described the route as having good rock but also some wet spots and moss.

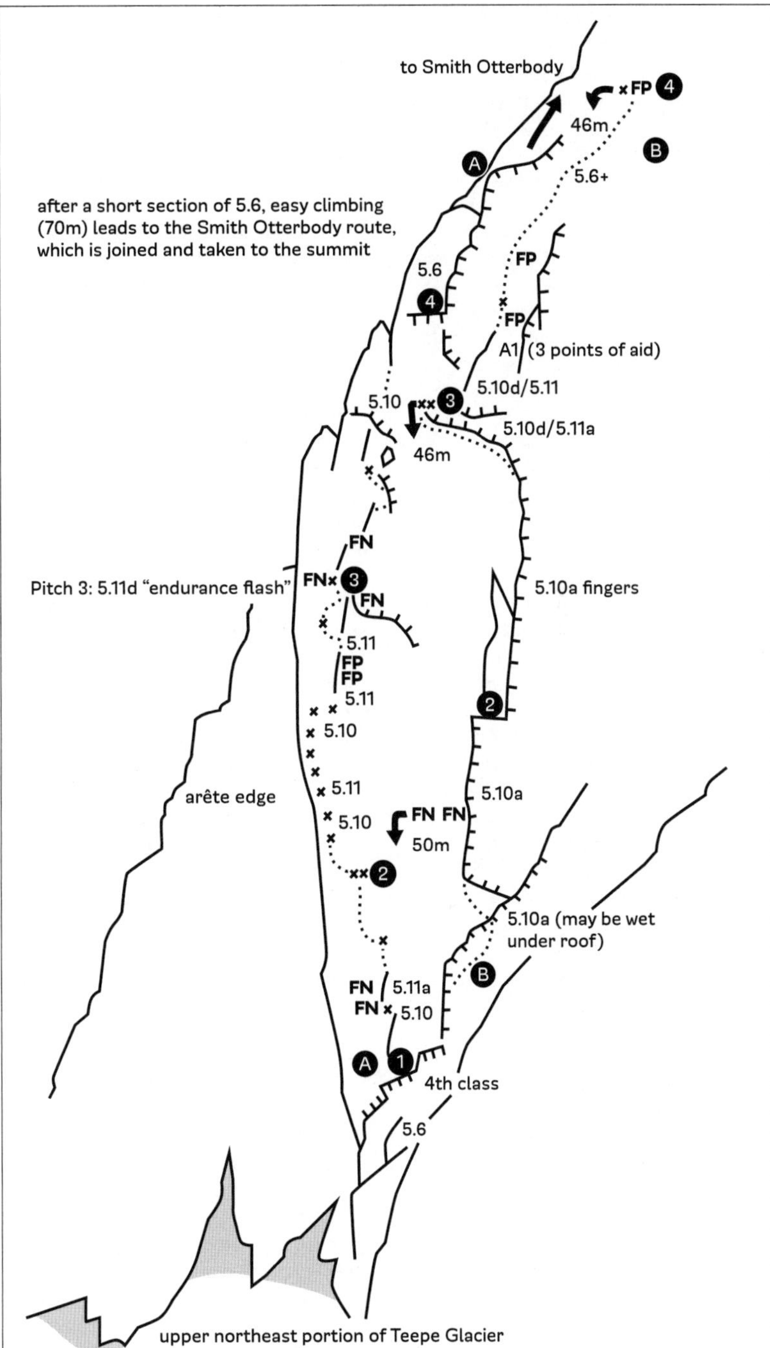

FIGURE 4-28. Grand Teton, east aspect. (A) Golden Arête *(Route 29)*, IV, 5.11d; (B) Variation: Offspring, III, 5.11, A1

ROUTE 30. PETZOLDT-LOOMIS OTTERBODY. III, 5.1. First ascent August 2, 1935, by Paul Petzoldt and William Loomis; first descent (and second ascent) September 10, 1936, by Paul Stettner and Art Lehnebach. Although Petzoldt ranks this as one of the easiest routes on the Grand Teton, this is perhaps true only in good conditions and only for a small party of experienced mountaineers adept at routefinding and snow climbing. Also, there is substantial danger from rockfall, which is significantly increased during wet, warm weather. Climb directly up the Teepe Glacier (ice axe and crampons recommended) as rapidly as possible. Leave the snow at its upper right (northwest) corner and gain the rocks just to the right (east) of the large couloir that comes down from above the Second Tower on the east ridge of the Grand Teton. Work up these scree-covered ledges (somewhat rotten), crossing left (west) into the upper, wet portion of the couloir. Ascend and ultimately cross the couloir to the left (southwest) onto the slabs on the outside of the Otterbody Snowfield. Traverse left (south) on these slabs below the snowfield, past the "hind legs" of the Otterbody; then kick or cut steps to the wide chimney leading up from the "shoulder" of the Otterbody. After a few pitches in this chimney, one will emerge onto the main upper southeast face of the Grand Teton at the point where the chimney opens out to the left (west). In early season this will be mainly a large snowfield; in late season the underlying slabs will be exposed. For the three options to the summit from this point, see *Route 28*. **Time:** 5¼ hours from the Caves. See *Appalachia* 20, no. 7 (November 1935): p. 420. **Note:** This route is perhaps best known as being the scene of the infamous Appalachian Mountain Club rescue of 1962, which was chronicled in a two-part *Sports Illustrated* feature by James Lipscomb: "72 Hours of Terror" (June 14, 1965; vol. 22, no. 24) and "Night of the One-Eyed Devils" (June 21, 1965; vol. 22, no. 25).

Variation: III, 5.1. First ascent August 6, 1961, by J. Gordon Edwards and Kenneth Proctor. This variation, a better alternate route to the "tail" of the Otterbody, follows the left (west) side of the couloir. Because it reduces the danger of rockfall, it is recommended in preference to the original route. Leave the snow about 8m to the left (west) of the couloir that comes down from above the Second Tower on the east ridge of the Grand Teton. Climb the slabs that angle up to the right (northeast), but stay well out of the couloir until about two-thirds of the way to the large snow patch high in the couloir. At the steepest part of the couloir climb over to the right (east) side; the stream that drains the snow patch must be crossed just below a 3m waterfall. After a short climb up the east side to the snow patch, cross quickly back to the left (south and west); from this point it is but a short scramble up slabs to the "tail" of the Otterbody Snowfield. See *Chicago Mountaineering Club Newsletter* 15, no. 5 (December 1961): pp. 1–3.

Variation: III, 5.1. First ascent August 6, 1961, by J. Gordon Edwards and Kenneth Proctor. Since this party observed a rock avalanche in the wide chimney leading above the "shoulder" of the Otterbody onto the upper southeast face, they were motivated to pursue a different exit from the Otterbody. Instead of climbing up the snow to the top of the "shoulder," continue to the "nose" of the Otterbody. From here climb a series of narrow ledges to the shallow col separating the final tower on the Underhill Ridge from the upper southeast face. For routes to the summit from here, see *Route 28*.

ROUTE 31. OTTERBODY CHIMNEYS. III, 5.7, WI3–WI4. First ascent September 14, 1979, by Kim Schmitz; first winter ascent December 29, 1985, by Renny Jackson and Dan Burgette. Rising from the upper right (north) corner of the Teepe Glacier is a long, steep couloir/chimney system between the vertical southwest walls of the Second Tower and the main southeast face of the Grand Teton below the East Ridge Snowfield. The lower 120+m forms the initial broken rock of the Petzoldt-Loomis Otterbody (*Route 30*). This route ascends the very steep upper portion of the same chimney system directly to the crest of the east ridge just above the Second Tower. Due to the rotten nature of this upper section, this climb should not be undertaken except in very cold conditions, such as winter, when the rock is frozen in place by ice and crampons can be worn. Approach this route via the Teepe Glacier in the same manner as for *Route 30*. Climb about 120m to an easy section of snow at the extreme right end of the Otterbody "tail," leading toward the final, very steep, poorly protected chimney below the ridge. A total of six leads of mixed ice and rock, with sections of thin snow over rotten rock as well as vertical ice, will be found on this route. In summer conditions this upper section will be heinous with much loose rock, mud, and running water. Once the crest of the east ridge is reached, proceed to the summit as in *Route 32*.

Grand Teton, East Ridge and North Face Routes

Rising high above Teton Glacier at the head of Glacier Gulch is the north face of the Grand Teton, one of the most famous and picturesque walls in the United States. This huge north wall is bounded by the Grand's eastern and northern ridges, and this next section covers the wide expanse of the many and varied routes contained within. The normal approach for these routes is by way of Glacier Gulch (see Section 7), and the most efficient means of accessing this drainage has evolved over the years. Due to the popularization of the Delta Lake area through social media, many boots have worn an unofficial, unmaintained trail to this picturesque alpine lake. This access route takes off from the north end of the first switchback along the trail to Surprise and Amphitheater Lakes, about 3.2 miles from the Lupine Meadows trailhead and just above the junction where the left fork of the trail splits off into Garnet Canyon. This 0.5-mile social trail may now be the most direct way of getting to any of the routes at the upper end of Glacier Gulch, making it a good option for one-day ascents. For those on a multiday outing, camping is available at Surprise Lake (three sites) or the Teton Glacier. From Surprise Lake, one can continue up to Amphitheater Lake and follow the traditional approach up and over the col north of the lake into Glacier Gulch.

On the afternoon of September 6, 2022, a large dust cloud was observed rising from Teton Glacier. This may have marked the day when a significant portion of the Second Tower on the East Ridge route fell away. Over the next several days rockfall from the decomposing Tower continued to occur off both sides of the ridge. Climbers should take note of the possibility of additional rockfall in this area and its effect on routes that come up from below. The climbing routes that were most likely affected by this

significant event are: Routes 32, 35, and 38 on the north side and Route 31 to the south. Any of the climbs on the north side of the East Ridge route that are located beneath the Second Tower may have been affected, however.

ROUTE 32. EAST RIDGE. III, 5.7. First ascent July 22, 1929, by Robert Underhill and Kenneth Henderson; first descent August 2, 1935, by Paul Petzoldt and William Loomis (six rappels); first winter ascent February 16–18, 1973, by George and David Lowe and Jock Glidden. This fine ridge, the first new route on the mountain after the discovery of the Owen-Spalding route in 1898, remains today a significant mountaineering objective. The variety of rock, the interesting routefinding problems, the snowfield near the summit, and the absence of extreme difficulty make this 1,200m ridge one of the most satisfying climbs on the Grand Teton. Although it was attempted several times in the 1920s, the exceptional skills of Robert Underhill and Kenneth Henderson, who were in fact trained in climbing in the Alps, were required to overcome the Molar Tooth, the first and main obstacle on the ridge. Today, the standard East Ridge route is not considered to be exceptionally difficult, but the two main towers, the Molar Tooth and the Second Tower, provide routefinding challenges.

The initial section is but a scramble, but the original northern passage of the Molar Tooth requires one or two rappels with great exposure, followed by an icy climb with loose rock to reach the notch behind the tower. The southern passage of the tower is both faster and free of the mental stress that comes with the cold and shade of the north side. Either method requires careful route selection and immediately presents the climber with an interesting pitch up out of the notch. Once the slabs are passed, the interesting climbing continues with the northern traverse of the Second Tower. For enterprising climbers seeking a greater challenge than the normal route, one or both of these towers can be climbed en route, although this option is rarely done. Above the Second Tower, the East Ridge Snowfield stretches to the summit, providing a long, exhilarating finish to this classic climb.

History: As seen from Jackson Hole, the east ridge of the Grand Teton is the most obvious and enticing route to the summit of the mountain. The relatively easy beginning of the ridge encouraged a long sequence of early attempts. It is possible that Edmond Kelly and Richard W. G. Welling followed this ridge on August 21, 1894, but the information regarding their route is vague and their high point is unknown; they did "proceed to one of the high peaks," perhaps the Molar Tooth, before turning back. The ridge attracted the attention of Franklin Spalding after his 1898 ascent of the Grand Teton. He wrote in 1899, "If I ever have a chance to try the mountain again, I would like to make the attempt from the east side." In September 1907, William Stroud attempted the peak from Jenny Lake, again reaching an uncertain high point, probably on the east ridge, which he claimed to be "80–100 feet from the top."

When Paul Petzoldt was just 16, he attempted the ridge with Ralph Herron on July 23, 1924, during his first visit to the range, but they were defeated by the passage of the Molar Tooth and, lacking equipment, narrowly escaped with their lives. Petzoldt and Herron returned, along with Harold Criger and Melvin Whitehead, for another attempt on July 27, 1925. This attempt also failed after Herron sustained serious injuries in a spectacular fall held by the belay rope, which the resourceful Petzoldt had hurriedly wrapped around a substantial rock when he saw that his partner was about to pitch off. On August 31, 1926, Phil Smith attempted the peak—with William Gilman, Melvin Nevitt, and George Behen (and two dogs)—probably via the east ridge. Four years after their successful fourth ascent of the Grand Teton in 1923, Albert R. Ellingwood and Eleanor Davis (Ehrman) returned to try the east ridge with Colorado Springs climbers Robert Ormes and Eleanor Bartlett. This effort was also stymied by the Molar Tooth, although they may have reached the top of this imposing tower. On about August 24, 1928, two European mountaineers, Ulrich Wieland and Fredi Luce, took a stab at the east ridge but failed after a serious effort.

Success finally came the following summer. On July 19, 1929, New England climbers Robert Underhill and Kenneth Henderson established a camp (assisted by horse packers) at Amphitheater Lake. The next day the pair descended into Garnet Canyon (then known as Bradley Canyon), proceeded up to the Lower Saddle, and climbed the Owen-Spalding route—both to familiarize themselves with the mountain and to scope out the upper reaches of the east ridge for their attempt. After resting on the 21st, they set off at 6 AM on July 22 for the ridge. The problem of the Molar Tooth was finally "solved" (as the logician and philosopher Underhill would have liked for it to be stated) when they succeeded in passing the tower on the north by means of a rappel from a horn, which they slung with a section of lariat their horse packer had given them. Beyond this, after traversing west along a ledge and by chopping a few steps in a couloir they intersected, they reached the notch past the Molar Tooth and the crux moves of the climb. These led to the next intimidating section: "Five hundred feet or more above us loomed smooth, overhanging, down-sloping slabs," Underhill later wrote. "Henderson now took over the lead and gave a brilliant exhibition of slab climbing." Above these slabs they were able to pass the Second Tower, again on the north side, and the route was open to the summit. The snowfield above led to the summit block, which they climbed via a chimney that required a *courte-échelle*—a shoulder stand—to pass.[1] They arrived at the top at 4 PM, after 10 hours of climbing.

The next attempt, on July 7, 1934, by Fred Ohlendorff and Helmut Leese, ended in spectacular tragedy with one of their bodies being recovered on the Teepe Glacier and the other on the Teton Glacier. During the second successful ascent on August 21, 1934, by Fritiof Fryxell and Fred Ayres, two cairns, one containing a faded fragment of coarse-weave cloth, were found about 6m below and south of the notch separating the gendarme from the Second Tower. Henderson and Underhill disclaimed responsibility for the cairns, and the condition of the cloth suggested that it much antedated even the 1929 first ascent. The identity of the

1. Underhill once defined a *courte-échelle* in a humorously matter-of-fact way as "The Procedure of the Leader's Mounting upon the Second Man's Shoulders." See "Mountaineering Vocabulary," *Appalachia 18* (1930–31): 296–302; *24* (1942–43): 72–78.

early climber to this very high point on the Grand Teton remains unknown—a lingering mystery.

Strategy: The best way to climb the East Ridge route is as a day trip from the valley floor, but this requires ideal weather, a high level of fitness, good routefinding ability, and preferably some prior knowledge of and experience on the mountain. Camping at Surprise Lake saves only a couple of hours, and carrying bivy gear up the climb and over the summit slows the process way down (and just isn't that much fun). Light and fast is the way to go!

Route Description: Refer to *Figure 4-29* for a photographic overview of key route details. From Amphitheater Lake, head up and over the col north of the lake and take the route beneath the north face of Disappointment Peak toward the Teton Glacier (see *Glacier Gulch* in Section 7). The southern arm of the terminal moraine of the Teton Glacier offers the primary access to the base of the East Ridge

FIGURE 4-29. Grand Teton, East Ridge *(Route 32)*, III, 5.7

route, as the climb begins only 15m south of the moraine crest. Scramble up the first 600m well left (south) of the crest of the east ridge. The smooth yellow walls of the first tower, the Molar Tooth, loom above. As described in the history section above, this tower blocked several early attempts to scale the Grand Teton's east ridge, and even today it is a formidable obstacle if the route is lost; see *Molar Tooth* in Section 6. The original East Ridge route, the Northern Traverse of the Molar Tooth, is described below but it is *not* recommended: there have been a number of accidents there. Instead, bear left (south) of the crest of the ridge and aim for the bowl below the Molar Tooth. From this bowl head for the broken chimney located approximately 90m south of a prominent 60m smooth-walled chimney; this latter chimney has only been descended by rappel. Climb up and left (south) past the bottom of the broken chimney. Proceed up on the left side of the chimney for a ropelength until it is possible to cut right around a corner to an obvious ledge that allows entry into the upper narrow section of the chimney (one or two pitches, 5.6–5.7). This is climbed without difficulty to the window in the sharp ridge crest that overlooks the great couloir leading north from the Teepe Glacier to the main notch between the Molar Tooth and the Grand Teton. Traverse the Molar Tooth on its south side using either the Southern Traverse variation (described below) or the preferred alternative known as the Tricky Traverse, detailed here.

Variation: **TRICKY TRAVERSE OF THE MOLAR TOOTH (RECOMMENDED).** III, 5.7. First ascent July 9, 1972, by Robert Irvine, David Lowe, and Jim "Ole" Olson. (See *Figure 4-30*.) This variation provides a relatively slick method of passing the Molar Tooth in the course of an East Ridge climb and can provide a drier alternative to the sometimes unpleasant (verglas) wall to the right of the giant chockstone mentioned in the Southern Traverse variation. From the window notch on the south ridge of the Tooth, gained as in the 1935 Southern Traverse variation, follow an obvious 5.7 crack system leading up and left around a corner to a large ramp. Take this ramp to its left (north) end and then climb a wide crack (5.7) to a ledge slanting up to the left. From the left end of this ledge traverse across a short, steep face up to an area of broken rock at a corner of the ridge. From here an easy, downward-trending horizontal lead goes across a scree ledge to the top of the giant chockstone just below the main notch behind the Molar Tooth. This notch is then easily reached. Some loose rock will be encountered on this variation.

The first short pitch directly up out of the notch behind the Molar Tooth is difficult: it is the route's technical crux at 5.7 and may require aid if it is wet. For the next 100m belay positions are scarce, but the climbing—up a series of slabs leading up the east side of the Second Tower—is not difficult. From the top of the short pitch out of the notch, bear slightly right up some easy slabs to a chimney leading to an alcove about 40m above the notch. Climb right (north) out of this alcove and up one step to the beginning of about 90m of slabs. Angle slightly left (south) for several ropelengths to reach a break in the small ridge that descends to the south from the gendarme preceding the Second Tower. From the far (west) side of this small ridge ascend north up the gully (snow-filled in early season) that leads to the sharp notch between the gendarme and the Second Tower.

Figure 4-31 shows the route from this point to the summit. To reach the far (west) side of the Second Tower, traverse around its north side on adequate ledges. About halfway around the Tower descend about 3m and pass behind a very large upright flake. Then climb a 12m chimney (5.6) filled with many flakes. Once up this chimney, one can easily reach the notch between the Second Tower and the Grand Teton. Wet, scree-covered slabs (covered with snow in early season) lead up to the East Ridge Snowfield, which is climbed along its right (north) edge. Extreme caution should be exercised while climbing these hazardous slabs, because belay positions are either poor or nonexistent and the exposure is considerable. In late season the rock to the right (north) of

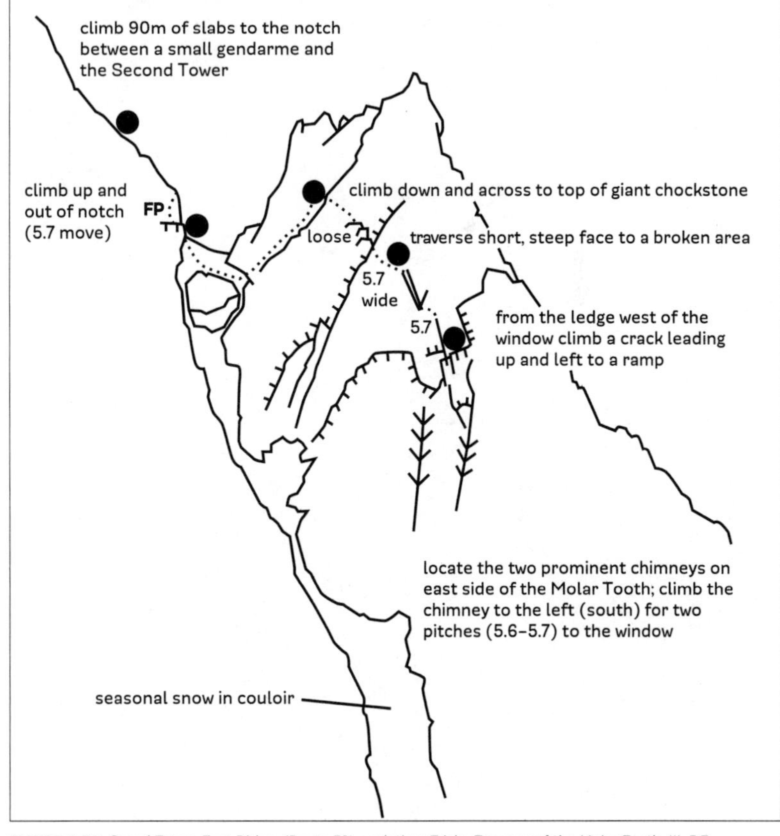

FIGURE 4-30. Grand Teton, East Ridge *(Route 32)*, variation: Tricky Traverse of the Molar Tooth, III, 5.7. **Note:** This topo shows the upper portion of the Molar Tooth as viewed from the south.

the snowfield, along the edge of the great north face, provides a route to the summit block. During the rest of the season, an ice axe is required to negotiate the East Ridge Snowfield safely; crampons are convenient.

From the top of the snowfield there are four ways to attack the summit block. The first is the traditional route and is the most difficult and direct. The fourth is more commonly used—and is the one this author (R. Jackson) would recommend.

(1) Reach the summit directly from the east via the large chimney in the center of the summit block. To access this chimney pitch, climb a 24m blocky section. The pitch itself consists of four short subchimneys yielding some of the most enjoyable climbing of the route, but one must pass a number of old tin cans from earlier days. (*Figure 4-31* shows this option.) (2) Another option is to contour around to the left below the summit block and join the top part of the Exum Ridge route *(Route 8)*. On the second ascent of the ridge, completed in one day on August 21, 1934, Fritiof Fryxell and Fred Ayres used this alternative. (3) It is possible to contour around the right (north) side of the summit block along an interesting ledge system at the extreme top of the north face, emerging at the upper end of the "V" (see the Direct Finish variation of *Route 43*). One awkward and strenuous chimney must then be climbed to reach the last blocks leading to the summit. This alternative was first climbed on August 12, 1935, by Paul Petzoldt, Glenn Exum, and Elizabeth Cowles (Partridge) during the third ascent of the ridge. (4) A prominent chimney in the right (north) half of the summit block comes out on the north ridge only 30m below the summit. Once on the ridge, weave in and out of the boulders to the summit. **Time:** 10¾ to 13 hours from Amphitheater Lake. See *Alpine Journal* 42, no. 241 (November 1930): pp. 267–77, illus.; *American Alpine Journal* 1, no. 2 (1930): pp. 138–39, illus.; 5, no. 2 (1944): pp. 220–32, illus.; *Appalachia* 18, no. 3 (June 1931): pp. 209–32, illus.; 23, no. 4 (December 1941): p. 534; *Canadian Alpine Journal* 18 (1929): pp. 96–97, illus.; *Mazama* 31, no. 13 (December 1949): pp. 20–23, illus.; *Trail and Timberline*, no. 141 (July 1930): pp. 5–7, illus.; no. 205 (November 1935): pp. 126–31, illus.; no. 237 (August 1938): pp. 87–89, illus.; no. 415 (July 1953): pp. 95–97, illus.

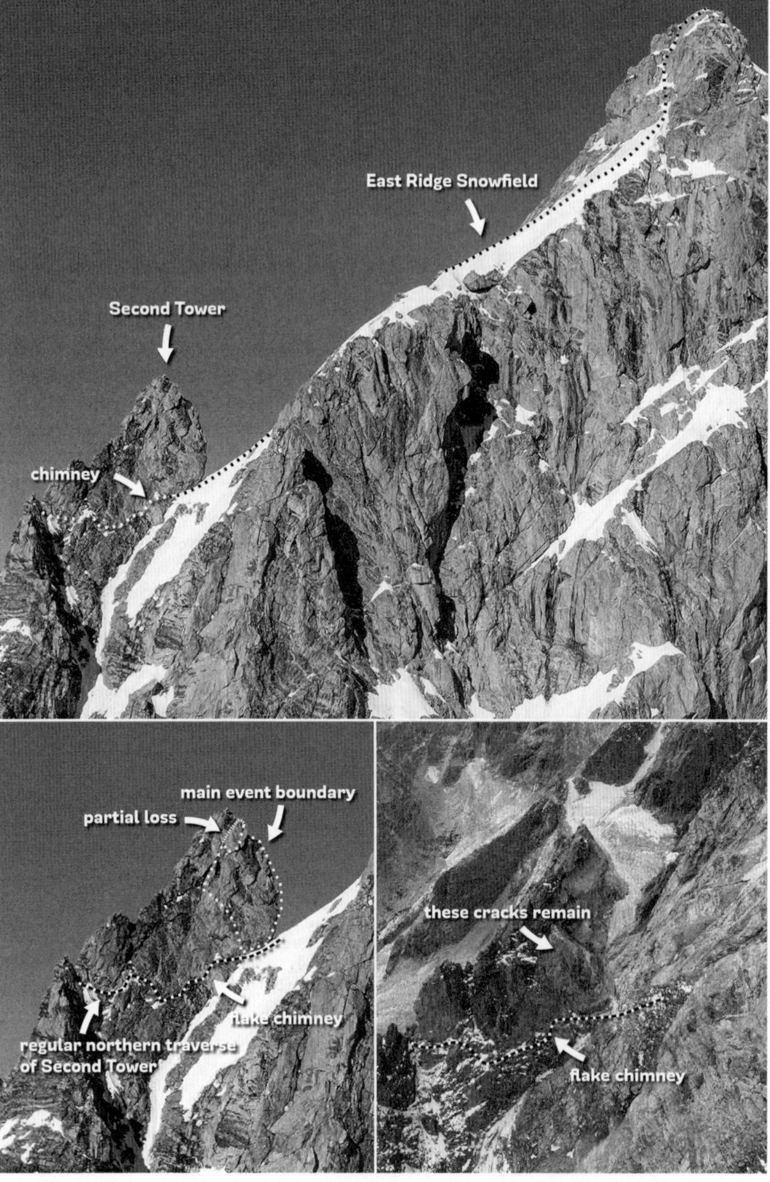

FIGURE 4-31. *Top:* Grand Teton, East Ridge *(Route 32)*, northern traverse of the Second Tower detail and summit; *bottom, l to r:* before and after close-ups of the Second Tower after the rockfall events of September 2022

Original Route: **NORTHERN TRAVERSE OF THE MOLAR TOOTH (NOT RECOMMENDED).** Scramble to the bowl, which is 90m below and just east of the Molar Tooth; the bowl is bounded on the north by the crest of the east ridge. Climb to the right (north) to gain the narrow crest of the ridge at a point just west of the first gendarmes on the crest. Proceed along the ridge crest to the northeast corner of the Molar Tooth. The objective now is to reach the main notch separating the Molar Tooth from the upper portions of the east ridge. Climb down the steep and exposed north side of the Molar Tooth about 15m–30m, depending on the amount of snow present, until it is possible to make an 18m diagonal rappel down and across an ice gully to a small ledge on the far (west) side of the gully. From this ledge scramble right (west) for perhaps 30m (exposed and loose) over to the rotten yellow couloir that leads up to the main notch.

This section may be partially covered by snow and ice. Two pitches up the yellow couloir, either directly up from the bottom (loose rock) or up its left (east) side (also loose), then take one to the notch.

***Variation:* SOUTHERN TRAVERSE OF THE MOLAR TOOTH.** III, 5.7. First ascent August 12, 1935, by Paul Petzoldt, Glenn Exum, and Elizabeth Cowles (Partridge). This route was discovered, but not climbed, by Petzoldt and Ralph Herron in 1924 on their first attempt to climb the Grand Teton. From the window in the sharp ridge crest above the broken chimney, descend about 30m on rotten and broken rock, then climb the great couloir that leads north from the Teepe Glacier to the main notch between the Molar Tooth and the Grand Teton. Depending on the season, steep snow and even ice may be involved; some have found crampons useful here. Pass the enormous chockstone that completely blocks the couloir just short of the notch by climbing the steep wall on the right (east). Depending on conditions this climbing can be quite difficult with either wet or verglas-covered rock. The chockstone may well be the largest in the Teton Range. The notch is then attained after 21m of scrambling over scree or steep snow depending on the time of year. See *Chicago Mountaineering Club Newsletter* 2, no. 5 (January–July 1948): pp. 5–7; *Trail and Timberline*, no. 205 (November 1935): pp. 126–31, illus.

***Variation:* SOUTH MOLAR TOOTH COULOIR.** III, 5.7. First ascent July 28, 1936, by Paul Petzoldt, Karl Keuffel, and James Monroe. This variation has been used at least a few times during winter ascents of the East Ridge route. From the right (east) edge of the Teepe Glacier, ascend the great couloir leading to the notch behind the Molar Tooth on the east ridge of the Grand Teton. For most of the summer this couloir will be filled with very steep snow. In late season it will no doubt contain steep, loose rock. Pass the same enormous chockstone mentioned in the preceding Southern Traverse variation and join the main East Ridge route at the notch.

Variation: III, 5.4. First ascent July 28, 1936, by Paul Petzoldt, Karl Keuffel, and James Monroe. This seldom-climbed variation starts at the Molar Tooth and does not rejoin the regular upper East Ridge route until it reaches the sharp notch between the Second Tower and the gendarme immediately to the east. From the window in the south ridge of the Molar Tooth, descend the rotten chute to the great couloir leading from the Teepe Glacier to the notch between the Molar Tooth and the upper portions of the east ridge. Instead of following this couloir up to the enormous chockstone, cross the couloir and climb a rotten chute on the other (west) side to gain the obvious ledge system leading horizontally left (south) out to the crest of the skyline ridge (this is the south ridge of the gendarme that precedes the Second Tower). The high ledges are most suitable for getting around the corner at the ridge crest and into the next couloir, which runs up the south face of the Second Tower. A neat horizontal ledge leads from the corner into this scree- and rock-filled couloir. Scramble up this loose material to the steep rock at the head of the couloir. It is apparently possible to climb directly up this rock on the left (west) if one wants to climb the Second Tower en route to the summit of the Grand Teton; see *Second Tower, Route 5*. Otherwise, cut right (east) from the head of the couloir up a short chimney. From the top of this chimney, walk up the snow (rock in late season) to the sharp notch between the gendarme and the Second Tower and follow the regular East Ridge route to the summit. This variation is not as difficult as the usual route, but it contains more loose rock and requires some routefinding skill.

Variation: III, 5.7. First ascent September 7, 1955, by Leigh Ortenburger and Irene Beardsley (Ortenburger). This intriguing variation starts from Dike Col, goes over the top of the pinnacle known as Okie's Thorn, and reaches the window in the south ridge crest of the Molar Tooth. From Dike Col climb Okie's Thorn by its Southeast Ridge route (see Section 6, *Okie's Thorn, Route 1*); this will be the most difficult part of the climb. Downclimb the southwest ridge a short distance and make a 37m rappel to the black schist slabs on the west face of the pinnacle, about even with the very sharp notch between Okie's Thorn and the Grand Teton. This notch, formed by the weathering away of a rotten red dike, is only about 2m wide. On the first ascent of this variation a Tyrolean traverse was arranged across this obstacle. Do not descend the chute leading west onto the Teepe Glacier; it is exceedingly rotten and dangerous—perhaps the worst such place in the park (and that is really saying something!).

On the Grand Teton side of this notch a wide ledge leads left (west) for about 30m. The wall above this ledge is almost vertical but not difficult, having many large holds. After about three ropelengths, angle right to gain the east side of the ridge (the south ridge of the Molar Tooth). Ascend the first chimney (counting from the south), which leads up to the crest of the south ridge of the Molar Tooth. For the route to the summit, follow either the Southern Traverse variation or the Tricky Traverse variation.

Variation: III, 5.6. First ascent August 11, 1957, by James Langford and William Cropper. A large couloir or gully descends the south face of the Second Tower onto the right (north) margin of the Teepe Glacier. This gully is bounded on the left (west) by the true south ridge of the Second Tower and on the right by the south ridge of the distinct large gendarme just east of the Second Tower. This variation starts from the Teepe Glacier and reaches the usual East Ridge route, utilizing this south ridge of the gendarme. The chief obstacle is a 240m vertical section of smooth gray rock, which is passed by following a diagonal, high-angle, 90m shelf leading from left to right (west to east) across the crest. The end of this shelf brings the climber to about 120m of easier climbing; the remainder of the ridge is climbed mostly on the right (east) side close to the crest until the usual East Ridge route is joined at the notch between the gendarme and the Second Tower. See *American Alpine Journal* 11, no. 1 (1958): pp. 85–88.

Variation: III, 5.7. First ascent July 25, 1977, by Jon King and Chuck Fitch. This variation provides a much more difficult start to the standard East Ridge route. Take the traditional approach from Amphitheater Lake out onto the Teton Glacier (see *Glacier Gulch* in Section 7). Shortly after descending from the crest of the moraine onto the glacier, look up at the eastern end of the north face of the Grand Teton. A broad but vertical rock buttress will be seen between the easternmost two gullies that lead from the glacier back onto the east ridge. This buttress lies well to the east of the large northeast couloir. A broad, smooth 45° ramp ascending this buttress from lower left to upper right forms the beginning of this variation. After gaining the ramp from the glacier, climb only a short distance before turning directly up the wall above the ramp. The difficulty is about 5.6 or 5.7, and passage of some overhangs is involved. Once the east ridge is reached, about halfway up the lower portion of the ridge, join the standard route to continue to the summit.

***Variation:* NORTH MOLAR TOOTH COULOIR.** III, 5.8, WI3+. First ascent January 31, 1984, by Alex Lowe. (See *Figure 4-32.*) This significant variation, one of the few new climbs in the range first done in the winter, attains the notch behind the Molar Tooth directly from the north. The climb begins with the first portion of the Hossack-MacGowan Couloir *(Route 35)*. During the first ascent this involved climbing rock steps and some sections of good, but thin, water ice. At the point where *Route 35* moves right out onto the slabs leading to the upper Hossack-MacGowan Couloir, this variation continues up the main steep couloir that descends from the Molar Tooth–Second Tower notch. Lowe then climbed four difficult pitches of rock, along with about 60m of water ice, which reached 70° for 15+m. This route is most suitable for climbing when there is sufficient snow and ice to cement in place the loose rock of the couloir. Even in winter Lowe encountered some loose rock, although overall the rock was predominantly sound.

ROUTE 33. NO NAME GULLY. III, 5.7, WI4+. First ascent in 1979 or 1980, by Steve Shea. This very steep gully rises from the Teton Glacier about 60m east of the Hossack MacGowan Couloir. It is separated from both branches of that northeast couloir (including the Route Canal, *Route 34*) by a substantial rock ridge or buttress. When formed, this gully contains two pitches of water ice climbing, but this is probably a rare event these days. From the Teton Glacier climb the steep snow apron leading to the first of these water ice pitches. A difficult pitch is followed by an easier section that leads to the second steep water ice pitch. Once past this obstacle, climb several ropelengths to the top of the route, a notch behind a very sharp needle on the east ridge of the Grand Teton, located at the top of *Route 34*. This route was done during an exceptionally rare alpine season in the Tetons, when many of the chutes and couloirs throughout the range were well covered with ice.

ROUTE 34. ROUTE CANAL. IV, 5.9, WI5. First ascent June 17, 1979, by Jeff Lowe and Charlie Fowler. (See *Figure 4-32.*) This difficult ice route reaches the crest of the east ridge from the north at a small notch just east of the Molar Tooth, utilizing the narrow and nearly vertical chute that forms the left (east) branch of the Hossack-MacGowan Couloir (see *Route 35*). Approach this route from Amphitheater Lake via the Teton Glacier (see *Glacier Gulch* in Section 7) and aim for the north edge of the glacier to reach the base of the Hossack-MacGowan. Climb the lower portion of that route to the point where this chute diverges out to the east. This serious climb of six pitches comprises vertical ice, 5.9 rock, and difficult mixed ground. The route usually comes into shape in the spring (or less often in the fall) when there is sufficient meltwater in

FIGURE 4-32. Grand Teton, overview of north face ice routes. (A) East Ridge *(Route 32)*, variation: North Molar Tooth Couloir, III, 5.8, WI3+; (B) Route Canal *(Route 34)*, IV, 5.9, WI5; (C) Hossack-MacGowan Couloir *(Route 35)*, IV, 5.6 (in summer); (D) Grand North Couloir (Shea's Chute; *Route 37*), IV, 5.8, WI5; (E) Squeeze Box *(Route 39)*, IV, M7, A0; (F) Alex Lowe Memorial Route *(Route 40)*, V, WI5, M6

this chimney system that then freezes and forms the climb.

ROUTE 35. HOSSACK-MACGOWAN COULOIR. IV, 5.6, high-angle snow. First ascent August 8, 1939, by Jack Hossack and George MacGowan; the fast time of the first-ascent party—6¾ hours from the Teton Glacier—is noteworthy. Mark Newcomb and Hans Johnstone nabbed both the first winter ascent and first ski descent on February 16, 1996. (See *Figure 4-32.*) This remarkable and long route, largely on the north face of the mountain, does not join the regular East Ridge route *(Route 32)* until the notch above the Second Tower. Evidence easily observed on the Teton Glacier at the base of this northeast couloir shows that hazardous rockfall occurs in it. Select a day for the climb when there is no party on the East Ridge route. This route is perhaps best viewed as an early-season climb when it is largely snow and ice and overnight low temperatures are well below freezing. As is the case with many of the couloir routes in the Tetons, during warm periods or when precipitation is likely, this route becomes a veritable bowling alley.

Approach the Teton Glacier from Amphitheater Lake (see *Glacier Gulch* in Section 7), walking toward the north edge of the glacier in order to be certain of selecting the right couloir. The correct couloir leads to the notch separating the Molar Tooth from the Grand Teton. The bergschrund is crossed near its left (east) edge. Usually a snow tongue will extend some distance up the couloir. Quickly climb either up the snow or up the rocks on the left (east) edge of the snow tongue to the point where the couloir forks. Continue another 90m or 120m up the right (west) branch of the couloir. In early season some steep ice may be encountered in this section. A great deal of rock debris will be found on the ledges in this area. At an obvious point, one or two leads above a snow patch, traverse out on the right (northwest) wall of the couloir on good ledges. Climb and scramble out to a shoulder from which the upper Hossack-MacGowan Couloir—the couloir descending from the notch above the Second Tower—can be reached. Snow and steep ice will be found in the bottom of this upper couloir, and usually it cannot be avoided. In late season, however, it is possible to climb the rock on the right side of the couloir all the way to the notch; parts of this are steep, but for the most part just scrambling is required. Follow the East Ridge route, which is intersected just above the Second Tower, to the summit. See *The Mountaineer* 32, no. 1 (December 1939): pp. 25–26, illus.

Variation: IV, 5.8. First ascent August 24, 1962, by Pete Sinclair and Leigh Ortenburger. This variation reaches the bottom the upper portion of the Hossack-MacGowan Couloir from the west by starting the climb on the regular North Face route (see *Route 43*). In this way the lower portion of the couloir and its rockfall problems are entirely avoided. Climb the first four pitches of the North Face route, up the left-slanting chimney to the point where one would begin the "obvious traverse . . . to the right toward the First Ledge." At this point, turn left and climb up to the left (east) on broken rock for three leads or so. The problem ahead is to get around the obvious corner at the east edge of the north face and into the upper Hossack-MacGowan. A small ice chute protects this corner, and one must climb a pitch up the right (west) side of the chute before crossing it (this is likely part of *Route 40*). The final lead crosses this narrow chute and goes up and around the very exposed corner into a short but smooth-walled dihedral (5.8). Were it not for this pitch, this variation would be among the least difficult (technically, at least) of those that approach the summit of the Grand Teton from the north. Once the upper couloir is reached, proceed as in the standard Hossack-MacGowan route. See *American Alpine Journal* 14, no. 1 (1964): pp. 185–86.

Variation: IV, 5.7, AI4. First ascent June 25–26, 1990, by Todd Cozzens and James Earl. This variation is quite similar to the preceding one. Proceed as described to the area of the ice chute. This party rappelled 6m into the chute, which was then followed for three pitches. At that point one is about 23m from the bottom of the upper portion of the Hossack-MacGowan, by which this route finishes.

ROUTE 36. NORTHEAST BUTTRESS. IV, 5.8, A4, or IV, 5.10+. First ascent August 24–25, 1970, by Paul Myhre and Dale Sommers; first free ascent on about July 30, 1978, by Jon King and Charles Foster. This route ascends the entire buttress immediately to the right (west) of the lower two-thirds of the Hossack-MacGowan Couloir (see *Route 35*). This buttress is bounded on the right (west) by a prominent ice chute, the Grand North Couloir (see *Route 37*), a major feature of the lower north face. The approach to the buttress is made via the Teton Glacier, heading toward the steep, conical snow slope below the bergschrund at the base of the Hossack-MacGowan. Gain the rock from the lower right (west) side of this snow slope, well below the entry into the couloir, on a wide ledge system leading diagonally out to the right in dark-colored rock. This ledge system ends about 9m short of the steep Grand North Couloir, on the right side of the buttress. From here a large system of flakes (5.7) leads up to a narrow ledge after 23m. The next pitch goes up and right with some aid (5.8, A2) to a small ramp that continues diagonally up and right to a belay ledge. The crux of this route is a 1.5m–2.5m ceiling, which was climbed using aid to traverse up and right on the first ascent. This was accomplished using tied-off 2"–3" bongs in reportedly poor rock. Continue on aid above the ceiling to the right on broken but steep rock to a wide, high-angle ramp (5.8) that takes one through a small overhang to the bottom of the prominent chimney that is visible from the glacier. On the first ascent a bivouac was made at this point. Two pitches in the chimney then lead to a very slick wall, which is avoided by scrambling right into the chute on the right of the buttress and then back left (5.8) and up a short wall to return to the face of the buttress. One more pitch (5.6) then leads to the top of the buttress where the normal Hossack-MacGowan route is joined as it traverses right on slabs to gain the upper couloir descending from the notch above the Second Tower.

***Variation:* LITTLE WING.** IV, 5.8. First ascent July 16–17, 1976, by Tom Deuchler and Dave Moerman. The northeast buttress contains three prominent, smooth ramps slanting up and right. This climb, which ascends the upper half of the buttress, begins in the Hossack-MacGowan Couloir (see *Route 35*), ascending the steep snow for about 100m to the base of the second ramp. Two pitches of 5.6 face or slab climbing lead to a large ledge at the top west end of the ramp. From the outside edge of the ramp, two moderate pitches on rotten rock provide access to the base of the large chimney near the right edge of the buttress; this chimney is easily seen from the glacier below and forms the upper part of the main Northeast Buttress route. This 1976 variation apparently joins that route at about this point, and both proceed in slightly different ways to the top of the buttress to join

Route 35. The rock on this variation varies from poor to excellent, making it difficult to obtain adequate belay anchors.

ROUTE 37. GRAND NORTH COULOIR (SHEA'S CHUTE). IV, 5.8, WI5. First ascent (mostly on rock) on about August 1, 1978, by Jon King and Charles Foster; Steve Shea climbed it mostly on ice on June 6, 1980. **Note:** This route is commonly referred to as Shea's Chute, even though Shea's ascent was two years after the 1978 climb. (See *Figure 4-32.*) This formidable couloir or chute is immediately to the right (west) of the northeast buttress, described in *Route 36*. In midseason or late season its ascent will be a mixed climb, involving both rock and ice. In some early seasons it is a major ice climb, ranking with the Route Canal *(Route 34)* as one of the most difficult ice climbs in the range. This chute has important similarities with Mount Owen's Run-Don't-Walk Couloir (see Section 7, *Mount Owen, Route 10*) in that one must wait for exactly the right conditions for the climb. An extremely early start is recommended to minimize the objective hazard from falling rock and ice. The approach is via the Teton Glacier, across the bergschrund, and up a relatively low-angle gully leading to the base of the chute. Climb this lower section (5.6 to 5.7) and gain access to the chute itself. The climb contains five or six pitches, entirely on ice, up the frozen waterfall of the chute, which rises in a series of vertical tiers. After the first four or five pitches the angle in the chute eases somewhat, but the final ice lead is again very steep. The route ends as one emerges out of the chute onto the broad, slabby apron where the Hossack-MacGowan Couloir route *(Route 35)* traverses right to gain the upper couloir leading up toward the Second Tower. In midseason or late season, when more rock is exposed, this will be a very difficult mixed climb.

ROUTE 38. NORTH BUTTRESS DIRECT. IV, 5.10+R. First ascent August 15, 2020, by Mark Jenkins and Justin Bowen. (See *Figure 4-33.*) This long route on the lower portion of the Grand Tetons's north face lies between the Hossack-McGowan Couloir *(Route 35)* and the regular North Face route *(Route 43)*. Remarkably, it remained undiscovered (or at least unclimbed) until the motivated pair of Jenkins and Bowen found and climbed it in 2020. They began climbing at 4 AM and found the bergschrund below the northeast buttress "deep and wide," which forced

FIGURE 4-33. Grand Teton, North Buttress Direct *(Route 38)*, IV, 5.10+R

the pair to gain a rocky ledge system at its far eastern end, near the bottom of the Hossack-McGowan. Traversing the ledge system to the west required five pitches of easy 4th- and 5th-class simul-climbing, some downclimbing, and one short rappel to get to the start of this long 14-pitch route. **Pitch 1:** Begin with face climbing; some gear placements are possible in discontinuous cracks (5.9PG-13). **Pitch 2:** Climb a right-leaning finger crack followed by a left-leaning finger crack (5.10). **Pitch 3:** Climb a "scary, dirty crack with unprotected face moves to the left over a bulge" (5.10+R). **Pitch 4:** Continue up and to the west on ramps into the ice-filled gully that is part of *Route 39* (5.7). **Pitch 5:** Climb on wet, chossy rock to the top of the gully (5.6). **Pitch 6:** Head left (east) out of the gully to a good hand crack (5.7). **Pitches 7–9:** Simul-climb up 4th- and easy 5th-class terrain to the base of the second tower on the route. **Pitch 10:** Continue up via 5.7 crack climbing. **Pitch 11:** Climb another crack to the top of the tower (5.9). **Pitch 12:** Ascend a "chossy" dihedral (5.7). **Pitch 13:** Climb a crack through an overhang (5.9), then continue up for several ropelengths of scrambling. **Pitch 14:** Go up a crack (5.7) at the edge of the north face. At this point the route joins the East Ridge route *(Route 32)*. The pair continued up the snowy ridge crest to the summit block, completing the route in 13 hours, and then descended via the Owen-Spalding route *(Route 1)*.

ROUTE 39. SQUEEZE BOX. IV, M7, A0. First ascent February 6, 2007, by Hans Johnstone and Stephen Koch. (See *Figure 4-32.*) This difficult mixed route ascends a line of weakness between the Grand North Couloir (see *Route 37*) and the Alex Lowe Memorial Route *(Route 40)*. The line was spotted by Koch while skiing the Koven Couloir in January 2007, and he made his first attempt on the climb with Brian Harder. Koch returned with Johnstone to complete the route. A challenging squeeze chimney low on the route, too narrow to climb facing in, led to a beautiful ice gully. This was climbed to a black chimney, followed by two ropelengths of rock climbing. The second-to-last pitch involved a tension traverse across smooth slabs to reach "another set of bottomed-out seams that offered slightly more opportunity for the metal to catch on the minuscule and insecure features." One more mixed pitch brought the pair to the top of the climb, and they rappelled the 305m route to get down. (Souce: Alpinist.com)

ROUTE 40. ALEX LOWE MEMORIAL ROUTE. V, WI5, M6. First ascent October 5, 2004, by Stephen Koch and Mark Newcomb. (See *Figure 4-32.*) This route begins just east of the start of the original 1936 North Face route (see *Route 43*) and just west of the Squeeze Box *(Route 39)*. After 300m, it joins the upper portion of the Hossack-McGowan Couloir route *(Route 35)*. The second pitch was the crux, presenting a thin veneer of chandelier ice with no protection. Koch retreated into a "womb-like feature," broke through the back of the chandelier, and climbed out and over a small roof, allowing access to lower-angle terrain. Having climbed through a small waterfall on that pitch, he spent some time at the belay wringing out his clothes and "dumping water" out of his boots. A spectacular storm then ensued, with great quantities of graupel cascading down over the climbers. This ended after about 25 minutes, and Koch and Newcomb continued up several more pitches, including one WI5 pitch through steep granite, to the Hossack-McGowan. The pair intersected the east ridge and traversed across and around to the upper Ford Couloir and then on to the summit.

FIGURE 4-34. Grand Teton, north aspect, Simpleton's Pillar *(Route 41)*, IV, 5.9+

ROUTE 41. SIMPLETON'S PILLAR. IV, 5.9+. June 16–17, 1972, by Jeff Lowe. (See *Figure 4-34.*) This interesting and seldom-climbed route uses the normal start for the standard North Face route *(Route 43)* to gain a left-slanting chimney on the lower face. Watch for this chimney system cutting up and to the left rather than continuing up and right to the Guano Chimney of *Route 43*. In early season ice will force the climber to use the outer lip of the couloir/chimney system. Follow this system for approximately 75m to the lower of two right-leaning, right-facing corners. (A descent bolt, dating from repeated attempts [1959–1970] by Ray Jacquot on a still uncompleted route, will be found here along with a fixed pin or two near the base of the corner.) Climb four pitches in this corner to its top and then up a short but steep wall above. Continue up the broken wall above, reaching a left-trending crack system that leads up to near the top of the buttress or pillar. Follow this crack system until it rounds the left corner of the buttress and becomes a ledge. Once around this corner easier climbing up and right takes one onto the east ridge, where the climb can be finished to the summit via *Route 32.*

ROUTE 42. GOODRO-SHANE. IV, 5.8, A1. First ascent August 9, 1953, by Harold Goodro and Jim Shane. (See *Figure 4-35.*) Follow *Route 43* to the First Ledge on the north face. Instead of traversing this ledge to its west end, stay on the left (east) edge of the snow and continue straight up. Climb 30m up a chimney to a smooth 3.5m wall. This very exposed pitch, the most difficult on the climb, required the leader to stand on the outstretched hands of his second man. From the top of this pitch move slightly to the right where a series of small ledges and terraces leads upward for about 90m. Continue up and to the right (west); some ice patches must be crossed. Then climb directly up a steep, loose ridge for about 46m until one can cut left (east) into a shallow couloir filled with very loose rock. This couloir leads directly to the enormous boulder, perched at the edge of the east ridge, that hangs over the north face. Gain the east ridge and follow *Route 32* to the summit. See *American Alpine Journal* 9, no. 2 (1955): pp. 147–49.

Variation: IV, 5.8. First ascent July 2, 1961, by Tom Spencer and Ron Perla. (See *Figure 4-35.*) This variation also utilizes the large indentation near the eastern edge of the upper north face. It is possible to enter this indentation from the beginning of the Second Ledge instead of attacking it directly from the First Ledge, as was done in 1953. Use the 1941 variation of *Route 43* to reach the east end of the Second Ledge. A short distance up this ledge a high-angle crack leads slightly left (east) and up the wall above the ledge for about 30m to an excellent belay stance; this pitch was reported to be very strenuous with protection difficult to obtain. Midway through the next lead, which continues up the same crack, is a sequence of 5.8 moves onto a block and then up off the block in order to make a traverse left (east) to the second excellent belay position. Make a short lead up and right to the easy slabs that meet the Goodro-Shane route in a gully in the aforementioned indentation. This ice gully can be followed up to the east ridge or, after 6m, one can climb up and left, hand traversing a difficult slab. This avoids further climbing

FIGURE 4-35. Grand Teton, overview of upper north face routes. (A) North Face with Direct Finish variation *(Route 43)*, IV, 5.8; (B) Goodro-Shane *(Route 42)*, IV, 5.8, A1; (C) Goodro-Shane, variation: 1961, IV, 5.8; (D) Golden Pillar *(Route 44)*, V, 5.12-; (E) Medrick-Ortenburger *(Route 45)*, IV, 5.8, A2; (F) North Ridge *(Route 47)*, IV, 5.8+; (G) American Cracks *(Route 46)*, IV, 5.9; (H) North Ridge, variation: Italian Cracks, IV, 5.7/5.8

in the gully and gives access to a series of easy slabs that lead to the east ridge.

ROUTE 43. NORTH FACE. IV, 5.8. First ascent August 25, 1936, by Paul Petzoldt, Eldon Petzoldt, and Jack Durrance; first direct ascent August 13, 1949, by Richard Pownall, Ray Garner, and Art Gilkey; first free ascent July 24, 1953, by Richard Emerson, Willi Unsoeld, and Leigh Ortenburger; first winter ascent February 28–March 2, 1968, by George Lowe, Mike and Greg Lowe, and Maurice Horn. First winter ascent with Direct Finish January 1–3, 1987, by Alex Lowe and Jack Tackle. (See *Figures 4-35, 4-36*, and *4-37*.) This imposing wall, seen and admired by millions of tourists, is *the* north face in the United States. Although not as well-known as the Eiger Nordwand in Switzerland or some of the other great north faces of the Alps, the north face of the Grand Teton is one of the most famous mountain features in this country. A climb of the North Face route is not as highly coveted as it once was, its rating being fairly easy by today's standards, but it was a clear object of fear in the 1950s and 1960s. A common question during the time period, posed jokingly—yet not—among Teton climbers, was "When are you going up to do the North Face?" Yvon Chouinard, in his classic *Climbing Ice*, described it this way:

In the 1950s the goal of every Alpine climber was to do one or more of the great north walls in the Alps—the Matterhorn, Eiger, or Grandes Jorasses. In the States there was but one north wall and that was on the Grand Teton. It had seen very few ascents, and most of these had involved a bivouac somewhere on the mountain. Those fortunate few who managed an ascent came back with stories of terrible rockfall, iced-over rocks, routefinding problems, and all the usual troubles one finds on a typical big north wall. It was the premier American alpine climb, and, of course, was a dream of mine ever since I began climbing in 1955.

This captures what it is about going into the unknown that fascinates alpinists—and will continue to fascinate future alpinists.

As one stands beneath the north face preparing for the climb, one cannot help but be overcome by a sense of awe and fear. The approach—the crossing of the Teton Glacier to the base of the route and the negotiating of the tricky bergschrund—necessitates bringing ice-climbing gear, even as climate change has had its effect on the range. Because it is a north face, this aspect of the Grand will always be subject to serious consequences in the event of bad weather; climbers will need good judgment and adequate gear to cope with this possibility. Even with good conditions, the length of the climb demands efficiency to avoid benightment. The initial portion of the face is not difficult, but the routefinding is notoriously tricky, and the rockfall hazard is significant—especially in the region below the First Ledge. (The rock quality on the lower two-thirds of the route is not great.)

Climbing ranger Dick Emerson leading the Pendulum Pitch free during the first ascent of the Grand Teton's Direct North Face, July 24, 1953 (Photo by Leigh Ortenburger)

Over the years there have been remarkably few accidents from such acts of nature. Still, two major rescue operations were conducted on the face during the latter part of the 20th century. The first, in 1967, involved a series of lowerings from the vicinity of the Second Ledge all the way down to the Teton Glacier far below. This epic rescue has become legendary and was featured in a 2013

FIGURE 4-36. Grand Teton, North Face with Direct Finish variation *(Route 43)*, IV, 5.8

docudrama called *The Grand Rescue.* The second operation, conducted in 1980, consisted of a 180m raising of two stranded climbers and a climbing ranger up a very iced-up north face to the upper East Ridge Snowfield, done during an intense lightning storm. A third rescue, in 2002, demonstrated the dramatic evolution of the helicopter short-haul technique: rescuers were delivered to the base of the Guano Chimney, where they spent the night in a storm with an injured climber and his partner, and were then extracted from their aerie by helicopter the next day, thus avoiding the risk of an extended ground-based operation.

The North Face route presents a variety of problems for the seasoned mountaineer to overcome. While the Guano Chimney has endured a bad reputation over the years, the Pendulum Pitch high on the wall is a genuine classic of American mountaineering in terms of its position, history, and difficulty. Except for one, all variations on the face funnel through this pitch. Richard Pownall needed exceptional courage to attack this lead in 1948 via the pendulum, and Richard Emerson's free lead of the pitch in 1953 was a tour de force for the time.

For those returning for a second climb on the face or just wishing for more than what the normal route offers, there are several other routes that have been worked out on the north face over the years. Some of these are not easy. The major climb to the upper east ridge, the Goodro-Shane *(Route 42)*, is icy and difficult and has seldom been repeated. The direct approach to the Second Ledge from the Grandstand, the Medrick-Ortenburger *(Route 45)*, is another major route, which only recently received a repeat ascent. The same is true of the three climbs on the eastern portions of the wall—the Northeast Buttress route *(Route 36)*, the Northeast Buttress's Little Wing variation, and Simpleton's Pillar *(Route 41)*. For those interested in alpine ice there are a number of steep chutes and gullies on the north face, among them the Route Canal *(Route 34)* and the Grand North Couloir (Shea's Chute; *Route 37*), though their existence is fleeting in light of climate change. The Golden Pillar *(Route 44)* will no doubt stand as *the* classic of the north face for future generations.

History: The long history of the north face of the Grand Teton began on July 6, 1933, when Paul Petzoldt and Sterling Hendricks descended about 300m down the north ridge of the mountain to explore the north face in the vicinity of the Second Ledge. This exploration led Petzoldt to think that there was probably a feasible route up the north side. Three years later, on August 25, 1936, he partnered with his brother Eldon and Jack Durrance to pioneer the first actual climb on the face. The trio left very early in the morning from the valley in order to sneak past another strong team camped at Amphitheater Lake, who they knew were up there for the same climb. It was late by the time Durrance and the Petzoldt brothers reached the Third Ledge. They made a short rappel to the Second Ledge, traversed this ledge to the north ridge, and then followed *Route 47* to the summit.

The team that had been given the slip included Fritz Wiessner, William "Bill" House, and Elizabeth "Betty" Woolsey. House and Wiessner were fresh off their first ascent of the South Face route of Mount Waddington—the hardest climb in North America at the time. After realizing that Durrance and the Petzoldts had done the North Face, Wiessner turned his attention to the North Ridge route *(Route 47)* and managed its first free ascent.

On August 14, 1941, Paul and Bernice Petzoldt, Glenn Exum, and Hans Kraus repeated the North Face route (with one important variation). Both of these early climbs, however, avoided the upper portion of the face. In 1946 Ray Garner, with Jim Smith and Kirk Smith, attempted the face but retreated from a point above the First Ledge. Another three years passed before the direct route that includes the upper portion was finally climbed on August 13, 1949, by the strong party of Garner, Richard Pownall, and Art Gilkey. Then on July 24, 1953, the final step in the evolution of the now-classic North Face route with the Direct Finish was made when Richard Emerson, Willi Unsoeld, and Leigh Ortenburger did the first free ascent. Emerson freed the Pendulum Pitch, previously pioneered by Pownall, and was also the first to lead the delicate traverse into the "V" at the very top of the face.

Other remarkable achievements followed. A decade later, on July 21, 1963, Tom Cochrane made a solo ascent of this standard route. Another five years passed before the first winter ascent of the face was completed—from February 28 to March 2, 1968—by George Lowe, Mike and Greg Lowe, and Maurice Horn. This group finished their climb by climbing the last two pitches of the North Ridge route from the Second Ledge. It was then up to the hardy twosome of Jack Tackle and Alex Lowe to make the first winter ascent of the face with the 1953 Direct Finish, which they did from January 1 to 3, 1987. On December 28, 1992, Alex Lowe soloed the

FIGURE 4-37. Grand Teton, detail of upper North Face with Direct Finish variation *(Route 43)*

North Face route (with a traverse to the Owen-Spalding from the Second Ledge) in an astonishing 20-hour day from the valley floor to the summit and back.

Strategy: Five schemes have been used to climb this face: (1) from the valley in one day, facilitated perhaps by the new social trail to Delta Lake; (2) from a camp at Surprise Lake; (3) from a camp on the Teton Glacier or just west of its terminal moraine; (4) with a planned bivouac on the face, usually on the First Ledge; and (5) from Garnet Canyon via the Black Dike Traverse or by descent from Dike Col. Each of these has its advantages and disadvantages. The best method will depend on the speed and experience of the party, the condition of the bergschrund, and the time of year.

Route Description: See *Figure 4-36* for an overview of the modern North Face route, which follows the original 1936 route to the Third Ledge, the 1949 variation to the Fourth Ledge, and the

1953 Direct Finish (the traverse into the "V") to the summit. While the North Face has lost some of its attraction over the years, it remains a worthwhile mountaineering objective involving a variety of terrain including glacier ice, wet chimneys, and rock climbing on an impressive, exposed face.

From Amphitheater Lake take the traditional approach out to the Teton Glacier (see *Glacier Gulch* in Section 7) and climb onto the upper section of the glacier, passing the crevassed section on the right (north). Bare ice is commonly encountered in this region. From the upper glacier two chimneys can be seen on the bottom part of the face. Avoid the right (west) vertical chimney containing rotten yellow rock; this truly bad chimney leads straight up the face from the bottom of the Grandstand and is off-route. The initial section of the North Face route ascends the left-slanting chimney on the left (east); this chimney can be reached in various ways, determined by the manner in which the bergschrund is passed. Depending on the route taken, 5.7–5.8 climbing will be encountered and there are several old to ancient fixed pins in this area. The bergschrund presents a significant problem on this route and considerable time can be lost in its passage; some ice gear, particularly for the leader, will be useful. (**Note:** A major but rarely used variant to gain the base of this chimney and bypass the entire upper glacier is to take the wide but tricky ledge that diagonals up, from left to right, along the base of the face on the viewer's left [east] side of the icefall.)

Once the left-slanting chimney is reached, climb several ropelengths up it until it is possible to see an obvious traverse on easy ledges and slabs up to the right toward the First Ledge. To reach the ledge, climb the large chimney (the Guano Chimney) that goes back into the wall on the left (east) edge of the steep beginning of the ledge. This chimney is 5.6 in difficulty; in some years it is icy. An unpleasant feature of this chimney (unique in the Tetons, fortunately) is the accumulation of bird (or perhaps bat) droppings through which one must climb. Exit to the right at the top of this chimney onto the First Ledge. If a bivouac is planned on the First Ledge, a good place is at its lower end about 30m above the end of the chimney. A suitable cave will be found here.

Scramble to just short of the west end of the First Ledge and make a 37m high-angle lead up a shallow corner (5.6), followed by another moderate lead up a friction face (5.7) to the Second Ledge. Avoid the large, ice-filled chimney a meter to the west of the shallow corner. If desired, it is now possible to traverse out to the right on the Second Ledge all the way to the North Ridge route *(Route 47)*, but a slippery section of water-covered slabs below the small snow patch on the Second Ledge must be negotiated. To continue the North Face route, proceed out on the Second Ledge for only two or three ropelengths and then climb up and slightly right directly onto the Third Ledge. Traverse right (west) up the Third Ledge until about 90m from the north ridge. An obvious rappel point will be found here near the base of the 1949 Pendulum Pitch, which ascends a right-facing corner in the steep wall above. If time or weather is an issue, one can rappel 34m down to the Second Ledge, which is then easily followed a short distance out to the north ridge.

See *Figure 4-37* for a breakdown of the upper part of the route. The Pendulum Pitch is one of the two most difficult pitches on the route, and it is significantly more difficult than those preceding it. Climb the right-facing corner (5.7) for 18m until it is possible to traverse out and left on a downsloping, narrowing ledge. The climb then moves left (east) on this ledge, around the corner (5.8) where the ledge inverts, and up to a black alcove at the beginning of the Fourth Ledge. In early season and midseason these final rocks will usually be wet, making the last meter or so difficult. A number of fixed pitons will be passed on this pitch. Beware of the sharp crack at the corner, which presents a rope-jamming hazard. Now traverse 37m up the Fourth Ledge to the right (west); the north ridge is now only about 15m away. For the 1953 Direct Finish, at the end of this lead traverse back to the left (east) and then turn upward in a small right-facing corner. At this point one is only about 9m west of the bottom of the "V" (a V-shaped gully). Make a delicate friction traverse across a 75° face to finish the climb. Once in the gully, scramble up blocks and chimneys to the summit.

In the event one is seeking escape from the face because of time considerations or bad weather, the original 1936 route, rather than any of the following variations, is the quick and easy solution: from the point where the Second Ledge meets the north ridge, one can contour easily around the mountain to the Upper Saddle. From the north ridge, a short, ice-filled gully must be crossed just west of the ridge (more properly called a "corner") in order to reach the main, broad ledge leading around the west face of the Grand Teton. Follow the ledge to the Great West Chimney, where a few moves around the outside of a chockstone lead down (about 4.5m) into and across the chimney to the Crawl of the Owen-Spalding route *(Route 1)*. It is now possible to descend to the Lower Saddle from this point. To return to the Teton Glacier or to Surprise Lake to pack up camp, follow the Black Dike Traverse along the south side of the Grand Teton (see *Glacier Gulch* in Section 7), though this may involve some steep snow in crossing the Stettner Couloir, descending the Teepe Glacier, and descending from Dike Col to the Teton Glacier. To return to Surprise Lake from the vicinity of the Teton Glacier, climb back up along the traditional route to Amphitheater Lake and continue down the trail to Surprise Lake. **Time (with the Direct Finish):** 8 to 11½ hours from the upper Teton Glacier; 10½ to 13½ hours from Amphitheater Lake. See *American Alpine Journal* 3, no. 1 (1937): pp. 105–6; *Appalachia* 21, no. 2 (December 1936): p. 268; 21, no. 3 (June 1937): pp. 425–26, illus.; *Dartmouth Mountaineering Club Journal*, 1961: pp. 40–48, illus.

Variation: IV, 5.6. First ascent August 14, 1941, by Paul and Bernice Petzoldt, Glenn Exum, and Hans Kraus. Instead of going all the way out to the west end of the First Ledge, climb straight up the snow on this ledge and start working up the broken rock leading to the left (east) end of the Second Ledge. This is the easiest method of reaching the Second Ledge.

Variation: IV, 5.7, A1, or IV, 5.8. First ascent August 13, 1949, by Richard Pownall, Ray Garner, and Art Gilkey; first free ascent July 24, 1953, by Richard Emerson, Willi Unsoeld, and Leigh Ortenburger (with the Direct Finish, below). This direct variation ascends the upper portion of the north face, through the famous Pendulum Pitch above the Third Ledge, and is detailed in the main route description. See *American Alpine Journal* 8, no. 1 (1951): pp.

61–70; *University of Wyoming Outing Club Journal,* 1959–1960: pp. 64–70, illus.

Variation: **DIRECT FINISH.** IV, 5.8. First ascent July 24, 1953, by Richard Emerson, Willi Unsoeld, and Leigh Ortenburger. This variation is detailed in the main route description, above; it leads into the V-shaped gully at the very top of the face. At the end of the 37m lead up the Fourth Ledge, traverse back to the left (east) and then turn upward in a small right-facing corner. At this point one is only about 9m west of the bottom of the "V". Make a delicate friction traverse across a 75° face in order to finish the climb. Once in the gully, scramble up blocks and chimneys to the summit. See *American Alpine Journal,* 1954: pp. 172–84, illus.; *Dartmouth Mountaineering Club Journal,* 1958: pp. 17, 47, illus.; *Sierra Club Bulletin* 39, no. 6 (June 1954): pp. 27–33.

Variation: IV, 5.7. First ascent July 9, 1954, by William Buckingham and Fred Ford. It is possible to reach the north ridge (see *Route 47*) by traversing out on the Third Ledge. Near the ridge this ledge inverts and becomes a horizontal chimney just large enough to crawl along. It is necessary to pass on the outside of a boulder in this chimney, where the exposure is considerable.

Variation: IV, 5.7. First ascent August 24, 1955, by Willi Unsoeld and Frank Ewing. Reach the Second Ledge from the First Ledge via the 1941 variation. From a point just above the lower of two snowfields, which remain on the Second Ledge throughout most of the summer (this point can also be identified as being directly above the west end of the First Ledge), climb the deep chimney that forms the extreme left (east) end of the Third Ledge. This chimney soon turns up to the right to join the main portion of the Third Ledge.

Variation: IV, 5.8, A2. First ascent September 2, 1955, by Willi and Jolene Unsoeld. This is the only known alternative to Richard Pownall's Pendulum Pitch for reaching the Fourth Ledge from the Third. The eastern extension of the Fourth Ledge has the same property as the western extension of the Third Ledge—it inverts, becoming a ceiling instead of a ledge. There are three such inversions on this variation. When the Third Ledge is reached, cross it instead of walking out to the right (west). A very steep and difficult pitch

Jack Tackle on the Pendulum Pitch during the first winter ascent of the Direct North Face (Photo by Alex Lowe)

leads to the Fourth Ledge at a point about 4.5m to the right (west) of the first large inversion. After 12m the Fourth Ledge terminates in an abrupt wall; the ledge is reduced to a sharply ascending crack in an otherwise smooth wall. This difficult crack was climbed by the use of an aid sling as a foothold for a long upward step across a smooth section. The two inversions in the remaining 46m leading to the intersection of the Pendulum Pitch and the Fourth Ledge are passed by very delicate traverses out on the face proper. See *American Alpine Journal* 10, no. 1 (1956): pp. 116–19.

Variation: **UPPER SADDLE START.** III, 5.8. First ascent July 31, 1960, by Bill Echo, John Waage, Keith Staley, and Dean Millsap. This enterprising party accessed the Direct Finish of the North Face route from a standard camp on the Lower Saddle. Follow the Owen-Spalding route to the Upper Saddle (see *Route 1*) and take the ledge system all the way out to the north ridge from the Crawl. Small difficulties will be met in crossing the Great West Chimney and in passing the final icy gully just before reaching the north corner at the end of the Second Ledge. From the west end of the Second Ledge, two large dihedrals about 24m apart, leading up to the west end of the Third Ledge, will be seen above. Climb the shallow, black-rock chimney (5.7, 27m) that lies between these two dihedrals. Once on the Third Ledge, traverse about 6m back to the left (east) to the base of the Pendulum Pitch and join the upper North Face route at this point.

Variation: **NORTH RIDGE START.** IV, 5.8. First ascent August 11, 1976, by Jim Donini, Rick Black, and Michael Cole (using the original 1931 North Ridge route *[Route 47]*), and July 20, 1977, by George Montopoli and Ralph Baldwin (using the Italian Cracks variation, which was named by this party). The difficult climbing of the 1953 North Face route with the Direct Finish can be effectively doubled by the devious method of using one of the North Ridge variations to gain the Second Ledge. Both first-ascent parties gained access to the Grandstand by way of the Valhalla Traverse from the Lower Saddle, which is discussed in *Route 47.* In addition to increasing the magnitude of either route, this variation bypasses the rockfall-prone portions of the standard North Face route below the First Ledge. This advantage is offset, however, by the alpine nature of the Valhalla Traverse as well as the effect climate change has had on it. Upon reaching the point on the Second Ledge where the North Ridge route's Slab Pitch emerges, one can gain the Third Ledge by climbing the black-rock area mentioned in the Upper Saddle Start variation, above.

ROUTE 44. GOLDEN PILLAR. V, 5.12-. First ascent July 11, 2003, by Greg Collins and Hans Johnstone; the two started working on the route in 2002, and at the time of this writing, it has had just a couple of ascents. (See *Figures 4-35*, *4-38*, and *4-39*.) Established by an indomitable pair of local alpinists, this modern Teton classic continues the tradition of talented locals putting up cutting-edge routes. Purity of line, exceptional rock quality, and difficult rock climbing characterize this beautiful route. Depending on the year, getting across the bergschrund and onto the Grandstand can be very difficult. Once onto the lower Grandstand, stay close in to the wall and scramble up to a point directly below the west end of the First Ledge, high above. The first pitch will vary according to the time of year and the extent of snow on the Grandstand, but scrambling will lead up to a belay beneath the Golden Pillar—a distinctive section of golden rock.

Pitch 1: Climb up and right and then back left to a belay with a fixed pin at the base of a long gold crack (5.7, 20m). **Pitch 2 (Golden Pillar Pitch):** Ascend the beautiful crack via a strenuous lieback (fixed Z piton) and sustained jamming to a belay on a good ledge (5.11c, 48m). **Pitch 3:** Climb a crack above the belay, step left onto a slab, and set a belay below the roof crack (5.10b). **Pitch 4 (Roof Pitch):** Go through the roof via a fist crack, then jam through a crack to the First Ledge (5.12-, 46m). **Pitches 5–6:** Continue up the North Face route *(Route 43)* to the Second Ledge (5.7) and then up 3rd- and 4th-class terrain to the Third Ledge. Belay below a steep left-facing corner about 40m east of the Pendulum Pitch on the North Face route; some fixed pins should be visible in this corner. Two more difficult pitches remain at this point. **Pitch 7 (Rugged Prima Donna Pitch):** Climb a 5.9R face up to the steep left-facing corner, the Rugged Prima Donna, and climb it up to the lower (east) end of the Fourth Ledge to a belay on a ledge with two fixed pins. Two Lost Arrow and two knifeblade pitons are suggested to protect this pitch. **Pitch 8 (Boulder Problem Pitch):** This final difficult pitch ascends a thin corner on small crimps and then perfect finger locks and ends with steep stemming and wild jamming (5.12-). Fourth- and 5th-class climbing (5.8) then leads to the summit of the Grand Teton. **Gear:** For protection take two full sets of cams from micro to 4", including half sizes, and a set of nuts with several of the larger sizes. In addition, bring at least six pitons including two Lost Arrows, two knifeblades, and two baby angles. The first-ascent party also suggests crampons, helmets, tape, and "plenty of chalk!" A 60m rope will be adequate for the climb and the rappel along the descent to the Upper Saddle.

FIGURE 4-38. Grand Teton, north aspect, Golden Pillar *(Route 44)*, V, 5.12-

ROUTE 45. MEDRICK-ORTENBURGER. IV, 5.8, A2. First ascent August 14–15, 1963, by Rick Medrick and Leigh Ortenburger. (See *Figure 4-35* for an approximate route line.) This major route of 10 pitches avoids the First Ledge completely by ascending the face directly to the middle of the Second Ledge. Below the western half of the Second Ledge, there are three huge, parallel chimney systems. This route ascends the easternmost of the three; the American Cracks route *(Route 46)* ascends the westernmost chimney. From the upper glacier above the icefall, climb onto the slabs of the Grandstand as in *Route 47*, staying near the wall on the south edge. Approximately halfway to the top of the Grandstand, a small buttress forces one away from the wall. This route begins at the top of this buttress, which is gained from the right (north). The first ropelength leads back slightly to the left (east) over somewhat rotten rock to a prominent black cave, usually wet. The second lead traverses left (east) from this cave, past some loose gray rocks and around a corner to the beginning of a large shelf that angles steeply up and back to the right. Climb this shelf for about 15m, then head out to the right edge and go up a short, vertical wall (5.8) to the end of this 46m lead. The next pitch continues up and right on good rock over two overhangs (5.6 and 5.7). The fourth pitch angles back to the left toward a wet, narrow chimney leading toward the base of two of the huge chimneys already mentioned—the eastern one and the central one. This 24m pitch past loose, yellow blocks perched on the ledges is unpleasant. Go another 18m. Just short of the wet, narrow chimney turn up and right onto a large shelf that angles up to the right; this shelf more or less parallels the first such shelf mentioned above.

Proceed about 9m up this shelf, climb an A2 crack in the 6m wall directly above the shelf, then continue back to the left (east) to the start of a clearly defined 15m chimney containing ice and loose flakes. From this point it is possible to reach either the eastern or central huge chimney. Climb the 15m chimney, past loose rocks that are a hazard to the belayer, to the eastern chimney. Considerable ice was found in the bottom of this chimney during the first ascent, making crampons useful here. Alternatively, this eighth lead can be made on rock on the left (east) side of the chimney. Aid was used here to reach a belay point about 9m below the first major chockstone. The ninth pitch attacks the right-hand wall of the chimney (wet, slabby). An incredible flake with no visible means of support hangs on the upper part of this pitch. This flake may last for many ascents if climbers are careful not to dislodge it. From the belay position, climb an A1 crack on the left edge of this slab/wall and step across to the lower end of the flake. Climb to the top of this flake, then across to the right onto the wall itself. An adequate belay position out of the confines of the chimney will be found 6m above.

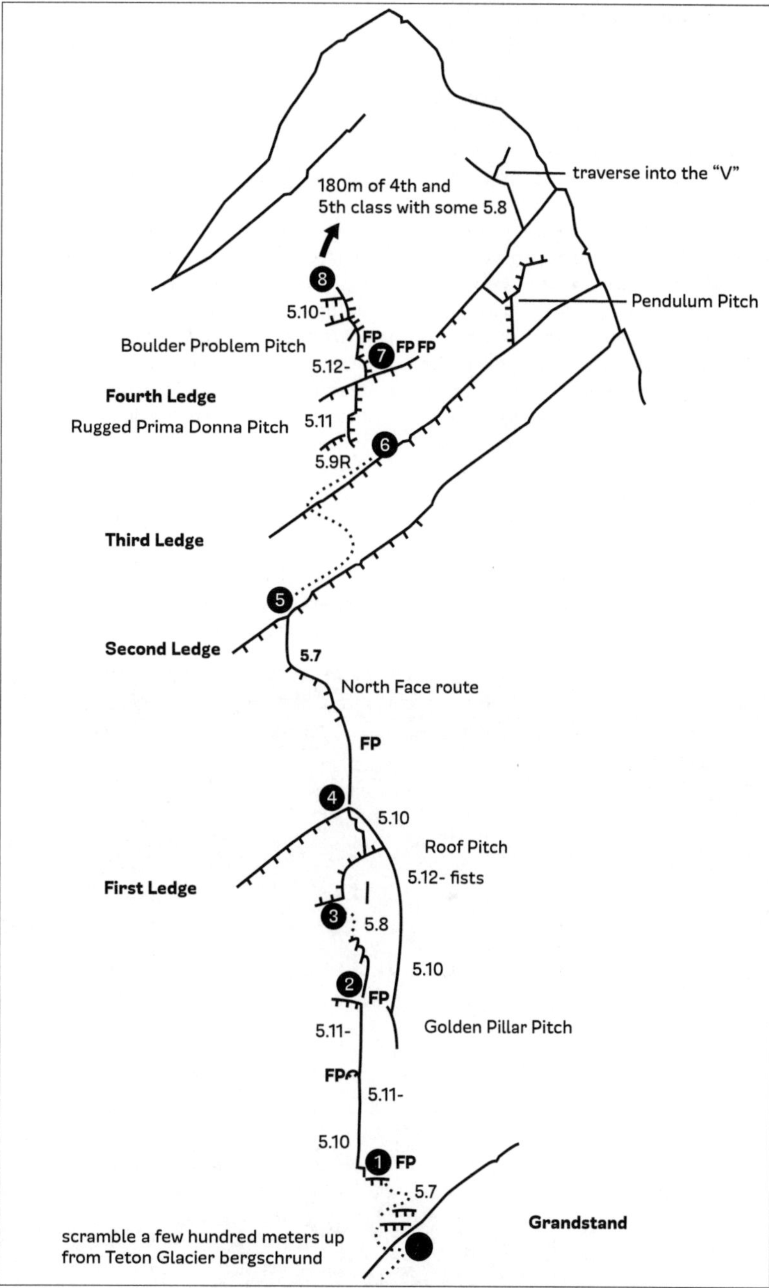

FIGURE 4-39. Grand Teton, north aspect, Golden Pillar *(Route 44)*, V, 5.12-

The last lead is long (46m) and ascends easier rock slightly back to the left to the Second Ledge of the standard North Face route *(Route 43)*, which is followed to the summit. This approach to the Second Ledge is considerably more direct than the standard route and approximately doubles the difficult climbing. Much loose rock must be passed in the course of the climb. When combined with the Direct Finish—the Pendulum Pitch and the traverse into the "V"—this is one of the more difficult routes on the Grand Teton. See *American Alpine Journal* 14, no. 1 (1964): pp. 186–88, illus.

ROUTE 46. AMERICAN CRACKS. IV, 5.9. Attempted on July 7, 1988, by Mike Colacino and Calvin Hebert; first complete ascent July 14, 1988, by Mike Colacino and Jim Earl (to Second Ledge). Colacino and Earl attempted to push the route higher, up to the Fourth Ledge, but this was not successful. (See *Figures 4-35* and *4-40.*) This route provides a more difficult way to reach the Second Ledge from the Grandstand and explores a crack system parallel to but east of its neighbor, the Italian Cracks variation (see *Route 47*). **Pitch 1:** Begin with the first pitch of the the regular North Ridge route *(Route 47)*. From behind the large block 6m above the top of the Grandstand, climb up and east past an old fixed pin (5.7) and proceed east to where *Route 47* continues up a the gully to the right (south). Belay here. **Pitch 2:** Instead of going up the gully, drop down on another ledge system from the belay point and make a traverse horizontally left for 30m on a 4th-class ledge. Belay from a ramp leading up and right from the end of this traverse. **Pitch 3:** The next lead is short but difficult, starting directly up a right-facing corner (5.8) below a hanging flake to get into the 5.9 crack (wide hands) above; after 21m reach a good belay. **Pitch 4:** Continue 30m up the same crack system (5.7 hands) to a huge ledge (with block)—the same ledge from which the Italian Cracks variation starts, only a few meters to the right (west); move down and east a short distance to a corner and belay. **Pitch 5:** Climb the corner (5.7) and belay on the next ledge. **Pitch 6:** The next long lead (5.9), the crux of this route, is a large chimney that curves slightly to the right; this is the westernmost of the three chimneys described under *Route 45*. Halfway up this difficult chimney is a set of platelike chockstones that must be passed. **Pitch 7:** From the belay at the top of the chimney, head up and then back left to emerge onto the Second Ledge. Follow this out to the north ridge and rejoin *Route 47*.

Figure 4-40. Grand Teton, north aspect, American Cracks *(Route 46)*, IV, 5.9

ROUTE 47. NORTH RIDGE. IV, 5.8+. First ascent July 19, 1931, by Robert Underhill and Fritiof Fryxell; first free ascent August 30, 1936, by Fritz Wiessner, William House, Percy Olton, and Beckett Howorth; first descent of upper half July 6, 1933, by Paul Petzoldt and Sterling Hendricks (summit to Second Ledge); first descent of lower half September 3, 1955, by Willi and Jolene Unsoeld (Second Ledge to the Teton Glacier); first winter ascent March 20–22, 1975, by Dave Carman and George Lowe. (See *Figures 4-35* and *4-41.*) Even though it was pioneered nearly eight decades ago, the North Ridge of the Grand Teton remains today one of the great mountaineering routes in the range, a tribute to the vision and skill of the first-ascent party. It stands as an enduring classic—a touchstone for generations of Teton climbers. This alpine route, which averages over 63° for 360m, is better described as the intersection of two high-angle faces than as a ridge; a more accurate name, preferred by Fryxell, would be the "North Corner."

The old standard approach via the Teton Glacier from the east is a mountaineering task, replete with routefinding issues and noticeable danger from rockfall off the face above. In some years passage from the bergschrund onto the rock presents a substantial problem. Even the climb up to the top of the Grandstand is not trivial. The ridge above is impressive, and the famous Chockstone Chimney is challenging even by today's standards. Opinions vary widely as to its technical difficulty, from the classic Teton sandbag 5.7 all the way to 5.10- (it was first free climbed by Fritz Wiessner in 1936). In bad or even slightly bad weather, the Chockstone Chimney pitch and the two above it are serious endeavors. The North Ridge is not a climb to be undertaken in unfavorable conditions. When the Slab Pitch on the very corner of the ridge is covered with verglas, it can be nearly impossible without crampons.

History: At the time of its first ascent in 1931, with a rating of IV, 5.7, A0, the North Ridge of the Grand Teton was perhaps the most difficult climb in the country. It had previously been considered impossible, but Robert Underhill's solo reconnaissance of the route in 1930 led him to believe it was worth a try. His and Fritiof Fryxell's gear was primitive by today's standards: Underhill wore nailed

FIGURE 4-41. Grand Teton, North Ridge *(Route 47)*, IV, 5.8+

boots and Fryxell had the impediment of leather-soled work boots. These pioneers earned their accolades. See *The Golden Age* in the History chapter for the story of their climb and how it got its initial 5.7, A0 rating.

On August 30, 1936, the route was repeated by Fritz Wiessner, William House, Percy Olton, and Beckett Howorth. Wiessner free climbed the Chockstone Chimney on his second attempt "by spreading across in front of it and edging up and over the sloping outer margin"[2]

The first winter ascent of the route by George Lowe and Dave Carman, although technically done outside the "official" winter season (December 20–March 20), was made during a nearly continuous storm that effectively shut down the neighboring Jackson Hole Mountain Resort. Carman's description from the top of the infamous Slab Pitch conveys the wildness of their undertaking:

> *It couldn't have been a much crazier situation. I was straddling a saddle of rock on the edge of a steep slab, some two thousand feet above the canyons, in the middle of a winter storm. I'd arrived there with just a couple of pitons left on my rack and only one that fit. So I anchored the fixed rope to myself, as well, in order to hold some of the load on my waist. My stance was good, and the weight wouldn't really be much, or critical, until George got close and there were no more pitons between us. In the meantime, I leaned back against the mountain, duvet drawn snug around my head. My right leg dangled over the North Face, and my left pointed into Valhalla Canyon. I couldn't see the vast space around me and below me, but I could sense it, and I was happy.* This is OK, *I thought.* Hell, this is more than OK; this is great!
>
> —Dave Carman, "Good Medicine," *Alpinist* 33 (Winter 2010–11), p. 48

Strategy: There are four ways to approach the top of the Grandstand, from which the upper technical portion of the North Ridge route can be climbed: (1) via the original, classic approach from the Teton Glacier onto and up the east face of the Grandstand; (2) from the west side of the Grandstand, either from Valhalla Canyon or by way of the Lower Saddle and the Valhalla Traverse; (3) by way of Gunsight Notch as part of the Cathedral Traverse or the Grand Traverse (this alternative is especially popular with those parties who go on to climb the Italian Cracks variation); and (4) by rappelling from the Second Ledge after traversing out across the upper west face from the Upper Saddle—a somewhat irregular and impure method that has become popular to the point of rappel anchors being established in the vicinity of where the Slab Pitch tops out on the Second Ledge.

The original approach, described below, is directly up from the east, up the Teton Glacier and then onto the east ledges and slabs of the Grandstand. While this option is very scenic, expect some danger from rockfall from the north face. For those who wish to bivouac on the climb, there

2. Fritiof Fryxell, *Mountaineering in the Tetons: The Pioneer Period 1898–1940*, edited by Phil Smith.

are a few spots right near the top of the Grandstand, but it is often quite windy at this exposed location.

Route Description: Proceed to the Teton Glacier (see *Glacier Gulch* in Section 7) and climb to the upper glacier, passing the crevassed section on the right (north). Cross the bergschrund—or *randkluft*, as the case may be—somewhere near the bottom corner of the north face and the Grandstand. The difficulty of getting started up the Grandstand varies with the year and the snow conditions; in some years this will be a challenging and time-consuming proposition. There is some danger from falling rocks during the ascent of the Grandstand. Climb to the top of the Grandstand, either next to the wall on the left (south) edge or via a zigzag on ledges farther out on the Grandstand.

See *Figure 4-41* for the details of this classic route above the Grandstand. From the top of the Grandstand proceed up and south to a large block for the first belay. Climb behind the block and then out and left (5.7) past an old fixed pin on steep rock

A climber emerges from the top of the Chockstone Chimney pitch during an ascent of the Grand Teton's North Ridge route. (Photo by Renny Jackson)

for 6m or so. Continue angling up and left to a steep gully and belay. Ascend the gully and belay again just below an abrupt step. The next short pitch continues up and right over steep black rock (5.7) to the belay at the base of the famous Chockstone Chimney. The final portion of this lead often involves climbing a small ice sheet to the bottom of the chimney. Climb up the first part of the pitch on gradually steepening rock until it is possible to swing into the subsidiary chimney on the left (5.8+) and then gain the top of the main chockstone. One can also climb up and over the chockstone using hand jams and then stem across to the opposite wall (5.8+). The next lead, an enjoyable large chimney (5.7) in an area of black rock, brings one to the 24m Slab Pitch. This Slab Pitch can be extremely difficult when coated with ice, so consider weather conditions carefully before attempting this climb.

Climb up and then to the left across the slab (5.7) to the very exposed corner of the ridge and then continue up and right to the west side of the ridge. This point marks the west end of the Second Ledge of the north face. From here there are three ways to finish the climb: (1) Two obvious chimneys of moderate difficulty lead up just to the right (west) of the ridge crest to a point where the Fourth Ledge on the north face joins the north ridge. If this alternative (the most direct) is chosen, the remaining fairly difficult pitch ascends an 8m face just to the right of the crest. Above this pitch, easy scrambling leads to the summit. (2) One can avoid the upper ridge by traversing right (south) toward the Great West Chimney and from there scrambling quickly to the summit via the Owen-Spalding route (*Route 1*). (3) If it is late or the weather is bad, a fast descent can be made without going to the summit, by making a traverse almost horizontally south all the way over to the Owen-Spalding route and then reversing the Crawl and the Belly Roll to get to the Upper Saddle.

The classic North Ridge route can also be expanded in a major way by combining it with the Direct Finish to the North Face (see *Route 43*), adding a great finish to what is already an outstanding route; this is described under the 1976 North Ridge Start variation of *Route 43*. If the original North Ridge is not in good condition due to recent precipitation, the 1971 Italian Cracks variation, described below, is an excellent alternative to the chimneys of the standard route, because they are less of a major drainage and are generally drier. **Time:** 12 to 13½ hours from Amphitheater Lake. See *American Alpine Journal* 1, no. 4 (1932): pp. 465–69, illus.; 9, no. 1 (1954): pp. 172–84, illus.; *Appalachia*, 21, no. 2 (December 1936): pp. 216–24, illus.; *Canadian Alpine Journal*, 1931: pp. 72–86, illus.; *Harvard Mountaineering* 16 (May 1963): pp. 82–83; *Trail and Timberline*, no. 354 (June 1948): pp. 79–83, illus.

Variation: **EAST GUNSIGHT APPROACH.** IV, 5.8, A1. First ascent on about August 22, 1936, by Fritz Wiessner, Paul Petzoldt, Brad Gilman, Beckett Howorth, William House, and Elizabeth Woolsey. Instead of gaining the Grandstand at its base, this party attempted to reach Gunsight Notch directly from the east, via the gully from the upper Teton Glacier. About 60m above the upper glacier the gully is blocked by an enormous chockstone, which required a three-person shoulder stand—Woolsey on Wiessner on House—to pass. "At one point we made a triple courte echelle to get over a chockstone," Woolsey later wrote. "I stood on Fritz's shoulders who was standing on Bill's shoulders. As Fritz was wearing boots studded with tricouni nails, this was an uncomfortable few minutes for Bill." The rock above the chockstone became looser, wetter, and steeper until the gully narrowed to a width of about a meter and 10m of vertical ice was encountered. At this point they made a delicate traverse left across the south wall of the gully and around the corner onto the Grandstand, where two difficult chimneys were then climbed. The top of the Grandstand was then easily reached. (Source: Elizabeth D. Woolsey, *Off the Beaten Track* [Wilson, WY: Wilson Bench Press, 1984])

Variation: **WEST GUNSIGHT APPROACH.** IV, 5.8. First ascent August 6, 1940, by Jack Durrance, Henry Coulter, Merrill McLane, and Chap Cranmer. The top of the Grandstand can be reached by first ascending the West Gunsight Couloir out of Valhalla Canyon (see *Valhalla Canyon*) and then climbing up and left (southeast) out of Gunsight Notch to gain the Grandstand, which is then followed up to its top. Apparently, this party encountered difficult, rotten rock directly up from the south side of the notch.

If one is traversing to the Grand Teton from Mount Owen, the top of the Grandstand can be gained using a different and better option out of Gunsight Notch. From the notch climb down to the left (east) on ledges for about 30m to the base of a crack system that leans slightly to the right, leading to a small notch. Ascend this crack (5.7) for 24m on excellent rock up to the notch. Scramble for 120m to the top of the Grandstand.

***Variation:* VALHALLA APPROACH.** IV, 5.8. First ascent July 31, 1960, by Jake Breitenbach, Pete Sinclair, Leigh Ortenburger, and Irene Beardsley (Ortenburger). The top of the Grandstand can be reached directly from Valhalla Canyon or, in combination with the Valhalla Traverse, from the Lower Saddle (see *Valhalla Canyon* and *Figure 4-47*). Although it misses the alpine aspect of glacier travel involved in the standard eastern approach, climbing in the upper Valhalla drainage with the imposing west face of the Grand looming above is certainly a worthwhile alternative.

From Valhalla Canyon it is possible to see that the First Shelf of the West Face route *(Route 50)* leads directly to the top of the Grandstand. If starting from Valhalla, proceed as in *Route 50* toward the wall protecting access to the Second Shelf. The aim here is to get to the lower (west) end of the First Shelf. Most often, when conditions are the driest, this will require climbing a pitch of rock that is at least wet and about 5.6 in difficulty. This pitch is in an area of black rock. The amount and difficulty of ice and wet rock encountered on the shelf proper will depend on the year and the season; an ice axe is commonly required. In early season crampons will be useful, if not completely necessary. Climb eastward up the shelf, staying well out to the left (north) on the dry rock. With good routefinding, little more than scrambling is required to attain the top of the Grandstand. Some loose rock will be encountered, but there is little danger from falling rock once past the area below the Black Ice Couloir (see *Route 51*).

If the Valhalla Traverse from the Lower Saddle is used, one will climb down the ramp shown in *Figure 4-47* (snow-covered in early season; wet and littered with loose rock later on), exit the traverse ledge beneath the shelves of the west face, and then cross the snow/icefield to reach the west end of the First Shelf. This is a very efficient approach to the North Ridge route, though it is fraught with its own hazards. See *American Alpine Journal* 12, no. 2 (1961): pp. 373–77.

***Variation:* ITALIAN CRACKS.** IV, 5.7/8. First ascent August 19, 1971, by Howard Friedman and Peter Wollan. (See *Figures 4-35* and *4-42*.) This important variation of the original North Ridge route lies around the corner and out on the north face, providing an excellent alternative to the famous Chockstone Chimney pitch. It is easier than the classic ridge and hence is the most commonly used route for Grand Traverse climbers (see Section 5). It has a completely different character than the North Ridge route since it consists of crack climbing out on the face rather than in a deep, shady chimney system.

Climb the first pitch of the original route up from the top of the Grandstand and belay where convenient in the easy gully. For the second pitch continue up the gully until the first obvious ledge system leading left (east) appears. Traverse out east on the ledge (feels exposed) to a point where the blackish rock turns white and set up a belay beneath a short crack

FIGURE 4-42. Grand Teton, North Ridge *(Route 47)*, variation: Italian Cracks, IV, 5.7/5.8

A climbing ranger on a mountain patrol following the crux sixth pitch of the Grand's West Face route (Photo by Vic Zeilman)

leading upward. Climb the crack (5.6, 5m) and then walk left on a ledge until it is possible to climb up and right to a corner; go up the corner (5.7) to a short 5.8 exit. Climb up another 5m to a black, commonly wet alcove. For the fifth pitch climb the roof out of the alcove (5.8 stem) and continue up 7m–10m where left-trending face climbing leads to a short corner that trends back slightly right. Continue up (5.7–5.8) toward the Second Ledge and belay where convenient. An easier alternative for this pitch climbs out and to the east from the alcove, into and out of a gully and then up to intersect the Second Ledge at a slightly lower point. Traverse right on the ledge to rejoin the standard North Ridge route at the exposed corner of the ridge. From here nearly everyone traverses over to the Owen-Spalding route *(Route 1)* to get to the summit of the Grand. *Figure 4-42* also shows the original North Ridge finish.

Variation: **CHOCKSTONE BYPASS.** IV, 5.7. First ascent August 10, 1974, by Jim McCarthy and Gerald Barnard. This variation bypasses the famous chockstone of the classic North Ridge route. From the belay point at the base of the Chockstone Chimney, traverse right 15m, stepping around a corner, to a large ledge below a steep 30m wall. Climb straight up from this ledge, first on blocks and then via face climbing, to a short, curving 5.7 crack leading onto a slab. At the top of this lead the slab gives access to a ledge that can be taken back left (east) to rejoin the standard route, above the chockstone.

Variation: **ODETTE-SHERNER.** IV, 5.10+. First ascent August 7, 1994, by Chuck Odette and Jim Sherner. This variation of three pitches ascends the dark crack system between the classic North Ridge route and the Italian Cracks variation. The first pitch is 5.10 in difficulty; the second is 5.10+; and the third is 5.8–5.9. The second pitch was described as being "loose and dangerous" with a "huge death-flake on it."

Grand Teton, West Face Climbs

Because of its aspect, relative remoteness, and size, the west face of the Grand Teton offers some of the most difficult alpine routes in the entire range. The region that is situated between the Grand Teton's north and northwest ridges is as mysterious as it is huge, the face being nearly 900m in height. It beckons the alpinist from far below in Cascade Canyon and it sits proudly at the head of the impressive Valhalla Canyon. See *Figure 4-43* for an overview of this facet of the peak. The west face was first approached by walking up Cascade Canyon for 4 miles before turning south to begin the steep climb into Valhalla Canyon. After the discovery of the Valhalla Traverse, which provides access from Garnet Canyon and the Lower Saddle, that became the preferred method of reaching all the climbs on this side of the Grand Teton. Climate change has negatively affected the traverse, like many other areas in the Tetons, but for a number of reasons it remains the recommended approach for several of these climbs, especially during early season. Expect loose rock, exposure, and mixed-terrain challenges on this traverse. See *Valhalla Canyon* and *Figure 4-47* for details of both approaches.

The West Face route *(Route 50)*, one of the greatest of the early Teton climbs, was pioneered in 1940 by the

outstanding team of Jack Durrance and Henry "Hank" Coulter. As with the other major lines, several variations are available. Alternative methods of passing the upper chimney problems have been found, but some seem largely to provide escape routes, such as to the Owen-Spalding route *(Route 1)* or to the Upper Saddle. A significant exception is Alberich's Alley (see *Route 51*), the difficult rock-and-ice chute to the south of the main West Face line. The foremost variation, however, starts the West Face climb with the lower section of the Black Ice Couloir *(Route 51)*, thus upgrading an already major route into the upper realm of Teton alpine climbs. While the normal West Face route does involve some ice, especially on the lower shelves, the lengthy initial ice of this variation dominates the climb and changes its character from one requiring mostly rock skills to one demanding extended competence on both rock and ice.

Other completely independent climbs of equal stature have been worked out near the north end of the west face. The first of these, and the second route on the Grand Teton out of Valhalla Canyon, was the huge Northwest Chimney *(Route 49)*, which ascends one of the most conspicuous features of this side of the mountain. David Dornan, Leigh Ortenburger, and Irene Beardsley (Ortenburger) followed the same initial approach as for the West Face, then climbed the wall guarding the chimney base and were soon enmeshed in its difficulties—including, as with the best of these alpine routes, a length of ice. The depth of this chimney combined with its aspect seems to imply that its inner portions have never seen the rays of the sun. It is indeed one of the coldest climbs on the mountain, so be prepared. The major West Face Finish variation of this route, first climbed by Royal Robbins, Joe Fitschen, and Yvon Chouinard only nine days after the 1960 first ascent, combines the most difficult parts of the Northwest Chimney route with those of the West Face route, creating a climb of exceptional proportions.

Then in 1980, Renny Jackson and Tom Kimbrough added the Black Ice Couloir start to the combination Northwest Chimney and West Face climb (see the Jackson-Kimbrough Contortion variation of *Route 49*). By taking the ice to the base of the upper West Face route, then downclimbing the Rotten Yellow Chimney to the base of the Northwest Chimney route, the pair created a formidable Teton alpine climb.

The last line worked out, Loki's Tower *(Route 48)*, is at the far north edge of the west face, on the massive buttress between the north ridge and the northwest chimney. Involving vertical and at times unprotected rock leads up solid Teton rock with very few cracks and weaknesses, this extreme route is perhaps the most difficult of these west face climbs. The line ascended is certainly improbable to the untrained eye.

FIGURE 4-43. Grand Teton, west aspect, overview of west face routes

FIGURE 4-44. Grand Teton, west aspect. (A) Loki's Tower *(Route 48)*, IV, 5.9+; (B) Variation: 1984, IV, 5.9+

ROUTE 48. LOKI'S TOWER. IV, 5.9+. First ascent August 2, 1981, by Mark Whiton and Michael Stern. (See *Figure 4-44.*) This improbable route was discovered on the massive buttress between the north ridge and the northwest chimney. The buttress itself is composed of solid Teton rock with very few cracks and weaknesses; routefinding is difficult on this somewhat featureless formation. From the Lower Saddle use the standard Valhalla Traverse Ledge to gain the lowest of the three shelves leading up and onto the west face of the Grandstand (see *Figure 4-47*). This route begins at the top of this First Shelf with two pitches of climbing (5.6) to the left (north) of the ramp that leads to the crux pitch of the Northwest Chimney route *(Route 49)*. The third lead passes a small overhang up into a corner with a 5.8 hand crack, followed by a 5.9 right-facing shallow corner, from the top of which face climbing leads left onto a belay ledge. The next difficult lead—the crux pitch of the route, with only marginal protection—involves steep and delicate face climbing (5.9+) followed by a vertical straight-in corner (5.9). A pitch of strenuous face climbing (5.9) past two small overhangs follows. The sixth lead goes up and somewhat right to a belay at a ledge that is below and to the right (west) of the base of the Chockstone Chimney of the North Ridge route *(Route 47)*. The final lead (5.7) of this route goes directly up, via face climbing and cracks, to the top of the tower or buttress. From this point the Northwest Chimney route is joined at the exit from the Black Rock Bowl. The icy upper cracks/chimneys of that route are

FIGURE 4-45. Grand Teton, west aspect. (A) Northwest Chimney *(Route 49)*, IV, 5.9; (B) Variation: Hummingbird Wall, IV, 5.10-; (C) Variation: West Face Finish, IV, 5.9

now climbed for two long pitches, leading upward to the extension of the Second Ledge of the north face.

Variation: IV, 5.9+. First ascent July 17, 1984, by Renny Jackson and Steve Rickert. (See *Figure 4-44*.) This variation of five pitches provides a distinct start to Loki's Tower and includes a spectacular traverse. Use the same approach as for the standard Loki's Tower route to gain the base of the tower or buttress. The first pitch begins to the right of the lower extension of the northwest chimney with a 5.9 mantel into a right-facing corner (5.8) that leads up to the belay near the chimney extension. Two ropelengths along the right side of the ramp (5.6) bring one to the ice of the northwest chimney immediately below the crux of *Route 49*. An unlikely exit to the left (north), up and across the blank-looking wall, is largely face climbing (5.9) on small holds followed by a difficult hand traverse to gain the ledge at the end of the crux pitch of the main Loki's Tower route. This is a spectacular lead, initially under a line of overhangs, on the best solid Teton rock.

ROUTE 49. NORTHWEST CHIMNEY. IV, 5.8, A1, or IV, 5.9. First ascent July 26, 1960, by David Dornan, Leigh Ortenburger, and Irene Beardsley (Ortenburger); first free ascent August 4, 1960, by Royal Robbins, Joe Fitschen, and Yvon Chouinard; attempted July 15, 1957, by Fred Ayres, Leigh Ortenburger, and Irene Beardsley (Ortenburger); first winter ascent December 21, 1991, by Alex Lowe and Renny Jackson. (See *Figure 4-45*.) This large chimney, lying between the north ridge and the Great West Chimney, is perhaps the most conspicuous feature of the Grand Teton when viewed from the northwest. Because of its orientation, this is a dark and cold climb where the sun is never seen. Crampons are useful because of the mixed nature of the climbing. This route can be combined with two other Valhalla climbs to create what is perhaps one of the finest of all the alpine routes in the Tetons: the Jackson-Kimbrough Contortion variation, described below. On the 1960 first ascent of the main Northwest Chimney route, this climb was approached from Cascade Canyon into Valhalla Canyon. The recommended, modern approach is the Valhalla Traverse Ledge from the Lower Saddle (see *Figure 4-47*)—provided one is familiar with it and the preferred campsite is the Lower Saddle.

Approach as for the West Face *(Route 50)* to the far (east) end of the Second Shelf. To the left of the Rotten Yellow Chimney (of the West Face route) two cracks can be seen in the massive section of rock that separates the end of this shelf from the bottom of the chimney proper. This route begins in the left-hand crack. Climb this wide crack (5.8), which often contains ice-cold running water. From the end of this first 37m lead, climb one more ropelength up somewhat easier steep slabs to a perch along the right side of the 12m-wide sheet of ice in the bottom of the chimney. Cross the ice to a spot suitable for belaying the next pitch, which goes directly up the nearly vertical beginning of the chimney proper. Aid was used originally on the first portion of this pitch; at little over a week after the first ascent, it went free at 5.9. Some loose rock will be encountered along this lead. Continue up difficult rock (a nasty 5.8 flared chimney) until above the large chockstone seen from below. Now climb 24m of ice above this chockstone to reach the steep section of the chimney above. A final lead past a 5.7 overhang ends where the chimney opens out into the Black Rock Bowl. With some difficulty a belay stance can be found in the bowl. Above this point the chimney overhangs and then disappears in the smooth west face so traverse left (north) in the black rock to a crack/chimney system (often containing ice) near the extreme left (north) edge of the west face. Two pitches directly up these cracks/chimneys top out on a wide scree bench that leads from the end of the Second Ledge of the north face all the way over to the Crawl of the Owen-Spalding route *(Route 1)*. The West Face route meets this same bench 46m to the right (south).

There are a few options from the bench to the summit. To finish the route via the North Ridge *(Route 47)*, go left (north) and continue up to the final two pitches of that route (5.7). This is perhaps the most logical extension of the Northwest Chimney route. It is also possible to follow this bench south past the Great West Chimney all the way over to the Double Chimney of the Owen-Spalding and finish the climb by that route. If time does not permit continuing to the summit of the Grand Teton and an escape is needed, this same scheme can be used to reach and then descend the initial portion of the Owen-Spalding route to the Upper Saddle. See *American Alpine Journal* 12, no. 2 (1961): pp. 373–77.

***Variation:* WEST FACE FINISH.** IV, 5.9. First ascent August 4, 1960, by Royal Robbins, Joe Fitschen, and Yvon Chouinard. (See *Figure 4-45.*) From the Black Rock Bowl traverse right, instead of left, and up to the flake at the beginning of the first of the two difficult pitches of the West Face route *(Route 50)*. Two leads of 5.7 face and crack climbing are involved to reach the flake. Use the West Face for the remainder of the ascent. This fine variation combines the most difficult portions of these two routes. See *Sierra Club Bulletin* 46, no. 8 (October 1961): pp. 53–54.

***Variation:* JACKSON-KIMBROUGH CONTORTION.** V, 5.9, AI3. First ascent August 9, 1980, by Renny Jackson and Tom Kimbrough. This devious variation combines parts of three routes to create an extended alpine climb. Begin by climbing the 1967 Black Ice–West Face Combination (see *Route 50*) to the base of the rock of the West Face route. Then invert the West Face approach by traversing left (north) along the upper edge of the ice to the top of the Rotten Yellow Chimney. Downclimb or rappel this chimney and traverse over to the beginning of the Northwest Chimney route. Climb the 1960 finish up the West Face (see above) that connects with the upper difficult portion of the West Face and finish the climb by that route. This combination produces the longest climb of all the variations on the west side of the Grand Teton.

***Variation:* HUMMINGBIRD WALL.** IV, 5.10-. First ascent in August 1990, by Beverly Boynton and Ted Kerasote. (See *Figure 4-45.*) This three-pitch variation likely ascends the right-hand of the two cracks mentioned at the beginning of *Route 49*. Starting at the base of the Rotten Yellow Chimney, the first pitch follows a 5.9 crack for 24m; pass an old fixed piton near the start. The second pitch, somewhat lichen covered, climbs a 5.10- hand and finger crack for 30m. From an alcove at the top of the second pitch, climb up and right over 5.9 and then 5.8 terrain to the large ledge that divides the west face into two sections. Join the regular West Face route *(Route 50)* and follow it to the summit.

ROUTE 50. WEST FACE. IV, 5.8. First ascent August 14, 1940, by Jack Durrance and Henry Coulter; first winter ascent February 19–24, 1972, by George Lowe and Jeff Lowe. (See *Figure 4-46.*) Like the North Ridge *(Route 47)*, this groundbreaking climb seems today to have been 10 or even 20 years ahead of its time, as it was the first time this great alpine face had been confronted by mountaineers. Jack Durrance and Henry "Hank" Coulter approached the climb by way of the mysterious hanging canyon that led to its base, to which they bestowed the name "Valhalla." The initial problem of this west wall of the Grand is the approach to its base, because the rock portion begins at the upper lip of the main section of the Black Ice Couloir *(Route 51)*. Durrance solved this via the Rotten Yellow Chimney, an interesting and not very solid feature of the mountain. The route attacks the center of the wall above, trying to follow the Great West Chimney, a major feature of the mountain. The West Face is a beautiful climb with continual interest. In early season, or after precipitation, the first pitches may be covered with verglas, making these leads truly desperate. Once on the summit, the climber feels the accomplishment of having gained a more complete understanding of this grand mountain.

History: Robert Underhill once remarked that the Great West Chimney "presented the most obvious and direct route to the summit" up the west face of the Grand Teton. When asked whether he was interested in establishing a route up the face, Underhill said that he "would leave it to some of the younger climbers." Dartmouth

College students Jack Durrance and Hank Coulter answered the call.

Durrance was uniquely positioned for this route, having scoped it out two years before during his climb with Michael Davis of the Northwest Ridge of the Enclosure *(The Enclosure, Route 5)*. Waiting for the driest conditions possible, Coulter and Durrance headed up Cascade Canyon on August 13, 1940, accompanied by five others who helped them carry loads and establish their first campsite in the pristine Vallhalla Canyon. The pair were away by 3:30 the following morning. They proceeded up the West Gunsight Couloir for about 120m before veering off to the south toward the imposing face, which towered nearly 900m above them.

They made their way over to the First Shelf, climbed one rock pitch, traversed east, and then climbed another rock pitch that provided access to the Second Shelf. Climbing quickly along this shelf, Durrance narrowly missed getting hit with a chunk of ice. At the upper end of the shelf they spent 20 minutes in their bivouac sack as a snow squall passed. Durrance then led up the Rotten Yellow Chimney and out across the top of the main icefield of what is now known as the Black Ice Couloir. Around noon they decided to press upward in what appeared to be the only reasonable break in the wall

FIGURE 4-46. Grand Teton, west aspect, West Face *(Route 50)*. (A) Variation: Black Ice–West Face Combination, IV, 5.8, AI3; (B) Variation: Neutron Burn, IV, 5.9+; (C) Variation: Tilley-Nicholson Traverse, IV, 5.9

above—a difficult crack (5.8) leading up from a large triangular flake. Nearby was the first of three battered hats that the pair found, dropped from above over the years by climbers on the Owen-Spalding route *(Route 1)*. Durrance had to use three pitons for protection on the pitch and they ended up hauling their packs. The modern climber is often impressed with the difficulty of this pitch, for it is frequently wet; the great alpinist Alex Lowe once took a fall while leading it!

Durrance and Coulter completed two additional pitches to reach the broad shelf that leads over toward the Upper Saddle and the base of the Great West Chimney. Three pitches up the left side of the chimney brought them to a ledge just below and north of the Owen-Spalding. The wall above was devoid of cracks. As Durrance prepared to climb the two crux pitches of the route, he glanced back at an exhausted Coulter on the ledge and found that he was sound asleep and snoring. In Coulter's words, he "was quickly restored by a tirade of highly abusive language." Durrance led off into a series of two mantels and then traversed south, where he set a belay and brought Coulter up. At this point Bob Bates, a member of the 1938 K2 expedition, appeared on the Owen-Spalding route above them; he saw that the traverse would go and would eventually lead up and onto the great chockstone at the top of the Great West Chimney. Durrance used several pitons for protection on this delicate pitch, which would prove to be the last difficult one on the route (5.8). It was 7:30 PM when they started up the left side of the continuation of the chimney, and they reached the summit 35 minutes later, just as darkness came. They then descended into Garnet Canyon in the moonlight and spent the night at the Dartmouth Mountaineering Club (DMC) campsite in the Meadows.

Strategy: Without a doubt, the best way to do this route is via the Black Ice–West Face Combination, first done by George Lowe and Mike Lowe in 1967 (see variation below). In the era of climate change, however, this strategy presumes that the Black Ice Couloir *(Route 51)* is in and has not melted out completely. For this combination one must also be familiar with the Valhalla Traverse from the Lower Saddle (see *Figure 4-47*). There are numerous advantages to doing the climb in this fashion: there is less exposure to rockfall; it is more direct, with the first 180m of the Black Ice Couloir leading directly to the start of the rock climbing on the West Face route; and it is possible to do the climb from a camp on the Lower Saddle, leaving bivouac gear, etc., and picking it up on the way down. If the climb is done in the classic fashion, using the Cascade Canyon–Valhalla Canyon approach, consider trying to go light and fast as a day climb from the valley floor to avoid having to pick up a camp in Valhalla at some later date. This latter strategy presumes that the climbing team is familiar with the crossing of Cascade Creek and the "trail" into Valhalla Canyon, and that they can find their way through these obstacles in the dark.

Route Description: From the upper reaches of Valhalla Canyon, three distinct diagonal shelves can be seen extending across the bottom part of the west face of the Grandstand. The initial climbing and routefinding task is to gain the upper (eastern) end of the Second Shelf, where the Rotten Yellow Chimney begins. Depending on the year and season, the climbing encountered getting to and up these shelves can include anything from pure ice to iced rock, wet rock, and on rare occasions, dry rock. The main route described below is appropriate when the Cascade Canyon–Valhalla Canyon approach is used. In recent years, however, the standard approach to this route has been from the Lower Saddle via the Valhalla Traverse Ledge to the lower end of the First Shelf (see *Figure 4-47*), at which point the original route is joined.

Climb partway up the snow couloir that descends from Gunsight Notch between Mount Owen and the Grand Teton. To the right (south) of the couloir is what appears from below to be a round-topped rock tower; it is, in fact, only a broad buttress extending in a northwest direction from the wide bench above. Exit from the snow couloir on an easy system of ledges leading around the left (northeast) side of this buttress. Continue up easy ledges and slabs, bearing slightly right (south) to connect with the black rock at the lower end of the three conspicuous shelves; this black rock, which can be seen from the floor of Valhalla Canyon, runs along the bottom of the first two shelves and affords a route from the First Shelf to the Second Shelf. Some routefinding skill will be useful here.

After gaining the Second Shelf, climb left (east) and up several ropelengths of wet friction slabs and ice patches to the upper end of the shelf. A second band of black rock connecting the Second and Third Shelves will be found here. From the east end of the Second Shelf, climb the Rotten Yellow Chimney leading south and up to the Third (uppermost) Shelf, which is actually the edge of the main icefield of the Black Ice Couloir (see *Route 51*). This brings one to a ledge at the top of

The last few moves of the Grand's West Face route with the Cascade Canyon visible far below (Photo by Renny Jackson)

this icefield (a bivouac site has been constructed here). Traverse right (south) for perhaps 60m, first on this ledge and later along the top edge of the icefield, to a crack that is the second major break in the smooth wall above. A huge triangular flake sits at the base of this crack, which is the start of the main upper part of the West Face route. Not infrequently this initial crack will be wet or covered with verglas, greatly increasing its difficulty.

Pitch 1: Climb this difficult crack (5.8) past two old fixed pitons and continue up and into a slot that leans left. Climb the slot (5.7) and belay on a ledge. **Pitch 2:** Continue up the crack system above the belay (often wet or icy) and belay where convenient on a large ledge. **Pitch 3:** Move to the northern end of the ledge and climb a 5.5 weakness to the main broad ledge that bisects the west face and belay. From here one can escape to the Upper Saddle if the need arises (see the 1971 variation, below). Move the belay up and into the intimidating Great West Chimney. **Pitch 4:** Climb mid-5th-class terrain on the left side of the chimney to a short, steep crack (5.7) that leads to a 4th-class ramp and the belay. **Pitch 5:** Follow the ramp up and to the north to a large flake/block, then hand traverse over to the belay at a fixed pin on the other side (5.7). **Pitch 6 (crux):** Start climbing straight up the exposed face (5.7 mantels), aiming for the left side of the huge overhang above. When a flake is reached (20m above the belay), move right along a sloping traverse that is well below the overhang. Follow the sloping ramp until it disappears, passing a few fixed pins along the way. Interesting and exposed 5.8+ climbing leads around the corner (hand traverse, step down) and into the Great West Chimney. Climb up and around a chockstone (5.8) and belay. Beware of serious rope drag on this wandering pitch. From here it is but a short traverse to the south to the Owen-Spalding route *(Route 1)*, intersecting it at the Double Chimney. One can also continue up the Great West Chimney—not commonly done, but it contains interesting mixed climbing. If time does not permit continuing to the summit of the Grand Teton, traverse south to the Owen-Spalding route, descend to the Upper Saddle, and then head down to the Lower Saddle and Garnet Canyon. **Time:** 13¼ hours from Valhalla Canyon. See *American Alpine Journal* 4, no. 2 (1941): pp. 234–38, illus.; 9, no. 1 (1954): pp. 172–84, illus.

Variation: **DIRECT WEST CHIMNEY.** IV, 5.8, A1. First ascent August 13, 1960, by Tom and William Spencer. Instead of making the detour out to the left (north) and then back into the Great West Chimney, it is possible to climb straight up the chimney, using aid to pass the first large chockstone. Ice, the chockstone, wet rock, poor protection, and a waterfall combine to make this an undesirable substitute for the original West Face route.

Variation: **BLACK ICE–WEST FACE COMBINATION.** IV, 5.8, AI3. First ascent July 23, 1967, by George Lowe and Mike Lowe. (See *Figure 4-46*.) This superb combination joins, in a natural way, two of the finest Teton routes. The result is one of the great alpine climbs of the range. Approach from the Lower Saddle via the Valhalla Traverse Ledge around the north side of the Enclosure to the start of the Black Ice Couloir (see *Route 51*). Climb the initial 180m of ice (55°), angling slightly left on the main icefield to reach the huge triangular flake at the start of the rock of the upper West Face route. Out on the center of this icefield one is totally exposed to any rockfall that occurs. In the event of bad weather or lateness of the hour, there are two alternatives to completing the entire long West Face route: one can continue up the normal Black Ice Couloir route to the Upper Saddle, or one can follow the 1971 variation, described below. The first option, while not easy, should take somewhat less time, and it has the advantage that the difficulty of ice is not greatly increased by new snow, whereas rock climbing may become enormously more difficult. The second option is also not an easy one, because it involves some serious climbing including more ice.

Variation: **TRAVERSE TO UPPER SADDLE.** IV, 5.7, AI3. First ascent February 2–4, 1971, by George and David Lowe and Jeff and Greg Lowe. From the broad scree ledge at the end of the third lead of the West Face route, it is possible, but not easy, to reach the Upper Saddle directly. A horizontal traverse from the extreme south end of this ledge or bench leads to a final section of ice and difficult rock guarding access to the north edge of the Upper Saddle. About three leads are involved in this variation, which is useful if an escape from the standard West Face route is required.

Variation: **DIRECT APPROACH.** IV, 5.8. First ascent August 28, 1973, by Jim "Ole" Olson and Doyle Nelson. This variation bypasses completely the climbing up the Second Shelf, instead climbing out to the far (east) end of the First Shelf before turning up and right (south) to join the original route near the base of the Rotten Yellow Chimney. This is the preferred method of approach to the face if the lower portion of the Black Ice Couloir is not used. From the broad buttress at the start of the original route, a section of black rock can be seen cutting across the base of the first two diagonal shelves on the lower portion of the West Face route. Use this black rock to gain the lower end of the First (lower) Shelf. Climb or scramble up this shelf, staying (if possible) out on ledges to the left (north) of the ice that, through most of the season, occupies the right portion of the shelf. In early season one may have to climb directly up the snow or ice on the shelf, hugging the right-hand wall, which separates the First Shelf from the Second Shelf. After about 120m up the shelf, near its end, a second area of black rock is reached where the terrain steepens. Ledges in this section permit a traverse back to an area of steep cracks and chimneys in the right wall; a section of ice will probably have to be crossed here. One ropelength up an easy chimney system takes one to the Second Shelf and the Rotten Yellow Chimney. This variation offers a relatively quick method to reach this chimney, is less subject to rockfall than the lower end of the Second Shelf, and affords an expedient descent route in bad weather.

Variation: **TILLEY-NICHOLSON TRAVERSE.** IV, 5.9. First ascent July 20, 1978, by Buck Tilley and Bill Nicholson. (See *Figure 4-46*.) This difficult variation departs from the standard West Face route at the large scree ledge in the middle of the route. From this ledge, start from flakes up and to the right (south) of the Great West Chimney. Climb one pitch up a rotten, yellow left-facing corner (5.8) to a ledge system on which a traverse 60m to the right can be made to an alcove about even with the Upper Saddle. From here climb a 5.9 hand crack and the face above it, which leads eventually onto a talus slope and then to the Upper Saddle.

***Variation:* NEUTRON BURN.** IV, 5.9+. First ascent August 7, 1989, by Jon Patterson and Pete Keane. (See *Figure 4-46.*) From the ledge that runs along the top of the main icefield of the Black Ice Couloir (see *Route 51*), this surprising variation provides a two-pitch alternative to the upper West Face route. From the top of the Rotten Yellow Chimney proceed along the ledge south to a very large detached flake, where this variation begins. Move up and left to a right-facing corner (overhanging), which is climbed (5.9+) onto a small ledge for the first belay. The second pitch continues up this corner (5.8) and exits to the right onto a sloping ledge for the second belay stance. Now make an easy traverse right to join the standard West Face route.

ROUTE 51. BLACK ICE COULOIR. IV, 5.7, AI3+. First ascent July 29, 1961, by Ray Jacquot and Herb Swedlund; first winter ascent January 1, 1981, by Mark Bennett, Dave Bjorkman, and Kent Jamison (to top of climb only). (See *Figures 4-47* and *4-53.*) This relatively long and predominantly narrow couloir, which sharply separates the Enclosure from the west face of the Grand Teton, has in the past 60 years become the best known of the Teton ice climbs—an American classic. This sweep of ice curves upward for 360m along the eastern edge of the imposing north buttress of the Enclosure. The Black Ice Couloir proper, where current climbing interest centers, consists of the upper two of four icefields on this part of the mountain. The lowest ice is found just above the floor of Valhalla Canyon and extends up toward the broad bench at the east end of the Valhalla Traverse Ledge. The second section consists of an easy ice slope, and the rock walls above that guard the entrance to the main (third) icefield. The final (fourth) section is the steepest, narrowing considerably before meeting the Upper Saddle. The most difficult climbing is in this final section.

The nature of the ascent depends on the time of year and conditions; in early season, a portion of the couloir may have snow cover, but crampons will always be desired. Due to climate change, the Black Ice Couloir has all but completely disappeared at times during the last decade.

History: The history of ice climbing in the Teton Range very nearly begins with the ascent of the Black Ice Couloir. In earlier years very little alpine ice climbing had been done, other than what was normally required on the Teton Glacier to reach the base of the north face or north ridge of the Grand Teton. Generations of climbers had peered into the depths of this dark chute from the Upper Saddle, but it was long believed that the couloir was too dangerous to be considered seriously as a climbing route. The first attempt, on July 7, 1958, seemed to verify this opinion: Ken Weeks, Yvon Chouinard, and Frank Garneau started at the very bottom but retreated from just above the first section because of a significant fall of rock and ice fragments. A second attempt—on June 26, 1961, by Fred Beckey and Charlie Bell—also failed.

It was something of a breakthrough in Teton climbing when Ray Jacquot and Herbert Swedlund succeeded on the route in 1961, exemplifying unusual courage in the face of the unknown. Their method of approach, via the entire length of Valhalla Canyon and the rock wall below and left of the second icefield, surely contributed to the difficulties of the route. The pair bypassed a considerable portion of the ice, entered the couloir halfway up the main or third icefield, and completed the final crux section to reach the Upper Saddle from the north for the first time. Their route started from the right (west) end of the Second Shelf of the West Face route (see *Route 50*) and moved up and east along this shelf for about 150m on wet slabs and ice patches, past some smooth yellow buttresses, to an area of black rock. Two moderate rock pitches up and back to the right (west) then led onto the Third Shelf, which is the edge of the main (third) icefield.

The second ascent, on August 18, 1963, by Ken Weeks and Jim May, followed the first-ascent line. Then on July 23, 1967, when George Lowe and Mike Lowe pioneered the Black Ice–West Face Combination variation (see *Route 50*), they also became the first to link together the first three icefields, entering the main icefield near its base. The modern approach into the very bottom of the main (third) icefield from the Valhalla Traverse was first done on August 10, 1968, by Leigh Ortenburger and Rick Reese. One year later, on July 22, 1969, George Lowe and Yvon Chouinard climbed the couloir in its entirety—all four icefields—from the floor of Valhalla Canyon. (**Note:** This lower approach is not recommended because it exposes the climbers to objective hazards for a greater period of time. The more modern route, which enters at the very beginning of the main icefield, is given in the route description that follows.)

On one occasion, the base of the main (third) icefield was reached by rappelling from the Upper Saddle, a novel and devious scheme to start the climb. In 1994, Mark Newcomb (on skis) and Stephen Koch (on snowboard) descended the Black Ice Couloir, using ropes, belays, and rappels to safeguard much of the riding.

Herb Swedlund follows the crux pitch of the Black Ice Couloir during the first ascent, July 29, 1961. (Photo by Ray Jacquot)

Sandy Stewart during the first one-day ascent of the Black Ice–West Face route (Photo by Renny Jackson)

FIGURE 4-47. Grand Teton, northwest aspect, Valhalla Traverse to the Black Ice Couloir *(Route 51)* and the west face of the Grand. (A) Aim for this corner of the upper northwest ridge of the Grand Teton (just past the stone-walled bivouac site). Continue north from the corner to a small "ridgelet" of shattered rock. (B) Cross the ridgelet. (C) Descend into a snow- and ice-filled bowl (early season; in late season this bowl contains mud the consistency of wet cement). **To reach *Route 51* (and routes on the north/northwest aspect of the Enclosure):** (D) Traverse near the top of the bowl—stay high!—and climb over a small step (4th class, *very exposed*). (E) After a short descent, reach the Enclosure Ice Couloir. Descend to and cross this couloir. (F) Climb 60m–90m of rock on this larger, lower ramp (possibly snow-covered) to the bottom of the main icefield of the Black Ice Couloir (5.7 just below the start of the ice). (G) Take this smaller, upper ramp for Emotional Rescue *(The Enclosure, Route 12)*. **To reach *Routes 47–50* on the west face of the Grand Teton:** (H) After crossing the ridgelet, descend a narrowing and very exposed scree-and-ice-covered ramp to the east; this is the original Valhalla Traverse. (I) Cross this snow/icefield quickly! (J) Gain the bottom of the First Shelf (ice/wet rock; one pitch, 5.6) to access the west side of the Grandstand.

Strategy: This climb is best approached from Garnet Canyon with a bivouac on the Lower Saddle to ensure an alpine start the next day. Given the effects of climate change, late spring/early summer (May/early June) is the window in which ice conditions are likely to be the best. Checking out the Valhalla Traverse approach the afternoon before can make it much easier to negotiate in the early hours of the following day; it is common for climbers to become lost on this approach and never make it to the ice! Rockfall, which discouraged early attempts, does occur frequently, sometimes in large volume. These rockfall events are either natural or the result of carelessness on the part of climbers on the Owen-Spalding route *(Route 1)*. Safety is increased by staying near the right edge of the ice, because the main line of rockfall is farther out on the face of the ice. There are several protected belay positions along the way.

Route Description: See *Figure 4-47* for an overview of the approach and the climb. The current standard approach to this route is as follows: Take the Valhalla Traverse Ledge to the corner of the upper northwest ridge of the Enclosure. A faint trail continues down along the ledge for a short distance until a "ridgelet" that forms the right (west) edge of a small bowl is met. Traverse across this bowl for a ropelength, maintaining elevation; this strange little bowl contains occasional rock outcrops stuck in a matrix of what appears to be wet cement. Continue traversing for another ropelength, again maintaining elevation, to the west edge of the Enclosure Ice Couloir *(The Enclosure, Route 7)*. On the far (east) side of this ice couloir two small, diagonal shelves will be seen at the base of the impressive north buttress of the Enclosure. The object now is to traverse up and around the base of this buttress on the lower of these two diagonal shelves. Climb for two pitches up this lower shelf, with the final 6m being the most difficult (5.7), to the start of the ice climbing at the base of the main icefield. Timing and speed can minimize the objective hazards: Begin the climb at a very early hour, aiming to reach the Upper Saddle before the sun strikes the west and northwest faces of the Grand Teton. The lower portion, where most of the rockfall is funneled, should be climbed as rapidly as possible. **Gear:** Ice screws are required for protection on the ice, and in addition to the usual rack, pitons may be found useful in the poor rock along the main icefield. See *American Alpine Journal* 13, no. 1 (1962): pp. 216–20.

Variation: **ALBERICH'S ALLEY.** IV, 5.9, AI4. First ascent July 22, 1982, by Peter Hollis and Renny Jackson; first winter ascent February 28–March 2, 1990, by Renny Jackson and Jim Woodmencey (to summit). (See *Figures 4-47* and *4-53*.) Like the Black Ice–West Face Combination variation of *Route 50*, this major variation starts at the base of the main icefield of the Black Ice Couloir. Instead of climbing the icefield up and left toward the rock of the upper West Face route, this variation heads toward the regular Black Ice Couloir crux and ascends a thin ice runnel to the left (east) of the upper Black Ice Couloir; this runnel or ice chute is in the first chimney system to the right (south) of the West Face route.

Pitch 1: The initial lead goes up the narrow ice chute, which becomes vertical for a 6m section, to reach a chockstone in the chimney. Climb in behind this chockstone and consider setting up a belay on top of it. **Pitch 2 (crux):** Continue up and slightly left on very steep ice and rock (5.9) toward the giant jammed chockstone. Ice conditions can vary considerably here and affect the difficulty; it can be as hard as WI4. Climb from under this huge boulder on thin ice out to the left to gain the southern end of the main bench that cuts across the middle of the West Face route. **Pitch 3:** One can either traverse south on this bench to the Upper Saddle or climb directly up, past another chockstone, and exit in an ice chute that leads to a point located 30m to the east of the Black Ice Couloir finish. A total of 180m of climbing is involved from the beginning of the narrow ice runnel to the Upper Saddle. This is a good technical climb and is highly recommended.

Valhalla Canyon

Valhalla Canyon is perhaps the most impressive and majestic of all the canyons in the park. Nestled between the northwest ridge of the Enclosure and the west faces of the Grand Teton and Mount Owen, this high canyon was named with admirable sensitivity in 1940 by Henry Coulter, Jack Durrance, and the small group of climbers who helped carry loads for their historic first ascent of the West Face route *(Grand Teton, Route 50)*. Nowadays the canyon is rarely entered except for those few mountaineers intent on one of the major routes on the west sides of Mount Owen or the Grand Teton. This is a special place and may it ever be so. Entrance to the canyon is guarded by an arduous 600m climb up out of Cascade Canyon that requires a crossing of the cold Cascade Creek and some challenging bushwhacking.

Hike up the Cascade Canyon trail (see *Cascade Canyon* in Section 8) until the stream descending from Valhalla Canyon is in sight. The problem of crossing Cascade Creek remains, and because the existence and location of suitable logs spanning the creek are dependent on the year, the best recommendation is to make an inquiry at the Jenny Lake Ranger Station. In almost all years some manner of log can be found, usually near the woods approximately 180m above the stream junction with Cascade Creek. If necessary, the main creek can be waded, but in early season this is not easy and is somewhat dangerous. Once on the brushy alluvial fan immediately below the entrance to Valhalla Canyon, head toward the main stream draining the canyon. A more or less adequate trail will be found close to the right (west) side of the stream, taking the climber up past the main cliff band guarding access to the upper canyon. Once past this section, pieces of trail can be found in the line of trees to the west. Once through the treed section the "trail" brings one out into the open on steep, sparsely vegetated terrain. There are several fine campsites on the floor of the canyon, and the views of the faces and pinnacles above are very impressive. The upper section of the canyon consists of sloping talus, but one good campsite for two or three climbers has been constructed at about 11,000 feet. This site is located at the base of the first cliff (as one approaches from the floor of the canyon) immediately to the left (north) of the West Gunsight Couloir, the main snow couloir leading to Gunsight Notch between Mount Owen and the Grand Teton. Water is available at the West Gunsight Couloir.

The canyon was reached at least once from the south fork of Cascade Canyon by ascending to the crest of the northwest ridge of the Enclosure and then descending the loose rubble into the head of the

A climber nearing the summit of the Enclosure after an ascent of Jim's Big Day (Photo by Eric Bissell)

canyon. This is, however, hardly the route of choice.

On July 25, 1960, Leigh Ortenburger and Irene Beardsley (Ortenburger) discovered a completely different route into the uppermost reaches of Valhalla Canyon from the Lower Saddle: the Valhalla Traverse. This traverse has proved to be both convenient and popular for experienced climbers setting out to climb one of the routes on the west/northwest aspect of the Grand Teton and the northern side of the Enclosure. This access route, detailed in *Figure 4-47*, requires only a few hours, allowing one to camp on the Lower Saddle and return to the same camp after completing one of these climbs. It must be stressed, however, that the Valhalla Traverse is a serious undertaking, as even in the driest of conditions one can expect to find ice and wet rock. In certain sections the rock is of the poorest quality, and belay anchors and protection are difficult or impossible to obtain.

From the Lower Saddle it should be possible to see the large cairn constructed at a principal step on the crest of the southwest ridge of the Enclosure; for the convenience of others, such cairns should be maintained. Hike north up the main trail from the saddle and veer off to the west (a small trail can be found) at a point about halfway to the Black Dike. Contour around and down into a gully of red rock. Follow a faint trail across this gully, around two small ridges, and then up a final gully, which leads to the cairn on the southwest ridge of the Enclosure. From the cairn, contour north along the very broad shelf leading across the west face of the Enclosure to the far (north) end of this shelf at the upper northwest ridge of the Enclosure (see *The Enclosure, Route 5*). Some icy snow patches will usually be encountered on this shelf. There is a stone-walled bivouac site at the base of the steep wall before this corner; water is usually available at the snow patches. The crucial continuation of the Valhalla Traverse Ledge starts at this corner. Continue around the corner for 23m–30m until a small "ridgelet" is encountered. The traverse becomes a very serious proposition from this point on. From this ridgelet a small bowl can be seen immediately down and to the east. (In this bowl in midseason climbers will encounter a curious, yellow, muddy sand that is the texture of wet cement; in early or late season the bowl will contain snow or even water ice.) Here the route splits, depending on one's objective.

If one wishes to gain access to Valhalla Canyon itself or the west face of the Grandstand for routes such as the North Ridge *(Grand Teton, Route 47)*, Loki's Tower *(Grand Teton, Route 48)*, the Northwest Chimney *(Grand Teton, Route 49)*, or the West Face *(Grand Teton, Route 50)*, climb carefully down into this bowl. At the bottom of the bowl a narrowing scree- and ice-covered ramp will be seen descending to the east. Continue (with great caution) down along this ramp to its lower end, where an expanse of ice or snow must be crossed to gain the shelves leading toward the Grandstand. This snowfield (ice in late season) is immediately beneath the Enclosure Ice Couloir *(The Enclosure, Route 7)* and the fall line of the Black Ice Couloir *(Grand Teton, Route 51)* on the north side of the Upper Saddle. *Beware of rockfall at this point.* Cross as rapidly as possible to the shelves directly west of the Grandstand, where the selected ascent route can be started.

If the objective is to descend into Valhalla Canyon, proceed down to the end of the ramp mentioned above and then down and across the ice/snowfield beneath the Black Ice Couloir. Continue about 120m down toward a broad, relatively flat promontory. From the promontory, scramble down to the northeast into the West Gunsight Couloir, the snow chute that descends from Gunsight Notch. Take the snow chute or the rocks along its southern edge all the way down to the floor of Valhalla Canyon. Note that a high bivouac site is located 60m to the north along the base of the wall that forms the northern boundary of the snow chute.

For other routes such as the Enclosure Ice Couloir, the Black Ice Couloir, or the north buttress routes on the Enclosure, a secondary exit from the small bowl mentioned earlier is taken. Traverse across the bowl, maintaining elevation until considerably better rock on the other side of it is met. Continue around (still maintaining elevation) for two traversing pitches (5.4) to the west edge of the Enclosure Ice Couloir, which leads back up and right to the northwest ridge. On the far (east) side of this ice couloir two small, diagonal shelves will be seen at the base of the north buttress of the Enclosure, the major and most impressive feature rising above and to the east. The smaller (upper) of the two diagonal shelves leads directly up to the base of Emotional Rescue *(The Enclosure, Route 12)* and the Lowe Route *(The Enclosure, Route 11)*. If the objective is the Black Ice Couloir, cross the Enclosure Ice Couloir and continue up and left (on the larger and lower of the two shelves) around the base of the north buttress for about 90m; this starts out loose but gets better and harder. The last ropelength (5.7 for a few moves just below the ice) up this shelf brings one to the base of the main icefield of the Black Ice Couloir.

THE ENCLOSURE (13,280+)

(0.17 mi W of the Grand Teton)
Map: Grand Teton

The western spur of the Grand Teton, the second-highest point in the Teton Range, holds a curious manmade structure within a meter of its summit. Nathaniel P. Langford and James Stevenson came across this unique feature during their attempt to climb the Grand Teton on July 29, 1872. "We found on one of the buttresses, a little lower than the extreme top of the mountain, evidence that at some former period it had been visited by human beings," Langford wrote in his now-famous 1873 article about the climb for *Scribner's Monthly*. "There was a circular inclosure about seven feet in diameter, formed by vertical slabs of rough granite, and about three feet in height, the interior of which was half filled with the detritus that long exposure to the elements had worn from these walls." The site was still in near-pristine condition when Albert R. Ellingwood visited it in 1923 and confirmed Langford's description. Even today, after more than a century of disturbance by a multitude of mountaineers, one can see the remnants of the original circular arrangement.

Speculation regarding the origin of this structure revolves around two possibilities: that it was built by a trapper named Michaud, the only white man reported to have made an attempt to scale the Grand Teton prior to 1872, or that it was built by one or more indigenous persons, probably Shoshone and may be ancient or more recent (19th century), perhaps as a part of their vision quest ceremony. The latter seems far more probable. Regardless of how it got there, since the late 1930s the name "the Enclosure" has been applied to the entire formation, not just to the structure on its summit.

The depth of the Upper Saddle that separates the Enclosure from the Grand Teton is insufficient to qualify this western spur as an official peak. In this guidebook, its route descriptions have nevertheless been separated from those of the Grand Teton. There are two primary reasons for this division: First, most of the 14 routes (plus variations) described here were not intended as routes to the top of the Grand Teton, although a few of the first-ascent parties did continue to the summit via the Owen-Spalding route *(Grand Teton, Route 1)*. Two exceptions are the Jack Durrance routes—the Northwest Ridge *(Route 5)* and the Southwest Ridge *(Route 3)*—which were continued to the summit of the Grand during their first ascents. Second, when adverse conditions prevail, the Enclosure serves as an alternative, easier summit when one has intended to climb the Grand. The route descriptions are arranged in clockwise order, with the easiest (and original) route listed first.

An ascent of the Enclosure is a worthwhile and recommended side trip during an ascent or descent of its larger neighbor, the Grand Teton. From the Upper Saddle it requires only 15 minutes to scramble to its summit, where one will be fully repaid with a spectacular view of the entire west face of the Grand Teton, extending from the Exum Ridge to the north ridge. Moreover, the unique enclosure on the summit is the only such human-made structure to be found in the range.

To approach the Enclosure from Garnet Canyon, see *Garnet Canyon* in Section 3; to approach from Valhalla Canyon, see *Valhalla Canyon*, above; and to approach from Dartmouth Basin, see *Cascade Canyon, South Fork* in Section 8.

Chronology

SOUTH COULOIR: Pre-1872, presumably by an indigenous person(s); July 29, 1872, James Stevenson, Nathaniel Pitt Langford
NORTHWEST RIDGE: August 8–10, 1938, Jack Durrance, Michael Davis
var—**KIMBROUGH-OLSON CRACK:** July 21, 1976, Tom Kimbrough, Jim "Ole" Olson
var—**JACKSON-JOHNSON:** August 17, 1994, Renny Jackson, Ron Johnson
var—**LARSON-MONTOPOLI:** July 8, 2000, Leo Larson, George Montopoli
var—**NORTHERN CORNERS:** July 25, 2000, Paul Horton, Georgie Stanley
SOUTHWEST RIDGE: July 29, 1940, Jack Durrance, Henry Coulter, Fred Ayres
ENCLOSURE ICE COULOIR: July 22, 1962, Al Read, Peter Lev, Jim Greig
WEST FACE: August 13, 1965, Leigh Ortenburger, John Whitesel
var—**RIGHT EDGE:** August 1980, Kent Lugbill, Phil Pearl
LOWE ROUTE: August 22, 1969, George Lowe, Mike Lowe; FFA August 5, 1977, Jim Donini, Rick Black
HIGH ROUTE: August 8, 1977, Charlie Fowler, Steve Glenn
var—**PISS AND VENOM:** July 1998, John Kelley, Jason Strickland (partial); July 2001, John Kelley, Chris Sheridan (complete)
VISIONQUEST COULOIR: August 10, 1981, Michael Stern, Steve Quinlan
var—**TRAINING WHEELS:** August 2009, Landon Wiedeman, Paul Rachele
EMOTIONAL RESCUE: July 26, 1985, Renny Jackson, Steve Rickert; FFA ca. August 1, 1988, Alex Lowe, Jim "Jaime" Olson
var—**DIRECT:** August 16, 1988, Renny Jackson, Jim Woodmencey, Steve Rickert
JIM'S BIG DAY: August 3, 1989, Jim Woodmencey, Renny Jackson
LOOKIN' FOR TROUBLE: July 4–5, 1991, Jim Beyer (solo)
RHINELANDER-JORDAN: April 16, 1994, Marcus Rhinelander, Travis Jordan
PROSPECT OF AN END: September 1, 2002, John Kelley, Sune Tamm-Buckle
THREE SHOTS IN THE DIZZY WIND: September 20, 2002, John Kelley, Kevin Mahoney

ROUTE 1. ▲ SOUTH COULOIR. II, 3.0. First ascent pre-1872, by an indigenous person(s), probably Shoshone; first recorded ascent July 29, 1872, by James Stevenson and Nathaniel Pitt Langford. From the Lower Saddle of the Grand Teton the Enclosure is seen to harbor on its south slope a large couloir, snow-filled during much of the season, extending from

Dartmouth Basin below the Lower Saddle to the Upper Saddle. This couloir can be entered from the rocks above the Black Dike and below the Needle and climbed directly toward the Upper Saddle. This, however, is not recommended: in early season the snow in the couloir is steep with no runout, and hence dangerous, and in late season, steep, loose rock will be encountered. The better alternative is to use the Owen-Spalding route *(Grand Teton, Route 1)* until only about 100 vertical feet short of the Upper Saddle. Instead of continuing all the way to the saddle, turn up and left (northwest) and scramble up easy boulders and chutes on the southeast side of the Enclosure to the summit. If ascending this route during a descent from the Grand Teton, remember that the ascent of the Enclosure does not start at the Upper Saddle because there is a vertical rock step in the connecting ridge. Descend from the Upper Saddle about 30m to the southwest, along what has become almost a trail on the standard Owen-Spalding descent, until around the south side of the vertical step. Then scramble up the southeast side to the summit.

ROUTE 2. JIM'S BIG DAY. III, 5.10-. First ascent August 3, 1989, by Jim Woodmencey and Renny Jackson. (See *Figure 4-48.*) From the Lower Saddle the upper portion of the southwest ridge of the Enclosure has the appearance of a smooth slab with a large overhang at its top. This six-pitch route ascends the middle of the slab and escapes through the left side of the overhang. This is one of the most spectacular and scenic rock pitches in the range. As for the Owen-Spalding route *(Route 1)*, proceed from the Lower Saddle to the base of the Needle, and then turn off to the left toward the southwest ridge. Pass below the small rock knob that is seen up and to the left of the couloir (snow in early season) that goes up along the west side of the Needle. Cross the gully on the far (west) side to gain a section of good gray rock.

Pitch 1: This first short lead (5.8) goes up onto a ledge system that heads west easily toward the southwest ridge. Move the belay 21m farther along this ledge system to the base of a wall with a vertical crack system that leads up and right toward the large slab beneath the main overhang. **Pitch 2:** Pull through a short bulge in black rock (5.8) and head for the obvious weakness above. **Pitch 3:** Climb straight up through 5.7 terrain and belay out to the west beneath the slab and main overhang. **Pitch 4:** Continue up the right edge of the slab to a belay at a stance beneath the main overhang. **Pitch 5:** Stem, jam, lieback, and fight up the overhanging corner of beautiful, golden rock (5.10-). End the pitch on a sizable belay ledge near the end of the rope. **Pitch 6:** Directly above the belay ledge climb an awesome slabby face (5.5R) that eventually turns into an exposed 4th-class ridge scramble. Climb a chimney between the last towers of the southwest ridge and scramble to the top of the Enclosure. **Gear:** For protection take doubles from finger size to 3.5", a few smaller cams, and one 4" cam; a few mid-size stoppers; and a few long runners.

ROUTE 3. SOUTHWEST RIDGE. III, 5.7. First ascent July 29, 1940, by Jack Durrance,

FIGURE 4-48. The Enclosure, south aspect, Jim's Big Day *(Route 2)*, III, 5.10-

Henry Coulter, and Fred Ayres. (See *Figure 4-49.*) This long route contains some excellent rock with many interesting features and is a very enjoyable climb. The ridge begins at about 9,600 feet in the lower reaches of Dartmouth Basin and forms the north rim of the basin. The first 670m is just scrambling. Because the Lower Saddle is a standard focal point for Teton climbing, it is perhaps the best starting point for this route. On the other hand, the approach from Cascade Canyon will reveal new vistas, and lower Dartmouth Basin makes an excellent, beautiful, and wild camping site. Traces of previous human passage are rare—a stark contrast to the heavily traveled Garnet Canyon.

From the Lower Saddle one can see the horizontal section of the ridge about 150m below the Lower Saddle. Hike up the crest of the Lower Saddle until just short of the Black Dike, then contour left (northwest) toward the section of red rock that is immediately south of the Black Dike. Here descend an easy, loose-rock couloir below the cliffs that protect the southwest ridge, then continue west along the base of these cliffs, ultimately reaching the crest of the southwest ridge at the horizontal section. The first 300m of climbing on the ridge involves no serious difficulties, but the scrambling is interesting, especially if an effort is made to stay on the crest. This type of climbing ends abruptly at the second horizontal section, where the Valhalla Traverse Ledge, leading to Valhalla Canyon, crosses the ridge. The cairn that marks this traverse can be seen from

FIGURE 4-49. The Enclosure, west aspect. (A) Southwest Ridge *(Route 3)*, III, 5.7; (B) unnamed variation, III, 5.9+

the Lower Saddle. Scramble on the left (north) side of the crest to pass the short, but steeper, portion above. The top of the slope above this step in the ridge meets directly the first major tower of the ridge about 120m above the Valhalla Traverse. The route depicted in *Figure 4-49* begins at this point.

Pitches 1–2: Climb onto the last boulder and start the roped climbing by stepping across to the rock on the right (south) side of the tower. Continue up and around the south side of this tower on a Wall Street–like shelf to a giant flake that is passed by jamming on its right side. Continue up the crack system/corner, past a fixed pin, and climb through a steep bulge via hand jams and jugs on the face (5.7). **Pitches 3–4:** From the comfortable belay stance above the steep 5.7 bulge, avoid continuing up the easier, low-angle ramp directly ahead, and instead quickly move left into the first prominent weakness/chimney system that accesses the ridgeline proper. These two pitches can be linked (rope-stretcher) or done separately; either way, they end in some loose, low-5th-class terrain that deposits one on a large ledge. **Pitch 5:** This is a fairly short pitch. Move the belay to the far side of the terrace, then climb the cleft/chimney in the next prominent high point in the ridge. Start up the chimney, then move left onto the face (fun 5.7). Belay in a notch in the disintegrating black-rock gully above. **Pitch 6:** Watch for rope drag on this short pitch, which begins with a traverse to the right across a red-rock wall (5.4). Find the path of least resistance, moving up and right along a hand traverse below a massive overhang. This pitch culminates in an awkward (and surprisingly difficult) downclimb to the other side of the major break/notch in the black-rock gully; belay on a large ledge. **Pitches 7–9:** Many belay options exist for this sizable stretch of the route, but basically cruise up loose 4th- and low-5th-class terrain, trending left toward the ridgeline proper (5.6). Once a large ledge on climber's left is reached, move along the terrace and belay below a wide crack. **Pitches 10–11:** Climb the 5.7 wide crack straight up the face, eventually making some awkward moves to the right around a small bulge/chockstone, then continue up easier terrain above (5.6). Belay or simul-climb until the terrain eases at the top of the ridgeline leading toward the summit of the Enclosure. **Gear:** For protection bring a single rack of cams to 3.5", with doubles in the 1"–2" range; a set of stoppers; many shoulder-length runners; and a 60m rope.

Variation: III, 5.9+. First-ascent unknown. (See *Figure 4-49.*) This four-pitch variation to the start of the original Southwest Ridge route appears like it would be quite good. Look for a smooth orange wall out to the north of the start of the regular route. The first pitch of this variation begins in the first crack system to the north of the orange wall. **Pitch 1:** Climb 5.9+ fingers and then 5.9 hands to a ledge and belay (43m). **Pitch 2:** From the belay climb up and right to a triangular pillar, then continue straight up to a stem/squeeze chimney (5.7). A 5.6 finger traverse leads up and right to a belay. **Pitch 3:** Climb up and left on a 5.4 face and belay next to a flake on a ledge. **Pitch 4:** Climb a short right-facing corner to some flakes, then head straight up through a small overhang, joining *Route 3* at the top of its fourth pitch.

ROUTE 4. WEST FACE. III, 5.7, A1. First ascent August 13, 1965, by Leigh Ortenburger and John Whitesel. The major portion of this face, which is bounded by the northwest and southwest ridges, lies above the main Valhalla Traverse Ledge system, which could be used to approach the middle of this route. The complete climb, however, begins in the lower reaches of Dartmouth Basin and uses the west ridge of the Enclosure to reach the Valhalla Traverse Ledge. This ridge lies south of the main stream draining the small icefield or glacier that nestles at the base of the lower west face of the Enclosure; it is separated from the lower extension of the southwest ridge by a rotten rock gully. Climb this ridge directly via a 5.4 chimney near the right edge of the initial broken face. Three towers will be encountered along this ridge; bypass the latter two on the south. Easy slabs are then reached, leading onto the main (upper) west slope of the Enclosure at the Valhalla Traverse Ledge somewhat north of the southwest ridge. Looking up, one will see the next objective: a significant chimney with a large black chockstone in the middle of the upper vertical section of the face. Ascend the next 150m with considerable caution, mostly scrambling up a connecting series of ledges, slabs, and chimneys near the middle of the face; some rockfall may be encountered. Various routes can be found in this section, up to 5.6 in difficulty. Two small snowfields can be utilized or avoided, as desired, while following ledges generally covered with rocks and scree.

The difficult climbing commences on the vertical wall above the final scree ledge that leads left (north) toward the col behind the Great Tower of the northwest ridge. The chimney with the black chockstone is on the right (south) side of a small buttress projecting from the base of the face above. Traverse right on a ledge along the base of the face past the small buttress. Belay in the alcove on the right (south) side of the buttress, and climb the difficult chimney past the chockstone using a combination of techniques (5.7, A1). Continue up and slightly left (north) in a second chimney of similar difficulty to a stance below and to the right of an obvious hand traverse. Make this traverse (strenuous) 4.5m left to a second stance where an easier 12m section of free climbing leads to the base of an open book with cracks in its left wall. This short pitch is climbed using aid to a belay on the large, scree-covered ledge at the top of the vertical portion of the west face of the Enclosure. The upper section of the face above, much of it composed of black rock, lies back at a more reasonable angle. The final chimney, now just above, is seen to be capped by a large, black-bottomed chockstone. Climb one ropelength up to the right, then cut back into the chimney about 6m below the chockstone. Continue up the chimney and exit to the left to reach the final easy rock leading to the summit ridge. Scramble up to the square notch just right of the summit. Some difficulties will be found gaining the top of this notch. From the Valhalla Traverse Ledge, this route generally stays in the middle of the face, never close to either of the bounding ridges.

***Variation:* RIGHT EDGE.** III, 5.8. First ascent in August 1980, by Kent Lugbill and Phil Pearl. This variation lies to the right (south) of the preceding main route and emerges onto the upper southwest ridge. Start from the Valhalla Traverse Ledge and climb and scramble easily up toward a prominent chimney in the right edge of the west face of the Enclosure. A total of four pitches are climbed to attain the southwest ridge crest. The second lead is the chimney (5.8).

ROUTE 5. NORTHWEST RIDGE. V, 5.7. First ascent August 8–10, 1938, by Jack Durrance and Michael Davis. This long northwest ridge, perhaps the largest single feature of the Grand Teton, rises from the floor of Cascade Canyon over 5,500 vertical feet to the summit of the Enclosure in a spectacular 2-mile sweep. The ridge contains three distinct sections that, if done in their entirety, produce the longest climb in the park. The initial part of the ridge—a roughly horizontal section containing several subpeaks, towers, and pinnacles—is the longest, rising from Cascade Canyon before ending at the southwest corner of Valhalla Canyon. Here a fault passes through the ridge at a vertical step. This fault divides the poor rock of this lower initial section from the high-quality rock of the upper two-thirds of the ridge. The second section marks the beginning of the difficult climbing, rising steeply to meet first a talus slope and then a long section of low-angle, downsloping slabs that ends at the corner of the north end of the Valhalla Traverse Ledge. The final section, which rises abruptly above the traverse ledge, is the main attraction (see *Figures 4-47, 4-50,* and *4-52* for two aspects of this upper ridge). Because the rock here is excellent, most ascents of the ridge begin with this section. The major tower on this section is separated from the uppermost ridge by a col at the head of the Enclosure Ice Couloir. The ridge then veers off to meet the southwest ridge 46m below the summit. Combining the ice couloir with the uppermost section of the ridge produces one of the most classic alpine climbs in the range.

History: The winter of 1937–1938 had been a particularly heavy snow year, so Dartmouth climbers Michael Davis and Jack Durrance delayed their attempt on the northwest ridge until late in the summer. Prepared for a two- or three-day climb, they left Jenny Lake at 2 AM on August 8. About a half mile up the south fork of Cascade Canyon they crossed the creek and wandered up to the foot of the first tower. By 3:30 PM they had climbed three major towers and several smaller ones along the ridge crest including one of the prominent Rabbit Ears, twin pinnacles that are conspicuous from the road as one approaches String Lake. A thunderstorm was in progress and the pair sought shelter under a large boulder where they brewed some "delicious tea," ate lunch, and

FIGURE 4-50. The Enclosure, west aspect, upper Northwest Ridge *(Route 5)*, variation: Kimbrough-Olson Crack, IV, 5.8

napped for a while, as Davis later noted in a typewritten account of the climb. By 5 PM the rain had stopped and they carried on, traversing around or climbing up two or three more small towers.

Only one tower remained, and once past this obstacle they knew that they could make it up to what is now known as the Valhalla Traverse. The rock was reddish in color and looked extremely rotten. In fact, it has stopped a few modern-day climbers in their tracks. Davis described it quite vividly in his account: "In front of us was a tower about 18m high made up of some of the most abominable rock any mountaineer would want to use. It was just a pile of small red blocks perched on top of one another like a red brick fireplace chimney without any mortar between the bricks, each one ready to fall out." For this intimidating pitch (5.7R) Durrance changed into his "sneakers"—a pair of basic rubber-soled canvas shoes that would have offered more precision and frictioning capability than clumsy mountain boots, especially nailed ones! He climbed up to a large overhang, traversed beneath it out to the right about 4m, placed a piton, and then made it to a belay. After hauling both of their packs, Durrance belayed Davis up to the ledge. Now they were at the base of a large talus slope. The hour was late, so they took shelter under a large boulder for the night. With one bivouac sack and one sleeping bag between them, Davis won the draw, sleeping warm on that first night.

Durrance and Davis got under way again at 8:30 the next morning, after "leaving a note in a little bottle in the cave" and naming their spot "the Double D Bivouac." Some 62 years later, with luck and a little planning, two Jenny Lake climbing rangers—Tom Kimbrough and David Bywater—discovered this site and recovered the bottle and its contents, which now reside in the Grand Teton National Park archives. Still legible after six decades, the note described the conditions that the pair had encountered and their feelings as they prepared to spend the night. Also found with the note was a small stamp with the symbol of the Dartmouth Mountaineering Club (DMC) plainly visible.

The pair carried on, climbing up to and past what is now the Valhalla Traverse to the more difficult uppermost portion of the ridge. Nearing the top of this section, just below the top of the Great Tower located just west of the Enclosure Couloir Col, the pair again sought shelter under a huge block, which they named "Dartmouth Symbol." It was 6:30 PM, another storm was approaching, and they found a small cave to the northeast of the "Symbol." Later that night the skies cleared and, as Davis recalled, the "moonlight glittered down and flooded the whole range with a superb glow." In the morning they left another note and completed their ascent, climbing the Owen-Spalding route to the summit of the Grand Teton. In 1994 this author (R. Jackson) tried to find this second note to no avail; but I did come across an ancient soft-iron piton with lichen on it sitting on a small ledge in what may have been their second bivouac cave. Perhaps someday that note will be found!

Strategy: A true adventure is in store for those wishing to complete an ascent of the entire ridge—good luck! These days, most people access the Northwest Ridge route from a camp on the Lower Saddle, prepared for a day climb with light packs. This is true for the Enclosure Ice Couloir–upper Northwest Ridge or one of the Northwest Ridge variations from the Valhalla Traverse. These are all superb alpine climbs.

Route Description: The following description is for the complete Northwest Ridge route; if taking the Valhalla Traverse Ledge, skip ahead to the fifth paragraph in this section.

Follow the Cascade Canyon trail to a point just below the forks. Cross Cascade Creek and bushwhack directly up the north slope of the first and lowest tower on the ridge. Follow a large shelf up to the right-hand (northwest) ridge of the tower. From the end of this shelf a near-vertical pitch up solid rock leads to an awkward chimney. Above this, scramble to the summit of the first tower, Peak 10,405. The second tower, Peak 10,640+, is climbed from the col to the south by a large left-facing corner system leading up and left for two pitches. A steep downclimb leads to the col between the second and third towers. The third tower is climbed directly from this col: Traverse left (east) out on a diagonal ledge to a band of black rock that allows a traverse back to the right on a small ledge. This gives access to a second ledge leading left toward the summit of the tower.

There is little or no notch behind this tower, and mere scrambling takes one past two small gendarmes to the Rabbit Ears. The first "ear," the more northerly one, overhangs on all four sides and is one of the more difficult pinnacles in the park. The first three ascents of this ridge bypassed this North Ear. For details, see *Rabbit Ears* in Section 7. The second "ear"—the South Ear—is much easier. The next tower, or step, south of the Rabbit Ears must be contoured on the west side in order to reach the col beyond. The remainder of the horizontal section of the ridge involves indistinct towers and steps of no great difficulty.

The notch at the base of the initially steep second section of the ridge (at the south end of the horizontal section) contains rotten rock, and a small, rotten red pinnacle rises directly above. A fault passes through this notch, and the character of the rock changes abruptly. This fault extends from Valhalla Canyon around the base of the west side of the Enclosure and ends at the lower, western extension of the Black Dike on the south side of the Grand Teton. Climb directly up the pinnacle from the notch to a belay position below a large flake. Above the flake is a 3m overhang with a steep, short face below. With protection in place climb to the right-hand edge of the overhang, where it narrows. A key handhold on the face above the overhang allows the passage of this 5.7 pitch. Steep but easy and fairly solid rock then leads directly above to the 90m talus slope. A cliff band above this slope can be climbed directly at its left (north) corner up chimneys to the slabs above. Alternatively, from the upper right corner of this talus slope, two 18m pitches up cracks lead to easy scrambling up the scree-covered slabs for about 150m.

The slabs end on the Lower Saddle–Valhalla Traverse Ledge, which lies at the base of the Great Tower—an impressive pinnacle that is the apex of the steep upper section of the northwest ridge. If the entire northwest ridge is addressed as a two-day climb, this large ledge provides a good place to bivouac: water can be found (except in late season) 90m to the right (south) of the ridge, and a small stone-walled bivy site has been constructed near the northern corner of the ridge.

The west face of the Great Tower above is marked by two sections of black rock, one about a quarter of the way up the tower and the other, halfway up the tower. Start the tower at the first reasonable crack (it has the appearance of a lieback crack) south of the north corner of the ridge. The first 6m of this lead is difficult, but the angle eases, and after another 18m–24m climb slightly to the left. This pitch ends with a short lieback and easier black rock. Then scramble for three ropelengths over excellent rock. Ultimately, as high as possible, a traverse must be made up and around the right edge of the face into a shallow gully that leads back toward the crest. This gully should be reached only about 15m short of its top. Ascend the left side of the gully to the top, cross to the right, climb a short chimney, and traverse around the south side of the tower to a long, large crack or chimney that leads to the crest of the ridge at the col behind the tower. This is the same col—the Enclosure Couloir Col—that is reached from the other (north) side via the Enclosure Ice Couloir *(Route 7)*. Attaining the summit of the Great Tower, a solid yellow monolith, is part of the complete Northwest Ridge route from a purist's standpoint. To do this, scramble back to the tower, which is climbed by its south face. There apparently is no rappel anchor at the top of this tower.

The col at the base of the second tower (actually a buttress) is easily reached after negotiating the descent from the Great Tower. The first two ascents passed this buttress on the right, traversing beneath the overhanging face to a difficult water-worn crack that was ascended to reach the ridge behind the buttress. The better alternative is to climb it directly, up the obvious ledge and crack that slants up and left from the base of the buttress. The rock here is outstanding. One lead up this crack (5.7) and the face just to the left places the party beneath an overhang. Pass this overhang on the right, using beautiful holds, and ascend the short face above to easier ground, which again leads to the crest behind the buttress; the overhang can also be passed on the left. The third tower, just a step in the ridge, is climbed via a crack system on the right side of the face. A tricky horizontal step leads to an awkward overhang; exit to the right onto easier rock. Then scramble to the black-rock region just beneath the summit of the Enclosure. The northwest ridge does not lead directly to the summit but ends at the southwest ridge, about 46m below the top. Before reaching the southwest ridge it is advisable to traverse left under a yellow wall to a black-rock talus slope leading to the crest of the southwest ridge just below and south of the summit of the Enclosure. Alternatively, scramble up to the final wall, where 5.8 moves on good rock lead around to the right of a fixed piton and the top of the climb. It is then but a short walk to the true summit of the Enclosure. See *American Alpine Journal* 3, no. 3 (1939): pp. 364–65, illus.; *Dartmouth Mountaineering Club Journal*, 1938: pp. 29–36.

Variation: **KIMBROUGH-OLSON CRACK.** IV, 5.8. First ascent July 21, 1976, by Tom Kimbrough and Jim "Ole" Olson. (See *Figures 4-50* and *4-51*.) On the Valhalla Traverse, prior to rounding the corner of the northwest ridge, there is a very built-up bivouac site that is occasionally used. This climb begins in a prominent right-facing corner in good rock just before reaching the bivy site. Climb this vertical right-facing corner (5.7) to an easier right-trending flake. The second lead goes up the flake (5.6) onto face climbing on black rock to a belay at the beginning of a second flake, which forms a right-facing corner. The

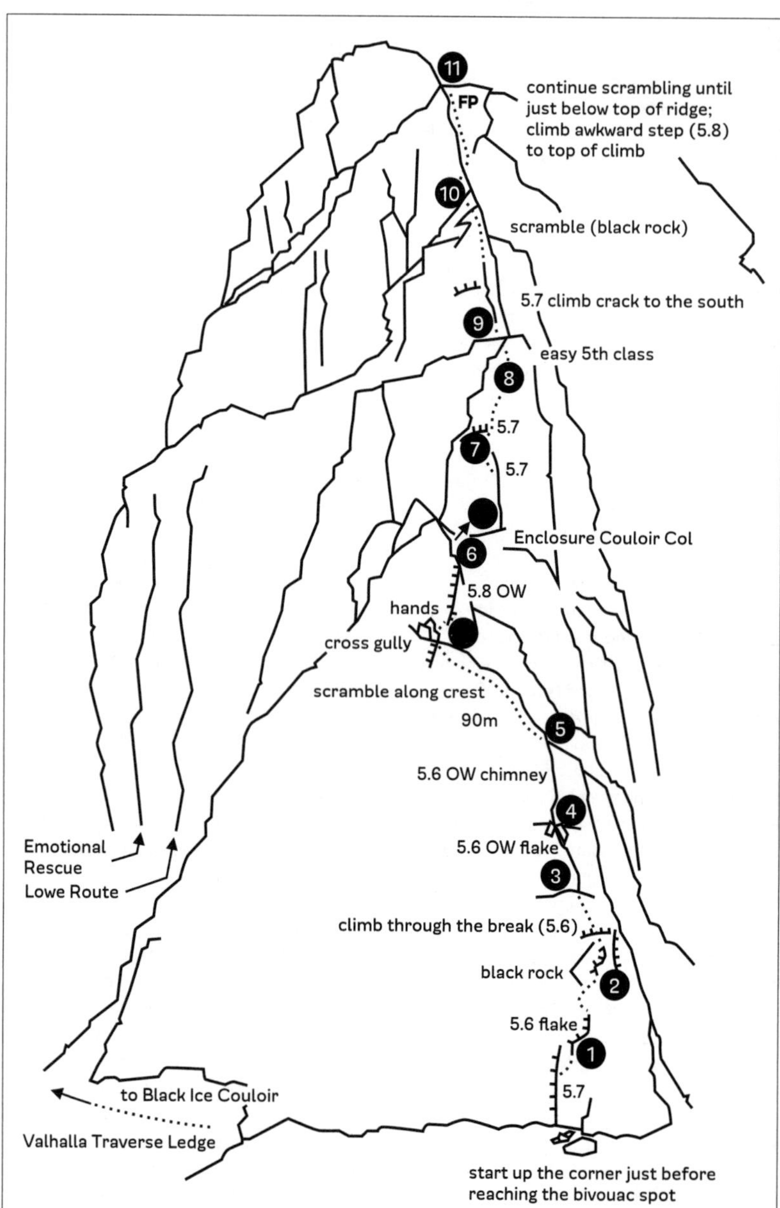

FIGURE 4-51. The Enclosure, west aspect, upper Northwest Ridge *(Route 5)*, varation: Kimbrough-Olson Crack, IV, 5.8

next pitch ascends the edge of this flake and continues up a steep, black-rock face (5.6) through a break in the wall. From the belay ledge, go for two leads straight up an offwidth flake past some large flakes, and end with an offwidth chimney. The angle eases here and simple scrambling up and slightly left for 90m leads to a shallow gully that diagonals up from right to left. From here continue up and left (north) to join the Northern Corners variation, or traverse a bit higher out to the right to a hand crack that leads to a 5.8 offwidth. Either way, the Northwest Ridge route can be rejoined on the east side of the Enclosure Couloir Col.

***Variation:* JACKSON-JOHNSON.** IV, 5.8. First ascent August 17, 1994, by Renny Jackson and Ron Johnson. This two-pitch variation to the upper Northwest Ridge route is located on the south side of the ridge on excellent rock. From the Enclosure Couloir Col, climb down the gully to the south (as if going down to the rappel; see *Route 7*) approximately 30m until it is possible to scramble up and left to the base of an amazing wide crack (would require cleaning) that is visible from the Valhalla Traverse far below. Climb two pitches (5.8) up the right-facing corner system to the east of the crack, then join the main Northwest Ridge route and follow it to the summit of the Enclosure.

***Variation:* LARSON-MONTOPOLI.** IV, 5.8. First ascent July 8, 2000, by Leo Larson and George Montopoli. On the Valhalla Traverse, prior to rounding the corner of the northwest ridge, there is a very built-up bivouac site that is occasionally used. This five-pitch variation begins just past (a few meters north of) this bivy site. Look for a double-crack system that starts about 3m above the Valhalla Traverse Ledge. **Pitch 1:** Climb directly up the intermittent right-hand crack system for 60m (5.7) to a belay at the base of a well-defined vertical hand crack. **Pitch 2:** Climb the crack and then continue up through black rock (loose blocks in this area) and belay (5.8, 60m). **Pitch 3:** Continue up and to the southeast and join the Kimbrough-Olson Crack variation (5.6, 60m). **Pitch 4:** Climb the fourth pitch of that route (5.6, 60m). **Pitch 5:** Continue up the Kimbrough-Olson Crack variation to and past the 5.8 offwidth along a ramp until it ends. Climb straight up through broken terrain and wet slabs to the first break in the wall to the west. This break leads to a ledge system that traverses horizontally to the top of the Enclosure Ice Couloir *(Route 7)*. From here the uppermost portion of the main Northwest Ridge route can be taken to the summit of the Enclosure.

***Variation:* NORTHERN CORNERS.** IV, 5.8. First ascent July 25, 2000, by Paul Horton and Georgie Stanley. (See *Figure 4-52*.) This variation starts on the "ridgelet" described in *Valhalla Canyon* and shown

FIGURE 4-52. The Enclosure, west aspect, upper Northwest Ridge *(Route 5)*, variation: Northern Corners, IV, 5.8

in *Figures 4-47* and *4-52*, continues up a prominent corner system in predominantly white rock, and then follows the ridge leading to the top of the Great Tower. **Pitch 1:** Begin with pleasant climbing up the ridgelet to a large ledge (5.7, 60m); move the belay to the west to the base of a ramp. **Pitch 2:** Ascend the 4th-class ramp, cross a rib, and follow ledges to an obvious crack in white rock. Climb this steep crack (5.8) to a belay on small ledges (5.8, 60m). **Pitch 3:** Continue up the crack/open book (5.6) and pull a small overhang (5.7). Climb easier terrain through bands of black rock, then go up a corner. Belay on a prow to the left (5.7, 50m). **Pitch 4:** Climb fun slabs to a nice crack, then move left and up via face moves (5.8, 60m). **Pitch 5:** Climb up and left through a 5.7 step via cracks and continue to the ridge crest. Fourth-class climbing leads to a belay on the crest (5.7, 40m). **Pitch 6:** Follow easy ledges to the west side of a huge block, then climb to the snow-filled gully above the block. Ascend the gully to exit right on an unprotected slab (5.8, 55m). Scramble east through a slot in the ridge to easy terrain on the east side of the Great Tower and continue down to the Enclosure Couloir Col. Join the upper section of the regular Northwest Ridge route here and follow it to the summit of the Enclosure. **Gear:** Bring a 60m rope and an alpine rack.

ROUTE 6. RHINELANDER-JORDAN. IV, 5.6, A1, WI3+. First ascent April 16, 1994, by Marcus Rhinelander and Travis Jordan. (See *Figure 4-53*.) This is another of the Teton ice lines whose existence is somewhat fleeting; it probably comes

FIGURE 4-53. The Enclosure, overview of northwest face ice routes. (A) Valhalla Traverse; (B) Rhinelander-Jordan *(Route 6)*, IV, 5.6, A1, WI3+; (C) Enclosure Ice Couloir *(Route 7)*, IV, 5.7, AI3; (D) High Route *(Route 10)*, IV, 5.9; (E) Prospect of an End *(Route 9)*, IV, 5.10X, AI3, M4; (F) Three Shots in the Dizzy Wind *(Route 8)*, IV, AI5, M6; (G) Black Ice Couloir *(Grand Teton, Route 51)*, IV, 5.7, AI3+; (H) Black Ice Couloir, variation: Alberich's Alley, IV, 5.9, AI4; (I) Visionquest Couloir *(Route 14)*, IV, 5.8, AI3+; (J) Visionquest Couloir, variation: Training Wheels, IV, 5.7, A1, AI3, M4

in only during brief periods in the early spring or, under the right conditions, at times in the fall months. On the first ascent it was discovered accidentally. To reach the start of the climb, proceed around the Valhalla Traverse Ledge to the section that descends steeply from the bowl located just around the corner from the upper northwest ridge. Traverse across this bowl, staying high near the base of the steep rock. At about the point where one turns the corner and catches a glimpse of the Enclosure Ice Couloir, look for two parallel cracks going up to the south. Climb the left-hand crack (5.6) to a ledge, then continue up past a fixed piton to a belay on the left at the base of a slabby area. Proceed up the slabs to the base of the first ice pitch. Steep ice will be encountered on this lead, and the belay is located in an alcove. Continue up the gully and belay in another alcove located on the left. The first-ascent party encountered an overhanging chockstone on the fifth pitch that required aid to pass. Three more mixed pitches bring one to an unusual keyhole finish and the top of the climb. One can then continue up the Northwest Ridge route *(Route 5)* to the summit of the Enclosure; this combination is an excellent alpine Grade IV.

ROUTE 7. ENCLOSURE ICE COULOIR. IV, 5.7, AI3 (to summit of the Enclosure), or III, 5.6, AI3 (with rappel descent). First ascent July 22, 1962, by Al Read, Peter Lev, and Jim Greig. (See *Figure 4-53*.) On the north side of the Enclosure is a prominent ice couloir diagonaling up to the right (west) to meet the northwest ridge at the col that separates the Great Tower of the steep section of the ridge from the uppermost ridge. The route has become one of the three most popular ice climbs in the Teton Range. The standard and recommended approach (also that of the first-ascent party) is from the Lower Saddle via the Valhalla Traverse (see *Figure 4-47*). By using the same approach as for the Black Ice Couloir *(Grand Teton, Route 51)*, one will enter the Enclosure Ice Couloir about 60m above its beginning. If approaching from Cascade and Valhalla Canyons (rarely done), one can climb diagonally up and right (west) across the second icefield of the Black Ice Couloir onto the rocks just above and left of the extreme bottom end of the Enclosure Ice Couloir. These rocks, while not pleasant, lead to the lower reaches of the couloir and the start of the ice climb. In early season, the ice in the couloir may continue down into a narrow chimney that can also be climbed.

Stephen Koch following a pitch on the High Route in mixed conditions (Photo by Alex Lowe)

The angle of the ice in the couloir is about 50°; during early season it can, for the most part, be snow climbing. Some falling ice blocks and rocks must be expected, but the danger is less than in the Black Ice Couloir (mainly because one does not usually have to worry about climbers dislodging rocks from above). Depending on ropelength and choice of belay stances, this route delivers six or seven pitches of snow and ice climbing. Once the Enclosure Couloir Col is reached, follow the uppermost Northwest Ridge route (see *Route 5*) to the summit of the Enclosure. This excellent mixed route is highly recommended. If a shorter climb is desired or if the hour is late, descent can be made via rappel down the west face of the Enclosure to regain the Valhalla Traverse Ledge. Start by climbing down from the col in a gully to the south for approximately 60m to where the first of the rappel stations can be seen. **Gear:** For protection bring a number of screws and an alpine rack. See *American Alpine Journal* 13, no. 2 (1963): pp. 487–89.

ROUTE 8. THREE SHOTS IN THE DIZZY WIND. IV, AI5, M6. First ascent September 20, 2002, by John Kelley and Kevin Mahoney. (See *Figure 4-53.*) Climb the Enclosure Ice Couloir *(Route 7)* to about 46m below the Enclosure Couloir Col; the first pitch of this ice route begins at a belay at a horn. Traverse left into a left-facing corner, pull a roof (M6), and continue up the corner on thin ice (AI5) for 55m to a belay. The second pitch proceeds up and right in an easy slot filled with snow to an overhanging straight-in corner. Pull an overhang (M6) and continue up a thinly plastered corner (AI5) to a belay at the base of a chimney (55m). Climb up and left in the obvious ice-plastered left-facing corner to the top of the headwall (M5, then AI4 in corner). Traverse left and finish on the High Route *(Route 10)* as it goes up and to the south to the northwest ridge and then the summit. **Gear:** Bring a 60m rope; cams from ⅜" to 3.5"; stoppers from tiny to 1"; and slings.

ROUTE 9. PROSPECT OF AN END. IV, 5.10X, AI3, M4. First ascent September 1, 2002, by John Kelley and Sune Tamm-Buckle. (See *Figure 4-53.*) Climb the initial 180m of the Enclosure Ice Couloir *(Route 7)*. Begin the climb just off the couloir, as shown in *Figure 4-53*, below a large boulder on the east side. The first-ascent party encountered M4 conditions on their first pitch, which goes up and left to a belay on a ledge. The second pitch ascends a 5.8 crack to another ledge with a fixed pin at the belay. From the left side of the belay ledge, climb a steep face up and right to another belay ledge (5.9R). The fourth pitch proceeds up and right on a 5.8 ramp until it is possible to climb up and left to a belay (the last 9m is rated 5.10X). With no protection for 15m, the fifth pitch is rated 5.8X, although there *may* be a fixed pin and two fixed heads (if they are still there); it attains a ledge for the belay at another fixed pin. The sixth pitch consists of M4 climbing to the ice apron that leads up and to the south to the northwest ridge, which can be followed to the summit (see *Route 5*). **Gear:** Bring a 60m rope; stoppers; and cams to 4".

ROUTE 10. HIGH ROUTE. IV, 5.9. First ascent August 8, 1977, by Charlie Fowler and Steve Glenn. (See *Figures 4-53* and *4-54.*) This route ascends the crack and chimney

FIGURE 4-54. The Enclosure, west aspect. (A) High Route *(Route 10)*, IV, 5.9; (B) Variation: Piss and Venom, IV, 5.10R

system at the intersection of the main north buttress of the Enclosure with the northwest ridge of the Grand Teton. The High Route, which stays completely to the right (west) of the earlier Lowe Route *(Route 11)*, may be slightly more prone to icing than its neighbors to the north, as it tops out near the lowest point of the snow/ice apron above. Expect mixed climbing, including 50° ice. To approach, take the Valhalla Traverse from the Lower Saddle to the bottom of the Enclosure Ice Couloir (see *Route 7* and *Figure 4-47*). The first-ascent party began by climbing up and right from near the start of the Lowe Route, but it is also possible to climb about two pitches of ice in the Enclosure Ice Couloir and then cut left to the start of the route. The details of the route are shown in *Figure 4-54*. Six difficult pitches are required to reach the top of the main buttress, at which point one reaches—but does not cross—the same downsloping ledge crossed by the Lowe Route and Emotional Rescue *(Route 12)*. Instead, follow this ledge out to the right (west) for several pitches, past a 46m ice apron, to reach the crest of the northwest ridge. During very dry seasons most of this ice melts away, and what remains can be avoided by climbing along the side of it. From the northwest ridge, some 90m of scrambling up the upper west face of the Enclosure leads to the summit. **Gear:** For protection take a standard rack to 3.5".

Variation: **PISS AND VENOM.** IV, 5.10R. First partial ascent in July 1998, by John Kelley and Jason Strickland; first complete ascent in July 2001, by John Kelley and Chris Sheridan. (See *Figure 4-54*.) This three-pitch variation (150m) to the normal start of the High Route is located in the next crack system to the south.

ROUTE 11. LOWE ROUTE. IV, 5.9, A2, or IV, 5.10+. First ascent August 22, 1969, by George Lowe and Mike Lowe; first free ascent August 5, 1977, by Jim Donini and Rick Black. The initial four pitches were first climbed during an attempt on August 6, 1969, by George Lowe, Jack Turner, and Leigh Ortenburger. (See *Figures 4-55* and *4-56*.) This pioneering route, the first established on the impressive north face of the Enclosure, was in its day probably the most difficult route on either the Grand Teton or the Enclosure. A mixed climb like the other two routes on this face of the Enclosure, it follows in part a major drainage, so climbers are advised to try for conditions as dry as possible. The initial attempt approached this climb from Valhalla Canyon, which added a considerable amount of climbing to a very serious and strenuous route; the first-ascent party used the standard Valhalla Traverse from the Lower Saddle (see *Figures 4-47* and *4-55*). After reaching the Enclosure Ice Couloir *(Route 7)* on the Valhalla Traverse, climb at least one pitch of ice before traversing up toward this crack and chimney system, the most obvious line on the face. Refer to *Figures 4-55* and *4-56* for the details of the lower and upper sections of this route. The top of the main buttress is reached at the end of the eighth lead. The final section to the summit involves a direct attack via the leftmost (eastern) of three chimneys that penetrate the summit block. A tunnel in this chimney provides a neat ending to an outstanding mountaineering route. (**Note:** This author—R. Jackson—has done all three of the climbs on this face and this one is by far the most strenuous.)

FIGURE 4-55. The Enclosure, north and west aspects, overview of the Lowe Route *(Route 11)*, IV, 5.10+

FIGURE 4-56. The Enclosure, west aspect, Lowe Route *(Route 11)*, IV, 5.10+

Gear: For protection take a small piton selection, plus a standard rack with many small nuts. A few large cams (4.5"–7.5") will be very useful.

ROUTE 12. EMOTIONAL RESCUE. IV, 5.10-, A2, or IV, 5.11c. First ascent July 26, 1985, by Renny Jackson and Steve Rickert; first free ascent on about August 1, 1988, by Alex Lowe and Jim "Jaime" Olson. (See *Figure 4-57* for an overview and *Figure 4-58* for the route details.) On the north side of the Enclosure, between the Black Ice Couloir *(Grand Teton, Route 51)* and the Enclosure Ice Couloir *(Route 7)*, is a huge buttress of excellent yellow Teton rock. The formidable lower portion rises vertically from the junction of the two couloirs, with major faces on its eastern, northern, and western exposures. This climb is located on a line to the left of the earlier Lowe Route *(Route 11)* and High Route *(Route 10)*, near the left-hand prow of the northwest facet of the buttress. It starts at the upper (smaller) of the two diagonal ramps used for entry into the Black Ice Couloir. Because there are natural lines of drainage on this face, this route should be climbed in the driest possible conditions; it would be very difficult with any ice. A total of 12 pitches are required, with eight on the initial steep buttress. Take the Valhalla Traverse from the Lower Saddle to the Enclosure Ice Couloir (see *Figures 4-47* and *4-57*), then angle up and left to

Climbing ranger Peter Hollis on the second ascent of the Visionquest Couloir, North Face of the Enclosure, August 11, 1981 (Photo by Renny Jackson)

150m 4th/easy 5th class to summit of the Enclosure
5.8 OW
5.9
scrambling or snow and ice, depending on season
cross Enclosure Ice Couloir and climb up to base of climb

FIGURE 4-57. The Enclosure, west aspect, overview of Emotional Rescue *(Route 12)*, variation: Direct, IV, 5.10-

The first pitch of Emotional Rescue (Photo by Vic Zeilman)

near the northern margin of the face of the buttress. The initial double-crack pitch rises directly above. Note that hanging belays are needed at the ends of the second, third, and fifth pitches. **Gear:** For protection take a standard rack to 3.5", with RPs and small wired nuts.

***Variation:* DIRECT.** IV, 5.10-. First ascent August 16, 1988, by Renny Jackson, Jim Woodmencey, and Steve Rickert. (See *Figures* 4-57 and 4-58.) This variation follows the drainage line of this part of the face, while the original Emotional Rescue route avoids it to the right. Consequently, *very* dry conditions are needed for this variation. It is highly recommended. **Pitch 1:** Climb double cracks (5.8) that lead up the steep wall to a squeeze chimney; continue up this short chimney (5.7) to the belay (40m). **Pitch 2:** A few moves of 5.10- (steep fingers) off the belay lead to a long stretch of 5.9 hands (3"–3.5" pro). Pull through a final overhanging section of 5.10- hands and set up an awkward hanging belay below a small roof (37m). **Pitch 3:** Undercling to the right along the base of the roof, then head straight up toward a large roof/overlap to reach another hanging belay in a small alcove with a small left-facing corner (24m). **Pitch 4:** Instead of following the original Emotional Rescue line out to the right from the belay, pull through some 5.9 moves near the corner and trend left up onto the weakness in the face above, heading straight up toward the next overhang/double roof. Set up another hanging belay below the double-roof overlap (30m). **Pitch 5:** Traverse right below the overhang for a few body lengths, then pull over the lip on good holds. Move back hard left (directly above the belay) and continue up a fun 5.9 weakness of flakes and corners. Belay on a comfortable ledge (40m). **Pitch 6:** Move right on a wildly exposed hand traverse (5.8+) for 10m–12m (don't pull through the first bulge that is approximately 3m up and right from the belay ledge). Solid hand jams and good feet lead to an awkward 5.8 move around a flake/knob. Continue up the large 5.7 right-facing corner (which cannot be seen from the belay) and belay on a large ledge, where the original Emotional Rescue route is joined near the top

FIGURE 4-58. The Enclosure, west aspect. (A) Emotional Rescue *(Route 12)*, IV, 5.11c; (B) Variation: Direct, IV, 5.10-

of its seventh pitch (46m). **Pitch 7:** Move the belay a short distance up and left to the base of a prominent chimney/weakness. **Pitch 8:** Continue up this chimney (5.6) and belay on the large terrace above. Coil the rope and wander up 4th-class terrain (or snow) to a high point below a prominent left-facing corner. **Pitch 9:** Either climb the wide left-facing corner (5.8 offwidth) or continue up and left along a ramp and pull through some 5.9 moves in a stack of solid chockstones leading to a notch. From here climb up and right for approximately 150m (4th and easy 5th class) along a ridge, past the top of the Visionquest Couloir, to the summit of the Enclosure. **Gear:** For protection take a double rack of cams to 3.5" plus a single set of smaller cams and stoppers. A 4" piece is needed for the optional offwidth finish to the ninth pitch.

ROUTE 13. LOOKIN' FOR TROUBLE. V, 5.11, A3. First ascent July 4–5, 1991, by Jim Beyer (solo); probable second ascent July 4, 2021, by Ryan Little and Sam Stuckey. (See *Figure 4-59*.) The rating reflects both mandatory free climbing that is required and the free climbing done by Beyer on the first ascent. This impressive route, one of the most difficult thus far completed on the Grand Teton or the Enclosure, was an exceptional tour de force by this talented climber from Colorado. No bolts were placed on the route. Approach this imposing wall via the Valhalla Traverse (see *Figure 4-47*), passing the Enclosure Ice Couloir *(Route 7)* and then continuing up and around toward the beginning of the Black Ice Couloir *(Grand Teton, Route 51)*. The route begins just around the prow from Emotional Rescue *(Route 12)* on the northeast facet of the wall and approximately 10 meters up the rock pitch leading to the start of the Black Ice. **Pitch 1:** Mixed free and aid climbing in a corner (awkward) leads upward to the top of a left-facing flake with a fixed pin. Above the pin locate a fixed head from which a pendulum to the right is made to a horn. Belay as far to the right as possible (5.10, A2, 25m). **Pitch 2:** Lower off and tension right to a left-facing flake system that becomes a left-facing corner and aid climb to a roof. Traverse left under the roof (hand size cams) and

Steve Rickert on the second pitch of Emotional Rescue during the first ascent, July 26, 1985 (Photo by Renny Jackson)

continue up to a belay. This pitch ends about 15 meters above the belay after 25+ meters of climbing (5.10/.11, A2+). **Pitch 3:** Easier aid and free climbing (juggy) leads to a blank section that is aided using beaks, followed by a tension traverse left to a large horn (A2+, 25m). (Note: a 70m rope fixed here just gets to the ground.) **Pitch 4:** This is the crux pitch, labeled by Beyer as a "5.10- shakefest!" Mandatory free climbing (5.10R) leads up and left toward the left end of a roof about 18m away. At the roof, aid climbing on heads and beaks leads to a good cam placement and a tension traverse to the left. Clip another head and tension farther left to a right-facing 5.9 corner. Climb approximately 12m up the corner and belay (5.10R, A3, 50m). **Pitch 5:** Free climb up the crack and chimney to a small ledge and traverse right to another crack. Climb the crack and the easier face above to a ledge and belay (5.9, 50m). **Pitch 6:** Climb a crack to another ledge with a large boulder on it (5.9+, 18m). **Pitch 7:** From the left side of the ledge, climb another crack to the talus field above (5.9+, 18m). *Figure 4-59* illustrates this somewhat complex route. Note that hanging belays were used on the first, second, third, and fifth pitches. On the first ascent, Beyer climbed the initial three pitches during the first day, with the first pitch taking about six and a half hours. He bivouacked at the base of the climb after leaving fixed ropes to the top of the third pitch. He then completed the climb the next day, reaching the summit of the Enclosure in 14 hours, with the fourth pitch taking the longest (five to six hours). This route joins Emotional Rescue at the top of its eighth pitch and then follows that line to the top. **Gear:** For protection the second ascent party suggests the following (all are BD sizes): one set offset cams, one each at 0.1" and 0.2", 2 each at 0.3" to 3", and one at 4"; copperhead kit; three large beaks; three medium beaks; wired nuts and a small pin selection. An axe and crampons are useful if done in early season. *(Source: Little/Stuckey correspondence.)*

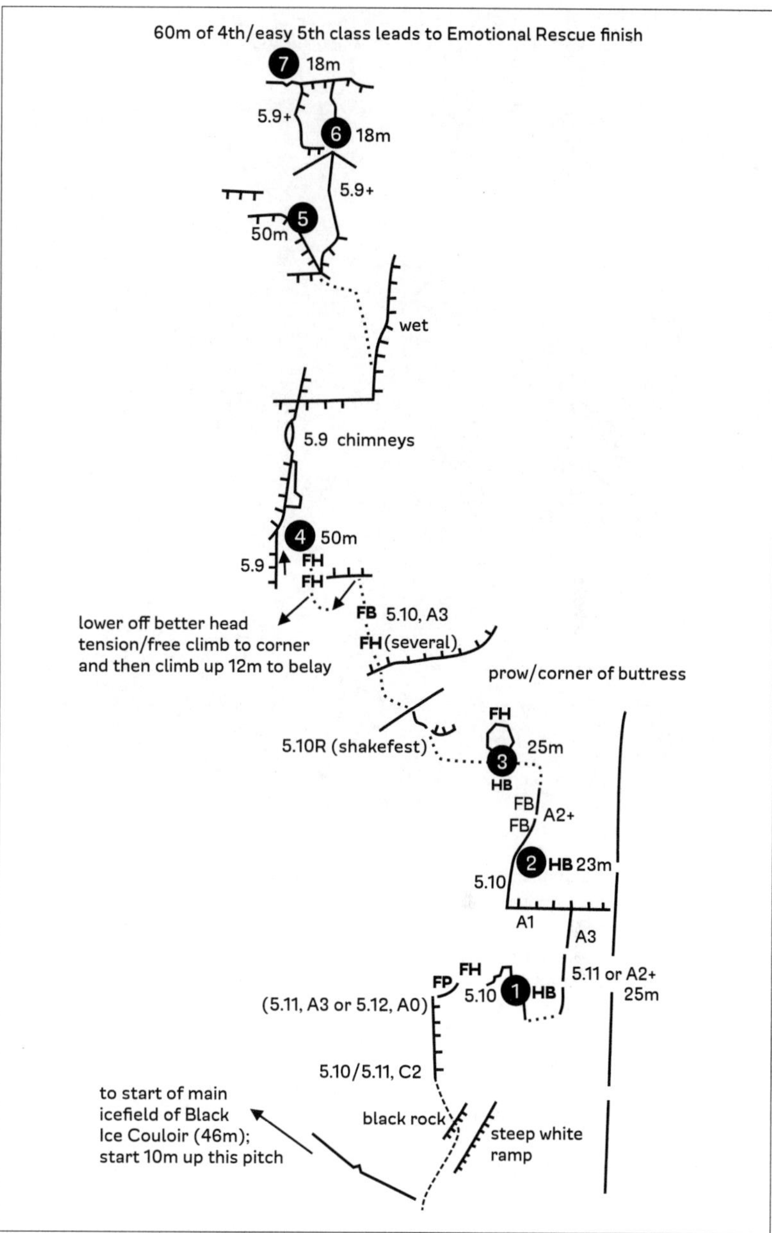

FIGURE 4-59. The Enclosure, west aspect, Lookin' for Trouble *(Route 13)*, V, 5.11, A3. Note: FB = fixed beak.

ROUTE 14. VISIONQUEST COULOIR. IV, 5.8, AI3+. First ascent August 10, 1981, by Michael Stern and Steve Quinlan. (See *Figure 4-53.*) Directly across the Black Ice Couloir from the west face of the Grand Teton is the Visionquest Couloir, a narrow ice gully that provides 180m of excellent climbing. Take the Black Ice Couloir *(Grand Teton, Route 51)* for about 180m to the top of the main (third) icefield and cut right (west) into the steep initial chimney of the couloir. The first two ropelengths are the most difficult, consisting initially of 12m of mixed rock and ice runnels (5.8), followed by a narrow ribbon of steep 60° ice. This narrow section leads to a wide ice sheet of about 55°. The next 90m ascends the left margin of this ice slope, continuing to a large chockstone jammed in the gully. Climb around this chockstone on the right and continue up, partly on ice, bearing right (west) and winding around to the northwest ridge just below the summit. Gain the summit from the west. Once the initial couloir has been entered from the Black Ice Couloir, the route is difficult to lose. This is an excellent climb and is

Ryan Little on the second pitch of Lookin' For Trouble, North Face of the Enclosure during the second ascent, July 3–4, 2021 (Photo by Samuel Stuckey)

slightly more difficult than the standard Black Ice Couloir route. Conditions should be carefully selected for the climb; major rockfalls have been observed in this chute.

***Variation:* TRAINING WHEELS.** IV, 5.7, A1, AI3, M4. First ascent in August 2009, by Landon Wiedeman and Paul Rachele. Conditions will vary dramatically on this route depending on the year and the season in which the climb is undertaken. As shown in *Figure 4-53*, three steep ramps take off to the west from the middle portion of the Black Ice Couloir *(Grand Teton, Route 51)*. The uppermost ramp, the broadest of the three, is the Visionquest Couloir. This variation ascends the middle ramp after climbing the first 150m or so of the Black Ice Couloir. It consists of four mixed pitches before joining the Visionquest Couloir. Wiedeman and Rachele encountered thin ice on the first pitch and gave it an M4 rating (30m). Their second pitch began with a short section of easy ice (AI2) and then continued up a chimney (5.7, M3, 21m). On the third pitch they would have liked to have had a large cam (4.5"–7.5" range) to protect face climbing that led to a roof, which was passed by means of an aid pin (a knifeblade). This was followed by 5.6 climbing on loose rock to a belay. The fourth pitch (60m) went up a loose gully, past a huge flake or block, before joining the Visionquest Couloir. (**Note:** One can apparently avoid the loose gully by climbing solid rock to climber's right.)

SECTION 5

The Grand Traverse

The Grand Teton and the other peaks that make up the heart of the Teton Range are linked together in a great 6-mile arc that forms the upper reaches of Garnet Canyon and Glacier Gulch. Surrounding these peaks are the glaciated Cascade and Avalanche Canyons. This iconic skyline comprises a range of geographical features including a spectacular collection of knife-edge ridge crests, exquisite rocky summits, and needlelike spires—all complemented by an equally stunning array of broad, windswept saddles, narrow cols, and sharp notches. Travel across this serrated crest has come to be known among climbers as the Grand Traverse. Those who undertake this adventure reach 11 summits along the way, with all but one rising above 12,000 feet, and they accumulate nearly 25,000 painful feet of elevation gain and loss.

History

The climbing history of the Grand Traverse is lengthy, and the individuals who feature in it also helped shape the greater history of climbing in the United States and abroad. Fred Ayres climbed from the Middle Teton to Nez Perce during the summer of 1932, thus completing the first and easiest section. The first attempt at the entire Traverse occurred on July 14, 1950, when Michael Brewer and Richard Pownall left Lupine Meadows at midnight and reached the summit of Nez Perce a little under four hours later. A close examination of Pownall's personal scrapbook revealed not only the audacity of this attempt but also the self-admitted mistakes that he and Brewer had made.

After climbing Cloudveil Dome, the pair traversed to its western saddle. "We made a quick scramble up what we thought was the South Teton," wrote Pownall. "We were dismayed to find ourselves hung up on a large pinnacle on the ridge between Cloudveil and the South." They were on the summit of Spalding Peak and were no doubt looking over toward Gilkey Tower and the Icecream Cone, barring easy passage to the South Teton. (**Note:** Gilkey Tower had not yet received its name, as Art Gilkey was to perish on the American attempt on K2 in 1953.) The pair decided that it would be best to descend to the floor of the south fork of Garnet Canyon and scurry up the regular Northwest Couloir route of the South Teton. After losing an hour and several hundred feet of precious altitude, they still managed to reach the summit at 7:30 AM. It was here that they were hit with the first snowstorm of the day. Carrying on, Pownall and Brewer reached the summit of the Middle Teton at 9:30 AM and then began a harrowing descent of the north ridge. They were buffeted by a strong, cold wind and ended up doing six rappels, with the ropes sometimes blowing back up over their heads. "The descent of this ridge cannot be adequately described. It was more of a nightmare than a pleasant mountaineering adventure," Pownall wrote afterward in understated terms.

After recovering and having something to eat at the Lower Saddle, they quickly climbed the Grand Teton via the Owen-Spalding route and were on the summit at 2:30 PM. Presumably, the thought of descending the technical North Ridge route, and then doing the daunting high traverse of the Grandstand to Mount Owen, led them to believe that the best way to go would be down the East Ridge route, onto the Teton Glacier, and then over to the Koven Couloir. After committing to this equally audacious plan, they soon realized that it was a mistake and would take much longer than they had anticipated. The snow conditions were quite bad and a storm was once again

Overview

- **Rating:** VI, 5.8
- **Elevation gain/loss:** 24,712 feet (7,532m)
- **Total distance:** 18.6 miles (30 km)
- **Traverse distance** *(from Teewinot Mountain summit to Nez Perce summit)*: 5.7 miles (9.2 km)
- **Approach and descent distance** *(mainly on trail; includes Lupine Meadows trailhead to Teewinot summit and from Nez Perce summit to Platforms and then Lupine Meadows trailhead)*: 12.9 miles (20.8 km)
- **Ideal season:** Midsummer, when most of the snow is gone from the crest of the Traverse

upon them. As they made their way along the northern side of the Second Tower on the east ridge, lightning forced a short bivouac. "It began to snow again and the wind was blowing all directions at once," wrote Pownall. "Conditions couldn't be much worse." Keep in mind that their biggest self-admitted mistake was taking "nothing but shorts and light weight parkas" for this adventure—hardmen indeed! After a traumatic five hours, the pair reached the Teton Glacier and decided that it was too late in the day to continue; they descended to the valley.

When did the idea of a traverse of all of the peaks in the heart of the range become the Grand Traverse? It is this author's (R. Jackson's) belief that Pownall, a driving force behind the earliest attempts to complete the Traverse, deserves credit for the original idea. On August 8, 1959, he returned, this time with mountaineers Pete Schoening and Willi Unsoeld, to tackle the Traverse in the now-standard order, beginning with Teewinot Mountain. The entry in the Teewinot summit register, made at 4:45 AM, simply reads, "Grand Traverse." By the time they reached the top of Mount Owen at 8:30 AM, perhaps overcome with the magnitude of their endeavor, Pownall's summit register entry had transformed to "The Grand Traverse," the name by which it is known today. It may be the case that this was simply the title of the register entry, but this author likes to think that Pownall came up with the name. The group reached the summit of the Grand at 4 PM, at which point they abandoned their attempt and returned to the valley floor. Although they were disappointed, their effort had resulted in the first ascent of the acclaimed Cathedral Traverse.

The first successful Grand Traverse was accomplished by Richard Long, John Evans, and Allen Steck in 20 hours, 30 minutes on August 12, 1963, only a few days after their first attempt, which came just short of the summit of Mount Owen. On the advice of Unsoeld, the party started at Nez Perce and rappelled the north ridge of the Grand, which "would be less complex than its ascent" and thus would save time. Detailing their climb in an article entitled "A Traverse of the Grand Tetons" in the 1965 *American Alpine Journal*, Steck set the bar high for all subsequent Grand Traverse aspirants:

> ***I am not aware of the origins of the insidious schedule, though I do detect a certain Unsoeldian flavor in the following: from the Jenny Lake parking lot ascend Teewinot, traverse in order: Mount Owen — the Grand, Middle and South Tetons — Cloudveil Dome — Nez Perce, and struggle as best you can back to the car. Any route or time of day is acceptable, however, only be sure to finish within 24 hours.***

The first to actually accomplish the Grand Traverse in Steck's described order were Jim McCarthy and Lito Tejada-Flores, in August of 1966. The pair did the climb in a respectable two days with a bivouac just

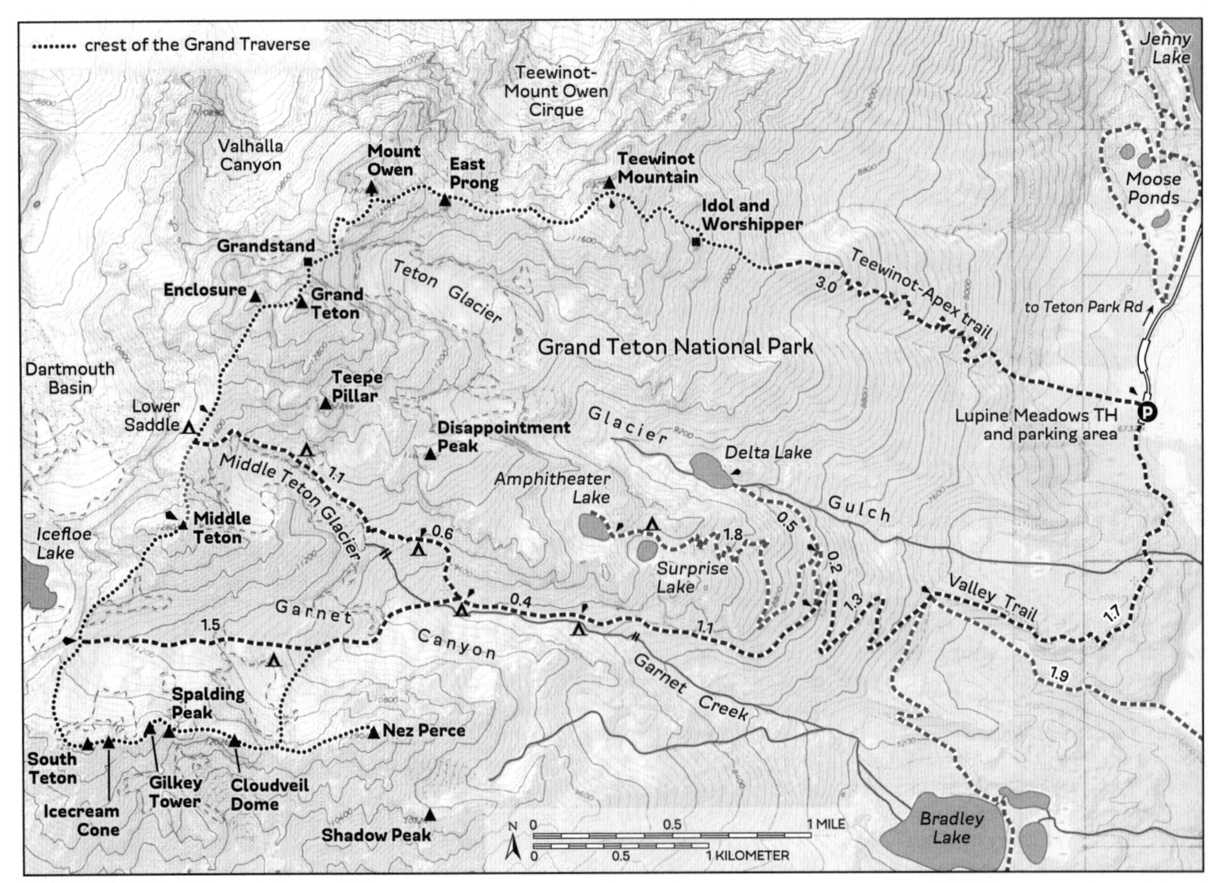

below the summit of the Grand. Before they started, Tejada-Flores remarked sarcastically to McCarthy, "Jim, if we do this, we won't have to climb any of these peaks ever again!"

The Grand Traverse is now a highly sought-after climbing objective. Popularized by the speedy summertime exploits of Alex Lowe and Rolando Garibotti, it is a worthy goal and there is a good deal of traffic on it during the main climbing season. Lowe shattered the original 24-hour time limit in 1988 with a time of 8 hours, 40 minutes, and then Garibotti lowered it further on August 26, 2000, with the mind-boggling time of 6 hours, 49 minutes. Records are made to be broken, and this one is no exception: on August 13, 2016, Canadian climber and runner Nick Elson completed the Traverse in 6 hours, 30 minutes, 49 seconds.

The first winter ascent of the Grand Traverse was a strange and brutally harsh step in the evolution of alpine climbing in the range. As with the summer Traverse, a major piece fell into place with the first winter ascent of the Cathedral Traverse—by Greg Collins, Phil Powers, and Gary Wilmot over a three-day period in January of 1993. Less than a week later Alex Lowe and Andrew McLean repeated this feat from the valley floor and back in just under 24 hours—an incredible effort. Then at 3:50 AM on January 17, 2004, Hans Johnstone and Renny Jackson began the Traverse after two prior failed attempts. They were joined later in the day by friends and fellow mountaineers Mark Newcomb and Stephen Koch near the summit of Mount Owen. After a cold open bivouac on top of the Grandstand, the team climbed the Italian Cracks variation of the North Ridge route and then summited the Grand. At the Lower Saddle Newcomb and Koch carried on while the Johnstone/Jackson party waited a day due to issues with Jackson's boots. Newcomb and Koch completed the first winter Traverse on January 20, and Johnstone and Jackson finished on the 21st.

Strategy

The Grand Traverse is typically done in a north-to-south direction, beginning with Teewinot Mountain and finishing with Nez Perce. As the route evolved, climbers began to use the Italian Cracks variation instead of the regular North Ridge route of the Grand Teton, thus avoiding the chimneys and the more difficult climbing of that route; this is now the way nearly everyone goes. Magazine articles, aggressive marketing by guide services, and social media attention have all contributed to the increased popularity of the Traverse. Yet it remains a serious endeavor that requires significant routefinding skill, sound judgment, confidence on poor-quality rock ("Teton choss"), and an ability to move quickly over exposed, technical terrain.

The most important ingredient for success on the Traverse is familiarity with each segment of the route. For example, it helps to know the Owen-Spalding route on the Grand, which is used for the descent. Prior experience with the trickier parts of the Traverse, such as the section between Mount Owen and the Grandstand, will pay huge dividends in terms of time. It is also extremely useful to study the escape routes from some of the more isolated sections.

For those coming to the Tetons for the first time hoping to onsight the Traverse, perhaps the most valuable resource will be the Jenny Lake Ranger Station, which is also the place to obtain the mandatory overnight backcountry permits. The rangers there can provide up-to-date information on route conditions and explain some of the trickier routefinding problems.

In general, a fit party who is unfamiliar with the terrain can expect to take a total of three days, which can be broken up any number of ways. For a sample three-day Traverse, a worthy first-day goal is to reach the Grandstand; having negotiated the trickiest portion of the Traverse, the party will be in the best position the following morning to get up and down the Grand quickly. Then the second night could be spent at the saddle between the Middle and South Tetons, which would provide for a pleasant final-day traverse of the section from the South Teton to Nez Perce.

Hans Johnstone on the upper east ridge snowfield of Mount Owen during the first winter ascent of the Grand Traverse, January 17, 2004 (Photo by Renny Jackson)

Equipment

(assuming ideal dry summer conditions):

- **Lightweight bivouac gear**
- **Sticky-rubber approach shoes for climbing**
- **A lightweight pair of rock shoes for the leader (if they are not comfortable leading in approach shoes)**
- **One 60m rope**
- **One set of stoppers**
- **A single set of cams from 0.4" to 3.5"**
- **6–10 alpine draws**
- **A lightweight pair of crampons**
- **A short ice tool with adze for chopping steps (conditions dependent)**

Approach

Begin at the Lupine Meadows trailhead. To reach this trailhead, turn west off Teton Park Road at the Lupine Meadows junction, cross the bridge over Cottonwood Creek, and proceed 1.5 miles (west and then south) on the dirt road that leads to the trailhead. Near the middle of the northern portion of the main parking area, look for the Teewinot Apex trail (unmaintained) leading west. Take this trail to Teewinot Mountain and climb its East Face route.

Teewinot Mountain to Mount Owen

See *Figure 5-1* for an overview of this section. From the summit of Teewinot Mountain, climb back down a few hundred meters on the east side until it is possible to traverse back to the huge notch immediately south of the summit. (See *Figure 5-2*.) Descend to the west a short distance until a traverse to the southwest is possible. Traverse 50m and gain a small saddle that leads down and onto the expansive and beautiful plateau on the west side of Teewinot. Walk west on the plateau toward Peak 11,840+.

FIGURE 5-1. Overview of the Grand Traverse, Teewinot Mountain to Mount Owen

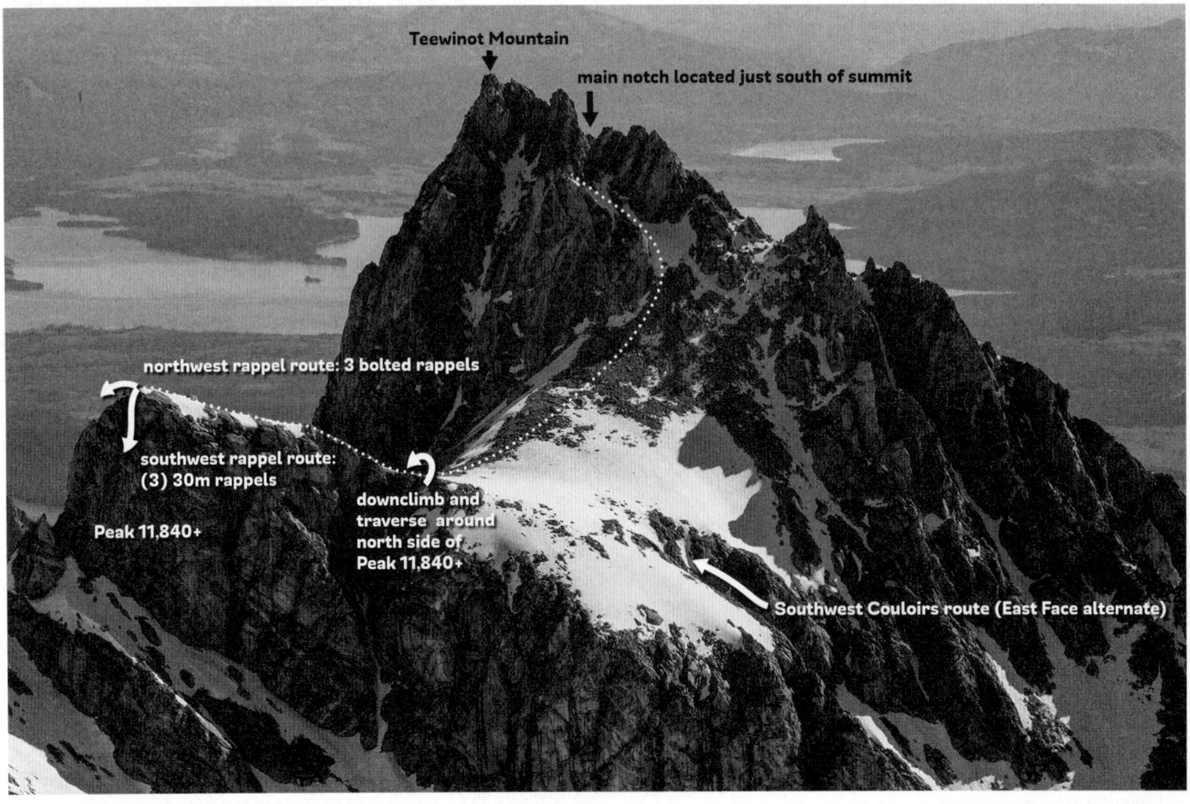

FIGURE 5-2. The Grand Traverse, southwest aspect, Teewinot Mountain to Peak 11,840+

FIGURE 5-3. The Grand Traverse, Peak 11,840+, west aspect

There are three possible ways around Peak 11,840+ (see *Figure 5-3*), with the second and third options being the ones that are currently used: (1) Descend to the north a few hundred meters and pass the peak on its north side. This involves steep snow (early season) and/or loose rock (later in the season). Although this is probably the fastest way around the peak, the terrain hazards can be significant depending on the year and the time of year. (2) Descend a large corner system on the northwest side, which in 2019 was equipped with bolts, cord, and rings for three rappels. **Note:** Although these can be done with a 40m rope, the recommendation here is for a lightweight 60m rope. This will probably become the preferred descent method. (3) Descend a short distance to the southwest from the top of Peak 11,840+ and make three 30m rappels from established anchors down a corner system. (**Note:** The last rappel may be slightly longer than 30m—caution is advised!) For the second and third options, check the anchors and take normal rappel precautions.

From here to the East Prong, the easiest route consists of 4th- and easy 5th-class climbing and walking, keeping generally on the north side of the crest. The East Prong is passed either by downclimbing its northwest side (easy 5th class with potential late-season snow and patchy ice) or by making two 30m rappels from just below the summit to reach the East Prong Col—the col at the top of the Koven Couloir.

Just above the col is a large chimney system that is often a good place to get water. Climb partway up this system until an obvious escape out to the north leads to the top of the chimney. Walk around and up on the south side of the summit block until one reaches another chimney system. Leave packs here and tag the summit of Mount Owen via scrambling (4th and easy 5th class) up and around to the west side, where the Koven Chimney takes one to the top. Reverse this, return to the packs, and prepare for the trickiest part of the Traverse.

- **Mount Owen, Koven** *(Route 6)*: 5.4, steep snow; see *Figures 7-9* and *7-10*.

Mount Owen to the Grandstand

A prominent U-shaped notch, visible from the valley, is part of the key to the Traverse, as it provides access to the west side of the southwest ridge of Mount Owen and eventually to Gunsight Notch. (See *Figure 5-4*.) Downclimb and traverse to this U-shaped notch on the east side of the ridge. Once there, either downclimb (intimidating 5.6ish terrain) on the west side or rappel from two bolts (30m) down a steep chimney system that eventually becomes more of a gully. A descending traverse to the south on scree- or snow-covered ledges leads toward Gunsight Notch. Follow a faint ledge around to the east. When the ledge disappears, a few climbing moves lead to a point just above Gunsight Notch, and a short (8m) rappel gets one into the notch. Alternatively, skip the ledge and the rappel and simply scramble down and into the West Gunsight Couloir where convenient, then climb up to the notch.

An alternative route from the summit of Mount Owen is to proceed down to the first notch in the south ridge, just above an obvious bivouac site on the east side of the ridge; this is Rolando Garibotti's preferred route (see "Garibotti route" in *Figure 5-4*). From the notch, rappel or downclimb into a loose gully for 60m and then proceed down to the southwest toward Gunsight Notch as described above.

A second alternative, shown as a solid black line in *Figure 5-4*, gains Gunsight Notch using a higher traverse. From the bottom of the 30m rappel from the U-shaped notch, traverse to the south and find a small ledge that provides a way through a small cliff band. Either downclimb (5.5) or do a short rappel (10m) and then continue south, over to a point where one becomes cliffed out above Gunsight Notch. Three rappels are then necessary to gain the notch.

Once in Gunsight Notch, climb up approximately 12m–15m on the south side until it is possible to descend to the east on a ledge. Go down the ledge a short

FIGURE 5-4. The Grand Traverse, Mount Owen to the Grandstand, west aspect

distance until a nice-looking crack in good rock is found leading up to the shoulder of the Grandstand. Climb the crack (5.7–5.8) to the shoulder and belay. A second pitch (5.7) can be done here up the shoulder on knobby, golden Teton rock. Or traverse out onto the east face of the Grandstand and follow the path of least resistance upward. There is often running water in a few places in the area of the east face, just below the flat bivouac spots near the top.

Grand Teton: Italian Cracks to Owen-Spalding

The Italian Cracks variation to the North Ridge route on the Grand Teton is the easiest—and by far the preferred—way to get to the Second Ledge on the north face. The Second Ledge permits a traverse over to the Owen-Spalding route and the quickest way to the summit of the Grand. Leave packs and extra gear near the base of Sargent's Chimney, where they can be picked up on the way back down to the rappel. After tagging the summit of the Grand, descend to the Upper Saddle. (**Note:** Use the standard rappel—not the bolted anchors! The standard rappel is 30m; be sure to throw ropes to the south—skier's left.) Continue down to the Lower Saddle, where water can be found near its lower eastern edge.

- **North Ridge** *(Route 47)*, **variation:** Italian Cracks: 5.7/5.8; see *Figure 4-42*.
- **Owen-Spalding** *(Route 1)*: 5.4; see *Figures 4-3* and 4-4.

Middle Teton: North Ridge to Southwest Couloir

The North Ridge route up the Middle Teton is the next part of the Traverse; it is fairly straightforward once the notch behind Bonney's Pinnacle is attained. Use the southwest couloir to descend to the saddle that separates the Middle Teton from the South Teton.

- **North Ridge** *(Route 32)*: 5.6; see *Figure 3-27*.
- **Southwest Couloir** *(Route 1)*: 3.0; see *Figure 3-14*.

South Teton to Nez Perce

Proceed up the Northwest Couloir route of the South Teton and descend the East Ridge route; both are 4th class. From the notch between the South Teton and the Icecream Cone, either climb a chimney on the steep west face of the small tower or traverse around on the north side and tag the summit via the easier East Face route. The summits of Gilkey Tower, Spalding Peak, and Cloudveil Dome can be easily traversed by staying on or near the crest (3rd and 4th class); see *Figure 5-5*. The descent from Cloudveil Dome along its east ridge is the trickiest part of this

All of the peaks of The Grand Traverse

FIGURE 5-5. The Grand Traverse, South Teton to Cloudveil Dome, northeast aspect

FIGURE 5-6. The Grand Traverse, Cloudveil Dome to Nez Perce

section of the Traverse. It is exposed 4th or easy/moderate 5th class, depending upon which route is taken—caution is advised! Some may prefer to rappel. (See *Figure 5-6.*) The ascent of Nez Perce, the final peak of the Traverse, is by the Northwest Couloirs route.

- **South Teton, Northwest Couloir** *(Route 7)*: 4.0; see *Figure 3-13.*
- **South Teton, East Ridge** *(Route 4)*: 4.0
- **Icecream Cone, West Face** *(Route 1)*: 5.6
- **Icecream Cone, East Face** *(Route 2)*: 3.0
- **Gilkey Tower, West Ridge** *(Route 1)*: 4.0
- **Gilkey Tower, East Face** *(Route 3)*: 3.0
- **Spalding Peak, West Ridge** *(Route 1)*: 4.0
- **Spalding Peak, East Ridge** *(Route 4)*: 3.0
- **Cloudveil Dome, East Ridge** *(Route 10)*: 5.0; see *Figure 3-11.*
- **Nez Perce, Northwest Couloirs** *(Route 1)*: 4.0; see *Figure 3-2.*

Descent

Reverse the Northwest Couloirs route and descend from the col between Cloudveil Dome and Nez Perce into the south fork of Garnet Canyon. Follow the climbers' trail down to the main Garnet Canyon trail and return to the Lupine Meadows trailhead.

Hans Johnstone rapelling into the notch between Gilkey Tower and Spalding Peak during the first winter ascent of the Grand Traverse (Photo by Renny Jackson)

SECTION 6

Garnet Canyon to Glacier Gulch

Disappointment Peak, Southern Arêtes, Couloirs, and Ridges

Garnet Canyon and Glacier Gulch are the two major drainages that flank the Grand Teton on the east side of the Teton Range. They are separated from one another by Disappointment Peak, with its many southern arêtes, ridges, and couloirs rising above the Garnet Canyon trail and its magnificent north wall that towers over the south side of Glacier Gulch. At the head of the north fork of Garnet Canyon and the head of Glacier Gulch lie two of the largest remaining active glaciers in the park: the Middle Teton Glacier and the Teton Glacier. The serrated skyline of the Grand Traverse (see Section 5), comprising an array of iconic peaks, encircles these two major canyons. This section describes the myriad pinnacles, spires, and towers associated with the Grand Teton as well as the many shorter rock climbs that have been done over the years. See the introduction to Section 3 for Garnet Canyon approach information; and see *Figure 6-1*, which shows the trail from the upper Meadows in the north fork of the canyon as well as several of the climbs, pinnacles, and other features described in this section. The introduction to Section 7 contains Glacier Gulch approach information.

GLENCOE SPIRE (ca. 12,320)

(0.3 mi S of the Grand Teton)

Map: Grand Teton

This spire, one of two large towers on the south flank of the Grand Teton, lies due west of Teepe Pillar and is about the same altitude. The name is derived from Glencoe, Illinois, the hometown of Jack Lewis, one of the first ascensionists. In the early days of the park, Glencoe Spire was known as the "Red Sentinel," and Glencoe Col, formed by the weathering out of the Black Dike between the spire and the Grand Teton, was "Sentinel Col." The switch in names was probably due to Haldon Smith, who joined Hans Kraus in 1947 in his attempts on the pinnacle that is now known as the Red Sentinel. From Teepe Col, Glencoe Spire appears difficult but is actually a short, easy climb up from Glencoe Col at the base of the Underhill Ridge. Glencoe Col can be reached either by traversing the Black Dike from the Lower Saddle or by approaching from the Teepe Glacier. The south face of Glencoe Spire extends for almost 300m upward from the Middle Teton Glacier moraine. This face is flanked on the left (west) during most of the season by a waterfall draining the Stettner Couloir of the Grand Teton and on the right (east) by a steep, rotten gully separating Glencoe Spire from Teepe Pillar.

Chronology

NORTH AND WEST FACES: July 25, 1947, Jack Lewis, Haldon Smith
SOUTH FACE: July 29, 1959, William Buckingham, Beatrice Vogel
GLENCOE-TEEPE GULLY: August 6, 1963, Dallas Kloke, Mike Killien
DIRECT NORTH FACE: August 11, 1967, Dave Foster, Ray Palmer
DIRECT SOUTH FACE: August 28, 1974, Michel DeRoy, Alain Henault
var—September 8, 1988, Paul Horton, Brent Bishop
SOUTHWEST RIDGE: July 1990, George Montopoli, Leo Larson

ROUTE 1. SOUTH FACE. II, 5.6. First ascent July 29, 1959, by William Buckingham and Beatrice Vogel. Below (south of) the Black Dike that cuts across the south side of the Grand Teton is a wall extending from Teepe Pillar to the Lower Saddle and forming the north rim of the uppermost north fork of Garnet Canyon. At the base of this wall below the Petzoldt Ridge is a small, nearly circular basin marked by black stains from a small waterfall draining the Beckey and Stettner Couloirs. This route begins at the right (east) side of this basin on the western part of the south ridge of Glencoe Spire. One can start either from the Lower Saddle or from the Caves.

From the Lower Saddle descend to the basin, cross the stream, and climb about 120m out of the basin up a series of loose, black chimneys on the right (east) side to the small terrace on the south face proper. From here 76m of easy chimneys and slabs leads to the base of the large slab below the "prow." Climb about 24m up the

FIGURE 6-1. Garnet Canyon, north fork overview

slab to the base of the prow. The next pitch zigzags upward, with an initial zig to the right along the top edge of the slab and then a zag back to the left to a belay platform. The next pitch is long and steep and goes almost directly up the wall. It begins slightly left of the crest, traverses under an overhang to just right of the crest, and ends with a short jam crack that leads to a belay position in a pile of boulders on a sloping ledge. Climb through one of the breaks in the overhanging wall above for 46m to a broad ledge beneath the final steep wall. At the right edge of this ledge, climb 12m up a distinct black chimney and then traverse 18m left on a sloping ledge. After another 24m up the steep wall (good holds), a short eastward scramble leads to the summit. See *American Alpine Journal* 12, no. 1 (1960): pp. 125–27.

ROUTE 2. DIRECT SOUTH FACE. III, 5.9. First ascent August 28, 1974, by Michel DeRoy and Alain Henault. This fine route of 10 pitches starts from the very bottom of the south face and follows a line distinct from the 1959 route. At the base of the face a corner is seen as the main break in the initial wall. Climb the crack (5.6) 4.5m left (west) of the corner for 23m until one can traverse horizontally back into the corner, gaining a big scree ledge for the belay. The next lead (5.7) starts in the center of the face 6m left (west) of an obvious corner, goes diagonally left, and passes a small overhang. The third ropelength (5.7) slants up and right onto the wall with two liebacks, just to the right of the obvious corner that contains loose rock and a large black crack. The next two pitches are easier, continuing the previous line for 9m, then proceeding up to the top of the large, obvious gully above to a large crack. The sixth lead traverses left (west) on easy slabs at the base of the wall to reach an obvious crack under the summit block. The next pitch of 23m is the most difficult (5.9); it starts on the wall 6m left of the obvious crack and joins the crack after 18m and a small traverse. Now follow the crack upward for about 18m and then continue up to and left along the base of the summit block. The final pitch leads easily onto the summit. The rock on this route is in general solid, and the climb is clean, except for the scree ledge and the main lower gully.

Variation: III, 5.9. First ascent September 8, 1988, by Paul Horton and Brent Bishop. The upper portion of this variation is apparently the same as the main Direct South Face. Look for a prominent chimney at the right (east) side of the upper portion of the south face, above a big ramp that bisects the face. This chimney becomes a gully that continues down from the ramp to the base of the face. Begin by scrambling up from below toward a ridge that is to the right (east) of this gully. The first three pitches ascend this ridge via easy 5th-class climbing and some 5.6, heading up and to the left (west) until the gully is intersected. Third- and 4th-class climbing then leads up the gully for another ropelength. Next, climb onto and across the ramp for a pitch until just below the obvious crack under the summit block. Continue up the Direct South Face to the summit.

ROUTE 3. GLENCOE-TEEPE GULLY. II, 5.4. First ascent August 6, 1963, by Dallas Kloke and Mike Killien (in conjunction with an ascent of Glencoe Spire). This gully, located between Glencoe Spire and Teepe Pillar, had been climbed four years earlier as part of an ascent of Teepe Pillar; see *Teepe Pillar, Route 2*. For their ascent, Kloke and Killien climbed the gully to the Black Dike, where they took the regular North and West Faces route *(Route 5)* to the summit. Not unexpectedly the party reported the gully to be "very rotten, rockfall danger extreme." This is a gully to avoid, although it may yield a reasonable ice climb if all the rocks are frozen in place.

ROUTE 4. DIRECT NORTH FACE. II, 5.6. First ascent August 11, 1967, by Dave Foster and Ray Palmer. From directly at the top of Glencoe Col climb 3m up and left on an easy ledge to the base of a left-facing open book, which is then climbed for 12m to a broad ledge. Continue past an overhang and up a wide chimney for 21m to another ledge. Nine meters of easy climbing up yet another wide chimney leads to the north summit. After a short descent to the notch, the main summit is then easily reached.

ROUTE 5. ▲ NORTH AND WEST FACES. I, 5.1. First ascent July 25, 1947, by Jack Lewis and Haldon Smith. About 15m down to the right (west) from Glencoe Col, climb a wide vertical chimney on the otherwise smooth north face. Scramble up a small gully in the west face to a small notch in the south ridge only a meter from the summit. Descent can be made from the summit directly down to the col in two single-rope rappels. **Time:** 1½ hours from the Lower Saddle.

ROUTE 6. SOUTHWEST RIDGE. II, 5.9+. First ascent in July 1990, by George Montopoli and Leo Larson. This is an enjoyable four-pitch route that is easily accessed from the Lower Saddle, if one happens to be camped up there with some extra time. It begins just west of where the southwest ridge of Glencoe Spire intersects the terminus of the Stettner Couloir, just before it drops off steeply into the upper north fork of Garnet Canyon. It is suggested that climbers harness up and rack up below the base of the Petzoldt Ridge before dropping down to the start of the route, in order to begin climbing without delay. There is potential rockfall hazard on this approach, especially since the huge rockfall event of 2007 (see *Grand Teton, Southern Ridges*). At the bottom of the approach gully, just before it drops into Garnet Canyon, a rock slab divides

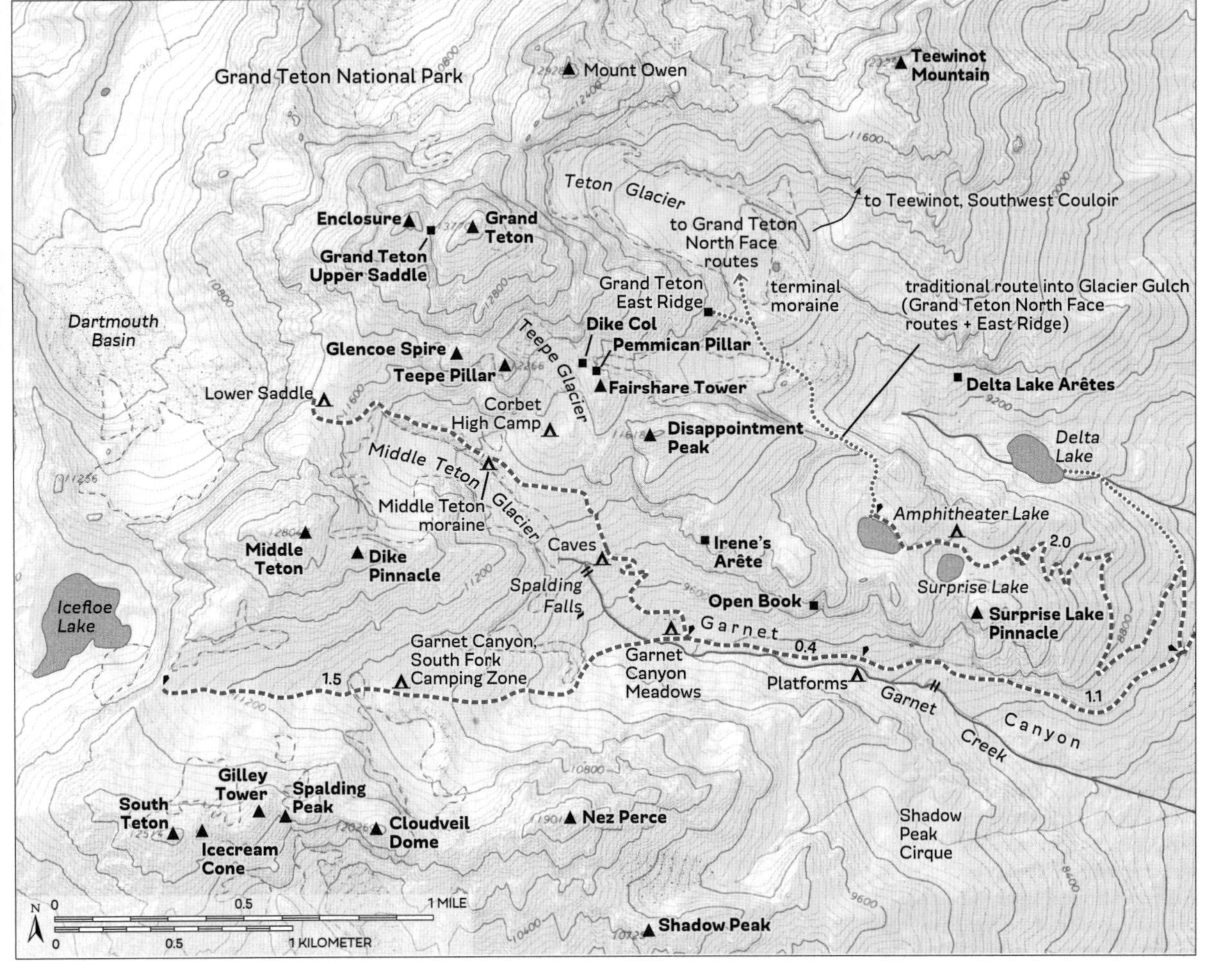

the couloir into west and east branches. Descend the east branch until it ends, and at this point scramble up approximately 12m on easy terrain to the base of the first pitch. **Pitch 1:** Climb up steep rock with intermittent short cracks and some meandering (5.6, 46m). **Pitch 2:** Ascend 12m up and left to the base of a steep crack in a shallow left-facing corner. The initial move into the corner is the crux (5.9+), but the rest of the crack is in the 5.7–5.8 range. At the top of the corner, continue up easy ground for another 12m to a belay (5.9+, 35m). **Pitch 3:** Go up moderate terrain for 15m on the left side of the ridge until the ridge itself is attained. Then continue up the ridge for another 30m to a large belay ledge (5.6). **Pitch 4:** Climb directly up the southwest ridge to the summit. The climbing is easy but quite pleasant on spectacularly colored rock (5.6, 46m).

TEEPE PILLAR (12,266)

(0.4 mi SE of the Grand Teton)
Map: Grand Teton

This major pinnacle, separated by the Black Dike from the southeast side of the Grand Teton, is the largest and most prominent of those that surround the peak. Teepe Pillar was named for Theodore Teepe, who was killed on August 4, 1925, while descending the Teepe Glacier after a successful ascent of the Grand Teton. (Teepe was the first known person to perish while climbing in the Teton Range.) In recent years the Teepe Pillar has become a popular short climb. The view from the airy summit shows the southeast face of the Grand Teton at very close range. Teepe Pillar can be approached from the Lower Saddle or from the cirque below the Teepe Glacier. The recommended descent is made by rappelling the West Ridge route *(Route 1)*, which involves four 30m rappels. However, this descent places one at Teepe Col, necessitating either a traverse back to the Lower Saddle or a downclimb of the Teepe Glacier. Another rappel route is being developed on the east face; it requires two ropes, and the approximate positions of the anchors are shown in *Figure 6-3*. Note that several of these eight rappels are 60m in length, so two ropes are necessary. There is a bit of downclimbing at the bottom of the fourth rappel.

Chronology

UNDERHILL-HENDERSON: July 18, 1930, Robert Underhill, Kenneth Henderson
WEST RIDGE: August 5, 1941, Hans Kraus, Susanne Kruger-Simon
var—July 1970, Ray Jacquot, Henry Siracusian
DIRECT EAST FACE: August 27, 1952, Robert Merriam, Steve Jervis, Chris Marshall
SOUTHWEST RIDGE: August 1, 1956, David Anderson, David Dornan
SOUTH RIDGE: August 10, 1957, Willi and Jolene Unsoeld, Norman Lee
NORTH FACE: July 21, 1958, Yvon Chouinard, Ken Weeks
GLENCOE-TEEPE GULLY: July 5, 1959, Tim Bond, Richard Pittman
NORTHEAST FACE: August 24, 1961, Royal Robbins, Jane Taylor
SOUTH FACE: August 10, 1978, David Beneman, Steven Winnett
SOUTH FACE (HOWE-KEITH): July 1999, Jim Howe, Jason Keith
D IS FOR DIZZLE: June 28, 2015, Emma Williams, Sam Macke
SOUTH FACE (OPP-HENNESSEY): September 2015, Nate Opp, Sam Hennessey
EAST FACE, CENTER: Date and party unknown

ROUTE 1. ▲ WEST RIDGE. II, 5.4. First ascent August 5, 1941, by Hans Kraus and Susanne Kruger-Simon. This is a short but pleasant route to an airy summit. It is best climbed as a secondary ascent from the Lower Saddle or the Caves, rather than as a separate endeavor all the way from the valley. Although the route name has become fixed as the West Ridge, strictly speaking it is the northwest ridge. The route, the most popular one on the pinnacle, starts from the high col formed by the weathering out of the Black Dike, which separates the Pillar from the Grand Teton. This col can be reached either from the Lower Saddle (easy), by traversing the Black Dike, or by climbing up the Teepe Glacier. The route is much easier than its fearsome appearance from the col would suggest. The first ropelength is up the jam cracks just right of the left (north) edge of the ridge. Continue up the ridge another ropelength or two until it is possible to traverse right over to the south ridge, which is then followed to the summit. In all, only four short pitches are required to reach the summit from the col. **Time:** 6 hours from Garnet Canyon. See *American Alpine Journal* 10, no. 1 (1956): pp. 116–19; *Appalachia* 24, no. 4 (December 1943): pp. 528–30; *Dartmouth Mountaineering Club Journal*, 1956: pp. 34–38.

Variation: II, 5.6. First ascent in July 1970, by Ray Jacquot and Henry Siracusian. This one-pitch variation starts the West Ridge route from the col with a 12m traverse down and left onto the north face to a steep jam crack. Climb this crack, which widens into a chimney, exiting at the top of the first pitch of the regular West Ridge route.

ROUTE 2. GLENCOE-TEEPE GULLY. II, 5.4. First ascent July 5, 1959, by Tim Bond and Richard Pittman. The steep south couloir separating Glencoe Spire from Teepe Pillar has two branches. This variation ascends the right (east) branch—this contains loose, rotten rock (and snow and ice in early season)—to Teepe Col, from which the standard West Ridge route *(Route 1)* is climbed. This alternative approach to the Black Dike and Teepe Col is unpleasant, hazardous, and not recommended.

ROUTE 3. SOUTH FACE. II, 5.8. First ascent August 10, 1978, by David Beneman and Steven Winnett. The exact location of this climb is uncertain. Starting from the moraines, scramble up a talus slope to a chimney that leads onto a rock plateau. Continue upward until it steepens, and then take a narrow ledge all the way around to the left to Teepe Col. This ledge cuts diagonally across the large west-southwest face of Teepe Pillar. Because the face above overhangs, the climb occasionally becomes a crawl along a "tunnel." This traverse contains several difficult places (5.8), with the crux move coming near the end of the traverse. From the col take the regular West Ridge route *(Route 1)* to the summit.

ROUTE 4. SOUTHWEST RIDGE. II, 5.6. First ascent August 1, 1956, by David Anderson and David Dornan. Approach from the Caves and start around and up the couloir just west of the Pillar. From a point well below Teepe Col climb two 5.6 pitches in order to reach the south ridge above. Once on the ridge the remainder of the route to the summit is enjoyable 4.0 climbing.

ROUTE 5. D IS FOR DIZZLE. III, 5.11b/c. First ascent June 28, 2015, by Emma Williams and Sam Macke. This climb is located on the southwest face of Teepe Pillar and is approached by going up the gully between the Pillar and Glencoe Spire. This route comprises three difficult pitches, after which it joins the upper south ridge. The climbing is atypical of the Tetons in that it follows good cracks through beautiful, gray-colored granite. To find the start, look for a prominent, light-colored pillar immediately right of a black-and-white-striped headwall. **Pitch 1:** Begin by climbing up and right just to the right of a crack system in red-colored rock for 20m until just below a short left-facing corner (5.7). **Pitch 2:** Go up the corner and then through a bulge to a belay beneath a large roof with two parallel cracks in it (5.9, 30m). **Pitch 3:** This crux pitch goes up and over the roof via the left-hand crack; the crack widens from hands to fists through the roof. Once above the roof, continue up to a wide crack that leans to the left and is slightly overhanging (5" piece useful here). Once above this difficult section, ascend vertical terrain via cracks and blocks to a large ledge. The route joins the south ridge here and follows it to the summit. **Gear:** For protection take a set of stoppers, a set of cams to 4" (with extras in the 2.5"–3.5" range), and a 5" piece. (Source: Mountain Project)

ROUTE 6. SOUTH FACE (HOWE-KEITH). III, 5.10c/d. First ascent in July 1999, by Jim Howe and Jason Keith. (See *Figure 6-2*.) This route is distinctive because of an "A-frame" roof on the second pitch that one can see on the approach. Also look for a chimney system just to the west of the steep, smooth lower portion of the south face. Begin climbing on the right side of this chimney system on easy 5th-class terrain (5.6). The crux moves (5.10c/d) are at the beginning of the second pitch, right off the belay ledge, and are protected by either a bolt or a pin. The pitch then goes up to and through the A-frame roof (5.8). The third pitch consists of moderate climbing directly up the ridge crest. The fourth pitch continues up via moderate climbing, and the route finishes with a long scramble to the summit.

ROUTE 7. SOUTH FACE (OPP-HENNESSEY). III, 5.12aR. First ascent in September 2015, by Nate Opp and Sam Hennessey. (See *Figure 6-2*.) This is a high-quality, very difficult route. **Pitch 1:** Begin by scrambling up a ramp/ledge system to the middle of the south face. From this ramp locate a small, left-arching dihedral and reach as high as possible to clip a bolt that protects the initial difficult moves. Then climb straight up for 23m through a break in the roof above and then slightly left to a fixed anchor at a ledge beneath a small roof. Although the technical crux of the pitch is down low, the entire pitch is very pumpy without any rests. It is well protected with a few bolts and some fixed pins (5.12a, 30m). **Pitch 2:** Climb straight up from the belay to a bolt, then make a hard move aiming for a big handrail. Mantel up on the handrail, where protection again becomes available (4.5m runout!). Now climb the big right-facing corner above up to two fixed pitons. Tricky stemming, protected by the pins and a micro stopper, leads up to a step left followed by face climbing up to another small ledge and a fixed anchor for the belay (5.11aR, 30m). **Pitch 3:** Proceed up and left from the belay past a flake (micro cams are nice to have here), then climb up and right to a wide crack through a roof (5.10-, 40m). Above the roof this route joins the major gully on the upper half of Teepe Pillar and the climbing eases off. Follow this gully system for a few hundred meters to the summit via easy

FIGURE 6-2. Teepe Pillar, south aspect. (A) South Face (Howe-Keith; *Route 6*), III, 5.10c/d; (B) South Face (Opp-Hennessey; *Route 7*), III, 5.12aR

5th-class climbing. The first-ascent team rappelled the east face (see *Figure 6-3*), a descent they described as "surprisingly easy and straightforward." The West Ridge route *(Route 1)* could also be rappelled for the descent. **Gear:** For protection take a standard rack with micro cams and quickdraws.

ROUTE 8. SOUTH RIDGE. III, 5.8. First ascent August 10, 1957, by Willi and Jolene Unsoeld and Norman Lee. This ridge is most conveniently approached from the Caves. The route follows the extreme southeast edge of the large, triangular south face, utilizing small ledges that overhang the south face. After four leads, the third being the most difficult, the climbing eases off somewhat and eventually joins and follows the Underhill-Henderson route *(Route 9)* to the summit. **Time:** 8¾ hours from the Caves. See *American Alpine Journal* 11, no. 1 (1958): pp. 85–88.

ROUTE 9. UNDERHILL-HENDERSON. II, 5.4, A1, or II, 5.7. First ascent July 18, 1930, by Robert Underhill and Kenneth Henderson. (See *Figure 6-3.*) This climb starts at the base of the east face. Two intersecting chimneys cut the east face, one leading right toward the summit and the other leading left to the south ridge. To reach the grassy ledge at the base of the left (south) chimney, climb about 46m up a slab. (**Note:** *Figure 6-3* shows this route following the 5.5 start for *Route 10.*) From a ledge at the top of the slab climb 9m up to the large overhang at the base of the chimney. The first-ascent party used a shoulder stand on the south wall of the chimney to pass this overhang, but a few moves of 5.7 now suffice. Small holds then permit a traverse back into the chimney above the overhang. The next overhang, some 12m farther up the chimney, is easily passed on the right (north). Pass the large chockstone above (shown in *Figure 6-3*) by climbing on the south wall. Eighteen meters of easy climbing leads to the south ridge. Follow this about 90m to the summit. **Time:** 5¾ hours from the Caves. See *Appalachia* 18, no. 3 (June 1931): pp. 209–32, illus.; *Canadian Alpine Journal* 19 (1930): pp. 84–91, illus.

ROUTE 10. DIRECT EAST FACE. III, 5.8. First partial ascent August 21, 1938, by Bert Jensen, William Rice, William Bigelow, and Harry Kornberg; first complete ascent August 27, 1952, by Robert Merriam, Steve Jervis, and Chris Marshall. (See *Figure 6-3.*) The 1938 second ascent of Teepe Pillar did not follow the 1930 Underhill-Henderson route exactly but utilized a portion of the east face before eventually cutting left onto the south ridge and face. This direct route of 1952 follows the right (north) of the two major intersecting chimney systems on the east face; it leads almost directly to the summit. This is a fine climb on good rock.

Near the base of the Pillar, aim for the large squeeze chimney that is the common base of the two main east chimney systems. To start, either climb this old-school chimney (5.8) to a wide ledge or ascend a 5.5 face to the right of the chimney. From the top of the chimney,

FIGURE 6-3. Teepe Pillar, east aspect. (A) Underhill-Henderson *(Route 9)*, II, 5.7; (B) East Face, Center *(Route 11)*, III, 5.9; (C) Direct East Face *(Route 10)*, III, 5.8

it is possible to make an exposed traverse to the left into the chimney of *Route 9*; one could also traverse to *Route 9* from the 5.5 start. For this Direct East Face route, however, continue nearly straight up on enjoyable rock, staying slightly to the right (north) of the main east chimney. The natural line leads to the foot of the double-crack pitch (5.7), shown in *Figure 6-3*. From the top of this crux lead, move left (south) over a small overhang to a broken area affording a good belay position. After passing a small nose, keep to the right (north) of the main vertical chimney and continue all the way to the bottom of the final chimney with a chockstone at its top. This chimney is just left (south) of the large, smooth, overhanging face near the top of the Pillar. Climb this chimney and emerge onto the rock above, which leads easily to the summit. See *American Alpine Journal* 3, no. 3 (1939): pp. 361–65.

ROUTE 11. EAST FACE, CENTER. III, 5.9. First ascent unknown; this information was provided by Sean McLane, who climbed the route with Maria Bisaga in August 2020. (See *Figure 6-3*.) This route is commonly guided by Jackson Hole Mountain Guides and is reported to be pretty good. **Pitch 1:** Climb up an easy gully between the squeeze chimney and the 5.5 start of *Route 10* to access the leftmost of several broken left-facing corners. Ascend this corner, and at its top climb up and left onto the arête, finishing on a ledge 5m to the right of the top of the squeeze chimney (5.8, 65m). **Pitch 2:** Climb the hand crack in the right wall of the dihedral above the belay. Move hard left in the large right-facing corner/chimney. Exit right and then follow a left-trending crack to a belay (5.8, 65m). **Pitch 3:** Follow the left-trending crack over a short arête and into a large left-facing dihedral. Climb a flake using jugs into a wide lieback. Exit left on face moves at the top of the dihedral and continue straight up on broken terrain (5.9, 70m). **Pitch 4:** Climb broken terrain onto a large ledge, then continue into the large left-facing chimney. Belay at the base of the headwall (5.6, 60m). **Pitch 5:** Climb a crack (thin hands) just to the right of large blocks to another ledge and belay (5.9, 35m). **Pitch 6:** Climb the face between the ridge and the central gully and then follow the ridge to the summit.

ROUTE 12. NORTHEAST FACE. IV, 5.1, A3. First ascent August 24, 1961, by Royal Robbins and Jane Taylor. This route lies between the Direct East Face *(Route 10)* and the North Face route *(Route 13)*. From the right edge of the east shoulder, climb diagonally up to the right over easy rock to a right-angle recess, which is directly below a huge roof on the east ridge. Ascend this recess for about 30m, then diagonal off to the right to a steep, sloping ledge leading up to the right. Follow this ledge to its end; then cut back left for 9m up to a second sloping ledge, where the difficult climbing begins. Traverse right to piton cracks in a smooth face. Proceed directly up using aid pitons (the last 9m is free) to a sharp orange overhang. Pass this overhang on the right and turn a corner into a recess containing two black overhangs. Ascend this recess and exit to the right above. Now follow a depression up to the right to a small notch, beyond which is a ledge connecting with the North Face route. From the notch, move left and then up a face, using aid in the cracks. Above these cracks, face climbing leads to a broad, sloping ledge. From this ledge, turn a corner to the left and climb two easier east face pitches to the summit. See *American Alpine Journal* 13, no. 1 (1962): pp. 216–20; *Sierra Club Bulletin* 46, no. 8 (October 1961): pp. 53–54.

ROUTE 13. NORTH FACE. III, 5.8. First ascent July 21, 1958, by Yvon Chouinard and Ken Weeks. From Teepe Col, at the base of the West Ridge route *(Route 1)*, easily descend diagonally left (east) and out onto the north face to a difficult overhanging block. This is about 30m above the Teepe Glacier. Descend a meter or so from the top of this block and then climb around a difficult corner to a belay ledge 1m above. Now climb directly above this ledge, following an obvious ledge that slants up to the right. The next pitch continues a little farther on the ledge before striking vertically upward and slightly back to the left until a traverse to the left becomes obvious. This traverse starts on a 2-inch ledge that disappears; continue to a belay spot. The next-to-last pitch goes up from the belay spot on broken blocks until a very comfortable belay ledge with loose rocks is reached. Here one is directly below the conspicuous open book, which is the main feature of the upper north face. Climb the corner until it is necessary to exit onto the overhanging face to the right. This face leads directly to the summit. This somewhat intricate route is not recommended because of the broken and loose nature of the rock. See *American Alpine Journal* 11, no. 2 (1959): pp. 307–9; *Sierra Club Bulletin* 46, no. 8 (October 1961): pp. 53–54.

SECOND TOWER (12,960+)

(0.2 mi E of the Grand Teton)
Map: Grand Teton

This is the higher of the two main towers on the long east ridge of the Grand Teton (see Section 4, *Grand Teton, Route 32*); it rises at the lower edge of the East Ridge Snowfield. The west and southwest faces are sheer, and there is no possibility of bypassing the Second Tower on the south without extensive rappelling. The Second Tower is preceded on the east by a large gendarme that was first climbed on July 29, 1941, by Norman Dyhrenfurth, James Ramsey Ullman, and Donald Gardner.

On or around September 6, 2022, a significant portion of the western side of the Second Tower collapsed, creating a large rockfall event on either side of the East Ridge route of the Grand Teton. Please refer to Section 4, Figure 4-31, for a before and after photo.

Chronology

NORTH CHIMNEY: July 18, 1951, Richard Irvin, John Mowat, Nick Clinch, Leigh Ortenburger
SOUTHEAST FACE: August 19, 1956, Barry Corbet, Gerry Cabaniss
SOUTH RIDGE, BRIMSTONE CHIMNEY: August 2, 1970, Dave Ingalls, Scott Brim
SOUTH FACE, CENTRAL DIHEDRAL: August 1988, John Kelley
var—**GARY'S ROUTE:** September 2011, Mike Abbey, Gary Falk
TOWER TWO CHUTE: June 14, 1993, Renny Jackson, Ron Johnson
SOUTH RIDGE, ABBEY-MACKE: June 2017, Mike Abbey, Sam Macke

ROUTE 1. SOUTH RIDGE, BRIMSTONE CHIMNEY. III, 5.8, A1. First ascent August 2, 1970, by Dave Ingalls and Scott Brim. This is the lower of the two main chimneys, which might be described as large left-facing dihedrals, on the left (southwest) side of the south ridge of the Second Tower. The general route should be studied from the upper edge of the Teepe Glacier: look for a large, reddish corner containing the narrowing chimney. From the top of the Teepe Glacier, climb the lower portion of the Petzoldt-Loomis Otterbody couloir *(Grand Teton, Route 30)*, using slabs on its left side until past the initial steep section. Traverse for two pitches across and right to the left side of the south ridge of the Second Tower. Climb another 46m diagonally up and right on broken, dirt-covered rock to the small gully leading to the base of the reddish corner. Climb the corner (5.8) and its right wall for 24m to a belay stance above a bulge. The next pitch continues up the corner, exiting with one move of aid. Climb up and right through a boulder field to a 5.4 pitch (46m) that goes up and left in a large crack breaking the low-angle slabs. Finish by climbing out and up to the right to the 3rd-class upper end of the ridge above. From this point the Southeast Face route *(Route 5)* can be taken to the summit of the Second Tower. The East Ridge route of the Grand Teton *(Grand Teton, Route 32)* could be joined by a short traverse to the right (east). **Gear:** A regular hardware assortment will suffice, but there are several cracks in the 1" to 1.5" category.

ROUTE 2. SOUTH RIDGE, ABBEY-MACKE. IV, 5.10. First ascent in June 2017, by Mike Abbey and Sam Macke. (See *Figure 6-4.*) This major route ascends the south ridge of the Second Tower, which leads directly to its summit. It may have intersected *Route 1*, but details of both routes are limited. (Note that the line in *Figure 6-4* is approximate.) The first-ascent party climbed to the point where it would have been possible to traverse over to the East Ridge route of the Grand Teton *(Grand Teton, Route 32)*; they elected to rappel instead. This climb is not recommended due to "lots of loose rock and death flakes."

ROUTE 3. TOWER TWO CHUTE. IV, 5.9, A1, WI4. First ascent June 14, 1993, by Renny Jackson and Ron Johnson. (See *Figure 6-4.*) This route is rarely in shape and its existence is fleeting, but it provides a great alpine climb to the summit of the Grand Teton when combined with the upper East Ridge route *(Grand Teton, Route 32)*. On the southern side of the Second Tower, two prominent ridges rise from the upper section of the Teepe Glacier. These ridges flank a steep chute that provides a convenient path for the considerable meltwater that then freezes and forms the climb. The first-ascent party encountered nine pitches of mixed climbing, the quality and difficulty of which will certainly vary from year to year. This climb joins the East Ridge route at the small eastern notch where one normally begins the northern traverse of the Second Tower.

ROUTE 4. SOUTH FACE, CENTRAL DIHEDRAL. IV, 5.11-. First ascent in August 1998, by John Kelley (roped solo). Kelley had worked on this route previously with Jeff Wilson, but they were stormed off it after doing the first pitch. (See *Figure 6-4.*) This line follows the large dihedral to the right of the Tower Two Chute *(Route 3)*. **Pitch 1:** Climb a short finger crack that leads up to a large ledge (5.9). **Pitch 2:** Climb up from the belay to a hand traverse (5.8) leading left to a finger crack (5.11-) that takes one to a belay in the main corner. Another option is to continue farther left on the hand traverse to an easier finger crack (5.10-) that leads up to the same belay. **Pitch 3:** Proceed up the corner to a large roof, where a traverse right (5.10-)

FIGURE 6-4. Second Tower, south aspect. (A) South Ridge, Abbey-Macke *(Route 2)*, IV, 5.10; (B) Tower Two Chute *(Route 3)*, IV, 5.9, A1, WI4; (C) South Face, Central Dihedral *(Route 4)*, IV, 5.11-; (D) South Face, Central Dihedral, variation: Gary's Route, IV, 5.10

leads up via 5.7 climbing to another belay. **Pitch 4:** Face climb up and right to a left-facing, left-leaning corner that is climbed to a belay ledge (5.10). **Pitch 5:** Climb straight up via discontinuous cracks and face climbing for a ropelength to a belay. **Pitch 6:** Slab climbing (5.6) leads to a point where the climbing difficulty eases. It is now possible to reach the top of the Tower via 4th- and easy 5th-class climbing or join the East Ridge route *(Grand Teton, Route 32)* and climb to the summit of the Grand Teton. **Gear:** For protection take one set of stoppers; one set of small cams; and one set of cams from 0.75" to 4".

***Variation:* GARY'S ROUTE.** IV, 5.10. First ascent in September 2011, by Mike Abbey and Gary Falk. (See *Figure 6-4*.) This route was named in honor of Exum guide and climber Gary Falk, who died tragically on the Grand Teton in 2015. Approach is made by way of the Teepe Glacier from the regular Garnet Canyon trail. After about four or five pitches it joins John Kelley's Central Dihedral route, which is followed to its intersection with the East Ridge route of the Grand Teton *(Grand Teton, Route 32)*. That route is then taken to the summit of the Grand. According to Abbey, the first two pitches are "loose, dirty, and scary!" But after those initial pitches the quality of the route changes dramatically for the better, and the rock climbing appears to be stellar. The third pitch—the crux—is a 5.10 finger crack.

ROUTE 5. SOUTHEAST FACE. III, 5.4. First ascent August 19, 1956, by Barry Corbet and Gerry Cabaniss. On an ascent of the East Ridge route of the Grand Teton *(Grand Teton, Route 32)*, when one reaches the south ridge of the gendarme just east of the Second Tower, instead of climbing up to the notch between it and the Tower, descend about 1m and scramble around the corner to the left into the small bowl on the southeast side of the Tower. The steep face above is broken by cracks and ledges; climb it more or less directly to the leftward traverse to the south ridge described in *Route 6*. Once on the knife-edge south ridge, follow it to the summit of the Tower. See *Dartmouth Mountaineering Club Journal*, 1957: pp. 22–23, 50–51.

ROUTE 6. NORTH CHIMNEY. III, 5.6. First ascent July 18, 1951, by Richard Irvin, John Mowat, Nick Clinch, and Leigh Ortenburger. When one traverses around the north side of the Second Tower (see *Grand Teton, Route 32*), a shallow chimney will be seen leading up to a small notch east of the summit. Climb this chimney to the notch. Then traverse left (south) and up a steep series of ledges and slabs to the knife-edge south ridge and follow the ridge to the summit of the Tower. One of the more difficult problems of this climb is getting off the Tower. Climb down for about 30m to the last small ledge on the west side (facing the Grand). A spectacular double-rope rappel deposits one at the notch that separates the Tower from the Grand. Alternatively, the North Chimney route can be rappelled with a single 60m rope.

MOLAR TOOTH (12,320+)

(0.35 mi E of the Grand Teton)

Map: Grand Teton

This unsymmetrical tower on the east ridge of the Grand Teton is actually one of the major features of the peak. Historically, the Molar Tooth is also important, having stopped several early attempts to reach the summit of the Grand Teton. For additional information regarding the Molar Tooth, see *Grand Teton, Route 32*—in particular the Southern Traverse and Tricky Traverse variations. Although directly in the path of the East Ridge route, the Tooth is seldom climbed. The actual summit is a shaky stack of boulders.

The Molar Tooth is also a significant obstacle for those descending the east ridge of the Grand Teton. Perhaps the fastest method of passing the Tooth on descent is to climb from the main notch up and to the southeast for about 30m, reaching easily a notch in the upper south ridge of the Tooth. Two 46m rappels down the east face from this notch end the difficult part of this descent route.

Chronology

NORTHEAST CRACKS: [probable] Early August 1927, Albert R. Ellingwood, Eleanor Davis (Ehrman), Robert Ormes, Eleanor Bartlett; August 4, 1939, Norman Dyhrenfurth, Elpenor Ohle

SOUTHWEST LEDGES: August 4, 1939, Norman Dyhrenfurth, Elpenor Ohle (descent)

SOUTH RIDGE: June 23, 1955, Richard Long, Leigh Ortenburger, Donald Monk

EAST CHIMNEY: August 8, 1955, Bill Briggs, Yves Erickson

DIRECT SOUTH FACE: September 1, 1971, Gordon Parham, Terry Grainger

ROUTE 1. SOUTHWEST LEDGES. II, 5.1. First descent August 4, 1939, by Norman Dyhrenfurth and Elpenor Ohle. This route starts from the main notch separating the Molar Tooth from the Grand Teton. See *Grand Teton, Route 32* for the northern and southern approaches to this notch. Climb up and to the right (south) from the notch onto a series of ledges and chimneys leading to a small notch between the two summits of the Molar Tooth. The route is hard to find but is not difficult. It is also the best method of descent from the Tooth if one wishes to continue from its summit up the East Ridge route of the Grand Teton.

ROUTE 2. DIRECT SOUTH FACE. III, 5.7. First ascent September 1, 1971, by Gordon Parham and Terry Grainger. This route starts from the Teepe Glacier and ascends the main snow (and chockstone) couloir descending from the notch behind the Molar Tooth. In late season one can scramble up this couloir to the third talus- and scree-covered platform; in early season this platform will be covered with snow. From the platform, face climb for two pitches up and left to a good ledge. An easy crack leads up and left to a headwall that blocks progress. Here make a step-around to the left onto a narrow ledge. From the end of the ledge a broken chimney is climbed to the next belay ledge. The next pitch goes up a dihedral and squeeze chimney, then cuts back left. Face climbing then leads to the crux pitch, an overhanging crack that takes one to the ridge between the two small summits. Scramble to the eastern, true summit.

ROUTE 3. SOUTH RIDGE. III, 5.7, A2. First ascent June 23, 1955, by Richard Long, Leigh Ortenburger, and Donald Monk. Follow the East Ridge route of the Grand Teton *(Grand Teton, Route 32)* toward the Southern and Tricky Traverse variations to reach the window notch in the south ridge of the Molar Tooth. From this sharp notch, climb directly up the ridge for 37m. Continue 18m up and slightly right (east) on easier rock to the knife-edge ridge crest. The next 24m pitch is difficult. Climb about 6m up a slab to a point where it is just possible to slither around the corner to the left (south) onto a small, exposed ledge. At the end of this ledge climb upward and then left using aid. Regain the crest and walk to the base of a small chute (snow in early season) that leads up to the very small notch between the two summits. The base of this chute is the top of the 60m vertical, smooth-walled chimney referred to in *Grand Teton, Route*

32. From this small notch it is but a short distance to the summit.

ROUTE 4. EAST CHIMNEY. II, 5.7. First ascent August 8, 1955, by Bill Briggs and Yves Erickson. Climb the first 600m of the east ridge of the Grand Teton (see *Grand Teton, Route 32*). Keep left (south) of the ridge crest. As the Molar Tooth is approached, two large chimneys with a common base will be seen in its east face. The left (south) vertical chimney ends at a horizontal step and window in the south ridge and is used to access the Tricky Traverse of the Molar Tooth during an ascent of the East Ridge route. The right (north) one diagonals up to the right to meet a band of black rock 46m below the summit of the Tooth. Climb the slabs (sometimes wet) leading to the base of the right (north) chimney. The first lead goes straight up the chimney. The second lead is on the right (north) wall of the chimney and passes an overhang. Then scramble to the well-defined ledge leading back to the left (south). Walk left on this ledge and up to the base of the small chimney or jam crack that leads to the highest small notch in the south ridge, just short of the summit of the Molar Tooth. The 35m lead up the face to the left (south) of this crack is 5.7. From the crest of the ridge it is an easy scramble north and east up to the shaky summit. See *American Alpine Journal* 10, no. 1 (1956): pp. 116–19.

ROUTE 5. NORTHEAST CRACKS. III, 5.6. Probable first ascent in early August 1927, by Albert R. Ellingwood, Eleanor Davis, Eleanor Bartlett, and Robert Ormes; first known ascent August 4, 1939, by Norman Dyhrenfurth and Elpenor Ohle. For a description of the route up to the base of the northeast corner of the Molar Tooth, see the Northern Traverse of the Molar Tooth variation in *Grand Teton, Route 32*. From this point climb the chimney that slants up and right; then proceed out on a face until it is possible to work left onto easier rocks and up to a belay position. The first lead is of 5.6 difficulty. On the second pitch climb up and right (west; 4th class) to a place from which scrambling leads to the notch between the two small summits of the Tooth. The eastern summit, which is the higher of the two, is easily reached from the notch. Two 46m rappels from the notch suffice to descend this route.

OKIE'S THORN (11,840+)

(0.4 mi SE of the Grand Teton)

Map: Grand Teton

This sharp pinnacle, although providing one of the better pinnacle climbs in the park, is little known, perhaps due to its inconspicuous position on the southeast flank of the Grand Teton. The southeast ridge provides a good route. The name is derived from the fact that Willi Unsoeld nabbed the first ascent from Leigh Ortenburger, who had told him of the spire's existence. Ortenburger was born in Norman, Oklahoma. See the 1955 variation of the East Ridge route on the Grand Teton *(Grand Teton, Route 32)* for additional information regarding Okie's Thorn.

The descent of this pinnacle is by no means simple. Probably the only method that can be recommended is to rappel back down the southeast ridge to Dike Col. Four double-rope rappels are necessary to get off the climb. This pinnacle gets climbed very rarely, so check the anchors carefully before using them. The narrow, steep, and extremely rotten couloir descending west from the notch should be avoided at all costs. The couloir descending to the east, although not so steep, is very nearly as dangerous because of rockfall and is also not recommended.

Chronology

NORTHEAST FACE: September 5, 1953, Willi Unsoeld
SOUTHEAST RIDGE: August 29, 1954, William Buckingham, George Houghton, James Butler, Elsa Schmieger, Margaret Mulligan, Edgar Jenkins
var—July 4, 1998, Andy Byerly, Leo Larson

ROUTE 1. ▲ SOUTHEAST RIDGE. II, 5.6. First ascent August 29, 1954, by William Buckingham, George Houghton, James Butler, Elsa Schmieger, Margaret Mulligan, and Edgar Jenkins. This ridge, leading directly up Okie's Thorn from Dike Col, is the most obvious route on the pinnacle. The pinnacle, however, is usually difficult to distinguish from the rock mass behind it when viewed from this angle. The first two ropelengths from the col require little more than scrambling. The south face, now above and left, is a steep, smooth wall cut only by a few cracks. The east face, to the right, is also relatively smooth but it lies back at a slightly gentler angle. Climb this face for 15m on small, rounded holds to a point where a short traverse can be made into the small chimney that separates the south and east faces. This short chimney leads easily to a broad, sloping ledge. After another ropelength make a delicate traverse left (south) around a corner and across a smooth face to the easy ledges of the upper south face. From this point one can either climb right and up, reaching the summit from the east, or else cut left (west) over to the southwest ridge and follow it to the summit. The cracks out on the south face are of excellent quality and numerous difficult (5.9 to 5.10) variations are possible.

Variation: II, 5.10a/b. First ascent July 4, 1998, by Andy Byerly and Leo Larson. This one-pitch variation provides a good alternate start to the Southeast Ridge route. Instead of scrambling up the first pitch, traverse right to a finger crack just below a roof. Climb the finger crack (5.10a/b) to a section of offwidth (5.9+) that leads up to the roof, which is climbed via a crack to the right (5.9). Continue up via blocky climbing (easy 5th class) to a broad, flat ledge and belay at two fixed pins.

ROUTE 2. NORTHEAST FACE. II, 5.4. First ascent September 5, 1953, by Willi and Jolene Unsoeld and Stanley Bishoprick (Willi ascended the final pitch alone). From Amphitheater Lake follow the traditional route into Glacier Gulch and then head up toward Dike Col (see *Glacier Gulch* in Section 7); about 90m below the col, cut right and head directly for the sharp notch between Okie's Thorn and the Grand Teton. Use the more southerly of two large, prominent chimneys. As the notch is neared, turn onto the wall left (south) of the large chimney and climb a 9m chimney to a sharp cleft formed by the separation of a large flake from the main wall. Ascend this flake, then span the gap (a meter and a half) and climb a shallow groove in the delicate opposite wall to the ample ledges above. At this point it is possible to turn left (south) and reach the Southeast Ridge route *(Route 1)* after 37m. To reach the notch, however, move right (north) and up over loose and rotten rock. From the notch climb 2.5m up on the Grand side; then bridge across and swing over onto the Thorn. One ropelength to the right, first across the slabs of the west face of the Thorn and finally up some steep walls, places one on the southwest ridge. Climb one ropelength up this distinct ridge to the summit.

PEMMICAN PILLAR (11,520+)

(0.25 mi E of Teepe Pillar)
Map: Grand Teton

This is the first pinnacle east of Dike Col on the ridge connecting Disappointment Peak with the Grand Teton.

ROUTE 1. WEST SIDE. I, 3.0. First ascent August 23, 1936, by Fred and Irene Ayres and Kenneth Henderson. This is a straightforward climb from Dike Col.

ROUTE 2. EAST RIDGE. I, 3.0. First ascent July 19, 1951, by Richard Irvin and Leigh Ortenburger. This ridge involves only scrambling and is ordinarily used only for a traverse to or from Fairshare Tower.

FAIRSHARE TOWER (11,520+)

(0.3 mi E of Teepe Pillar)
Map: Grand Teton

This is the central of the three towers on the ridge between Dike Col and Disappointment Peak. All three—the Red Sentinel, Fairshare Tower, and Pemmican Pillar—present impressive north faces when viewed from the Amphitheater Lake–Teton Glacier approach route. The south ridge of this tower contains a broad, easy saddle that separates the Watchtower, a subpeak, from the upper ridge and main summit. This saddle provides an easy route to pass from the vicinity of the Teepe Glacier over into the couloirs leading to the Red Sentinel. Jackson Hole Mountain Guides (JHMG) utilize the west buttress of the Watchtower for short instructional ascents. The nonsummit rock climbs on the south side of this tower are described under *Fairshare Tower, Watchtower*. Descent of Fairshare Tower is normally made to the west over the top of Pemmican Pillar down to Dike Col.

In a story about her historic 1957 first ascent of her namesake arête (see *Disappointment Peak, Route 29*), Irene Beardsley (Ortenburger) included a humorous aside about the origin of the names Fairshare Tower and Pemmican Pillar:

> *[John Dietschy and I] spent the first day on leisurely ascents of Fairshare Tower and its sub-pinnacle, the Watchtower, right above the Caves," she wrote. "Pemmican Pillar and Fairshare Tower . . . mark an earlier SAC [Stanford Alpine Club] escapade. Leigh [Ortenburger], Dick Irvin, Nick Clinch, and John Mowat were returning along the Black Dike the next day after climbing the East Ridge [of the Grand] in 1951. Leigh spotted the possibly unclimbed pinnacles and asked Nick to open his emergency can of pemmican. When it was passed around, Leigh said he might take a small bite, whereupon Nick, realizing what was up, said 'Hell, no, you'll eat your fair share!' Leigh and Dick went off to bag new routes, left the can as a summit register, and named the pinnacles.*
>
> —Irene Beardsley, "Irene's Arête, Again," *The Stanford Alpine Journal*, 2003–2004: p. 6

Chronology

WEST RIDGE: July 19, 1951, Leigh Ortenburger, Richard Irvin
EAST RIDGE: July 21, 1951, Nick Clinch, Peter Robinson
SOUTH RIDGE: July 9, 1957, John Dietschy, Irene Beardsley (Ortenburger)

ROUTE 1. WEST RIDGE. I, 3.0. First ascent July 19, 1951, by Leigh Ortenburger and Richard Irvin. From the summit of Pemmican Pillar it is an easy scramble to the summit of Fairshare Tower.

ROUTE 2. SOUTH RIDGE. II, 5.1. First ascent July 9, 1957, by John Dietschy and Irene Beardsley (Ortenburger). As seen from the Caves, the double southern end of this ridge appears as two vertical buttresses. The first ascensionists did 12 pitches; the first of these commences on good rock at the right edge of the eastern buttress, which lies just to the left (west) of the gully leading to the Red Sentinel. Stay on the east side of this south buttress until the ridge crest is reached just past the main south tower (the Watchtower) of this ridge. Then follow the crest to the broad saddle and on to the summit. For a shorter version of this route, approach the saddle from the snout of the Teepe Glacier; this leaves a climb of just 150m to the summit. The rock on this ridge is excellent, and escape into the gully on the right is possible from almost any point along the climb. See *American Alpine Journal* 11, no. 1 (1958): pp. 85–88.

ROUTE 3. EAST RIDGE. I, 3.0. First ascent July 21, 1951, by Nick Clinch and Peter Robinson. Start from the notch between the Red Sentinel and Fairshare Tower. This notch is reached from the south via the usual couloir approach to the Red Sentinel, immediately west of Disappointment Peak.

FAIRSHARE TOWER, WATCHTOWER

(0.3 mi E of Teepe Pillar)

The precipitous southern extremity of Fairshare Tower is known as the Watchtower and is divided by a very steep, narrow chimney into a large buttress on the right (east) and a narrow, high-angle arête on the left (west). Most of this rock is of good quality. The following routes lead to this prominent subpeak. The approach is from the Garnet Canyon trail above the Caves. Proceed up the switchbacks and leave the trail where it begins the long horizontal traverse toward the outlet stream from the Teepe Glacier. The south ridge is a short distance from the trail.

Chronology

NORTH RIDGE: July 9, 1957, John Dietschy, Irene Beardsley (Ortenburger) (descent)
DIRECT SOUTH RIDGE: August 2, 1958, John Gill, Bill Mason
CORKSCREW: July 25, 1969, Steve Wunsch, Diana Hunter
var—**FNG:** 1991, Bill Alexander, John Carr
WEST ARÊTE: July 9, 1975, Bob Crawford, Kurt Mendenhall
WEST FACE, CHUBBY BUNNY: 1989, Greg Collins
var—**BUNNY LOVE:** Date unknown, Bean Bowers
MALBEC CORNER: September 2011, Mike Abbey, Josh Beckner
BROWN WALL: July 2016, Nate Opp, Steve Quinlan

ROUTE 1. BROWN WALL. II, 5.11-. First ascent in July 2016, by Nate Opp and Steve Quinlan. (See *Figure 6-5*.) This brown wall, located just west of the Corkscrew, is composed of some of the best-quality rock in this area. To locate the start of the climb, descend approximately 100m below the Big Guy Boulder (see *Garnet Canyon, North Side Rock Climbs, Route 1*) to the cleanest-looking section of brown rock. Start up a low-angle crack and face, trending just slightly left. The wall becomes progressively steeper and blanker until a bolt is reached. Clip the bolt and make a low, slabby traverse out and right to better holds and another bolt. From the bolt, climb straight up, finding good protection until the angle lessens and a fixed anchor is reached (5.11-, 60m). A double-rope rappel leads back down to the ground from here, or one can climb an additional pitch (easier) to a point that allows a traverse off below the Watchtower. **Gear:** For protection take one set of cams from micro sizes to 3.5", three each from 0.3" to 0.5", and two each from 0.75" to 2.5", plus one set of stoppers.

A climber follows the second pitch of the Corkscrew. (Photo by Vic Zeilman)

Disappointment Peak
Fairshare Tower
Pemmican Pillar
Watchtower
Red Sentinel
west face climbs
The Big Guy Boulder
A
B
C
D
E

FIGURE 6-5. Watchtower, south aspect. (A) The Big Guy Boulder, II, 5.11+; (B) The Big Guy Boulder, Good Over Evil, II, 5.13; (C) Brown Wall *(Route 1)*, II, 5.11-; (D) Malbec Corner *(Route 2)*, II, 5.10+; (E) Corkscrew *(Route 3)*, II, 5.8

ROUTE 2. MALBEC CORNER. II, 5.10+. First ascent in September 2011, by Mike Abbey and Josh Beckner. (See *Figure 6-5*.) This climb is located up and around to the west from the toe of the buttress, a short distance from the beginning of the Corkscrew *(Route 3)*. **Pitch 1:** Climb a short, easy chimney (5.6). **Pitch 2:** Follow a crack system up and left and leave it by way of steep face climbing that leads to a crack to the right and eventually to a belay on a good ledge at the base of a large left-facing corner (5.10). **Pitch 3:** Climb the corner (5.10+) to a ledge and belay. **Pitch 4:** A short, easy pitch leads to the top of the climb and a scramble off on the west side.

ROUTE 3. CORKSCREW. II, 5.8. First ascent July 25, 1969, by Steve Wunsch and Diana Hunter. (See *Figures 6-5* and *6-6*.) This fun, readily accessible route lies on the arête left (west) of the very steep, narrow chimney that splits the end of the south ridge. One of the better rock climbs in Garnet Canyon, it is not subject to the weather problems of higher routes, and it has relatively easy retreat options. The route starts on the south side of the arête, just right of center, and then angles up slightly left for the next five pitches, ending on the west face of the arête. **Pitch 1:** The first lead goes up and right from the bottom of the arête, past a small left-facing corner, to a large belay ledge in the main left-facing dihedral. **Pitch 2:** From the ledge climb the dihedral to an exit onto low-angle slabs to the left. **Pitch 3:** Climb a jam crack (5.6) on the south face to a stance at the corner of the arête; go around onto the left (west)

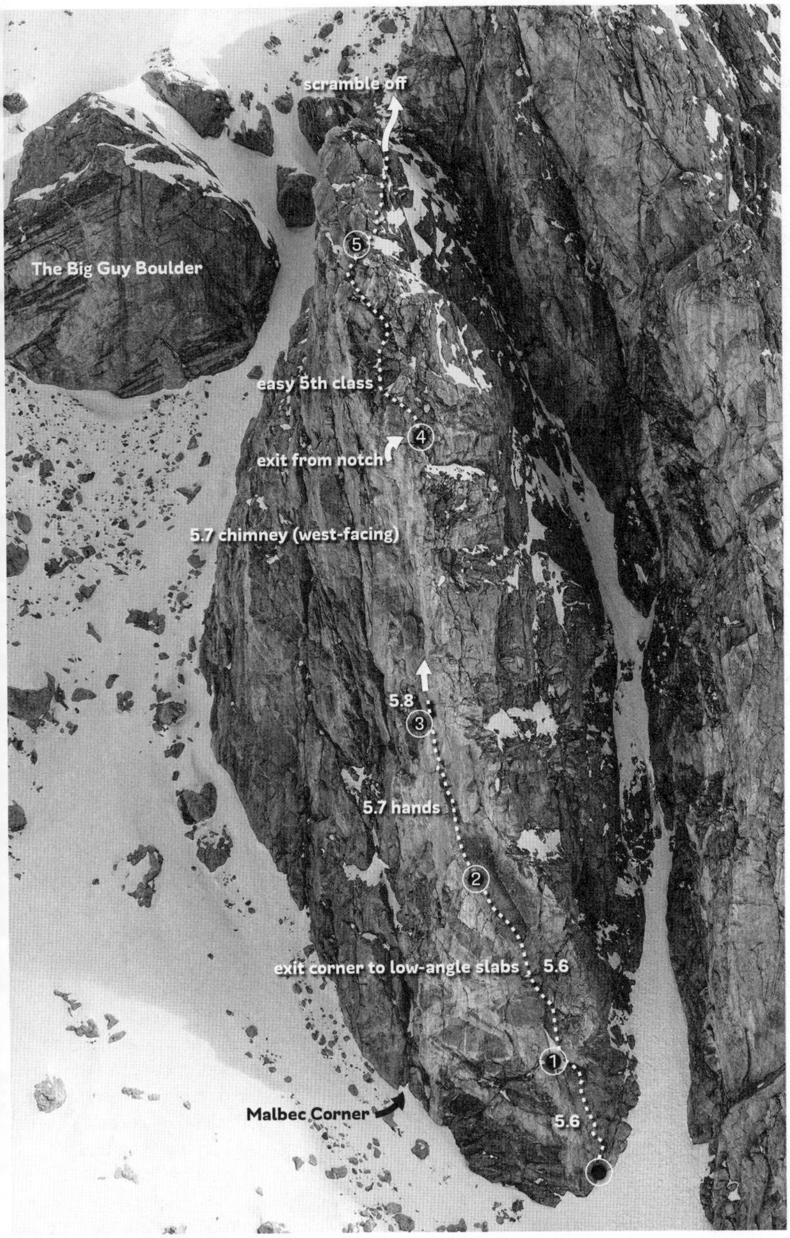

FIGURE 6-6. Watchtower, south aspect, Corkscrew *(Route 3)*, II, 5.8

side of the arête and continue up steep cracks (5.7) to a square-cut belay ledge. **Pitch 4:** A short 5.8 section is required to reach a chimney up and left, which is then climbed (5.7) to a notch behind a tower. **Pitch 5:** The final pitch presents easier climbing upward until one can scramble off the arête toward the west face (see *Figure 6-7*). **Gear:** For protection take a standard rack up to 3".

Variation: **FNG.** II, 5.8+. First ascent in 1991, by Bill Alexander and John Carr. Begin up and east of the start of the Corkscrew. The first pitch ascends a 5.8 right-facing dihedral that is somewhat tricky to protect. From the top of this dihedral climb a bulge via a hand crack (5.8) to a belay on a terrace. Face climbing (5.7+) leads up to a short offwidth with a chockstone at the bottom of it. Climb

Ranger Phil Edmonds enjoying the excellent rock on the Crystal Tower, Grand Teton (Photo by Vic Zeilman)

the offwidth (5.8+) and then continue up into a left-facing corner via 5.8 hands to a belay on another series of terraces. Move the belay up and left (west) and then face climb (5.8) to intersect the upper part of the Corkscrew route.

FIGURE 6-7. Watchtower, west face. (A) Cole Traverse, 5.8R; (B) Blunt Arête, 5.9; (C) Jed Workman Arête, 5.10; (D) Little Bunny, 5.8; (E) Chubby Bunny *(Route 4)*, II, 5.10b; (F) Bunny Love, II, 5.10d; (G) Right Side Arête, 5.7

ROUTE 4. WEST FACE, CHUBBY BUNNY. II, 5.10b. First ascent in 1989, by Greg Collins (free solo). (See *Figure 6-7.*) This climb provides an excellent, more difficult finish to the Corkscrew *(Route 3)*. From midway along the escape ledge at the top of that climb, look for a left-facing corner that defines the first pitch of Chubby Bunny. Climb the corner and then continue with face climbing past fixed pins to a ledge and belay at a fixed baby angle (5.7). The next pitch ascends the stellar finger crack above, through an overhang and then directly to the summit (5.10b). A 50m rappel takes one back down to the starting ledge. The North Ridge route *(Route 7)* can also be used to get down. **Gear:** For protection take one set of stoppers, one set of cams from finger to hand size, and quickdraws.

Note: This area features several additional climbs not described in detail here but illustrated in *Figure 6-7*. There are two to three bolts on the Blunt Arête (5.9) and the Jed Workman Arête (5.10); for both of these climbs, it is suggested that one also take quite a few supplemental cams. There are no bolts along the Right Side Arête (5.7). The Cole Traverse is a south-to-north traverse of the Watchtower that can include the summit of the Watchtower. If one stays as close to the crest as possible, one will encounter a short but stout 5.8 south-facing boulder problem on beautiful red-orange rock along the way. (It is possible to access this traverse from the Teepe Glacier using the 4th-/easy 5th-class route shown in *Figure 6-7*.) Please understand and be mindful of the fact that this area is used by Jackson Hole Mountain Guides for instruction throughout the summer. Their base camp, Corbet High Camp, is located just a short distance to the west. It is a very special place, and hopefully it will remain so.

***Variation:* BUNNY LOVE.** II, 5.10d. First ascent by Bean Bowers (date unknown). (See *Figure 6-7*.) This one-pitch variation to Chubby Bunny is located to its right and is more difficult. From the belay at the base of the second pitch of Chubby Bunny, climb out and right to finger cracks that lead to a slot in the roof above. Climb through the overhang and up the short headwall above (5.10d). **Gear:** Protection consists of pieces from finger to hand size, with one fist-size piece.

ROUTE 5. DIRECT SOUTH RIDGE. II, 5.8. First ascent August 2, 1958, by John Gill and Bill Mason. The Watchtower is the only large tower on the south ridge of Fairshare Tower. The difficulty of this route depends on its directness; easier climbing can usually be found to the right (east) of the ridge crest. Start the climb from the upper corner of a gigantic gray boulder that is located just right (east) of the steep, narrow chimney that splits the end of the ridge. After one ropelength in a prominent chimney near the crest of the ridge, diagonal left and pass under a small roof to a 9m open chimney adjacent to the crest. Climb a pitch up the center of a slabby face and then move around a corner to the left into an open chimney on the crest. The roof and the difficult overhang above the roof are both climbed directly. Next climb a 15m crack on the right side of the crest. After some easier climbing to a small overhang, the final pitch containing an overhanging flake goes directly up the crest. Scramble to the summit.

ROUTE 6. WEST ARÊTE. II, 5.9. First ascent July 9, 1975, by Bob Crawford and Kurt Mendenhall. The exact location of this five-pitch route is uncertain, but it lies on an arête, separated from the west side of the Watchtower by a snow gully. The initial lead of 30m, up a 5.8 face, is followed by an easier lead (5.6) of 40m up the same line. At this point make a 12m traverse (5.7) to the right to ledges, from which a 27m lead turns directly upward. At the belay two cracks diverge upward, one angling right and the other slightly left. Take the left crack, 5.9 offwidth, for 37m onto the ridge crest, which is then followed easily back to the right to the summit of the Watchtower.

ROUTE 7. NORTH RIDGE. II, 4.0. First descent July 9, 1957, by John Dietschy and Irene Beardsley (Ortenburger). This narrow ridge is the natural route on the Watchtower and can be climbed without difficulty from the broad saddle that connects with the main summit of Fairshare Tower. It can be gained either from the east or from the west.

RED SENTINEL (11,200+)

(0.1 mi W of Disappointment Peak)

Map: Grand Teton

This remarkable, chisel-like pinnacle lies on the ridge connecting Disappointment Peak with the Grand Teton. Of the four pinnacles on this ridge, the Red Sentinel is the most easterly, lying directly under the west face of Disappointment Peak. The most spectacular view of the Sentinel is the one obtained by looking straight down from the summit of Disappointment. This sharp pinnacle underwent a change of names at some point after the early 1930s. Previously, the highest col on the Black Dike (Glencoe Col) was known as "Sentinel Col," and Glencoe Spire was the "Red Sentinel." The current Red Sentinel was first attempted on August 6, 1941, by Hans Kraus and Susan Simon; they reached a point on the northwest ridge only 9m below the summit. Kraus returned six years later on August 12, 1947, with Donald Brown, Adolf Snow, and Haldon Smith, but was again stopped after 6m of aid climbing on the northwest ridge by the last 9m—"no cracks, no holds."

The approach is the same for the following climbs: from the Garnet Canyon trail above the Caves, take the large talus gully (the Red Sentinel gully) next to the west face of Disappointment Peak up to the notch to the east of the Sentinel. (Vertical gain from Caves to Red Sentinel is 400 meters.) During much of this approach the Sentinel itself will not be visible. It is also possible, but more difficult, to approach the Sentinel from the north, but steep snow will be encountered.

The descent from the Sentinel involves a spectacular free-hanging rappel down the south face from a bolt and the slung summit horn. This is a two-rope rappel of nearly 60m to get all the way down to easy terrain. (**Note:** Opinions differ as to the exact length of this rappel; when this author—R. Jackson—asked a number of friends who guide this frequently, the concensus was 60m.)

Chronology

EAST FACE AND NORTH FACE: July 11, 1950, Robert Merriam, Richard Pownall, Michael Brewer, Leigh Ortenburger

NORTH FACE: August 22, 1956, Barry Corbet, Gerry Cabaniss

NORTHWEST CORNER: August 8, 1966, Dave Ingalls, Greg Joiner; FFA June 26, 1988, Renny Jackson, Jim Woodmencey

SOUTHWEST DIHEDRAL (KLIGFIELD ARCH): July 27, 1968, Dave Ingalls, Roy Kligfield, Charles Bookman; FFA summer 2008, Nate Opp, Julia Niles

RED ALERT: June 29, 2008, Greg Collins, Sue Miller, Hans Johnstone

ROUTE 1. SOUTHWEST DIHEDRAL (KLIGFIELD ARCH). II, 5.7, A3, or II, 5.11-R. First ascent July 27, 1968, by Dave Ingalls, Roy Kligfield, and Charles Bookman; first free ascent in summer 2008, by Nate Opp and Julia Niles. Both Opp and Niles led the route free, and their line varied slightly from the original aid line; they renamed the route Kligfield Arch. (See *Figures 6-8* and *6-11*.) Originally

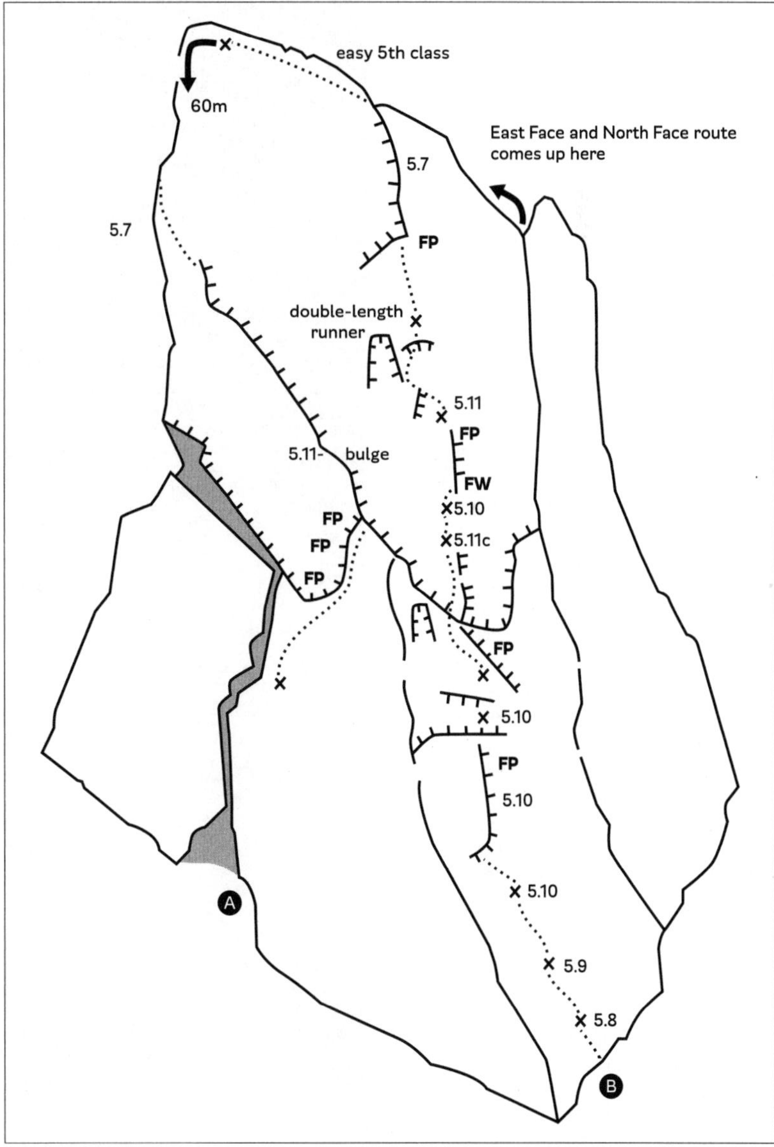

FIGURE 6-8. Red Sentinel, south aspect. (A) Southwest Dihedral (Kligfield Arch; *Route 1*), II, 5.11-R; (B) Red Alert *(Route 2)*, II, 5.11b/c

done in three pitches, and now done as a long single-pitch climb, this route ascends an overhanging corner on the southwest side of the Red Sentinel. It can be started either by climbing (5.6) to a belay stance in a cave or, better, by working around the left shoulder to the north face so that this cave can be entered from the rear. **Gear:** Bring two ropes for the 60m rappel down the south face.

ROUTE 2. RED ALERT. II, 5.11b/c. First ascent June 29, 2008, by Greg Collins, Sue Miller, and Hans Johnstone. (See *Figures 6-8* and *6-11.*) This modern single-pitch route is located on the red-colored face just to the right of *Route 1*. This is a good face climb on excellent rock with great protection. **Gear:** For protection take one set of cams, medium stoppers, 18 quickdraws, and one double-length runner. Two ropes are necessary for the 60m rappel down the south side of the Sentinel.

ROUTE 3. ▲ EAST FACE AND NORTH FACE. II, 5.7. First ascent July 11, 1950, by Robert Merriam, Richard Pownall, Michael Brewer, and Leigh Ortenburger. (See *Figures 6-9* and *6-10.*) From the notch on the eastern side of the Sentinel, the jam crack leading up the center of the east face is obvious. Climb this crack for 18m to its end, where a delicate friction traverse right leads to the northeast corner. Belay the next pitch at this corner. From the corner, face climb out onto the edge of the sheer north face up to a secure position behind a flake. Early in the season these ledges may be damp or wet. Then go à cheval up the sharp ridge to the small summit. **Gear:** A 4"–5" piece is useful for the jam crack on the east face, and the cracks on the north face are thin, requiring small nuts. Two ropes are necessary for the 60m rappel down the south side of the Sentinel. **Time:** 3½ hours from the Caves. See *American Alpine Journal* 8, no. 1 (1951): pp. 176–81; *Dartmouth Mountaineering Club Journal*, 1957: pp. 22–23, 28, 50–51; *Harvard Mountaineering* 12 (May 1955): pp. 57–58.

ROUTE 4. NORTH FACE. II, 5.8. First ascent August 22, 1956, by Barry Corbet and Gerry Cabaniss. The first-ascent party apparently approached this route from Amphitheater Lake, going around the bottom of the north face of Disappointment Peak and up to the subsidiary glacier at the bases of the Red Sentinel, Fairshare Tower, and Pemmican Pillar. They then ascended the steep snow to the base of the north face of the Sentinel. A more logical approach is from the Caves in Garnet Canyon. Starting 6m east of the chimney that forms the northwest corner of the Sentinel, climb up and left (east) until the crest of a small nose is reached. Climbing up this nose and then back to the right leads to a comfortable ledge containing a large belay boulder. From this boulder proceed upward to a wide ledge that permits a hand traverse left to an obvious 6-inch shelf. Traverse left again on sloping ledges that ultimately peter out about 2.5m from the flake of *Route 3*. This gap is difficult. From the flake, join *Route 3* and follow it to the summit. **Gear:** Two

FIGURE 6-9. Red Sentinel, east aspect, East Face and North Face *(Route 3)*, II, 5.7

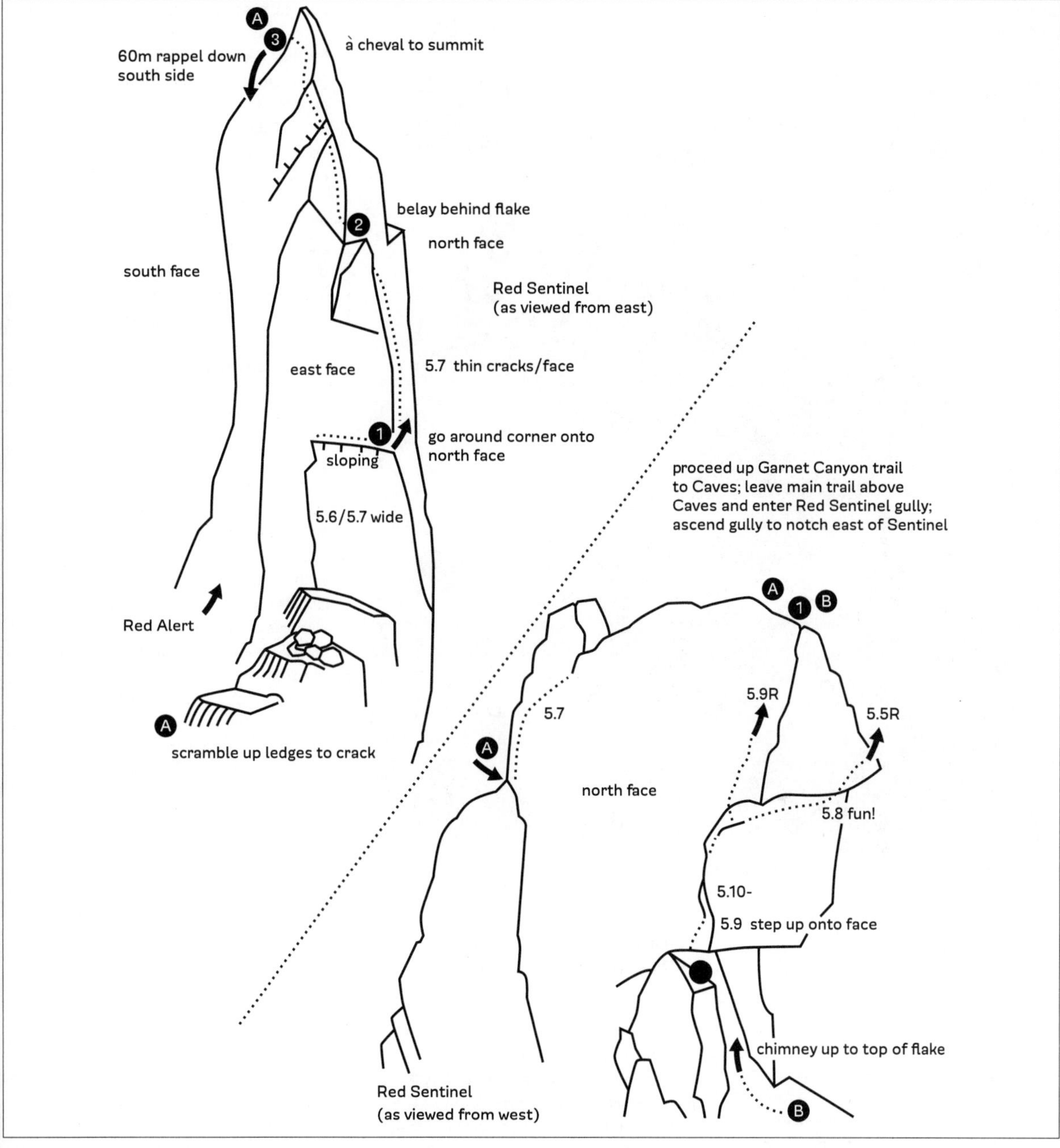

FIGURE 6-10. Red Sentinel. (A) East Face and North Face *(Route 3)*, II, 5.7; (B) Northwest Corner *(Route 5)*, II, 5.10-

ropes are necessary for the 60m rappel down the south side of the Sentinel. **Time:** 9 hours from Jenny Lake. See *Dartmouth Mountaineering Club Journal*, 1957: pp. 22–23, 28, 50–51.

ROUTE 5. NORTHWEST CORNER. II, 5.10- (5.9R if using the first-ascent finish). First ascent August 8, 1966, by Dave Ingalls and Greg Joiner; first free ascent June 26, 1988, by Renny Jackson and Jim Woodmencey. (See *Figures 6-10* and *6-11*.) Access the chimney that forms the northwest corner of the Red Sentinel from the west. Climb the back of this chimney up and onto the top of the enormous flake that forms the north wall of the chimney and belay. Using small holds make the tenuous step up and onto the exposed face and climb up to a flake with a ring angle piton on its right edge. Turn the corner around to the right and climb a 1-inch crack (5.10-)

FIGURE 6-11. Red Sentinel. (A) Northwest Corner *(Route 5)*, II, 5.10-; (B) Southwest Dihedral (Kligfield Arch; *Route 1*), II, 5.11-R; (C) Red Alert *(Route 2)*, II, 5.11b/c

to an adequate ledge. At this point there are two options for finishing the pitch. The first-ascent party climbed up 4.5m of rounded slabs to a small ledge and then continued up the right edge of the north face to the summit. This option involves runout face climbing (5.9R) on small holds and angles to the right edge of the formation when possible. For the second alternative proceed out and right (south) on an airy 12m traverse (5.8) to the southwest edge of the Sentinel. Once around the corner climb the unprotected face (5.5R) above to the summit. **Gear:** For protection take RPs and a selection of wired nuts and camming devices to 2.5". Two ropes are necessary for the 60m rappel down the south side of the Sentinel.

GARNET CANYON, NORTH SIDE ROCK CLIMBS

Map: Grand Teton

The following climbs are on the difficult side of the scale, all put up by off-duty mountain guides in their spare time. Magpie Acres is especially prominent to the east when traveling up or down the trail above the Caves.

Chronology

DEVIL'S SEED: July 1999, Jim Howe, Jason Keith
MAGPIE ACRES: July 1999, Jim Howe, Jason Keith
THE BIG GUY BOULDER, GOOD OVER EVIL: Late 1990s or 2000, Greg Collins
THE BIG GUY BOULDER: August 2017, Nate Opp, Michael Gardner

ROUTE 1. THE BIG GUY BOULDER. II, 5.11+. First ascent in August 2017, by Nate Opp and Michael Gardner, who both redpointed. (See *Figure 6-5.*) This "boulder" is actually an interesting mass of rock located just west of the Watchtower and on the eastern edge of the Teepe Glacier terminal moraine. The face that the climbs are on faces south, and there are two very difficult routes located here. This leftmost route, which leads to the apex of the boulder, was initially worked on by Kim Schmitz and Steve Quinlan. Begin the climb in the middle of the face by crawling out on a ledge, protected by a #1 Camalot and a double-length runner. Clip a bolt (while crawling) and then stand up and "wander around in a sea of slab" for about 60m (5.11+). **Gear:** Two 60m ropes are required for the descent from this climb. For protection take a single set of cams to 3", a set of stoppers, and quickdraws.

ROUTE 2. THE BIG GUY BOULDER, GOOD OVER EVIL. II, 5.13. First ascent in the late 1990s or 2000, by Greg Collins. (See *Figure 6-5.*) Collins has described this short (17m) climb as a "beautiful arête boulder problem." Somewhat hidden, it is located on the southeast prow of the rock just below the west face of the Watchtower, and it begins in a steep, loose gully. Overhanging jumps and campus moves lead to edge pinching and liebacking up the arête on very high-quality rock. There is a two-bolt anchor at the top. **Gear:** For protection take six quickdraws.

ROUTE 3. DEVIL'S SEED. II, 5.10a. First ascent in July 1999, by Jim Howe and Jason Keith. (See *Figure 6-24.*) This is the awkward hand crack located immediately left of *Route 4*. The crack was described as being pretty licheny on the first ascent, but it should clean up as it gets climbed more. Descent is made via rappel from a small tree at the top.

ROUTE 4. MAGPIE ACRES. II, 5.11+. First ascent in July 1999, by Jim Howe and Jason Keith. (See *Figure 6-24.*) This difficult one-pitch climb is located near the base of the southwest ridge of Disappointment Peak and is visible to the east of the initial switchback leading up from the Caves. The route consists of a hand crack (5.11+) that splits the gently overhanging west-facing wall, as seen from the trail, with anchor slings visible at the top. **Gear:** Suggested protection includes a double set of cams with extras in the hand size.

ROUTE 5. Y SLAB. II, 5.5–5.10. (See *Figure 6-1.*) This large, striped slab is located just a few hundred meters to the west of the base of Spalding Falls above the Meadows in Garnet Canyon and is comprised of beautiful, banded gneiss. The easiest approach consists of an upward traverse from the west end of the switchback nearest to the bottom of the falls. Because of its position relatively low in the track of the main avalanche path that begins high on the east face of the Grand Teton, this slab has been scrubbed clean by moving snow over the eons. Several routes have been done, with the slab's numerous jugs and pockets for protection making for fun climbing. The Right Y is a beautiful pitch of 5.5. To the left of the Left Y is a classic 5.8-, and the Left Arête is 5.6. Even the overhang has big holds and good protection. A second easy pitch (4th class) leads up to a point where one can scramble up to the Petzoldt Caves. **Note:** Located just to the west around the corner from the Y Slab is Crack in the Track, which is situated on a west-facing wall that has endured the wrath of avalanches off the east face of the Grand Teton. There are currently nine protection bolts on this 5.13+ project—bring a stick clip!

DISAPPOINTMENT PEAK (11,618)

Map: Grand Teton

Disappointment Peak is unique in the Tetons in that it harbors two delightful lakes, Surprise and Amphitheater, high on its east slopes. The peak is ringed by cliffs on the south, west, and north; only the eastern approach is gradual, and even there the glacial action that formed Amphitheater Lake left a considerable headwall between the lake and the summit plateau, a remnant of an ancient peneplain surface. The trail to Amphitheater Lake, constructed in 1923 by J. G. (Gibb) Scott and Homer Richards as a commercial venture to allow guided trips onto the Teton Glacier, was much used in the 1920s because it was almost the only trail that penetrated the mountains. Because of the existence of this "Glacier Trail," Amphitheater Lake was used as the starting point for several early climbs of the Grand Teton. It was more than 10 years later that the Garnet Canyon trail was completed.

The members of the Disappointment Peak first-ascent party were unfamiliar with the topography of the Grand Teton area and had thought that they might be able to reach the summit of the Grand Teton by climbing directly from Amphitheater Lake. Upon reaching Disappointment Peak's summit and seeing the great gap between them and the Grand Teton, they attempted, but failed, to traverse farther toward their objective; Phil Smith and Walter Harvey named the peak on their return.

Disappointment Peak has proved popular as a relatively easy, readily accessible peak with a spectacular view. This summit vista is truly remarkable, showcasing all of the peaks and pinnacles surrounding Garnet Canyon and Glacier Gulch, the heart of the Tetons, to great advantage. By peering over the edge to the west, it is possible to see the impressive, slender splinter of the Red Sentinel from an unusual angle. Easy access via the Garnet Canyon trail to the southern routes and via the Surprise and Amphitheater Lakes trail to the eastern and northern routes contributes to the popularity of this peak. In recent years the numerous southern ridges, and to a lesser extent the north face, have been the scene of considerable rock-climbing activity, because they provide a large selection of high-angle rock routes.

The Disappointment Peak routes are grouped here according to the aspect of the peak on which they are located. The first group begins with the Southeast Ridge *(Route 1)*, which has become the regular scrambling route up the peak. The routes in this group and the second group, located on the east and north aspects of the peak, are listed in counterclockwise fashion. The routes in the third and fourth groups, which include the arêtes and ridges on the south and west aspects of the peak, are listed in clockwise fashion, as one would encounter them while walking up Garnet Canyon. The primary access to Garnet Canyon is from the Lupine Meadows trailhead. To reach this trailhead, turn west off Teton Park Road at the Lupine Meadows junction, cross the bridge over Cottonwood Creek, and proceed 1.5 miles (west and then south) on the dirt road that leads to the trailhead.

Note that the southeast ridge and the southwest couloir (see *Routes 1* and *31*) are the two most commonly used routes of descent from all of the routes on Disappointment Peak that end up on the summit plateau.

Chronology

LAKE LEDGES: August 20, 1925, Phil Smith, Walter Harvey
SPOON COULOIR: August 20, 1925, Phil Smith, Walter Harvey (descent)
NORTHWEST SHELF: August 20, 1925, Phil Smith, Walter Harvey (partial descent); August 11, 1953, Robert Brooke, Rob Day (complete descent)
SOUTHWEST COULOIR: July 14, 1926, Norman Clyde, Ernest Dawson, Alice Carter, Julie Mortimer, J. C. Downing (ascent and descent)
SOUTHEAST RIDGE: [probable] August 12, 1935, Perry W. Gilbert
EAST RIDGE: September 2, 1937, Jack Durrance, George Sheldon, Percy Rideout
WEST FACE: August 14, 1947, Hans Kraus, Donald Brown
MERRIAM COULOIR: July 17, 1950, Robert and Doris Merriam
var—July 30, 1973, Robert Fenichel, Richard Schmitz
SOUTHWEST RIDGE: July 9, 1952, Robert Merriam, Richard Emerson
var—July 5, 1957, Art Gran, Robert Chambers, Paul Calcaterra
var—August 8, 2014, Keith Hadley, Peter Rowat, Tom Hunt, Taryn Hunt-Smith
DIRECT NORTH FACE: August 4, 1955, John Dietschy, William Cropper
NORTHWEST CRACK: August 15, 1955, John Dietschy, William Cropper
SATISFACTION ARÊTE: August 20, 1955, Richard Pownall, Allen Steck
POWNALL-UNSOELD NORTH FACE (PIN TIME): July 27, 1956, Richard Pownall, Willi Unsoeld; FFA August 6, 1979, Mike Munger, Bill Feiges
SATISFACTION CRACK: August 19, 1956, John Gill, Gene Davant, Tom Clohessy
EAST CHIMNEY: September 5, 1956, Harvey T. Carter, Robert Beck
SOUTH CENTRAL BUTTRESS: June 29, 1957, William and Evelyn Cropper, James Langford
var—July 23, 1957, John Dietschy, James Langford
var—**DIRECT EAST CORNER:** August 5, 1958, John Gill, Bill Mason
var—August 9, 1966, Sherman Lehman, William Hooker, William Kirkpatrick
IRENE'S ARÊTE: July 10, 1957, John Dietschy, Irene Beardsley (Ortenburger)
var—July 2, 1970, Jim "Ole" Olson, Mark Chapman
GRUNT ARÊTE: July 22, 1957, John Dietschy, James Langford
var—**SOUTH FACE:** July 6, 1958, John Gill, Paul Rieche
CAVES ARÊTE: August 7, 1957, John Dietschy, Robert Larson
var—**WEST FACE:** July 11, 1970, Thomas Dunwiddie, Scott Stewart, Roger Zimmerman
ALMOST ARÊTE: July 15, 1958, John Gill, Fred Truslow
var—**GRAY SLAB:** July 23, 1963, Richard Goldstone, Peter Gardiner, Steven Derenzo
var—**ALMOST OVERHANGING:** August 20, 1972, Howard Friedman, Henry Mitchell
var—1980, Andy Carson, Jim Evangelista
var—July 13, 1985, Steve Saez, Mark Golde
FIFTH COLUMN: July 17, 1958, John Gill, James Langford
var—**THE KNOB:** July 25, 1958, John Gill, Yvon Chouinard
var—**HUMMINGBIRD FACE:** July 12, 1981, Rich Perch, Mike Beiser
BEELZEBUB ARÊTE: July 19, 1958, John Gill, Fred Truslow
SATISFACTION BUTTRESS: July 28 and August 1, 1958, Yvon Chouinard, Bob Kamps; FFA July 15, 1977, Rich Perch, Mike Munger
LANCE'S ARÊTE: July 28, 1958, John Gill, Dave Jones
HIDDEN ARÊTE: July 31, 1958, John Gill, Bill Mason
DELICATE ARÊTE: August 16, 1958, John Gill, Fred Wright
GRAN: July 5, 1962, Art Gran, John Hudson

CHOUINARD-FROST CHIMNEY: August 13, 1962, Yvon Chouinard, Tom Frost; FFA August 19, 1970, Dave Ingalls, Dave Loeks, or August 3, 1994, Tom Kimbrough, Andy Byerly
GRUNT ARÊTE, OPEN BOOK: August 21, 1963, Philip Jacobus, Steve Larsen; FFA June 26, 1977, Jim Donini, Mike Munger
var—**LEFT OF OPEN BOOK:** July 28, 1977, Mike Munger, Ed Sessions
var—**RIGHT OF OPEN BOOK:** July 1983, Kim Schmitz, Jim Donini
GREAT WEST CHIMNEY: July 17, 1964, Richard Goldstone, Raymond Schrag, Fred Pfahler
NO NAME COULOIR: August 20, 1973, Randy Jamieson, Dave Alvestad
WEST SIDE STORY: August 23, 1977, George Montopoli, Keith Hadley
WEST ARÊTE: July 17, 1979, Jim Beyer, Joanne Urioste
WHITON-WIGGINS: September 19, 1981, Mark Whiton, Earl Wiggins
var—**SACCO-VANZETTI MEMORIAL:** Spring 1992, Jay Pistono, Keith Cattabriga, Ray Warburton
JERN-WIGGINS: September 11, 1983, Ken Jern, Earl Wiggins
WEST BUTTRESS: September 24, 1986, Ken Jern, Jay Pistono
KIMBROUGH-RICKERT: August 1994, Tom Kimbrough, Steve Rickert
YODEL THIS: September 1996, Mike Fischer, Sam Lightner Jr.
CARSON ROUTE: August 15, 1998, Andy Carson, Dan Carson
SOUTHERN EDGE: June 27, 1999, Paul Horton, Mark Daverin
KIM SCHMITZ MEMORIAL ROUTE: Summer 2017, Mike Abbey, Sam Macke

Disappointment Peak, East Face Routes

These routes are situated above the Amphitheater Lake cirque and are approached via the popular Surprise and Amphitheater Lakes trail. From the Lupine Meadows trailhead, take the Garnet Canyon–Surprise and Amphitheater Lakes trail 1.7 miles south and then west to a junction. Instead of continuing to the left (south) along the Valley Trail, stay straight and begin climbing the switchbacks up to a second junction at 3 miles, where the Garnet Canyon trail splits off to the left (south). Stay right (north) and continue up several more switchbacks to Surprise Lake at 5 miles. Amphitheater Lake is located a quarter mile above Surprise Lake, and a total of 3,000 feet of elevation is gained along the hike. The following five routes are listed from left to right as viewed from Amphitheater Lake. Descent from these routes is made via the southeast ridge (see *Route 1*).

ROUTE 1. ▲ SOUTHEAST RIDGE. II, 4.0. Probable first ascent August 12, 1935, by Perry W. Gilbert. (See *Figure 6-12.*) This long ridge, which bounds Surprise Lake and Amphitheater Lake on the south, provides the most straightforward route to the summit of Disappointment Peak from the east and is the recommended route of descent if doing one of the southern rock climbs in the area. Cross the outlet stream from Amphitheater Lake and hike up grassy slopes, covered with snow in early season, to the saddle in the ridge south of the lake. Contour north along the base of the cliffs, which form the west side of the saddle, to a large, wide chimney—seen from below to be blocked by two giant chockstones. Climb this chimney, passing the first chockstone by means of a tunnel, an uncommon feature. The second chockstone is turned via easy rock on the left (south). The gully above is then easily followed up to the eastern extension of the summit plateau. Proceed west to the summit along the flat ridgetop, passing the various towers on this ridge, which are the "summits" of the more easterly southern ridges rising from Garnet Canyon. Note that if the ridge crest itself, which

FIGURE 6-12. Disappointment Peak, east aspect overview

lies south of the wide chimney, is followed from the initial saddle, several pitches of greater difficulty will be encountered. On descent, a trail will be found leading from the low point of the summit plateau through the low, wind-deformed trees to the head of the aforementioned gully. Follow the gully down to the large chockstones. Remember that the ridge crest itself is more difficult and, if it is followed, will require some rappelling.

ROUTE 2. ▲ LAKE LEDGES. II, 4.0. First ascent August 20, 1925, by Phil Smith and Walter Harvey. (See *Figure 6-12*.) From Amphitheater Lake a prominent snow couloir leads in a southwest direction up to the summit plateau. To the left (east) of this couloir a series of ledges and short cliffs leads to the ridge extending east from the southern edge of this plateau. These can be climbed in many places, so the difficulty of the route will depend on the routefinding ability of the party. Some of the alternatives are moderately difficult. Once on the plateau, hike west and north to the summit blocks, which require a bit of scrambling. A 5.1 pitch must be climbed if these blocks are attacked directly from the southeast. **Time:** 2 to 4 hours from Amphitheater Lake; 6½ to 7½ hours from Jenny Lake.

ROUTE 3. SPOON COULOIR. II, 4.0. First descent August 20, 1925, by Phil Smith and Walter Harvey; first ascent uncertain. (See *Figures 6-12* and *6-14*.) The long snow couloir leading southwest from Amphitheater Lake up to the summit plateau is referred to as the Spoon Couloir because of its distinctive shape. In early season it is a long, moderately steep snow climb all the way from Amphitheater Lake to the plateau. Numerous accidents, including at least one fatality, have occurred in this couloir during all of the seasons of the year. Most of these have involved parties hoping to find a quicker, less complicated descent to Amphitheater Lake. If there is snow in the couloir, it can be quite hard; having an ice axe—along with the corresponding knowledge of how to use it for self-arrest in the event of a fall—is mandatory. Beware!

ROUTE 4. EAST CHIMNEY. II, 5.7. First ascent September 5, 1956, by Harvey T. Carter and Robert Beck. Above Amphitheater Lake a band of slabby cliffs extends from the Spoon Couloir on the south to the east ridge on the north, effectively blocking access to the upper plateau of Disappointment Peak. The left (southern) section of this band is a nearly blank wall with vertical water stains. The right section, about 60m–90m high, is more broken with cracks, ledges, and chimneys. Two chimneys or open-book formations cut up through the lower portion of this right section. This East Chimney route goes up the left (south) of these two chimney systems. In early season a small snow patch lies below and slightly left of this chimney. Scramble up a series of easy blocks and ledges for 46m to the base of the first section of the chimney. The first long lead goes directly up the chimney or inside corner, past two small overhangs (5.6) to easier ground, ending at a comfortable ledge with a very small tree. There is a fixed piton about 1m above this tree. From the belay move right and then left across slabs to a small alcove, then go out right to reach the main wide crack of the chimney. This long pitch begins with an awkward 5.7 bulge and ends on the large tree-, grass-, and talus-covered shelf that extends from the east ridge all the way south along the top of the main cliff band to the southeast ridge. One can walk south along this shelf and reach the summit plateau by one short pitch near the south end of the shelf. The original climb of this route, however, apparently continued up near the north end of the rock above. The rock on this route is good and solid. See *American Alpine Journal* 11, no. 1 (1958): p. 84.

ROUTE 5. EAST RIDGE. II, 5.6/5.7. First ascent September 2, 1937, by Jack Durrance, George Sheldon, and Percy Rideout. (See *Figures 6-12, 6-13*, and *6-14*.) This is a short, enjoyable climb on excellent rock leading to one of the finest viewpoints in the range—the summit of Disappointment Peak. From Amphitheater Lake hike north to the col overlooking Glacier Gulch and then follow the ridge left (west) through the trees to the start of the climb. The difficulty

FIGURE 6-13. Disappointment Peak, East Ridge *(Route 5)*, II, 5.6/5.7

FIGURE 6-14. Disappointment Peak, east-northeast aspect. (A) Spoon Couloir *(Route 3)*, II, 4.0; (B) East Ridge *(Route 5)*, II, 5.6/5.7; (C) ice lines (winter); (D) Pownall-Unsoeld North Face (Pin Time; *Route 6*), III, 5.10+; (E) Chouinard-Frost Chimney *(Route 7)*, IV, 5.9+; (F) Kimbrough-Rickert *(Route 8)*, III, 5.10-; (G) Direct North Face *(Route 9)*, III, 5.8; (H) Northwest Crack and Gran *(Routes 10–11)* up and around corner

of this route depends on how closely the crest of the ridge is followed. **Pitch 1:** After stepping around to the south side of the ridge, begin climbing up a ramp that steepens and becomes a left-facing corner. Continue up and left until a traverse left into a gully is possible. Walk up the gully and belay at a tree (5.6, 60m). (Alternatively, climb directly up the ridge via an initial section of face climbing that leads to a right-facing corner and a belay near the next horizontal section of the ridge.) Walk along the ridge crest and move the belay up to the base of a short, steep face. **Pitch 2:** Climb the steep face through a small overhang and then up easy climbing to a right-facing corner system. Climb a thin crack for 4m and belay just above (5.6). **Pitch 3:** Proceed up the corner, which becomes less distinct, and belay in blocks near the edge of the north face (5.5). **Pitch 4:** Climb straight up and slightly left (5.6) until midway up this pitch. Now climb a 5.7 crack or go up and left via easier climbing. At the top of this pitch climb a short 5.5 chimney with good holds and emerge out onto the summit plateau of the peak; belay here. Now above the steep portion of the ridge, one can either follow the somewhat jagged ridge to the summit or traverse south to the main trail up the steepening summit plateau; both options are easy. For descent take the southeast ridge (see *Route 1*). One should avoid the steep, east-facing Spoon Couloir (*Route 3*)—unless one has an ice axe and is knowledgeable in its use. **Time:** 3 to 4 hours from Amphitheater Lake; 6¾ to 9 hours from Jenny Lake.

Disappointment Peak, Northern Routes

The north face of Disappointment Peak is a beautiful wall nestled midway up the south side of Glacier Gulch. A wide terrace that narrows to a ledge cuts almost all the way across this face, dividing it nearly in half. The first three routes are usually approached by climbing the first pitch of the East Ridge route *(Route 5)* and then traversing west across the ledge. The other routes are approached by descending from the col above and north of Amphitheater Lake into Glacier Gulch and then walking along the base of the face to the west. (See *East Face Routes*, above, for approach details to Amphitheater Lake.) This is an intimidating north wall, but the rock is surprisingly good. *Figure 6-14* presents an overview of the routes.

ROUTE 6. POWNALL-UNSOELD NORTH FACE (PIN TIME). III, 5.8, A2, or III, 5.10+. First ascent July 27, 1956, by Richard Pownall and Willi Unsoeld; first free ascent August 6, 1979, by Mike Munger and Bill Feiges, at which time the name Pin Time was applied. (See *Figures 6-14, 6-15,* and *6-16*.) Because of loose rock, scary traverses, and the degree to which the final pitch is vegetated, this route is best left to the true aficionado of the obscure. The north face of Disappointment Peak is divided horizontally by a broad terrace that cuts across the eastern half of the face about halfway up from the bottom; this terrace narrows to a ledge as it proceeds west, eventually blending into the face about halfway across before reemerging farther west. This difficult route diagonals from left to right up the indented eastern portion of the north face above this terrace. Climb to the top of the first step of the East Ridge route (*Route 5*). Two diagonal ramps, which are the major features of this route, should be visible from the top of this step. To find the base of the climb, traverse out across the terrace until just past a large overhang that usually has water dripping inside it (a waterfall in early season). The first pitch begins just to the east of a second overhang (containing freshly fallen rock) in a nice finger crack that one must step up into. After about 9m of climbing, this crack begins to flare. At this point one is forced to exit right across a short section of face climbing (5.9) that leads to a right-facing corner. Follow the corner up (3m) and then onto a ledge that leads back left (east) past an old ring angle piton to a step that must be climbed (5.8) to allow access to the beginning of the first ramp. After a 5.7 crawl, follow the ramp (5.6) up and right for about 60m to a good belay ledge. Move the belay up and right to the east end of this first ramp, to beneath a chimney that slants off and to the right. (**Note:** With a 60m rope, this move might not be necessary.) Climb the chimney and a nice crack to the left of it for about 12m until it is possible to traverse left across a short section of face climbing (5.9). Then climb up and left to a prow, around which can be seen a narrow ledge, about 6 inches wide and 6m long, that goes out to the east. Proceed out across this ledge, the Plank, without protection to its eastern end, where an exciting 5.8 move permits access to the second of the two ramps. Continue up the ramp (5.10, RPs useful) until the difficulty eases off and belay. The remainder of the ramp is much easier (5.6). The last lead (5.10+) up a vertical right-facing corner and cracks to the right is strenuous, and the difficulties are compounded by the fact that the corner is vegetated and the cracks filled with dirt. Near the top, exit to the right near a small pine and continue up right-facing corners to the top of the climb. The first-ascent party used aid on the first and last pitches. As with any of these north face routes it is suggested that one seek conditions that are as dry as possible. See *American Alpine Journal* 10, no. 2 (1957): p. 148.

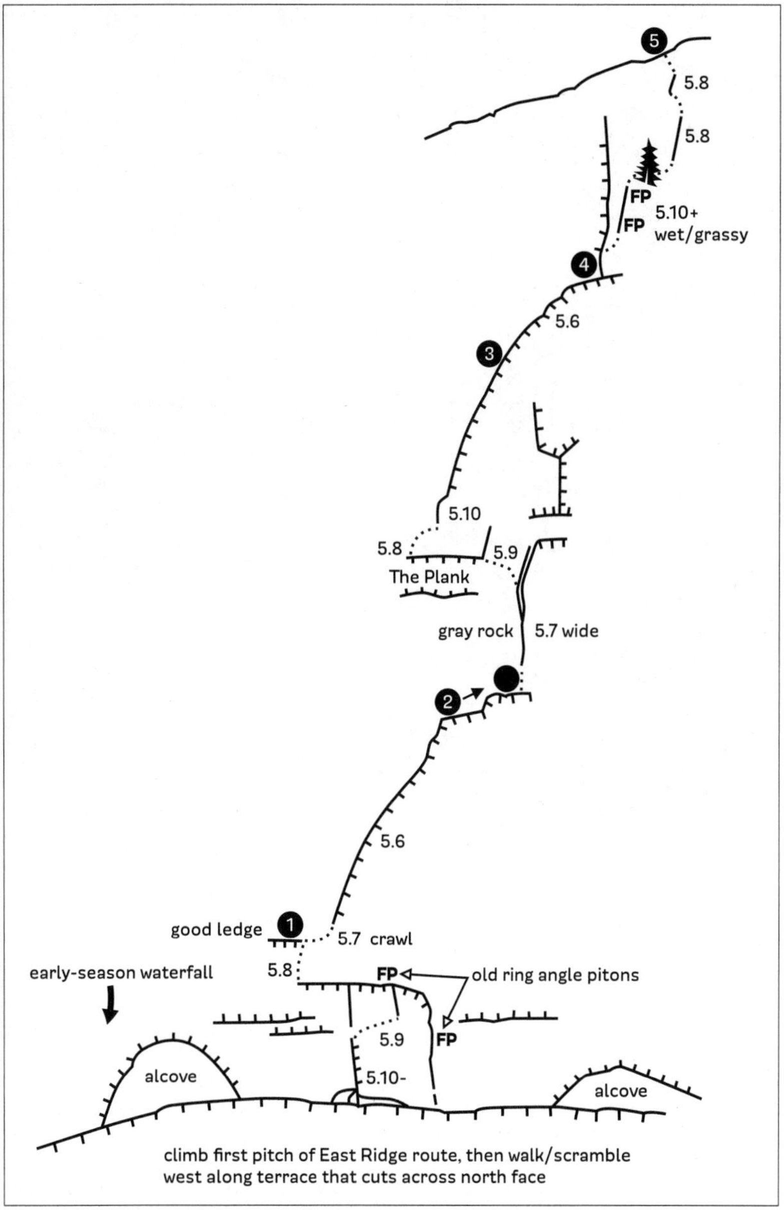

ROUTE 7. CHOUINARD-FROST CHIMNEY. IV, 5.9, A3, or IV, 5.9+. First ascent August 13, 1962, by Yvon Chouinard and Tom Frost; first free ascent August 19, 1970, by Dave Ingalls and Dave Loeks, or August 3, 1994, by Tom Kimbrough and Andy Byerly. **Note:** It is unknown whether the 1970 party free climbed the last pitch of the original route; it is this author's (R. Jackson's) belief that the 1994 party did, and therefore both ascents are listed. Also note that this is the author's best guess as to how the original line finished. (See *Figures 6-14* and *6-16*.) The eastern portion of the north face of Disappointment Peak is a

FIGURE 6-15. Disappointment Peak, Pownall-Unsoeld North Face (Pin Time; *Route 6*), III, 5.10+

FIGURE 6-16. Disappointment Peak, north aspect. (A) Pownall-Unsoeld North Face (Pin Time; *Route 6*), III, 5.10+; (B) Chouinard-Frost Chimney *(Route 7)*, IV, 5.9+

massive wall broken about halfway up by a broad horizontal terrace that extends west from the east ridge. This excellent route begins on the terrace and follows a prominent curving chimney system up the upper part of the wall, eventually reaching the crest of the east ridge. Chouinard and Frost started about 137m below the terrace—a three-pitch direct start that is reported to be unpleasant and is thus not recommended. (To reach this direct start, go past Amphitheater Lake to the col to the north that overlooks Glacier Gulch, then descend to the base of the north face and start the climb at a point 180m west of the old section—just one or two large iron bolts remain—on the lower portion of the face. **Note:** During some late-fall/winter seasons this lower portion of the face occasionally forms up as a significant waterfall ice climb. Several lines are possible, generally in the WI5 difficulty range.) This was a significant climb when it was put up by the Chouinard-Frost team in 1962, ranking with Satisfaction Buttress as one of the two most difficult routes on Disappointment Peak. Seventy-two pitons were used on the ascent, including 24 placed for direct aid. With modern gear it stands as a highly recommended free climb.

To reach the upper start of this route, climb the first pitch of the East Ridge route *(Route 5)* from the col north of Amphitheater Lake, then traverse west along the horizontal terrace, as depicted in *Figures 6-14* and *6-16*. The climb begins in a spectacular chimney system that curves gently to the right. **Pitch 1:** Climb up and around an initial chockstone via 5.9 hands, then negotiate a 5.8 squeeze. Belay in an alcove above a chockstone, just after a 5.7 section. **Pitch 2:** Continue up the chimney system for another ropelength to its upper end and belay on a ledge (5.6). **Pitch 3:** Steep and difficult cracks (5.9) lead up and right to a ramp that is followed past some blocks. End with a 15m traverse right (5.8) to the belay. **Pitch 4:** Climb a large left-facing corner, moving out left past a few fixed pins as it becomes an overhang (5.9). Belay on a nice ledge on top of the overhang. **Pitch 5:** Climb easy 5th-class terrain up and right to a ledge. This ledge becomes a ramp leading up to the right (west). From here there are two ways to finish the climb. For the easiest and quickest way off, follow the ramp up to a short slabby section of rock that leads to easier scrambling toward the summit. For the original finish to the climb, head left before the short slabby section, climbing directly up to a belay beneath a final overhang. **Pitch 6:** Climb up and left to the overhang (5.9) and then around its left edge (5.9+). Follow a corner to the top of the face and belay. Easy scrambling leads to the upper east ridge and the summit. Climb this route only in late season or when there is no chance of its being wet. **Gear:** For protection take a standard rack to 4". For descent, use the southeast ridge (see *Route 1*). See *American Alpine Journal* 13, no. 2 (1963): pp. 487–89.

ROUTE 8. KIMBROUGH-RICKERT. III, 5.10-. First ascent in August 1994, by Tom Kimbrough and Steve Rickert. (See *Figure 6-14.*) This route follows a line of weakness just to the east of the main large chimney system on the north face (not the Chouinard-Frost of *Route 7*). Access to the route is gained by climbing the first pitch of the East Ridge route *(Route 5)* to the terrace that cuts across the north face. Just past *Route 7*, climbing is required (two to three pitches, 5.7) to continue farther along to the base of this route, which is located at the bottom of the aforementioned chimney system. Begin by climbing up into the main drainage and then traverse up and east for over two pitches (5.6), heading for an arch in an area of black rock. The third pitch consists of a 5.10- finger crack that leads up and left from near the bottom of the arch to a belay ledge. Now follow a big chimney or gully (5.4) up and right for two pitches. Near the top of the second of these pitches, 5.9 face climbing permits access to a large ledge system. Traverse up and east on the ledge until a big left-facing corner appears. Climb the corner (5.7) and belay where one can see a wild hand traverse leading to the east once again. For the seventh pitch, begin with this wild hand traverse (5.9 to 5.10-) over to a right-facing corner and then continue up and into a steep left-facing corner (5.9), belaying beneath an overhang. Climb this overhang (5.9) up and onto the summit plateau.

ROUTE 9. DIRECT NORTH FACE. III, 5.8. First ascent August 4, 1955, by John Dietschy and William Cropper. (See *Figure 6-14.*) This difficult route goes up the right (west) portion of the main north face between two overhanging bulges. The face climbing on the first, third, and fourth pitches is superb. Descend from the col above and north of Amphitheater Lake into Glacier Gulch to reach the base of the north face, then approach this route via the snow below the Red Sentinel. After leaving the snow (at the point indicated in *Figure 6-14*), scramble back eastward for about 100m. The first three pitches lead upward over broken cliffs toward the ceiling-type overhang that can be seen above. From a comfortable ledge just below the overhang, the smooth outside wall to the left looks promising, but there are no cracks for protection. Hence, the overhang must be attacked directly. Climb the back wall beneath the overhang for 8m, then traverse 1m to the left until immediately below the horizontal 1.5m ceiling of the overhang. Now make a hand traverse on a flake, which is detached from the ceiling, out to the lip of the overhang. Once established on the face above the overhang, make a very thin traverse (5.8) to the left (east) before climbing upward to a good belay stance on a downsloping ledge below a second overhang. Two short pitches slightly to the right place one on a 10-inch ledge at the base of a very shallow gully bordered on the left by a 40m crack and on the right (west) by a steep chimney. The chimney is not recommended because of its steepness and its wet moss. The next lead, up a 40m lieback crack, is 5.6 and provides access to a broken ledge. From this ledge it is just a scramble to the east ridge and the summit. **Time:** 8 hours from Amphitheater Lake. See *American Alpine Journal* 10, no. 1 (1956): pp. 116–19.

ROUTE 10. NORTHWEST CRACK. II, 5.4. First ascent August 15, 1955, by John Dietschy and William Cropper. On the western portion of the north face of Disappointment Peak are three main shelves that angle left (east) up to the east ridge. The lower right (west) end of the lowest of the three shelves dwindles down to a crack in a steep wall. To approach this route, descend from the col above and north of Amphitheater Lake into Glacier Gulch, then ascend toward the notch separating the Red Sentinel from the west face of Disappointment Peak (steep snow and/or loose scree); leave this couloir at the base of the aforementioned crack. If this crack is wet, make two short leads on the wall to the right (west) before traversing back left into the crack. Climb the next three ropelengths up the crack, sometimes using the wall to the left. The crack narrows to about 10 inches on the last pitch, and wedged chockstones must be used for holds. To reach the wide shelf above, climb right (west) out of the top of the crack. Scramble up the shelf to the east ridge, reaching the summit via the easy summit plateau. **Time:** 7 hours from Amphitheater Lake. See *American Alpine Journal* 10, no. 1 (1956): pp. 116–19.

ROUTE 11. GRAN. II, 5.8. First ascent July 5, 1962, by Art Gran and John Hudson. This route, which lies between the Northwest Crack *(Route 10)* and the Northwest Shelf *(Route 12)*, uses the central of the three shelf and chimney systems that slant from lower right to upper left to meet the east ridge. Approach as for *Route 10* and head up the couloir (steep snow and/or loose scree) toward the notch separating the Red Sentinel from the west face of Disappointment Peak. This route ascends the shelf that starts about 76m below the notch. Walk out left (east) on the shelf and scramble up a short wall to a higher ledge at the base of a large, steep open book. Climb the left wall for about 6m to a ledge where it is possible to enter the open book and reach another ledge. Ascend a crack in the right wall, cross to the left wall up past chockstones, and then step left around a corner to a belay ledge. The next pitch traverses left (east) and goes up and over a difficult bulge. The roof formed by the chockstone above is passed on its right side to a ledge that is reached after 27m. Now climb and scramble up to the east for about 52m until the ledge ends. A final scramble up to the right below the ridge leads to a small notch in the crest of the east ridge. Follow the ridge to the summit. See *American Alpine Journal* 13, no. 2 (1963): pp. 487–89.

ROUTE 12. NORTHWEST SHELF. II, 5.1. First partial descent August 20, 1925, by Phil Smith and Walter Harvey; first complete descent August 11, 1953, by Robert Brooke and Rob Day. As a means of ascent, this route should be approached from Garnet Canyon up to the notch between the Red Sentinel and the west face of Disappointment Peak. On the western portion of the north face of Disappointment Peak there are three main shelves that angle up to the left (east) to meet the long east ridge. From the notch a narrow ledge leads out on the north face to connect with the highest of these shelves. It may be necessary to descend slightly to reach the ledge. One can climb the shelf with no great difficulty by keeping to the right, next to the wall. The series of ledges and short faces that form the shelf are connected by a rotten chimney, which can be climbed. The shelf comes out on the east ridge at the first prominent notch east (about 60m) of the summit.

Disappointment Peak, Southern Arêtes, Couloirs, and Ridges

The following 21 routes are listed from east to west (as one walks up Garnet Canyon), beginning with Hidden Arête *(Route 13)*—the first arête visible after turning the corner into Garnet Canyon—and ending with the Southwest Ridge *(Route 33)*. The boundary of the west facet of the peak is the Red Sentinel gully, which leads to the notch between Disappointment Peak and the Red Sentinel. The two most popular rock climbs in this array are Irene's Arête *(Route 29)* and the Open Book *(Route 23)*, both with well-deserved reputations and worthy of many repeat ascents. All of these routes are located above the main Garnet Canyon trail, starting from where one enters the canyon and extending all the way up to the Caves. See *Figure 6-17* for an overview.

ROUTE 13. HIDDEN ARÊTE. II, 5.9. First ascent July 31, 1958, by John Gill and Bill Mason. This ridge lies to the east of the Fifth Column and Lance's Arête, and its lower portion is not easily discerned. Hidden Arête is a 46m buttress with several overhanging steps, giving the appearance of an inverted staircase. The climbing begins on the steep, solid face of a short ridge immediately to the left (west) of the main mass of the ridge and to the right (east) of the upper switchback

FIGURE 6-17. Disappointment Peak, southern arêtes and Garnet Canyon detail. (A) Hidden Arête *(Route 13)*, II, 5.9; (B) Surprise Lake Pinnacle, I, 1.0; (C) Lance's Arête *(Route 14)*, II, 5.6; (D) Fifth Column *(Route 16)*, II, 5.9; (E) Satisfaction Buttress *(Route 17)*, IV, 5.10-; (F) Satisfaction Arête *(Route 18)*, II, 5.6; (G) Almost Arête *(Route 21)*, II, 5.7; (H) Grunt Arête, Open Book *(Route 23)*, III, 5.9; (I) South Central Buttress *(Route 26)*, II, 5.1; (J) Delicate Arête *(Route 27)*, II, 5.9; (K) Beelzebub Arête *(Route 28)*, II, 5.7; (L) Irene's Arête *(Route 29)*, III, 5.8; (M) Caves Arête *(Route 30)*, II, 5.4; (N) Southwest Ridge *(Route 33)*, II, 5.6; (O) Watchtower, II, 5.8; (P) Fairshare Tower, Corkscrew, II, 5.8

corner on the Garnet Canyon trail. Climb directly up this face and the overhang at its top. Scramble—or climb by choosing short, interesting pitches—up and right (east) to reach the base of the arête proper. Climb the overhangs on the buttress as directly as possible, even though easier rock can be found to the right or left.

ROUTE 14. LANCE'S ARÊTE. II, 5.6. First ascent July 28, 1958, by John Gill and Dave Jones. This short ridge rises directly above the top corner of the first switchback in the Garnet Canyon trail. Scramble 1m up a broken chimney and then move left and up a small face. Stay directly on the crest for the next moves up a slab with a small overhang at the top. The next ropelength stays very nearly on the crest, to gain a level area. Here the route moves horizontally left across the crest, around a corner and up a slightly overhanging crack to a small notch in the crest. Continue to the top of the ridge. The route in general seeks out difficulty to provide interest; six pitches of 5.4 to 5.7 climbing can be found if one tries. **Time:** 4 hours from Jenny Lake.

ROUTE 15. YODEL THIS. III, 5.12b/c. First ascent in September 1996, by Mike Fischer and Sam Lightner Jr., with help from Steve Bechtel, Shep Vail, Susie Schenk, Scott Morley, Steve Bullock, and Chip Brejc. (See *Figure 6-18.*) This climb was established using ground-up tactics, and all bolt placements were hand-drilled. All the anchors, except for those at the top of the fifth pitch, are fixed and chained. Note that the bolts have been painted to match the color of the rock. Approach as for *Route 16*. The climb is located on the south side of the Fifth Column, 30m to the west of a large corner system that runs up most of the buttress. Begin by scrambling 8m up to a ledge that is accessed from the left. The obvious corner, located 8m to the east, is loose and dangerous at the top and is 5.8 in difficulty. **Pitch 1:** Face climb steeply (5.11a) for 30m past four bolts, two fixed pitons, and a fixed #2.5 Friend to a two-bolt belay anchor. **Pitch 2:** Follow a crack up and left (at a roof) to a belay ledge (5.7, 18m, natural pro). **Pitch 3:** This crux pitch consists of steep face climbing past seven bolts (24m). Begin by placing a 4" cam in a horizontal crack under a small right-facing corner. The most difficult climbing is getting past the first four bolts; it eases off slightly to 5.11R after that (large fall possible here!). **Pitch 4:** This lead moves onto the main face for steep 5.10b on big holds along the right side of the Elephant's Trunk, a unique feature (15m). **Pitch 5:** Thrash up a 5.5 choss gully and belay at a couple of fixed pins. **Pitch 6:** This final pitch (5.11b) goes up a corner system before moving out onto a clean face with two bolts (30m). **Gear:** Suggested protection includes slings and draws, a small assortment of stoppers, and a few cams to 4". (Source: Sam Lightner Jr.)

ROUTE 16. FIFTH COLUMN. II, 5.9. First ascent July 17, 1958, by John Gill and James Langford. (See *Figure 6-18.*) This ridge, or rounded corner, just east of the Surprise Lake outlet, is climbed directly up its very steep crest to the giant flake at its top. From the intersection of the Garnet Canyon trail and the drainage from Surprise Lake, scramble up to the right to the base of this route. A total of six leads are required to reach the base of the summit flake. Climb the large overhanging

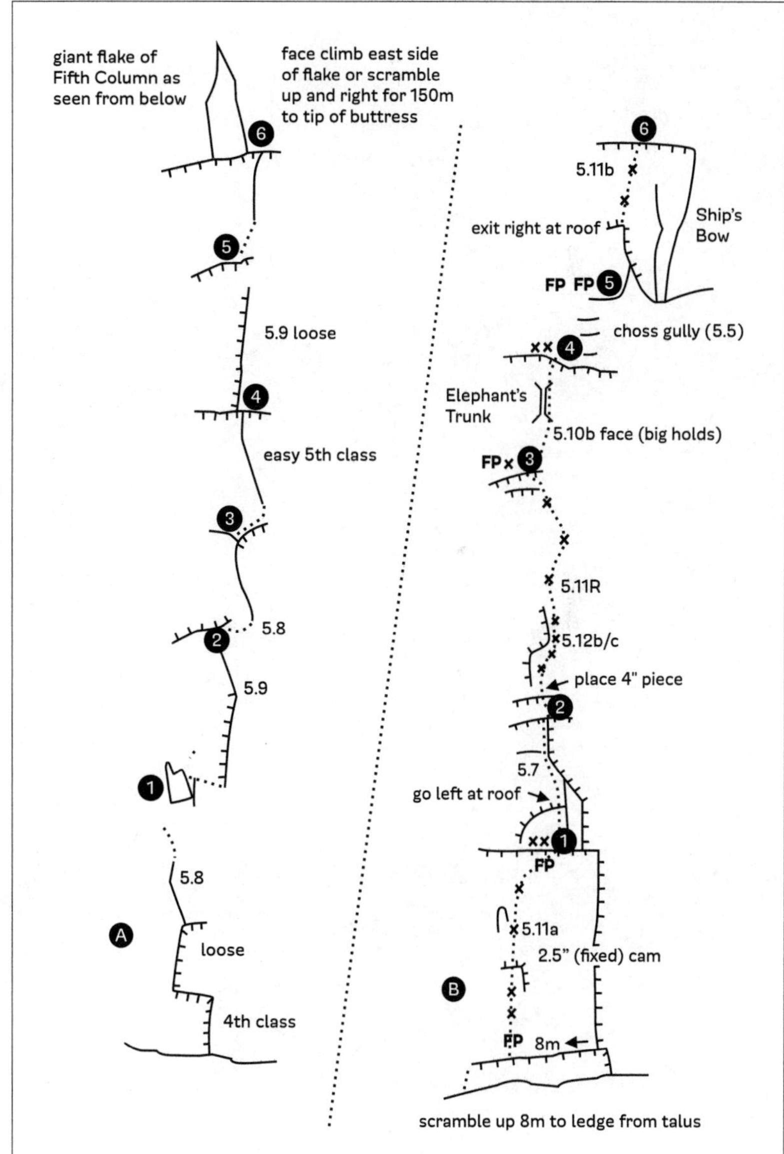

FIGURE 6-18. Disappointment Peak, southern arêtes. (A) Fifth Column *(Route 16)*, II, 5.9; (B) Yodel This *(Route 15)*, III, 5.12b/c

flake, directly above, via balance holds on its east face. Scramble up and right for 100+m to the top of the buttress. Descent can be made easily to Surprise Lake. The rock is generally loose on this route and therefore it is not recommended. **Time:** 5½ hours from Jenny Lake.

Variation: **THE KNOB.** I, 5.9. First ascent July 25, 1958, by John Gill and Yvon Chouinard. To the right (southeast) of the Fifth Column is a small tower, the Knob, which can be approached via a 60m scramble from the Garnet Canyon trail. The route on the south face moves from right to left, then up a very difficult open chimney to a short, broken face that leads to the top. Protection in this last chimney is difficult to obtain.

Variation: **HUMMINGBIRD FACE.** Rating unknown. First ascent July 12, 1981, by Rich Perch and Mike Beiser. This variation is east of the Fifth Column.

FIGURE 6-19. Disappointment Peak, southern arêtes, Almost Arête and Satisfaction Arête. (A) Satisfaction Buttress *(Route 17)*, IV, 5.10-; (B) Satisfaction Arête *(Route 18)*, II, 5.6; (C) Carson Route *(Route 19)*, III, 5.8/5.9; (D) Satisfaction Crack *(Route 20)*, II, 5.9+; (E) Almost Arête, variation: Almost Overhanging, III, 5.8; (F) Almost Arête *(Route 21)*, II, 5.7; (G) Carson-Evangelista, variation: 1980, II, 5.9; (H) Almost Arête, variation: Gray Slab, II, 5.4

ROUTE 17. SATISFACTION BUTTRESS. IV, 5.9, A2, or IV, 5.10-. First ascent July 28 and August 1, 1958, by Yvon Chouinard and Robert Kamps; first free ascent July 15, 1977, by Rich Perch and Mike Munger. (See *Figures 6-19* and *20*.) The first broad ridge west of the Surprise Lake outlet stream harbors both this Satisfaction Buttress route and Satisfaction Arête *(Route 18)*. Instead of reaching the ridge crest from the west, as in *Route 18*, this route follows a line starting from the base of the ridge. This is a serious route with difficult climbing on loose rock on the first three pitches. Although the topo delineates just one line, it appears that climbers have taken more than one path up this buttress. The first-ascent party used a different start for the first pitch. From the Garnet Canyon trail, scramble up talus to the first buttress west of the Surprise Lake outlet stream.

Start at the left edge of the buttress in an area of rotten black rock and climb this corner to a belay ledge. The second short lead is up rotten 5.8 rock, past an overhang to another ledge. The third difficult lead (5.9) starts with a 5.8 left-facing corner to a roof, which is passed on the left on decomposing white rock to a sling belay under a square-cut roof. Passing this roof on the left is the crux of the route (5.10-); this fourth pitch ends with a belay under the next roof. Turn this roof on the left to gain a 5.8 hand crack leading onto a large belay ledge. Move the belay to the right 15m on this ledge before starting up the face above. The next two leads wander up a steep face to the base of an inside corner below a huge roof. Climb this corner as a lieback to the roof, then traverse out to the right edge of the roof before turning up onto a belay ledge. From here the difficulty eases and the remainder of the route is 4th-class climbing to the top of the ridge. For the descent scramble north down to Surprise Lake and take the trail back to the Lupine Meadows trailhead, or return to Garnet Canyon via the Surprise Lake outlet drainage. **Gear:** For protection take a standard rack to 4" with small nuts.

ROUTE 18. SATISFACTION ARÊTE. II, 5.6. First ascent August 20, 1955, by Richard Pownall and Allen Steck. (See *Figure 6-19*.) The first ridge west of the Surprise Lake outlet stream, prominent from the Garnet Canyon trail, was named Satisfaction Arête by the first-ascent party. Although "arête" is a misnomer because the ridge is broad and not sharp, the name has been retained to distinguish this route from the more difficult later route, Satisfaction Buttress *(Route 17)*. Both routes, however, are on the same ridge. After crossing the Surprise Lake outlet stream on the Garnet Canyon trail, leave the trail around the next trail corner and scramble up the talus slope along the west side of the ridge to the beginning of the major chimney, Satisfaction Crack *(Route 20)*, on the left side of this face. Start the climb here, well left (west) of the crest of the ridge, and head up and slightly right in a chimney system for three leads. Traverse right under a prominent overhang on a broken ledge that crosses the crest at a band of white rock. The only difficult lead of this indirect route is the last one, up over the white rock and around the corner to the right (east). From this point one can contour on around, reaching the outlet stream from Surprise Lake. The complete ridge, however, culminates at one of the towers south of Surprise and Amphitheater Lakes. Descent can be made easily either to Surprise Lake or back to Garnet Canyon. See *American Alpine Journal* 10, no. 1 (1956): pp. 116–19.

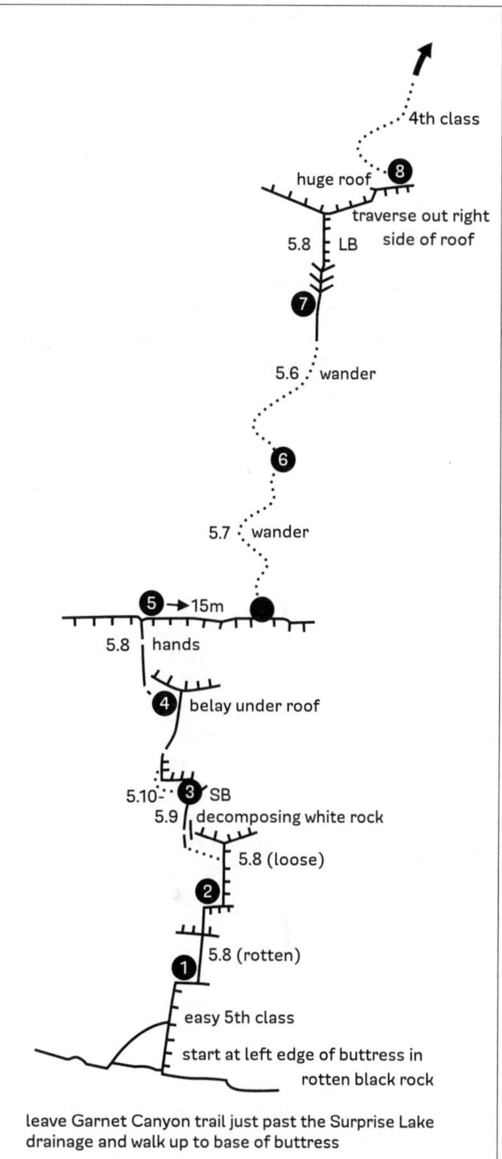

FIGURE 6-20. Disappointment Peak, southern arêtes, Satisfaction Buttress *(Route 17)*, IV, 5.10-

ROUTE 19. CARSON ROUTE. III, 5.8/5.9. First ascent August 15, 1998, by Andy Carson and Dan Carson. (See *Figure 6-19*.) This climb is located between Satisfaction Crack *(Route 20)* and the upper Satisfaction Arête route *(Route 18)*. It follows a conspicuous and continuous crack/chimney system on the left side of the buttress that angles from lower right to upper left. The system ends on a big ledge and is marked by a large whitebark pine tree—an unmistakable landmark (unless it has died, as so many of these magnificent trees have). It intersects Satisfaction Arête on the second pitch. The first-ascent party did the climb in eight pitches, although they believe it could go in six. The rock quality oscillates between poor and very good, and due to the leaning nature of the route, there are some awkward moves. Once the ledge with the tree is reached, scrambling brings one north to the slopes above Surprise Lake.

ROUTE 20. SATISFACTION CRACK. II, 5.9+. First ascent August 19, 1956, by John Gill, Gene Davant, and Tom Clohessy. (See *Figure 6-19*.) This crack—actually a major chimney system—just left (west) of Satisfaction Arête separates that ridge on the east from Almost Arête on the west. Six pitches are required to ascend this crack/chimney. Easy scrambling just to the west of the main crack/chimney system leads up to the east and then back west on a ledge for the first belay. **Pitch 1:** Climb up and right (5.4) to the main crack and continue up (5.7) to a belay in an alcove at the base of an overhanging corner. **Pitch 2:** Exit to the left out of the alcove and face climb back up into the main corner system, into a crack that progresses from 5.7 to 5.8 in difficulty; belay on a ledge (expect some loose rock at the beginning of the pitch). **Pitch 3:** This pitch starts with easy 5th class (loose) and then becomes sustained 5.9+ in the crack system while passing a fixed piton. The climbing eases to 5.6 after the crack opens up into a chimney. Belay on a ledge where the chimney widens significantly. **Pitch 4:** This pitch involves climbing past the two large chockstones visible from below. Begin on the left side of the chimney, climbing up past a fixed piton (easy 5th class), then move out right to a point beneath the left side of the lower chockstone. Pass this obstacle on its left side (5.6). Continue up to the next huge chockstone, past a fixed pin, and face climb around to the right (5.8) of this second obstacle. A short chimney leads to a belay at the bottom of a large scree amphitheater. Move the belay up the scree to the base of an easy slab. **Pitch 5:** Climb the 5.4 slab to a ledge with a tree on it and belay. **Pitch 6:** Face climb up to a short 5.7 crack and belay on a ledge at the top of the crack. Easy scrambling then leads upward to a point from which one can descend to Surprise Lake and the trail.

ROUTE 21. ALMOST ARÊTE. II, 5.7. First ascent July 15, 1958, by John Gill and Fred Truslow. (See *Figure 6-19*.) This is the somewhat indistinct ridge between Satisfaction Arête and Grunt Arête; the upper portions ultimately taper to form a ridge crest. Satisfaction Crack *(Route 20)* is the demarcation line between Almost and Satisfaction Arêtes. The lower portion of Almost Arête is split in half vertically by a prominent chimney; to the right (east) of this chimney is a rectangular region of yellow-white overhanging rock known as the Postage Stamp. The first few leads of this route go up the left wall of the chimney. A scramble up and right then leads to the base of the smooth, slablike, very steep upper crest. Start at the right side of this slab and diagonal to the left underneath the overhang that caps the face. After climbing the overhang directly, the route stays within 3m of the crest to the top of the arête. One short pinnacle is climbed directly along the way.

***Variation:* GRAY SLAB.** II, 5.4. First ascent July 23, 1963, by Richard Goldstone, Peter Gardiner, and Steven Derenzo. (See *Figure 6-19*.) This variation of several pitches ascends the rock near the left (west) edge of the lower buttress of Almost Arête to gain the Gray Slab, an area of uniformly gray rock on the upper left shoulder of the arête. Hike up the talus, then scramble up the lowest broken rocks to the left of the central chimney until the rock steepens. At this point, follow for one ropelength a shallow depression that diagonals up and left on steep rock with rounded holds. Nine meters beyond is a grassy platform at the west end of the first wide ramp that slopes back up to the right (east). Walk up the ramp for about 15m to the east end of a narrow ledge that leads back west above some overhangs. This ledge is traversed left for about 18m until it ends at a vertical chimney/crack. The next short lead first goes up the crack and then up the wall on the right to a comfortable belay ledge. After another 18m up broken, slightly overhanging rock, the second wide ramp cutting across the arête is reached. Scramble up, crossing the ramp, for about 46m onto the lower portion of the Gray Slab. Continue another 46m up the slab on small but adequate holds to a stance above some bushes at the lower end of a groove of white rock. Climb this easy groove up and right until it opens out into the third large ramp, which is followed back to what is now a well-defined ridge crest. At this point join the 1958 route and follow it for three leads over excellent exposed rock within inches of the crest to the top of the arête.

***Variation:* ALMOST OVERHANGING.** III, 5.8. First ascent August 20, 1972, by Howard Friedman and Henry Mitchell. (See *Figure 6-19*.) The lower half of Almost Arête is a buttress barred by overhangs and the rectangular yellow-white area known as the Postage Stamp. This variation heads up the buttress just to the right (east) of the Postage Stamp and goes through the overhangs. Begin this climb 30m–40m to the west of Satisfaction Crack *(Route 20)*; scramble up and onto a ledge and belay on its far right side. **Pitch 1:** Climb a chimney that narrows to a jam crack past two overhanging sections, eventually reaching a rock-strewn ledge (5.6). **Pitch 2:** Continue up to where the crack forks and take the left fork to a ledge holding a tree with rappel slings; belay here (5.5). **Pitch 3:** Continue straight up and belay under a small, gray roof (5.6). **Pitch 4:** Traverse right under the roof and climb the crack farthest to the right up to a "jutting nose of yellow rock." Pass the nose on its left side and climb up to a large flake (5.7). Lieback around the flake's left side and climb cracks (5.7) to a "bulging wall"—the crux (5.8). Belay at the top of the wall (25m). **Pitches 5+:** A sloping ramp is then climbed up and right for a few pitches of easy 5th class. After reaching a rocky, treed bench, an exit can be made up a gully to a point above Surprise Lake. Alternatively, there are a number of additional ropelengths of easy climbing to the extreme top of the arête. This route follows a logical line on predominantly sound rock.

Variation: II, 5.9. First ascent in 1980, by Andy Carson and Jim Evangelista. (See *Figure 6-19*.) This difficult variation provides a distinct three-pitch start to the left of the standard Almost Arête route. The initial lead goes up a large chimney capped by an overhang. The next pitch is up a steep wall to the right via a 5.9 crack. The easy third pitch is up and out to the right onto a steep red slab, containing a crack, on the ridge crest. One pitch up the crest completes the climb, as exit to the right is possible at this point.

Variation: II, 5.7. First ascent July 13, 1985, by Steve Saez and Mark Golde. This two-pitch variation provides an alternate start to the Almost Overhanging variation. Climb a large chimney to the left (west) of that described in Almost Overhanging for 24m of easy 5th class to a belay ledge. The second pitch (40m) continues up this chimney, with large, loose blocks in its bottom, to an overhang; pass the overhang on the right side (5.7) and continue up to a belay ledge that contains a tree with rappel slings. The next lead joins the preceding Almost Overhanging variation. **Gear:** For protection bring a standard rack up to 3.5".

ROUTE 22. NO NAME COULOIR. II, 4.0. First ascent August 20, 1973, by Randy Jamieson and Dave Alvestad. The first-ascent party, who described this climb simply as "the gully west of the Surprise Lake outlet stream," apparently ascended the couloir separating Almost Arête on the east from Grunt Arête on the west. Leave the Garnet Canyon trail as it crosses the broad talus slope west of the Surprise Lake outlet stream and head for this gully. The lower portion of the gully consists of an easy scree slope. The exit at the upper end requires a 4th-class scramble up through a chimney. This couloir is used as a descent route from the Open Book *(Route 23)* for those wishing to return to the Garnet Canyon trail.

ROUTE 23. GRUNT ARÊTE, OPEN BOOK. III, 5.8, A3, or III, 5.9. First ascent August 21, 1963, by Philip Jacobus and Steve Larsen; first free ascent June 26, 1977, by Jim Donini and Mike Munger. First winter ascent January 22, 2001, by Hans Johnstone and Rolando Garibotti. (See *Figure 6-21.*) This six-pitch route is one of the better rock climbs in the Tetons. The best approach is by way of a climbers' trail that begins just before the main Garnet Canyon trail diverts into the boulder field near the Platforms. This trail heads immediately up toward Grunt Arête, passing to the right (east) of a small cliff band to reach, at its top, a flat area with boulders and some withering whitebark pines. From here head straight up the slope to a point on the left side of the arête where careful scrambling along a ledge system out to the right (east) leads to the start of the climb. (One can also climb straight up to this same ledge via approximately 60m of 4th- and easy 5th-class terrain.) Once on the ledge, pass a popular alternate start that ascends a finger and hand crack (5.9), ending at the belay at the top of the first pitch. For the traditional start, continue along the ledge to a large flake at the base of an easy ramp that leads up and left (west).

FIGURE 6-21. Disappointment Peak, southern arêtes, Grunt Arête, Open Book *(Route 23)*, III, 5.9

Pitch 1: Follow the ramp up and left, then head up into the main corner through blocky terrain to a belay beneath an overhang (5.6). **Pitch 2:** The second lead goes straight up to a second overhang in gray rock, which is passed on its right side. Belay at the top of a large detached flake. **Pitch 3:** Undercling out and around to the right using a flake (5.8) and then continue up the corner, passing through a thin crack section (5.9), to a sloping belay ledge beneath the huge overhang visible from below. **Pitch 4:** This overhang is normally passed on its right side via 5.8 face climbing and jamming; one can also go out to the west from the belay and join the regular Grunt Arête route *(Route 24)*—either way this is a memorable pitch. **Pitch 5:** The fifth lead can be taken off to the right on easy 5th-class rock, but one can also continue straight up the crack in a left-facing corner to a small roof that requires a 5.9+ move to escape out its left side. **Pitch 6:** Climb up from the large belay ledge on sloping holds and over a small roof (5.7). A short distance above, look for an escape out and to the east leading to a belay in some small trees. Partway along this traverse to the east is a final (optional) left-facing corner (5.8). Loose rock makes this alternate finish unappealing.

Descent from the top of the climb begins as a traverse on the east side of the arête, which is followed by an easy walk down to Amphitheater Lake and then back down the trail to the Lupine Meadows trailhead. Alternatively, one can downclimb into the gully to the east *(Route 22)* and descend back to the Garnet Canyon trail. This is especially useful if the party has left extra gear near the base of the climb. **Gear:** For protection take a standard rack to 3", mostly medium nuts. See *American Alpine Journal* 14, no. 1 (1964): p. 188.

***Variation:* LEFT OF OPEN BOOK.** III, 5.8. First ascent July 28, 1977, by Mike Munger and Ed Sessions. This variation starts at the first obvious ramp to the left (west) of the Open Book, just left of some trees and bushes; this ramp diagonals up and left. Climb 30m (5.6) up this ramp and exit to the right to a belay. Make an easy traverse (loose) right and then up to gain the base of a corner. The third long lead goes up this corner, passes an awkward roof, then continues up a 5.8 crack in a steep face. The next pitch continues up easier (5.6) rock for 46m onto a belay ledge. Easy escape could be made to the right from this ledge, but this variation continues up one more pitch past two 5.8 roofs to easier 3rd- and 4th-class climbing and the top of the arête.

***Variation:* RIGHT OF OPEN BOOK.** II, 5.10+. First ascent in July 1983, by Kim Schmitz and Jim Donini. This variation goes up the obvious crack system to the right of the Open Book, starting with a steep 5.8 pitch. The second lead goes easily up to an overhang, which is turned on the left with difficulty (5.10+). Two more short pitches, containing overhangs, complete the variation. The difficult overhang lead was by far the hardest climbing encountered.

ROUTE 24. GRUNT ARÊTE. II, 5.6, A1. First ascent July 22, 1957, by John Dietschy and James Langford. This route may have been climbed free in 1977 (see the Left of Open Book variation in *Route 23*). Grunt Arête is the first ridge east of the south central buttress and is easily viewed from the Garnet Canyon Platforms. Use the same approach as described for the Open Book *(Route 23)*; this route begins 30m to the west of that route, and it stays near the crest at the left (west) edge of the buttress. Three enjoyable and steep leads go directly up the crest of the ridge to an obvious overhang.

The first pitch provides a 5.8 move only 6m off the ground. After reaching the first overhang, traverse onto the west wall and head up for one pitch to meet a second overhang, which is passed using aid for about 4.5m. The next lead continues up the west wall and regains the crest at a belay position on a steep slab (fixed pins here). The first-ascent party climbed the start of the next lead by means of a tension traverse across a 3m overhanging wall. They then encountered a vertical section with downsloping holds. This 34m pitch finished with an upward traverse on a very steep, smooth, exposed slab to a small shelf. An easier lead around the corner to the east brings one to easy ground near the top of the ridge. The remainder of the climb is not difficult. The rock quality on this route varies, and the protection is sometimes poor. For descent from the top of the climb, traverse across a ledge system to the north until above Amphitheater Lake. Walk down the ridge to the east and drop into a large chimney system to the south. Downclimb and scramble around some large chockstones and eventually end up in the major drainage to the east of Grunt Arête (see *Route 24*). Alternatively, one could scramble down to Amphitheater Lake and walk down the trail. **Time:** 5½ hours from the Caves. See *American Alpine Journal* 11, no. 1 (1958): pp. 85–88.

***Variation:* SOUTH FACE.** II, 5.7. First ascent July 6, 1958, by John Gill and Paul Rieche. This climb, starting about 120m east of the preceding route, is completely separate from the first climb on this ridge until the uppermost portions are reached. After two or three ropelengths up a large chimney, continue up a flakelike ridge to a belay stance. A diagonal traverse up and to the left under a large overhang leads to a belay position on a 2-foot downsloping ledge. Now climb the right side of this overhang until beneath a second large overhang, where a hand traverse to the right leads to a detached nubbin. A 2-foot ledge now diagonals up to the right to a belay stance beneath the large black overhang that caps this entire portion of the face. After swinging directly up over this, climb a series of open chimneys and minor walls and rejoin the main route near the top of the arête.

ROUTE 25. MERRIAM COULOIR. II, 5.1. First ascent July 17, 1950, by Robert and Doris Merriam. This couloir, which separates the south central buttress from Grunt Arête, provides a moderate yet interesting route to the summit of Disappointment Peak. Start the climb a short distance up the canyon from the Platforms. Some 4.0 climbing is required to pass the initial cliff band below the couloir. Ascend a short talus section and enter the moderately steep couloir proper. After about 75m the couloir narrows to a steep chimney, blocked by chockstones at two levels. The original ascent apparently continued to the top of the couloir, where a sloping slab provides an interesting lieback exit onto the southeast ridge (see *Route 1*). The summit can be reached after a long walk.

Variation: II, 5.6. First ascent July 30, 1973, by Robert Fenichel and Richard Schmitz. When confronted by the chockstones, move left (west) around the corner for 60m to the base of a brick-red wall. Climb this wall to a point in its upper left end that is near a chimney, then follow a steep fingertip crack up and right until one can scramble left into a large couloir. Ascend this couloir for about 120m to its end at a tight chimney. Scramble up and right to near the top of an open chimney in black rock. The next pitch traverses straight left on chicken heads around the corner, then farther left (5.6) across a steep face back into the original tight chimney for the belay. Climb the remainder of the chimney onto the southeast ridge (see *Route 1*).

ROUTE 26. SOUTH CENTRAL BUTTRESS. II, 5.1. First ascent June 29, 1957, by William and Evelyn Cropper and James Langford. This route curves up from east to west and then, in the upper part, back to the crest of the ridge. Starting from a large, treed ledge, climb up and west on the buttress to a steep section of smooth yellow rock. Traverse left (west) on easy slabs and then back to the crest for the final portion of the climb. There are about five pitches on this route. **Time:** 9 hours from Jenny Lake. See *American Alpine Journal* 11, no. 1 (1958): pp. 85–88.

Variation: II, 5.8. First ascent July 23, 1957, by John Dietschy and James Langford. This essentially distinct route on the south central buttress angles up from west to east, in the opposite direction

Irene Beardsley on the third pitch of her arête during the fiftieth anniversary ascent, July, 2007 (Photo by Renny Jackson)

from the first route, and hence crosses it. Begin roped climbing at the base of a steep gully just west of the buttress. After two pitches a large chockstone is passed, and the route leads onto the west face of the buttress for two more ropelengths. The crest is then reached. Make two leads in the section of smooth yellow slabs; then follow several small ledges around to the east side of the ridge and up to the top of the buttress. **Time:** 5½ hours from the Caves. See *American Alpine Journal* 11, no. 1 (1958): pp. 85–88.

Variation: **DIRECT EAST CORNER.** II, 5.7. First ascent August 5, 1958, by John Gill and Bill Mason. This route lies on the east edge of the broad south central buttress, but it is west of the large chimney that separates the buttress from Grunt Arête. It is, in fact, almost completely distinct from either of the two routes described above. From the lower portions of this large chimney, traverse 30m to the west, then climb up and right (east) in a break in the smooth face above. The first-ascent party avoided the easy rock by climbing more or less straight up from this point. After several pitches, climb a 5.7 roof directly. Above this overhang, scrambling leads to the top of the buttress.

Variation: II, 5.4. First ascent August 9, 1966, by Sherman Lehman, William Hooker, and William Kirkpatrick. About eight pitches are involved in this variation, which is similar to the preceding 1957 variation. From below the bottom of the Merriam Couloir *(Route 25)*, follow a red ledge leading left across the base of the buttress until it ends near the left side of the buttress. Climb the red chimney above for two pitches to an area of small pine bushes. Avoid the gray gully above by climbing up and right to a small cave, then continue on to the right below a prominent yellow nose and across a horizontal section. The ridge of the Direct East Corner is now just to the east. Pass the yellow tower above on the left, gain a knife-edge ridge, and finally turn a corner to the left to the grassy slope leading to the main summit plateau.

ROUTE 27. DELICATE ARÊTE. II, 5.9. First ascent August 16, 1958, by John Gill and Fred Wright. This small ridge lies immediately west of the south central buttress and is separated from it by a large chute. Several ropelengths lead up the lower crest and then into and up a short section of this chute, which contains a large chockstone. After securing a belay stance (a bolt will be found here) at the base of the large slablike section of the crest above, avoid the temptation to move right onto easy rock. Instead, move about 1m left onto the eastern edge of this face, then around the corner, continuing up with very little protection for about 40m to a large ledge. Easier climbing can be found in a crack system located even farther east. As done on the first ascent, however, this significant lead requires very difficult balance climbing on exposed and poorly protected rock. Above this crux pitch climb directly up the crest to the large roof that caps the arête. This can be passed on the right via a smooth face to the left of a slanting crack. A short scramble then leads to the top of the ridge. **Time:** 6½ hours from Jenny Lake.

ROUTE 28. BEELZEBUB ARÊTE. II, 5.7. First ascent July 19, 1958, by John Gill and Fred Truslow. This small ridge can be described as the second arête west of the large south central buttress and the second arête east of Irene's Arête. The route starts close to the crest and follows it to the top of the arête. A 5.7 overhang was climbed during the first ascent on the final summit pitch.

ROUTE 29. IRENE'S ARÊTE. III, 5.8. First ascent July 10, 1957, by John Dietschy and Irene Beardsley (Ortenburger). First winter ascent March 14, 1985, by Renny Jackson and Larry Detrick. (See *Figure 6-22*.) This beautiful knife-edge ridge is one of the finest rock climbs in the Tetons. Purity of line and excellence of rock and position combine to create a route that is worthy of climbing again and again. This ridge is the one seen in profile when looking east from the Caves, and from the Meadows it appears razor sharp as it pierces the sky above the heart of Garnet Canyon. The route stays directly on or very near the crest of the arête for six pitches. Many excellent variations are possible on this route, and some are marked in *Figure 6-22*.

Approach via the Garnet Canyon trail from the Lupine Meadows trailhead, continuing to the Caves; leave the trail here. Scramble up and to the east (4.0), following some evidence of a climbers' trail in the whitebark pine forest up and around to intersect the arête just above its base. A couple of short sections of scrambling as well as one short, slabby downclimb (facilitated by grabbing some branches) will be encountered on this approach. Belay in a small alcove at the crest of the arête. (**Note:** An alternate, lower approach brings one to a medium-size pine tree located approximately 25m–30m below the alcove.)

Pitch 1: From the alcove, step around the arête crest and climb shallow cracks (5.7) up and right of the crest to a belay at a small ledge, above some large blocks and beneath a crack in golden rock. **Pitch 2:** The second lead up the hand crack above passes a fixed pin just above the belay (5.8) and continues straight up to a large ledge. Belay on top of a large boulder at the arête crest. An easier alternative leads up and right from the belay to intersect the large ledge earlier. **Pitch 3:** The next pitch begins just left of the crest with a few face-climbing moves. Now step around right across the arête and climb up to a left-facing corner in a black-rock area. Continue up the arête crest, and then slightly on the west side, via fun climbing to a good belay ledge on the crest. A more difficult variation begins a few meters east of the arête crest: climb directly up via a somewhat gritty crack (5.9) and then intersect the regular route at the left-facing corner. **Pitch 4:** The original line goes up and left for a few moves directly above the belay (5.8, protected by a wire or two or a small cam) and then continues with easier climbing to an area of black rock just right of the arête crest. Climb fun, juggy rock up to the golden rock above, where a beautiful white crystal foothold provides access to a curiously difficult groove. Climb the groove past two fixed pitons (5.8) and up to a belay on a wide, sloping ledge. An alternate start is again available just a few meters to the right of the crest via a nice crack (5.8+). **Pitch 5:** The next pitch is normally climbed on the left side of the crest via cracks and face climbing to gain the horizontal knife-edge section of the ridge. A more difficult variation can be taken directly upward (short 5.9 corner, fingers and stemming); continue up and right around the crest and then along the sharp arête. Be sure to look for the many garnets embedded here along the crest. Belay on the crest at a deep cleft in the ridge. An intimidating alternate finish (5.10-) departs here: stem across the cleft and climb the steep wall above it, then continue up to the crest and belay where convenient. The usual scheme, however, is to move the belay down off the ridge crest and into the gully to the right (east), descending 30m–40m. Partway down this gully a steep hand-and-fist crack provides another alternate—and burly—means of reaching the crest. **Pitch 6:** From the moved belay, climb up and around to the right (5.6–5.7) and then up the east face of the arête to a belay on the crest. Easier climbing followed

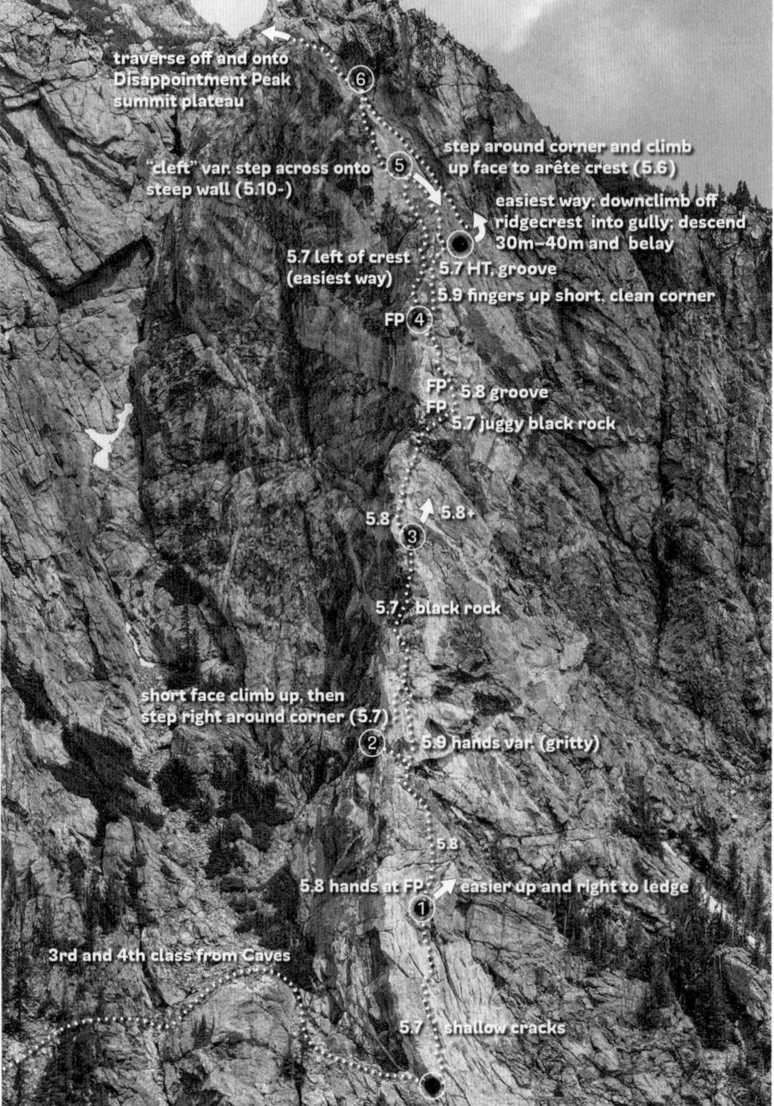

FIGURE 6-22. Disappointment Peak, southern arêtes, Irene's Arête *(Route 29)*, III, 5.8

by a traverse to the north provides access to the summit plateau. For descent, scramble to the west, past one small gully, over to the first major gully—the southwest couloir (see *Route 31*)—which is easily descended. Alternatively, one could descend the southeast ridge (see *Route 1*) to Amphitheater Lake and the trail. **Time:** 10½ hours from the Caves. See *American Alpine Journal* 11, no. 1 (1958): pp. 85–88; *Harvard Mountaineering* 16 (May 1963): pp. 82–83.

Variation: III, 5.7. First ascent July 2, 1970, by Jim Olson and Mark Chapman. This variation begins at the step in the ridge crest midway up the fourth pitch. Instead of traversing right to gain the 5.8 groove, move left on the west face of the arête and slightly down to a ledge system, past the beginning of some overhanging jam cracks. (One of these has apparently been climbed at 5.10.) Continue north for two leads in shallow gullies to a rotten belay alcove. The final lead goes 3m above the alcove, heads right and slightly down past a downward mantel, climbs up past the right side of an overhang (5.7), and finishes with an exposed friction face up and right onto the ridge crest. This variation reaches the ridge crest about 90m east of the prominent tower at the summit plateau and so avoids the notch to the east.

ROUTE 30. CAVES ARÊTE. II, 5.4. First ascent August 7, 1957, by John Dietschy and Robert Larson. This ridge forms the right (east) upper edge of the southwest couloir of Disappointment Peak (see *Route 31*) and lies west of the more distinct Irene's Arête *(Route 29)*. The lower 100m involves nothing more than scrambling. The upper portion includes three pitches, which for the most part stay near the crest and are steep and exposed. **Time:** 3½ hours from Garnet Canyon. See *American Alpine Journal* 11, no. 1 (1958): pp. 85–88.

Variation: **WEST FACE.** II, 5.6. First ascent July 11, 1970, by Thomas Dunwiddie, Scott Stewart, and Roger Zimmerman. Scramble up to the highest trees on the southwest corner of the arête. Now climb 12m and make a long 5.4 traverse into a grassy couloir. Follow this couloir for about 100m, staying next to the west face of the arête, to reach a platform with a small tree. Resume climbing directly up the face (5.6) with a long lead up a lieback crack, a slab, and a nose onto a grassy belay ledge. Continue up to a row of overhangs that guards the top of the face. Passing these overhangs is only of 5.6 difficulty. This indirect variation has little to recommend it.

ROUTE 31. ▲ SOUTHWEST COULOIR. I, 4.0. First ascent and descent July 14, 1926, by Norman Clyde, Ernest Dawson, Alice Carter, Julie Mortimer, and J. C. Downing. Although the first use of this route to reach the Lower Saddle and the Grand Teton from a camp at Amphitheater Lake was somewhat by accident, this couloir does provide the easiest route from Garnet Canyon to the summit of Disappointment Peak. From the vicinity of the Caves this very large couloir leads northeast up to the summit plateau of Disappointment Peak. The first large chockstone is easily passed, but the second requires some scrambling on the right (south). From the plateau it is little more than a walk to the summit. As a descent route, this couloir is simple and fast down to the Caves. When the upper chockstone is reached, cross a rib into a subsidiary smaller couloir to the left (south) and scramble down to a steep 6m wall, which can be downclimbed, or rappelled with a single rope, to regain the main couloir. **Time:** 2¾ hours from the Caves. See *Sierra Club Bulletin* 12, no. 4 (1927): pp. 356–64, illus.

ROUTE 32. SOUTHERN EDGE. II, 5.9. First ascent June 27, 1999, by Paul Horton and Mark Daverin. (See *Figure 6-23.*) This climb is located just to the east of the southwest ridge of Disappointment Peak (see *Route 33*) on a spur of nice-looking rock. For

FIGURE 6-23. Disappointment Peak, Southern Edge *(Route 32)*, II, 5.9

the approach, scramble up a chimney/gully system above the Caves, west of the southwest couloir (see *Route 31*). At the top of the scree look for a thin crack going up the crest of the buttress above. For the first pitch, climb this thin crack up to a belay on a sloping ledge (5.9, 40m). The second pitch consists of easy climbing on the crest of the buttress to a short, steep face. Pull onto the face (5.9 move) and ascend it to a large diagonal crack, then follow the crack to the belay in the chimney above (46m). A short, easy pitch climbs the chimney onto the rib crest, followed by broken ground and ledges (easy 5th class, 15m). The fourth pitch is just right of the rib crest and includes face climbing, cracks, and liebacks; belay at the west end of a ledge at the base of a small open book on the rib crest (5.8, 40m). Climb the open book (5.6), then go up and right across a face and up the crest (5.7R); cracks, ramps, and increasingly broken terrain lead to ledges and a belay (50m). Easy scrambling brings one to the summit plateau.

ROUTE 33. SOUTHWEST RIDGE. II, 5.6. First ascent July 9, 1952, by Robert Merriam and Richard Emerson. This ridge—the westernmost of the myriad south ridges and faces of Disappointment Peak—is better described as the broad, indistinct corner where the west and south faces intersect. It rises in two sections: the first section rises about 240m to the flat shoulder formed by the summit plateau, and the second section extends another 90m from this plateau to the summit. From the Caves a talus hike of about 30 minutes brings one to the base of the ridge. A multitude of routes on this broad but very steep ridge can be climbed, and there almost always seem to be ample good holds. During the approach, look for an initial face with western exposure that rises about 60m, giving access to the south face of the ridge. Climb broken rock on this face to a Wall Street–like ledge. Follow this ledge back onto the crest. Climb about 9m out onto the west face until a V chimney offers a route up over a short overhang. Traverse a bit farther left and follow an upward-sloping ledge back to the crest. The remainder of this first section is enjoyable and not difficult, staying near the crest. Easier climbing can be found out to the right (east) on the south face. Most of the alternatives on this upper part seem to converge at a chimney (5.6) with an old fixed piton.

Once reached, the summit plateau offers an easy route to the summit; one can detour out to the right (east) and approach the summit from that direction. The proper route, however, continues on the upper south face as close to the west face as possible. The angle decreases after the first pitch in this section and the climbing is easy. When the weather is good, this high-angle route stays in the sun for most of the day, and the predominantly good rock assures a pleasant climb. **Time:**

A climber on the final pitch of Irene's Arête (Photo by Eric Bissell)

6¼ hours from the Caves. See *American Alpine Journal* 9, no. 2 (1955): pp. 147–49.

Variation: II, 5.6. First ascent July 5, 1957, by Art Gran, Robert Chambers, and Paul Calcaterra. Most of this variation lies on the west face of the southwest ridge. Start on the crest of the ridge, then bear up and left to an exposed traverse leading onto the west face above the overhangs. Follow this traverse for about 55m to a slight break leading upward and follow the break for 43m to a ceiling. Pass this obstacle 9m to the left. Eighteen meters above, an obvious traverse leads back to the crest of the plateau. Reach the summit plateau in one more pitch.

Variation: II, 5.10aR. First ascent August 8, 2014, by Keith Hadley, Peter Rowat, Tom Hunt, and Taryn Hunt-Smith. (See *Figure 6-24*.) This route begins below the southwest ridge of Disappointment Peak, approximately 10m east of the left side of the lower rock band's overhanging west edge. The start may be hidden during the early season by a snowbank. The first pitch ascends a distinct left-facing corner via face climbing and a hand-to-fist-size crack (5.7). Near the top of the corner, angle up and right to a belay ledge. For the second pitch, climb over an easy 5th-class step along a stepped, tree-covered ledge to a belay near the bottom of a large left-facing corner. The third pitch begins with easy 5th-class rock for about 15m, followed by a short traverse to the right into the main corner. Above the corner move left (5.8) into a parallel crack for a few moves before moving back right to a small roof. Undercling the roof to the left where a thin finger crack leads over another roof to a larger, left-trending crack system (5.9). Belay below a crack that heads up and right. The fourth pitch goes up the right-trending crack system to a small ledge (5.5). Above this ledge, make a difficult move up and right (5.10aR) using a shallow corner. This corner leads to thin face climbing and the top of the route. A 5.6 alternate finish goes up and left using a crack system (5.6) to a tree-covered traverse back to the right and the top of the climb. For the descent, follow a 3rd- to 4th-class corner to the east. A tree anchor will be found on the approach slabs that lead into this corner. A 60m rappel from the anchor takes one to the talus slope at the base of the climb. **Gear:** For protection take a standard rack to 3".

FIGURE 6-24. Disappointment Peak, southwest aspect. (A) Great West Chimney *(Route 38)*, II, 5.4; (B) Kim Schmitz Memorial Route *(Route 36)*, IV, 5.11dR; (C) Whiton-Wiggins *(Route 35)*, III, 5.9; (D) Whiton-Wiggins, variation: Sacco-Vanzetti Memorial, III, 5.10; (E) Jern-Wiggins *(Route 34)*, III, 5.9; (F) Devil's Seed, II, 5.10a; (G) Magpie Acres, II, 5.11+; (H) Southwest Ridge *(Route 33)*, variation: 2014, II, 5.10aR

Disappointment Peak, West Face Routes

Approach all of the following climbs from the vicinity of the Caves in Garnet Canyon. Continue along the Garnet Canyon trail past the Caves to a point where it is possible to angle north up the Red Sentinel gully—the large talus gully (snow-filled in early season) next to the west face of Disappointment Peak that eventually leads up to the notch between the peak and the Red Sentinel. These climbs are located on the expansive face above the gully.

ROUTE 34. JERN-WIGGINS. III, 5.9. First ascent September 11, 1983, by Ken Jern and Earl Wiggins. (See *Figure 6-24*.) This five-pitch route on the west face of the southwest ridge is to the right (south and east) of the Whiton-Wiggins route *(Route 35)*. It starts a short distance up the Red Sentinel gully, just to the right of a very large right-facing corner that rises immediately above the talus (or snow in early season). The first pitch angles right, up toward but passing below a higher, yet equally large, overhanging right-facing corner. The roofs to the right of this corner are passed on the right to gain the steep wall above, which is then climbed more or less straight up. Near the top a band of light-colored rock between two sections of black rock is climbed via a good vertical crack near its center.

ROUTE 35. WHITON-WIGGINS. III, 5.9. First ascent September 19, 1981, by Mark Whiton and Earl Wiggins. (See *Figure 6-24.*) High on the face to the right (south) of the West Side Story line *(Route 37)* is another large corner formation that is visible from below. This eight-pitch route ascends a crack system up to this corner. The climb starts from the vicinity of a very large right-facing corner that rises immediately above the talus a short distance up the Red Sentinel gully. Ascend the talus of the gully and turn up the wall just past this corner. Several leads of 5.7 and 5.8 difficulty go mostly straight up toward the right-facing corner high on the face, with some angling left in steep cracks and past bulges. The two leads up the corner are the crux of the route. These pitches involve climbing a large black slot (5.8) and climbing left around a gray roof into a strenuous offwidth crack (5.9). One final pitch of easier rock then leads to the top of the route, from which the upper plateau is easily reached. On the first ascent of this route the Great West Chimney *(Route 38)* was downclimbed with difficulty; one rappel was required to return to the talus of the Red Sentinel gully.

***Variation:* SACCO-VANZETTI MEMORIAL.** III, 5.10. First ascent in spring 1992, by Jay Pistono, Keith Cattabriga, and Ray Warburton. (See *Figures 6-24* and *6-25.*) This six-pitch variation starts just to the right (south) of the original Whiton-Wiggins route. The first two pitches go up the "very large right-facing corner" (5.10) mentioned in the main *Route 35* description, at which point the variation joins the Whiton-Wiggins for the middle three leads. At the gray roof on the final pitch, this variation avoids the offwidth by face climbing out around to the right and then finishes with 5.9+ stemming up to the summit plateau.

Pitch 1: The crux pitch comes early on this climb. Start in the right-leaning dihedral that leads to a wider crack/bulge about 10m–15m up the wall. Climb some off-balance lieback moves (5.9, thin fingers to fingertips) to reach the bulge. Pull through this overhanging 5.10 section, which is steep and awkward but eventually gives way to big holds. Foot traverse right along the face to reach another right-leaning crack system. Continue up this crack (5.8–5.9), then move back left along a ramping ledge. Follow this ledge

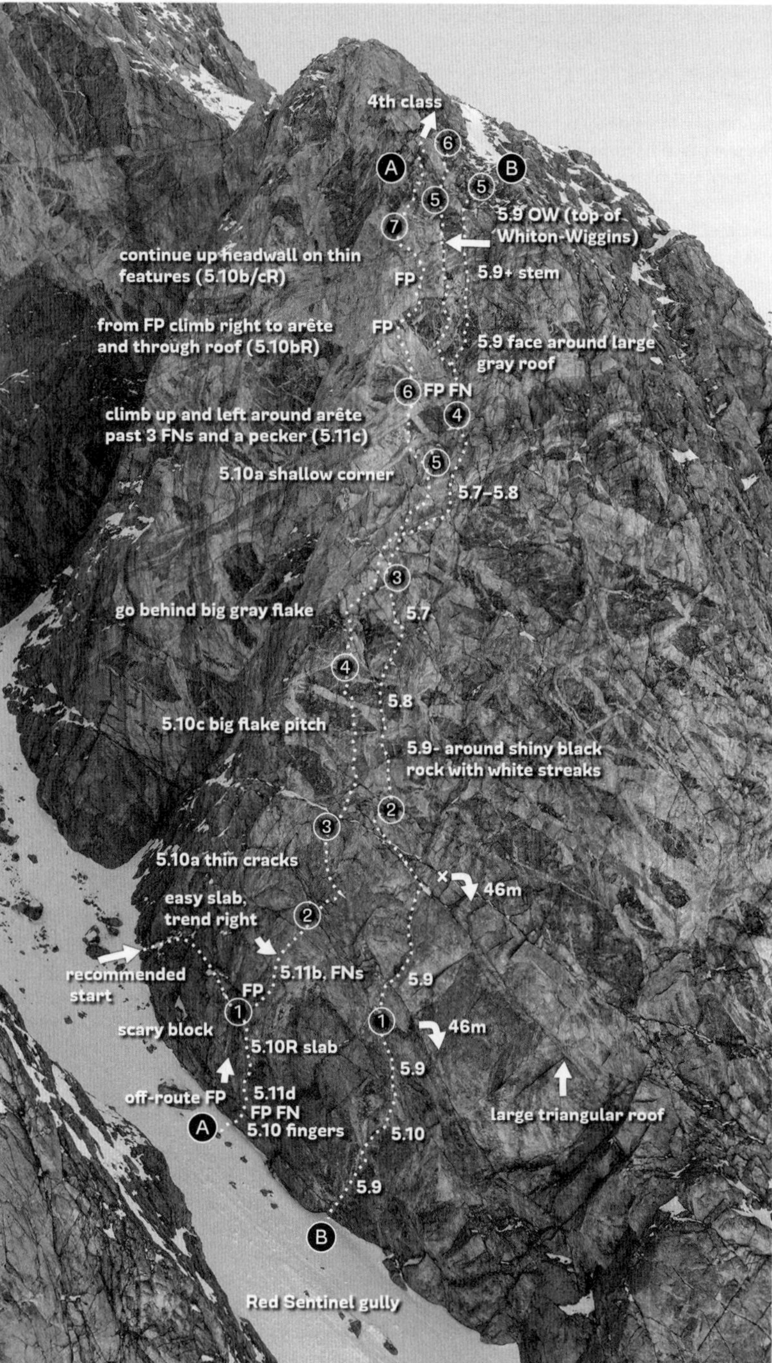

FIGURE 6-25. Disappointment Peak, southwest aspect. (A) Kim Schmitz Memorial Route *(Route 36)*, IV, 5.11dR; (B) Whiton-Wiggins *(Route 35)*, variation: Sacco-Vanzetti Memorial, III, 5.10

up and left, clip a fixed pin, execute a few moves, and belay on the far left edge of a ledge with a lone pine tree beneath an obvious wide corner. **Pitch 2:** Climb the slightly overhanging wide corner/dihedral through awkward jamming, stemming, and liebacking (5.9). Exit right to a good stance, then continue up and right in a prominent weakness (5.6–5.7). At a sloping ledge with a piece of ancient tat hanging from a bolt, move up and left along the ramp to belay at the upper end of the ledge. **Pitch 3:** Aim for a large open-book weakness with white streaks on dark rock and a large chunk of black rock protruding from the wall at the top of the climb. Move directly up from the belay and climb around the left side of a shiny black rock with white streaks (5.9) and then into blocky terrain in a black-rock area (5.8); belay where convenient after a section of 5.7.

Pitch 4: Wander up 5.7–5.8 terrain that can be a little runout depending on the chosen path. Continue to aim for the prominent open-book weakness at the end of the climb. Belay near the end of the rope on a small, grassy perch below a steep corner with a large roof. **Pitch 5:** Gear management is key on this pitch as it is sustained 5.9/5.9+ climbing to the top. Start up the dihedral/open book toward the roof, staying primarily on the face to the right. Good incuts and edges appear, but the gear can be somewhat tricky. Pull around the right edge of the roof and launch into the final section of steep stemming, moving up and right. This last 10m–12m of slightly overhanging and exposed climbing is perhaps the best part of the whole climb. Fourth-class terrain leads to a belay at the top of the climb. One can either scramble up to the summit or walk down to the east and find the descent gully leading back down south to the Caves in Garnet Canyon. Another descent option is to follow the southeast ridge (see *Route 1*) down to the Surprise and Amphitheater Lakes trail.

ROUTE 36. KIM SCHMITZ MEMORIAL ROUTE. IV, 5.11dR. First ascent in summer 2017, by Mike Abbey and Sam Macke. (See *Figures 6-24* and *6-25*.) This difficult, serious, and sustained route on the west side of the southwest ridge of Disappointment Peak features several runout sections of climbing. It begins several meters upslope of the conspicuous triangular roof in the Red Sentinel gully. Look for a 5.10 finger crack with a fixed pin and fixed nut at its top. Just above this are the crux moves of the climb (5.11d), followed by 5.10R slab climbing up and left toward a "scary block." Once past the block, belay at a fixed pin on a ledge. **Note:** It is recommended that one skip this difficult pitch—and avoid the block and the runout—by traversing in from the left (north) on ledges. The second pitch climbs the right-facing corner above (5.11b) past three fixed nuts on red-colored rock. Above the corner climb up and right on a slab to another belay at a fixed piton. For the third pitch, climb straight up via small seams and cracks (5.10a) to a belay on a large ledge at the base of a big flake. The fourth pitch goes up the big flake (5.10c), past a fixed piton and nut, to a belay on another large ledge. Now climb up and left, passing behind a gray flake, and then trend up and right to a shallow corner. Ascend the corner (5.10a) and belay on a ledge located about 15m left of the Sacco-Vanzetti Memorial corner system (see *Route 35*). The sixth pitch climbs up and around the arête to the left past three fixed nuts and a fixed pecker (5.11c); this is just left of a prominent black rock with a white stripe. Belay at a fixed pin and a fixed nut. The seventh lead proceeds up the headwall to a fixed pin, then goes right to the arête and through the roof above (5.10bR) to another fixed piton. Once past the piton continue up on thin features (5.10b/cR) to a black roof. Climb up and right around the roof and belay on the blocky ridge crest at the end of the difficulties. A short 4th-class section leads to the top of the climb. **Gear:** For protection take a double rack with extras in the small sizes. (Sources: Mike Abbey; Mountain Project)

ROUTE 37. WEST SIDE STORY. II, 5.8. First ascent August 23, 1977, by George Montopoli and Keith Hadley. (See *Figure 6-26*.) This route lies on the west side of the southwest ridge of Disappointment Peak where a large dihedral system begins about 180m past (north of) the base of the ridge. From the vicinity of the Caves, proceed about 120m up the Red Sentinel gully to this major right-facing corner or dihedral, located down and to the south of the Great West Chimney route (*Route 38*). Begin by scrambling 46m up and right along a ramp, away from the dihedral, to the base of the first pitch—5.7 double cracks. The second lead traverses left back into the dihedral itself. The next two leads ascend the dihedral proper to the final pitch, which passes an overhang on the left to exit onto a 5.8 face; climb the face to the top, where the dihedral system intersects the upper southwest ridge (see *Route 33*) and the summit plateau. To return to Garnet Canyon, descend via the southwest couloir (see *Route 31*); to reach the Surprise and Amphitheater Lakes trail, descend the southeast ridge (see *Route 1*). Some loose rock is to be expected on this route.

ROUTE 38. GREAT WEST CHIMNEY. II, 5.4. First ascent July 17, 1964, by Richard Goldstone, Raymond Schrag, and Fred Pfahler. (See *Figure 6-24*.) About halfway between the southwest ridge of Disappointment Peak and the notch at the Red Sentinel is a huge right-facing corner, a major feature of this western aspect of the mountain. An identifying feature of this corner is the dark-colored rock that forms the lower half of the corner's left (north) face. The Great West Chimney is in the corner itself.

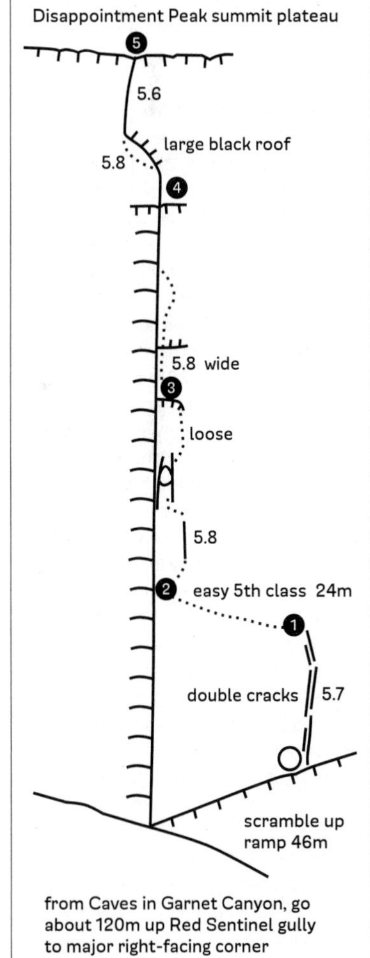

FIGURE 6-26. Disappointment Peak, West Side Story *(Route 37)*, II, 5.8

Approach the base of the chimney from the vicinity of the Caves via the Red Sentinel gully. The climbing up the chimney is not difficult, skirting overhangs and chockstones out on the right (south), but some loose rock will be encountered. The top of the chimney emerges onto the summit plateau at the north end of the horizontal step in the southwest ridge.

ROUTE 39. WEST BUTTRESS. II, 5.7. First ascent September 24, 1986, by Ken Jern and Jay Pistono. This route is on the left (north) portion of the wall that forms the left (north) boundary of the Great West Chimney *(Route 38)*. From the vicinity of the Caves proceed north up the Red Sentinel gully, passing the Great West Chimney and the massive wall on its left (north) side. Near the left edge of this wall turn up and climb on good rock for the first of four pitches. The top of this route emerges onto the uppermost plateau just below the final summit blocks.

ROUTE 40. WEST ARÊTE. II, 5.9. First ascent July 17, 1979, by Jim Beyer and Joanne Urioste. (See *Figure 6-27*.) This route, which might better be described as a face climb rather than an arête, can be climbed in various ways in the lower portion, but the options all lead into the one difficult pitch near the top. From the vicinity of the Caves, ascend the Red Sentinel gully to the start of the route, which is about 90m south of the notch between the Red Sentinel and the west face of Disappointment Peak. The first pitch goes straight up a crack. Next, continue up a right-facing corner, past two overhangs. This is followed by a face-climbing pitch that ends with a 5.5 chimney onto the belay ledge. Move right and up through an overhang and pass a second overhang on the right to gain a right-facing corner (5.7 face climbing); the lead ends with a left-facing corner to the belay. The fifth lead is the crux pitch: climb a 5.9 hand crack past a white flake and continue up onto a ramp that angles up and right. One final pitch of easier climbing exits onto the summit ridge about 180m south of the top. For descent back to the Caves, use the southwest couloir (see *Route 31*). **Gear:** For protection take a rack up to 3" with many small wired nuts.

ROUTE 41. WEST FACE. II, 5.4. First ascent August 14, 1947, by Hans Kraus and Donald Brown. This impressive face has the pleasant characteristic of appearing more difficult than it is. The route is recommended to those seeking a steep, enjoyable rock route that is easily accessible from the Caves. The route starts from the notch between the Red Sentinel and Disappointment Peak. This notch is most easily approached from the south via the Red Sentinel gully. If approached from the north, steep snow and some loose rock will be encountered. This route involves only four pitches but is moderately high angle and exposed. From the notch, climb easy downsloping black slabs and ledges, then diagonal up and slightly right (south) over steep rock that continues for two more ropelengths. There are, in general, several variations available on each pitch, and the difficulty will depend on which is chosen. The fourth lead is up a chimney to black slabs located below the crest. To maximize the climbing make a deliberate traverse back to the left on this lead. The edge of the summit plateau will be reached about 60m south of the summit. To descend, take the southwest couloir (see *Route 31*) directly back to the Caves.

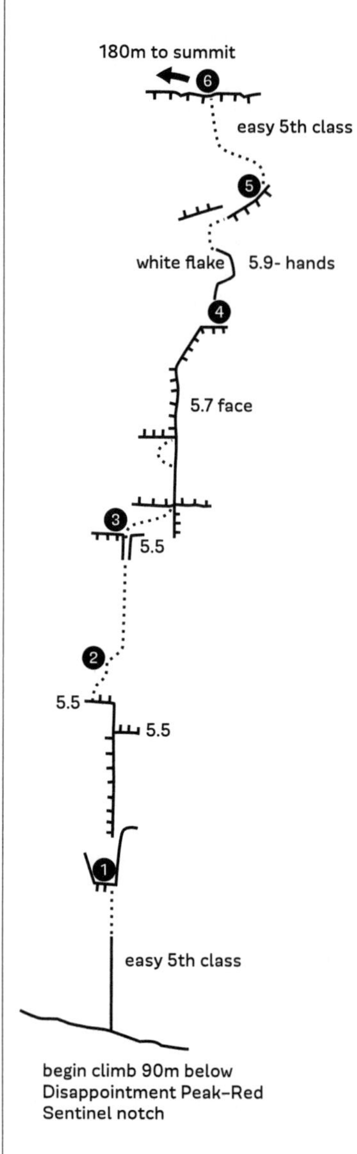

FIGURE 6-27. Disappointment Peak, West Arête *(Route 40)*, II, 5.9

PEAK 10,080+

(0.8 mi ESE of Disappointment Peak)
Map: Grand Teton

This minor summit is due south of the east end of Amphitheater Lake.

ROUTE 1. NORTH SLOPE. I, 4.0. First ascent unknown, probably in the 1920s when the first trail to Surprise and Amphitheater Lakes was completed. This high point is easily approached from Amphitheater Lake. The summit block requires a short section of exposed scrambling.

SURPRISE LAKE PINNACLE (9,760+)

(1.0 mi ESE of Disappointment Peak)
Map: Grand Teton

Although Surprise Lake Pinnacle rises only 60m above the lake, the view from the top is much more expansive than that obtained from the lakeshore, so the few minutes required to reach the top are well spent. This has become a popular destination for skiers and riders, and the National Park Service maintains a weather instrument on the summit during the winter months.

ROUTE 1. NORTH SLOPE. I, 1.0. First ascent unknown, probably in the 1920s when the first trail to Surprise and Amphitheater Lakes was completed. The summit is easily reached directly via the pinnacle's northwest side.

SECTION 7

Glacier Gulch to Cascade Canyon

Teewinot Mountain from the East

Glacier Gulch

Separating Disappointment Peak from Teewinot Mountain and the Grand Teton from Mount Owen, Glacier Gulch leads from the flats south of Lupine Meadows past beautiful Delta Lake to the Teton Glacier and ends at the sharp Gunsight Notch. For those who do not mind bushwhacking, the direct approach is interesting and wild; there are a few game trails leading up this canyon from both the north and south. Delta Lake, turquoise green from the glacial flour ground by the Teton Glacier and nestled beneath the northern ramparts of Disappointment Peak, has become an overvisited backcountry destination, made popular across various social media platforms.

The traditional approach into upper Glacier Gulch is via Amphitheater Lake, which is best accessed from the Lupine Meadows trailhead. To reach this trailhead, turn west off Teton Park Road at the Lupine Meadows junction, cross the bridge over Cottonwood Creek, and proceed 1.5 miles (west and then south) on the dirt road that leads to the trailhead. From the parking area, take the Garnet Canyon–Surprise and Amphitheater Lakes trail 1.7 miles to the first junction, where the Valley Trail continues left (south) to Bradley and Taggart Lakes. Stay straight and switchback 1.3 miles up to the second junction, where the trail to Garnet Canyon turns left (south). From here, take the right (north) fork toward Surprise and Amphitheater Lakes. Surprise Lake is reached after 19 switchbacks, 5 miles from the trailhead. Three designated backcountry campsites—and a fine view of the Grand Teton and Mount Owen—are found just to the north. Continue another 0.25 mile to Amphitheater Lake.

The most popular route to Delta Lake leaves the main trail at the northern end of the first long switchback corner above the second junction, about 3.2 miles from the Lupine Meadows trailhead. A heavily used social trail leads west from this point, reaching the lake in 0.5 mile. This may now be the most direct means of accessing the routes at the upper end of Glacier Gulch, making it a good option for one-day ascents. But tread gently through the fragile Delta Lake area, given the heavy use it already receives. (It is recommended that one use the traditional Amphitheater Lake approach into Glacier Gulch—described below—for multiday outings.)

To reach the upper portion of Glacier Gulch and the Teton Glacier from Amphitheater Lake, head up the trail to the col above and north of the lake. Follow this trail down the far (north) side of the col as it angles left (west) directly under the sheer north cliffs of Disappointment Peak (some exposure here). This traverse can be treacherous in early season when covered with snow; one should have an ice axe and be experienced in its use. Later in the season after the snow melts, the trail leads to a short downclimb (a few moves) and then a traverse over to the first moraine, formed by the snow/icefield that originates high above in the Dike Couloir. Climb up and over this moraine into the small bowl between Disappointment Peak and the Grand Teton. Cross this bowl to reach the terminal moraine of Teton Glacier, aiming for the left (west) edge of the moraine, which is next to the base of the east ridge of the Grand Teton. The glacier has receded considerably since the 1920s, when it was possible to step down a few feet from the crest of the moraine onto the surface of the glacier.

There is also an alternative direct approach up Glacier Gulch to Delta Lake and the glacier—a route that is useful for descent back to the valley. Leave the standard Garnet Canyon–Surprise and Amphitheater Lakes trail shortly after leaving the Lupine Meadows trailhead to gain the crest of the moraine on the north side of the Glacier Gulch drainage. Wait until it is possible to see a more or less open route through the trees to reach this moraine; some bushwhacking will be necessary. A small game trail will be found along the morainal crest. Follow the crest west until it steepens and then cut left (south) into the gulch, not far below Delta Lake.

Another approach utilizes the Teewinot Apex trail. This trail begins midway along the northern portion of the main Lupine Meadows trailhead parking area and heads west to the vicinity of the small waterfall located just south of the trail, about a third of the way up to the Apex. Game trails provide a traverse into Glacier Gulch to the south from just below the waterfall.

To reach the surface of the Teton Glacier from Delta Lake, aim for the bowl on the left (south) side of its terminal moraine and proceed as in the traditional approach from Amphitheater Lake described above. It is also possible to circle around the north side of the large terminal moraine and gain the glacier from that direction. Because the eastern approach to Gunsight Notch at the head of the canyon is protected by a steep, difficult, and dangerous (rockfall) chute, it is not feasible to pass out of the canyon by that route.

It is frequently desirable to return to a camp on the Teton Glacier or at Surprise Lake from the Lower Saddle via the Black Dike, which cuts across the south side of the Grand Teton; this interesting and direct traverse is also occasionally used from Glacier Gulch to reach the Lower Saddle before an ascent of the Grand Teton. To take this Black Dike Traverse, ascend the long snow couloir leading southwest out of the bowl between Disappointment Peak and the Grand Teton; an ice axe—plus the knowledge of how to use it—is essential here. This couloir ends at Dike Col between Pemmican Pillar and Okie's Thorn; the col is on the divide between Glacier Gulch and Garnet Canyon. To continue to the Lower Saddle, make an upward crossing of the Teepe Glacier to Teepe Col, which separates Teepe Pillar from the southeastern cliffs of the Grand Teton. In late season the snow covering this remnant glacier may disappear and it will show bare ice. The dike itself passes beneath the glacier and reappears at Teepe Col. Now follow the dike to the Lower Saddle, crossing over Glencoe Col on the way. In general, the loose rock encountered on this traverse is most stable at the extreme right (north) edge, immediately beneath the walls of the Grand Teton, and a faint trail can be found there. There are no great difficulties in this traverse, but it is a bit time-consuming and, as stated above, an ice axe is necessary for safety. Early in the day, when the snow is frozen hard, crampons may be useful on both the Teepe Glacier and the Dike Couloir.

GLACIER GULCH, SOUTH SIDE ROCK CLIMBS (ca. 9,800)

Map: Grand Teton

The lower section of Glacier Gulch contains significant buttresses on both the north and south sides, but only a single rock-climbing route has been worked out on the south walls.

ROUTE 1. ANOTHER TRAILSIDE ATTRACTION. II, 5.8. First ascent August 24, 1986, by Yvon Chouinard, Roch Horton, and Alberto Bendinger. The approach to this route is from Amphitheater Lake. Take the small trail north from the lake over the col, as if heading to the Teton Glacier. The route ascends the wall just east of this trail, down on the north side from the col. Four pitches of excellent climbing will be found along with opportunities for spectacular photographs.

Early season calm and quiet at Delta Lake in Glacier Gulch

GLACIER GULCH, NORTH SIDE ROCK CLIMBS (ca. 10,200)

Map: Grand Teton

The terminus of the south ridge of Teewinot Mountain consists of a set of buttresses that rise above the west end of Delta Lake. See *Figure 7-1* for an overview. The routes that have been worked out on these readily accessible rocks lie between about 9,500 and 10,200 feet. There are five buttresses, sometimes referred to as arêtes, but they are not all well defined. In order to identify them and their corresponding descriptions listed below, they are—from west to east—the Western Arête, the Olson-Nelson Tower, the Chouinard Buttress, the Delta Lake Tower, and the Red Arête. The location is scenic, providing direct views of the north face of Disappointment Peak and the east ridge of the Grand Teton. The quality of the rock is not always good. See *Glacier Gulch* for the approach to these buttresses.

Chronology

RED ARÊTE: September 4, 1968, Ted Wilson, Dick Ream
var—**LEFT BUTTRESS:** August 1977, Yvon Chouinard, Steve Wunsch
var—**RIGHT BUTTRESS:** August 1977, Jim Donini, Rick Black
CHOUINARD BUTTRESS: September 4, 1972, Yvon Chouinard
OLSON-NELSON TOWER: August 14, 1974, Jim "Ole" Olson, Doyle Nelson
DELTA LAKE TOWER: July 17, 1979, Paul Horton, Renny Jackson
WESTERN ARÊTE: August 3, 2016, Paul Horton, Jennifer Crawford, Mike Werner

ROUTE 1. WESTERN ARÊTE. II, 5.7. First ascent August 3, 2016, by Paul Horton, Jennifer Crawford, and Mike Werner. This ridge or arête is the farthest left (westernmost) of the arêtes above and north of Delta Lake. When viewed from the lake the lower parts of this and other nearby ridges and towers blend together and are hard to distinguish as individual formations. Easy scrambling up the gully that separates this ridge from the Olson-Nelson Tower leads to the start of the climb, just below the notch between these formations. The first pitch traverses horizontally across a nice slab to easy ground leading up to a lone pine tree on the rib. The second pitch follows a left-trending weakness on the west edge of the ridge to an alcove. Pitch number three continues to the top of the weakness and then heads right, up a slab to a steep step on the skyline, where a short wall with dubious rock leads to a chimney and the belay on the left side of the crest. The final three pitches stay on or near the scenic crest of the arête on progressively easier terrain to the top. Descent is to the west via scree gullies with short cliff bands.

ROUTE 2. OLSON-NELSON TOWER. II, 5.7. First ascent August 14, 1974, by Jim "Ole" Olson and Doyle Nelson. This four-pitch climb goes up the small tower immediately to the right (east) of and below the Western Arête. Scramble for 46m to the southeast base of the tower, which is just left of the prominent gully separating the tower from the large arête—the Chouinard Buttress—on the right (east). Continue past a steep section to sloping ramps at a small pine tree. Climb past loose blocks to a large, sloping ramp beneath a large overhang. The last lead traverses left on a short wall around the overhang (5.7) to the crest of the tower. An open book then leads to the summit. To descend, scramble down the back side of the tower to a notch separating it from the Western Arête.

ROUTE 3. CHOUINARD BUTTRESS. III, 5.8. First ascent September 4, 1972, by Yvon Chouinard. This buttress is the third from the left (west) and the third from the right of the arêtes above and north of Delta Lake. It is also reported to be the best of these climbs above Delta Lake. The original route followed the left skyline to the top of the

FIGURE 7-1. Teewinot, south aspect, Delta Lake arêtes

buttress on excellent rock. A more recent ascent yielded the following description: Start at the left-hand edge of the steep south face of the buttress. Climb 43m or so to overhangs, then go left around the edge to the west side and a belay below a corner (5.8). The second pitch ascends the corner to cracks and ledges that lead right; follow them around the edge back onto the south face and climb up to the belay. The third lead trends up and right to easier climbing into an alcove/gully at the top of the steep face. Above the belay, the buttress narrows into an arête. Sixty to seventy meters of moderate climbing leads to an impressive window through the ridge, where a huge block forms an arch. Climb over the block on its east side. The sixth pitch goes up the steep step above via a prominent offwidth, which requires just a few moves of 5.7 but offers little or no pro. A couple more pitches of easy 5th-class climbing and some scrambling follow the ridge to its end on the slopes of Teewinot Mountain. Traverse east to the large, easy descent gully.

ROUTE 4. DELTA LAKE TOWER. II, 5.7. First known ascent July 17, 1979, by Paul Horton and Renny Jackson; Horton and Jackson found a rappel sling of unknown origin on the summit. This spire is located to the right (east) of the Chouinard Buttress. The first of three pitches begins near the eastern margin of the south face and gains easy slabs along the intersection of the east and south faces. The second lead stays somewhat right of the edge. The final pitch, easily the best of the route, climbs up and left into a chimney and crack system splitting the top of the south face and follows it directly to the summit. Descend via rappel from blocks into the gully to the west. A short, tricky scramble then leads back to the base of the route.

ROUTE 5. RED ARÊTE. II, 5.7. First ascent September 4, 1968, by Ted Wilson and Dick Ream. This arête is the easternmost of the small ridges and towers at the base of the south ridge of Teewinot Mountain; it is quite distinct when viewed from Delta Lake. A red face (or slab), easily seen from the lake, is the main feature of the climb. The two variations done in 1977 are both located left (west) of this original route. Start below the red face on a big, grassy ledge with trees and climb a rounded prow (5.4) to an easy ramp leading up and left to a good ledge at the base of the red face (40m). Then ascend the red face via an obvious 5.7 crack up its center to a belay on a flat section of the ridge crest (30m). The third pitch begins with a series of ledges (5.4) on the crest and then goes left (5.6) beneath a steeper section of the ridge. It then trends up and left (5.6) to a belay at the crest (60m). Other belay options are available to shorten this long pitch if desired. The finish involves about 100m of 4th- and easy 5th-class climbing on or near the crest. From the top, hike upward on the slopes of Teewinot and look for a large gully to the east that provides a straightforward descent.

***Variation:* LEFT BUTTRESS.** III, 5.10. First ascent in August 1977, by Yvon Chouinard and Steve Wunsch. This variation, also on the Red Arête, begins on the face that lies between an obvious large dihedral and the left (west) corner of the buttress. The initial lead up the left of two possible lines is 5.10 and can be well protected. The second lead goes over a difficult overhang and then straight up. The remainder of the climb is easier and the route is readily followed to the top of the buttress. Descent can be made to the right (east).

***Variation:* RIGHT BUTTRESS.** II, 5.9. First ascent in August 1977, by Jim Donini and Rick Black. This variation, also on the Red Arête, parallels the Left Buttress variation and was climbed on the same day. It apparently took the right of the two possible lines and was slightly less difficult. This variation was probably the one that was climbed on August 5, 1981, by Renny Jackson and Jim "Ole" Olson. They reported four pitches, some of which were on poor rock.

WORSHIPPER (10,880+)

(0.4 mi ESE of Teewinot Mountain)
Map: Grand Teton

This is the lower and thinner of the two pinnacles about two-thirds of the way up the east face of Teewinot Mountain (see *Figure 7-4*); the other is the Idol, described below. The name, according to early Teton climber Phil Smith, was suggested by the relative height and proportion of these two spires. Although very few of those who climb Teewinot notice it, the Worshipper has a large rectangular window just below the summit. This unique feature adds considerable interest to climbs of the pinnacle. On August 21, 1934, during an ascent of Teewinot, Ernest Scheeff climbed a tower that might have been the Worshipper.

Chronology

EAST RIDGE: August 8, 1936, Jack Durrance, Fred Ayres, Walter Spofford
WEST FACE: July 16, 1953, Leigh Ortenburger, William Buckingham
NORTHEAST FACE: August 3, 1957, Yvon Chouinard, John Lowry

ROUTE 1. ▲ WEST FACE. I, 5.4. First ascent July 16, 1953, by Leigh Ortenburger and William Buckingham. The Worshipper is separated from the Idol by a col that can be easily reached from the couloir of Teewinot's East Face route *(Teewinot Mountain, Route 3)*. Much loose rock is present. A slightly overhanging chimney leads up the west face from this col directly to the window. Climb through the window and reach the summit from the northeast.

ROUTE 2. EAST RIDGE. I, 5.1. First ascent August 8, 1936, by Jack Durrance, Fred Ayres, and Walter Spofford. Follow the east ridge, which commences just south of the couloir of Teewinot's East Face route *(Teewinot Mountain, Route 3)*. Near the summit traverse south to avoid loose blocks.

ROUTE 3. NORTHEAST FACE. II, 5.6, A1. First ascent August 3, 1957, by Yvon Chouinard and John Lowry. Start on the northeast face and climb easily about 46m to a belay ledge. After another 12m up to a small ledge, traverse up and right on more difficult rock to the north ridge and a belay spot under an overhang. Climb this overhang directly (A1).

IDOL (10,880+)

(0.4 mi ESE of Teewinot Mountain)
Map: Grand Teton

The Idol is the larger and higher of the two towers about two-thirds of the way up the broad east face of Teewinot Mountain (see *Figure 7-4*). These two towers, the Idol and Worshipper, are passed on the north by every climber of the standard East Face route on the mountain *(Teewinot Mountain, Route 3)*. If time permits during the descent of that route, these towers make a pleasant addition to the day. The smaller pinnacles southwest of the Idol were climbed on August 3, 1957, by Yvon Chouinard and John Lowry. The taller of these (estimated at about 12m) was climbed on January 11, 2022, by Greg Collins and Eric Boomer during a ski excursion, earning the name the "Supplicant."

Chronology

NORTHWEST FACE: August 20, 1931, George Goldthwaite
SOUTH FACE: July 3, 1982, Andy Carson, Jorge Colon

ROUTE 1. SOUTH FACE. II, 5.8. First ascent July 3, 1982, by Andy Carson and Jorge Colon. This face of the Idol consists of a large mass of loose, white rock. The three-pitch route, which doesn't follow an obvious line, consists of face climbing on the left edge of the face, using discontinuous cracks.

ROUTE 2. ▲ NORTHWEST FACE. I, 5.1. First ascent August 20, 1931, by George Goldthwaite. The chimney on the western portion of the north face is the natural route if the pinnacle is approached from the couloir of the East Face route on Teewinot *(Teewinot Mountain, Route 3)*. After one 9m pitch up the chimney (5.1), climb down and around to the right (south) in order to make the second lead straight up the west face to the summit. An excellent view of the window in the Worshipper can be obtained from the summit of the Idol.

CROOKED THUMB (11,680+)

(0.15 mi NNE of Teewinot Mountain)
Map: Grand Teton

This is the spectacular pinnacle on the skyline ridge just north of the summit of Teewinot Mountain. From the summit an excellent view is obtained of the impressive north faces of Teewinot, Mount Owen, and the Grand Teton. Its overhanging northwest face is seen to best advantage from the northeast.

Chronology

SOUTHWEST RIDGE: [probable] July 26, 1935, William Loomis; [certain] July 30, 1936, Fred Ayres
var—August 17, 1944, John and Ruth Mendenhall
var—September 2, 1959, Robert Toepel, Ruth Kirtland
DIRECT NORTH FACE: August 11–13, 1966, Peter Cleveland, Don Storjohann
WEST RIDGE: July 28, 1981, Robert Irvine, Tom Kimbrough
NORTH RIDGE: September 1, 1991, Tom Turiano, Stephen Koch

ROUTE 1. WEST RIDGE. III, 5.7. First ascent July 28, 1981, by Robert Irvine and Tom Kimbrough. (See *Figure 7-2.*) With an early start, approach via the Teewinot–Owen cirque (see *Mount Owen, Route 8*) and scramble up the drainage of the couloir that separates the northwest ridge of Teewinot from the Crooked Thumb. A considerable distance of exposed 3rd-class scrambling leads to the start of the climb, a short distance above the base of the ridge itself. The first full ropelength on very steep and loose rock is unprotected and subject to some rockfall from the northwest face of Teewinot. The route improves, with occasional difficult sections interspersed with more moderate climbing and even some occasional scrambling. The next-to-last pitch is continuous 5.6 for a full ropelength on steep, enjoyable rock; it is the best of the route. A total of nine pitches are involved in this route out of the beautiful and seldom-visited cirque.

FIGURE 7-2. Teewinot Mountain and Crooked Thumb, northwest aspect. (A) Direct North Face *(Crooked Thumb, Route 4)*, V, 5.9, A3; (B) West Ridge *(Crooked Thumb, Route 1)*, III, 5.7; (C) Northwest Ridge *(Teewinot, Route 14)*, III, 5.4; (D) Northwest Ridge, variation: Direct Buttress, III, 5.7; (E) Northwest Couloir *(Teewinot, Route 15)*, II, 5.1; (F) Southwest Couloirs *(Teewinot, Route 1)*, II, 4.0

ROUTE 2. ▲ SOUTHWEST RIDGE. II, 4.0. Probable first ascent July 26, 1935, by William Loomis; first known ascent July 30, 1936, by Fred Ayres. This short ridge is climbed, via a short 4.0 southwest chimney, from the Crooked Thumb Col—the col between the Thumb and the upper north ridge of Teewinot. For the approach to this col, see *Teewinot Mountain, Route 10*.

Variation: II, 4.0. First ascent August 17, 1944, by John and Ruth Mendenhall. The Crooked Thumb Col can be reached directly from Cascade Canyon (see *Cascade Canyon* in Section 8), but this has been done on very few occasions. It requires a long approach on the northwest side in the loose rock couloirs from the Teewinot–Owen cirque.

Variation: II, 5.1. First ascent September 2, 1959, by Robert Toepel and Ruth Kirtland. The Crooked Thumb Col can also be reached from the north side of the Thumb. Approach the Thumb from the north (or

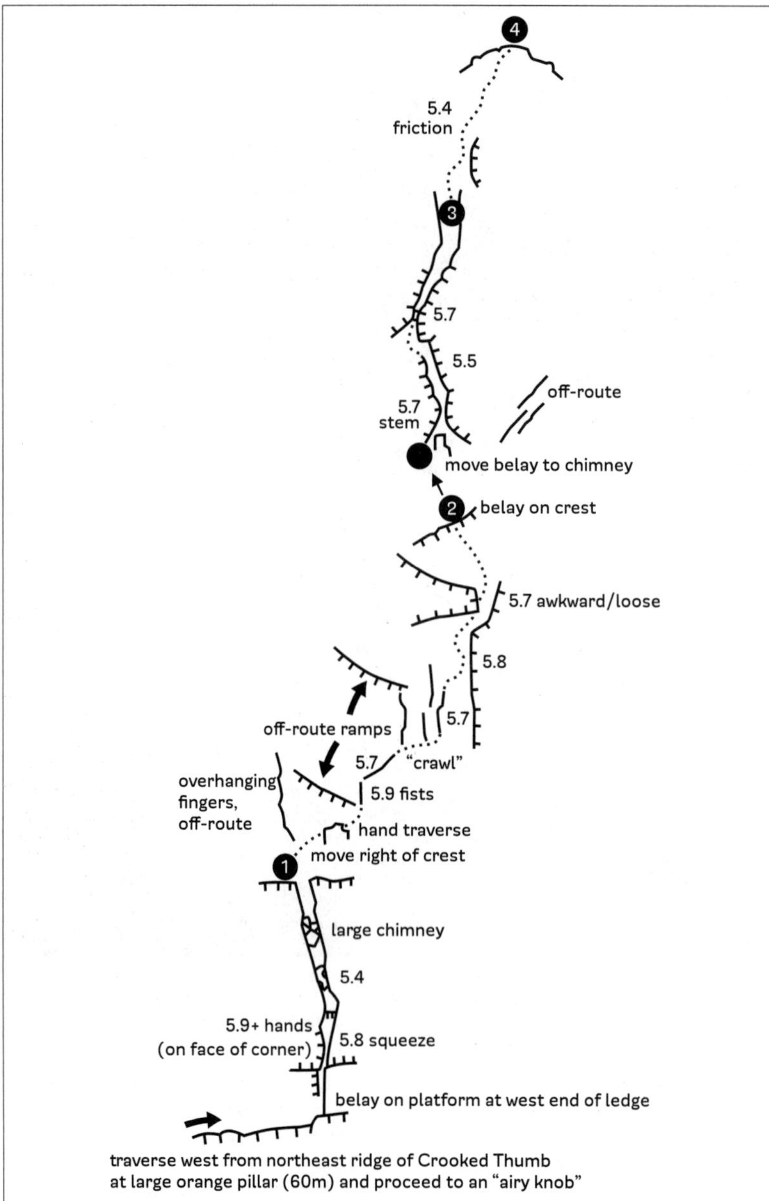

FIGURE 7-3. Crooked Thumb, North Ridge *(Route 3)*, II, 5.9+

east) and climb one small open-book pitch on the northeast corner onto a ledge on the north face. Traverse about 9m on the ledge and then ascend an easy, rotten chimney, from which it is but a walk around the corner to the col and the main Southwest Ridge route. **Time:** 6 hours from Jenny Lake.

ROUTE 3. NORTH RIDGE. II, 5.9+. First ascent September 1, 1991, by Tom Turiano and Stephen Koch. (See *Figures 7-3* and *7-5*.) Climb the couloir that leads to the Crooked Thumb Col—the col between the Crooked Thumb and the upper north ridge of Teewinot—and traverse out and right (north) early enough to reach the base of the northeast ridge of the Thumb. From a large orange pillar, traverse west along a ledge system on the north side to an "airy knob," where the climb begins. The first pitch starts with 5.7 face climbing to a 2m ceiling with a slot on its left (east) side. This awkward slot (5.9+) is negotiated by hand jams, stemming, and a squeeze chimney and eventually finishes via a large 5.4 chimney (55m). The second pitch proceeds up just west of the crest and again begins with face climbing that leads right to a hand-traverse flake. Continue up and right to a 5.9 fist crack, across an awkward 5.7 "crawl" section, and then farther right to a left-facing corner. Belay on the ridge crest. The third pitch ascends the large, classic chimney system directly above the belay and is 5.7 in difficulty. From the top of the chimney, an unprotected 5.4 slab leads to the summit.

ROUTE 4. DIRECT NORTH FACE. V, 5.9, A3. First ascent August 11–13, 1966, by Peter Cleveland and Don Storjohann. (See *Figure 7-2*. [Teewinot Mountain and Crooked Thumb, Northwest Aspect]) The first attempt on this imposing face, by Yvon Chouinard and Bob Kamps on August 9, 1959, ended with a 46m leader fall. This determined party returned three weeks later on September 2 and climbed the first 240m to the large ledge some 90m below the summit, only to be stopped again by the apparent lack of cracks in the overhanging upper wall. The face is divided into an upper third and lower two-thirds by a huge, horizontal ledge. The successful climb, considered by Cleveland as his most difficult Teton ascent, encompassed 18 pitches and spanned three days.

Approach via the Teewinot–Owen cirque (see *Mount Owen, Route 8*). When this face is viewed from the west, two large, black-stained overhangs—the key to the route—will be seen on the wall below the final, pointed section of the Crooked Thumb. Scramble up the main gully on the west and climb three pitches to the bottom of these black stains and the first overhang. After one pitch (30m) that traverses to the left, the next lead goes up a vertical crack to a downsloping ledge, which was traversed left on aid to a hanging belay. The third pitch continues left and then up into an open book under a small roof and then moves left around a bulge and up over an overhang (5.9) to a belay stance. Next go left up a gray face beneath a huge roof, passed by a hand traverse right until the crack runs out, where a pendulum is necessary to reach holds and a small ledge. Now continue slightly up and into a corner beneath an overhang to another hanging belay. The difficult overhang above is passed via aid using knifeblade pitons and RURPs. Mixed free and aid climbing then takes one across a sloping ledge to the base of a steep wall. An easier friction pitch goes left 30m and up 6m to a small ledge. The 10th lead traverses right 6m and up 6m to a ledge that is followed up and right past wet, difficult rock to a belay ledge on black, water-stained rock. The next easy lead goes right and up, finally providing access to the huge, rock-strewn ledge beneath the final triangular face.

From the far side of this ledge the 12th lead starts up the middle of the face to a belay stance on a large, black block beside a loosely attached flake. The next pitch ascends this flake, continuing up and right over enjoyable rock to a belay beside another large flake. Climb this flake and continue right into a steep open book, climbed with aid to a small roof that is passed on the left to a third hanging belay. The 15th lead traverses left (overhanging) toward the base of overhanging rock below a conspicuous chimney; continue up a lieback crack to a belay below and left of the severely overhanging and fractured brown rock band. Climb this section on aid until it is possible to enter a deep, guano-filled chimney. The 17th pitch goes 3m up this chimney, traverses out right and up a crawl ledge, then moves right into a deep chimney above. The final lead goes up this chimney and emerges onto the west ridge about 15m below the summit, which is then easily reached. Cleveland and Storjohann took a total of 20 hours to climb the route, and they required 15 aid pitons to pass the difficulties of the upper face. (**Note:** These pitches were defined in terms of the first-ascent party's 37m ropes. With a longer rope, the number of leads and the location of belay points will be different.)

TEEWINOT MOUNTAIN (12,325)

Map: Grand Teton

The name for this salient peak was bestowed by the first-ascent party of Fritiof Fryxell and Phil Smith. According to them, *Tee-Win-At*, as it was originally spelled, is a Shoshone word meaning "pinnacles." Teewinot is certainly one of the most important of the Teton peaks, both in placement and in size. From the Jenny Lake campground, the original and most ideally located of the campgrounds in the park, this mountain is the highest one visible to the south, leading some visitors to mistake it for the Grand Teton. Although it entails a long climb with 5,600 feet of elevation gain, Teewinot is one of the more popular summits. The routes on the east face can be studied at length from the highway with binoculars or a telescope. An ascent of Teewinot, however, should be taken seriously because the moderately steep snow in the east face couloir (see *Route 3*) has been the site of several accidents. An ice axe—and the knowledge of how to use it—is essential for early- and midseason climbs.

The view from the summit is one of the finest in the park, taking in the nearby north face of the Grand Teton (see *Grand Teton, Route 43*) and the northeast snowfields of Mount Owen (see *Mount Owen, Route 8*). The summit itself, a large monolith with room at its uppermost corner for only one person, is a spectacular place. From this airy perch the exposure down the northwest side of the mountain is sensational. Most of the routes on the mountain require one long day for the ascent.

In August 1980, the Apex trail—the climbers' trail to the apex of the triangular, tree-covered east slope of Teewinot—was completed. This unmaintained trail begins midway along the northern portion of the main Lupine Meadows trailhead parking area. It heads west through bushes and willows up a broad alluvial fan and then through two rock bands, staying just north of but fairly close to the creek. Above the second rock band, adjacent to a waterfall, the trail leads farther north and ascends many switchbacks that eventually lead to the Apex. Although not commonly used, an excellent but waterless campsite will be found on the crest near tree line at the Apex; water can usually be obtained from the drainage to the north.

Chronology

EAST FACE: August 14, 1929, Fritiof Fryxell, Phil Smith
var—**NORTHERN APPROACH:** July 4, 1931, S. John Ebert
var—**SOUTHEAST APPROACH:** August 8, 1940, Paul Petzoldt, Elizabeth Cowles (Partridge)
var—September 20, 1980, David and Jon Baddley
SOUTHWEST COULOIRS: September 13, 1930, Paul Petzoldt, Maynard Barrows (descent); June 22, 1931, Fritiof Fryxell, Frank Smith (ascent)
NORTHWEST COULOIR: July 4, 1931, Fritiof Fryxell, Rudolph Edmund, Theodore Anderson, Harold Hendrickson (descent)
EAST RIDGE: ca. August 6, 1933, Angus Roy, Gordon Sutherland; [possible] August 24, 1933, John McCrumm
var—**BLACK CHIMNEY:** [probable] July 22, 1939, Anne Sharples, Mary Whittemore, Philip Davis; [certain] July 10, 1940, Robert Bear, William Plumley
SOUTH RIDGE: June 16, 1935, Malcolm Smith, Norman Dole
var—**SOUTHEAST COULOIR:** [possible] July 20, 1932, Glenn Exum, Edward Woolf, C. F. Jehlan; [possible] August 4, 1933, Floyd Wilson, Burl Bandel
var—**SOUTHEAST FACE:** June 2000, George Montopoli, Leo Larson
NORTHEAST CHIMNEY: July 26, 1935, William Loomis (upper); July 30, 1936, Fred Ayres (complete)
LOWER NORTHEAST RIDGE: July 14, 1938, Jack Durrance, Michael Davis, Harry Butterworth (to the Crooked Thumb Col)
var—July 1, 1963, Tom Cochrane, Jim Mays
var—**LEDGER BOOK:** May 15, 1971, David Boyd, Chuck Schaap
UPPER NORTH RIDGE: September 4, 1938, William Rice, Robert Bishop, Donald Grant
NORTH FACE: August 17, 1944, John and Ruth Mendenhall
var—**EMERSON'S CHIMNEY:** August 24, 1948, Richard Emerson, Pete Owen
var—**TEEWINOT TUNNEL:** August 30, 1948, Charles Crush, Graham McNear
var—**REESE ARÊTE:** July 28, 1965, Rick Reese, Mike Ermarth, Ralph Tingey
var—**GARDNER-HEADLY:** July 9, 2021, Michael Gardner, Dean Headly
NORTHWEST RIDGE: September 7, 1954, John and Jean Fonda, Don Decker, Martin Benham
var—**DIRECT BUTTRESS:** July 29, 1967, Leigh Ortenburger, John Whitesel
var—**CHOCKSTONE CHIMNEY:** July 26, 1975, Tom Burns, Bill Katra
NORTHEAST FACE: July 13, 1957, John Dietschy, William and Evelyn Cropper
DIRECT NORTH RIDGE: July 28, 1957, John Breitenbach, Barry Corbet
DIRECT EAST RIDGE: [probable] August 30, 1959, Rick Medrick, Sterling Neale; [certain] August 9, 1986, Renny Jackson, Leigh Ortenburger
NORTHWEST FACE: August 22–23, 1961, David Dornan, Barry Corbet, Richard Emerson
NORTHEAST FACE DIRECT: July 3, 2005, Jim Beyer, Dan Petrus

ROUTE 1. ▲ SOUTHWEST COULOIRS. II, 4.0. First descent September 13, 1930, by Paul Petzoldt and Maynard Barrows; first ascent June 22, 1931, by Fritiof Fryxell and Frank Smith. See *Figure 7-1* for an overview. This route provides a somewhat safer means of access for a winter ascent of Teewinot than the imposing East Face route *(Route 3)*. The traditional approach to this route is from Amphitheater Lake into Glacier Gulch, but the Delta Lake approach or the direct approach up Glacier Gulch could also be used. From the lower section of the Teton Glacier, climb out over the north edge of the terminal moraine where it abuts against the walls of Mount Owen. Contour east for about 120m before turning up to the high, flat plateau west and slightly south of the summit of Teewinot. Some of the couloirs leading to this plateau are difficult and require careful routefinding. Once the plateau is reached, climb the easy slopes to the northeast to reach the small west ridge of the first large tower south of the true summit. Some scrambling is necessary to cross this ridge to the north and to reach the couloir that leads east to the large main notch just south of the summit. Avoid turning up from the plateau too soon (too far south) or else the south ridge of Teewinot will be reached south of the large tower. This final tower of the south ridge is separated from the summit by the large notch and is somewhat difficult. From the large main notch, descend easily 30m down the east side and reach the summit as in *Route 3*. Alternatively, instead of climbing all the way up to the large notch from the west, from slightly west of and below the notch climb northward to the summit ridge only a short distance east of the summit. The rock here is steep but not difficult. In early season the southwest couloirs provide a fast method of descent to Delta Lake, provided that one is knowledgeable in the art of glissading. **Time:** 4 to 5¼ hours from Amphitheater Lake. See *Appalachia* 18, no. 4 (December 1931): pp. 388–408, illus.; *Chicago Mountaineering Club Newsletter* 2, no. 5 (January–July 1948): pp. 5–7.

ROUTE 2. SOUTH RIDGE. II, 5.4. First ascent June 16, 1935, by Malcolm Smith and Norman Dole; on July 20, 1933, W. T. Allemann climbed one of the towers on this ridge from the west. This route was first used as a substitute for the East Face route *(Route 3)* in early season to avoid the very long snow couloir, which in that era involved tedious step-cutting. To start the climb just north of Delta Lake, one possible approach to the ridge is from Glacier Gulch. A more devious method is to take the standard Teewinot trail to the Apex and then cut left (south) across the large, open southern basin on the east face of Teewinot, crossing the stream, to reach the south ridge at a somewhat higher point. Either way the initial buttresses (see *Glacier Gulch, North Side Rock Climbs*) at the base of the ridge are avoided on the east. There are many towers along this ridge and some of these can be climbed directly, but most are bypassed on their east sides. It is unlikely that any one party has climbed over all the towers and pinnacles. At the first major notch, just above a big monolith on the ridge crest, stay on the ridge using 5.4 crack and ledge systems on the northeast flank. Regain the crest and continue along the ridge, staying near the crest and zigzagging over and around a half dozen towers, to eventually reach the top of the final large tower immediately south of a second major notch in the south ridge, just short of the summit of the mountain. Either rappel (25m) directly to the notch or go back down 46m to the south base of this tower and, from there, traverse around to the east to gain the notch. From the notch descend a short distance to the east and join the East Face route *(Route 3)* to the summit. The rock on the ridge is mostly good and the views are excellent. **Time:** 9 hours from Lupine Meadows.

***Variation:* SOUTHEAST COULOIR.** II, 5.1. Possible first ascent July 20, 1932, by Glenn Exum, Edward Woolf, and C. F. Jehlan, or August 4, 1933, by Floyd Wilson and Burl Bandel; or it may have been used by Malcolm Smith and Norman Dole in 1935. This minor variation gains the south ridge via the obvious broad slope and couloir on the southeast side of the mountain, thereby avoiding the lower section of the ridge. This couloir is the upper extension of the southern basin on the east face, lying south of the Idol and Worshipper pinnacles. The couloir can be gained either by traversing around (east and north) from Delta Lake or by going directly up from Lupine Meadows via the Apex trail. It ends at the first major notch along the South Ridge route, which is then followed to the summit.

***Variation:* SOUTHEAST FACE.** II, 5.8, steep snow. First ascent in June 2000, by George Montopoli and Leo Larson. This variation was put up by two Jenny Lake climbing rangers during an early-season patrol. Follow the regular route up to the Teewinot Apex and then traverse over to the steep couloir that goes up past the Worshipper and the Idol on their south sides. Depending on the time of year, this couloir may consist of approximately 150m of steep snow climbing. A short, easy climb over a rocky step at the top of the couloir leads to a larger rock band. The first pitch up this 120m rock band is the most difficult (5.8). Although still steep, the climbing above it is easier, bringing one to the intersection with the south ridge. Follow the ridge (4th class), bypassing one tower, to reach the final large tower. Downclimb or rappel (25m) into the large notch located just south of the summit of Teewinot. Follow the final portion of *Route 3* to the summit.

ROUTE 3. ▲ EAST FACE. II, 4.0 PG-13. First ascent August 14, 1929, by Fritiof Fryxell and Phil Smith. (See *Figure 7-4*.) From the vicinity of Jenny Lake the most prominent mountain of the Teton Range is Teewinot, and its east face seems to irresistibly beckon climbers as the most obvious route to its sharp, pointed summit. The 4th-class rating for this route belies the fact that the easiest way is somewhat difficult to follow, as it wanders back and forth across the upper face, following the path of least resistance. There have been numerous accidents over the years on this route, many consisting of slips on the substantial snowfields that cover the face sometimes well into the summer climbing season. Basic mountaineering skill in the use of the ice axe for self-arrest is absolutely essential for an early-season ascent. Later on, when the snowfields melt away, a trail wanders up the face. Even then, several cliff bands must be negotiated, and for this routefinding skill again comes into play. ***Caution is advised!*** Areas of particular concern are marked as "PG-13" in *Figure 7-4*.

From the Lupine Meadows trailhead, take the Apex trail to the Apex, the top of the triangular, treed lower east slope of Teewinot. From the Apex the climbers' trail continues up and right (north) to get into the main couloir, passing first below and then to the north of the Idol and the Worshipper. Climb either up the snowfields, avoiding the center (where rockfall may occur), or up the rocks on either side of the couloir. In early season even this second alternative is mainly covered with snow and will involve step-kicking. In late season when the snow remnants can be avoided it is a scramble up scree and ledges with an occasional 4th-class rock section. During most of an ordinary season, the climb is somewhere between these extremes, but careful routefinding is always essential.

Keep in mind that the summit lies to the right (north) as the main notch in the summit ridge is approached. About 30m below this notch, turn right up easy ledges toward the summit. Cross a short knife-edge to the summit monolith. On the long descent, continual care must be taken with the small, exposed, scree-covered ledges on both sides of the main couloir. **Time:** 6½ to 8 hours from Lupine Meadows. See *Appalachia* 18,

FIGURE 7-4. Teewinot Mountain, East Face *(Route 3)*, II, 4.0 PG-13

no. 4 (December 1931): pp. 388–408, illus.; *Chicago Mountaineering Club Newsletter* 2, no. 5 (January–July 1948): pp. 5–7; 2, no. 6 (July–December 1948): p. 5; *Trail and Timberline*, no. 148 (February 1931): pp. 22–24, illus.

***Variation:* NORTHERN APPROACH.** II, 4.0. First ascent July 4, 1931, by S. John Ebert. This variation essentially inverts the recommended approach to the Crooked Thumb Col; see *Route 10*. From Lupine Meadows ascend the large couloir on the right (north) of the wooded Apex; this open couloir leads to the col between the Crooked Thumb and the upper north ridge of Teewinot. Some bushwhacking is required in the lower reaches of the couloir, and in early season the upper portion will be largely a snow climb. From the Crooked Thumb Col it is possible to traverse almost horizontally left (east) across the bottom of the northeast face to the corner, which is the northeast ridge. This traverse is exposed but not difficult. Once around the corner, traverse across the eastern slopes of the mountain to reach the couloir on the regular East Face route.

***Variation:* SOUTHEAST APPROACH.** II, 4.0. First ascent August 8, 1940, by Paul Petzoldt and Elizabeth Cowles (Partridge). The broad southeast side of Teewinot can be approached from the east or from the Amphitheater Lake area. From Amphitheater Lake drop down to the vicinity of Delta Lake (or approach Delta Lake by way of the newer social trail; see *Glacier Gulch*). Then angle right (east) up to the south ridge and cross to the southeast side, which is an open talus and scree slope. From this slope there are several options. One of these is to contour around the mountain at a level below the base of the Worshipper to reach the beginning of the couloir on the East Face route. Another, which is a little more enterprising, is to ascend to a point near the upper right (northwest) corner of this slope and gain, via a couloir, the broad subsidiary ridge that connects the Idol and the Worshipper with the main south ridge; this is the route Malcolm Smith and Norman Dole took in 1935 (see *Route 2*). It is then possible to climb this subsidiary ridge to the south ridge and follow *Route 2* to the summit over and around the many towers that remain. Finally, if one climbs upward from the southeast slope, the south ridge is soon reached and can be followed north to the summit (again, see *Route 2*). See *Trail and Timberline*, no. 353 (May 1948): pp. 67–70, illus.

Variation: II, 5.6. First ascent September 20, 1980, by David and Jon Baddley. Between the upper narrow extension (a deep and wide chimney) of the east face snow couloir and the Black Chimney (see *Route 4*) is a small ridge ascending the summit mass. This variation goes up the right side of this small ridge but stays well left (south) of the Black Chimney. As the upper narrow extension is approached, a small notch will be seen on this small ridge to the right (north). Traverse over to this notch, which is where the climbing begins. The first full lead (5.6) goes up a crack and then a slab to the base of a large, overhanging block. The next pitch (5.4) passes this block on the right, goes around the corner onto the north face of the ridge, and then proceeds up two vertical sections to finish in a crack system angling up and right (west) to a belay just below an overhang. Traverse right below this overhang until it is possible to climb to the crest of the ridge. It is then but a scramble to reach the summit of Teewinot.

ROUTE 4. EAST RIDGE. II, 5.4. First ascent on about August 6, 1933, by Angus Roy and Gordon Sutherland; possible first ascent August 24, 1933, by John McCrumm. After the first ascent of the mountain in 1929, several early climbs were described as "east ridge" rather than "east face." Because it is reasonably certain that none of these ascents followed the ridge directly, this terminology has resulted in serious confusion. It is likely that none of these ascents took the exact same line. They probably all followed some portion of the ridge to the right (north) of the main east face couloir (see *Route 3*) and ultimately gained the easier ground to the south of the ridge crest, thus avoiding the prominent, very steep step in the ridge.

After reaching the beginning of the main east couloir, traverse right (north) as soon as practicable onto the east ridge. The difficulty of the route depends on how closely the crest is followed. Shortly after roping up, ascend a 10m pitch on the crest; at a higher point some buttresses can be climbed or avoided as desired. Generally, however, the climbing is easy until the ridge steepens abruptly about 200m below the summit. Abandon the crest of the ridge here to get onto easier ground to the left (south) and join the regular East Face route to reach the summit. **Time:** 6¾ to 9 hours from Lupine Meadows.

Variation: **BLACK CHIMNEY.** II, 5.6. Probable first ascent July 22, 1939, by Anne Sharples, Mary Whittemore, and Philip Davis; first known ascent July 10, 1940, by Robert Bear and William Plumley. It is also possible that this chimney was climbed by one or more of the earlier parties who described their route as "east ridge." This distinctive chimney in the main summit mass of Teewinot lies to the right (north) of the standard east face snow couloir (see *Route 3*) but left (south) of the well-defined upper east ridge. It is easily seen from Lupine Meadows. Follow the general East Ridge route to the base of the steep section about 200m below the summit. Abandon the crest of the ridge here in order to get into the beginning of the Black Chimney 30m to the left (south) of the ridge. (This chimney leads to a small notch in the crest of the east ridge; the same notch is reached from the north via *Route 6*.) Above the two chockstones in the lower section of the Black Chimney is a steep, rotten section that often has black ice in it. After three or four ropelengths, traverse left (south) out of the chimney onto the easier rock leading up to the summit. This route is not recommended for early season because running water pours over the chockstones as waterfalls. At best, the Black Chimney is a treacherous place because of the rotten rock.

ROUTE 5. DIRECT EAST RIDGE. III, 5.8. Probable first ascent August 30, 1959, by Rick Medrick and Sterling Neale; first recorded ascent August 9, 1986, by Renny Jackson and Leigh Ortenburger. The 1959 party found cairns and rusty pitons on this route, indicating that others had gone before but very likely had bypassed some or all of the more difficult climbing. This ridge can also be described as the east edge of the northeast face, when viewed from the north. In profile, the east ridge of Teewinot contains a prominent steep section of massive yellow rock about 90m below the summit. The East Ridge route *(Route 4)* bypasses this section on the south. The lower ridge can be accessed from the north, as done in 1959, at a point below the steep section; for this approach, use the north couloir that leads to the Crooked Thumb Col (see *Route 10*). Or take the Apex trail to the Apex, the top of the tree-covered slope on the east face of Teewinot, and then traverse horizontally north to attain the extreme base of the east ridge. If this is done, the initial, smaller steep section of the ridge is climbed in two leads using cracks (5.8) on its left (south) side. A section of scrambling then provides access to the base of the main, steep rock section of the ridge, which is broken by five cracks in the nearly vertical, yellow rock. Exactly how the 1959 party climbed this buttress has been lost in the mists of time. However, in 1986, Jackson and Ortenburger selected the crack nearest the nose of the ridge, the second from the right (north). From the end of this pitch, two small steps broken by horizontal sections led to the final three towers that guard the summit. Each was either climbed directly or passed on the right (north).

ROUTE 6. NORTHEAST CHIMNEY. II, 5.4. First ascent July 26, 1935, by William Loomis (upper chimney); first complete ascent July 30, 1936, by Fred Ayres. The eastern facet of the north face of Teewinot holds, near its left (east) edge, a large chimney. This northeast chimney is the only large one that cuts up this face to a small notch in the uppermost east ridge. This climb is approached via the long couloir extending down from the Crooked Thumb Col between the Crooked Thumb and the upper north ridge of Teewinot; see *Route 10* for the approach to this couloir. Although for most of the season the upper part of this couloir is a snow climb, some bushwhacking is necessary in the lower part. One could climb directly from the upper couloir to the bottom of the obvious northeast chimney; however, it is better to proceed all the way to the col first. (Once at the col, the Crooked Thumb can be climbed for an excellent view from its summit of this Northeast Chimney route and the rest of the northern aspect of Teewinot.) It is a slightly upward traverse left (east) on ledges from the col to the middle of the northeast chimney. On his ascent in 1936, Fred Ayres apparently made a horizontal traverse, with perhaps a slight descent, to reach the bottom of the chimney; this adds two or three pitches to the climb. Climb the chimney past the chockstone. Some loose rock will be encountered. The top of the chimney brings one out at a small notch above the steep section of the east ridge. A short scramble up and left (south) leads to the summit knife-edge. **Time:** 5¾ hours from Lupine Meadows.

ROUTE 7. NORTHEAST FACE. III, 5.7. First ascent July 13, 1957, by John Dietschy and William and Evelyn Cropper. (See *Figure 7-5*.) This fine route ascends the middle of the east facet of the north face of Teewinot between two overhanging bulges. Ascend the couloir as in *Route 10* toward the Crooked Thumb Col, the col between the Crooked Thumb and the upper north ridge of Teewinot. From a point about 60m short of the col, an obvious ramp leads diagonally about 60m onto the northeast face where a definite break in the wall above can be found. Climb two or three pitches almost straight up from this point, generally following a narrow crack. A prominent feature of this face is a giant flake or detached block about three-quarters of the way to the top, somewhat right of center. This route apparently goes up left (east) of this block, perhaps the right of the two overhanging bulges described by the 1957 first-ascent party. Other climbs of this face have attempted the small chimney behind the block unsuccessfully and have had to resort to a crack on the right to reach the top of the block. The route leaves the face just below its apex. This is a delightful climb on good rock. **Time:** 10¾ hours from Lupine Meadows. See *American Alpine Journal* 11, no. 1 (1958): pp. 85–88.

ROUTE 8. NORTHEAST FACE DIRECT. IV, 5.10. First ascent July 3, 2005, by Jim Beyer and Dan Petrus. (See *Figure 7-5*.) This route intersects the ramp mentioned in *Route 7* after two pitches and then continues up the face, eventually trending east and intersecting *Route 5* approximately 30m below the summit. (**Note:** The line shown in *Figure 7-5* is a best guess, especially after it crosses the ramp.) From the couloir leading to the Crooked Thumb Col, climb up (3rd class) to the base of a right-facing corner and belay. Climb the right-facing corner, which starts out at 5.9 and then becomes more difficult (5.10), up to a ledge and belay. The second pitch consists of easy 5th-class climbing up to and across the ramp and then up to a belay ledge. The third pitch goes up a left-leaning crack until it is possible to break out to the west via 5.8 face climbing up to another belay ledge next to a large flake. The fourth pitch goes up and slightly east via face climbing to a right-facing corner that is climbed (5.8) to a belay ledge beneath an overhang. On the fifth pitch, climb the overhang (5.8) and then begin working out to the east via cracks and then a ledge system, which leads to an alcove and the belay. The sixth pitch climbs up and out of the alcove (5.8+) and into a flaring crack that leads up and east to a belay at the base of another right-facing corner. The final pitch continues out to the east via a 4th-class ledge that joins *Route 5*. Thirty meters of 3rd-class climbing then leads to the summit.

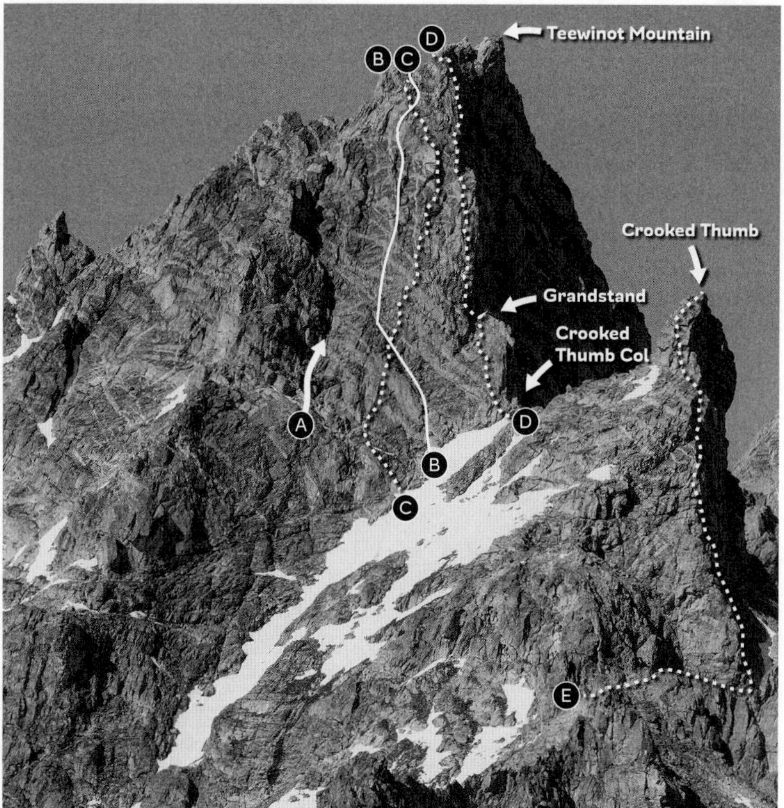

FIGURE 7-5. Teewinot Mountain and Crooked Thumb, northeast aspect. (A) Northeast Chimney, *(Teewinot, Route 6)*, II, 5.4; (B) Northeast Face *(Teewinot, Route 7)*, III, 5.7; (C) Northeast Face Direct (approximate; *Teewinot, Route 8*), IV, 5.10; (D) Direct North Ridge *(Teewinot, Route 11)*, III, 5.8; (E) North Ridge *(Crooked Thumb, Route 3)*, II, 5.9+

ROUTE 9. LOWER NORTHEAST RIDGE. II, 4.0. First ascent July 14, 1938, by Jack Durrance, Michael Davis, and Harry Butterworth (to the Crooked Thumb Col); an earlier attempt the same year by Jack and Jim Durrance and George Kingsbury resulted in the first ascent of Elizabeth's Needle, one of the towers on this ridge. This very long, generally easy ridge rises from the mouth of Cascade Canyon and leads past the Crooked Thumb to the abrupt final north face of Teewinot. The climb starts from the Hidden Falls trail just south of the Cascade Creek crossing (see *Cascade Canyon* in Section 8). Bushwhack directly up through trees onto the open ridge and over various pinnacles to a point just northeast of the Crooked Thumb. At this point the few parties who have climbed this ridge have scrambled up and across the eastern slopes of the Thumb to reach the Crooked Thumb Col, the col separating it from the upper north ridge of Teewinot. To reach the summit of Teewinot, one must take one of several routes that begin at or near the col: see *Routes 6, 7, 8, 10, 11,* and *12*, as well as *Crooked Thumb*. See *Harvard Mountaineering* 16 (May 1963): pp. 83–84.

Variation: II, 5.7. First ascent July 1, 1963, by Tom Cochrane and Jim Mays. Little information is available concerning the exact location of this variation, but it is on a small arête or wall in Cascade Canyon about one-quarter of the way up the north side of Teewinot. It is on the west side of the lower northeast ridge. Cross Cascade Creek and bushwhack to the base of the arête or wall. Climb three pitches of 5.5, 5.6, and 5.7 to the top of the route. Descent is complicated by lack of usable cracks at the second rappel point.

Variation: **LEDGER BOOK.** III, 5.6. First ascent May 15, 1971, by David Boyd and Chuck Schaap. The crest of the lower northeast ridge consists of the tops of a series of steep buttresses rising from the base of its northwest face. From the Cascade Canyon trail just west of the cutoff to the west shore boat dock (the trail that leads past the Symmetry Couloir and Baxter's Pinnacle), two wide, parallel shelves at the bottom of the first buttress east of the Crooked Thumb will be seen angling up from left to right toward the col north of the Thumb. This variation, an early-season snow-and-ice climb, ascends the left of these two shelves. Cross Cascade Creek and scramble or kick steps in the snow to the base of the left shelf. Climb directly up the shelf, at times only 4.5m wide, to the small notch at its head. Now traverse left across two ridges and gullies to a couloir leading back left to the northeast ridge crest only a short distance from the col north of the Crooked Thumb. Scramble to the col, traverse around the east side of the Crooked Thumb, and reach the Crooked Thumb Col, from which various routes lead to the summit of Teewinot. This climb is comparable to the Northwest Ice Couloir of the Middle Teton *(Middle Teton, Route 33)* or the Northeast Snowfields route of Mount Owen *(Mount Owen, Route 8)*. **Gear:** Crampons are recommended for the ice.

ROUTE 10. UPPER NORTH RIDGE. II, 5.6. First ascent September 4, 1938, by William Rice, Robert Bishop, and Donald Grant. (See *Figure 7-7.*) As seen from the valley, this imposing high-angle ridge, which divides the north face of Teewinot into eastern and western facets, rises in three sections from the Crooked Thumb Col. The first shoulder is the top of the small Grandstand from which the north face routes lead out right (west) onto the west facet. At the top of the second section is a broad, scree-covered ledge that again provides access to the west facet of the north face. The third and final section of the north ridge ends at a high point about 90m east of the summit.

From Lupine Meadows take the Apex trail up toward the regular East Face route *(Route 3)* and exit to the north in its upper reaches before reaching the Apex. Traverse across the basin and ascend the couloir to the Crooked Thumb Col. An ice axe will be required in early season and midseason when the couloir is snow-filled. Alternatively (and preferably), the Crooked Thumb Col can be reached from the Apex: Take the first part of the east face couloir to a point about 90m above the Idol and the Worshipper, then move out to the right on ledges to a flat step in the east ridge. From the crest of the ridge a ledge system leads around to the north and gives access to the upper snow, or rocks in late season, just below the col. From the col gain the top of the Grandstand in two ropelengths of 5.6 climbing on its east side. The second section is more difficult and is climbed by staying left (east) of the crest in a series of cracks and open chimneys until the broad, scree-covered ledge is reached. Follow this ledge to the right (west), out onto the west facet of the north face, where the rock is loose; the ledge narrows into a nearly horizontal crack. Climb along the crack and continue up, angling west past a steep V-shaped crack with a chockstone at its top. The final wide chimney, which is filled with loose rock, brings one out on the summit ridge only 30m east of the summit. **Time:** 7¼ hours from Lupine Meadows.

ROUTE 11. DIRECT NORTH RIDGE. III, 5.8. First ascent July 28, 1957, by John Breitenbach and Barry Corbet. (See *Figures 7-5, 7-6,* and *7-7.*) A splendid but strenuous climb is available on this excellent ridge if one stays within 6m to 9m of the actual crest of the ridge. In general, it is possible to find easier rock by climbing farther out to the left (east) along the second steep

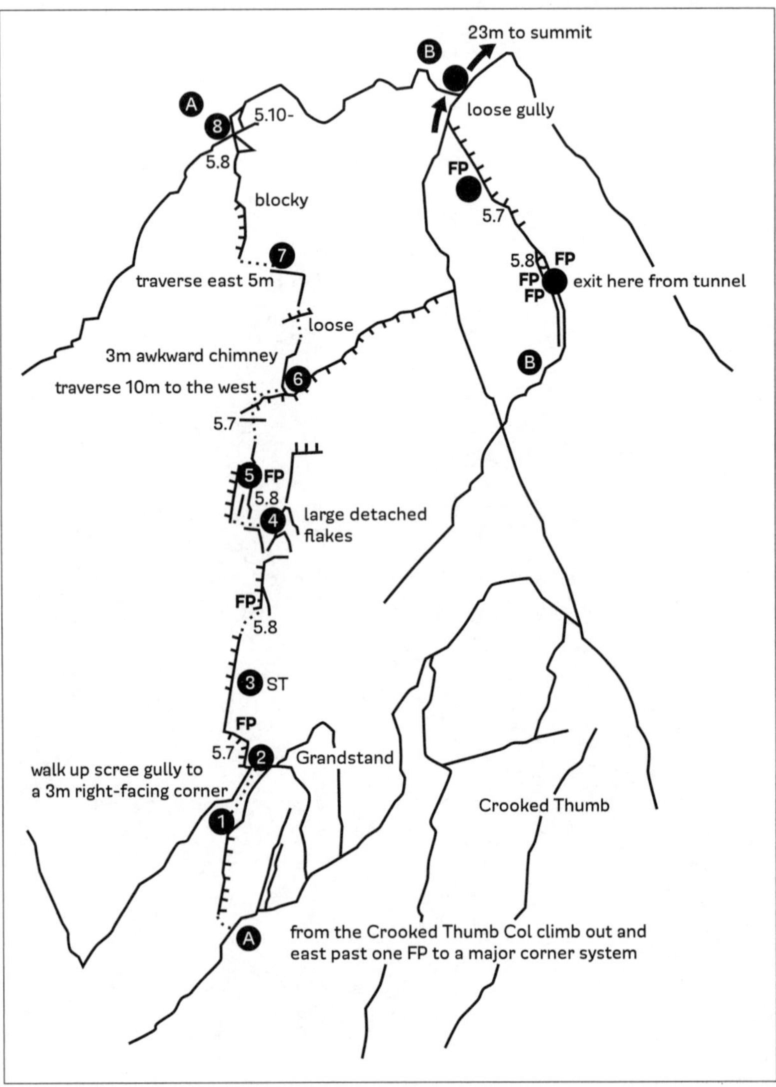

FIGURE 7-6. Teewinot Mountain. (A) Direct North Ridge *(Route 11)*, III, 5.8; (B) North Face *(Route 12)*, variation: Emerson's Chimney, III, 5.8

FIGURE 7-7. Teewinot Mountain, north aspect. (A) Direct North Ridge *(Route 11)*, III, 5.8; (B) North Face *(Route 12)*, II, 5.6; (C) Upper North Ridge *(Route 10)*, II, 5.6; (D) North Face, variation: Gardner-Headly, III, 5.9; (E) North Face, variation: Reese Arête, III, 5.7; (F) North Face, variation: Emerson's Chimney, III, 5.8; (G) Northwest Face *(Route 13)*, IV, 5.8, A3

section and out to the right (west) above that section. Follow *Route 10* to reach the top of the first step, the Grandstand. This direct route begins at the top of the Grandstand in a short (3m) right-facing corner slightly west of the crest; it then goes up to the left, about 6m east of the crest, to the edge of the first large overhang and a stance. At this point angle right and up a dihedral between two overhangs. Traverse west past a fixed piton around a small corner and then up two parallel cracks (5.8) to a piton belay on a slab. Climb out and west to a jam crack on the outside of the slab. This crack leads to a small overhang at the top of the second step. The route then traverses 8m west and up to an awkward chimney. Climb the chimney for 3m and then continue up through an overhang past easy ledges to a point where a traverse to the east is possible. Climb a large right-facing corner above this traverse, which leads to a few 5.8 exit moves and the summit ridge. One is now about 90m–120m east of the actual summit. Either scramble easily to the top or, if more fun is desired, climb a short 5.10- crack just to the right of the ridge crest. Six pitches of excellent rock are found on this route above the Grandstand; the trick is to stay as close as possible to the crest. **Time:** 10½ hours from Lupine Meadows. See *Dartmouth Mountaineering Club Journal*, 1958: pp. 7, 50, illus.

ROUTE 12. NORTH FACE. II, 5.6. First ascent August 17, 1944, by John and Ruth Mendenhall. (See *Figure 7-7*.) This interesting route, which starts from the Crooked Thumb Col, traverses the west facet of the north face, reaching the northwest ridge not far below the summit. This col is most easily attained from the east (see *Route 10*); it can also be reached from Cascade Canyon to the west (see *Cascade Canyon* in Section 8), as was done by the first-ascent party, but the northwest couloirs leading to the col are long, contain much loose rock, and are not recommended. From the col one can reach the top of a shoulder, the Grandstand, which abuts the north face, in two ropelengths of 5.6 climbing up its east side. From here three ledges can be seen leading up and to the right (west). Climb along this ledge system across the west facet all the way to its right (west) edge; there is some choice in this section, but with careful routefinding it should involve easy 5th-class climbing. Climb directly up the northwest ridge to the summit, which is then attained from the west.

***Variation:* EMERSON'S CHIMNEY.** III, 5.8. First ascent August 24, 1948, by Richard Emerson and Pete Owen. (See *Figures 7-6* and *7-7*.) This variation is perhaps done more often than any of the other north face routes. Emerson's Chimney is the second (westernmost) of the two left-slanting chimney/crack systems on the west facet of the north face. Proceed to the top of the Grandstand, which is reached as in *Route 10*, and climb to the highest of the three ledges that lead to the right (west) across the west facet of the north face. Make a diagonal traverse out on this ledge past the first (eastern) of the left-slanting chimney systems. A total of three to four ropelengths of easy 5th-class climbing lead to the base of Emerson's Chimney. Start up the chimney. About halfway up one can see the remarkable tunnel that leads all the way through Teewinot and opens out on the south face. Continue up the chimney to a small ledge on its left (east) wall beneath the extremely narrow upper portion. On the face outside the chimney, up and to the left (east), is a shelf that leads diagonally up for 37m to the summit ridge. The problem is to reach this shelf. Make a strenuous and exposed move (5.8) onto the outside face, using some small chockstones as handholds to get up and out of the chimney onto the shelf. Once on the shelf, climb enjoyable but tricky slabs for 37m to a short, loose rock gully that leads to the summit knife-edge, only 23m east of the summit. The upper end of this shelf is the hardest. This entire climb from the Crooked Thumb Col is in shadow and is likely to be cold. **Time:** 10½ hours from Lupine Meadows. See *American Alpine Journal* 9, no. 2 (1955): pp. 147–49; *Stanford Alpine Club Journal*, 1955: pp. 48–50.

Variation: **TEEWINOT TUNNEL.** II, 5.6. First ascent August 30, 1948, by Charles Crush and Graham McNear. It is possible to walk and crawl all the way through the tunnel from Emerson's Chimney on the north face and finish the climb by the easier south face. It is also possible to reverse this procedure (if one can find the tunnel) and crawl from the sunny south side out to the belay below the crux of the chimney, then finish by that variation. This tunnel feature seems to be unique in the Teton Range.

Variation: **REESE ARÊTE.** III, 5.7. First ascent July 28, 1965, by Rick Reese, Mike Ermarth, and Ralph Tingey. This variation is on a small arête on the north face of Teewinot about halfway between Emerson's Chimney and the north ridge crest. Some loose rock will be encountered. Approach as for the Emerson's Chimney variation to a point about 37m before (northeast of) the chimney. A chimney system that starts as a small couloir leads from here back toward the left (east), culminating in a very high-angle chimney. After 15m up this couloir, climb left onto the left (north) wall of the couloir. The first lead on this wall ascends an awkward jam crack (5.7) that slants up and left across the smooth face to a large chimney filled with loose blocks. The next lead goes 18m up this chimney before cutting right around a corner to large, steep blocks. The final lead goes directly up over a small overhang onto the summit ridge, about 24m east of the summit itself.

Variation: **GARDNER-HEADLY.** III, 5.9. First ascent July 9, 2021, by Michael Gardner and Dean Headly. (See *Figure* 7-7.) The first-ascent party approached via the Apex trail and then a traverse north to the Crooked Thumb Col. From the col, traverse around the north side of the Grandstand and ascend it by climbing the first corner system (5.8) to the lowest of the three ledges that traverse upward from left to right across the north face. Continue up for one ropelength to gain the highest ledge, then proceed up this ledge for another pitch and belay just before the arête that is the right-hand boundary of the main north face (see the Reese Arête variation, above). Climb straight up to the ridge crest for two pitches (5.9), following the path of least resistance on rock that varies at times from very good to somewhat questionable. Continue a short distance to the summit.

ROUTE 13. NORTHWEST FACE. IV, 5.8, A3. First ascent August 22–23, 1961, by David Dornan, Barry Corbet, and Richard Emerson. (See *Figure 7-7*.) This long and difficult route was named the Northwest Face by the first ascent party. This is somewhat misleading since the climb is actually located on the same facet of the peak as *Route 12* and its variations, between the north and northwest ridges. As shown in the figure it surmounts the bulge of the lower portion of the north face. One crack system, initially two parallel cracks, cuts through the bulge. This crack, which is partly wet and icy even at the end of a dry season, is easily distinguished from a distance. It slants up from right to left near the center of the north face and reaches the summit ridge about 90m to the left (east) of the summit. This particular facet of Teewinot is composed of many bands of light and dark rock that dip slightly to the west and cross this main crack system. Some of the belays on this route are hanging belays.

Hike up the Cascade Canyon trail, cross the creek, and bushwhack into the cirque between Teewinot and Mount Owen (see *Cascade Canyon* in Section 8 and *Mount Owen, Route 8*). The first task is to reach the base of the crack system described above. An obvious couloir leads to the Crooked Thumb Col, the col between the Crooked Thumb and the upper north ridge of Teewinot. The ascent of this long, deep couloir involves nothing more than 3.0 or 4.0 climbing, with the exception of a 24m 5.6 pitch (poorly protected) that leads past a chockstone on the left side about one-quarter of the way up the couloir. Leave the couloir to the right (south) before reaching the col and wind back and forth on a series of easy ledges that lead to the plainly visible base of the cracks. There are two parallel cracks at the start that join higher up. The right crack was the object of aid attempts in 1949 or 1950 by Richard Emerson and William Byrd, who were defeated by their lack of knifeblades and bongs, neither of which were available at the time. This route utilizes the left crack.

Pitch 1: Begin by climbing a short, easy 5th-class chimney and belay at the top. **Pitch 2:** This crux pitch begins with aid over a roof, then continues with aid up a crack for 9m (or as high as possible) to enable a difficult pendulum around the corner to the left; a knifeblade piton was used here just before the corner. From the corner, traverse 3m left (5.8) to another aid crack and ascend it for 9m to a sling belay at a questionable bolt. (**Note**: Fifteen-plus aid pitons were used on this pitch.) **Pitch 3:** Continue up the aid crack, using knifeblades, for 18m to a good belay stance. **Pitch 4:** Climb up a "rather smooth face" (5.8) to the left of a chimney to a large ledge; protection is described as being "poor." **Pitch 5:** Head up from the belay ledge to a bolt (5.6) and then transition back to aid climbing (10 pitons), eventually reaching a belay at a "shaky flake." **Pitch 6:** Continue up the same crack system—using a mix of free climbing (5.6) and aid—for 30m to the next belay. **Pitches 7–8:** One or two leads of easy 5th-class climbing will now bring one onto the easy ledge that diagonals up and right to the beginning of Emerson's Chimney (see *Route 12*); climb this chimney to the summit.

From a high bivouac this route can perhaps be climbed in one day. The base of the cracks could also be approached by ascending to the Crooked Thumb Col from the east and then descending the upper portion of the northwest couloir (see *Route 15*) to reach the ledges that lead to the cracks. It is worth noting that while this route tackles the most difficult portion of the northwest face—the bulge—the section below the base of the two parallel cracks (which was the object of an attempt on August 2, 1960, by Gary Hemming, Rick Medrick, and Ken Weeks) and the final section of the crack system, above the diagonal ledges leading to Emerson's Chimney, have not yet been climbed. The lower of these two sections is very steep and contains rotten rock, whereas the upper should not prove very difficult.

ROUTE 14. NORTHWEST RIDGE. III, 5.4. First ascent September 7, 1954, by John and Jean Fonda, Don Decker, and Martin Benham. (See *Figure 7-2*.) Follow the trail up Cascade Canyon and cross Cascade Creek where streams descending from the northeast snowfields of Mount Owen empty into the creek (see *Cascade Canyon* in Section 8 and *Mount Owen, Route 8*). Logs spanning the stream should be found in this area. Bushwhacking can be minimized by linking game and climbers' trails up the right (west) side of the drainage into the large basin that is enclosed by Mount Owen and Teewinot. Two parallel ridges descend into this basin from the main ridge connecting Teewinot and Mount Owen. Walk up the talus to the base of the western ridge, scramble up this ridge for about 150m, and then cross the northwest couloir (see *Route 15*) to the eastern ridge, which is the northwest ridge of Teewinot. In this lower part the climbing is easy but much of the rock is loose. Continue scrambling on poor rock until this ridge steepens and the nature of the rock abruptly changes for the better. At this point, where this ridge intersects the north and west faces, cut right (south) across the base of the west face on a series of ledges. The uppermost of these ledges terminates at the base of a chimney. Climb 60m up this chimney to a broad ledge; turn left (north) and climb directly up a rib for 90m to the small overhang near its top. The first-ascent party used a shoulder stand to surmount this overhang. At the top of this rib veer left again and climb over the top of the large chimney that separates the rib from the northwest ridge. After regaining the ridge, follow it directly to the summit monolith. **Time:** 11½ hours from Jenny Lake. See *American Alpine Journal* 9, no. 2 (1955): pp. 147–49.

***Variation:* DIRECT BUTTRESS.** III, 5.7. First ascent July 29, 1967, by Leigh Ortenburger and John Whitesel. (See *Figure 7-2*.) The initial ascent of the northwest ridge made a substantial horizontal traverse right (south) at the point where the steep section of the ridge with solid yellow rock was encountered. This variation continues directly up this steep section near the crest of the ridge, past a small tower, followed by a difficult (5.7) left-facing chimney. Three pitches of near-vertical, beautiful knobby rock (5.1) lead to the top of a second tower, which is separated from the remainder of the ridge by an impassable notch. At this point a descent of about 46m to the right, which includes a 9m rappel, permits access to a rib on the right (south) side of the main chimney, which leads back up to the aforementioned notch. This rib is then climbed to reach the summit from the northwest.

***Variation:* CHOCKSTONE CHIMNEY.** III, 5.8. First ascent July 26, 1975, Tom Burns and Bill Katra. During the horizontal traverse right (south) along the base of the west face, a deep, 3m-wide, vertical chimney containing a large chockstone will be found about 9m north of the shallower chimney of the original route. This variation follows this chimney, which is easily distinguished as the deepest break in the middle of the smoothest and most nearly vertical section of the west face. The top of the chimney breaks into two roughly parallel cracks that continue upward. The first 5.8 lead (40m) climbs past the chockstone on the left, going over a small overhang and up the left-hand crack of the chimney to a good belay. Then scramble for 24m to a good ledge about 12m below a huge, overhanging chimney. Go up this chimney and directly over the overhang. A step left provides access to face and crack climbing to a good belay stance. The fourth pitch continues up a 9m vertical lieback/jam crack combination (5.8) followed by easier climbing to the northwest ridge crest and a solid belay. From this point easier climbing leads to the summit.

ROUTE 15. NORTHWEST COULOIR. II, 5.1. First descent July 4, 1931, by Fritiof Fryxell, Rudolph Edmund, Theodore Anderson, and Harold Hendrickson. (See *Figure 7-2*.) This route starts from the Teewinot–Owen cirque and ascends the major wide couloir leading to the high plateau west of Teewinot's summit; this couloir is just to the right (west) of the northwest ridge of Teewinot. (For the approach to the Teewinot–Owen cirque, see *Route 14* and *Cascade Canyon* in Section 8.) Moderately steep scrambling is required to pass the lower portion of the couloir. During most of the season the upper portion will be steep snow. Edge left (east) while approaching the plateau; leave the couloir about 120m below the plateau and enter a steep chimney, which is the beginning of the V-shaped couloir that descends west from the large main notch just south of the summit of Teewinot. Some difficulty should be expected initially in this chimney, but after two large chockstones it opens out into an easier couloir. Loose rock will be encountered as the main notch is approached. When about 60m short of the main notch, cut left (north) up the steep, but not difficult, rock leading to the ridge crest about 1m east of the summit monolith. See *Appalachia* 18, no. 4 (December 1931): pp. 388–408, illus.

PEAK 11,840+

(0.3 mi WSW of Teewinot Mountain)
Map: Grand Teton

This peak is the high point on the west end of the broad plateau due west of the summit of Teewinot Mountain and is the first obstacle to be negotiated on the traverse to Mount Owen (see Section 5). It provides an excellent viewpoint of the impressive north precipice of the Grand Teton.

ROUTE 1. EAST SLOPE. II, 3.0. First ascent August 18, 1940, by Edward McNeill and Thomson Edwards; this ascent was made in the course of the first traverse from Teewinot to Mount Owen. The high plateau to the east can be reached from the summit of Teewinot by descending the standard East Face route (*Teewinot Mountain, Route 3*) until the main notch in the ridge south of the summit can be reached from the east. From the notch one can easily descend 150m to the plateau. From the plateau it is but a scramble to the summit of this peak. The plateau, however, can also be reached directly from Glacier Gulch as in *Teewinot Mountain, Route 1*.

EAST PRONG (12,000+)

Map: Grand Teton

The East Prong is the first major tower east of Mount Owen on the ridge connecting that peak with Teewinot Mountain. It is separated from the east ridge of Mount Owen by the East Prong Col. Although it provides an excellent viewpoint from which to take in all the peaks and faces surrounding Glacier Gulch and the Teton Glacier, the East Prong is usually climbed only in conjunction with an ascent of Mount Owen or in the course of the ridge traverse between Mount Owen and Teewinot (see Section 5). It

was the location of Fritiof Fryxell's widely published photograph showing a young Paul Petzoldt in the foreground with the north face of the Grand Teton looming in the background.

Chronology

SOUTH COULOIR AND EAST RIDGE: August 1, 1927, Paul Petzoldt, Fritiof Fryxell, Robert Spahr
WEST RIDGE: August 27, 1934, George Goldthwaite (descent); July 28, 1941, Orrin Bonney, Margaret Hawkes (ascent)
SOUTH FACE: August 2, 1966, Peter Cleveland, Don Storjohann

ROUTE 1. WEST RIDGE. II, 5.4. First descent August 27, 1934, by George Goldthwaite; first ascent July 28, 1941, by Orrin Bonney and Margaret Hawkes. Approach the East Prong Col as in *Mount Owen, Route 7*. Throughout most of the summer some ice climbing will be required to reach the summit of the East Prong from the col. The steepest part can be avoided if one climbs onto the rocks of the west ridge about 30m below the summit. When using this route for descent, start by descending to the north for a short distance before turning west toward the col. See *Appalachia* 20, no. 7 (November 1935): p. 421.

ROUTE 2. SOUTH FACE. II, 5.8. First ascent August 2, 1966, by Peter Cleveland and Don Storjohann. This is a short, straightforward climb with considerable exposure. Climb the initial face without great difficulty to the base of a large, diamond-shaped face. The diagonal crack in this face is the one difficult pitch on the route. The top of the East Prong is then easily reached.

ROUTE 3. SOUTH COULOIR AND EAST RIDGE. II, 4.0. First ascent August 1, 1927, by Paul Petzoldt, Fritiof Fryxell, and Robert Spahr. From the northeastern edge of the Teton Glacier climb one of the couloirs that lead up to the east ridge of the East Prong. These couloirs are straightforward, and once one is on the ridge, no further difficulty will be experienced. See *Appalachia* 18, no. 3 (June 1931): pp. 209–32, illus.

MOUNT OWEN (12,928)

Map: Grand Teton

Mount Owen is one of the greatest of the Teton peaks in height, beauty, and climbing interest. Named for William O. Owen, pioneer Wyoming surveyor and organizer of the 1898 ascent of the Grand Teton, it was one of the last of the high peaks to be ascended, having resisted several early attempts. The first attempt was made on August 1, 1927, by Fritiof Fryxell, Paul Petzoldt, and Robert Spahr, but they chose the wrong couloir from Glacier Gulch and soon found themselves on the summit of the East Prong. Eight days later Phil Smith and Ben Lengel were stopped at about 11,500 feet. In the same week Albert R. Ellingwood and Robert Ormes also attempted the peak. In 1928 Owen urged Fryxell and Smith, this time with William Gilman, to try once again to reach the summit. On July 28 this trio attained the base of the summit knob, only 30m below the summit, but they were unable to scale its smooth face; Gilman reached a new high point about 15m up the face of the knob. The next year, on July 26, J. D. Hunter and Notsie Garnick made an attempt on the peak but apparently reached only the first bench on the south face. Not until 1930 did the very strong first-ascent party of Fryxell, Smith, Robert Underhill, and Kenneth Henderson solve the problem of the summit knob.

Even today there is no easy way to the summit, for every route requires mountaineering skill. Thus, Mount Owen remains one of the most appealing goals in the range. The spectacular view of the north face of the Grand Teton from the summit is most impressive.

Many of the routes on Mount Owen can be climbed in one day from the valley, but this requires a strong, fast party and an early start. If this is attempted, expect a *very* long day. A high camp, usually near Surprise Lake, is desirable for any of the routes approached from the east or southeast across the Teton Glacier. Similarly, a camp in Valhalla Canyon, either high or low, is recommended for the west and northwest routes; however, retrieval of this camp can be a problem, depending on one's itinerary. For the northeast routes, it is best to camp in the Teewinot–Owen cirque. Note that the routes approached from the west, northwest, north, or northeast require a potentially challenging crossing of the swift and cold Cascade Creek. With luck and some advance searching, a log can often be located, permitting a dry crossing. But sometimes one must wade across the creek, which can be difficult and dangerous in early season when the water is high. If one wishes to make a north side climb in one day, the crossing point should be reconnoitered in advance to avoid losing time on the climbing day.

These routes are arranged in counterclockwise fashion, beginning with the Southwest Ridge route at Gunsight Notch.

Chronology

EAST RIDGE: July 16, 1930, Robert Underhill, Kenneth Henderson, Fritiof Fryxell, Phil Smith
var—August 28, 1935, Paul Petzoldt, H. K. Hartline, A. Curtis Smith
var—September 7, 1937, Joseph and Paul Stettner
var—September 2, 1946, Willi Unsoeld, Herbert Rickert
KOVEN: July 20, 1931, Paul Petzoldt, Glenn Exum, Theodore and Gustav Koven
NORTHEAST SNOWFIELDS: August 7, 1931, Paul Petzoldt
var—**EAST RIDGE FINISH:** July 25, 1976, Rich Page, Corky Marshall, Phil Arnold
var—September 1977, George Montopoli
var—September 24, 1983, Norm Larson, Steve Quinlan
FRYXELL: August 18, 1931, Fritiof Fryxell, Frank Smith
WEST LEDGES: July 28, 1932, Paul Petzoldt, Edward Woolf
SOUTHWEST RIDGE: September 3, 1937, Jack Durrance, George Sheldon, Percy Rideout
NORTHWEST RIDGE: August 5, 1941, Jack Durrance, Henry Coulter, Merrill McLane
NORTH FACE: August 21, 1945, Hans Kraus, Harrison Snyder
var—July 16, 1989, Randy Harrington, Leo Larson
BUNTON: August 16, 1949, C. A. Bunton, George Lucas
NORTH RIDGE: July 31, 1951, Richard Emerson, William Clayton
var—**CRESCENT ARÊTE DIRECT:** June 1994, Greg Collins, Stephen Koch
SOUTH CHIMNEY: August 6, 1957, Yvon Chouinard, John Lowry, Tink Thompson
SERENDIPITY ARÊTE: August 8, 1959, William Buckingham, Rick Medrick, Sterling Neale, Frank Magary; FFA July 14, 1965, Henry Mitchell, George Griffin
var—**JENNI'S WAY:** August 4, 1996, Alex Lowe
CRESCENT ARÊTE: September 9, 1959, Fred Beckey, Yvon Chouinard
var—July 24, 1960, Ray Jacquot, Peter Lev
SOUTH FACE: August 18, 1962, Ants Leemets, John Hudson
NORTHWEST FACE: August 4, 1965, Leigh Ortenburger, Herb Swedlund
var—August 20–21, 1982, Rick Reese, David Susong
RUN-DON'T-WALK COULOIR: July 6, 1972, Stephen Arsenault, John Bouchard
INTREPIDITY ARÊTE: August 18, 1990, Tom Turiano, Matthew Goewert
var—**MAS INTREPIDO:** August 1994, Matthew Goewert, Mark Limage
NORTH FACE DIRECT: August 15, 2001, Nate Brown, Tobey Carmen, Eric Draper
NORTH RIDGE RIGHT (ESCAPE): July 18–19, 2020, Mike Abbey, Matt Meinzer
RENNY TAKE THE WHEEL: July 25, 2020, Michael Gardner, Michael Hutchins
var—August 9, 1985, Paul Gagner, Renny Jackson

ROUTE 1. SOUTHWEST RIDGE. III, 5.6. First ascent September 3, 1937, by Jack Durrance, George Sheldon, and Percy Rideout; though the ridge was climbed, electricity stopped them within "a short stone's throw of the summit." (See *Figure 7-8.*) This is an excellent route containing some of the most enjoyable rock in the Tetons. The base of the southwest ridge of Mount Owen is in the spectacular Gunsight Notch. The recommended approach to Gunsight Notch is from the west via a straightforward but moderately steep snow-and-ice climb (see *Valhalla Canyon* in Section 4). Rockfall, rotten rock, and wet and icy rock are good arguments against the direct approach up the East Gunsight Couloir to the notch; this was first done on about August 22, 1936, by Fritz Wiessner, Paul Petzoldt, Brad Gilman, Beckett Howorth, William House, and Elizabeth Woolsey by means of a

Figure 7-8. Mount Owen, southeast aspect. (A) Koven *(Route 6)*, II, 5.5 steep snow; (B) Fryxell *(Route 4)*, II, 5.5; (C) Bunton *(Route 5)*, II, 5.6; (D) East Ridge *(Route 7)*, II, 5.6; (E) South Chimney *(Route 3)*, III, 5.6; (F) South Face *(Route 2)*, III, 5.6, A1; (G) Southwest Ridge *(Route 1)*, III, 5.6

three-person shoulder stand—Woolsey on Wiessner on House—to pass a large chockstone. The first-ascent party for this Southwest Ridge route, however, used another approach, a bit circuitous and difficult: From the upper Teton Glacier on the east, cross the bergschrund onto the Grandstand and climb to the second scree-covered shelf, which diagonals up and right toward Gunsight Notch. Follow this shelf out to its upper end, where the traverse can be continued for a pitch or two to a point where descent into the notch is possible. This approach, while feasible, makes for a long day, and some may wish to rappel in order to reach the notch.

From the notch the first pitch is 5.6, starting a meter or so to the right of the nose. In the next few leads the route reaches the top of the first tower from the left (west) side of the crest over excellent rock. The sequence of towers leading to the junction with the Fryxell route *(Route 4)* can be climbed in various ways, but the most interesting is to keep as close as possible to the crest. At the north end of the first large horizontal step after passing these towers, *Route 4* is joined and followed to the summit. **Time:** 8½ hours from Valhalla Canyon. See *Dartmouth Mountaineering Club Journal,* 1938: pp. 37–41.

ROUTE 2. SOUTH FACE. III, 5.6, A1. First ascent August 18, 1962, by Ants Leemets and John Hudson. (See *Figure 7-8.*) On the easily approached south or southeast face of Mount Owen there is an expanse of rock between the southwest ridge (see *Route 1*) and the south chimney (see *Route 3*) that can be climbed more or less directly to the upper snowfield. Make the usual approach to the Teton Glacier (see *Glacier Gulch*) and climb above the crevassed section toward its extreme western extension in the East Gunsight Couloir. This route begins on broken rock in watercourses just to the right of a large buttress at the base of the rock wall to the right (north) of the East Gunsight Couloir; the exact start will vary according to the snow level on the glacier. The following leads to the first snowfield bench are all about 40m in length.

The first lead bears slightly left on wet rock to a flake and then right and up to a belay under an obvious 4.5m corner. Climb this corner and scramble up slabs, zigging left and zagging right, to a small belay ledge underneath a second corner of the same size. After ascending this, exit right and scramble left to a watercourse that is followed by a wet corner. The fourth pitch starts with an 8m corner to the right of a large slab and leads, after zigzag scrambling, to a belay stance at the base of a slab capped by a small overhang. The next lead goes up to and diagonally left under the overhang, then heads up and right, past a small face to the left of a corner to a belay on large ledges. Walk right 23m and work up over some overhanging flakes to a scramble up to a large ledge. Two more scrambling pitches up and to the right under a vertical face lead to the lower snowfield on the Fryxell route bench (see *Route 4*). Scramble about 60m back to the left (west) on the bench, then gain a smaller ledge above the bench. Climb the left of two corners above for 9m before scrambling right and up a large, broken dihedral. An easy ledge now leads left and up for 18m to a large, sloping ledge. After a slight downward traverse on this ledge, use some aid to climb an overhanging wall to the base of a chimney, which is climbed to a stance below an overhang. Move right to an easy chimney leading to approximately 100m of 4.0 climbing in a shallow couloir that ends in the vicinity of the southwest ridge, at the upper snowfield of Mount Owen. Join the Koven route *(Route 6)* at this point. **Gear:** For protection take a standard rack with some wide (3" to 4") devices. See *American Alpine Journal* 13, no. 2 (1963): pp. 487–89.

ROUTE 3. SOUTH CHIMNEY. III, 5.6. First ascent August 6, 1957, by Yvon Chouinard, John Lowry, and Tink Thompson. (See *Figure 7-8.*) This route goes directly from the Teton Glacier to the upper snowfield of Mount Owen without touching the south ridge or the regular East Ridge route *(Route 7)*. Reach the lower portion of the Teton Glacier (see *Glacier Gulch*) and continue up the glacier beyond the crevassed section (crampons useful) until underneath the center of the south face, at the base of the prominent, large chimney containing a large chockstone about 46m above. Depending on the year, some difficulty should be expected in crossing the *randkluft* guarding the entrance to the chimney. Two 5.6 pitches lead to a belay point from which an exposed lead is made out of the chimney to the right and then back into it again above the chockstone. A short lead to the right brings one to easy ledges just below the Fryxell route bench (see *Route 4*), which is then crossed. After a slight traverse to the right, the route ascends the continuation of the chimney, which is now a deep chute that descends from the upper snowfield and forms a distinctive feature of the mountain. This chute can be climbed directly on steep snow or on the easy rock of the left wall. From the upper snowfield, follow either the Koven route *(Route 6)* or the East Ridge route to the summit. See *American Alpine Journal* 12, no. 1 (1960): pp. 125–27.

ROUTE 4. FRYXELL. II, 5.5. First ascent August 18, 1931, by Fritiof Fryxell and Frank Smith. (See *Figure 7-8.*) This clever early route takes the lower broad bench and shelf on the south face of Mount Owen from the standard Koven Couloir on the east over to the southwest ridge on the west; it combines parts of *Route 1* and *Route 6* but is easier than either. From the Teton Glacier, climb the standard Koven Couloir (see *Route 6*) to the first broad bench. Instead of continuing up the couloir, turn left (west) and follow the bench itself—a snow traverse in early season and midseason. This bench soon ends at a slabby step that is passed via a chimney near the right edge to gain the wide shelf that now extends all the way to the south ridge. Follow the shelf west on snow or easy rock until the angle increases and downsloping slabs dominate; this is just past (west of) the point where the large chute of *Route 3* crosses the shelf. Climb this step on slabs about 46m out from the right corner. Continue out along this shelf on easy slabs until the final steep section is encountered short of the southwest ridge. Surmount this step via a short face pitch about 15m left (south) of the chimney in the right corner. A short scramble brings one to the crest, which is attained at a notch at the extreme right (north) end of the relatively level lower section of the southwest ridge. From this notch a single lead on the left (west) side of the tower above brings one to easier, enjoyable climbing over, around, and through the various remaining towers on the ridge.

Ultimately this ridge climb meets the Koven route, which crosses the southwest ridge very near its upper end above the upper snowfield at the summit knob. Reach the summit either by the Koven Chimney or by the difficult chimney in the southwest corner of the summit knob (first climbed on August 9, 1953, by William Buckingham and Rob Day). This is a pleasant mountaineering route, without great difficulty, in one of the most scenic areas in the range. The north face of the Grand Teton dominates the view across the glacier, which lies 300m below. **Time:** 10¼ hours from Amphitheater Lake. See *Appalachia* 19, no. 1 (June 1932): pp. 86–96; *Trail and Timberline*, no. 175 (May 1933): pp. 62–66, illus.

ROUTE 5. BUNTON. II, 5.6. First ascent August 16, 1949, by C. A. Bunton and George Lucas. (See *Figure 7-8*.) This route, not well understood, reaches the upper snowfield without using the regular Koven Couloir to the East Prong Col. Take the Fryxell route *(Route 4)* to the bench above the glacier and out left to the vicinity of the first slabby step at the west end of the bench. At this point, about 90m west of the standard Koven Couloir and past a triangular wall, a smaller couloir, commonly snow-filled, leads up and right (northeast) back toward the East Prong Col. Take this couloir a short distance (apparently to the point where it forks) and then move left (west) to a "ledged rock wall" that, via a series of cracks on the right, leads toward the upper snowfield of the Koven route *(Route 6)*. This part of the route contains several pitches of 5.6 climbing on an open and comparatively exposed face. Easy slabs lead onto the snowfield, where either *Route 6* or *Route 7* can be joined and followed to the summit. In early season and midseason some snow and ice must be expected on this route, but when the regular Koven Couloir is dangerous because of poor snow conditions, this route may provide an accessible alternative.

ROUTE 6. ▲ KOVEN. II, 5.5, steep snow. First ascent July 20, 1931, by Paul Petzoldt, Glenn Exum, and Theodore and Gustav Koven. (See *Figures 7-8, 7-9*, and *7-10*.) As one of the least difficult climbs accessed from the east, the Koven route has become the most popular early-season mountaineering objective on the peak. Before undertaking this climb, however, one should know how to use an ice axe for self-arrest. Although Mount Owen can be easier to climb in late season, the lower portion of the Koven Couloir (shown as melted out in *Figure 7-9*) can become an unpleasant mix of mud and loose rock; an early-season ascent with firm snow conditions is therefore recommended.

FIGURE 7-9. Mount Owen, southeast aspect, Koven *(Route 6)*, II, 5.5, steep snow

Follow the East Ridge route *(Route 7)* to the upper snowfield. Instead of cutting back onto the ridge crest when traversing the upper snowfield on the south side of the east ridge, continue west until due south of the summit. See *Figure 7-10*, which details the upper Koven route. In early season this upward traverse will be entirely on snow—somewhat hazardous because the snowfield ends below with cliffs. In midseason or late season it is much easier to skirt the snow using bare rock ledges along its bottom edge. When directly south of the summit knob near the southwest ridge, one will see large, easy chimneys leading up to the left (west) to a small notch in the uppermost southwest ridge just below the summit knob. Climb to this notch and then traverse north around the west side of the summit knob on an easy ledge until the big west chimney is seen. It is an easy climb up this chimney (5.5) to the top. Do not turn up one of the smaller west chimneys. The proper one is a few meters across, very deep, and due west of the summit.

While this Koven route is the usual descent route on the mountain, it is not fast: care must be taken—both on the traverse of the upper snowfield and in the Koven Couloir leading down to the glacier. Many parties will wish to remain roped during the majority of the climb. An early start will prevent potential time problems on this long route. **Time:** 6 to 7½ hours from Amphitheater Lake; 7¾ to 9 hours

FIGURE 7-10. Mount Owen, east aspect, upper Koven detail *(Route 6)*

from Jenny Lake. See *Appalachia* 19, no. 1 (June 1932): pp. 86–96; *Chicago Mountaineering Club Newsletter* 2, no. 6 (July–December 1948): p. 9; *Trail and Timberline*, no. 175 (May 1933): pp. 62–66, illus.; no. 491 (November 1959): pp. 168, 171.

ROUTE 7. EAST RIDGE. II, 5.6. First ascent July 16, 1930, by Robert Underhill, Kenneth Henderson, Fritiof Fryxell, and Phil Smith. (See *Figure 7-8*.) The successful first ascent of Mount Owen by this route marked a major threshold in Teton climbing history. Not only did the first-ascent party overcome significant technical difficulty, but this was also the last of the high peaks to be climbed. And this East Ridge route remains a fine mountaineering objective, combining excellent rock pitches with significant snow climbing. For the approach see *Glacier Gulch*. From the middle of the lower portion of the Teton Glacier, the Koven Couloir leading to the East Prong Col between the East Prong and Mount Owen is easily seen. About one-third of the way to the col, the two sections of this couloir are broken by a broad talus-and-scree bench that extends across the southeast flank of the mountain below the East Prong. This bench will be at least partially covered with snow in early season and midseason (see *Figure 7-9*). The first section of this couloir, containing rotten rock, is usually capped by a small waterfall from the melting snow on the bench. Climb to the waterfall and traverse left to easier ground on the left wall that takes one to the bench. Walk or kick steps up the bench, depending on the time of year. Ascend the upper section of the couloir for about 60m before turning left onto the rock forming its left (west) edge. Under good conditions late in the season, this rock is a scramble on small ledges all the way to the col. In early season, however, almost all this rock will be covered with snow, and many steps will have to be kicked in the steep upper part of the couloir to reach the col. Crampons can be useful here.

From the East Prong Col turn abruptly left (west) up the ridge. The 37m band of rock that must be climbed to reach the upper snowfield can be passed in several places. These four options are listed from left to right, with the third being the preferred method: (1) From the crest of the ridge traverse left (south) around a corner just at the base of this rock band. Only a meter or so around this corner, climb steep slabs to the snowfield in two ropelengths. This is one of the more difficult possibilities because the rock is commonly wet from the melting snow above. (2) The face directly above the crest of the ridge can be climbed, but this is even more difficult. (3) The standard scheme is to traverse 15m down to the right (north) of the ridge crest along the base of this rock band and enter a large chimney. Climb the chimney and exit up and right before reaching the chockstone at the top. In early season this chimney will be either wet or a snow climb. (4) Traverse even farther right to a series of ledges leading up to the base of the snowfield.

Two possibilities of about equal difficulty present themselves once the upper snowfield is reached. The east ridge, now directly above, ends in a vertical drop, so the object is to traverse around either the south or north side of this nose before turning up to regain the ridge crest. *South side:* Traverse left (south), staying on the bare rock ledges at the lower edge of the snow if possible. If these rocks are covered with snow, cut diagonally up the snow until 60m–90m past the nose of the ridge. A series of shallow chimneys and ledges will be seen leading back onto the ridge. If these are climbed at their left (west) edge, one will come out 30m below the ridge crest, where two pitches lead westward to the base of the summit knob. If the chimneys and ledges are climbed at their right (east) edge, one will reach the actual crest of the ridge, which at this point is composed of smooth slabs. Climb these smooth slabs via cracks in the center for several ropelengths, angling slightly left (south) to the base of the summit knob. *North side:* Traverse right (north) around the nose, diagonaling up the snow about 60m past the nose until ledges lead back south to the ridge crest at the beginning of the aforementioned smooth slabs. In late season more rock will be exposed on this north side, increasing the difficulty somewhat.

Once the smooth and near-vertical east face of the summit knob is reached, there are three possible ways to proceed: (1) The standard route goes directly up the difficult face on small holds for about 8m. Once this somewhat runout section has been passed, climb upward 1m before traversing left (south) to the easy rock at the summit. Little protection is available for this lead. (2) Traverse left (south) along the base of the knob to the southeast corner, where a large flake is detached from the knob itself. Climb the corner across from the flake using the crack. When the crack runs out, make a delicate traverse to the left (south) for 2m to gain a broad ledge just below the summit. This pitch is slightly less difficult than the standard direct route, and it has the advantage that some protection can be placed. (3) The devious route of the first ascent requires a 9m rappel to the north and then a traverse along a shelf extending completely around the summit knob to the Koven Chimney. The great cleft of this chimney extends deep into the summit knob and is the only easy way to the summit.

The suggested route of descent is the Koven route *(Route 6)*; another option is to rappel down the east ridge, which is more complicated. Caution must be exercised when climbing back down the main couloir. **Time:** 6 to 7¾ hours from Amphitheater Lake. See *American Alpine Journal* 1, no. 3 (1931): pp. 320–26, illus.; *Appalachia* 18, no. 3 (June 1931): pp. 209–32, illus.; *Canadian Alpine Journal* 19 (1930): pp. 84–91, illus.; *Trail and Timberline*, no. 447 (March 1956): pp. 47–48.

Variation: III, 5.6, A1. First ascent August 28, 1935, by Paul Petzoldt, H. K. Hartline, and A. Curtis Smith. From the East Prong Col, the first-ascent party traversed across the "bottom of snowfields to north ridge"; exactly how this was done is uncertain. There are several possibilities, but unless one wants to engage in long, steep horizontal snow traverses, this variation is probably best done in late season when more rock will be exposed. From the col one can descend a meter or so and head northwest along the top edge of the steep snowfield past the initial wall to its right (north) edge, where a snow chute of moderate angle (a rock ledge in late season) leads back due west to gain the edge of the next snowfield. This snowfield, sometimes ice in late season, must be crossed one way or another to reach the cliffs guarding, at this level, access to the north ridge. These cliffs, which appear difficult, form the east wall of the Great Yellow Tower of the north ridge. Once above this cliff band, which appears to harbor excellent but steep cracks or chimneys in good rock, the upper north ridge is at hand and is climbed to the summit knob, passing a moderately difficult chimney along the way. The summit can be attained by traversing to the right to gain the standard Koven Chimney (see *Route 6*), or a difficult chimney on the northwest corner of the knob can be climbed.

An almost completely different alternative is to start the traverse toward the north ridge from *above* the first cliff band above the East Prong Col. One could then traverse northwest along the bottom edge of the uppermost of the northeast snowfields. This scheme would also involve crossing some snow, perhaps ice in late season, to attain the north ridge at some point above the first step above the notch separating the Great Yellow Tower from the upper north ridge.

Variation: III, 5.6, A1. First ascent September 7, 1937, by Joseph and Paul Stettner; a similar route was climbed on August 19, 1952, by Willi Unsoeld, Ellis Blade, Steve Jervis, and Tom Klemens. It is possible to attack the nose at the end of the upper east ridge above the upper snowfield more or less directly. Ascend the snowfield directly to the extreme eastern point of the ridge. Climb broken ledges on the north side of the ridge for 6m–15m (depending on the depth of the snow) to the big overhang that spans the entire width of the ridge. At the extreme north end of this overhang is a climbable corner reached by traversing about 4m to the right on a vertical face. At this corner aid was used to reach the ledge sloping up to the west just above the overhang. From this ledge climb a steep 9m wall to the block of rock at the top of the ridge, which is commonly used as a rappel point for the descent to the snowfield.

Variation: III, 5.6. First ascent September 2, 1946, by Willi Unsoeld and Herbert Rickert. The low point (11,440+) of the ridge between Mount Owen and Teewinot Mountain can be reached directly from Cascade Canyon (see *Cascade Canyon* in Section 8) via a long, obvious snow couloir. In late season the upper portions of this couloir will be rock; beware of falling rock here. To reach the east ridge of Mount Owen from this saddle, traverse west over the East Prong and descend to the East Prong Col, where *Route 6* or *Route 7* is joined.

Chris Figenshau on the east ridge snowfield, Mount Owen (Photo by Jimmy Chin)

ROUTE 8. NORTHEAST SNOWFIELDS. III, 5.6, steep snow. First ascent August 7, 1931, by Paul Petzoldt. (See *Figure 7-11.*) This very long and varied route provides one of the finest snow climbs in the range. The several early ascents of this route did not record their exact lines, so the history of the three significant variations of the main route is uncertain. It is difficult to pinpoint precisely when conditions on this route are the best; the right combination may exist during late spring, well after the final avalanche cycle, and when low overnight temperatures allow for a hard freeze of the snow on this vast face. Because of the steepness and constant angle, there is some danger from rockfall on this route. Crampons are useful for the hard snow that is likely to be encountered in the early morning hours.

FIGURE 7-11. Mount Owen, northeast aspect. (A) Northeast Snowfields *(Route 8)*, III, 5.6, steep snow; (B) Northeast Snowfields, variation: 1983, III, 5.8, WI3+/WI4; (C) Northeast Snowfields, variation: 1977, III, 5.9; (D) Crescent Arête *(Route 9)*, IV, 5.7; (E) Run-Don't-Walk Couloir *(Route 10)*, IV, 5.5, WI4+/WI5

Approach via the Cascade Canyon trail (see *Cascade Canyon* in Section 8) and continue past the point where the streams descending from the northeast snowfields of Mount Owen empty into Cascade Creek. Cross the creek in the vicinity of a very large boulder on its north side. Logs spanning the creek can sometimes be found in this area; scouting the situation the day before the proposed ascent is recommended. The bushwhacking up into the Teewinot–Owen cirque is not easy, but one can often link up game trails and utilize the trees on the right (west) side of the drainage, or trend into the boulder-filled gully just west of the trees. Whatever path is taken, scramble up the talus below the first snowfield.

Proceed up the snow, keeping in mind that the obvious couloirs leading up from the upper southwest corner of this snowfield serve as funnels for falling rocks. It is recommended that this portion be passed very early in the morning before the sun starts melting the snow above. Avoid the easier climbing in these dangerous couloirs by accepting the increased difficulty of staying to the right to pass the initial cliffs. Some moderately difficult friction pitches will be met in this section.

Proceed upward until one has a choice of two routes—shown in *Figure 7-11* —for getting past the next vertical section of rock to the second major snowfield: (1) The most obvious and standard route is up to the right (west) over wet rock (some snow in early season) onto the lower right (west) corner of the second snowfield. Then climb up and slightly left (east) on this steep snowfield to the next and final rock band. (2) The other possibility is to climb the steep rock wall to the left (east) and thereby gain the small snowfield that descends from the East Prong Col. Climb along the right edge of this snowfield until above the initial wall, reaching a large rock ledge (snow in early season) that leads back right (west) to near the upper left corner of the second snowfield. Cross the upper portion of this snowfield to reach the same rock band as in the first option.

Cross this final rock band. Its difficulty depends on the quantity of snow present; in early season this may be completely covered by snow, simplifying matters. The third, last, and steepest snowfield is now at hand and is climbed diagonally right (west) up to the summit rock mass. From the highest point of the snow an interesting chimney leads up to the north ridge, ending at the base of the summit knob. The summit is then attained either directly from the northwest via a difficult chimney or, after a slight traverse to the right, via the Koven Chimney (see *Route 6*).

If the second major snowfield is reached as in the first option described above, it is possible to climb this snowfield by staying right (west) and passing beneath a wall—the east face of the Great Yellow Tower. Then climb a steep crack or chimney near the left edge of this face to gain the extreme lower right corner of the third and final snowfield, which is then climbed to the summit rock mass.

It is also possible to bypass completely the first snowfield and initial rock band: Continue up Cascade Canyon until under the main north walls of Mount Owen at about 7,600 feet, cross Cascade Creek, and bushwhack up toward the base of the north ridge of Mount Owen. A continuous bench that diagonals up and left along the base of these cliffs is easily followed left (east) toward the bottom end of the Crescent Arête (see *Route 9*). Some scrambling is required to continue this traverse east past the bottom of the arête. Ledges then take one into the main couloir system of the northeast face between the first and second major snowfields. **Time:** 13¼ hours from Cascade Canyon. See *Appalachia* 19, no. 1 (June 1932): pp. 86–96; *Trail and Timberline,* no. 175 (May 1933): pp. 62–66, illus.

Variation: **EAST RIDGE FINISH.** III, 5.6. First ascent July 25, 1976, by Rich Page, Corky Marshall, and Phil Arnold. This variation follows the standard Northeast Snowfields route to the final snowfield. Instead of continuing up to the highest point (the upper right corner) of this snowfield, head for the lowest point of rock jutting down into the snowfield left of center. The initial rock lead (40m) goes up an obvious crack to its end, where a traverse right under an upside-down flake permits a move up to a small ledge. The next ropelength follows a line up and right, to and over a small bulge onto a grassy ledge for the belay. The third short lead (18m) goes up the rightmost groove above to a large, grassy ledge. Now scramble up and farther right to a large ledge with snow. The final lead goes up this section of snow and traverses left

Climbing ranger Noah Ronczkowski in the Run-Don't-Walk Couloir, Mount Owen. (Photo by Vic Zeilman)

into an ice gully that is climbed onto the east ridge, apparently above the section of slabs. Follow the East Ridge route *(Route 7)* to the summit.

Variation: III, 5.9. First ascent in September 1977, by George Montopoli. (See *Figure 7-11.*) This variation links the various upper snowfields via the rock bands. Follow the regular Northeast Snowfields route to the point where one is presented with two options for passing a vertical section of rock. Take the second option, climbing a 5.6 corner system that is nearly a ropelength in height. Traverse up and left across snow to a second small cliff band (easy 5th class) that permits access to the small snowfield directly below the East Prong Col. The third cliff band has a large overhang near its eastern end. This variation ascends a left-facing corner for two or three pitches (5.9) to the west of the overhang. The East Ridge route *(Route 7)* is then followed to the summit.

Variation: III, 5.8, WI3+/WI4. First ascent September 24, 1983, by Norm Larson and Steve Quinlan. (See *Figure 7-11.*) This difficult variation reaches the East Prong Col directly from the north. The first-ascent party surmounted two pitches of near-vertical ice before reaching the small snowfield below the col via the leftmost narrow couloir. It is possible that this section of ice forms only very late in the season.

ROUTE 9. CRESCENT ARÊTE. IV, 5.7. First ascent September 9, 1959, by Fred Beckey and Yvon Chouinard. (See *Figure 7-11.*) This prominent, well-defined subsidiary ridge lies between the northeast snowfields (see *Route 8*) and the true north ridge of Mount Owen. It is separated from the main north ridge to the west by a sharp, steep couloir (the Run-Don't-Walk Couloir; see *Route 10*). The upper end of this ridge curves west and joins the north ridge at the northeastern base of the Great Yellow Tower. The fitting name—Crescent Arête—is derived from the combined appearance of the ridge and its lower extension, which also curves back to the west. This route is approached via the Teewinot-Owen cirque and then the start of the Northeast Snowfields route. Look for a ramp leading up and to the west toward the crest of the arête. Climb several pitches of good rock on or near the occasionally difficult crest until the north ridge is reached below the Great Yellow Tower. Then follow *Route 11* to the summit. There are apparently several ways to climb this arête since the difficulty reported by different parties has varied from 5.6 to aid; many climbers have encountered 5.8 pitches. Instead of continuing from the top of the arête to the summit of Mount Owen, some parties opt to descend to the east, down the lower northeast snowfields back to Cascade Canyon. **Time:** 8 hours from Jenny Lake. See *American Alpine Journal* 12, no. 1 (1960): pp. 125–27.

Variation: IV, 5.7, A1. First ascent July 24, 1960, by Ray Jacquot and Peter Lev (also the second ascent of the Crescent Arête). This variation consists of a more difficult three-pitch start to the original route. Aid was used on the second pitch and the party continued to the summit via *Route 8*.

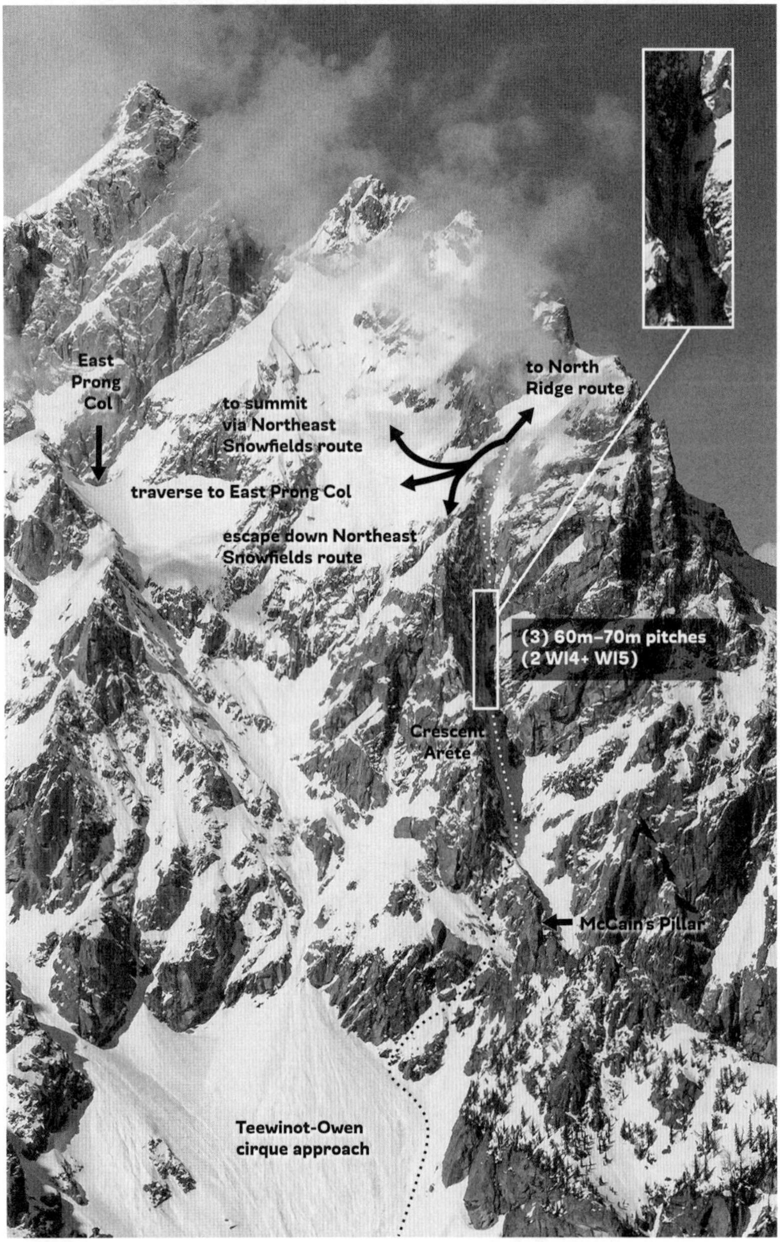

ROUTE 10. RUN-DON'T-WALK COULOIR. IV, 5.9, A3, WI5 (first ascent), or IV, 5.5, WI4+/WI5 (normal conditions with Koven finish). First ascent July 6, 1972, by Stephen Arsenault and John Bouchard. (See *Figures 7-11* and *7-12.*) This very steep, narrow ice couloir lies to the east of the rather broad north ridge of Mount Owen and is bounded on its left side by the Crescent Arête *(Route 9)*. The couloir provides two or three pitches of difficult ice climbing, but significant objective hazards exist, warranting an alpine start, close attention to conditions and temperature, and a skilled party that is capable of moving quickly up this type of terrain. The best time to find good ice conditions seems to be in late spring or very early summer—after the spring avalanche cycle but when cold temperatures still permit the ice sections to form. The portion of the northeast snowfields that lies above the upper couloir is a significant avalanche starting zone. Route conditions can be checked with a spotting scope from the valley in the vicinity of the Cathedral Group turnout.

First-Ascent History: Stephen Arsenault wrote the following in his report for the 1973 *American Alpine Journal*:

Named from a distance several years ago, this couloir which lies between the north ridge and the Crescent Arête of Mount Owen has a particularly evil appearance, marked by rock scars and running water when it is not filled with ice. It was first climbed on July 6 by John Bouchard and me. The couloir was approached via the northeast snowfields to a point where we could traverse right to a narrow ridge, just left of the couloir. After a bivouac on this ridge, we started at five AM, climbing the couloir until just below the first ice bulge. This

FIGURE 7-12. Mount Owen, north aspect, Run-Don't-Walk Couloir *(Route 10)*, IV, 5.5, WI4+/WI5 (normal conditions with Koven finish)

30-foot overhanging ice bulge had melted through, leaving an impassable gap of 15 feet. This section was bypassed by climbing a very difficult rock pitch to the left (F9-A3). We continued up the extremely narrow couloir (some objective dangers from falling ice if the weather is warm), encountering three more steep ice bulges before emerging onto the upper section of the couloir. Moderate-angle snow was then followed for six pitches. From near the top of the couloir we traversed left to the northeast snowfields which we followed to the summit, arriving at seven PM. For optimum conditions this route should be done earlier in the season when the ice would still be intact.

Approach: Take the Cascade Canyon trail (see *Cascade Canyon* in Section 8), cross the creek (logs can usually be found), and hike up into the Teewinot–Owen cirque to where good camping spots can be found near its lower edge. Climb easily up the right side of the large snowfield below the main northeast face of Mount Owen until it is possible to traverse and climb up and right (west) to the base of the Crescent Arête. Traverse farther west into the Run-Don't-Walk Couloir and climb steep snow to the start of the first ice pitch.

A second approach option is to locate the lower drainage of the Run-Don't-Walk Couloir, which originates farther up Cascade Canyon (it eventually flows into Cascade Creek) and is on the west side of the ridge that culminates in the Crescent Arête. If one can find this point, cross the creek here—sometimes easier said than done, though in some years one can find a log on which to cross—and then climb directly up the couloir from the bottom.

Route Description: The crux of the climb consists of three difficult leads up the narrowest part of the couloir; these pitches vary in technical difficulty from year to year as well as seasonally with changes in ice quality. In some years the first pitch will involve climbing a short rock step to reach a protected belay for the beginning of the steep ice climbing. The next two pitches can range from WI4+ to WI5 and are 60m–70m in length. After emerging from the technical difficulties, continue up for a few hundred meters on steep snow to the top of the Crescent Arête. From here there are four options: (1) Traverse the northeast snowfields over to the East Prong Col and follow either the Koven route *(Route 6)* or the East Ridge route *(Route 7)* to the summit. (2) Climb the Northeast Snowfields route *(Route 8)* to the summit. (3) Join the North Ridge route *(Route 11)*, though this adds considerable climbing, including the Great Yellow Tower, before the summit is reached. (4) Downclimb the Northeast Snowfields route as an escape route. A very early start is suggested for this route. Careful attention to—and selection of—conditions in the couloir is highly recommended in order to minimize the objective hazards. **Gear:** For protection take a regular Teton alpine rack including a set of stoppers and cams from small to 3.5". Pitons, especially knifeblades and Lost Arrows, can also prove useful.

FIGURE 7-13. Mount Owen, northwest aspect. (A) North Ridge *(Route 11)*, IV, 5.7, A1, or IV, 5.9; (B) North Ridge Direct *(Route 12)*, V, 5.9; (C) North Ridge Right (Escape; *Route 13*), V, 5.10; (D) North Face *(Route 14)*, III, 5.6; (E) North Face, variation: 1989, III, 5.8; (F) Northwest Ridge *(Route 15)*, III, 5.7; (G) Northwest Face *(Route 16)*, III, 5.6; (H) Renny Take the Wheel *(Route 17)*, IV, 5.11a; (I) Renny Take the Wheel, variation: 1985, III, 5.9

ROUTE 11. NORTH RIDGE. IV, 5.7, A1, or IV, 5.9. First ascent July 31, 1951, by Richard Emerson and William Clayton; first winter ascent March 18–19, 2007, by Hans Johnstone and Greg Collins. (See *Figures 7-13* and *7-14*.) The North Ridge, one of the finest routes on this major Teton peak, is a very long route; climbers must get an early start and move rapidly or expect to be benighted. The major feature on the route is a conspicuous 150m right-facing corner just left (east) of the crest of the ridge and just below the main tower on the ridge, the Great Yellow Tower (12,400+). This steep right-facing corner system is the key to the route.

For the approach options for this climb, see *Route 10*. At a point where the

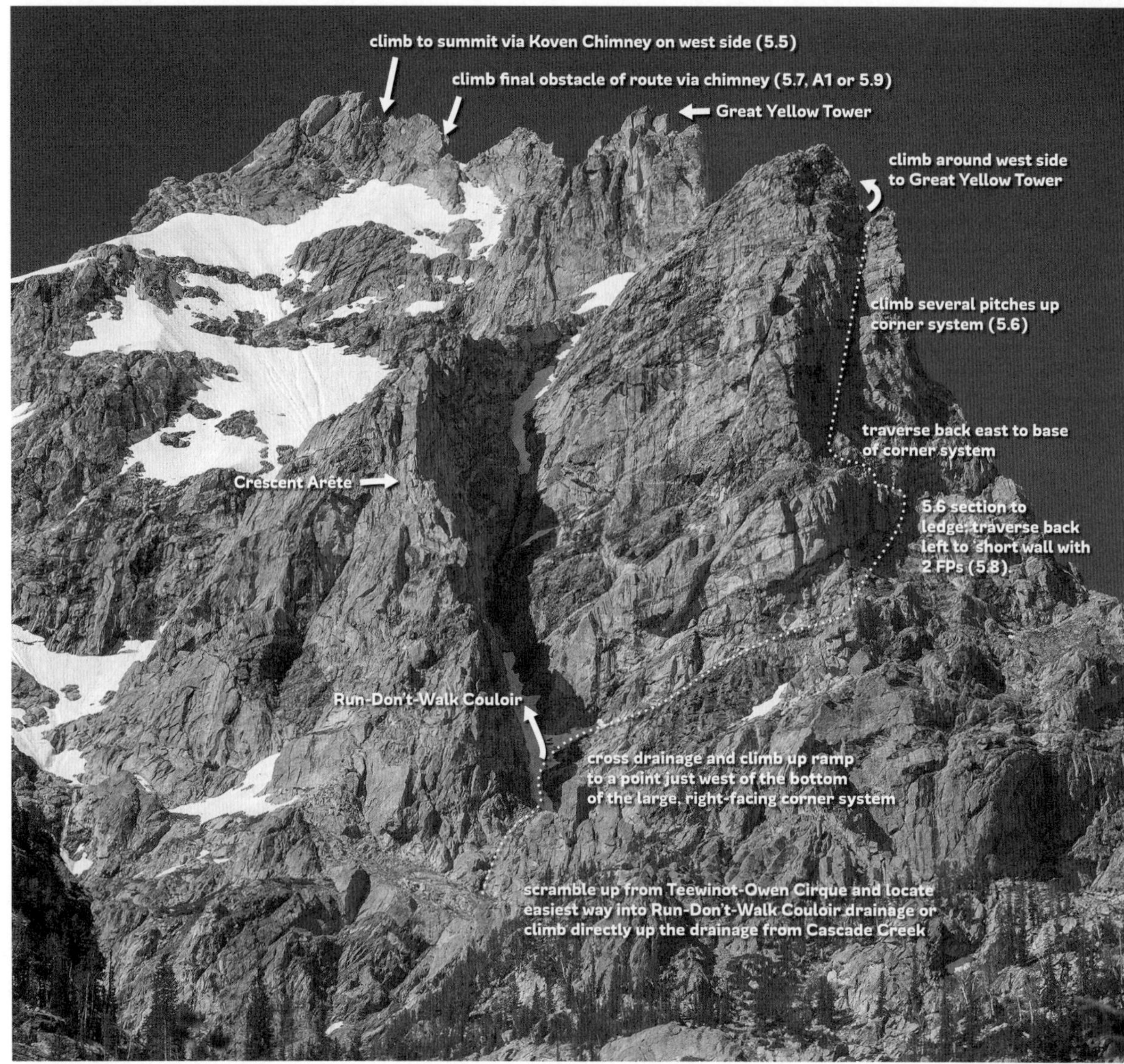

FIGURE 7-14. Mount Owen, North Ridge *(Route 11)*, IV, 5.7, A1, or IV, 5.9

Run-Don't-Walk Couloir steepens and leads to the steep ice climbing (early season), locate a ramp that leads up and west beneath a band of light-colored rock. Proceed out west on this ramp until just west of the upper corner system. Climb a short 5.6 section to a ledge. Follow the ledge back left (east) for 23m to a vertical wall with a crack and two fixed pitons. Climb up 6m (5.8), after which a pitch of easy 5th-class climbing leads to the bottom of the main corner. Once in the main corner system, several pitches of enjoyable climbing (4th and easy 5th class) lead to the small notch on the ridge at its head. Now climb easy ledges around on the west side until the crest is regained just short of the Great Yellow Tower.

There are two ways to attack this formidable tower, which very effectively blocks further passage along the ridge: (1) Traverse around and under the tower on the right (west) side on a sloping ramp, beginning on easy ledges with great exposure. Continue along this ramp, heading toward the notch separating the tower from the remainder of the ridge. An overhang 15m short of this notch can be passed by a very difficult lead to the right and then back left across its top up to the ridge crest on the tower side of the notch. Climb back down to the notch along the east side. Note that the notch cannot be reached directly from the west. (2) See *Figure 7-15* for this recommended option: On the northwest corner of the tower is a steep chimney/corner that extends upward for about 30m. Climb the crack system (5.9 wide) in this chimney/corner directly, exiting on the north face of the tower about 12m below the summit, where ledges will be found leading around the north and upper east walls of the tower to the sloping slabs that lead to the notch separating the tower from the ridge.

The remainder of the ridge usually involves a mixture of snow and rock climbing. Depending on the amount of snow, one can scramble via a series of slabs and easy chimneys to the summit of the Fourth Tower (the apex of Serendipity Arête), or one can climb straight up to the notch to the east of the tower. (If one summits the Fourth Tower, descend 15m to the notch to the east.) At the notch one is confronted with a large, deep chimney. The initial moves in this chimney (5.7, A1 or 5.9) are probably the most difficult of the route. From the top of the chimney, either climb several pitches directly up the ridge above, and reach the summit from the northwest, or continue up and to the south and climb the Koven Chimney to the summit (see *Route 6*); the latter option is shown in *Figures 7-14* and *7-15*. This is a climb of major proportions, containing more roped pitches than is usually the case for Teton climbing. **Time:** 15½ hours from Jenny Lake. See *American Alpine Journal* 9, no. 2 (1955): pp. 147–49. See also the *Alpinist* Newswire by Erik Lambert posted on April 4, 2007.

Variation: **CRESCENT ARÊTE DIRECT.** IV, 510+R, A1. First ascent in June 1994, by Greg Collins and Stephen Koch. This two-pitch climb is listed as a variation on the North Ridge route simply because it provides an unusual means of accessing the uppermost portion of the route—that is, by first climbing the Crescent Arête and then continuing directly up the Great Yellow Tower. From the top of the Crescent Arête, walk directly up to the base of a thin, black left-facing corner on the northeast side of the tower and belay on a grassy ledge. Climb the first portion of the corner (5.7) and then pass a block on the right (5.9). Continue up and over a bulge (5.10, A1) and belay in an alcove (anchor protection difficult). The second ropelength goes directly up the remainder of the dihedral (5.10+R) to a belay ledge. It is then 3.0 climbing to the top of the Great Yellow Tower. Follow the remainder of the North Ridge route to the summit. **Gear:** For protection take a regular rock rack with extras in thin sizes. Pitons may be useful for the first belay and the crux.

ROUTE 12. NORTH RIDGE DIRECT. V, 5.9. First ascent August 15, 2001, by Nate Brown, Tobey Carmen, and Eric Draper. (See *Figure 7-13*.) The little information available about this route comes from Brown's report for the 2002 *American Alpine Journal*: "We began climbing a hundred feet or so to the west of the lowest point of rock on the north face. We belayed about ten pitches of 5.9 and easier climbing, through mostly clean and enjoyable rock, from the ground to the point where we joined the established North Ridge Route and continued to the summit. It took us roughly 20 hours to complete the ascent and descent, car to car."

FIGURE 7-15. Mount Owen, west aspect, North Ridge *(Route 11)*, Great Yellow Tower detail

FIGURE 7-16. Mount Owen, northwest aspect, North Ridge Right (Escape; *Route 13*), V, 5.10

ROUTE 13. NORTH RIDGE RIGHT (ESCAPE). V, 5.10. First ascent July 18–19, 2020, by Mike Abbey and Matt Meinzer. (See *Figures 7-13* and *7-16*.) This very long route was accomplished by the first-ascent party with one bivouac. They continued on to the summit of Mount Owen after joining the North Ridge route at the Great Yellow Tower (see *Route 11*). There are two possible approaches from the floor of Cascade Canyon: (1) use the lower drainage of the Run-Don't-Walk Couloir (see *Route 10*) to gain the toe of this ridge; or (2) traverse over to it from the west after going up the Valhalla Canyon "trail" (see *Valhalla Canyon* in Section 4). Either way, begin climbing just west of the toe of the ridge. Follow easy 5th-class ledges up and east to gain the ridge proper.

This is an adventure climb, reflected in the scarcity of information provided in *Figure 7-16*. The six numbered arrows applied to the photo point out key pitches and other features of the route. Arrow 1: Belay near the crest to the left of ledges that lead to a prominent dihedral located about 30m to the right of the crest. Stay to the left on the arête. Steep climbing just right of the arête (5.10) leads through a steep overhang and then to a small right-facing corner and the ridge. Arrow 2: Follow cracks (5.9) just right of the crest up through a steep left-facing corner (5.10) to gain the ridge. Arrow 3: Easy terrain just right of the crest leads to a large chimney/dihedral with a short overhang at its top (5.10-). This pitch tops out on a big ledge on the crest of the ridge. Arrow 4: Just across a small scree gully on the ledge is a headwall with an obvious offwidth crack through its middle. A small cairn of black rocks marks the base of this crack. This offwidth was attempted on the first ascent but was not climbed. Instead, continue up the ledge/scree slope to the right where it turns the corner of the crest on a band of black rock. This weakness creates a small ledge system that diagonals to the right across the west face; follow it for three or more pitches on poor rock (easy 5th class). Very little upward progress is made during this traverse. Arrow 5: After a few sideways pitches, reach a cave in a prominent chimney. Snow in this chimney provided water for the first-ascent party when they bivouacked here. Climb up and right out of the chimney and continue up ramps and easier climbing to the huge west face ledge. Arrow 6: Follow this ledge (the arrow points to where it begins) up and to the south to a point where this route nearly converges with the Northwest Ridge route (*Route 15*). Climb the obvious dihedrals located left (north) of that route to arrive just below the Great Yellow Tower. Climb the tower and continue to the summit via the North Ridge route.

Expect a good, long Teton adventure. Either the West Ledges (*Route 20*) or the Koven route (*Route 6*) can be used for the descent.

ROUTE 14. NORTH FACE. III, 5.6. First ascent August 21, 1945, by Hans Kraus and Harrison Snyder. Note that the line shown in *Figure 7-13* is this author's (R. Jackson's) best guess as to where this route goes. This huge, roughly triangular face is located between the North Ridge route (*Route 11*) and the Northwest Ridge route (*Route 15*); it starts from the 10,000-foot level and extends some 2,400 feet to the north ridge at the Great Yellow Tower, after merging with *Route 15* at about mid-height. These two routes then continue to the summit via *Route 11*. The broad north face contains considerable rock that has been seldom explored and hence is not well known. The base of the face, which slants up from lower left to upper right, meets the upper end of the long talus slope east of the mouth of Valhalla Canyon.

For the approach to this route, take the Cascade Canyon trail (see *Cascade Canyon* in Section 8) and cross Cascade Creek at about the 7,600-foot level. Climb the talus, bearing right (west) of the north ridge until under the middle of the north face. Look for a large, gray, slabby triangular projection near the middle of the face. The right side of this triangular projection is a steep ramp, clearly defined by a 60m large crack/chimney system. The climbing begins in this crack/chimney system;

scramble and climb up for a total of about 120m until it is possible to move out left to the top of the triangular projection. At this point the scree bench that cuts across the upper face is still 240m above, and there are likely a few different ways to proceed.

The first-ascent route apparently went almost straight up for about 90m before angling up and right in a succession of cracks for another 90m. Easy climbing then led up and slightly right for approximately 60m to the upper scree bench. From the top of the triangular projection, another party utilized the major crack system that can be seen angling up and right (west) across the face to a band of black rock at the top of this first section of the north face. The major obstacles are two short, slightly overhanging jam cracks, separated by about 30m and also visible from the top of the projection. Climb a series of pitches angling up and right, past these jam cracks, and gain the scree bench.

This scree and talus bench is bounded on the right (south) by a small secondary ridge leading up to and joining the northwest ridge just below its final step to the base of the Great Yellow Tower. Scramble to the upper right corner of the bench and climb a shallow gully to the point where this subridge and the northwest ridge meet. Follow *Route 15* for several pitches of easy climbing to the sloping ramp at the west base of the Great Yellow Tower, then climb the tower as in *Route 11*. Continue up *Route 11* to the summit. As with the other north side routes of Mount Owen, this is a very long climb if pursued to the summit; the first-ascent party did not continue beyond the Great Yellow Tower. See *Appalachia* 26, no. 1 (June 1946): pp. 105–8.

Variation: III, 5.8. First ascent July 16, 1989, by Randy Harrington and Leo Larson. (See *Figure 7-13.*) To the right (west) of the initial crack/couloir of the 1945 route is a steep wall bounded on the right by a steep indentation or near-vertical couloir. This five-pitch variation starts midway between these boundaries. The first lead is the most difficult, up a crack to and past a small roof (5.8) with an additional crack above leading to the belay. A pitch of scrambling up and left ends at the base of a second vertical crack in the wall above. The third and fourth leads go directly up this crack, past another small overhang (5.7). A final pitch of easier rock (4.0) moves up and left to join the original route along the diagonal scramble up and right toward the northwest ridge.

ROUTE 15. NORTHWEST RIDGE. III, 5.7. First ascent August 5, 1941, by Jack Durrance, Henry Coulter, and Merrill McLane. (See *Figure 7-13.*) This stepped ridge leads from Valhalla Canyon east to the prominent Great Yellow Tower on the north ridge of Mount Owen. It forms the left (northern) boundary of the large but very steep northwest couloir leading to the notch in the north ridge that separates the Great Yellow Tower from the remainder of the north ridge above; this couloir is at the north edge of the main west face of Mount Owen. Some upper sections of this ridge are rather broad and ill defined. The northeastern boundary of Valhalla Canyon, however, is a well-defined ridge starting from the final trees above Cascade Canyon and extending directly to the first tower or buttress of this northwest ridge. See *Valhalla Canyon* in Section 4 for the approach into the canyon.

From the floor of the canyon ascend about 120m of scree and talus to the base of the first tower on the ridge. The climb begins very near a small, fingerlike pinnacle that can be seen in profile from the Cascade Canyon trail. Scramble as high as possible and climb at least two pitches around the left side of the tower on ledges to reach the notch behind this tower. Bypass the initial blank wall of the second tower on the right to gain a crack/chimney leading in three pitches to the top of the second tower or buttress, which is the beginning of a major talus bench. Above this bench the rock is divided into two sections, one over to the left (apparently the third tower encountered by the first-ascent party) and another on the right, more or less directly above. Climb this right section, which contains two bands of black rock, in three to four pitches—first around to the right, then up the steep black-rock wall of this section, and finally back to the left on a long traverse toward a small saddle at the top of the third tower. From the saddle pass through a vertical window and traverse right to the beginning of a difficult crack (5.7, 37m), one of the landmarks of this route. The remainder of the climbing to the base of the Great Yellow Tower is little more than scrambling. See *Route 11* for the passage of the Great Yellow Tower and the balance of the upper north ridge to the summit. **Time:** 13¾ hours from Valhalla Canyon. See *American Alpine Journal* 5, no. 1 (1943): pp. 71–75. illus.

ROUTE 16. NORTHWEST FACE. III, 5.6. First ascent August 4, 1965, by Leigh Ortenburger and Herb Swedlund. (See *Figure 7-13.*) This terraced face rises from the lower Valhalla Canyon to the Fourth Tower, the last large tower on the north ridge of Mount Owen and the apex of Serendipity Arête. It is bounded on the right (south) by Serendipity Arête and on the left by the northwest couloir, the deep and near-vertical chute that defines the northwest ridge and separates the Great Yellow Tower from the remainder of the north ridge above. This is a broad face that supports more than a single route or line, as evidenced by the distinct variations taken by the first three parties on the face. The main steep portion of this face, which contains the primary climbing interest, lies above the upper of two huge horizontal talus and scree benches that extend across the entire western aspect of Mount Owen; two more scree ledge systems, smaller but prominent, are found in this upper portion.

From lower Valhalla Canyon (see *Valhalla Canyon* in Section 4), take the obvious couloir (snow-filled in early season) through the initial broken cliff band. Head toward the black, water-streaked cliff band above, which may contain a small waterfall. If desired, suitable bivouac sites can be found here. Reach the second huge scree bench by scrambling to the left (north), between the waterfall and the northwest couloir itself. Continue scrambling for about 100m in a zigzag, perhaps partially on snow, up and left to easy (5.1 to 5.6) rock that will lead onto the next large horizontal scree ledge (covered with snow in early season or midseason) near its left (north) end.

The wall directly above this ledge is steep and cut by only a few cracks. Traverse right (south) along the ledge about 30m past an obvious jam crack until one can turn up the wall in a crack system for 23m and then cut back left (5.6 to 5.8) to easier rock. A second pitch, of similar difficulty, brings one to the large ledge just below the final huge open book of the upper face. An immense flake with a chimney behind it will be seen above. Traverse right along this ledge to an area of black rock well to the right of the massive yellow rock containing the flake. There are several alternatives for climbing this section, depending on how far right one traverses. A chimney can be found leading upward, with strenuous 5.6 at the top. Continue for another 60m on the left (north) side of Serendipity Arête (*Route 18*), finally joining that route near its last towers.

Variation: III, 5.8. First ascent August 20–21, 1982, by Rick Reese and David Susong. This variation used a different line up from the large horizontal scree ledge. From this ledge, one pitch leads up and right and then back left to the base of a steep, narrow, difficult ramp. After 12m this ramp turns into a chimney and finally a mere crack. Just below the crack, stretch left across a face on small holds (5.8) and then climb up to a belay ledge. Easier rock then leads to a bivouac ledge from which a traverse right for some 75m provides access to an easy chimney. Climb this chimney and then 60m more to a rib from which Serendipity Arête is easily reached at the base of its Third Tower (see *Route 18*).

ROUTE 17. RENNY TAKE THE WHEEL. IV, 5.11a. First ascent July 25, 2020, by Michael Gardner and Michael Hutchins. (See *Figures 7-13* and *7-17*.) Any Teton Grade IV is an undertaking, and this route is no exception. Although Renny Take the Wheel consists of just eight pitches of roped climbing, the approach via Cascade and Valhalla Canyons, the several hundred meters of scrambling to the base, and the complex descent of the West Ledges all make for an extended outing and a true wilderness adventure. The first ascent was accomplished in a long 17-hour day—a testament to the motivation and experience of the two young first ascensionists.

On the approach the crossing of Cascade Creek can be the initial crux, depending on the time of year. Once up in Valhalla Canyon, head up from the small bivy meadow (located just above where the canyon drops steeply to the north into Cascade Canyon) toward the bottom of the West Gunsight Couloir coming down from Gunsight Notch. Scramble up on the north side of the lower portion of the couloir to a huge, scree-covered ledge with a large boulder on it. This is the base

FIGURE 7-17. Mount Owen, northwest aspect, Renny Take the Wheel *(Route 17)*, IV, 5.11a

of the West Ledges route *(Route 20)*. (For additional approach details see *Figure 7-18*; *Cascade Canyon* in Section 8; and *Valhalla Canyon* in Section 4.)

Follow this ledge to the north, angling upslope until the terrain becomes 5th class. Look straight up and the third pitch with the large left-facing corner should be easy to spot. **Pitch 1:** From the start of the climb, shown in *Figure 7-17*, climb a slabby face (5.9) up to the next big ledge and belay. **Pitch 2:** Continue up, heading for the big left-facing corner above via incipient cracks with some face climbing. Pass another big ledge to reach a belay in an alcove below the corner. **Pitch 3:** Climb the corner past a bulge at the top (5.9) and belay on the next ledge above. **Pitch 4:** Easy, broken terrain leads to a terrace located below the main upper headwall. Move the belay north approximately 30m. **Pitch 5:** This long pitch leads up and right (5.8) to a belay beneath roofs composed of black rock with "wildly bright green lichen" decorating them. **Pitch 6:** The Smoke 'Em If Ya Got 'Em Pitch goes up through the initial black roofs and then to another feature—the Ear Roof (5.11a). Continue up the Mega Flake to a belay alcove at the base of a chimney. **Pitch 7:** The Shotgun Rider Pitch follows the right-slanting crack system that is the prominent feature of this headwall. Climb the offwidth above the belay (#4 Camalot useful) and continue up the crack system, to and through a bulge via hands/fingers (5.10), to a belay on a ledge. Scrambling now leads to the top of the Fourth Tower of *Route 18*. Instead of finishing with the final difficult chimney of the North Ridge route *(Route 11)*, the first ascensionists descended from the Fourth Tower to the highest ledge on the west side and traversed horizontally southward to the base of a steep crack. **Pitch 9:** Climb this crack (5.8) to the ledge above and belay. To finish, scramble up and left to the Koven Chimney (see *Route 6*) and climb that to the summit. *Route 20* was used for the descent. **Gear:** For protection take a double rack of cams with one 4" piece and several runners.

Variation: III, 5.9. First ascent August 9, 1985, by Paul Gagner and Renny Jackson. This variation traverses to the south below the final headwall that Renny Take the Wheel ascends directly. It is likely that the first four pitches of that later route were climbed during this ascent. Traverse to the south along the big ledge above the fourth pitch a short distance to the black-rock area, then turn up and climb a small dihedral (5.9). Two more leads (5.8 and 5.7) continue up the face itself before finally joining Serendipity Arête *(Route 18)* only one pitch short of its top.

ROUTE 18. SERENDIPITY ARÊTE. IV, 5.7, A1, or IV, 5.9. First ascent August 8, 1959, by William Buckingham, Frederick Medrick, Sterling Neale, and Frank Magary (this group used a few moves of A1 on the second pitch); first free ascent July 14, 1965, by Henry Mitchell and George Griffin; first winter ascent March 10 or 11, 1994, by Jack Tackle. (See *Figures 7-18, 7-19,* and *7-20.*)

FIGURE 7-18. Mount Owen, west face. (A) Serendipity Arête *(Route 18)*, IV, 5.7, A1, or IV, 5.9; (B) West Ledges *(Route 20)*, II, 5.1; (C) start of Intrepidity Arête *(Route 19)*, IV, 5.10b

FIGURE 7-19. Mount Owen, northwest aspect, Serendipity Arête *(Route 18)*, IV, 5.7, A1, or IV, 5.9

Serendipity Arête is a recommended climb in a remote, spectacular setting. The approach is via Cascade Canyon and Valhalla Canyon (see *Cascade Canyon* in Section 8 and *Valhalla Canyon* in Section 4); the structure of the west side of Mount Owen as viewed from Valhalla Canyon is complex but must be understood to find this route. The west face is bounded on the south by the West Gunsight Couloir and on the north by the large northwest couloir that separates the northwest ridge and the Great Yellow Tower from the principal mountain mass. Between these bounds and rising above the floor of Valhalla Canyon is a broad talus and scree slope that leads to the first cliff band. This initial cliff band attains maximum height at its northern extremity (north of the northwest ridge), forming the north face of Mount Owen. On the south this band narrows and ends at the West Gunsight Couloir. The major talus and scree bench above this cliff band lies about one-third of the way up the west face from the bottom and can be reached easily from the vicinity of the West Gunsight Couloir. It extends all the way across the face.

Serendipity Arête rises abruptly from this scree bench, just to the left (north) of a shallow drainage gully (both water and rock funnel through here), and it leads diagonally upward to culminate at the last tower, the Fourth Tower, on the north ridge of Mount Owen. The arête can be identified by the huge, orange left-facing dihedral on the left side of its initial steep section, the lowest of its four towers. This conspicuous dihedral has a square-cut ceiling on its lower left corner, and the bottom of it is actually a great ceiling as well. While the bulk of the arête is recognizable, its beginnings are unfortunately somewhat indistinct.

Approach from the floor of Valhalla Canyon via scree and talus slopes, ledges, and gullies onto the major talus bench described above, starting with either the lowest portion of the West Gunsight Couloir or the next small gully to the north. (See *Figure 7-18* for the details of this approach.) Begin a long traverse to the north on the large talus bench and then zigzag back south. After reaching a small crest, cut back north again below a big triangular roof. Continue up easy cracks and broken terrain just left of a long, thin black roof and set up a belay for the first pitch.

Easy climbing and scrambling leads to the base of the First Tower, which is ascended along its southern side in four to five pitches. **Pitch 1:** Traverse south across an easy slab to a hand traverse leading right (5.7). Step down and belay on ledges below the right-hand crack. **Pitch 2:** Climb the right-hand crack (5.8 hands) and then a 10m slab (5.5R) to the belay. **Pitch 3:** A short section of stemming (5.7) leads to a bulge and then easier climbing. **Pitch 4:** Negotiate 4th- and easy 5th-class terrain along the arête crest to a short knife-edge leading to the notch at the base of the Second Tower.

Pitch 5: From the base of the Second Tower, descend diagonally to the right for 12m on a narrow ledge and belay at the base of a crack. **Pitch 6:** Climb a corner in black rock (5.7) and then another corner in lighter rock above to reach the notch behind the Second Tower. **Pitch 7:** The Third Tower, about 24m high, is climbed directly from the notch by way of 5.7 crack and face climbing on the prow of the tower. **Pitch 8:** About 60m of scrambling leads to the base of the final tower on the ridge, the Fourth Tower, whose crest here has a fearsome appearance. **Pitch 9:** Proceed 5m around to the left (north) and climb up the first crack system left of the crest (5.7). **Pitches 10–11:** Scramble (3rd and 4th class) up along the crest and then up and around the Fourth Tower on its north side to the sharp notch behind it. **Pitch 12:** A chimney, located just above this notch, is the final remaining obstacle of the climb. The most difficult moves of the route (5.7, A1 or 5.9) are located a short distance up this chimney. **Pitch 13:** From the top of the chimney continue up and to the south and climb the Koven Chimney to the summit (see *Route* 6).

This long and enjoyable climb is consistently interesting, and nowhere is it excessively difficult. For descent back into Valhalla Canyon, the recommended route is the West Ledges *(Route 20)*. **Time:** 12 hours from Valhalla Canyon. See *American Alpine Journal* 12, no. 1 (1960): pp. 125–27; *Dartmouth Mountaineering Club Journal*, 1960: pp. 79–89, illus.

***Variation:* JENNI'S WAY.** IV, 5.10. First ascent August 4, 1996, by Alex Lowe (free solo). This not-to-be-missed variation to the start of Serendipity Arête ascends the prominent crack system on the west face of the First Tower of that route; see *Figure 7-20* for the details of this excellent climb. Alex Lowe, who perished in an avalanche on Shishapangma in 1999, was more than just a superb technical climber and cutting-edge alpinist. He was also a loving father, husband, and friend. Always humble despite his widespread fame, he was generally more interested in hearing what his friends had been up to than in talking about his own incredible accomplishments. This variation was the result of one of Alex's many solo exploratory forays into the Teton Range. Impressively, after his first ascent of Jenni's Way, he traversed over to and climbed the North Ridge of the Grand Teton *(Grand Teton, Route 47)*—all in one day!

Pitch 1: Climb the first pitch of Serendipity Arête and set up a belay just after the 5.7 hand traverse. The first pitch of this variation is directly above. **Pitch 2:**

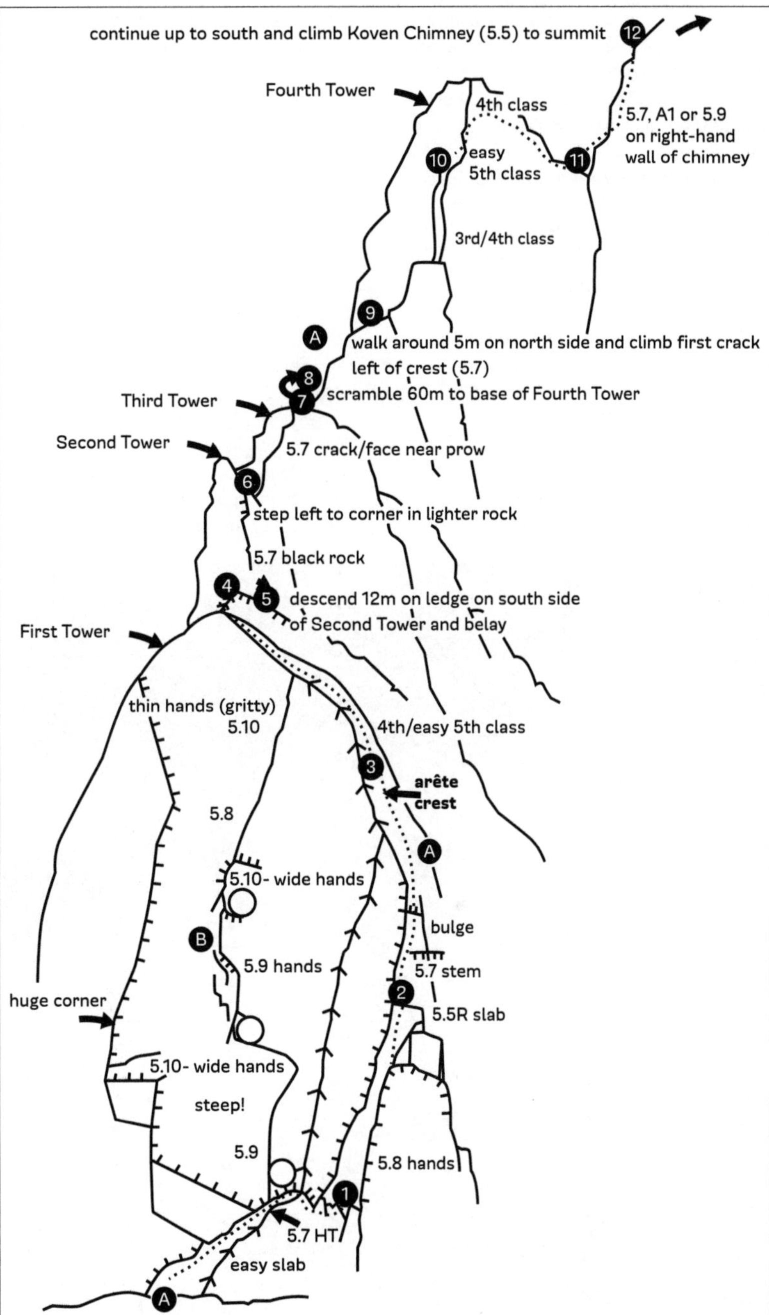

FIGURE 7-20. Mount Owen, west aspect. (A) Serendipity Arête *(Route 18)*, IV, 5.7, A1, or IV, 5.9; (B) Variation: Jenni's Way, IV, 5.10

Climb the steep crack above until it jogs hard left (5.10-) and belay in an alcove. **Pitch 3:** Continue up and left along a discontinuous, broken crack system (5.9) and belay at a small stance below a small overhang. **Pitch 4:** Climb through the roof (5.10- wide hands) and continue up the beautiful crack that eventually becomes slightly gritty and tapers to thin hands (5.10). Belay in the notch at the base of the Second Tower. Finish with the remainder of Serendipity Arête to the summit of Mount Owen. Descend via the Koven route *(Route 6)* or the West Ledges route *(Route 20)*. **Gear:** For protection take a standard Teton rack with stoppers, a double set of cams from 0.5" to 3.5", and alpine draws.

ROUTE 19. INTREPIDITY ARÊTE. IV, 5.10b. First ascent August 18, 1990, by Tom Turiano and Matthew Goewert. (See *Figures 7-18, 7-21,* and *7-22.*) According to the first-ascent party, as the leader was proceeding up the crux pitch of this climb, a wild electric hail/rainstorm blew in. The intrepid climber fought his way up the pitch and then belayed his second from the summit of the "Electrode," with hair standing straight out and gear buzzing with electricity. Immediately to the right (south) of Serendipity Arête *(Route 18)* and slightly higher is an immense rock wall that culminates in the summit of Mount Owen. This route ascends the southern edge of this wall and, like its northern neighbor, passes four towers along the way. Use the same approach as outlined for Serendipity Arête, along the northern edge of the West Gunsight Couloir. Continue up the lower portion of *Route 20* and traverse left (north) over to the start of this route as shown in *Figures 7-18* and *7-21.* The first pitch begins on top of a huge block at the base of the arête and wanders back and forth across the crest. For specific route details, refer to *Figure 7-22.* The Electrode, the first tower on the route, is four pitches up. Use the Koven route *(Route 6)* or the West Ledges route *(Route 20)* for descent. The rock on this route is reported to be of exceptional quality, and the climb was done in a 14½-hour round-trip from Jenny Lake. This route comes highly recommended, with Teton aficionado and prolific first ascensionist Jim Beyer giving it five stars. (**Note:** On the fourth pitch Beyer went up and left from the belay, as shown in *Figure 7-22,* encountering 5.9+ face climbing before joining the original route just below the top of the Electrode.)

FIGURE 7-21. Mount Owen, west aspect. (A) Intrepidity Arête *(Route 19)*, IV, 5.10b; (B) Variation: Mas Intrepido, IV, 5.10-

***Variation:* MAS INTREPIDO.** IV, 5.10-. First ascent in August 1994, by Matthew Goewert and Mark Limage. (See *Figures 7-21* and *7-22.*) This three-pitch variation to Intrepidity Arête provides an alternate means of reaching the top of the Electrode. The first pitch begins 9m to the left (north) of the start of Intrepidity Arête and ascends a 37m left-facing corner (5.10-). This pitch was described as a sustained lieback on an "elephant ear" flake with the crux consisting of a thin 5.10- traverse left to a belay at the base of a fist crack. The first ascensionists noted on their topo that this first pitch rates as "one of the ten best in the range." From a hanging belay, climb the fist crack (5.9) to a belay ledge. The third ropelength is a dirty left-facing corner (5.8) that ends atop the Electrode. Continue up the main Intrepidity Arête route to the summit.

ROUTE 20. WEST LEDGES. II, 5.1. First ascent July 28, 1932, by Paul Petzoldt and Edward Woolf. (See *Figures 7-18* and *7-21.*) This long route was the first one to start from Valhalla Canyon, the beautiful high cirque lying beneath the west faces of the Grand Teton and Mount Owen. The west side of Mount Owen has a complex structure and is difficult to describe, but it has an obvious southern boundary at the long, straight snow couloir, the West Gunsight Couloir, leading to Gunsight Notch. The West Ledges route ascends the region just north (left) of this snow couloir, negotiating a series of cliff bands, talus and scree slopes, and sloping ledges, plus a few ill-defined couloirs; it terminates at the crest of the southwest ridge of Mount Owen.

Approach via Cascade Canyon, cross Cascade Creek, and climb into the upper Valhalla Canyon (see *Cascade Canyon* in Section 8 and *Valhalla Canyon* in Section 4). The initial cliff band just above the upper Valhalla bivouac site is easily passed by climbing near the West Gunsight Couloir or by ascending the couloir that begins just left (north) of the bivouac site. By either route the talus and scree slope leading to the second large, jumbled cliff band is reached and then climbed. Near the right (south) edge of this cliff band, just left of the West Gunsight Couloir, is a steep section of black rock capped by a vertical wall of light-colored rock. Climb the broken rock to the left of this wall to gain access to a section of moderate slabs. There are two alternatives at this point. (1) One can make a lengthy scramble up and right (southeast) to the uppermost part of these slabs, skirting a cliff on the right, until a more broken area is found near the couloir. Climb for 30m or more in this area before turning back left (north) to reach the lower southwest edge of the final large area of slabs and snow patches just below the southwest ridge. (2) The second alternative is to move up and slightly left to the base of a smaller cliff; traverse left (north) under this wall until broken rock is reached just short (south) of a large couloir. Climb to reach the lower northwest edge of the same final area of slabs and snow patches.

Now scramble to the central, topmost point of these extensive slabs, beneath the cliffs that prevent easy access to the southwest ridge crest. Climb a short chimney, then traverse left and up to reach the prominent couloir forming the left (north) boundary of the west ledges region. Climb this couloir to the crest at a large notch between two of the largest towers on the southwest ridge; this is the distinctly U-shaped notch as seen from the east. At this point traverse around to the east side of the southwest ridge and follow that route to the summit (see *Route 1*). Other routes can be worked out, for there are many possible variations. With either talent or luck in the routefinding, the West Ledges route provides both a relatively easy means of ascent and a fast means of descent because most of the route is scrambling.

When descending from the summit along the upper southwest ridge and looking for this route, remember that it strikes the ridge relatively low on the crest. It is important to avoid the temptation to turn off the ridge crest too early down to the west. Error slings for rappelling will be found in one or more notches too far to the north along the crest; ignore these mistakes and continue downclimbing the

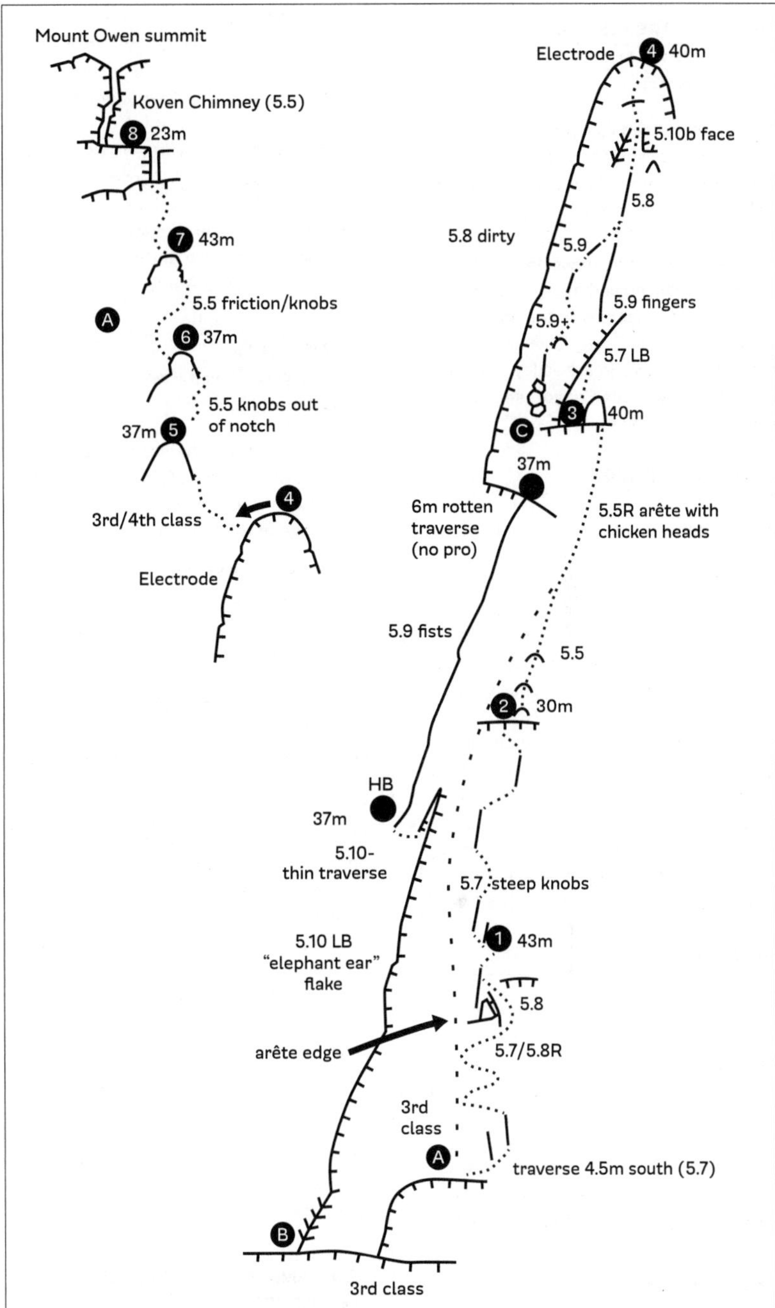

FIGURE 7-22. Mount Owen, west aspect. (A) Intrepidity Arête *(Route 19)*, IV, 5.10b; (B) Variation: Mas Intrepido, IV, 5.10-; (C) Variation: Beyer, 5.10b

ridge until there is a significant increase in the difficulty. At this point it is possible to downclimb onto the upper West Ledges route without having to rappel (though some may wish to commence this descent to the west with a rappel).

For those skilled in the use of an ice axe, there is an advantage in early season or midseason in seeking out an early entry into the steep West Gunsight Couloir. A fast descent can be made with the right snow conditions.

RABBIT EARS (10,880+)

(0.7 mi WNW of Mount Owen)
Map: Grand Teton

These well-named twin pinnacles are on the northwest ridge of the Grand Teton, which forms the west boundary of Valhalla Canyon; they are almost due west of Mount Owen. Of the various peaks and towers on this ridge, these are the smallest, most difficult, and most distinctive. They are easily seen from the northern approach road to String Lake and from many other places in the valley. For the approach to Valhalla Canyon, see *Valhalla Canyon* in Section 4.

North Ear (10,880+)

ROUTE 1. NORTH RIDGE. II, 5.4, A2, or II, 5.7. First ascent July 17, 1957, by Fred Ayres, Leigh Ortenburger, and Irene Beardsley (Ortenburger); first free ascent July 31, 1968, by Dave Ingalls and Roy Kligfield. This remarkable pinnacle overhangs on all four sides. Approach from Valhalla Canyon through the col north of the North Ear. On the west side, negotiate a prominent downsloping shelf leading left to the north ridge. From the platform at its end, surmount the bulging overhang above to the sharp summit crest. A rappel is required for descent of the west face. See *American Alpine Journal* 11, no. 1 (1958): pp. 85–88.

South Ear (10,880+)

ROUTE 1. SOUTH RIDGE. II, 4.0. First ascent August 8–10, 1938, by Jack Durrance and Michael Davis. Approach from Valhalla Canyon through the col north of the North Ear. Bypass the North Ear on the west to reach the west side of the South Ear. Climb the last meter to the summit via the south ridge. See *Dartmouth Mountaineering Club Journal,* 1938: pp. 29–36.

PEAK 10,640+

(0.8 mi WNW of Mount Owen)
Map: Mount Moran

The col between this peak and the next peak to the north, Peak 10,405, can be reached either directly from the west via the couloir leading up to it (reached after crossing the south fork of Cascade Creek) or by descending south from Peak 10,405.

ROUTE 1. NORTH RIDGE. II, 5.1. First ascent August 8, 1938, by Jack Durrance and Michael Davis. From the col between Peak 10,640+ and Peak 10,405, the north ridge is climbed directly.

ROUTE 2. SOUTH RIDGE. II, 3.0. First descent August 8, 1938, by Jack Durrance and Michael Davis. This ridge is easily descended during an ascent of the complete northwest ridge of the Enclosure (see *The Enclosure, Route 5*).

PEAK 10,405

(0.7 mi NW of Mount Owen)
Map: Mount Moran

This easy peak, which rises to the southeast above the forks of Cascade Canyon, constitutes the extremity of the northwest ridge of the Enclosure.

ROUTE 1. NORTHWEST RIDGE. II, 5.1. First ascent August 8, 1938, by Jack Durrance and Michael Davis. Cross the south fork of Cascade Creek (see *Cascade Canyon* in Section 8) to approach this ridge, which is then easily followed on loose rock to the summit of the peak.

ROUTE 2. SOUTH RIDGE. II, 5.1. First descent August 8, 1938, by Jack Durrance and Michael Davis. This ridge is used to descend into the col between this peak and Peak 10,640+, which is the next tower on the northwest ridge of the Enclosure (see *The Enclosure, Route 5*). No problems, other than loose rock, will be encountered.

ROUTE 3. EAST FACE. I, 4.0. First ascent September 4, 2000, by Paul Horton and Heather Paul. Wander up easy slabs above the meadows in Valhalla Canyon (for the approach to this canyon, see *Valhalla Canyon* in Section 4). This party continued to Peak 10,640+ and then returned to camp via downclimbing and a couple of rappels down the east side of the ridge.

ART-AND-BRENT PINNACLE (ca. 9,600)

(0.6 mi NE of Teewinot Mountain)
Map: Mount Moran

This obscure pinnacle on the south side of Cascade Canyon is very difficult to find or even see. It is located on a lower north ridge of Teewinot Mountain, opposite Guides' Wall on the southwest ridge of Storm Point.

ROUTE 1. NORTH FACE. II, 5.10-, A1. First ascent September 20, 1984, by Renny Jackson and Tom Kimbrough. Cross Cascade Creek just below the small pond (Perch Pond) that was formed by a rockslide that came down from the southwest couloir of Storm Point (see *Cascade Canyon* in Section 8). Hike up about 300m of scree toward a large ramp angling steeply upward, from which the pinnacle rises. The climb begins with a few aid moves (or 5.11- free) on the northeast side of the pinnacle. Then climb up and left into a 5.9 groove on the east side to a belay below a small roof. The second short pitch goes up and over the roof (5.10-) and then follows good cracks to the summit. Although the first pitch has been freed (by Dennis Sanders), aid was used on the second lead, so the pinnacle awaits a free ascent. **Gear:** Two ropes are needed to rappel off the north side.

MCCAIN'S PILLAR (10,400+)

(0.55 mi NE of Mount Owen)
Map: Mount Moran

Near the base of the northeastern aspect of Mount Owen, this 46m black pinnacle lies on the ridge that forms the lower extension of the Crescent Arête (see *Mount Owen, Route 9*). Approach via the Teewinot–Owen cirque (see *Cascade Canyon* in Section 8), gaining the ridge about 300m north of the pinnacle. The pinnacle could also be approached via the couloir west of it or—best—from the first northeast snowfield on Mount Owen, from which it is clearly visible.

ROUTE 1. EAST FACE AND SOUTH FACE. II, 5.10, A1. First ascent September 3, 1969, by Rick Reese and John Whitesel. Scramble to the vicinity of the base of the east face. Climb a series of furrows and cracks on the east face to a slanting shelf just below the final 21m south face. Climb 6m up this wall to a small ledge where a protection bolt will be found. The first-ascent party used aid on tied-off knifeblade pitons in an 8m crack to get to a small ledge—efforts they considered worthy of an A3 rating. With modern equipment, however, the ledge can be accessed via a few moves of A1 (this section will probably go free at 5.10+). An overhanging face then leads free to the summit. The first-ascent party looped a sling carefully around the summit as a rappel anchor.

FAULTLINE (10,640+)

(0.95 mi W of Middle Teton)
Map: Grand Teton

Immediately west of and below Icefloe Lake in the upper south fork of Cascade Canyon (see *Cascade Canyon* in Section 8) is a prominent buttress with a sheer west wall. This small yet intriguing diamond-shaped wall is split by a huge vertical dihedral near its center. The base of the buttress is easily reached from the canyon via scree slopes.

ROUTE 1. WEST FACE. II, 5.9. First ascent July 31, 1978, by Tom and Barry Rugo. (See *Figure 7-23.*) Climb the lower third of the face via broken and somewhat loose rock (5.7), angling up and right to the large platform ledge to the left (north) of the huge dihedral. On the extreme right end of this ledge is a large left-facing corner that is part of the main dihedral; on the extreme left end a jam crack heads up and through an overhang. This route climbs a 6m face to the start of another jam crack that lies midway between these extremes. Ascend this well-protected crack, which contains three strenuous 5.9 sections, for about 40m to a good belay "hole" (the term used on the original topo). Although the crack continues to the top of the buttress, the third lead (5.6) angles up and right to the dihedral, which is followed for 30m to the top. Descent can be made easily to the north. **Gear:** For protection take a regular rack with camming devices in the 2"–4" range for the jam crack.

FIGURE 7-23. Faultline, west aspect, West Face *(Route 1)*, II, 5.9

THE WALL (11,108)

Map: Grand Teton

Viewed from the east from one of the high central peaks of the range, the Wall appears as a sheer, 150m wall of sedimentary rock on the divide at the head of the north fork of Avalanche Canyon above Snowdrift Lake. The west side of the peak slopes off gently toward Sunset Lake, Alaska Basin, and the Teton Crest Trail. The original "Skyline Trail," constructed in the 1930s south from the Cascade-Avalanche divide, was built along the shelf at the base of the east cliffs and emerged onto the west side of the divide through the saddle (10,640+) separating the Wall from the northwest ridge of Veiled Peak. This trail was abandoned in 1938 when the magnitude of rockfall and rockslides from the cliffs immediately above became evident; the section of this trail leading to the Cascade-Avalanche divide is still intact. The cliff band contains several indentations or caves, one of which extends for a few hundred meters back into the Death Canyon Limestone. While not significant as a technical mountaineering objective, this minor sedimentary summit has the distinction of (probably) being the first Teton peak with a documented ascent. On an exploratory scouting trip prior to their ascent of, or attempt on, the Grand Teton on July 29, 1872, Nathaniel P. Langford and James Stevenson reached the top of a peak on the divide, almost surely this one. It provides an excellent vantage point for the three Tetons and is a recommended side

trip for hikers of the Teton Crest Trail. Although it is not indicated on the map, there is reportedly another benchmark (BM 10,953) on top of the Wall, located about 0.5 mile south of the highest point; this was probably placed by the T. F. Murphy topographic party in 1934 or 1935.

ROUTE 1. WEST SIDE. I, 1.0. Probable first ascent July 24, 1872, by Nathaniel P. Langford and James Stevenson; this peak was also presumably climbed by the T. M. Bannon topographic party in 1899, as their map indicates a benchmark on the summit. Although this peak is well guarded on the east by sedimentary cliffs, the ascent from the west from the trail in Alaska Basin is easy. The approach to all of these peaks along the divide is ordinarily made via the Teton Crest Trail, starting either at Jenny Lake and entering via Cascade Canyon (see *Cascade Canyon* in Section 8) or from the Death Canyon trailhead and entering via Death Canyon (see *Death Canyon* in Section 2).

PEAK 10,635

(0.9 mi S of Table Mountain)
Map: Grand Teton

This sedimentary ridge forms the divide on the west side of the south fork of Cascade Canyon. Rising only 300 feet above and immediately north of Hurricane Pass (10,320+), where the Teton Crest Trail crosses from Cascade Canyon to Alaska Basin, it is easily reached. This peak may have been the objective reached on July 28, 1872, by two members of the Snake River Division of the 1872 Hayden Survey Expedition—general assistant Robert Adams Jr. and assistant geologist William R. Taggart—while exploring the upper reaches of Teton Canyon (although it is likelier that they climbed another point on the divide, 10,800+, which is 0.6 mile southwest of the pass). Adams and Taggart were probably trying to determine the best way to get down into the south fork of Cascade Canyon and over to Dartmouth Basin, which the division was eventually successful at doing.

ROUTE 1. SOUTH RIDGE. I, 1.0. First known descent in late July 1958, by Howard R. Stagner Jr. and Richard Byrd; first known ascent August 20, 1960, by Arthur J. Reyman. No difficulties will be encountered on this easy ridge.

ROUTE 2. NORTH RIDGE. I, 1.0. First known ascent in late July 1958, by Howard R. Stagner Jr. and Richard Byrd. This party found a hollow, circular 2-foot cairn on the summit.

TABLE MOUNTAIN (11,106)

Map: Grand Teton

This flat-topped summit is capped by only a thin layer of sedimentary rock; the excellent Precambrian rock is exposed down the 430m east face in the south fork of Cascade Canyon. One of the first peaks in the range to be ascended, Table Mountain has become famous as the viewpoint from which William Henry Jackson, the pioneer photographer with the Hayden Surveys, obtained the first photographs of the Grand Teton in late July 1872. The peak is most easily reached from Teton Canyon to the west, where a popular US Forest Service (USFS) trail leads up the north fork of the canyon onto and up the long, gentle west ridge.

On the other side of the formation, the impressive east face (see *Figures 7-24* and *7-27*) is divided into three main sections or buttresses: The southern section is the most prominent buttress looming over the Cascade Canyon trail. A large chimney or chute separates this south buttress from the central buttress, which is somewhat inset and not clearly seen from some angles. From this main chimney a second chute branches off to the right and separates the central and north buttresses. The routes on this aspect of the peak—*Routes 2–11*— are approached via the trail in the south fork of Cascade Canyon (see *Cascade Canyon* in Section 8) or from the Idaho side via Teton Canyon.

Chronology

WEST SLOPE: ca. July 27, 1872, William Henry Jackson, Charles Campbell, Philo J. Beveridge, Alexander Sibley (and perhaps John M. Coulter)
SOUTH RIDGE: July 23, 1934, Fritiof Fryxell, Reynold Holmen, Harry Thayer, Eugene Beattie
EAST FACE, EAST LEDGES: September 6, 1959, Steve Jervis, Robert Page
EAST FACE, CENTRAL BUTTRESS I: September 7, 1959, Fred Beckey, Yvon Chouinard, Ken Weeks
EAST FACE, SOUTH BUTTRESS: June 15, 1961, Maurice Horn, Pete Sinclair
NORTH RIDGE: August 3, 1967, Leigh Ortenburger, John Lemon
SOUTHEAST COULOIR: July 4, 1980, Jack Tackle, George Barnett
HEARTBREAK RIDGE: July 28, 1995, Paul Horton, Jon Stuart
LINE OF FIRE: August 4, 2013, Paul Kimbrough, Brandon Gust; FFA September 8, 2013, Paul Kimbrough, Brandon Gust
KINDRED SPIRITS (EAST FACE, NORTH BUTTRESS): August 16, 2021, Rich Baerwald, James Pfeifer
29 FINGERS: September 29–30, 2021, Jamison Johnson, Grant Burson, Thomas Ney

ROUTE 1. ▲ WEST SLOPE. I, 1.0. First ascent on about July 27, 1872, by William Henry Jackson, Charles Campbell, Philo J. Beveridge, and Alexander Sibley (and perhaps John M. Coulter); in 1899 T. M. Bannon and party placed a benchmark on the summit, probably by some variation of this route. From the campground parking area at the (east) end of the road in Teton Canyon, a good trail leads northeast into the north fork of the canyon, ultimately turning south to gain the west end (9,900) of the summit plateau, which is followed easily to the summit block. Ever since Jackson's time, when pack animals were required to carry his heavy and bulky wet-plate photographic equipment to the summit plateau, horses have been used on this trail to the base of the summit block.

ROUTE 2. SOUTH RIDGE. I, 2.0. First recorded ascent July 23, 1934, by Fritiof Fryxell, Reynold Holmen, Harry Thayer, and Eugene Beattie. This route is approached from Jenny Lake via the Cascade Canyon trail into the south fork of the canyon. Leave the trail at 9,000 feet, turning west up the open slope and drainage just past (south of) the south buttress on the east side of Table Mountain. This drainage is easily followed to the saddle (10,120) south of the mountain. The broad ridge above is then easily followed to the summit plateau and final summit block. **Time:** 5½ hours from Jenny Lake.

ROUTE 3. 29 FINGERS. III, 5.10+ PG-13. First ascent September 29–30, 2021, by Jamison Johnson, Grant Burson, and Thomas Ney. This route of approximately 200 meters is located on the south side of the southern buttress and was approached via Teton Canyon. The beginning of the climb is located a few hundred meters to the southwest of *Route 5* and less than one-half mile east of the Park boundary. Look for a right-trending ramp leading through easy terrain to a left-facing corner. **Pitch 1:** Climb up through easy terrain on the ramp and belay at the base of a left-facing corner (5.5, 50m). **Pitch 2:** Jam up a crack in the corner until it widens and a roof is encountered; then head left and lieback a thin flake to a nice stance and a good belay (5.7, 35m). **Pitch 3:** Scramble through easier loose rock to another good stance at the base of a squeeze chimney (easy 5th, 25m). **Pitch 4:** Climb the first few feet of the chimney just left of a golden block and then continue further left for quality climbing and a comfortable ledge. Belay at the base of a golden face (5.8, 45m). **Pitch 5:** From the left end of the ledge climb multiple cracks to and over a small roof (crux) and a belay at a stance (5.9, 30m). **Pitch 6:** From the belay stance move left around a corner and continue up a chossy ramp to an exit move (5.8, stemming/double cracks) that provides access to a large ledge that was used for a bivouac on the first ascent (5.8, 20m). **Pitch 7:** Climb the perfect crack directly above the ledge up a golden face toward a small chimney and an exciting roof. Belay from the left side of the ledge (5.10+, 25m). **Pitch 8:** Follow the right-facing corner above the ledge to and through another roof (fixed nut) to a small ledge. Trend left for a micro seam and a heady finish to this quality pitch (5.10+ PG-13, 30m). **Pitch 9:** Walk up and right easy 3rd-class terrain to a corner system just to the left of a gully. Ascend the corner system stemming and jamming until 3rd-class terrain is reached (5.7, 35m). Walking then leads to the summit. **Gear:** For protection take a double set of cams 0.1" to 3" and a single 4" piece, a set of stoppers, and 10 alpine draws.

ROUTE 4. SOUTHEAST COULOIR. II, 5.8. First ascent July 4, 1980, by Jack Tackle and George Barnett. This large and distinct couloir, containing some snow in early season, lies on the left (west) side of Table Mountain's south buttress. Gain the base of the couloir (ca. 10,000) from the southeast, using the south fork of the Cascade Canyon trail for the approach. This route involves 180m of straightforward but sustained climbing. The first and third leads require passing large chockstones on the right (east). The move past the second chockstone was the crux of the route for the first-ascent party because it was slippery from running water. Beyond the fourth pitch, the duo followed snow for 30m before moving right onto easier rock, which they climbed up to a drop-off. From this point traverse left (west) for a few hundred meters to gain the summit plateau.

Climber on the first pitch of Jenni's Way, Serendipity Arête, Mount Owen (Photo by Renny Jackson)

FIGURE 7-24. Table Mountain, east aspect. (A) Heartbreak Ridge *(Route 5)*, III, 5.7; (B) East Face, South Buttress *(Route 6)*, III, 5.8+; (C) Line of Fire *(Route 7)*, III, 5.10c

ROUTE 5. HEARTBREAK RIDGE. III, 5.7. First ascent July 28, 1995, by Paul Horton and Jon Stuart. (See *Figures 7-24* and *7-25*.) From the trail in the south fork of Cascade Canyon, below the impressive east face of Table Mountain, this route is visible as the left-hand skyline. The rib it ascends forms the left-hand (south) border of the south buttress of the face. It is distinguished by a veneer of golden rock along the crest of the lower ridge. For those seeking moderate routes containing excellent rock, both this ridge and *Route 5* are highly recommended. **Pitch 1:** Start at the toe of the rib on golden rock and climb 46m up a slab (5.6). **Pitch 2:** Ascend a ramp and corner on the left side of the crest or a 5.8 crack on the ridge crest itself. **Pitch 3:** This lead starts up 5.7 cracks and then turns to 4th class up the crest. **Pitch 4:** Another 4th-class section up the stepped crest leads to a corner just to the right of the crest. Climb partway up this corner (5.6) to a belay. **Pitch 5:** Continue up the corner (5.6) to where more 3rd- and 4th-class climbing leads to the next belay. Then move the belay north on a big ledge to the base of the steep section of the ridge. **Pitch 6:** Ascend a crack and then traverse left across a black face to a belay on the prow immediately below a "nose." **Pitch 7:** This lead climbs either the left side of the nose (5.7) or the right side (5.9) before regaining the crest (46m). **Pitch 8:** Continue up and climb a short face (5.6) that gives way to easier ground. Third- and 4th-class slabs lead to the top of the climb. Use the South Ridge route *(Route 2)* to descend to Cascade Canyon or take the west slope trail (see *Route 1*) to go down into Teton Canyon.

ROUTE 6. EAST FACE, SOUTH BUTTRESS. III, 5.8+. First ascent June 15, 1961, by Maurice Horn and Pete Sinclair; the initial portion of this route was first climbed on September 8, 1960, by Maurice Horn and Ken Weeks. (See *Figures 7-24* and *7-25*.) The imposing south buttress contains the steepest rock on Table Mountain. The approach is the same as for the other eastern routes—via the trail in the south fork of Cascade Canyon. The route starts from the north end of a wide bench at the base of the face, where 46m of easy face

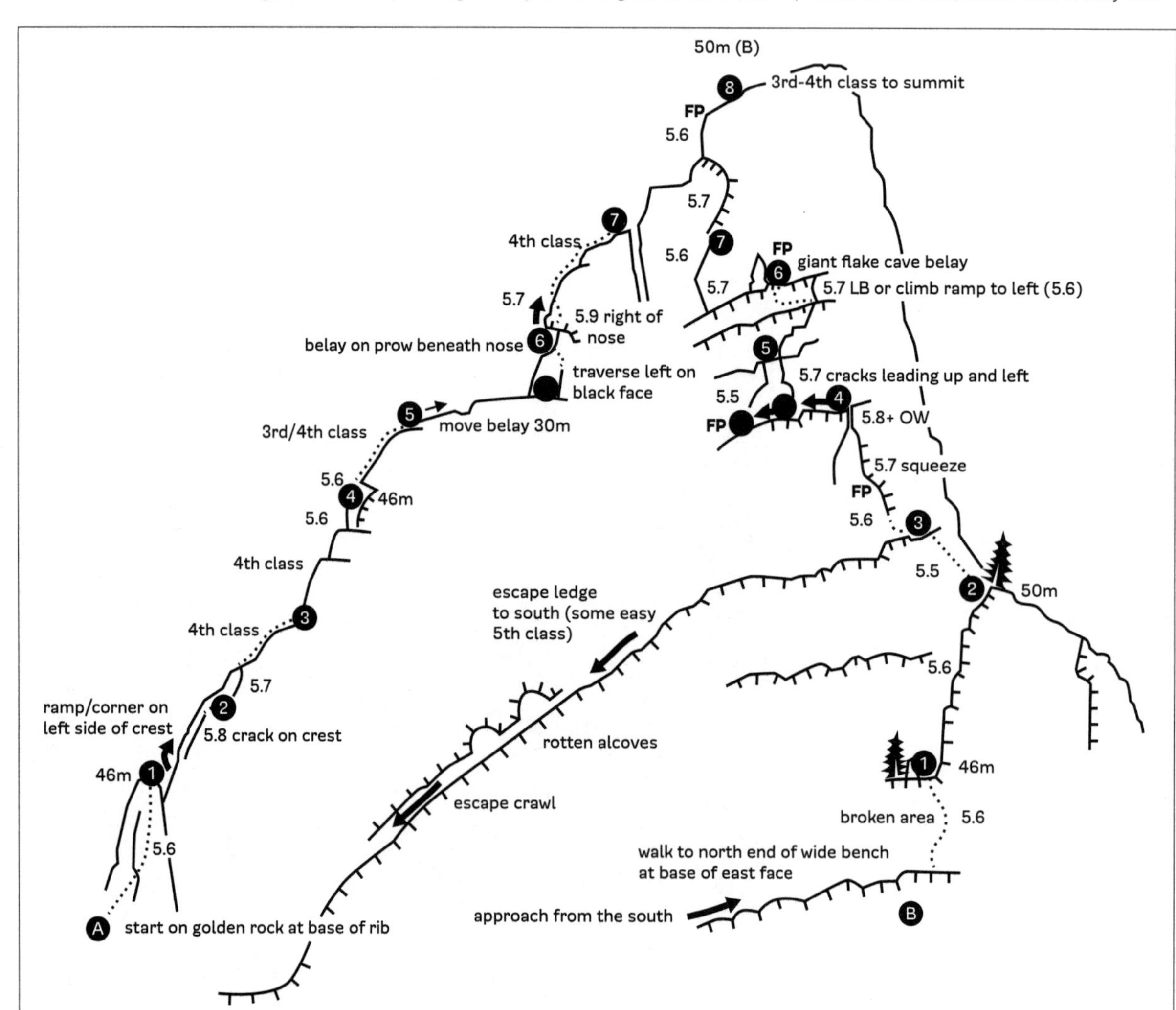

FIGURE 7-25. Table Mountain, east aspect. (A) Heartbreak Ridge *(Route 5)*, III, 5.7; (B) East Face, South Buttress *(Route 6)*, III, 5.8+

climbing on broken rock leads to a belay near a tree and boulder. The second pitch is a left-facing corner (5.6) that takes one to a tree for the next belay stance. More face climbing provides access to a wide diagonal ledge that allows an escape to the south, if needed. The fourth lead starts 1m to the left up 5.6 face climbing to a squeeze chimney (5.7) and then an offwidth (5.8+) that ends at a narrow ledge. Move the belay to the south to cracks leading up and left or over to a belay at a fixed pin. Either way, a short pitch ends on a ledge at the base of a right-trending crack. The next lead follows the crack up and right to a ledge and then continues up to another ledge using either a 5.6 ramp leading up and right or a 5.7 vertical lieback crack. Belay behind a giant flake near another fixed pin. From the far (south) side of the flake the seventh pitch descends slightly and goes up a face (5.7) and crack, angling slightly to the right. The final long lead (50m) starts up a 5.7 left-facing corner and ends by moving left up the face (5.6) on the left side of this corner. The summit is then reached by a scramble up and left. The upper part of the route has some spectacular exposure that is very enjoyable because the rock is good and the belay positions are secure. See *American Alpine Journal* 13, no. 1 (1962): pp. 216–20.

ROUTE 7. LINE OF FIRE. III, 5.10c. First ascent August 4, 2013, by Paul Kimbrough and Brandon Gust; the pair did the first free ascent about a month later on September 8, 2013. This climb is located just to the north of *Route 6*, very near the prow of the south buttress. See *Figures 7-24* and *7-26* for the details of this route. It is a good climb, for the most part on sound rock.

ROUTE 8. EAST FACE, CENTRAL BUTTRESS I. II, 5.6. First ascent September 7, 1959, by Fred Beckey, Yvon Chouinard, and Ken Weeks. Ascend the south fork of Cascade Canyon to the large chute that separates the south buttress of Table Mountain from the central buttress. Climb this chute and begin the ascent of the second chute, which branches out to the right and separates the central buttress from the north buttress. Traverse out on the first small, sloping ledge leading left, onto the face of the central buttress. A prominent open book is encountered in the first pitch on the buttress. In general, the route from here stays in the middle of the face and consists of roped climbing all the way to the summit plateau. See *American Alpine Journal* 12, no. 1 (1960): pp. 125–27.

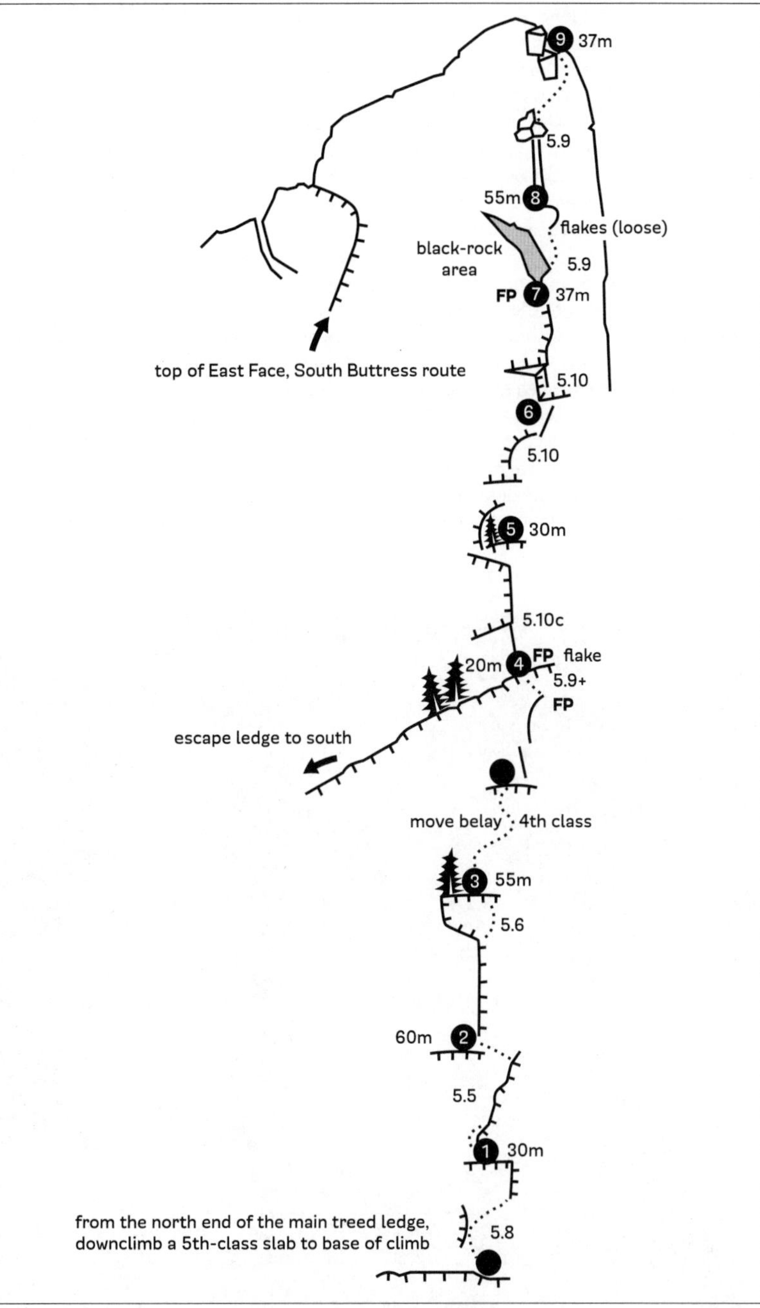

FIGURE 7-26. Table Mountain, east aspect, Line of Fire *(Route 7)*, III, 5.10c

ROUTE 9. EAST FACE, EAST LEDGES. II, 5.1. First ascent September 6, 1959, by Steve Jervis and Robert Page. This route ascends the left (south) edge of the north buttress. Walk 2 miles up the south fork of Cascade Canyon, leaving the trail after one can clearly see that there are three buttresses; there appear to be only two until one is rather high up into the south fork. Angle up and right to the first conspicuous tree-lined ledge at the base of the north buttress. Walk south along this ledge to within about 100m of the large chute that separates the left (south) buttress from the central buttress. Follow more ledges up and right to a broad, sloping meadow. Go about 60m up the obvious chute separating the north and central buttresses. At this point the chute steepens, so work up the right wall until a traverse to the left is possible. After about 15m of climbing, simply follow the good rock on the right side of the chute all the way to the summit plateau. See *American Alpine Journal* 12, no. 1 (1960): pp. 125–27.

ROUTE 10. KINDRED SPIRITS (EAST FACE, NORTH BUTTRESS). III, 5.11. First ascent August 16, 2021, by Rich Baerwald and James Pfeifer. (See *Figure 7-27.*) This remote route is located on the northeast shoulder or prow of the north buttress of Table Mountain and was approached via Teton Canyon. Ledges on the north side of the buttress lead down from a shoulder near the summit of Table Mountain to the base of the climb. The start is found to the right of a large roof and is accessed by a series of 4th-class ledges. **Pitch 1:** Angle left toward a right-facing corner, then face climb right and head up a series of thin cracks (5.11, 35m). Move right and up to another thin crack (5.10-), then traverse left. Find a good stance in the black rock. **Pitch 2:** Continue left, turn the corner, and climb up into a bowl (5.7). Locate a good stance below boulders and belay (35m). **Pitch 3:** Follow the right side of the "boot," a large, boot-shaped flake. Climb a finger crack to a wild hand traverse that goes left along the "boot top" (5.10). Continue up a right-facing corner. Move left at a small roof to a narrow ledge and belay (5.9, 50m). **Pitch 4:** Start to the left where a right-facing corner leads to a large flake and a white triangular block. Continue past these features, trending right and up double cracks (5.8) into black rock. A short right-facing corner (5.9) ends at a small stance (46m). **Pitch 5:** Begin with a hard move left to a right-facing corner. Pass loose black rock to reach the start of double hand cracks (5.7). Belay here to avoid loose rock (20m). **Pitch 6:** Follow the double hand cracks to a big ledge (5.9, 20m). **Pitch 7:** Climb a left-angling dihedral (5.7) past big blocks to its end and a good stance below more double cracks (35m). **Pitch 8:** Climb these exit cracks into and out of a chimney box (5.9). Scramble up to the top of the north buttress and belay (40m). The descent is described as a "walk-off." It is suggested that this climb be undertaken in late summer when the snow has disappeared from the ledges on this northeast-facing buttress.

ROUTE 11. NORTH RIDGE. II, 2.0. First ascent August 3, 1967, by Leigh Ortenburger and John Lemon. This ridge is encountered if one traverses along the main divide separating Teton Basin on the west from Jackson Hole on the east. From the east it is approached via Alpha-and-Omega Basin, just above the Cascade Canyon patrol cabin. One steep, shattered section of this ridge, between about 10,400 and 10,700 feet, must be negotiated. It is a dangerous undertaking and is not recommended. A snowfield lingers through most of the summer on the plateau just northeast of the summit and can provide sufficient water for an exposed bivouac on the plateau.

FIGURE 7-27. Table Mountain, east aspect, Kindred Spirits (East Face, North Buttress; *Route 10*), III, 5.11

YOSEMITE PEAK (10,015)

(1.6 mi NE of Table Mountain)

Map: Mount Moran

This prominent point forms the northeast end of a long and nearly horizontal ridge extending out from the divide north of Table Mountain. It rises almost directly above the forks of Cascade Canyon. The steep but sloping east face, which resembles the granite rocks of Yosemite, suggested the name for this point. The diminutive north face is also impressive when viewed from the slopes above and north of the forks of the canyon. The highest point of the peak is not easy to find because the summit ridge is almost level. The rarely attained summit provides a fine viewpoint of the west faces of Mount Owen and the Grand and Middle Tetons.

The peak is easily approached via the Cascade Canyon trail from Jenny Lake (see *Cascade Canyon* in Section 8). For the east face routes, continue on the trail into the south fork of the canyon for 0.5 mile, then leave the trail at the north end of a small switchback where one can easily hike up the talus to the base of the face.

Chronology

EAST FACE, WEEKS' CHIMNEY: September 6, 1959, Fred Beckey, Ken Weeks
var—August 19, 1974, Dave Anderson, Mark Jonas, Todd Chavez, Dale Tomrdle
EAST FACE, CHOUINARD: September 4–5, 1961, Yvon Chouinard, Charles Ostin; FFA August 13, 1969, Steve Wunsch, Jim Erickson
var—August 12, 1967, Jim Erickson, Sheldon Smith
NORTH FACE: August 4, 1963, Peter Koedt, Rich Kettler
var—August 22, 1974, Rich Halgren, Jim Wheeler, Gene Francis
var—**SOMETHING YOSEMITE LIKE:** Date unknown, David Bywater, Helen Bowers
WEST LEDGES: August 4, 1963, Peter Koedt, Rich Kettler (descent)
EAST FACE, TREE SURGEON: July 27, 1974, Lincoln Freeze, Bob Horton
PENSIVE: August 1986, Dave Carman, Bill Givens
THE SNAKE: August 31, 1988, Jim Woodmencey, John Carr
NORTH BUTTRESS: July 1, 2015, Paul Horton, Carol Viau, Mike Werner

ROUTE 1. WEST LEDGES. II, 2.0. First descent August 4, 1963, by Peter Koedt and Rich Kettler. From the patrol cabin near the forks of the Cascade Canyon trail, bushwhack southwest up into the drainage below Alpha-and-Omega Lakes. This attractive, small canyon opens out below the west slope of Yosemite Peak. Various routes are available on this slope to gain the nearly level summit ridge; the original line was described as a couloir. All will lead to the ridge crest somewhat south or southwest of the highest point, for which a diligent search must be made.

ROUTE 2. THE SNAKE. III, 5.10. First ascent August 31, 1988, by Jim Woodmencey and John Carr. (See *Figure 7-28*.) Near the lower left (south) edge of the main east face is a horizontal inclusion of black rock that conveys the appearance of the head of a snake. It begins just to the right (north) of the gully forming the extreme south edge of the face. This route of four leads starts at the left (south) end of the "snake" with a 5.9 mantel move to get into a left-facing corner (5.10-); climb up to and through the black rock to the upper edge of the snake for the belay. The second lead traverses right (5.6) to a right-facing dihedral and face that is climbed up to a belay ledge with a fixed piton. The next pitch starts with a 5.8 wide crack up to an overhanging block, which is passed on the left into a series of sloping ledges, cracks, and faces to a belay ledge below the upper left-facing corner system. The fourth pitch begins with a 5.7 hand crack, which then leads up to a difficult undercling and lieback (5.10). If desired, a 5.5 escape that avoids the difficult finish is available at the right edge of the large, sloping belay ledge. For descent scramble up and left to treed ledges, cross the gully, and descend grassy slopes (with intermittent slabs) until it is possible to cut back north to the bottom of the gully and the base of the route. The rock is very solid on this route but expect some vegetation. **Gear:** For protection take a regular rack to 3.5" with doubles of 2.5" to 3".

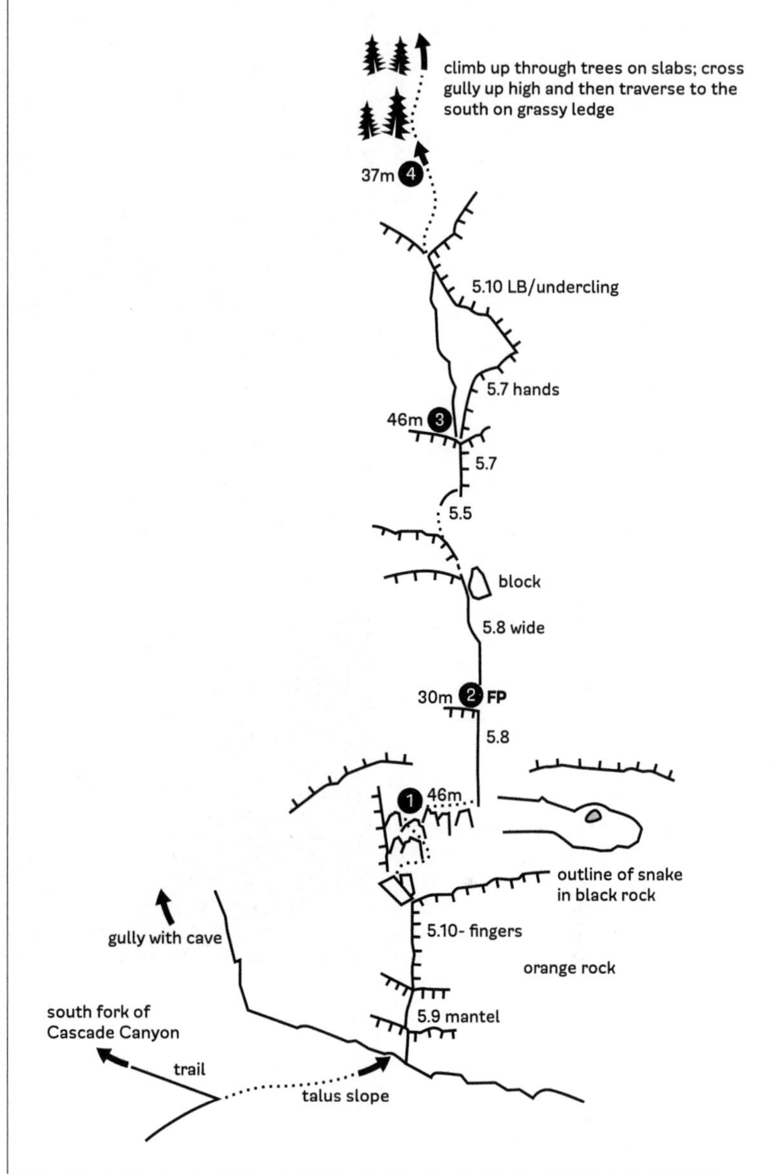

FIGURE 7-28. Yosemite Peak, east face, The Snake *(Route 2)*, III, 5.10

ROUTE 3. EAST FACE, TREE SURGEON. II, 5.8. First ascent July 27, 1974, by Lincoln

Freeze and Bob Horton. This route starts in a broken chimney in the main east face about 120m left (south) of the obvious chimney that cuts up through the entire face. Perhaps the best identifier of the route is a large, cave-like overhang directly above, with some small trees and bushes to the left. Climb the chimney and move up into the cave-like structure for the belay. Now climb the face, head around the corner to the left, and then go up cracks into a chimney, belaying as high up as possible. The third lead climbs up out of the chimney (5.6) and follows a crack up sloping slabs until directly beneath an overhang with a thin crack in it. From a belay under the overhang move left 6m, then follow a corner and cracks above, ultimately climbing a crack on the left (5.8) to a ledge; then step right into a dirty chimney that is climbed up to trees. Climb over trees to a large ledge. From here scramble left up a corner to a second large ledge. Directly above is a 3rd-class gully that is easily climbed. **Gear:** For protection take a regular rack including a selection of wired stoppers and cams to 4".

ROUTE 4. PENSIVE. III, 5.10. First ascent in August 1986, by Dave Carman and Bill Givens. The name of this route adequately describes how others have felt on this particular wall while contemplating the upper overhangs. The route starts approximately 60m to the south of *Route 5*. Begin by climbing a perfect lieback crack located left (south) of a large left-facing corner. The lieback crack leads upward through some slightly loose blocks to a belay on a ledge left of a large flake. Traverse south (5.8, then 5.6) to a grassy ledge that leads up and right. Continue up and right and then straight up on grassy ledges. Move the belay up and left to a pillar that is situated below and left of a big roof. From the pillar climb up and left over a small roof and up a slab to a belay beneath a slot. The crux fifth pitch goes up through this slot (5.9) and then up via 5.10 face climbing (marginal protection) to a very large, tree-covered ledge. For the descent proceed south along this ledge until easy scrambling takes one back to the trail in the south fork of Cascade Canyon.

ROUTE 5. EAST FACE, CHOUINARD. IV, 5.9, A3, or IV, 5.10-. First ascent September 4–5, 1961, by Yvon Chouinard and Charles Ostin; first free ascent August 13, 1969, by Steve Wunsch and Jim Erickson. (See *Figures 7-29* and *7-30*.) This route can be found by looking for a gray right-facing corner just left of an orange pillar at the base of the face. A short pitch (5.6) angling left on ledges leads to the start of this 5.9 corner pitch. The third lead continues up the corner for 6m and then traverses right (5.8) and up across a face to a belay ledge. The next pitch goes up via face climbing to the left of and then around to the right of (5.9) an amazing flake, finishing on a diagonal ramp sloping up and left. The fifth lead, the Jungle Pitch, is very strenuous (5.10-) and at best unpleasant, going up a dirt- and moss-filled right-facing corner past a fixed piton onto a belay ledge. Now climb left past a small corner and up a right-facing corner to a ledge and onto the top of a large block where a belay can be made. The seventh pitch angles right past another fixed piton up a left-facing corner and onto the first major horizontal ledge that extends all the way across the face. Climb a vertical hand crack above the ledge, using a hand traverse at its top to pass a small overhang to gain a belay ledge above, just below the second major horizontal ledge or terrace. The ninth lead goes up a large chimney above the terrace to a belay ledge. The final pitch goes up through a section of overhangs on poor rock, weaving right and then left to a right-facing corner; hand traverses are used to reach and then exit from this

FIGURE 7-29. Yosemite Peak, northeast aspect. (A) East Face, Chouinard *(Route 5)*, IV, 5.10-; (B) East Face, Weeks' Chimney *(Route 6)*, III, 5.7; (C) North Face *(Route 7)*, variation: Something Yosemite Like, II, 5.9; (D) North Buttress *(Route 8)*, II, 5.7

corner. The rock eases off at the top of this pitch and the climbing is much easier up and right to the summit. For descent, use the large couloir that cuts through the middle of the entire east face back down to the trail. See *American Alpine Journal* 13, no. 1 (1962): pp. 216–20.

Variation: IV, 5.10-, A2. First ascent August 12, 1967, by Jim Erickson and Sheldon Smith. This major variation of six pitches starts about 30m to the left (south) of the Chouinard route; goes up to a huge, impassable roof; and traverses 30m to the right to join the original 1961 route. The first lead (37m) begins with a short jam crack (5.7) up the left side of a large pillar on the face, leading into a dark, overhanging chimney for the belay. The next pitch (30m) ascends two thin cracks (5.6) up and right until the chimney opens onto smooth, low-angle slabs. The third lead (5.8, 30m) goes up the short, damp, overhanging cleft in the wall to the left and then traverses across slabs to a small belay stance. The next lead (18m) is severe, moving right and then up a very thin, poorly protected crack (5.10-) on small holds over a small overhang to a downsloping belay position under a wet roof. The roof and the dihedral above are then climbed (18m) on aid (A2) to a pitifully small belay stance just under the huge roof. The final exciting pitch (37m) traverses under the roof overhangs for 24m on very small holds (5.9) across wicked, short slabs to a crack that leads up to a belay stance; protection on this lead is poor. From the end of this lead one can step around the corner to the right to join the Chouinard route at an undetermined location (it is possible that this is at the base of the seventh pitch or simply on the first major ledge). **Gear:** Knifeblade pitons and very small nuts are useful on this climb.

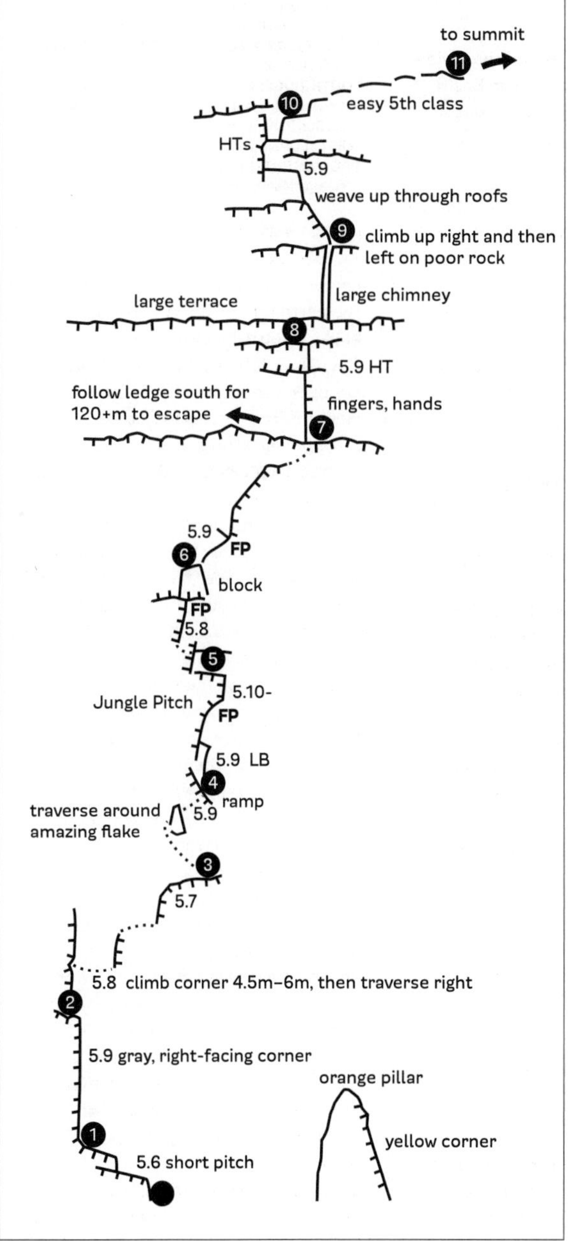

FIGURE 7-30. Yosemite Peak, East Face, Chouinard *(Route 5)*, IV, 5.10-

ROUTE 6. EAST FACE, WEEKS' CHIMNEY. III, 5.7. First ascent September 6, 1959, by Fred Beckey and Ken Weeks. (See *Figure 7-29.*) Two broad, tree-covered ledges divide the smooth east face of Yosemite Peak into three equal horizontal sections. Rising diagonally from lower left to upper right is a long chimney or crack that intersects the lower of these ledges and comes close to the bottom (northern) end of the upper ledge; this chimney is a major feature of the right-hand (northern) portion of the east face. The first 30m of this chimney is 5.7. Follow the chimney to the second ledge, then traverse out to the right on this ledge to the crest of the ridge that marks the extreme right edge of the east face. Follow this ridge to the summit. See *American Alpine Journal* 12, no. 1 (1960): pp. 125–27.

Variation: III, 5.8, A1. First ascent August 19, 1974, by Dave Anderson, Mark Jonas, Todd Chavez, and Dale Tomrdle. The first three pitches of this route are on the ramp to the right of Weeks' Chimney, intersecting the chimney where it turns straight up the face. Here is the crux of this variation, which evidently required some A1 on the first and likely only ascent of this route. Two pitches then go up the wall to the right of the chimney to the first large ledge. Scramble up the northeast ridge to within two leads of the top, then climb on the left side of the ridge (5.8) to the summit slabs. One needs a wide selection of protection devices on this climb.

ROUTE 7. NORTH FACE. II, 5.8. First ascent August 4, 1963, by Peter Koedt and Rich Kettler. From the trail in the vicinity of the patrol cabin at the forks of Cascade Canyon, bushwhack up the drainage just north of Yosemite Peak toward the north face rising directly above, surmounting a broken abutment and the diagonal chimney system beyond, to reach a large tree below the middle of the face. The first 46m pitch starts 6m above, behind a large block/flake, and leads up an open book that has a jam crack in its right face. Climb this jam crack or the face to the left to some broken rock; bear slightly right to reach a belay stance on a large ledge. Proceed up a large, obvious open book for 6m, cut back slightly to the left, and then climb up a system of parallel jam cracks in high-angle rock for 6m until it is possible to traverse onto a small, grassy ledge. After another 5m on easy, broken rock, reach a large, grassy belay ledge. From the left end of this ledge, climb directly up an obvious 90° open book to a large ledge, about 10m left of the large tree at the top of the face. From here, easy scrambling to the right along the ledge and then up leads to the summit. For descent, the first-ascent party utilized a west couloir that heads about 100m south of the summit. The couloir ends in a drop-off, which is avoided by taking a ledge back to the right (north) over to the base of the north face.

Variation: II, 5.8. First ascent August 22, 1974, by Rich Halgren, Jim Wheeler, and Gene Francis. This variation was described as the "right corner of the east buttress." For the approach, scramble up the middle of the face and work toward the left. A chimney/offwidth formed by a large flake near the top of the face will be seen approximately 60m east of the summit. This climb trends up and left toward this flake and consists of two pitches (both 5.8) of crack and face climbing.

Variation: **SOMETHING YOSEMITE LIKE.** II, 5.9. First ascent by David Bywater and Helen Bowers (date unknown). (See *Figure 7-29.*) **Pitch 1:** Begin to the right of the main North Face route at the lowest portion of the face, just left of the couloir dividing the face from a buttress at the western end of the face. Face climb up on good rock to the rightmost (westernmost) of two left-facing corners midway up the face. Belay at the base of this corner (5.8, 30m). **Pitch 2:** Climb the corner until it ends, then continue up and left to a small, grassy ledge (5.9, 37m). At this point the route joins the main North Face route to the summit. This party descended off the south shoulder of the peak into the south fork of Cascade Canyon.

ROUTE 8. NORTH BUTTRESS. II, 5.7. First ascent July 1, 2015, by Paul Horton, Carol Viau, and Mike Werner. (See *Figure 7-29.*) The north buttress of Yosemite Peak is separated from the north face by a deep couloir. Start this route near the base of the couloir and ascend a blunt arête to right-leaning ramps that lead up to a nice ledge at the bottom of a dihedral. Climb the dihedral to the overhang at its head; traverse right to attain a large, prominent curving crack; and follow the crack to its end at a ledge with big blocks. At the left end of the ledge, face climb and follow shallow grooves up and right to the top of the steep buttress. Scramble about 100m on or near the ridge up to the nearly level summit crest. The rock on the route is generally sound but often dirty.

PEAK 10,650

(0.9 mi N of Table Mountain)
Map: Mount Moran

This easily climbed peak lies on the divide at the head of Alpha-and-Omega Basin, the delightful upper canyon just south of the Wigwams that harbors the twin Alpha-and-Omega Lakes.

ROUTE 1. SOUTH RIDGE. I, 1.0. First recorded descent August 3, 1967, by Leigh Ortenburger and John Lemon. Climb or descend this easy ridge.

ROUTE 2. NORTH RIDGE. I, 1.0. First recorded ascent August 3, 1967, by Leigh Ortenburger and John Lemon. The pair found an unusual cairn with no record on the summit.

SOUTH WIGWAM (10,840)

Map: Mount Moran

West of the Grand Teton on the ridge crest that forms the hydrographic divide between Jackson Hole and Teton Basin is a series of peaks (Mount Owen Quartz Monzonite formation) that have a conical or wigwam appearance when viewed from the east. These were named by Fritiof Fryxell in the first years of Grand Teton National Park. It is not known how many wigwams Fryxell had in mind, but two are listed in this book. This southern peak is in fact a double peak with a northern subsummit (10,800+).

ROUTE 1. SOUTH RIDGE. I, 2.0. First recorded ascent August 3, 1967, by Leigh Ortenburger and John Lemon. This ridge is easier than the north ridge.

NORTH WIGWAM (10,855)

(2.0 mi N of Table Mountain)
Map: Mount Moran

This peak is the highest of the Wigwams, and although records do not indicate an ascent prior to 1954, it offers little difficulty from either the west or the south. There are two cairns on the summit. The east ridge is the most prominent feature of the peak, ending with a separate tower (10,480+) and a sharp drop-off into Cascade Canyon.

Chronology

NORTHWEST RIDGE: [probable] August 3, 1954, Richard Armstrong, Hugh Rollins
EAST RIDGE: [probable] August 3, 1954, Richard Armstrong, Hugh Rollins (descent); August 18, 1957, William and Evelyn Cropper (ascent)
var—**EAST TOWER:** July 28, 1947, E. W. Marshall, H. D. Holland
SOUTH RIDGE: August 18, 1957, William and Evelyn Cropper (descent); [probable] 1958, Howard Stagner Jr., Bob Perkins (ascent)
WEST SLOPE: July 12, 1960, Arthur J. Reyman
WIGWAM BUTTRESS: July 23, 1990, Leo Larson, George Montopoli

ROUTE 1. WEST SLOPE. I, 2.0. First ascent July 12, 1960, by Arthur J. Reyman. This slope can be easily approached from the trail in the north fork of Teton Canyon.

ROUTE 2. SOUTH RIDGE. I, 1.0. First descent August 18, 1957, by William and Evelyn Cropper; probable first ascent in 1958, by Howard Stagner Jr. and Bob Perkins. This ridge presents no difficulties.

ROUTE 3. EAST RIDGE. I, 3.0. Probable first descent August 3, 1954, by Richard Armstrong and Hugh Rollins; first ascent August 18, 1957, by William and Evelyn Cropper. The upper flat crest of this ridge can be easily attained from either Mica Lake to the north or the basin to the south after an approach via the north fork of Cascade Canyon (see *Cascade Canyon* in Section 8). It can also be reached from the north ridge by traversing around on a snowfield below the uppermost north face.

Variation: **EAST TOWER.** I, 4.0. First ascent July 28, 1947, by E. W. Marshall and H. D. Holland. This prominent tower is climbed from the notch separating it from the upper east ridge. There are minor towers both on the west of this larger tower and on the east.

ROUTE 4. NORTHWEST RIDGE. I, 3.0. Probable first ascent August 3, 1954, by Richard Armstrong and Hugh Rollins. This ridge must be negotiated if one traverses the divide between Littles Peak and Table Mountain. However, it consists of steep, shattered sedimentary rock and is not recommended.

ROUTE 5. WIGWAM BUTTRESS. III, 5.9. First ascent July 23, 1990, by Leo Larson and

George Montopoli. This is the prominent buttress to the south when viewed from a point that is approximately 1.25 miles up the north fork of Cascade Canyon, just after the second footbridge (see *Cascade Canyon* in Section 8). Leave the trail here and proceed up a talus field from which a tree-covered ledge is accessed; continue back east on this ledge to locate a dihedral, encountered just before reaching the corner of the buttress at a dead snag. Climb the dihedral and 5.6 cracks above to another tree-covered ledge. Walk right a short distance to a crack system that goes up and right. Climb this pitch, which ends with a 5.8 traverse back left (east) to a belay at a big flake. The third pitch continues straight up (5.5, no protection) to an alcove and then ends with a 5.7 traverse west below a number of overhangs. Now climb a corner that avoids two overhangs (the second one is large) on their eastern edges. The 50m fourth pitch climbs the 5.9 dihedral above (obvious from below). From the belay at the top, climb up and right on easy 5th-class terrain and then up via a 5.8 face to a belay on much easier ground. Scramble 15m to the east to a number of large flakes. The sixth and final pitch begins in a 5.8 jam crack, and then easier climbing leads to the top of "GeoLeo Pinnacle." From here a 15m rappel leads to a notch. One hundred and fifty meters of easy- to mid-5th-class scrambling provides access to the summit of the buttress. Exit to the south and descend the drainage to the east.

PEAK 10,720+

(1.85 mi SW of Littles Peak)
Map: Mount Moran

This unmarked high point due west of Mica Lake on the divide achieves peak status, while Point 10,686 just north does not. The easiest way to get to Mica Lake is via the north fork of Cascade Canyon (see *Cascade Canyon* in Section 8): Take the trail to just below Lake Solitude, where the drainage coming down from Mica Lake is encountered. Follow the drainage to the lake, then continue up the peak.

ROUTE 1. SOUTH RIDGE. I, 1.0. First recorded descent August 3, 1954, by Richard Armstrong and Hugh Rollins. This is an easy ridge.

ROUTE 2. NORTH RIDGE. I, 1.0. First recorded ascent August 3, 1954, by Richard Armstrong and Hugh Rollins. This ridge is easily climbed as one marches along the divide south of Littles Peak.

LITTLES PEAK (10,712)

Map: Mount Moran

This peak, while minor in terms of its height and aspect, is a major Teton summit because of its location. Littles Peak is something of a landmark for traffic out of Cascade Canyon headed north on a high-level approach to the heads of Leigh Canyon, Moran Canyon, or even Moose Basin. Easily accessible from the west as well as from Lake Solitude to the east, it was one of the earlier high peaks in the range to be climbed. A few decades later, on October 16, 1931, Littles Peak was ascended by Earl M. Buckingham, who established a triangulation station, known as "Leigh Station," on the summit.

ROUTE 1. WEST RIDGE. I, 1.0. Probable first ascent in 1899, by T. M. Bannon and party, or August 24, 1912, by Eliot Blackwelder and Mack Lake. The original quadrangle map, issued in 1901, indicates a benchmark on the summit, so Bannon's topographic party must have climbed the peak. The geologist Blackwelder and his assistant also climbed the peak during the course of his geological study of the west slope of the Teton Range. The west ridge of this peak is easily reached and climbed from the trail in Granite Basin.

ROUTE 2. ▲ EAST RIDGE. I, 2.0. First recorded ascent September 1, 1933, by Dudley Hayden, who was on official duty as a park ranger to intercept a herd of sheep illegally crossing the divide into Leigh Canyon. (It is felt by some that perhaps the sheep should be credited with the first ascent.) This narrow horizontal ridge connects the summit of Littles Peak with the extensive, high, flat plateau above and west of Lake Solitude. Hayden reached this plateau in 1933 by ascending the slopes due west of the lake to the saddle (10,320+) that marks the south end of the plateau. It is now more commonly reached via the large couloir that leads northwest from the lake, providing a straightforward route past the headwall up onto the plateau, about 1 mile east of the summit. Proceed west to the summit along the slender but easy ridge. In descending from Littles Peak to the lake, remember that this couloir heads near the southeastern edge of the plateau. The portion of the headwall south of this couloir can be negotiated on either the ascent or the descent but requires adroit routefinding and some serious scrambling among the wet cliffs. **Time:** 1 hour from Lake Solitude.

ROUTE 3. NORTH RIDGE. I, 1.0. First descent September 1, 1933, by Dudley Hayden; first ascent September 1, 1941, by Fritiof Fryxell and Bob Crist, in one day after hiking up Moran Canyon from String Lake. This ridge has become the standard route for access into the south fork of Moran Canyon from the east side of the range. There are no difficulties, and a rough trail can be found from the saddle (10,000+) at the head of Leigh Canyon.

PEAK 10,245

(1.8 mi ESE of Littles Peak)
Map: Mount Moran

This minor peak is a high point on the ridge between Littles Peak and Paintbrush Divide north of Cascade Canyon. The higher point to the west, Point 10,538, was climbed on July 12, 1960, by Arthur J. Reyman.

Chronology

WEST RIDGE: July 11, 1960, Arthur J. Reyman
NORTHEAST CHUTE: August 14, 1961, Ed Bellero, Ingmar Olafson, Rolf Schette
EAST RIDGE: September 2, 1976, Leigh Ortenburger

ROUTE 1. WEST RIDGE. I, 1.0. First known ascent July 11, 1960, by Arthur J. Reyman. The southwest slope leading to this ridge and the ridge itself are easily climbed directly from Lake Solitude.

ROUTE 2. EAST RIDGE. I, 1.0. First ascent September 2, 1976, by Leigh Ortenburger. From the trail at Paintbrush Divide proceed westward easily along this rocky ridge to the summit.

ROUTE 3. NORTHEAST CHUTE. I, 2.0. First ascent August 14, 1961, by Ed Bellero, Ingmar Olafson, and Rolf Schette. Proceed from the high basin northwest of Paintbrush Divide.

PEAK 10,880+

(1.25 mi WSW of Mount Woodring)
Map: Mount Moran

This easy summit lies but a short distance north of Paintbrush Divide, which is reached by trail from either the north fork of Cascade Canyon or Paintbrush Canyon (see Section 8).

Chronology

NORTHWEST SLOPE: August 1, 1954, William Buckingham, Betty Bierer
SOUTH RIDGE: ca. August 23, 1958, Howard R. Stagner Jr., Richard Byrd

ROUTE 1. ▲ SOUTH RIDGE. I, 1.0. First recorded ascent on about August 23, 1958, by Howard R. Stagner Jr. and Richard Byrd. This is an easy hike from the trail, which is only 60m below the summit.

ROUTE 2. NORTHWEST SLOPE. I, 1.0. First ascent August 1, 1954, by William Buckingham and Betty Bierer. This pair likely wandered up from the upper reaches of Leigh Canyon as they traversed across Paintbrush Divide and over to Mount Fryxell.

MOUNT FRYXELL (PEAK 11,270)

(1.5 mi NW of the Jaw)
Map: Mount Moran

Although not usually an objective by itself, this high peak with a double summit forms a good viewpoint if one has time to spare while hiking the trail from Cascade Canyon to Paintbrush Canyon. It is also climbed by energetic climbers making the traverse from the Jaw at the head of Hanging Canyon to Paintbrush Divide. During their August 1, 1954, ascent of the northwest ridge, William Buckingham and Betty Bierer found an empty cairn on the point (10,960+) just northwest of the summit; this was probably the summit reached by William Shand on August 4, 1943. Although this peak is now commonly referred to as Mount Fryxell, in honor of prolific Teton first ascensionist, geologist, and writer Fritiof Fryxell, that is not its official name. It is truly astonishing as well as a serious omission that no summit in the Teton Range *officially* bears the name of such a towering figure in Teton climbing history. This author (R. Jackson) would like to see "Mount Fryxell" become firmly established in the coming years.

ROUTE 1. SOUTHEAST RIDGE. I, 2.0. First descent August 1, 1954, by William Buckingham and Betty Bierer; first ascent August 2, 1958, by Paul Salstrom and Robert Marshall. The ridge from the saddle (10,480+) between this peak and McClintock Peak is straightforward. From this saddle, the gully with the stream descending to the southwest toward the bridge over Cascade Creek makes a fast descent route. Stay west of the stream.

ROUTE 2. LEAPING DEER COULOIR. II, 3.0, snow. First known ascent July 21, 2017, by Vivian Lee and Peter Lenz. With snow, this steep eastern couloir leading directly to the summit is a worthy climb. Beware of rockfall. The upper section sometimes melts into the shape of a leaping deer. (Source: Mountain Project)

ROUTE 3. ▲ NORTHWEST RIDGE. I, 2.0. First known ascent August 1, 1954, by William Buckingham and Betty Bierer. Take either the Cascade Canyon trail or the Paintbrush Canyon trail (see *Cascade Canyon* and *Paintbrush Canyon* in Section 8) to Paintbrush Divide, from which this ridge is a straightforward scramble. A cairn but no record was found on the summit. When snow is present, the upper part of the ridge can be attained directly from Paintbrush Canyon via a steep snowfield and couloir.

MCCLINTOCK PEAK (10,960+)

(1.2 mi W of the Jaw)
Map: Mount Moran

The only intriguing feature of this otherwise undistinguished peak is its conspicuous rocky south ridge, which contains a number of small towers and apparently some pretty rotten rock. One of these small towers was climbed by Eddie and Trevor Bowman on June 16, 2000, at which time it earned the name "Toppling."

ROUTE 1. EAST RIDGE. I, 2.0. First descent June 23, 1931, by H. L. and Frank McClintock and Carl Sampson; first ascent August 2, 1958, by Paul Salstrom and Robert Marshall. Climb the easy ridge from the saddle (10,480+) separating this peak from Buckingham Palace. This ridge is commonly done as part of a traverse westward from the Jaw and Hanging Canyon (see *Hanging Canyon* in Section 8).

ROUTE 2. NORTH RIDGE. I, 3.0. First ascent June 23, 1931, by H. L. and Frank McClintock and Carl Sampson; Frank was 10 years old at the time. From Paintbrush Canyon (see *Paintbrush Canyon* in Section 8), ascend the gully leading to the saddle west of this peak. An ice axe will be useful in early season. From the saddle the summit is reached by ascending the easy ridge above.

BUCKINGHAM PALACE (11,097)

(0.7 mi W of the Jaw)
Map: Mount Moran

This peak, which apparently remained unclimbed until 1958, consists of three summits; the west summit is the highest.

ROUTE 1. EAST RIDGE. I, 3.0. First ascent June 21, 1958, by William Buckingham and Margaret West. After climbing the Jaw from Hanging Canyon (see *The Jaw* in Section 8), continue traversing west, passing over Window Point (11,120+) on the way. The ridge can also be reached from the south by scrambling up the steep slopes above the Cascade Canyon trail (see *Cascade Canyon* in Section 8). The ridge itself from the high saddle (10,640+) to the east is an easy scramble; the part between the central and western summits is the most interesting. See *American Alpine Journal* 11, no. 2 (1959): pp. 307–9.

ROUTE 2. NORTHWEST RIDGE. I, 3.0. First ascent August 1, 1958, by Paul Salstrom and Robert Marshall. Leave the Paintbrush Canyon trail (see *Paintbrush Canyon* in Section 8) at about 9,500 feet and ascend the loose rock and steep snow to the saddle between McClintock Peak and Buckingham Palace. From the col walk up to the summit.

SECTION 8

Cascade Canyon to Leigh Canyon

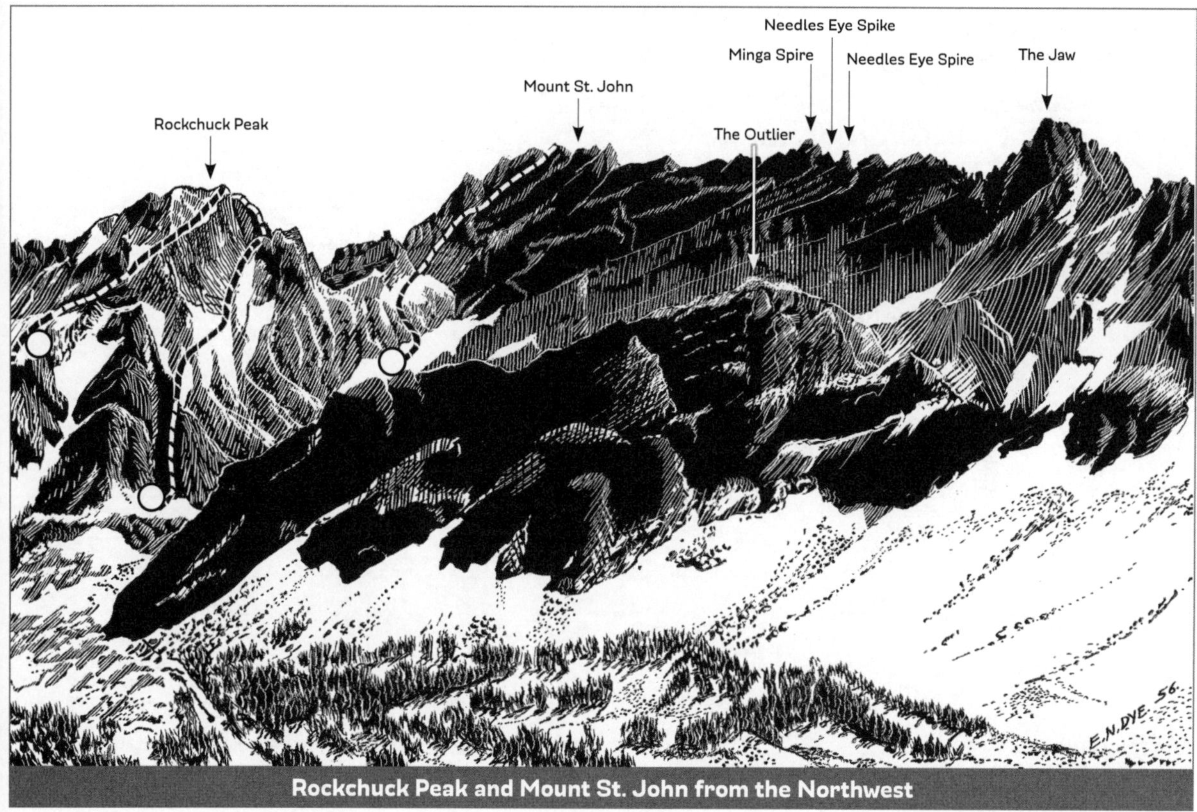

Rockchuck Peak and Mount St. John from the Northwest

Cascade Canyon

Cascade Canyon is the central, largest, and best-known canyon in the Teton Range. It contains the most heavily traveled trails, with Lake Solitude, at the head of the north fork, being a principal tourist attraction. The Cascade Canyon south fork trail connects with the Death Canyon trail via Hurricane Pass (10,320+) and Alaska Basin, and the north fork trail joins the trail in Paintbrush Canyon by way of the high Paintbrush Divide (10,560+). This system is known as the Teton Crest Trail. The Cascade Canyon trail provides, as described here, access to the Symmetry Couloir, the Teewinot–Owen cirque, and Dartmouth Basin. These in turn can be used to approach Teewinot Mountain, Mount Owen, the three Tetons, the peaks along the divide, and all the peaks and pinnacles on the ridge north of Cascade Canyon, such as Storm Point and Symmetry Spire. Valhalla Canyon, also accessed from Cascade Canyon, is discussed separately (see *Valhalla Canyon* in Section 4).

The spectacular Hidden Falls, near the beginning of the Cascade Canyon trail, can be reached in three ways. (1) The easiest option is to take the boat across Jenny Lake from the boat dock at the south end of the Jenny Lake campground area and hike 0.5 mile from the west shore boat dock. (2) Another option is to hike 2.5 miles from the east shore boat dock around the south side of Jenny Lake via the trail past Moose Ponds to the falls. (3) It is also possible to start from String Lake, cross the bridge at the southern end of that lake, and hike 2.2 miles around the north and northwest sides of Jenny Lake. From the cutoff for the Hidden Falls viewpoint, the Cascade Canyon trail crosses Cascade Creek, switchbacks above the cutoff for 0.3 mile to Inspiration Point (7,200), and then pushes beyond into Cascade Canyon. Because this segment of the trail can be extremely congested, from the west shore boat dock the fastest route for climbers going farther west into the canyon is to use the horse trail: Hike north approximately 0.2 mile on the Valley Trail to where the horse trail (marked) takes off to the west through the trees for 0.7 mile. After emerging from the last trees, the final upper section of the horse trail traverses horizontally south to join the level portion of the main Cascade Canyon trail beyond Inspiration Point. It is easy and fast going on this horizontal section of the trail to the forks (4.5 miles from the boat dock).

Symmetry Couloir: About halfway along the upper horizontal section (above the switchbacks) of the horse trail, a stream that descends from the main drainage between Ice Point/Storm Point and

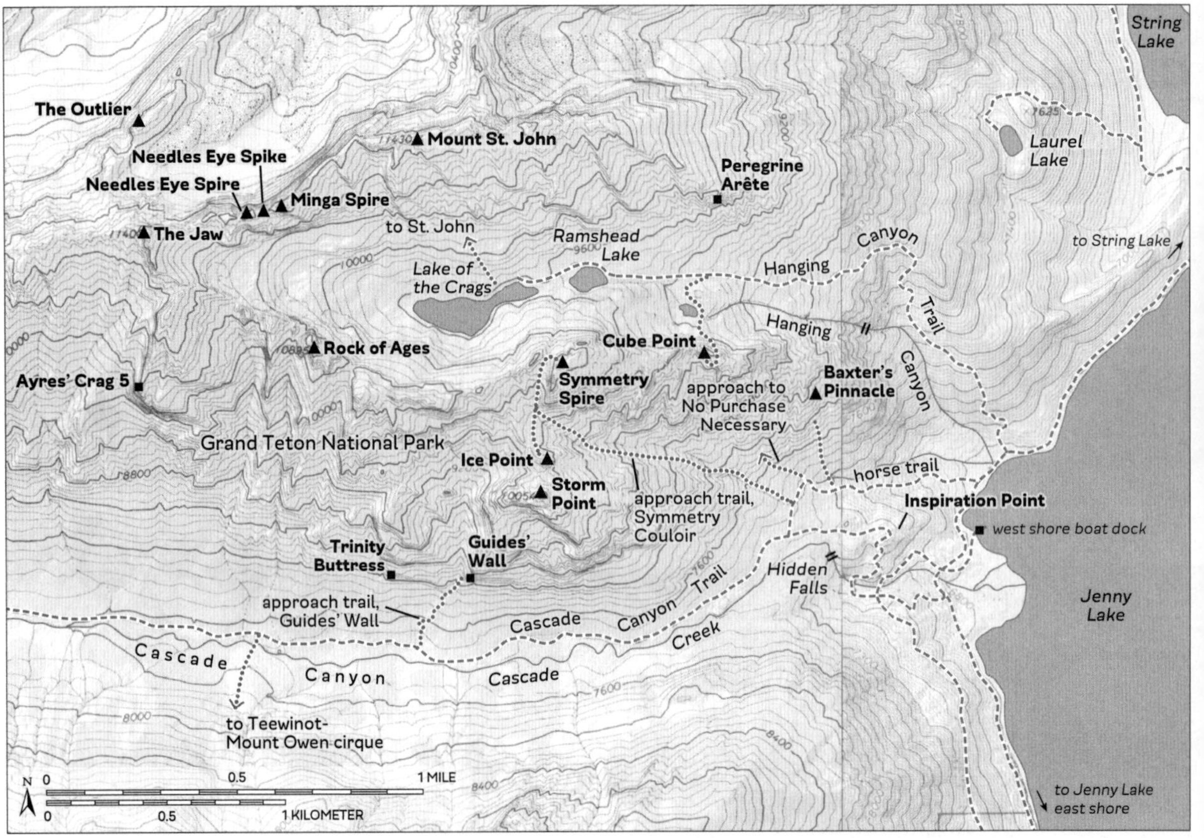

Symmetry Spire will be crossed. Just before (north of) this stream a small climbers' trail leads uphill to the right (west) through bushes and boulders, paralleling the streambed, toward a small cliff band. Upon reaching the cliff band, bear right into a secondary cul-de-sac where a short (5m) scramble accesses the top of the cliff band. Follow the trail as it leads left (south) along the top of this band, cross the main drainage, and zigzag up the open slopes above, following a climbers' trail.

In late season this broad couloir, which narrows at its top, is just talus and scree, but in early season and midseason it contains a moderately steep snowfield. This has been the scene of many accidents, some fatal. The moats that open up in early season are commonly in the main fall line and are especially dangerous. *Beware.* A rope and an ice axe, plus the knowledge of how to use it for self-arrest, are essential for safety in this heavily traveled couloir.

At the apex of the snowfield or the trail (depending upon the season), look for a secondary gully out to the north that comes down from the main Ice Point–Symmetry Spire saddle (there is a small waterfall here, again seasonally dependent). Head right (north) and scramble up a low-angle cliffband, following bits of trail here and there (there is loose, shattered rock in this area). One can now proceed easily up to the saddle using the slope to the right (north) of the gully. The base of Symmetry Spire's south face and its southern ridges are also readily reached by bearing right up past a few scattered trees.

Teewinot–Owen Cirque: The major cirque between Teewinot Mountain and Mount Owen provides access to the north, northwest, and west routes on Teewinot and the Crooked Thumb and to the northeast and north routes on Mount Owen. Climbers should expect some problems in crossing Cascade Creek, but with luck and some advance searching a log can often be located, permitting a dry passage. Inquire at the Jenny Lake Ranger Station as to the location of a suitable log. One suggestion is to hike west on the Cascade Canyon trail until past the point where the streams descending from the northeast snowfields of Mount Owen empty into the creek, and then cross where there is a very large boulder on the south side of the creek. Logs spanning the creek can sometimes be found in this area, but scouting the situation the day before the proposed ascent is recommended. Sometimes one must wade across the swift and cold creek, which can be difficult and dangerous, especially in early season when the water is high. The bushwhacking up into the Teewinot–Owen cirque is not easy. Early routes used the left (east) side of the drainage, but most parties now hike up through the trees on the right (west) side of the drainage or in a boulder-filled gully just to the west of the trees. Either way, scramble up the talus below the first snowfield. A campsite can be found in the lower reaches of the cirque beneath a very large boulder.

South Fork: At the head of the south fork of Cascade Canyon is a subsidiary trail leading to the saddle (10,560+) west of the South Teton; this provides climbers with a route into the north fork of Avalanche Canyon.

The south fork of Cascade Canyon can also be used to access Dartmouth Basin, which offers climbers an interesting alternative to the customary Garnet Canyon approach to the Lower Saddle. About 1 mile south of the forks of the canyon, leave the trail and cross the creek; turn left (east) up the ravine leading toward Dartmouth Basin, which lies immediately west of the Lower Saddle. A small bit of bushwhacking is necessary, but after the initial waterfall is passed on the left (north) the going is easier. A beautiful, unspoiled, grassy meadow for camping is passed at about 9,600 feet before the basin itself is reached. The west side of the Lower Saddle is protected by cliffs containing loose rock; these cliffs have been climbed (first by Hayden Survey geologist Frank Bradley in 1872) but are not recommended for either ascent or descent. The preferable route goes to the left (northeast) up a long, easy couloir that passes through the Black Dike and leads to the slopes north of the Lower Saddle. In early season this couloir will be filled with steep snow, requiring caution. To descend via this route from the Lower Saddle, climb toward the Grand Teton almost up to the Black Dike, then contour left (west) to a region of red rock, where the upper reaches of the couloir can be easily entered. There is loose rock in this couloir and caution should be exercised, especially if there is more than one party in it.

North Fork: The main trail provides complete access to this portion of the Teton backcountry. Camping is permitted in specified areas only and a permit is required.

Hanging Canyon

Hanging Canyon, an attractive canyon conveniently located near Jenny Lake, is encircled by the many peaks and crags of the Symmetry Spire–Mount St. John group. It harbors three beautiful alpine lakes—Arrowhead Pool, Ramshead Lake, and Lake of the Crags—which themselves are worthwhile objectives. The usual approach into the canyon is from the boat dock on the west side of Jenny Lake. Take the Valley Trail north past the main stream draining Hanging Canyon. After entering the trees, pass two small bridges before turning left (northwest) onto a small but distinct trail heading off through the trees toward the main open slope leading up into the canyon. The upper section of this unmaintained trail into Hanging Canyon ascends an eroded hillside. To minimize erosional damage caused by multiple social trails, the National Park Service (NPS) has improved this trail; stay on the existing NPS trail to prevent the creation of parallel ruts. At the top of this slope the trail swings left, crosses a small watercourse, and proceeds upward into the canyon, staying on the right (north) side of the stream and the lakes. In early season an ice axe will be useful for the snow that lingers in this area. Fine campsites will be found just east of Ramshead Lake among the charred skeletons of trees. Small campsites can also be found at Lake of the Crags.

Although more tedious and involving some bushwhacking, another approach to the lakes is to contour into the canyon from the north. From the String Lake trailhead, cross the bridge and follow the trail that swings around the west side of String Lake; this trail crosses an open slope on the east side of St. John. Climb up this slope, using a pretty good trail, to and past Laurel Lake. A few hundred feet above Laurel Lake, traverse left (south) toward Hanging Canyon. Some bushwhacking and boulder hopping will be encountered along the way, but the main Hanging Canyon trail should be easy to link up with.

Paintbrush Canyon

The trail in the easily accessible Paintbrush Canyon forms the northern end of the main Teton Crest Trail system and provides easy access to the few peaks of this region. The beginning of the Paintbrush Canyon trail is reached by driving to the Leigh Lake trailhead parking area and taking the String Lake Trail (on the east side of String Lake) to the bridge at the north end of the lake. Cross the bridge and follow the main trail to the left to the first junction; the right fork at this junction is the Paintbrush Canyon trail. The trail in the upper portion of the canyon bifurcates, with the right branch leading to a beautiful tarn, Holly Lake. There are fine campsites in designated locations near this lake. The upper stretches of the trail over Paintbrush Divide (10,560+) into Cascade Canyon will be covered with snow until late season; throughout most of the summer an ice axe will be needed to cross safely over to Lake Solitude.

To reach solitary Grizzly Bear Lake from Paintbrush Canyon, do not aim for the low point of the divide between Holly Lake and Grizzly Bear Lake because the north side of this saddle is ringed with cliffs. Instead, take the trail to a point (about 10,160+) above and west of this saddle, and from there descend easy slopes into the Grizzly Bear cirque.

To reach the upper portions of Leigh Canyon from Paintbrush Canyon, either descend from Paintbrush Divide into Blister Basin to the northwest or descend the drainage from Grizzly Bear Lake to the floor of Leigh Canyon.

FOURTEEN-HOUR PINNACLE (9,280+)

(0.95 mi SW of the Jaw)
Map: Mount Moran

Bracing the north side of Cascade Canyon, opposite the mouth of Valhalla Canyon, lies this salient pinnacle or pillar. Located about 0.7 mile east of the trail junction in the canyon, Fourteen-Hour Pinnacle forms the extreme end of the south ridge of Buckingham Palace (11,097). From some angles, the notch separating the summit from the wall above cannot be seen, but the pillar still appears as a prominent buttress. Steep and rotten couloirs descend to the east and to the west from the notch. The name, given in advance of the first ascent, reflects the amount of time the team expected the climb would take. The base of the pinnacle is easily approached via the Cascade Canyon trail.

Chronology

SOUTHEAST RIDGE: August 3, 1960, Jake Breitenbach, Sterling Neale
var—**SOUTHEAST FACE:** August 11, 1960, Dick Bonker, William Crowther
SOUTHWEST COULOIR: August 5, 1966, Alan Rubin, Dennis Memhet
DIRECT SOUTH RIDGE: September 7, 1977, George Montopoli, Mugs Stump
SOUTHEAST COULOIR: August 30, 1978, Keith Hadley, Lars Holbeck
EAST FACE, TWENTY-FOUR-HOUR CRACK: August 11, 1983, Peter Koedt, Kevin Dye

ROUTE 1. SOUTHWEST COULOIR. II, 5.6. First ascent August 5, 1966, by Alan Rubin and Dennis Memhet. From the Cascade Canyon trail scramble up the gully to the left (west) of the pinnacle. At the first step, about one-third of the way up the couloir, rope up and climb (5.6) the center of the rock. Scramble up to the next step, and then climb the left corner and in the center for the next four and a half leads. This section contains occasional 5.6 climbing and is very rotten. It leads to the ridge crest, from which one can scramble and climb left to the summit. This route contains much loose rock and is not recommended. There is also natural rockfall on the right side of the gully.

ROUTE 2. DIRECT SOUTH RIDGE. III, 5.10. First ascent September 7, 1977, by George Montopoli and Mugs Stump. See *Figure 8-1* for the line of this eight-pitch route—a recommended climb on good rock. From the Cascade Canyon trail approach the lower end of the south ridge of the pinnacle. Move west along the base until the best steep black rock is found. Begin the climb here above a few obvious large boulders in a gully and approximately 50m west of the toe of the south ridge. **Pitch 1:** Climb straight up through sound black rock that offers good gear and decent holds (5.8); belay just above and west of a large white boulder. **Pitch 2:** Continue up, trending left into a 5.7 corner with good holds, and pass an arête at the top of the corner. Climb out of sight of the belay in a good jam crack, aiming for a 5.8 chimney that is passed on its right at its top, and belay in the sun. **Pitch 3:** Move up through blocky terrain until it steepens, then move right and face climb (airy 5.9, good gear) until it is possible to move back left in a crack and gain a decent ledge with a straight-in jam crack above it in golden rock. Belay just below this crack. **Pitch 4:** Climb the jam crack and pull a bulgy roof (5.10) to gain easier ground. Continue crack climbing, and belay where appropriate. **Pitches 5–6:** This terrain can be broken into two pitches or simul-climbed at 5.7. Belay below a wider section of dirty black rock after about 90m. **Pitch 7:** Climb up clean gray rock (5.7) just to the right of the dirty black rock. Protection for the pitch consists of small cams and wires. Exit the gray rock and trend back left, using a large handrail, to a belay at the base of a chimney. **Pitch 8:** Avoid the chimney by climbing the arête (5.6), then continue up on easier ground to where more simul-climbing leads to the summit. For the descent, continue north along the summit ridge, aiming for the southwest couloir (see *Route 1*). This is a very loose and exposed descent consisting of long sections of downclimbing. Rappels from trees may also be necessary.

ROUTE 3. EAST FACE, TWENTY-FOUR-HOUR CRACK. II, 5.9. First ascent August 11, 1983, by Peter Koedt and Kevin Dye. This entire route stays to the right (east) of the south ridge. From the Cascade Canyon trail approach the pinnacle from the east to gain the bottom of the initial gray-white slabs at the base of this face. Proceed partway up these slabs to a belay "dish" at the right edge, just below the first wall. The first short lead (5.8) goes up and right to the top of a flake. Next, pass two red roofs—the first on the right and the second on the left—via 5.8 climbing to the belay. The crux crack above ascends a section of polished white rock to the left of a dihedral; this polished white rock is separated from the south ridge by a section of red rock. This third pitch starts

FIGURE 8-1. Fourteen-Hour Pinnacle, Direct South Ridge *(Route 2)*, III, 5.10

as 5.8 but becomes 5.9 above and is a sustained, hard-to-protect lead. The next lead, after a short section of 5.8, becomes much easier (5.5) and angles up and left. Two more leads (5.6) bring one to a ledge. After belaying on this ledge, move out right and up for two more leads of similar difficulty to the summit.

ROUTE 4. SOUTHEAST RIDGE. II, 5.6, A1. First ascent August 3, 1960, by Jake Breitenbach and Sterling Neale. This ridge is marked by three overhangs. The first is passed by climbing the white rock to the right. Then climb the crest to the base of the second overhang, which is passed around the corner to the left. The third overhang is also passed on the left. From here the crest of the ridge is followed to the summit. This route involves one direct-aid pitch. See *American Alpine Journal* 12, no. 2 (1961): pp. 373–79.

***Variation:* SOUTHEAST FACE.** II, 5.6, A2. First ascent August 11, 1960, by Dick Bonker and William Crowther. Ascend the lower face and reach a large pulpit-like feature from the right. The face above is marked by two parallel cracks angling up to the right. Climb the lower crack and then go up the overhanging face to a friction pitch. Three of the nine pitches required extensive use of aid. See *American Alpine Journal* 12, no. 2 (1961): pp. 373–79.

ROUTE 5. SOUTHEAST COULOIR. II, 5.6. First ascent August 30, 1978, by Keith Hadley and Lars Holbeck. The couloir on the east or southeast side leading to the notch behind the summit was apparently climbed by this party.

CASCADE CANYON, NORTH SIDE ROCK CLIMBS

Map: Mount Moran

Assembled here, from west to east, are routes that have been climbed on the walls on the north side of Cascade Canyon. These routes are attractive both for their accessibility and their (usually good) rock quality. The lack of exact information concerning the numerous early climbs made in this area in the 1950s and 1960s implies that the attribution of first ascents is doubtful in many cases. As will be seen in the following descriptions, old pitons have been encountered on several of these "new" routes.

Yellow-Bellied Buttress (10,810)

(1.25 mi WSW of the Jaw)

The Yellow-Bellied Buttress is a large, prominent, west-facing buttress that lies north-northeast of the forks of Cascade Canyon, about 300m to 400m above the trail. Hike about two-thirds of a mile up the north fork trail to the point where one emerges from the forested area and the buttress is clearly visible. One can either contour up the hillside above or hike directly up a drainage to the base of the buttress.

ROUTE 1. WEST FACE. III, 5.9. First ascent July 5, 1997, by George Montopoli and Jim Phillips. The base of this climb lies just to the right (south) of the ridge that flanks the north side of the buttress. The first pitch begins on a steep ramp containing several cracks, just to the left of a large detached block (6m by 6m) with a large crack in the middle of it. **Pitch 1:** Climb 20m up cracks in the middle of the ramp (5.6) to a horizontal crack. Step onto the horizontal crack (delicate balance move) and traverse left (5.7, no handholds) until more vertical cracks are reached at the left end of the horizontal crack. Climb these cracks (5.6) to a large belay ledge (50m). A large alcove lies to the right (south). **Pitch 2:** Continue up cracks on the right side of a large detached flake. To reach this flake, from the right end of the belay ledge climb straight up tricky face moves (5.7, 6m) until it is possible to work left to the base of the flake. Ascend the crack on its right side to the top of the flake (5.9 offwidth), then make a difficult finger traverse (5.9, 3m) to easier ground that leads up and right to a belay ledge (46m). **Pitch 3:** From the belay ledge, climb a left-facing corner containing double cracks (5.7, 10m). From the top of the corner scramble up and slightly right to an obvious crack system. Climb this crack system via a series of jamming, liebacking, and offwidth moves (5.8+). At the top of the crack system, climb a steep wall—actually the left side of a deep chimney—to a large belay ledge (50m). **Pitch 4:** Climb a left-facing corner for 15m (5.8), then scramble to another crack system in blocky rock. Ascend this crack system and continue up easy 5th-class rock toward the summit to another large belay ledge (50m). **Pitch 5:** Continue up easy rock to, and through, a 5.5 step-across move just below the top (30m). For the descent use gully systems to the southeast until it is possible to traverse back to the start of the climb. **Gear:** For protection bring a standard rack with stoppers and camming devices to 3".

Banded Buttress

(1.8 mi WSW of the Jaw)

This 300m buttress is located behind and east of Fourteen-Hour Pinnacle. When viewed from Cascade Canyon, it has a moderate eastern edge, a smooth slab halfway up the west edge, and a series of black-and-white bands on the west edge. Also visible from below are two corners in the central part of the buttress and nice-looking cracks in brownish-gold rock near the base.

ROUTE 1. SOUTH FACE. III, 5.9. First ascent July 28, 2001, by Trevor Bowman and Reed Finlay. Approach this climb by ascending the slopes beneath the buttress, aiming for the nice-looking cracks in brownish-gold rock. The first pitch is short, climbing a moderate crack (5.5) to a belay ledge. The second pitch goes up the easternmost crack in the corner to a belay ledge with trees (5.7+, 50m). Traverse about halfway across this ledge (to the west) to a chimney; climb the chimney, then work up and right via easier climbing for a few ropelengths, avoiding the overhangs above. The sixth pitch, the crux for the first-ascent party, goes to the right of the roofs and ascends the leftmost corner to a ledge with a thin flake (5.9, 50m). Several more pitches lead to the flat summit of the buttress. Descent is made to the north down a chossy gully leading to the larger gully between McClintock Peak and Buckingham Palace; go down that gully to reach the trail in Cascade Canyon. **Gear:** A 4" piece was useful on this climb.

Ayres' Crag 5 (11,040+)

(0.2 mi S of the Jaw)

The south wall of Ayres' Crag 5 is the most imposing of those forming the north rim of Cascade Canyon. For the approach, hike about 4 miles up the Cascade Canyon trail to a point directly opposite the north face of Mount Owen. Above and to the north is this nearly vertical south face, which starts at about 9,600 feet. It is bounded on the left (west) by the large open couloir that descends from the

vicinity of the Jaw. (See *Ayres' Crags* later in this section for a route to the top of this buttress.)

ROUTE 1. WEST FACE. II, 5.9. First ascent August 23, 2005, by David Bywater, Leo Larson, and Helen Motter. This climb ascends a right-facing corner system and was the first route on the west face of Ayres' Crag 5. Head up from the Cascade Canyon trail toward the south face of the formation, moving up and west into a gully below the west face and passing a giant chockstone on its left side. Begin the first pitch just up from the chockstone, heading up via wandering face climbing on the left side of a prominent column. This column is situated just below and left of a right-facing corner system that comprises the bulk of the route. Belay on a good ledge on top of the column (5.6, 56m). The second pitch moves up and right into the right-facing corner in a band of dark rock. Climb the corner, via finger locks and stems, until another good belay ledge is encountered at the end of the dark rock and the beginning of a section of lighter rock (5.9, 55m). The third and last pitch ascends a hand-and-fist crack through the light-colored rock to an exit through a short section of loose, blocky, dark rock. From the top of the climb descend by walking off along a ledge system that continues north, past a steep gully, into a broad, low-angle talus field. Go down the talus field to the base of the route.

ROUTE 2. SOUTH FACE. IV, 5.8, A4. First ascent June 23–26, 1963, by Fred Beckey and Steve Marts; attempted September 8, 1960, by Ed Cooper and Ron Niccoli. This original route follows approximately the left skyline of the south face, as seen from the trail when the crag first comes into full view. The main south wall actually faces somewhat southwest and has two apparent summits; the left one is the highest. This somewhat dish-shaped wall has water stains down the middle, and this route lies to the left (west) of these water stains. Ascend the talus directly beneath the highest summit. An overhanging band that bisects the face will be seen slanting upward from left to right. After the first two pitches, which go up and slightly to the right, make a very difficult aid lead, requiring three bolts to pass a slab and ending in a hanging belay. The fourth pitch takes one up to the overhang, which is attacked via an open book, both walls of which overhang. The one rotten piton crack ultimately bottoms out, and three more bolts are required to reach a small belay ledge. With inadequate protection, the next delicate lead works upward, free and slightly left, to a rocky ledge about halfway up the face. The route proceeds up and right again, using difficult cracks, to a second ample ledge about 60m below the upper rim of the face. A lead up steep but broken rock ends at a cul-de-sac with vertical, rotten rock on the left and a great overhanging wall on the right. Traverse right on pitons for about 18m (very exposed) until it is possible to pendulum into an open book. Climb about 30m of exposed slabs and flakes on the right side of this open book to the rim. See *American Alpine Journal* 14, no. 1 (1964): pp. 184–85.

Variation: IV, 5.8. First ascent July 28–29, 1966, by Peter Cleveland and Don Storjohann. On this variation fewer difficulties were reported, partially because the first-ascent party avoided the third pitch and its bolts by climbing to the right of the aid crack. At the cul-de-sac at the top of the wall, instead of traversing right, climb directly up on 5.8 rock.

Variation: IV, 5.10. First ascent in June 1979, by Ron Matous and Keith Hadley. Although this climb was largely a free repetition of the original 1963 route, its description differs in some regards and so is given here. **Pitch 1:** From the talus climb 60m of easy rock (5.1 to 5.4) to a ledge just right of a small overhang. **Pitch 2:** This lead, up and slightly left toward the set of three bolts, is difficult (5.10, 23m). **Pitch 3:** Equally difficult, this lead passes the bolts (and possibly a fixed pin) and continues for 46m toward the base of an obvious dihedral below the main diagonal overhang of the face. **Pitch 4:** Climb the dihedral to and past the overhang, then pass a bolt above the overhang and find a decent belay for the next pitch (5.10, 46m). **Pitch 5:** This pitch is easier (5.6) but unprotected, up and slightly left to a good belay ledge (37m). **Pitch 6:** Continue up the face to a belay stance (5.6–5.7, 50m). **Pitch 7:** This pitch contains loose rock (5.6, 37m). **Pitch 8:** A difficult, short lead brings one out at the top of the wall (5.9, 23m).

ROUTE 3. SOUTH FACE DIHEDRAL. IV, 5.8. First ascent August 4, 1979, by Peter Koedt and Kent Lugbill. This climb lies to the right (east) of the water stains in the middle of the main south face. In this area, climb an obvious large dihedral that arches up from lower right to upper left (5.7). Some rotten rock will be found in this dihedral, but at its top there is good climbing, with considerable exposure while traversing out left over the face. The protection here is not good. From the top of the dihedral, climb straight up for 23m over good black rock, then make a horizontal traverse up and right around the eastern edge of the face. There are about two pitches (5.8) from the dihedral to the top of the face; protection is again not good in this section.

Symmetry Crag 4 (10,720+)

(0.45 mi W of Symmetry Spire)

The southern battlements of the Symmetry Crags extend all the way down to the floor of Cascade Canyon. The most impressive of these is the sequence of steep cliffs forming the south buttress of Crag 4. Appropriately named Trinity Buttress in 1970, it is the first obvious wall beyond Storm Point and is divided horizontally into three sections by two large, prominent ledges with trees. It is located to the left (west) of the large rockslide issuing from the gully immediately west of the southwest ridge of Storm Point (and Guides' Wall). For the approach, hike up Cascade Canyon and leave the trail just beyond this rockslide, where the trees begin again. (See *Symmetry Crag 4* later in this section for two routes to the summit of this formation.)

ROUTE 1. LOWER SOUTH BUTTRESS. II, 5.8. First ascent September 4, 1961, by Fred Beckey and John Hudson. From the trail climb into the gully along the left side of the First Tier of the crag. Climb easily up the very steep rock on the nose that leads directly upward from the gully on the left (west) side of the buttress. From the first treed ledge, work left along a black-dike chimney; then climb right and up, when the wall permits, to the second treed ledge. Traverse right (east) along the ledge (and slightly downhill) for about 120m to the definite corner of the buttress. From this point the route goes directly upward, remaining slightly left of this corner. The first roped pitch leads up a crack system. A short overhang is encountered near the end of this pitch. Next, work slightly right and up. The third pitch stays within a meter of the corner, using an obvious

1-foot-wide, slightly overhanging chimney, which is very strenuous. Work diagonally left on the next lead over an overhang and then up a difficult, shallow groove, which contains nothing but rounded holds. The next pitch goes directly upward on very small holds to an obvious dead snag that points about 45° to the right; this snag, which can be seen from the trail, marks the end of the technical climbing. Because the rock presents more than a single possibility at various points on the route, it is likely that the most difficult pitches can be avoided, if desired. This buttress ends about halfway to the summit of the crag from Cascade Canyon; the route was not pursued beyond the dead snag. See *American Alpine Journal* 13, no. 1 (1962): pp. 216–20.

ROUTE 2. TRINITY BUTTRESS. III, 5.9–5.10+. First ascent August 1, 1970, by Yvon Chouinard and T. M. Herbert. As shown in *Figure 8-2*, there are many route possibilities on this buttress, with the most consistently difficult climbing found on and to the left of the sunlight/shadow line visible in the figure. The one route done by this author (R. Jackson)—marked in the figure with the letter *A* —stays near the crest and is on predominantly good rock. Eight pitches of climbing are involved if one goes all the way to the top of the Third Tier. A recommended way of accessing the buttress is to climb the first pitch of Guides' Wall *(Storm Point Cliffs, Route 1)* and then cross the main couloir to the west and traverse over to this buttress. Descent is via a ledge system down to the east that leads into the same couloir as for the old Guides' Wall walk-off descent. (Source: Jack Tackle, for the other route lines, difficulty ratings, etc.)

FIGURE 8-2. Symmetry Crag 4, Trinity Buttress routes *(Route 2)*, III, 5.9–5.10+. **Note:** The one route done by this author (R. Jackson) is marked with an *A*.

Storm Point Cliffs

Near the mouth of Cascade Canyon and featuring one of the shortest Teton approaches, the cliffs at the base of Storm Point offer a surprising variety of climbing compressed into a relatively small area. (See *Storm Point* later in this section for routes to the summit. *Figure 8-8* presents an overview of key features and routes on the south face of this peak, including a few of the rock climbs detailed here.)

Chronology

GUIDES' WALL: August 3, 1949, Richard Pownall, Art Gilkey
var—**BLOBULAR OSCILLATIONS:** August 25, 1984, Renny Jackson, Larry Detrick
var—**ATTRITUS:** October 2019, Ben Hoiness, Benja Glatz, Justin Willis
SOUTH CENTRAL BUTTRESS: August 18, 1958, John Gill, Rick Lloyd
BUM'S WALL: July 24, 1970, George Meyers, Andrew Cox

PICNIC AND PARANOIA: August 29, 1970, Jeb Schenck, Mike Henderson, Fred Long
SOUTH FACE OF GUIDES' WALL: July 11, 1971, Yvon Chouinard, T. M. Herbert, Juris Krisjansons
NO FRIENDS: August 1979, Jim Williams, friend
VIEUX GUIDE: July 22, 1980, Yvon Chouinard, Jim Donini
MORNING THUNDER: July 9, 1985, Paul Gagner, Dan Burgette
BAT ATTACK CRACK: July 4, 1986, Paul Gagner, Renny Jackson
HOT DOGS: ca. July 11, 1986, Paul Gagner, Jim Woodmencey
THE JONES SISTERS: August 13, 1987, Paul Gagner, Jim Woodmencey
NO MORE MR. NICE GUY: September 15, 1987, Paul Gagner, Jim Woodmencey
SKINNY DIP: July 10, 1989, Dave Carman et al.
RAGS-TO-RICHES: August 19, 1989, Tom Turiano, Harry Hollis

ROUTE 1. GUIDES' WALL. II, 5.8. First ascent August 3, 1949, by Richard Pownall and Art Gilkey. More than 70 years after this pioneering climb, one cannot be certain whether all of the pitches of the current Guides' Wall were included in the 1949 ascent. The present route was worked out over the ensuing decade: subsequent early climbs in this area were made on September 4, 1953, by Richard Emerson and William Wallace; on June 29, 1954, by William Buckingham and Gary Hemming; on August 16, 1954, by Steve Jervis, Mike Wortis, and John Mann; on July 30, 1955, by William Cropper, John Dietschy, Steve Jervis, and Mike Wortis; and on July 22, 1956, by Willi Unsoeld and R. L. Evans. The ascent that led to the current name, however, appears to have been made on September 5, 1959, by Barry Corbet, Jake Breitenbach, Sterling Neale, Carlos Plummer, Willi Unsoeld, and Fred Beckey.

The southwest ridge of Storm Point has the exceptionally attractive combination of easy access and excellent rock. Guides' Wall, the first seven pitches of this ridge (although only six are now commonly done), has over the years become one of the most popular rock climbs in the park. (See *Figures 8-3* and *8-4*.) Variations are possible, although any direct climb of the ridge must funnel through the 5.8 crux pitch, described below. There are several possible escapes from this route into the southwest couloir (see *Storm Point, Route 3*) to the left (north). During most of the climb this couloir is in sight; hence, the route is at or near the western edge of the main southwest buttress.

From Inspiration Point, hike up the Cascade Canyon trail about 1.5 miles until, past the southwest ridge, one can look up into the major southwest couloir immediately west of Storm Point. There is a small pond here, known as Perch Pond; it was formed in the early 1980s by a microburst-induced rockslide that came down from the north side of the canyon. At this point look for a climbers' trail leading north through a boulder field, up across a small cliff band, and then west through large trees to the start of the climbing at the corner of the steep, continuous section.

The first pitch starts right on the corner and ends at a bolted anchor (5.7). Take care climbing over the small tree at the base of this pitch. The next four ropelengths are most easily done on the ridge crest, but there are alternate routes on both sides. These pitches lead to the Flake Ledge, the first broad ledge of the

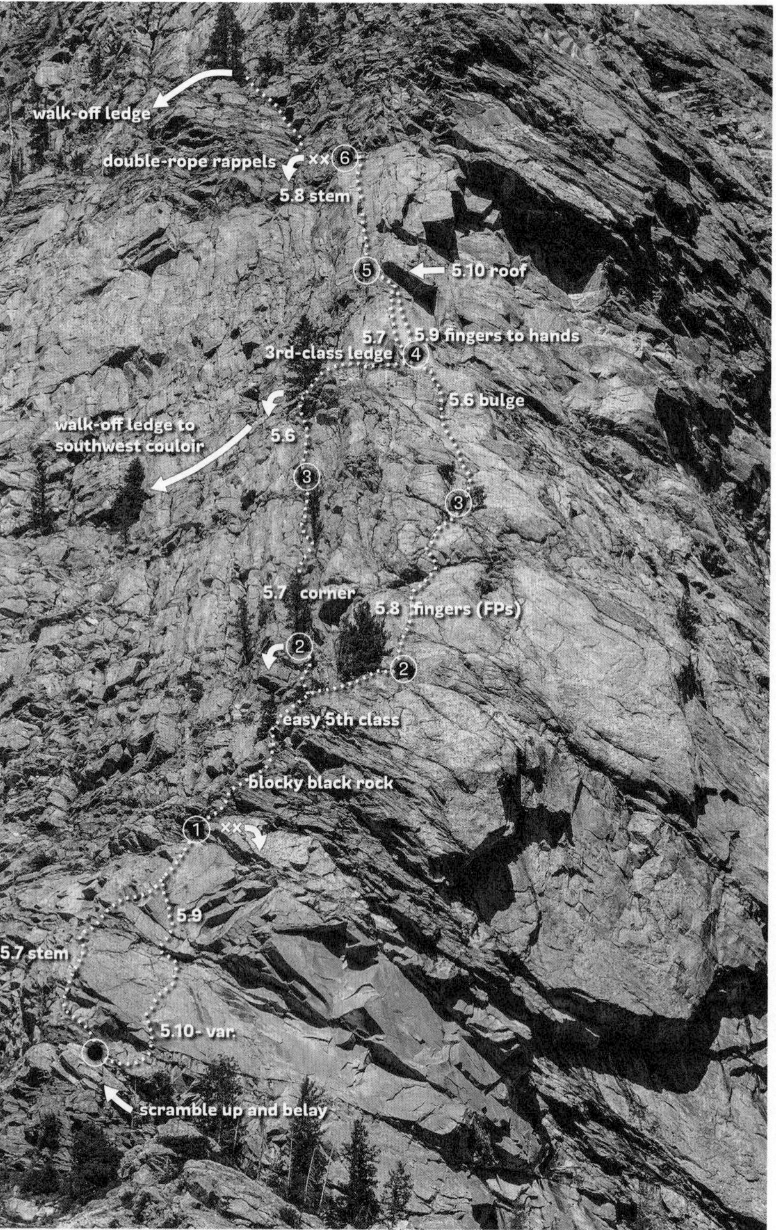

FIGURE 8-3. Storm Point, southwest ridge, Guides' Wall *(Route 1)*, II, 5.8

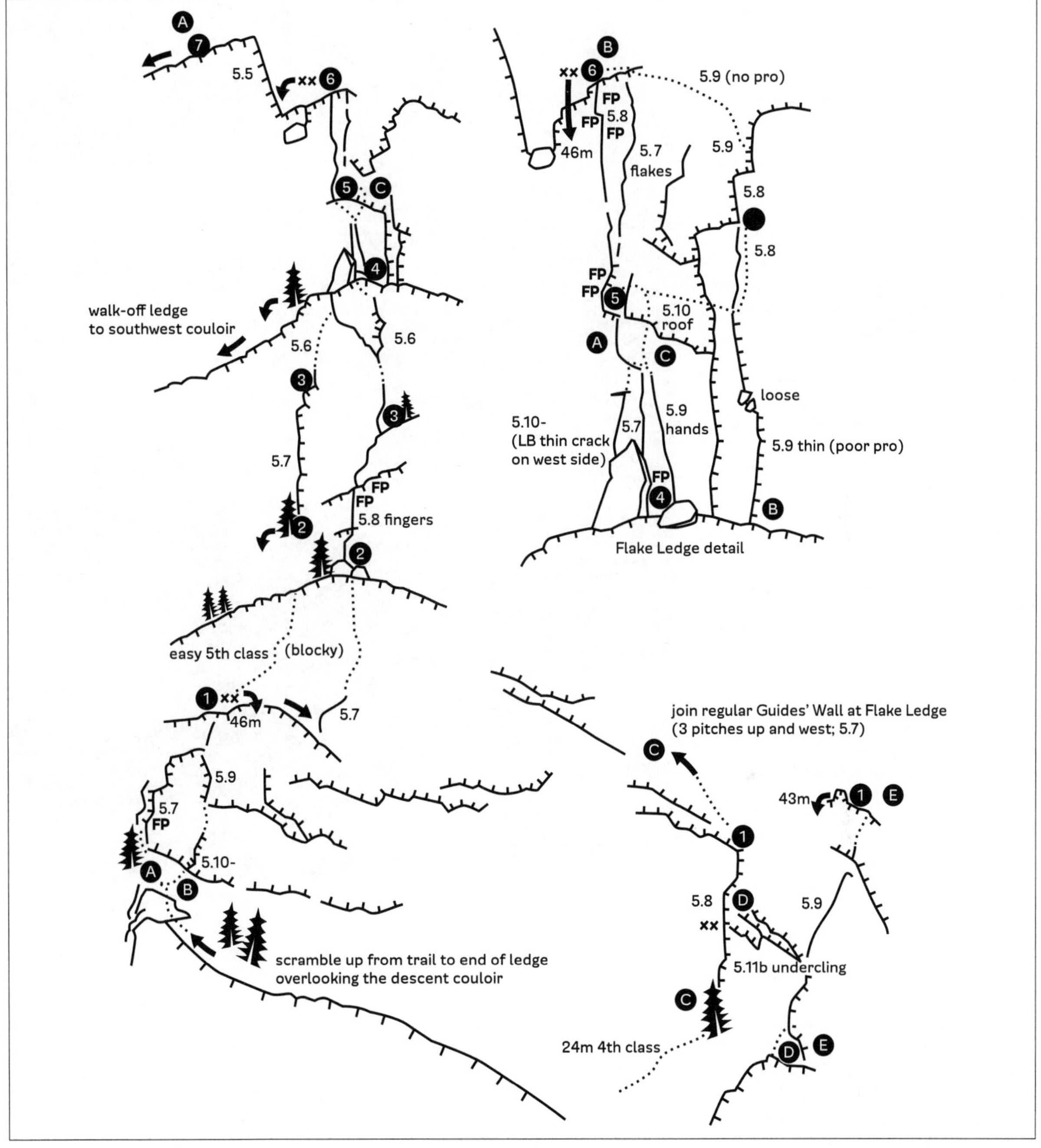

FIGURE 8-4. Storm Point, southwest ridge. (A) Guides' Wall *(Route 1)*, II, 5.8; (B) Guides' Wall, variation: Blobular Oscillations, II, 5.10-; (C) Vieux Guide *(Route 2)*, II, 5.10; (D) Bat Attack Crack *(Route 3)*, I, 5.11b; (E) Hot Dogs *(Route 4)*, I, 5.9. **Note:** The pitches on the left side of the topo are on the west side of the ridge, and the pitches on the right side are south-facing.

ridge just below a very large flake on the crest. The flake can be seen in profile from the trail. This ledge provides an escape route into the southwest couloir, if desired. Reach the top of the flake by climbing a crack and flake system on the east side (5.7). Then move left (west) and up to a comfortable belay ledge at the base of the crux sixth pitch. Follow the obvious crack upward, face climbing at the top on very enjoyable rock (5.8). These final two pitches are usually run together. A bolted anchor at the top of the sixth pitch marks the end of the Guides' Wall route as it is commonly done today. **Gear:** For protection take a standard rack to 2.5" and quickdraws.

Most parties rappel down, starting from the bolted anchors at the top of the sixth pitch. The first 46m rappel reaches the Flake Ledge. Two additional 46m rappels (from tree anchors) bring one down to the bolted anchors at the top of the first pitch, where another 46m rappel reaches the start. To access the walk-off descent instead, one must climb another easy pitch (5.5) to a ledge that leads out north and west into the southwest couloir. This ledge is easy, but caution is required because of the considerable exposure. Then follow a steep trail down the southwest couloir back to the base of the climb, staying on the west side of the drainage.

***Variation:* BLOBULAR OSCILLATIONS.** II, 5.10-. First ascent August 25, 1984, by Renny Jackson and Larry Detrick. (See *Figures 8-4* and *8-5*.) This variation provides a much more difficult start and finish for the regular Guides' Wall route. From the belay for the first pitch, move up and right over an overhang (5.10-) and then into and up a left-facing corner (5.9). This corner intersects the main Guides' Wall route about 6m below the rappel bolts at the top of its first pitch; continue up to that anchor and belay. Two pitches were climbed above and right (east) of the Flake Ledge on the first ascent, but they are not recommended.

***Variation:* ATTRITUS.** III, 5.12-. First ascent in October 2019, by Ben Hoiness, Benja Glatz, and Justin Willis. (See *Figure 8-5*.) Over the years, climbers have gazed at the beautiful rock just east of the beginning pitches of the regular Guides' Wall and wondered about new route potential. Credit goes to this trio with their establishment of Attritus, which is the Latin word for the action or process of rubbing or grinding—put more simply, friction! It is an apt description of the difficulties of the climb. This variation begins just a few meters east of Blobular Oscillations and joins its first pitch about halfway up. The route then continues to stay to the east of the regular Guides' Wall route for four more enjoyable and varied pitches of difficult climbing. **Pitch 1:** Climb broken rock to a fixed pin, then continue up via very difficult friction moves (5.12-) past two protection bolts to join Blobular Oscillations below the 5.9 left-facing corner. Climb the corner and belay at the bolted anchor at the top of the first pitch of Guides' Wall (37m). **Pitch 2:** Climb up to a broken ledge and traverse down and to the east to the base of a large, golden right-facing dihedral. Build an anchor near the end of the ledge (easy 5th class, 30m). **Pitch 3:** Step right past a bolt and climb a big lieback flake that gives way to a flaring slot and eventually a stemming dihedral that accepts small wires for pro. The pitch ends at a ledge with a fixed pin and a bolt for the anchor (5.11, 40m). **Pitch 4:** Climb up past a bolt and a fixed pin (5.12-) to an easy, right-angling flake that ends, and then proceed to the right past a second bolt via an unlikely lunge to a jug. The pitch ends at an anchor with two bolts (5.12-, 37m). **Pitch 5:** Climb past a bolt above the belay (5.10+) and continue to easier ground; belay on the Flake Ledge of the regular Guides' Wall route. **Gear:** Suggested protection includes four quickdraws; six alpine draws; doubles in micro and small cams; one set of regular cams to 3.5"; and small wires. **Note:** The first-ascent party drilled the bolts by hand after obtaining permission from National Park Service (NPS) climbing management staff, following a review process.

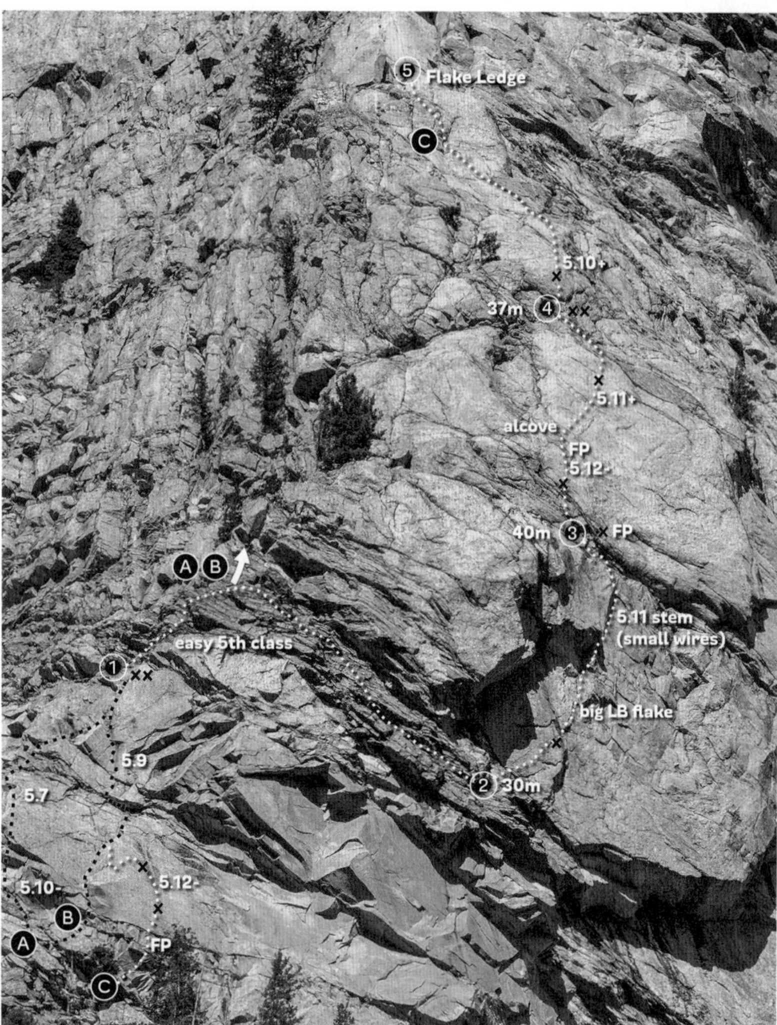

FIGURE 8-5. Storm Point, southwest ridge. (A) Guides' Wall *(Route 1)*, II, 5.8; (B) Variation: Blobular Oscillations, II, 5.10-; (C) Variation: Attritus, III, 5.12-

ROUTE 2. VIEUX GUIDE. II, 5.10. First ascent July 22, 1980, by Yvon Chouinard and Jim Donini. (See *Figure 8-4*.) The beginning of this route is marked by a prominent left-facing corner located 60m to the right (east) of the regular Guides' Wall start (see *Route 1*). Climb 24m (4.0) past a tree to reach the base of this corner, which is then climbed (5.8) to a belay to the right of some overhangs. From the top of this corner the route continues up and left for three pitches (5.7) to the Flake Ledge of the regular Guides' Wall route. The small roof directly above the 5.9 hand crack above the Flake Ledge was climbed on the first ascent of this route (5.10).

ROUTE 3. BAT ATTACK CRACK. I, 5.11b. First ascent July 4, 1986, by Paul Gagner and Renny Jackson. (See *Figure 8-4*.) Located to the right of the left-facing corner of Vieux Guide (see *Route 2*) is a difficult ceiling or arching crack known as Bat Attack Crack. Begin by scrambling up and right on an easy ramp to where a belay can be set just below the arch that forms the route. Very difficult jamming and the crux undercling then take one to the left, where a steep corner provides an exit at the top of the first pitch of Vieux Guide. Rappel anchors (two bolts) at the top of the pitch provide an escape from this one-pitch climb. **Gear:** For protection bring a double set of cams from 0.5" to 3", medium to large stoppers, and a 60m rope.

ROUTE 4. HOT DOGS. I, 5.9. First ascent on about July 11, 1986, by Paul Gagner and Jim Woodmencey. (See *Figure 8-4*.) This excellent one-pitch climb begins at the same spot as Bat Attack Crack. Climb up to the beginning of the hard jamming and then exit out right (east) via a 5.9 jam crack.

ROUTE 5. BUM'S WALL. III, 5.8, A3. First ascent July 24, 1970, by George Meyers and Andrew Cox. Start in the center of the broad face to the right of the Guides' Wall route (*Route 1*) and directly below a large right-facing corner. Work up to the start of this corner from the right; some aid will be needed in this section. Climb this corner until one can exit left below a chimney slot and follow a series of dihedrals to a large ledge. From here scramble 8m up to the right to the base of an obvious crack and corner system. Climb this corner and exit at the top, using pitons for aid (A3), to a ledge. The next pitch goes up pleasant rock for 24m to the large ledge that traverses the entire face. Take this ledge west to the regular Guides' Wall route.

ROUTE 6. PICNIC AND PARANOIA. II, 5.8. First ascent August 29, 1970, by Jeb Schenck, Mike Henderson, and Fred Long. This six-pitch route ascends the first rock buttress to the right (east) of the right end of Guides' Wall (*Route 1*). It lies to the right of a prominent, left-arching black chimney. Start by scrambling up to a large chockstone for a belay stance. Climb loose blocks (5.6) and slabs until just left of a steep open-book chimney. Exit from the belay ledge to the right (east) around an overhang. Now climb a chimney for 3m until a crack in the left face of the chimney is visible. Traverse to the crack and climb to a small ledge near the top of the chimney (5.7). Go back into the chimney, then right to a small ledge, and exit around a difficult block with poor protection to a belay ledge. Scramble up and right on easy holds to a large tree and then cut under the tree (left) to a large ledge. Now climb the nearly vertical slab above on small flakes and crystals for 6m (unprotected 5.8). Directly above is a 12m corner with a large, shifting flake on its right side. Climb about one-third of the corner on good protection, then traverse right to the loose flake. Taking care not to dislodge it, jam up the flake to a ceiling, avoiding the loose blocks as handholds; protection is scarce on this lead. Traverse left to the opposite side of the ceiling. The next pitch is the crux: exit left around "a horrifying holdless block," using only a hand jam up in the ceiling (5.8); around the corner are good ledges and the next belay point. Now climb an easy corner, exit right, and then move up to a left-slanting crack. Climb this lieback crack (5.6), then a very thin flake, and traverse right until directly above the belay. Continue up and right on the flake on chicken heads. Continue up and right of an overhanging block until directly right of the block. Climb to the right side via friction moves and knobs. Exit straight up (5.7) to the end of the climb. On the first ascent pitons were used extensively for protection, including thin horizontals. Descent is to the right (east) along the face.

ROUTE 7. SOUTH FACE OF GUIDES' WALL. III, 5.9. First ascent July 11, 1971, by Yvon Chouinard, T. M. Herbert, and Juris Krisjansons. This 10-pitch route is located east of Guides' Wall in the middle of the broad south face of Storm Point. It consists of a steep lower section, a middle easy ramp section, and a final very steep and overhanging wall. Start at the middle of the face under some overhangs and climb up and right on a hand traverse (5.7) to a grassy ramp that angles back to the left. From a belay at the end of this ramp, start up a corner and then cross over to the left to another corner and finish the lead (5.7) at an obvious ledge. The third short pitch goes up and right on easy broken rock (4.0). Now climb a shallow, rounded crack straight up to an easy broken ledge system that permits access to the large ledges at the top of the steep lower section of the route. The next two pitches take easy ramps, first to the right and then back left, passing a flat, blank alcove. The seventh lead (5.9), which was originally marked by a small cairn, goes up and over some overhangs and then angles right over another roof. Once over the top of this roof, traverse left under some more overhangs and finish by climbing directly up a steep wall to a small belay stance. The next short pitch starts out to the right and goes up a shallow trough, ending on a large, sloping ledge. The ninth lead (5.6) goes mostly straight up, following the easiest line to a good belay ledge. The final pitch begins slightly to the left, turns up over a small overhang, and finishes up and right in a broken section. Some 60m of scrambling takes one to the end of the upper steep section of this route. For the descent traverse over to the southwest couloir. **Gear:** The first-ascent party used protection to 1.5".

ROUTE 8. NO FRIENDS. II, 5.9+. First ascent in August 1979, by Jim Williams and friend. This route surmounts the initial south buttress of Storm Point well to the east of Guides' Wall (*Route 1*). The start of the climb is about 120m from the ridge crest, below overhangs at the lower edge of a broad, slabby region that is bordered on the left (west) by a large right-facing corner formation. The first pitch, the most difficult, goes up toward and past these overhangs on the right, passing some small caves, to gain a shallow corner on the face above. Belay partway up this corner, which slants up and left. Climb to the top of the corner, then cut back right up a major right-facing corner that diagonals up and right. The final lead continues up in cracks and chimneys to the broad ledge that is taken all the way west to the southwest ridge and the Guides' Wall route (at the Flake Ledge).

ROUTE 9. RAGS-TO-RICHES. II, 5.7, A1. First ascent August 19, 1989, by Tom Turiano and Harry Hollis. This route on the lower south buttress of Storm Point lies 0.25 mile east of Guides' Wall *(Route 1)* and is approached via the Cascade Canyon trail. On the eastern portion of the buttress, proceed north up the talus to an obvious gully system in the lower orangish section of the wall. The large triangular section of the wall above the grassy talus is attacked from the center of the base; the route aims for the huge black bulge at the top of the buttress. From the top of the gully the first lead goes up a sequence of open or flaring chimneys, past an overhang (5.7), and then past some trees and a final loose 5.6 wall to a huge ledge. Walk left past another tree to the large chimney with chockstones that can be seen from the trail near Guides' Wall. Climb the left side of this chimney to the chockstone and fixed piton, then move out on the face to the left to belay at a tree. Next get back into the main chimney to the right and work upward, taking the left fork (5.7 stemming) when it narrows, to the belay above the end of the chimney. Gain a large ledge, then move the belay to the left past a tree. Do not take the obvious flake up from this ledge as it leads to dangerously loose blocks. Instead, climb the crack (5.7) in the wall to the left of a right-facing corner. Climb a 3m aid section (a knifeblade piton would be handy here) and continue up the easier face above to gain the belay ledge. The fourth lead starts up a crack and continues up classic knobs (5.6) below and to the right of a right-facing triangular roof and corner. Move up and back toward this corner (fixed piton here), exiting past a small roof (5.7) onto the ledge near the top of the buttress. The end of this lead is a short distance to the right of the huge black bulge. For descent hike east down the ramp at the top of the buttress. Rappels may be necessary if the ramp is followed and are certainly needed if one wishes to return to the base of the climb. Numerous trees are available for these rappels.

ROUTE 10. SKINNY DIP. II, 5.7. First ascent July 10, 1989, by Dave Carman et al. This route lies on the main buttress at the base of the south face of Storm Point, well east of Guides' Wall *(Route 1)*. Take the Cascade Canyon trail to a small gully about 90m past the end of the rapids of Cascade Creek and the beginning of the meandering section. Turn up here and scramble toward the start of the climb, on the right (east) of steep, rusty cliffs that appear rotten. Hike up the final scree, boulders, and bushes to the large, treed ledge that diagonals up and left to the drainage just below the climb. Scramble up and right of the drainage on ledges with scattered trees, then traverse left and up to the start of the first pitch. Begin to the right of a rock scar and climb 46m on 5.6 rock (two fixed pitons) past a very small tree to a small belay ledge. A short lead on broken and easier rock takes one to a large ledge. Move this belay about 9m left to start the third pitch, which climbs up to and beyond two left-facing corners (fixed piton) to a sloping ledge for the belay (5.7, 46m). The fourth and fifth pitches, which are short (23m each) and on broken rock (5.6), lead to the large terrace, a major feature of this route. Move the belay up to a large tree and climb 46m on dark, classic Teton rock (5.6) past an old piton to a belay on a ledge that slopes off to the right (east). Sixty meters of easier rock (3.0 and 4.0) up and left takes one to the end of this pleasant route. Descent is made via down-climbing and rappels (23m), mostly to the right (east) of the ascent route.

ROUTE 11. THE JONES SISTERS. II, 5.8. First ascent August 13, 1987, by Paul Gagner and Jim Woodmencey. (See *Figure 8-6.*) There are three major ramps (see *Storm Point, Route 7*) that sweep up and left (west) across the crest of the southeast ridge of Storm Point. The first, the lowest and most westerly of these ramps, begins near the base of the ridge and gives access to the bottom of the gully in the central bowl if followed westward. The middle ramp ends abruptly at the west face of the southeast ridge. This two-pitch climb lies on the steep buttress between the first and middle ramps. The top of the buttress, the end of the climb, is the edge of the middle ramp, which diagonals steeply down to the right (east). From the talus slope with trees at the beginning of the first ramp, take this ramp up and left to the start of this route on the left edge of the buttress, past the left-facing corner of *Route 12*. The climb begins near an old fixed piton below a pair of left-facing corners. Move to the right from the piton to the right-hand corner. Climb this corner (5.7, 50m) to a belay at its top. The second pitch goes up to and along the right side of a flake, then cuts right past another fixed piton under a small roof, passing the roof on the right (5.8). Now climb the wall to and past two more overhangs (5.7), eventually exiting onto the ramp edge. For protection take a standard rack.

ROUTE 12. NO MORE MR. NICE GUY. II, 5.11-, A1. First ascent September 15, 1987, Paul Gagner and Jim Woodmencey. (See *Figure 8-6.*) This three-pitch route is located on

Julia Heemstra on Baxter's Pinnacle (Photo by David Bowers)

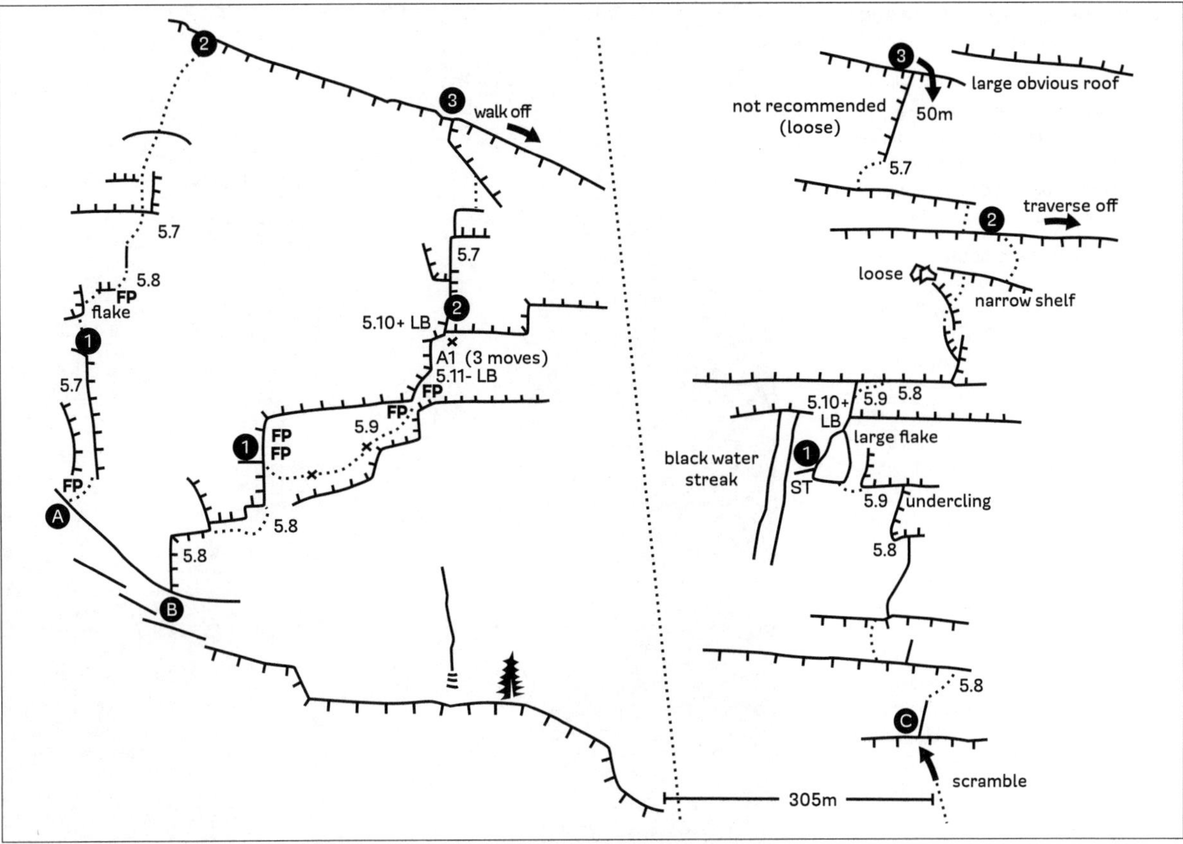

FIGURE 8-6. Storm Point, southeast side. (A) The Jones Sisters *(Route 11)*, II, 5.8; (B) No More Mr. Nice Guy *(Route 12)*, II, 5.11-, A1; (C) Morning Thunder *(Route 13)*, II, 5.10+

the same buttress as *Route 11*; approach as for that route. The climb starts with a left-facing corner (5.8) to a ledge. Move right along this ledge and under a roof to gain a right-facing corner. Belay from halfway up this corner, where two fixed pitons will be found. The wall to the right is undercut by an overhang, and the corner above converts into an overhang above this wall. The second intricate lead moves slightly down and across this wall to the right to a bolt, continues to a second bolt (5.9), and then proceeds on and up to the right edge of the overhang (two fixed pitons will be found here), which here converts to a right-facing corner again. Lieback this corner (5.11-), then use three points of aid (A1) to reach a third bolt below another overhang. The last part of the lead passes through this overhang via 5.10+ liebacking to the belay on a small ledge. The final pitch, less difficult, goes up a left-facing corner past two small roofs to a diagonal left-facing corner, which provides access to the edge of the major middle ramp. Descent is easily made by walking off down to the right (east). **Gear:** For protection take tiny nuts and camming devices up to 4".

ROUTE 13. MORNING THUNDER. II, 5.10+. First ascent July 9, 1985, by Paul Gagner and Dan Burgette. (See *Figure 8-6*.) As described under *Storm Point, Route 7*, there are three major ramps that sweep up and left (west) across the crest of the southeast ridge of Storm Point. This three-pitch route lies between the first ramp (the lowest and most westerly—the one that ends up in the central bowl) and the middle ramp. It can also be located just to the right of a black water streak on the cliff. Approach via the Cascade Canyon trail and turn up just beyond the lowest rockslide coming down from the north. Scramble to the start of the first pitch, a short 5.8 wall leading up to an initial ledge and then a second ledge, both slanting down from left (west) to right (east). From the second ledge climb into and up a left-facing corner that turns into a small roof. Climb over the roof and up the wall above to another overhang where 5.9 undercling holds permit one to move left to a belay stance on the left side of a large flake. Immediately above this block, on the second lead, pass a very difficult bulge (5.10+) using lieback holds, then continue up to a second overhang; move right along this overhang (5.9) to a break, then head up the left-facing corner above, curving left to some loose blocks. This last section is sparsely protected. Finish the pitch by first descending slightly to the right on a ledge and then climbing a face to the belay on a large ledge, from which one could exit the route to the right. The third pitch moves left along this ledge and then up to a second ledge to a sequence of two right-facing corners, which contain some loose rock. These end at another large ledge—the top of the climb. To descend, make one long (50m) rappel to easier ground, from which it is possible to hike down to the trail. **Gear:** For protection take devices to 3.5".

East Cascade Buttresses (ca. 8,600)

(0.65 mi E of Symmetry Spire)

The following climb, No Perches Necessary, is located on a small buttress up and left (west) of the southwest descent couloir of Baxter's Pinnacle. Due to their proximity, this route is often combined with a climb of Baxter's Pinnacle.

ROUTE 1. NO PERCHES NECESSARY. I, 5.9. First ascent in August 1989, by Renny Jackson and Evelyn Lees; it was partially climbed September 18, 1987, by Rich Perch and Jim Woodmencey, and in 1988 by Rich Perch, Renny Jackson, and Jim Woodmencey. (See *Figure 8-7.*) Leave the horse trail at the north end of the final switchback (just before the trail levels out and crosses the Symmetry Couloir drainage). A faint climbers' trail should be visible taking off from this switchback. Scramble up a short distance to the base of the first pitch. **Pitch 1:** Climb up and left for a few meters before heading right to a large flake. Climb the left side of the flake toward a wide crack that begins on the right side of the roof above. Pull up into the slot above the roof (3.5" pro) and climb the wide-hands/fist crack (4" pro useful in spots). Belay in a small alcove at a bolted anchor with chains, which was added sometime after the first ascent (5.9, 30m). **Pitch 2:** Step left and climb a small left-facing corner, stemming off a large detached flake. At the top of the corner, step around right (small cam or offset brass placement) and continue up to the first of two bolts. The tricky move right above the bolt is the most difficult of the pitch. Continue up to the next bolt and eventually the top of the climb via excellent face climbing. Nutcraft skill, a set of brass offsets, and a couple of small cams will keep the runouts on the second pitch to a minimum. A double-rope rappel (55m) from a two-bolt anchor at the top brings one back to the base. Alternatively, two rappels can be made using bolted anchors at the tops of both pitches; a 60m rope will suffice for this option. **Gear:** For protection bring a set of cams with doubles in the 3.5" to 4" range, as well as some small cams; a set of wired brass offsets; and a set of stoppers.

FIGURE 8-7. East Cascade Buttresses, No Perches Necessary *(Route 1)*, I, 5.9

STORM POINT (10,054)

Map: Mount Moran

High above the mouth of Cascade Canyon, this small but conspicuous point gives the finest view in the park of the Cathedral Group—Teewinot Mountain, the Grand Teton, and Mount Owen. In particular the steep northwest face of Teewinot and the impressive northeast snowfields of Mount Owen are seen to close advantage. This magnificent summit view combined with the ease and shortness of the ascent makes Storm Point a preferred one-day climb from Jenny Lake.

During the first ascent in 1931, the determined party of Fritiof Fryxell and Frank Smith started in a steady rain, climbing the Symmetry Couloir with 15m–30m of visibility. By the time they reached the top of the couloir, the rain had turned to snow and sleet and the wind was whipping over the divide "with gale velocity." The name—Storm Point—was thus well earned. In recent years the south side of this peak with its considerable expanse of excellent and challenging rock has received the most attention. Much of this interest has

concentrated on the lower portion of the southwest ridge, known as Guides' Wall, which has become one of the most popular rock climbs in the range (see *Cascade Canyon, North Side Rock Climbs, Storm Point Cliffs, Route 1*). In early season the south-facing routes on Storm Point are among the first to be clear of snow and so are especially attractive. See *Figure 8-8* for an overview of key routes and features on this broad—and complex—southern aspect.

Despite its proximity to Jenny Lake, the epicenter of climbing activity, the south side of Storm Point remains inadequately known, persisting as something of an embarrassment for a Teton geographer. Knowledge seems to have advanced but little in the decades since Willi Unsoeld described it as "a real wilderness of broken walls, ridges which disappear, and gullies which lead nowhere"; William Buckingham observed that the impression was one of "bewildering confusion." This side of Storm Point is bounded by two ridges, the southwest and the southeast, both of which rise irregularly in a series of steps to the summit. Between these ridges is a large central bowl (or gully); access to the bottom of this bowl is cut off by a considerable wall that extends entirely across the base of the south face. The angle and height of this initial wall or buttress decreases from west to east. Near its eastern end it meets a steep chute that extends downward from the bowl toward the talus slope just above the Cascade Canyon trail. The southwest ridge is a large, triangular facet bounded on the right by this central bowl and on the left by the west wall of Storm Point, which rises directly above the main southwest couloir. The crest of the southeast ridge is most easily reached from the east via one of the ramps or shelves that diagonal up to meet it. Above the basal south buttress, the upper west face of the southeast ridge drops very steeply into the large central bowl. This bowl, which apparently can be easily ascended past its trees and bushes once the lower end of it is gained, leads diagonally below the true upper south face of Storm Point onto the relatively flat section of the upper southwest ridge, about 500 vertical feet below the summit. Between this flat section and the summit is the West Knob, defined by a distinct col on the southwest ridge.

The climbing history of Storm Point is especially difficult to convey because of the confused state of the terminology used in the early years of exploration and route development. The term "south

FIGURE 8-8. Storm Point, south face overview

face" was applied to various climbs on the southwest ridge and Guides' Wall; "south couloir" was sometimes used for the south bowl and sometimes for the southwest couloir; and "west face" at times meant the regular route via the Symmetry Couloir with the finish on the west face. At this late date it is impossible to be certain where some of these early climbs took place. Additionally, few of the many climbs made on the south side of the peak since 1937 have been carefully described, so not all of the many variations that have probably been climbed are listed here. Attributions of first ascents of routes or variations are necessarily left somewhat vague because some of the more recent routes may well have first been done in the enthusiasm of the two decades from 1945 to 1965; at least 65 climbs were made on the south side in those early years.

The nonsummit rock climbs are listed separately: see *Cascade Canyon, North Side Rock Climbs, Storm Point Cliffs*.

Chronology

SYMMETRY COULOIR AND UPPER WEST FACE: August 13, 1931, Fritiof Fryxell, Frank Smith
SOUTHWEST COULOIR: August 13, 1931, Fritiof Fryxell, Frank Smith (descent); August 1, 1940, C. Grove McCown, Thomson Edwards (ascent)
EAST RIDGE, SYMMETRY COULOIR: August 31, 1931, Arthur Kleinschmidt, or July 23, 1936, Jack Durrance, James Monroe
var—**EAST RIDGE, SOUTHEAST COULOIR:** August 31, 1934, Whipple Andrews, Reynold Holmen
var—**DIRECT EAST RIDGE:** August 22, 1940, John and Elizabeth Buck
SOUTHEAST RIDGE: August 17, 1938, Bert Jensen, William Rice, William Bigelow
WEST FACE: June 26, 1948, William McMorris, James Colburn, or July 1, 1963, Peter Gardiner, Robert Williams
SOUTH BOWL: August 18, 1948, Martin Murie, Dick Nabors, Desmond Watt, George and John Bascom, or August 24, 1955, William Cropper, Richard Bonker, Brad Pearson, Tom McCalla, or July 31, 1958, Yvon Chouinard, Marliese Braitinger, or August 23, 1965, Rick Reese, Rich Ream
SOUTHWEST RIDGE: August 3, 1949, Richard Pownall, Art Gilkey
WEST RIDGE: June 30, 1963, Steven Derenzo, Peter Gardiner
COMPLETE SOUTHEAST RIDGE, HIGHWAY TO HEAVEN: June 30, 2014, Nobuyuki "Yuki" Fujita, Ron Watters (lower portion); July 21, 2015, Pete Walka, Ron Watters (upper section to summit)

ROUTE 1. WEST RIDGE. II, 5.6. First ascent June 30, 1963, by Steven Derenzo and Peter Gardiner. This indistinct ridge is roughly due west of the summit of Storm Point and is separated from the west face (see *Route 2*) by a steep couloir or two. It is on the right (south) side of the main southwest couloir (see *Route 3*), which is used to approach the base of this ridge. The climbing on the ridge itself contains little of interest with the exception of one 18m step of yellow rock. This is climbed by a very delicate lead on its northwest corner.

ROUTE 2. WEST FACE. II, 5.6. First ascent June 26, 1948, by William McMorris and James Colburn, or July 1, 1963, by Peter Gardiner and Robert Williams. There is a considerable quantity of rock rising above and east of the southwest couloir (see *Route 3*), which leads from Cascade Canyon to the Ice Point–Symmetry Spire saddle. Its features are as obscure as those of the south face of Storm Point, but some general statements can be made. The principal face is the west face of the southwest ridge, and it culminates at the West Knob of that ridge, about 200 vertical feet below the summit. To the left (north) of this steep face lie at least two ill-defined ridges and two steep couloirs leading up in the general direction of Ice Point. More than one climb has been made on the main west face, but detailed information is available only for the 1963 ascent, described below.

In early season the lower end of the southwest couloir funnels into a series of vertical waterfalls a short distance above the Cascade Canyon trail. Avoid these by zigzagging up the slabby slope east of the falls, angling west to the top of the highest one. Hike about 90m up the couloir past a slimy vertical chimney that drains the shallow bowl underneath the west face. Continue about 30m up the couloir until an exposed ledge is found leading back south to the top of the slimy chimney. From this point climb a crumbly red-rock chute up and left. Continue in the same direction past the end of the chute, eventually reaching a grassy platform only 15m from the left (north) edge of the west face. After a 15m scramble upward, a full ropelength of steep rock gives access to a broad, tree-covered ledge angling slightly back across the face to the south. Just above the right (south) end of the ledge, reached after some bushwhacking and a delicate traverse, a deep fissure angles up and back to the left (north). Follow this general line for about two pitches to the top of the face and join one of the variations on the upper southwest ridge below the West Knob. Climb over the West Knob, staying on or near the crest, on enjoyable knobby rock, in places considerably exposed on either side.

ROUTE 3. SOUTHWEST COULOIR. II, 4.0. First descent August 13, 1931, by Fritiof Fryxell and Frank Smith; first ascent August 1, 1940, by C. Grove McCown and Thomson Edwards. An alternative to the direct eastern approach to the Ice Point–Symmetry Spire saddle is the large southwest couloir, which leads to this same saddle from the west via Cascade Canyon. Hike into the canyon on the trail until a large talus fan issuing from the southwest couloir is reached. This talus fan is immediately west of the prominent southwest ridge of Storm Point. At the top of the talus fan, the bottom of the couloir is blocked by a short cliff band, which can be passed at its left edge by a series of ledges containing trees, bushes, and dirt. Once above this section, the couloir is followed without difficulty to the saddle. From the saddle, follow the upper part of *Route 10*. Note that the lower portion of the southwest couloir offers a walk-off descent (and an escape option) from Guides' Wall (see *Cascade Canyon, North Side Rock Climbs, Storm Point Cliffs, Route 1*).

ROUTE 4. SOUTHWEST RIDGE. III, 5.8. First ascent August 3, 1949, by Richard Pownall and Art Gilkey. The southwest ridge of Storm Point has the exceptionally attractive combination of easy access and excellent rock. These features have made the routes and variations on this ridge some of the most popular in the park. Although rarely done in its entirety, this 600m ridge is an enjoyable outing. The first six pitches, which surmount the difficult initial pyramidal buttress now known as Guides' Wall, are often done as a separate rock climb. See *Cascade Canyon, North Side Rock Climbs, Storm Point Cliffs, Route 1* for the approach to and description of this initial section.

From the top of Guides' Wall, at the end of the sixth pitch, it is still a long climb to the summit of Storm Point. Surmount the difficulties of the formidable wall above by using a series of downsloping slabs that cut across the face diagonally up to the right. After two pitches a Wall Street–type ledge leads around the corner to easy ground. From here to the summit the climbing is easier, and a route can be found along or beside the meandering crest. About 120m below the summit there is a pinnacle that is passed by a vertical 24m lead on the face to the left of the pinnacle. The uppermost portion of the ridge leads almost due east to the summit. **Time:** 11½ to 12¼ hours from Jenny Lake. See *American Alpine Journal* 8, no. 1 (1951): pp. 176–81.

ROUTE 5. SOUTH CENTRAL BUTTRESS. II, 5.7. First ascent August 18, 1958, by John Gill and Rick Lloyd. There is a large central bowl (or gully) between the southwest and southeast ridges of Storm Point. Directly beneath this bowl lies the center section of the buttress at the base of the south face of Storm Point. The upper portion of this section appears smooth and white and is capped by a large overhang. From the Cascade Canyon trail diagonal up tree-covered shelves from the east to the large gully just right (east) of the base of this section of the buttress. An obvious jam crack facing east in the middle of the lower section is the key to this climb and should be located before starting. Traverse an obvious ledge out to a point about 24m beneath this crack. Climb directly up for one pitch, making one small zigzag before reaching a belay stance. Friction climb around the corner to the right for 9m, then ascend the jam crack. The next lead moves up the center of the face, passing to the right of a small tree, to a large ledge bisecting the buttress. Traverse left (west) on this ledge to a shallow chimney that is capped by an overhang centered 18m above in the smooth white face. Using a crack in this chimney, climb directly up to the overhang and make a difficult traverse to the left (west) to gain a 12m crack. This crack leads to a belay ledge just above the overhang. The next ropelength goes directly up enjoyable rock, passing the first roof above on the left and climbing a thin and difficult 9m section to an open chimney beneath the large roof capping the buttress. After climbing about 1m up from the belay stance, begin a very exposed and delicate 21m hand traverse to the right across a vertical face to the east edge of the buttress wall; move up this edge to a belay. The final pitch zigzags left and then right before going straight up over an overhang, finishing with some slabs to the top of the buttress. Now scramble easily up the central bowl (or gully) to the Southwest Ridge route *(Route 4)*, which is followed to the summit. The rock on this South Central Buttress route is excellent.

ROUTE 6. SOUTH BOWL. II, 5.1. First ascent uncertain, perhaps August 18, 1948, by Martin Murie, Dick Nabors, Desmond Watt, and George and John Bascom, or August 24, 1955, by William Cropper, Richard Bonker, Brad Pearson, and Tom McCalla, or July 31, 1958, by Yvon Chouinard and Marliese Braitinger, or August 23, 1965, by Rick Reese and Rich Ream. The main central bowl (or gully) in the upper south face of Storm Point is composed of two sections separated by some steep rock. The lower section is just above the initial rock buttress that extends along the base of the entire south face of Storm Point. The upper section holds a tree-covered shelf that diagonals from lower right to upper left to meet the upper end of the southwest ridge. Routes have been made in this region by climbing one or both of these sections. Access to the lower section of the gully apparently is possible via climbing the broken cliffs just below the lowest point of the gully near its eastern end. Once these cliffs have been passed and the lower section of the bowl has been gained, one can traverse left (west) all the way out to the crest of the southwest ridge.

However, to continue this route one must gain entry into the upper section of the bowl. This can apparently be done via either the left (west) edge of the lower section or a large chimney in the right (east) edge, or more directly up a prominent, slanting chimney/crack system that leads all the way up the rock wall above. An alternative approach into this upper section is provided by the lowest of the three ramps that angle in from the east toward the crest of the southeast ridge. Once on the main shelf in this upper section one can scramble west and up along the shelf to its end at the uppermost southwest ridge. Follow *Route 4* to the summit.

ROUTE 7. SOUTHEAST RIDGE. II, 5.6, A1. First ascent August 17, 1938, by Bert Jensen, William Rice, and William Bigelow. The length and difficulty of this route depend on both the point at which the crest is attained and the closeness with which it is followed to the summit. Many climbs have been made on the southeast side of Storm Point, but perhaps no two have been identical, and perhaps none has followed exactly the ridge crest from the base to the summit. It is not easy even to define the beginning of the ridge, which is lost in the basal buttress of the south side of Storm Point.

There are three major shelves or ramps that diagonal from lower right to upper left (west) across the southeast face to meet the southeast ridge. The southeast ridge can be said to have its true beginning just above the lowest and farthest west of these shelves; for the complete ridge see *Route 8*, below. If followed westward, this lowest ramp gives access to the bottom of the gully in the central bowl. The next shelf up is easily gained from the talus above the Cascade Canyon trail and, by moving up and out to the left (south) past a few trees, one can reach the ridge crest. However, this second ramp ends abruptly at the west face of the southeast ridge. The difficulties of the steep step in the ridge above this bench are not known but are probably considerable. One can progress toward the summit by climbing out to the west, where apparently a narrow couloir will be found leading downward to the central treed gully or bowl, which is followed out to the upper part of the southwest ridge (see *Route 4*).

The first-ascent party accessed this climb by way of the third, highest, and largest of the ramps, bypassing the seven initial pitches of climbing described in *Route 8*. The beginning of this shelf is just left (west) of a prominent black-rock wall immediately above the talus slope above the trail. Follow this shelf west to the ridge crest (this may be the point referred to as "Tranquility Point" in *Route 8*), directly below a large overhang, which is avoided by traversing around the corner to the left on easy ledges. This traverse can be continued a considerable distance before one turns up to regain the ridge. Or, more directly, one can turn up after one traversing lead, regaining the ridge just above the overhang. If this alternative is chosen, continue up the ridge to the base of a pitch, the top of which overhangs; this is the most difficult pitch of the ridge. Aid climbing (A1) may be necessary to climb the first part of this pitch to the point where the overhang begins. Then traverse left 2m to a small ledge, from which a traverse left on small holds around a corner leads to easier ground. Keep somewhat to the right (east) of the actual crest, and ascend the remainder of the ridge, scrambling most of the way. Despite the details provided above, the exact line of the 1938 party has been lost to the mists of time. Note that *Route 8* describes going straight up from "Tranquility Point." **Time:** 6½ to 8¼ hours from Jenny Lake. See *American Alpine Journal* 3, no. 3 (1939): p. 363.

ROUTE 8. COMPLETE SOUTHEAST RIDGE, HIGHWAY TO HEAVEN. III, 5.10. First ascent June 30, 2014, by Nobuyuki "Yuki" Fujita and Ron Watters (lower portion), and July 21, 2015, by Pete Walka and Ron Watters (upper section to summit). Fujita and Watters began working on this route on the southeast face of Storm Point in June 2012. The pair encountered seven pitches of climbing, 5.7–5.8 in difficulty. It is likely that most—or even all—of these pitches had been climbed at some point before, given the route's proximity to Jenny Lake and its relatively easy approach; in his write-up of the upper Highway to Heaven route, completed with Walka in 2015, Watters stated that the complete Highway to Heaven could fairly be called a "newly described" route. (In the spirit of having new, updated information for this area, perhaps the term "newly *re*described" route could be used here.) To get to the climb, proceed up the Cascade Canyon trail from Inspiration Point (or slightly above, from where the horse trail intersects it) approximately 0.6 mile. Just past where the trail breaks out into the open after being in trees, and across from where Cascade Creek turns to flat water meandering through willows, look for a small ramp to the north that slants upward from right (east) to left (west) at the top of the scree slope. Ascend the boulder field and scree slope to the ramp and proceed to its top.

Pitch 1: Climb a southeast-facing slab that extends upward for about 60m. **Pitch 2:** Continue up the slab, aiming for the west end of a large roof where a few moves (5.8) around a flake lead up to a roomy belay ledge. A few variations are possible on these first two pitches, but all end on this comfortable ledge above and to the west of the initial large roof. **Pitch 3:** From the west end of the ledge, climb up black slabs (5.7) for 35m and through two small roofs, located close together, to the belay. **Pitch 4:** Climb a few 5.8 moves not far above the belay and continue up to the far end of a large ledge (with live conifers on its eastern end); belay on the upper end of this ledge. One can exit here by going down and to the east. **Pitch 5:** Proceed directly above the belay and then move west to a wide chimney, which narrows for a short distance into a corner (5.7+). Continue above the corner, trending slightly to the right on easy terrain until just beneath a smooth face with overhanging blocks on its right edge; belay here. **Pitch 6:** Ascend the wall immediately above (5.8)—the crux of the route. A fixed pin was found on this wall. Continue climbing above the wall on easier terrain for nearly a ropelength. **Pitch 7:** Scrambling leads to the high point of the lower portion of the climb (referred to as "Tranquility Point" by Fujita and Watters); take in the scenic view. To return to the base of the route from here, do four 60m double-rope rappels, located generally to the east of the route.

To continue to the summit of Storm Point, climb down to the col located at the base of the next wall and belay. A large roof looms a couple pitches above: the route goes straight up to the base of this roof and around its west edge. **Pitch 8:** Climb up to a house-size block, which forms one side of a left-facing corner, and ascend the corner (12m). Continue up through blocky terrain to another left-facing corner, followed by a traverse left to a belay (5.10, 55m). **Pitch 9:** Climb straight up from the belay to a short corner, then climb the corner (5.10, past three fixed pins) until directly beneath the large roof seen from below. Traverse left (west) for a few meters and climb a short face on white-colored rock to another corner. Climb the corner to a small overhang and continue up to a large, treed belay ledge (5.10, 50m). From the ledge easy climbing (mostly 4th class) leads upward to a short section of 5.8 to a false summit seen from below. Beyond this, scrambling leads to the true summit of Storm Point. Refer to *Route 10* for the descent. See *American Alpine Journal* 57, no. 89 (2015): p. 136; www.ronwatters.com/Climbs_HighwayLower.html and /Climbs_HighwayUpper.html.

ROUTE 9. EAST RIDGE, SYMMETRY COULOIR. II, 4.0. First ascent either August 31, 1931, by Arthur Kleinschmidt, or July 23, 1936, by Jack Durrance and James Monroe. The east side of Storm Point south of the standard Symmetry Couloir route *(Route 10)* is a hodgepodge of couloirs, cliffs, trees, and talus. Many variations are possible on this side of the peak, and because there have been numerous climbs in this region over the years, it is likely that most of these options have been explored, either intentionally or inadvertently; the route described here appears to have been the one followed by the Durrance party. Take the standard route to gain the Symmetry Couloir (see *Cascade Canyon, Symmetry Couloir*). Climb this couloir to the first large snowfield. Instead of continuing into the upper section of the main couloir and snowfield, cut out to the left (southwest) into the first and larger of two smaller, less well-defined couloirs. This couloir, which has a bush- and tree-covered slope bordering it to the southeast, leads up toward the Ice Point–Storm Point col, from which the upper part of *Route 10* can be followed to the summit. This approach to the col is slightly more difficult than the standard route described below.

Variation: **EAST RIDGE, SOUTHEAST COULOIR.** II, 4.0. First ascent August 31, 1934, by Whipple Andrews and Reynold Holmen. The broad east side of Storm Point can also be reached using a major couloir on the southeast side of the peak. Hike up the Cascade Canyon trail about 0.3 mile above the top of Hidden Falls, just past the junction with the bypass or horse trail, to a large, open talus slope leading up to the first cliffs of the southeast side of Storm Point. A small creek (may be dry in late season) forms the west edge of this somewhat bushy talus slope and leads directly to the large couloir that is used to pass this cliff band. Ascend this couloir, which is plainly visible from Jenny Lake, in a northwesterly direction for about 60m until it opens out to the left. (The narrow right-hand continuation of this couloir, walled vertically on the right [northeast], provides access to the bush- and tree-covered northeast slope of Storm Point utilized by the main *Route 9*.) Leave the couloir to the left and scramble up for about 120m until past a major eastern buttress. The original variation apparently cut back right (north) onto the upper eastern slope after passing to the south of this buttress. The summit is then attained directly from the east. One might also continue due west near the extreme south edge of the upper couloir to a small notch in the southeast ridge. If one proceeds all the way to this notch, some steep rock above the notch must be climbed in order to reach the summit.

***Variation:* DIRECT EAST RIDGE.** II, 5.1. First ascent August 22, 1940, by John and Elizabeth Buck. Both the main *Route 9* and the East Ridge, Southeast Couloir variation bypass the lower two-thirds of the east ridge of Storm Point. This lower section is unattractive, however, because it consists of trees interspersed with short, broad cliff bands, without anything like a clear line. It forms the left (south) boundary of the main Symmetry Couloir. The beginning of the ridge can be gained from the southeast or directly from the east by working up through the bushes, trees, and cliff bands south of the main stream draining the Symmetry Couloir. Scramble up, partly among the trees, and pass the head of the southeast couloir, mentioned in the preceding variation, still among trees, until the moderately steep rock due east of the summit is reached. Climb the center of this face to the summit.

ROUTE 10. ▲ SYMMETRY COULOIR AND UPPER WEST FACE. II, 4.0. First ascent August 13, 1931, by Fritiof Fryxell and Frank Smith. For the route to the saddle between Symmetry Spire and Ice Point, see *Cascade Canyon, Symmetry Couloir.* From the trees at the saddle, proceed around the right (west) side of Ice Point on a faint trail along some obvious ledges just below the cliffs of Ice Point. This will require a descent of about 1m from the level of the saddle. From the Ice Point–Storm Point col climb directly up the north ridge of Storm Point for about 15m to a very wide ledge that leads around to the right (west) side. After climbing up the 6m corner at the end of the ledge, the easiest way to the summit, now only about 60m above, is a zigzagging route through the west chimneys. It is also possible to continue traversing around the peak and reach the summit from the south or even from the east. On descent inexperienced climbers may wish to make a short rappel. **Time:** 4 to 6 hours from Jenny Lake; 60 to 90 minutes from the summit of Ice Point (see *Ice Point, Route 5*). See *Appalachia* 18, no. 4 (December 1931): pp. 388–408, illus.

ICE POINT (9,920+)

Map: Mount Moran

This small pinnacle has an enjoyable, short, and exposed summit ridge, which is usually combined with a traverse to Storm Point or Symmetry Spire, or both, making for a pleasant conditioning climb at the beginning of a climbing season. The small summit affords an excellent close-up view of the south side of Symmetry Spire. Fritiof Fryxell and Frank Smith, who did the first ascent of Ice Point on the same day as Storm Point, named these two peaks in recognition of the weather of the day—rain, wind, snow, and sleet—which made the ascent significantly more difficult than it is in dry conditions. On July 23, 1931, an attempt by Anderson and Inez M. Hilding and David Tilderquist failed only 12m from the summit on the northwest ridge. The approach for Ice Point is the same as for the regular routes on Storm Point or Symmetry Spire; see *Cascade Canyon* for a description of the route to and up the Symmetry Couloir to the saddle between Ice Point and Symmetry Spire from Jenny Lake.

Chronology

NORTHWEST RIDGE: August 13, 1931, Fritiof Fryxell, Frank Smith

SOUTHWEST RIDGE: August 13, 1931, Fritiof Fryxell, Frank Smith (descent); August 30, 1948, John Holyoke, John Churchill, or June 21, 1949, Robert Brooke, Pete Brown (ascent)
var—July 22, 1960, Bill Wentworth, Alan Feltman

NORTH FACE: August 8, 1952, Gary Driggs, David Sowles, Jim Fisk, Marcia Newell

EAST CHIMNEY: August 12, 1952, William Byrd, S. Blain St. Clair

SOUTH FACE: September 5, 1953, Dmitri Nabokov, Robert Kubie, Dave Arnold

ROUTE 1. SOUTHWEST RIDGE. II, 4.0. First descent August 13, 1931, by Fritiof Fryxell and Frank Smith; first ascent either August 30, 1948, by John Holyoke and John Churchill, or June 21, 1949, by Robert Brooke and Pete Brown. From the Ice Point–Storm Point col a series of large, downsloping steps leads up to the right directly to the summit. Some routefinding ability is required but nowhere is the route difficult.

Variation: II, 5.4. First ascent July 22, 1960, by Bill Wentworth and Alan Feltman. The southwest ridge can be attained from the east using the large eastern couloir. Follow the standard Symmetry Couloir approach up past the initial waterfall to the main snowfield in the couloir. Instead of proceeding up this snowfield (in late season, a loose scree slope with a trail) toward the Ice Point–Symmetry Spire saddle, cut left into the next large couloir to the south, which heads toward the Ice Point–Storm Point col. The talus and rock in the couloir are easily climbed for 90m until one can diagonal right onto a brushy ridge where the roped climbing begins. Climb this ridge to a platform, then move right to and climb up an obvious jam crack, finishing at a tree on a second platform ledge. Move right and up along a ramp and then over a small overhang. One can now climb directly along the southwest ridge to the summit.

ROUTE 2. SOUTH FACE. II, 5.4, A1. First ascent September 5, 1953, by Dmitri Nabokov, Robert Kubie, and Dave Arnold. This route lies to the right (east) of the southwest ridge. The south face consists of downsloping slabs with some loose rock as well. On the first ascent one section involved a piton for aid.

ROUTE 3. EAST CHIMNEY. II, 5.6. First ascent August 12, 1952, by William Byrd and S. Blain St. Clair. From the Ice Point–Symmetry Spire saddle, traverse out past the north face on the one large, obvious ledge to the base of the prominent east chimney. Climb this chimney to the summit.

ROUTE 4. NORTH FACE. II, 5.4. First ascent August 8, 1952, by Gary Driggs, David Sowles, Jim Fisk, and Marcia Newell. This is an alternative route from the Ice Point–Symmetry Spire saddle. Traverse out on the large, obvious ledge near the base of the north face to a point below and somewhat to the right (west) of the summit. Climb the face above, past a small tree, meeting the knife-edge northwest ridge only about 9m west of the summit block. The downsloping holds are intermixed with some vegetated sections.

ROUTE 5. ▲ NORTHWEST RIDGE. II, 4.0. First ascent August 13, 1931, by Fritiof Fryxell and Frank Smith. From the Ice Point–Symmetry Spire saddle, this route follows the obvious ridge curling upward to the summit of Ice Point. The first abrupt step in this ridge can be climbed via a small chimney just to the right (west) of the crest, but one can avoid this section by traversing out on a ledge on the left flank of the ridge to a series of easy ledges that lead back to the crest above this step. From this point to the summit closely follow the knife-edge crest. On descent no rappels are required. To climb Storm Point on the same day, as is easily and commonly done, descend this ridge to the small notch where the ridge turns northward to the Ice Point–Symmetry Spire saddle. From this notch it is an easy matter to descend south to the Ice Point–Storm Point col via the southwest ridge. To approach the base of this ridge from Storm Point, a trail can be easily followed around the west base of Ice Point from the Ice Point–Storm Point col. **Time:** 4½ to 5½ hours from Jenny Lake; 60–90 minutes from the summit of Storm Point. See *Appalachia* 18, no. 4 (December 1931): pp. 388–408, illus.; *Trail and Timberline,* no. 447 (March 1956): pp. 47–48.

HANGOVER PINNACLE (ca. 8,800)

(0.3 mi SE of Symmetry Spire)
Map: Mount Moran

This small but distinctive pinnacle is on the right (north) edge of the main east couloir that leads to the saddle between Ice Point and Symmetry Spire (see *Cascade Canyon, Symmetry Couloir*). Hangover Pinnacle is about one-quarter of the way up the couloir and is easily seen after one enters the area of the main snowfield above the initial shoulder, which is above the top edge of the waterfall (see *Figures 8-13 and 8-14*). The pinnacle, composed of excellent solid rock, has significant overhangs on all sides except the north aspect. Easily approached from Jenny Lake, it achieved considerable early popularity as a rock climb. (It has since been eclipsed by Baxter's Pinnacle, which is an even shorter hike.) Using a top rope, climbers have worked out various more difficult routes on all four faces; Robert Merriam, Willi Unsoeld, and Leigh Ortenburger established the first of these lines on July 15, 1951. For those interested in photographs, it is possible to establish an impressive Tyrolean traverse from the pinnacle to the slope of Symmetry Spire, rising above.

Chronology

NORTH FACE: August 1948, Richard Pownall, Mickey Thomas, Leigh Ortenburger
SOUTHWEST RIDGE: August 20, 1956, Richard Pownall, Marian Macy, Van Hellar

ROUTE 1. SOUTHWEST RIDGE. II, 5.6, A2. First ascent August 20, 1956, by Richard Pownall, Marian Macy, and Van Hellar. Aid was used to lead and climb this overhanging ridge.

ROUTE 2. ▲ NORTH FACE. I, 5.6. First ascent in August 1948, by Richard Pownall, Mickey Thomas, and Leigh Ortenburger. From the main Symmetry Couloir some scrambling is required to reach the notch separating Hangover Pinnacle from the main mass of Symmetry Spire. From the notch the route lies up the downsloping slabs of the north face and angles left to reach the final summit block from the east. For descent, a rappel is necessary down either the regular route of ascent or the spectacular south face. **Time:** 3 hours from Jenny Lake.

BAXTER'S PINNACLE (ca. 8,000)

(0.65 mi E of Symmetry Spire)
Map: Mount Moran

This minor spire has a history unique in the Tetons and perhaps in the United States. For 10 years after its discovery and first ascent in 1947 by Alfred Baxter and Ulf Ramm-Ericson, it was lost. At the time of the first edition of this book (published by the Sierra Club in 1956), Teton climbers were aware of the note that had appeared in the *Sierra Club Bulletin* concerning the pinnacle's first ascent, and queries had been made of members of the first-ascent party as to its location. Several parties searched for it, climbing some minor points in the area around Storm Point and Symmetry Spire, but it remained for John Gill, Rick Lloyd, and Douglas Jefferson to rediscover the pinnacle on July 25, 1957. The second ascent was made a few days later on July 29 by Yvon Chouinard and John Lowry.

Originally named Stanford Pinnacle, in honor of the school of the first-ascent party, Baxter's received its current name by editorial happenstance: The 1965 revised edition of this guidebook was also published by the Sierra Club, and a member of its editorial staff, a friend of Al Baxter's, saw fit to change the name after the manuscript had been submitted for

The final pitch of Baxter's Pinnacle (Photo by Vic Zeilman)

publication. Such is the crooked historical course of toponymy. (Another unfortunate and tragic twist occurred during the Oakland Hills Firestorm on October 20, 1991. Leigh Ortenburger, co-author of this guidebook, was visiting friends Al and Gail Baxter at their Berkeley home when the fire swept through. He and Gail were killed, and Al survived with severe burns.)

The approach to this small, distinctively yellow pinnacle requires so little time that any one of its upper routes is entirely appropriate for an afternoon rock climb. The original 1947 route up the upper south face, *Route 4*, combined with the pitches of the south ridge leading up to it, is a fun, short, yet distinctly difficult climb to a genuine summit, which requires a rappel to leave. The nearby small ridge east of Baxter's Pinnacle has also been climbed at least once.

Baxter's Pinnacle is located on the second lowest (counting from the east) of the south ridges of Cube Point, just above a large, open talus slope that extends almost all the way down to the trail on the west side of Jenny Lake. For the approach, walk north from the west shore boat dock on the Valley Trail a short distance, about 0.2 mile, to the horse trail (with sign) leading off to the west. Take this wide trail about 0.5 mile to a grove of trees where the trail makes a right-angle bend back to the left (south). From this point the south ridge of Baxter's Pinnacle can be seen rising above to the north. A climbers' trail turns off here and leads up through scree and talus to the start of the South Ridge route *(Route 5)*. The horse trail can also be reached by hiking south on the Valley Trail, starting at the south String Lake parking lot.

The southwest couloir leading down from the notch behind the pinnacle is the standard route of descent. Great care must be taken in this couloir because there are likely to be other climbers below in the couloir and much of the rock is loose. An alternative scheme for descent is to scramble a short distance up from the notch onto the ridge above and descend the far (northeast) side to a talus slope, which will bring one back to the horse trail.

A climb of Baxter's Pinnacle is often combined with No Perches Necessary, a two-pitch route located on a small buttress up and left (west) of the southwest descent couloir (see *Cascade Canyon, North Side Rock Climbs, East Cascade Buttresses*). **Note:** Baxter's Pinnacle and the area around it, including the approach and the descent gully, is often closed during the spring season because of nesting peregrine falcons. Inquire about its status at the Jenny Lake Ranger Station.

Chronology

UPPER SOUTH FACE: June 26, 1947, Alfred Baxter, Ulf Ramm-Ericson; FFA August 1957, John Gill, partner
var—**GILL:** July 10, 1958, John Gill, Gordon Sutton
EAST FACE: July 18, 1958, Yvon Chouinard, David Craft; FFA ca. July 17, 1975, Jeb Schenck, partner
SOUTH RIDGE: July 27, 1958, Barry Corbet, Robert French
var—**GRAY RAMP:** September 8, 1968, Peter Koedt, William Miller
var—**SEIZURE DISORDER:** September 5, 1989, Jim Springer, Lanny Johnson
var—**SOUTHEAST FACE:** June 2, 2001, Trevor Bowman, Nick Stayner
NORTHWEST CORNER: August 7, 1958, Yvon Chouinard, Bob Kamps
NORTH FACE: August 11, 1958, Richard Pownall, Paul Kenworthy; FFA July 19, 1960, Royal Robbins, Joe Fitschen, Robert Toepel, Ken Weeks
NORTHEAST RIDGE: August 1959, Barry Corbet, Julie Peterson
SOUTHWEST FACE: Early July 1963, Rick Medrick, Barry Corbet, Sterling Neale
HOWARD: June 9, 1971, George Hurley, Dennis Wignall
WEST FACE I: July 1971, Yvon Chouinard, Juris Krisjansons
WEST FACE II: September 7, 1978, Yvon Chouinard, Mike Munger

ROUTE 1. WEST FACE I. II, 5.8. First ascent in July 1971, by Yvon Chouinard and Juris Krisjansons. The west face of Baxter's Pinnacle rises from the southwest couloir, which is the standard, if unpleasant, descent route. From the col behind the pinnacle at the top of the couloir, a large ledge system cuts horizontally across this west face over to the base of the upper south face. From a point almost directly below the summit, an intermediate ledge harboring a flake will be seen about halfway between the couloir and the upper ledge system. Climb directly up from the descent gully on a dark, high-angle face to this lower ledge, just to the right of the flake, and continue up the face (5.7) to gain the main ledge system. The second lead (5.8) goes slightly left and then up a 2.5-inch slanting jam crack to the prominent horn on the northwest ridge; this same horn is attained from the col on the Northwest Corner route *(Route 10)*. From the horn climb directly up to the summit. **Gear:** For protection take a regular rack of nuts, quickdraws, and camming devices to 2.5"–3".

ROUTE 2. WEST FACE II. II, 5.10. First ascent September 7, 1978, by Yvon Chouinard and Mike Munger. This route starts in the southwest descent couloir about 60m up from the base of the South Ridge route *(Route 5)*. Climb (4.0) up to the west base of an obvious fin on the crest of the south ridge. The first lead, on the left (west) side of the fin, goes up a left-facing corner (5.8) past some fixed pitons to a belay ledge. The second pitch moves left to a smooth right-facing corner, which is climbed (5.10) to its top. The next lead also stays out on the face to the left of the regular South Ridge route up to the crest of the ridge. An easier pitch takes one to the base of the upper south face, where a descending traverse to the left of the summit block takes one to the west face crack (5.8) leading up toward the prominent horn on the northwest ridge (see *Route 10*). From the horn and bolt (may have been removed and/or replaced) move out right and up to the summit instead of climbing straight up.

ROUTE 3. SOUTHWEST FACE. II, 5.8. First ascent in early July 1963, by Rick Medrick, Barry Corbet, and Sterling Neale. This three-pitch route starts out of the southwest descent couloir, as do *Routes 1* and *2*, and ascends the southwest face of the south ridge. The first pitch begins in the first large open book to the west of the crest of the south ridge, proceeds up about 9m toward the large overhang that caps the book, and then traverses left 4.5m on thin holds (5.8) to a belay stance on a downsloping ledge where anchor placements are difficult to obtain. The next lead (5.8) goes up 6m to a loose block and then traverses slightly down and left for 4.5m around a bulge to a crack leading diagonally back up to the right for another 4.5m; now climb back left and up across the face, stepping around a corner to an easier crack that is followed, amid loose rock, for 12m to the belay. The final pitch turns left around a corner and continues up a short but strenuous overhang to the main west face ledge system at the base of the summit block. One can continue to the summit via *Route 1* or *Route 4*.

ROUTE 4. ▲ UPPER SOUTH FACE. II, 5.6, A1, or II, 5.9. First ascent June 26, 1947, by Alfred Baxter and Ulf Ramm-Ericson; first free ascent in August 1957, by John Gill and partner. (See *Figures 8-9* and *8-10*.) From the talus slope south of Baxter's Pinnacle, the notch separating the pinnacle from the remainder of the ridge above is reached by ascending the southwest couloir (loose rock) on the left (west) side of the pinnacle. From this notch a series of ledges leads without difficulty around the exposed west face to the small notch at the base of the upper south face of the final yellow tower. The first- and second-ascent parties, and many parties even today, pull up on the piton buried in the crack at the base of the final pitch in order to reach the easier rock that leads to the large flake just above. The initial part of the pitch is the most difficult, and most people find that dropping down to the right (east) about 1m and then climbing the wall directly up to the flake is the easiest way. This still requires a few 5.9 moves, however. From the flake climb up and left, liebacking up a steep ramp past old fixed pins, a maneuver that

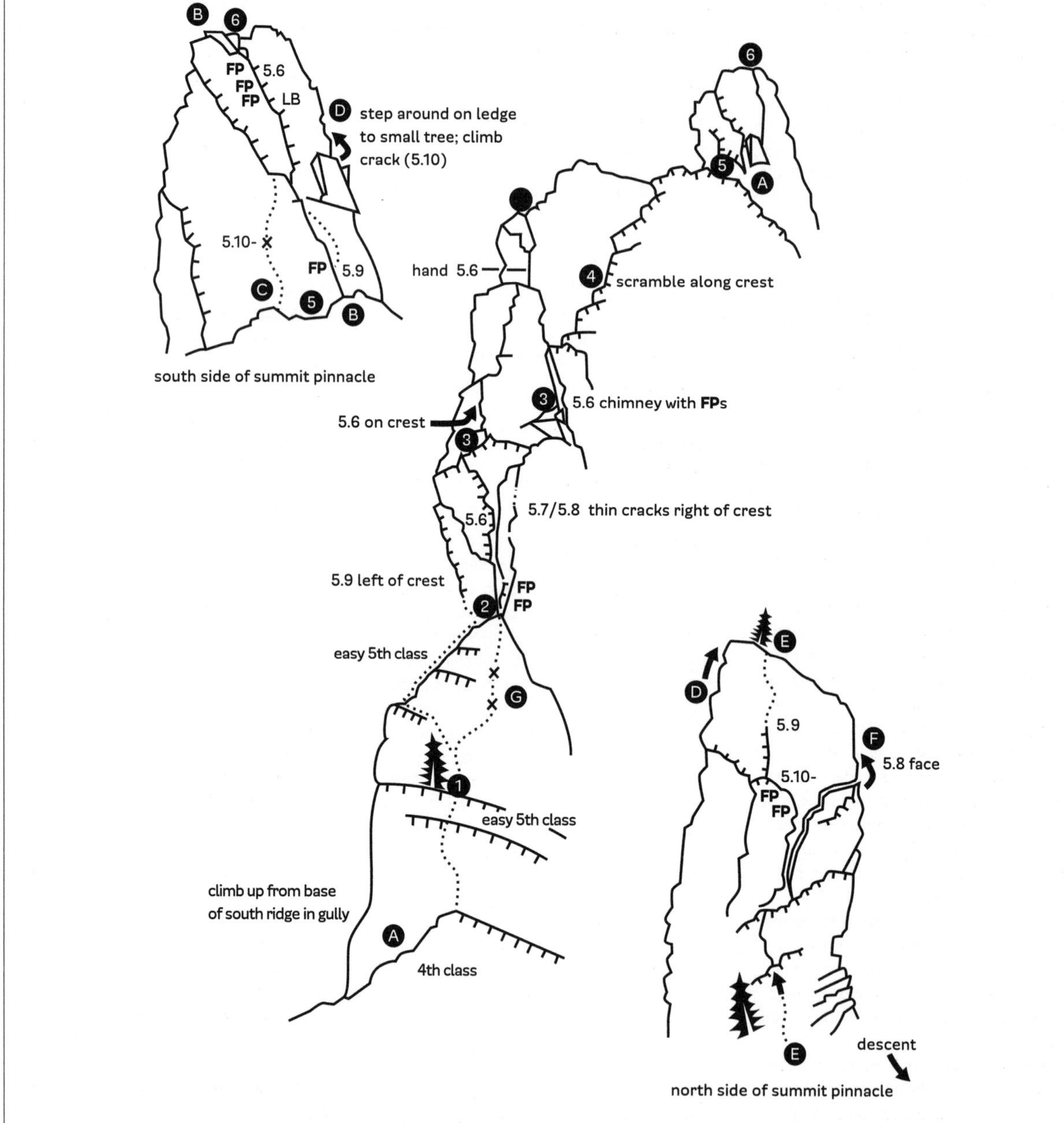

FIGURE 8-9. Baxter's Pinnacle. (A) South Ridge *(Route 5)*, II, 5.6; (B) Upper South Face *(Route 4)*, II, 5.6, A1 or II, 5.9; (C) Upper South Face, variation: Gill, II, 5.10-R; (D) East Face *(Route 7)*, II, 5.10; (E) North Face *(Route 9)*, II, 5.10; (F) Northwest Corner *(Route 10)*, II, 5.8; (G) South Ridge, variation: Seizure Disorder, II, 5.10

is fortunately somewhat easier than it appears. The final short vertical wall to the summit is exposed. An established anchor on top facilitates a 25m rappel (partly free) into the notch on the north side. Descend the southwest couloir back to the base of the pinnacle. *Use great care* in this descent because there are likely to be other climbers below in the couloir and much of the rock is loose. **Time:** 3¼ to 5 hours from Jenny Lake. See *Sierra Club Bulletin* 33, no. 3 (March 1948): p. 121.

***Variation:* GILL.** II, 5.10-R. First ascent July 10, 1958, by John Gill and Gordon Sutton. (See *Figures 8-9* and *8-10.*) This difficult variation ascends the face immediately left of the regular Upper South Face route on the final tower. Move up on thin holds for about 6m, clipping a bolt about 3m above the ledge, and then diagonal to the flake to the right. Follow the remainder of the Upper South Face route to the summit.

ROUTE 5. ▲ SOUTH RIDGE. II, 5.6. First ascent July 27, 1958, by Barry Corbet and Robert French. (See *Figures 8-9* and *8-10.*) This popular route is perhaps the most enjoyable climb on the pinnacle and certainly contains the most pitches. It starts at the base of the well-defined lower south ridge of the pinnacle at the upper end of the talus slope and stays on the crest for about five pitches, until the final tower is reached, at which point the Upper South Face route *(Route 4)* is followed to the summit. Begin the route by climbing up from the base in a gully. From the top of the gully continue up some 15m of 4.0 and 5.1 climbing to gain a ledge next to a large tree; belay here. The Seizure Disorder variation is just above on an orange face. Easier climbing around to the west leads to the next belay, beneath parallel cracks with a few old fixed pins. The third pitch begins with these cracks just right of the crest and eventually reaches a lieback flake. After the flake climb up and right to the base of a short chimney and belay. (**Note:** As an alternative to the parallel cracks, it is possible to climb 5.7/5.8 thin cracks farther to the right. Additionally, belaying on the crest at the top of the third pitch permits one to stay on the crest [5.6] for the fourth lead.) From the belay at the top of the third pitch, stem up the short chimney (5.6) to where easier climbing along the ridge crest leads to a belay on a ledge with trees. One more pitch of scrambling reaches the base of the summit pinnacle. Climb the final pinnacle as in *Route 4.*

FIGURE 8-10. Baxter's Pinnacle, South Ridge *(Route 5)*, II, 5.6, to Upper South Face *(Route 4)*, II, 5.9

***Variation:* GRAY RAMP.** II, 5.9. First ascent September 8, 1968, by Peter Koedt and William Miller. On the first pitch of the South Ridge route, follow a gray ramp below and to the left (west) of the blade of the ridge crest for one pitch.

***Variation:* SEIZURE DISORDER.** II, 5.10. First ascent September 5, 1989, by Jim Springer and Lanny Johnson. (See *Figures 8-9* and *8-10.*) After the first pitch up from the base of the south ridge, mostly in a gully, this difficult one-pitch variation starts on the southeast-facing wall to the right of the ridge crest near a large tree. Climb this wall to the left of a large detached pedestal toward and past a diagonal crack, moving right and up past two bolts (5.10) to a ledge. This brings one to the base of the third pitch of the standard South Ridge route.

Variation: **SOUTHEAST FACE.** II, 5.8. First ascent June 2, 2001, by Trevor Bowman and Nick Stayner. This three-pitch variation begins on the lower east face of Baxter's Pinnacle, north of the starts of *Routes 5* and *6*. The first pitch is short and takes a direct line up the face to a belay on the same ledge system shared with *Route 6* (easy 5th class). The second pitch goes up a crack (5.7, 3m) to a ledge with two corners rising from it. Continue up the right-hand corner (5.8, 8m) to easier ground leading to the "ledge with a large tree" mentioned in *Route 6*. Climb a short chimney to a belay ledge with a second, smaller tree on it (5.8, 50m). The third pitch climbs the face directly above via a flake system (5.6) to the large roof and then bypasses the roof by means of a hand traverse left (5.5) to join the standard South Ridge route. **Gear:** Long runners are needed for this route, along with a regular Teton rack.

ROUTE 6. HOWARD. II, 5.8. First ascent June 9, 1971, by George Hurley and Dennis Wignall. This route stays on the east side of the south ridge to the base of the summit block. The first pitch (5.1, 40m) starts below and to the right of the tree at the top of the first pitch of the South Ridge route *(Route 5)*. Follow an obvious lieback/jam crack for 9m; continue up, angling right to easy (4.0) ledges, to the belay at the base of a short headwall. The next lead (40m) proceeds up and slightly right in the obvious crack past a ledge with a large tree; go right of the tree to and across easy (4.0) ledges for the belay at another headwall. The third pitch (5.8, 46m) ascends the crack in this headwall into and up the rotten dihedral above to a large belay ledge. Next traverse left (west) for 6m to an obvious lieback/jam crack in the wall; climb this crack to easy ledges (4.0) and trees on the upper portion of the South Ridge route. The next two leads stay on the right side of the ridge crest up to the summit block. The summit is attained by *Route 4*.

ROUTE 7. EAST FACE. I, 5.6, A1, or II, 5.10. First ascent July 18, 1958, by Yvon Chouinard and David Craft; first free ascent on about July 17, 1975, by Jeb Schenck and partner. (See *Figures 8-9* and *8-10*.) Start from the base of the south face of the final tower and climb to the flake, as in *Route 4*. From the flake, traverse around to the right to the east face and climb the steep, short face/crack above (5.10). **Gear:** Tiny to small offsets are useful in the hard section.

ROUTE 8. NORTHEAST RIDGE. II, 5.9. First ascent in August 1959, by Barry Corbet and Julie Peterson. Start as in *Route 7*, traversing around to the right (north) from the flake, but continue past the east face to the northeast ridge, which is climbed to the summit.

ROUTE 9. NORTH FACE. II, 5.6, A2, or II, 5.10. First ascent August 11, 1958, by Richard Pownall and Paul Kenworthy; first free ascent July 19, 1960, by Royal Robbins, Joe Fitschen, Robert Toepel, and Ken Weeks. (See *Figure 8-9*.) This route starts from the main col separating the pinnacle from the mountain and stays near the center, or slightly left of the center, of the north face. The obvious crack, which parallels *Route 10* and then cuts left into a right-angle alcove, is utilized for either aid or difficult free climbing. Leave the alcove to the right to reach easier free climbing above.

ROUTE 10. NORTHWEST CORNER. II, 5.8. First ascent August 7, 1958, by Yvon Chouinard and Bob Kamps. (See *Figure 8-9*.) Start from the main col at the base of the north face where a prominent, wide crack goes first up and then horizontally out to the right (northwest) corner and a prominent horn. Climb this crack using jam holds and hand traverse out to the corner. Step up on top of the flake at the corner and climb the face above (5.8); then angle slightly to the left and directly up the corner to the summit. A protection bolt for this lead may have been removed and/or replaced.

CUBE POINT (9,600+)

(0.4 mi E of Symmetry Spire)

Map: Mount Moran

This is the prominent tower at the lower end of the east ridge of Symmetry Spire. It is separated from the spire by a deep, sharp notch. Cube Point furnishes a fine summit and an interesting, easily approached, short one-day climb. The first climbs of this peak are a bit confused. Having found no evidence of a previous ascent, the 1938 party of Jack Fralick and Harold and William Plumley claimed the first ascent. Then at some point in the ensuing years, a note turned up among the summit register records: "August 5, 1937, Norton Nelson and Carroll Saffell. We came up the gully just to the south." This note presumably was not found on the highest point, or else the 1938 party would have reported it. Originally it was thought that Fralick and the Plumleys had named the peak after the cubical shape of the summit block. However, after a discussion with Fralick some years later, it was determined that they were simply living on cube steaks purchased at the Jenny Lake Store at the time.

The combined East Couloir/East Ridge route (see *Routes 4* and *5*) has become popular, especially for guided parties, because it affords an enjoyable climb on moderate but exposed rock. To approach this regular route, take the climbers' trail into Hanging Canyon to Arrowhead Pool (see *Figure 8-11*). Approach information for the other routes is discussed in detail below.

Chronology

EAST COULOIR: June 25, 1938, Harold and William Plumley, Jack Fralick, or August 5, 1937, Norton Nelson, Carroll Saffell (probably partial)
var—[probable] June 29, 1957, Dean Millsap, Bill Echo, Sam Mitchell, Anthony Lagani, S. Bostwick

WEST CHIMNEY: 1939, John and George Holyoke (descent); July 6, 1940, Paul Petzoldt, Joseph Hawkes, Bernhard Nebel (ascent)
var—[probable] July 12, 1960, Charles and Cora Sanders, A. Maram (descent)

EAST RIDGE: [probable] August 17, 1945, Joseph and Edith Stettner, John Speck, Alan Stiles, Rex Parks, B. Hicks, Anna Gay, Betty Burno, Elv Bushman, Mary Tremaine, T. A. Campbell; [possible] July 1, 1938, Carl Heeschen, Clyde Havenstot, Robert Rynot

SOUTH RIDGE: June 15, 1958, Walter Gove, Karl Ross, or July 16, 1959, Barry Corbet, Robert French
var—September 4, 1966, Barry Corbet, Chuck Satterfield
var—**WALL OF LEO:** July 24, 1990, Leo Larson, Jim Woodmencey (first pitch); August 10, 1990, Brent Finley, George Montopoli (second and third pitches)
var—**CON GUSANO:** August 7, 2021, Michael Gardner, Elliot Gaddy, with Jimmy Voorhis

NORTH FACE: July 15, 1971, Mark Chapman, Bruce Patterson

BREACHING WHALE TOWER, SOUTH FACE: July 2005, David Bywater, Martin Vidak

ROUTE 1. WEST CHIMNEY. II, 5.1. First descent in 1939, by John and George Holyoke; first ascent July 6, 1940, by Paul Petzoldt, Joseph Hawkes, and Bernhard Nebel. (See *Figure 8-12*.) From the vicinity of Arrowhead Pool, go to the notch between Cube Point and Symmetry Spire. Just left (north) of the notch is a steep-walled chimney or couloir that provides a chockstone route up through the first cliffs. From the top of this chimney, scramble along the narrow ridge to the summit. No rappel is actually needed to descend this chimney, although it may be desired.

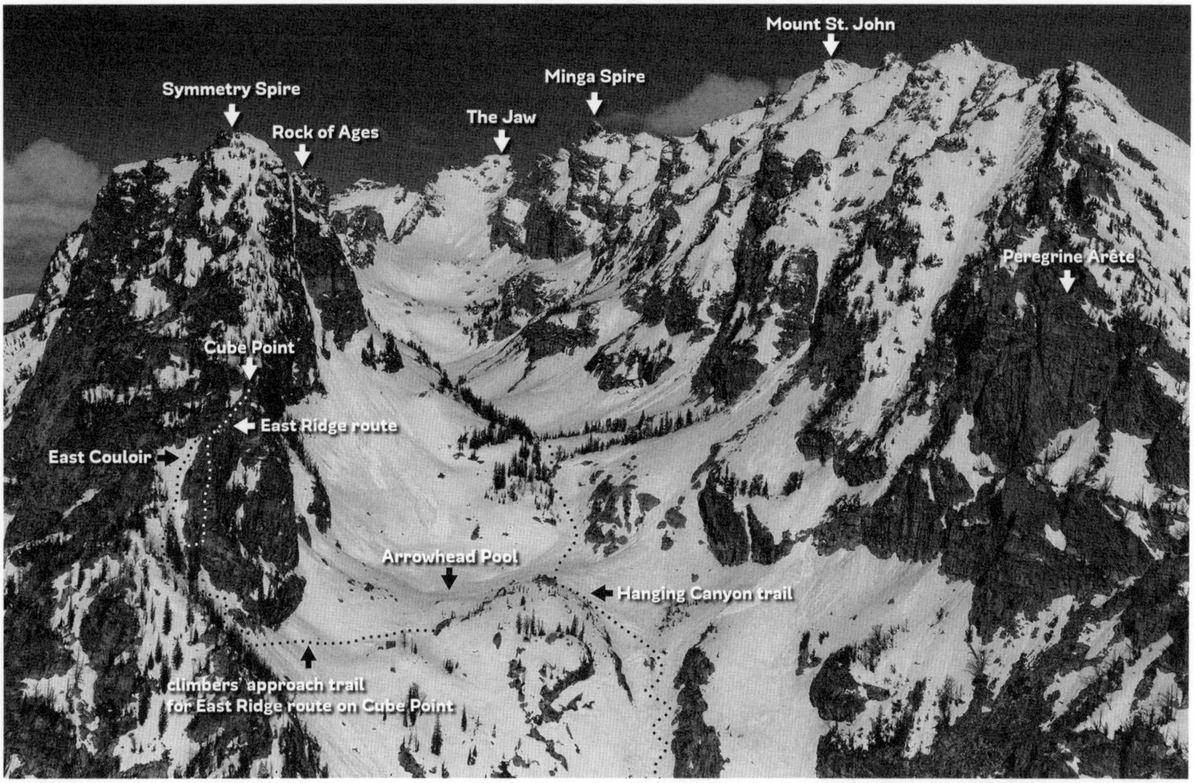

FIGURE 8-11. Hanging Canyon overview

Variation: II, 5.1. Probable first descent July 12, 1960, by Charles and Cora Sanders and A. Maram. The notch immediately west of Cube Point can also be reached from the south. To enter the couloir that leads to this notch, start the climb via the usual route up the Symmetry Couloir (see *Cascade Canyon*). Along the beginning of that route, after climbing the short cliff and cutting back left along the top of this cliff, cross a small stream. This stream drains the two couloirs. Ascend the left (western) of these two couloirs up to the notch in the ridge.

ROUTE 2. SOUTH RIDGE. II, 5.4. First ascent June 15, 1958, by Walter Gove and Karl Ross, or July 16, 1959, by Barry Corbet and Robert French; on June 15, 1938, Jack Fralick and Harold and William Plumley attempted this side of the peak but retreated from a point on the lower east ridge. The main south ridge of Cube Point lies between the two couloirs drained by the stream that one crosses in the short traverse left at the top of the initial cliff of the regular route up the Symmetry Couloir (see *Cascade Canyon*). Several climbs have been made on the south side of the pinnacle, but the exact locations of the routes are not accurately known. The 1959 ascent started with 150m of scrambling up into a bowl of white rock on the right side of one of the south ridges; this main south ridge may have been the one described, or it may have been the next one to the east (the southeast ridge). The bowl was abandoned when it became easier to climb the ridge itself. The top of the ridge ended at a south peak, separated from the main summit by the top of the east couloir (see *Route 4*). Scramble across this to the true summit.

Variation: II, 5.8, A2. First ascent September 4, 1966, by Barry Corbet and Chuck Satterfield. The start of this variation at the base of the south ridge is reached by scrambling up and to the far right side of the ridge toward a tree on a slanting apron. The first pitch starts up a 15m open book, exiting to the left to a small ledge containing several blocks, then heads back to the right to a continuation of the open book; now move up and left over a 3m bulge (5.8) onto a downsloping

FIGURE 8-12. Cube Point, west aspect

ledge, the belay spot. The next short lead moves up and slightly left over slightly loose rock for 15m to a belay stance below a dark overhang. The third pitch, the crux, starts 3m left of the belay, goes up a difficult friction slab to the lower of two bulging troughs, and continues straight up the slab above to the slight bulge at its top; pass this bulge with aid to the belay stance. The next lead goes up a 6m tight chimney to the base of a ramp, where one continues left to the nose of the ridge, which is climbed on small, delicate holds to the belay position. An easier pitch (4.0) leads after 30m to a smooth 9m face, which is climbed with some difficulty to a belay ledge. One more lead (4.0) allows exit from the ridge to the false summit, the southwest apex. From this point to the main summit is but a scramble.

***Variation:* WALL OF LEO.** II, 5.10-. First ascent July 24, 1990, by Jim Woodmencey and Leo Larson (first pitch), and August 10, 1990, by Brent Finley and George Montopoli (second and third pitches). (See *Figure 8-13.*) The southern side of Cube Point is an area that is complicated by numerous walls and smaller cliff bands. When one looks up the Symmetry Couloir, a steep gully is seen dropping down from Cube Point. At the point where this gully intersects the Symmetry Couloir, an upward-slanting, continuous line of trees is apparent. The Wall of Leo is a smooth-looking wall directly above the highest of these trees. In the center of this wall there are a number of shallow, right-facing corners located just to the north of a recent rockfall scar. Climb up to the base of the first corner north of this scar and look for a bolt a few meters up. Continue past the bolt (5.10-) and two fixed pitons, then at its top step over to the west (5.9) to another right-facing corner. Continue up a lieback crack (5.7 to 5.8) to a belay at another bolt. The second pitch ascends an easy face to a 5.8 finger crack and then proceeds up to a ledge for the belay. Diagonal right on a 6- to 12-inch ledge (5.7) and then climb a flaring crack that ends on the ramp that marks the top of the climb. For the descent go up and east to a treed ledge that leads into the gully that comes down from Cube Point. Note that this climb can be done in two pitches. **Gear:** For protection take a regular rack with several additional small camming devices.

FIGURE 8-13. Cube Point, South Ridge *(Route 2)*. (A) Variation: Wall of Leo, II, 5.10-; (B) Variation: Con Gusano, II, 5.11-

***Variation:* CON GUSANO.** II, 5.11-. First ascent August 7, 2021, by Michael Gardner and Elliot Gaddy, with Jimmy Voorhis on an intial foray. (See *Figure 8-13.*) This variation rises above the Wall of Leo walk-off descent. It makes for an interesting linkup with that route for those desiring wide, overhanging crack climbing. **Pitch 1:** Pull through overlaps off the ground to gain a low-angle slab that rises up to meet the wildly overhanging wide crack. Thoughtful gear placements are essential to avoid rope drag later on. Climb the crack (5.11-), saving the big cams for the end. Belay on a horselike feature, using a crack in the headwall for an anchor. **Pitch 2:** Worm along the horselike feature to the obvious weakness that breaks the steep headwall. Climb balancy slabs, trending up and left for 55m (5.9). Belay out left before the final pitch of golden rock. **Pitch 3:** Traverse a short distance over to the next step, climb straight up, and pull a small roof on the left side (5.9). From here sail up through a sea of classic Teton granite, following the path of least resistance. Belay near a big tree on an obvious ledge. Descent is made via rappel, beginning skier's right (west) of the tree: One 30m rappel off a slung block leads to a large ledge. Walk down, skier's left, to the next anchor, where another 30m rappel takes one to the base of the first pitch. Now follow the walk-off descent for Wall of Leo, trending east into the gully that comes down from Cube Point. **Gear:** Recommended protection includes two sets of cams up to 2", one 3.5" cam, two 4" cams, and one #5 Camalot C4, plus micro cams and a set of nuts.

ROUTE 3. BREACHING WHALE TOWER, SOUTH FACE. II, 5.9. First ascent in July 2005, by David Bywater and Martin Vidak. Breaching Whale Tower, which looks much like a breaching whale, is a freestanding pinnacle located on the south side of Cube Point, directly above No Perches Necessary *(Cascade Canyon, North Side Rock Climbs, East Cascade Buttresses, Route 1)* and at an elevation of approximately 8,250 feet. To approach, proceed up the Symmetry Couloir climbers' trail (see *Cascade Canyon, Symmetry Couloir*) a short distance to a point below a large drainage, which is followed upward to the base of the tower. This drainage is located about 150m up from No Perches Necessary and just before the first scrambling section of the Symmetry Couloir climbers' trail. **Pitch 1:** From the toe of the south-facing side of the tower, climb a shallow crack system past a fixed nut to a belay stance below a roof (5.8, 30m; two fixed pins at the belay). **Pitch 2:** Climb up and right through the right-hand side of the roof onto the southeast face. Then climb straight up smooth, solid granite on small face holds, reaching the crux just before the top of the tower. Protection is thin on the upper face (5.9, 21m). Small nuts and cams are useful. To descend, scramble and downclimb off the northwest side and then scramble down along the west side of the tower to the base of the climb; descend the drainage used for the approach.

ROUTE 4. ▲ EAST COULOIR. II, 4.0. First ascent June 25, 1938, by Harold and William Plumley and Jack Fralick, or August 5, 1937, by Norton Nelson and Carroll Saffell (probably partial). (See *Figure 8-11.*) *Routes 4* and *5* in combination have become the standard route on Cube Point. Together, they provide a great day in the mountains to a worthy summit featuring excellent views. Prior to the improvements to the old climbers' trail in Hanging Canyon, early ascents entered this couloir lower down in the canyon. These days simply take the climbers' trail to Arrowhead Pool and cross the outlet stream, heading south and up along a trail that switchbacks toward the ridge crest. Near the crest the trail turns west and wanders up parallel to and south of the distinct east ridge. Along the way, a cutoff to the north leads to the base of that climb (see *Route 5*); from this point on, one is on the normal descent route from *Route 5*. Continue scrambling up this gully/couloir to a notch at its head and turn right (north) to reach the summit block from the east. The summit "cube" can then be climbed from either the south or the west. Use caution with the loose rock in this couloir because other climbers may be below.

Variation: II, 4.0. Probable first ascent June 29, 1957, by Dean Millsap, Bill Echo, Sam Mitchell, Anthony Lagani, and S. Bostwick. The east couloir can also be reached indirectly from the south. From the approach to the Symmetry Couloir (see *Cascade Canyon*), take the main couloir leading onto the lower east ridge of Cube Point. It is located about halfway between Baxter's Pinnacle and the couloir (see the 1960 variation to *Route 1*) that leads to the notch west of Cube Point. Once the east ridge is reached, one can contour around on the north side and scramble into the upper east couloir.

ROUTE 5. ▲ EAST RIDGE. II, 5.4. Probable first ascent August 17, 1945, by Joseph and Edith Stettner, John Speck, Alan Stiles, Rex Parks, B. Hicks, Anna Gay, Betty Burno, Elv Bushman, Mary Tremaine, and T. A. Campbell; possible first ascent July 1, 1938, by Carl Heeschen, Clyde Havenstot, and Robert Rynot. (See *Figures 8-11* and *8-12.*) This airy ridge is now the popular route on this small peak, providing an enjoyable short day of easy rock climbing. It has the advantage that the descent route, the east couloir (see *Route 4*), passes by the start of the steep rock on the east ridge, so one can leave packs and extra gear near the beginning of this climb. Approach as described in *Route 4*. Three to four pitches of enjoyable climbing on the narrow ridge crest lead to the summit "cube," which can be climbed from either the south or the west. Some fixed pitons will be encountered. Several small variations on the crest are possible. To descend by way of the east couloir, first scramble down to the southeast a short distance to the notch mentioned in *Route 4*, then head down the 4th-class gully/couloir to return to Arrowhead Pool. Be mindful of loose rock on this descent. **Time:** 5½ to 6 hours from Jenny Lake.

ROUTE 6. NORTH FACE. II, 5.6. First ascent July 15, 1971, by Mark Chapman and Bruce Patterson. Approach this face from Arrowhead Pool and start the climb near the northeast corner. Climb toward the center of the face.

SYMMETRY SPIRE (10,560+)

Map: Mount Moran

Symmetry Spire, rising immediately above Jenny Lake, appears insignificant when the entire range is viewed from a distance, but this small peak played a major role in the development and history of Teton mountaineering. Originally climbed in the opening wave of first ascents in the initial year of the new Grand Teton National Park, the peak became the locus of difficult rock-climbing activity. The routes pioneered by Jack Durrance and Bert Jensen were early classics of the range and served as standard objectives for enterprising climbers who wished to apply their skills to Teton rock. In the 1950s the impressive Direct Jensen Ridge *(Route 9)* was one of the area's major testpieces, attracting the best climbers of the day. For a time, this little peak was more popular with the climbers who visited Grand Teton National Park than any other peak except the Grand Teton itself.

The establishment of newer, more difficult rock climbs in Death, Garnet, and Cascade Canyons eventually diverted attention from Symmetry Spire. Despite this reduced activity, the south side routes remain fine objectives and even today can be recommended as an enjoyable way to spend a day on Teton rock. One of the challenges for a chronicler of climbing history is deciphering and interpreting from now-ancient route descriptions where climbers went at the height of the spire's popularity. The cautious reader must realize that venturing onto any route other than one of the three that currently see the most traffic—the Southwest Ridge *(Route 4)*, the Durrance Ridge *(Route 7)*, and the Direct Jensen Ridge—will involve some adventure.

As with all mountain routes, there is an occasional loose block here and there, but the rock is predominantly good with ample cracks available for protection. This peak is easily accessible from Jenny Lake; only two hours are required to reach the base of the high-angle rock climbs on its south side. From these south-side climbs, climbers have the advantage of being able to easily see the approach of bad weather. Another plus is the spire's fast, easy route of descent—helpful in the event the summit is reached at a late hour. Although it is primarily a rock climber's peak, ice axes must usually be taken for the moderately steep snow in the Symmetry Couloir in early season and in the upper couloir even in midseason.

See *Figure 8-14* for an overview of the upper Symmetry Spire drainage, including the locations of several of the climbs described below. The usual approach for the regular Southwest Couloir route *(Route 3)* is via the Symmetry Couloir to the Ice Point–Symmetry Spire saddle; see *Cascade Canyon, Symmetry Couloir* for directions into and up this couloir. Also see *Figure 8-15* for an overview of climbs on the south side of Symmetry Spire: The Southwest Ridge *(Route 4)*, perhaps the best route on the peak, is shown on the left side of the figure with its two noteworthy pitches. Also shown for reference is the Durrance Ridge, which ascends the right-hand side of the same face.

For the scenic approach to the north side of Symmetry Spire, see *Hanging Canyon*. The standard route of descent from the summit of Symmetry Spire is via the southwest couloir.

FIGURE 8-14. Symmetry Spire and Symmetry Couloir overview

Chronology

EAST RIDGE: August 20, 1929, Fritiof Fryxell, Phil Smith
var—[probable] July 30, 1935, M. N. Schell, R. L. Harrington, P. E. Griffith
var—**NORTHERN COULOIR:** July 27, 1954, William Cropper, Ellis Blade, Bob and Anne Larsen
var—August 16, 1955, Beatrice Burford, Gene Schlichter
var—**STAIRCASE RIDGE:** July 5, 1963, Rich Ream, J. Gully
var—**SOUTHERN COULOIR:** Date and party unknown
var—**SAM'S TOWER RIDGE:** Date uncertain, Barry Corbet et al.

NORTHWEST COULOIR AND LEDGES: July 13, 1931, Fritiof Fryxell, Leland Horberg, Rudolph Edmund, William Cederberg, Neuman Kerndt, Elof Petersen

SOUTHWEST COULOIR: July 8, 1935, Eldon Petzoldt

DURRANCE RIDGE: August 7, 1936, Jack Durrance, Walter Spofford
var—**SOUTH FACE START:** August 25, 1950, Leigh Ortenburger, James Collison
var—**TRAVERSE TO SOUTHWEST RIDGE:** June 30, 1952, Robert Merriam, Charles Wilder, Roger Nichols, Ulrich Kruse

JENSEN COULOIR: July 28, 1938, Bert Jensen, Fred Brown, David Davis (lower section); September 6, 1954, Gary Hemming, Leigh Ortenburger (upper section)

DIRECT JENSEN RIDGE: July 28, 1938, Bert Jensen, Fred Brown, David Davis (upper portion from east); August 5, 1952, Willi Unsoeld, Norman Lee, Tony Mueller, Sandy Gregory (upper portion from west); August 14, 1953, Willi Unsoeld, Norman Lee (lower portion, with aid); FFA August 16, 1953, Willi Unsoeld, Mary Sylvander, Steve Jervis (complete)

SOUTHWEST RIDGE: July 30, 1938, Bert Jensen, Walter Spofford
var—July 7, 1957, Al Read, Bob Kamps

TEMPLETON'S CRACK: July 1943, Fritz Wiessner, James Huidekoper, Hank Geering (attempt); July 18, 1946, Robin Hansen, Fritz Lippmann (partial); July 13, 1949, Lee Pedrick, Richard Pownall (to Bowl); July 24, 1949, Richard Pownall, Red Austin, Harvey and Jewel Templeton (complete to summit ridge)
var—**LOWER CHIMNEY:** August 30, 1951, Robert and Doris Merriam, Leigh Ortenburger
var—August 17, 1961, Ray Jacquot, Robert Scott

NORTHEAST CHIMNEY: July 19, 1949, Richard Pownall, Art Gilkey, Red Austin

SOUTH FACE: July 3, 1950, Richard Pownall, Leigh Ortenburger
var—August 1, 1954, William Cropper, Ellis Blade
var—June 25, 1962, Herb Swedlund, Mike Borghoff

NORTH FACE: July 20, 1953, Roald Fryxell, Ronald Cullen
var—**CUPA KAVA:** August 1975, Bruce and Brent Weide, Mark Sixel
var—August 28, 1989, Tom Turiano, Phil McBride

WEST FACE, NORTH EDGE: August 26, 1955, William Cropper, Yves Erickson, Ron Chapman

DIRECT SOUTH FACE: August 8, 1956, Richard Pownall, Willi Unsoeld, Norman Lee
var—August 30, 1958, William Buckingham, Barry Corbet, Pete Sinclair
var—July 1978, Yvon Chouinard, T. M. Herbert

NORTHEAST FACE: July 24, 1957, John Dietschy, David Dingman

DIRECT WEST FACE: July 27, 1957, John Dietschy, David Dingman

DIETSCHY RIDGE: July 30, 1957, John Dietschy, David Dingman, Karl Pfiffner

NORTHWEST FACE: July 15, 1974, John Cain, Tim East

RETICENT SLABS: October 28, 1998, Ryan Hokanson, Paul Horton (original route); October 23, 1999, Paul Horton, Andy Carson (modern route)
var—**INCOGNITO BUTTRESS:** September 2018, Vic Zeilman, Ken Kreis

ROUTE 1. WEST FACE, NORTH EDGE. II, 5.1. First ascent August 26, 1955, by William Cropper, Yves Erickson, and Ron Chapman. The west face of Symmetry Spire rises above the southwest couloir (see *Route 3*), which leads to the high col between the peak and Symmetry Crag 1, the first of the Symmetry Crags to the west. This very short route starts on the face only a short distance below (south of) the col. Two pitches lead easily to the top of the wall, well north of the top of the southwest ridge (see *Route 4*).

ROUTE 2. DIRECT WEST FACE. II, 5.6. First ascent July 27, 1957, by John Dietschy and David Dingman. This face is approached via the regular Symmetry Couloir to the saddle connecting Ice Point with Symmetry Spire. From the saddle, scramble north up the southwest couloir leading to the col between Symmetry Spire and Symmetry Crag 1 until just past the first pitch of the Southwest Ridge *(Route 4)*. About nine pitches, including two overhanging cracks, rise more or less straight up to end at the apex of the face, about 60m left (north) of the top of the Southwest Ridge route (the Flake Pitch).

ROUTE 3. ▲ SOUTHWEST COULOIR. II, 4.0. First ascent July 8, 1935, by Eldon Petzoldt, who pieced together two earlier Fritiof Fryxell routes into what has become the regular route on the peak. The Ice Point–Symmetry Spire saddle was first reached by Fryxell and Frank Smith on August 13, 1931, in the course of their first ascents of Ice and Storm Points. The higher col immediately west of the summit was reached by Fryxell and his party on July 13, 1931, during a west-to-east traverse of Symmetry Spire and the pinnacles on either side of it. (See *Figure 8-15*.) Approach via the Symmetry Couloir to the Ice Point–Symmetry Spire saddle. The large southwest couloir below the west face of Symmetry Spire leads directly to the high col west of the summit; this same col is reached from the north via the Northwest Couloir and Ledges route *(Route 17)*—the one Fryxell et al. established during their aforementioned July 1931 traverse. A substantial stream drains the southwest couloir, which harbors snow of moderate steepness during the early part of the summer and then deteriorates to loose rubble later on. Climb this couloir to the high col at its head. From the col climb right (east) up the ridge for about 30m before following easy but exposed ledges out to the left (north) and up the northwest side of the peak to the summit. There is virtually a trail now, worn by the boots of climbers over the past 85-plus years.

FIGURE 8-15. Symmetry Spire, south face overview. (A) Southwest Couloir *(Route 3)*, II, 4.0; (B) Southwest Ridge *(Route 4)*, II, 5.7; (C) Southwest Ridge, variation: 1957, II, 5.7; (D) Direct South Face *(Route 5)*, III, 5.9; (E) Direct South Face, variation: 1958, III, 5.9; (F) South Face *(Route 6)*, II, 5.8; (G) Durrance Ridge *(Route 7)*, II, 5.6; (H) Templeton's Crack *(Route 8)*, II, 5.6; (I) Direct Jensen Ridge *(Route 9)*, III, 5.7+/5.8; (J) Jensen Couloir *(Route 10)*, II, 5.6; (K) Dietschy Ridge *(Route 11)*, II, 5.6

When using this couloir as a descent route, scramble from the summit down the exposed northwest side on the small path, angling west and down toward the col to the west. From the col descend the southwest couloir to the main saddle between Symmetry Spire and Ice Point. Use care with the loose rock in the couloir because other climbers may be below and in the fall line. In early season or midseason an ice axe will be needed for this descent, but by late season the snow in this upper couloir can usually be avoided by downclimbing on the ledges on the couloir's west side. **Time:** 5 to 5¾ hours from Jenny Lake.

ROUTE 4. SOUTHWEST RIDGE. II, 5.7. First ascent July 30, 1938, by Bert Jensen and Walter Spofford. (See *Figures 8-15* and *8-16*.) This beautifully direct and impressively steep route is probably the most pleasant climb on Symmetry Spire. Approach to just below the saddle between Symmetry Spire and Ice Point, from which the spectacular southwest ridge is seen, forming the extreme left edge of the south face. The route can be done in five pitches using a 60m rope. The first pitch begins at the toe of the ridge. Climb up through blocky terrain situated just west of an open corner on a steep, brownish wall (easy 5th class). The second pitch begins with a short section of double cracks and then goes up through excellent orange-yellow rock in a right-facing corner past some fixed pins. Partway up the corner, traverse out to a thin crack on a smooth orange face and proceed upward to a belay at the top (5.7). Move the belay up 10m to the base of the Nose Pitch. Climb up and left past fixed pins (5.7) to a big ledge; exiting right is a bit easier than going straight up. Walk 5m right (east) on the ledge to a point beneath a small roof. Climb up through the roof (5.6) and then through a fun section of black rock to a good belay ledge. From the belay the fourth pitch—the Flake Pitch, the last major pitch of the climb—leads out left for 3m to a fun right-facing corner. Take the corner up and right past a few fixed pins and then up to the Flake, a large chockstone in the chimney above. From a block just below the Flake, climb either out and left around the Flake (5.7 move) or out and up easier terrain on its right side (5.6), then continue up to a belay. Follow the easier but still exposed ridge above to the summit, staying mostly on the right (east) side of the crest. For descent, take the regular northwest ledges (see *Route 17*) and the southwest couloir (see *Route 3*) back to the Ice Point–Symmetry Spire saddle. **Time:** 6¼ to 7¾ hours from Jenny Lake. See *American Alpine Journal* 3, no. 3 (1939): pp. 361–65; *Chicago Mountaineering Club Newsletter* 5, no. 1 (January 1951): p. 5.

Variation: II, 5.7. First ascent July 7, 1957, by Al Read and Bob Kamps. A more difficult beginning of about two pitches can be made around the corner to the right (east); see *Figure 8-15* for this author's (R. Jackson's) best guess as to where this variation starts. From the trees about 21m east of a small, shallow chimney system on the south face that leads to the southwest ridge, climb slightly to the right over two black overhangs; the upper one is prominent. Now traverse left under a white wall to the slightly overhanging chimney, which is followed up to meet the ridge.

ROUTE 5. DIRECT SOUTH FACE. III, 5.8, A2, or III, 5.9. First ascent August 8, 1956, by Richard Pownall, Willi Unsoeld, and Norman Lee. (See *Figure 8-15* for a best guess as to where this route starts.) The Direct South Face lies between the southwest ridge on the left (west) and the long left-facing

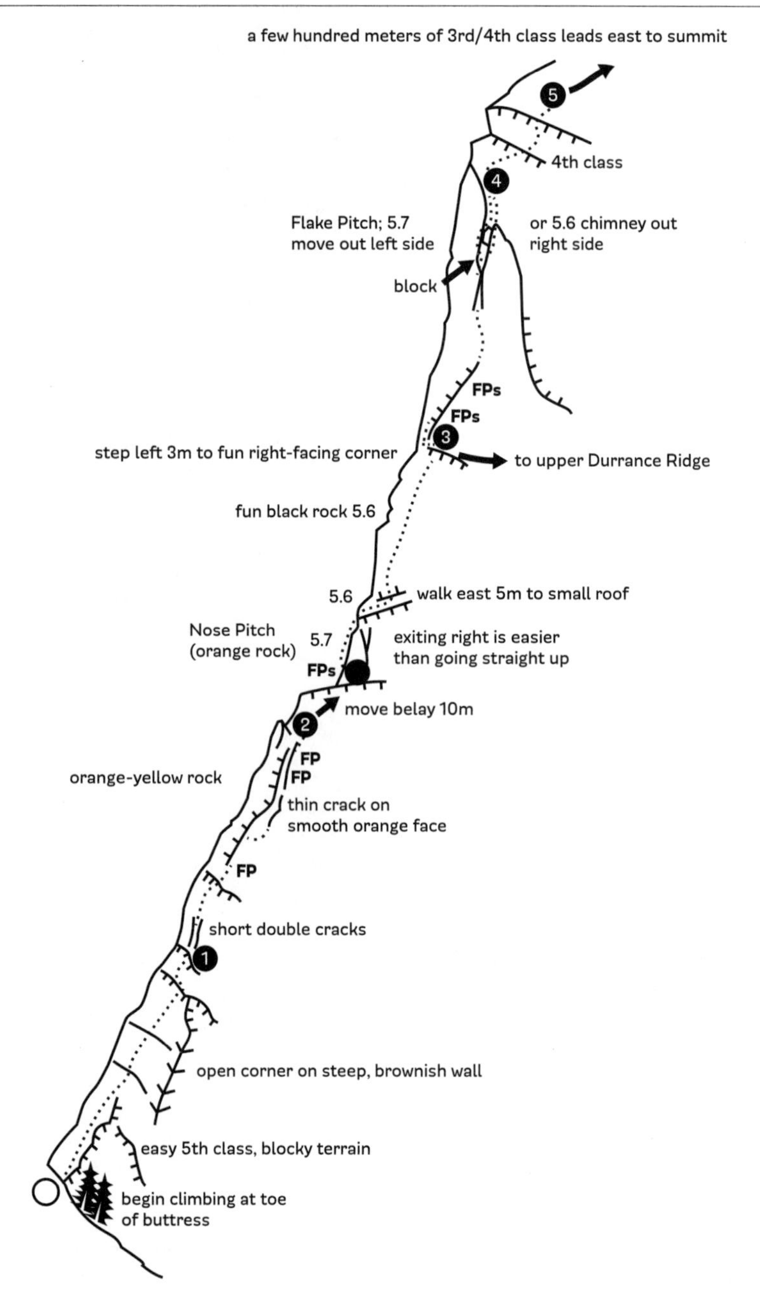

FIGURE 8-16. Symmetry Spire, Southwest Ridge *(Route 4)*, II, 5.7

corner of the original 1950 South Face route *(Route 6)* on the right (east). The considerable expanse of wall in this region saw a number of early climbs—some distinct, some not—but this 1956 route was the first. In addition to the 1958 and 1978 variations described below, the 1954 and 1962 variations listed under the South Face route merge with this 1956 route in their upper sections. Most ascents on this sector of the south face combine one or more of these variations.

This direct route starts in a prominent dihedral about halfway between the southwest ridge and the left-facing corner of the original South Face route. Angle up and slightly left on good rock for about two pitches to a belay platform. Now traverse up and right until one can turn straight up once more in the center of the face for two leads to a prominent 1+m ceiling. This serious obstacle can be passed using a crack on the left or, as originally done, it can be climbed directly using aid. It is uncertain whether or not this ceiling has been free climbed via the original aid line. Now continue up the narrowing face to the traverse ledge, which extends from the Durrance Ridge (see *Route 7*) to the southwest ridge, and avoid being forced out to the right onto the Durrance Ridge. Just above is the large final overhang that extends across the top of the south face immediately left (west) of the final pitch of the Durrance Ridge. This overhang was surmounted directly using aid on the first ascent in 1956; for a free bypass, see the following 1958 variation. **Time:** 10 hours from Jenny Lake. See *American Alpine Journal* 10, no. 2 (1957): pp. 148–49.

Variation: III, 5.9. First ascent August 30, 1958, by William Buckingham, Barry Corbet, and Pete Sinclair. (See *Figure 8-15.*) This pitch is worth doing as a more difficult finish to either *Route 4* or *Route 7*. Just above the traverse ledge described in the original route is the large final overhang that extends across the top of the south face immediately left (west) of the final pitch of the Durrance Ridge. Pass this overhang on the left, up a large, obvious open-book chimney that faces left (west) and is some 18m to the east of the Flake Pitch of the Southwest Ridge *(Route 4)*. This is a difficult pitch involving many small overhangs, but it does not require aid.

Variation: III, 5.9. First ascent in July 1978, by Yvon Chouinard and T. M. Herbert. Starting at some small pine trees, this variation apparently begins and remains somewhat to the right (east) of the main route. Climb two pitches of excellent vertical rock (5.8), continue up to the traverse ledge, and finish using the 1958 variation. The 1+m ceiling of the main route is avoided using this variation.

ROUTE 6. SOUTH FACE. II, 5.8. First ascent July 3, 1950, by Richard Pownall and Leigh Ortenburger. (See *Figure 8-15.*) The south face of Symmetry Spire extends from the southwest ridge to the Durrance Ridge. A prominent left-facing corner, curiously described in earlier editions of this book as a "vertical ledge," runs up the center of the face to an obvious overhang. This route follows the crack in the corner and sometimes uses the face to its left. The rock is steep and solid but belay positions are exposed, requiring good anchors for safety. To pass the overhang at the top of the corner, climb up and out on the face until even with its top, then make a spectacular step back to the right onto the top of the overhang. The line of least resistance now leads in one ropelength up to the right to join the Durrance Ridge *(Route 7)*, which is then followed to the summit. This is an enjoyable high-angle climb on good rock. **Time:** 9 hours from Jenny Lake. See *American Alpine Journal* 9, no. 2 (1955): pp. 147–49.

Variation: II, 5.6. First ascent August 1, 1954, by William Cropper and Ellis Blade. From the top of the final overhang mentioned in the standard route, one can continue up without touching the Durrance Ridge. Traverse left (west) for about 18m from the top of the overhang to a roomy platform, then go up and left in a band of broken rock to join the Southwest Ridge route *(Route 4)*. There seems to be more than one possible line, and the difficulty will vary depending on which is chosen.

Variation: II, 5.6. First ascent June 25, 1962, by Herb Swedlund and Mike Borghoff. (**Note:** This route is not well understood with respect to other routes in the immediate vicinity.) From the final overhang of the main route, continue up for 18m on steep rock to a small ledge. Start the next pitch on 5.6 rock, which is avoided after 6m by a traverse left on good handholds, then climb for 37m, easily bearing left to avoid the Durrance Ridge, until about 9m below a prominent roof. This roof apparently can be bypassed on the left by a difficult fingertip traverse or on the right (east). This is followed by a friction move and a strenuous move up a secondary overhang to a vertical crack with adequate holds. One full ropelength on steep, exposed rock then leads to a point below the final overhang where one can traverse either to the Durrance Ridge or to the Southwest Ridge route, or finish by one of the methods described under *Route 5*.

ROUTE 7. DURRANCE RIDGE. II, 5.6. First ascent August 7, 1936, by Jack Durrance and Walter Spofford, after climbing Storm and Ice Points earlier the same day. (See *Figure 8-15.*) The southeast side of Symmetry Spire is deeply cut by a great chimney system (see *Route 8*), and this, the first of the south side rock climbs, goes directly up the ridge forming its left (west) edge. The Durrance Ridge is a very enjoyable but relatively long climb on steep, solid rock. This route, which contains five to six pitches, depending upon how it is climbed, can serve as an excellent introduction to Teton climbing. The base of the Durrance Ridge is easily reached from the slope just below the Ice Point–Symmetry Spire saddle. Many variations can be made, because one can climb almost anywhere on the ridge. The route is best initiated at the extreme toe of the ridge. After one pitch of easy climbing, this original route and the variations seem to funnel into a vertical pitch that consists of a crack to the right of a dihedral with a steep, yellow left wall. This is one of the route's two crux pitches; a fixed piton may still be found here. Above, the climbing becomes easier and includes one 60m section of scrambling to reach the steeper upper section of the ridge. The final lead, which lies slightly left of the rounded ridge crest, is the most interesting and difficult but can be well protected; some fixed pitons will be found here. It consists of a 30m system of cracks and a small chimney that exits at the top of the ridge. This point is at the lower edge of the Bowl, the upper basin that drains into *Routes 8* and *10*, some 90m below the summit. The objective here is to scramble left (west) over to the crest of the upper southwest ridge. From the top of the Durrance Ridge, climb one long or two short additional pitches up and left across a section of downsloping black slabs to gain the upper southwest ridge, which is followed to the summit, either on the crest itself or slightly on the right (east) side (see *Route 4*). For descent, see the Northwest Couloir and Ledges route *(Route 17)*. **Time:** 7 to 8½ hours from Jenny Lake. See *Chicago Mountaineering Club Newsletter* 15, no. 1 (February 1961): pp. 4–7.

Variation: **SOUTH FACE START.** II, 5.4. First ascent August 25, 1950, by Leigh Ortenburger and James Collison. Instead of starting directly from the bottom of the ridge, climb the south face between *Route 6* and the Durrance Ridge via a left-facing corner. After about three ropelengths, a smooth wall above forces one to traverse to the right to the Durrance Ridge.

Variation: **TRAVERSE TO SOUTHWEST RIDGE.** II, 5.6. First ascent June 30, 1952, by Robert Merriam, Charles Wilder, Roger Nichols, and Ulrich Kruse. (See *Figure 8-15.*) About one pitch from the top of the ridge, a ledge below the overhang at the top of the south face diagonals up and to the left (west) across the south face all the way to the southwest ridge. Hence, this climb can be completed on the Southwest Ridge route *(Route 4)* by following this ledge, which meets the ridge just below the Flake Pitch.

ROUTE 8. TEMPLETON'S CRACK. II, 5.6. First ascent July 13, 1949, by Lee Pedrick and Richard Pownall. The first attempt on this prominent feature was made in July 1943, by Fritz Wiessner, James Huidekoper, and Hank Geering. On July 18, 1946, Robin Hansen and Fritz Lippmann made a partial ascent of this crack, bypassing one 90m section with a 46m traverse out to the left onto the Durrance Ridge *(Route 7)*. On July 13, 1949, Pedrick and Pownall climbed the crack directly to the Bowl; the upper continuation of the crack to the summit ridge was first climbed on July 24, 1949, by Pownall, Red Austin, and Harvey and Jewel Templeton. (See *Figure 8-15.*) This climb, consisting of a series of scree walks and difficult chockstones, goes up the great chimney that cuts the southeast face of Symmetry Spire. The usual approach is from the slope just below the Ice Point–Symmetry Spire saddle to the base of the Durrance Ridge, from which one can scramble down into the chimney and walk to the base of the first overhang. Climb the first three overhangs in the first ropelength and pass the fourth overhang by climbing the right wall of the chimney. Another scree walk leads to a 24m chimney, at the top of which is a small cave. The 30m difficult chimney above is known as the Green Chimney because of the slippery green slime on its walls in early season. Pass outside the chockstone at the top of this chimney and, after another scree walk, ascend some 75m in moderate chimneys, climbing the vertical section on the right wall. Go up and to the right to a downsloping ledge. The 4.5m pitch directly off this ledge, the Harvey Pitch, is the most difficult of the route. The main chimney, which is 4.5m to the left of the Harvey Pitch, has also been climbed, but the rock is rotten and it is not easier than the Harvey Pitch. Above this pitch, easier climbing leads to the Bowl, from which most parties traverse left (west) to follow the Southwest Ridge route *(Route 4)* to the summit. However, in order to complete the entire chimney, it is necessary to climb another two ropelengths up its continuation. On the right wall there are adequate holds on the downsloping, slabby rock. This section appears more difficult than it is and leads to the ridge about 15m west of the summit. **Time:** 7½ to 9½ hours from Jenny Lake. See *American Alpine Journal* 8, no. 1 (1951): pp. 176–81; *Sierra Club Bulletin* 32, no. 5 (May 1917): pp. 128–29.

Variation: **LOWER CHIMNEY.** II, 5.6. First ascent August 30, 1951, by Robert and Doris Merriam and Leigh Ortenburger. A longer climb can be obtained by beginning the climb in the lower extension of the chimney, which starts from the upper right corner of the snowfield in the Symmetry Couloir. In late season several ropelengths on rock of poor quality are required to reach the initial overhang of the regular Templeton's Crack route. In early season this 150m lower extension will be almost entirely on snow.

Variation: II, 5.6. First ascent August 17, 1961, by Ray Jacquot and Robert Scott. Above the scree above the Green Chimney, face climb out on the right (north) wall instead of staying in or near the main chimney. The sloping ledge at the base of the Harvey Pitch will be reached from the right instead of from the left.

ROUTE 9. DIRECT JENSEN RIDGE. III, 5.7+/5.8. First complete ascent August 16, 1953, by Willi Unsoeld, Mary Sylvander, and Steve Jervis. The upper portion of this ridge, gained from the couloir to the right (east), was ascended on July 28, 1938, by Bert Jensen, Fred Brown, and David Davis; this upper section, gained from Templeton's Crack on the west, was climbed on August 5, 1952, by Willi Unsoeld, Norman Lee, Tony Mueller, and Sandy Gregory; the lower section was first climbed (with aid) on August 14, 1953, by Willi Unsoeld and Norman Lee. The complete climb two days later was done free. (See *Figures 8-15, 8-17,* and *8-18.*) The Jensen Ridge forms the right (eastern) boundary of Templeton's Crack *(Route 8)*. The ridge, very impressive when seen from any angle, was considered one of the better rock climbs of its day. It is a more difficult climb than either of the two Symmetry Spire standards, the Durrance Ridge *(Route 7)* and the Southwest Ridge *(Route 4)*, and it has been the scene of several bad accidents, some involving very good climbers. The base of the Jensen Ridge is approached by descending into Templeton's Crack from the base of the Durrance Ridge and then scrambling up the smooth, slabby rock on the far (east) side. The lower section of this ridge rises at a very high angle and is capped by a large overhang. After 10 pitches (fewer with a 60m rope), traverse west over to the Southwest Ridge route and follow that line to the summit. **Time:** 7 to 10 hours from Jenny Lake. See *American Alpine Journal* 9, no. 1 (1954): pp. 172–84, illus.

ROUTE 10. JENSEN COULOIR. II, 5.6. First ascent July 28, 1938, by Bert Jensen, Fred Brown, and David Davis (lower section), and September 6, 1954, by Gary Hemming and Leigh Ortenburger (upper section). (See *Figure 8-15.*) This distinct couloir is just to the right (east) of the Jensen Ridge, separating it from the next ridge to the east, the Dietschy Ridge *(Route 11)*. The difficult entrance to the Jensen Couloir was first climbed by the 1938 party, who traversed left onto the Jensen Ridge after climbing only 60m up the couloir. Approach as for *Route 9*; from where that route starts, climb up and to the right 24m to a poor belay position. The next pitch, which is just left of the overhanging right wall of the couloir, is difficult because of the smooth, downsloping rock. Few, if any, cracks are available for protection. The upper portion of the couloir is just a scramble. See *American Alpine Journal* 3, no. 3 (1939): pp. 361–65.

ROUTE 11. DIETSCHY RIDGE. II, 5.6. First ascent July 30, 1957, by John Dietschy, David

Dingman, and Karl Pfiffner. (See *Figure 8-15.*) This ridge of good rock lies just east of the Jensen Ridge; the Jensen Couloir separates the upper portions of the two ridges. At the bottom, where the lower portion of this southeast ridge is a 60m wall (not visible in the phototopo), all three of these features blend together. This ridge is best approached the same way as the Jensen Ridge (see *Route 9*). The first lead traverses low across the broad nose of the ridge onto and up its right (east) flank. Three additional short pitches (4.0 to 5.6) of interesting climbing on good rock remain slightly on the right side of the crest. The fifth lead brings one back to the crest; follow the crest to the knife-edge horizontal section, which can be done à cheval. Immediately above the knife-edge is a steep, yellow 60m step in the ridge that is visible from Jenny Lake.

FIGURE 8-17. Symmetry Spire, south aspect, Direct Jensen Ridge *(Route 9)*, III, 5.7+/5.8

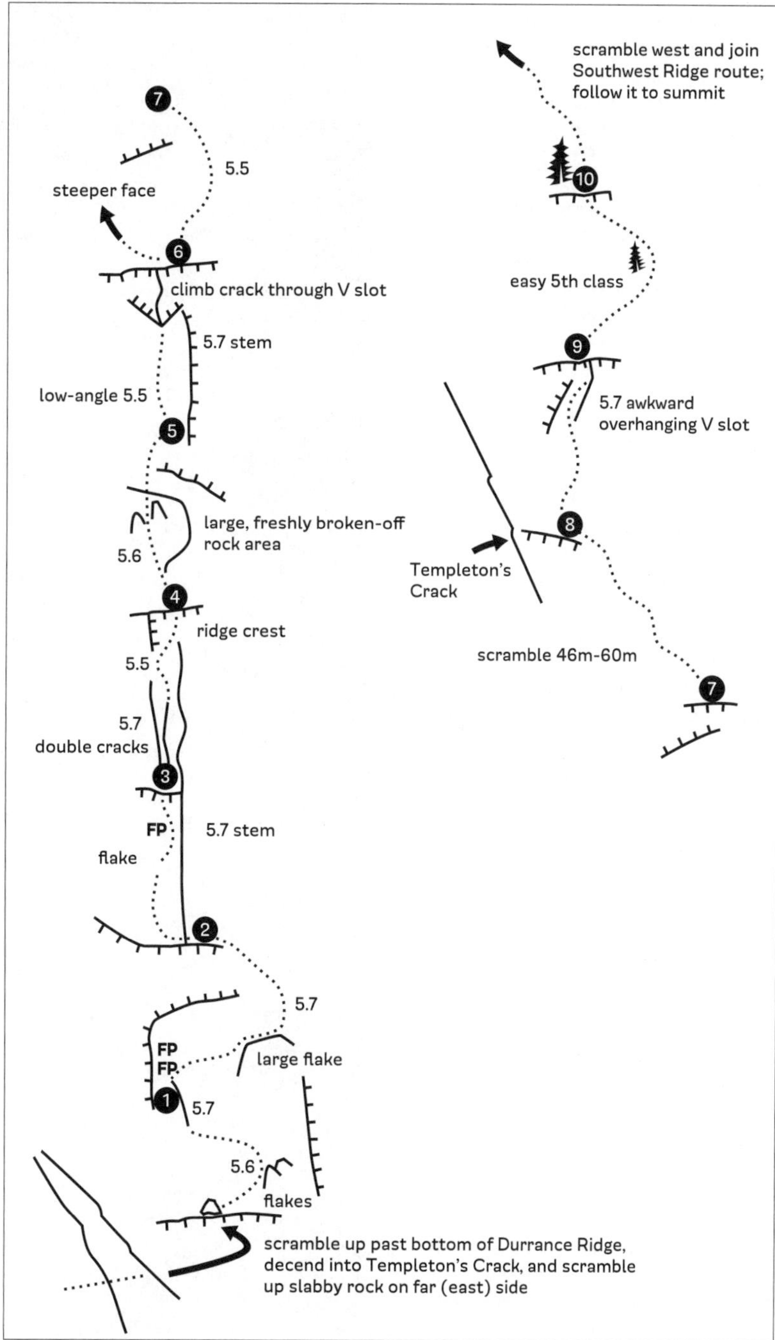

FIGURE 8-18. Symmetry Spire, south aspect, Direct Jensen Ridge *(Route 9)*, III, 5.7+/5.8

Although it is possible to traverse left into the top of the Jensen Couloir at this point, the step is usually passed on the right (east) side. A short lead around to the east brings one to easy ground, where steep scrambling leads directly up to the east ridge of Symmetry Spire, from which the nearby summit is easily attained.

ROUTE 12. RETICENT SLABS. III, 5.8. First ascent October 28, 1998, by Ryan Hokanson and Paul Horton (with different first and third pitches); first ascent of the modern route October 23, 1999, by Paul Horton and Andy Carson. (See *Figures 8-14* and *8-19*.) From the semipermanent snowfield about halfway up the Symmetry Couloir, scramble about 120m up a steep, tricky 4th-class gully to the base of these slabs. This approach may contain high-angle snow and/or wet rock, depending on the season. The route begins from small ledges on the steep slopes beneath clean gray flakes and slabs, under a large overhang. **Pitch 1:** The long first pitch liebacks up thin flakes (5.7), then exits horizontally left across the slab via a 5.8 finger traverse along a horizontal crack. Continue left around a blunt nose (5.8) and work up a face and corner to a belay on a good ledge with trees (58m). **Pitch 2:** Ascend beautiful cracks up a corner, step left under a small overhang, and climb up parallel cracks to a comfortable, grassy ledge (5.8, 30m). **Pitch 3:** Step right to a crack and bulky flake, then ascend the steep corner above (5.8) via liebacks and jams to a pedestal. Trend right, up a face, to a belay on a sloping ledge (40m). **Pitch 4:** From the sloping ledge, climb a short wall, pass to the right of a flared overhang, and continue up the wide, flared crack above. Follow the narrowing crack to a short friction face leading to a large ledge and the belay (5.8, 35m). Alternatively, climb the short wall, trending a few meters right of the flared overhang, to finger cracks leading up a clean, slabby face to the belay on the large ledge (5.7, 35m). **Pitch 5:** Ascend dirtier rock, angling up and right under a large bulge. Continue up via corners and wide cracks to the belay in trees and rubble on the ridge crest at the top of the wall (5.7, 50m).

(**Pitches 3–5 option:** Instead of stopping at the belay on the sloping ledge at the end of the third pitch, continue trending right, then head straight up moderate cracks to a belay at the small evergreen where one of the two-nut rappel stations is located [57m]. From there, climb a nice pitch [5.7, 58m] up clean slabs, followed by steeper rock, to join the traditional route high up the fifth pitch. This is the best alternative, and it allows for the combining of the fourth and fifth pitches, if desired.)

Pitch 6: Ramble up the fun, rounded ridge to the belay at a step (5.6, 50m).

FIGURE 8-19. Symmetry Spire. (A) Reticent Slabs *(Route 12)*, III, 5.8; (B) Variation: Incognito Buttress, III, 5.8+, A0

Pitch 7: Follow the ridge to a slot that exits to forested slopes (5.6, 30m). From the end of the roped climbing, traverse right and up grassy slopes, scree, slabs, and steps to terrain near the east ridge of Symmetry Spire. With good routefinding, a 3rd-class route can be followed to the summit. Some parties choose to rappel the route, starting from the trees on the crest at the top of the fifth pitch (two ropes required). A couple of fixed-nut anchor stations slightly north (climber's right) of the ascent line provide access to the final rappel, from a tree at the top of the first pitch.

***Variation:* INCOGNITO BUTTRESS.** III, 5.8+, A0. First ascent in September 2018, by Vic Zeilman and Ken Kreis. (See *Figure 8-19.*) This variation adds four pitches of good climbing to the exceptional rock found in this out-of-the-way nook of Symmetry Spire. (The possibility of a little more climbing on a day's outing also helps ease the pain of the approach.) Incognito Buttress begins on broken 3rd-class ledges about 70m north of the Reticent Slabs start. Look for a right-facing feature in an area of light-colored rock. **Pitch 1:** Climb a small, broken right-facing corner in a band of light-colored rock, then venture onto 5.7 face climbing in dark rock. Move up and right onto the face, clip a bolt, and continue up and right on the excellent face climbing above. Eventually trend back left to a semi-hanging belay on the lip of the giant roof system, beneath a prominent corner (5.7, 30m). **Pitch 2:** Stem/lieback up the corner (5.8+), then climb around the left side of a roof and transition into a hand crack that leads up to a fixed pin at the base of a 5.8+ left-facing corner. This corner ultimately goes up to an off-route roof. Instead, look for a bolt off to the right and exit the corner here. The moves at the bolt are A0, with the first ascensionists speculating that this section may go free at 5.11+. Continue right to easier terrain leading up to a belay on a large, sloping ledge (5.8+, A0, 40m). **Pitch 3:** Climb up and left, staying on better rock in a left-facing feature (5.7). Exit this feature and face climb straight up; at this point the first-ascent party tied off a marginal pin and executed a "delicate foot traverse" hard left to a flared seam with knobs. Climb the seam (5.7R, "cool, well-featured stemming") and then continue up to a belay at a fixed piton at the left side of a huge roof (55m). **Pitch 4:** Get a high piece off the belay before venturing left into nondescript slabby terrain with sparse pro (5.7). The general path is marked with a fixed pin somewhere midpitch. Stay beneath all of the prominent roofs overhead and eventually meet Reticent Slabs along its fifth pitch. Belay at a rap station on a ledge near a dead tree (60m). It is possible to get down to the base from here via three double-rope rappels, or one can continue up Reticent Slabs and then to the summit of Symmetry Spire. **Gear:** The first-ascent party suggests a double set of cams from 0.5" to 2", one 3" cam, and one 4" cam; a good selection of micro cams; small to medium stoppers; and RPs or offsets. Also bring two ropes if rappelling.

ROUTE 13. EAST RIDGE. II, 4.0. First ascent August 20, 1929, by Fritiof Fryxell and Phil Smith. This pleasant scrambling ridge is the most obvious route on the peak, especially when viewed from the north. It is not a difficult climb and can be enjoyed by almost any mountaineer seeking a pleasurable outing in the mountains. For those who have climbed the peak more than once, the east ridge can serve as an alternate route of descent. On its south side there is a considerable degree of complexity. In all there are five ridges and five couloirs between Templeton's Crack (*Route 8*) and Cube Point. Approach via Hanging Canyon; from the canyon, cross the stream between Arrowhead Pool and Ramshead Lake and follow a distinct grassy horizontal ledge on the northeast face of Symmetry Spire out to the east ridge. Between Cube Point, the peak on the lower end of this ridge, and the summit of Symmetry Spire there is another large gendarme, Sam's Tower. This ledge brings one onto the ridge just above this tower. From this point to the summit the route requires little more than scrambling. Near the summit, a short knife-edge ridge adds interest to the route. **Time:** 5 to 6½ hours from Jenny Lake. See *Appalachia* 18, no. 4 (December 1931): pp. 388–408, illus.; *Chicago Mountaineering Club Journal* 2, no. 5 (January–July 1948): pp. 5–7.

Variation: II, 4.0. Probable first ascent July 30, 1935, by M. N. Schell, R. L. Harrington, and P. E. Griffith; it is possible that this party climbed one of the two couloirs to the east of the one described here. From the upper (west) end of the snowfield that persists throughout most of the summer in the Symmetry Couloir, a narrow couloir leads directly north to the crest of the east ridge, well to the west of Sam's Tower. This couloir begins very near the base of the lower extension of Templeton's Crack (see the Lower Chimney variation of *Route 8*). For the purposes of identification, the correct couloir is the first one west of the large couloir above Hangover Pinnacle. A short wall prevents easy access to the beginning of the couloir, but it can be climbed near its left end, which forms the north wall of the lower extension of Templeton's Crack. Once in the couloir, scramble to the east ridge; in early season snow will be encountered.

***Variation:* NORTHERN COULOIR.** II, 5.4. First ascent July 27, 1954, by William Cropper, Ellis Blade, and Bob and Anne Larsen. The crest of the east ridge can also be gained from the north at the col just west of Cube Point via a scree couloir. To reach the upper east ridge of Symmetry Spire, it is necessary to pass Sam's Tower. This traverse involves two awkward pitches that include some 5.4 climbing and perhaps a rappel down the gendarme's west face.

Variation: II, 5.1. First ascent August 16, 1955, by Beatrice Burford and Gene Schlichter. Leave the regular Symmetry Couloir at Hangover Pinnacle, which stands at the entrance to a large subsidiary couloir running north to the crest of the east ridge. This couloir can very likely be ascended without great difficulty all the way to the east ridge, but this party, after scrambling up three-quarters of the couloir, turned horizontally left (west) on a treed ledge for about 90m. This ledge widens out into a broad slope bounded on the right by an overhanging buttress. Three steep pitches somewhat to the right lead to a notch in the Staircase Ridge (see the Staircase Ridge variation, below), of which this buttress is a part. Traverse into the next couloir to the west (the preceding 1935 variation) and climb to the east ridge, which leads to the summit.

***Variation:* STAIRCASE RIDGE.** II, 5.4. First known ascent July 5, 1963, by Richard Ream Jr. and J. Gully. Staircase Ridge is the second ridge east of the Dietschy Ridge and it rises immediately west of Hangover Pinnacle, leading north to the east ridge with one large, flat step approximately halfway up the ridge. The climbing is easy, the only difficulties being two short walls; the first is climbed up the middle and the second is climbed up the left (west) edge. This ridge climb can be easily combined with an ascent of Hangover Pinnacle at the base.

***Variation:* SOUTHERN COULOIR.** II, 5.1. First ascent unknown. It is also possible to reach the east ridge via this southern couloir, which leads to the col immediately west of Cube Point. This large couloir is the first one east of Hangover Pinnacle and is easily reached by following the main drainage of a small stream upward. This is the same stream ordinarily crossed (from north to south) just after scaling the short cliff on the west wall of the cul-de-sac on the approach to the regular Symmetry Couloir. There is little information available concerning this couloir, but it has very likely been ascended or descended and should not prove difficult. From the col, one will be faced with the task of passing the gendarme, Sam's Tower, between the col and the upper east ridge of Symmetry Spire; see the Northern Couloir variation.

***Variation:* SAM'S TOWER RIDGE.** II, 5.8. First ascent uncertain, but at some point it was climbed by Barry Corbet and party. Sam's Tower, the large gendarme on the east ridge of Symmetry Spire just west of Cube Point, has a south ridge that extends down toward the regular Symmetry Couloir. The ridge is the one immediately west of the large couloir that descends from the col separating this large tower from Cube Point. In the lower portion of the ridge, a 5.1 corner will be found on the second pitch. About halfway up the ridge a ledge 15m wide will be reached. Just above this ledge is an overhang with a chimney piercing it. This 6m pitch is difficult, 5.8 or A1, and apparently cannot be bypassed on either side. The remainder of the climb can be as easy as desired because one can just scramble to the top of the tower by avoiding the exact crest, which contains the more interesting climbing.

ROUTE 14. NORTHEAST CHIMNEY. II, 5.6. First ascent July 19, 1949, by Richard Pownall, Art Gilkey, and Red Austin. This deep chimney is as conspicuous from the northeast as Templeton's Crack *(Route 8)* is from the southeast. At its top it forms a small but distinct notch separating the north pinnacle of Symmetry Spire from the spire itself. Approach from Hanging Canyon and gain the base of the chimney by crossing the stream between Arrowhead Pool and Ramshead Lake. Scrambling and easy climbing take one about three-quarters of the way up the chimney, to the point where it narrows—the one difficult pitch of the climb. Climb perhaps 3m in the narrow section until it is possible to climb to the outside; then cross over to the right (north) wall. A 5m 5.6 chimney is then ascended to a wide ledge. The 9m step above the ledge is also difficult, but above that it is just a scramble to the notch at the top of the chimney. The first-ascent party climbed the north pinnacle, and most parties usually include it. From the notch scramble up and to the right (south and west) on easy ledges to the summit. **Time:** 6 hours from Jenny Lake. See *American Alpine Journal* 8, no. 1 (1951): pp. 176–81.

ROUTE 15. NORTHEAST FACE. II, 5.7, A1, or II, 5.8. First ascent July 24, 1957, by John Dietschy and David Dingman. Just to the right (north) of the prominent northeast chimney (see *Route 14*) is a face containing a light-colored bulge of rock about halfway up. Approach this route via Hanging Canyon. From the bottom of the face below the overhanging bulge, the first two pitches angle off to the west. The next pitch goes straight up for 12m to a shelf, from which a thin traverse back to the east leads to a good belay stance below the bulge. The overhanging corner that bisects the bulge is difficult and was first climbed by tension from three pitons; it has been done free (5.8). An additional difficult pitch, followed by several easier leads, puts one on top of the north pinnacle of Symmetry Spire. Scramble down to the south and then up the north ledges to the main summit. This is an excellent, enjoyable rock climb of eight pitches, but the routefinding is not easy. See *American Alpine Journal* 11, no. l (1958): pp. 85–88.

ROUTE 16. NORTH FACE. II, 5.1. First ascent July 20, 1953, by Roald Fryxell and Ronald Cullen. From Ramshead Lake in Hanging Canyon, scramble to the highest snow patch near the right (west) base of the face, where a wide ramp leads back left and upward across the wall. Rope up where this ledge narrows and continue 18m around a bulge in the face. Once past this bulge, the face slopes back, and easy climbing leads to a ledge system that can be followed diagonally up to the right (west) to the west ridge of the north pinnacle (10,400+) of Symmetry Spire. The short pitch up this ridge to the summit of the pinnacle is perhaps the most difficult of the climb. After descending into the cleft that isolates this small pinnacle, scramble easily up to the right (west) to the main summit.

***Variation:* CUPA KAVA.** II, 5.7. First ascent in August 1975, by Bruce and Brent Weide and Mark Sixel. Instead of starting with the diagonal ledge leading left, make a direct ascent aiming at an overhanging point above. The first lead goes up a very shallow dihedral on small holds (5.7) over a bulge onto a ledge. Now angle slightly right and up either a chimney or the overhang at its left edge (5.7). A slightly overhanging lieback and then a jam crack lead onto big ledges with trees. After one easier pitch, climb the face above directly, passing a small, nearly holdless overhang; this takes one into the gully below the summit overhangs—the overhanging point seen from the beginning of the climb. Now climb over the point to the right and continue to the summit of the north pinnacle.

Variation: II, 5.7. First ascent August 28, 1989, by Tom Turiano and Phil McBride. This variation, while similar to Cupa Kava above, differs in that the north pinnacle of Symmetry Spire is reached more directly from its north face. From Arrowhead Lake hike to a large ramp under the base of the north face that leads from left (east) to right (west); this ramp narrows to 18 inches wide for a 6m section and then widens out again. Start this route at a small bush at the narrowest part of the ramp. The first short lead goes up and left over 5.4 rock to a belay ledge. The next pitch goes up between two overhangs and past a fixed piton into a lieback (5.7) with thin protection; from the top of the lieback, continue up a 5.6 face to the right of some flakes and blocks, finishing on a short belay ledge just left of a small arête. Now climb a face (5.7) between two right-facing corners to the large ramp that diagonals down to the right (west) to the base of the face; one can escape the route easily here. Continue this third lead, moving up and left, passing two right-facing corners with a fine 5.7 face with edge holds between them, to a belay ledge where an old fixed piton will be found. The fourth pitch moves up the face (5.6) above the ledge and past a small overhang into a set of black-rock cracks, which diagonal up and right to a sloping ledge that holds a large block; follow this ledge left past the block and climb the face above to a right-facing corner. The corner (5.7) takes one to the belay at a broken, mossy ledge. From here one can scramble onto the left (east) ridge of the north pinnacle and follow it to the summit.

ROUTE 17. NORTHWEST COULOIR AND LEDGES. II, 4.0. First ascent July 13, 1931, by Fritiof Fryxell, Leland Horberg, Rudolph Edmund, William Cederberg, Neuman Kerndt, and Elof Petersen. Approach this route from Hanging Canyon. Cross the stream between Ramshead Lake and Lake of the Crags and climb directly up the main couloir to the col between Symmetry Spire and the Symmetry Crags to the west. This is the same col as reached from the south via the Southwest Couloir route *(Route 3)*. During most of the summer this northwest couloir is filled with steep snow and sometimes ice, so the knowledge of how to use an ice axe is essential. From the col climb left (east) up the ridge for about 30m before following easy but sometimes exposed ledges out to the left (north) and up the northwest side of the peak to the summit. There is almost a trail now in this final section of ledges. Given good snow conditions, this route is also useful for a descent into Hanging Canyon, but the uppermost snow is very steep and should not be attempted unless one is experienced on such hazardous ground. **Time:** 5¼ to 6¼ hours from Jenny Lake. See *Appalachia* 18, no. 4 (December 1931): pp. 388–408, illus.

ROUTE 18. NORTHWEST FACE. II, 5.6. First ascent July 15, 1974, by John Cain and Tim East. This route apparently ascends the face to the left (east) of the northwest couloir and below the final northwest ledges (see *Route 17*). From Hanging Canyon climb the snow and ice of the couloir for about 90m to an obvious point that provides access to this face. The first lead is face climbing to a grassy belay ledge. The next two pitches lead toward a huge face of overhanging rock. Now traverse right and up for the next lead to a large belay ledge. The next pitch continues straight up to another belay ledge. Three pitches of scrambling then lead to the summit.

SYMMETRY CRAGS (10,320+ TO 10,400+)

Map: Mount Moran

All the pinnacles of the series extending west from Symmetry Spire to Rock of Ages have gentle east slopes and precipitous west faces. The exact number of summits depends on who is counting; the numbering from east to west, which is given here, is one approximation. However, the first pinnacle west of Symmetry Spire and the first two pinnacles east of Rock of Ages are quite distinct. Only these latter two qualify as peaks and are treated separately (see *Symmetry Crag 4* and *Symmetry Crag 5*, below). On the south slopes of the Symmetry Crags, and west of the Ice Point–Symmetry Spire saddle, are three small pinnacles that were climbed on July 22, 1957, by Fred Ayres and Ellis Blade during the search for the lost Baxter's Pinnacle. The first is in the main couloir west of Storm Point, about 120m below the saddle, and the other two are on the crest of the next ridge to the west; all are short, easy climbs. Cutting across the lower southern slopes of the western crags is a line of weakness in the rocks that forms a wide, continuous, and shallow couloir running in a southwest–northeast direction. Although not specifically recognized as a fault, it forms a conspicuous feature from the proper viewpoint; it isolates the pinnacles climbed in 1957.

Crag 1. I, 3.0. First ascent July 13, 1931, by Fritiof Fryxell, Leland Horberg, Rudolph Edmund, William Cederberg, Neuman Kerndt, and Elof Petersen. This crag is climbed by its east ridge, starting from the high col just west of Symmetry Spire, which is reached by *Route 3* or *Route 17* for that peak. It is a short scramble from the col to the summit.

Crag 2. I, 3.0. First ascent July 26, 1934, by Fred Ayres. This pinnacle is reached by dropping down from Crag 1 and climbing up a steep southern couloir to the east ridge, which is followed west to the summit. A climb of the north ridge of this crag on July 26, 1971, after an ascent of Crag 1, was reported by Mark Chapman.

Crag 3. I, 3.0. First ascent July 26, 1934, by Fred Ayres. From Crag 2 drop down to the north on ledges to gain the notch between Crags 2 and 3, and then climb the east ridge of Crag 3 to its summit.

On August 8, 1973, Tom Kimbrough and Bob Greenspan climbed the north slope directly from Hanging Canyon onto the east ridge, which they followed to the summit.

SYMMETRY CRAG 4 (10,720+)

(0.45 mi W of Symmetry Spire)
Map: Mount Moran

Crag 4 denotes the second summit east of Rock of Ages. Protected by crags on either side, this summit is seldom climbed even though it is readily accessible. Its west face, like the other crags of this series, is indeed steep, discouraging the casual climber.

Chronology

EAST RIDGE: July 26, 1934, Fred Ayres
UPPER SOUTH FACE: July 12, 1959, William Buckingham, Fred Wright

ROUTE 1. UPPER SOUTH FACE. II, 5.4. First ascent July 12, 1959, by William Buckingham and Fred Wright. From the Ice Point–Symmetry Spire saddle, traverse west across several gullies to the long scree shelf that angles upward along the base of the nearly vertical upper south face of Crag 4. Begin the ascent in the obvious line of weakness near the center of the face in a very shallow and deceptive gully. One ropelength up this depression leads to a grassy ledge. Traverse right on this ledge for about 60m to the point where it intersects another large ledge that diagonals upward to the left. Follow this ledge back for 46m to a point where two chimneys form a break in the wall above. Climb one of these chimneys for one ropelength; an easy pitch then leads to the summit ridge 60m east of the summit. See *American Alpine Journal* 12, no. 1 (1960): pp. 125–27.

ROUTE 2. EAST RIDGE. I, 3.0. First ascent July 26, 1934, by Fred Ayres. As is the case for the crags to the east of Rock of Ages, there are no difficulties on this ridge once it is attained. One method is to start from the Ice Point–Symmetry Spire saddle, stay below (south of) the main ridge crest, and then gain the ridge just west of Crag 3. From the summit of Crag 3 the easiest method of reaching Crag 4 is to return to the notch between Crags 2 and 3, drop down around the south cliffs of Crag 3, regain the ridge crest at the notch between Crags 3 and 4, and continue on the east ridge to the summit of Crag 4. A direct descent of the west face of Crag 3 to reach the start of this ridge may involve rappelling.

SYMMETRY CRAG 5 (10,720+)

(0.55 mi W of Symmetry Spire)
Map: Mount Moran

Immediately to the east of Rock of Ages, Crag 5 presents a very steep west face with rock of dubious quality.

Chronology

EAST RIDGE: June 19, 1936, Fred and Irene Ayres
SOUTH COULOIR: August 12, 1947, George Bell, Austen Riggs II, Rolfe Glover III, Wayland Griffith

ROUTE 1. SOUTH COULOIR. II, 5.6. First ascent August 12, 1947, by George Bell, Austen Riggs II, Rolfe Glover III, and Wayland Griffith. This climb starts from Cascade Canyon and probably ascends the couloir located immediately beyond (west of) Trinity Buttress. At some point the shallow couloir below the upper south side of this crag must be crossed or ascended partway. The left (west) face of the couloir is climbed and a western branch is then followed to the summit, which is attained from the southeast.

ROUTE 2. EAST RIDGE. I, 3.0. First ascent June 19, 1936, by Fred and Irene Ayres. Approach via Hanging Canyon. Above and south of Lake of the Crags is a wide ledge that angles from lower left (east) to upper right (west) and joins the east ridge of Crag 5 immediately west of Crag 4. In early season this ledge will be covered with snow. The ridge itself offers no problems. The short east ridge can probably also be reached from the south, using the wide diagonal shelf that passes under the south face of Crag 4. This shelf can be gained from the Ice Point–Symmetry Spire saddle. A traverse west from Crag 4 requires a rappel down the steep west face of that crag.

ROCK OF AGES (10,895)

Map: Mount Moran

This curiously flat-topped peak gained its maximum popularity decades ago. Many of the routes are as challenging as those on the south side of Symmetry Spire, and the approach is only a little longer. The nine routes range from easy to difficult, and like Symmetry Spire, Rock of Ages has one easy descent route, the South Couloir *(Route 2)*. The rock is usually sound and in places is outstanding. The features of the north face of Rock of Ages can be described in terms of two major V-shaped indentations. The western V is larger and more distinct; it lies directly below the summit and contains prominent black water stains on the rock at its bottom. The eastern V is less distinct and begins just above a small Wall Street–like ledge that diagonals up across the face from left to right.

The best approach is from Hanging Canyon. Take the climbers' trail into the canyon and continue past the meadow on the west side of Lake of the Crags. Because the slopes and chutes leading up to the notches to the east and west of Rock of Ages are very rotten, there is a definite advantage in making the ascent in early season when the rubble is covered by snow, even though the snow is steep. In midseason or late season there are significant difficulties (5.4) in climbing the treacherous rock just below these notches.

It is also possible to approach Rock of Ages from Cascade Canyon, but the couloirs are long and not easy to find, and they steepen considerably in their upper reaches. Go up Cascade Canyon, past the drainage west of Trinity Buttress, to the next major stream draining a relatively narrow couloir; this couloir (with a short dogleg to the right) leads to the notch east of the peak. It is relatively free of loose rock and provides good rock scrambling. Near the notch the couloir narrows to a cleft 2m wide with multiple chockstones that are passed on the left wall. The next couloir to the west, also narrow, leads toward the notch west of Rock of Ages. About 60m short of the ridge crest, this open couloir narrows and splits, with the right branch leading up to the desired notch and the left branch leading more easily to the col west of the Schoolhouse (Ayres' Crag 1). Both of these couloirs are directly opposite the falls (on the opposite [south] side of the canyon) in the stream that drains the northeast snowfields of Mount Owen.

Chronology

EAST CHIMNEYS: August 14, 1934, Fred and Irene Ayres
NORTHWEST CORNER: July 23, 1935, Paul Petzoldt, Phil Smith, Herman Petzoldt
var—**NORTHWEST FACE:** August 26, 1972, Tom Kreuzer, John Waldvogel
SOUTH COULOIR: July 23, 1935, Paul Petzoldt, Phil Smith, Herman Petzoldt (descent); August 14, 1947, Ronald K. Smith, James T. Smith, Donald F. Smith, Bruce Edwards (ascent)
STETTNER: August 21, 1941, Joseph and Paul Stettner
var—August 8, 1949, Joseph Murphy, John Rouson
EAST RIDGE: August 8, 1946, James T. Smith, Ronald K. Smith, Donald Caruthers
SOUTHWEST COULOIR: August 14, 1947, George Bell, Rolfe Glover III
NORTHEAST FACE: August 25, 1949, William Primak, Reinhold Mankau, Peter Pfister
var—July 24, 1951, Robert and Doris Merriam, Leigh Ortenburger
NORTHEAST CHIMNEY: July 30, 1951, Peter Robinson, Jim Cooke, Percy Crosby
SOUTHEAST RIDGE: June 24, 1979, George Montopoli, Tim Hogan
var—July 1993, Jim Howe, Mark Rump

ROUTE 1. SOUTHWEST COULOIR. II, 5.4. First ascent August 14, 1947, by George Bell and Rolfe Glover III. This route ascends the westernmost couloir on the upper south side of Rock of Ages; this couloir leads to the west ridge just below the flat summit block. The base of this couloir can be reached via the long couloir extending upward from Cascade Canyon, or it can be gained by traversing other crags along the ridge to the west and passing the Schoolhouse (Ayres' Crag 1) on the south. If coming up from Cascade Canyon, take the last branch of the long couloir to the right (east) before attaining the notch west of Rock of Ages; this eastern branch is more of a broad ledge than a couloir. If starting from the notch west of Rock of Ages, scramble or rappel south down the very steep couloir and gain this same broad ledge system. Either way, climb up and east along the ledges to gain the west edge of the upper south face and climb directly upward to reach the uppermost west ridge of Rock of Ages. One 5.4 pitch is encountered just below the ridge crest. Follow the west ridge to the summit.

ROUTE 2. ▲ SOUTH COULOIR. II, 4.0. First descent July 23, 1935, by Paul Petzoldt, Phil Smith, and Herman Petzoldt; first ascent August 14, 1947, by Ronald K. Smith, James T. Smith, Donald F. Smith, and Bruce Edwards. This short couloir is the one major break in the upper defenses of Rock of Ages. One can reach it via one of the long couloirs out of Cascade Canyon, but it is usually approached from the notch east of Rock of Ages after a

Hanging Canyon approach. From this notch, traverse west underneath the south walls of Rock of Ages to the crest of the small south ridge. Climb the ridge until it is possible to work up and slightly to the right (east) over easy blocks and chimneys into the south couloir. Scramble up to its head, then climb easy slabs leading right (east) up to the sloping summit ridge; follow this back (west) to the summit block. This south couloir is also the standard route of descent. To locate it from the summit, walk east down the broad summit ridge until just past the small evergreen bushes, then cut back downward south and west on the aforementioned slabs.

ROUTE 3. SOUTHEAST RIDGE. III, 5.9. First ascent June 24, 1979, by George Montopoli and Tim Hogan. (See *Figures 8-20* and *8-21*.) This route lies very close to the crest of the southeast ridge, which is left (south) of the notch east of Rock of Ages. Descend a short distance from the notch and climb the initial section, over a pointed flake that hangs down, and then continue up (5.4) to the first belay point at the base of a steep face. The second lead goes up a flake (5.6 hand crack) past a curious round, gray projection (about 1 foot in diameter) and into and up cracks (5.8) to the next belay stance, located just to the right of a hollow flake. The third pitch starts by passing a roof on the right (5.6), and then a short, overhanging flake move (5.9) is followed by an unprotected friction traverse (4.5m) to the right to a shallow dihedral (5.7); climb the dihedral up and left to the next belay. The last lead climbs an overhanging crack (5.8) up onto an easier face that ends at the broad summit ridge. Scramble to the summit. The route contains good, solid rock. **Gear:** Devices up to 4" are useful.

Variation: III, 5.9. First ascent in July 1993, by Jim Howe and Mark Rump. This variation takes off from the second pitch of the original Southeast Ridge route. The crux third pitch ascends a thin finger crack on excellent rock to a steep (vertical), blocky face.

ROUTE 4. ▲ EAST CHIMNEYS. II, 5.6. First ascent August 14, 1934, by Fred and Irene Ayres (from Cascade Canyon); they had attempted the route from Hanging Canyon on July 16, 1934. (See *Figure 8-21*.) This climb starts from the notch just east of Rock of Ages. Directly above the notch is the east ridge. An indentation containing a series of steep chimneys begins a little left (about 24m south) of the notch. Climb these chimneys on good rock (during the first ascent a *courte-échelle* —a shoulder stand—was used at one overhang) for several pitches. Near the top, traverse to the right on a ledge out onto the east face and climb the last meter onto the gently sloping, grass-covered summit ridge. Stroll westward to the unusual flat summit block, which can be climbed via a crack near its north end or by a lieback on its

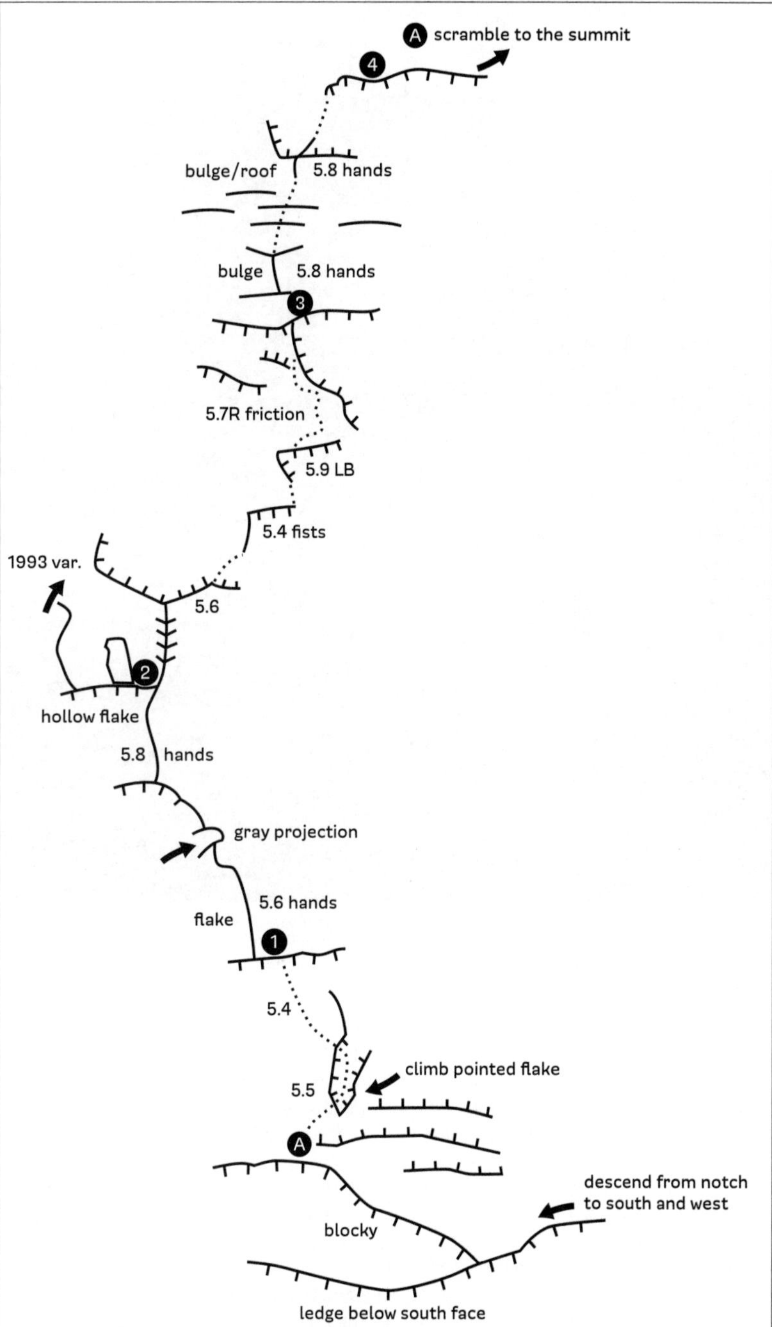

FIGURE 8-20. Rock of Ages (A), Southeast Ridge *(Route 3)*, III, 5.9; variation: 1993, III, 5.9

FIGURE 8-21. Rock of Ages, northeast aspect. (A) Southeast Ridge *(Route 3)*, III, 5.9; (B) East Chimneys *(Route 4)*, II, 5.6; (C) East Ridge *(Route 5)*, II, 5.8; (D) Northeast Chimney *(Route 6)*, II, 5.6; (E) Northeast Face *(Route 7)*, II, 5.6; (F) Northeast Face, variation: 1951, II, 5.6; (G) Stettner *(Route 8)*, II, 5.7; (H) Northwest Corner *(Route 9)*, II, 5.7

east face (more difficult). Many variations are possible in the chimneys, and the climbing is steep and not too difficult. **Time:** 7¾ hours from Jenny Lake. See *Chicago Mountaineering Club Newsletter* 2, no. 5 (January–July 1948): pp. 5–7; *Trail and Timberline*, no. 196 (February 1935): p. 18; no. 223 (May 1937): p. 56.

ROUTE 5. EAST RIDGE. II, 5.8. First ascent August 8, 1946, by James T. Smith, Ronald K. Smith, and Donald Caruthers. (See *Figure 8-21.*) From the notch, one can stay directly on the east ridge and never enter the couloir or chimneys of the regular East Chimneys route *(Route 4)*, but this is significantly more difficult.

ROUTE 6. NORTHEAST CHIMNEY. II, 5.6. First ascent July 30, 1951, by Peter Robinson, Jim Cooke, and Percy Crosby. (See *Figure 8-21.*) From the meadow west of Lake of the Crags, climb (snow in early season) toward the notch east of Rock of Ages; cut right (west) onto the north face by means of the small, Wall Street–like ledge that slopes up to the right and narrows at the end. From this point climb over an overhang to a shelf that leads steeply up to the right toward the bottom of the eastern V. Instead of following this shelf out to the right, climb 6m left (east) to a chimney. On the first ascent this next pitch began with a shoulder stand. Climb 18m up the chimney past another overhang, then continue up the chimney to a large chockstone, which can be passed either by a steep ledge on the left side (this may be wet) or on the right wall. Climb left onto the summit ridge and follow it westward to the summit block. See *Dartmouth Mountaineering Club Journal*, 1951: pp. 11–15, illus.

ROUTE 7. NORTHEAST FACE. II, 5.6. First ascent August 25, 1949, by William Primak, Reinhold Mankau, and Peter Pfister. (See *Figure 8-21.*) This route utilizes the right (west) branch of the less distinct eastern V on the north face of Rock of Ages. Reach the lower end of this V, which is about 90m above the slabs and snow at the base of the north face, via a series of chimneys well east of the water stains of *Route 8*. Three short pitches, including the passage of a chockstone, lead to a 3m-wide grassy ledge. (**Note:** Because it is not known precisely which line the first-ascent party took to reach this point, *Figure 8-21* shows this route beginning with the Wall Street–like ledge of *Route 6*.) From the broken rock of the V, a sequence of chimneys and ledges angles up slightly to the right (west). After five short leads the easy summit ridge is attained through a chimney near the right edge of the V. See *Chicago Mountaineering Club Newsletter* 3, no. 6 (August 1949): pp. 26–27.

Variation: II, 5.6. First ascent July 24, 1951, by Robert and Doris Merriam and Leigh Ortenburger. (See *Figure 8-21.*) This climb starts as in *Route 6*, using the same small, Wall Street–like ledge. At its west end climb over the same overhang to the same shelf, and follow it steeply up to the right toward the bottom of the eastern V. An awkward step with considerable exposure is required to complete the traverse into the V. This variation provides an alternate to the chimneys used by the 1949 party. **Time:** 8½ hours from Jenny Lake. See *Stanford Alpine Club Journal*, 1955: pp. 48–50.

ROUTE 8. STETTNER. II, 5.7. First ascent August 21, 1941, by Joseph and Paul Stettner. (See *Figure 8-21.*) This route is fortunately unique in the Tetons in that its starting point was originally marked by a circular blaze of red paint on the rock; this circle was found in 1948 on the second ascent but has not been seen since. It was also an early scene of a 9m leader fall, successfully held by a sitting belay. This route goes up the western V. Below the bottom of this V are prominent black water stains on the rock. The climb starts in a narrow chimney about 15m to the right (west) of these black markings. Climb about 46m up this wet chimney on steep and exposed rock. Because the chimney terminates in an impossible-looking narrow crack that slants to the left, climb out about 4.5m on the difficult open wall to a grassy shelf at the bottom of the V. Follow the steep ledges of the right (west) section of the V and reach the summit ridge at a point north and west of the summit block. Traverse around underneath the summit block on the west and climb to the summit from the south. Some rotten rock can be expected on this route.

Variation: II, 5.1. First ascent August 8, 1949, by Joseph Murphy and John Rouson. Instead of climbing up and to the right (west) from the bottom of the V, walk down and to the left (east) along an obvious ledge to join *Route 7* about two pitches above the first overhang. Follow that route to the summit.

ROUTE 9. NORTHWEST CORNER. II, 5.7. First ascent July 23, 1935, by Paul Petzoldt, Phil Smith, and Herman Petzoldt. (See *Figure 8-21.*) This six-pitch climb on uniformly excellent rock is recommended as an early-season climb for those who can pass the first lead safely. It is not as well protected as one might wish. From the meadow at the west end of Lake of the Crags, proceed up the talus and snow to the notch between the Schoolhouse (Ayres' Crag 1) and Rock of Ages. This is much more easily and safely done in early season when snow will extend all the way to the notch; otherwise, steep, loose, and hazardous rock must be negotiated. The first-ascent party climbed about 46m out to the left onto the north face in order to avoid the smooth face rising out of the notch. Once above this face, they cut back right (west) onto the northwest face, which they climbed up and left to a small platform on the northwest corner of the peak.

It is possible to take a more direct route out of and only 1m left of the notch. From a belay at its base, climb the initial slightly overhanging section on small holds up and right past a small, strenuous, very awkward corner (5.7) onto easier rock that angles up and slightly left to a stance near the north edge of the main wall above the notch. Protection here is difficult to place, but a large camming device can be placed up and left of the awkward corner. An alternative to this corner is an overhanging crack (5.7) about 4.5m to the right (south).

The second pitch rejoins the original route, going up and right around the main corner of the ridge to a sequence of vertical jam cracks (5.6) that lead to the belay at the base of an outstanding steep, slabby wall of excellent rock. Climb directly up this wall (5.4) on good holds, even though the absence of cracks makes protection scarce. The fourth lead goes up and slightly left around an overhanging section to a belay well around on the north side. Next, continue in a crack up and left out to an exposed point at the upper end of the Stettner route *(Route 8)*. Easier climbing in cracks and blocks then takes one to within 30m of the summit. Scramble to the top via the northern break in the summit block. See *Harvard Mountaineering* 12 (May 1955): pp. 57–58.

Variation: **NORTHWEST FACE.** II, 5.8. First ascent August 26, 1972, by Tom Kreuzer and John Waldvogel. From the platform out on the northwest corner, one can climb straight up for 30m and then continue up and slightly right until the easier rock below the summit block is reached. Most of the climbing is 5.6, but two sections of 5.8 will be encountered below the final overhang of the summit block.

AYRES' CRAGS (10,640+ TO 10,720+)

Map: Mount Moran

On the ridge immediately west of Rock of Ages and numbered from east to west, the five Ayres' Crags contain some of the better climbing around Lake of the Crags. These pinnacles, as well as several others on the rim of Hanging Canyon, were first climbed by Fred Ayres, who modestly objected to the name Ayres' Crags, saying it was "hardly euphonious." A traverse of the crags along with Rock of Ages provides a full day of good climbing—or ridge running, as Ayres would say. All are normally reached from Hanging Canyon, but long couloirs from Cascade Canyon do provide direct access to Crags 4 and 5. The proper couloir, more open than those to the east, leads due north from the eastern edge of a barren talus slope just beyond (west of) a section of trees. This proper couloir lies just west of the falls—on the opposite (south) side of the canyon—in the stream that drains the northeast snowfields of Mount Owen. To reach Crag 1 or 2 from the south, take the next couloir to the east (see *Rock of Ages, Route 1*), which ends at the notch just west of Rock of Ages.

The Schoolhouse (Ayres' Crag 1) (10,640+)

(0.05 mi W of Rock of Ages)

The Schoolhouse, the smallest and sharpest of the Ayres' Crags, is the first pinnacle west of Rock of Ages. Originally called "The Old Setting Hen" in the 1930s, this pinnacle was renamed by Fred Ayres, who felt that the first name was "hardly dignified enough for an official name." It is not easy to find today such a concern for dignity in nomenclature.

ROUTE 1. WEST FACE. I, 5.4. First ascent July 8, 1940, by Fred and Irene Ayres and Margaret Smith (Craighead); attempted on July 22, 1936, by Fred Ayres (solo). From the col west of the Schoolhouse, first climb over the large boulder that rests directly on the ridge. The lower part of the west face, which is now directly above, is a very large detached slab. The first-ascent party climbed the high-angle outside face of the slab; the chimney between the slab and the face itself may possibly be climbable for a small person. The first part of this pitch is very exposed. From the top of the slab climb a series of cracks to the knife-edge summit. **Time:** 4½ hours from Ramshead Lake.

ROUTE 2. EAST RIDGE. I, 5.6. First ascent June 17, 1958, by William Buckingham, Karl Ross, and Walter Gove. From the notch east of the Schoolhouse (and west of Rock of Ages) climb two pitches up the east ridge, the second of which is a pleasant jam crack, to the platform just south of the summit. One short, slightly overhanging pitch then leads to the summit. See *American Alpine Journal* 11, no. 2 (1959): pp. 307–9.

ROUTE 3. THE WINDOWSILL. II, 5.6. First ascent August 12, 1966, by Robert Fenichel, Mary Louise Denman, and Robert Hoguet III. Beneath the large boulder at the base of the west face of the Schoolhouse is a tunnel or window some 4m in length; it is large enough for a crouching climber to pass through. This four-pitch route provides access to this window from the north, using the face just to the right of the extremely loose chute that leads to the notch between Rock of Ages and the Schoolhouse. The first pitch goes approximately straight up from the right of the chute for 30m on downsloping holds to a good ledge for a belay. Now move right from the ledge to an overhang, which is passed by way of a V cleft (5.6), and finish the lead (43m) over very poor rock to a 2-square-meter square ledge. The third pitch (5.1, 37m) exits right from this ledge. Climb up to a long ledge and then go out to and up a short, steep open book near the right end of this ledge. From the top of this corner move right to an enormous detached block. The final lead (43m) starts left from the top of the block, goes up 4m, continues left to a corner overlooking the original chute, and then ends with a scramble up to the window.

Ayres' Crag 2 (10,720+)

(0.15 mi W of Rock of Ages)

This is the major summit between Rock of Ages and the Blockhouse (Ayres' Crag 4), higher and larger than the smaller crags (Crags 1 and 3) to either side.

ROUTE 1. EAST FACE. II, 3.0. First ascent July 22, 1936, by Fred Ayres. The ascent or descent of the sloping east face involves no difficulties.

ROUTE 2. WEST FACE. II, 4.0. First descent July 22, 1936, by Fred Ayres; first ascent August 3, 1950, by Jack "Jiggs" and Ted Lewis and Jim Smith. This broad and slabby face can be readily climbed on good holds near its north edge.

Ayres' Crag 3 (10,640+)

(0.16 mi W of Rock of Ages)

ROUTE 1. WEST RIDGE. I, 3.0. First ascent July 22, 1936, by Fred Ayres. From the notch west of this small pinnacle climb directly up the knife-edge west ridge leading to the summit until a traverse can be made to the right (south), down onto a shelf, which leads around the south side of the pinnacle. Continue along this shelf until due south of the summit; then climb blocks leading back to the west ridge and follow it to the summit. If approaching this pinnacle from the east, contour around its south ridge and reach the summit in a similar manner.

The Blockhouse (Ayres' Crag 4) (10,720+)

(0.2 mi W of Rock of Ages)

This significant tower rises steeply on all sides, with the northeast face providing the only break in the otherwise serious defenses. It was first explored by Fred Ayres on July 22, 1936, who wisely decided that the climbing was too exposed for a solo climber. It provides an interesting multipitch climb worthy of the approach hike into Hanging Canyon.

Chronology

NORTHEAST FACE: August 1, 1940, Fred Ayres, John Oberlin, Orrin Bonney, Margaret Smith (Craighead)
SOUTH RIDGE: August 15, 1959, Barry Corbet, Frederick Medrick
SOUTHWEST FACE: August 15, 1959, William Buckingham, Al Read, Frank Magary
WEST FACE: July 8, 1960, Al Read, Sterling Neale
var—July 14, 2003, Tom Turiano, Corey Johnson

ROUTE 1. WEST FACE. II, 5.6. First ascent July 8, 1960, by Al Read and Sterling Neale. Approach the col between the Blockhouse and the Canine Tooth via Hanging Canyon and Lake of the Crags. From the base of the west face of the Blockhouse, traverse right on easy rock around to the edge of the southwest face. Climb directly up and to the left until a ledge is reached about 24m above the belayer. Now move left and up for 4.5m on very small holds to a broad ledge. The second pitch goes directly up the corner formed by the west and south faces. After 30m one can scramble along the level ridge to the summit block; attain the summit from the north. See *American Alpine Journal* 12, no. 2 (1961): pp. 373–79.

Variation: II, 5.7. First ascent July 14, 2003, by Tom Turiano and Corey Johnson. From the col at the base of the west face this party climbed straight up, encountering a difficult finger crack (5.7) located about 5m right of the northwest arête of the Blockhouse.

ROUTE 2. SOUTHWEST FACE. II, 5.7. First ascent August 15, 1959, by William Buckingham, Al Read, and Frank Magary. This route ascends a crack system near the center of the face; the crack is reached by angling left from a point near the south edge of the face. This difficult pitch is nearly vertical and poorly protected. After 46m an adequate belay stance on a broad ledge is reached. The final 60m section is moderate 4.0 climbing in a shallow couloir that leads right and up to the summit.

ROUTE 3. SOUTH RIDGE. II, 5.7. First ascent August 15, 1959, by Barry Corbet and Frederick Medrick. The south face of the Blockhouse, which faces Cascade Canyon, is divided by the sharp south ridge, containing a huge ceiling near the summit. This climb stays slightly left (west) of the ridge crest; a traverse to the left is required just below the ceiling. This enjoyable ridge can be approached directly from Cascade Canyon or from Hanging Canyon via a slight descent from the Canine Tooth–Blockhouse saddle.

ROUTE 4. ▲ NORTHEAST FACE. II, 5.1. First ascent August 1, 1940, by Fred Ayres, John Oberlin, Orrin Bonney, and Margaret Smith (Craighead); attempted on July 22, 1936, by Fred Ayres (solo). From the notch east of this pinnacle, scramble up to a large black ledge where the climbing begins. Descend a meter to the left (south) in order to reach a small chimney. Ascend this chimney and pass the chockstone; then use the face to the right to regain the east ridge. Scramble up some very large, loose blocks to a ledge containing a thin 1.5m flake set on edge. The next lead traverses about 15m out on the north face on a 2-foot ledge and then diagonals up to the right (west). The last ropelength that leads to the summit also angles up to the right on ledges and chimneys. Descend by several short rappels.

Ayres' Crag 5 (11,040+)

(0.2 mi S of the Jaw)

This solitary high point lies at the end of a ridge extending south of the rest of the pinnacles that surround Lake of the Crags. From Cascade Canyon, Ayres' Crag 5 is seen as a prominent buttress with a sheer south face (see *Cascade Canyon, North Side Rock Climbs*). From the summit, the major couloir west of this crag appears to offer a fast descent route down to Cascade Canyon. However, the bottom of it drops off, entailing at least one rappel, so it is preferable to cut left (east) out of the main couloir just below the imposing south face of the crag.

ROUTE 1. NORTHEAST RIDGE. I, 3.0. First ascent July 22, 1936, by Fred Ayres. This ridge connects with the east ridge of the Canine Tooth about halfway to its summit. Climb the slope from Hanging Canyon to the col west of the Blockhouse (Ayres' Crag 4) and ascend the east ridge of the Canine Tooth until it is easy to get onto the northeast ridge of Ayres' Crag 5. Follow this ridge to the summit, which consists of loose boulders.

JAW CRAGS (ca. 11,200+)

(0.8 mi WSW of Mount St. John)
Map: Mount Moran

This group of pinnacles at the western end of Hanging Canyon extending west and north from the Ayres' Crags forms the south ridge of the Jaw. Together with the Jaw, which is the highest of the group, they present a profile for which the name is apt when viewed from Lake of the Crags. The Grinders, although small, contain some difficult and exposed climbing. They are numbered from south to north. See *Dartmouth Mountaineering Club Journal*, 1952: pp. 45–46, illus.

Canine Tooth. I, 3.0. First ascent July 5, 1940, by Robert Bear and William Plumley. This is the first high point west of the Blockhouse (Ayres' Crag 4). It is an easy climb from the east or the west.

Grinder 1. I, 3.0. First ascent July 4, 1952, by Peter Robinson, Brian Brett, Percy Crosby, and Bill and John Briggs. This easy climb from the north uses a series of ledges.

Grinder 2. I, 5.4. First ascent July 4, 1952, by Peter Robinson. Climb the chimney separating this pinnacle from Grinder 3 until it is possible to climb out on friction holds on the east face, which leads to the summit. Another route, first climbed on September 9, 1954, by Gary Hemming and Leigh Ortenburger, leads up the prominent shelf on the south face. From the exposed end of this shelf climb a crack to the summit.

Grinder 3. I, 5.1. First ascent September 9, 1954, by Leigh Ortenburger and Gary Hemming. This is climbed from Grinder 4 via the sharp north ridge.

Grinder 4. I, 5.1. First ascent September 9, 1954, by Gary Hemming and Leigh Ortenburger. Climb the north ridge from the notch between this pinnacle and Grinder 5. Descent can be made via Grinder 3.

Grinder 5. I, 4.0. First ascent July 5, 1940, by Robert Bear and William Plumley. This pinnacle was first climbed by the chimney in the middle of its east face. On July 4, 1952, Peter Robinson, Brian Brett, Percy Crosby, and Bill and John Briggs climbed this pinnacle by its easy north ridge.

THE JAW (11,400)

Map: Mount Moran

At the extreme west end of Hanging Canyon lies the Jaw, which is only 30 feet lower than Mount St. John, the highest point of those that surround this canyon. (See *Figure 8-11* for an early-season view of Hanging Canyon.) The Jaw is easily approached from Lake of the Crags, and its summit affords an excellent view of the impressive north and northwest faces of Teewinot Mountain, Mount Owen, and the Grand Teton.

Chronology

EAST FACE: August 29, 1931, Frank Smith, Eccles Johnson
WEST RIDGE: June 21, 1958, William Buckingham, Robert and Margaret West, Robert Keyes (descent); July 30, 1989, Susie Harrington (ascent)
NORTH RIDGE: August 21, 1960, Loring Woodman, Duncan Cameron

ROUTE 1. WEST RIDGE. I, 5.6. First descent June 21, 1958, by William Buckingham, Robert and Margaret West, and Robert Keyes; first ascent July 30, 1989, by Susie Harrington. This ridge begins just east of Buckingham Palace (11,097) at the saddle (10,640+), which can be reached either from the north via a snow slope from Paintbrush Canyon or from the south via a 900m couloir from Cascade Canyon. At the base of the north approach is an interesting example of a rock glacier, perhaps the most accessible example in the range. Scramble easily from the saddle to the first high point, Point 11,120+, which contains a natural window. The remainder of the pinnacle ridge consists of scrambling until the uppermost steep section is reached. If this is climbed directly (as on the first ascent), a dihedral (5.6) with very loose rock in places leads to the summit. This section can be bypassed (as on the first descent) on the south to a small notch between the Jaw and the Grinders; the summit is then easily attained. As a descent route for a traverse continuing to the west, the southern bypass is recommended. See *American Alpine Journal* 11, no. 2 (1959): pp. 307–9.

ROUTE 2. ▲ EAST FACE. I, 2.0. First ascent August 29, 1931, by Frank Smith and Eccles Johnson. From Lake of the Crags continue up the benches and talus slopes of western Hanging Canyon to the summit. No difficulties will be met except for some snow climbing early in the season. **Time:** 4½ hours from Ramshead Lake.

ROUTE 3. NORTH RIDGE. I, 4.0. First ascent August 21, 1960, by Loring Woodman and Duncan Cameron. Approach via Paintbrush Canyon into the cirque between the Outlier (10,560+) and Mount St. John to the saddle separating the Outlier and the Jaw. Scramble up the north ridge to a col just below the steep section of the main west ridge. Climb the first nearly vertical 15m directly. Twenty-seven meters of scrambling on loose rock brings one to the base of a slight overhang, which is climbed by a crack on the left. On the next pitch pass the "Man," a pinnacle named for its appearance from the northeast, on the right. The final pitch follows the corner of the open chimney just to the right of the summit ridge; the jam crack on the left (the smaller of two) leads to a large depression just below the overhanging part of the chimney. A small horizontal ledge or crack then provides a hand traverse to the top of the chimney on the right. A short scramble then brings one to the top. See *American Alpine Journal* 12, no. 2 (1961): pp. 373–79.

CAMELS HEAD (11,200+)

(0.7 mi WSW of Mount St. John)
Map: Mount Moran

This very small pinnacle (only about 18m high) is located a short distance east of the first saddle east of the Jaw. It is the only difficult part of the ridge between Needles Eye Spire and the Jaw and can be approached from the upper east slopes of the Jaw.

ROUTE 1. EAST FACE. I, 5.4. First ascent September 9, 1954, by Gary Hemming and Leigh Ortenburger. The route starts on the left (south) edge of the smooth east face (5.4). Climb until the holds run out (about 6m), then traverse right (north) across the face and finish the short climb by the northeast ridge. The first-ascent party used interesting tactics to get off the pinnacle. One climber was belayed down, and then the rope was fixed and the second climber rappelled off the opposite side. A very long sling wrapped around the summit has also been used for the rappel. There are no nubs or cracks at the summit.

NEEDLES EYE SPIRE (11,200+)

(0.6 mi WSW of Mount St. John)
Map: Mount Moran

This spectacular finger is immediately west of the window, or "needle's eye," in the Mount St. John–Jaw ridge. The direct southern approach from Hanging Canyon is guarded by a cliff band that extends across the south side of Minga Spire.

ROUTE 1. EAST FACE. I, 5.7. First ascent August 9, 1946, by Fred Ayres and John Oberlin. Pass the series of cliffs, which prevent a direct approach to the spire from Hanging Canyon, by ascending the first (eastern) couloir of Minga Spire. Once past these cliffs, turn abruptly left (west) and scramble up and left along the top of the cliffs past the south buttress of Minga Spire. One can now climb a very steep 37m chimney to reach the notch just east of Needles Eye Spire. An easier approach is to go first to the col west of Needles Eye Spire and then circle in back (north) of the spire to reach this same notch. The almost-vertical east face is climbed by a series of small ledges and large flakes. An 18m rappel is just adequate for descent.

NEEDLES EYE SPIKE (11,150)

(0.5 mi WSW of Mount St. John)
Map: Mount Moran

This curious rock formation, precariously perched as if misplaced out of a Dr. Seuss book, forms the actual window—the "needle's eye." It is a landmark to which the eye is drawn from many different locations.

ROUTE 1. WEST FACE. I, 5.7. First ascent unknown; first known ascent July 1, 2006, by Paul Horton and Carol Viau. The 1946 party that climbed Needles Eye Spire noted climbing two other pinnacles en route, possibly including Needles Eye Spike. However, they made no mention of a traverse from the notch or of the unique nature of this spectacular little pinnacle, which is the one actually penetrated by the eye. The opening is surprisingly large, 3+m wide by perhaps 10m tall. The route starts on the west face, a short distance to the right of the chimney leading to the notch east of Needles Eye Spire. Climb a moderate face directly up to the eye, then continue left of the opening to a belay on or near the ridge crest. The second pitch, 5.7 and very short, goes up a tight chimney on the north side of the ridge to a short face, which is followed by a mantel onto the top of the Spike. The summit block has no cracks, but it can be wrapped with a long sling for an anchor. Rappel the route or join the 1946 route on Needles Eye Spire by descending to the belay, following the ridge a short distance, and dropping into the notch at the top of the steep chimney of that route.

MINGA SPIRE (11,360+)

(0.5 mi WSW of Mount St. John)
Map: Mount Moran

This is the most prominent high point on the ridge between Mount St. John and the Jaw; it lies immediately east of the window, or "needle's eye," on that ridge. From the highway just south of the Jenny Lake campground, this section of ridge is seen as the skyline between Storm Point and Symmetry Spire.

ROUTE 1. EAST RIDGE. I, 3.0. First ascent July 9, 1940, by Paul Petzoldt, Elizabeth Cowles (Partridge), and Anthony Whittemore. From Hanging Canyon proceed west past Lake of the Crags and climb the couloir leading toward the low point in the flat east ridge; follow this easy ridge west to the summit.

ROUTE 2. SOUTH BUTTRESS. IV, 5.10. First ascent August 5, 2004, by Alan and Keith Cattabriga. Despite its location in an accessible canyon, this apparently enjoyable climb comes with a feeling of remoteness. The first-ascent party reported excellent rock for the most part, although they did encounter a "crumble traverse" and some vegetation on the first pitch. The climb begins by ascending a large left-facing corner system on the southern prow of Minga Spire. **Pitch 1:** Enter the corner system with good protection. Move left after the initial short prow of the corner (the 5.10 "crumble traverse") and enter a vegetated section of the corner, passing a fixed pin. Move left beneath an overhang (5.10) and set up a hanging belay (55m). **Pitch 2:** Continue up the corner until face moves (5.10) provide access left to a crack that is followed to a good ledge and a belay (12m). **Pitch 3:** This long pitch continues up the corner (5.9) and finishes at a big ledge with krummholz on it. **Pitch 4:** Ascend just right of the arête edge, up a series of weird groove-type cracks and fins. This is reported to be more difficult than it looks (5.8+). **Pitch 5:** Stay right of the ridge crest, passing a few "precariously perched blocks," and belay on the huge step in the buttress. **Pitch 6:** Move the belay over to the base of the next section. Climb up past a few "cool flakes" through a small overlap, then traverse out left on overhanging rock (5.10) to easier cracks that lead up to a belay. **Pitch 7:** Continue up on lower-angle terrain past a few overlaps to another big step in the buttress. **Pitch 8:** Move the belay over to the base of a chimney. This final lead ascends this chimney—sometimes in the chimney itself and sometimes on the outside—to the summit (5.8, 60m). This climb took the first-ascent party a little over 12 hours to complete, up from and back to Jenny Lake. **Gear:** A full rack to 4" is suggested, with extra medium and large stoppers, small cams, and long slings.

ROUTE 3. WEST RIDGE. II, 5.6. First descent September 9, 1954, by Gary Hemming and Leigh Ortenburger. In the course of a traverse west to the Jaw, Hemming and Ortenburger descended the west ridge of Minga Spire to the window, but a rappel was required.

MOUNT ST. JOHN (11,430)

Map: Mount Moran

This peak, the highest point among the numerous towers and pinnacles that surround the alpine lakes of the beautiful Hanging Canyon (see *Figure 8-11*), was named after Orestes H. St. John, the geologist of the Teton Division of the Hayden Survey of 1877. The popular Mount St. John is one of the easier peaks in the park, and only one short day is required for its ascent. In early season, however, some snow slopes must be negotiated; an ice axe, plus the knowledge of how

to use it, is advised. Its long, serrated summit ridge contains several peaks, all very nearly the same altitude, which makes it difficult to select the proper couloir to ascend from Hanging Canyon. Efforts to reach the summit began in late September 1925 with a solo attempt by Phil Smith, in which he reached the most easterly of the subsummits. Other easterly subsummits were reached on August 20, 1926, by H. C. Forman; on July 9, 1928, by Fritiof Fryxell and Floyd Steele; and on July 14, 1929, by Phil Smith and Arthur Montgomery. On the first ascent repeated sightings with a Brunton Transit were required to verify that the highest point had finally been reached.

Chronology

SOUTH COULOIR, WEST RIDGE: August 20, 1929, Fritiof Fryxell, Phil Smith

EAST RIDGE: July 10, 1931, Robert Underhill (partial descent); June 16, 1934, Hans Fuhrer, Alfred Roovers (ascent, probably bypassed some subsummits)

SOUTH COULOIR, EAST RIDGE: Date and party unknown

NORTH RIDGE AND NORTH FACE: July 2, 1936, Wayne Thompson, Ralph Sinsheimer; July 2, 1939, Francis Hendricks, Adam Koj, Stanley Grites (descent)

NORTH FACE, EAST COULOIR: August 19, 1939, Arthur Guyer, C. Barber Moseley, or August 21, 1940, Bud Garnaas, Theodore Brandon, Robert Anderson, Tim Ramsland, Frank Blake

ROUTE 1. ▲ SOUTH COULOIR, WEST RIDGE. I, 3.0. First ascent August 20, 1929, by Fritiof Fryxell and Phil Smith. The entire south side of Mount St. John, rising above Hanging Canyon, is covered with couloirs leading up to the summit ridge. For this route, one is attempting to find the couloir that emerges just west of the summit. Hike up Hanging Canyon and continue past Lake of the Crags along its north shore. From the meadows at the west end of the lake, scramble due north, turning up either of the couloirs west of the prominent steep buttress in the lowest portion of the south face of St. John. In early season some steep snow must be expected in these couloirs; by midseason it is usually possible to avoid these snow patches. Depending on which couloir is chosen, one or more steps in the west ridge itself will have to be climbed. The major step rises about 75m, is steep and exposed on the north, and involves some 4.0 climbing. This west ridge is seldom intentionally climbed because the east ridge alternative (see *Route 2*) has become the regular route. The ridge would be encountered, however, along a traverse from the Jaw to St. John. For time and references, see *Route 2*.

ROUTE 2. ▲ SOUTH COULOIR, EAST RIDGE. I, 3.0. First ascent unknown. As already noted, the entire south side of Mount St. John is covered with couloirs leading up to the summit ridge. The principal difficulty with this route is the selection of the proper couloir. Proceed up Hanging Canyon to Lake of the Crags. From the north shore of the lake start up the talus where the lake is the narrowest and proceed up toward the ridge, occasionally moving left (west) into the adjacent couloir when it becomes convenient. In early season some steep snow must be expected in these couloirs; by midseason it is usually possible to avoid these snow patches. If the proper couloir is followed—and there are several possibilities on the upper third of the peak—the summit ridge will be reached at a broad col from which it is but a short scramble east to the summit. If the next couloir east has been inadvertently taken, the first subsummit east of the true summit must be traversed, and this will involve some 4.0 climbing and perhaps a rappel. A combination of the second couloir east and its associated ridge, climbed on July 14, 1971, by John Kevin Fox and Steven Doyle, provides a long, mixed rock-and-snow climb that ends at the second eastern subsummit, requiring an even longer traverse west to the true summit. **Time:** 5½ to 6¾ hours from Jenny Lake. See *Appalachia* 18, no. 4 (December 1931): pp. 388–408, illus.; *Chicago Mountaineering Club Newsletter* 2, no. 5 (January–July 1948): pp. 5–7; 2, no. 6 (July–December 1948): pp. 4–5; *Trail and Timberline*, no. 491 (November 1959): pp. 153–56.

ROUTE 3. EAST RIDGE. II, 5.1. First partial descent July 10, 1931, by Robert Underhill; first ascent June 16, 1934, by Hans Fuhrer and Alfred Roovers, although this climb apparently bypassed some of the subsummits. There are two approaches to the base of this ridge. One is to take the trail into the beginning of Hanging Canyon and cut north onto the broad east face or ridge as soon as it is convenient to do so. Another less heavily traveled approach is to cross the bridge at the south end of String Lake and take the trail north around its west shore until the first open slope is reached only a short distance from the south end of the lake. A small trail heading upward through the low bushes of this slope will be found; it leads to the picturesque Laurel Lake (7,400+). From the lake take the long open couloir near the right (north) edge of the east face; this couloir ultimately blends in with the upper ridge, well short of the first subsummit. This couloir is discernible on the Grand Teton quadrangle. There are five distinct subsummits on this ridge and one deep notch between the first and second. If one follows the ridge closely, this is an enjoyable climb; one or more rappels may be desired, depending on one's downclimbing limits. It is easy enough to bypass the notch and most of the subsummits by climbing along the south side of the ridge. **Time:** 6¾ to 8¾ hours from Jenny Lake. See *Appalachia* 18, no. 4 (December 1931): pp. 388–408, illus.

ROUTE 4. NORTH RIDGE AND NORTH FACE. II, 5.1. First ascent July 2, 1936, by Wayne Thompson and Ralph Sinsheimer; first descent July 2, 1939, by Francis Hendricks, Adam Koj, and Stanley Grites. The structure of this face can be characterized as a sequence of diagonal benches or broad ledges, leading up from lower left to upper right, separated by very steep, commonly vertical walls. The climbs of Mount St. John from the north by necessity take somewhat zigzagging lines, moving upward from bench to bench whenever a break in the next wall permits. These benches harbor quantities of loose rock but in early season will be covered with snow. It also appears that every ascent of the north side of St. John has utilized at least part of the north ridge that connects with Rockchuck Peak. The difficulty encountered is very sensitive to the routefinding. In recent years this route from the col separating Rockchuck from St. John has been used primarily in connection with the traverse from Rockchuck. The first route described below approximates that of the first-ascent party; the third option describes the traverse to the summit of St. John from the col. Descents of this face have been made (rarely) by rappel directly into Paintbrush Canyon. Keep in mind that the summit of St. John is just a short distance west of the ridge joining it with Rockchuck. The Jaw is misleading when seen from the north, as it appears higher than St. John. (See *Figure 8-22* for a view of these peaks from Paintbrush Canyon.)

Hike to Laurel Lake from String Lake (see *Route 3*) and continue up the cirque between Rockchuck and St. John. Climb up and west out of the southwest corner of this cirque, usually on snow, onto a broad bench leading to the north ridge. Scramble up loose rock to the crest of the north ridge, then continue out to the west to a sequence of diagonal shelves (snow-covered in early season, scree-covered in late season) that lead up toward the summit ridge of St. John. There is considerable exposure off the right (north) edge down into Paintbrush Canyon. If the proper sequence is selected, one will emerge onto the summit ridge about 60m east of the summit.

A second alternative is to follow the route described above onto the north ridge, and then climb back up and left (east) over loose rock to the most westerly of the three slanting (from lower left to upper right) ledges that lead to the summit ridge of St. John. Climb this wide ledge to the ridge, where the one tower lying between the climber and the summit can be either climbed over or bypassed on the left (south). This alternative can be very difficult if the easiest line is not found.

The third alternative is to start the climb from the main U-shaped col separating St. John from Rockchuck. This col will ordinarily be approached from the east via the same cirque described in the first alternative. Climb out of the col on the left (east) side on grassy ledges and then cut up onto the ridge crest over wet rock slabs. To reach the notch on the other side of a large, knoblike tower, clearly seen from the valley, either bypass the tower on the left (east) or climb it. The buttress on the far (south) side of this notch can be climbed directly (difficult) or passed on the left (wet, narrow, mossy ledges) or the right (recommended). After about 100m along the base of the west side of this buttress, enter a narrow couloir angling up to the left. In early season or midseason this couloir will be filled with snow. The large chockstone at the upper end of this couloir is passed by climbing a steep 12m pitch on the right (south) wall. One can now scramble up to the left (east) to a slanting ledge and follow it to the summit ridge. (**Note:** This third alternative also can be reached from the west via the Paintbrush Canyon trail, which begins at the south end of String Lake. From about the 8,600-foot level, cross the stream and ascend the talus in the cirque below the north face of St. John and the west face of Rockchuck. Either proceed to the initial col or join this option at the narrow diagonal couloir beyond the buttress; the latter would be the more obvious choice.)

ROUTE 5. NORTH FACE, EAST COULOIR. II, 5.4. First ascent August 19, 1939, by Arthur Guyer and C. Barber Moseley, or August 21, 1940, by Bud Garnaas, Theodore Brandon, Robert Anderson, Tim Ramsland, and Frank Blake. The upper east ridge of Mount St. John apparently can be reached from the north, via the cirque between St. John and Rockchuck Peak, without using the north ridge. Proceed as in *Route 4* up the cirque until past the first buttresses. Well before reaching the north ridge connecting St. John and Rockchuck, a large talus cone will be seen leading south toward the main notch in the east ridge. Climb this cone to its upper end where a cliff band will be encountered, guarding access to the notch and the three parallel shelves that slant up and right (west) to the summit ridge. The route ascended was one of these shelves, probably the most westerly one, although the notch itself might have been reached.

HANGING CANYON, NORTH SIDE ROCK CLIMBS (ca. 10,240+)

Map: Mount Moran

These rock climbs on the north side of lower Hanging Canyon are listed from west to east. While there is some good rock on these routes, the largely mediocre quality is perhaps compensated for by the relatively short Teton approach.

FIGURE 8-22. Paintbrush Canyon, north aspect overview

ROUTE 1. TREELINE. II, 5.7, A1. First ascent September 8, 1968, by George Goedecke, Bill Hackett, Bill Cooper, and Rick Thomas. This route is on one of the easterly south arêtes of Mount St. John, but apparently west of the Bird Arêtes (see *Routes 3–5*). Start from about the elevation of Arrowhead Pool and climb a 4.0 couloir to the left of the arête. Move right to start the climb at about the elevation of Cube Point. The first pitch (5.6), just left of an overhang, goes up to a belay below a second overhang that extends across the face of the arête. Move right and climb past this difficult overhang (5.7, A1), then move right again to a belay from a tree. The next lead goes up and slightly right to another tree belay. The fourth pitch passes a second overhang (5.7) to a third tree on the right edge of the arête, from which two easy leads take one to the top of the arête. Descent is back to the east down to the lower Hanging Canyon.

ROUTE 2. ST. John's Wart. II, 5.6. Probable first ascent July 17, 1980, by William Soller and Jonathan Hollin, or June 3, 1981, by Chuck Harris. This small, freestanding pinnacle at the base of a south ridge of Mount St. John is located about 0.3 mile north-northeast of the outlet of Ramshead Lake. Several routes are available on the pinnacle, ranging from 5.4 to 5.7.

ROUTE 3. AVOCET ARÊTE. II, 5.7. First ascent 1980, by unknown climbers; partial ascent in 1977, by Al Read and Rod Newcomb. Containing six pitches, Avocet Arête is the left-hand (western) of the Bird Arêtes, the three small ridges located on the southeast side of Mount St. John. See *Route 5* for the approach. The first pitch begins with a right-facing corner (5.7), which is ascended for 23m to a belay ledge. A ropelength of 4th-class climbing leads back to the left to a belay on the crest. The third pitch ascends the crest for 30m and consists of blocky corners. The fourth pitch consists of a 12m hand crack (5.7). Then wander up through ledges and trees and belay at the base of the final pitch, 15m of 5.6 climbing. Scrambling then leads to the top of the climb, which is situated at the base of a nice-looking wall.

ROUTE 4. OSTRICH ARÊTE. II, 5.8. First ascent June 5, 1981, by Chuck Harris and Steve Rickert. This is the central, white arête of the three Bird Arêtes. See *Route 5* for the approach. The first pitch goes up steep cracks on the arête to a belay, which is moved up and left for the beginning of the second lead. Now climb a steep, overhanging corner, containing loose blocks, to the left of a chimney. The third lead moves up around to the left of a flake on a pedestal and then up a lieback crack to a belay. The final pitch ascends a knobby face up and then left to finish the route. The climb is consistently in the 5.6 to 5.8 range, but a quantity of loose rock will be encountered. To descend, rappel 15m to the notch to the north, then scramble down a gully and traverse east to the notch situated above the top of Peregrine Arête. Continue down to Laurel and String Lakes from there.

ROUTE 5. PEREGRINE ARÊTE. II, 5.7. First ascent July 1, 1981, by Chuck Harris and Leo Larson, and on July 26, 1981, by Jack Tackle, Jim Donini, and Yvon Chouinard, by a slightly different variation. This is the right-hand (eastern), as well as the most popular, of the three Bird Arêtes on the southeast side of Mount St. John. *Figure 8-23* offers an oblique view of the route that is most commonly done. Approach

FIGURE 8-23. Mount St. John, southeast aspect, Peregrine Arête *(Route 5)*, II, 5.7

via Hanging Canyon to Arrowhead Pool. From Arrowhead Pool walk up scree slopes to the north onto the grassy talus bench from which this arête and the other two Bird Arêtes can be seen rising above. **Pitch 1:** To start this route one has the choice of a 5.10 roof near the crest; a 5.4 slab leading to a 5.7 face on the right (east) side of the arête; or a 4th-class ramp farther right. **Pitch 2:** Start with a 5.7 crack/lieback up a right-facing corner to the crest, then follow the crest, eventually trending right up a face and corner to the belay at a gully/ramp. **Pitch 3:** Traverse right to the out-of-view chimney east of the crest and climb to a broad ledge with trees. **Pitch 4:** This final pitch ascends the 5.4 face and ridge leading to the summit pinnacle. There are more difficult variations possible on each of the pitches. To descend, either downclimb (5.1) or make a short (20m) rappel into the notch to the east of the summit pinnacle, then walk down to the northeast where there are a few gullies. If the correct one is chosen, one can reach the base of the climb without a rappel and then return to the trail on the slopes to the south. A gully to the southwest of the summit pinnacle provides another descent option, but it involves 5th-class downclimbing and at least one rappel.

ROUTE 6. HAWKEYE. II, 5.9. First ascent September 5, 1980, by Leo Larson, Chuck Harris, and Mike Beiser. This three-pitch climb is on the south-facing buttress just below (east of) Peregrine Arête. The first 46m pitch (loose) starts to the right of a large snag with face climbing that leads to a left-facing corner. Continue past an overhang to a belay at a flake. The next pitch begins in a right-facing corner that leads to a roof, which is passed on the right to reach a second roof; climb over this roof and left onto the ridge crest for the belay. Protection on this second lead is minimal. The final 42m lead proceeds almost on the crest to the top of the buttress. **Gear:** Large devices are useful.

ROCKCHUCK PEAK (11,144)

Map: Mount Moran

This inconspicuous peak has, reasonably enough, attracted little attention from mountaineers seeking technical routes. However, for climbers with more modest ambitions, the eastern routes offer a pleasant and relatively short climb, readily accessible from String Lake. The traverse from Rockchuck Peak to Mount St. John, or vice versa, provides a longer and more challenging day. Rockchuck is separated from St. John to the south by a cirque leading to a distinctive U-shaped col (10,560+). Surprisingly, this cirque and col were the location of one of the earliest penetrations, probably the third by Euro-American explorers (counting that of Englishman William A. Baillie-Grohman), into the Teton Range from the east. The col was apparently first reached on August 14, 1888, by Owen Wister, famous author of *The Virginian*, and George West, who visited Laurel Lake en route. However, the knoblike pinnacle south of this col, on the ridge connecting Rockchuck with St. John, was not climbed until August 17, 1959, by William Cropper and Sam Tanner.

A distraction for today's climbers—and a hindrance for Fritiof Fryxell on his first ascent in 1929—is the plentitude of huckleberries available on the eastern slopes.

"The lower slopes of the mountain are thickly overgrown with huckleberry bushes, the finest in the Tetons," Fryxell later wrote in Mountaineering in the Tetons, *"and higher up are numerous raspberry patches clustered among the boulder fields, nor must one fail to mention the occasional clumps of serviceberry. An ascent of Rockchuck Peak in berry time (which usually spans the month of August) calls for great tenacity of purpose and self-mastery on the part of the mountaineer, lest he lose sight of his lofty goal and give himself up to the lusts of the flesh. The writer knows, since he once climbed this mountain (August 16, 1929), both hands and mouth busy all the way to timberline. Let it be known that he did reach the top, though the time consumed in making the ascent must never be disclosed. That this was the first complete ascent on record may perhaps be attributed to the failure of other climbers to get beyond the berry patches."*

Another feature of interest is the recent fault scarp that is passed early in the ascent from the east; it is readily seen at an elevation of about 7,200 feet as a brief steepening of the otherwise uniform slope. The scarp makes a step of about 20m, indicating movement along the main Teton fault within the last 15,000 years, since the underlying slope is of recent glacial origin. The eastern routes (see *Routes 3, 4,* and *5*) are all immediately available from the String Lake trailhead, whereas the approach for the western routes (see *Routes 1* and *6*) is via Paintbrush Canyon.

Rangers on an early morning search and rescue operation in Hanging Canyon above the Lake of the Crags (Photo by Vic Zeilman)

Chronology

EAST SLOPES: August 16, 1929, Fritiof Fryxell
NORTHWEST SIDE: August 1, 1932, Fred Ayres (descent); August 6, 1952, Theodore Brandon, Clement Ramsland, Frederick Tillotson (ascent)
NORTHEAST RIDGE: June 27, 1933, Fritiof Fryxell, Frank Swenson
WEST FACE: August 20, 1935, Phil Smith, Floyd Wilson
var—July 7, 1960, Tim and Sally Bond
EAST RIDGE: August 16, 1940, Judy Peterson, Beatrice Burford, Rick Hemmenway
var—**SOUTHEAST COULOIR:** August 28, 1941, Theodore Brandon, Robert Anderson, John Dewey
var—**SOUTHEAST FACE:** July 1987, George Montopoli, Leo Larson (descent)
SOUTH RIDGE: August 11, 1946, Michael and John Ladd, Helen and Anne Pratt, Mary Bartlett (descent)

ROUTE 1. WEST FACE. II, 5.4, A1. First ascent August 20, 1935, by Phil Smith and Floyd Wilson. The first two-thirds of this route was climbed on August 13, 1935, by the same party; they returned to complete it a week later. From about 8,600 feet on the Paintbrush Canyon trail, turn up past a small lake into the canyon on the west side of Rockchuck Peak. The climb begins by ascending the smooth, downsloping rock of a wide couloir; at the top, 180m of talus leads to a dish-shaped 250m section of steep rock. This second wide couloir gradually narrows into the final 9m chimney. On the first ascent an aid piton was required to surmount the chimney. From this point it is possible to traverse up and right (south) to the southwest corner. The last portion ascends a broken ridge to the summit.

Variation: II, 5.1. First ascent July 7, 1960, by Tim and Sally Bond. From String Lake ascend the cirque above Laurel Lake to the col separating Mount St. John and Rockchuck Peak. Descend on the far (west) side of the col, traversing around to the second couloir north of the col. This couloir leads up on good rock to the southwest ridge, which is followed to the summit via *Route 1*.

ROUTE 2. SOUTH RIDGE. II, 4.0. First descent August 11, 1946, by Michael and John Ladd, Helen and Anne Pratt, and Mary Bartlett. This ridge is ordinarily used only when traversing from Rockchuck Peak to Mount St. John; the traverse in the other direction has apparently not been done. From the summit of Rockchuck, the objective is to reach the U-shaped col separating it from St. John. This can probably be done in various ways, some of which will stay more nearly on the crest of the south ridge than the route described here. From the summit of Rockchuck descend the west side until a break in the ridgeline to the left (south) is seen. This break is the top of a steep, rotten couloir about 46m below the summit; descend this couloir for about 75m, cutting out left on rotten ledges to a small notch. Some scrambling on the far side of the notch will bring the climber onto the south ridge proper. The U-shaped col is now reached by passing the first large step in the ridge on the left (east) and the second on the right (west). This col can also be reached directly from String Lake by ascending the cirque separating St. John from Rockchuck. Others, to make the Rockchuck–St. John traverse, have descended from the summit down the west side for 120m and then traversed on easy ledges to the U-shaped col. For ascent either of these descent schemes would be reversed.

A climber approaches the summit of the Jaw in Hanging Canyon on a stellar summer's day.

ROUTE 3. EAST RIDGE. II, 5.1. First ascent August 16, 1940, by Beatrice Burford, Judy Peterson, and Rick Hemmenway. This major ridge forms both the northern boundary of the prominent cirque that separates Mount St. John from Rockchuck Peak and the southern boundary of the main east couloir used in *Route 4*. It provides an enjoyable day of rock scrambling, especially if one stays directly on the crest of the often sharp ridge. The ridge is not continuous and it does contain some loose rock, although it is mostly sound. Beware of the lichenous rock when it is wet. Some pinnacles will be found near the upper end of the ridge, which does not lead directly to the summit but intersects the main northeast ridge about 100m north of the summit. The pinnacles provide the most interesting climbing on the ridge and one may wish to rappel for descent from their summits.

***Variation:* SOUTHEAST COULOIR.** I, 5.1. First ascent August 28, 1941, by Theodore Brandon, Robert Anderson, and John Dewey. From String Lake hike into the cirque between Mount St. John and Rockchuck Peak. After passing the large, broad tower on the east ridge of Rockchuck, turn up the southeast wall of the peak to reach the east ridge just left (west) of the westernmost pinnacle of the ridge. Follow the upper east ridge to the main northeast ridge to the summit. This variation can also be used for the traverse from Rockchuck to St. John.

***Variation:* SOUTHEAST FACE.** II, 5.1. First descent in July 1987, by George Montopoli and Leo Larson. (**Note:** This pair is perhaps the world's authority on this traverse, having done it many, many times over the years.) The southeast face, which lies between the couloir described in the 1941 Southeast Couloir variation and the South Ridge route *(Route 2)*, can be used for the traverse from Rockchuck Peak to Mount St. John. From the summit of Rockchuck descend this face, containing easy 5th-class rock, to a point below a shoulder on the Rockchuck side of the U-shaped col. Climb back up to this shoulder and then descend a gully on the west side until one can traverse south over to the col.

ROUTE 4. ▲ EAST SLOPES. I, 3.0. First ascent August 16, 1929, by Fritiof Fryxell. From the String Lake trailhead, cross the bridge and continue along the trail on the west side of String Lake until the trail crosses the open slope that leads up into the broad east couloir of Rockchuck Peak. Climb the couloir until it steepens, then angle slightly left onto the upper east ridge and follow it to its intersection with the main northeast ridge. Climb south along this bouldery ridge to the summit. Like Teewinot Mountain, in early season this climb is mostly on snow, but later it is mostly talus and scree. **Time:** 4½ to 6 hours from Jenny Lake. See *Appalachia* 18, no. 4 (December 1931): pp. 388–408, illus.; *Chicago Mountaineering Club Newsletter* 15, no. 5 (December 1961): pp. 6–8.

ROUTE 5. NORTHEAST RIDGE. I, 5.1. First ascent June 27, 1933, by Fritiof Fryxell and Frank Swenson; one of the high points on this ridge had been reached on July 28, 1931, by Ray King and Edna Olson. This prominent ridge is reached from the trail that leads around the west side of String Lake. The lower portion of this major ridge is easy, but higher up it flattens into a section containing many towers. Some difficulty will be experienced in passing these towers, some of which are turned on the left (east). **Time:** 8¼ hours from Jenny Lake.

ROUTE 6. NORTHWEST SIDE. I, 3.0. First descent August 1, 1932, by Fred Ayres; first ascent August 6, 1952, by Theodore Brandon, Clement Ramsland, and Frederick Tillotson. Follow the trail up Paintbrush Canyon to about 8,600 feet, then turn south past a small lake into the canyon on the west side of Rockchuck Peak. Climb over talus and boulders up the northwest side of the peak, working right (south) near the top to avoid some cliffs. It is probable that one could also turn sooner up the northwest slopes of Rockchuck from the Paintbrush Canyon trail and climb the peak by a parallel route to the left (north) of the route described here. Either route is recommended for those who desire a traverse of the mountain; using the trail in Paintbrush Canyon, the descent of this route does not take much more time than a descent of the East Slopes *(Route 4)*.

ICE MAN PINNACLE (8,180)

(1.0 mi NE of Rockchuck Peak)
Map: Mount Moran

This obscure pinnacle was discovered and climbed in 2019 by longtime Jenny Lake Ranger Rich Baerwald and his wife, Maura. It is located on the lower northern slopes of Rockchuck Peak above the Paintbrush Canyon trail. From the String Lake trailhead, follow the trail into the canyon and, about 3 miles from the trailhead, where the trail levels off immediately before the Lower Paintbrush Canyon camping zone, leave the trail and head upward to the south. Pass by a seasonal pond in the boulder field and proceed upward through a band of trees and then through larger boulders for about a half hour. The pinnacle will come into view as one nears the lowest cliff band. This approach should take about one and a half hours from the trailhead.

ROUTE 1. SOUTH AND EAST FACES. I, 5.9. First ascent in August 2019, by Rich Baerwald and Maura Longden. (See *Figure 8-24.*) From the base of the pinnacle on the west side, climb a short step (5.6) into a notch and belay. Step out right and climb up the east side of the pinnacle, near the eastern arête, for about 24m of mixed crack and face climbing (5.9). Another 6m of easier climbing leads to the top. **Gear:** A range of gear is recommended including one set of stoppers; one set of micro cams; and larger cams from 0.5" to 2".

THE OUTLIER (10,560+)

(0.8 mi W of Mount St. John)
Map: Mount Moran

Rising above Paintbrush Canyon on the south is a salient ridge (running from the northeast to the southwest) that isolates the considerable cirque lying below the northwest face of Mount St. John. This ridge, named the Outlier because of its remote position, has the topographical prominence to justify its separate treatment even though it does not qualify as a peak. The seldom-entered cirque contains a rock glacier that is quite extensive, at the head of which is the north face of the Jaw. The approach for all the routes is via Paintbrush Canyon, along the trail to the vicinity of the forks (from 8,100 to 8,800 feet).

Chronology

NORTHWEST FACE: August 15, 1956, Roald and Redwood Fryxell, Julia Peterson
EAST SIDE: August 15, 1956, Roald and Redwood Fryxell, Julia Peterson (descent); July 27, 1958, Paul Salstrom, Robert Marshall (ascent)
SOUTHWEST RIDGE: July 16, 1966, Michael Petrilak, J. Curtiss Sinclear, Sherman Heller

ROUTE 1. SOUTHWEST RIDGE. I, 3.0. First ascent July 16, 1966, by Michael Petrilak, J. Curtiss Sinclear, and Sherman Heller. From Paintbrush Canyon ascend into the cirque between Mount St. John and the Outlier. Continue to the col (10,400+) at the upper west margin of the cirque. From the col climb this easy ridge, which contains loose rock, to the summit.

ROUTE 2. EAST SIDE. I, 2.0. First descent August 15, 1956, by Roald and Redwood Fryxell and Julia Peterson; first ascent July 27, 1958, by Paul Salstrom and Robert Marshall. From Paintbrush Canyon ascend into the cirque between Mount St. John and the Outlier. Scramble up the east side onto the ridge north of the summit. The summit is reached with no significant difficulties.

ROUTE 3. NORTHWEST FACE. I, 3.0. First ascent August 15, 1956, by Roald and Redwood Fryxell and Julia Peterson. From Paintbrush Canyon ascend an easy diagonal ramp on the northwest face to the col (10,080+) between the lower northwest summit and the main summit. From the col the ridge is followed easily to the main summit as well as to the northwest summit if desired.

PEAK 10,919

(0.8 mi NE of Mount Woodring)
Map: Mount Moran

At the end of the east ridge of Mount Woodring lies this seldom-visited high point. From its summit a fine view of the entire southern battlements of Mount Moran is available.

ROUTE 1. SOUTHEAST COULOIR. I, 2.0. First ascent June 25, 1939, by Francis Hendricks and Stanley Grites. Immediately after crossing the bridge over the main stream in Paintbrush Canyon head north up the drainage that leads to this peak.

FIGURE 8-24. Ice Man Pinnacle, South and East Faces *(Route 1)*, I, 5.9

MOUNT WOODRING (11,590)

Map: Mount Moran

After making the first ascent of this rounded peak, Fritiof Fryxell and Phil Smith named it in honor of their boss, Samuel T. Woodring, the first superintendent of Grand Teton National Park. Woodring's story is a controversial one;[1] Paul Horton recounts it in his book *Names on the Range*. (unpublished as this book goes to press)

Mount Woodring is one possible objective for those who would like to reach a major Teton summit as easily as possible. While the regular route from the south, which consists of loose talus and scree, is perhaps not appealing to the discriminating mountaineer, the standard approach to Mount Woodring provides a pleasant day's hike up through the attractive Paintbrush Canyon. The view of Mount Moran and Thor Peak from the summit is especially good. This technically easy peak, like a few other summits in the range, was found to have a cairn on top when the "first-ascent" party arrived in 1929. This cairn was very likely built by members of the crew that constructed the trail in Paintbrush Canyon in the mid-1920s for the US Forest Service (USFS). For the topographically inquisitive, most of the north side of this peak remains to be explored, partly because of the loose rock that it appears to hold. For the approach to the north side of this mountain, see *Leigh Canyon* in Section 9. On August 12, 1937, Edmund Lowe and Rainer Schickele descended from Mount Woodring via Grizzly Bear Lake into the "utterly wild and unspoiled" Leigh Canyon, where they found remnants of the old horse trail that had been built in the 1920s.

Chronology

SOUTHEAST SLOPE: July 24, 1929, Fritiof Fryxell, Everett Norling, Kenneth Landon, Roland McCannon, Roy Swanberg
SOUTHWEST SLOPE: June 15, 1930, Fritiof Fryxell, Phil Smith
EAST RIDGE: July 31, 1932, Phil Smith, William Rea (ascent); August 15, 1953, John Dorsey, Leigh Ortenburger (descent)
NORTH RIDGE: August 16, 1957, William Buckingham, Barry Corbet
WEST RIDGE: September 24, 1960, Gordon Fish, Gordon Esden, or September 5, 1973, Ron and Gretchen Perla
NORTH FACE: August 5, 1963, John Reed, David Steller
NORTH COULOIR: June 1, 1985, Andy Carson, R. Harris, S. Beitzel
SOUTH RIB: September 14, 1989, Andy Carson, Paul Horton

ROUTE 1. WEST RIDGE. II, 3.0. First ascent September 24, 1960, by Gordon Fish and Gordon Esden, or September 5, 1973, by Ron and Gretchen Perla. During the descent from the Paintbrush–Leigh divide toward the beautiful Grizzly Bear Lake, an initial plateau at about 9,700 feet must be crossed. The west ridges and couloirs rise above this plateau and are bounded on the right by the southwest ridge that forms the divide. One of these indistinct ridges was apparently climbed but is not recommended because of rotten rock.

ROUTE 2. ▲ SOUTHWEST SLOPE. I, 2.0. First ascent June 15, 1930, by Fritiof Fryxell and Phil Smith. This is the easiest route on the peak. Follow the Paintbrush Canyon trail to Holly Lake. Walk around the left (west) side of the lake and start up the talus and scree slope leading to the summit. Angle slightly right (east) to avoid the southwest ridge; this ridge can be followed but it is slightly harder. In early season some snow of moderate angle will be encountered and an ice axe will be needed. **Time:** 6 to 7¼ hours from String Lake; 2½ to 3¼ hours from Holly Lake. See *Appalachia* 18, no. 4 (December 1931): pp. 388–408, illus.

ROUTE 3. SOUTHEAST SLOPE. I, 2.0. First known ascent July 24, 1929, by Fritiof Fryxell, Everett Norling, Kenneth Landon, Roland McCannon, and Roy Swanberg, who found an empty cairn on the summit. From the trail in Paintbrush Canyon, one can start climbing the southeast side of the peak at almost any place. One method is to follow the left (west) side of the main drainage on the southeast side that ends in a small permanent snowfield, as shown on the USGS quadrangle map. Mount Woodring has three subsidiary east peaks, so head toward the highest peak, which is the one farthest west. See *Appalachia* 18, no. 4 (December 1931): pp. 388–408, illus.

ROUTE 4. SOUTH RIB. II, 5.8. First ascent September 14, 1989, by Andy Carson and Paul Horton. This well-defined, stepped rib of surprisingly good rock extends from just above the highest trees northeast of Holly Lake to about 90m below and southeast of the summit. From Holly Lake hike up scree, past a small buttress and across a gully, to the obvious ridge and the start of

1. Mike Koshmrl, "Disgraced park boss gave name to Mount Woodring," *Jackson Hole News&Guide*, September 20, 2017. Robert Righter, an esteemed Teton historian and author of *Crucible for Conservation: The Creation of Grand Teton National Park*, was interviewed for the piece. "[Woodring] was involved in sexual harassment, and we really ought to rename it," he said of the peak. While doing research for his 1982 book, Righter uncovered letters in the National Archives alleging that Woodring had touched a babysitter inappropriately while giving her a ride from Moose to Jackson—accusations that apparently prompted his firing but were kept under wraps.

this route, which is about 30m above the very beginning of the rib. This eight-pitch climb stays on or near the crest of the rib, following the line of least resistance. The first lead starts near the crest and moves right on a ledge to and up a chimney (5.6) to the belay. Now move left around the crest and climb cracks (5.6) and ledges, ending on the right side at a ledge with a large block. Walk 15m to begin the third pitch just left of the crest on poor rock (5.8); then continue out right and up good cracks (5.6) to an overhang that is passed on the right to reach the belay on the crest. Walk along the level crest here for 30m and climb the next step (12m). Again walk 30m to the start of the next step and climb up and onto a ramp on the left side of the ridge, exiting on cracks (5.4) to a belay ledge. The sixth lead climbs up to a crack/chimney, which must be climbed (5.7) to get through a prominent overhang; then continue up to complete the lead at the top of this step in the rib. Now scramble for about 60m to the start of the next step, where a 12m open chimney with truly bad rock (5.6) leads to the top of this step. The final lead is easier climbing on the right side of the crest. Scramble about 90m to the summit. **Gear:** A standard rack suffices for protection on this route.

ROUTE 5. EAST RIDGE. I, 5.1. First ascent July 31, 1932, by Phil Smith and William Rea; first descent August 15, 1953, by John Dorsey and Leigh Ortenburger. This ridge, which contains one distinct peak—Peak 10,919—and two major, separate subsummits, offers an interesting day of ridge scrambling. Where the Paintbrush Canyon trail crosses to the north side of the main stream, climb from the southeast directly up to Peak 10,919, the most easterly of the three high points on this ridge. From here the crest of the ridge can be followed all the way to the summit, although the first-ascent party apparently bypassed a direct descent of the second point (11,120+), instead reaching the col between the third point (11,200+) and the main summit by contouring around the south side. The short, steep section on the ridge crest above this final col was also avoided by the 1932 party by working out on the north slope of the mountain to the northwest corner and probably to the upper portion of the north ridge (see *Route 8*). A short, broad couloir led from this corner to the summit. On the east ridge itself the schistose rock of this last steep section is very rotten, although it is probably climbable; on descent a rappel is desirable.

ROUTE 6. NORTH COULOIR. II, 4.0. First ascent June 1, 1985, by Andy Carson, R. Harris, and S. Beitzel. This route leads from the far (west) end of the second lake (7,785) in Leigh Canyon to the col (10,480+) in the east ridge of Mount Woodring separating the peak from Peak 10,919. This couloir was climbed as a snow route, and as such it is a fine route. Later in the season there may be difficulties with what will probably prove to be loose rock in the couloir. The first-ascent party did not continue on the east ridge to the summit of the peak.

ROUTE 7. NORTH FACE. II, 3.0. First ascent August 5, 1963, by John Reed and David Steller. From the lower lake in Leigh Canyon, climb diagonally up to the first col east of the summit on the east ridge. Significant routefinding skill is needed in order to minimize the difficulties on the face. Depending on the time of year and the exact route selected, some snow climbing may be involved. The final ridge to the summit will involve the steep, rotten section referred to in *Route 5*.

ROUTE 8. NORTH RIDGE. II, 5.6. First ascent August 16, 1957, by William Buckingham and Barry Corbet. From a half mile above the lakes in Leigh Canyon, Mount Woodring is seen to have two prominent faces, the concave north face and the northwest face. Both appear to contain much rotten rock. This route ascends the ridge that separates these two faces; it leads directly to the summit. The ridge, composed of good rock, rises in four steps from the canyon floor. The climbing is straightforward to the base of the third step, where there is a small but spectacular pinnacle (Corbuck Pinnacle). Scramble to the base of the chimney that separates the pinnacle from the ridge on the west side. Climb two pitches up this chimney to the notch. To climb the pinnacle, one enjoyable corkscrew pitch starts at the south side of the notch, circles around the east to the north, and finishes on the northwest corner. From the notch, more enjoyable climbing leads to the summit wall, which is climbed directly over steep slabs to the summit ridge. See *American Alpine Journal* 11, no. 1 (1958): pp. 85–88; *Dartmouth Mountaineering Club Journal,* 1958: p. 21.

MOUNT KIMBURGER (10,080+)

(1.1 mi W of Mount Woodring)

Map: Mount Moran

Rising immediately above and west of Grizzly Bear Lake is an impressive and massive cliff band capped by a flat summit ridge with occasional pinnacles. Thought to be the last unclimbed peak in the Teton Range, this summit remained unvisited until 1986. It is surprisingly well protected on all sides from casual ascent; it appears to have no easy route to the summit. The north ridge rises in tiers for over 460m from Leigh Canyon, its east face is a substantial wall, and the southwest ridge is very sharp. Only its west face is accessible and broken. The peak is readily approached via the Paintbrush Canyon trail to the divide leading over to Grizzly Bear Lake and the Leigh Canyon drainage. The rounded point (10,240+) to the southwest was climbed on July 7, 1984, by William Dennis via its west slope.

ROUTE 1. WEST FACE AND NORTH RIDGE. II, 5.7. First ascent July 29, 1986, by Tom Kimbrough and Leigh Ortenburger. From the divide above Grizzly Bear Lake make a slight descent and climb loose scree to the saddle (9,920+) southwest of this point. Scramble directly up the ridge above the saddle for 30m on loose rock to a ledge system leading left (north) out onto the main west face of the peak. Belay from the end of this ledge for the lead, which zigs out and then zags back to gain an awkward, left-slanting squeeze chimney (5.7). From the top of this chimney continue up and left for two more pitches over easier but steep ground to gain the center of the summit ridge. Scramble along the narrow ridge past a *2001*-esque monolith toward the north end of the ridge, where a short wall on the east side leads to the extreme northeast corner of the summit block. Climb this block (5.7) by small cracks and ledges on the face.

ROUTE 2. NORTHWEST LEDGES. I, 5.7. First ascent July 19, 1994, by Paul Horton and Jon Stuart. From the vicinity of Grizzly Bear Lake scramble onto the north ridge and continue to the base of the summit walls. Traverse via the highest ledge onto the west face. Zigzag up wooded ramps to the summit block. The only technical pitch of the route ascends this block from the north and west.

SECTION 9

Leigh Canyon to Moran Canyon

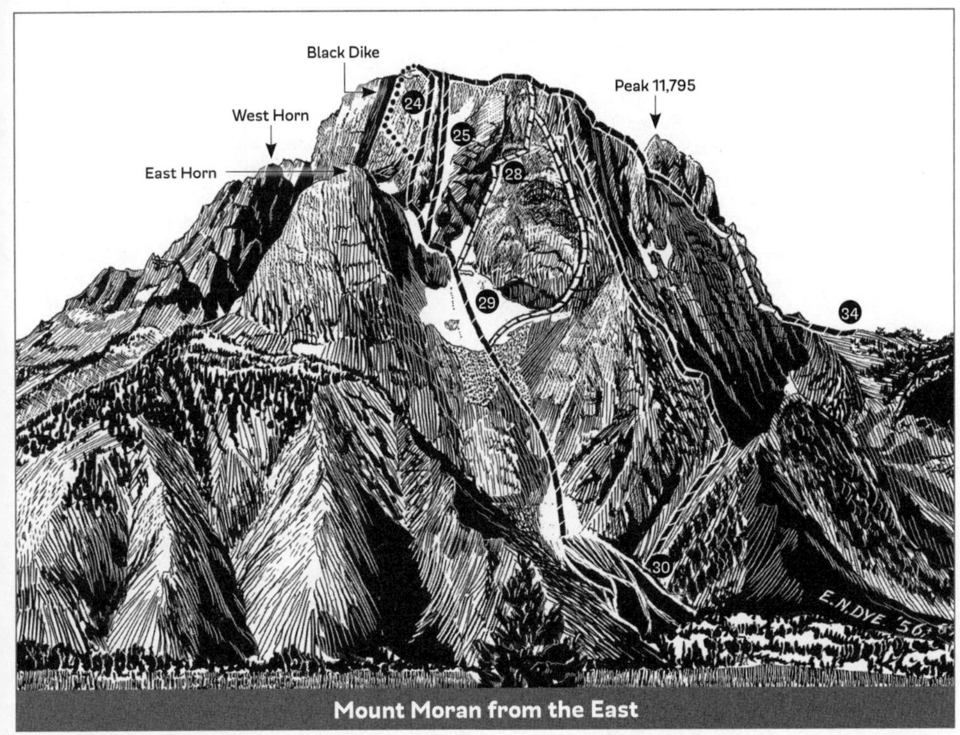

Mount Moran from the East

Leigh Canyon

Leigh Canyon is one of the longer Teton canyons, cutting almost straight through the range from Leigh Lake to the divide. Many important climbs, most notably the major routes on the south side of Mount Moran, start from Leigh Canyon. Because it is currently without a trail, this canyon is not a common backpackers' destination. A very early horse trail once extended into the canyon, but almost all traces of it have been lost over many subsequent decades. The National Park Service (NPS) has also abandoned the good foot and horse trails that used to contour both the southwest and northwest shores of Leigh Lake, leading to the mouth of the canyon. Lack of maintenance has rendered these valuable trails nearly useless for man or beast. The old trail around the southwest shore of the lake is nonexistent, totally blocked by large quantities of deadfall as well as the bogs.

As a result, canoeing across Leigh Lake is currently the *strongly* recommended method for those seeking entry into Leigh Canyon. Begin by putting the canoe (they can be rented in Jackson or in Moose) into String Lake at the String Lake boat launch and paddling to the north end of the lake (about 1 mile). Make the short portage to Leigh Lake, then paddle the 2.5 miles to the mouth of the canyon to the two designated campsites (14A and 14B) located on the lakeshore on either side of the outlet of Leigh Creek. Depending on one's objectives, these campsites can be used as a base of operations in Leigh Canyon.

Without canoe but with noticeably more exertion, hike from the Leigh Lake trailhead along the trail on the east sides of String and Leigh Lakes to the patrol cabin at the north end of Leigh Lake. Beyond (west of) the cabin the remnants of the once-good trail, at times overgrown by lush vegetation, can usually, with effort, be followed to the two campsites at the mouth of the canyon.

The rather dense vegetation in initial sections of the canyon can be passed via a climbers' trail that starts directly upcanyon from campsite 14B (the one on the north side of the Leigh Creek outlet). This trail is not that easy to follow, mainly because it sees relatively little use and vegetation and avalanche debris make navigation difficult. An occasional cairn will be seen along the way.

Once past the initial rocky outcrops near the mouth of the canyon, the trail veers toward Leigh Creek. In the autumn months, when the creek is very low, it is almost easier to stay in the creek bed until an exit can be made to the talus below the south buttress of Mount Moran. Campsites can be found in this region near the stream. The two shallow lakes just beyond this point should be passed on their north sides. These are commonly known as the Spectacle Lakes, although in the summit register for Pinetop, first climbed by the Petzoldts et al. in 1935, that party referred to at least one of these as "Laughing Water Lake." There seem to be no well-defined game trails from the lakes to the upper end of the canyon, but the traveling is not too difficult. Some fording of the stream is necessary to avoid the dense willow thickets and scrub pine. It will usually be most expedient to stay near the stream before turning up at right angles into a desired side canyon.

The seldom-visited upper section of the canyon can also be reached by descending from the Paintbrush Canyon trail to Grizzly Bear Lake and then climbing down on the west side of the stream draining from the lake. This involves some bushwhacking. More easily, the upper canyon can be gained from Paintbrush Divide by descending the isolated Blister Basin northwest toward Mink Lake. This remote region can also be reached from Cascade Canyon and Lake Solitude by climbing Littles Peak, traversing north along the divide, and then descending into Leigh Canyon from the low saddle 0.5 mile north of the summit. Campsites can be found here and there along the upper canyon floor.

LEIGH CANYON, NORTH SIDE ROCK CLIMBS

Map: Mount Moran

The entire collection of these routes out of Leigh Canyon, including the major southern routes on Mount Moran, contain many of the finest difficult rock climbs of the Teton Range. The rock is massive, generally of excellent quality, and commonly exceedingly steep. The earliest difficult routes on Mount Moran as well as some of the more recent ones on the north side of Leigh Canyon were first done as summit climbs. These and the other summit routes are described later under *Mount Moran*, even though several, such as the Direct South Buttress (*Mount Moran, Route 10*), are now usually climbed as rock routes—with descent after the finish of the initial difficult sections. The imposing northern walls and ridges, listed here from east to west as one would encounter them while hiking west up Leigh Canyon, do not lead to a summit in any direct fashion. These rock-climbing routes have a relatively short approach and are often done in a single day by a fast party with an early start.

No Escape Buttress, the location of *Routes 1–8*, is the first significant wall rising to the north from the mouth of Leigh Canyon. See *Figure 9-1* for an overview of this sector. The name was derived from the fact that a descent of the buttress could be difficult, the

FIGURE 9-1. Mount Moran, No Escape Buttress overview. (A) West Arête *(Route 8)*, IV, 5.10b; (B) Smoke and Mirrors *(Route 7)*, IV+, 5.10, C2; (C) Direct South Face *(Route 6)*, IV, 5.9R; (D) Direct South Face, variation: Direct Finish, IV, 5.9R; (E) No Escape Slabs *(Route 1)*, I, 5.8 to 5.10; (F) start of No Survivors *(Route 4)*, III, 5.10R

ceilings making rappelling uncertain. *Figure 9-25* offers a view of No Escape Buttress from the west, with the bulk of Mount Moran rising above it.

Chronology

SOUTHEAST RIDGE: July 6, 1957, John Dietschy, William Cropper
STAIRCASE ARÊTE: August 28, 1959, David Dornan, Al Read
NO ESCAPE BUTTRESS, WEST ARÊTE: August 21, 1960, Al Read, Peter Lev (lower half); September 11, 1960, Al Read, David Dornan (upper half); FFA August 1, 1977, Buck Tilley, Ivan Rezucha
var—July 16, 1969, Rick Reese, Ted Wilson
var—August 1, 1977, Buck Tilley, Ivan Rezucha
NO ESCAPE BUTTRESS, DIRECT SOUTH FACE: August 17, 1962, David Dornan, Yvon Chouinard, Jim McCarthy
var—**DIRECT FINISH:** July 30, 1977, Mike Munger, Rich Perch
NO ESCAPE SLABS: August 1970, Alan Rubin, Charles Jackson (discovered); August 14, 1977, Mike Munger, Charlie Fowler (first friction climbs)
NO SURVIVORS: August 6, 1977, Mike Munger, Jim Donini, Steve Wunsch
GIN AND TONIC: August 23, 1977, Mike Munger, Charlie Fowler
NO ESCAPE BUTTRESS, EAST EDGE: July 30, 1978, Andy Carson, Jorge Colon
DIRECT AVOIDANCE: July 31, 1978, Dieter Klose, Mike Kehoe
SPREADEAGLE: August 1, 1978, Dieter Klose, Mike Kehoe
var—May 21, 2001, Paul Horton, Heather Paul
IRVINE ARÊTE: August 13, 1982, Leo Larson, Ed Thompson
FORGOTTEN ARÊTE: September 14, 2003, Paul Horton, Charlie Thomas
SMOKE AND MIRRORS: September 23, 2008, Aaron Gams, Toby Stegman

ROUTE 1. NO ESCAPE SLABS. I, 5.8 to 5.10. (See *Figure 9-2*.) These beautiful slabs, located immediately below No Escape Buttress, are a great place to spend a day of climbing on excellent rock in a scenic location. The first climb appears to have been done by Alan Rubin and Charles Jackson in August 1970. This was probably the 5.8 crack located in the center section. The name Easy Escape Slabs was applied to the area at that time. The pure friction-climbing potential of the slabs was realized somewhat later by Rich Perch and Mike Munger, on July 30, 1977. Pure friction climbing is a rarity in the Tetons. Some 14 different lines are available, and many more possibilities exist. From the west shore of Leigh Lake take the climbers' trail about 0.5 mile into Leigh Canyon. No Escape Slabs will be seen at the base of No Escape Buttress, which is the first major rock feature on the southeast side

A climber on the Direct South Face of No Escape Buttress (Photo by Renny Jackson)

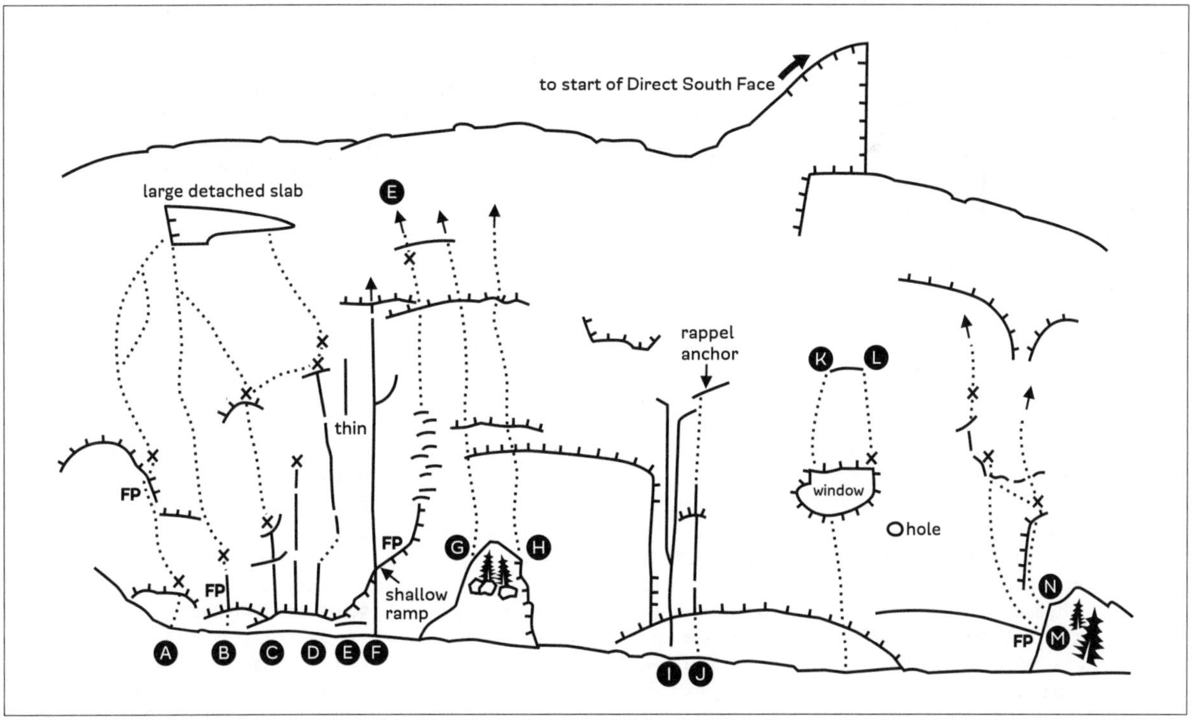

FIGURE 9-2. Mount Moran, No Escape Buttress, No Escape Slabs *(Route 1)*. (A) Last Chance Texaco, 5.9; (B) Facts and Friction, 5.10; (C) Stranger Than Friction, 5.10; (D) Scared and Profane, 5.10; (E) Youth Challenge, 5.9; (F) Tsutsugamushi Fever, 5.10; (G) Tugboat, 5.8; (H) Departure, 5.8; (I) No Name 1, 5.8; (J) No Name 2, 5.10; (K) Window, 5.9; (L) Greaser Right, 5.10; (M) Slip Sliding Away, 5.9; (N) Don't Sweat It, 5.9

of Mount Moran. Two ropes for top-roping are recommended for these climbs. Some routes can be led, but top-roping them first is strongly suggested because the protection for some routes is marginal or nonexistent. For descent walk back down around the sides to the base of the slabs.

ROUTE 2. NO ESCAPE BUTTRESS, EAST EDGE. III, 5.7. First ascent July 30, 1978, by Andy Carson and Jorge Colon. This route contains six pitches with rock of fair quality, sometimes wet and licheny. It starts from trees near the right (east) edge of the main face and goes up a series of chimneys and corners. One 5.7 chimney will be encountered near the beginning, prior to the traverse to the left (west) to gain the indentation, which is the only line of weakness in this part of the face. In a band of white rock higher on the route another chimney of similar difficulty must also be climbed.

ROUTE 3. DIRECT AVOIDANCE. III, 5.10. First ascent July 31, 1978, Dieter Klose and Mike Kehoe. The exact location of this route is uncertain, but it apparently starts 120m to the right of the Direct South Face (*Route 6*); the description is somewhat similar to the line of *Route 2*, which was climbed the day before. Perhaps it can be identified by the first lead—5.10 on good granite. After two pitches up the wall, traverse left (west) for 60m. Now climb up a short offwidth crack and into a system of cracks. Next move left up to the crux overhang and then back right to a sloping ledge. Climb right up through the overhang and move left on the face above, finishing back to the right to a belay point. Descend 3m and climb 12m to the right, up through another overhang, and then move left to the belay. Two additional pitches lead to the top of the buttress. Because the rock was not good after the first pitch, this route is not greatly recommended.

ROUTE 4. NO SURVIVORS. III, 5.10R. First ascent August 6, 1977, by Mike Munger, Jim Donini, and Steve Wunsch. (See *Figure 9-1* for the location of the start and *Figure 9-3* for the route topo.) No Survivors begins to the east of Gin and Tonic (*Route 5*) and, like that route, is poorly understood, so finding and climbing it will be a challenge. It starts on a large, square-cut ledge "with large blocks sitting on it." This ledge curves up at its left end, forming a left-facing corner that gets smaller as it goes up. Directly above the ledge are some roofs. The first pitch (crux 5.10R) goes up the corner at the left end of the ledge until it is possible to traverse right to a small right-facing corner. This is a very intimidating traverse, given the lack of protection and the large ledge above which one is climbing. Zig first up and right and then zag back left under a roof, passing it just left of a loose flake to a belay below a huge block. For the second pitch climb to the top of the block and traverse right to a long roof, crossing it via an awkward move, and continue right to a large, easy corner with a ledge on the right. The third lead can be made up the corner, which angles left, or one can go left and cross a roof on bucket holds. Now move the belay up and right to the highest grassy terrace. The next pitch goes up to the left of a left-facing corner at the left edge of a white streak in the rock and past a loose flake to a ramp that leads up and left; follow this ramp until it is possible to climb to a large ledge for the belay. The fifth lead follows a dihedral above this ledge to another ledge below a ceiling; this ledge goes left around a corner and eventually up to a terrace. The final rock is easier and leads up and right to the top of the buttress.

ROUTE 5. GIN AND TONIC. III, 5.9. First ascent August 23, 1977, by Mike Munger and Charlie Fowler. (See *Figure 9-3*.) This route begins to the right (east) of the original 1962 Direct South Face (*Route 6*) and to the left (west) of No Survivors (*Route 4*). Because this route has apparently not

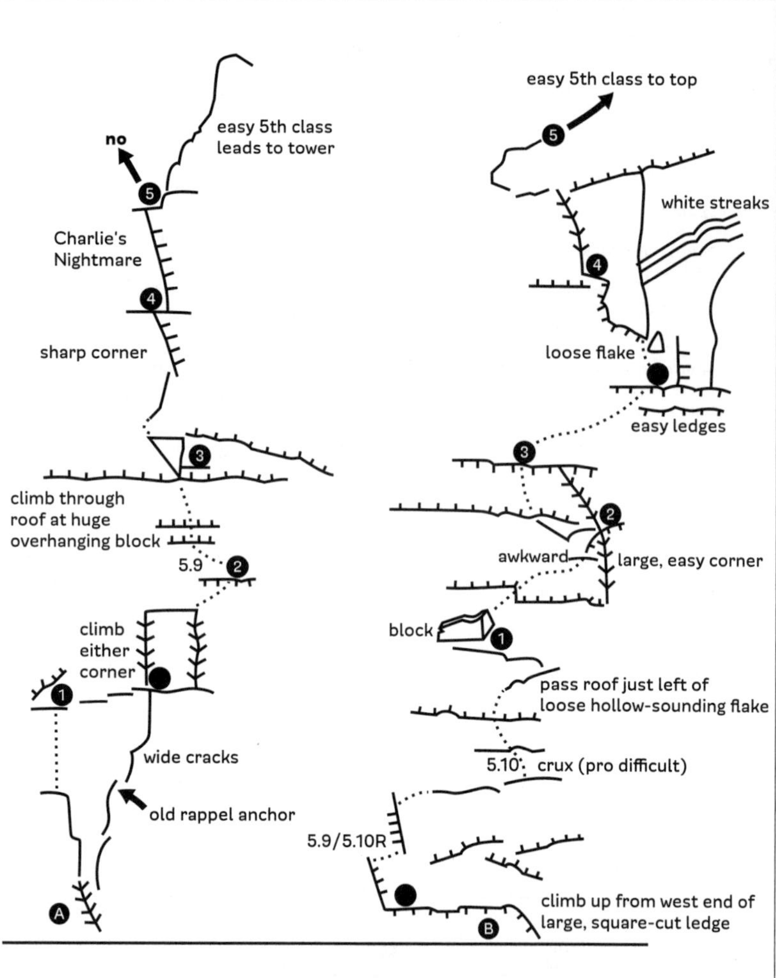

FIGURE 9-3. Mount Moran, No Escape Buttress. (A) Gin and Tonic *(Route 5)*, III, 5.9; (B) No Survivors *(Route 4)*, III, 5.10R

been repeated, it may be difficult to locate and its ascent should be a challenge. The route starts up a corner, with the first long lead (52m) finishing with a difficult, unprotected 10m face; perhaps this pitch can be recognized by the old rappel anchor out to the right in a system of wide cracks. Move the belay to the right to a pair of corners, either of which can be climbed straight up, and then trend right onto a belay ledge below a series of roofs. The third pitch goes up through the roofs at a huge overhanging block (5.9). The actual break through which one escapes through the roofs is difficult to find. The next lead starts with a crack (5.9) past the left edge of another roof to and up a sharp left-leaning, left-facing corner ending at a belay ledge. The final difficult pitch, Charlie's Nightmare, is a full lead up a left-facing corner (5.9). From the top of this corner, easier climbing goes up and right to the top of a tower and the end of the route.

ROUTE 6. NO ESCAPE BUTTRESS, DIRECT SOUTH FACE. IV, 5.9R. First ascent August 17, 1962, by David Dornan, Yvon Chouinard, and Jim McCarthy. (See *Figures 9-4* and 9-5.) This difficult rock climb goes more or less directly up the south face of No Escape Buttress. Because the approach is relatively short, the route has been climbed many times and is now well understood, but climbers should appreciate that routefinding on this complex buttress can be difficult. It is also important to note that the bolts on the route were placed by others subsequent to the first ascent. This is a testament to the impressive abilities of McCarthy, who led the fourth pitch without protection. From the west shore of Leigh Lake take the climbers' trail about 0.5 mile into Leigh Canyon. No Escape Buttress, the first major rock feature on the southeast side of Mount Moran, and the slabs at its base will be seen rising above on the north. Walk up the boulder field to the base of the buttress.

The route begins from the top of the small pedestal located a bit left (west) of the center of the face. Approach and climb to the top of this pedestal from the west. The first short lead (20m) goes up to a small belay ledge (with a small flake) directly above the belayer. The second pitch goes right and up, involving some tricky traverses and a small inside corner (5.8), to gain a ledge that is followed to its top. The next lead goes up past a fixed pin around the left edge of a pair of small ceilings to a block and ends at a ledge and belay bolt. The crux fourth pitch moves right on friction past another bolt and then up a difficult corner that is difficult to protect (5.9R). Continue up right-facing corners in dark, broken rock using liebacks

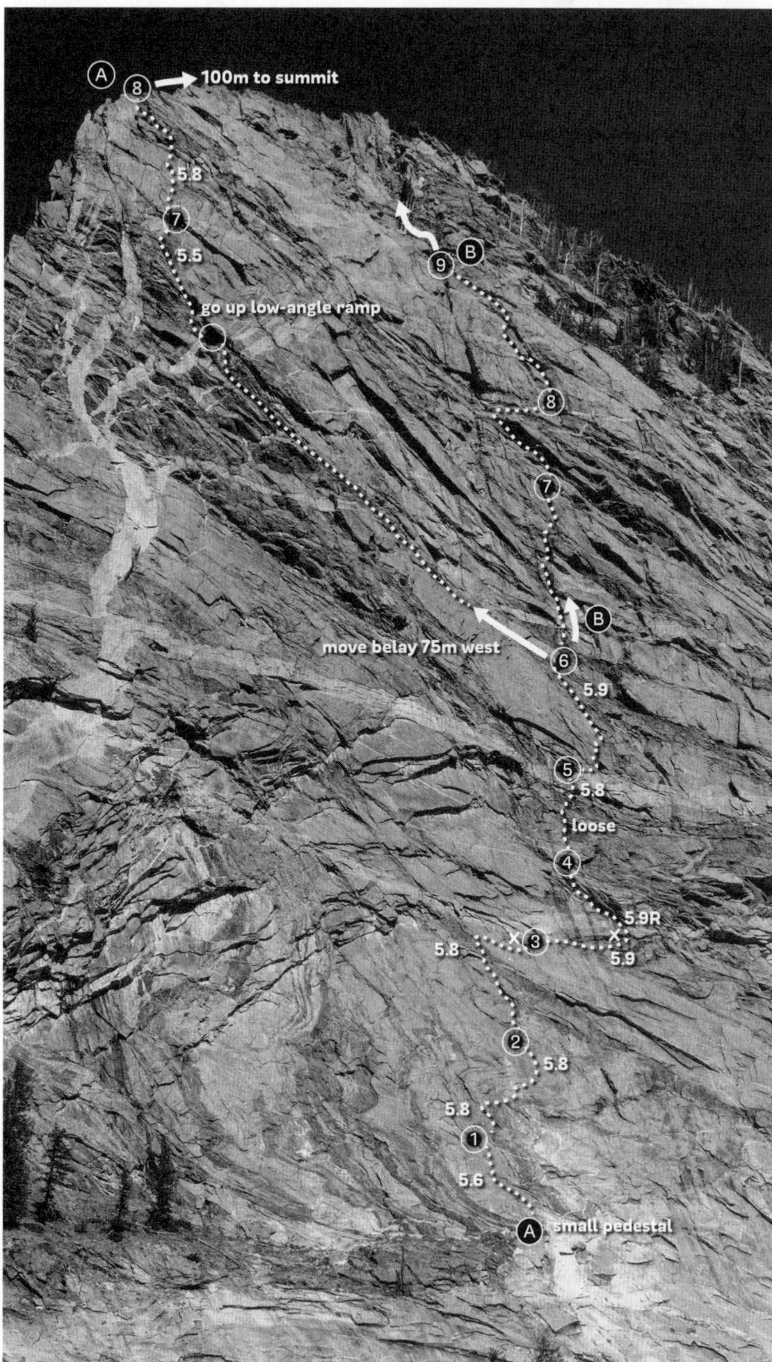

FIGURE 9-4. Mount Moran, No Escape Buttress. (A) Direct South Face *(Route 6)*, IV, 5.9R; (B) Variation: Direct Finish, IV, 5.9R

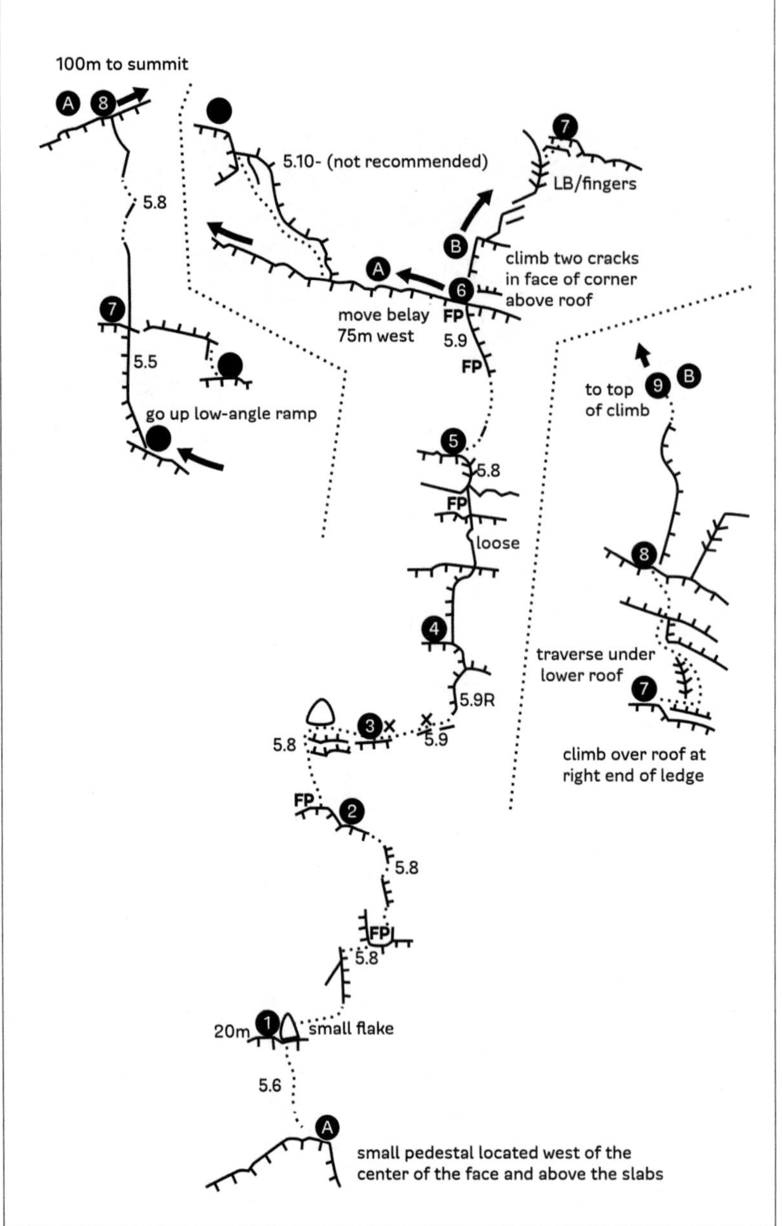

FIGURE 9-5. Mount Moran, No Escape Buttress. (A) Direct South Face *(Route 6)*, IV, 5.9R; (B) Variation: Direct Finish, IV, 5.9R

and stemming, finishing in a short, steep slot (5.8) past a fixed piton onto the belay ledge. The final lead onto the ramp goes directly up the steep face into a steep, slanting crack (5.9) containing flakes and chockstones and fixed pitons. Once on the broad ramp, walk up to the left (west) for about 75m and then climb a low-angle higher ramp that turns into a right-facing corner (46m). The eighth pitch (46m) continues up this corner over a difficult 5.8 bulge to the top of the buttress. Easy climbing now takes one up to the crest. An alternative finish or escape avoids these last two pitches and takes the broad ramp all the way left to the west corner of the face before turning up to reach the top of the buttress. To descend back to Leigh Lake from the top of the buttress, proceed down the grassy slopes to the east. See *American Alpine Journal* 13, no. 2 (1963): pp. 410–20, illus.

***Variation:* DIRECT FINISH.** IV, 5.9R. First ascent July 30, 1977, by Mike Munger and Rich Perch. (See *Figures 9-4* and *9-5*.) From the top of the sixth pitch at the broad ramp, this variation continues straight up for three additional pitches instead of making the 75m traverse out to the left on the ramp. The first lead (43m) up from the ramp uses two cracks in the face of a corner above a roof and then moves right across a face to a corner, which is climbed using a thin lieback, exiting to the right at the top. The next pitch moves around and past two roofs onto a big ledge. The easier final lead continues up a left-facing corner and then left to the top of the buttress.

ROUTE 7. SMOKE AND MIRRORS. IV+, 5.10, C2. First ascent September 23, 2008, by Aaron Gams and Toby Stegman. (See *Figure 9-6*.) This route was established over a period of two years and multiple attempts, with additional assistance from Charlie Thomas and Brian Mulvihill. The climb ascends the steepest portion of the face, with the second pitch leading up to and through the enormous stepped roof that cuts upward across the base of the face from left (west) to right (east). Gams described his first time through this feature as "an epic 60m, 3-hour lead": "[I] gained a small ledge where I fixed the line and collapsed. Brian jugged the roof without the benefit of any fixed gear and, after about two hours and several terrifying swings into space, joined me in the dark."

Start about 75m west of the small pedestal where the Direct South Face route (*Route 6*) begins. The enormous roof of the second pitch is directly overhead, and the left-leaning crack that cuts through it is visible. **Pitch 1:** Some loose rock leads to a small left-facing corner/lieback (5.7). Traverse right on a broken ledge to a good, slightly tilted ledge. Belay from a few small nuts (35m). **Pitch 2:** Step right and up over a couple of blocks, then continue up on rock that improves in quality (5.7) to the base of the roof. This C2 awkward roof crack leans left and overhangs nearly 12m. The three fixed pins are located for the best lowering-out for the second. Some mandatory 5.7 near the end of the pitch leads to a belay at an

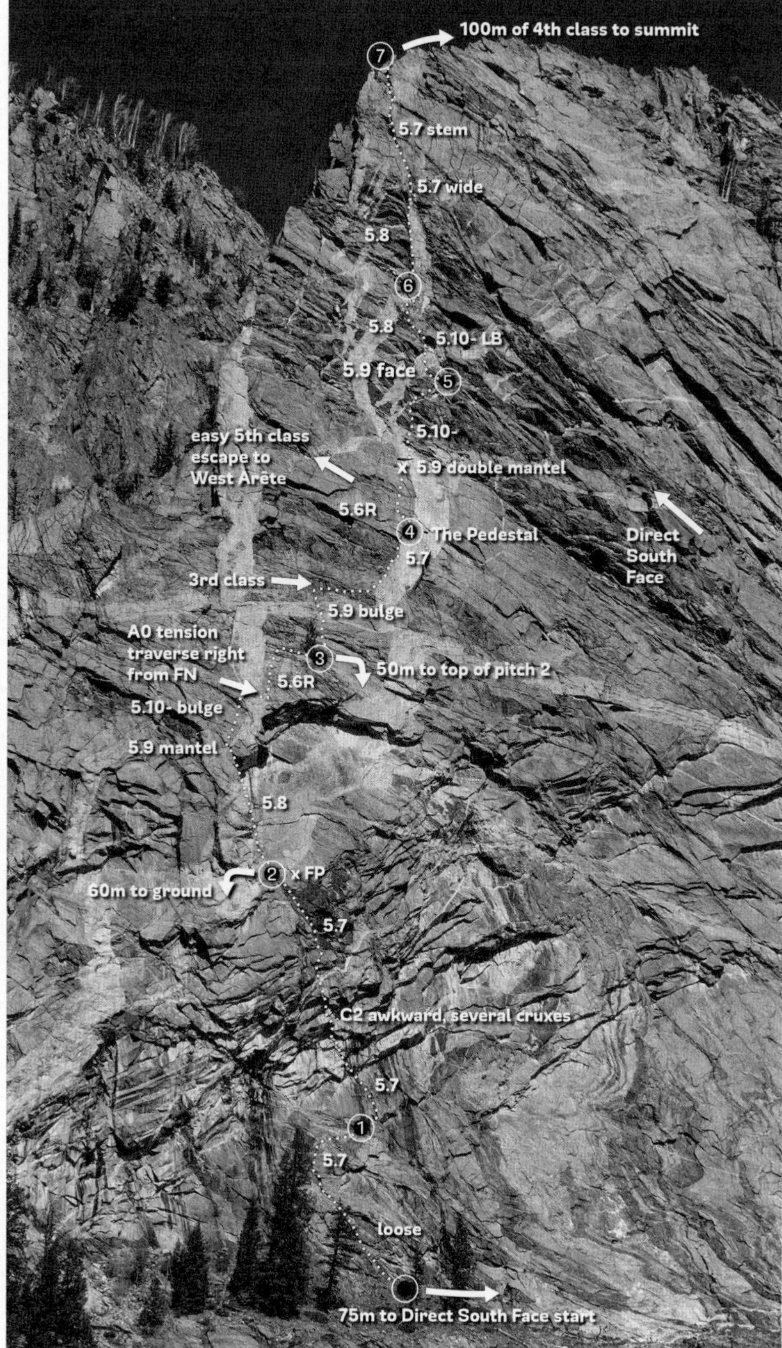

FIGURE 9-6. Mount Moran, No Escape Buttress, Smoke and Mirrors *(Route 7)*, IV+, 5.10, C2

anchor with a bolt and a fixed pin (55m). **Pitch 3:** Climb the dihedral to the roof (5.8). Do not undercling right; instead, traverse left past a piton and out onto the exposed face. Reach through a big move (5.9), find good gear, then step right into the white dike; go up, then step back left to good gear. Go over the bulge (5.10-) and tension right from a fixed nut across the white dike (A0). Climb up on steep buckets (5.6R) to a pin, then traverse right to a ledge with a tree and belay (50+m). **Pitch 4:** Climb straight up from right of the tree to a short, shallow right-facing corner. Continue straight up on superb stone through a 5.9 bulge. Traverse right on a 3rd-class ledge to a short 5.7 corner to a belay on top of the Pedestal (46m). **Pitch 5:** Above the belay, climb the left of two microcracks (5.6R) just left of the white dike to a bolt. A 5.9 double mantel leads to a lieback move through the white dike to a bold 5.10- bulge into dark rock. Stem up through steep terrain (5.9) on tiny gear past a large, loose block. Step right to a sloping belay ledge (35m). **Pitch 6:** Climb the face (5.9) straight up from the belay to an easy traverse left across the white dike. Go up the left margin of the dike through a jam/lieback bulge (5.10-), step left on a thin ramp, and then climb up (5.8) to a pin. A 5.7 hand traverse leads right across the white dike to a short hand crack. Scramble up to the broad ramp that extends across the buttress and belay (35m). **Pitch 7:** This 60m final pitch continues straight up the left side of the tapering white dike (5.8) into a wide constriction (5.7). Then stem straight up (5.7) for over 30m to end on the sharp, exposed western ridge of the buttress. Fourth-class scrambling for 100m brings one to the summit. **Gear:** Two 60m ropes are needed for retreat from the second or third pitch; because of a few sharp edges on the roof pitch, a larger-diameter (10mm) rope is recommended. Also bring two sets of small nuts, including one set of offsets; a double set of cams from #0 Camalot C3 (black Alien) to #2 Camalot; and several singles—specifically one #00 Camalot C3, one #000 Camalot C3, one #3 Camalot, and one #4 Camalot. (Source: correspondence with Aaron Gams)

ROUTE 8. NO ESCAPE BUTTRESS, WEST ARÊTE. IV, 5.10b. First ascent of the lower half August 21, 1960, by Al Read and Peter Lev; first ascent of the upper half September 11, 1960, by Al Read and David Dornan; first free ascent August 1, 1977, by Buck Tilley and Ivan Rezucha (entire route). (See *Figures 9-7* and *9-8*.) The West Arête route ascends the left (west) edge of No Escape Buttress. Take the Leigh Canyon climbers' trail 0.5 mile into the canyon; the climb begins at the base of the couloir immediately northwest of the buttress. Angle up and right to a very wide platform.

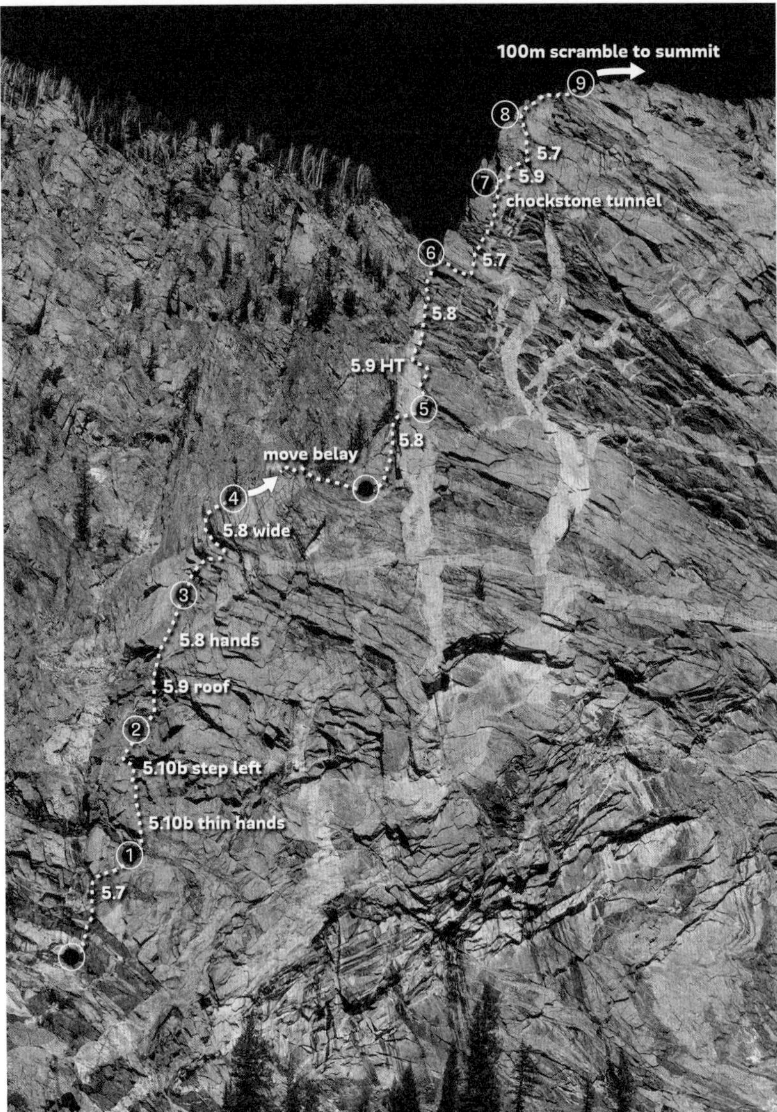

FIGURE 9-7. Mount Moran, No Escape Buttress, West Arête *(Route 8)*, IV, 5.10b

The objective is to reach an obvious jam crack that angles slightly left but begins above an overhang. The first-ascent party climbed a corner about 4.5m to the right of this crack for about 6m until a piton placed in a ceiling allowed a pendulum to the base of the jam crack. After about 9m up this crack they again used a pendulum to access the crescent-shaped crack beneath the small overhang to the left. Direct aid (pitons and one wooden wedge) was used to surmount difficulties on a few of the pitches above. Refer to *Figures 9-7* and *9-8* for a general representation of how the climb is done today. There are nine pitches of roped climbing to the top of the buttress. The grassy slopes on the eastern side of the buttress can be used for descent. See *American Alpine Journal* 13, no. 2 (1963): pp. 487–89. (Sources: correspondence with Norm Larson and Martin Vidak regarding topo corrections)

Variation: III, 5.8, A2. First ascent July 16, 1969, by Rick Reese and Ted Wilson. This variation is but one of several possibilities on this arête. To reach the obvious jam crack at the beginning of the route, the first-ascent party overcame the initial overhang by aiding (overhanging) directly up the crack, rather than using a pendulum. When the edge of the arête is reached at the end of the second lead, continue directly up the crest instead of traversing out onto the face to the right (east). The first lead (5.7) up this crest (the third lead of the route) goes up 4.5m and then requires a hand traverse left for 2.5m to gain a slightly overhanging crack just left of the crest; climb this crack for 9m to a belay in easier rock. To regain the crest on the next pitch climb a 9m wall to the left of a chimney that has a large jam crack up one side; scrambling to the east through some trees puts one back on the crest at the end of the 1960 route. Continue scrambling for about a ropelength along the crest over easy blocks and then low-angle slabs to the base of a steep wall. The route now goes up this wall, starting next to a dead gray tree, for 6m (5.7) until one can enter a very steep left-leaning wide crack. Climb this strenuous (5.8 or 5.9) crack for 9m and then traverse left across a smooth face on a small ledge. The arête continues from this point, but the 1969 party was deterred by the weather; the 1977 variation, described next, probably climbed this last portion.

Variation: IV, 5.10-. First ascent August 1, 1977, by Buck Tilley and Ivan Rezucha. The description of this "variation" bears some similarity to what is now the recommended way to climb the arête, as represented in *Figures* 9-7 and 9-8. From the end of the last pitch of the 1960 route at the top of a large step in the ridge, the first lead (5.8, 30m) of this variation starts from the right edge of the step, goes up a corner and a chimney to gain a ledge on the south face, and then moves right 4.5m and up 4.5m in steep cracks to a good ledge. The next pitch (43m) of similar difficulty (5.8–5.9) continues up cracks for 4.5m, moves up and left on chicken heads to a notch in the skyline, and then climbs the arête to a belay stance. The third long lead starts with a traverse down and right for 6m across a face to a chimney and then goes up this chimney to black ramps that lead to a large ledge. Now climb a corner behind a large chockstone and another corner above to a belay tree on the ridge crest. The final pitch traverses right around the crest up moderate slabs to finish with easy climbing.

ROUTE 9. SPREADEAGLE. II, 5.10. First ascent August 1, 1978, by Dieter Klose and Mike Kehoe. (See *Figure 9-9* in the Mount Moran section.) Little information is available regarding this route, but the light-colored dihedrals on the prominent crest described under *Route 10* are a likely location for the climb; a cairn was found in 2001 at the base of the dihedrals. Use the same approach as for Forgotten Arête to the bowl at the junction of the big rocky couloirs; Spreadeagle is directly above, between the couloirs. Scramble up the left couloir to the base of a dirty corner, where two easy pitches lead to a big, forested ledge at the base of the light-colored dihedrals. The first difficult lead (5.10) is up a large, left-facing gray-and-orange corner to an overhanging jam crack; climb 3m up this crack to the belay. The next pitch, also 5.10, starts with a step 3m to the right and up the right-hand crack to the belay. The next lead (5.8) moves left and up a crack in the face above to the end of the technical climbing. Scramble the remainder of the now low-angle ridge to the slopes leading to the CMC campsite.

Variation: II, 5.7. First ascent May 21, 2001, by Paul Horton and Heather Paul. From the big, forested ledge at the base of the difficult dihedrals ascend a clean lower-angle corner on the left, which leads up to a crest. The next pitch follows this crest. Finally, ascend chimneys, the last 15m of which is nasty and loose, and rejoin the main route at the start of the scrambling.

ROUTE 10. FORGOTTEN ARÊTE. III, 5.9. First ascent September 14, 2003, by Paul Horton and Charlie Thomas. (See *Figure 9-9* in the Mount Moran section.) On the north side of Leigh Canyon, about 0.25 mile east of Laughing Lions Falls, a large talus cone and stream lie beneath the couloir system east of Mount Moran's southeast ridge (see *Route 11*). The talus, which goes down nearly to the main canyon stream, extends up to a headwall with a seasonal waterfall. Far above are ridges; Forgotten Arête is the one to the left and is marked by a large nose of orange rock near the top. (Spreadeagle—*Route 9*—is apparently located at the light-colored dihedrals on a prominent crest to the east.)

Proceed up Leigh Canyon and ascend the talus cone. From the top of the talus work up a gully to the right of the headwall for about 100m. When feasible, traverse exposed ledges and ramps left to a bowl above the headwall, at the top of the waterfall. The bowl lies at the junction of big, rocky couloirs; Forgotten Arête is above and to the west. Complicated scrambling—first up big slopes west of the bowl, then to the right across slabs and ribs, then back left up a forested ramp—eventually leads to the base of the steeper arête and the first belay. The arête itself is straightforward climbing, compared with the intricate approach. About five long, enjoyable pitches follow cracks and weaknesses on or near the crest. The crux (5.9) is a short, awkward chimney to the right of the crest, about halfway up. The huge, overhanging orange nose lurking near the top of the ridge is passed easily and pleasantly on the left. The ridge ends in blocky talus slopes that provide a simple traverse to the CMC campsite.

ROUTE 11. SOUTHEAST RIDGE. II, 5.4. First ascent July 6, 1957, by John Dietschy and William Cropper. (See *Figure 9-9* in the Mount Moran section.) This long ridge leads directly from Leigh Canyon to the summit of Drizzlepuss, a large tower between the West Horn and the main east face of Mount Moran. The ridge is paralleled on the west by an equally long

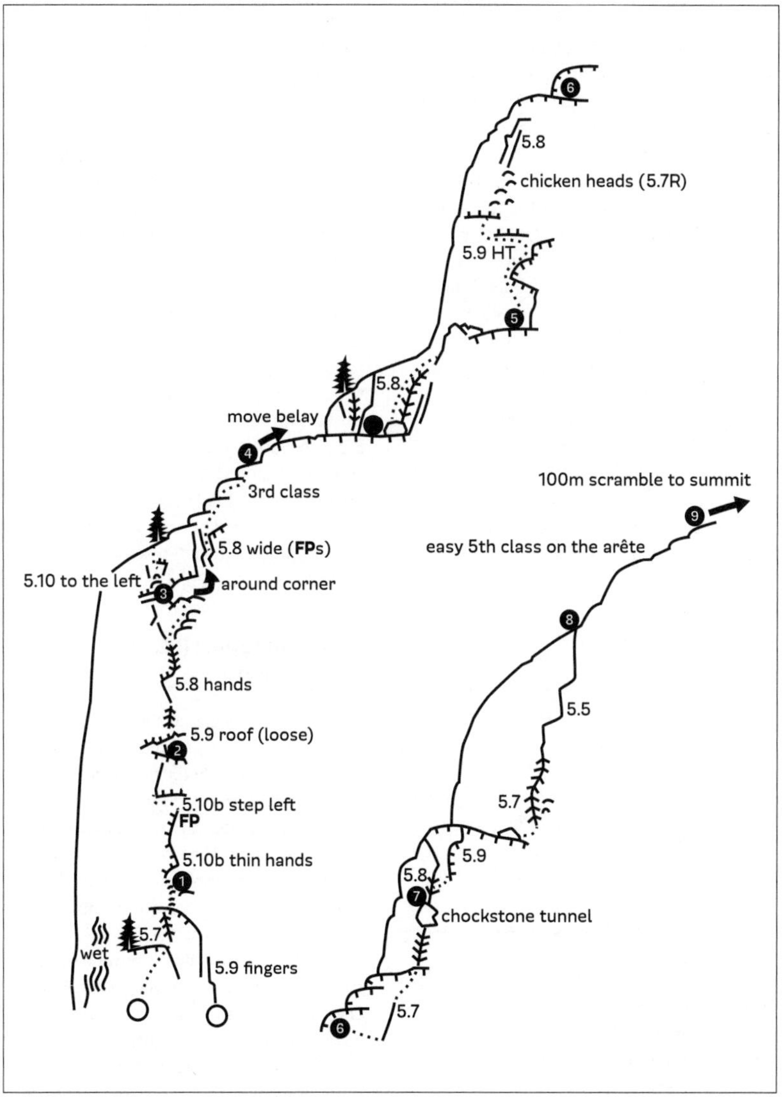

FIGURE 9-8. Mount Moran, No Escape Buttress, West Arête *(Route 8)*, IV, 5.10b

gully, which contains at least two waterfalls (this is the Laughing Lions Falls drainage) in the lower section and opens out in the upper section to form the main large bowl beneath the final south walls of Mount Moran. The only other ridge of this length on the south side of Mount Moran is the main south buttress (see *Mount Moran, Routes 10* and *11*). Take the climbers' trail into Leigh Canyon and approach the bottom of the ridge from the east along treed ledges. The ridge presents easy scrambling to the first large step. Use a diagonal ledge on the east side of the step to pass this obstacle and regain the crest. Follow a knife-edge to the base of the second step. An unusual 90m horizontal cave on the west side provides an easy traverse into a gully, from which an easy walk leads back to the crest. Then scramble to the summit of Drizzlepuss, where the CMC route (*Mount Moran, Route 20*) is joined. See *American Alpine Journal* 11, no. 1 (1958): pp. 85–88.

ROUTE 12. IRVINE ARÊTE. III, 5.9, A1. First ascent August 13, 1982, by Leo Larson and Ed Thompson. The initial 1957 ascent of the Southeast Ridge route (*Route 11*) stayed primarily on the east side of the crest to the end of the second step. This much more difficult route, containing interesting and tricky pitches, starts on the left (west) side of the crest and ends just above the junction of Staircase Arête (*Route 13*) with the southeast ridge. Approach from Leigh Canyon to a point due east of the base of Laughing Lions Falls, the prominent waterfall on the south side of Mount Moran east of the south buttress. Scramble up the rocky couloir between Staircase Arête and the southeast ridge to the chockstone where the couloir narrows. The first lead starts out to the right at a large tree in a difficult 15m jam crack to a ledge followed by a narrow chimney. At the top of this chimney a bulge forces a series of 5.9 moves on thin friction and loose blocks to a belay position. A chimney then leads to the next belay ledge. Continue up to a large ledge below a short, vertical wall. Climb this wall using a fine parallel-sided jam crack to the next belay stance at a large tree. The sixth lead ascends the right side of the steep wall above using shallow cracks and thin flakes. Now move right from the small belay ledge over broken rock and short walls to a small belay tree. The steep, smooth wall above, broken by a thin, shallow crack, is climbed along the left side toward the tapering overhang at its top. At the overhang, pendulum 3m to the right to easier ground and then climb up over loose rock with poor protection to yet another large tree. The final three pitches involve moderate scrambling to join the main Southeast Ridge route. This route could be followed to the summit of Drizzlepuss, or descent can be made down the large couloir (much loose rock) to the east, angling east from time to time, ultimately reaching the next crest, which is the first "ridgelet" west of No Escape Buttress. Downclimb this slender ridge to a tree from which three rappels of 23m suffice to reach the talus below.

ROUTE 13. STAIRCASE ARÊTE. III, 5.6, A1, or III, 5.8. First ascent August 28, 1959, by David Dornan and Al Read; the same party had attempted the route on July 21, 1957. (See *Figure 9-9* in the Mount Moran section.) On the lower south side of Mount Moran, to the east of the south buttress, is a prominent waterfall named Laughing Lions Falls. This beautiful waterfall drains the bowl in the upper portion of the south face of the mountain, between the upper south ridge (see *Mount Moran, Routes 10* and *11*) and Drizzlepuss. Immediately to the right of these falls, at an altitude of about 7,800 feet, the slender Staircase Arête begins. It ascends in three large steps and many smaller ones for about 350m and ends in a final steep wall, where it joins the long southeast ridge (see *Route 11*). Take the climbers' trail into Leigh Canyon for about 1 mile to the waterfall. The route begins with a traverse to the right from the falls on a nonobvious ledge to the face of the first step. (**Note:** An alternate start to the climb can be obtained by climbing corner systems on the south face of the first step. The rock is superb, and nearly three additional pitches of climbing can be done, generally 5.9 to 5.10 in difficulty.)

At the end of the nonobvious ledge, climb 35m straight up a corner over moderate rock and through a small V to a fine belay ledge. Continue up a crack system, but work right as soon as possible to gain the large chimney leading to the crest of the arête. From the top of the chimney, scramble 46m to the second great step. From a wide platform, traverse left a meter and turn up over an awkward step at the obvious bush. The first-ascent party used aid for about 4.5m at this point to get up the steep, leaning corner (5.8). A short scramble leads to the third step. Climb a corner to the left of the crest by means of a 7m lieback. Complete this lead up a chimney with a difficult overhang at its top, which again required aid on the first ascent. The next pitch leads straight up smooth slabs in moderate cracks; after about 25m it is possible to exit to the right. At this point one can also scramble off to the left and traverse to the lower Blackfin rappels (see *Mount Moran, Route 1*). This is most likely the easiest way off the climb. From the top of this fourth step, climb a series of slabs, liebacks, short steps, cracks, and one overhang on or near the crest for about 75m to a good belay position at the base of the last step. The final 50m wall of the arête is avoided by a traverse left on a large ledge, allowing access to about 60m of easy climbing back toward the right to the very top of the arête, where a cairn should be found. Most of the southeast ridge lies above this junction point.

The descent from this point to Leigh Canyon is complex, requiring careful routefinding. From the cairn, descend the southeast couloir on the east side of the southeast ridge about 350m to a grass-covered slope that leads east above the lower cliff band. Follow this slope until an easy couloir leads down into Leigh Canyon. If the correct route is found, no rappels are required. See *American Alpine Journal* 13, no. 2 (1963): pp. 487–89.

MOUNT MORAN (12,605)

Map: Mount Moran

Among all the peaks of the Teton Range, Mount Moran may justifiably be considered as second only to the Grand Teton. If the range is approached from the north or northeast, Mount Moran easily dominates the scene. The primary impression conveyed by the mountain is that of massiveness, and when one climbs on the mountain this impression is reinforced. The singular, nearly flat summit marks the boundary between the Precambrian crystalline gneiss rock of Mount Moran's bulk and the thin sedimentary sandstone cap marking the highest rounded point; it measures some 200m by 500m, covering more than 15 acres. It is a big

mountain in every respect and a most worthy objective for the Teton mountaineer. Like several other peaks in the range, Mount Moran affords no truly easy route to the summit, but there is a wide range of difficulty—from the moderate Northeast Ridge route *(Route 30)* to the very difficult routes from the south and north. Mount Moran's five glaciers provide extensive opportunity for snow and ice climbing and, in combination with adjacent rock walls, significant mixed routes. In addition to massive rock walls, the prolific mountain contains numerous ridges and couloirs, some of which have been investigated only in recent years, resulting in several routes of the first order. Many years still remain, however, before the

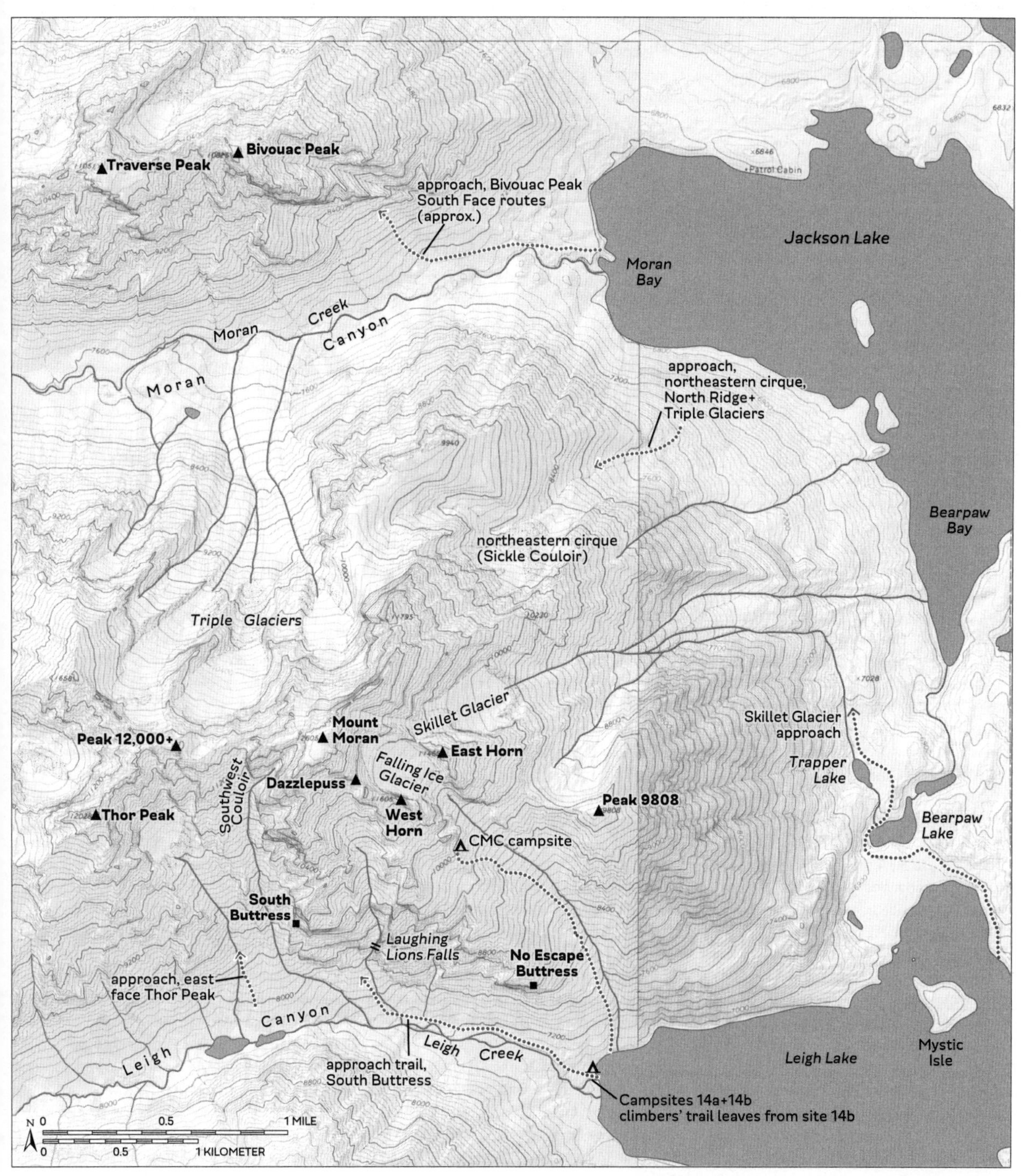

last sector of Mount Moran will have been explored. A number of the more recent routes that have gone up on the south side of Mount Moran are rock climbs that do not lead to the summit (see *Leigh Canyon, North Side Rock Climbs* for descriptions of some of these routes).

Structure of the Peak

On the north and south, Mount Moran is confined by Moran and Leigh Canyons, but to the west there is a well-defined ridge that soon deteriorates into a sequence of complexities. About 800m above the floor of Moran Canyon, three large but seldom-visited glaciers sweep up to meet the complex west ridge. In contrast, above Leigh Canyon the imposing south walls rise abruptly to provide very steep ground for some of the finest rock routes in the park. The southwest aspect of Moran contains a very large expanse of rock forming the west face of the main south ridge as it rises from the initial buttress to the summit. Not visible from the valley floor, and hence underappreciated by many visiting climbers, this section contains several clearly defined ridges and steep couloirs between the southwest couloir on the north and the south buttress on the south. Extending eastward from the south ridge and above the major basal buttresses on the south is the considerable bowl of the upper south face. The right (east) edge of this rarely visited face is the left (south) edge of the east face.

The remarkable black dike that cleaves the east face into two unequal sections measures about 40m in width. This dike continues through the mountain to the west and can be traced for 7 miles all the way to the divide at the head of Moran Canyon. The two major glaciers below the east face, the Skillet Glacier and the Falling Ice Glacier, are guarded by the salient East and West Horns. Around on the northeast side of the mountain, lying below the northeast ridge and the east face of the north ridge of Mount Moran, is a most interesting cirque seldom visited by mountaineers. From the snowfield and the expanse of morainal boulders in the cirque, rock walls cut by four large parallel couloirs diagonal up from east to west to join these ridges. The northwest aspect of Mount Moran encompasses both the west face of the north ridge and the north face and is bounded on the right by the upper snow arm of the easternmost Triple Glacier. Three couloirs cut the left (northern) half of the face below the north ridge. The north buttress or pillar is a prominent vertical feature in the center (southeast corner) of the face to the right (south) of the third couloir (see *Route 35*).

History

Mount Moran, named by members of the 1872 Hayden Survey for the famous landscape artist Thomas Moran, was the second great peak of the Tetons to attract the attention of mountaineers. Moran himself never saw his mountain from Jackson Hole but caught a brief glimpse from the west through smoky skies during his one visit to the range in late August of 1879. This view provided the basis for his prophetic pronouncement: "The Tetons here loomed up grandly against the sky & from this point it is perhaps the finest pictorial range in the United States or even in N. America." As early as 1886 the north shoulder of the peak was reached by the geologist Joseph P. Iddings on a short side trip from the geologic mapping of Yellowstone National Park. In 1915 the first semiserious effort to attain the summit was made by John Shive, veteran of the 1898 ascent of the Grand Teton, with his daughter Carrie, Tom Tracy, and Marguerite Clark. They were turned back by lack of time at a point apparently above the Skillet Glacier some 180m below the summit.

An outing to one of the eastern glaciers in August of 1917 by the manager of the Yellowstone Park Transportation Company, Huntley Child, with a retinue of photographers and writers, resulted in an article in *Scientific American* ("The Jackson Hole Country of Wyoming," March 30, 1918, p. 272) with this tantalizing sentence: "The summit has never been attained and probably never will, as the last 3,000 feet of the mountain are sheer perpendicular walls of rock." Almost surely inspired by this self-defeating prophecy, LeRoy Jeffers, a mountaineer well known in his day, on August 11, 1919, reached the lower north summit at 9 PM in a sleet storm after a remarkable solo climb of a variant of the northeast ridge. There is little doubt that he would have continued to the higher south summit had the weather been better and the day longer. With at least some competitive motivation, Dr. LeGrand Haven Hardy and Ben C. Rich came to Jackson Hole in 1922 to climb the mountain and, after meeting Bennet McNulty, formed a party of three to attain the summit via an impressive ascent of the Skillet Glacier (*Route 25*) on July 27. It was indeed impressive, considering the party had no ice axes and instead used "short tough sticks . . . and two short auto shovels" to negotiate the steep snow and ice. Curiously, their summit note remained undiscovered until August 25, 1964, when it was found intact in its half-pint whiskey bottle by W. Bousman and John Bousman. Jeffers returned with Warren Loyster only 10 days later, on August 6, 1922, and this time reached the main south summit but was most disappointed to succeed with only the second ascent of the mountain.

From this point on Mount Moran's climbing history parallels that of the rest of the Teton Range. Routes such as the entire Northeast Ridge, the black dike (see *Route 21*), and the East Ridge (*Route 24*) were worked out by such pioneers as Albert R. Ellingwood and Carl Blaurock, Hans Wittich and Otto Stegmaier, and Robert Underhill and Paul Petzoldt. On September 5, 1926, three years after she became the first woman to climb the Grand Teton and the South Teton, Eleanor Davis (Ehrman) added Mount Moran to that list, reaching the summit via the Northeast Ridge route. Four adventurous climbs of 1935—the West Ridge (*Route 19*) from Thor Peak by P. Petzoldt and H. K. Hartline, the easterly Triple Glacier (*Route 38*) by Malcolm Smith, the Upper South Ridge (*Route 11*) by Phil Smith and Eldon Petzoldt, and the descent of the CMC route (*Route 20*) by Chris Scoredos and Joe Merhar—contributed significantly to the knowledge of the other sides of this massive mountain. In 1940 and 1941, before the war brought a pause to climbing in the mountains, Paul Petzoldt pioneered the North Ridge (*Route 34*) and the CMC route, both outstanding if not overly difficult climbs; routefinding was Paul's forte. Tragedy in the form of an airplane crash high on the northeast ridge occasioned a dangerous and very difficult climb to the site of the wreck on November 21, 1950, by Petzoldt and party.

After the war, climbers seemed content with the normal routes, until Richard Emerson decided in 1953 that the south ridge from Leigh Canyon should be examined carefully. His optimism resulted in the now-classic Direct South Buttress and ridge (*Route 10*), which he led from August 29 to 30, 1953, with Don Decker and Leigh Ortenburger. This ascent signaled a new era, marking the first major climb in the Tetons requiring the use of a considerable amount of direct aid; at the time it was the most difficult technical climb in the park. Technical rockwork was beginning its meteoric rise elsewhere, most notably in Yosemite Valley. Yet four years passed before the ascent was repeated by David Dornan, Al Read, and Bob Kamps in the summer of 1957. That same summer saw renewed investigations of Mount Moran's other southern ridges. John Dietschy and William Cropper climbed the ridge leading to Drizzlepuss (the large tower between the West Horn and the main east face of Moran) from Leigh Canyon, while John Fonda led David Dingman and Karl Pfiffner up the long and difficult southwest ridge (see *Route 17*), requiring two days for the ascent.

In the late 1950s and early 1960s the principal driver of route development was Dornan, who on his ascent of the Direct South Buttress noticed several ridges paralleling the south buttress on the east. Dornan pioneered the first of these, Staircase Arête (see *Leigh Canyon, North Side Rock Climbs, Route 13*), in 1959 with Read; they found a delicate, difficult, and delightful ridge leading toward Drizzlepuss. He climbed the second, known now as the Blackfin (*Route 1*) because of the first black tower on the ridge, in 1960 with Ortenburger. Requiring two days, it proved to be a long and difficult climb, ultimately joining the south ridge near the summit of the mountain. Dornan's third new route, the West Arête of No Escape Buttress (see *Leigh Canyon, North Side Rock Climbs, Route 8*), again climbed with Read, involved considerable difficulty on excellent rock. In 1961 Dornan and Herb Swedlund established the now-classic South Buttress Right (*Route 3*), using a fair amount of direct aid in the process. A year later, Dornan returned to No Escape Buttress, this time teaming up with Yvon Chouinard and visiting climber Jim McCarthy to put up a stellar climb on the feature's south face. McCarthy flawlessly led the unprotected 5.9 face-climbing pitch (see *Leigh Canyon, North Side Rock Climbs, Route 6*).

The 1970s saw outstanding efforts by a few motivated individuals to free climb existing stretches of aid climbing on some of the early classic rock climbs. Stan Mish was responsible for freeing the Direct South Buttress, while the South Buttress Right fell to Art Higbee and Steve Wunsch via a bypass, and later to Buck Tilley and Jim Mullin on the original line. Mike Munger, who was perhaps the most talented free climber of this period, explored new routes on No Escape Buttress as well as in many other areas of the park. Jim Beyer visited the Tetons late in the decade and struck up a long relationship with Mount Moran, beginning with his West Dihedrals route (*Route 14*) on the western aspect of the south buttress. Beyer continued to explore the peak in the 1980s, 1990s, and beyond, sometimes with partners and sometimes solo, establishing five other major routes over the ensuing decades.

Montana climbers Alex Lowe and Jack Tackle made astonishing first winter ascents in the 1980s of the Staircase Arête, the Direct South Buttress, and the South Buttress Right, defining a new level of alpinism on some of the more difficult walls in the range. This pair teamed up with Wilson, Wyoming, local Andy Carson to make the first complete winter ascent of Laughing Lions Falls in 1985. Attempted several times over the preceding decades, the first complete winter ascent of the Direct South Buttress to the summit of Mount Moran finally came together in 2001, when local climbers Hans Johnstone, Mark Newcomb, and Renny Jackson experienced perfect conditions for the climb. Around the same time, ski mountaineering skyrocketed to an extraordinary level when Johnstone, Bill Dyer, Kent McBride, and Doug Coombs descended the CMC route on May 16, 2002, after two previous attempts. Fourteen years later Johnstone returned with Dan Corn and Adam Fabrikant to make the first ski descent of Mount Moran's major south side drainage (Laughing Lions Falls) on March 8, 2016.

The last few decades have seen a resurgence of interest in the south buttress, primarily because it contains some of the best rock in the range. In 1998 Beyer established Whirl of Hate (*Route 2*) and the South Buttress Drifter (*Route 7*)—both solo. Two years later he put up yet another line, this time with John Kelley, a talented alpinist and rock climber who has opened difficult new routes from the Tetons to the Himalaya. Their combined effort—the Kelley-Beyer route (*Route 6*)—features runout face climbing at the 5.11+ level. In 2006, Johnstone and fellow Teton local Greg Collins, accompanied by the late Bean Bowers, put up the South Buttress Prow (*Route 9*), a technically very difficult route, all free and in a day. Johnstone and Collins added the South Buttress Houdini line (*Route 4*) the following year over just three days. These routes are major excursions and were pioneered at a very high standard. There is no doubt that much more exploration and difficult climbing possibilities remain.

Approaches

To approach the southeastern side of Mount Moran, as for an ascent of the CMC route or either the West or East Horn, there are three methods available: (1) The best by far is to canoe from the String Lake boat launch north for a mile along String Lake, do a short portage to Leigh Lake, and then paddle over to the Falling Ice Glacier drainage; this involves 3.5 miles of paddling. (2) Without a canoe but with noticeably more exertion, one can follow the remnants of the once-good but now-abandoned trail around the northwest side of Leigh Lake (with bushwhacking) to the same drainage. Begin this hike from the Leigh Lake trailhead, following the maintained trail along the east sides of String and Leigh Lakes. (3) It is also possible, but *not recommended*, to hike around the southwest side of Leigh Lake on yet another NPS-abandoned trail—now nearly impassable with years of deadfall—to the mouth of Leigh Canyon. Continue around the northwest shore of the lake to reach the same stream from the Falling Ice Glacier.

Whichever way is taken, from the lakeshore hike up the boulder-strewn stream gully, gaining some 2,500 feet, to the open, semigrassy slope due east of and below the West Horn, just south of the glacier. (**Note:** This author, R. Jackson, has seen the major remnants of icefalls from the glacier all the way down this stream gully to the lake!) An improved climbers' trail will be found on this slope leading up to the outstanding CMC campsite (ca. 10,000), located on the flat ridge up to the left (south) in the large trees, one step down (about 30m) from the last trees. Excellent flat areas will be found among the trees on the ridge crest, and except in late season during dry years, there is water in the boulder field 30m to the south.

To approach the northeastern side of Mount Moran, as for an ascent of the Skillet Glacier or Northeast Ridge routes, there are also three methods available: (1) The first is by canoe across Leigh Lake from the String Lake portage. One can head for the north shore of the lake (3.1 miles of paddling) and continue by hiking north on the final portion of the maintained NPS trail to Bearpaw Lake. To reach the northeastern base of the mountain or the mouth of Moran Canyon, fierce bushwhacking will be encountered not far beyond Bearpaw Lake. Maintenance of the trail that once led easily to the mouth of Moran Canyon was abandoned by the NPS many decades ago, and now the trail can scarcely be found amid the avalanche debris. (2) Instead of canoeing, one can hike along the trail around the east sides of String and Leigh Lakes to reach the north end of Leigh Lake in about the same amount of time but with noticeably greater exertion. (3) The best approach to the northern or northeastern routes on the mountain is across Jackson Lake, either by powerboat from Colter Bay or Signal Mountain Lodge or by canoe (4 miles of paddling) from Spalding Bay. (For more information on these options, see *Moran Canyon* in Section 10.) All of these schemes are time-consuming, so the first of two climbing days is normally devoted to packing in to a high camp. Compensating for the effort is the picturesque and remote setting of some of the high campsites.

Chronology

SKILLET GLACIER: July 27, 1922, LeGrand Haven Hardy, Ben C. Rich, Bennet McNulty
NORTHEAST RIDGE: August 19, 1924, Albert R. Ellingwood, Carl Blaurock
var—August 11, 1919, LeRoy Jeffers
var—August 25, 1939, Earl Clark, Donald Grant
var—**NORTHEAST BUTTRESS COULOIR:** July 16, 1971, Gale Long, Robert Frisby
DIKE: June 23, 1931, Hans Wittich, Otto Stegmaier
var—August 14, 1946, Gerald Brandon, Theodore Brandon (descent); August 12, 1952, Theodore Brandon, Tim Ramsland, Willis Wood, Don and Ivan Zastrow (ascent)
EAST RIDGE: July 24, 1931, Robert Underhill, Paul Petzoldt
var—July 24, 1931, Paul Petzoldt, Robert Underhill (descent)
var—July 18, 1951, Peter Robinson, Bill Briggs, Brian Brett
UPPER SOUTH RIDGE: June 30, 1935, Phil Smith, Eldon Petzoldt
CMC: July 14, 1935, Chris Scoredos, Joe Merhar (descent); June 25, 1941, Paul Petzoldt, Joseph Hawkes, Earl Clark, Harold Plumley
var—July 23, 1952, Richard Emerson, Walt Sticker
var—August 17, 1952, Martin Benham, Dmitri Nabokov (descent)
WEST RIDGE: August 26, 1935, Paul Petzoldt, H. K. Hartline
TRIPLE GLACIER: September 8, 1935, Malcolm Smith
NORTH RIDGE: July 5, 1939, Paul Petzoldt, William Ringler
var—July 27, 1956, Richard Emerson, Robert Bowen (partial); September 13, 1957, Bill Pope, Mary Kay Pottinger (complete)
DIRECT SOUTH BUTTRESS: August 29–30, 1953, Richard Emerson, Don Decker, Leigh Ortenburger; FFA July 3, 1979, Stan Mish, with Hal Gribble
var—September 9, 1958, Richard Sykes, Bill Briggs
VAR: August 12–13, 1965, Peter Cleveland, Roland Fleck, Jack Stauffer
var—**SOUTH BUTTRESS WRONG:** Date unknown, Ken Sims, Rick Reese
EAST CHIMNEY: July 9, 1956, Rob Day, Peter Lipman, Alan Williamson
FONDA RIDGE: August 22–23, 1957, John Fonda, David Dingman, Karl Pfiffner
THE BLACKFIN: July 4–5, 1960, David Dornan, Leigh Ortenburger
SOUTH BUTTRESS RIGHT: July 14, 1961, David Dornan, Peter Lev (attempt); July 25, 1961, David Dornan, Herb Swedlund; July 18, 1973, Steve Wunsch, Art Higbee (FFA via nail-up bypass); August 2, 1978, Buck Tilley, Jim Mullin (FFA via original route)
var—**HABELER:** July 13, 1969, Peter Habeler, Juris Krisjansons
var—**DELIVERANCE:** July 6, 1990, James Earl, Todd Cozzens
var—**KELLEY:** Late August 1998, John Kelley (solo)
NORTH FACE: June 29, 1962, Pete Sinclair, Peter Lev, William Buckingham, Leigh Ortenburger
SKILLET GLACIER HEADWALL: July 27, 1962, Don Anderson, Larry Scott
SOUTHWEST COULOIR: August 17, 1962, Ted Vaill, Stuart Kearns
SOUTH BUTTRESS, WEST FACE: August 25–26, 1962, Art Gran, John Hudson
NORTHEAST SLABS: September 10, 1962, Fred Beckey, Dan Davis
SICKLE COULOIR: August 8, 1964, Gary Cole, Ray Jacquot
SOUTH BUTTRESS CENTRAL: July 16, 1967, Peter Koedt, Keith Becker; FFA summer 1984, Eric Breitenberger, Bill Trull
PIKA BUTTRESS: July 27–28, 1968, Jim Kanzler, Paul Myhre, John Neal
WESTERN BUTTRESS: August 6–7, 1968, Peter Cleveland, Bill Widule
NORTH BUTTRESS: July 18, 1969, Peter Habeler, George Lowe
NORTHWEST RIDGE: July 17, 1977, Paul Horton, Lew Hitchner
SKILLET CHIMNEY: October 13, 1978, Paul Horton, W. D. Horton
WEST DIHEDRALS: June 28, 1979, Jim Beyer
REVOLUTIONARY CREST: July 15, 1982, Jim Beyer, David Koch
SANDINISTA COULOIR: Late June 1983 (or 1984), Jim Beyer
WISE BURGETTES GO BY WATER: June 28, 1997, Gary Wise, Dan Burgette, Lane Burgette, David Bywater
SOUTH BUTTRESS DRIFTER: July 1998, Jim Beyer (solo)
WHIRL OF HATE: October 1998, Jim Beyer (solo)
SKILLET BUTTRESS: August 19, 1999, Paul Horton, John Britton
KELLEY-BEYER: July 2000, John Kelley, Jim Beyer
MINOR FOURTH COULOIR: October 2002, John Kelley, Bob Webster
STUCK PIG: August 11–12, 2004, Nate Fuller, Patrick Wright
EUDEMONIA (HAPPINESS): July 27, 2005, George Montopoli, David Bywater, Martin Vidak
SOUTH BUTTRESS PROW: September 29, 2006, Bean Bowers, Greg Collins, Hans Johnstone
SOUTH BUTTRESS HOUDINI: October 2007, Greg Collins, Hans Johnstone

Mount Moran, South Buttress (South Aspect)

The south buttress of Mount Moran comprises a vast amount of terrain and is home to some of the longest and most difficult climbs in the range. For the most part the climbing is on fine-grained granitic rock, and the rock quality is exceptional. From the floor of Leigh Canyon, the southern aspect of this buttress is impressive, with the line of the Direct South Buttress *(Route 10)* and upper south ridge (see *Route 11*) rising in a series of towers to the summit, nearly 5,000 feet above. On the eastern side of the buttress is the beautiful Laughing Lions Falls, a good landmark and water source. Just west of the falls, two ramps rise from east to west, up and across the base of the buttress. These features—the First Ramp and the Second Ramp—provide access to nearly all the climbs on this aspect of the peak. A short distance west of the bottom of the falls is the short first pitch of the Blackfin *(Route 1)*: Look for a clean right-facing corner (5.8 wide) in excellent rock that leads to the eastern end of the Second Ramp. This pitch is the best (and recommended) way to reach the Second Ramp and *Routes 2–10*.

The following climbs are listed from east to west, ending with the corner of the Direct South Buttress, which eventually meets the upper south ridge. See *Figures 9-9* and *9-10* for an overview of route locations on this facet of Mount Moran.

Moran Memories by David "Dave" Dornan

In the summer of 1957 Al Read and I had summer jobs in Yellowstone working for the Park Service's trail crew. We were undergraduates at the University of Colorado and eager to spend our weekends climbing in the Teton Range. In June of that year, the first edition of Leigh Ortenburger's A Climber's Guide to the Teton Range came out and Al and I pored over it to prioritize what we wanted to climb. My suggestion was to climb the Direct South Buttress of Mount Moran, which since its first ascent in 1953 had not been repeated and had a fearsome reputation. Since neither one of us had climbed Mount Moran, our first venture was to climb the CMC route to learn the standard decent route off the mountain. We climbed to the top of Drizzlepuss but when we saw the amount of snow on the CMC slabs, we said forget it and came down. The next weekend we hiked into Leigh Canyon by following the old trail around the south side of Leigh Lake. In the 1950s there were no canoes that we could rent to paddle across Leigh Lake. We discovered that the trail turned into bogs and deadfall without any bridge across Leigh Creek. The crux for us was balancing on a log to cross the creek that finally allowed us access to the canyon. Unfortunately we only had time to climb the ramp and chimney that were the first three pitches of the route. We stopped at the end of a long ledge system where we could see how the route continued up much steeper rock. The next weekend we returned to Leigh Canyon since Al had spotted a slender arête that begged to be climbed. We did the first seven pitches of this arête, which Al had named Staircase Arête, and which started near a waterfall.

It wasn't until July 27 before we returned to the Direct South Buttress with Bob Kamps, whom we'd met at Fishing Bridge where he had a job pumping gas. On the climb we switched leads but in my memory Al and I did most of the leading. I recall Bob leading a flake pitch and the pitch that ended on the narrow ledge below the pendulum pitch. I led the pendulum pitch since I had the only bolt kit and had been told by Dick Emerson to replace his wafer piton that he used to pendulum from. The tip of his piton was wedged into a crack about three-quarters of an inch but seemed fairly secure. It took me nearly an hour to drill a hole for the bolt, and by the time I finished it was getting dark so we bivouacked on the small ledge. The next morning I led the pendulum and Al did the aid pitch. I think Bob led the hand traverse to the bowl. We were all badly dehydrated at this point and could barely talk, so we decided to untie and traverse off toward Drizzlepuss and descend to the lake. The famous wafer piton and carabiner I mailed to Emerson in Seattle, but I never heard back from him. I don't know if this was the first bolt placed on a climb in the Tetons, but it was the first and only bolt that I ever placed on a climb. I learned on this climb that we were capable of doing the more difficult climbs, and that the south side of Mount Moran had a lot of great potential rock climbs to do someday.

After the Direct South Buttress, Al and I did several other climbs but we didn't go back to Moran. As far as I know Barry Corbet and Jake Breitenbach did the third ascent of the buttress that year. In 1958 I climbed Mount McKinley with Jake and Dave Dingman, and while they left Alaska to guide for Exum in the Tetons, I stayed in Alaska and Canada to do more climbing. In 1959 Al Read and I climbed the entire Staircase Arête and we found it to be quite a fun climb. We were both still in college and I had started reading philosophy, which inspired me to name the waterfall near the arête Laughing Lions Falls, from a passage in Nietzsche's The Will to Power.

The year 1960 was another turning point for me in my climbing career. I had a job as a Jenny Lake Ranger, which gave me two days a week off to climb. I was still excited about Leigh Canyon and the south side of Mount Moran and eager to do more climbs there. John Fonda in 1957 had shown me an aerial photo of Mount Moran and he pointed to a ridge that merged into the south ridge of Moran and said, "This is a possible route." This ridge began to the east of the south buttress and had a prominent black diorite tower. In 1960 I climbed this new route to the summit with Leigh Ortenburger, and I named it the Blackfin after its most prominent feature. Also that year I climbed what we were calling the west ridge [now the West Arête] of No Escape Buttress with Al Read. On this climb I did what was my most difficult lead to date, climbing an overhang about three pitches below the top. The name No Escape Buttress was one I gave the buttress early in our 1957 explorations of Leigh Canyon.

In 1961 Herb Swedlund and I climbed the South Buttress Right, which I had previously tried with Peter Lev. On this first attempt I took a leader fall on the third pitch (the 5.11a/b one) and we rapped off. With Herb we finished the climb and rappelled down the Blackfin route. Herb put the bolts in on the pitch above the wide ledge near the top. The name was one I gave to distinguish it from the Direct South Buttress. In some ways I wish I had thought of a better name since it is such a great climb. In 1962 I climbed it again and led the pitches that Herb had led on the first ascent.

My last Leigh Canyon first ascent was in 1962 on No Escape Buttress, going up the center of the buttress. I had started the climb a couple of weeks earlier with Pete Sinclair, but we were rained off. I invited Yvon Chouinard and he invited Jim McCarthy, who ended up leading the crux pitch with no protection. Except for that pitch, Yvon and I alternated the leading. It is also a favorite climb of mine, but repeating it years later, I was distressed to see that bolts had been added. We had only used pitons for anchors and protection.

FIGURE 9-9. Mount Moran, south aspect overview. (A) approach to upper arêtes (complex); (B) Spreadeagle, II, 5.10; (C) Forgotten Arête, III, 5.9; (D) Southeast Ridge, II, 5.4; (E) Staircase Arête, III, 5.8; (F) Direct South Buttress *(Route 10), V, 5.8, A1, or V, 5.12a,* to Upper South Ridge *(Route 11)*; (G) The Blackfin *(Route 1)*, V, 5.8; (H) traverse to/from CMC campsite; (I) Direct South Buttress, start of original descent; (J) Upper South Ridge *(Route 11)*, II, 5.4

ROUTE 1. THE BLACKFIN. V, 5.8, A1, or V, 5.8. First ascent July 4–5, 1960, by David Dornan and Leigh Ortenburger; previously attempted by Dornan and Peter Lev. (See *Figures 9-9* and *9-10*.) This fine ridge, immediately to the right (east) of the main south ridge of Mount Moran, is a very long route if continued to the summit. It begins with a tower of dark rock, aptly named the Blackfin. This tower is visible in *Figure 9-10*, directly east of the large bowl that is gained after the first eight pitches of the Direct South Buttress route (*Route 10*). It is the first of five towers on the distinct ridge that curves upward to the west to join the main south ridge about 300m below the summit. The initial challenge is to reach the base of this first tower. The route begins immediately to the left (west) of the bottom section of Laughing Lions Falls. Climb a clean right-facing corner (5.8 wide) that becomes a short, easy chimney at the top; a 4" piece is useful for this pitch. Now scramble left (west) along the large Second Ramp, past a tree, to the beginning of an obvious crack and chimney system. Four leads upward (one place was originally passed using aid) bring one out on a large platform at the lower edge of the south face bowl. Scramble up and left to the beginning of a difficult friction pitch. Four 5th-class pitches, always bearing left (west) toward the Blackfin, which is now in full view above, lead to the area below the Blackfin itself. Pass the nose of the Blackfin on the left and scramble up to a large, nearly horizontal quartz vein. Follow this vein, which lies in the west face of the Blackfin, back to the right (east) for two leads, to the top of the Blackfin.

The second tower, or more properly step, is climbed directly. The second lead is about 42m and of 5.6 difficulty. The third involves some scrambling to the summit of the tower. The buttress of the third tower begins with a crack system in a steep but short face. The top of this tower can very likely be attained directly, but on the first ascent, a small detour was made to the left (west), from which side the top was reached. The descent to the notch is not difficult. In early season, the area near this notch makes a good bivouac spot, because there is water and some level ground. The escape route to the east from the south buttress crosses the Blackfin at this point. The fourth tower starts with a small overhang and slabs for about 25m. Then a chimney must be climbed, perhaps most easily by the use of lieback technique. Moderate climbing leads to the top of this step. The fifth and final tower is even easier. The Blackfin joins the south ridge just after this last tower. This last 300m of the south ridge is climbed by staying mostly on the right (east) side of the crest until the final steep section is reached. Bypass this section on the left (west) and reach the summit plateau from the west by climbing one pitch. This route is a long climb on rock that is good, once the initial chimney/corner system is passed. Two days are recommended for this climb. See *American Alpine Journal* 12, no. 2 (1961): pp. 373–77.

ROUTE 2. WHIRL OF HATE. VI, 5.10, A4. First ascent in October 1998, by Jim Beyer (solo). This big route was put up by Beyer over a period of seven days. We all climb for different reasons; for many, climbing can be a salve for the various wounds of heart and soul. It certainly has been for this author (R. Jackson) over the years. The following is excerpted (with permission) from an article Beyer wrote for the 2001 *American Alpine Journal*:

The government had taken control of my house and possessions, and I was living out of my car. I got a cell phone, so my last customers could contact me as my business collapsed. Should I bring my cell phone on the route? The weather had been stormy; I could get weather reports. I left it behind.

I spent seven days and 14 nights in rainy weather on Whirl of Hate (VI 5.10 A4). It was quality: runout face climbing up big slabbers, some nailing out a big roof, more 5.10 face, some easy aid, days on end climbing alone. There was no place I'd rather have been, and I didn't want to go back to civilization anyway.

It was good until about October 6, when a big snowstorm rolled in with high winds. My sunny south face turned into the ice planet. I was one pitch of friction from the top of the wall and out of food. I spent three hungry days trapped in my leaking portaledge buffeted by high winds and pummeled by falling ice. I was gripped that my ledgefly would tear, leaving me exposed to the storm. Retreat was impossible, as my ropes and the rock that I had to rappel and pendulum down were all covered in thick ice.

It was a very dark side as I shivered in my sodden pit. I remember spending a whole day debating whether or not I should just untie and jump.

The sun returned, and I gaped in wonder at the changes below. In two days, the foliage in Leigh Canyon went green to red, and now elk were bugling with need. My stomach was also bugling, so I hoofed it to Leigh Lake and my food cache at my canoe, happy to have a simple goal, even if it was in the wrong direction. But I had rapped off with my bag, and I was crestfallen to have missed my main goal: the top of the wall.

FIGURE 9-10. Mount Moran, south buttress overview. (A) South Buttress Right, variation: Habeler, IV, 5.8, A1; (B) South Buttress Right, variation: Kelley, IV, 5.10X; (C) Whirl of Hate *(Route 2)*, VI, 5.10, A4; (D) South Buttress Right, variation: Deliverance, IV, 5.10-, A3; (E) South Buttress Houdini *(Route 4)*, V, 5.11d; (F) South Buttress Right *(Route 3)*, IV, 5.11a/b; (G) Kelley-Beyer *(Route 6)*, VI, 5.12-R/X, A0; (H) South Buttress Drifter *(Route 7)*, V, 5.10c; (I) South Buttress Central *(Route 8)*, IV, 5.10R; (J) South Buttress Prow *(Route 9)*, IV, 5.12b; (K) Direct South Buttress *(Route 10)*, V, 5.8, A1, or V, 5.12a

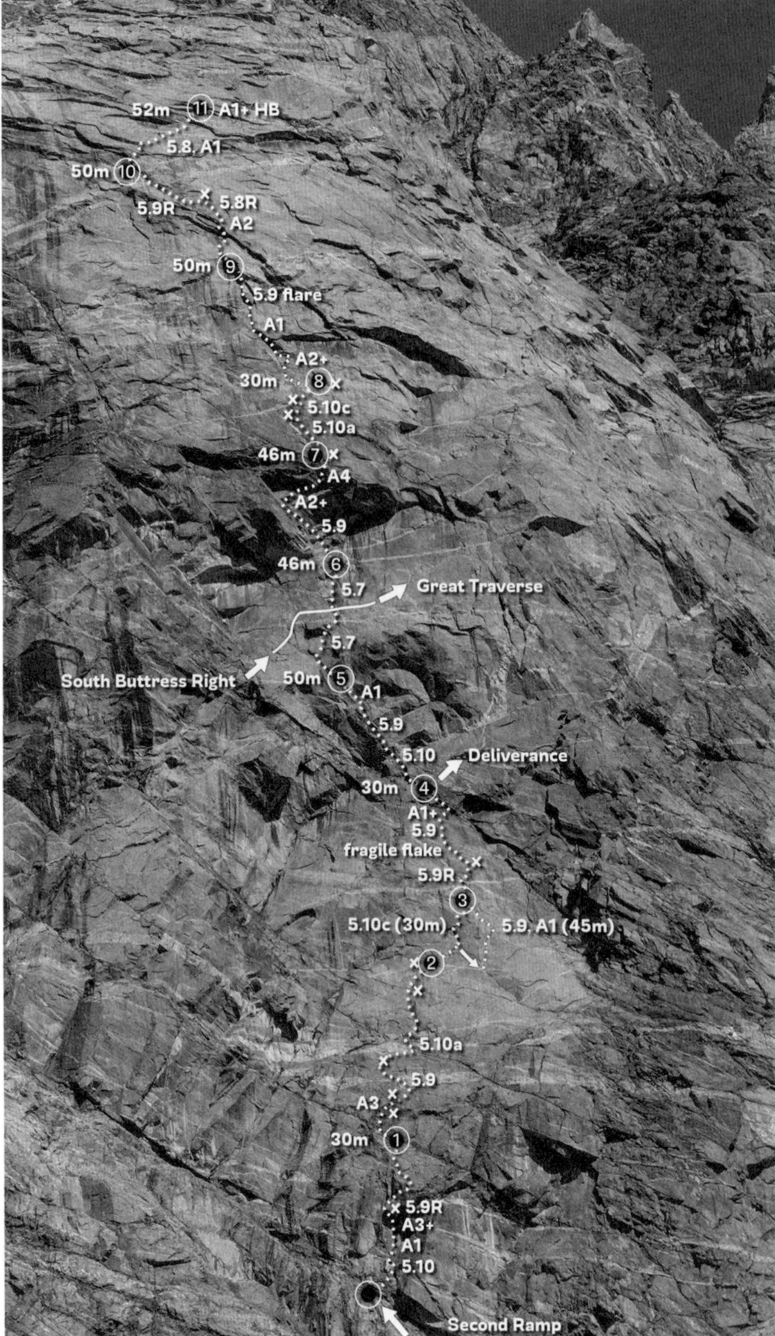

FIGURE 9-11. Mount Moran, south buttress, Whirl of Hate *(Route 2)*, VI, 5.10, A4

See *Figures 9-10*, *9-11*, and *9-12* for the location of the climb and the details of the route. Note that Beyer did two 5.6 pitches to access the Second Ramp from the huge, grassy First Ramp. These two pitches are located directly below the start of the difficult climbing and are not shown on the topos. Also note that the line in *Figure 9-11* is approximate, as are the locations of the bolts. **Gear:** Beyer suggests bringing three sets of cams to 3"; one 4.5" cam; 20 wires to 1"; 15 blades to Bugaboos; eight Lost Arrow pitons; one set of angle pitons to 1"; five Leepers; 10 heads; seven beaks; RURPs, mini-beaks, and hooks; two ⅜" bolt hangers; and one set of hexes from #5 to #10. (Sources: Correspondence with Jim Beyer; "The Tetons, Revisited," *American Alpine Journal* 43, no. 75 [2001]: pp. 116–121)

ROUTE 3. SOUTH BUTTRESS RIGHT. IV, 5.8, A1, or IV, 5.11a/b. First ascent July 25, 1961, by David Dornan and Herb Swedlund. This early Teton classic reaches the top of the south buttress from the southeast rather than directly from the south as in the 1953 route (*Route 10*). It is located to the right of a prominent set of water streaks on the buttress. The South Buttress Right is one of the finest pure rock climbs in the Tetons and has justifiably achieved popularity among those seeking a difficult climb in a truly wild and beautiful setting. All the pitches are quite good, and the rock is exceptional for the Teton Range, composed for the most part of a fine-grained granite. The Great Traverse, with huge overhangs above and below, is an unforgettable pitch featuring impressive exposure.

History: David Dornan submitted this short description for the 1962 *American Alpine Journal*:

The long first lead ended with a few direct-aid pitons; the second was a beautiful, moderate jam crack. The third presented perhaps the only route-finding problem, following the direct-aid crack on the right instead of going straight up. The fourth lead took us onto the great slab, which was easier to traverse than it looked; then we passed the overhangs with fifth and sixth class climbing to reach a square-cut ledge. The lead off this ledge ends in a blank wall that required a four-bolt ladder and a knife-blade piton. The remainder of the climbing was pleasant fifth class mainly in cracks. The climb ends in an arête, a parallel feature to the top of the South Buttress route. Climbing time was eleven hours. We used about 50 pitons, some 20 for direct aid.

Four days after completing the first ascent of this route with Dornan, Herb Swedlund did the highly sought-after first ascent of the Grand Teton's Black Ice

Couloir (*Grand Teton, Route 51*) with Ray Jacquot, thus snagging two super-classic Teton climbs. Dornan had previously attempted the South Buttress Right with Peter Lev, but the pair retreated after he took a fall while leading the third pitch—the 5.11a/b free crux. On July 18, 1973, hardmen Steve Wunsch and Art Higbee made the first free ascent using a flake variation to avoid the difficult undercling pitch, but the flake on this alternative route subsequently fell off. The first free ascent of the original route fell to Buck Tilley and Jim Mullin on August 2, 1978, with Stan Mish and Renny Jackson repeating the feat just a day later. Montana super-alpinists Alex Lowe and Jack Tackle accomplished the first winter ascent of the route from December 16 to 22, 1985.

Strategy: With a canoe, this is an excellent day climb. Camping below the south buttress or on Leigh Lake is also quite enjoyable.

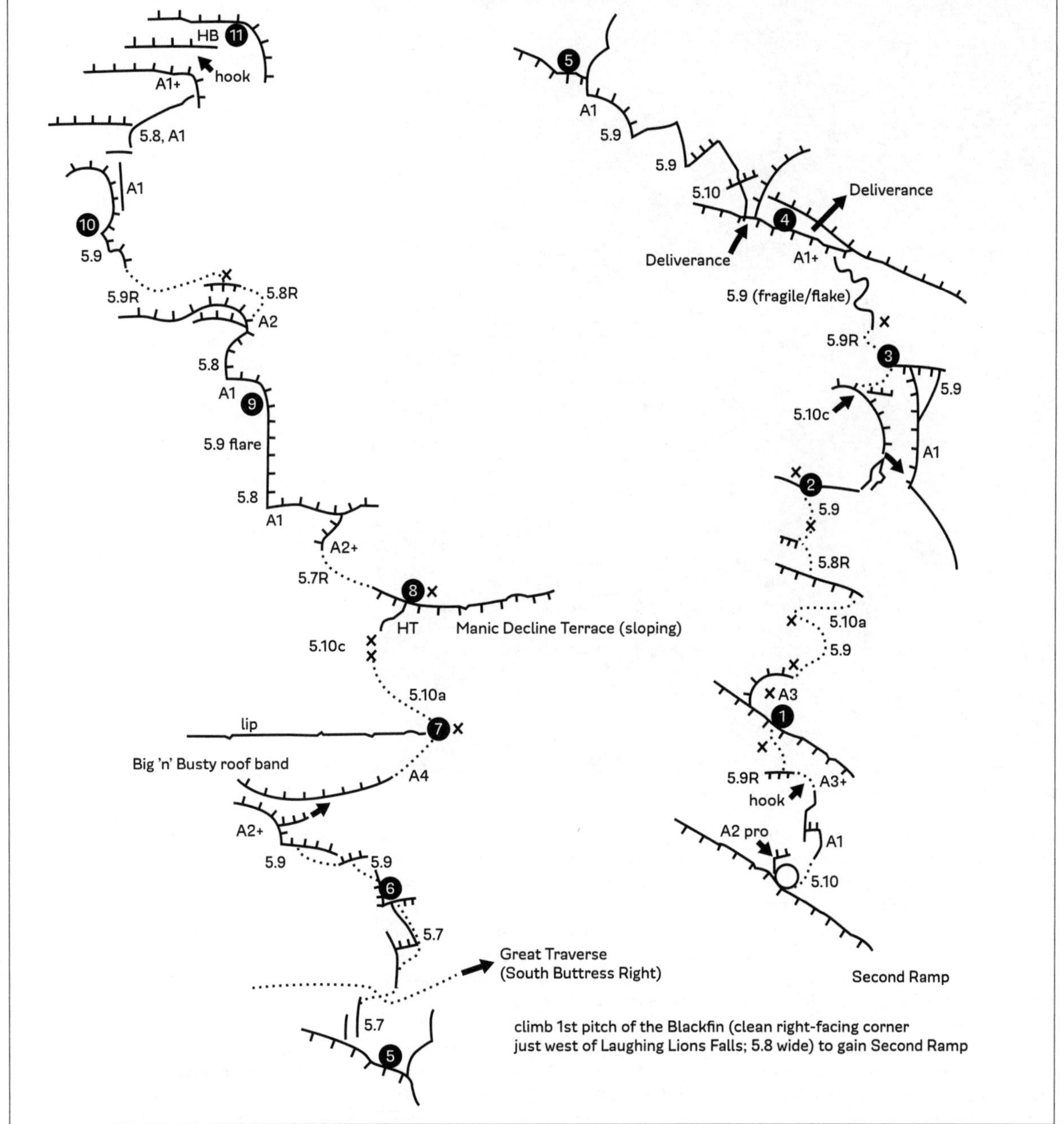

FIGURE 9-12. Mount Moran, south buttress, Whirl of Hate *(Route 2)*, VI, 5.10, A4

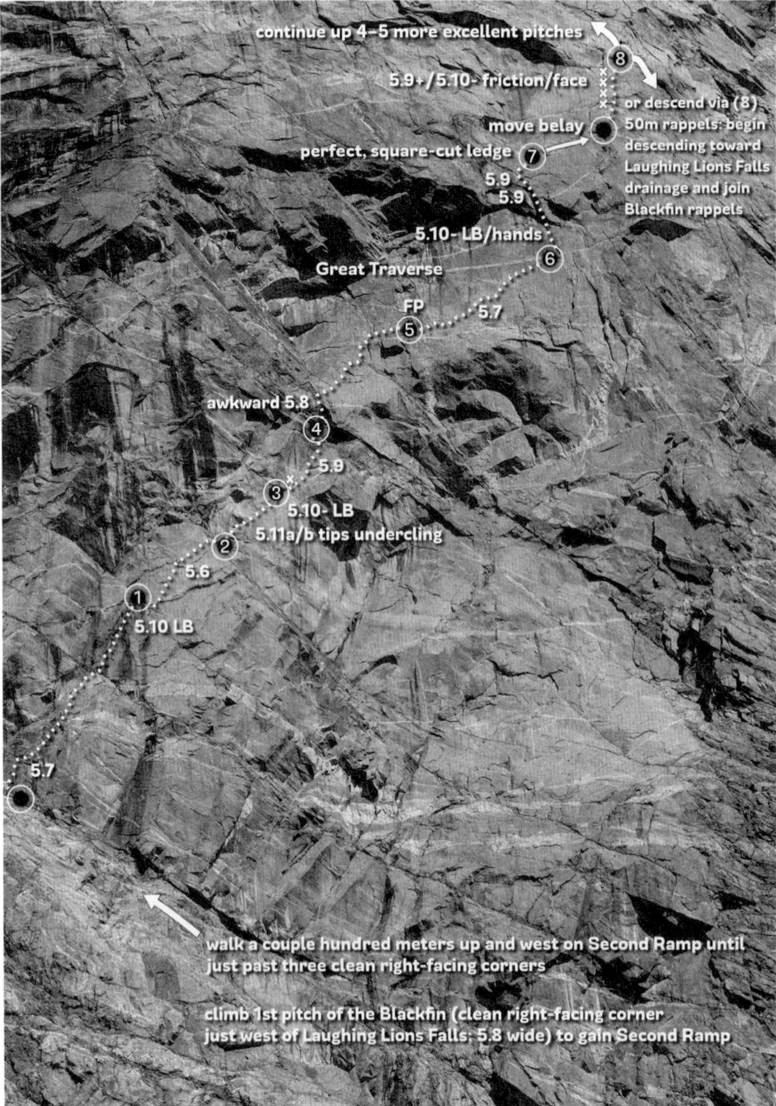

FIGURE 9-13. Mount Moran, South Buttress Right *(Route 3)*, IV, 5.11a/b

Route Description: The approach is the same as for the Direct South Buttress (see *Route 10*). The technical details of the route are presented in *Figure 9-13*; also see *Figure 9-10* for the location of the start of the climb. The South Buttress Right proper begins on the Second Ramp above the base of the buttress. This ramp is usually gained by means of the first pitch of the Blackfin route (*Route 1*), a clean right-facing corner (5.8 wide) just left (west) of Laughing Lions Falls; at the top the crack widens to a short, easy chimney. Once on the Second Ramp, scramble easily a couple hundred meters west along the ramp, passing the Blackfin corner system (recognized as being a large, loose-looking left-facing corner and chimney system) and then three prominent, sharp-featured right-facing corners. The beginning of the route, which is just past the third of these clean corners, is marked by a sharply pointed flake just above the terrace. The short third pitch holds the 5.11a/b crux, climbed by means of a fingertip undercling. There may be a few fixed pins on this pitch and one bolt (placed by an unknown climber in recent years). Two pitches above is the spectacular Great Traverse, which goes horizontally right across smooth slabs, using small flakes and hand traverses, for 30m to a good belay stance at a group of flakes. It is one of the most memorable pitches in the Teton Range and is as exciting to follow as it is to lead.

The seventh lead up from the end of the traverse originally used aid for 10m, with mixed aid and free climbing to turn the ceiling system above; this crack is now freed via 5.10- hand jamming/liebacking. This pitch ends on a perfect, square-cut belay ledge, the first roomy and comfortable area on the climb. Move the belay to the right end of this ledge and climb a thin crack and flakes to a blank wall with a four-bolt ladder (5.9+/5.10-; it is suitable for a museum display—*caution is advised*).

From the broad ledge at the end of this difficult lead many climbers make their descent to the right (east), as shown in *Figure 9-13*, but the original route continued up excellent rock—mainly in cracks—for four to five more pitches. The initial pitch consists of great face climbing up a blunt arête immediately above the belay (5.7+). A few more pitches continue up an arête that parallels the top of the Direct South Buttress route. The climbing finishes at a tree-covered ledge, from which one can descend to the right toward the Blackfin. This extension produces one of the most enjoyable rock climbs in the park. The now-standard descent from the top of the bolt ladder pitch leads off down to the east to the first of eight double-rope 50m rappels alongside and then down the Blackfin route. Some scrambling and downclimbing is necessary to link them together. The lower rappels go down the left-facing chimney system of the Blackfin route, and the final rappel is from a small tree on the ramp near the top of the first pitch of the Blackfin. **Gear:** For protection bring a double set of cams to 3", a 4" piece, and a few small cams and/or nuts for the undercling pitch. See *American Alpine Journal* 13, no. 1 (1962): pp. 216–20.

Variation: **DELIVERANCE.** IV, 5.10-, A3. First ascent July 6, 1990, by James Earl and Todd Cozzens. (See *Figure 9-14.*) The

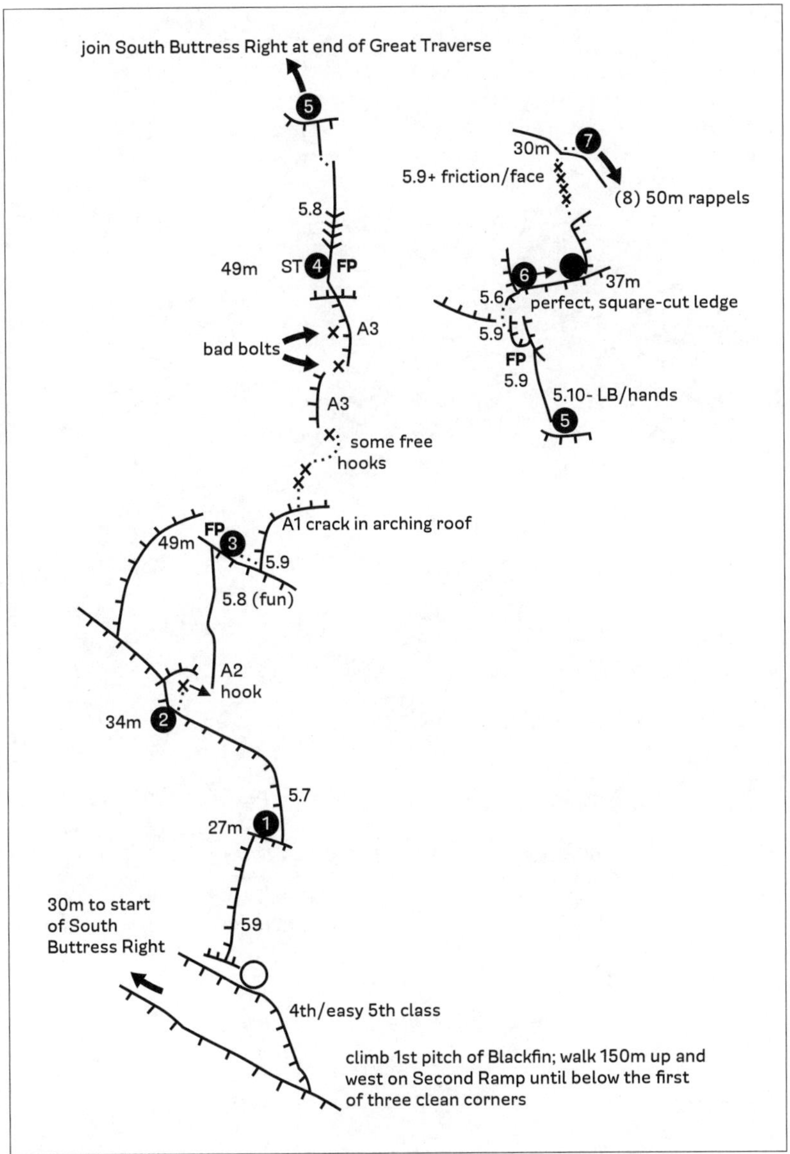

FIGURE 9-14. Mount Moran, South Buttress Right *(Route 3)*, variation: Deliverance, IV, 5.10-, A3

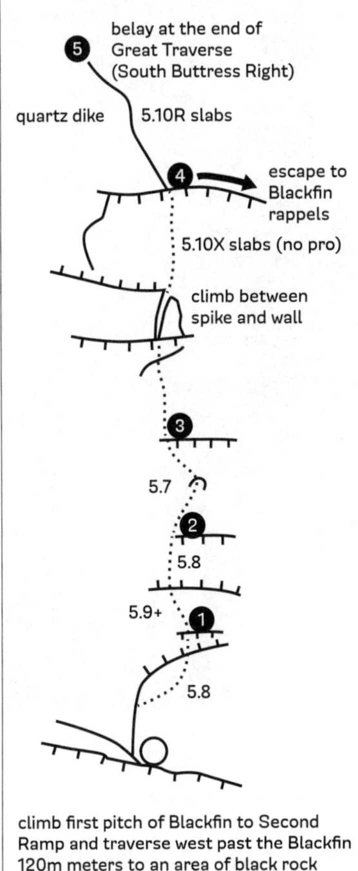

FIGURE 9-15. Mount Moran, South Buttress Right *(Route 3)*, variation: Kelley, IV, 5.10X

approach is the same as for the main South Buttress Right route. Once on the Second Ramp, scramble about 150m up and west until below the first of the three prominent, sharp-featured right-facing corners mentioned in the description of the original route. The first pitch begins by climbing this clean corner (5.9, 27m). Note that this variation and the two following variations join the South Buttress Right at the end of the Great Traverse, each by apparently different means. **Gear:** The first-ascent party suggests a "standard clean aid rack" plus six copperheads, four knifeblades, several Lost Arrow pitons, two RURPs, and hooks (including one large).

***Variation:* KELLEY.** IV, 5.10X. First ascent in late August 1998, by John Kelley (solo). This bold variation is located between the Deliverance and Habeler lines, and it joins the South Buttress Right at the eastern end of the Great Traverse; see *Figure 9-10* for the location of the start. As shown in *Figure 9-15*, the fourth and fifth pitches consist of runout slab climbing, the last of which is on a quartz dike. One can apparently escape from the final pitch by traversing over to the east to the Blackfin rappels. **Gear:** For protection a standard rack to 4" is suggested. (Source: correspondence with John Kelley)

***Variation:* HABELER.** IV, 5.8, A1. First ascent July 13, 1969, by Peter Habeler and Juris Krisjansons. This variation begins off the Second Ramp in a section of darker rock well to the east of the South Buttress Right. Use the first pitch of the Blackfin to access the Second Ramp and the start of the route. This was reported to be "an enjoyable climb without severe difficulties." The route has apparently not been repeated in the last several decades, so little information is available

Steve Rickert on pitch four of the South Buttress Right (Photo by Lanny Johnson)

aside from the entry in the 1971 *American Alpine Journal*:

Mount Moran, South Buttress Right, variation. On July 13, 1969, Juris Krisjansons and Peter Habeler made a significant new variation of this massive buttress by climbing the rock between the Black Fin and the South Buttress Right route. Six leads in this section of broken rock went generally straight up, involving F6 and occasionally F7 pitches [5.6–5.8]. The variation ends with a pendulum to the left (west) to join the normal South Buttress Right at the east end of the Great Traverse. This fine variation (F7 [5.8], A1) is more direct than the normal route, but it has the defect of missing the Great Traverse pitch which is one of the main attractions of the normal route.

Descend as described in the main South Buttress Right route.

ROUTE 4. SOUTH BUTTRESS HOUDINI. V, 5.11d. First ascent in October 2007, by Greg Collins and Hans Johnstone. (See *Figure 9-16*.) With this climb, prolific Teton alpinists Collins and Johnstone established an alternate start of two very difficult free pitches to the South Buttress Right (*Route 3*). They then joined that route for its crux pitch and finished by free climbing the upper pitches of Stuck Pig (see *Route 5*). After gaining access to the Second Ramp via the first pitch of the Blackfin—a clean right-facing corner (5.8 wide) that becomes a short, easy chimney at the top; see *Route 1*—proceed up to a clean, black right-facing corner 15m east of the start of the South Buttress Right. **Pitch 1:** Stem

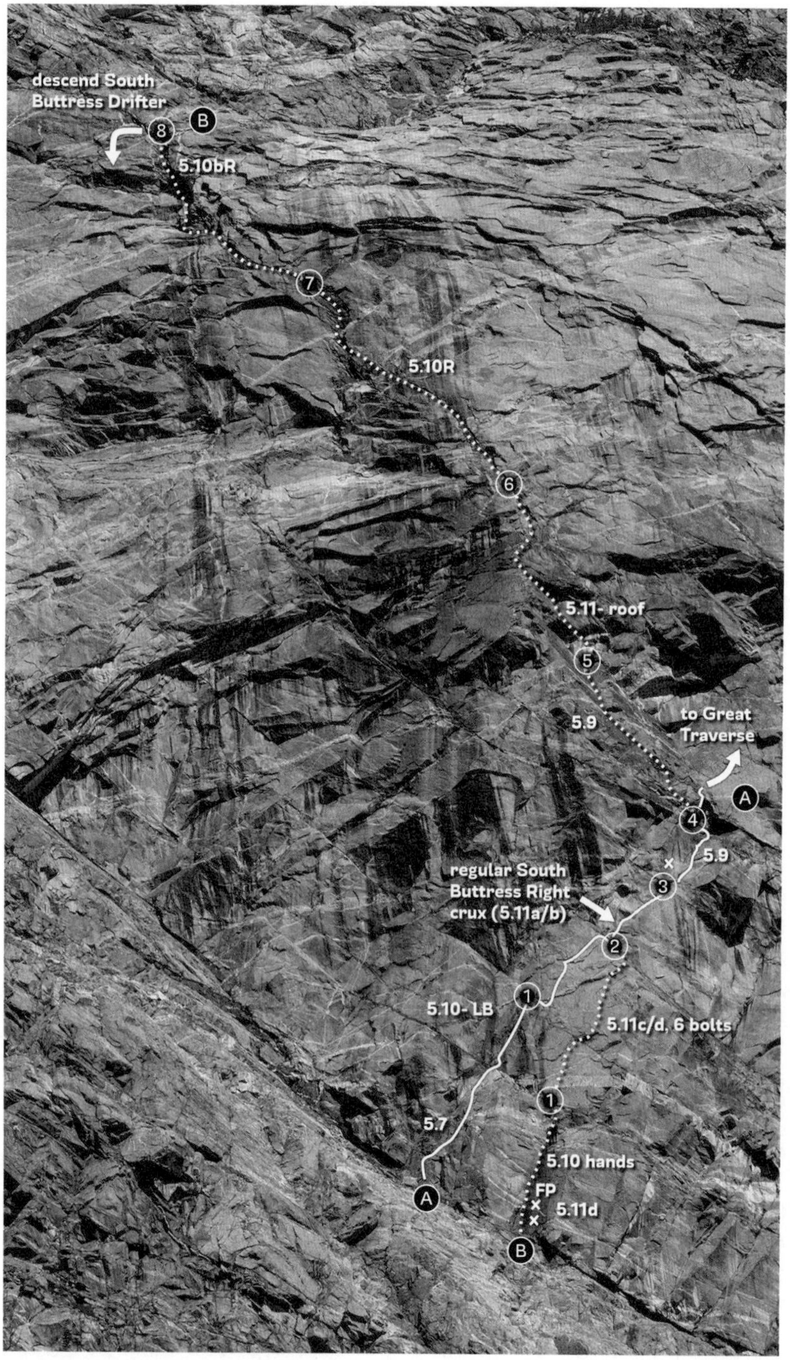

FIGURE 9-16. Mount Moran. (A) South Buttress Right *(Route 3)*, IV, 5.11a/b; (B) South Buttress Houdini *(Route 4)*, V, 5.11d

and lieback (5.11d) past two bolts and then up and into a splitter corner crack (5.10), protected with finger- to hand-size cams, and belay on a sloping ramp (28m). **Pitch 2:** Climb a short slab to a horizontal crack (5.7) and then move up and into a blank right-facing corner past six bolts (5.11c/d). Belay on a ramp or under the South Buttress Right crux (32m–44m). **Pitches 3–4:** Continue up through the South Buttress Right crux (5.11a/b) and that route's fourth pitch. **Pitch 5:** Climb up and left on left-facing black flakes and belay under a roof (5.9, 25m). **Pitch 6:** Climb the overhang/roof (5.11-), moving left, and belay on a ledge located left of a crack (25m, expect some lichen). **Pitch 7:** Climb a short wall up and into a left-trending crack feature (5.10R, 55m). **Pitch 8:** Continue up the left-trending crack feature, which contains vertical black flakes, and then go up and over the slot near the top (5.10bR, 60m). Descend the South Buttress Drifter (*Route 7*) via four double-rope rappels; see *Figure 9-20* for a depiction of this rappel route. **Gear:** For protection take two sets of cams from small to 3", plus one 4" piece for the Blackfin pitch. (Sources: interviews and correspondence with Greg Collins and Hans Johnstone)

ROUTE 5. STUCK PIG. V, 5.11a/b, C1+. First ascent August 11–12, 2004, by Nate Fuller and Patrick Wright. (See *Figure 9-17.*) This route and the South Buttress Houdini (*Route 4*) share the same upper half but are presented here as separate climbs. This route is really a variation on the South Buttress Right (*Route 3*), proceeding up and west from its crux pitch instead of heading east toward the Great Traverse. The name is derived from Fuller and Wright's decision to use big-wall tactics to establish the climb. (Sources: interview and correspondence with Patrick Wright and Nate Fuller)

ROUTE 6. KELLEY-BEYER. VI, 5.12-R/X, A0. First ascent in July 2000, by John Kelley and Jim Beyer, who established the route over six days and two attempts. See *Figure 9-18* for a general idea of where the initial portion of this big route goes and *Figure 9-19* for a topo, courtesy of Beyer. Not much is known about this route on the south buttress other than that it was an exceptional tour de force by these two climbers. It begins on the First Ramp and reaches the Second Ramp in three pitches. The fourth pitch goes to the same higher ramp as the South Buttress Drifter

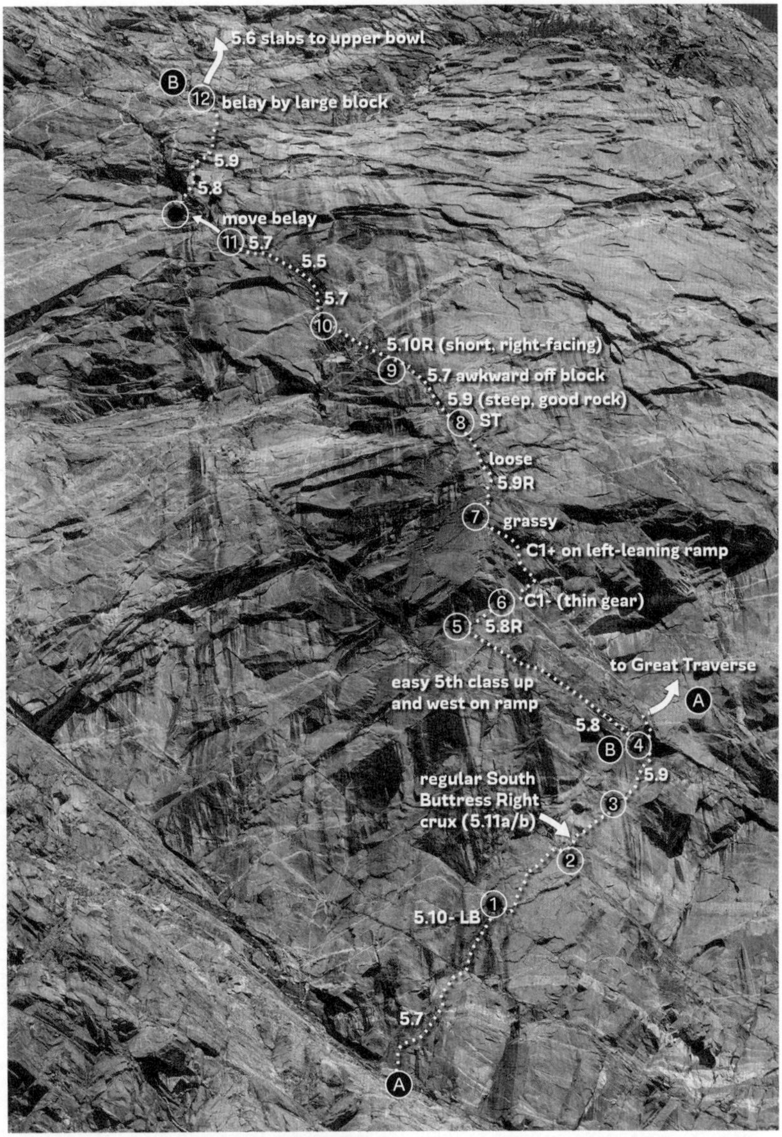

FIGURE 9-17. Mount Moran. (A) South Buttress Right *(Route 3)*, IV, 5.11a/b; (B) Stuck Pig *(Route 5)*, V, 5.11a/b, C1+

Jack Tackle on the first winter ascent of the South Buttress Right, December 16–22, 1985 (Photo by Alex Lowe)

(*Route 7*), at which point the Drifter route cuts up and west. Kelley and Beyer did 10 pitches of bold climbing to reach the bowl of the south buttress, with four of these rated R or X. They continued to the summit via the remainder of the Direct South Buttress (*Route 10*) and then descended the CMC route (*Route 20*). Some of the flavor of the climb is captured in Beyer's 2001 *American Alpine Journal* article, excerpted here with permission:

Just right of Drifter's fourth pitch, John led a blank corner with ledge-fall potential off the 5.10 crux. Above, I led a 5.11 bulge up into an arch. The arch looked too blank to free, so I banged in a good knifeblade and top-stepped to preview my options. The blade blew, and I took a 20-footer, landing on my back on a slab. I locked eyes with John and saw apprehension. It was the moment of truth. I started laughing like a psycho, and the moment passed.

I abandoned the arch. I could have traversed left to easier ground and an all-free pitch, but didn't—it was too close to Drifter. Instead, I traversed right to a spectacular arête. I drilled two aid bolts to reach the free climbing. . . .

Higher up the route is our ambitious goal: a big, blank, high-angle slab. It was John's lead, and he pulled a 5.11 crux right off my one-bolt belay. An overhanging corner was protected by sketchy wires on screamers and one bolt went in free onsight at continuous, contortionist 5.11, with a spot of 5.12.

The roof above went easily, and John was on the Great Slab. After drilling one bolt, he traversed right on fragile 5.10 crystals right above the very sharp edge of the roof below. After this super scary traverse, he finished the pitch on continuous 5.11/5.11+ with 20- to 25-foot runouts between bolts. This pitch is probably the hardest bold lead in the range. South Buttress Central crosses the Great Slab a bit higher and we traversed off and rappelled down Drifter because we were down to our last two bolts.

A few days later we were back, and I led a dangerous 5.10a pitch protected by sketchy aluminum heads and two bolts. John flashed the roof (5.11) at the top of the Great Slab and then avoided an easy shattered chimney with a clean 5.11 bulge. We bivied at the top of the face

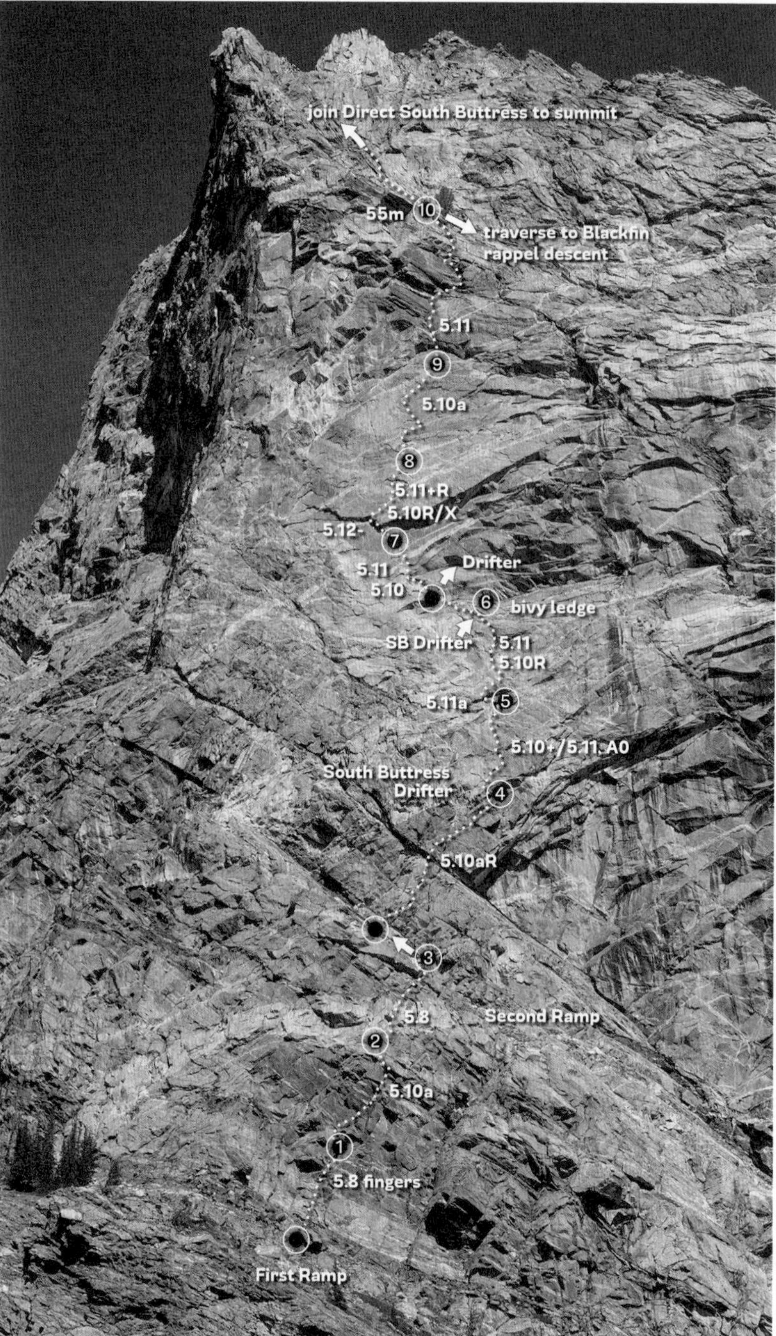

FIGURE 9-18. Mount Moran, south buttress, Kelley-Beyer *(Route 6)*, VI, 5.12-R/X, A0

and then continued 4,000 to 5,000 feet up the South Ridge on generally easy (5.6-5.8) soloing and some four to five roped pitches (one directly out of a notch at 5.9/5.10) to the summit of Mt. Moran.

We rushed down the CMC route (which is some 3,000 feet of scrambling) in the hopes of getting to our bivy gear before dark. We didn't make it and spent a memorable night in the rain without it.

Gear: Beyer recommends two sets of nuts, tiny to 1"; two sets of cams to 2.5", plus one 3" cam; and hammer and heads (optional). See *American Alpine Journal* 43, no. 75 (2001): pp. 116–121.

ROUTE 7. SOUTH BUTTRESS DRIFTER. V, 5.10c. First ascent in July 1998, by Jim Beyer (solo); second ascent in August 1998, by Jim Beyer and John Kelley. (See *Figure 9-20.*) This was the first major route to go up on the south buttress in three decades, following the establishment of the South Buttress Central (*Route 8*). Beyer climbed solo on the first ascent, putting up the route over "three days and five nights" [sic] and placing only three bolts. He likened it "in quality and effort to the Black Canyon [of the Gunnison]'s Scenic Cruise." Note that the topo reflects starting from the Second Ramp approximately 60m east of the beginning of *Route 10* and 60m west of the start of the South Buttress Right (*Route 3*). On the first ascent Beyer climbed three pitches—5.7, 5.6, and easy 5th class—from the First Ramp to the Second Ramp. A double-rope rappel route (shown on the topo) was established to facilitate descent from the western end of the large bowl on the buttress. **Gear:** For protection bring two to three sets of cams to 2", one 3" cam, and one 4" cam; many wires, from tiny to 1"; and alpine draws and quickdraws. (Sources: Jim Beyer and John Kelley; "The Tetons, Revisited," *American Alpine Journal* 43, no. 75 [2001]: pp. 116–121)

ROUTE 8. SOUTH BUTTRESS CENTRAL. IV, 5.8, A3, or IV, 5.10R. First ascent July 16, 1967, by Peter Koedt and Keith Becker; three earlier attempts on this route had been made by Koedt in 1966: on June 19 with Ken Fisher and Lynn Swanson, on July 30 and 31 with Will Bassett, and on August 6, also with Bassett; first free ascent in summer 1984, by Eric Breitenberger and Bill Trull. (See *Figure 9-21* for the technical details of the route.) The South Buttress Central is flanked by the South Buttress Prow (*Route 9*) on the west and the South Buttress Drifter (*Route 7*) on the east. Regrettably overlooked for decades, this climb is recognized now as a very difficult and daring route, especially considering the era in which it was established. Major features of the route include three horizontal quartz dikes cutting through "a great smooth slab some 300 feet across"

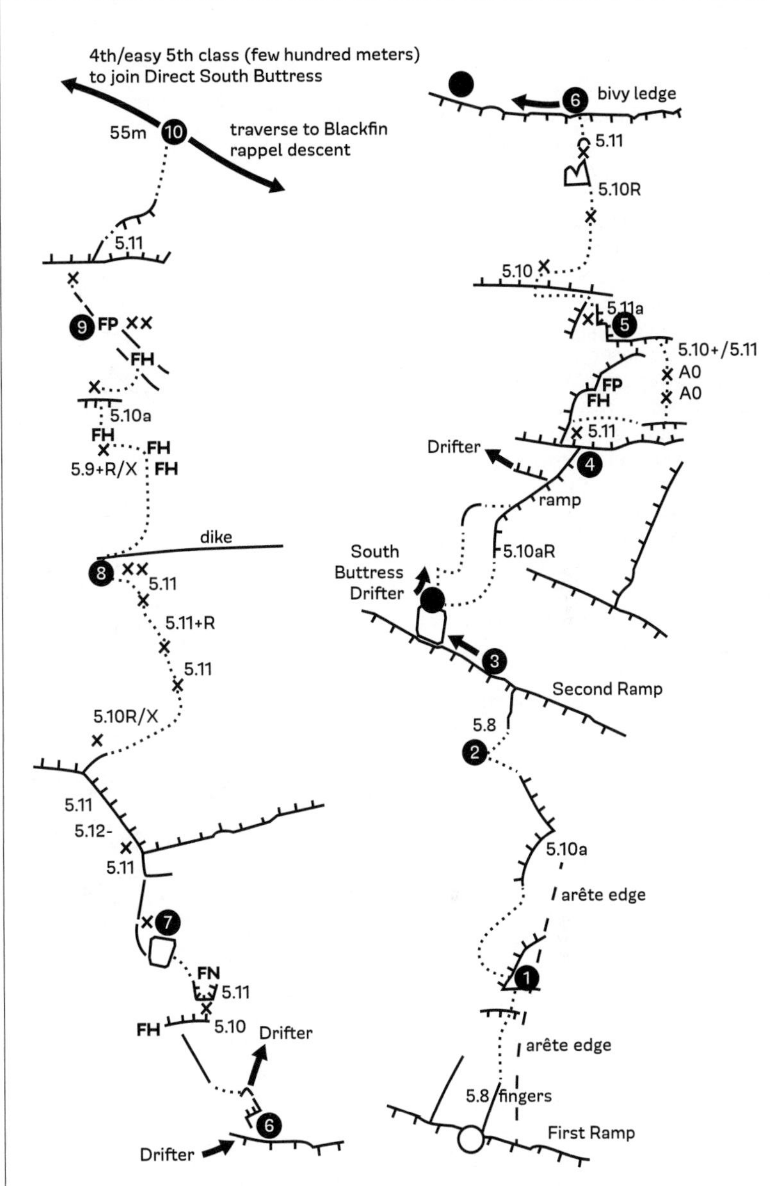

FIGURE 9-19. Mount Moran, south buttress, Kelley-Beyer *(Route 6)*, VI, 5.12-R/X, A0

found midway up the climb. This slab is similar to, but two or three times larger than, the Great Traverse slab of the South Buttress Right (*Route 3*). The Kelley-Beyer (*Route 6*) crosses this route in the vicinity of the dike traverse across the slab.

Proceed as in the Direct South Buttress route (*Route 10*) one pitch above the Second Ramp onto the main ledge system, which leads around on the west side of the buttress. As shown in *Figure 9-21*, four leads up and left take one to a belay just right of a huge right-facing corner system that arches up and to the right over the great, smooth slab cut by the three prominent horizontal quartz dikes. The South Buttress Prow continues up this corner system. Instead, climb up and to the right across the first two dikes—the crux lead of the route. The passage between the first and second dikes is especially serious: if this is done with aid, as on the first ascent, the absence of cracks makes the aid difficult to place, and if it is done free, there is also little protection available on the section of 5.10. This runout lead is a perilous undertaking, even though there are two bolts (dating from 1967) available. The sixth lead proceeds horizontally along the dike past a fixed piton to a belay at the end. From here there are two options for completing the route, based on two subsequent ascents. Both initially go up a right-facing corner and face to gain a ledge, at which point one alternative moves left and up a 5.9 wall and finishes in a V slot; the other alternative moves up and right past a bolt along a system of ledges to gain the bowl at the top of the south buttress. The original climb of the route apparently made yet a third finish, but its location is not clear. See *Route 10* for descent options from the bowl.

ROUTE 9. SOUTH BUTTRESS PROW. IV, 512b. First ascent September 29, 2006, by Bean Bowers, Greg Collins, and Hans Johnstone. This incredibly strong team of seasoned Teton hardmen put up this proud route onsight—perhaps the most difficult one-day effort the range has seen to date. Their eight-pitch climb is located on the left wall of a large right-facing corner system east of the Direct South Buttress (*Route 10*); see *Figure 9-22* for route details. This wall diverges to the west from the initial corners and huge slabs and dikes that make up the South Buttress Central (*Route 8*). Begin by climbing the first pitch of the Blackfin (5.8 wide; see *Route 1*) to gain access to the Second Ramp. Continue out to the west end of the ramp. **Pitch 1:** Climb the initial pitch of the Direct South Buttress (5.7). **Pitch 2:** Follow the path of least resistance to the base of the main corner system. **Pitch 3:** At the point where the South Buttress Central route leads out and east across an immense slab, head straight up an initial corner (5.10bR) to a belay at a "cryptic corner." **Pitch 4:** Climb the cryptic corner (5.9R/X), which is the key to getting to the overhanging crack on the main white wall of the corner system. Belay at the base of the crack, just right of the prow of the buttress. **Pitch 5:** This crux pitch consists of sustained, partly overhanging 5.11+ off-fingers jamming, giving it an overall rating of 5.12b—a testament to the considerable abilities of Bean Bowers, who got the onsight. Bowers described it as "mostly one and a half to tight, two-inch jams with a technical endurance crux at the end as you pull the final lip on rattly finger locks and smeary feet." **Pitch 6:** Climb a corner and face (5.10b, somewhat licheny) and exit left around two large, wedged blocks to a stance in a small corner. **Pitch 7:** Climb around a final small roof on its left side, then cross over its top and back right up steep and exposed finger locks, exiting directly on the prow of the buttress (5.11-). **Pitch 8:** Climb the final 5.5 hand-traverse pitch of the Direct South Buttress and exit into the huge bowl at the top. For descent the first-ascent party used the South Buttress Drifter rappels (see *Figure 9-20*). *Route 10* describes additional descent options accessed from this bowl, including the Blackfin rappel route. (Sources: Interviews with Greg Collins and Hans Johnstone; Alpinist.com)

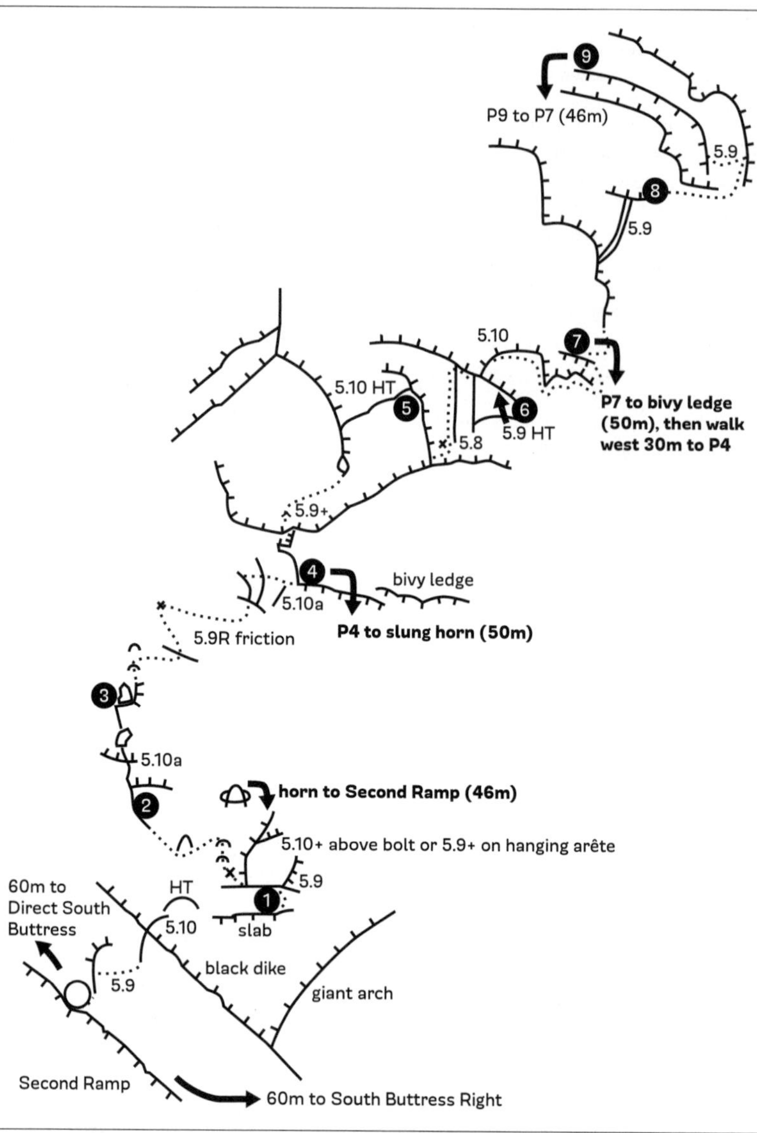

FIGURE 9-20. Mount Moran, South Buttress Drifter *(Route 7)*, V, 5.10c

ROUTE 10. DIRECT SOUTH BUTTRESS. V, 5.8, A1, or V, 5.12a. (**Note:** The Grade V rating for this climb reflects the overall difficulty of the ascent if one goes to the summit; the climb was originally rated IV, 5.7, A3 due

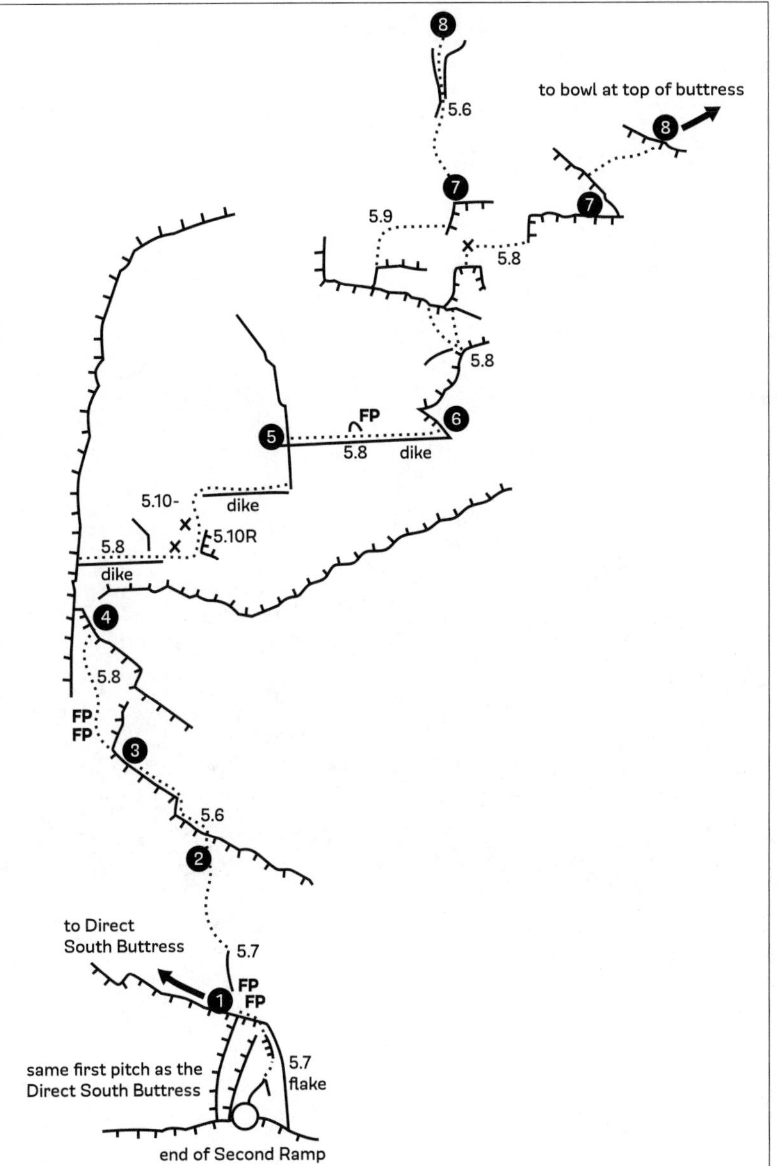

FIGURE 9-21. Mount Moran, South Buttress Central *(Route 8)*, IV, 5.10R

to the dubious quality of the piton used for the pendulums.) First ascent August 29–30, 1953, by Richard Emerson, Don Decker, and Leigh Ortenburger; first free ascent July 3, 1979, by Stan Mish, with Hal Gribble; first winter ascent January 5, 1988, by Jack Tackle and Alex Lowe (to top of climb only); first winter ascent to summit March 5–7, 2001, by Hans Johnstone, Mark Newcomb, and Renny Jackson. The Direct South Buttress of Mount Moran with its southern aspect, fine rock, and airy exposure has become a Teton classic. At the time of its first ascent, the route was one of the longest roped climbs in the country. The prospective climber now has the option of doing the route as a pure rock climb, by descending from the top of the buttress—or one can embark on one of the longer Teton routes by continuing to the summit of Mount Moran.

History: In 1935 Phil Smith and Eldon Petzoldt climbed the upper portion of the great south buttress of Mount Moran (see *Route 11*), utilizing an intricate traverse from the CMC campsite across the vast southern bastions of the peak. They had thought about attempting the ridge from the bottom of Leigh Canyon, but the formidable lower buttress didn't seem possible given its length, numerous towers, and smooth-looking verticality. Nearly 20 years later, in 1953, Leigh Ortenburger and prolific Teton first ascensionist William Buckingham conducted a reconnaissance and decided the same thing, estimating that nearly 150m of direct aid climbing would be required. That same year, Jenny Lake climbing ranger Richard Emerson, one of the strongest rock climbers of the day, went into Leigh Canyon twice and scoped out a possible line on the daunting lower buttress. He recruited Don Decker for an August 14 attempt, and to everyone's astonishment the pair established a high point on a 4-inch ledge at the beginning of what would become the crux pendulum and aid pitch—after free climbing some 600m up the wall, and before retreating in the face of a Teton hailstorm.

On the evening of August 28, 1953, Emerson and Decker were camped below the buttress with Ortenburger, prepared for a full-on assault in the morning. When the trio reached Emerson and Decker's previous high point, Ortenburger noted that "the face to their right was smooth granite, about 60 feet across and at an angle of 80°." On the far side of the face they could see a perfect aid crack—if only they could get to it! Emerson tried a line up and to the left of the huge overhangs above. Realizing it wouldn't go, he lowered Ortenburger nearly 15m from the previous high point so Ortenburger could check a possible traverse of the face below. He found nothing there; they would have to engineer a way over to the aid crack. Emerson once again took the lead, moving out of sight of Ortenburger, who was belaying. Two hours later, after doing two separate pendulums from dubiously placed wafer pitons, Emerson yelled, "Off belay!" at the base of the crack. Another six hours passed while Emerson aided the crack (with seven pin placements) and then the others followed his impressive technical lead. In fading daylight the team tried to go straight up to escape their precarious position, but when this didn't work, Decker found a hand traverse leading east and into the huge bowl at the top of

Bean Bowers onsighting the crux 5.12b pitch of the South Buttress Prow (Photo courtesy of Helen Bowers)

the buttress. Here they bivouacked in "a friendly grove of pine trees," as Ortenburger later wrote in the 1954 *American Alpine Journal*. "With a good fire they passed a comfortable night on a mattress above pine needles." The following day they reached the summit at 2 PM after climbing the upper 800m of the ridge. Then they scurried down the CMC route and continued down to the lake and their trusty rowboat.

The first free ascent of the route was accomplished on July 3, 1979, by Stan Mish and Hal Gribble, with Mish leading a low traverse across the pendulum slab at 5.9 and the short aid crack at 5.12a. He had missed the first free ascent of the South Buttress Right by a day in 1978. The second known free ascent occurred seven years later in August 1986, by Steve Petro and Jack Tackle. Tackle teamed up with Montana super-alpinist Alex Lowe for the first winter ascent of the initial buttress on January 5, 1988. Lowe returned during the late winter of 1999 and repeated the initial buttress with Renny Jackson. Many others tried to complete the entire climb to the summit over the years. This first winter ascent was finally achieved by Jackson, Hans Johnstone, and Mark Newcomb from March 5 to 7, 2001.

Strategy: As a rule, two days should be allowed for the complete ascent of the south buttress and ridge to the summit, although it has been done as a day climb several times. Camping in Leigh Canyon is not only wild and beautiful but also convenient, providing the opportunity to study the ridge from below and get an alpine start in the morning. A rock climb of the initial buttress makes for a great day in a wilderness setting, facilitated by the established Blackfin rappel route.

Route Description: See *Figure 9-9* for an overview of the route, *Figure 9-10* for the location of the start, and *Figures 9-23* and *9-24* for route details. Hike into Leigh Canyon to the stream below Laughing Lions Falls. Here one will see two conspicuous grassy ramps cutting across the lower part of the south buttress to the left of the falls. The original climb took the First Ramp to its far (western) end and then climbed two pitches up a moderate chimney slightly on the west side of the ridge crest (some loose rock) to gain the west end of the Second Ramp. *That approach is no longer recommended.* Instead, climb

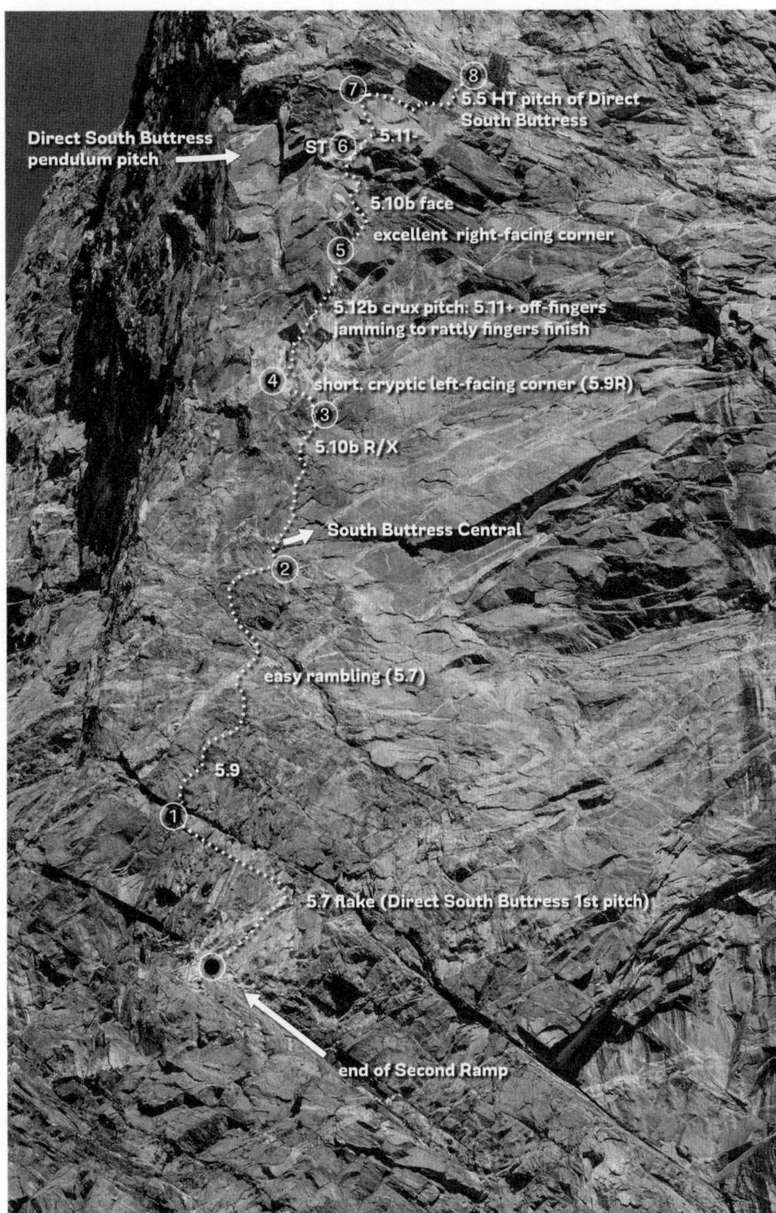

FIGURE 9-22. Mount Moran, South Buttress Prow *(Route 9)*, IV, 5.12b

the first pitch of the Blackfin (*Route 1*) —a clean right-facing corner (5.8 wide) located just west of Laughing Lions Falls—to reach the eastern end of the Second Ramp. Note the small tree that provides the final anchor of the Blackfin rappel route near the top of the corner. Located just a few meters to the west is the Blackfin chimney system. Proceed up and west along the Second Ramp for approximately 300m to near its west end, where one easy 5th-class section leads to the end of the ramp and the start of the climb.

The long first pitch (5.7) heads up, right, and then back left onto a ledge system that curves up to the left (west) side of the crest (40m). Continue out along this ledge for another 40m or so and belay after a short downclimb. The next pitch

FIGURE 9-23. Mount Moran, Direct South Buttress *(Route 10)*, V, 5.8, A1, or V, 5.12a

Climber on the eighth pitch of Mount Moran's Direct South Buttress (Renny Jackson archive)

zigzags out left across a slabby 4th-class section and then back up on a ramp to avoid a loose 5.8 corner. Looking back toward the ridge crest, two large flakes will be seen: the lower is gray and separated from the mountain by a fine chimney, and the upper is capped by white rock and is to the right of the first. Try to avoid turning up the wall too soon. The seventh lead as shown in *Figure 9-24* starts with a climb up to and then off of a remarkably thin flake. Proceed up to a 4-inch ledge and, from this ledge, traverse up and right via tricky balance moves to the very edge of the ridge crest. Step around the corner

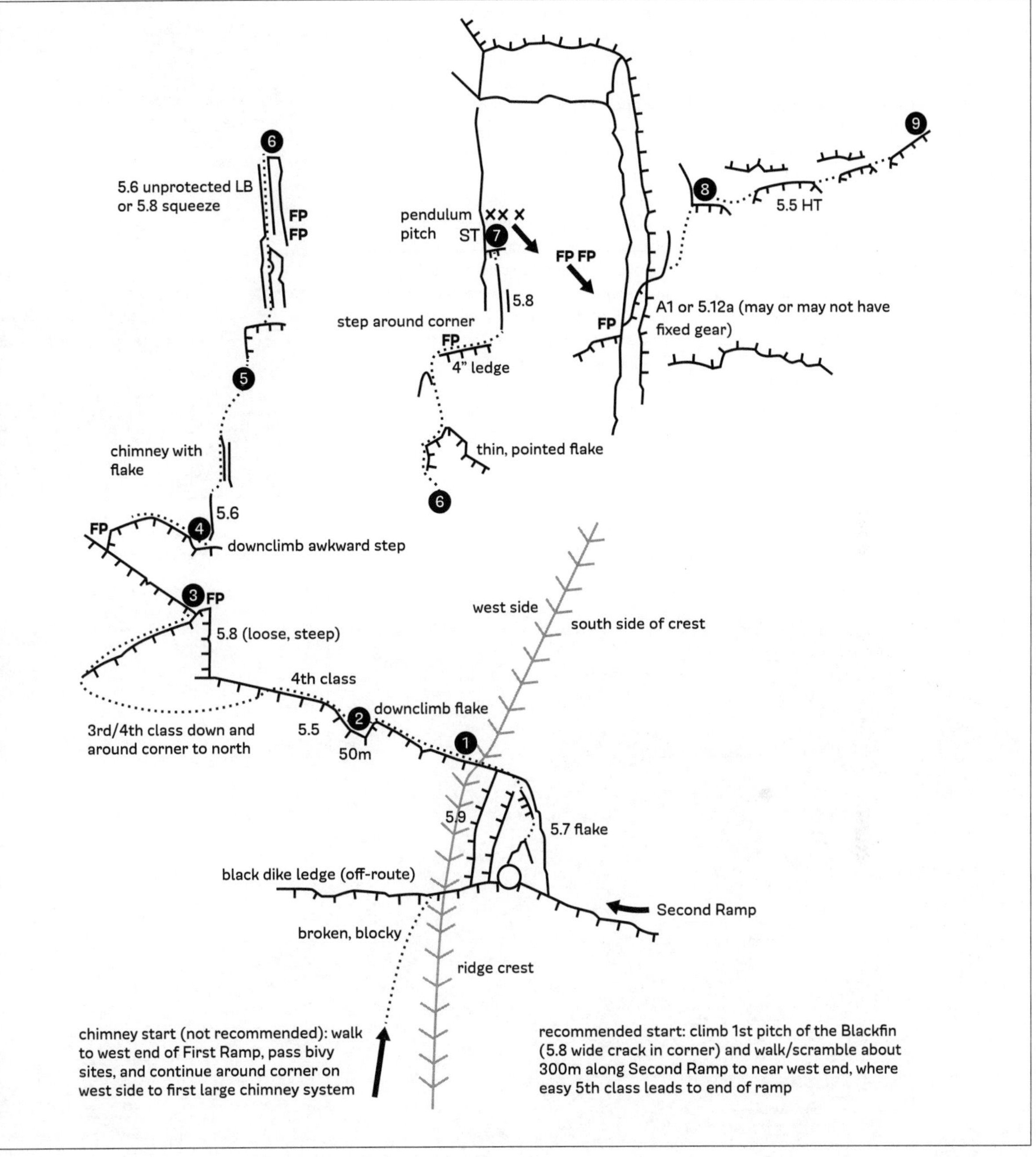

FIGURE 9-24. Mount Moran, Direct South Buttress *(Route 10)*, V, 5.8, A1, or V, 5.12a

and continue up (5.8) to a stance for the two-bolt belay. (**Note:** These were replaced in 2016 with two stainless steel 3.8" bolts.) This spectacular position at the left edge of the now-famous 80° face is located just below the large ceiling-like overhang that caps the initial 500m high-angle portion of the buttress. Across this face a beautiful thin crack will be seen leading up and over the overhanging corner at the right (east) edge of the face. The problem is reaching it.

Using a couple of intermediate fixed pitons, one can tension traverse down and over to the 3-inch ledge at the base of the thin crack. Alternatively, by dropping down lower, one can use holds at the lower edge of the undercut face to pull across onto the 3-inch ledge (reported to be 5.9 face climbing during the first free ascent). (**Note:** In 1953 this entire pendulum was done from a single, partially driven wafer piton.) If one is aiming to free the thin crack (5.12a), most parties bring the belayer over to the stance at the base of the crack. If one is aiding, simply continue up the crack and around the overhang to the right (A1). This pitch has now seen several free ascents. An exposed but comfortable 2-foot ledge is reached at the end of this lead. The last pitch of the difficult section of this route consists of a fun hand traverse out of sight around to the right (east). This finally puts one above the buttress in a large, open bowl just below and east of the first level section of the ridge.

Here, one is presented with several options. (**Note:** If needed, an excellent bivouac can be made among the pine trees in this bowl, although water may be scarce in late season.) (1) *To descend via the Blackfin rappels,* proceed 75m–100m to the upper eastern edge of the bowl. From there, several double-rope rappels from trees and other fixed anchors will bring one to the usual multiple-rappel route for the South Buttress Right, down the Blackfin chimneys (see *Routes 1* and *3*). (2) *To continue to the summit of Mount Moran,* continue upward on the left (west) edge of the bowl and exit onto the horizontal ridge crest at the very top of the main buttress. This entire horizontal section must be negotiated, involving numerous pitches of enjoyable but sometimes exposed climbing over or around towers to reach the final sharp tower on the crest. From the summit of this tower, a 20m rappel on the east side permits one to reach the notch beyond (north of) the tower. Now traverse slightly to the right (east) and climb the long (650m) but easier ridge above, keeping generally on the right (east) side of the crest. The 1935 Upper South Ridge route (*Route 11*) is joined in this section. Combined with the south buttress below, the complete south ridge does indeed provide a long climb. (3) *To access the*

Renny Jackson on the hand traverse (pitch 9) during the first winter ascent of the South Buttress Direct route (Photo by Mark Newcomb)

FIGURE 9-25. Mount Moran, south buttress, west aspect, overview of western routes *(Routes 12–19)*

original descent route, proceed as in the second option to the notch north of the final sharp tower on the ridge crest. The original descent starts here and involves two steep parallel couloirs or gullies that descend to the west (see *Figures 9-25* and *9-26*). The notch is at the head of the first (the more southerly) of these couloirs. *Do not* continue along the crest and attempt to climb down directly into the second (more northerly) of these couloirs. Instead, climb down into the first couloir for 60m to 90m until one can conveniently cross the separating rib into the more northerly couloir; from above, this part of the descent looks worse than it is. With adroit routefinding this main western couloir permits downclimbing and scrambling all the way into the main drainage separating Mount Moran from Thor Peak. No rappels are required. As Leigh Ortenburger said in his classic way, "No matter what, do *not* try to continue all the way down the first southern couloir, for it is blocked by huge overhanging chockstones, and terrifying rappels into outer space are required."

(4) *To descend by way of the CMC campsite*, proceed as in the second option to the notch north of the final sharp tower on the ridge crest. This effective but

FIGURE 9-26. Mount Moran, south buttress, west aspect, overview of western routes *(Routes 12–19)*

seldom-used route of descent involves a traverse (roughly horizontally) east (see *Figure 9-9*), first across the notch in the Blackfin above the third tower and then across various gullies (some of which may contain snow) and the south ridge of Drizzlepuss. It eventually emerges on the southeast side of Drizzlepuss at the CMC campsite. One can follow the climbers' trail down from there. **Gear:** For protection on this route take a standard rack to 4", with small wireds and RPs. See *American Alpine Journal* 9, no. 1 (1954): pp. 172–84, illus.; *Harvard Mountaineering* 16 (May 1963): pp. 82–83; *Sierra Club Bulletin* 39, no. 6 (June 1954): pp. 27–33.

Variation: IV, 5.7, A3, or IV, 5.10. First ascent September 9, 1958, by Richard Sykes and William Briggs. Near the top of the south buttress, from the 2-foot ledge at the end of the final aid crack and before making the final long hand traverse, one can turn upward and complete the climb in a slightly more direct manner. This lead goes up over a sequence of small bulges in difficult and uncompromising rock.

Variation: V, 5.9, A1. First ascent August 12–13, 1965, by Peter Cleveland, Roland Fleck, and Jack Stauffer. From the west end of the Second Ramp, this variation, which is not well understood, follows a line between the standard Direct South Buttress route and the South Buttress, West Face (*Route 12*), emerging at the top of the first step on the south ridge. Begin by traversing west from the end of the Second Ramp for one ropelength, then scramble farther west to the beginning of a gully. Climb half a lead up this gully and then one and a half leads up and left on a sloping ledge. The route now passes up and right over three steps of increasing difficulty, the last via a strenuous jam crack to a good belay ledge on the corner of the south face west of the south ridge. The next pitch traverses right for 6m and then diagonally up and right for 18m (5.9) over a thin face to a wall below a sloping ledge. Aid was used to pass this wall. Now traverse left 6m to a good belay ledge. After a small overhang, climb right to an open book well below a large, black overhang. One more lead plus some scrambling places one on top of the first step of the south buttress. Two days were spent on this long climb to the summit of Mount Moran.

***Variation:* SOUTH BUTTRESS WRONG.** IV, 5.11-, A1. First ascent by Ken Sims and Rick Reese (date unknown). It is unclear exactly when this climb was done and whether the first ascensionists joined the Direct South Buttress route, but a topo was drawn up after the climb entitled "South Buttress Wrong." It is located roughly between *Routes 9* and *10* and proceeds upward for four pitches, joining the regular Direct South Buttress at the pendulum. Reaching the start apparently involves a traverse above the Second Ramp. **Pitch 1:** Face climb directly up from a block with slings (5.8, marginal pro) to an open corner (5.9+) that leads to a belay in an alcove. **Pitch 2:** Climb a right-trending finger crack to its top, then pendulum right (5.9, A1) to a right-leaning hand crack. Partway up this crack head left via thin crack and face climbing (5.9) to a small ledge. Continue up and right and belay where possible. **Pitch 3:** Proceed up through a small roof to a thin crack (described as an "RP crack") that is climbed via face moves (5.10+/5.11-) to a ledge. Continue up a short distance (5.10) and belay. **Pitch 4:** From the belay face climb out and right to an open corner. Ascend this corner (5.9) to a roof that is immediately below the pendulum pitch of the Direct South Buttress. Join that route here, at the base of the 5.12a/A1 pitch.

ROUTE 11. UPPER SOUTH RIDGE. II, 5.4. First ascent June 30, 1935, by Phil Smith and Eldon Petzoldt. (See *Figure 9-9*.) The principal south ridge of Mount Moran, as seen from the west or east in profile, has two distinct sections. The buttress forming the bottom 500m rises smoothly at a very high angle to its overhanging cap. The upper south ridge sweeps up to the summit in a series of giant steps, each adorned with pinnacles. This route avoids the lower buttress by contouring in above it from the east. From the usual CMC campsite, traverse left and up over grass- and tree-covered ledges along the south edge of the talus slope to the crest of the south ridge of Drizzlepuss. Climb down northward into the large bowl of the upper south face of Mount Moran. Below, toward Leigh Canyon, this bowl funnels into the narrow and steep drainage of Laughing Lions Falls. Scramble west, crossing the bowl into and up a rotten gully leading to the notch in the upper Blackfin ridge; this is the same notch crossed from west to east during an escape from the top of the south buttress routes to the CMC campsite. From the notch descend slightly on the far (west) side to a grassy bench and continue on to the south ridge, which is then followed to the summit. Most parties stay somewhat on the right (east) side of the crest of the south ridge until the final step is reached. This final step, which leads onto the southwest corner of the summit plateau, is steeper than those below and contains difficult rock that can be avoided by traversing left to the west side of the ridge, where two moderate pitches (5.4) lead to the summit plateau.

Although not difficult, this route is an interesting and challenging climb partly because much of the route cannot be seen at the start. The rock is solid and enjoyable and the terrain is not on the beaten path of the standard routes. Along the traverse to gain the south ridge, rather than crossing the Blackfin one can climb its upper part and join the south ridge higher up. This alternative may have been selected by the first-ascent party, who indicated that they stayed somewhat on the left (west) of the crest of the south ridge rather than on right (east). **Time:** 8 hours from the CMC campsite.

Mount Moran, South Buttress (West Aspect)

The western aspect of the south buttress and south ridge of Mount Moran represents an immense amount of terrain—huge faces, major couloirs, minor gullies, and several fine subridges. This sector is bounded on the west by the southwest couloir (see *Route 18*), which leads directly up to the west ridge (see *Route 19*). Because of the difficulty in accessing this side of the peak, climbing here has a strong wilderness feel. For those contemplating an ascent of one of these seldom-traveled routes, *Route 18* provides an excellent opportunity to survey this mysterious zone. See *Figures 9-25* and *9-26* for an overview of the following climbs.

ROUTE 12. SOUTH BUTTRESS, WEST FACE. IV, 5.7, A3. First ascent August 25–26, 1962, by Art Gran and John Hudson. (See *Figures 9-25* and *9-26*.) This very long route, which lies well around on the west face of the south buttress, is continuously steep and difficult. Little is known about this climb other than what was reported by the first-ascent party, which is presented here; a second ascent has probably not been done. From Leigh Canyon ascend the talus, go around left under the beginnings of the south buttress, and enter the north–south side canyon described in *Route 18*. Continue about 100m up the gully to the second rotten inside corner, which is climbed for 10m to a belay position beneath a bulge on the left. This point marks the start of the climb, and unless it is found the following route description cannot be understood. The first pitch goes 42m up the inside corner to a belay on top of a capping chockstone. Now climb diagonally up the right wall and around the corner to and past a large ledge, ending the ropelength on a higher ledge. The large ledge is the westward continuation of the First Ramp of the south buttress. Below this large ledge the rock is somewhat rotten, but it is noticeably better above. Climb the nose above, then go up a shallow groove to an overhang from which one exits to the right and up, to a belay ledge. The fourth pitch ascends the inside corner above until it becomes overhanging, at which point the route moves left and up to a flake. From its top traverse 8m right and up to a ledge at the end of a 34m lead. The next long lead takes one up past another large ledge to the beginning of a small ramp leading left and up; this large ledge is the westward continuation of the Second Ramp of the south buttress.

After 12m up this ramp, climb up and right over a bulge, passing one ledge, and continue up and right to another at the end of 30m. Now gain the slab above and ascend to a belay under an overhang. The eighth lead starts to the right, then goes up a steep wall, and finishes by moving left and up, first with a hand traverse and then with a crack and two inside corners, to the beginning of a second large ramp. Climb up and left one long pitch on the ramp, past a short wall, ultimately going around the corner to a large block. The 10th lead continues up and left on the ramp, reaching a flake, from the top of which another ramp is gained and followed out left to its end. Now climb a steep corner and exit to the right to a nose; move up and left and climb another corner to a roof, where one exits to the left to a small ramp. The 12th pitch goes up over a bulge, left on a ramp, around a corner, and then straight up to a bulge, where a traverse to the right leads to a large ledge. Scramble right on this ledge around the corner and then up to the right, entering a chimney. The final pitch goes up this long chimney all the way to the crest of a west spur of the south buttress. From this point one can traverse over to the uppermost part of the Direct South Buttress (*Route 10*) on the level section at the top of the buttress. The ascent can be continued to the summit of Mount Moran via the Upper South Ridge route (*Route 11*), or one can descend via one of the methods outlined under *Route 10*. This climb required knifeblade pitons and many angle pitons to 2" on the first ascent. Many parties will find two days necessary for this climb, especially if the ridge is completed to the summit. See *American Alpine Journal* 13, no. 2 (1963): pp. 410–20, illus.

ROUTE 13. REVOLUTIONARY CREST. IV, 5.8, or V, 5.8 (to the summit). First ascent July 15, 1982, by Jim Beyer and Dave Koch. Note that the route line in *Figure 9-26* is approximate; also see *Figure 9-25*. This is an exceptionally long climb, involving 16 pitches just to gain the crest of the south ridge about 600m below the summit. The Revolutionary Crest is the buttress to the right (south) of the indentation of the West Dihedrals route (*Route 14*). The climb starts about halfway along the first broad wall past (north of) the original descent route from the Direct South Buttress (see *Route 10*) and stays on the southwest aspect of this part of the west side of Mount Moran's south ridge. This initial wall separates the Direct South Buttress descent couloirs from the conspicuous curving black arch that dominates the beginning of the West Dihedrals route.

From Leigh Canyon use the same approach as for *Route 14*. Some easy climbing (5.1) is involved in reaching a suitable bivouac spot for this route on a flat shoulder near the beginning of the major ramp that lies along the base of the west face of the south ridge of Moran. The route begins a short distance up this ramp beyond the mouth of the lower Direct South Buttress descent couloir. The first two pitches (5.1) on the broken wall above the ramp angle up and right to a small ridge crest and a belay just right of a cluster of small roofs. Two moderate pitches then go straight up this ridge that forms the top edge of the initial wall. After a lead (5.4) up and right to a belay below an overhanging block, the sixth pitch traverses horizontally right around the crest (5.6), then up and right to an overhang. Take a line to the right of this overhang, make a short hand traverse (5.6) right, and then climb left and straight up to the base of a long band of overhangs, finally traversing right across a slab to a belay ledge. To pass this band of overhangs, traverse right for 27m to the first nonoverhanging dihedral and climb this crackless left-facing dihedral (5.8) to easier ground. A ropelength on a 4th-class ramp now leads left. The 10th lead ascends a second crackless left-facing dihedral (5.7) that angles left to a ridge crest. Climb 4th-class ground to the col between the overhanging wall on the left and a pinnacle to the right (south). The 12th lead goes horizontally right to a belay in a chimney just right of an 8-inch crack. Climb about 1m to the right of this offwidth crack, then step into it at the first chockstone and continue up the chimney above. The next two moderate leads attain the ridge crest and continue along the crest. The final pitch (5.4) goes up, traversing right over a rib. One can unrope here and climb the snow-and-rock gully on the right of the ridge, eventually regaining the crest. Now climb with an occasional bit of 5.4 to the summit. Water can usually be found 150m below the summit near the upper reaches of the main south ridge. The southwest couloir (see *Route 18*) is a convenient means of descent for returning to the bivouac site. Although this route can be climbed in one extremely long day, two days will be preferred by many climbers.

ROUTE 14. WEST DIHEDRALS. IV, 5.9. First ascent June 28, 1979, by Jim Beyer. The expanse of rock forming the upper west face of the main south ridge is best understood by studying *Figures 9-25* and *9-26*, as well as *Routes 15, 16,* and *17*. There are several important features in the central section between the Western Buttress (*Route 15*) on the left and the two parallel steep couloirs involved in the original descent route from the Direct South Buttress (see *Route 10*) in the lower right (south) portion of the face. Across the lower portion of this entire section is a major ramp or bench paralleling the base, slanting up from right (south) to left (north). In the wall immediately above the far (north) end of this major ramp is

Colby Stetson begins a ski descent of Mount Moran's CMC route. (Photo courtesy of Fabrikant collection)

a huge, conspicuous curving black arch containing a second, smaller arch with a 12m roof. Above and to the right of these arches is an indentation containing two large left-facing dihedral formations—the left relatively clean, the right blocky—that reach the crest of the south ridge. This 13-pitch route begins below and right of the huge arch and ends with the left dihedral to gain the ridge.

From Leigh Canyon ascend the side canyon on the west side of the south ridge of Mount Moran (see *Route 18*) to the last break in the wall short of the Western Buttress. This point is recognizable as a steep secondary ramp that leads from the talus up toward the midpoint of the huge arch. A bivouac site can be found near the trees just above the beginning of this ramp. The route should be scouted during the approach up the side canyon because most of it cannot be seen from the base of the secondary ramp where the climbing begins. The first two pitches up the ramp are easy climbing (4.0 and 5.1), using a dihedral that diagonals left to gain the main bench of orange rock, where one can contour left toward the huge arch. Traverse some tricky slabs and continue up to the base of the first left-facing dihedral to the right (south) of the huge arch. This 37m dihedral (5.6) is climbed to a ledge at its top, from which 5.6 cracks, first on the left and then on the right, lead to a belay at the top of a buttress. The next lead begins with an easy traverse down and right before turning up to a cramped belay near the base of an obvious, black left-facing dihedral. Climb the crack to the right over a 5.7 overhang up to the base of a short ramp that slants up and left. Go up this ramp to the next lead, the most difficult of this route. It does not go up to the roof in the dihedral (where a huge, loose flake will be seen) but instead climbs a face (5.9) on the slightly overhanging wall to the left. Traverse left, then diagonal back right on easy rock to a belay below a small roof containing a hand crack.

Climb this roof and traverse right on an easy, unprotected face to a dihedral that is climbed to a belay ledge below a large left-facing open book. The ninth lead (5.6) is liebacked and jammed up this open book. The next very long pitch wanders up and right, then back left into the dihedral, and finally traverses up and right into an area of broken black rock, where a belay piton should be found. Climb the next dihedral, over a 5.8 roof, to the "Pillar of Fate," a precarious stack of loose blocks, passing to the left around the pillar to a belay 5m left of the dihedral crack. The 12th lead follows the left-angling, left-facing dihedral to its top, continuing up cracks and blocks to the belay. The final 12m up exposed 5.1 slabs takes one onto the ridge crest, which is then followed to the summit as in *Route 11*. On the second known ascent of this route, this author (R. Jackson) encountered some loose rock, particularly on the crux pitch—no surprise for the Tetons! For our descent we rappelled and downclimbed back to the original descent route for the Direct South Buttress (see *Route 10*, as well as *Figures 9-25* and *9-26*). **Gear:** In addition to the usual set of nuts and devices to 3", this very long climb may require pitons for adequate protection, as well as an ice axe if one descends the southwest couloir (see *Route 18*).

ROUTE 15. WESTERN BUTTRESS. IV, 5.8. First ascent August 6–7, 1968, by Peter Cleveland and Bill Widule. (See *Figures 9-25* and *9-26*.) The southwest aspect of Mount Moran contains a very large expanse of rock forming the west face of the main south ridge as it rises from the initial buttress to the summit. Clearly defined features include the following, listed from south to north: the west face of the south buttress (see *Route 12*), the Revolutionary Crest (*Route 13*), the Western Buttress, the Sandinista Couloir (*Route 16*), the Fonda Ridge (*Route 17*), and the upper portion of the southwest couloir (see *Route 18*). This Western Buttress route ascends the well-defined buttress forming the right (south) edge of the Sandinista Couloir, but little detailed information is available because the route diagram that was prepared at the time of the first ascent has apparently been lost. The top of this route meets the crest of the south ridge at the same point where the Blackfin (*Route 1*) joins the ridge from the other (east) side. The nature of the climb is sensitive to the exact route selected. The first-ascent party reported mostly face climbing of 5.8 difficulty on solid rock in about nine pitches up a series of steps. The second ascent in 1978 found moderate rock, 5.6 or perhaps 5.7, and 12 or 13 pitches.

ROUTE 16. SANDINISTA COULOIR. II, 5.6. First ascent in late June 1983 (or 1984), by Jim Beyer. (See *Figures 9-25* and *9-26*.) This short but well-defined couloir, which forms the right (south) boundary of the Fonda Ridge (*Route 17*), ends at the last notch on the south ridge of Mount Moran 300+m below the summit. One-third of the way up the couloir there is a split, with the main left branch forming the base of the south face of the Fonda Ridge and the smaller right branch angling back to hit the south ridge crest about 80m lower. The route goes up the left branch, which is in its best climbing condition in early summer. The approach from Leigh Canyon into and up the north–south side canyon is described under *Route 18*. Just short (south) of the Fonda Ridge, enter the initial narrow section of the Sandinista Couloir. On the first ascent Beyer climbed this section on snow that steepened to 80° or more for about 8m. The climbing was on an unusual fin of snow, freestanding from the sides of the couloir. From the top of this fin he made a 5.6 dogleg traverse left and gained the main couloir, which he then followed all the way to the crest of the south ridge. The upper portion was straightforward 45° snow. Two final 5.6 rock pitches then provided access to the south ridge, which he followed to the summit. It appears that there is less rockfall in this couloir than in the southwest couloir. For reasons that are not clear, near the bottom of the couloir the rock has been rent asunder by two bolts, placed by nameless, faceless climbers.

ROUTE 17. FONDA RIDGE. III, 5.6. First ascent August 22–23, 1957, by John Fonda, David Dingman, and Karl Pfiffner. (See *Figures 9-25* and *9-26*.) The sector of Mount Moran that lies between the south ridge and the west ridge contains several ridges and buttresses, but only one—the Fonda Ridge—leads directly to the summit plateau. The approach is the same as that described for the southwest couloir (see *Route 18*). Because this is a long ridge (600+m), a camp or bivouac is essential either at the cave in the side canyon (also described below) or down in Leigh Canyon at the first lake. From the lake, climb the huge talus slope up into the north–south side canyon. A major problem now is the selection of the proper ridge. By moving to the left side of the drainage below the western buttresses of the south ridge of Moran, one obtains a better view of the complexities above. The Fonda Ridge can be identified by its solid midsection, which is composed of lighter-colored rock than either of the two flanking ridges. The high-angle flanking ridge on the right (south) ends on the main south ridge; the flanking ridge on the left (north) connects with the west ridge of Mount Moran.

There are many possible routes up the first 180+m section of the Fonda Ridge. This section is very rotten and great caution must be exercised in climbing and in selecting belay positions under overhangs. Perhaps the least dangerous route lies up a small subsidiary abutment on the right (south) of the main base of the ridge. Climb directly up this abutment for about 150m to the large amphitheater that separates the Fonda Ridge from the ridge flanking it on the south. Regain the ridge proper here, and climb onto the second section of the ridge, which angles north toward the crest. This section is not as steep as the first section, and the rock is solid, comparable to the steeper parts of the Exum Ridge of the Grand Teton (*Grand Teton, Route 8*). After the crest is reached, the first towers and steps of the third and last section of the ridge are in sight. In general, these towers and steps are most easily turned on the right (south). The final two or three steps, however, are passed on the left. A final pitch will place the party on the summit plateau. Two days were required by the first-ascent party. This ridge is primarily a mountaineering and routefinding problem.

ROUTE 18. SOUTHWEST COULOIR. II, 5.4. First ascent August 17, 1962, by Ted Vaill and Stuart Kearns. (See *Figures 9-25* and *9-26*.) Rising from the floor of Leigh Canyon at a remarkable, nearly constant angle (36°) is a north–south side canyon. Bounded on the right (east) by the various western cliffs of the long south ridge of Mount Moran and on the left (west) by the impressive east side of Thor Peak, this side canyon contains two separate and parallel drainages. The western stream originates at the glacier below the east face of Thor Peak, and the other (eastern) stream descends from the snows of the upper southwest couloir. To reach this well-defined couloir, ascend Leigh Canyon to the huge talus cone that rises above the first lakes in the canyon. Hike north up the talus, passing the first cliff band by a rotten rock chute on the right (east) side. The side canyon then opens out, and just scrambling is involved all the way up to the point where it splits. About halfway up the couloir, at 10,000 feet, is an excellent bivouac spot on the left (west) side of the couloir in a wind- and rainproof cave that is some 8m deep, providing ample space for five; the opening of the cave is easily seen as one ascends the open slopes. A V-shaped notch above and about 60m west of the cave assists in locating this cave. (**Note:** This author, R. Jackson, searched for this cave and was unable to find it—good luck!)

At the point of bifurcation (at about 11,000 feet), the main left branch goes north to meet the west ridge, and the other turns right (northeast) almost directly toward the summit of Mount Moran. Both branches contain snow until late season. This route follows the right (northeast) branch, which is bounded on the right (south) by the Fonda Ridge. Do not turn up and right too soon; the correct couloir is the last possibility before reaching the west ridge. The black dike crosses the couloir near its top, having passed completely through the mountain from the east side where it is a more familiar sight. Climb 300m or more of steep snow (35°–55°) in this couloir to its upper end, which narrows to a small, steep, icy chimney only a short distance below the summit. Climb the exposed left wall of this chimney (expect some loose rock) to pass the first large chockstone, and then stem past the two final chockstones. Scramble to the notch in the west ridge above and gain the summit plateau either by climbing the final step of the west ridge directly (5.4) or by working diagonally up the north slope left of the ridge. This southwest couloir, while requiring mountaineering skill, is at no point very difficult; for those experienced with an ice axe, it can provide a fast method of descent to Leigh Canyon as long as snow remains in the upper couloir. Most climbers will probably want to begin this descent with two rappels—one from the summit down the final step of the west ridge and a second down the uppermost chimney of the couloir. Because this is an enclosed, narrow, and steep couloir, there is some, but apparently not excessive, rockfall danger on this route. See *American Alpine Journal* 13, no. 2 (1963): pp. 410–20, illus.

ROUTE 19. WEST RIDGE. III, 5.4. First ascent August 26, 1935, by Paul Petzoldt and H. K. Hartline. (See *Figure 9-26*.) This long ridge, one of the major but seldom-seen features of the mountain, extends west from the summit to a point west of Peak 12,000+, where it splits into a northwest branch leading to the Rotten Thumb (11,658) and a southwest branch leading to Thor Peak. The first ascent commenced with the first ascent of the South Slope route on Thor Peak (*Thor Peak, Route 1*), from which the ridge looks more fearsome than it actually is. There is, however, a certain unavoidable amount of loose rock. (**Note:** This is putting it mildly!) Descend from the summit of Thor Peak toward the ridge and Peak 11,840+; avoid much of the worst section, which contains apparently unstable pinnacles, by following a ledge (apparently) on the left (northwest) side 15m–30m below the crest until it seems wise to cut back up onto the crest. It appears that the 1935 party climbed over Peak 11,840+ along the way. In general, the route to Peak 12,000+ goes partly along the crest but mostly along ledges on the north side and, after crossing to the right (southeast) side, ultimately emerges on the broad east face of the peak. To reach the summit of Peak 12,000+ one must then backtrack slightly. Walk down to the saddle (11,680+) that separates Peak 12,000+ from Mount Moran and climb the next portion of ridge that consists of dike rock and rises rather steeply; care must be taken with the loose rock here, but it is not difficult. One is now on the broad, flat final portion of the west ridge, which is separated from the summit of Moran by a notch at the head of the southwest couloir (see *Route 18*). Descend to the notch, then climb the short, steep pitch on good rock to the summit.

If one does not want to traverse the entire ridge, it is possible to attain the crest from either the north or the south. From the north one can (1) start with an ascent of Peak 12,000+ via its west or north ridge and then continue east toward the summit of Moran or (2) reach the saddle between Peak 12,000+ and Mount Moran directly from the central Triple Glacier. This second alternative, a route apparently not yet done, will require climbing a substantial, and probably unpleasantly loose, wall above the glacier. From the south there are three large couloirs that provide access to the west ridge, listed here from west to east: (1) the steep couloir (see *Peak 11,840+, Route 2*) that leads to the low point (11,600+) of the ridge connecting Peak 11,840+ with Peak 12,000+; (2) a couloir turning into a shelf that diagonals up from right to left (east to west) to meet the crest (and black dike) just west of Peak 12,000+; and (3) the main south couloir, the upper extension of the main drainage just west of the south ridge of Moran, which leads to the saddle (11,680+) between Peak 12,000+ and Moran. Only the third alternative is straightforward, and even then some routefinding is required to find the easiest way up the drainage and couloir. In early season or midseason all of these couloirs will contain moderately steep snow.

Note: The following three descriptions are inserted here because of their location on the east face of Mount Moran. Mount Moran routes continue on page 453.

EAST HORN (11,465)

Map: Mount Moran

The East Horn is more easily recognized as the northern of the two horns that flank the Falling Ice Glacier on the southeast side of Mount Moran (see *Figure 9-28*). It also forms the southern boundary for the Skillet Glacier and so separates the two major glaciers on the east side of Mount Moran. Although Teton glaciers normally lurk below the dark north faces of the mountains, the Falling Ice Glacier is unique in the range in that it faces southeast. As Fritiof Fryxell wrote, it is able to persist because of the topography: ". . . so deep is the cleft in which it lies and so well do its two horns protect it that the sun reaches its surface only a few hours each day." (*The Tetons: Interpretations of a Mountain Landscape*, pp. 58–59). During his solo first ascent in 1931, Fryxell noted eight different types of ripe berries on his approach hike; mountaineering sometimes has unanticipated benefits. The summit of the East Horn offers a comprehensive view of the east faces of Moran, extending from the northeast ridge to the south edge of the CMC face. The eastern extension of the prominent black dike on the east face of Mount Moran passes along the base of the north face of the West Horn at the south edge of the Falling Ice Glacier and is then lost beneath the rubble below the snout of the glacier. It reappears below the southeast wall of the East Horn and finally crosses the south ridge of Point 9,808 among the trees.

The easiest method of approach is the same as for the CMC route (*Mount Moran, Route 20*), which is via the stream gully below the Falling Ice Glacier: see *Approaches* in the Mount Moran introduction. Hike up the stream drainage to about 8,800 feet and cut north to the saddle (9,600+) that separates Point 9,808 to the east from the east slopes of the East Horn. Alternatively, one could use one of the northeastern approaches and hike and bushwhack up the stream drainage below the Skillet Glacier to reach the same saddle from the north.

Chronology

EAST FACE: July 30, 1931, Fritiof Fryxell
WEST RIDGE: July 18, 1951, Peter Robinson, Bill Briggs, Brian Brett (descent); August 31, 1954, Stanley and Virginia Boucher, Sayre Rodman, Jean Winne (ascent)
SOUTH FACE: November 14, 1976, Paul Horton, Hal Gribble
SOUTHEAST BUTTRESS: July 25, 1978, Yvon Chouinard, Juris Krisjansons
NORTH FACE: August 9, 1984, Yvon Chouinard, Naoe Sakashita

ROUTE 1. WEST RIDGE. II, 5.6. First descent July 18, 1951, by Peter Robinson, Bill Briggs, and Brian Brett; first ascent August 31, 1954, by Stanley and Virginia Boucher, Sayre Rodman, and Jean Winne. This sharp ridge is significantly more difficult than the East Face route (*Route 4*). The West Ridge route was first utilized for a traverse to the summit of Mount Moran via its east ridge. From the summit of the East Horn, climb down the ridge to a rotten pinnacle. Because a rappel is undesirable from here, descend about 60m toward the Falling Ice Glacier, where a ledge system leads back and slightly up to the ridge crest. After an 18m rappel from this point, easy scrambling places one on the col between the East Horn and the east ridge of Mount Moran. To ascend this West Ridge route, the col can be reached from the north via the Skillet Glacier. It is also possible to reach the col from the south via the Falling Ice Glacier through a chimney leading to the low point in the col, but getting onto the surface of the glacier is not a simple matter. Direct approach from the glacier snout is possible but very hazardous, unless it is done when the ice blocks and rocks are frozen in place; steep ice requiring crampons is usually encountered. Descent from the Drizzlepuss notch (see *Mount Moran, Route 21*) onto the glacier is also possible but not pleasant. See *Dartmouth Mountaineering Club Journal*, 1952: pp. 8–11, illus.

ROUTE 2. SOUTH FACE. II, 5.4, AI2+. First ascent November 14, 1976, by Paul Horton and

Hal Gribble. From Leigh Lake follow the main gully containing the stream draining the Falling Ice Glacier to the snout of the glacier. Attain the upper flat section of the glacier by four ice pitches near its right (north) edge. Discretion must be used here, because at times ice avalanches have occurred at the glacier snout; some years will be more dangerous than others. Just east of the summit of the East Horn is a sharp notch from which a large chimney extends down to the glacier below. This route generally follows the right (east) edge of the face to the left of this large chimney. This edge becomes a small ridge halfway up the face, curving slightly west and ending at the summit. Start about 60m left of the chimney and diagonal right and up for one and a half pitches to reach the edge of the face, which is then followed to the summit in six pitches. Most of the climb is 4.0 on broken, blocky rock that, while somewhat loose, is not especially dangerous.

ROUTE 3. SOUTHEAST BUTTRESS. III, 5.8. First ascent July 25, 1978, by Yvon Chouinard and Juris Krisjansons. (See *Figure 9-27.*) This reportedly excellent route starts at the lowest point of the southeast buttress to the right (east) of the snout of the Falling Ice Glacier, which has melted back considerably over the past few decades. **Pitch 1:** Climb up to and then ascend a left-facing corner (5.7) to a ledge and the belay. Move the belay up and west past the nose of the buttress, encountering some easy 5th class getting to a belay beneath three overhangs. **Pitch 2:** Climb an open corner (5.8) to the right of three overhangs and just left of the nose of the buttress to a large ledge and the belay. Move the belay up and west along the ledge (3rd class, 60m). **Pitch 3:** Continue along the ledge for 24m before turning up and climbing to the base of a small right-facing feature with a flake at the top; belay here. **Pitch 4:** Climb the right-facing feature and then continue up via good face climbing to a belay below a small roof. **Pitch 5:** Climb up through the overhang (5.8) and then face climb up to an open corner and belay partway up this corner. **Pitch 6:** Exit the flared crack and face climb up and left for a ropelength (5.7). **Pitch 7:** Continue up for another ropelength of climbing (5.6). **Pitch 8:** Fourth-class climbing leads to the southeast summit. From here descend 30m and then continue another 100m (3rd class) to the summit of the East Horn. Descent is made via *Route*

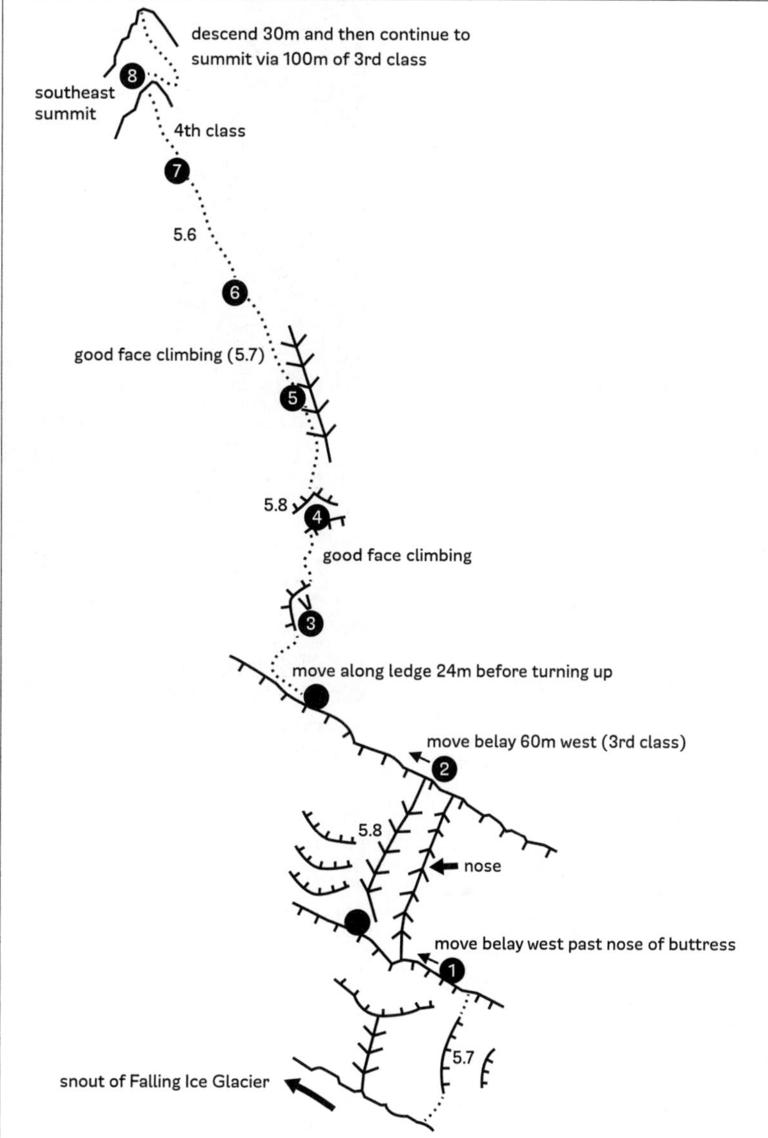

FIGURE 9-27. Mount Moran, East Horn, Southeast Buttress *(Route 3)*, III, 5.8

4 (3rd class). (Source: Nate Opp, who provided the accompanying topo)

ROUTE 4. ▲ EAST FACE. II, 3.0. First ascent July 30, 1931, by Fritiof Fryxell. From the saddle (9,600+) to the east, separating Point 9,808 from the East Horn, the broad east face above can be climbed in various ways, all of which involve moving somewhat out to the right (north) from this saddle. Easy routes can be worked out by linking together ledges intermixed with slabs in the middle of the face. If the south edge of the east face (this could be called the southeast ridge) is followed closely over the various gendarmes, interesting climbing of somewhat greater difficulty (5.1) will be found. **Time:** 5½ hours from the north end of Leigh Lake. See *Appalachia* 18, no. 4 (December 1931): pp. 388–408, illus.

ROUTE 5. NORTH FACE. II, 5.4. First ascent August 9, 1984, by Yvon Chouinard and Naoe Sakashita. This climb, involving crampons and ice axes, started from the Skillet Glacier and reached the summit of the East Horn from the north.

WEST HORN (11,605)

Map: Mount Moran

This splendid pinnacle is the more southerly of the two that flank the Falling Ice Glacier (see *Figure 9-28*). The north and south faces are remarkably sheer, the west ridge is a knife-edge, and the slightly broader east ridge harbors excellent rock. Although every party that climbs the popular CMC route on Mount Moran *(Mount Moran, Route 20)* passes the base of this horn, it is seldom climbed, very likely due to its forbidding appearance from the south or west. Its overall thinness, combined with the great overhang on its west ridge, leads one to believe that its ascent is a major undertaking. However, the West Horn is a short, exciting climb and is recommended as a viewpoint before or after a climb of the CMC route. The view of the east face of Mount Moran from the summit of the West Horn is especially impressive, the slabs of the CMC route appearing absolutely sheer and smooth. One can also look vertically down on the surface of the Falling Ice Glacier, for which Fryxell gave this apt description: "This glacier lies in its cleft [between the two horns] like a beast in its lair."

The pioneering Teton mountaineer Fred Ayres was especially intrigued by this region of the horns of Mount Moran. On August 13, 1934, "a tremendous mass of ice" broke off the snout of the Falling Ice Glacier, leaving a trail of ice fragments 400m long. On August 18 and 19, Ayres twice explored this ice avalanche, climbing partway up the lower extension of the black dike on the south edge of the glacier. On June 29, 1936, he made a solo attempt on the west ridge of the West Horn, but without a rope he was stopped by the "terrific overhang" on the ridge crest. On July 10, 1936, he made the second ascent (solo) of the East Horn and on the same day attacked the West Horn again, this time by the east ridge, but retreated at the steep and exposed slabs about 120m below the summit. His third effort on August 28 via the west ridge—with companions and rope—was finally rewarded with success. He returned 15 years later, in 1951, to make the second (perhaps third) ascent of the West Horn by its west ridge, and on July 24, 1953, he completed his explorations with the first ascent of the east ridge.

Re-climbing Drizzlepuss following an ascent of the CMC route (Photo by Eric Bissell)

The approach is the same as for the CMC route: see *Approaches* in the Mount Moran introduction.

ROUTE 1. ▲ WEST RIDGE. II, 5.4. First ascent August 28, 1936, by Fred and Irene Ayres, Donald Grant, and J. Keith Anderson. The west ridge of the West Horn is separated from the main col between the West Horn and Drizzlepuss by an incredible gendarme with a rock balanced on its top. Reach this col by scrambling from the CMC campsite as in the CMC route (see *Figure 9-28*). From the col climb along ledges on the right (south) side of this gendarme to the small notch between the gendarme and the spectacular overhang on the west ridge of the West Horn. Avoid this overhang by ascending a small, easy chimney on its right (south) flank for a ropelength before turning up ledges to the knife-edge west ridge, which is followed to the summit. Both the north and south faces drop off very steeply from this narrow ridge. For the descent, climb back down the west ridge until just above an overhang in the knife-edge, where old slings will be found. A full-length rappel down the south face is followed by exposed downclimbing and a second (and perhaps third) rappel, all the while angling west to minimize the distance to the talus. Once the talus is reached follow the usual climbers' trail back to the CMC campsite. **Time:** 7½ hours from the north end of Leigh Lake.

ROUTE 2. EAST RIDGE. II, 5.6. First ascent July 24, 1953, by Fred Ayres and A. E. Creswell. From the CMC campsite, climb the talus slope south of the West Horn until the big gash that slices across the east ridge in a north–south direction can be seen. This gash separates a distinct, eastern high point (10,560+) from the main West Horn summit. It is probably possible to go to the col at the head of this gash and start the east ridge of the West Horn by climbing up and out to the right on ledges with krummholz. A better scheme is to continue 60m–100m west beyond this gash to a break in the wall, leading to a small notch in the ridge; a short 5.6 pitch is climbed to reach this notch. The ridge from here to the summit is enjoyable climbing of 5.4 difficulty, and there are a variety of ways to proceed, mostly edging right (north) when the opportunity presents itself. Four or five pitches are involved, containing intervals of slabs and some excellent rock, especially in one knobby section. One eastern subsummit with a knife-edge is passed just before reaching the summit.

UNSOELD'S NEEDLE (11,680+)

(0.2 mi SE of Mount Moran)

Map: Mount Moran

This slender pinnacle stands at the left (south) edge of the east face of Mount Moran, south of the black dike (see *Figure 9-29*). It is west of and about 30m above the notch behind (west of) Drizzlepuss. The approach is the same as for the CMC route: see *Approaches* in the Mount Moran introduction. This pinnacle, although difficult, can be ascended en route to the summit of Mount Moran via that route.

ROUTE 1. EAST RIDGE. I, 5.4. First ascent July 31, 1952, by Willi Unsoeld, Robert Moffitt, Elias Gregory, and Gilbert Mueller. From the notch between Drizzlepuss and the beginning of the east face, climb about 15m up out of the notch. Now instead of traversing right (north), climb about 12m straight up the sharp east ridge of Unsoeld's Needle, now directly above, to a vertical, crackless band. Swing left (south) off the crest to climb around the band, up a 5.4 break, and out onto the shoulder immediately below the summit. An 18m rappel reaches the notch to the west.

Mount Moran, Southeast and East Aspects

When viewed from the east in Jackson Hole, Mount Moran is the dominant northern peak, perhaps bringing to mind a massive fortress of stone. The huge vertical black dike bisects the upper east face, and on the left is the improbable-looking CMC route *(Route 20)*, which has become the regular route of ascent on this magnificent Teton peak. The remainder of the routes on Mount Moran are listed here from south to north in counterclockwise fashion, beginning with the popular CMC route. This makes sense in that this is how one views these routes from left to right. (The numbering is continued from the preceding section of Mount Moran routes—the ones on the west aspect of the south buttress—even though those routes are ordered in clockwise fashion, from east to west.)

ROUTE 20. ▲ CMC. II, 5.5. First descent July 14, 1935, by Chris Scoredos and Joe Merhar; first ascent June 25, 1941, by Paul Petzoldt, Joseph Hawkes, Earl Clark, and Harold Plumley of the Chicago Mountaineering Club. (See *Figures 9-28* and *9-29*.) This pleasant climb, with one of the finest campsites in the range, has become the most commonly used route for reaching the summit of Mount Moran. It is a varied climb on good rock that enjoys—if one owns, rents, or borrows a canoe (highly recommended!)—a relatively short approach with little bushwhacking. The ascent nevertheless typically requires two days.

To approach via canoe (3.5 miles of paddling), put in at the String Lake boat launch and proceed to the portage at the north end of the lake. Then canoe across Leigh Lake to the mouth of the stream descending from the Falling Ice Glacier. Alternatively, one can hike along the east sides of String and Leigh Lakes to the north end of Leigh Lake, where with some effort (and bushwhacking) the abandoned trail around the northwest side of the lake can be followed to the stream; begin this approach from the Leigh Lake trailhead. Ascend the boulder-strewn stream gully, gaining some 2,500 feet, to the open, semigrassy slope due east of and below the West Horn, just south of the glacier. (**Note:** This author, R. Jackson, has seen the major remnants of icefalls from the glacier all the way down this stream gully to the lake!) An improved climbers' trail will be found on this slope leading up to the outstanding CMC campsite (ca. 10,000), located on the flat ridge up to the left (south) in the large trees, one step down (about 30m) from the last trees. Excellent flat areas will be found among the trees on the ridge crest, and except in late season during dry years, there is water in the boulder field 30m to the south.

During early summer a snow tongue extends up toward the col between the West Horn and Drizzlepuss, the large tower between the West Horn and the main east face of Mount Moran. Paul Petzoldt's name for this tower was inspired by the wet conditions he and his party encountered during their first ascent. One route follows the ridge a short distance above the camping spot and then cuts left (south) to the bottom of the snow tongue, then follows the small gully in which the snow tongue lies and continues up toward the col east of Drizzlepuss. Another more direct method, which has the advantage of avoiding most of the snow if one does

FIGURE 9-28. Mount Moran, southeast aspect, CMC *(Route 20)* approach and campsite

FIGURE 9-29. Mount Moran, southeast aspect, CMC *(Route 20)*, II, 5.5

not want to carry an ice axe, is to follow the ridge up above the camping spot until it disappears and then cut slightly to the right (north) onto another smaller rocky ridge with some bushes. If the proper tricky route is selected, easy scrambling will bring one to the desired col. Do not get too close to the southern cliffs of the West Horn. One does not have to proceed all the way to the col because the objective is the summit of Drizzlepuss, the tower on the west side of the col. Scramble easily up its east face to its top.

From here there is a terrifying view of the CMC route, which goes more or less up the middle of the face to the left (south) of the black dike; see *Figure 9-29* for the approximate lines of ascent and descent on this face. Most of the slabs appear impossible. However, take heart and downclimb the very steep west face of Drizzlepuss toward the notch separating it from the main east face of Mount Moran. One can also rappel into this notch; to find the fixed rappel anchor, climb down the obvious weakness from the top of Drizzlepuss and, after a zigzagging descent on ledges, look for the anchor on the north side. The rappel leads to the narrow notch (only 3m–5m wide here). From the notch, climb about 15m up the left (south) edge of the main east face of the mountain until it is possible to traverse 35m horizontally out to the middle of the face, using a little friction work. One can now see plainly the last remaining pinnacle, Unsoeld's Needle, on the south edge of the east face.

Climb diagonally toward the notch between the Needle and the east face, but before reaching it traverse back out onto the face. From here to the summit not much description is needed. The climbing is exposed all the way because there are no very large ledges, yet at no place is there a shortage of holds. The last section of the face has a gentler angle; if one moves somewhat closer to the dike than before, the climb can be easily completed to the rounded summit area. The highest point on the spacious summit plateau is about 100m to the north and is easily recognized by its large cairn. The summit views are quite unlike those obtained from the more frequently trodden summits farther to the south.

For the descent one can simply retrace the ascent route all the way to the Drizzlepuss notch. One may wish to rappel in a number of places, depending on the downclimbing abilities of the party. It is easier to keep to skier's right (south) when descending from the plateau, and to stay near the south edge of the CMC face until just above Unsoeld's Needle; this section can usually be downclimbed, if the easiest route is found, without the need for rappels. The last portion of this descent is in a shallow gully/corner system just off (south of) the edge of the face and will lead naturally to a mass of slings, from which two rappels down the main CMC face to the left (north) bring one to the vicinity of the Drizzlepuss notch; this section can also be downclimbed with effort and care.

To climb back up Drizzlepuss from the notch, there are three possibilities: (1) The easiest scheme is to climb out of the notch to the right, traversing out on a ledge on the west wall of Drizzlepuss (5.5). Turn up to the next ledge at the first likely opportunity, as difficulties increase the farther out one traverses. From this second ledge ascend without difficulty the remainder of the steep ledges to the top of Drizzlepuss. (2) Another method is to climb directly up out of the notch. If this option is selected, it will be the most difficult (5.7) pitch of the climb, involving a few overhanging moves. (3) It is also possible, *but not recommended*, to go down the steep couloir leading south from the Drizzlepuss notch toward Leigh Canyon. Because this ultimately leads to the south cliffs of Mount Moran, bear left (east) after about 90m, cross the south ridge of Drizzlepuss, and continue contouring to the vicinity of the CMC campsite, from which the rest of the descent is easy. **Time:** 5½ to 6¾ hours from the CMC campsite. See *Appalachia* 25, no. 2 (December 1944): pp. 239–41, illus.; *Dartmouth Mountaineering Club Journal*, 1956: pp. 34–38; *Trail and Timberline*, no. 285 (September 1942): pp. 115–18, illus.

Variation: II, 5.5. First ascent July 23, 1952, by Richard Emerson and Walt Sticker. The notch between Drizzlepuss and the main east face of Mount Moran can also be reached from the CMC campsite by climbing up the snout of the Falling Ice Glacier. The difficulties depend on the year, and the route is potentially threatened by serac fall. Ice-climbing equipment is necessary for this variation. The final snow-and-ice chute leading to the notch from the main portion of the glacier is usually protected by a small bergschrund.

Variation: II, 5.6. First descent August 17, 1952, by Martin Benham and Dmitri Nabokov. From the col between Drizzlepuss and the West Horn it is possible, although difficult, to descend to the south edge of the Falling Ice Glacier and follow it to the Drizzlepuss notch, thereby bypassing Drizzlepuss on the north. This variation was originally used on descent to avoid the overhang out of the notch, but it is equally difficult from that direction.

ROUTE 21. DIKE. II, 5.4. First ascent June 23, 1931, by Hans Wittich and Otto Stegmaier. This remarkable early route goes up the face of the black dike that cuts the east face of Mount Moran so prominently (see *Figure 9-29*). The first problem is to reach the base of the dike where it meets the Falling Ice Glacier. The direct approach is to climb the snout of the glacier on its right (north) side to the flat section above. Depending on the year and the season, there may be both difficulty and danger associated with this part of the route. At the upper end of the glacier some difficulty can be expected crossing the *randkluft*, which widens as the season advances, between the rock and the ice. A more roundabout route—the one used on the first ascent—is to proceed as in *Route 20* up over Drizzlepuss (this was the first ascent of Drizzlepuss) and down into the notch; then traverse horizontally to the right (north) all the way over to the dike. The lower portion of the dike offers no great difficulty, although one must be on guard for loose rock. Because the dike is only about 38m wide, it is not possible to stray very far off the route. The final 60m–90m of the dike stands away from the main face of the mountain and must be climbed with caution owing to the downsloping nature of the rock. See *American Alpine Journal* 9, no. 2 (1955): pp. 147–49; *Appalachia* 18, no. 4 (Dec. 1931): pp. 388–408, illus.; *Nature Friend* 25, no. 6 (June 1947): pp. 3–4.

Variation: II, 5.4. First descent August 14, 1946, by Gerald Brandon and Theodore Brandon; first ascent August 12, 1952, by Theodore Brandon, Tim Ramsland, Willis Wood, and Don and Ivan Zastrow. The flat portion of the Falling Ice Glacier can be reached by ascending a 60m chimney on the left (south) side of the snout of the glacier where the dike again outcrops. Because of its loose and rotten rock, this chimney is not recommended.

ROUTE 22. EUDEMONIA (HAPPINESS). III, 5.9. First ascent July 27, 2005, by George Montopoli, David Bywater, and Martin Vidak, all three Grand Teton National Park climbing rangers at the time. (See *Figure 9-30*.) This route is located in a spectacular setting above the Falling Ice Glacier and is characterized by mostly moderate climbing on excellent rock. Follow the normal approach to the CMC campsite (see *Route 20*) until the point where it is possible to traverse right (east) over to the toe of the glacier. The easiest way to get up to the flat portion of the glacier is

FIGURE 9-30. Mount Moran, east aspect, Eudemonia (Happiness; *Route 22*), III, 5.9

on the northeast flank. Later in the season this may involve ascending a few hundred meters of 45° ice. Once on the flat portion of the glacier, cross over to the expansive rock face right (north) of the black dike. Look for a large, prominent left-facing corner on the wall above the glacier (pitches 3–4). Depending on the time of year, getting onto the rock may involve a descent into the bergschrund. **Pitch 1:** Climb out of the bergschrund and traverse up and left (south) on small ledges for 30m (5.8); belay on the right-hand edge of the black dike. **Pitch 2:** Climb up and right (north) toward a short left-facing corner (5.7), then continue up and right to the base of the main left-facing corner and belay (50m). **Pitch 3:** Climb the first section of the corner to a belay beneath a small roof (5.6, 50m). **Pitch 4:** Climb the roof (5.9 crux) and continue up the corner system to easier climbing (5.6). **Pitch 5:** Continue up in the corner system for half a pitch and then move onto and up easy slabs (easy 5th class). **Pitch 6:** Slab climbing leads up and right toward an open chimney that separates the face from a huge buttress to the north of the chimney (easy 5th class, 50m). **Pitch 7:** Climb the steep face to the left of the open chimney via small ledges and cracks to a notch (5.6, 50m). **Pitch 8:** From the notch, drop down slightly into the open chimney and climb the left-hand side to the summit plateau (5.9, 40m). This pitch can be wet, and the rock quality is the poorest encountered on the route. The first-ascent party descended the CMC route (*Route 20*); however, note the early-season cornice hazard above this route, as shown in *Figure 9-30*. The backdrop for this climb is spectacular, with the West and East Horns of Mount Moran framing the view far below to Leigh Lake. This inspired the name Eudemonia, which is synonymous with happiness, well-being, and finding fulfillment in life.

ROUTE 23. EAST CHIMNEY. II, 5.4. First ascent July 9, 1956, by Rob Day, Peter Lipman, and Alan Williamson. From the usual campsite for the CMC route (see *Route 20*), climb onto the Falling Ice Glacier; this is discussed under *Route 21*. Ascend the glacier to its upper right (northwest) corner, then climb the large chimney or crack that leads from the glacier to the summit plateau. This chimney lies between the east ridge (which connects with the East Horn) and the black dike and consists of easy 5th-class climbing. It begins about 150m north of and is roughly parallel to the dike.

ROUTE 24. EAST RIDGE. II, 4.0. First ascent July 24, 1931, by Robert Underhill and Paul Petzoldt. This ridge forms the left (south) edge of the "handle" of the Skillet Glacier; it begins at the col separating the East Horn from the mountain and is reached from the north via the glacier. For the approach to the glacier see *Route 25*. From a campsite below the moraine of the Skillet Glacier, climb over the moraine onto the "pan" of the glacier. A bergschrund separates the lower and larger section from the upper section. During most of the summer the slabby rocks to the left (southeast) of the bergschrund are exposed and provide an easy but wet route past this obstacle. Above these rocks, continue up the snow and climb onto the right (north) flank of the east ridge of Mount Moran (immediately south of the Skillet's "handle"), some 60m above the col between the East Horn and Moran. Some rotten rock will be met before one reaches the crest of the ridge, three ropelengths above the glacier. The ridge is straightforward climbing all the way to its top, which is only about 60m north of the summit. **Time:** 5¾ hours from a camp below the glacier. See *Appalachia* 18, no. 4 (December 1931): pp. 388–408, illus.

Variation: II, 4.0. First descent July 24, 1931, by Paul Petzoldt and Robert Underhill. After climbing up the ridge a short distance, cut left (south) across the slabby face, passing a chimney (see *Route 23*), and finish the climb on the rock near the black dike.

Variation: II, 4.0. First ascent July 18, 1951, by Peter Robinson, Bill Briggs, and Brian Brett. This longer variation combines the climb of the East Horn with the east ridge of Mount Moran. Ascend the east ridge of the East Horn to its summit, and then descend its west ridge to the col separating the East Horn from the mountain; for this route description see *East Horn, Route 1*. From the col ascend the east ridge of Mount Moran as already described. The summit of the East Horn can also be bypassed on the south; this unlikely and tricky maneuver was first done on September 15, 1954, by Craig Merrihue and William Hooker. Stay near the left (south) edge of the east ridge of the East Horn, and when confronted by a pinnacle move left on a ledge system across the south face of the East Horn to the vicinity of the col between the East Horn and Moran. Near the beginning of the traverse it may prove necessary to drop down about 1m onto a second set of ledges before continuing. See *Dartmouth Mountaineering Club Journal*, 1952: pp. 8–11, illus.

ROUTE 25. SKILLET GLACIER. II, 5.4, AI2+. First ascent July 27, 1922, by LeGrand Haven Hardy, Ben C. Rich, and Bennet McNulty. (See *Figure 9-31*.) The Skillet Glacier route is one of the few long snow-and-ice climbs in the Tetons, and it has been climbed and skied quite often in recent years. As seen from the valley, this well-named glacier provides a very obvious line through the imposing precipices that protect the summit plateau from easy access. But the route has also produced a disproportionate number of serious accidents and fatalities, perhaps because of its deceptive appearance. This is *not* a route for beginning climbers inexperienced in the use of an ice axe and the rope. The "handle" of the glacier is very steep and must be ascended and descended with great care. Do *not* undertake a descent by glissade unless snow conditions are exactly right and one is truly expert in this demanding and hazardous form of snow travel. The large crevasse that opens at the lower end of the "handle" forms a great mouth ready to swallow any climber who slips on the snow above.

Two days are normally required to climb this long route, and the approach to a campsite can be made by land, by water, or by a combination of the two; see *Approaches* in the Mount Moran introduction. As stated there, the best approach is across Jackson Lake by powerboat from Colter Bay or Signal Mountain Lodge or by canoe (4 miles of paddling) from Spalding Bay. The traditional method of approach, which involves serious bushwhacking, is to hike from the Leigh Lake trailhead around the east shores of String and Leigh Lakes to Bearpaw Lake, which marks the end of the maintained trail. Continue north past Trapper Lake and around the east side of Mount Moran to the main creek descending from the Skillet Glacier; cross to the north side of the stream and cut left (west) up the timbered slope. This portion (1 mile) of the approach is neither easy nor pleasant because many years ago

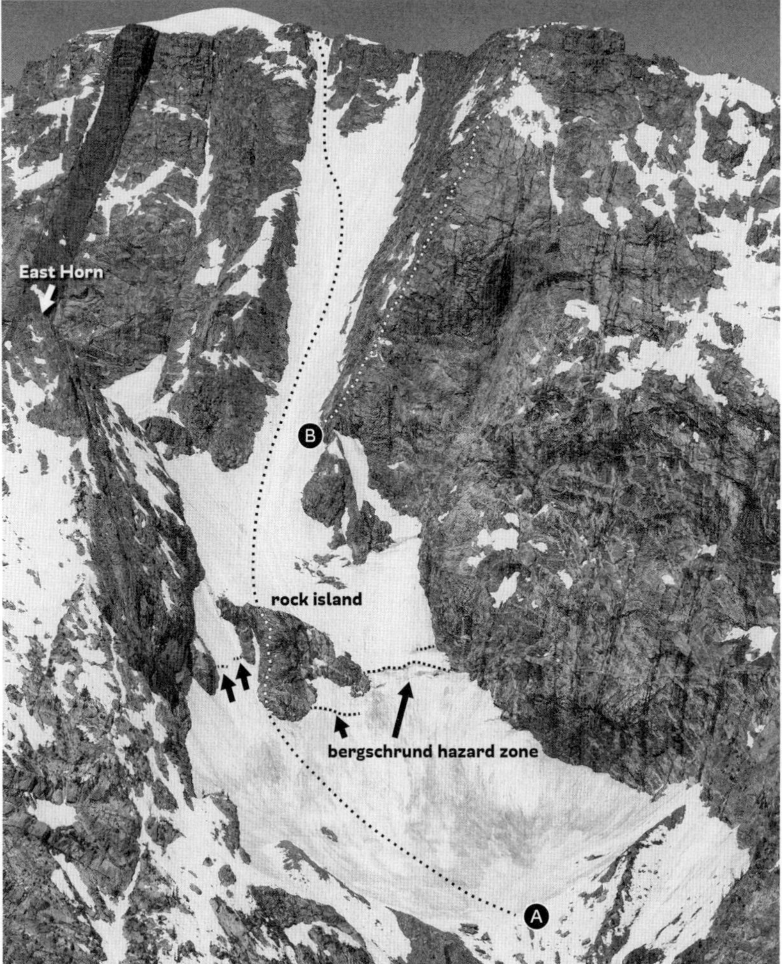

FIGURE 9-31. Mount Moran, east aspect. (A) Skillet Glacier *(Route 25)*, II, 5.4, AI2+; (B) Skillet Buttress *(Route 27)*, II, 5.4, AI2+

the National Park Service (NPS) abandoned the maintenance of the once-good trail to Moran Creek and beyond, and winter avalanches have since left a broad area of flattened tree debris. No specific recommendation can be given to simplify this section, as serious bushwhacking is impossible to avoid. Some game trails will usually be found leading up to the morainal basin below the Skillet Glacier, although even here some bushwhacking must be expected. The boulder-strewn main streambed can then be followed to within 90m of the moraine.

Another scheme to reach the Skillet Glacier, which minimizes the bushwhacking, is to canoe across Leigh Lake to the mouth of the stream that descends from the Falling Ice Glacier, hike up the drainage of that stream, and cut right (north) to the broad saddle (9,600+) connecting the treed eastern Point 9,808 with the East Horn. From this saddle drop down on the north side only about 75m and contour around the eastern base of the East Horn to gain access to the moraine below the Skillet Glacier. Below the moraine and a short distance to the right (north) is a clump of trees that makes a suitable campsite.

Cross the moraine and ascend the Skillet Glacier to the bergschrund that separates the lower, large portions of the "pan" of the glacier from the upper portion. This obstacle can be passed on the left (south), using the rock island of wet slabs that are exposed during most of the summer; it is also possible to use the rock on the right (north) end of the bergschrund, but this is more difficult. Now continue on the glacier, and proceed directly up the narrow "handle" to the summit plateau. This is a straightforward but steep snow-and-ice climb. Be constantly alert for falling rock while on the "handle." Near the summit, steep snow in the left (south) fork of the upper "handle" couloir leads almost all the way to the flat summit. For competent and experienced mountaineers, the Skillet Glacier can serve as a fast descent route in early season. It has the advantage of very simple routefinding and can be found even in the dark if absolutely necessary. **Time:** 6¾ hours from a camp below the glacier. See *Appalachia* 18, no. 4 (December 1931): pp. 388–408, illus.; *Canadian Alpine Journal* 19 (1930): pp. 84–91, illus.; *Chicago Mountaineering Club Newsletter* 12, no. 6 (November 1958): pp. 5–9; *Sierra Club Bulletin* 12, no. 4 (1927): pp. 356–64, illus.

ROUTE 26. SKILLET CHIMNEY. II, 5.4, AI2+. First ascent October 13, 1978, by Paul Horton and W. D. Horton. In the rock wall on the north side of the lower end of the "handle" of the Skillet Glacier is an indentation leading directly to the north summit. This becomes a well-defined chimney and this route follows the line of the chimney. Proceed to and up the Skillet Glacier as in *Route 25*, past the bergschrund to the narrowing at the beginning of the "handle." Exit from the snow and ice onto the rock to the right (north) and start up the chimney. The rock is sound and the climbing is mainly on the left (west) side of the chimney, although much of the route is in the chimney itself. While there is a considerable extent of exposed climbing, the difficulty is never greater than 5.4 and much of it can be done by careful scrambling.

ROUTE 27. SKILLET BUTTRESS. II, 5.4, AI2+. First ascent August 19, 1999, by Paul Horton and John Britton. This route ascends the buttress or ridge formed by the intersection of the rock wall on the north side of the "handle" of the Skillet Glacier with the northeast slabs. It lies to the right (north) of the Skillet Chimney (*Route 26*) and leads to the north summit. Proceed to and up the Skillet Glacier as in *Route 25*, past the bergschrund to the narrowing at the beginning of the "handle." Exit from the snow and ice onto the rock to the right (north) a few meters past the steep toe of the buttress and below the start of the Skillet Chimney. A steep pitch diagonals right (north) to the crest of the buttress. The exposed crest is then followed all the way to the north summit, with minor variations to the left or right as desired. An overhang apparent from below is easily bypassed on the left. The rock is generally reliable (and very slabby in some areas), the routefinding is straightforward, and the climbing is never difficult.

ROUTE 28. NORTHEAST SLABS. III, 5.7, AI2+. First ascent September 10, 1962, by Fred Beckey and Dan Davis. This route starts well left of *Route 29*, makes a considerable horizontal traverse midway up the northeast face, and reaches the uppermost northeast ridge a short distance from the north summit in a manner similar to the Skillet Buttress (*Route 27*). Proceed to the lower portion of the Skillet Glacier, as in *Route 25*, and ascend toward the "handle" in the upper left corner. Cross the bergschrund, then climb the snow and ice (crampons useful) to the highest point of the glacier to the right (north) of the "handle" proper, directly below a prominent vertical headwall about 100m above. Climb a short, steep wall and enter the obvious open gully, which is followed for about four leads up and slightly right (north) until a headwall blocks progress. It may be possible to continue directly upward at this point, but the first-ascent party angled up and left for about 50m before diagonaling back right. Now make an exposed, nearly horizontal traverse to the north of several leads, crossing over very steep slabs beneath a series of overhangs and occasionally losing some altitude until it is possible to climb over a short overhang to the rock above. From this point climb nearly directly upward for four ropelengths on steep, smooth slabs, occasionally climbing some short overhangs formed by huge slabs overlapping those below. The final section is more broken, and a large chimney or gully will be found that leads easily to the ridge crest north of the north summit. See *American Alpine Journal* 13, no. 2 (1963): pp. 410–20, illus.

ROUTE 29. SKILLET GLACIER HEADWALL. III, 5.7, A1, AI2+. First ascent July 27, 1962, by Don Anderson and Larry Scott. There is a considerable expanse of steep, slabby rock between the "handle" of the Skillet Glacier and the northeast ridge of Mount Moran. This long route, the first to penetrate this region, starts from the lower portion of the Skillet Glacier (see *Route 25*) and ascends nearly a direct line to the uppermost crest of the northeast ridge, just short of the north summit. Leave the glacier near its upper right (northwest) margin, cross the *randkluft*, and climb the wall above, which is immediately left (south) of a prominent gully in the main headwall. When the wall steepens, traverse right into the gully and follow it upward. A vertical wall will be met, where one traverses slightly left (south) and up to a belay on a steep slab. Now work back right (north) across a delicate, sometimes wet, slab to a deep crack, which leads to an awkward chimney. Climb easier rock above the chimney, keeping a large wall about 8m to the left (south). A difficult lieback crack in the steepening main wall above provides the most difficult pitch of the route. An overhanging wall higher up forces a slightly descending traverse 46m to the right (north). Climb out to a small rib on the skyline and then up until past the overhanging wall. Work back to the left to a gully that provides an easy upward route. Climb this gully and the slabs to the left, bypassing two bulging buttresses on the left (south). Several pitches (wet) on the left of the final buttress provide the concluding problems; the final pitch required aid. The crest is reached just 46m north of the north summit. See *American Alpine Journal* 13, no. 2 (1963): pp. 410–20, illus.

Mount Moran, Northeast and North Aspects

The routes described in this section are accessible by way of a seldom-visited northeastern cirque, situated about 2,000 feet above the shore of Jackson Lake. This beautiful cirque is bounded on the south by the northeast ridge of Mount Moran (see *Route 30*) and on the north by the north ridge (see *Route 34*). Serious bushwhacking up from the lakeshore is necessary to access the talus slope that leads into the area. The various north face routes as well as the eastern Triple Glacier are perhaps more easily accessed by entering this cirque from below and then traversing up and over Moran's north shoulder. The northern routes could also be approached more directly from Moran Canyon. The following climbs are listed in counterclockwise fashion, beginning with the northeastern routes, arranged from south to north, and turning the corner at the north ridge. *Figure 9-32* presents an overview of the locations of *Routes 30–34*, and *Figure 9-33* shows *Routes 34–39*.

ROUTE 30. ▲ NORTHEAST RIDGE. II, 5.4. First complete ascent August 19, 1924, by Albert R. Ellingwood and Carl Blaurock; on August 11, 1919, LeRoy Jeffers climbed a variant of this ridge to the lower north summit. Before the closing of the road to the north end of Leigh Lake and the discovery of the CMC route (*Route 20*), the Northeast Ridge was the popular route to the summit of Mount Moran. It is a pleasant climb on good rock of modest difficulty, but one should carefully consider the weather prior to starting for the summit because storms coming in from the west are not visible while climbing this route. The ridge is an exposed and frightening place during a thunderstorm. The approach options for this route are roughly the same as those described for the Skillet Glacier (see *Route 25*). One way or another the stream descending from the Skillet Glacier must be reached at or near the shore of Jackson Lake. Stay out of the avalanche thickets. Much of the uphill bushwhacking can be avoided if one can piece together game trails on the right (north) side of this stream. With skill or luck these can be followed to the open slope, which is then taken to the ridge crest. The usual camping spot for this climb is in or near the last trees on the ridge. Water is usually obtained from a nearby snowfield but may be difficult to find in late season.

The first and principal obstacle on the ridge is the Great Gendarme (10,230), which is easily reached a short distance above camp. It is usually bypassed on the right (north) using a broad but somewhat insecure ledge; one can also climb it directly and make a tricky rappel down the far (west) side. The route from the tower to the north summit of Mount Moran requires little description, as the ridge is well defined and the climbing is not difficult. A macabre point of interest partway up this ridge is the wreckage of the airplane crash that occurred on November 21, 1950. In general stay on the ridge, sometimes climbing on the slabs just left (south) of the crest, until the

FIGURE 9-32. Mount Moran, northeast aspect. (A) Northeast Ridge *(Route 30)*, II, 5.4; (B) Northeast Ridge, variation: 1939, II, 5.4; (C) Sickle Couloir *(Route 31)*, III, 5.4; (D) Pika Buttress *(Route 32)*, III, 5.4; (E) Northeast Ridge, variation: Northeast Buttress Couloir, III, 5.4; (F) Minor Fourth Couloir *(Route 33)*, IV, WI6, AI5, M6; (G) North Ridge *(Route 34)*, III, 5.4

steep section below the north summit is reached. Although it is possible to climb this section directly, it is simpler to traverse left (south) for about 30m to a prominent chimney, which brings one out on the flat north summit; either way one pitch of 5.4 difficulty will be encountered. Traverse the narrow ridge leading to the main (south) summit, which is about 46m higher and 0.25 mile away. This route offers few technical difficulties, but it is a long climb. Get an early start. **Time:** 4 to 7⅓ hours from a timberline camp on the ridge; 6¼ to 8½ hours from a camp below the glacier; 8 to 11 hours from Leigh Lake. See *American Alpine Journal*, 2, no. 3 (1935): pp. 312–14; *Appalachia* 18, no. 4 (December 1931): pp. 388–408, illus.; *Canadian Alpine Journal* 19 (1930): pp. 84–91, illus.; *Chicago Mountaineering Club Newsletter* 12, no. 6 (November 1958): pp. 5–9; *Harvard Mountaineering* 1 (June 1927): pp. 12–17; *Summit* 6, no. 9 (September 1960): pp. 16–17, illus.; *Trail and Timberline*, no. 83 (August 1925): pp. 1–8, illus.

Variation: II, 5.4. First ascent August 11, 1919, by LeRoy Jeffers; an early descent in this region was made with difficulty on September 15, 1931, by Harvey Sethman and John Seerley. The crest of the northeast ridge can be gained from the south at a point above (west of) the Great Gendarme. Use one of the approach options outlined in *Route 25* to reach the area below the terminal moraine of the Skillet Glacier. To the right (north), on the eastern portion of the south face of the northeast ridge, one or more diagonal couloirs will be seen leading up to the ridge crest. One of these apparently provides a relatively easy but probably loose route; little information is available. In 1978 the gully and slabs immediately west of the Great Gendarme were descended by a competent party with no particular difficulties. See LeRoy Jeffers, chapter 2 in *The Call of the Mountains* (New York: Dodd, Mead, 1922); *Appalachia* 15, no. 1 (November 1920): pp. 108–9; 18, no. 4 (December 1931): pp. 388–408, illus.; *Canadian Alpine Journal* 11 (1920): pp. 49–55, illus.; *Sierra Club Bulletin* 11, no. 2 (January 1921): pp. 161–66, illus.; *Trail and Timberline*, no. 23 (August 1920): pp. 2–5, illus.; no. 148 (February 1931): pp. 16–20, illus.

Variation: II, 5.4. First ascent August 25, 1939, by Earl Clark and Donald Grant. The upper northeast ridge can be reached via an interesting variation from the large cirque just north of the ridge. For the approach to this cirque see *Route 31*; a campsite is available to the north of the main snowfield in the cirque. Of the five snow couloirs that extend upward from the cirque, the most southerly—the first one described under *Route 31* —can be climbed to reach the crest of the northeast ridge about 100m above the Great Gendarme. Entry into the couloir (see *Figure 9-32*) is gained from the upper left corner of the snow-filled cirque. It is probably best climbed in early season or midseason, because in late season the floor of the cirque is filled with steep black ice and is swept by rockfall. While ascending the couloir under these conditions, one must stay high on the left (east) wall, which is composed of loose debris. The top of the couloir narrows. After passing a moat, climb a short, awkward 5.1 corner to exit the couloir. About 100m of open slopes with ledges and scrambling leads onto the northeast ridge at the site of the airplane wreckage. This variation is the probable route Paul Petzoldt and Blake Vandewater used on November 25, 1950, to investigate the airplane crash that had occurred four days earlier; needless to say, this climb in winter conditions was much more difficult than normal.

***Variation:* NORTHEAST BUTTRESS COULOIR.** III, 5.4. First ascent July 16, 1971, by Gale Long and Robert Frisby. This variation

FIGURE 9-33. Mount Moran, north aspect. (A) North Ridge *(Route 34)*, III, 5.4; (B) Peak 11,795, West Face, III, 5.8; (C) Wise Burgettes Go by Water *(Route 35)*, III, 5.4, AI2; (D) North Buttress *(Route 36)*, IV, 5.8; (E) North Face *(Route 37)*, IV, 5.8; (F) Triple Glacier *(Route 38)*, II, 5.6, AI2+; (G) Northwest Ridge *(Route 39)*, II, 5.1, AI2; (H) Peak 12,000+, North Ridge, II, 5.4

begins in the first couloir to the right (north) of the Sickle Couloir (see *Figure 9-32*); it is the third of the snow couloirs described under *Route 31*, and it leads to the notch that separates Peak 11,795 from the upper north ridge of Mount Moran. Climb this couloir to the large bench area about halfway up the buttress. From the bench angle almost horizontally left across early-season snowfields to gain the northeast ridge in the vicinity of the airplane wreckage. Later in the season the absence of these snowfields would make this traverse much more difficult. Follow the Northeast Ridge route to the summit.

ROUTE 31. SICKLE COULOIR. III, 5.4. First ascent August 8, 1964, by Gary Cole and Ray Jacquot. Between the northeast ridge and north ridge of Mount Moran is a significant but seldom-visited morainal cirque from which five major couloirs rise toward the ridges. These couloirs can be identified from left (south) to right (north); see *Figure 9-32*. The first, the 1939 variation of *Route 30*, leads to a point about halfway up the northeast ridge in the general vicinity of the airplane crash site. The second is the Sickle Couloir—the major couloir, snow-filled except in late season, that ends at the last notch on the north ridge before its final rise to the north summit. The third couloir (see the Northeast Buttress Couloir variation to *Route 30*) follows a line to reach the first and main notch separating Peak 11,795 from the upper sections of the north ridge. The fourth is a minor couloir or chimney that disappears in a face on the northeast ridge of Peak 11,795 (see *Route 33*; although "minor," it is the most difficult route on this face). The fifth is just a steep bench, mostly talus in the lower sections, that ends low on the northeast ridge of Peak 11,795.

Extending for nearly 900m, the Sickle Couloir is one of the major Teton snow-and-ice climbs. The route is best done in early season while there is snow to cover the ice. It can be climbed by a fast party in a single day from the shore of Jackson Lake, or a high camp can be placed to the north of the snowfield in the cirque. The base of the Sickle Couloir is reached from the shore of Jackson Lake by bushwhacking through the timber to the talus slope leading into the cirque. Climb the southwest corner of the snowfield in the cirque up into the couloir and proceed directly up the couloir. After about 100m the couloir steepens and splits. Climb the wet chimney left of the rock bulge between the two branches. Reenter the couloir and continue up past the bench area of the northeast buttress and climb another 460m to the notch in the north ridge. Follow the North Ridge route (*Route 34*) to the summit.

ROUTE 32. PIKA BUTTRESS. III, 5.4. First ascent July 27–28, 1968, by Jim Kanzler, Paul

Myhre, and John Neal. (See *Figure 9-32*.) This long route ascends the broad ridge or buttress separating the Sickle Couloir from the next couloir to the north. The approach is the same as for the Sickle Couloir (*Route 31*) to the base of the buttress. At no point difficult, the route features enjoyable climbing on good rock. The North Ridge route (*Route 34*) is joined just north of the Sickle Couloir notch and is followed to the summit. The buttress seems to be a haven for friendly pikas (*Ochotona princeps*). Two days may be desired for this route; the first-ascent party bivouacked on the bench about halfway up to the ridge.

ROUTE 33. MINOR FOURTH COULOIR. IV, WI6, AI5, M6. First ascent in October 2002, by John Kelley and Bob Webster. (See *Figure 9-32*.) Located approximately 450m to the north of the Sickle Couloir, this wild route ascends a feature described somewhat dismissively under *Route 31*: "The fourth is a minor couloir or chimney." No doubt this was a ready source for the name of the route, a tongue-in-cheek counterpoint considering its difficulty as well as its length—approximately 550m! This is a conditions-dependent climb and one that is difficult to catch "in shape." Nevertheless, when combined with the upper North Ridge route (*Route 34*), it is a climb of major proportions. It was a significant Teton first ascent.

Approach this climb as for *Route 31*. **Pitch 1:** From the cirque climb up increasingly steep terrain and moderate ice (AI3) and belay in a cave beneath the large chockstone seen from below. **Pitch 2:** Exit out the right side of the chockstone on mixed terrain (M5) and continue up on moderate ice (AI3) to a belay beneath a pillar/curtain. **Pitch 3:** Climb the WI5 pillar/curtain and belay on top. **Pitch 4:** Climb a ropelength of moderate ice and belay at a fixed piton and stopper (WI3). **Pitch 5:** Ascend a squeeze chimney (M5/AI5), which is followed by about 120m of easy snow climbing leading to the base of a thin smear. **Pitch 6:** Climb the thin smear of ice (WI4), located in the middle of the lower bowl. **Pitch 7 (crux):** Two thin mixed corners, the lower right-facing and the upper left-facing (M6), provide access to the hanging curtain above, which is climbed to its top and a belay (WI5+/WI6). Ninety meters of easy snow and WI3 ice bulges then leads up to the intersection with the North Ridge route. The difficulty rating reflects the conditions the first-ascent party encountered. (Source: correspondence with John Kelley)

ROUTE 34. NORTH RIDGE. III, 5.4. First ascent July 5, 1939, by Paul Petzoldt and William Ringler. (See *Figures 9-32* and *9-33*.) This ridge, a major feature of Mount Moran, rises at a steady angle from Moran Canyon until it passes over Peak 9,940 and flattens out at approximately 9,800 feet, forming a large shoulder or bench. The dominant steep section above this bench provides the standard north ridge ascent; the lower 900m has so far been ignored. Moran's North Ridge route is a worthwhile mountaineering objective in a wild section of the park.

To approach this route, one must first reach the northeast base of Mount Moran. This is done by one of the alternatives described in the Mount Moran introduction and in *Moran Canyon* in Section 10: hike from the Leigh Lake trailhead by String Lake; canoe across Leigh Lake and hike and bushwhack the remainder of the distance; canoe on Jackson Lake from Spalding Bay; or take a powerboat from Colter Bay or Signal Mountain Lodge. From the shore of Jackson Lake, the starting point for working uphill is one of the streams draining the large, open cirque on the north side of the northeast ridge of Mount Moran. One must bushwhack directly up through the timber for an hour or more to gain the open slope leading to the talus bowl beneath the northeast ridge. Once through the trees the rest of the approach is one of the most attractive features of this climb. Follow along the right side of the small stream through a sequence of superb alpine meadows with many exquisite flowers. Continue to the broad crest of the north shoulder of Moran and camp in the last trees, at about 9,800 feet. Melting snow will provide water during early season; later it may be necessary to camp somewhat lower in order to obtain water. This is a most scenic location, one of the finest in the range. Retrieval of this camp after the ascent, however, involves some problems because the ridge has never been descended directly. If the Northeast Ridge route (*Route 30*) is to be used for the descent, there is an alternative campsite about 250m below the shoulder in the trees on the north margin of the talus bowl that lies at the northern base of the northeast ridge of Mount Moran. Camp retrieval then involves little or no uphill travel; descend the northeast ridge past the Great Gendarme until a couloir is reached leading down to the west into the talus bowl.

The northernmost point of the upper north ridge, Peak 11,795, is a distinct peak. This summit possesses a north-northwest face, the base of which is reached via a talus slope above the north shoulder. The north ridge is considered to be the left (east) edge of this face, separating it from the main east (or slightly northeast) face of the mountain. Start at the base of this edge; climb up and left on easy exposed ledges to a wide ledge. Three or four pitches then lead up and to the right, back toward the ridge crest. One can proceed to the crest, but the easiest route involves a long scramble up and diagonally left. There are many possibilities in this region that involve crossing couloirs and climbing ribs, all ultimately reaching the distinct couloir (snow-filled most of the season) that leads to the first notch south of Peak 11,795. Along this easy upward diagonal traverse, the entire east face of Peak 11,795 will be skirted. Most parties bypass this summit, but it can be bagged with only small additional effort as part of this north ridge climb; see *Peak 11,795* for further information about this peak and its routes.

From the first notch south of Peak 11,795, remain on the crest and climb a small gendarme, which is separated from the remainder of the ridge by a second notch at the head of large and prominent couloirs ascending from both the east and the west. The western couloir, the one taken in *Route 35*, drops to the snow band above the lower portion of the eastern Triple Glacier. The eastern couloir is the Sickle Couloir (*Route 31*), which lies at the base of the north face of the northeast ridge. Descend to the second notch and climb two easy pitches on loose rock directly up out of the notch. After a section of scrambling, two somewhat more difficult pitches on good rock will put one well up the north ridge, where it levels off and joins the northeast ridge. The north summit is then reached by that route without further difficulty, and the usual traverse to the main south summit is made. This is a long and enjoyable climb on predominantly good rock, although there is one section of loose rock above the second notch. **Time:** 7 hours from a camp at timberline. See *Sierra Club Bulletin* 32, no. 5 (May 1947): pp. 128–29; *Summit* 6, no. 9 (September 1960): pp. 16–17, illus.; *Trail and Timberline*, no. 354 (June 1948): pp. 79–83, illus.

Variation: III, 5.6. First partial ascent July 27, 1956, by Richard Emerson and Robert Bowen, who made the first climb of the difficult portion of this face but did not finish the last easy portion to the summit of Peak 11,795. On September 13, 1957, Bill Pope and Mary Kay Pottinger made the first complete ascent; a similar route was climbed on September 10, 1960, by Peter Gardiner, Frank Knight, and Mihaly Csikszentmihalyi. The route described is the one that was taken by the 1960 party. On the regular North Ridge route of Mount Moran, after the initial traverse left, climb up and back to the right (west) for about four pitches all the way up to the ridge crest. Gain the ridge at the relatively level section below the final steep rise of the north ridge and northwest face, which culminates at the summit of Peak 11,795. This level section is somewhat more than halfway from the base of the ridge to the summit of Peak 11,795. From the point where the ridge meets the left edge of this final north face, a narrow diagonal ledge system of broken rock will be seen stretching up and right (west) across the entire face. Follow this delightfully exposed, but relatively easy, ledge system for three or four ropelengths until it begins to peter out at a point after the Triple Glaciers have come into clear view. Now turn straight up for two leads on very steep, solid rock to the top of this north face; the 1957 party encountered a large chockstone in this section. Scramble south to the base of a short headwall containing an 8m jam crack, which is easier than it appears. From the summit of Peak 11,795, a short distance above this headwall, descend easily to the notch to rejoin the main route described earlier.

ROUTE 35. WISE BURGETTES GO BY WATER. III, 5.4, AI2. June 28, 1997, by Gary Wise, Dan Burgette, Lane Burgette, and David Bywater. (See *Figure 9-33.*) This route ascends the diagonal snow couloir that slants from lower right to upper left on the left-hand margin of the north face of Mount Moran. The approach for the climb is the same as for the North Face route (*Route 37*), via the north shoulder of the peak and the lower portion of the eastern Triple Glacier. After passing the bergschrund in the middle of the glacier, traverse left (east) above the bergschrund to the snow gully marking the northern edge of the cliff band that separates the glacier from the upper reaches of the Triple Glacier route (*Route 38*). Once above the overhangs in the cliff band, follow a snowy ledge to the south. This snow traverse above the cliff band connects with the snow couloir leading to the notch on the north ridge where the Sickle Couloir (*Route 31*) meets the ridge from the east. This couloir is not as steep as the Sickle Couloir and it stays in the shade, thereby lessening the softening problems that occur on the upper portion of the Triple Glacier route. This climb is recommended as an easy mountaineering route in a wilderness setting with spectacular scenery. The first-ascent party did not rope up until the rock of the north ridge (see *Route 34*).

ROUTE 36. NORTH BUTTRESS. IV, 5.8. First ascent July 18, 1969, by Peter Habeler and George Lowe. (See *Figure 9-33.*) The northwest aspect of Mount Moran encompasses both the west face of the north ridge (see *Route 34*) and the North Face route (*Route 37*) and is bounded on the right by the upper snow arm of the easternmost Triple Glacier (see *Route 38*). Three couloirs cut the left (northern) half of the face below the north ridge: The first, if counting from north to south, is nearly vertical, descending from the notch immediately south of Peak 11,795. The third (see *Route 35*) is the largest and is snow-filled; it descends diagonally to the right (south) from the notch at the head of the Sickle Couloir, just below the final rise to the north summit, to connect with the upper snow band above the eastern Triple Glacier. The second couloir, rising at an intermediate angle, divides the face between the other two. The north buttress or pillar is the main prominent vertical feature in the center (southeast corner) of the face to the right (south) of the third couloir; it leads directly to the north summit of Mount Moran.

Approach the eastern Triple Glacier as in *Route 37* and continue up to and across the upper snow band above the glacier proper. To reach the base of the north buttress above, climb in the general line of the main chimney system, which descends from the left (north) face of the buttress. This section is not easy. The main portion of the climb goes straight up the crack and chimney system on the left (north) side of the well-defined pillar. The climbing is continuously difficult, requiring a mix of techniques, but is mostly in cracks, including two 5.8 pitches. Some of the rock is not good. The route exits onto the flat summit by going left around the final bulge that separates the split in the uppermost end of the chimney system.

ROUTE 37. NORTH FACE. IV, 5.8. First ascent June 29, 1962, by Pete Sinclair, Peter Lev, William Buckingham, and Leigh Ortenburger. (See *Figure 9-33.*) Between the upper snow arm of the easternmost of the Triple Glaciers and the north ridge of Mount Moran lies a considerable face containing small ridges, snow chutes, and walls. This route, the first on this portion of the mountain, goes approximately up the center of the face that rises directly above the lower portion of the eastern Triple Glacier. The face could be approached directly up from Moran Canyon (see *Route 38*), but a far better method is to use the same approach as for the North Ridge route (*Route 34*) up to the north shoulder, where an excellent camp can be placed. From the shoulder it is an easy matter to descend about 30m onto the level of the lower eastern Triple Glacier.

Ascend the glacier past the bergschrund toward the one crack in the first wall above; this crack diagonals up and left toward the upper snow band, which is completely separated from the main body of the glacier. In late season this snow band may disappear, leaving a sloping scree ledge. At the base of the crack traverse left (east) along a very wet ledge (in early season, through a waterfall) to its end, about 46m. Then turn up and right across difficult wet rock to reach the edge of the upper ledge, which parallels the smaller first ledge. Take this second ledge up and to the left until it is possible to scramble up to the edge of the snow band. Cut steps more or less straight up the snow band to reach the upper rock.

Cutting up through the entire face above, and slanting from lower right to upper left, is a prominent chimney with overhangs in the upper portions. Start on the rocks about 60m to the right of the chimney and traverse easily up and left toward the chimney. Moderate climbing for about three long ropelengths leads back to the chimney just beneath an overhanging section of the wall. Climb 46m up the rock to the left (north) of the chimney to a large area suitable for lunch. The next two pitches go up and right over difficult and somewhat loose rock. The climbing from here to the upper ramps becomes progressively steeper. At this point it appears that it should be possible to go up and left, but after about 25m in this direction the rock becomes excessively overhanging. Instead, one must make a difficult traverse to the right; a piton will be found at the beginning of this 8m traverse. There is some degree of commitment once this traverse has been made because the face below and to the right of the traverse is overhanging; retreat would be difficult. After negotiating the traverse, continue up and right to the end of the rope. The next lead is also difficult, ascending an ill-defined chimney (an angle piton will be found here) for about 20m before continuing upward to the right, again to the end of the rope. Two more ropelengths diagonal out in the same direction. The first is moderate, but the end of the second is difficult. A wafer piton will be found in the belay position at the end of this pitch. The final pitch of 46m leads again up and to the right and is of sustained difficulty, consisting of a series of small, bulging overhangs before ending on the upper right edge of the face. Protection is difficult to obtain on this vertical and overhanging pitch because cracks are scarce. This pitch exits onto the upper ramps leading to the summit ridge; these ramps lie back at a much more reasonable angle, and three relatively easy ropelengths lead to the ridge connecting the north summit to the main (south) summit. See *American Alpine Journal* 13, no. 2 (1963): pp. 410–20, illus.

ROUTE 38. TRIPLE GLACIER. II, 5.6, AI2+. First ascent September 8, 1935, by Malcolm Smith. (See *Figure 9-33*.) This climb was an achievement, considering it was a solo ascent that required a variety of climbing skills on an unexplored section of a major Teton peak. In early season it is a moderate snow-and-ice climb, but in midseason and late season there is serious climbing on the wet, downsloping rocks that will be found between the main lower section and the upper arm of the glacier. The traditional approach to this route is from Moran Canyon; see *Moran Canyon* in Section 10 for several options for reaching the mouth of this canyon, with the best being by powerboat from Colter Bay or Signal Mountain Lodge. About 1 mile up the canyon, where the streams descending from the Triple Glaciers meet the main Moran Creek, bushwhack up the talus to the terminal moraines of the three glaciers, then scramble up onto the easternmost glacier. The crossing of Moran Creek will present a problem best solved the night before the climb. A much better option is to approach from the east via the north shoulder of Mount Moran and establish a camp in the last trees on the shoulder (see *Route 34*). A descent of about 30m will then be required to reach the lower portion of the eastern Triple Glacier.

From the lower edge of the glacier, the upper arm or snow tongue (which does not actually connect with the main lower glacier) will be seen leading to the west ridge of Mount Moran just a short distance from the summit. Climb directly up the snow toward this snow tongue. Crossing the bergschrund of this glacier is the first problem, the severity of which will depend on the season. In early season there is usually a bridge near the middle of the glacier, but in late season it may be necessary to climb onto the rocks at the left (east) edge of the glacier to pass the bergschrund and gain the upper ice. Crampons will be very useful. Climb to the steep upper right (southwest) corner of the glacier above the bergschrund and onto the rock band separating the glacier from the snow tongue. While not overly difficult, this rock is unpleasant because it is all downsloping slabs, many of which are wet with running water. The snow tongue itself involves straightforward but moderately steep snow climbing to the crest of the west ridge, meeting the ridge a short distance west of the notch at the head of the Southwest Couloir route (*Route 18*). Descend into the notch, then climb the pitch out of it onto the flat summit of Mount Moran.

ROUTE 39. NORTHWEST RIDGE. II, 5.1, AI2. First ascent July 17, 1977, by Paul Horton and Lew Hitchner. (See *Figure 9-33*.) Between the eastern and central Triple Glaciers lies this major ridge, which rises in a series of sloping shelves to the final broad portion of the west ridge of Mount Moran. It is mostly easily approached from the east over the north shoulder of Mount Moran (see *Route 34*) and across the lower portion of the eastern Triple Glacier, although the base of the ridge could be reached by hiking directly up from Moran Canyon, gaining about 2,800 feet. An excellent campsite can be found at the base of the ridge. The route stays on or near the crest, and most of it consists of exposed scrambling up very broken rock of generally poor quality. The first roped pitch occurs low on the route, where the climbing out of a notch behind a small tower is steep and exposed. About two-thirds of the way up the ridge, two more pitches will be found on the face of a step where the rock quality is surprisingly good. After joining the west ridge, follow that route (*Route 19*) to the summit.

MOUNT MORAN, NORTH SUMMIT (12,400+)

Map: Mount Moran

Separated from the main (south) summit of Mount Moran by a flat ridge about 500m in length, the north summit was one of the earliest Teton peaks to be ascended. The first ascent took place on August 11, 1919, when LeRoy Jeffers reached this high point during his solo climb of a variant of Mount Moran's northeast ridge (see *Mount Moran, Route 30*)—a feat he publicized widely in several magazine articles and described in his book *The Call of the Mountains*. Most of the routes on Mount Moran from the north or northeast pass across the top of this flat subsummit, so no separate route descriptions will be given here.

PEAK 11,795

(0.5 mi NNE of Mount Moran)

Map: Mount Moran

This conspicuous subsummit high on the north ridge of Mount Moran is ordinarily climbed only during an ascent of that ridge (see *Mount Moran, Route 34*). By chance, the first four ascents of the north ridge of Moran apparently bypassed the top of this peak on the east. A mapping curiosity is the large 167-foot change in elevation of this point between the 1948 and 1968 USGS maps, perhaps the largest such shift between the two editions.

Chronology

UPPER EAST FACE: July 13, 1957, Yvon Chouinard, Duane Ewers
NORTH FACE: July 27, 1956, Richard Emerson, Robert Bowen (partial); September 13, 1957, Bill Pope, Mary Kay Pottinger (complete)
NORTH PROW ARÊTE: September 2, 1986, Steve Walker, Hugh Phillips, Bert Stolp
EAST BUTTRESS: September 2, 1986, Steve Walker, Hugh Phillips, Bert Stolp (descent)
WEST FACE: 2002, Jim Beyer

ROUTE 1. UPPER EAST FACE. II, 4.0. First ascent July 13, 1957, by Yvon Chouinard and Duane Ewers. On the usual traverse around the east side of Peak 11,795 during an ascent of the North Ridge route of Mount Moran (see *Mount Moran, Route 34*), one can scramble carefully upward and reach the summit of this peak. The difficulty is about the same whether one begins the traverse from the east, the southeast, or even the south. See *American Alpine Journal* 11, no. 1 (1958): pp. 85–88.

ROUTE 2. EAST BUTTRESS. II, 5.7. First descent September 2, 1986, by Steve Walker, Hugh Phillips, and Bert Stolp. The continuous couloir or chute that descends from the notch separating Peak 11,795 from the upper north ridge of Mount Moran forms the right (north) boundary of the Pika Buttress (see the Northeast Buttress Couloir variation under *Mount Moran, Route 30* for more on this couloir). To the right (north) of that couloir is a second well-defined buttress that was used as a direct route of descent from the summit of Peak 11,795. The complex and diverse terrain of this buttress necessitates careful routefinding. One 46m rappel was required, so the difficulty of this buttress for ascent can only be estimated.

ROUTE 3. NORTH FACE. II, 5.6. First partial ascent July 27, 1956, by Richard Emerson and Robert Bowen, who made the first climb of the difficult portion of this face but did not finish the last easy portion to the summit of Peak 11,795. On September 13, 1957, Bill Pope and Mary Kay Pottinger made the first complete ascent; a similar route was climbed on September 10, 1960, by Peter Gardiner, Frank Knight, and Mihaly Csikszentmihalyi. This route is described as a variation under *Mount Moran, Route 34*.

ROUTE 4. NORTH PROW ARÊTE. III, 5.8. First ascent September 2, 1986, by Steve Walker, Hugh Phillips, and Bert Stolp. When Peak 11,795 is viewed from the north, the steep north face or prow is seen to be bordered on the lower right by a subsidiary "ridgelet" or arête that leads south and terminates at the main arête forming the western edge of the main north face. From the north shoulder of Mount Moran, gain this initial subsidiary arête, which is then climbed easily (4.0) in several pitches to reach the main arête. Climb two pitches up this arête (5.6 and 5.7) to a belay stance from which one can go around the corner to the right. Climb the steep face (5.8) above for the third lead to gain a bowl. Several easier pitches up and slightly left lead to the top of the face or prow. After emerging north of the summit, scramble up along the crest of the ridge above to the top.

ROUTE 5. WEST FACE. III, 5.8. First ascent in 2002, by Jim Beyer. (See *Figure 9-33*. [Mt. Moran, North Aspect]) This route takes a direct line up the center of the west face of Peak 11,795 from the high meadow below. Little is known about this route other than that it contains short sections of steep to overhanging rock.

PEAK 9,940

(2.0 mi NNE of Mount Moran)
Map: Mount Moran

Rising 3,200 feet directly above the mouth of Moran Canyon is this high point at the end of the north shoulder of Mount Moran. It is well off the beaten path and has been visited very few times. The flat crest leading southwest to join that ridge is an attractive place to stroll, through a sparse grove of timberline trees. At the saddle (9,680+) a dike comes up from the west along the line of drainage and meets this ridge.

ROUTE 1. SOUTHWEST RIDGE. I, 2.0. First recorded ascent July 19, 1962, by John C. Reed Jr., who found a cairn but no record. The connecting ridge to Mount Moran is most directly approached from Jackson Lake up the main couloir leading to the base of the north ridge of Mount Moran. Reed, however, attained this ridge from the eastern Triple Glacier after hiking up from Moran Canyon. Either approach offers no technical difficulty, but some bushwhacking will be involved; see *Moran Canyon* in Section 10.

PEAK 12,000+

(0.6 mi W of Mount Moran)
Map: Mount Moran

This remote peak, which lies about halfway along the ridge connecting Mount Moran with Thor Peak, is unique in that it is composed largely of the black dike that extends from the east side of Mount Moran all the way west to the divide. It is ordinarily climbed only in conjunction with the ascent of Mount Moran via its West Ridge route *(Mount Moran, Route 19)*. The distance from the valley to this peak is sufficient to suggest a high camp prior to the ascent to the summit. See *Leigh Canyon* for the southern approach and *Moran Canyon* (in Section 10) for the northern approach.

Chronology

EAST RIDGE: August 26, 1935, Paul Petzoldt, H. K. Hartline
WEST RIDGE: August 24, 1964, Peter Cleveland, James Gregg
NORTH RIDGE: September 12, 1977, Norm Larson, Kevin Tischer

ROUTE 1. WEST RIDGE. II, 5.1. First ascent August 24, 1964, by Peter Cleveland and James Gregg. From about 7,300 feet in Moran Canyon ascend the very long slope up to the central Triple Glacier, passing the extensive moraines at the base of the glacier. This glacier could also be approached, perhaps with less effort, by hiking first to the north shoulder of Mount Moran (as in *Mount Moran, Route 34*) and then, with a slight descent, contouring west across the eastern Triple Glacier and the intervening ridge. Once on the central glacier climb to the highest point of the glacier at its left (east) side, where a snow bridge may be found to facilitate getting over the bergschrund. Ice axes will be necessary on the glacier, and in late season crampons will be useful on the bare ice. Then gain a broad ledge, which traverses Peak 12,000+ from east to west. Take this ledge right (west) to emerge on the ridge (rotten rock) west of the summit. Climb the first blocky pinnacle, descend 60m to the right (south), and traverse east to a snow couloir leading back onto the ridge. Climb the couloir to the ridge and follow it east to the summit on a mixture of better rock (5.1) and easy scrambling.

ROUTE 2. EAST RIDGE. II, 3.0. First ascent August 26, 1935, by Paul Petzoldt and

H. K. Hartline. In the course of their long traverse from the summit of Thor Peak to Mount Moran via its west ridge, Petzoldt and Hartline incidentally climbed Peak 12,000+. Approaching this peak along its west ridge, the duo contoured around the north side of the peak on ledges until the east ridge was reached. It was then an easy matter to scramble up the east ridge to the summit of the peak. More directly, from Leigh Canyon two separate drainages will be seen leading up into the large side canyon between Thor Peak and the south ridge of Mount Moran. Scramble up the right-hand (eastern) drainage toward the ridge connecting Mount Moran with Peak 12,000+. While this can be done without difficulty, some routefinding skills will be needed and an ice axe will be useful on some steep snow chutes during most of the season. The crest of the east ridge will be reached near its lowest point and then can be followed west to the summit. With an early start it is possible to reach the summit of this peak in one day, but a camp or bivouac will be required before the return.

ROUTE 3. NORTH RIDGE. II, 5.4. First ascent September 12, 1977, by Norm Larson and Kevin Tischer. (See *Figure 9-33*.) This major ridge, which separates the western and central Triple Glaciers, has an imposing appearance but contains some rock of less than high quality. Approach as for the West Ridge route (*Route 1*). The ridge begins between the considerable terminal moraines of the adjacent glaciers. Start this scenic climb on the crest of the ridge up to the first high point (10,640+). The significant sharp tower above, capped by good yellow rock, is bypassed on the left (east) until one can scramble back up to the crest south of its summit. The remainder of the climb to the summit of Peak 12,000+ is scrambling, largely up loose scree.

THE ZEBRA (11,680+)

(0.45 mi N of Thor Peak)
Map: Mount Moran

This remarkable and isolated peak lies on the northwest spur of the west ridge of Mount Moran. From a distance it appears as a group of unstable pinnacles, an impression based on the generally rotten nature of the rock in this area and the fact that there is an impressive hole or window in the ridge. The northeast and southwest faces of the peak are sheer, and the northwest ridge connecting to the Rotten Thumb also has a vertical step. These conditions led the few mountaineers who had seen the peak to steer clear because it was believed that the towers would probably collapse if an ascent was attempted. It was indeed a surprise to find that the summit block of the peak is formed from the finest Teton crystalline rock, of the same nature as Cleaver Peak. The southwest face of the Zebra features "stripes" of alternating white and black rock, 30m thick, which inspired the name for the peak.

ROUTE 1. SOUTHWEST COULOIR AND SOUTHEAST RIDGE. III, 5.4. First ascent July 26, 1989, by Leigh Ortenburger and Paul Horton. From Leigh Canyon ascend the side drainage on the west side of Thor Peak. Before turning north up into this drainage, it is best to stay near the creek in Leigh Canyon until the stream from this drainage is met. This avoids the grievous bushwhacking that would be encountered on an upward diagonal approach. In early season moderately steep snow will be encountered in some chutes before reaching the high plateau (ca. 10,800) just west of the summit of Thor Peak; ice axes and crampons will be required. Two cliff bands in this drainage are passed by some tricky routefinding on the left (west) side. The high plateau provides an adequate campsite with outstanding and unique views of the Teton Range. From this plateau ascend slightly to the upper left bounding ridge, from which a view can be had across the little-known cirque below the northwest face of Thor Peak. This cirque harbors a significant remnant glacier (see *Thor Peak*) that must be crossed to reach the Zebra. Descend from the ridge onto the snowfield, cross to the far northeast edge, pass the crest of the lateral moraine, and head toward one of the black-rock couloirs descending from the northeast.

Start in a couloir that leads toward the col to the right (east) of the summit of the Zebra, but switch to other subsidiary couloirs when the going becomes difficult or unpleasant. Some steep snow will be involved. If the correct route up the couloirs is found, the roped climbing does not begin until the col on the summit ridge is reached. (In early season a better approach might be directly up the western Triple Glacier to this col. In late season, however, an ascent of the glacier will be a serious undertaking, involving significant ice climbing and the passage of large crevasses.)

Almost immediately the good yellow crystalline rock will be found, as one climbs northwest along the ridge crest toward the summit. Five leads are involved, some short, mostly staying on the right side of the crest on ledges. At times the top edge of the snowfield will be used. The final pitch to the small summit involves enjoyable friction. A rappel was needed for descent from the summit; an anchor will be found at the summit for this initial rappel back down the southeast ridge. A second rappel along the ridge leads to the initial small notch in the ridge, then a long rappel straight down the southwest face takes one past the "stripes." Scrambling then permits a traverse left (east) to the couloirs used for the ascent.

ROTTEN THUMB (11,658)

(1.1 mi WNW of Mount Moran)
Map: Mount Moran

The vagaries of topographic mapping initially indicated, on the 1948 USGS quadrangle map, that this prominent high point culminating the northwest spur of the west ridge of Mount Moran was indeed a peak—that is, it had five closed 50-foot contour lines. The 1968 USGS quadrangle map changed contour intervals and the Rotten Thumb lost its peak status while its more impressive neighbor, the Zebra, gained peak status by holding three closed 80-foot contour lines. In any event, this isolated point was a climbing objective in the early 1960s, and even today it is not easily reached. Moran Canyon is the obvious method of approach (see *Moran Canyon* in Section 10), but an alternative worth considering is via Leigh Canyon and then up over the ridge into the largely unknown canyon west of Thor Peak and the Rotten Thumb. Only one route has been used to reach the summit, and it is probably neither the easiest nor the most pleasant.

ROUTE 1. EAST FACE. II, 5.1. First ascent August 31, 1962, by Ted Vaill, Stuart Kearns, and Ben Shapiro. From Moran Bay on Jackson Lake hike into Moran Canyon along the north side about 1.5 miles to the point where the stream draining the western Triple Glacier joins Moran Creek. On the first ascent the talus was ascended to the apex of the tree-covered triangle just below the western Triple Glacier, where a large boulder (visible from Moran Canyon) provides an adequate campsite for two. Above this camping area, the glacier was reached and climbed along its right side toward the east face of the Rotten Thumb.

An ascent done in 1988 suggests proceeding up the same talus slope while keeping to the right (west) of the stream until the lowest edge of the lateral moraine from the glacier is encountered. It is possible to gain and stay on the crest of this moraine all the way to its upper end at a clearly evident cliff band. This is not recommended, however, because this moraine crest is extremely sharp and, as with all moraines, is composed of crumbly morainal dirt, scree, and rocks. Of all the glacial moraines in the park this is probably the sharpest and best defined, reminiscent of Andean moraines. It is better to keep to the slope to the right of this moraine until meeting the cliff band, where exit can be made onto the uppermost flat end of the moraine. A campsite can be found at this point. The difficulty of the remainder of the climb is somewhat dependent on the time of year. In early season snow will be available, requiring ice axes to ascend the relatively low-angle right (west) edge of the glacier to sneak around the south end of the cliff band. In late season this will be bare ice, requiring crampons as well. Some rockfall can be expected from the slabs above the glacier.

When convenient, leave the glacier and head onto the talus, scree, and downsloping slabs of the east face of the Rotten Thumb and make an upward traverse toward the ridge just north of the summit block. This traverse is unpleasant going—loose, slippery, and exposed on thin scree on downsloping slabs. The final ascent to the summit can be made in two ways: For the original route, traverse left (east) around to the east face and climb an exposed, rotten chimney to the top. More easily one can simply continue up the north ridge, bypassing the final steep step on the right (west) to gain the summit via a short chimney on the northwest side. See *American Alpine Journal* 13, no. 2 (1963): pp. 487–89.

PEAK 11,840+
(0.2 mi NE of Thor Peak)
Map: Mount Moran

This peak lies on the north ridge of Thor Peak, rising about halfway toward the point where this ridge joins the west ridge of Mount Moran. Not usually an objective in itself, this point is generally climbed only in the course of the rarely done traverse from Thor Peak to Mount Moran or vice versa. The rock is not solid.

ROUTE 1. SOUTH RIDGE. II, 4.0. Probable first ascent August 26, 1935, by Paul Petzoldt and H. K. Hartline. This crumbly ridge has been gained only directly from the summit of Thor Peak and the connecting col (11,600+). There are blocky towers on this ridge that must be passed.

ROUTE 2. HEATHER'S COULOIR. II, 4.0. First ascent June 14, 2003, by Heather Paul and Paul Horton. This large southeast couloir leads to the low point on the ridge between Peak 11,840+ and Peak 12,000+. Proceed to the permanent snow/icefield below the east face of Thor Peak and continue up the obvious couloir above. With suitable conditions the ascent is a straightforward snow climb; Heather Paul kicked all the steps on the first ascent. Near the top of the couloir follow a steep branch leading west to a sharp notch in the main ridge. To reach the summit from the notch, climb up and right on an exposed and tricky rock face before regaining the ridge just below the top. In midseason and late season this couloir melts out because of its sunny exposure.

ROUTE 3. NORTH RIDGE. II, 4.0. Probable first descent August 26, 1935, by Paul Petzoldt and H. K. Hartline; possible first ascent June 30, 1966, by Don Storjohann, Pres Ellsworth, and Gunther Schlader. Like the South Ridge route (*Route 1*), this route is climbed only during a traverse, or attempted traverse, between Thor Peak and Mount Moran.

THOR PEAK (12,028)
Map: Mount Moran

This fine peak—one of the few in the park rising to more than 12,000 feet—has received little attention from climbers, largely because it is overshadowed by the massive Mount Moran. Thor Peak is one of the major Teton summits, harboring a permanent snow/icefield on its east side and a remnant glacier on its more remote northwest side. It is a challenging climb and should not be overlooked by visiting mountaineers. Thor Peak is readily approached via Leigh Canyon, but one very long day must be allowed for the ascent of the mountain. Some climbing is involved in ascending the steep valley on the west side of the peak, and in early season ice axes and even crampons will be required. A campsite with an extensive view can be found on the high plateau (10,800) west of the summit. The eastern approach toward the snowfield at the base of the east face is not as difficult, involving scrambling up the slope and talus near the stream from the bottom of Leigh Canyon.

The remnant glacier at the northwest base of the peak has ice, crevasses, moraines, and a bergschrund, but in 1963 no evidence of movement was found. It was first visited three years earlier, in 1960, and the remote and unnamed north–south drainage west of Thor Peak, between it and Peak 11,126, was probably first entered at that time. *Routes 4, 5,* and *6* all begin by ascending a slabby section of rock below the right-hand margin of the east face. What is thought to be the easiest route is depicted in *Figure 9-34*; it is not known *exactly* where the three different first-ascent parties went in this section.

Chronology

NORTHEAST COULOIR: Late August 1930, Paul Petzoldt, Bruton Strange
SOUTH SLOPE: Late August 1930, Paul Petzoldt, Bruton Strange (descent); August 26, 1935, Paul Petzoldt, H. K. Hartline (ascent)
EAST FACE: July 22, 1950, Glenn Exum, Michael Brewer, Richard Pownall
var—August 15, 1957, Yvon Chouinard, Ken Weeks
var—August 1, 1994, Beverly Boynton, Rob Mahoney
SOUTHEAST RIDGE: September 28, 1954, Keith Jones, Martin Benham
EAST FACE, SOUTH CHIMNEY: September 2, 1957, Ken Weeks, Curt Butler
NORTHWEST FACE: August 13, 1960, Leigh Ortenburger, Irene Beardsley (Ortenburger), Pete Sinclair, Ray Jacquot
EAST FACE ARÊTE: June 19, 1966, Don Storjohann, Pres Ellsworth
HIDDEN COULOIR: September 6, 1975, Paul Horton, Renny Jackson

ROUTE 1. ▲ SOUTH SLOPE. II, 4.0. First descent in late August 1930, by Paul Petzoldt and Bruton Strange; first ascent August 26, 1935, by Paul Petzoldt and H. K. Hartline. There are two principal southern

FIGURE 9-34. Thor Peak, east aspect. (A) Southeast Ridge *(Route 2)*, II, 5.4; (B) East Face, South Chimney *(Route 3)*, II, 5.6; (C) East Face *(Route 4)*, IV, 5.8; (D) East Face, variation: 1957, IV, 5.8; (E) East Face, variation: 1994, IV, 5.9; (F) East Face Arête *(Route 5)*, III, 5.6; (G) Hidden Couloir *(Route 6)*, III, 5.6, AI3

approaches to the upper portions of Thor Peak. Both ultimately take the climber to a large talus couloir that leads in a southwest–northeast direction from the saddle between Thor Peak and Peak 11,126 to the notch on the southeast ridge a few meters from the summit. The very steep, diagonal east face snow chute leads to this same notch from the other side (see *Route 6*). This easy talus couloir, which contains much loose rock, can be reached by first ascending Leigh Canyon past the side canyon between Mount Moran and Thor Peak, and past the southeast ridge of Thor Peak. Then turn up and west to gain the main south talus and scree slope. Some cliff bands will be encountered on this slope, and routefinding skill will be required while diagonaling up and west. This slope ultimately leads to the talus couloir, which takes one almost directly to the summit.

To reach this couloir more directly, continue up Leigh Canyon until the stream descending from the steep drainage between Thor Peak and Peak 11,126 is reached. In general, the route ascends this drainage to the saddle and then cuts right (northeast) up the obvious talus couloir that leads to within a few meters of the summit. The first headwall in the drainage can be passed near the stream or on the left (west) side; either way involves scrambling up a steep pitch or two. A second headwall blocks the drainage about halfway up; it can be climbed to the left (west) of the stream or to the right (east). Some routefinding is necessary on both of these headwalls. To avoid having to rappel on the descent, one should remember where these obstacles were passed on the ascent. Continue to the gentle saddle and then turn up the talus couloir that leads to the small notch in the southeast ridge; the summit is quickly reached from this notch by scrambling along the ridge. On the descent from the summit, take the talus couloir down to the saddle; if one tries to descend more directly to the southwest, cliffs requiring rappelling will be unavoidable.

ROUTE 2. SOUTHEAST RIDGE. II, 5.4. First ascent September 28, 1954, by Keith Jones and Martin Benham. (See *Figure 9-34.*) Bushwhack up Leigh Canyon about 2 miles to the large talus fan on the north side of the canyon just west of the south buttress of Mount Moran. Ascend this fan, bearing left (west) toward Thor Peak's southeast ridge, which forms the left edge of the prominent east face. Cross the creek from the permanent snow/icefield that lies beneath the east face and climb a grassy slope and boulders to the point where the crest of the glacial moraine meets the southeast ridge. At this point the ridge broadens into a face bisected by a large crack. Climb a section of rotten rock, traversing left across the face to the large crack. Enter the crack and ascend it for about 46m, or use the slabs to the left (south) that are covered with loose scree. Continue to a small notch overlooking the steep snow couloir that leads upward from the left (south) edge of the east face permanent snow/icefield. A short traverse on a narrow ledge leads to the col at the head of this couloir. Now scramble over easy rocks up the remainder of the ridge to the summit. It would also be possible to traverse west to *Route 1*.

ROUTE 3. EAST FACE, SOUTH CHIMNEY. II, 5.6. First ascent September 2, 1957, by Ken Weeks and Curt Butler. (See *Figure 9-34.*) Like *Route 4*, this route starts at the top of the permanent snow/icefield beneath the east face. Once on the rock above the snow/icefield, a difficult friction pitch must be negotiated to gain access to the large chimney leading upward and slightly left (south) to the southeast ridge. About one-third of the way up the chimney, climb out on the face to the right (north) for about one ropelength before returning to the chimney. Once the ridge is attained, follow *Route 2* without difficulty to the summit.

ROUTE 4. EAST FACE. IV, 5.8. First ascent July 22, 1950, by Glenn Exum, Michael Brewer, and Richard Pownall. (See *Figure 9-34.*) This impressive climb is an example of true exploration and adventure in the Tetons. Pownall and Brewer had noticed the face from the summit of Mount Moran while guiding an ascent of that peak. They thought Thor Peak had probably been climbed but were quite sure that its east face had not been touched. They underestimated the size of the wall on their first attempt, thinking that it could be about 200m in height. Finding it to be nearly twice that size, the pair retreated, reasoning that they did not have enough time to complete the climb after negotiating the difficult approach. For their successful ascent they conscripted their boss, Glenn Exum, deciding that "to do this ascent safely would require at least a three-man party." On the evening of July 21, the trio paddled across Leigh Lake in Brewer's vintage two-person Folbot folding kayak, towing a small inflatable raft holding their climbing equipment. After spending the night fighting off porcupines at the mouth of Leigh Creek, they made quick time and arrived at the small snowfield below the face a little after 9 AM. They climbed the 400m face in 16 pitches, each 37m in length. With the face surprisingly lacking in suitable piton cracks, they didn't place their first protection pin until the 13th pitch! Exum was given the honor of the final crux lead of the day. After Exum managed the difficult overhang (5.8) directly above the belay, "it was only a matter of minutes before he had 120 feet of rope out and yelled down that he was on the summit ridge," Pownall recalled in his report for the 1951 *American Alpine Journal*. "Glenn's last lead was one of the finest I have seen—the highlight of the climb."

To approach the east face of Thor Peak, proceed as in *Route 7* into the side canyon between Thor Peak and the south ridge of Mount Moran and ascend to the apex of the small permanent snow/icefield at the base of the east face. The first lead from the top of the ice goes up rather smooth friction slabs to a broad belay ledge. After the second lead, up a series of broken chimneys and slabs to a grassy ledge, a 30m chimney is climbed. The fourth pitch ascends a series of ledges, climaxed by a 15m chimney containing running water. A ropelength of friction slabs traverses slightly to the right (north). The sixth lead climbs short, vertical faces up and slightly left (south) to a broad ledge from which a large open book, or V chimney, in orange rock can be seen above near the top of the face. The next portion of the route is an upward traverse to the left toward the bottom of this easily recognized open book. Scramble for a ropelength and then climb some broken faces including a difficult, crackless 12m chimney. The ninth pitch ascends a 15m chimney, makes an upward traverse to the right, and finishes with an 8m vertical chimney. The next short lead goes up a 4m chimney, traverses left (south) for 6m, and reaches a beautiful, flower-covered, grassy ledge after passing a 3m wall. Traverse up and left for about 145m toward the base of the open book, which the first-ascent party attempted but did not climb. Instead, attack a nearly vertical 25m chimney about 15m to the right of the main open book. The upper portion of this chimney is difficult, as is the exit that is made to the right across a vertical face. After this traverse right, climb about 3m up on good rock to a good belay anchor ledge. Now climb 15m in a vertical chimney to a chockstone anchor. The next lead goes directly upward for 37m; the final 12m is on downsloping and loose rock to a perch beneath a band of overhanging yellow rock. The first 9m of the final pitch, directly up over several overhanging bulges in downsloping and loose rock, is the most difficult section of the climb; the lead ends on the upper "ridgelet" of the east face arête (see *Route 5*), which forms the outer border of the steep, diagonal snow couloir on the east face of Thor Peak (see *Route 6*). Follow this ridgelet easily up to the summit ridge, from which the summit is gained. This long and complex route entails some rockfall danger in the lower sections as well as some loose rock, and it offers very few cracks for protection. See *American Alpine Journal* 8, no. 1 (1951): pp. 71–77.

Variation: IV, 5.8. First ascent August 15, 1957, by Yvon Chouinard and Ken Weeks. (See *Figure 9-34.*) This variation begins by going up two friction pitches just left of *Route 3*. Three pitches then follow in the chimney of *Route 3* before a traverse to the right is made to easy scrambling on whitish rock. The original East Face route is then joined approximately 60m below the open book/V chimney.

Variation: IV, 5.9. First ascent August 1, 1994, by Beverly Boynton and Rob Mahoney. (See *Figure 9-34.*) This important variation marked the first time that the large open book, or V chimney, so conspicuous from below, was climbed. This open book and its orange rock are easily visible from the cirque. Directly below this prominent feature one can see a large, light-colored, dish-like area of rock. The main objective in the lower portion of the route is to reach this dish-like area. From the upper left (west) portion of the permanent snow/icefield beneath the east face, the first-ascent party went up the first pitch of *Route 3* and then traversed up and east for two ropelengths to join the original East Face route. They climbed two pitches up and then back to the west into the dish. Scramble up for approximately 90m along the east side of the dish, heading for the open book and the large chimney to the right. Two roped pitches (5.6 to 5.7) lead up and left to the base of the open book. Three spectacular 30m pitches (5.8 to 5.9) lead up this main corner system. The climbing consists of jamming and delicate stemming with good protection (except for a moderate runout on the final pitch). Easy climbing leads up the final portion of *Route 5* and the top of the Hidden Couloir (*Route 6*) to the summit of the peak.

ROUTE 5. EAST FACE ARÊTE. III, 5.6. First ascent June 19, 1966, by Don Storjohann and Pres Ellsworth. (See *Figure 9-34.*) The major feature of the east face of Thor Peak is the Hidden Couloir (*Route 6*), which diagonals up from lower right to upper left, reaching the southeast ridge 30m short of the summit. The east face arête forms the left edge of this couloir; the uppermost part of this arête is used by the East Face route (*Route 4*). Approach the permanent snow/icefield lying at the base of the east face of Thor Peak as in the Northeast Couloir route (*Route 7*). From the apex of the snow/icefield, start up the slabs of *Route 4*, eventually breaking right to reach the bowl at the beginning of the arête. The arête is then climbed on broken rock.

ROUTE 6. HIDDEN COULOIR. III, 5.6, AI3. First ascent September 6, 1975, by Paul Horton and Renny Jackson. (See *Figure 9-34.*) This major, well-defined diagonal couloir is readily seen from the summit plateau of Mount Moran, but it is not visible from Jackson Hole. Entry to the couloir is gained in the same manner as the east face arête (see *Route* 5), which forms the left edge of the couloir. The climbing in the couloir itself consists of eight or nine pitches (approximately 350m) of 40°–50° snow and ice, the proportion of ice depending on the year and time of year. Belay anchors can be obtained by climbing near the right side of the couloir, though the rock quality is not all that great. While rockfall danger must exist in such a steep and narrow chute, very little has been observed in the ascents to date. **Gear:** An assortment of hardware, including nuts, pitons, and ice screws, was used on the first ascent.

ROUTE 7. NORTHEAST COULOIR. II, 5.6. First ascent in late August 1930, by Paul Petzoldt and Bruton Strange. The name of this route is somewhat misleading because the couloir faces southeast but reaches the summit ridge north or north-east of the summit. Proceed up Leigh Canyon for about 2 miles, past the south ridge of Mount Moran; then turn right (north) up into the side canyon between the east face of Thor Peak and the south ridge of Mount Moran. From the vicinity of the permanent snow/icefield, a shallow couloir (or a concave face) leads north-west up to the ridge that joins Thor Peak with Mount Moran. This couloir is at the right (north) edge of the main east face and ends at the col (11,600+) between Thor Peak and Peak 11,840+. Some 5.6 climbing leads to the ridge crest north of the summit of Thor Peak. Follow the ridge south to the summit. See *Appalachia* 18, no. 4 (December 1931): pp. 388–408, illus.

ROUTE 8. NORTHWEST FACE. III, 5.4. First ascent August 13, 1960, by Leigh Ortenburger, Irene Beardsley (Ortenburger), Pete Sinclair, and Ray Jacquot. There are three possible approaches to the base of this obscure 350+m face; more than one day will be required to reach and climb this face, so a campsite must be selected. (1) One can ascend Moran Canyon (see *Moran Canyon* in Section 10) and turn up the unnamed north–south subsidiary canyon that leads to this side of Thor Peak; it is not known if this has been done yet, but in theory it should work well. (2) Or one can ascend Leigh Canyon, climb its north slope between Peak 11,126 and Point 10,805, and drop down into the head of the same unnamed canyon. For this alternative there is an excellent camping site at 9,400 feet in the highest trees on the north side of the 10,000+-foot col between the unnamed canyon and Leigh Canyon. From this site make a gradual upward traverse to reach the high plateau west of Thor Peak, from which it is possible to descend 120m to the remnant glacier at the base of the face. Ice axes are required for this descent. (3) Finally, one can ascend Leigh Canyon and climb the steep drainage between Thor Peak and Peak 11,126 to the high plateau, and then descend the far (north) side to the base of the northwest face. This alternative is most direct but will also require ice axes for the steep snow.

An obvious moraine leads around the left edge of the remnant glacier to the base of the face. From the top end of the moraine climb up and then slightly to the right, following a line of weakness to about 60m below the summit. This final portion could be climbed directly, but the first-ascent party veered slightly left here and reached the northeast ridge of Thor Peak about 46m below the summit. A considerable quantity of rotten and loose rock must be expected on this climb, although this route, which actually stays generally left of center, does not seem to be subject to much falling rock. Routes farther to the right would be both more difficult and more dangerous. This climb is not recommended due to the unpleasant nature of the rock, even though it is a 350+m high-angle face. See *American Alpine Journal* 12, no. 2 (1961): pp. 373–79.

PINETOP (9680+) AND POINT 10,000+

(east slopes of Thor Peak)
Map: Mount Moran

These two points are located on a ridge below the east face of Thor Peak, to the west of the stream running from the permanent snow/icefield at the base of the face to the upper, or more westerly, of the two lakes midway up Leigh Canyon (7,785). Pinetop is distinguished by a summit pine tree that is prominent when viewed from certain angles. Point 10,000+ is the more ragged summit above. Approach from the floor of Leigh Canyon by ascending the scree and cliff bands of the side canyon.

Pinetop

ROUTE 1. EAST RIDGE. I, 5.6. First ascent July 26, 1935, by Paul and Eldon Petzoldt, Edward Lorenz, and Dan Webster. This is presumably the route that the Petzoldts et al. used long ago. In the summit register they referred to one of the two lakes below in Leigh Canyon as "Laughing Water Lake." Scramble to a ledge with trees on the right side of the ridge and just to the right of the darker rock. The first pitch attains the broad ridge and ascends it via shallow cracks. The second pitch follows cracks to easier steps and ledges. The third pitch consists of 3rd- and 4th-class scrambling to the summit with its pine tree and empty cairn. Descend by down-climbing the west ridge to the notch, then drop to the slopes to the east.

Point 10,000+

ROUTE 1. EAST RIDGE. II, 5.6 (if combined with Pinetop). First known ascent June 22, 1997, by Paul Horton and Andy Carson. From the notch in the ridge west of Pinetop, scramble west to steeper terrain. The first pitch (5.6) starts left of the crest and crosses over to the right. The next pitch ascends a chimney to the broken summit area. The actual summit is a big block, surmounted with some boulder moves. To descend, follow the ridge connecting to the slopes of Thor Peak; a notch and short step are 5th class.

PEAK 11,126

(0.8 mi SW of Thor Peak)
Map: Mount Moran

Perhaps the least known of the Teton peaks in the formidable class, Peak 11,126 is ringed with barriers of difficulty even after the considerable approach up Leigh Canyon is overcome. Only the side of the first ascent is moderate. From the west the summit block is seen as a solid wedge resting in a V of couloirs. The cliff band above these couloirs extends around the east side and rises above extensive downsloping slabs. The steep western couloir that bounds the block on the north forms a distinct notch on the north ridge and continues with equal clarity down the east face of the mountain. It appears to be an important line of weakness in the structure, if not a fault line.

ROUTE 1. SOUTHWEST RIDGE. II, 5.1. First ascent June 28, 1953, by Leigh Ortenburger and William Buckingham, who climbed the peak from Cirque Lake via a traverse of its southwest ridge from Point 10,805. (See *Moran Canyon* in Section 10 for the approach to Cirque Lake.) The southwest ridge intersects the summit mass of Peak 11,126 just beyond a small 10,400+-foot col. From this point, a ramp allows one to contour around to the east side of the peak, crossing some small gullies and ridges. From the upper east side an easy scramble leads to the summit ridge just left (south) of the summit block. Traverse underneath the summit block on the west and reach the flat, slabby summit from the northwest. This route involves some tricky routefinding. It is also possible to intersect this climb on the upper east side of the peak by approaching via Leigh Canyon and the steep drainage separating Peak 11,126 from Thor Peak (see *Thor Peak, Route 1* and *The Zebra, Route 1* for information concerning this drainage). For descent, reverse the route onto the smooth slabs of the east face, then return to either the 10,400+-foot col or the upper end of the drainage separating this peak from Thor Peak. One party has reported a descent using a system of slabs toward the northeast.

Variation: II, 4.0. First ascent August 3, 1963, by John C. Reed Jr. and David Steller; this was also the second ascent of the peak. Gain the small 10,400+-foot col on the same southwest ridge directly from Leigh Canyon and follow the ridge toward Peak 11,126. However, instead of traversing around to the east side, climb the last 100m on the south face. This variation also involves tricky routefinding. Descent to Leigh Canyon was made via the south gully from the 10,400+-foot col, traversing west out of the gully at about 9,000 feet to avoid a waterfall. This same col was gained a year later, in August 1964, by Olton and Glenn Hewitt. They may have climbed a slight variant on the upper part of the peak above the col on the southeast side.

ROUTE 2. NORTH RIDGE. II, 5.6. First ascent July 25, 1998, by Paul Horton and Greg Fulkerson. The approach for this climb is from Leigh Canyon to the plateau west of Thor Peak, as for *The Zebra, Route 1*. Once on this saddle hike and scramble west toward the north ridge of Peak 11,126, at first on the crest and then below the crest on the east side. A distinct notch will be encountered just before the first pitch. **Pitch 1:** Climb broken ledges and a chimney to a belay on the west side of the ridge (easy 5th class, 46m). **Pitch 2:** Scramble up easy slabs to a belay at the base of the headwall (4th class, 23m). **Pitch 3:** Climb cracks and an offwidth on the headwall on the west side of the ridge (5.6, 23m). Easy scrambling on the western side of the ridge leads to the summit. The descent was made via downclimbing and scrambling on the south aspect of the peak. After losing approximately 1,500 feet of elevation it is easy to traverse back into the approach drainage and regain the floor of Leigh Canyon.

PEAK 10,952

(1.2 mi E of Cleaver Peak)
Map: Mount Moran

Between Cleaver Peak on the west and Mount Moran on the east lies a major north–south ridge separating the relatively well-known Cirque Lake from the almost unknown side canyon to the east. Geological peculiarities mark this ridge. Just north of and only 90m lower than the summit of Peak 10,952 are some curious depressions along the flat and broad ridge, perhaps attributable to the north–south fault in the region that crosses, at right angles, the east–west continuation of the black diabase dike of Mount Moran. The black dike here is offset some 0.2 mile from the east–west line of the dike to the east. The entire eastern side of this mountain is a dreadful continuous scree-and-talus slope, not to be considered for ascent and probably not pleasant even for descent. Jipe Lake, the small lake at 9,840+ feet on the west slope of this peak above Cirque Lake, makes a fine campsite. See *Moran Canyon* in Section 10 for the approach to Cirque Lake.

ROUTE 1. SOUTH RIDGE. I, 2.0. Probable first ascent in 1935, by T. F. Murphy and Mike Yokel Jr.; first recorded ascent June 27, 1953, by Leigh Ortenburger and William Buckingham. From a camp at Cirque Lake, ascend the easy slope to the col between Peak 10,952 and Point 10,805. A short section of the south ridge above the col involves 3.0 scrambling and is climbed on the right (east) side. An alternative is to diagonal left (north) when approaching this col from Cirque Lake and to reach the ridge crest above (north of) this section. A cairn but no record was found on the plateau that is 600 feet south of the summit and a few feet lower.

ROUTE 2. NORTH RIDGE. II, 2.0. First ascent July 13, 1963, by John C. Reed Jr. and David Steller. From Moran Canyon ascend into the unnamed canyon east of the peak to about 8,800 feet and then climb the easy but dreadful slope to the north ridge near the line of the dike. Follow the north ridge past the curious depressions to the summit.

PEAK 10,880+

(0.5 mi E of Maidenform Peak)
Map: Mount Moran

This is an unimportant high point on the ridge crest south of Cirque Lake. See *Moran Canyon* in Section 10 for the approach to Cirque Lake.

ROUTE 1. WEST RIDGE. I, 2.0. First ascent June 27, 1953, by Leigh Ortenburger and William Buckingham. This ridge is easily traversed from the summit of Maidenform Peak.

ROUTE 2. EAST RIDGE. I, 2.0. First descent June 27, 1953, by Leigh Ortenburger and William Buckingham. The crest of this ridge is readily traversed to Point 10,805 at the southeast corner of the Cirque Lake region.

MAIDENFORM PEAK (11,137)

Map: Mount Moran

This easy but isolated peak affords one of the most comprehensive views in the range. With the exception of Mount Wister, Shadow Peak, Nez Perce, Cloudveil Dome, and Disappointment Peak, every peak from Buck Mountain to Eagles Rest Peak and beyond is visible. The name, given in 1955, is derived from the remarkable appearance of the peak as seen from the north. The rock unfortunately is not sound. The most common method of approach is circuitous, via the Cascade Canyon trail, over Littles Peak, and on north and east to the saddle at the head of

the south fork of Moran Canyon (see *Moran Canyon* in Section 10); this route was discovered by Fred Ayres in the course of his first ascent. The direct but long approach via Leigh Canyon is fraught with bushwhacking. The easiest approach is from the west, utilizing the trails of the Caribou-Targhee National Forest/Jedediah Smith Wilderness (also see *Moran Canyon*). *Figure 9-35* shows the view to the southwest over Cleaver and Maidenform Peaks.

Chronology

NORTH RIDGE: August 7, 1941, Fred Ayres
EAST RIDGE: June 27, 1953, Leigh Ortenburger, William Buckingham (descent); July 25, 1973, Jim Bruggeman, Don Thompson (ascent)
SOUTHWEST RIDGE: August 7, 1941, Fred Ayres (descent); August 15, 1955, John and Jean Fonda, Roald Fryxell (ascent)

ROUTE 1. ▲ SOUTHWEST RIDGE. II, 3.0. First descent August 7, 1941, by Fred Ayres; first ascent August 15, 1955, by John and Jean Fonda and Roald Fryxell. From the saddle to the west of Maidenform Peak that separates the south fork of Moran Canyon from Leigh Canyon, scramble up this ridge to the summit. Of the three routes to the summit this is perhaps the most devious because one cannot easily stay directly on the ridge crest. The steeper and rotten sections are usually bypassed on the right (south).

ROUTE 2. EAST RIDGE. II, 2.0. First descent June 27, 1953, by Leigh Ortenburger and William Buckingham; first ascent July 25, 1973, by Jim Bruggeman and Don Thompson. This entire ridge was descended over Peak 10,880+ to Point 10,805. The east ridge has also been reached directly from the south by climbing the long slope out of upper Leigh Canyon.

ROUTE 3. NORTH RIDGE. II, 3.0. First ascent August 7, 1941, by Fred Ayres. This ridge can be easily reached from either the Cirque Lake side or the south fork of Moran Canyon (see *Moran Canyon* in Section 10). On the first ascent, this ridge was followed after a climb of Cleaver Peak.

CLEAVER PEAK (11,055)

Map: Mount Moran

The massive character of the rock makes aptly named Cleaver Peak conspicuous from most points, including the summit of the Grand Teton. The attractiveness of this double summit stems from the sharpness of its end-on profile and partially from its remoteness from standard tourist traffic. Furthermore, the rock of the upper peak is of the finest Teton type, golden and solid, in sharp contrast to the crumbly dark rock surrounding its base. Cleaver Peak comprises two separate peaks—a north peak and a south peak—of almost the same elevation; the US Geological Survey (USGS) strangely places the highest elevation, 11,055 feet, on the south peak, which is the lower of the two. A large rectangular notch separates the two peaks. The first ascent was made somewhat unintentionally following a remarkable early attempt on the south face of Bivouac Peak.

FIGURE 9-35. Maidenform Peak and Cleaver Peak, northeast aspect overview

See *Figures 9-35* and *9-36* for two views of Cleaver Peak.

From Jackson Hole there are three methods of approach, but all are long, requiring hours of hard work. The most obvious is the bushwhack directly up Moran Canyon from Moran Bay on Jackson Lake, as was done on the first ascent (see *Moran Canyon* in Section 10 for the possible approaches to this canyon). Continue to the south fork to reach the west side of the peak, or hike into the Cirque Lake basin for the eastern routes. One can also approach via Leigh Canyon, an equally difficult bushwhack, to the divide (9,920+) west of Maidenform Peak and thereby reach the upper south fork of Moran Canyon. Most commonly used, however, is the devious route that starts with the Cascade Canyon trail to Lake Solitude, goes up and over the top of Littles Peak and along the main divide north (easy), and then eventually turns right (east) to enter the uppermost south fork of Moran Canyon.

A sneaky scheme that requires less physical effort than any of the preceding approaches, perhaps first utilized by Marty Thompson in the early 1970s, involves the trails of the Caribou-Targhee National Forest/Jedediah Smith Wilderness on the west slope of the Teton Range. From Driggs, Idaho, drive to the US Forest Service (USFS) trailhead on North Leigh Creek at the edge of the wilderness area (see the USGS Granite Basin quadrangle). Take the Green Mountain trail to the basin above and beyond Green Lake, from which one can easily reach and cross the divide at the broad saddle (9,760+) due west of Cleaver Peak. The south fork of Moran Canyon is then easily crossed to reach the peak.

Chronology

NORTH PEAK, NORTHWEST CHIMNEY: August 9, 1940, John McCown II, C. Grove McCown, Edward McNeill, Thomson Edwards

NORTH PEAK, NORTHEAST CHIMNEY: August 9, 1940, John McCown II, C. Grove McCown, Edward McNeill, Thomson Edwards (descent); August 22, 1969, Charles Bockes, Marvin Conway, Judy and Maurice Horn (ascent)

NORTH PEAK, WEST CHIMNEY: August 7, 1941, Fred Ayres (descent); August 1992, Jim Springer (ascent)

SOUTH PEAK, SOUTHEAST SHOULDER: August 7, 1941, Fred Ayres (first ascent of south peak)

SOUTH PEAK, EAST FACE–SOUTH RIDGE: August 19, 1988, Jim and Kim Springer

NORTH PEAK, ANNATIA'S: August 11, 1990, Paul Horton, Marianne Fraser

NORTH PEAK, WAYNE'S WORLD: August 8, 1998, Wayne, Nils, Scott, and Markus Peterson

ROUTE 1. ▲ NORTH PEAK, NORTHWEST CHIMNEY. II, 5.4. First ascent August 9, 1940, by John McCown II, C. Grove McCown, Edward McNeill, and Thomson Edwards. The west side of the north peak has two distinct features: a small, sharp notch that bisects the summit block and a large, rounded notch farther north with a spire on its north side. From the west in the south fork of Moran Canyon, scramble up talus and ledges to a wide chimney leading to the large, rounded notch. About 15m short of the notch one is forced out onto the left (north) face of the wide chimney, where small holds and a jam crack (5.4) permit passage. One can also climb up in the right corner and do a hand traverse left (5.6) to gain the notch. From the notch climb (south) using a vertical face left of some large cracks. Mantel onto a ledge, then climb a steep east-facing slab (5.4) and scramble south to the higher north peak. From the notch, a small spire—"Jipe Point"—can be ascended (5.4) en route to the summit.

ROUTE 2. NORTH PEAK, WAYNE'S WORLD. II, 5.7. First ascent August 8, 1998, by Wayne, Nils, Scott, and Markus Peterson. This climb is located just to the right (southwest) of *Route 1* and consists of two reportedly excellent pitches. Move past the ledge leading right (south) to the West Chimney route (*Route 3*) to an obvious south-trending crack, less than halfway between the ledge and the beginning of *Route 1*. **Pitch 1:** Begin by climbing a steep face with a hand crack on the right, then move around a bulge to the left (east) on downsloping slabs with an undercling on

FIGURE 9-36. Cleaver Peak, east aspect, South Peak, East Face–South Ridge *(Route 6)*, III, 5.8

the left (5.5). Now climb the steep, somewhat runout west-facing wall above (5.5), trending right (south) to a belay on the extreme south end of the large, rounded notch. This belay is directly beneath two large cracks located just to the right of the third pitch of *Route 1*. **Pitch 2:** Face climb near the more easterly of the two cracks toward a large flake. Follow the crack and face along the left side of the flake to the obvious alcove above. Climb a short, tight chimney and pull the roof above using a good handhold (5.7). Scramble right (south) and across a smooth, downsloping slab (the top of *Route 3*), followed by a 4m vertical hand crack, and then scramble easily to the summit. For descent the Peterson party scrambled a short distance down *Route 3* to a ledge, from which a double-rope rappel (from anchor slings around a chockstone) deposited them on the access ledge for *Route 3*.

ROUTE 3. NORTH PEAK, WEST CHIMNEY. II, 5.4. First descent August 7, 1941, by Fred Ayres; first known ascent in August 1992, by Jim Springer. From the base of the wide chimney described in *Route 1*, ascend a corner up and right to the small, sharp notch that bisects the main summit block. At two points one is forced to traverse out right onto the face and then back left to the corner. At the top of the second detour there are two options: continue straight up a chimney to the notch and the nearby summit (the normal route), or traverse left (north) behind a gigantic flake, then climb up a slab to join *Route 1* just above the rounded notch. This route can be descended with two single-rope rappels, with an occasional section of easy downclimbing.

ROUTE 4. NORTH PEAK, ANNATIA'S. II, 5.6. First ascent August 11, 1990, by Paul Horton and Marianne Fraser. Scramble up the dark rock of the west face to the base of the gold rock. Traverse to a point beneath a crack and chimney system that leads up to the north end of the large rectangular notch between the peaks. **Pitch 1:** The initial pitch ascends cracks (5.6). **Pitch 2:** Climb to a broken area behind a large detached block. Take a narrowing ramp in the upper headwall out to and around a prow on the right, then immediately climb steep cracks to and above the headwall (5.6). **Pitch 3:** Follow ledges and steps up to the large rectangular notch between the peaks, then continue onto the face left of the steep south edge of the north peak (5.4). **Pitch 4:** Trend left up the face to a large ledge at the base of the summit headwall (5.1). Scramble north on this ledge, eventually reaching the small, sharp notch and the nearby summit. One can also climb directly up to the summit (5.7, no protection) from the south end of this ledge; this was done by Richard DuMais in the summer of 1993.

ROUTE 5. SOUTH PEAK, SOUTHEAST SHOULDER. II, 5.4. First ascent August 7, 1941, by Fred Ayres. The ridge between Maidenform Peak and the south peak can easily be gained from the east or west at a point just south of the south peak. From the small final notch in the black rock, avoid the short vertical section of the south ridge of the south peak (*Route 6*) by climbing down on the right (east) shoulder of the ridge and climbing up and right over a series of diagonal, narrow ledges and onto the south summit from the east side. To traverse to the large rectangular notch between the south and north peaks, keep on the east side of the connecting ridge. From the notch traverse down and left (west) around the west side of the north peak on obvious ledges to the base of the large northwest chimney (see *Route 1*). Ayres reported climbing to the north summit "from the south and west," a route that was perhaps distinct from *Route 3*. To descend the south ridge over the top of the south peak, a rappel will be needed to pass the vertical section on the south ridge of the south summit. **Time:** 11½ hours from Jenny Lake (via the "devious route" outlined in the peak intro).

ROUTE 6. SOUTH PEAK, EAST FACE–SOUTH RIDGE. III, 5.8. First ascent August 19, 1988, by Jim and Kim Springer. The east face of the south peak is bisected from the left at half-height by a grassy, tree-covered ledge. Hike to the south end of this ledge from Cirque Lake and traverse out along it to its highest point at a shallow, low-angle V of rock where a chimney slants up and left. Climb the face to the right up to a tree, and then up to a steep flake (5.7), until above a promontory that juts out from the face on the right. After moving the belay up 9m, climb the obvious ramp up and left onto a second ramp also leading up and left to a corner directly above. Rather than climbing the corner, move down and left (5.7) from a flat edge to the left of the corner and then across and up loose holds into the large chimney above. A short scramble up the remainder of the chimney leads to the small final notch in the south ridge. Now climb straight up on the left of a small tower and then left under a roof until it is possible to mantel (5.8) via rounded holds onto a ledge. Easy scrambling then leads to the summit of the south peak.

ROUTE 7. NORTH PEAK, NORTHEAST CHIMNEY. II, 5.4. First descent August 9, 1940, by John McCown II, C. Grove McCown, Edward McNeill, and Thomson Edwards; first ascent August 22, 1969, by Charles Bockes, Marvin Conway, and Judy and Maurice Horn. The northeast ridge of Cleaver Peak is easily reached from Cirque Lake at the saddle connecting to Dragon Peak. From this saddle climb and scramble up slabs to reach the large, rounded notch on the north ridge, attained from the west by *Route 1*. The final pitches of that route on the ridge are then followed south to the summit.

DRAGON PEAK (10,465)

(0.4 mi NE of Cleaver Peak)

Map: Mount Moran

This thin peak, when viewed broadside from the west, has the appearance of a humpbacked monster, hence the name. The summit ridge crest is very narrow and at places composed of precariously positioned rock splinters. The exact location of the highest point is very difficult to determine; it behooves one to bring a hand level. Both the west and east faces of the peak are steep crystalline rock; the west face appears to be very rotten.

ROUTE 1. SOUTHWEST RIDGE. II, 5.1. First ascent August 11, 1959, by W. V. Graham Matthews and Irene Beardsley (Ortenburger). The approach to the saddle separating Dragon Peak from Cleaver Peak can be made either from the northwest from Moran Canyon or from the southeast from Cirque Lake (see *Moran Canyon* in Section 10). The sharp southwest ridge provides an interesting, slightly crumbly climb. Care must be taken as one proceeds along the crest because it is not obvious that all the rock splinters are solid. Parts of the crest can be bypassed on steep ledges on the left (west) side. See *American Alpine Journal* 12, no. 1 (1960): pp. 125–27.

SECTION 10

Moran Canyon to Webb Canyon

Rolling Thunder Mountain

Moran Canyon

There are several possible approaches for Moran Canyon, none especially easy or short; the one that is selected depends on the starting point and whether one is aiming for the mouth or the head of the canyon. For several reasons, the passage up the length of Moran Canyon from Jackson Lake to the divide is recommended only for enterprising hikers and climbers: the trail is easily lost (and once it is lost, the bushwhacking is difficult); some of the stream fords can be very tricky, especially during times of high water; and to gain the mouth of the canyon between Mount Moran and Bivouac Peak is more difficult now than in previous years due to lack of trail maintenance. The best approach—by a wide margin—is to cross Jackson Lake by boat.

Without a boat, the traditional method is to hike north from the Leigh Lake trailhead around the east sides of String and Leigh Lakes to Bearpaw Lake, which marks the end of the maintained trail. Continue north past Trapper Lake around the east side of Mount Moran to the mouth of Moran Canyon. This last portion (3 miles) of the approach is neither easy nor pleasant, because many years ago the National Park Service (NPS) abandoned the maintenance of the once-good trail beyond Trapper Lake to Moran Creek. Winter avalanches have since left a broad area of flattened tree debris. No specific recommendation can be given to simplify this section since serious bushwhacking seems to be impossible to avoid. At times remnants of the old trail may be found. An alternative is to head cross-country toward the extreme south end of Bearpaw Bay on Jackson Lake from the end of the normal trail near the upper Bearpaw Lake. After a fairly short and moderate bushwhack to the lakeshore, the beach can be followed around to the mouth of the canyon. This route is longer than the direct route through the trees but has the advantage of little or no deadfall as well as the disadvantage of a slanting, sandy surface. Since the route up the canyon from its mouth is on the north side of Moran Creek, a final problem of the traditional foot approach from the south is the crossing of the creek. With luck a log may be found.

One can avoid the first portion of this hike by canoeing across Leigh Lake to the north shore and starting the hike from the Leigh Lake patrol cabin. This involves 3.1 miles of paddling plus the String Lake–Leigh Lake portage. The best approach to the mouth of Moran Canyon, however, is across Jackson Lake—via powerboat or canoe (on a day without excessive wind from the west). Powerboats can be rented at Colter Bay or Signal Mountain Lodge, or one can canoe (4 miles of paddling) from Spalding Bay. Disembark on the north side of Moran Creek.

To proceed upcanyon stay mostly on the north side of the creek. Using keen observation, one will find a game trail almost all the way to the forks of the canyon. One secret is to stay close to the creek and avoid the natural tendency at places to try to hike along the sidehill. With luck and a good eye, it is even possible to pick up faint traces of an old horse trail marked by partly overgrown blazes on trees and axe-cut deadfall. Most of the blazes are to be found on the upstream (west) side of the trees. Adding interest to the canyon are two old moldering log cabins, probably built by hunters, tuskers, or poachers from the Idaho side of the range. There is a substantial swamp before the forks of the canyon are reached. Getting past this swamp is a problem. There are faint traces of a trail along its northern edge, but it may well be simpler to wade directly through it, regaining the trail on the same (north) side of the stream at the upper (western) end of the swamp. In very late season or in a very dry season, this swamp dries up and it becomes easy to walk through its waist-high grass.

The remote Cirque Lake (9,605), one of the larger alpine lakes in the park, is reached by bushwhacking up the west side of its outlet stream from the floor of the south fork of Moran Canyon. The cirque provides numerous wild and beautiful camping sites. An alternative approach is to access the saddle between Maidenform and Cleaver Peaks from the upper south fork of Moran Canyon and then drop down 1,000 feet to the lake. Another route that has been used (sometimes in reverse for

FIGURE 10-1. Moran Canyon from the east

exit from Cirque Lake) is to hike into Leigh Canyon, scramble north up the interminable slope to the low point (10,000+) on the Leigh-Moran divide, and skirt west around the head of the unnamed canyon on the north side to the saddle (10,400+) southeast of the lake, where an easy descent leads to the destination.

South Fork: From the forks of Moran Creek, cross the north fork stream and continue up the open canyon to timberline. For those interested in wildflowers, the upper portions of the south fork provide an astonishing display. It is a beautiful place in early season or midseason. Maidenform and Cleaver Peaks are directly accessible from the south fork, and one can easily pass over the saddle west of Maidenform Peak and drop down into the head of Leigh Canyon.

This upper south fork area near the divide is most commonly reached not by ascending Moran Canyon but by hiking the Cascade Canyon trail to Lake Solitude, climbing over Littles Peak, continuing north along the divide, and then dropping down into the south fork over the Maidenform Peak saddle. Another scheme, which requires less physical effort, involves the trails of the Caribou-Targhee National Forest/Jedediah Smith Wilderness on the west slope of the Teton Range. From Driggs, Idaho, drive to the US Forest Service (USFS) trailhead on North Leigh Creek at the edge of the wilderness area (see the USGS Granite Basin quadrangle). Take the Green Mountain trail to the basin above and beyond Green Lake, from which one can easily reach and cross the divide at the broad saddle (9,760+) due west of Cleaver Peak. Drop from this saddle into the south fork of Moran Canyon.

North Fork: Travel up the north fork of Moran Canyon is relatively easy on either side of the stream. The cirque high above the north fork that holds Lake 9,610, also known as Ortenburger Lake, is an uncommonly beautiful location, with the waters of the lake providing a reflection of the Cathedral Group. At the extreme head of the south branch of the north fork is another rarely visited lake (9,680+) with the western extension of the Mount Moran dike exposed on its eastern shore. Entry into the head of the north fork can be gained from the west slope in a manner similar to that described earlier for the south fork. From Green Lake continue east and then north along the pack trail for about 2 miles and cross the divide at one of the low points south of Green Lakes Mountain.

Another method of reaching the north fork is via Webb Canyon (see *Webb Canyon* in Section 11) and the Lake 9,610 cirque. From the extreme southern end of Moose Basin in Webb Canyon, cross the saddle (10,320+) just east of Peak 10,880+ and drop into the upper end of the south fork of Snowshoe Canyon. Without losing much altitude one can skirt around the head of Snowshoe Canyon, cross the Snowshoe-Moran divide via the saddle (10,400+) on the southeast ridge of Doubtful Peak (10,852), and then drop down to Lake 9,610. This entails some scrambling, and an ice axe is required for safety on the snow slopes. This scheme of transit from Webb Canyon to Moran Canyon is commonly used in conjunction with the Littles Peak–Moran Canyon route by those who wish to make an extended north–south traverse of the range—for example, from Webb Canyon to Cascade Canyon (or farther south). See *Figure 10-1* for an overview of this area.

Snowshoe Canyon

Based on experience accumulated through the years, it seems not unreasonable to claim that Snowshoe Canyon is indeed the most difficult of all the Teton canyons. The already enormous bushwhacking problems of ascending the canyon from the shores of Jackson Lake were exacerbated by the winter avalanches of 1985–86, when forested sections were smashed and deposited like jackstraws on the bottom of the canyon. Simply put, there is no easy or even moderate route up the canyon to the forks. Nevertheless, the upper two forks of the canyon are ideal alpine valleys with outstandingly beautiful small lakes. And several important but rarely climbed peaks, such as Rolling Thunder Mountain and the twin summits of Eagles Rest Peak, are accessible from Snowshoe Canyon. But serious and exasperating effort must be made to reach these prizes.

Many years ago Snowshoe Canyon was the most northerly canyon readily reached by the trail that led from the Leigh Lake trailhead around the east side of Leigh Lake and Mount Moran all the way to the Moran Bay patrol cabin (a forest fire destroyed the cabin in 2000). Since the NPS abandoned maintenance of the trail north of Bearpaw and Trapper Lakes, this approach is no longer feasible. The only reasonable approach to the mouth of the canyon is by boat across Jackson Lake. Powerboats can be taken from Colter Bay or Signal Mountain Lodge, or one can canoe (4.9 miles) from Spalding Bay. From the shore in the vicinity of the old patrol cabin site, strike northwest through the trees, cross North Moran Creek, and try to enter the canyon. The usual advice to stay mostly on the north side of the creek is perhaps valid but cannot be strongly advocated. Some crossings of the creek may prove useful. Essentially, brute force must be applied to reach the forks of the canyon, at which point most of the troubles are over.

From the forks, travel up the north fork is now relatively easy, although two headwalls must be passed before Talus Lake is reached. The first, 0.75 mile above the forks, is probably best negotiated on the southwest side of the stream. The first lake (9,120+) in this fork is a rare jewel, surrounded by cliffs, near-timberline trees, and hundreds of alpine flowers. Admire but do not disturb. Pass this first lake on the right (north) and continue easily to gain the rocky shore of Talus Lake (9,670). Small campsites can be found along the east edge of the lake. Webb Canyon and Moose Basin can be easily reached either via the pass (9,920+) north of Talus Lake or simply by going over the ridge west of the lake.

To penetrate into the south fork of Snowshoe Canyon along North Moran Creek, follow faint game trails mostly on the right (north) side of the stream until above the first step in the canyon. Avoid trying to stay close to the stream. Above about 8,000 feet the south fork opens up and there are no difficulties to the secondary branching at about 9,000 feet. Above and south of the south fork are three major cirques with several snow/icefields that have seldom been visited—interesting country to explore. Moran Canyon can be entered by climbing over the pass (10,400+) at the head of the south branch and down to Lake 9,610 (Ortenburger Lake). Throughout most of the summer an ice axe will be desired to safely negotiate the snow slopes leading to this pass. Webb Canyon and Moose Basin are accessible via the north branch of the south fork using the pass (10,320+) just west of Peak 10,894. This pass is a major thoroughfare for enterprising hikers, climbers, and ultrarunners making a north–south traverse of the range. From this pass, by contouring high around the head of both forks of Snowshoe Canyon, one can traverse from Webb Canyon into Moran Canyon, or conversely.

Dudley Lake, perched up on the south side of the canyon above the forks of the canyon, was first explored by (and named for) early park ranger Dudley Hayden, in 1933. This remote lake provides a picturesque camping spot and so is a good but strenuous hiking objective. It is best reached by bushwhacking from the south fork stream up the wooded slopes northwest of the lake rather than by following directly up the stream draining the lake.

Waterfalls Canyon

The trailless Waterfalls Canyon, while providing access to the most spectacular waterfalls in the park, is very difficult to approach on foot. The northern approach along the west shore of Jackson Lake from the vicinity of the lower Berry patrol cabin involves several miles of difficult bushwhacking and may not have been used since the winter expedition of Lt. Gustavus Cheyney Doane in 1876. The southern approach, starting at the end of the trail at Trapper Lake, is equally long and even more exhausting, because the area at the eastern base of Eagles Rest Peak, between the mouths of Snowshoe Canyon and Waterfalls Canyon, is an incredible mass of mosquitoes, deadfalls, and nearly impenetrable forest. Thus, the only reasonable method for reaching the mouth of the canyon is via boat across Jackson Lake. Leave the shore of the lake north of the mouth of the stream and bushwhack west and up through the region burned by the fire of 1974; move west through the dead trees and small swamps, staying within 0.25 mile of the stream. Continue through meadows at about 7,200 feet to within 0.2 mile of the base of Columbine Cascade. Pass the cascade on the north, climbing up through some dense willow thickets to about 8,280 feet; then head diagonally upstream to the top of the cascade at 8,600 feet. The stream junction of the north and south forks is in a large bowl just below Wilderness Falls. A good campsite can be found here or at timberline near the relatively large lake (9,615) above the falls. This lake is most easily reached by climbing the slopes north of the falls, although with skillful routefinding and some moderate scrambling the falls can also be passed on the south. Easy slopes above this lake then lead to Ranger and Doane Peaks. The minuscule lake at 10,480+ feet high in the north fork can also be used for a campsite. The south fork of Waterfalls Canyon can be used to reach Anniversary Peak and the extensive ice-and-rock remnant glacier below the northwest face of Eagles Rest Peak. The head of the north fork of Waterfalls Canyon can also be easily entered from the southeast corner of Moose Basin in Webb Canyon via the broad saddle (10,800+) just north of Doane Peak (see *Webb Canyon* in Section 11).

Quartzite Canyon

Little-known Quartzite Canyon, immediately east of Ranger Peak, is valuable as the approach to the remarkably beautiful cirque on the east side of that peak. This canyon has gone by several names. The original name—Quartzite Canyon—was applied in 1942 by Fritiof Fryxell and Leland Horberg in an article for the *American Journal of Science*[1], a geological journal. Other names include Falcon Canyon and Osprey Canyon. According to climber and geologist John C. Reed Jr., the latter is used by local fishermen.

The only recommended approach is via boat across Jackson Lake to the shore north of the mouth of the stream. From the lakeshore bushwhack up and west through heavy timber and swamps, passing an abandoned cabin (unusable) at about 7,240 feet. Continue through open woods and grassy meadows. At about 7,600 feet climb up brushy slopes on the north side of the stream for about 400 feet before traversing back to the left (west) to reach the stream again at about 8,500 feet. Continue on the north side to 9,000 feet (campsite available here) and cross the stream here; move across brushy talus slopes on the south side and up a rock step to a good campsite at the first lake at 9,720+ feet. There are several small lakes in the remainder of the canyon, which ends at the east slopes of Ranger Peak.

1. 240, no. 6 (June 1942): pp. 385–93

Colter Canyon

Seldom-explored Colter Canyon holds no great interest for climbers, because it does not provide easy or direct access to any major peak, but it may be of interest to enterprising hikers seeking the wilderness. Cross Jackson Lake by boat or canoe and leave the lakeshore about 0.5 mile north of the mouth of the stream. Climb steep, heavily wooded slopes to the crest of the morainal ridge east of the prominent bend in the stream. This section will be difficult going because of all the trees downed as a result of the fire of 1974. Follow the crest of this ridge north and then northwest into the open meadows at about 7,300 feet. Stay on the north side of the canyon, reentering heavy woods at 7,500 feet, and follow game trails to open woods near timberline at about 8,500 feet. The upper canyon can be followed either south to Ranger Peak or north to Mount Robie.

PEAK 10,345

(1.5 mi N of Littles Peak)
Map: Mount Moran

This is the first rounded peak on the divide north of Littles Peak. The first ascent was inadvertent, made by a park ranger in the course of intercepting and ushering out of the park a band of sheep and their herder.

ROUTE 1. SOUTH RIDGE. I, 1.0. First ascent September 1, 1933, by Dudley Hayden. This is an easy scramble from Littles Peak and is easily gained from Leigh Canyon or from the west.

ROUTE 2. NORTH RIDGE. I, 3.0. First descent September 1, 1933, by Dudley Hayden; first ascent August 8, 1963, by Leigh Ortenburger, Irene Beardsley (Ortenburger), Julie Peterson, and Dennis Wilson. This ridge contains a steep, slabby section that requires care because of the unsound rock.

PEAK 10,484

(1.1 mi S of Green Lakes Mountain)
Map: Granite Basin

According to the first USGS Grand Teton quadrangle (1901), the T. M. Bannon topographic party in 1899 placed a benchmark on this peak, perhaps the most interesting of those on the northern divide. However, the benchmark found by a 1963 party seemed to date from the T. F. Murphy topographic party of the 1930s and was located on the central of five summits. It is believed that the highest point is the most northerly summit, although this is not known definitively; a hand level is necessary. However, the central summit is certainly not the highest point. The easiest approach for this peak is from the west via the Green Mountain trail in the Caribou-Targhee National Forest/ Jedediah Smith Wilderness (see *Moran Canyon, South Fork*).

Chronology

SOUTH RIDGE: August 14, 1954, Gene Balaz, Roald Fryxell (partial ascent, to south summit); August 7, 1963, Leigh Ortenburger, Irene Beardsley (Ortenburger), Julie Peterson, Dennis Wilson (complete descent)
NORTHEAST RIDGE: July 2, 1963, John C. Reed Jr., David Steller, Alfred Chidester (to north summit)
NORTH RIDGE: August 7, 1963, Leigh Ortenburger, Irene Beardsley (Ortenburger), Julie Peterson, Dennis Wilson (to all five summits)

ROUTE 1. SOUTH RIDGE. II, 4.0. First partial ascent August 14, 1954, by Gene Balaz and Roald Fryxell (to south summit); first complete descent August 7, 1963, by Leigh Ortenburger, Irene Beardsley (Ortenburger), Julie Peterson, and Dennis Wilson. Dudley Hayden may have also climbed this ridge on September 1, 1933. The ridge is easily climbed to the south summit from the broad expanse along the divide north of Littles Peak. The 1954 party found no cairn or record on the south summit. The traverse of the pinnacled summit ridge involves significant difficulties because the ridge is sharp and contains some distinct notches between pinnacles, and in places the rock is unsound, although not sedimentary. Some of the problems could be avoided by dropping down from the crest to the east side.

ROUTE 2. NORTHEAST RIDGE. I, 3.0. First known ascent July 2, 1963, by John C. Reed Jr., David Steller, and Alfred Chidester. This ridge, which connects with Window Peak (10,508), was climbed from a camp in Moran Canyon to the north summit only.

ROUTE 3. NORTH RIDGE. I, 3.0. First recorded ascent August 7, 1963, by Leigh Ortenburger, Irene Beardsley (Ortenburger), Julie Peterson, and Dennis Wilson. The north summit was reached by traversing the ridge from Green Lakes Mountain. No cairn, benchmark, or record was found, although this summit had been climbed a month earlier (see *Route 2*) and may have been reached by either the Bannon party or the Murphy party, or both. All five summits were traversed by the August 1963 party.

PEAK 10,300

(0.6 mi SW of Window Peak)
Map: Mount Moran

Separating this small high point from the divide is the western continuation of the main black dike of Mount Moran, which can be seen disappearing at the lake (9,680+) in the cirque to the northwest.

ROUTE 1. EAST RIDGE. II, 3.0. First recorded ascent September 3, 1988, by Leigh Ortenburger. The saddle separating this peak from Window Peak can be reached from either fork of Moran Canyon, although some scrambling is involved. The ridge itself is interesting, involving some climbing usually slightly on the right (north) side of the crest. The left (south) side contains some smooth slabs.

WINDOW PEAK (10,508)

Map: Mount Moran

A worthwhile objective, this prominent peak divides upper Moran Canyon into the north and south forks. The name is derived from a natural window said to be in a subsidiary south ridge.

ROUTE 1. SOUTHWEST RIDGE. II, 3.0. First recorded ascent August 10, 1959, by W. V. Graham Matthews and Irene Beardsley (Ortenburger), who found an empty cairn on the summit. From the south fork of Moran Canyon, climb past a very small lake (not shown on the map) to the saddle west of the peak where an interesting pinnacle will be found. Some scrambling, usually on the right (south) side of the crest, is required to negotiate the ridge to the large summit. See *American Alpine Journal* 12, no. 1 (1960): pp. 125–27.

GREEN LAKES MOUNTAIN (10,240+)

Map: Granite Basin

This peak is most easily approached from the west side of the Teton Range, via trails in the Caribou-Targhee National Forest/ Jedediah Smith Wilderness to the pass

(9,480+) west of the peak. It can also be reached, with more effort, by way of the north fork of Moran Canyon. The main distinction of Green Lakes Mountain is that it has been given a name, taken from the four lakes in the high cirque 2 miles to the southwest.

Chronology

NORTHEAST RIDGE: [probable] July 1935, T. F. Murphy, Mike Yokel Jr.
SOUTH RIDGE: August 7, 1963, Leigh Ortenburger, Irene Beardsley (Ortenburger), Julie Peterson, Dennis Wilson (descent)

ROUTE 1. SOUTH RIDGE. I, 1.0. First known descent August 7, 1963, by Leigh Ortenburger, Irene Beardsley (Ortenburger), Julie Peterson, and Dennis Wilson. There are no difficulties on this ridge.

ROUTE 2. NORTHEAST RIDGE. I, 1.0. Probable first ascent in July 1935, by T. F. Murphy and Mike Yokel Jr. This is an easy ridge that is reached directly from the north fork of Moran Canyon or via a traverse from Dry Ridge Mountain.

DRY RIDGE MOUNTAIN (10,321)

Map: Mount Moran

The name for this mountain is taken, curiously, from the ridge to the west in the Caribou-Targhee National Forest/ Jedediah Smith Wilderness, which meets the divide at Green Lakes Mountain. The T. M. Bannon topographic party presumably placed a benchmark on this summit in 1899. The 1952 party from the J Bar Y Ranch near Ashton, Idaho, built on the summit one of the largest cairns in the park.

ROUTE 1. SOUTHEAST SLOPE. I, 1.0. Probable first ascent in July, 1935, by T. F. Murphy and Mike Yokel Jr.; first recorded ascent August 7, 1963, by Leigh Ortenburger, Irene Beardsley (Ortenburger), Julie Peterson, and Dennis Wilson. No problems will be found on this peak, no matter which route is used from the north fork of Moran Canyon.

ROUTE 2. NORTHWEST RIDGE. I, 1.0. First known ascent August 11, 1952, by Jack and Frank Young, Henry Tausend, Roger Abelson, Richard Cohen, Kirby Orme, Frederick Berlinger, Richard Luria, and Roger and Peter Bensinger. This straightforward ridge is presumably the route that was used on the upper climb; the first-ascent party approached on horse to timberline, via Hidden Corral Basin in the south fork of Bitch Creek, then continued to the ridge above Dead Horse Pass (9,376).

PEAK 10,160+

(0.55 mi ENE of Dry Ridge Mountain)
Map: Ranger Peak

This is a small high point on the divide between the north fork of Moran Canyon and the south fork of Bitch Creek. During an extended exploratory traverse of peaks in the north end of the range in 1963, Leigh Ortenburger and party bypassed this summit via the bench to the south because on the old map (1948) it did not qualify as a peak. No information is available concerning ascents.

PEAK 10,474

(1.1 mi ENE of Dry Ridge Mountain)
Map: Ranger Peak

The main distinction of this peak above the north fork of Moran Canyon is that it is one of two enclosing the beautiful cirque containing the high Lake 9,610. In 1993 the US Board on Geographic Names regrettably rejected the proposal that this lake be renamed Ortenburger Lake in honor of Leigh N. Ortenburger; nevertheless, the name is in common use.

ROUTE 1. NORTH RIDGE. I, 2.0. First ascent August 7, 1963, by Leigh Ortenburger, Irene Beardsley (Ortenburger), Julie Peterson, and Dennis Wilson. From Lake 9,610 (Ortenburger Lake), which makes an ideal campsite, proceed easily up the slope to the saddle on the divide north of this peak. Once on the ridge, only 10 minutes are required to reach the summit.

DOUBTFUL PEAK (10,852)

(1.1 mi NW of Raynolds Peak)
Map: Ranger Peak

Named by the 1958 first-ascent party to reflect their uncertainty as to whether theirs was the true first ascent, Doubtful Peak is one of the highest points along the divide. It also stands as the dividing point between the two branches of the south fork of Snowshoe Canyon. Its appearance when viewed from the west in Bitch Creek has prompted the name Pyramid Peak, preferred by some over that given by the first ascensionists. When this peak is viewed from the north, as from the summit of Glacier Peak, the contact between the lighter Webb Canyon gneiss on the northern portion of the peak and the darker amphibolite that largely comprises the west ridge presents a stark, well-defined contrast. All approaches to Doubtful Peak are long. The shortest is probably from the Caribou-Targhee National Forest/Jedediah Smith Wilderness west of the Teton Range: Starting at the Forest Service trailhead north of South Badger Creek, take the Badger Creek trail to the Teton Crest Trail. Continue up and over Dead Horse Pass, then head cross-country over the intervening ridge to the basin just west of the peak. Coming directly up either Moran Canyon or Snowshoe Canyon will require considerable effort and heinous bushwhacking. Most of the rare climbs of Doubtful Peak have been made in the course of a north–south traverse of this part of the range—for example, from Berry Creek to Cascade Canyon, or conversely.

Chronology

NORTH RIDGE: July 23, 1958, Jack Davis, Julie Peterson, Silvia Prodan
SOUTHEAST RIDGE: July 23, 1958, Jack Davis, Julie Peterson, Silvia Prodan (descent)
WEST RIDGE: July 27, 1978, Gary Kofinas, Amy Wilbur, John Polstein, Jim Siesfield, Paul Sachs, Matthew Rice, Gordon Anteil, Jeff Garbaty, David Rattray, Liz Ganfort, Jim Verdone, Andy Sebesta

ROUTE 1. WEST RIDGE. II, 5.2. First ascent July 27, 1978, by Gary Kofinas, Amy Wilbur, John Polstein, Jim Siesfield, Paul Sachs, Matthew Rice, Gordon Anteil, Jeff Garbaty, David Rattray, Liz Ganfort, Jim Verdone, and Andy Sebesta. This ridge on the divide starts at the saddle (10,160+), which is crossed by an east–west dike, and leads directly to the summit. The saddle can be easily reached from the south (via Moran Canyon) or the north (via South Bitch Creek).

ROUTE 2. SOUTHEAST RIDGE. I, 4.0. First descent July 23, 1958, by Jack Davis, Julie Peterson, and Silvia Prodan. This ridge contains some of the excellent yellow Teton rock, much like that of the Exum Ridge of the Grand Teton *(Grand Teton, Route 8)* or Cleaver Peak on the south side of Moran Canyon. The first two parties who descended this ridge bypassed the steep, difficult section (about 46m long) on the west via a convenient gully.

A dike crosses the base of this ridge at about 10,480+ feet, a situation similar to the west ridge (see *Route 1*). The 1958 party continued east to Point 10,214 (named "Birthday Cake"), where they built an elaborate cairn prior to descending north into Snowshoe Canyon.

ROUTE 3. NORTH RIDGE. I, 3.0. First ascent July 23, 1958, by Jack Davis, Julie Peterson, and Silvia Prodan. The saddle between Doubtful Peak and Peak 10,480+ is easily reached from South Bitch Creek, but some 3rd-class gullies must be climbed to reach it from Snowshoe Canyon. Once on the ridge, steep rock and many sharp pinnacles restrict access to the west side of the ridge. Near the summit the slabs on the ridge provide enjoyable climbing. During the first ascent the entire ridge along the divide from Blackwelder Peak (10,800+) was traversed south over all the intervening pinnacles. The most southerly of these was shown as Point 10,445 on the original USGS Grand Teton quadrangle (1901) and as Point 10,480+ on the 1968 Ranger Peak quadrangle. The 1901 map indicated a benchmark on this point; the 1958 party found a cairn here, but a thorough search by the second-ascent party in 1963 failed to reveal any traces of it. It does seem likely that T. M. Bannon's topographic surveying party in 1899 reached at least the saddle north of Doubtful Peak from South Bitch Creek, and probably hiked up to this easy Point 10,480+. See *American Alpine Journal* 11, no. 2 (1959): pp. 307–9.

RAYNOLDS PEAK (10,910)

Map: Mount Moran

This fine, isolated peak is the highest point on the long ridge that extends west from Traverse Peak to the divide. It was named for Capt. William F. Raynolds, who in 1860 led the first scientifically oriented expedition of exploration into Jackson Hole. Raynolds, incidentally, had made the first ascent of Pico de Orizaba (18,491) in 1848 with some of his men while on duty in the Mexican-American War; this was very likely the American altitude record for the next half century. The general approach to this peak can be made from Moran Canyon, Snowshoe Canyon, or Cascade Canyon via Littles Peak. It is not clear that anyone has ever visited the three very small snow/icefields that lie along the north base of the mountain.

Chronology

SOUTHWEST SIDE: [probable] Summer 1935, T. F. Murphy's surveying party, perhaps Frank Somner; [certain] August 15, 1954, Roald Fryxell, Gene Balaz
EAST RIDGE: September 4, 1955, John Fonda, William Buckingham
WEST RIDGE: August 6, 1963, Leigh Ortenburger, Irene Beardsley (Ortenburger), Julie Peterson, Dennis Wilson

ROUTE 1. WEST RIDGE. II, 3.0. First ascent August 6, 1963, by Leigh Ortenburger, Irene Beardsley (Ortenburger), Julie Peterson, and Dennis Wilson. This is a long ridge containing many pinnacles, towers, and false summits, some of which can be avoided on the right (south), but it is usually simpler to climb over most of them.

ROUTE 2. SOUTHWEST SIDE. I, 2.0. Probable first ascent in summer 1935, by T. F. Murphy's surveying party, perhaps Frank Somner; first recorded ascent August 15, 1954, by Roald Fryxell and Gene Balaz. From the south base of the peak in Moran Canyon, obvious couloirs lead easily to the summit. On the summit Fryxell and Balaz discovered a large cairn composed half of white rocks and half of black rocks. It is reasonable to assume that the first ascent was actually made by surveyors; Frank Somner was working in this area in the summer of 1935 as an assistant to T. F. Murphy. The slender, fingerlike pinnacle standing just east of the summit was first climbed by Fryxell and Balaz. A climb of similar difficulty from the same direction, somewhat more on a ridge than in a couloir, was made on August 14, 1962, by J. H. Dieterich and T. B. Ranson. **Time:** 4½ hours from the forks of Moran Canyon.

ROUTE 3. EAST RIDGE. II, 5.1. First ascent September 4, 1955, by John Fonda and William Buckingham. This ascent, the third of the peak, was made via the very long traverse of the entire ridge from Traverse Peak. It was a tour de force, requiring a considerable amount of climbing effort and careful routefinding to climb all the many tall and impressive towers on the ridge. Several of the pinnacles near Traverse Peak are over 46m high. Many hours of 4.0 and 5.1 scrambling were involved. It is intriguing that a cairn was found on the summit of one of the towers. It should prove possible to gain this ridge from various points either in Moran Canyon or in Snowshoe Canyon. See *American Alpine Journal* 10, no. 1 (1956): pp. 116–19.

IMAGE (10,750)

(1.0 mi E of Raynolds Peak)
Map: Mount Moran

This pinnacle, the higher of the Images, lies on the north side of the ridge extending from Raynolds Peak to Traverse Peak. The name is derived from the fact that these peaks are reflected in the still waters of Dudley Lake (8,243), which provides a nifty wilderness campsite for these peaks. Passing through the saddle (10,560+) to the south is an east–west dike.

Chronology

NORTHEAST FACE: August 20, 1957, Jack Davis, Redwood Fryxell, Nick Ellena, Julie Peterson
SOUTHEAST FACE: August 15, 1962, John C. Reed Jr.
NORTH RIDGE: July 31, 1983, Leigh Ortenburger, Roman Laba

ROUTE 1. SOUTHEAST FACE. II, 3.0. First ascent August 15, 1962, by John C. Reed Jr. From the upper part of the south fork of Snowshoe Canyon, ascend into the cirque between the Images and Raynolds Peak. Climb to the col south of the summit and then up the southeast face.

ROUTE 2. NORTHEAST FACE. II, 3.0. First ascent August 20, 1957, by Jack Davis, Redwood Fryxell, Nick Ellena, and Julie Peterson. From Dudley Lake bushwhack up into the cirque east of the summit and ascend the northeast couloir, then scramble up a series of ledges to the summit.

ROUTE 3. NORTH RIDGE. II, 4.0. First ascent July 31, 1983, by Leigh Ortenburger and Roman Laba. Reach the notch between the two Images from the east, then climb the moderate north ridge to the summit.

COUNTERIMAGE (10,560+)

(1.0 mi E of Raynolds Peak)
Map: Mount Moran

This peak, the lower and northern Image, presents a striking appearance when seen from the west, as it is composed of a light-colored rock that contrasts with the black rock of the surrounding peaks. The name, in addition to its apparent meaning, also is a technical term in mathematical set theory, given appropriately by the first-ascent party—a mathematician and his wife.

Chronology

NORTHEAST RIDGE: August 9, 1956, Sherman and Lillian Lehman
WEST LEDGES: August 9, 1956, Sherman and Lillian Lehman (descent)
SOUTH RIDGE: July 31, 1983, Leigh Ortenburger, Roman Laba

ROUTE 1. WEST LEDGES. II, 4.0. First descent August 9, 1956, by Sherman and Lillian Lehman. This route is a comparatively easy rock climb, approached from the seldom-entered cirque between the Images and Raynolds Peak.

ROUTE 2. SOUTH RIDGE. II, 5.1. First ascent July 31, 1983, by Leigh Ortenburger and Roman Laba. Climb this ridge directly from the notch between the two Images. It is an interesting climb on good rock.

ROUTE 3. NORTHEAST RIDGE. II, 4.0. First ascent August 9, 1956, by Sherman and Lillian Lehman. Approach via Snowshoe Canyon to the couloir that leads from the east to the notch between the two Images. At the level of the lower slope of the higher Image traverse right (north) to the northeast ridge. Follow this moderate ridge to the summit, staying mostly left of the crest. This is not the prominent north ridge seen in outline from Dudley Lake.

TRAVERSE PEAK (11,051)

Map: Mount Moran

This flat-topped peak was incorrectly identified as "Bivouac Peak" on the 1948 USGS topographic map of Grand Teton National Park. The history of this error is worth noting. On Google Earth three high points are clearly shown within the plateau-like summit area. In 1916, A. C. Tate and Bill Scott climbed the easy east slope and stopped on the first east summit, which is nearly a hundred feet lower than the true summit and a thousand feet to the west. Then in 1930, Fritiof Fryxell and party repeated this climb but continued along the ridge leading west to a flat-topped summit, which is slightly higher than the easterly summit, but not quite as high as the true summit. Fryxell named this peak "Bivouac" because some members of the party were benighted before returning to Jackson Lake. The highest point, Traverse Peak, lies still farther west and was not climbed until 1934 (roundtrip in one day from Leigh Lake) by Fred and Irene Ayres, who named the peak. This discrepancy in names was not noticed until 1953, when the second ascent of Traverse Peak was made. In the course of their ascent in 1934, the Ayreses witnessed the "heavy, jarring rumble" of the collapse of a crevasse on the small snow/icefield on the northeast side of the peak. The southern aspect of this peak contains steep walls similar to, but not as extensive as, those on neighboring Bivouac Peak. See *Moran Canyon* for the approach to the south side of Traverse Peak or *Snowshoe Canyon* for the approach to the north side of the mountain. There is an excellent view of the northwest side of Mount Moran and the Triple Glaciers from the summit.

Chronology

EAST RIDGE: August 23, 1934, Fred and Irene Ayres
SOUTHEAST COULOIR: June 25, 1953, Leigh Ortenburger, William Buckingham
WEST RIDGE: September 4, 1955, William Buckingham, John Fonda (descent); August 8, 1956, Redwood and Roald Fryxell (ascent)
var—**NORTH APPROACH:** July 12, 1987, Doug Parker, Jim and Steve Herzog
SOUTHEAST RIB: June 7, 2003, Paul Horton

ROUTE 1. WEST RIDGE. II, 5.4. First descent September 4, 1955, by William Buckingham and John Fonda; first ascent August 8, 1956, by Redwood and Roald Fryxell. This ridge consists of very steep and loose scrambling; the route must be chosen with care to avoid difficult and dangerous sections. See *American Alpine Journal* 10, no. 1 (1956): pp. 116–19.

***Variation:* NORTH APPROACH.** II, 5.4. First ascent July 12, 1987, by Doug Parker and Jim and Steve Herzog. From the south fork of Snowshoe Canyon climb the snowfield at the base of the northwest face of Traverse Peak to gain the west ridge at a point 0.3 mile west of the summit. Pass over the top of a subsummit (10,880+), descend to the col, and continue up steep rock (5.4) to the main summit.

ROUTE 2. SOUTHEAST RIB. II, 3.0. First ascent June 7, 2003, by Paul Horton. There are a number of ribs on the southeast face. This is the longest one, and the first one to the right of the south ridge. Ascend the southeast couloir (see *Route 3*) to the base of the rib and then scramble up it, staying on or near the crest on good rock.

ROUTE 3. SOUTHEAST COULOIR. II, 3.0. First ascent June 25, 1953, by Leigh Ortenburger and William Buckingham. Proceed up Moran Canyon about 1.5 miles to the streams descending from the Triple Glaciers. A large, obvious couloir descends from the col between Traverse Peak and Bivouac Peak. In early season this is a 1,000m snow chute, making a rapid and enjoyable route of descent (glissaded all the way in 1953). To ascend Traverse Peak, turn left (west) up a subsidiary couloir about 60m before the top of the main couloir, thus avoiding the pinnacles on the ridge crest itself. The flat summit, unlike that of Bivouac Peak, has no bushes or trees.

ROUTE 4. ▲ EAST RIDGE. II, 3.0. First ascent August 23, 1934, by Fred and Irene Ayres. This route starts at the summit of Bivouac Peak, using the East Ridge route *(Bivouac Peak, Route 7)* to begin the ascent. From the Bivouac Peak summit continue traversing west, "threading in and out through a long array of splintered pinnacles," to the flat summit of Traverse Peak. **Time:** 10¾ hours from Leigh Lake.

PRIMROSE PEAK (10,800+)

(0.2 mi N of Traverse Peak)
Map: Mount Moran

Relatively small and obscure by most standards, this peak is prominent on the skyline as seen from the vicinity of Colter Bay. The notch separating Primrose Peak from the higher Traverse Peak is formed by an east–west black dike, which can be seen extending from the small snow/icefield on the east to the same feature on the west. The name arose from the astonishing multitude of the flower Parry's Primrose encountered on the slopes above Dudley Lake during the first ascent.

ROUTE 1. WEST COULOIR AND SOUTH RIDGE. II, 2.0. First descent August 14, 1975, by Leigh and Carolyn Ortenburger. This rotten couloir follows the line of the black dike from the left (east) edge of the small snow/icefield lying at the northwest base of Traverse Peak. Take the couloir to the notch and then follow the south ridge to the summit.

ROUTE 2. EAST FACE. II, 4.0. First ascent August 14, 1975, by Leigh and Carolyn Ortenburger. Climb directly up from Dudley Lake into the cirque east of this peak to gain the base of the east face well north of the summit. A few pitches in the chimney system in the slabs of the face are then climbed to reach the north ridge, which is followed to the summit. Some loose rock will be found on this route.

Ranger Jim Olson on the divide overlooking Lake 9610 in the upper north fork of Moran Canyon (Photo by Renny Jackson)

BIVOUAC PEAK (10,825)

Map: Mount Moran

Bivouac Peak on the north and Mount Woodring on the south provide a visual balance flanking the central bulk of Mount Moran. A lesser mountain than Moran, Bivouac Peak shares the same unusual feature of a flat summit area. In June of 1972 a mountain sheep and three lambs were seen on the summit. It is also similar to Mount Moran in that it harbors significant south walls, which in this case rise above Moran Canyon. As a climbing objective, Bivouac Peak was surprisingly one of the first in the range to be attempted. The ascent of the east peak in 1916 ranks as one of the first successfully attained Teton summits following the 1898 climbs of the Grand Teton by William O. Owen, Franklin Spalding, Frank Peterson, and John Shive (see *Grand Teton, Route 1*). And even as there was an early attempt on the south ridge of Mount Moran, so the south face of Bivouac Peak was nearly climbed at an early date. In early August 1940, three-quarters of the face was climbed by a group from the Philadelphia Alpine Club, John McCown II[1], C. Grove McCown, Edward McNeill, and Thomson Edwards; their remarkable attempt was stopped by lack of time and an understandable reluctance to spend the night on the face. This same party later continued up Moran Canyon to make the first ascent of Cleaver Peak.

The approach to Bivouac Peak begins at Moran Bay on Jackson Lake, but there are a couple of ways to reach the shore of the bay. The best is to boat across Jackson Lake; the put-in at Spalding Bay is perhaps the most commonly used. For some reason, either obtuseness or error, the road to the Spalding Bay put-in was omitted from the USGS Jenny Lake quadrangle, but it is shown on the overall Grand Teton National Park map. The other method, much less desirable, is to hike in from String Lake; this is a long hike, and the trail, which has not been maintained by the National Park Service (NPS) for many decades, gives out beyond Bearpaw and Trapper Lakes. Considerable deadfall will be encountered if one continues north to Moran Creek, but it can be done. An alternative from the vicinity of Bearpaw Lake, with less bushwhacking but much walking at an angle, is to head for the shore of Jackson Lake and follow that shoreline all the way north and west to Moran Bay. For the south face routes, bushwhack from the lakeshore up Moran Canyon on the north side of the creek for about 1 mile to the vicinity of the stream descending from the bench below the south face. Turn up here and hike up the long talus and scree slope to the base of the face. Venturing out onto one of the south face routes guarantees an adventurous day on one of the most impressive walls in the Tetons.

---

1. John McCown later became a First Lieutenant in the 10th Mountain Division (86th Mountain Infantry Regiment). He was killed on February 20, 1945, during the assault on Mount Belvedere, Italy. McCown was posthumously awarded the Silver Star for gallantry in action.

Chronology

EAST RIDGE: 1916, A. C. Tate, Bill Scott (partial, to east peak); July 12, 1930, Fritiof Fryxell, Theodore and Gustav Koven (complete)
var—August 3, 1948, Orrin and Roger Bonney
var—**NORTHEAST COULOIR:** July 29, 1956, Frank Ewing, Zach Stewart, or June 28, 1972, Doug Leen
WEST RIDGE: August 23, 1934, Fred and Irene Ayres
var—**SOUTH GULLY, WEST RIDGE:** July 14, 1985, Jim Lemmon, Merle King, Mark Wilk
SOUTH FACE I: August 19, 1947, Paul Kenworthy, Richard Pownall
EAST COULOIR: August 20, 1947, Paul Kenworthy, Richard Pownall (descent); June 19, 1994, Paul Horton, Cathy Mitchell (ascent)
NORTH SLOPE: July 29, 1956, Frank Ewing, Zach Stewart (descent), or June 28, 1972, Doug Leen (descent)
SOUTH FACE II: September 2, 1969, George Lowe, Juris Krisjansons
SOUTH FACE III: July 24, 1970, Yvon Chouinard, Juris Krisjansons
SOUTH FACE IV: August 22, 1981, Andy Carson, Jim Roscoe

ROUTE 1. WEST RIDGE. II, 4.0. First ascent August 23, 1934, by Fred and Irene Ayres. This ridge, which holds several shattered towers, has been used principally for traversing to Bivouac Peak after an ascent of Traverse Peak or vice versa. The rock is not always trustworthy on this ridge.

***Variation:* SOUTH GULLY, WEST RIDGE.** II, 4.0. First ascent July 14, 1985, by Jim Lemmon, Merle King, and Mark Wilk. From Moran Canyon take the second major drainage gully that meets Moran Creek at the same point as the stream descending from the eastern Triple Glacier on Mount Moran. Follow this gully, which contains a dogleg to the right, to its head at the crest of the west ridge. Some considerable scrambling will be involved in this gully and some moderately steep snow may be encountered. From the ridge crest it is only a short distance to the summit along the final west ridge.

ROUTE 2. SOUTH FACE II. IV, 5.7. First ascent September 2, 1969, by George Lowe and Juris Krisjansons. (See *Figure 10-2*.) This long route can be recognized and located by three features on the main south face of Bivouac Peak. Look for a large gray ceiling about 60m up and left of a small detached pillar at the base of the face. This small detached pillar is well left of the obvious black water streaks, where the South Face III starts. The third feature is the large buttress or pillar in the center of the face; this route starts and remains to the left of this pillar.

FIGURE 10-2. Bivouac Peak, south aspect. (A) South Face II (Lowe-Krisjansons; *Route 2*), IV, 5.7; (B) South Face III (Chouinard-Krisjansons; *Route 3*), IV, 5.10; (C) South Face IV (Carson-Roscoe; *Route 5*), IV, 5.10

The base of the climb is under the gray overhang (the largest on the face), which has a large, deep chimney in its right side. A dihedral, which begins just left of the small detached pillar, leads up toward the base of the overhang. The first pitch goes up this dihedral (5.4) on poor rock toward the gray overhang (some 60m above) to an alcove. Scramble up easy rock to the next belay in the large chimney already mentioned. The third lead climbs the right wall of the chimney to avoid poor rock in the chimney itself. Next, climb the chimney to the top and crawl through a horizontal continuation to the right. This is followed by a slightly downward hand traverse, followed by chimneying up a large crack to the belay. The fifth pitch goes to the top of the flake forming the chimney and then moves left up a small gully and back right through overhangs to the belay. Next climb the chimney and then traverse left on easier rock. Now continue up and left almost on the crest of a small ridge. The eighth lead ascends a large lieback flake followed by difficult cracks left and up to the belay, staying near the crest. Two more leads permit one to reach an alcove, moving out and left to avoid some difficult cracks. After a 25m jam crack pitch leading to a large ledge, scramble up and right, then ascend some 60m off to the left on easier ground. Avoid the obvious chimneys above, climbing instead on the difficult crest to the left. The final lead is up a lieback chimney, followed by a crack to a ledge with a hole in it. The rock on this long route is not the best.

ROUTE 3. SOUTH FACE III. IV, 5.10. First ascent July 24, 1970, by Yvon Chouinard and Juris Krisjansons. (See *Figures 10-2 and 10-3.*) Of the four south face routes on Bivouac Peak, this one—the third to be climbed—has seen the most ascents. It is a long and serious climb of around 11 pitches and makes for an adventurous day in a beautiful wilderness setting. The main feature available to locate the route is the large central buttress or pillar about halfway up this part of the face. This route goes up the wall to the right (east) and below this buttress, staying just left (west) of black water streaks on the steep rock. From the talus slope at the base of the face, climb a bit of 4th class and set up a belay. Proceed up and right under a band of overhangs, angling toward the vertical black water streak that is between two overhangs. The next five leads zigzag upward to avoid overhangs, following the line of least resistance up the middle of the steep and at times slightly overhanging face, staying left of the vertical black water streaks. This section contains sustained 5.8 to 5.10 climbing on high-angle rock with good belay ledges, but several of the leads require long runouts. Anchors and protection are at times hard to place, and knifeblade pitons were used in the old days in addition to the standard rack. The fifth pitch in the crux lower section of the route finishes on the first major feature of the climb, a huge ledge leading left (west) to meet the large central pillar.

Above this main ledge is a loose and rotten-looking wall. Scramble left on the ledge (3rd class) to the pillar, then climb the enjoyable chimney (5.6) behind the pillar. From the top of the pillar four more pitches lead to the top of the face and the upper portion of the southeast ridge, which must be traversed to reach the flat summit of Bivouac Peak. For descent, either take the East Ridge route *(Route 7)* or the east couloir that drops down to the east (slightly southeast) from the summit plateau (see *Route 6*). In early season this east couloir will contain snow, and there is a large chockstone that can be bypassed by a 13m rappel on its south side. **Gear:** For protection take small nuts (offsets useful) and a complete double set of cams, from very small to 3.5".

ROUTE 4. SOUTH FACE I. III, 5.6. First ascent August 19, 1947, by Paul Kenworthy and Richard Pownall. From the vicinity of Moran Bay on Jackson Lake one can see on the southeast side of Bivouac Peak the large, talus-filled couloir (see *Route 6*) that separates a southeast pinnacle ridge from the higher, flat north summit. Approaching the south face of Bivouac Peak from Moran Canyon, one will see a gendarme on the profile of the face. This route begins some 60m west of this gendarme and runs straight up to this southeast pinnacle ridge. Several overhangs will be encountered on this route and rotten rock must be expected for part of the climb. This route ends on the southeast pinnacle ridge, from which the main summit is reached by first descending about 60m into the upper end of the east couloir and then climbing west and up to the summit. See *The Iowa Climber* 2, no. 2 (Summer 1948): pp. 73–74, illus. (note that the photograph in this article is reversed).

ROUTE 5. SOUTH FACE IV. IV, 5.10. First ascent August 22, 1981, by Andy Carson and Jim Roscoe. (See *Figure 10-2.*) This more recent climb has several similarities with the South Face I route *(Route 4)*, and the two routes may even share some pitches or portions of pitches. Begin well east of the main face used by *Routes 2* and *3*. The initial climbing is 4th class up to a bench. Climb cracks above this bench. The second lead is a 5.9 crack. In all there are eight pitches of good rock on this route, with much continuous 5.7 and 5.8 climbing in cracks and corners. The climb ends about one-quarter of the way down from the top of the main face at the edge of the east couloir (see *Route 6*). The small ridge at the edge of the couloir here probably is the same as the "southeast pinnacle ridge" referred to in *Route 4*. Descend via the East Ridge route *(Route 7)* or the east couloir; two descent pitons were found in the latter in 1981.

ROUTE 6. EAST COULOIR. II, 5.4. First descent August 20, 1947, by Paul Kenworthy and Richard Pownall; first ascent June 19, 1994, by Paul Horton and Cathy Mitchell. Although this route had been used as a descent route a number of times, it was curiously overlooked as a way up the peak until 1994. This is the main large couloir on the east (slightly southeast) side of the peak that leads from the flat summit area directly down toward Moran Bay. At the bottom, access to this couloir is blocked by a large chockstone and an overhang; climb on the left (south) side (5.4) until it is possible to traverse right (northeast) into the couloir. Then scramble up the couloir, staying in the left branch, which goes in a straight line to the summit area. When this is used as a descent route, the chockstone and overhang must be avoided by moving right (south) out onto a ridge to the south of the couloir. Alternatively, the chockstone can be passed by means of a 13m rappel. Much of the couloir during the late season consists of talus, excessive brush, and loose and rotten rock and is therefore not recommended. It would be a good early-season snow climb were it not for the need to pass the chockstone. See *The Iowa Climber* 2, no. 2 (Summer 1948): pp. 73–74, illus. (note that the photograph in this article is reversed).

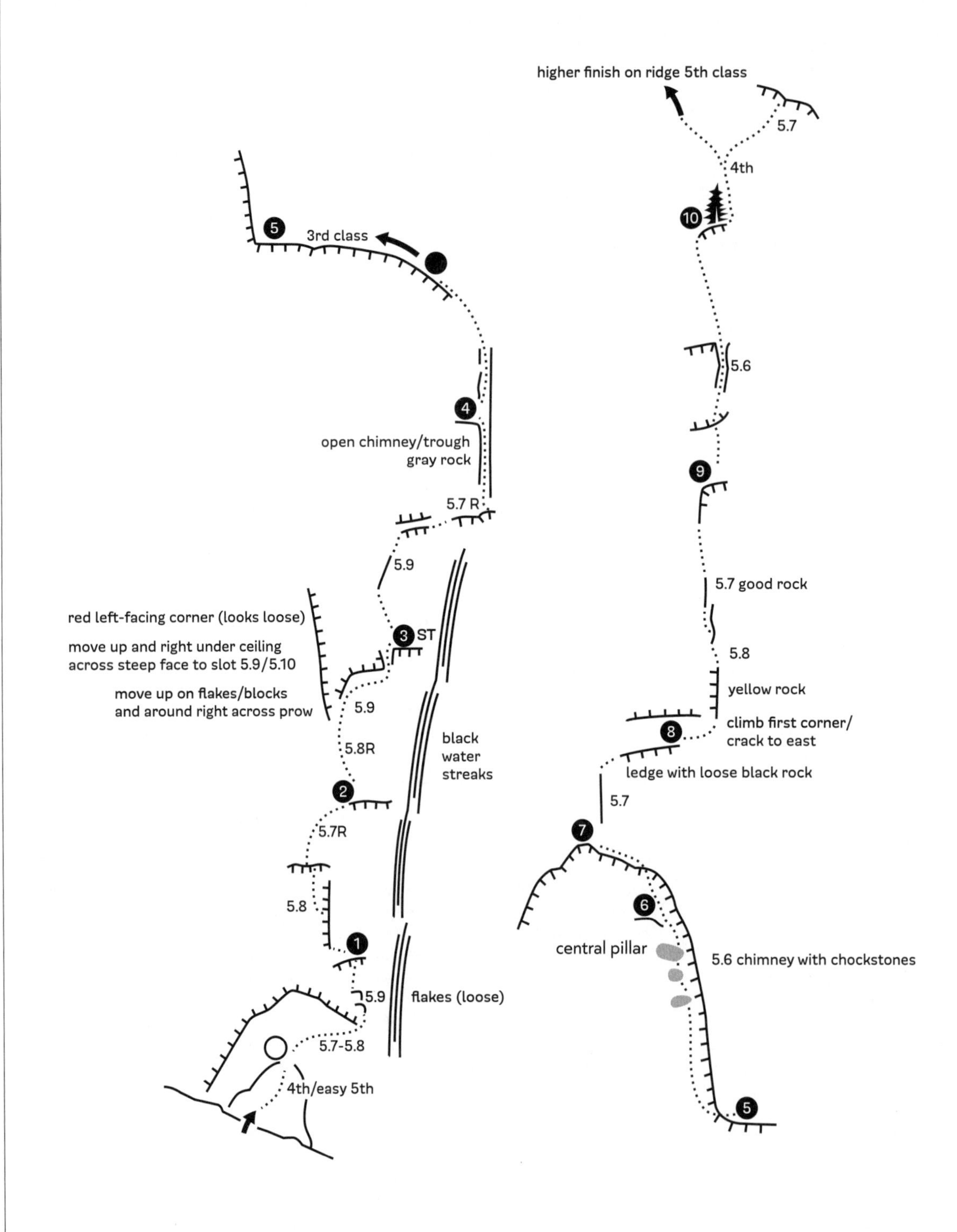

FIGURE 10-3. Bivouac Peak, south aspect, South Face III (Chouinard-Krisjansons, *Route 3*), IV, 5.10

ROUTE 7. ▲ EAST RIDGE. II, 3.0. First partial ascent in 1916, by A. C. Tate and Bill Scott (to east peak); first complete ascent July 12, 1930, by Fritiof Fryxell and Theodore and Gustav Koven. This is the standard route on a seldom-climbed Teton peak. From the west end of Moran Bay ascend the open slope on the southeast side of the wooded east ridge of Bivouac Peak; this will minimize the bushwhacking. Once the east ridge itself is gained above, follow it by scrambling among some giant boulders on the crest to the summit of the east peak. A short, steep descent to the col to the west is most easily made by taking an exposed shelf (3.0) immediately below and south of the east peak summit. Now scramble along the remaining ridge (3.0), past some dwarfed trees, to the main flat summit and cairn. **Time:** 4¾ hours from Moran Bay. See *Appalachia* 18, no. 4 (December 1931): pp. 388–408, illus.; *Chicago Mountaineering Club Newsletter* 2, no. 6 (July–December 1948): p. 4; *Trail and Timberline*, no. 157 (November 1931): pp. 177–78, illus.

Variation: II, 3.0. First ascent August 3, 1948, by Orrin and Roger Bonney. Contour north from the east slope and bypass the east peak to reach the main summit from the north.

Variation: **NORTHEAST COULOIR.** II, 3.0. First ascent July 29, 1956, by Frank Ewing and Zach Stewart, or June 28, 1972, by Doug Leen. From Moran Bay proceed (with difficulty) up Snowshoe Canyon through the initial trees to the avalanche slope below this rocky couloir that extends in a southwesterly direction straight toward the east peak. In early season this couloir is snow-filled and provides a relatively fast route of ascent. Join the standard East Ridge route at or near the east summit.

ROUTE 8. NORTH SLOPE. II, 4.0. First descent July 29, 1956, by Frank Ewing and Zach Stewart, or June 28, 1972, by Doug Leen. This descent was made almost directly down the north side, utilizing snow in the couloirs. The best route is not obvious; hence, some routefinding skill will be useful. In early season good glissading will be found down to Dudley Lake, where one turns east out Snowshoe Canyon to Moran Bay.

MORAN CANYON, NORTH SIDE ROCK CLIMBS: BIVOUAC PEAK, SOUTH SHOULDER (ca. 9,200)

(0.35 mi SSE of Bivouac Peak)

Map: Mount Moran

Rising immediately above and north of the floor of Moran Canyon from 7,300 feet is this initial buttress of Bivouac Peak, which mirrors on a smaller scale the north shoulder of Mount Moran on the other side of the canyon. It lies separate from and south of the base of the main south faces of the peak.

ROUTE 1. SOUTHWEST CORNER. II, 5.6. First ascent July 16, 1985, by Jim Lemmon, Merle King, and Mark Wilk. From Moran Canyon start by ascending the first (easternmost) drainage gully between Bivouac Peak and Traverse Peak. The protruding south shoulder of Bivouac Peak rises just above and to the right (east) of this gully. Take the talus slope east out of the gully onto a grassy slope just above a white-rock ledge. Several initial pitches of 5.1 climbing were required, first up and right and then back left to the southwest corner. The more interesting final four short leads begin at some trees where a large flake will be found. From the flake move right into a narrow chimney. Then climb on ledges right and up toward the top of the shoulder. The final pitch goes up some slabs to the shoulder. Descent is made back to the southeast via the large scree slope at the base of the main south face of Bivouac Peak.

PEAK 10,625

(0.8 mi E of Rolling Thunder Mountain)

Map: Ranger Peak

Dividing the two forks of Snowshoe Canyon, this modest peak is the high point at the end of the east ridge of Rolling Thunder Mountain. Tracks of mountain sheep were found within 15m of the summit in 1983.

Chronology

SOUTHEAST RIDGE: August 22, 1957, Jack Davis, Redwood Fryxell, Julie Peterson
WEST RIDGE: August 22, 1957, Jack Davis, Redwood Fryxell, Julie Peterson (descent)
SOUTH COULOIRS: August 1, 1983, Leigh Ortenburger, Roman Laba

ROUTE 1. WEST RIDGE. I, 3.0. First descent August 22, 1957, by Jack Davis, Redwood Fryxell, and Julie Peterson. This party traversed the entire ridge from the summit to Rolling Thunder Mountain.

ROUTE 2. SOUTH COULOIRS. I, 3.0. First ascent August 1, 1983, by Leigh Ortenburger and Roman Laba. A pair of couloirs, one narrow, leads from about 8,100 feet in the south fork of Snowshoe Canyon to the col west of the summit. Some routefinding is required in these couloirs. From the col the ridge is easily followed to the summit.

ROUTE 3. SOUTHEAST RIDGE. I, 3.0. First ascent August 22, 1957, by Jack Davis, Redwood Fryxell, and Julie Peterson, from a camp at Dudley Lake. This ridge, containing brush, scree, and talus, leads to the east ridge about 0.2 mile from the summit, which is then easily reached.

ROLLING THUNDER MOUNTAIN (10,908)

Map: Ranger Peak

Not only does this peak possess the finest name among the northern peaks, but it also presents the most alpine aspect. Except for the top 3m, the rock is crystalline. A snow/icefield exists at the northwest foot of the peak, and from the northeast Rolling Thunder Mountain appears astonishingly sharp. The cirque of lakes to the north and Dudley Lake to the southeast provide beautiful and pristine campsites. The approach, however, is long (see *Snowshoe Canyon*) and it may still be possible that only the first-ascent party has made the ascent and return in one day. The wedge-shaped high point (Peak 10,320+) at the end of the northeast ridge was first reached on August 5, 1963, by Leigh Ortenburger, Irene Beardsley (Ortenburger), Julie Peterson, and Dennis Wilson.

Chronology

SOUTHEAST RIDGE: August 15, 1933, Fritiof Fryxell, Phil Smith
SOUTHWEST COULOIR: August 15, 1933, Fritiof Fryxell, Phil Smith (descent); August 21, 1970, Leigh and Carolyn Ortenburger, Irene Beardsley (Ortenburger) (ascent)
WEST RIDGE: [probable] August 1935, T. F. Murphy, Mike Yokel Jr.; August 25, 1954, Roald and Redwood Fryxell, Earle McBride (descent); [certain] August 5, 1963, Leigh Ortenburger, Irene Beardsley (Ortenburger), Julie Peterson, Dennis Wilson (ascent)
NORTHEAST RIDGE: [probable] August 30, 1967, Hugh Scott, Harold Woodham; [certain] August 3, 1974, David Lowe, Leigh Ortenburger
RENNY'S ROUTE: July 9, 1980, Anne MacQuarrie, George Montopoli

ROUTE 1. WEST RIDGE. II, 5.1. Probable first ascent in August 1935, by T. F. Murphy and Mike Yokel Jr.; first descent August 25, 1954, by Roald and Redwood Fryxell and Earle McBride; first known ascent August 5, 1963, by Leigh Ortenburger, Irene Beardsley (Ortenburger), Julie Peterson, and Dennis Wilson. Although there are several towers and notches, there is no great difficulty in traversing this ridge from Peak 10,880+. It is easier to gain this ridge from the south than from the north where snow or ice must be crossed and the couloirs are steep.

ROUTE 2. SOUTHWEST COULOIR. II, 3.0. First descent August 15, 1933, by Fritiof Fryxell and Phil Smith; first ascent August 21, 1970, by Leigh and Carolyn Ortenburger and Irene Beardsley (Ortenburger). This couloir starts from the north branch of the south fork of Snowshoe Canyon at 9,100 feet and leads directly toward the summit. Some scrambling will be involved near the summit, but this is the easiest route on the peak. Numerous sheep beds will be passed along the way.

ROUTE 3. SOUTHEAST RIDGE. II, 4.0. First ascent August 15, 1933, by Fritiof Fryxell and Phil Smith. Ascend the north fork of Snowshoe Canyon to the high cirque directly east of the summit. Various couloirs provide access from the cirque to the ridge, which is then followed to the summit knob. The difficulty and length of the climb depend on which couloir is selected. One must expect to encounter snow in getting onto the ridge during most early-season climbs. On August 22, 1957, Jack Davis, Redwood Fryxell, and Julie Peterson climbed the entire southeast ridge, over all the intervening towers and subsummits. The two lakes in the cirque provide excellent campsites. **Time:** 3¼ hours from Talus Lake; 8¼ hours from Dudley Lake.

ROUTE 4. NORTHEAST RIDGE. II, 5.4. Probable first ascent August 30, 1967, by Hugh Scott and Harold Woodham; first known ascent August 3, 1974, by David Lowe and Leigh Ortenburger. This ridge is one of the major features of this isolated peak. Approach via Snowshoe Canyon to Talus Lake in the uppermost north fork, where campsites can be found. This splendid wilderness lake could also be reached from Moose Basin (see *Webb Canyon* in Section 11) by passing over one of the ridges to the west or north. From Talus Lake, the saddle on the ridge connecting with Peak 10,320+ is reached via snowfields on the northwest side of Rolling Thunder and a diagonal couloir. Scrambling or easy 4.0 climbing along the ridge, which at times is very narrow, leads to the last step to the flat summit. This step is not as difficult as it appears from below. It appears that the 1967 party stayed on the right (west) side of the ridge using slabs and chimneys but found loose rock.

ROUTE 5. RENNY'S ROUTE. III, 5.9. First ascent July 9, 1980, by Anne MacQuarrie and George Montopoli. Above Talus Lake in the north fork of Snowshoe Canyon on the north side of Rolling Thunder Mountain lies a considerable snow/icefield bounded on the right by the west ridge of the mountain and on the left by the northeast ridge. This difficult route follows a crack system in the north wall of the mountain, just right (west) of the intersection of the north face and the northeast ridge. The first pitch (5.9, 46m) off the snow steps onto face holds just right of this crack system. Then move up and left into the crack, where two mantels left of the crack lead to a big ledge. This is followed by 9m of offwidth crack to a belay stance on small ledges and a chockstone.

The next lead of equal difficulty and length ascends a lieback and a jam crack among loose flakes to a wet, mossy diagonal gully. Climb up and right along this gully for 9m and then straight up through a crack/dihedral system to a large platform belay. The next easy pitch goes straight up through loose blocks for 46m to the base of a 6m corner at the intersection of the northeast and north faces. Climb the corner and crack (which turns into a chimney) above, passing a chockstone to the end of the crack. Exit by a tricky move left onto a ledge, crawling until face holds are found that permit standing, to reach a belay at the base of a left-slanting dihedral. The final short lead goes up this dihedral for 9m until just below a roof. Step up and right on a brown wall to a ledge. Traverse right along this ledge past some blocks and then up a crack to the summit.

Dragon Peak and Cleaver Peak (foreground) frame the high peaks of the Teton Range to the south.

PEAK 10,880+

(0.8 mi NW of Rolling Thunder Mountain)
Map: Ranger Peak

Of all the crystalline peaks in the park, this long, nearly flat ridge is perhaps the least imposing in appearance. From almost any direction it presents no difficulties. In the course of their surveying in 1935 for the first USGS map of Grand Teton National Park, T. F. Murphy and Mike Yokel Jr. probably ascended this peak.

Chronology

EAST RIDGE: August 25, 1954, Roald and Redwood Fryxell, Earle McBride
WEST RIDGE: ca. August 15, 1960, Loring Woodman
SOUTH SLOPE: August 14, 1962, John C. Reed Jr.

ROUTE 1. WEST RIDGE. I, 1.0. First ascent on about August 15, 1960, by Loring Woodman. The saddle (10,320+) west of the summit provides the principal route for passing between the south fork of Snowshoe Canyon and the head of Webb Canyon. It is easily reached from both the north and the south, and the ridge above is equally simple.

ROUTE 2. SOUTH SLOPE. I, 1.0. First ascent August 14, 1962, by John C. Reed Jr. Approach via the north branch of the south fork of Snowshoe Canyon and turn north and climb the easy slope to the lower east summit; then follow the ridge to the main (west) summit.

ROUTE 3. EAST RIDGE. I, 2.0. First ascent August 25, 1954, by Roald and Redwood Fryxell and Earle McBride. This party traversed the entire ridge from the summit of Rolling Thunder Mountain.

BLACKWELDER PEAK (10,800+)

(0.55 mi SE of Glacier Peak)
Map: Ranger Peak

In 1912, during the course of his geological explorations of the west side of the Teton divide, Professor Eliot Blackwelder and his assistant ascended this point from South Bitch Creek. His field notes indicate: "From here we intended to climb the next peak north [Glacier Peak] but found the arête too dangerous." This arête and the east ridge both contain many towers and pinnacles. Besides being the intersection point of three canyons—Snowshoe, Webb, and South Bitch Creek—Blackwelder Peak has the added distinction of harboring one of the remaining glaciers north of those on Mount Moran. This may be a remnant glacier as it has receded significantly and there is a small lake at the snout.

ROUTE 1. SOUTH RIDGE. I, 2.0. First ascent August 12, 1912, by Eliot Blackwelder and Mack Lake. From a camp in the South Bitch Creek canyon, the saddle immediately south of this peak was easily reached. The ridge itself offers no significant difficulties.

ROUTE 2. EAST RIDGE. I, 3.0. First ascent July 23, 1958, by Jack Davis, Julie Peterson, and Silvia Prodan. Approach via the south fork of Snowshoe Canyon to the important 10,320+-foot saddle between this peak and Peak 10,880+. Climb west from this saddle over the first peak, "Crocodile Crag," along the pinnacled ridge connecting with the summit. Some of these towers are most easily bypassed by utilizing the top edge of the glacier along the north side.

EAGLES REST PEAK, EAST PEAK (PEAK 10,880+)

(0.2 mi E of Eagles Rest Peak)
Map: Ranger Peak

This eastern satellite of Eagles Rest Peak provides an impressive view of the main peak. It is climbed even less often than the seldom-visited main peak.

ROUTE 1. WEST RIDGE. I, 1.0. First ascent September 4, 1962, by John C. Reed Jr. From the vicinity of the Moran Bay patrol cabin (burned down, but located on the map), cross the creek that flows from Snowshoe Canyon just below the large swamp. Proceed up the southeast couloir of Eagles Rest Peak (see *Eagles Rest Peak, Route* 3) to the saddle (10,640+) that separates the two summits of Eagles Rest Peak from the east peak. Turn east up to the summit of the east peak, which can be reached in 30 minutes.

ROUTE 2. EAST RIDGE. I, 1.0. First descent September 4, 1962, by John C. Reed Jr. No significant obstacles were reported on this 1,200m ridge, which begins in the vicinity of North Moran Bay.

EAGLES REST PEAK (11,258)

Map: Ranger Peak

It is surprising that this attractive peak, which presents a double-summit skyline when viewed from Jenny Lake, is climbed so seldom. Following the first ascent, 21 years passed before the second ascent was made. It is one of the northernmost crystalline peaks, and the summit view presents the Tetons from an angle rarely seen. The peak *could* be reached on foot from the Leigh Lake trailhead by String Lake, but far better is to approach via boat across Jackson Lake. The west summit, only a few feet lower than the main (east) summit, was first attained on June 25, 1957, by Leigh Ortenburger and Irene Beardsley (Ortenburger).

Chronology

NORTHEAST CHIMNEY: August 30, 1932, Phil Smith, Walcott Watson, W. C. Lawrence
NORTH RIDGE: August 30, 1932, Phil Smith, Walcott Watson, W. C. Lawrence (partial descent); July 31, 1962, John C. Reed Jr., T. B. Ranson, J. H. Dieterich (ascent)
SOUTHEAST COULOIR AND EAST RIDGE: June 28, 1953, Fred Ayres, A. E. Creswell, Roald Fryxell
WEST RIDGE: June 25, 1957, Leigh Ortenburger, Irene Beardsley (Ortenburger)
var—**NORTH COULOIR-WEST RIDGE:** February 1991, Tom Turiano, Christoph Schork, Jim Schultz (descent); February 1991, Christoph Schork (ascent)
SOUTH RIDGE: September 10, 1976, Leigh Ortenburger

ROUTE 1. WEST RIDGE. II, 5.1. First ascent June 25, 1957, by Leigh Ortenburger and Irene Beardsley (Ortenburger). The high ridge that connects Anniversary Peak with Eagles Rest Peak can be attained from either the south or the north via one of several fairly steep couloirs. The first-ascent party traversed the entire ridge. The west summit was easily reached by scrambling. Descend to the col separating the two summits. From the col a chute filled with loose rocks will be seen somewhat to the left of the ridge crest. One or two pitches up this chute suffice to put one on the main summit. However, it is much easier (3.0) to traverse on the south side of the west ridge into a gully that leads to the summit. See *American Alpine Journal* 11, no. 1 (1958): pp. 85–88.

***Variation:* NORTH COULOIR-WEST RIDGE.** II, 50° snow. First descent in February 1991, by Tom Turiano, Christoph Schork, and Jim Schultz. From the base Schork turned around and climbed the couloir so he could ski it. From the high cirque northwest of Eagles Rest Peak, climb 50° snow for approximately 275m to the col between the east and west summits of the peak. Follow the West Ridge route *(Route 1)* to the summit.

ROUTE 2. SOUTH RIDGE. II, 4.0. First ascent September 10, 1976, by Leigh Ortenburger. The south side of this peak contains several somewhat indistinct ridges separated by somewhat indistinct couloirs. The final 330m funnels into a distinct south ridge that brings one onto the last short section of the West Ridge route *(Route 1)*. The climbing consists of 3.0 and 4.0 scrambling with considerable loose rock. The approach is similar to that for the Southeast Couloir and East Ridge route *(Route 3)*, except that one continues farther into Snowshoe Canyon before turning up the mountain.

ROUTE 3. ▲ SOUTHEAST COULOIR AND EAST RIDGE. II, 3.0. First ascent June 28, 1953, by Fred Ayres, A. E. Creswell, and Roald Fryxell. This route uses the large couloir that descends the southeast side of the peak from the saddle (10,640+) between the twin summits and the east peak. The primary difficulty is locating the proper couloir, because the first portion of the ascent is made in the trees with little visibility. Take a good look before starting. The final 180m up the east ridge to the main (east) summit is enjoyable scrambling.

ROUTE 4. NORTHEAST CHIMNEY. II, 4.0. First ascent August 30, 1932, by Phil Smith, Walcott Watson, and W. C. Lawrence. From Jackson Lake ascend Waterfalls Canyon about 1.5 miles before bearing left (southwest) up into the cirque northeast of the mountain. Ascend a scree slope that lies below the northeast face of the peak. Near the top of this slope a chimney, which is blocked at its base by a chockstone, leads to the north ridge just below the main (east) summit. A variation was climbed by Watson by moving left (east) from the chimney onto the upper east ridge, which was then followed to the summit.

ROUTE 5. NORTH RIDGE. II, 5.1. First partial descent August 30, 1932, by Phil Smith, Walcott Watson, and W. C. Lawrence; first ascent July 31, 1962, by John C. Reed Jr., T. B. Ranson, and J. H. Dieterich. From a camp at the foot of Wilderness Falls in Waterfalls Canyon, proceed up the east side of the rock glacier into the high valley northwest of the summit. Gain the notch (10,640+) in the north ridge from the west via a steep chimney, and then follow the ridge to the summit. Some exposed and loose climbing will be encountered. This same notch can also apparently be reached from the cirque to the east.

ANNIVERSARY PEAK (11,253)

(0.5 mi W of Eagles Rest Peak)

Map: Ranger Peak

Rising directly above the forks of Snowshoe Canyon, this high crystalline peak features a fine double summit.

ROUTE 1. EAST RIDGE. I, 2.0. First descent June 25, 1957, by Leigh Ortenburger and Irene Beardsley (Ortenburger). Descent of this ridge was made to Eagles Rest Peak. The couloirs descending from this ridge to the north and the south are rather steep but should be entirely feasible.

ROUTE 2. NORTHWEST RIDGE. I, 2.0. First ascent June 25, 1957, by Leigh Ortenburger and Irene Beardsley (Ortenburger). This party traversed the easy ridge from Doane Peak to the double summit. No great difficulty should be experienced in reaching this ridge from the north fork of Snowshoe Canyon, and it is easily attained from the south fork of Waterfalls Canyon.

PEAK 10,720+

(0.6 mi W of Doane Peak)

Map: Ranger Peak

The sedimentary capping of this peak forms a flat top, which makes the summit less attractive, but the lower slopes are composed of crystalline rock possessing some interesting features. The long southeast ridge has an inviting profile, while the southwest ridge rising east of Talus Lake contains the most garnetiferous rock this author (L. Ortenburger) had ever seen in the park. The unnamed lake (just below the 9,200-foot contour line) at the base of this ridge is one of the more secluded lakes in the range—and perhaps the most picturesque.

Chronology

WEST RIDGE: August 26, 1954, Roald and Redwood Fryxell, Earle McBride

NORTHEAST RIDGE: August 26, 1954, Roald and Redwood Fryxell, Earle McBride (descent); August 7, 1962, John C. Reed Jr., T. B. Ranson, J. H. Dieterich (ascent)

SOUTHWEST RIDGE: August 5, 1963, Leigh Ortenburger, Irene Beardsley (Ortenburger)

ROUTE 1. WEST RIDGE. I, 1.0. First ascent August 26, 1954, by Roald and Redwood Fryxell and Earle McBride. From Talus Lake ascend the easy slope leading north and east to the summit. It is difficult to say where the highest point on the long, flat summit is to be found, but it is perhaps at the location of the cairn.

ROUTE 2. SOUTHWEST RIDGE. I, 2.0. First ascent August 5, 1963, by Leigh Ortenburger and Irene Beardsley (Ortenburger). This is the ridge that forms the eastern boundary of Talus Lake. Although somewhat steeper than the west ridge, it offers no difficulties if the small cliff sections are bypassed on the right (east). Garnetiferous rock is to be found on the ridge itself and in the talus slope just west of the crest. Once the plateau of sedimentary rock is reached, only a stroll is required to reach the summit.

ROUTE 3. NORTHEAST RIDGE. I, 1.0. First descent August 26, 1954, by Roald and Redwood Fryxell and Earle McBride; first ascent August 7, 1962, by John C. Reed Jr., T. B. Ranson, and J. H. Dieterich. From the north fork of Snowshoe Canyon, ascend into the hanging canyon that leads to the saddle between Peak 10,720+ and Doane Peak. From the saddle scramble easily west and then south up the ridge to the summit.

DOANE PEAK (11,355)

Map: Ranger Peak

This summit is tied with Ranger Peak as the highest point north of Mount Moran. Its name was bestowed by Fritiof Fryxell in 1936 in recognition of the epic winter expedition led by Lt. Gustavus Cheyney Doane, which passed along the mouth of Waterfalls Canyon to the east on November 24, 1876. This replaced the temporary name "Moose Station," which Earl M. Buckingham had given the peak in 1931. The 3m cairn that Buckingham built on its flat summit was to facilitate his triangulation work. As with several of the other peaks in the north end of the range, Doane Peak is most easily approached by boat across Jackson Lake. Waterfalls Canyon provides the most direct eastern approach. Perched above Moose Basin, the remote Lake 10,032, 0.5 mile west of Doane Peak, is one of the higher lakes in the range.

Chronology

WEST SLOPE: September 10, 1931, Earl M. Buckingham

NORTH RIDGE: July 22, 1956, Zach Stewart, Eleanor Page, Neil Penry, Frank Ewing, Cecile Hilding, Jack Walther

SOUTHEAST RIDGE: July 22, 1956, Zach Stewart, Eleanor Page, Neil Penry, Jack Walther (descent), or June 25, 1957, Leigh Ortenburger, Irene Beardsley (Ortenburger) (descent)

var—**SOUTHEAST COULOIR:** February 1991, Tom Turiano, Christoph Schork, Jim Schultz

ROUTE 1. WEST SLOPE. I, 1.0. First ascent September 10, 1931, by Earl M. Buckingham; T. F. Murphy and Mike Yokel Jr. also climbed this general route on August 21, 1935, during the course of their topographic work. On August 26, 1954, Roald and Redwood Fryxell and Earle McBride ascended the west ridge from Peak 10,720+; this may have been a new route, because the exact routes of 1931 and 1935 are not known. This mountain presents no difficulties from the Moose Basin side. The northwest ridge is also an easy hike.

ROUTE 2. SOUTHEAST RIDGE. I, 2.0. First descent July 22, 1956, by Zach Stewart, Eleanor Page, Neil Penry, and Jack Walther, or June 25, 1957, by Leigh Ortenburger and Irene Beardsley (Ortenburger). Most of this easy ridge is sedimentary. The saddle (10,720+) at the base of the ridge can very likely be reached from either the east or the west without great difficulty.

Variation: **SOUTHEAST COULOIR.** I, steep snow. First ascent in February 1991, by Tom Turiano, Christoph Schork, and Jim Schultz. From the high cirque enclosed by Anniversary Peak and Doane Peak, climb directly toward the summit plateau via a 40° couloir.

ROUTE 3. NORTH RIDGE. I, 1.0. First ascent July 22, 1956, by Zach Stewart, Eleanor Page, Neil Penry, Frank Ewing, Cecile Hilding, and Jack Walther. This broad ridge can easily be reached from the upper end of the north fork of Waterfalls Canyon.

PEAK 11,200+

(0.8 mi WSW of Ranger Peak)
Map: Ranger Peak

Lying west of Ranger Peak and north of Doane Peak is a connecting ridge composed of massive limestone with three distinct summits.

ROUTE 1. SOUTH RIDGE. I, 1.0. First ascent June 26, 1957, by Leigh Ortenburger and Irene Beardsley (Ortenburger). This ridge is easily climbed from the small lake at 10,480+ feet in the north fork of Waterfalls Canyon.

PEAK 11,238

(0.5 mi W of Ranger Peak)
Map: Ranger Peak

This peak is situated above the upper south fork of Webb Canyon at the interesting convergence of Waterfalls and Colter Canyons.

ROUTE 1. SOUTH SLOPE. I, 1.0. First descent June 24, 1957, by Leigh Ortenburger and Irene Beardsley (Ortenburger). There are no difficulties on this slope, which is easily approached via the north fork of Waterfalls Canyon.

ROUTE 2. NORTH RIDGE. I, 2.0. First ascent June 24, 1957, by Leigh Ortenburger and Irene Beardsley (Ortenburger). This long ridge extends without difficulties from the saddle (10,480+) at the head of Colter Canyon for almost 1 mile over two high points (10,852 and 10,960+). The Forellen Peak fault, one of the major faults in the range, passes in a southeast–northwest direction through this saddle.

MARMOT POINT (11,200+)

(0.35 mi W of Ranger Peak)
Map: Ranger Peak

While this is the most interesting point on the sedimentary Ranger Peak–Doane Peak ridge, it does not qualify as a peak. Near-vertical cliffs guard both the south and north faces, and the west ridge is also steep and crumbly.

ROUTE 1. EAST RIDGE. I, 4.0. First ascent June 24, 1957, by Leigh Ortenburger and Irene Beardsley (Ortenburger). This attractive little point lies immediately west of Ranger Peak and was climbed by its crumbly east ridge.

RANGER PEAK (11,355)

Map: Ranger Peak

This peak, which according to the topographers is the same elevation as Doane Peak, takes its name from the members of the first-ascent party, all of whom were park rangers at the time. It is situated at the head of three of the most beautiful of the northern canyons: Waterfalls, Quartzite, and Colter. The climbing history of this peak is murky, but the following chronology seems to be the most likely reconstruction of the original routes. By far the best approach for this peak is by boat across Jackson Lake from the Colter Bay area. Because it is capped by sedimentary rocks, Ranger Peak holds little interest for the technical climber, but the unspoiled region surrounding it should attract the wilderness seeker. Worth quoting here is this striking passage from the book *Mountaineering in the Tetons: The Pioneer Period, 1898–1940*, by Fritiof Fryxell and Phil D. Smith, describing their first ascent:

> ***Our day seems memorable in retrospect chiefly by reason of the thrilling new country it revealed, a type of beauty in mountains and waterfalls very different from that of the severe alpine region to the south. It is the great matterhorn peaks that give distinction to the Teton Range, but one's appreciation of the major summits is broadened by acquaintance with the surrounding mountains from which they spring. Ventures afield, to outlying summits like Ranger Peak, never fail to make for new and richer understanding of these incomparable mountains.***

Chronology

NORTHEAST RIDGE: July 29, 1935, Fritiof Fryxell, Phil Smith, Allyn Hanks
SOUTH RIDGE: July 29, 1935, Fritiof Fryxell, Phil Smith, Allyn Hanks (descent); August 26, 1955, Roald and Redwood Fryxell, Bob Perkins (ascent)
WEST RIDGE: 1938 or 1939, Rudolph Edmund, or August 13, 1941, Fritiof Fryxell, Leland Horberg, Joe Hoare, Bob Crist
EAST SLOPE: August 26, 1955, Roald and Redwood Fryxell, Bob Perkins (descent); July 30, 1976, Ed Wilson, Elaine Gross (ascent)
SOUTHEAST RIDGE: July 22, 1956, Frank Ewing, Cecile Hilding (partial); July 25, 1962, John C. Reed Jr., T. B. Ranson, J. H. Dieterich (descent); September 9, 1976, Leigh Ortenburger, Patty McDonald (complete ascent)

ROUTE 1. WEST RIDGE. I, 1.0. First ascent in 1938 or 1939, by Rudolph Edmund, or August 13, 1941, by Fritiof Fryxell, Leland Horberg, Joe Hoare, and Bob Crist. This is an easy slope and a natural route from the upper part of the north fork of Waterfalls Canyon.

ROUTE 2. SOUTH RIDGE. I, 2.0. First descent July 29, 1935, by Fritiof Fryxell, Phil Smith, and Allyn Hanks; first ascent August 26, 1955, by Roald and Redwood Fryxell and Bob Perkins. Follow a semi-trail in Waterfalls Canyon from Jackson Lake up past Wilderness Falls to the scenic lake (9,615) in the north fork of the canyon. The south ridge starts at the east shore of this lake and leads directly to the summit.

ROUTE 3. SOUTHEAST RIDGE. I, 2.0. First partial ascent July 22, 1956, by Frank Ewing and Cecile Hilding; first descent July 25, 1962, John C. Reed Jr., T. B. Ranson, and J. H. Dieterich; first complete ascent September 9, 1976, by Leigh Ortenburger and Patty McDonald. The easy southeast ridge begins at the 10,240+-foot saddle separating Peak 10,716 from the main Ranger Peak and joins the upper south ridge at the high south shoulder (11,000). This saddle is most enjoyably reached from the shore of Jackson Lake through the untrammeled Quartzite Canyon due east of Ranger Peak. It could also be attained from the vicinity of Columbine Cascade in Waterfalls Canyon, and it has also been reached more directly by traversing over the top of Peak 10,716 from the east.

ROUTE 4. EAST SLOPE. I, 2.0. First descent August 26, 1955, by Roald and Redwood Fryxell and Bob Perkins; first ascent July 30, 1976, by Ed Wilson and Elaine Gross. This route starts from Jackson Lake and enters Quartzite Canyon immediately east of Ranger Peak. This canyon has seldom been entered and contains a succession of small lakes; from the highest lake, one can climb directly to the summit. Alternatively, by veering north or south, one can reach the northeast ridge (see *Route 5*) or the southeast ridge (see *Route 3*) and follow either one to the summit.

ROUTE 5. NORTHEAST RIDGE. I, 2.0. First ascent July 29, 1935, by Fritiof Fryxell, Phil Smith, and Allyn Hanks. The first-ascent party gained the beginning of this ridge by first climbing over the top of Peak 10,732 and descending to the 10,560+-foot saddle. The easy crest of the ridge was then followed without difficulty to the summit. Of considerable interest is the high saddle (11,120+) just east of the summit, formed by weathering and erosion of the shattered rock of the Forellen Peak fault.

PEAK 10,716

(0.85 mi ESE of Ranger Peak)
Map: Colter Bay

This high point, the westerly of the two peaks on the southeast ridge of Ranger Peak, is normally approached only in the course of an ascent of that peak.

Chronology

EAST RIDGE: July 22, 1956, Frank Ewing, Cecile Hilding
WEST RIDGE: July 25, 1962, John C. Reed Jr., T. B. Ranson, J. H. Dieterich

ROUTE 1. WEST RIDGE. I, 2.0. First ascent July 25, 1962, by John C. Reed Jr., T. B. Ranson, and J. H. Dieterich. This ridge was first climbed via a descent of the southeast ridge of Ranger Peak (see *Ranger Peak, Route 3*).

ROUTE 2. EAST RIDGE. I, 2.0. First ascent July 22, 1956, by Frank Ewing and Cecile Hilding. This ridge was reached via a traverse from Peak 10,686 toward the summit of Ranger Peak.

PEAK 10,686

(1.2 mi ESE of Ranger Peak)
Map: Colter Bay

While it is perhaps unimportant in itself, this peak forms the beginning of the long southeast ridge of Ranger Peak (see *Ranger Peak, Route 3*), whose traverse makes a pleasant day on easy ground.

ROUTE 1. WEST RIDGE. I, 1.0. First descent July 22, 1956, by Frank Ewing and Cecile Hilding. There are no difficulties on the 150m descent to the saddle west of this peak.

ROUTE 2. EAST RIDGE. I, 1.0. First ascent July 22, 1956, by Frank Ewing and Cecile Hilding. From Jackson Lake this ridge is a long 1,200m ascent with no difficulties. The lowest section above the shores of the lake shows the traces of the fire that burned from July to November in 1974.

PEAK 10,732

(1.0 mi NE of Ranger Peak)
Map: Colter Bay

Along the ridge separating Quartzite Canyon on the south from Colter Canyon on the north, Peak 10,732 is the high point. Surprisingly in this northern region of easy sedimentary peaks there is a sequence of towers on the east ridge of Peak 10,732 that offer some technical difficulty. These towers were first climbed directly on the ridge crest, from west to east, on September 9, 1976, by Leigh Ortenburger and Patty McDonald; a rappel was used to descend the last of these towers.

ROUTE 1. WEST RIDGE. I, 2.0. First descent July 29, 1935, by Fritiof Fryxell, Phil Smith, and Allyn Hanks; first ascent July 26, 1962, by John C. Reed Jr. and J. H. Dieterich. From the saddle west of the peak, the ridge leads easily to the summit.

ROUTE 2. EAST RIDGE. I, 2.0. First ascent July 29, 1935, by Fritiof Fryxell, Phil Smith, and Allyn Hanks. From Jackson Lake ascend into Quartzite Canyon, following the slope just north of the stream until past (west of) the pinnacled section of the ridge. Turn north to the ridge crest just east of the first lake in the canyon. Scramble west to the summit.

MOUNT ROBIE (10,881)

(1.5 mi N of Ranger Peak)
Map: Ranger Peak

This peak stands at the north end of the massif separating Moose Basin in Webb Canyon from Jackson Lake. It is probably most easily reached from Webb Canyon directly from the west (see *Webb Canyon* in Section 11 and *Route 3*). Point 10,515, 0.5 mile to the east, was first climbed on August 23, 1953, by Roald Fryxell and Charles McCary from Webb Canyon. An attempted ascent on September 7, 1958, by Frank Ewing and Keith Jones via the long ridge from Webb Canyon leading toward Point 10,298 was stalled by too much loose rock and too many kinds of ripe berries along the way. The line of the Forellen Peak fault coincides with the drainage just west of Mount Robie, from the saddle (10,480+) on the south ridge at the head of Colter Canyon all the way down to Moose Creek.

ROUTE 1. SOUTH RIDGE. I, 2.0. First descent June 23, 1957, by Leigh Ortenburger and Irene Beardsley (Ortenburger). No difficulties were encountered in traversing this ridge to Peak 11,238 and beyond. It could undoubtedly be attained from either Colter Canyon or Webb Canyon.

ROUTE 2. EAST RIDGE. I, 3.0. First known ascent June 23, 1957, by Leigh Ortenburger and Irene Beardsley (Ortenburger), who found on the summit a cairn but no record. From Jackson Lake ascend the entire east ridge directly over the top of Point 10,515. The summit is guarded by a sharp sedimentary tower (10,800+) immediately to the east. The first-ascent party, lacking the proper equipment to ascend this tower directly (likely 5th class), contoured around it on the south (this involved a short rappel) to reach the notch that separates the tower from the flat summit area. The tower was climbed by a chute containing loose rock. The main summit is very easily reached from the notch. See *American Alpine Journal* 11, no. 1 (1958): pp. 85–88.

ROUTE 3. WEST FACE. I. 2.0. First ascent July 15, 1997, by John R. Hall and Dana Reitz. Approach to the peak was made via Webb Canyon to the drainage (referred to by this pair as Fryxell Canyon) west of Mount Robie and north of Point 10,852. No difficulties aside from "hellish scree" were reported in the ascent of this side of the peak.

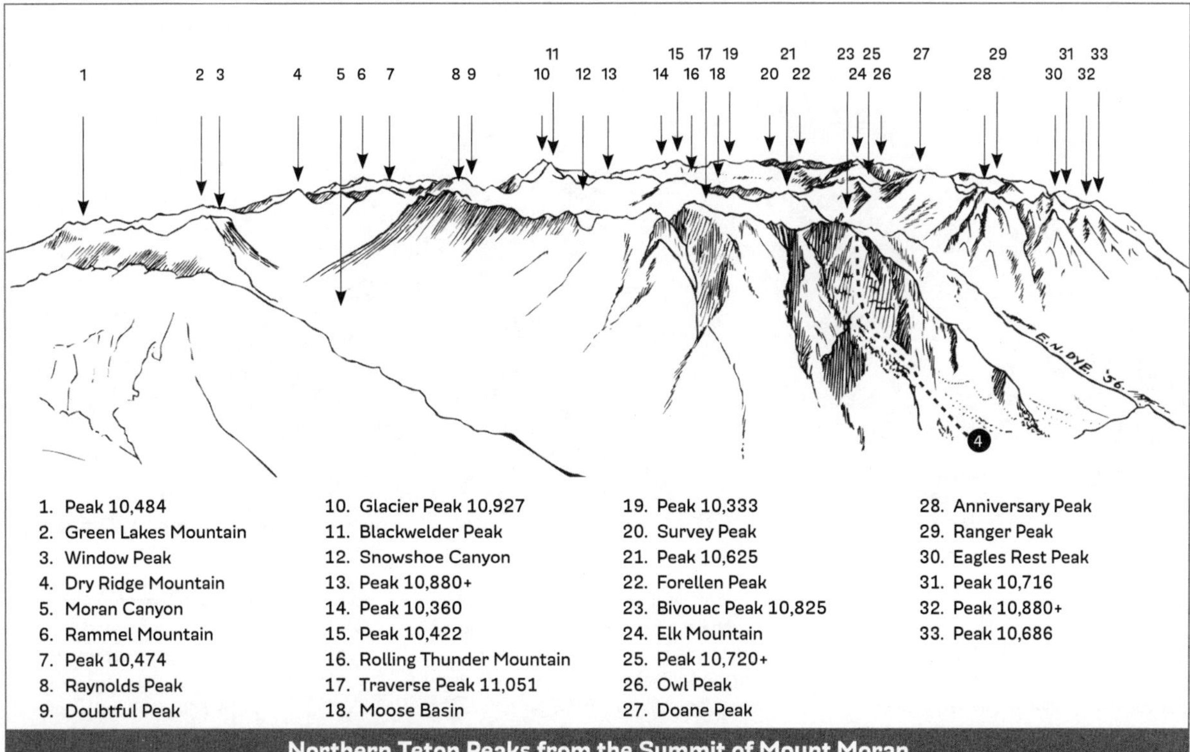

Northern Teton Peaks from the Summit of Mount Moran

SECTION 11

North of Webb Canyon

Webb Canyon

Webb Canyon is by far the largest canyon of the range in terms of area, containing much scenic open high country as well as one of the major climax forests in the park on its southeast side. Moose Basin is the name given to the upper open portion of the canyon east of the divide and west of the main creek. Curiously, the creek in Webb Canyon is called Moose Creek. Most of the canyon is hidden from view as seen from the valley and so is not appreciated until one hikes into its upper reaches. It is one of the great wilderness resources of the park even if the climbing opportunities on the surrounding peaks are limited. Of geological interest as well, the striking display of the Owl Peak fault on the north side of the canyon attracts the eye even of the unobservant.

Other than Berry Creek, Webb Canyon probably saw more early-day traffic than any canyon in the range. In the 1880s it became known as a haven for mountain sheep, and so was originally named Sheep Canyon. Because of this good fortune and relative ease of access, the canyon attracted many big-game hunting parties, some guided by Richard "Beaver Dick" Leigh in his last years. Two well-known parties, under the sponsorship of William Seward Webb, were in the canyon in 1896 and 1897. (These years are correct according to *Along the Ramparts of the Tetons: The Saga of Jackson Hole, Wyoming*, by Robert B. Betts.) Not long after, the US Geological Survey (USGS) topographic party that had begun work for the 1901 Grand Teton quadrangle named the canyon in Webb's honor. Prior to the completion of the dam on Jackson Lake, access by horse from the east into Webb Canyon was immediate because the lake ended at the mouth of the canyon.

Today Webb Canyon and Moose Basin are approached by trail from the lower Berry Creek patrol cabin on the west side of Jackson Lake near the mouths of Berry Creek and Moose Creek. The patrol cabin can be reached on foot from Grassy Lake Road (the Ashton–Flagg Ranch road), as described under *Berry Creek*, but this is a long hike (about 7.5 miles). It is far better to take a boat or canoe across the lake (0.7 mile) from Fonda Point at the Lizard Creek campground. Either way the Webb Canyon trail moves south across Berry Creek less than 0.2 mile west of the patrol cabin. This trail, maintained and easy to follow into Webb Canyon, has been rerouted: contrary to the USGS map, it now lies north of the stream, so stream crossings are not required. At about 7,680 feet, the location of one of the original Webb camps, the trail starts up the slope past the Moose Basin patrol cabin and continues to Moose Basin Divide (9,800+). Moose Basin is open-meadow country and so is easy and very scenic ground for cross-country hiking.

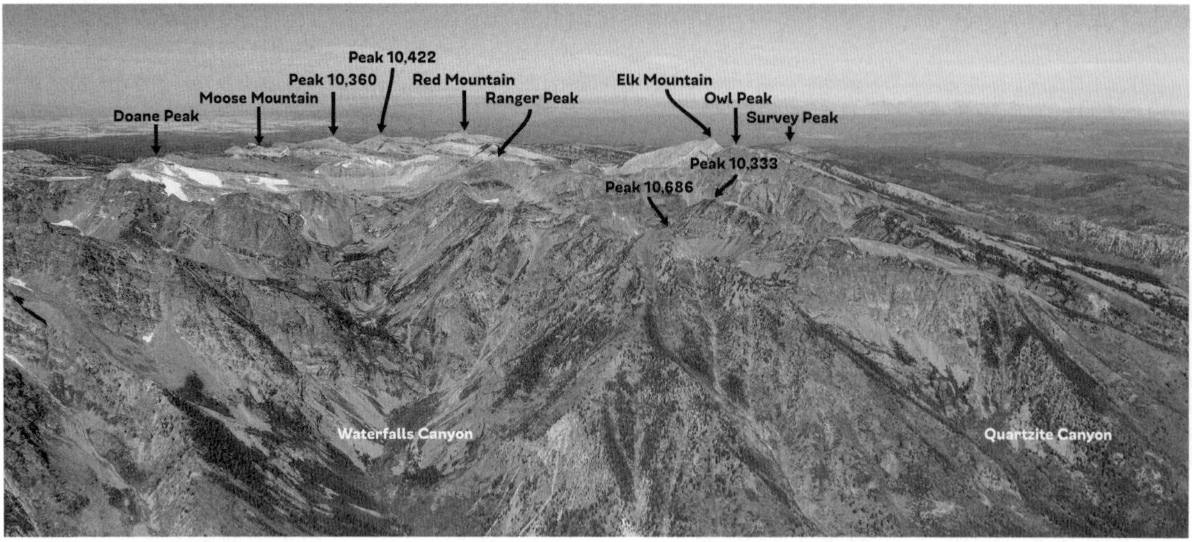

FIGURE 11-1. Waterfalls Canyon from the east

Exit from (or entry into) the upper Webb Canyon is available to the north at Moose Basin Divide into Owl Canyon; to the south into the south fork of Snowshoe Canyon via the saddle (10,320+) west of Peak 10,880+; into the north fork of Snowshoe Canyon via one of two passes (9,920+ and 10,000+) north and west of Talus Lake; or to the west via the US Forest Service (USFS) trail that comes from the north fork of Bitch Creek over Nord Pass to the divide at the saddle (9,680+) between Moose Mountain and Peak 9,970. With somewhat more exertion, one can also exit due east over the main ridge of Doane and Ranger Peaks into Waterfalls Canyon or Colter Canyon using one of the available high passes (10,800+ and 10,720+). The lower saddle (10,480+) near the north end of this main ridge is feasible only if one deliberately ascends the long northwest–southeast valley; the ridge bounding this valley on the west contains much sharp and shattered rock.

Owl Canyon

The main Owl Creek trail in Owl Canyon is maintained by the National Park Service (NPS), but the trail markings are sometimes inadequate, meaning use of the map is important. The main difficulty is caused by lack of bridges at stream crossings; this is especially notable in early season when the streams are high. The standard access is via the trail from the trailhead on Grassy Lake Road west of Flagg Ranch (see *Berry Creek* below). It is also easily reached via Jackson Lake from Fonda Point at the Lizard Creek campground. Canoe across (0.7 mile) to the vicinity of the lower Berry Creek patrol cabin near the lakeshore. At the patrol cabin, find the Berry Creek trail and follow it west into and up the narrows of lower Berry Creek to a junction; take the left branch into Owl Canyon. The Owl Creek trail then leads south to Moose Basin Divide (9,800+), where it joins the Webb Canyon trail. From upper Owl Canyon there is no trail connection to the saddle west of Forellen Peak where the upper Berry Creek trail ends.

If one is making a high traverse across the head of Owl Canyon from Webb Canyon to Berry Creek or in the reverse, it is best not to drop all the way down into Owl Canyon. Instead, stay high and contour as much as possible around the open country at the head of Owl Canyon between the two passes. The best route involves passing near the summit of Point 9,682 just west of the Berry-Owl divide. Because of limestone formations on the final portion of the trail to Moose Basin Divide, little drinking water will be found since water from the melting snow disappears into crevices in the rock. Hence, there is some difficulty in locating a suitable campsite in the upper elevations away from the main streams.

Berry Creek

Of all the canyons penetrating the Teton Range, Berry Creek was probably the first to be explored by European Americans. Originally an indigenous people's route, it was one of the trails of the fur-trapper era and later was an early scene of big-game hunting. The original north boundary of Grand Teton National Park as established in 1929 did not include this region; it remained under USFS control until 1943, then became part of the Jackson Hole National Monument and was incorporated into the park with the rest of the monument in 1950. Because the peaks surrounding the canyon are unspectacular and largely sedimentary, Berry Creek is of more interest to the backcountry hiker than to the mountaineer. The full USGS Grand Teton National Park map (1:62,500) can be used here, but some may prefer the 7.5-minute series topographic sheets (1:24,000)—Flagg Ranch, Survey Peak, and Hominy Peak. These are valuable since they are very detailed and show nearly all the trails.

The most northerly canyon in the range, Berry Creek is accessible by many different trails. The principal method of approach is from Grassy Lake Road (the Ashton–Flagg Ranch road), which passes around the north end of the range. From the junction immediately north of Flagg Ranch on the main highway leading to the Yellowstone National Park south entrance, take Grassy Lake Road west. After about 4 miles the small Berry Creek trailhead parking area will be seen on the south side of the road. The Berry Creek trail leads south, skirts the swamps near the Snake

River, and when the head of Jackson Lake is reached, moves west over a small pass (7,000+) to drop into an unnamed drainage. The trail then passes two junctions with trails leading south and, after crossing a second low pass (7,440+), finally enters the canyon. (Just after going over the second low pass and before entering Berry Creek, one can turn south on a trail and enter Owl Canyon just west of Elk Ridge.)

To pass the swampy main section of the canyon, the trail stays on the north side until reaching the east base of Survey Peak. The upper Berry Creek patrol cabin, as shown on the map, was removed and a new larger structure was constructed in 1987 at the same location. The entire region to the north, including the minor peaks at the extreme north edge of the park, is covered with dense lodgepole pine, making cross-country travel difficult. The divide north of Survey Peak can be gained by using the trail that heads north up the last drainage prior to reaching the base of Survey Peak. Two additional trails depart from this same area. One leads south to the Forellen Divide (8,840+), which is southwest of Forellen Peak. The other heads west over the divide at what is marked on the map as "Jackass Pass" (8,480); this is a misnomer because this location is very likely the historical Conant Pass, which is shown as being some 2 miles farther south on the map.

This upper portion of Berry Creek can also be reached from the west, starting from Ashton, Idaho, via the Ashton–Flagg Ranch road and then the Jackass road, which heads toward Hominy Peak. With the establishment of the Jedediah Smith Wilderness in 1984, one can no longer drive all the way to Hominy Peak or beyond. From the Hominy trailhead, a USFS trail leads to Hominy Peak and along the narrow ridge connecting with the divide at "Jackass Pass" (5.2 miles).

An easier method of reaching the mouth of Berry Creek is via the northern arm of Jackson Lake. From Fonda Point at the Lizard Creek campground it is a short (0.7-mile) canoe trip across to the vicinity of the lower Berry Creek patrol cabin near the lakeshore. At the cabin locate the Berry Creek trail and follow it either north—to join the trail already described from Grassy Lake Road (the Ashton–Flagg Ranch road)—or west, into and up the narrows of lower Berry Creek where one may branch north into Berry Creek or farther west into Owl Canyon. (See *Figure 11-1* for an overview of some of the peaks in this area.) **Note:** The "T" following some elevations means that a spot elevation was determined by photogrammetric methods.

GLACIER PEAK (10,927)

(2.0 mi NW of Rolling Thunder Mountain)
Map: Ranger Peak

As the highest peak on the divide north of Table Mountain between Teton Basin and Jackson Hole, Glacier Peak is an outstanding viewpoint for the entire north end of the Teton Range. It was named "Glacier Station" in 1931 by Earl M. Buckingham, who occupied it as a triangulation point. Although the summit is graced by a large cairn, Buckingham placed the benchmark, which is not easily found, some 60m to the north. Just east of the summit at the extreme southwest head of Webb Canyon is the glacier—now a remnant—that gave rise to the name of the peak. A lake has formed at the snout of this remnant glacier as it gradually succumbs to climate change. This high peak was known to, but probably not climbed by, the various hunting parties in Moose Basin in the 1890s. Because it is on the northern section of the divide, Glacier Peak is a good example of those peaks that are perhaps most easily approached from the Caribou-Targhee National Forest/Jedediah Smith Wilderness west of the range. From Teton Basin the closest approach appears to be from the US Forest Service (USFS) trailhead on the north side of South Badger Creek: take the Badger Creek trail east up South Badger Creek, turn north onto the Teton Crest Trail over Dead Horse Pass, and then drop down into the head of South Bitch Creek at a point 1.1 miles west of Glacier Peak.

ROUTE 1. NORTH RIDGE. I, 2.0. First ascent September 9, 1931, by Earl M. Buckingham. This gentle ridge begins at the 9,600+-foot saddle and lake, which provides a good camping site, but it can be attained considerably higher from either side. Some scrambling is involved because the ridge consists of large blocks, but it is not difficult.

PEAK 10,010

(1.8 mi NW of Rolling Thunder Mountain)
Map: Ranger Peak

This peak, perhaps the least important of the Teton peaks, was easily reached from the small lake at 9,720+ feet.

ROUTE 1. EAST SLOPE. I, 1.0. First known ascent August 4, 1963, by Dennis Wilson. Some evidence of previous ascent was found.

PEAK 9,970

(0.6 mi SSE of Moose Mountain)
Map: Ranger Peak

This is the broad, rounded knoll on the divide between Glacier Peak and Moose Mountain.

Chronology

NORTH SLOPE: [probable] August 1935, T. F. Murphy, Mike Yokel Jr.; [certain] July 31, 1963, Loring Woodman
SOUTH RIDGE: August 4, 1963, Leigh Ortenburger, Irene Beardsley (Ortenburger), Julie Peterson, Dennis Wilson (descent)

ROUTE 1. SOUTH RIDGE. I, 2.0. First descent August 4, 1963, by Leigh Ortenburger, Irene Beardsley (Ortenburger), Julie Peterson, and Dennis Wilson. A sedimentary cliff band on this ridge can be bypassed by a couloir on the west side.

ROUTE 2. NORTH SLOPE. I, 1.0. Probable first ascent in August 1935, by T. F. Murphy and Mike Yokel Jr.; first known ascent July 31, 1963, by Loring Woodman, who found a cairn but no record on the flat, tree-covered summit.

MOOSE MOUNTAIN (10,054)

Map: Ranger Peak

About 0.3 mile to the north on the north ridge of this very easy peak are some interesting sedimentary pinnacles that rise 18m or more from their surroundings. Moose Mountain is easily approached from the US Forest Service (USFS) trail at Nord Pass, only 0.5 mile to the northwest.

Chronology

NORTH SLOPE: [probable] August 1935, T. F. Murphy, Mike Yokel Jr.; [certain] July 31, 1963, Loring Woodman
SOUTH SLOPE: July 31, 1963, Loring Woodman (descent)

ROUTE 1. SOUTH SLOPE. I, 2.0. First known descent July 31, 1963, by Loring Woodman.
ROUTE 2. NORTH SLOPE. I, 1.0. Probable first ascent in August 1935, by T. F. Murphy and Mike Yokel Jr.; first known ascent July 31, 1963, by Loring Woodman, who also first climbed the pinnacles to the north.

PEAK 10,360

(0.85 mi N of Moose Mountain)
Map: Ranger Peak

Lying on the main divide between Jackson Hole and Teton Basin, this peak forms a portion of the western boundary of Moose Basin.

ROUTE 1. SOUTH RIDGE. I, 3.0. Probable first ascent in August 1935, by T. F. Murphy and Mike Yokel Jr.; first known ascent July 31, 1963, by Loring Woodman. This ridge can be gained from the west, as was done in 1963, or it can be easily reached from Moose Basin Divide between Webb and Owl Canyons. However, if one starts at the saddle north of Moose Mountain, a cliff band will be encountered; it can be passed on the east with a short, exposed traverse on semistable rock.

William Owen and Fritiof Fryxell, circa 1930 (Photo courtesy of GTNP archive)

PEAK 10,422

(1.3 mi N of Moose Mountain)
Map: Ranger Peak

This is one of the more challenging of the sedimentary peaks because it is ringed, almost without break, by a prominent cliff band.

ROUTE 1. EAST RIDGE. I, 2.0. First ascent August 4, 1963, by Leigh Ortenburger, Irene Beardsley (Ortenburger), and Dennis Wilson. Moose Basin Divide, the important saddle just east of this peak, is easily reached by trail either from Owl Canyon or Webb Canyon. From this saddle, pass to the north (right) of the first buttress, which prevents a direct ascent of the east ridge. Gain the col behind this eastern buttress and follow the rest of the ridge to the summit. The eastern buttress involves short sections of 3.0 climbing on its western side.

PEAK 10,270

(2.1 mi WSW of Elk Mountain)
Map: Ranger Peak

This minor sedimentary peak is located just to the northeast above Moose Basin Divide and is a high point along the southwest ridge of Peak 10,333. Its first ascent is unknown, but it has surely been climbed many times from the divide. A cave in the west-facing cliff was found by the 1994 party.

ROUTE 1. EAST RIDGE. I, 2.0. First known ascent April 14, 1994, by Dave Moore, Tom Turiano, and Mike Whitehead. This party climbed the peak and skied the steep southeast-facing bowl between it and Peak 10,333. (Source: Thomas Turiano, *Teton Skiing: A History and Guide to the Teton Range* [Moose, WY: Homestead Pub., 1995])

PEAK 10,333

(1.75 mi WSW of Elk Mountain)
Map: Ranger Peak

From Moose Basin Divide an unbroken cliff band will be seen guarding this peak on the northwest and southwest. It should prove possible to climb past this obstacle (probably loose) at the nose where these two faces meet and then traverse the long ridge east to the summit.

ROUTE 1. EAST RIDGE. I, 2.0. First ascent August 3, 1963, by Leigh Ortenburger, Irene Beardsley (Ortenburger), Julie Peterson, and Dennis Wilson. After ascending Elk Mountain (10,720+), this party descended its southwest ridge and continued west over Peak 9,924. At this point they gained the east ridge of Peak 10,333 and followed it without difficulty to the summit.
ROUTE 2. NORTH RIDGE. I, 3.0. First descent August 3, 1963, by Leigh Ortenburger, Irene Beardsley (Ortenburger), Julie Peterson, and Dennis Wilson. From Owl Canyon this ridge can be attained by following the trail to about the 9,000-foot level and then cutting east up one of the few breaks near the north end of the cliff band that protects this peak on the northwest. Once the plateau at about 9,300 feet is reached, no further problems will be met.

PEAK 9,924

(0.9 mi SW of Elk Mountain)
Map: Ranger Peak

This minor peak lies on the ridge connecting Elk Mountain and Moose Basin Divide.

ROUTE 1. EAST RIDGE. I, 1.0. First ascent August 3, 1963, by Leigh Ortenburger, Irene Beardsley (Ortenburger), Julie Peterson, and Dennis Wilson. This tree-covered bump is easily climbed from any direction.
ROUTE 2. WEST RIDGE. I, 1.0. First descent August 3, 1963, by Leigh Ortenburger, Irene Beardsley (Ortenburger), Julie Peterson, and Dennis Wilson.

ELK MOUNTAIN (10,720+)

Map: Ranger Peak

Of all the sedimentary peaks north of Webb Canyon, this is the highest and it dominates the north end of the Teton Range. Protected on most sides by interminable sedimentary talus and scree slopes, Elk Mountain rises over 3,000 feet from either Owl Canyon to the north or Webb Canyon to the south. On August 23, 1955, the "Buster Point" triangulation station was established by Kenneth S. McLean on the summit. In 1963 Leigh Ortenburger and party found the pole signal, still held in place by surveyors' wires, in the summit cairn. Elk Mountain actually has two distinct summits separated by a 0.3-mile ridge. When one is standing on the north summit, it seems to be several feet higher

Climbing rangers Mik Shain and Casey Heerdt on a mountain patrol of Thor Peak's Hidden Couloir (Photo by Vic Zeilman)

than the more easily reached south summit; an older USGS map indicated that the south summit was at least 8 feet higher, and modern maps confirm this slight difference with an additional small closed contour line. Still, to be assured of success the cautious mountaineer will be obliged to climb both. The major and readily visible Forellen Peak fault runs through the high saddle just to the east that separates Elk Mountain from Owl Peak.

Chronology

SOUTHEAST RIDGE: [probable] August 23, 1955, Kenneth S. McLean

SOUTHWEST RIDGE: August 3, 1963, Leigh Ortenburger, Irene Beardsley (Ortenburger), Julie Peterson, Dennis Wilson

ROUTE 1. SOUTHWEST RIDGE. I, 3.0. First ascent August 3, 1963, by Leigh Ortenburger, Irene Beardsley (Ortenburger), Julie Peterson, and Dennis Wilson. This route begins at the saddle (9,680+) in the Owl-Webb divide just west and south of Elk Mountain. This saddle can be reached from either the north or the south, using the Webb Canyon trail or the Owl Creek trail. Either way about 600m of uphill scrambling will be involved. The south end of this ridge is easily attained from the saddle. The upper, more or less horizontal, section of the ridge that leads to the south summit (10,720+) involves some scrambling, either on the crest or very slightly to the right (east) of the crest. This section is very sharp and exposed and contains some equally sharp, although small, notches. The traverse from the south summit to the north summit (perhaps higher) does not share these problems.

ROUTE 2. SOUTHEAST RIDGE. I, 2.0. Probable first ascent August 23, 1955, by Kenneth S. McLean. This ridge leads directly up to the south summit of Elk Mountain from the saddle that separates Elk Mountain and Owl Peak. The saddle is most easily reached from the south from Webb Canyon. The southern approach requires some adroit routefinding to avoid the sedimentary cliff bands that sweep in from the west. During most of the summer the direct northern approach from lower Berry Creek is complicated by the presence of a snow slope; an ice axe may be desirable. The ridge itself is loose and there is rather steep talus from the saddle to the south summit. From the south summit to the north summit (perhaps higher) is a pleasant 10-minute ridge walk.

OWL PEAK (10,612)

Map: Ranger Peak

The 1901 USGS Grand Teton quadrangle indicates that the T. M. Bannon topographic party placed a benchmark on this summit, although it seems that when the letters *BM* appear on a USGS map this does not always mean that the summit was reached and a bronze marker placed. Earl M. Buckingham named this peak "Owl Station" while doing his triangulation work in 1931, but he did not occupy the site. T. F. Murphy may have been the first surveyor to visit the summit. The major Forellen Peak fault cuts through the saddle separating this peak from Elk Mountain. The dark crystalline rocks of this peak contrast strikingly with the lighter sedimentary rocks of Elk Mountain. Surveyors' paraphernalia, dating from Kenneth S. McLean's 1955 visit, will be found on the summit.

Chronology

SOUTH SLOPE, WEST RIDGE: [probable] August 1935, T. F. Murphy, Mike Yokel Jr.
NORTH-NORTHEAST RIDGE: August 22, 1955, Kenneth S. McLean
EAST RIDGE: July 8, 1963, John C. Reed Jr., J. H. Dieterich

ROUTE 1. SOUTH SLOPE, WEST RIDGE. I, 2.0. Probable first ascent in August 1935, by T. F. Murphy and Mike Yokel Jr. If the main couloir leading from Webb Canyon to the col west of the summit is used, some routefinding will be required to avoid the sedimentary cliff bands that approach the couloir from the west. From the col, easy scrambling up the dark rocks of the moderately sharp west ridge takes one to the summit.
ROUTE 2. EAST RIDGE. I, 2.0. First ascent July 8, 1963, by John C. Reed Jr. and J. H. Dieterich. From Webb Canyon climb a large southern couloir to gain the east ridge about 0.5 mile east of the summit; the east ridge is then easily followed to the summit. The correct couloir can be identified as the one starting at the "Webb" of "Webb Canyon Trail" on the USGS Ranger Peak quadrangle.
ROUTE 3. NORTH-NORTHEAST RIDGE. I, 1.0. First known ascent August 22, 1955, by Kenneth S. McLean. Although most of the possible eastern approaches to this peak are far more straightforward, the following tedious route has actually been climbed. From the patrol cabin near Jackson Lake hike up the Berry Creek trail to approximately 0.5 mile below the junction of Berry Creek and Owl Creek. Cross to the south side of Berry Creek and ascend the long timbered ridge in a southwest direction to the bare, rocky, rounded summit of dark-colored rock. This creek-crossing point on lower Berry Creek can be reached via the trail directly from Jackson Lake (if one takes a boat or canoe across the lake) or via the connecting trail between upper Berry Creek and Owl Creek (if one hikes in from the trailhead on Grassy Lake Road [the Ashton–Flagg Ranch road], which skirts the north end of the range).

PEAK 8,602

(3.25 mi ENE of Owl Peak)
Map: Colter Bay

This tree-covered high point on the extreme end of the east ridge of Owl Peak separates the lower reaches of Berry Creek from Moose Creek. A north–south fault lies just east of the summit, aligned with the open couloir that descends toward Webb Canyon. This couloir is a steep scramble (I, 2.0) and the east ridge is a bushy hike (I, 1.0).

WEBB CANYON, NORTH SIDE ROCK CLIMBS (8,080+)

Map: Ranger Peak

ROUTE 1. ALL IN A DAY'S WORK. II, 5.9. First ascent August 20, 1984, by Todd Swain and Ralph Moore. On the north side of Webb Canyon, about 3.5 miles west along the trail from the patrol cabin at the mouth of Berry Creek, is the Webb Wall of crystalline rock. This seven-pitch route ascends this wall, passing trees and a midway terrace to a single tree marking the top of the climb. The location of this wall seems to be in the vicinity of the C of "Moose Creek" on either the USGS Ranger Peak quadrangle or the USGS Grand Teton National Park map. From the trail scramble up a talus slope and grassy ledges to a dead tree on the middle west part of the cliff, where the route begins.

The first pitch (46m) starts at the tree and goes straight up slabs (21m) to and up a small left-facing corner (5.4) to broken ledges; then traverse 6m right to the belay in a large left-facing corner. Next, climb the broken corner (5.2) left of the obvious buttress until it is possible to traverse left and up toward three trees; belay at the highest tree just below two dihedrals. The third lead ascends either of the two dihedrals (right is better, 5.6) straight up to another tree belay at the end of 25m. Then climb the corner above the tree and take an obvious hand crack (5.7) out to the steep wall on the right to the belay on the midway terrace above. Move the belay about 30m out to the right to a point just uphill of an obvious right-facing corner. The next crux pitch starts about 9m left of the yellow left-facing corner and moves up a steep face to the right to a small left-facing corner. After placing high protection, downclimb and traverse right to an obvious crack system that leads to a chute. Climb the wall (5.9) to a beautiful 2-inch crack and then climb the crack (5.9) to the belay about 9m farther up on the left. The final lead goes easily up and left to a tree that marks the end of this route. For the descent make one 46m rappel from the tree down to the midway terrace, which is followed out and to the right (east) to regain the trail below.
ROUTE 2. AEOLIAN ARÊTE. III, 5.9, First complete ascent August 22, 1997, by Dan, Reed, and Lane Burgette. Approach this climb as for *Route 1*, but continue farther west along the trail up Webb Canyon. About 10 minutes past the waterfalls in Moose Creek, leave the trail at the first large talus slope that reaches the trail above the falls. Before heading up the talus, take in the arête, which is best seen with the morning sun hitting the crest. Prominent features include the chimney on the fifth pitch, which appears to be a large, shaded open book, and a knife-edge arête below a large double dihedral at the skyline. Hike up the talus through the lower cliff bands. The route starts above a massive, weather-beaten whitebark pine that is on the crest of the slight ridge between the two gullies flanking the arête. Just to the left of an eye-catching, reverse-J-shaped dihedral, look for a vertical groove with a small cairn at its base.

Pitch 1: Ascend the groove (5.5–5.6) to a small tree (34m). **Pitch 2:** Drop down from the tree slightly and climb the glacier-polished face above to a broken ledge, then continue up to a belay beneath a roof (5.7, 30m). **Note:** These first two pitches can be linked. **Pitch 3:** Climb a thin crack through the roof (5.7) and then face climb left (thin protection, 5.8 or easier to the right) to where the angle eases and small ledges are found. Bear right to a good ledge and belay. **Pitch 4:** To begin this crux pitch, ascend the groove above the belay, then traverse left to an obvious, steep finger crack in a right-facing corner. Climb the corner via liebacks and finger locks (5.9). Above the corner is a steep wall with some tricky climbing and a mantel at the top to the belay at the base of a chimney. **Pitch 5:** Ascend the dramatic chimney that caps this step of the arête. The 5m below the top of the chimney (where it narrows) is the crux of this section (5.7; if climbing with a pack, haul or dangle it below for this section). Continue up 10m from the top of the chimney and belay. **Pitch 6:** Climb up to the step below the knife-edge (3rd class). **Pitch 7:** Climb along the arête crest (5.5R). **Pitch 8:** Continue along the arête's right side and belay where it ends at a horizontal step. It is recommended to descend from here using a ramp leading down and into the gully to the west, which leads back to the base of the climb. One short section of downclimbing will be encountered. Alternatively, it is possible to climb two to three additional pitches, although these are not recommended due to loose rock.

PEAK 7,185

(1.6 mi SE of Elk Ridge)
Map: Flagg Ranch

Rising only about 300 feet above the mouth of Berry Creek, this small, forested hill has, reasonably enough, not yet attracted the attention of climbers. No information is available regarding ascents. I, 1.0.

ELK RIDGE (8,451T)

Map: Survey Peak

Elk Ridge is a relatively large, rounded formation separated from Owl Peak on the south by Owl Creek, from Forellen Peak on the west by the modern Berry Creek, and from Peak 9,047 on the north by the ancient, abandoned Berry Creek channel. It is awkwardly located at the intersection of four modern quadrangle sheets—Ranger Peak, Colter Bay, Flagg Ranch, and Survey Peak—with the summit found on the Survey Peak map. This wooded ridge was apparently first climbed by the geologists Joseph P. Iddings and Walter H. Weed in late August or early September 1886 during the course of their pioneering work on the geology of the old Shoshone quadrangle; they provided a description of the summit rocks in their monograph. Except for the somewhat precipitous west side, Elk Ridge does not present difficulties for the prospective climber. I, 1.0.

FORELLEN PEAK (9,772)

Map: Survey Peak

The first ascent of Forellen Peak was almost certainly made by Joseph P. Iddings and Walter H. Weed on September 4, 1886; the two men were studying the geology of the old Shoshone quadrangle, whose southern edge was 44° north latitude. These geologists may have been responsible for the unusual name, the German word for "trout," because this peak was known as Forellen Peak at least as early as 1886. However, Teton historian and climber Paul Horton believes that the surveyors of the 1886 Shoshone map, William H. Leffingwell and Stephen A. Alpen, likely named the peak, as they were working in this section of the range in 1884–85. T. F. Murphy and Mike Yokel Jr., in the course of their topographic work in 1935, also very likely climbed the peak. Another geologist, Rudolph Edmund, climbed the peak on August 11, 1938, and again in August 1939 while doing fieldwork for his geological thesis. Before the expansion of Grand Teton National Park in 1950 to include the northern end of the Teton Range, Forellen Peak was within the Teton National Forest and for at least a few years in the 1940s was used as a fire lookout station. Lookout and longtime Jackson Hole resident Dave Adams, who spent three summers on the summit during this period, was able to report by telephone to Moran. Until the middle of August, the southwest slope of this peak is covered with beautiful alpine flowers. A field identification guide is most useful when trying to decipher the many varieties.

ROUTE 1. SOUTHWEST SLOPE. I, 1.0. First ascent September 4, 1886, by Joseph P. Iddings and Walter H. Weed. The approach to the Berry-Owl divide (8,840+) west of Forellen Peak is best made using the trail from Berry Creek. South of the divide in Owl Canyon the trail soon becomes difficult or impossible to follow although one can hike cross-country up from the main Owl Creek trail. An older quadrangle map shows that there was something of a trail leading from the saddle to the summit and down the east ridge to Berry Creek; hence, there is no difficulty in climbing this route. This trail is no longer shown on the more recent Survey Peak quadrangle. The major north–south Forellen Peak fault crosses the line of ascent at about the 9,100-foot level.

ROUTE 2. EAST RIDGE. I, 1.0. First ascent unknown, perhaps in 1935, by T. F. Murphy and Mike Yokel Jr. An older quadrangle map indicated that the lower reaches of the Forellen Peak trail started at the base of this ridge, at the point where Berry Creek turns south to join Owl Creek. As an ascent route, this trail cannot be found. However, as a route of descent, the trail can be followed from the summit down to about 7,800 feet. The lower 120m of the ridge must be negotiated by bushwhacking through the timber. Just above the tiny lake at 8,364 feet a north–south fault crosses this trail.

RED MOUNTAIN (10,205 AND 10,177)

Map: Ranger Peak

Easily approached from the west and providing a good view of the region, this peak has long been a favorite of geologists. It is identifiable as "Station XXXII," established by Orestes St. John, the staff geologist who accompanied the Teton Division of the 1877 Hayden Survey Expedition. The first-ascent party undoubtedly included others, specifically Gustavus R. Bechler, the leader of the division. Bechler, along with Fred A. Clark, produced the first topographic (with contour lines) map of the Teton Range in 1878. The 19-year-old Stephen Kubel, who later figured in the controversy over the first ascent of the Grand Teton, was also probably on the ascent, as he served as one of Bechler's assistants in the summer of 1877. On September 3, 1886, during their geological explorations of the old Shoshone quadrangle, Joseph P. Iddings and Walter H. Weed reached the summit on horseback from Berry Creek. On August 14, 1912, the geologist Eliot Blackwelder and his assistant, Mack Lake, made the ascent by gaining the north ridge from the west. His description of the summit is worth repeating: "... flat grassy top strewn with beautifully rounded cobbles of yellow quartzite, a most surprising occurrence on top of a high peak." It is a large, bulky mountain with two summits connected by a 0.6-mile summit ridge.

The original name, Crimson Peak, was given by Iddings and Weed after the red color of the Late Mississippian shales that cap most of the peak and are interbedded with more resistant limestones. Unfortunately, this splendid name has been bowdlerized over the years, largely by the US Forest Service (USFS), into the prosaic "Red Mountain."

Chronology

NORTH RIDGE: August 1, 1877, Orestes St. John and [probable] Gustavus R. Bechler, Stephen Kubel
SOUTHEAST SLOPE: [probable] Summer 1935, T. F. Murphy, Mike Yokel Jr.

ROUTE 1. SOUTHEAST SLOPE. I, 1.0. Probable first ascent in summer 1935, by T. F. Murphy and Mike Yokel Jr. The higher summit is easily and directly climbed via this slope from the Owl Creek trail.

ROUTE 2. NORTH RIDGE. I, 1.0. First ascent August 1, 1877, by Orestes St. John and probably Gustavus R. Bechler and Stephen Kubel. This very long ridge forms the divide between Berry Creek on the east and North Bitch Creek (and its tributaries) on the west. It starts from the pass (8,720+) marked on the current USGS and USFS maps as "Conant Pass." This name, however, is very likely incorrectly placed, as the historic Conant Pass almost surely refers to the lower pass (8,480) just southwest of Survey Peak. The exact route taken in 1877 is unknown and might have been some combination of the west and north ridges. The geologist Eliot Blackwelder in 1912 apparently reached only the northwest end of this summit ridge (10,177). The traverse between the two summits is a pleasant stroll.

PEAK 8,688T

(1.65 mi SW of Survey Peak)
Map: Survey Peak

Although this small high point on the divide between Conant Pass and Jackass Pass features no record of ascents, its easy summit was probably reached during the fur-trapper era prior to 1850. I, 1.0.

The mysterious and remote Cirque Lake in Moran Canyon

SURVEY PEAK (9,277)

Map: Survey Peak

This easy, round-topped sedimentary peak may have been climbed in 1877 by the topographic unit of the Hayden Survey under Gustavus R. Bechler, but there appears to be no record of it. The origin of the name is not known, but this era of surveying and exploration seems to be a reasonable explanation. Hiram Chittenden's 1895 regional history, *The Yellowstone National Park*, included this note about Survey Peak on page 309: "1885—U. S. G. S. This mountain was a prominent signaling point for the Indians. It was first named Monument Peak by Richard Leigh who built a stone mound on its summit." The geologists Joseph P. Iddings and Walter H. Weed apparently reached the summit on August 31, 1886, during the course of their work on the geology of the Shoshone quadrangle; it was already known to them by the name Survey Peak. When Earl M. Buckingham established a triangulation station on its summit on September 11, 1931, there was a wagon road from the west that crossed the divide at the southern foot of the peak and led to an old mine at the head of Berry Creek. Fire lookout Dave Adams built a cabin (1 mile east of the summit) and a trail between it and the summit when he served for four or five years (around 1939) in this area for the US Forest Service (USFS).

One can approach this peak from the west via Grassy Lake Road (the Ashton–Flagg Ranch road), which leads around the north end of the range between Grand Teton National Park and Yellowstone National Park and connects Jackson Hole with Teton Basin in Idaho. Before reaching Squirrel Meadows, a side road leads south to two trailheads, one at South Boone Creek and the other near the head of Jackass Creek. Either could be used for the hike into Survey Peak. To approach this part of the range from the east, the Berry Creek trail can be followed from the shore of Jackson Lake. The low pass (8,480) just southwest of Survey Peak is misidentified on the current USGS and USFS maps as "Jackass Pass." The correct name for this pass is almost surely Conant Pass, the historical pass of the fur trappers of the early 19th century.

ROUTE 1. SOUTHWEST SLOPE. I, 1.0. Doubtlessly first ascended by indigenous people; probably ascended by Richard "Beaver Dick" Leigh in the 1860s and by Gustavus R. Bechler and party in 1877. From "Jackass Pass" (8,480) where the trail crosses the divide, this slope is an easy hike to the summit, where a quantity of surveyors' paraphernalia will be found.

ROUTE 2. NORTHEAST SLOPE. I, 1.0. First ascent unknown. Joseph P. Iddings and Walter H. Weed may have ascended it in 1886. The old trail constructed on this slope served to ease Dave Adams's daily trip to the summit from the cabin he built at 8,400 feet about 1 mile east of the summit. This cabin has been completely eliminated by the National Park Service (NPS).

PEAK 8,803T

(1.7 mi NE of Survey Peak)
Map: Survey Peak

This heavily forested hill forms the north wall above upper Berry Creek immediately east of Survey Peak. No information is available regarding ascents, although it may have been visited by the geologists Joseph P. Iddings and Walter H. Weed in 1886. I, 1.0.

PEAK 8,582T

(2.2 mi NE of Survey Peak)
Map: Survey Peak

Near the extreme north boundary of Grand Teton National Park, this minor wooded peak is unknown to climbers. Considerable bushwhacking would be required to reach its flat summit. No information is available regarding ascents. I, 1.0.

MOUNT BERRY (8,971T)

Map: Survey Peak

The original Grand Teton National Park map (1948) showed the summit of this tree-covered high point as being outside the park boundary, but more recent maps—Grassy Lake Reservoir (1956) and Survey Peak (1989 prov.)—show the summit as being 300 feet inside the park and with a different elevation. It appears that Earl M. Buckingham or some member of his triangulation party must have occupied this peak in 1931 because the records of the US Geological Survey (USGS) in Washington, DC, mention a "pole and cloth signal" and "standard tablet reference, Berry 1931" as being on the summit.

ROUTE 1. SOUTH RIDGE. I. 1.0. First ascent in mid-September 1931, by members of the triangulation party of Earl M. Buckingham. This ridge is easily approached from the Berry Creek trail leading to Hechtman Lake, which is perched 400 feet above the swamps of Berry Creek. This route was also used by Leland Horberg and Bob Crist on August 5, 1941, during a reconnaissance trip for the Geological Society of America. Note that this trail is not shown on the most recent map, Survey Peak (1989 prov.).

ROUTE 2. NORTH RIDGE. I. 1.0. First descent August 5, 1941, by Leland Horberg and Bob Crist. This gentle but almost unknown ridge appears to consist of seemingly endless pine forest, extending for 5 miles to Grassy Lake Road (the Ashton–Flagg Ranch road). Somewhat of a shortcut is available in the drainage (with a small pond at its head) leading southwest from the road to intersect the ridge.

DAVE ADAMS HILL (9,004)

Map: Survey Peak

As the highest point north of Berry Creek, this peak is well situated as a fire lookout station and may have been used for that purpose in the decades from 1930 to 1950. It forms the north wall of Berry Creek with clear views to the west up the canyon and south into the lower Owl Creek drainage. It is an easy, tree-covered summit. The glades and forest on the eastern aspect are pleasant hiking from the shores of Jackson Lake. I, 1.0.

HAREM HILL (7,326)

Map: Flagg Ranch

The first known ascent of this low, wooded hill rising directly from the west shore of the northernmost part of Jackson Lake was apparently made in late August or early September 1886, by the geologists Joseph P. Iddings and Walter H. Weed, because they give a description of the summit rocks in their geological monograph. The name presumably derives from elk, not humans. I, 1.0.

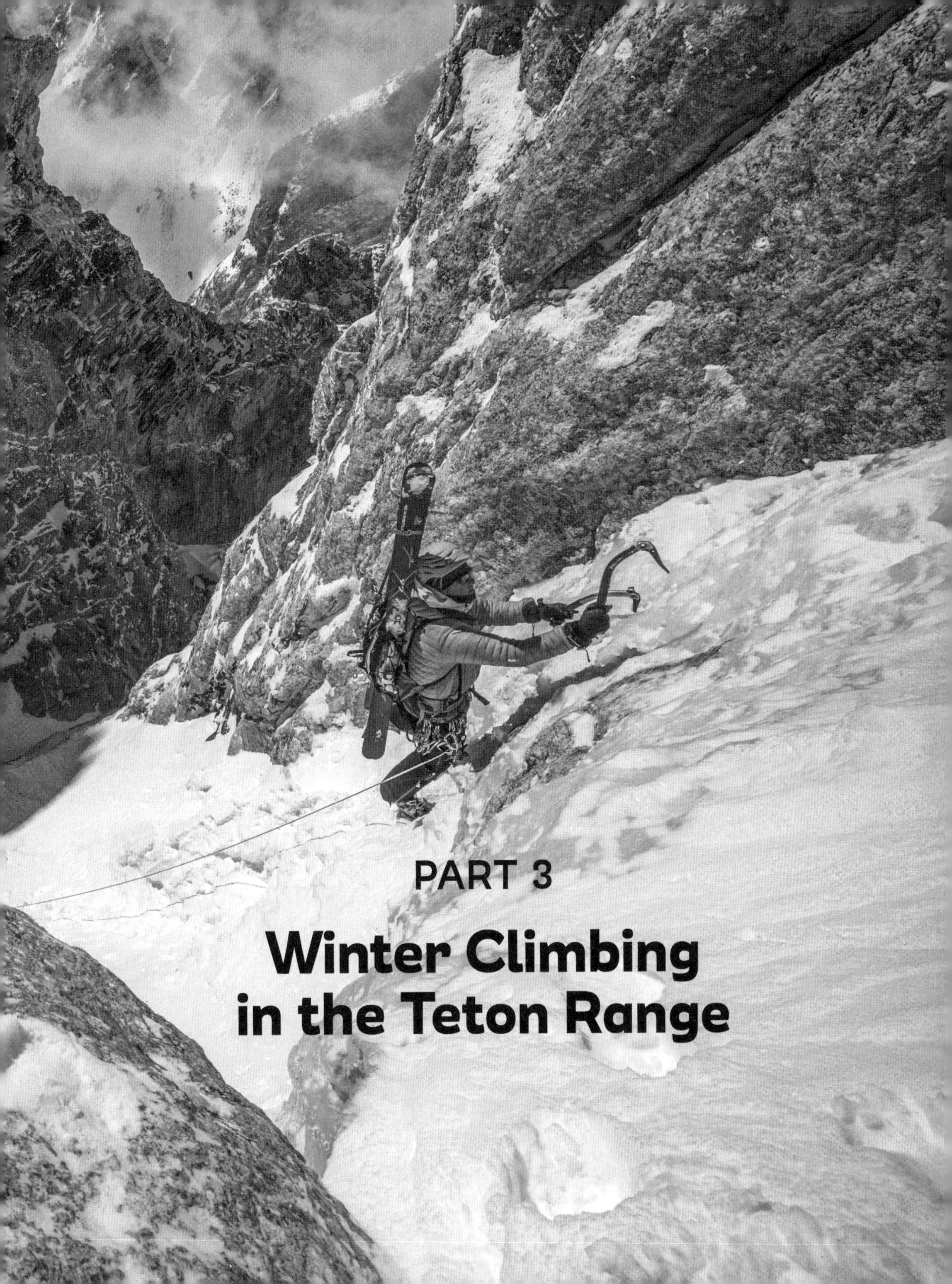

PART 3

Winter Climbing in the Teton Range

SECTION 12

Winter Climbing Overview and Routes

The Teton Range has long provided American mountaineers a convenient arena in which to develop the skills and experience necessary for challenging ascents in the great mountain ranges of the world. But it is during the winter months, when these peaks appear so magnificently remote, pristine, and untouchable, that this opportunity is greatly expanded. Climbers discovered winter climbing in the range nearly a century ago, but the relatively low number of winter ascents that were done over the ensuing several decades reflects the difficulty of the enterprise. Limiting factors include reduced travel options to isolated Jackson Hole during the winter and the difficulty of hitting weather and snow conditions just right. Yet the Tetons offer one of the finest areas in the country for difficult winter ascents of major mountaineering objectives. Traditionally, the winter season has been defined as the period between December 20 or 21 (the winter solstice) and March 20 or 21 (the vernal equinox). However, conditions commonly referred to as *winter*, which require some means of over-snow transport—skis, a splitboard, or, less commonly, snowshoes—for the approach portion of the climb, may occur as early as November and extend until late April.

History of Winter Climbing in the Teton Range

In the early decades of climbing in the Teton Range, the severity of the Wyoming winter, the manifest difficulty of the endeavor, and the simple challenge of winter living in Jackson Hole kept the peaks unmolested in the winter season. This changed in the 1930s, when enterprising rangers from the newly formed Grand Teton National Park initiated the winter exploration of the range. This generalization does neglect the probable prowling about the canyon entrances in near-winter conditions by the fur trappers in the 19th century. But the practical trappers had neither motivation nor time to explore the "useless" upper portions of the Teton Range.

To protect game animals from winter poaching, the staff of the new national park instituted a policy of winter snowshoe patrols along the base of the range in Jackson Hole. This justification for winter trips was then extended to provide an excuse for winter exploration of the high country; illegal hunters might well be coming into the heads of the canyons from the west. The first reported winter trip (almost surely on snowshoes) into the high country apparently was made in 1933 by National Park Service (NPS) rangers Allyn Hanks and Dudley Hayden, but no details are available. Such vigorous activity was not unnatural for the early NPS rangers, who commonly were skilled outdoorsmen.

The pioneering first winter ascent of the Grand Teton was made by Paul and Eldon Petzoldt and Fred Brown on December 19, 1935. After skiing to the caves in Garnet Canyon the first day, they spent two days relaying loads to the Lower Saddle, from which they climbed the Grand via the Owen-Spalding route. It was a near-perfect day with a large temperature inversion, permitting shirtsleeves on the summit while it was -20°F in Jackson. On March 5, 1949, Paul Petzoldt and John and Ted Lewis repeated this climb. This time they camped at the Platforms the first night and reached the Lower Saddle the second night. The third successful winter expedition (again on skis) was that of Leigh Ortenburger, William Dunmire, Richard Long, and Norman Goldstein, who on February 4, 1952, climbed the Middle Teton by the Southwest Couloir route in a blizzard. The remainder of the 1950s saw very little winter activity in the Tetons. Two attempts on the Grand Teton were made, but neither came close to the summit or even to the Lower Saddle. However, success in these early years was gained on two lesser peaks at the extremes of the range—Survey Peak and Rendezvous Peak—by Frank Ewing and Keith Jones (1957) and by Ewing and Rod Newcomb (1961), respectively.

Extended ski traverses in the range were initiated early in the climbing history of the park, partly because of the influence of Dartmouth College mountaineers and skiers in the mid-1930s. The route of the first such traverse started from the old park headquarters at Beaver Creek and went up Cascade Canyon, across Alaska Basin, down Granite Canyon, and then back to the starting point; it was carried out on skis from February 15 to 19, 1938, by Fred Brown of Dartmouth with NPS rangers Allyn Hanks and Howard Stagner. Food and equipment caches had been placed in the fall of 1937 at the forks of Cascade Canyon, Alaska Basin, and Marion Lake. The first known ski traverse of the crest of the range was done as a spring trip, from May 13 to 19, 1979, when Jeff Crabtree, Owen Anderson, and Greg Lawley started from Teton Pass, stayed close to the divide, and exited Berry Creek to Huckleberry Hot Springs. This major undertaking has been repeated in both directions. As a solo winter trip, in late December 1985 Peter Koedt made the south-north traverse in five days, entering at Phillips Canyon and emerging at Berry Creek. The trip was repeated in the reverse direction, from April 2 to 6, 1987, by George Lowe, Rich Henke, and Tom Dickey, who started from Flagg Ranch, entered the range at Owl Creek, stayed close to the divide, and exited via Phillips Canyon to Highway 22 east of Teton Pass.

It was another climb to the summit of the Grand Teton via the Owen-Spalding route, on January 2, 1964, that ushered in winter mountaineering as a standard

George Lowe on the summit of the Grand Teton after completing the first winter ascent of the North Ridge route with Dave Carman, March 20–22, 1975 (Photo by Dave Carman)

Brendan O'Neill during the first ski descent of the North Face of the Grand Teton, March 31, 2013 (Photo by Greg Collins)

pursuit. The party was composed of James Greig, Earl Lory, John Mugaas, Robert Napier, Rod Newcomb, and Heinie Nolden. Taking advantage of unusually light autumn and early-winter snowfalls, they camped at the Meadows in Garnet Canyon after a seven-hour trip from the old Jenny Lake Store; four of the party used snowshoes. The second night was spent on the Lower Saddle in a severe wind, and they reached the summit at 2 PM the next day.

After 1964 the pace of winter mountaineering accelerated, with most of the original impetus coming from Utah climbers who lived close enough to the Tetons to be able to take immediate advantage of a session of good weather. In 1965 the first winter ascents of the formidable Mount Owen were made by a party from Salt Lake City—George Lowe, Mike Lowe, Jon Marsh, Lenny Nelson, Tom Stevenson, and Steve Swanson—via the East Ridge and Koven routes. After three earlier failed attempts, success was finally gained on Mount Moran in 1966 by nine climbers from the Salt Lake area via the Northeast Ridge route. The myths about inaccessibility began to break down. Then from February 28 to March 2, 1968, the North Face of the Grand Teton was climbed in one alpine-style push by Maurice Horn, George Lowe, and Greg and Mike Lowe. This extraordinary climb shattered the psychological barriers. That same year first winter ascents were made of Teewinot Mountain and the South Teton, and the regular routes on the Middle and Grand Tetons were climbed again.

These last climbs introduced a final key element to the Teton winter mountaineering scene: local climbers from Jackson Hole, who had the advantage of being only minutes away from the base of the range. A new era of popularity in climbing, or at least attempting, the Grand Teton in winter began in 1969, exemplified by the near-annual expeditions patriarch Paul Petzoldt led into the range for his National Outdoor Leadership School (NOLS).

The 1970s saw numerous new winter climbs, including of major peaks and routes such as Mount Wister, the North Face of Cloudveil Dome, Nez Perce, the Middle Teton Glacier and North Ridge routes of the Middle Teton, Teepe Pillar, Disappointment Peak, the West Horn, the CMC route on Mount Moran, and even Thor Peak. The prize of the Exum Ridge of the Grand Teton was climbed in 1972. But, perhaps more importantly, the 1968 ascent of the North Face of the Grand encouraged other similarly challenging and daunting feats throughout the decade. Routes of great difficulty and commitment that were completed include the Black Ice–West Face Combination with the traverse to the Upper Saddle (1971), the West Face of the Grand Teton (1972), the East Ridge of the Grand Teton (1973), the North Ridge of the Grand Teton (1975), the Durrance Direct (Lower Exum Ridge) and the Petzoldt Ridge of the Grand Teton (1976), and the Enclosure Ice Couloir (1977).

Beginning in 1973, well-known Jackson climbers started searching for short, easy-to-access winter ice climbs in Death Canyon. Leading the charge were Pete and Dave Carman, Donnie Black, Jack Clinton, Norm Larson, Jim Roscoe, Jay Wilson, and Chuck Schaap. Their creative climbs, such as 737 Earful, Prospectors Falls, and Dread Falls, introduced a dedication to ice and mixed climbing that has expanded and now flourishes every winter. The pure ice-climbing tangent of this period inspired three forays up Laughing Lions Falls on the south wall of Mount Moran between 1983 and 1985: Jim Woodmencey, Dan Burgette, and Bill Pelander reached the top of the first pitch in March 1983; Renny Jackson, Burgette, Woodmencey, and Pelander pushed the route to the top of the main waterfall in January 1985; and Alex Lowe, Andy Carson, and Jack Tackle made it to the top of the climb the following month.

More winter first ascents on the high peaks were achieved during the 1980s and into 1990. These included routes on Buck, Prospectors, and Rolling Thunder Mountains; Mounts Hunt, Bannon, and Meek; and Static, Veiled, Shadow, Doane, and Forellen Peaks. These were done by a variety of climbers, with important contributions from Bob Graham, Ron Matous, Tom Turiano, and Donnie Black. Renny Jackson participated in two difficult winter ascents of Grand Teton routes—the Otterbody Chimneys and Alberich's Alley, the former with Dan Burgette and the latter with Jim Woodmencey. Jackson also teamed up with local climber/skier Larry Detrick to climb Irene's Arête, the summertime classic on Disappointment Peak, in March 1985. The prolific winter climber and guide Andy Carson did the first winter traverse from Cloudveil Dome to the South Teton two years later. But the major events of this period were carried out by Alex Lowe and Jack Tackle, who made concentrated efforts on some of the hardest climbs in the range. Together, the pair nabbed the second winter ascents of the Grand Teton's North Face and North Ridge routes and the first winter climbs of the Direct South Buttress and the South Buttress Right on Mount Moran.

Alex Lowe on the summit of the Grand Teton after the first complete ascent of the Direct North Face, January 1–3, 1987 (Photo by Jack Tackle)

Hans Johnstone during the first winter ascent and ski descent of the Hossack-McGowan Couloir on the Grand Teton, February 16, 1996 (Photo by Mark Newcomb)

The foreboding Northwest Chimney route on the Grand was climbed by Alex Lowe and Renny Jackson in December 1991, and Jackson and Larry Detrick did the Beyer East Face I in January 1993. Lander climbers Greg Collins, Phil Powers, and Gary Wilmot accomplished the impressive Cathedral Traverse in January 1993—a feat Lowe and Andrew McLean repeated a week later in an astonishing single day. No stranger to endurance efforts, Lowe had soloed the North Face of the Grand (with a traverse to the Owen-Spalding from the Second Ledge) in an unbelievable 20-hour day from the valley in December 1992. Other highlights include Tackle's solo climb of Serendipity Arête on Mount Owen in March 1994 and Mark Newcomb and Hans Johnstone's first winter ascent and ski descent of the Hossack-MacGowan Couloir on the Grand Teton in February 1996. But perhaps the culmination of winter climbing in the Tetons in the 1990s occurred in January 1997, when Norm Larson and Callum Mackay claimed the long-sought prize of Mount Wister's north face.

At the beginning of the new millennium, Jackson local and former Olympian Hans Johnstone emerged as the primary driving force behind difficult first winter ascents. Together with Rolando Garibotti and then Stephen Koch, Johnstone in quick succession climbed the summertime classic Open Book on Disappointment Peak (January 22, 2001) and then the difficult Sunshine Daydream on the Snaz Buttress (January 24, 2001) in Death Canyon. A month later he teamed up with fellow locals Newcomb and Jackson for the complete Direct South Buttress of Mount Moran—another highly sought-after winter route that had been attempted many times before. (Tackle and Lowe were the first to reach the top of the initial buttress in winter, in 1988.)

In 2003 visiting climbers John Kelley and Matt Nuner put up the 366m climb Tang-O-Max on the south side of Storm Point in Cascade Canyon, climbing six difficult ice and mixed pitches. In January 2004 another prized Teton first winter ascent was accomplished when two different teams—Johnstone and Jackson; Newcomb and Koch—made their way around the Grand Traverse, climbing the Cathedral Traverse portion together and then finishing a day apart on the remainder of the climb. In 2007 the 1,000m North Ridge of Mount Owen was climbed in winter by Greg Collins and Johnstone, who approached by way of the Koven Couloir and then descended the northeast snowfields. Johnstone and Koch had teamed up earlier in the year for Squeeze Box, a difficult mixed route on the Grand's north face. With Sam Magro, Koch climbed the Raven Crack in Death Canyon in January 2009, finding "1,200' of spectacular, sustained, mixed climbing at the WI5, M7 level."

More recently, in 2017, difficult mixed climbs have been discovered by Jackson locals Nate Brown, Brian Mulvihill, and Sam Macke and visiting climber Jackson Marvell on the dolomitic cliffs of Peak 10,450, conveniently accessed by the ski area's aerial tram.

Over the past decade, interest in winter first ascents has given way to ski mountaineering. The Grand sees more ascents in the winter now than ever before, with the majority of climbers seeking a descent of the peak on skis or snowboard. Many first winter ascents await a new generation of alpinists, and these represent the future of major Teton mountaineering.

See *American Alpine Journal* 2, no. 4 (1936): pp. 543–45; 7, no. 4 (1950): pp. 506–7; *Appalachia* 27, no. 4 (December 1949): p. 503, illus.; 28, no. 1 (June 1950): pp. 21–24, illus.; *Sierra Club Bulletin* 38, no. 8 (October 1953): pp. 72–73; *Summit*, 10, no. 8 (October 1964): pp. 24–27, illus.; *Trail and Timberline*, no. 211 (May 1936): pp. 43–44, illus.

National Park Service Winter Policy

Winter climbing in the Teton Range is a physically demanding but mentally exhilarating experience. The additional challenges imposed by the severe environmental conditions result in some limitations and a few additional regulations imposed by Grand Teton National Park. The winter ranger staff on hand to assist climbers and other park visitors is greatly reduced from that available in midsummer. Ranger stations and visitor centers are closed, which can be inconvenient when one is seeking information and/or permits. The rationale behind regulations, which the park tries to keep to a minimum, should be recognized as primarily the protection of park resources and secondarily the safety of the climber. There is an extra beauty available in the winter to the hardy outdoor traveler, but this beauty is fragile. Winter conditions place considerable stress on the climber and even more on the wildlife. View the winter animals from a distance and minimize their hardships.

GENERAL REGULATIONS

Beginning in 1994 the regulations that required registration for all climbs and for any over-snow travel away from the plowed roads in the park were abolished (see *National Park Service Policy* in the Climbing in the Tetons chapter). However, permits are required for all overnight backcountry trips. These are free and are available at the administration building at Park Headquarters in Moose, Wyoming, Monday through Friday 8:00 AM–4:30 PM. On weekends and federal holidays, visitors wanting a backcountry permit should call either the backcountry permits office (307-739-3309) or park dispatch (307-739-3301), at which point you may be redirected to one of the climbing rangers on staff. These rangers conduct regular patrols during the winter and are excellent sources of information about climbing in the range. Go to www.nps.gov/grte/planyourvisit/winter.htm for more information.

As a final note on winter rules, remember that garbage and human waste, which disappear so conveniently under a little blowing snow in the winter, reappear in full force in the heavily used summer Tetons. The use of human waste bags as a method of removal and disposal is highly recommended. All garbage must be carried out of the mountains.

WINTER RESCUE

Climbers planning winter ascents in the Teton Range should understand that rescue by the NPS in this season should not be presumed. Current and predicted weather as well as current or increasing

Greg Collins on the Cave Route (5.12b) in the upper Meadows, Garnet Canyon (Photo by Kent McBride)

avalanche hazard conditions may delay or even curtail any rescue effort. Storms or strong winds may prevent a speedy response by helicopter. Even in the best of conditions wintertime rescue is more time-consuming than in the summer. Climbing parties who come to these mountains in the winter should be equipped to deal with the possibility of an avalanche or climbing accident. Each climber or skier should carry an avalanche transceiver, a shovel, and a collapsible probe pole and should be trained in the use of such specialized equipment. Your best protection, however, consists of a cautious attitude and good judgment; these are by far the most important things that you can carry into the mountains.

Winter Access

Winter access to the mountains is necessarily more difficult than during the rest of the year when roads are not blocked by snow. The main eastside highway (US Highway 26/89/191) extending north from Jackson toward Yellowstone National Park is kept open and plowed as far as Flagg Ranch. From the Jackson Lake Junction it is plowed south only to Signal Mountain Lodge; from Moose north the plowed road ends at Cottonwood Creek just to the north of the Taggart Lake trailhead. From November 1 to May 1, Teton Park Road from the Taggart Lake trailhead to Signal Mountain Lodge is open for nonmotorized use only. Users can ski, walk, or snowshoe on the road, which is groomed a few times a week for skate and classic cross-country skiing. The Moose–Wilson road is also only partially plowed. From Wilson it is plowed north to the Granite Canyon trailhead. South from Moose, it is plowed only to the junction with the Death Canyon road.

For winter mountaineers, ski mountaineers, and backcountry skiers and riders looking to access the high country, the preferred entry points into the range are usually the plowed-out parking areas associated with the open roadways. The most popular of these are the Taggart Lake trailhead and the parking area just north of the Death Canyon road. An exception is the top of the tram at Jackson Hole Mountain Resort, which obviously represents a good starting point if one is interested in the southern peaks. Access from the tram, however, is under the control of the Jackson Hole Ski Corporation: you must exit the ski area through one of their designated gates. The daily backcountry avalanche forecast is available at each of these gates, which also feature an electronic indicator that informs you that your beacon is transmitting (or not) as you pass through the gate.

For the enterprising, the entire western slope of the Teton Range also offers access to the high peaks. Grand Targhee Resort, a ski area almost due west of the Grand Teton, has a "closed boundary/open gate" backcountry access policy, similar to that of Jackson Hole Mountain Resort. Access to the Caribou-Targhee National Forest is permitted in the resort's lift-served terrain through the backcountry access gates only. Contact the Teton Basin Ranger District office of the Caribou-Targhee National Forest in Driggs, Idaho, for advice and information on winter use regulations. Once one crosses the divide into the park, NPS regulations apply.

Berry Creek is most commonly entered by skiing due west from the turnout just south of the Lizard Creek campground. Access to Mount Moran and other peaks at the north end of the range is also available directly across the ice of Jackson Lake. The advisability of lake crossing is left to the climbers' judgment, but anyone contemplating this route should check with the NPS ranger staff at Colter Bay for information on current ice conditions and known hazard areas. Jackson Lake "flooding" with a few inches of water on top of the ice is common, can be widespread, and is obviously hazardous. Special precautions should also be taken with the dangerous thin ice at the Snake River inlet at the north end of the lake and at the Moran Creek inlet at the mouth of Moran Canyon.

Perhaps the most popular trail for touring and snowshoeing is the one that leads due west from the Taggart Lake trailhead. This ski trail soon turns north and heads up the moraine to a junction after about 1 mile. The left fork provides a loop tour of Taggart Lake. The right fork is more commonly used by climbers because it leads farther north to Bradley Lake. The main access route into Garnet Canyon is either directly across Bradley Lake (only when the ice is sufficiently thick) or on the north edge of the lake along the moraine. These days, given the popularity of backcountry skiing in the range, one can usually expect a pretty good broken trail leading up from Bradley Lake into Garnet Canyon. Note that the usual summer Garnet Canyon trail is not used in the winter. The preferred route into the canyon stays on the south side of the creek until just below the Platforms.

A third standard winter trail of value to climbers is the one to the Phelps Lake Overlook from the parking area on the Moose–Wilson road. This trail leads easily for 2 miles to the end of the current summer road and then continues up the summer trail to the overlook. Continuing safely beyond the overlook requires an understanding of current avalanche hazards on the slopes that must be traversed to gain entrance into Death Canyon.

Winter Hazards and Tactics

Climbing in the Teton Range in the winter season exposes the climber to hazards beyond those normally encountered in the summer. The first is avalanche hazard. Knowledge of recent snow conditions is essential to estimate local avalanche potential. The latest avalanche forecast is available from the Bridger-Teton Avalanche Center (BTAC)/US Forest Service (USFS): either call 307-733-2664 for a recording or visit www.jhavalanche.org. A winter meteorological technician position was recently added to the highly skilled Jenny Lake Rangers staff. In addition to contributing substantially to the BTAC/USFS forecast and online reports, this person spends a significant amount of time in the Teton Range gathering information and checking on weather instruments. There are two instruments located in the Surprise Lake area; data from these instruments and several others are also available on the BTAC website. Information gathered by these various instruments is invaluable to the winter traveler.

Mountaineering parties venturing into the Teton Range during the winter should also be capable of doing their own avalanche hazard estimation and snow-stability evaluation. Beyond those skills, careful routefinding is perhaps the most essential component of travel within the range. A trip up any of the canyons will necessarily involve crossing many different slide paths, some of immense proportions. A second major hazard is the thin or breakable ice at the various stream inlets or outlets from the larger lakes, such as Phelps, Bradley, Taggart, Jenny, Leigh, and

Jackson Lakes. Climbers should appreciate that any travel over lakes in wintertime is potentially hazardous. It is generally better to go around rather than risk your life on thin ice.

Methods that are successful in Teton winter climbing range from multiday tactics to light-and-fast trips on the highest peaks, up and down in a single day. The suitability of the selected method depends on the experience and strength of the climbing party, but the potential of weather changes to create major avalanche danger argues for as much speed as possible. Over the years there has been a trend toward light and fast to take full advantage of a spell of good weather. As one example, the West Face route of the Grand Teton was done by two climbers in four days, valley to valley. Another was Alex Lowe's solo winter ascent of the North Face of the Grand Teton in 20 hours. It is also possible, but not pleasant, to climb in reasonably bad weather. The first winter ascent of the North Ridge of the Grand Teton was climbed during a continuous storm that shut down Jackson Hole Mountain Resort. The trend lately has been toward one-day ascents of the major peaks, including Mount St. John, Teewinot Mountain, the South Teton, the Middle Teton, the Grand Teton, and even Mount Owen. However, there are both rewards and drawbacks to such exertions, as George Lowe has observed:

> ***[T]hese ascents have produced some of the most exhilarating times the writer has had in the mountains. It is difficult to top the sensation of moving rapidly in good weather amid the winterized peaks. But these efforts do tend to be physically exhausting!***

Climbing conditions on the west and east sides of the peaks may differ dramatically due to the prevailing winds coming from the west and southwest. Typically, the west sides of the peaks are covered with 12 inches or more of rime, and some slopes may be almost bare of snow due to the wind. This snow is, of course, deposited on the northeast-facing lee slopes, causing slab avalanche hazard that may persist for weeks. Snow conditions range from very hard slabs high in the canyons to light powder at medium altitudes. Except for the northwest sides of the Grand Teton and Enclosure, little ice is to be found mixed with the rock as it is rarely warm enough to allow the melting that is required. Additionally, much of the ice that is deposited disappears relatively quickly due to sublimation.

Winter Mountaineering Equipment

Equipment needed for winter climbing in the Tetons is generally equivalent to that required for Himalayan, Andean, or Alaskan conditions. An effective wind- and waterproof shell, insulated clothing, and warm mitts are needed to counter the cold except on the very finest of winter days. Double mountaineering boots or double alpine touring boots with effective, perhaps insulated, gaiters are recommended. After the skis are left behind, and if technical climbing is encountered, crampons are frequently necessary.

A strong, lightweight tent is a necessity for multiday climbs because adequate snow for caves cannot always be counted on. The Lower Saddle, for example, quite frequently is blown completely free of snow all winter long. A sturdy snow shovel should be part of every winter mountaineer's avalanche rescue kit, and knowing how to dig a snow cave can provide that extra margin of safety—even during a fast one-day trip.

Most backcountry users opt for a setup that includes alpine touring boots and skis with skins for uphill travel, although some prefer a snowboard that splits apart for the uphill portions. If one is contemplating a technical rock or mixed route and prefers climbing in double mountaineering boots, skis with some form of binding that accommodates the boots will need to be used. Being a strong skier or snowboarder helps enormously with the challenges of approach and descent in the Teton Range.

Ice screws are rarely needed, except for those routes that are ice climbs in the summer. The usual summer rack of rock protection, such as camming devices and nuts or chocks, works well for winter ascents. And while pitons are perhaps without honor in the summer, many times in winter conditions they will provide better anchors in the rime-filled cracks. An alpine hammer and an ice axe (or two ice tools) are useful for cleaning cracks and placing and removing protection.

Chronology of First Winter Ascents

Note: Ascents accomplished outside of the "official" winter season—December 20 to March 20—are enclosed in brackets.

Albright Peak (10,552)

EAST SLOPE: [probable] March 1974 or 1975, Steve Lundy, Dave Fox, Ed Lowton; [certain] March 15, 1979, John Connors, Larry Gilbert

SUNSHINE DAYDREAM (SNAZ BUTTRESS): January 24, 2001, Hans Johnstone, Stephen Koch

Baxter's Pinnacle (ca. 8,000)

SOUTH RIDGE: [April 4, 1976, Andy Carson, Jan Olson, Jug Bacon, Ben Toland]; March 20, 1986, John and Bruce Spitler; December 29, 1986, Jed Flanagan, Chuck Odette

Bivouac Peak (10,825)

EAST RIDGE, VARIATION: Northeast Couloir: February 9, 1991, Tom Turiano, Tom Bennett; February 25, 1991, Michael Best

Buck Mountain (11,938)

EAST FACE: Winter 1972, Callum Mackay, Jorge Colon

NORTH FACE, EAST COULOIR: January 9, 1981, Don Black, Scott Wade, Jim Humphries

NORTH CENTRAL RIDGE: January 10, 1981, Norm Larson, Jack Clinton (to North Face, East Couloir)

NORTH FACE, WEST COULOIR: February 26, 1982, Lyle Dean

EAST RIDGE: February 29, 1984, Ron Matous, Martin Springer

THE CATHEDRAL TRAVERSE (TEEWINOT MOUNTAIN, MOUNT OWEN, GRAND TETON): January 26–28, 1993, Greg Collins, Phil Powers, Gary Wilmot; February 4, 1993, Alex Lowe, Andrew McLean (one-day traverse)

Cleaver Peak (11,055)

NORTH PEAK, NORTHWEST CHIMNEY: January 26, 1994, Tom Turiano, Wesley Bunch, David Bowers

Cloudveil Dome (12,026)

NORTH FACE: March 8–10, 1972, Robert Redmayne, Ian Wade

EAST RIDGE: December 31, 1980, Rob Slater, Kirk Duffy

WEST RIDGE: [April 4–6, 1973, Vince Fayad, George Hunker, Jans Lund, Landry Corkery]; February 24, 1988, Norm Larson, Lorna Corson (ascent); February 18, 1987, Andy Carson, Gary Patton (descent)

TEMPORARY DISCOMFORT: February 11, 2001, Hans Johnstone, Norm Larson

Disappointment Peak (11,618)

WEST FACE: January 25 to February 2, 1973, Gene Forsythe, Stephen Bussell, Rod Ewald, Richard Kroll, Edwin Hinch

SOUTHWEST COULOIR: January 25 to February 2, 1973, Gene Forsythe, Stephen Bussell, Rod Ewald, Richard Kroll, Edwin Hinch (descent); January 29, 1976, Tom Milligan, Peter Hart, Jim "Ole" Olson, Ralph Tingey, Bill Conrod (ascent)

SOUTHWEST RIDGE: March 11–12, 1973, Richard Taplin, Chris Latour, Cecelle Brumder, Davie Agnew; March 11–13, 1973, Andy Carson, Pete Carman; January 23, 1981, Jeff Lowe, Kerry Shroyer (possible new route on southwest ridge)

LAKE LEDGES: [November 26, 1972, Clinton Blair, Jim Miller]; January 24, 1985, Ray Warburton, John Jakubowski

SOUTHEAST RIDGE: February 1985, Glenn Vitucci

SPOON COULOIR: February 1985, Glenn Vitucci (descent)
IRENE'S ARÊTE: March 14, 1985, Renny Jackson, Larry Detrick (to top of climb only)
OPEN BOOK: January 22, 2001, Hans Johnstone, Rolando Garibotti (to top of climb only)

Doane Peak (11,355)

NORTH RIDGE: March 1984, Peter Koedt, John Silverman
SOUTH COULOIRS: February 27, 1991, Tom Turiano, Christoph Schork, Jim Schultz

Doubtful Peak (10,852)

SOUTH COULOIRS: January 4, 1995, Tom Turiano, Wesley Bunch

Eagles Rest Peak (11,258)

NORTH RIDGE: February 27, 1991, Tom Turiano, Christoph Schork, Jim Schultz
WEST RIDGE: February 27, 1991, Tom Turiano, Christoph Schork, Jim Schultz (descent)

East Prong (12,000+)

WEST RIDGE: March 20, 1972, George Lowe

Elk Mountain (10,720+)

SOUTHEAST RIDGE: [March 26, 1994, Dave Moore, Dave Coon]

The Enclosure (13,280+)

SOUTH COULOIR: January 21, 1989, Ron Matous (to summit)
ENCLOSURE ICE COULOIR: February 1977, Dennis Turville, Dean Hannibal (to top of climb only)

Fairshare Tower (11,520+)

SOUTH RIDGE: February 8, 1976, Andy Carson, Swep Davis

Forellen Peak (9,772)

SOUTHWEST SLOPE: [(possible) 1957 or 1958, Frank Ewing, Keith Jones, Don Williams]; [(probable) early to mid-1980s, Steve Barnett]; [certain] February 10, 1989, John Carr, Chuck Schaap, Barbara Zimmer
EAST RIDGE: February 10, 1989, John Carr, Chuck Schaap, Barbara Zimmer (descent)

Fossil Mountain (10,916)

SOUTHEAST SIDE: January 1973, Callum Mackay, Ray White, Robbie Fuller

Gilkey Tower (12,320+)

SUNRISE RIDGE: February 27, 1975, Pete Carman, Jim Roscoe, Mike Fitzpatrick
EAST FACE: February 18, 1987, Andy Carson, Gary Patton (ascent); February 24, 1988, Norm Larson, Lorna Corson (descent)
WEST RIDGE: February 18, 1987, Andy Carson, Gary Patton (descent); February 24, 1988, Norm Larson, Lorna Corson (ascent)

Glacier Peak (10,927)

NORTH RIDGE: [April 4, 1974, John Carr, Susan Enger, Ted Shimo, George Bloom]; March 5, 1976, Bill Conrod, Jim Barmore

Glencoe Spire (ca. 12,320)

NORTH AND WEST FACES: January 29, 1973, Gene Forsythe, Stephen Bussell, Edwin Hinch, William McKinney

Grand Teton (13,770)

OWEN-SPALDING: [December 19, 1935, Paul and Eldon Petzoldt, Fred Brown]; March 3–6, 1949, Paul Petzoldt, John Lewis, Ted Lewis; January 3, 1974, Helen Higby (first female winter ascent of Grand Teton)
NORTH FACE: February 28–March 2, 1968, George Lowe, Mike and Greg Lowe, Maurice Horn; January 1–3, 1987, Jack Tackle, Alex Lowe
BLACK ICE–WEST FACE COMBINATION WITH TRAVERSE TO UPPER SADDLE: February 2–4, 1971, George and David Lowe, Greg and Jeff Lowe (to Upper Saddle only)
EXUM RIDGE: February 19–20, 1972, David Lowe, Jock Glidden, David Smith
WEST FACE: February 19–24, 1972, George Lowe, Jeff Lowe
EAST RIDGE: February 16–18, 1973, George and David Lowe, Jock Glidden
NORTH RIDGE: March 20–22, 1975, Dave Carman, George Lowe; January 3–4, 1985, Alex Lowe, Jack Tackle
PETZOLDT RIDGE: January 30, 1976, Glenn Milner, Don Black, Joseph Costello
DURRANCE DIRECT (LOWER EXUM RIDGE): February 2, 1976, Tom Ballard, Tom Shreve, Daniel Winner, Gregory Lee (to summit)
BLACK ICE COULOIR: January 1, 1981, Mark Bennett, Dave Bjorkman, Kent Jamison (to top of climb only)
STETTNER COULOIR: January 14, 1981, Bill Danford, Gene Forsythe
EAST RIDGE, VARIATION: North Molar Tooth Couloir: January 31, 1984, Alex Lowe (to east ridge only)
OTTERBODY CHIMNEYS: December 29, 1985, Renny Jackson, Dan Burgette
BLACK ICE COULOIR, VARIATION: Alberich's Alley: February 28–March 2, 1990, Renny Jackson, Jim Woodmencey (to summit)
NORTHWEST CHIMNEY: December 21, 1991, Alex Lowe, Renny Jackson
BEYER EAST FACE I: January 29, 1993, Renny Jackson, Larry Detrick (to top of climb only)
HOSSACK-MACGOWAN COULOIR: February 16, 1996, Mark Newcomb, Hans Johnstone (first winter ascent and first ski descent)
ROUTE CANAL: First week of March [year unknown], Mark Springer, Mike Anderson

The Grand Traverse

January 17–20, 2004, Mark Newcomb, Stephen Koch; January 17–21, 2004, Hans Johnstone, Renny Jackson

Green Lakes Mountain (10,240+)

NORTHEAST RIDGE: February 10, 1991, Tom Turiano, Tom Bennett

Housetop Mountain (10,537)

SOUTHEAST RIDGE: March 1967, Robbie Fuller, Juris Krisjansons, Robert Redmayne, Ray White, Bob Sartor

Icecream Cone (12,400+)

EAST FACE: February 18, 1987, Andy Carson, Gary Patton

Image (10,750)

SOUTHEAST FACE: March 15, 1994, Tom Turiano, Wesley Bunch, Christoph Schork, Scott McGee

The Jaw (11,400)

EAST FACE: March 17, 1990, Bob Graham

Littles Peak (10,712)

EAST RIDGE: [probable] 1947, Grant Hagen, Grover Bassett (during the first traverse of the crest of the Teton Range); [April 5, 1990, Tom Turiano, Tom Bennett, Gary Kofinas]

Maidenform Peak (11,137)

EAST RIDGE: [April 5–6, 1990, Tom Turiano, Tom Bennett, Gary Kofinas]
SOUTH COULOIR: [March 31, 1994, Christoph Schork]

Middle Teton (12,804)

SOUTHWEST COULOIR: February 4, 1952, Leigh Ortenburger, William Dunmire, Norman Goldstein, Richard Long
MIDDLE TETON GLACIER: January 27, 1973, Tom Warren, Lorni Brown, Jack Cockran, Michael McGowan, John Kirk
NORTHWEST ICE COULOIR: January 27, 1973, Tom Warren, Lorni Brown, Jack Cockran, Michael McGowan, John Kirk (descent); January 1, 1975, Dennis Turville, Dean Hannibal (ascent)
ELLINGWOOD COULOIR: February 23, 1975, Bill Rosqvist, Dave Bjorkman, Melvin Davis
CHOUINARD RIDGE: December 21, 1975, Glenn Milner, Joseph Costello, James Kilroy
NORTH RIDGE: [April 13–15, 1974, Pete Carman, Dave Carman]; February 7, 1976, Andy Carson, Swep Davis
DIKE: December 28–31, 1977, Dennis Turville, Dean Hannibal (to Dike Pinnacle only)
BUCKINGHAM (SOUTHEAST) RIDGE: January 31, 1994, Greg Collins, Ron Matous

Moose Mountain (10,054)

EAST SLOPES: January 20, 1985, Norm Larson, Martha Clarke
SOUTH RIDGE: February 1986, Ron Matous

Mount Bannon (10,966)

SOUTH SLOPE: January 28, 1989, Tom Turiano, Tom Bennett

Mount Hunt (10,783)

WEST RIDGE: January 1972, Callum Mackay, Jorge Colon
EAST RIDGE: January 12, 1986, Norm Larson, Martha Clark, Angus Thuermer, Linda Sternberg, George McClelland, Scott Berkenfield

Mount Meek (10,681)

SOUTHWEST SLOPE: January 28, 1989, Tom Turiano, Tom Bennett

Mount Moran (12,605)

NORTHEAST RIDGE: [December 19, 1966, Tom Stevenson, George Lowe, Mike Lowe, Dennis Caldwell, Tom Spencer, Court Richards, Bill Conrod]; December 20, 1966, George Lowe, Mike and Greg Lowe, George Gerhart
CMC: December 25, 1975, Dave Carman, Bob Graham, Charles Field
STAIRCASE ARÊTE: February 18, 1985, Jack Tackle, Alex Lowe (to top of climb only)
SOUTH BUTTRESS RIGHT: December 16–22, 1985, Alex Lowe, Jack Tackle (to top of climb only)
SKILLET GLACIER: February 1990, Keith Cattabriga

DIRECT SOUTH BUTTRESS: January 5, 1988, Jack Tackle, Alex Lowe (to top of climb only); March 5–7, 2001, Hans Johnstone, Mark Newcomb, Renny Jackson (complete)
SOUTHWEST COULOIR: January 28, 1989, Ron Matous

Mount Owen (12,928)

EAST RIDGE: [December 19, 1965, George Lowe, Lenny Nelson]; December 20, 1965, Tom Stevenson, Mike Lowe, Steve Swanson, Jon Marsh (all three parties on the East Ridge route climbed the southeast side of the summit knob)
KOVEN: [December 19, 1965, Mike Lowe, Steve Swanson]
SOUTH CHIMNEY: January 3–5, 1980, Jack Tackle, Pat Callis (to east ridge only)
FRYXELL: February 26, 1988, Steve Quinlan, Jim "Jaime" Olson
SERENDIPITY ARÊTE: March 10 or 11, 1994, Jack Tackle
NORTH RIDGE: March 18–19, 2007, Hans Johnstone, Greg Collins

Mount St. John (11,430)

SOUTH COULOIR, WEST/EAST RIDGE: February 12, 1972, Dennis and Karen Caldwell, David Smith, Milt Hollander, plus one other

Mount Wister (11,490)

NORTHEAST COULOIR, VARIATION: 1928: March 3–4, 1973, Chuck Schaap, Art Becker, Bob Stevenson
WEST RIDGE: 1984 or 1985, Bob Graham
SOUTH COULOIR: January 3, 1985, Ron Matous
NORTH FACE, SAVED BY THE SHEEP: January 19, 1997, Norm Larson, Callum Mackay

Mount Woodring (11,590)

SOUTHEAST SLOPE: [April 20, 1991, Tom Turiano (with a ski descent of the Southwest Slope route)]

Nez Perce (11,901)

NORTHWEST COULOIRS: February 6–8, 1972, George Lowe, David George
NORTHWEST COULOIRS, VARIATION: 1952: [December 10, 1988, Norm Larson, Jack Clinton]
SOUTH FACE: February 9–10, 1980, Mark Whiton, John Ninenger
SOUTHEAST FACE: February 9–10, 1980, Mark Whiton, John Ninenger (descent)

Owl Peak (10,612)

EAST RIDGE: February 10, 1979, Robbie Fuller, Ray White, Marty Krautter, Ken Thomasma

Peak 10,270

EAST RIDGE: [April 14, 1994, Dave Moore, Tom Turiano, Mike Whitehead]

Peak 10,333

WEST RIDGE: [April 14, 1994, Dave Moore, Tom Turiano, Mike Whitehead]

Peak 10,360

SOUTH RIDGE: [(certain) April 7, 1993, Tom Turiano, John Fettig, Forrest McCarthy]

Peak 10,422

SOUTH RIDGE: January 20, 1985, Norm Larson, Martha Clarke

EAST RIDGE: [April 7, 1993, Tom Turiano, John Fettig, Forrest McCarthy]

Peak 10,696

EAST RIDGE: Mid- to late 1970s, Bill Barmore, Dean Millsap, Joe Gale, Robert Hammer

Peak 12,000+

EAST RIDGE: February 22, 1988, Andy Carson, Gary Patton

Point 9,975 (25-Short)

EAST SLOPE: 1950s, NPS residents of Beaver Creek; 1960s, Barry Corbet; 1974–1977, Bill Barmore, Dean Millsap, Woody and Jim Barmore

Primrose Peak (10,800+)

WEST COULOIR AND SOUTH RIDGE: March 15, 1994, Tom Turiano, Wesley Bunch, Christoph Schork, Scott McGee

Prospectors Mountain (11,241)

SOUTHWEST RIDGE: January 17, 1990, Michael Best
RAVEN CRACK: January 2009, Stephen Koch, Sam Magro

Ranger Peak (11,355)

WEST RIDGE: [March 27, 1992, Tom Turiano, Matthew Goewert, Michael Keating, Wesley Bunch]
SOUTHEAST RIDGE: February 3, 1991, Dave Moore, Bill Stanley

Raynolds Peak (10,910)

EAST RIDGE: March 16, 1994, Tom Turiano, Wesley Bunch, Christoph Schork
WEST SUMMIT, NORTHWEST SIDE: January 4, 1995, Tom Turiano, Wesley Bunch

Red Mountain (10,205 and 10,177)

NORTH RIDGE: February 10, 1980, Bill and Woody Barmore, Mike Whitfield, Shari Gregory, Don Black; [April 15, 1994, Tom Turiano, Dave Moore (to 10,205-foot summit)]

Rendezvous Peak (10,927)

WEST RIDGE: January 25, 1961, Frank Ewing, Rod Newcomb

Rolling Thunder Mountain (10,908)

NORTH SNOWFIELD TO WEST RIDGE: March 20, 1990, Tom Turiano, Tom Bennett

Shadow Peak (10,725)

EAST RIDGE: January 3, 1988, Bob Graham

South Teton (12,514)

NORTHWEST COULOIR: January 22, 1968, Maurice Horn, Gary Cole, Frank Ewing, Denny Becker, Greg Bourassa, Peter Koedt, Keith Becker, John Walker, Don Ryan, John Horn
EAST RIDGE: December 21, 1975, Jim Roscoe (ascent); February 25, 1988, Norm Larson, Lorna Corson (descent)
SOUTH RIDGE: December 21, 1977, Bill Barmore, Craig George

WEST RIDGE: [November 23, 1972, Tom Warren, Gene Forsythe, Boots and Charla Brown, Jim Huntly, Judy Fox, Pat Viani]; December 20, 1972, Tom Warren, Gene Forsythe, Dan Miller, Roger Pope, Scott Russell, Sam Evans, Georgia and Stewart Silk, Cliff Berger

Spalding Peak (12,240+)

ZORRO SNOWFIELD: December 26, 1985, Craig Patterson, Roger Millward
EAST RIDGE: February 18, 1987, Andy Carson, Gary Patton (ascent); February 24, 1988, Norm Larson, Lorna Corson (descent)
WEST RIDGE: February 18, 1987, Andy Carson, Gary Patton (descent); February 24, 1988, Norm Larson, Lorna Corson (ascent)

Static Peak (11,303)

NORTH FACE: [October 27, 1976, Mike Volk, Dick Simmons]
EAST RIDGE: March 15, 1981, Steven Poole
SOUTHWEST RIDGE: [March 28, 1986, Chris Sabo, David Smith]

Survey Peak (9,277)

NORTHEAST SLOPE: December 1957, Frank Ewing, Keith Jones
SOUTHWEST SLOPE: March 16–18, 1973, Doug Leen, Jim "Ole" Olson

Symmetry Spire (10,560+)

SOUTHWEST COULOIR: [April 7, 1971, David Boyd, Owen Anderson]

Teepe Pillar (12,266)

WEST RIDGE: January 26, 1973, Tom Warren, Robert Gathercole

Teewinot Mountain (12,325)

SOUTHWEST COULOIRS: March 1, 1968, Denny Becker, Rex Alldredge
SOUTH RIDGE: December 26, 1977, Darvin Vandegrift, Tom Deuchler
SOUTH RIDGE, VARIATION: Southeast Couloir: [March 24, 1981, John Maniglia]; February 11, 1982, Hooman Aprin, John Callahan
EAST FACE: February 11, 1982, Kitty Calhoun, Len Wechter
NORTHWEST RIDGE: [March 21, 1986, Andy Carson, Gary Patton (via Teton Glacier)]

Thor Peak (12,028)

SOUTHEAST RIDGE: January 21–23, 1976, Jan Olson, Andy Carson, Jim Roscoe
SOUTH SLOPE: March 8, 1985, Andy Carson, Gary Patton

Tukuarika Peak (10,988)

NORTHEAST RIDGE: Late February 1990, Christoph Schork

Veiled Peak (11,330)

NORTHEAST LEDGES: December 21, 1985, Bob Graham

West Horn (11,605)

WEST RIDGE: December 25, 1975, Dave Carman, Charles Field

Winter Waterfall Ice and Mixed Climbing Routes

As interest in ice climbing developed in the United States in the 1970s, a few perceptive and energetic climbers who wintered in Jackson Hole saw that there were opportunities for this type of climbing in their home range. In the years since, winter ice climbing has gained considerable popularity in the Tetons, with most of the activity concentrated where ice is relatively accessible. These areas include Peak 10,450, Death Canyon, and Teton Canyon. While many of these routes reappear every winter, others are more transitory—the creatures of specific weather conditions. In any given winter, some ice sections will never form, while others will be suitable for climbing for only a few days or weeks. Local inquiry or telescopic viewing from the valley should precede the approach if one has a specific objective in mind. Ice climbing in the Tetons is more complex than in other popular US ice venues such as Hyalite Canyon (Montana), Cody (Wyoming), Provo Canyon (Utah), and Ouray (Colorado). The approaches here are substantial, and the addition of climbing gear to what is always carried for alpine touring only increases the challenge. Adventure awaits the intrepid, however!

Because most of the ice routes described below are of a high-angle nature, the risks associated with these climbs should be fully recognized by prospective climbers. Remember that it is frequently the case that ice screws are not quite as reliable as rock protection, meaning the implications of a leader fall can be more severe. Rescue is necessarily less efficient in winter for the many reasons listed under *National Park Service Winter Policy* earlier in this chapter.

Jackson Hole Mountain Resort Area

There are strategically placed backcountry gates along the roped and signed boundary line of Jackson Hole Mountain Resort. These allow access to a vast amount of "side country": to the south, one can enter areas administered by the Bridger-Teton National Forest, and to the north and west one can reach Granite Canyon in Grand Teton National Park.

PEAK 10,450 ICE AND MIXED CLIMBS

Map: Teton Village and Rendezvous Peak

Three mixed routes have been done on the north side of Peak 10,450. These were developed in recent years by local Jackson Hole climbers and are best approached with the assistance of the Jackson Hole Mountain Resort aerial tram. Note that there are also a few mixed climbs among the many great sport-climbing routes in the Rock Springs Buttress area south of the ski area. (See *Rock Climbing Jackson Hole & Pinedale, Wyoming*, by Wesley Gooch, for information on these climbs.)

ROUTE 1. SHATTER FACE. II, M6+R. This route was installed and later redpointed by Nate Brown in July or August 2015. Brown has described this route is as a "fantastic alpine trainer." It is located in a big corner between Corbet's Couloir and Chick Brain Couloir (the hanging couloir that originates immediately below the tram's tower #5). One can approach the climb by descending Corbet's or hiking around from the East Ridge trail. Continue west a short distance past Corbet's along the base of the cliff to the first break in the cliff band (Piggy's Pocket). Begin the climb on the west wall approximately 30m up into Piggy's Pocket. **Pitch 1:** This strenuous pitch on a mix of good and bad rock goes up past 10 bolts (great dry tooling and positive hooking) and finishes on an adequate ledge after stemming along an 8m bolt-protected dirt couloir. The crux is located around the seventh bolt (M6+R, 50m). **Pitch 2:** Climb up from the belay ledge past three bolts to a 75°, hummock-filled corner. These hummocks facilitate frontpointing, and the corner consists of excellent hooking with protection available along the right wall; reach a belay at the top at chain anchors (40m). This climb is reported to be well equipped for rope soloing or conventional top-roping. **Gear:** For protection take a small rack that includes a double set of small cams to 1.5", one 2" cam, and one 3" cam; several draws and slings; a few Spectre ice pitons; and the largest beaks. (Sources: Nate Brown; Mountain Project)

ROUTE 2. VILLAGE GHOST. II, 5.10, WI6. First ascent December 2, 2017, by Sam Macke, Jackson Marvell, and Nate Brown. This climb is located in the cirque to the west of Tensleep Bowl at the ski area and is approximately 150m west of the Horseshoe Couloir in Grand Teton National Park. The first pitch consists of mixed 5.10 rock climbing and WI6 ice climbing (55m). The second pitch involves WI5+ ice climbing (55m). The first-ascent party descended by way of *Route 3* and left no fixed gear on the route. (Source: correspondence with Nate Brown)

ROUTE 3. STATE OF EMERGENCY. II, WI4+, M6+. First ascent February 20, 2017, by Sam Macke, Nate Brown, and Brian Mulvihill. Located about 30m past *Route 2* and approximately 180m past the Horseshoe Couloir, this climb consists of three pitches of climbing. **Pitch 1:** Climb 30m of well-formed WI4 ice up black slabs. At the top of the slabs, traverse left via left-trending cracks (good cams and nuts) to a ledge with a good anchor (M6+, 50m). **Pitch 2:** Continue up via rock and ice-covered slabs. **Pitch 3:** Continue up to the top of the climb and then descend the route. (Source: correspondence with Nate Brown)

PEAK 10,753 (CODY PEAK)

(1.5 mi NNE of Rendezvous Peak)

Map: Rendezvous Peak

South of Jackson Hole Mountain Resort, in the uppermost portion of the Green River drainage and just below the eastern edge of Cody Bowl and the Powder 8 face, is a cliff band containing a fun mixed climb of three short pitches: Village Idiot. The ski-descent route Breakneck is adjacent to it just to the north.

ROUTE 1. VILLAGE IDIOT. II, WI4+, M4. First ascent unknown. Access for this route is via the tram at the ski area. Exit south from the bottom of Rendezvous Bowl through the gate that is provided. Ski down and across the Rock Springs drainage to the regular boot track that leads up into the Green River drainage. At the top of the track traverse out to the south and up to the base of the climb, which is located in the middle of the cliff band above (when it is in condition). The first pitch should be visible: it usually forms as an attached vertical pillar of ice approximately 15m–18m in height. **Pitch 1:** Climb the pillar and belay at the top (18m, WI4+). **Pitch 2:** Climb mixed terrain above to a ledge

Climbing ranger Noah Ronczkowski on a mountain patrol of Mount Owen's Run-Don't-Walk Couloir (Photo by Vic Zeilman)

below a left-leaning corner (M4). **Pitch 3:** Climb the corner to the top of the climb; grass hummocks are useful here (M4). Rappel the route. **Gear:** For protection take a few screws; a light rock rack including nuts, cams, and draws; and one Spectre ice piton.

Death Canyon

For the approach to the ice climbs in Death Canyon, drive south from Moose, Wyoming, on the Moose-Wilson road to a plowed turnout located just north of the spur road to the Death Canyon trailhead. (**Note:** The Moose-Wilson road is only plowed to this point during the winter, and the road to the Death Canyon trailhead is not plowed at all.) From this turnout there is then a 3.5- to 4.5-mile ski in to most of the Death Canyon ice climbs. Unless it is early enough in the season to walk in, skis are recommended for travel upcanyon and for getting back up to the crest of the Phelps Lake moraine. Depending on snow conditions, allow two to three hours to approach these ice climbs and about the same for the return to the Moose-Wilson road.

The season for these climbs is, in most years, late November to early April. The ice usually forms from the melting and refreezing of early-season snowfall (autumn). In an autumn drought these climbs may not form or can be marginal until a snowfall followed by a melt-freeze cycle occurs. The best conditions are usually from mid-December to mid-March. Prospectors Falls generally forms the earliest and stays the latest.

DEATH CANYON, SOUTH SIDE ICE CLIMBS (ca. 8,400)

Map: Grand Teton

ROUTE 1. RIMROCK FALLS. II, WI3–WI4. First ascent February 20, 1977, by Richard Rossiter and Jeff Splitgerber. This route ascends the ice formed by the outlet stream from Rimrock Lake. The climbing can be broken into two sections—the first is WI3 and consists of ice-covered slabs that are hard to protect. Then proceed up a long snow slope (370m; at times prone to avalanche) to the base of the second tier. This pitch is a 37m WI3+ to WI4 hose. To descend rappel from a tree near the top of the last pitch, walk down the middle section, and then rappel again from a tree on the west side of the first pitch. These are double-rope rappels.

ROUTE 2. THE NUGGET. I, WI4+. First ascent in January 1983, by Rex Hong and Tony Tulip. (See *Figure 12-1.*) Approach as for *Route 3*, then climb nearly 200m up the Apocalypse Couloir from the top of the snow/talus cone. Bear left at a dogleg in the couloir and begin this ice climb on the left side of the couloir shortly thereafter. It involves 34m of vertical and just off-vertical climbing. Anchors at the top are marginal. Beware of avalanches coming down the formidable Apocalypse Couloir.

ROUTE 3. PROSPECTORS FALLS. II, WI3+. First ascent in March 1973, by Pete Carman and Dave Carman. (See *Figure 12-1.*) This route, the most popular frozen waterfall climb in the canyon, was given the name Raven Falls by the first-ascent party. It is located at the base of the north face of Prospectors Mountain, immediately east of the Apocalypse Couloir, which is the most prominent winter feature of the mountain when viewed from Death Canyon. For the approach, leave the trail in the bottom of the canyon before starting up the lower switchbacks, cross the creek, and then ascend the snow cone that forms at the base of the falls. The route contains two pitches of 70°–80° ice with some vertical sections. During early season and/or some wetter winters, three additional pitches may be available. The fifth and highest ropelength consists at times of a narrow smear that steepens to vertical ice at the very top. To descend, rappel from trees on the right (northwest) side using two ropes. The avalanche hazard consists of heavy spindrift from above with some potential for larger slides from the Apocalypse Couloir, so cross the runout of this couloir as rapidly as possible. Once on the climb itself, the main danger is from spindrift, which can be significant at times.

FIGURE 12-1. Death Canyon, south side ice climbs, Prospectors Falls area overview

DEATH CANYON, NORTH SIDE ICE CLIMBS (ca. 8,000)

Map: Grand Teton

ROUTE 1. SENTINEL WINTER GULLY. II, WI3+. First ascent in winter 1978, by Norm Larson and Jack Clinton. (See *Figure 12-2.*) This moderate climb of one and a half pitches in a very scenic location ascends a section of ice just west of Sentinel Turret. It should be recognized that the name of this winter route differs from the summer terminology, which applies almost the same name—Sentinel Gully—to the large gully immediately east of Sentinel Turret. The first pitch on moderate-angle (60°) ice leads to the base of a short, steep section. Climb about 6m of steep ice (80°–85°) up into a small rock amphitheater containing a snowfield. Continue straight up the snow to the rock wall at the head of the amphitheater. Although fixed nuts and pitons can often be found here for rappelling (including an old Wort Hog pounded into the rock from the first-ascent party), bring some hardware just in case. One full-length double-rope rappel will put one

FIGURE 12-2. Death Canyon, north side ice climbs overview

about 9m from the snow at the base of the gully. Set up a second short rappel on ice or rock to reach the base, or downclimb the lower-angle ice. The avalanche potential is low because this is a well-protected route, with the only danger being a slide from the small snowfield at the top of the climb or during the canyon approach.

ROUTE 2. DREAD FALLS. III, WI3–WI4. First ascent in January 1982, by Rex Hong and Tony Tulip. (See *Figure 12-2.*) Earlier referred to as the "Curtain of Death," Dread Falls earned its name from an early attempt by Norm Larson, George Austigue, and Jack Clinton during which Clinton took a long fall. Hong and Tulip recovered gear from that previous ill-fated attempt during their successful first ascent. This is the most prominent ice climb on the north side of Death Canyon, and it can be climbed in at least two ways. For either method approach along the trail until about 0.25 mile past the Bulge *(Route 4)*. Minimal avalanche hazard exists on this climb besides that which is encountered on the approach.

(1) *Main falls.* This method is directed toward the climb of the upper section only, bypassing the lower section of mixed climbing. Approach by continuing upcanyon on the trail about 0.2 mile past Dread Falls, then angle back right and up to the base of the main falls on a large ramp. This route consists of one and a half pitches on ice that can often be of the hollow and "chandelier" variety. There are two methods of descent. One may rappel from a tree to the right of the top of the falls, using two 50m ropes, which will just reach the ground at the base of the falls; then retrace the route back to the trail. The avalanche gully to the east may be taken back down to the base of the climb as an alternative.

(2) *Direct approach.* From the trail directly below the falls start the climb by working up smears of mostly low-angle ice (often thin) to the base of Dread Falls. This method adds about 90m of additional mixed climbing. Routefinding up these lower slabs can be interesting, and rock protection is desirable.

ROUTE 3. THE THREE STOOGES. I, WI3. First ascent December 31, 1986, by Daniel Blumstein and Nancy Auerbach. Three prominent smears of moderate-angle ice form on the smooth rock slabs that are located about 50m left (west) of the Bulge. These smears are approximately 30m long with an angle of 60°–70°. To descend, rappel from a small tree at the top of the center smear. The avalanche potential consists of some sloughing and icefall from the ledges and snowfield above, but the route is generally sheltered. Because this route can be top-roped, it is a good area for practice.

ROUTE 4. THE BULGE. II, WI3–WI4. First ascent January 12, 1984, by Jim Woodmencey and Dan Burgette. This route is located on the south-facing side of Death Canyon just beyond the end of the first switchback as one goes upcanyon from Phelps Lake. The ice can be seen in a shallow right-facing corner. The first pitch has a 3m vertical section at the base, with lower-angle ice (often mixed) leading to the base of the Bulge itself (50m). Bring some rock protection for this section. The second pitch surmounts a 4m bulge of vertical ice to the lower-angle ice above, exiting right to a large tree. Use this tree for the upper belay and as the rappel point, using two 50m ropes. The avalanche hazard is the same as for *Route 3*.

ROUTE 5. CANADA REGIONAL AIR. III, 5.9, WI5, M4. First ascent November 25, 2017, by Hans Johnstone and Greg Collins. This modern mixed trad route rises out of the 747 Gully in three pitches. To find the 747 Gully, follow the main Death Canyon trail into the canyon from the Phelps Lake Overlook. This gully is located 200m to the east of Dihedral of Horrors on Ship's Prow Pillar (see *Omega Buttresses, Eastern Section/Ship's Prow*). It is difficult to see the climb from the trail, but proceed up through talus and vegetation into the runout from the gully, looking for the first pitch on the right side. This pitch is slabby with a vertical crack and hanging corner. Start up the first lead, which is dry 5.9—mostly on rock but with a bit of ice and snow. The second pitch involves an easy snow/slab ledge traverse (4th class). The third and final pitch is the main draw, described by Collins as "the marquee mixed/ice pitch." **Gear:** For protection bring a mixed rack, including stubby screws, cams, nuts, and a few pins, with an emphasis on thin gear. (Source: Mountain Project)

ROUTE 6. 737 EARFUL. I, WI3–WI4. First ascent in February 1973, by Pete Carman, Dave Carman, Jim Roscoe, Jay Wilson, and Chuck Schaap. Located at the base of a long drainage chute on the southeast corner of Albright Peak, this one-pitch climb was named for the excessive noise generated by jets departing from the Jackson

Hole Airport (the only one inside a national park). The acoustics here amplify the thunder of the engines, making one wonder whether it is a jet or an avalanche coming down the gully immediately above the climb.

The 737 Earful route is reached by descending the trail from the Phelps Lake Overlook to the end of the first switchback and then traversing to the west along the base of the south-facing rock. The main falls, containing 37m of 70°–90° ice, can be hollow at times, with running water underneath. The ice that forms to the left of the main falls over steeper rock and out of the main gully is generally thicker and less hollow; however, this does not always touch down and become continuous until later in the winter. There are numerous other short, sometimes narrow, or mixed possibilities to the right of the main falls in rock chimneys. Descent off the main falls or the variations to the left is made by walking up and left (west) in a gully to trees and then continuing left (west) and down to the base. Because it is located at the base of a 900m slide path, this climb is recommended *only* when the avalanche hazard is low or nonexistent.

ROUTE 6. SUNRISE PILLAR. I, WI3–WI4. First ascent January 29, 1980, by Randy Harrington, Shad Dusseau, and Jan Schofield. Seen from the Death Canyon trail before the Phelps Lake Overlook is reached, this short ice climb lies at the base of Albright Peak, facing east in the main gully coming down from the summit. It is approximately 12m high and is mostly vertical. For the descent one can walk off up and left out of the gully, or a rappel can be made from a small tree, which is sometimes buried. In late winter this ice route is often completely covered by avalanche debris.

Avalanche Canyon

Most of these little-known ice routes have been climbed only once, but they are readily accessible from the plowed parking area at the Taggart Lake trailhead. A number of other climbs have been discovered in the lower portion of the canyon on the south side of Shadow Peak. Note that all of these climbs are exposed to significant avalanche hazard from above.

ROUTE 1. WISTERSHEER FALLS. I, WI3+. First ascent in 1980 or 1981, by Rex Hong and Scott Lehman. This ice route of two pitches, one short (9m moderate angle) and one long (up to 80°), forms on the cliffs to the right of the large northwest couloir of Mount Wister; it is in the vicinity of the second line of drainage to the right of the couloir. Approach from Lake Taminah toward the left (southwest) edge of the headwall below Snowdrift Lake.

ROUTE 2. MOUNT WISTER, NORTH FACE ICE. II, WI3–WI4. First ascent in 1978 or 1979, by Jack and Bill Clinton, then repeated November 3, 1981, by Mike Fischer and Greg Miles. Information concerning the location of this two-pitch ice climb is sketchy. The first lead of 20m–25m was strenuous. The second pitch, also 20m–25m, goes up a narrow gully containing mixed climbing involving some rockwork. Exit by traversing on snow up and to the right to gain the crest of the east ridge of Mount Wister. One may then descend into the north fork of Avalanche Canyon via the standard snow slope, the northeast couloir (see *Mount Wister, Route 5*).

ROUTE 3. SHOSHOKO FALLS. I, WI2+. First ascent November 11, 1981, by Doug Speirs and Roger McMurtrey. One short pitch of ice was climbed near the base of the summertime Shoshoko Falls. Exit was made off on snow to the right.

ROUTE 4. THE TALON. III, WI3+. First ascent January 24, 1983, by Mark Whiton (though it is possible that Norm Larson preceded Whiton at some earlier point in time). On the right (north) side of Avalanche Canyon, about 1.5 miles west of Taggart Lake, is a prominent ice formation (in some winters) that starts as a single frozen waterfall and then splits into three twisted ice runnels or "talons" at the top. All three have been climbed. The first (easternmost) "talon" is the longest (110m total) and most exciting from a climbing standpoint. From the top traverse right to descend on snow—be aware that there is sometimes avalanche danger here—to a tree from which one or two rappels suffice to reach easier ground below.

Garnet Canyon

With Garnet Canyon being such a major area, the three climbs listed here represent a fraction of what is possible. There is little information available because these have seen only a single ascent or attempt; they are also somewhat rare, forming during only brief intervals in any given winter (if at all).

ROUTE 1. MIDDLE TETON, RIGHT OF DIKE. II, WI3–WI4. First ascent in about 1980, by Ron Matous and Mark Whiton. This climb is somewhat rare and forms at the base of the east ridge of the Middle Teton, just right of the black dike and to the left of the steep east buttress. Climb to the top of the snow cone at the base of the ice. The first 25m ice pitch contains a 6m vertical section. The second lead is a full ropelength on reasonable 60°–70° ice. From the top the first-ascent party traversed left across slabs to gain the dike, which they followed to the top of the Dike Pinnacle. Descent was made by rappel into the Ellingwood Couloir *(Middle Teton, Route 6)* and down into the south fork of Garnet Canyon.

ROUTE 2. GRAND TETON, LOWER STETTNER COULOIR ICE. First ascent in June 1978, by Steve Shea and David Breashears (to the Black Dike only). In some years there is sufficient ice formed from the melting in the Stettner Couloir and refreezing on the cliffs below the Black Dike to provide an ice climb. This route starts from the vicinity of the Middle Teton Glacier moraine. Information concerning the difficulty of the climbing is not available.

ROUTE 3. GRAND TETON, LOWER GLENCOE-TEEPE CHUTE. II, WI4+. First incomplete ascent in 1979, by Steve Shea and David Breashears; first known complete ascent June 12, 2012, by Keith Sidle and Sean O'Rourke; second known complete ascent—and first winter ascent (II, WI5, M5/M6)—in late February 2015, by Nate Brown and Sam Macke. The difference between the spring and winter ratings for this climb reflects the amount of ice seasonally present: because this drainage faces south, more water is available in spring for refreezing, thus forming thicker ice. Much loose rock is to be found here during the summer months. The following pitch descriptions convey what Sidle and O'Rourke encountered on their ascent. **Pitch 1:** Begin with a mixed climbing traverse from the right to get to the ice; a #0.75 cam was found to be "crucial" in this section (WI4+). **Pitch 2:** Climb a short column in a corner followed by an iced-up runnel, described as containing very aerated ice to "snice"' (WI4). **Pitch 3:** Continue up on snow to a final stretch of WI3 and then proceed a short distance to Teepe Col. After witnessing a "massive point release avalanche rip over the East Face of the Grand," Sidle and O'Rourke descended by way of the Teepe Glacier. Brown and Macke found mixed climbing and much thinner ice, and they used a variety of protection including beaks, a rock rack, and a selection of screws. (Sources: Mountain Project; correspondence with Keith Sidle and Nate Brown)

Disappointment Peak

This big ice climb occasionally forms up on the lower portion of the north face of Disappointment Peak, below the large terrace that cuts across the face. This is the terrace that is used to access the north face rock routes, such as the Chouinard-Frost Chimney.

ROUTE 1. NORTH FACE ICE. III, WI5. First known ascent November 22, 2004, by Hans Johnstone and Renny Jackson. When formed up, this climb on the lower north face of Disappointment Peak delivers about three to four pitches of steep ice and a small pillar or two, all in a spectacular setting. Although it rarely forms up completely, late fall seems to be the best time to catch it. It is possible to scope it out from US Highway 89, just north of the Teton Point turnout. If the line does come in, the best approach is up the Surprise and Amphitheater Lakes trail: from Amphitheater Lake, head up and over the col north of the lake into Glacier Gulch to the base of the face. The easiest means of descent after gaining the broad terrace about halfway up the face is to traverse over to the east ridge and rappel the first pitch of that route (see *Disappointment Peak, Route 5*). One can then walk back down the trail to the Lupine Meadows parking area. *Figure 12-3* illustrates one possible ascent line.

Teewinot Mountain

During the extremely dry winter of 1976–1977, Norm Larson and Forrest Rade climbed a few new routes on this peak that are normally covered with snow and avalanche debris. The first was the small waterfall in the drainage to the south of the Apex (WI3, 15m). On the north side of the mountain, near the mouth of Cascade Canyon, three gullies were also climbed (WI2+ or WI3, 90m–150m). These are located just west of a moss-covered rock outcrop that is 90m high.

Cascade Canyon

As with most of the other canyons during the winter months, Cascade is plagued with a long approach and, at times, significant avalanche hazard. The optimal time to climb some of these routes (when they come into condition) may be late in the fall, after the temperatures drop but before Teton Park Road closes.

ROUTE 1. PUTIN'S PICKLE. II, WI5. First ascent February 25, 2016, by Sam Macke and Emma Williams. This route ascends a short, steep pillar situated below the Teewinot-Owen cirque on the south side of Cascade Canyon. This climb was descended with one 70m rope from V-threads at the top.

ROUTE 2. LEFT PILLAR. II, WI5. First ascent in December 1991, by Jack Tackle. This route and its neighbor above, the Right Pillar *(Route 3)*, are both located to the west of Gorbachev Falls *(Route 5)* on the steep section of rock to the east of Guides' Wall *(Cascade Canyon, North Side Rock Climbs, Storm Point Cliffs, Route 1)*. The first pitch of this climb consists of 21m of vertical ice climbing on a prominent pillar. A section of mixed climbing is then encountered. Descent was accomplished by means of rappel anchors from the ice.

FIGURE 12-3. Disappointment Peak, North Face Ice, III, WI5

ROUTE 3. RIGHT PILLAR. I, WI5. First ascent in December 1991, by Jack Tackle. This pillar to the right of *Route 2* is a one-pitch climb that has a 12m vertical section. Descent was made via rappel anchors from the ice.

ROUTE 4. TANG-O-MAX. IV, WI5+, M6. First ascent January 20, 2003, by John Kelley and Matt Nuner; second ascent in January 2003, by Hans Johnstone and Renny Jackson. (See *Figure 8-8*.) This excellent mixed climb is located between *Routes 2* and *3* on a black, water-streaked wall on the south side of Storm Point near the mouth of Cascade Canyon. This 366m climb may share the first few pitches with the rock route Rags-to-Riches *(Cascade Canyon, North Side Rock Climbs, Storm Point Cliffs, Route 9)*. **Pitch 1:** Begin just east of an overhang with easy mixed climbing to a WI3 section leading to a belay on a ledge (60m). Continue up 120m of easier snow to a large ledge. **Pitch 2:** M6 climbing leads to a WI5 section of ice that reaches a belay at a tree. **Pitch 3:** Climb WI3 ice just left of a left-facing corner to a belay on a ledge with a tree on it. **Pitch 4 (crux):** Climb WI5+/M6 in the left-facing corner system that eventually leads to easier WI3 ice climbing. **Pitch 5:** Lower-angle ice leads to a short section of WI5- ice and the large ledge at the top of the climb. The descent from the climb involves a series of rappels from trees and V-threads. **Gear:** For protection the first-ascent party used 8–10 screws; a set of cams from 0.5" to 3"; one set of stoppers; and a 60m rope. Expect excellent protection (much of it using rock gear) on the climb depending upon how it has formed up.

ROUTE 5. GORBACHEV FALLS. II, WI3–WI4. First ascent December 24, 1991, by Jack Tackle. The name commemorates Gorbachev's fall from power. This climb of four or five pitches forms on the southeastern side of Storm Point near the eastern edge of the broad ledge on which one can traverse west all the way over to the Flake Ledge of the summertime Guides' Wall rock climb *(Cascade Canyon, North Side Rock Climbs, Storm Point Cliffs, Route 1)*. The first pitch begins with 8m of vertical ice and then eases off. The next pitch consists of snow- or ice-covered slabs for half a ropelength. The third pitch is a small curtain of ice that then continues off to the west where the climbing turns to slabs covered with thin ice. Pitch four begins with a vertical pillar and continues upward for 37m. Exit from the upper amphitheater via a chimney of ice. The first of the descent rappels (50m) is from fixed pins. The following three rappels are from pitons and trees.

ROUTE 6. LOWER SYMMETRY COULOIR ICE. I, WI3. First ascent in early December 1976, by Norm Larson and Forrest Rade. This route ascends the short 15m ice section that forms from the small waterfall that one passes on the standard summertime approach to the Symmetry Couloir. Follow the usual approach from the Cascade Canyon trail up into the cul-de-sac below the short cliff band (see *Cascade Canyon, Symmetry Couloir* in Section 8). This ice is immediately apparent on the wall to the left. In many years it will be covered with snow, but in dry winters it is bare ice. Note that this route is not in the main drainage from the Symmetry Couloir that separates Symmetry Spire from Storm Point.

Leigh Canyon

The approach to Leigh Canyon in winter is by usual standards long, requiring an 11-mile ski in from the end of the plowed road at the Taggart Lake trailhead, or 4 miles if one uses a snowmobile to reach the String Lake trailhead.

ROUTE 1. MOUNT WOODRING ICE. WI3+ or WI4. First ascent in January 1977, by Norm Larson and Will Mylander. This climb is located on the lower north side of Mount Woodring opposite Staircase Arête. Two 30m pitches were climbed.

ROUTE 2. LAUGHING LIONS FALLS. IV, WI4. First ascent March 8, 1983, by Jim Woodmencey, Dan Burgette, and Bill Pelander (to top of first pitch only); January 5, 1985, by Dan Burgette, Renny Jackson, Jim Woodmencey, and Bill Pelander (to top of main waterfall); February 19, 1985, by Jack Tackle, Alex Lowe, and Andy Carson (to top of climb). This major ice climb forms at the right (east) edge of the base of the south buttresses of Mount Moran. The first pitch consists of 50m of 70° ice (often thin) to a large snow ledge. The second and third pitches continue for 90m of 80°–90° ice. This is the top of the main continuous ice section. However, it is possible to climb another 30m of ice in the center of the large gully above the third pitch, or skirt it to the left toward an upper curtain of ice that rarely, if ever, touches down. Tackle, Lowe, and Carson managed to extend the route in February 1985 by using aid on the intervening rock to reach and then climb the final hanging ice section of 50m. The avalanche hazard on this climb can be significant and must be carefully evaluated before one commits to this very serious route.

ROUTE 3. NO ESCAPE ICE. Three smears were climbed on the No Escape Slabs in January 1977 by Norm Larson and Will Mylander.

Waterfalls Canyon

The winter approaches to any of the northern canyons in the Teton Range, including Waterfalls Canyon, entail crossing Jackson Lake. Getting to the base of Wilderness Falls, for example, requires a 3-mile ski across the lake from Colter Bay and then a 2.6-mile trek up Waterfalls Canyon.

Climbers on the first ascent of the initial pitches of Mount Moran's Laughing Lions Falls (Photo by Angus Thuermer, courtesy of *Jackson Hole News & Guide*)

ROUTE 1. DARKNESS FALLS. II, WI4+ or WI5. First ascent January 23, 1985, by Rex Hong and Jim "Jaime" Olson. (See *Figure 12-4.*) Described as the "first thing you come to" (just south of Columbine Cascade), this route is reached by going up the canyon to the base of a large, mostly vertical falls on the left. This requires passing some steep rock. The route consists of two 25m pitches of steep ice climbing. To descend, walk off to the east and rappel.

ROUTE 2. WILDERNESS FALLS. II, WI4. First ascent January 18, 1985, by Renny Jackson, Dan Burgette, and John Carr. (See *Figure 12-4.*) Near the head of Waterfalls Canyon, this route ascends the summer waterfall, which is readily seen from the highway in the valley. The route is about 90m in length. To descend from the top end of the ice, walk left (south) up to the top of the main cliff band and rappel, using two ropes, or walk off to the north and around the cliff band. The avalanche potential can be very high in the canyon on the approach but is greatly reduced once one is on the climb.

Teton Canyon

During cold, dry autumns, this west side canyon offers perhaps the most accessible array of ice climbs in the range. Numerous smears, curtains, hoses, fangs, and gullies stretch along the canyon's north-facing limestone rim between the Treasure Mountain Scout Camp and the Teton Canyon campground. Nice top-rope routes may be found near the forks, and a few ice climbs have even been explored farther up the immense south fork of the canyon.

Depending on the intended ice route, climbers may park in one of several pullouts along the Teton Canyon road until the road closes in mid-November or early December. After the road closes, parking may be found in a large plowed-out area 90m down the Teton Canyon road from its junction with the Freds Mountain road, 1 mile east of Alta, Wyoming. Most climbers approach by skiing along the snowbound road, but many use snowshoes or snowmobiles, or simply walk.

Teton Canyon is a sensitive winter range for deer, elk, moose, and bighorn sheep. Parties should stick to the road to minimize the impact of their passage.

TETON CANYON, SOUTH SIDE ICE CLIMBS (ca. 7,200)

Maps: Granite Basin and Mount Bannon

ROUTE 1. BOY SCOUT FALLS. II, WI3. First ascent unknown. This two-pitch route lies in the obvious gully past the Treasure Mountain Scout Camp. The first pitch (30m) ascends undulating moderate ice (40°–80°) to a belay niche below a steep rock wall with some fixed pitons, bolts, and old slings. Bring some rock protection to back up this belay and to help protect the next pitch in early season. The remainder of the climb may be done in one long pitch or in two short pitches with an intermediate belay on a good ledge. The second pitch ascends an 80° ice tongue, the crux, the width and thickness of which vary from year to year and month to month. The final 10m section ascends an 80° headwall to a large bush, which is suitable as a rappel anchor. Descend in one full double-rope rappel (60m) or two single-rope rappels. Avalanche danger is limited to the slope below the climb.

ROUTE 2. REUNION FALLS. These three adjacent 21m ice curtains form on the same limestone cliff band as Boy Scout Falls *(Route 1)* approximately 1 mile to the east. Rappels may be made from bushes near the tops of the climbs. Potential avalanche danger exists on slopes above and below the climbs.

(1) *LEFT ROUTE.* I, WI4. First ascent in February 1984, by Norm Larson and Andy Carson. This line contains one 6m section of vertical ice. Rappel from a bush.

(2) *CENTER ROUTE.* WI4+. First ascent December 14, 1993, by Tom Turiano and Stephen Koch. This center line ascends a rock overhang covered with thin ice in most years. Rock protection is useful. Rappel from a bush.

(3) *RIGHT ROUTE.* WI5+. First ascent December 14, 1993, by Stephen Koch and Tom Turiano. Forming irregularly, this difficult route ascends thin ice and a pair of icicles

FIGURE 12-4. Waterfalls Canyon ice overview

through a large rock overhang. Small cams and knifeblades help to protect the crux.

ROUTE 3. EAGLE SCOUT (A.K.A. MACK/TYSON PILLAR). I, WI5–WI6R (conditions dependent). First ascent November 23, 2011, by Ty Mack and Andy Tyson. This outstanding pillar consists of 50m of steep ice. It now seems to form more frequently, possibly due to changes in the drainage above the climb. On the day of its first ascent, however, the climb was anything but a pillar in the traditional sense. "I recall it being pretty scary," Mack later wrote. "We didn't have much rock gear (just a couple stoppers—no pins or cams) so I wasn't actually able to get any useful gear in until I was halfway up the route." Eagle Scout is located in the main cirque above the Treasure Mountain Scout Camp at the 7,600-foot level. If formed, it should be visible above the road, just west of the Scout camp bridge. This pillar used to fall down a few times per season but it now seems to form up "fat and solid," according to longtime Teton climber and Victor, Idaho, local Greg Collins. Also available in this area adjacent to the pillar are a few modern mixed climbs; see Mountain Project (mountainproject.com) for more information regarding these routes.

ROUTE 3. RIGHT GHOST. I, WI5. First ascent in the late 1970s or early 1980s, by Steve Shea and Whitney Thurlow. (See *Figure 12-5.*) Growing in a good year to 6m in diameter, this climb is reported to occasionally form a 30m, freestanding monolith. The approach can be arduous. Before embarking, scout the route with binoculars from just south of the practice rocks area to see if it is formed.

From the Teton Canyon campground, hike or ski to the first large meadow 0.25 mile up the south fork of Teton Canyon. Cross the meadow and Teton Creek and bushwhack and posthole 300m up steep and forested northeast-facing slopes and gullies to the overhanging limestone cove that houses the climb.

The ice begins vertical and then steepens to overhanging, often with brittle or rotten chandeliers. The bulge at the top makes this one of the endurance testpieces of the range. Water flows consistently during the winter, so be sure to climb during a solid freeze to avoid getting soaked. A shorter and easier second pitch may be done if climbers are still game after the first. Rappel on double ropes from a tree. Beware of avalanche danger in the approach gullies and from the huge, steep, wind-loaded slopes above the climb.

FIGURE 12-5. Teton Canyon, south side ice climbs, Right Ghost

There are also two bolted mixed climbs flanking the main pillar. These were equipped by Dean Lords in November 2004. Somewhere between Heaven and Hell (M7) is the bolted line on the left side of the pillar, and Poltergeist (WI5, M6) is the bolted line to the right of the pillar.

ROUTE 4. LEFT GHOST. I, WI4. First ascent in the late 1970s, by Steve Shea, or during the winter of 1982, by Rex Hong and Tony Tulip. This 20+m, nearly freestanding fang drips over a cove 180m to the southeast in the same cliff band as the Right Ghost *(Route 3)*. Ascend sustained near-vertical ice to the top section, which is often hollow. Belay and rappel from a tree at the top. Approach via the forested ridges immediately below or by traversing east from *Route 3*.

ROUTE 5. BIRDBRAINS ON ICE. II, WI4. First ascent in winter 1982, by Rex Hong and Tony Tulip. This climb is located 1 mile or more up the canyon past the two Ghosts (see *Routes 3* and *4*) and forms as water flows over the same cliff band. The first pitch is lower angle and leads up to the second, which is a 37m pillar. The rappel from the top of the climb was made from pitons.

TETON CANYON, EAST SIDE ICE CLIMBS (ca. 7,000)

Maps: Granite Basin and Mount Bannon

Several excellent top-roping areas may be found at the western foot of Table Mountain between the practice rocks and the mouth of Roaring Creek. Easy to moderate practice climbs may be found at the bottom of the long, treeless draw west of Table Mountain, while a small granite cove just to the north sports several more challenging options. Bring rock protection for the former area and long slings or a second anchor rope for the latter.

Darby Canyon

Like Teton Canyon, Darby Canyon is accessed from the west side of the range. Drive 5.3 miles north on Highway 33 from Victor, Idaho, then turn east on West 3000 South to get to the mouth of the canyon. A 30m WI5 pillar with a distinctive cone at its base forms occasionally in the south fork of the canyon. This pillar is reported to be best during early season. First-ascent information regarding this pillar is unknown.

Acknowledgments

All of this I have seen. Part of it I am.

This quote, from Virgil's *The Aeneid*, hung above Leigh Ortenburger's desk in Palo Alto as it now hangs above mine here in Kelly, Wyoming. I am now older than Leigh was when he perished in the Oakland Hills Firestorm in 1991, but his loss in that tragic event still haunts me. Mountaineer, historian, statistician, explorer, photographer, father, husband, Leigh was all of these and so much more. Much of his spirit dwells within these pages and I acknowledge Leigh and our friendship first and foremost.

I find myself in the unique position of being able to recognize certain individuals specifically for Leigh as well as many others who were known to both of us. This compilation of information over the past many decades has been possible only through the generous assistance of hundreds of people. Leigh would perhaps begin by mentioning his debt to Henry "Hank" Coulter and Merrill McLane, whose guidebook first inspired his own initial efforts. Richard Pownall also provided much of the original motivation toward a new climbing guide. As he mentioned in the 1965 edition, Leigh was indebted

A dreamlike aerial view of the Grand Teton and Mount Owen (Photo by Lanny Johnson)

to Phil Smith, Joseph Hawkes, and Jack Fralick in connection with the 1940 handwritten manuscript of Phil Smith's revision of the 1932 book by Fritiof Fryxell, *The Teton Peaks and Their Ascents*. The foreword for the third edition, by Jack Durrance and Hank Coulter, was not only greatly appreciated but is also highly treasured. Sadly, shortly after its completion, Coulter passed away, and Durrance followed a few years later in 2003.

I would like to thank Greg Winston for his friendship and for our collaboration on the photographs for this edition. Together we had many adventures, both on foot in the range and in the air above the peaks, trying to capture the very best images we could. The aerial images were obtained over a period of nearly five years with the generous help of Helicopter Express and the piloting skills of Jon Bourke and Steve Wilson. Many thanks to you both for those several memorable flights in which we juggled weather and decent flight conditions with trying to get just the right amount of good morning or evening light for the thousands of images that Greg was able to shoot. Thanks also to Lanny Johnson for his piloting skills and the images that Greg was able to obtain as a result.

My friendship with Paul Horton goes back to when I started climbing with the Wasatch Mountain Club in Salt Lake 50 years ago. I took the club's beginning climbing course in 1969 and Paul was one of the instructors. In the years since we have had many climbing adventures together and have maintained a friendship that continues to this day. This included a trip up the Exum Ridge in 2020 to celebrate the 50th anniversary of my first climb of the Grand Teton; Paul was on that 1970 ascent too. Taking time away from his own climbing and writing pursuits, he undertook the painful process of reading through the entire manuscript several times. Thank you for countless edits, corrections, and support as we wound our way through some pretty arcane history. History that is, without a doubt, of peculiar interest to only a few humans! Be sure to check out www.tetonclimbinghistory.com, a collection of digital images of Grand Teton National Park's Summit Register Archive. Paul took on the painstaking process of photographing and then organizing all of the old summit registers for the Teton peaks to make them available for anyone interested in the rich climbing history that exists here. Paul, I cannot thank you enough for all of your help.

Many thanks to Irene Beardsley for her invaluable help with the 1996 third edition of this book. Without your dedication, Irene, that project simply would not have been completed. And to Dan Bloomberg, thank you for the huge amount of help that you provided for the previous edition as well as the scans of the Eldon N. Dye drawings for this edition.

I would like to express my thanks to Jim Woodmencey for writing the informative section about Teton climatology and to George Montopoli for the hopefully lifesaving Staying Alive in the Tetons section. I worked for many years with both of them and together we have had many adventures. Many thanks as well to geologist Joe Stern for the fascinating chapter on Teton geology.

Speaking for both Leigh and myself, we would especially like to thank *all* of the Jenny Lake Rangers, past and present, as well as the many mountain guides whom each of us has known and climbed with over the years. The names are too many to mention here, but you know who you are and I salute you all. Within this group I have to say thanks to my mentors, Tom Kimbrough and Bob Irvine, as well as to especially mention my colleagues and climbing partners Steve Rickert and Jim Woodmencey. I would also like to recognize Nate Opp, Vic Zeilman, and Tom Turiano, who each provided a ton of information throughout the last few years based on their own significant forays into the mountains. Many thanks to Tom for keeping me on my toes with regard to Teton climbing history.

Much appreciation is extended to Eldon N. Dye, Jim Springer, and Rhiannon Klee for their incredible artwork and to Todd Cedarholm for his help with endless mapping history questions. In addition, for their generous photo contributions I would like to thank Eric Bissell, David Bowers, Helen Bowers, Dave Carman, Todd Cedarholm, Jimmy Chin, Greg Collins, Derek Craighead, Adam Fabrikant, Grand Teton National Park Archive, Jane Jackson, Jackson Hole Historical Society & Museum, Ray Jaquot, Lanny Johnson, Kent McBride, Mark Newcomb, Leigh Ortenburger family, Rich Perch, Samuel Stuckey, Jack Tackle, Angus Thuermer, Yellowstone Heritage and Research Center, and Vic Zeilman.

Without diminishing the important help of others, the following friends and contributors have recently been so generous with their time and assistance with route descriptions that they must be enumerated: Bill Anderson, Jim Beyer, Nate Brown, Keith Cattabriga, Greg Collins, Nate Fuller, Aaron Gams, Michael Gardner, Evan Howe, Hans Johnstone, Ray Jacquot, John Kelley, Paul Kimbrough, Norm Larson, Sam Lightner Jr., Jack McConnell, Mark Newcomb, Brendan O'Neill, Brian Smith, Tom Turiano, Lisa Van Sciver, Martin Vidak, and Patrick Wright.

I must also thank and praise the copyeditor, Laura Larson, who through her meticulous attention to detail and considerable expertise, mixed in with a great deal of patience, made this a much better book. Thanks, Laura!

I deeply thank my mother, Vivian, and my father, John, for instilling in me a love of mountains and of wild places. Many of the people mentioned above are those with whom I have ventured into the mountains over the years. The partnerships, adventures, epics, and climbs that we have had together account for some of the best experiences of my life and these are highly valued.

Finally, I wish to acknowledge the debt owed to my wife, Catherine, my daughter, Jane Jackson, and her husband, Eric Bissell. I have been consumed by the labor of love that this book has become over countless hours for several decades now. Only they know how much time and effort have been expended and I thank them sincerely for their patience and understanding. Let's go climbing now that this project is completed!

Since this book will be subject to revision in future years, it is very much the hope of the author that comments and corrections concerning the route descriptions, the climbing history, the difficulty ratings, the time information, and the bibliography will be sent to him at his home address (PO Box 35, Kelly, WY 83011) or via email (rennyjackson1952@gmail.com).

R.G.J.
Kelly, Wyoming

Appendix A: Staying Alive in the Tetons

George Montopoli

The Teton Range has attracted climbers for nearly a century and a half, providing a venue in which to learn basic mountaincraft or to prepare for more difficult ascents throughout the world. Unfortunately, climbing amid the splendor of these peaks can sometimes lead to accidents that result in serious injury or death. These incidents happen to those with little climbing experience as well as to highly experienced professional mountain guides. The following is a summary of recent accidents from 2000 through 2018. The data have been filtered to include only mountaineering and climbing accidents that occurred on the high Teton peaks; in approach canyons with unofficial, seldom-maintained trails; in trailed canyon areas where people have gone off-trail to scramble on slabs or over passes compromised by snow or other unusual circumstances; and at rock-climbing areas (which generally do not involve reaching a summit). Additionally, a separate summary of wintertime accidents and an analysis of fatality incidents are provided. It is the author's (G. Montopoli's) hope that by taking an in-depth look at where and how accidents have happened over the years, and by suggesting preventative actions, incidents such as these can be significantly reduced in the future.

Mountain Peaks

From 2000 to 2018, there were 172 incidents on the Teton peaks. Most accidents occurred on the Grand Teton (71), followed by the Middle Teton (24), Teewinot Mountain (19), Mount Moran (12), Albright Peak (8), Disappointment Peak and Symmetry Spire (7 each), Mount Owen (5), Nez Perce (4), and Baxter's Pinnacle and Cube Point (3 each). Seven other peaks had one or two incidents. (See *Figure A-1.*)

The majority of these incidents (103) involved individuals who were climbing unroped (53), climbing while roped together (43), or climbing (7) with no additional details provided. Additionally, 12 incidents occurred when climbers slipped while traveling on snow and were unable to self-arrest; 19 incidents involved uninjured climbers who became stuck while climbing and were unable to continue without assistance (11 incidents involved climbers who were roped together, and eight involved climbers who were unroped); six incidents occurred while rappelling; and three incidents occurred to climbers who lost control while glissading. Medical assists for conditions such as altitude sickness, dehydration, and cardiac concerns occurred 19 times at 11 different locations, most frequently at the Lower Saddle (5). Various trauma incidents (e.g., sprained ankles, falling rock injury, etc.) occurred six times at five different locations, and there was one search on Teewinot.

The five locations where most incidents occurred include:

The Grand Teton
(71 total incidents; see *Figure A-2*):

- 26 roped climbing incidents
- 19 unroped climbing incidents
- eight incidents of getting stuck while climbing roped
- seven medical incidents
- two incidents each involving: trauma assists, rappelling, lightning strikes while climbing roped, and climbing with no additional information provided
- one incident each involving: getting stuck while climbing unroped, a slip while traveling on snow while climbing unroped, and a lightning strike while climbing unroped

The Middle Teton (24 total incidents):

- eight unroped climbing incidents
- three incidents each involving: a slip while traveling on snow while climbing unroped, getting stuck while climbing unroped, glissading, and climbing with no additional information provided
- one incident each involving: roped climbing, getting stuck while climbing roped, a medical assist, and a trauma assist from rockfall

Mountain rescue on the Petzoldt Ridge, Grand Teton (Photo by Renny Jackson)

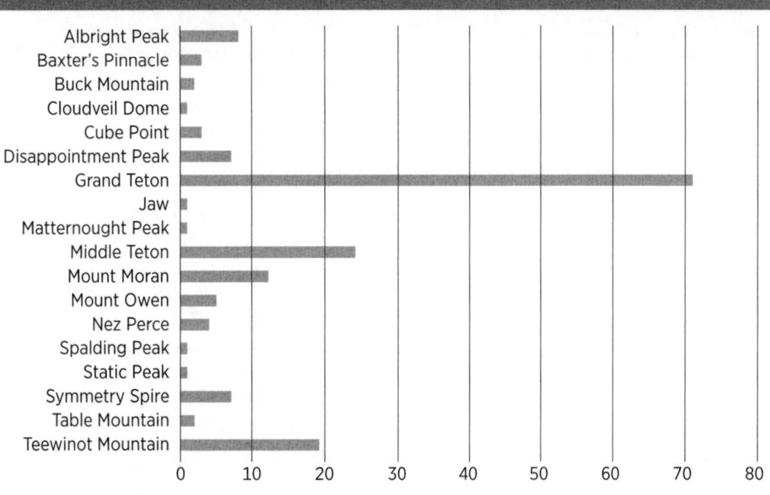

FIGURE A-2. Number of Incidents by Accident Category on the Grand Teton, 2000–2018, N = 71

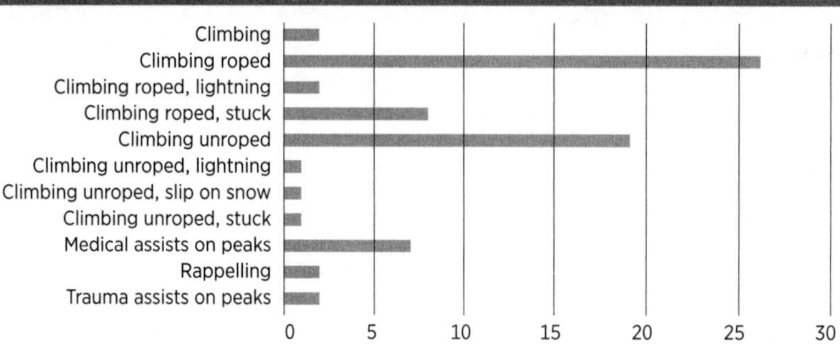

Teewinot Mountain (19 total incidents):

- eight unroped climbing incidents
- three slips while traveling on snow while climbing unroped
- two medical assists
- one incident each involving: getting stuck while climbing roped, getting stuck while climbing unroped, rappelling, a search, a trauma assist, and climbing with no additional information provided

Mount Moran (12 total incidents):

- four incidents while climbing unroped
- three medical assists
- two incidents while climbing roped
- one incident each involving: getting stuck while climbing roped, getting stuck while climbing unroped, and a trauma assist

Albright Peak (8 total incidents):

- three roped climbing incidents
- one incident each involving: a slip while traveling on snow, a stuck climber, a medical assist, rappelling, and climbing with no additional information provided

DISCUSSION

In general, most of the above accidents occurred when climbing unroped, except for on the Grand Teton, where the majority of accidents occurred while climbing roped—likely because most climbers ascend the Grand Teton using ropes. Therefore, one might think that the simple solution for avoiding accidents is to always climb roped. The issue is complex: in a mountain environment, there is a delicate balance between moving carefully (and more slowly) and moving expeditiously to avoid objective dangers such as avalanches, rockfall, or even afternoon thunderstorms. Mountaineers must decide between climbing with a rope using protection and belays, simul-climbing with a rope and limited protection (or no protection at all), and climbing unroped altogether. The decision must be based on environmental circumstances as well as the competency and ability of individual team members.

Is always climbing without a rope, or even soloing, the solution? The answer is obviously no, or at least not always. The mountain environment is dynamic: rain, snow, snowfall accumulation during the winter, storms, tremors (the Teton-Yellowstone area is a seismically active region), drought, a changing climate, etc., can all have localized effects on the areas through which climbers travel. In 2007, a house-size chockstone fell out of the Stettner Couloir on the south side of the Grand Teton into upper Garnet Canyon. During the last few years, the lower northwest slopes of Nez Perce have experienced unusual and substantial rockfall, resulting in crushing injuries to at least three different parties. These have occurred near the beginning of the south fork of Garnet Canyon, in an area where parties are often just hiking.

Traveling on 4th-class or easy 5th-class terrain without a rope can greatly speed up the ascent or descent of a peak. The decision of when to rope up is obviously an important one that should always be discussed and agreed upon by all members of the climbing team. If any member of the team becomes uncomfortable without a rope, the decision of whether to rope up should accommodate the uncomfortable member. In other words, the team should rope up or return. Likewise, simul-climbing with intermediate protection and running belays is a decision that the climbing team should agree upon, based on the relative competence and experience of team members. Strategies can vary during the day: the team can employ more conservative techniques over short sections of difficult terrain and then switch to less conservative techniques when the difficulty eases up.

Large climbing parties (more than three people) should be avoided if at all possible. These parties are often made up of one person who is competent, has some mountain experience, and acts as the leader and then two or more less experienced members. Progress can often be slow—a potentially dangerous situation in the mountains. At a minimum, if individuals are able to belay one another and keep the party progressing safely from anchor to anchor, the group may be able to move at a quicker rate and therefore reduce their exposure to rockfall or other objective hazards, such as lightning and rapid changes in weather.

In 2003, and again in 2010, several large groups of climbers attempting the Grand Teton ignored weather forecasts, started their ascents late in the morning, and progressed slowly. An intense afternoon thunderstorm with lightning hit several members of the groups, resulting in two fatalities and many injuries. The groups were led by experienced climbers but included members with limited experience. One group even deployed a metallic space blanket on the summit ridge to protect against the rain and sleet. Obviously, there was not a good outcome when lightning struck.

By getting an alpine start and reaching the summit before noon, a team can avoid afternoon thunderstorms. However, none of the above groups got an early start on their ascents, despite being advised by rangers to leave well before sunrise. With more preparation, more knowledge about the mountain environment, more experience with climbing techniques, and better decision-making, these mass casualty incidents might not have happened.

Group dynamics and impatience are contributing factors in many accidents. The relatively small size of the Teton Range as well as its accessibility can contribute to the misconception that the park is a giant playground, leading climbers to go in with a *What could possibly go wrong?* attitude. Images on social media depicting carefree folks on magical summits or at beautiful, remote mountain lakes belie the risk inherent in mountaineering and off-trail travel. Social media is also used to organize large group outings (e.g., school groups, church groups, Scouts), bringing together recreationists with different levels of experience, fitness, knowledge, and judgment. This unevenness can lead to dissent and division, with stronger members forging ahead while weaker members are left behind. The following scenarios often arise:

The stronger members forge ahead and the others wait or return to their point of origin. In some instances, the slower group may be left behind on their own to find their way back, which is especially dangerous if members are on perilous, unknown terrain outside of their comfort level and ability. This situation has led to several searches, many involving accidents.

The stronger members forge ahead while the others try desperately to keep up, often resulting in catastrophic outcomes. As those trying to keep up become fatigued and careless, they are more likely to succumb to injuries due to a misstep or a fall. Some individuals will attempt shortcuts on unknown terrain and become lost or injured. On a hot mountain day, a fatigued person trying to keep up can easily suffer from extreme dehydration and heat-related illness. Finally, when groups become separated, then overdue, they often request assistance from rescue teams. All of these situations have occurred, and several have led to fatal outcomes. In one instance, a group of three climbers attempted the Middle Teton by way of the regular route, the Southwest Couloir. The two stronger climbers arrived at the summit well ahead of the third climber. When the third climber arrived at the top, the other two immediately began their descent without waiting for him. A short distance from the summit, the third climber slipped and fell nearly a thousand feet to his death, most likely while trying to catch up with his faster friends.

A stronger member of the party, unhappy with the group's progress, ventures off on his/her own, most likely climbing unroped. This situation has occurred several times. In one case, a large group of teenagers set out to climb the Middle Teton. When they arrived at the saddle between the South and Middle Tetons, most were ready to head back, except for one of the leaders who was very physically fit and decided to climb to the summit. While the rest of the group was returning to the valley, she summited and, on the way back down, either lost her way or, most likely, took a shortcut to try and catch up to the group. Unfortunately, the shortcut ended at the top of a cliff, where she slipped and fell to her death.

Group dynamics played a role in the above situations. Individuals who organize and lead groups should be committed to maintaining the integrity of the group. The pace must accommodate all members of the group, and no one should be left behind. Impatience should have no role in the group's progress, and members must be willing to turn around and return without achieving their established goal. If the group does split up, which may be more desirable than pushing individuals beyond their physical capabilities, all must agree to the decision to separate, and a specific plan must be outlined and made known to all group members. The separated parties also should be able to communicate with one another in some manner at prearranged times.

In recent years, several mountaineering parties, both roped and unroped, have become stuck on routes. Most often the parties have climbed off-route, become lost or benighted, or found themselves subject to a significant weather change or event. If moving through unfamiliar terrain, be sure to continuously take note of the path of travel: look back frequently, build cairns if needed, and look for potential rappel stations in the event of a necessary retreat. When rescuers interviewed these stuck parties, they often heard some version of the following: "We wouldn't have continued but we knew we could always call the rangers for help." Good judgment and self-reliance are the keys here.

Before a party sets out on a climb, it is imperative that all members know how to retreat from a "stuck" situation and be willing to sacrifice gear to do so. Members should be capable of ascending a rope safely in the event they end up in a location where they must ascend the rope (for example, under an overhang). All members should also have appropriate clothing should they become benighted during a long ascent. Rescue rangers will assist a stuck party as soon as they are able to, but do not expect that to happen immediately. If a team becomes benighted on a route, it is very likely that rangers will not be able to respond until morning. If the party gets stuck during a thunderstorm, rangers will have to wait at least until the lightning stops before responding. If a storm is approaching, do not begin to climb or, if already on the route, follow a predetermined escape plan. The Teton Range is notorious for sometimes violent changes in weather that can happen during any time of the year.

A prior accident analysis report of the period from 1925 through 1995 found the primary cause of accidents to be falls from slips while traveling on snow while climbing unroped. Currently, the major cause of accidents is unroped climbing on rock, a switch that may be explained by the changing climate: there is some evidence that winter snow accumulation has decreased and that, due to generally warmer temperatures during the spring and summer climbing seasons, snowmelt in the range may occur earlier in the year. However, climate change is unpredictable, and some summers may exhibit deep, lingering snow accumulations resulting in a significant increase in incidents involving slips while traveling on snow while climbing unroped. Be sure to call the Jenny Lake Ranger Station (or check their blog) when planning a climb in the Teton Range.

The Probability of Getting Hurt while Climbing in the Tetons: A Statistical Analysis

During the late 1970s, human traffic counters were placed at trailheads and other locations throughout the park to determine how park resources were being utilized in the main hiking and climbing areas. That traffic-counter information, along with additional resource information (for example, that approximately 40 percent of people leaving the Lupine Meadows trailhead enter Garnet Canyon), was used to estimate the numbers of people in various locations, which then helped the National Park Service (NPS) determine risk of injury (expressed as probability and odds). Three counter locations of particular interest for calculating high-risk incident activity in the mountain peak areas included:

- **The Lupine Meadows trailhead and Garnet Canyon traffic counters—for estimating incident probabilities in Garnet Canyon and the surrounding mountains (Nez**

Perce, Cloudveil Dome, Spalding Peak, the South Teton, the Middle Teton, the Grand Teton, and routes on the south aspect of Disappointment Peak)
- The Teewinot Apex trail traffic counter—for estimating incident probabilities in the Teewinot Mountain area

Probability and odds calculations were based on two factors: estimates of the total number of individuals in the specified areas during the months of July and August from 2007 through 2014—which reflected peak hiking and climbing activity levels, and included complete, reliable data—and the number of search and rescue (SAR) incidents that occurred within the specified areas during the same time period. Table 1 summarizes the resulting calculations.

To put matters into perspective, consider the Garnet Canyon area with odds of 1:630. Suppose, for example, that during peak season an average of 250 people depart from the Lupine Meadows trailhead each day. About 100 of these people will take the Garnet Canyon trail (40 percent of 250). Over a period of 6.3 days, 630 people will enter Garnet Canyon and one incident is expected to occur.

Based on Table 1, about 85 people enter Garnet Canyon per day (42,198 total people/8 years/62 days per year). It would take about 7.4 days for 630 people to enter the canyon, at which time an incident would be expected to occur. Garnet Canyon, which attracts a substantial level of human activity and thus sees the highest number of incidents, has the highest odds of a SAR incident. In 2018, about 8,350 people entered Garnet Canyon during July and August, a 58.3 percent increase in activity when compared to the 2007–2014 period.

Applying the same calculations to the Teewinot area, about 22 people per day enter the area, and it would take about 70 days for 1,540 people to enter the area, during which time an incident would be expected. Teewinot offers easy access and an (allegedly) easy ascent, so most people, especially novices, climb the mountain unroped, which can result in a disastrous outcome. In 2018, about 875 people entered the Teewinot area during July and August, a 34.9 percent decrease in activity when compared to the 2007–2014 period.

Prior to the 1990s, both day-use, off-trail climbers and hikers and overnight-use climbers and hikers were required to register their activities with the NPS. Hence, detailed data were available for the numbers of climbers attempting peaks and off-trail hikes in all of Grand Teton National Park. One analysis determined that about three incidents occurred per 1,000 individuals who entered the Garnet Canyon area. The current odds of 1:630 is equivalent to about 1.6 incidents per 1,000 individuals entering the Garnet Canyon area, indicating that the current rate has dropped by about a factor of one-half from the historical rate. One can only speculate why, but possible explanations may include better equipment, better park informational services, a changing climate that has resulted in better climbing conditions, etc.

Approach Canyons

From 2000 to 2018, there were 99 incidents in approach canyons containing unofficial, minimally maintained trails and in trailed canyon areas where people went off-trail to scramble on slabs or over passes compromised by snow or other unusual circumstances. Most accidents occurred in Garnet Canyon (61), followed by Avalanche Canyon (7), the Delta Lake area (6), Paintbrush Divide (5), Hanging Canyon (4), and Glacier Gulch (3). Eight other canyon areas had one or two incidents.

The incidents that occurred in Garnet Canyon included 23 trauma incidents, 11 medical incidents, nine searches, six medical incidents at the Lower Saddle, three trauma incidents at the Lower Saddle (fall on snow, hit by rockfall at the fixed rope, lower leg injury while hiking), five falls due to slips while traveling on snow while climbing unroped, three rockfall incidents causing trauma, and one incident while climbing unroped. (See *Figure A-3*.)

Additionally, there were four unroped climbing incidents in other areas (one each in Cascade Canyon, Hanging Canyon, the Hidden Falls area, and the Inspiration Point area); one slip while traveling on snow on Paintbrush Divide; two incidents while glissading on snow (one each in Cascade Canyon and Hanging Canyon); four traumatic injuries and one lost person in the Delta Lake/Glacier Gulch area; four traumatic injuries in Avalanche Canyon; eight stuck parties (three in Avalanche Canyon, two on Paintbrush Divide, two in the Delta Lake area, and one in the Leigh Canyon area); and 14 incidents in other areas (seven traumatic incidents and seven medical incidents).

DISCUSSION

The majority of these incidents in approach canyons occurred because climbers (or advanced hikers) had underestimated the Teton terrain. The "trail" in Avalanche Canyon is unmaintained, and the canyon itself is a wilderness area with hundreds of downed trees, swampy areas, rugged and extensive boulder fields, cliff areas that often hold significant amounts of accumulated snow with moats, and subalpine shrub areas that are difficult to cross. Hanging Canyon is another rugged, U-shaped canyon flanked by high peaks, though it is not as demanding to navigate as Avalanche Canyon. The mystique of these areas and their surrounding peaks lures climbers to their slopes, and they often find themselves climbing unroped on steep rock or snow, which can result in a slip with serious consequences. Paintbrush Divide is a favorite destination of many trekkers, but when it is packed with snow (generally through July), it can be extremely dangerous for any novice or intermediate hiker.

Many of the individuals who suffered injuries were unprepared for the conditions; lacked the proper equipment (crampons, ice axe, etc.) or did not know how to use it (for example, could not perform a self-arrest using an ice axe); were carrying extremely heavy backpacks; or succumbed to a medical issue (high-altitude sickness) or a minor traumatic injury (sprained

Table 1. Probability and Odds Summary for Areas of Interest during July and August, 2007–2014

LOCATION	NUMBER OF INCIDENTS	NUMBER OF PEOPLE	PROBABILITY OF INCIDENT	ODDS OF INCIDENT
Garnet Canyon	67	42,198	0.0015878	1:630
Teewinot Mountain area	7	10,753	0.0006510	1:1,536

FIGURE A-3. Number of Incidents by Accident Category in Garnet Canyon, 2000–2018, N = 61

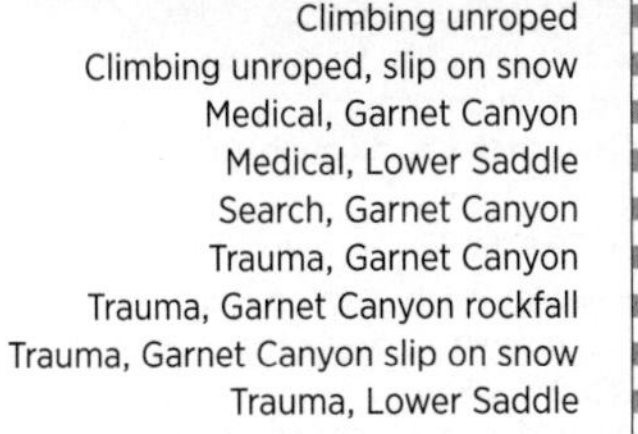

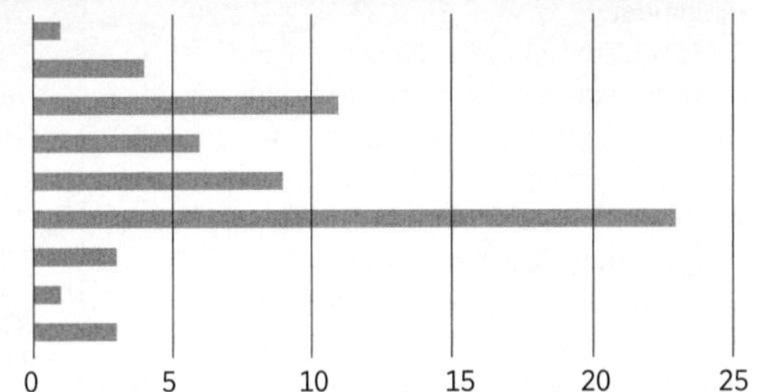

ankle). The Teton Range, although appealing and accessible, is characterized by rugged, steep terrain. The Lower Saddle is about 7.5 miles from the valley floor. If an individual averages one yard per step, they will take about 13,000 steps to reach the Lower Saddle. Add another 2,000 steps to get to the summit of the Grand Teton. Add in the return trip, and a minimum of 30,000 steps are taken during the endeavor of climbing the Grand Teton. All of this occurs on extremely rugged terrain while ascending, and then descending, 7,000 feet from the valley floor to the summit and back. Consider this: one misstep can have serious consequences, including death.

Finally, individuals undertaking treks must be physically and mentally prepared. A lack of physical fitness and pushing too hard can result in high-altitude sickness or other medical issues. Exhaustion can lead to carelessness while hiking on the trail, resulting in sprained ankles, falls, injuries to extremities, and other complications. On Paintbrush Divide, hikers can become mentally terrified or physically compromised, even when the trail is not covered with snow. Hikers need to be willing to turn around due to any alarming situation, whether it be lightning, steepness of the terrain, or snow.

In addition to having the proper gear for a given situation and knowing how to use it, remaining properly nourished and adequately hydrated is imperative. Many trekkers succumb to dehydration-related illnesses (high-altitude sickness, heat-related illness, etc.) because they run out of water. They are reluctant to drink from a mountain stream because they fear ingesting giardia, even though dehydration could kill them in hours, whereas giardia and other waterborne pathogens can take days to produce (curable) illnesses.

In general, before one undertakes excursions in the challenging environment of the Tetons, it can be advantageous to first gain experience in lower-altitude, more hospitable environments.

Rock-Climbing Areas

Grand Teton National Park contains several accessible rock-climbing and bouldering areas where one can gain strength and develop and hone climbing skill. These include the Blacktail Butte area (Lower and Upper Buttes), Boulder City, Exum Practice Rocks (Hidden Falls area), and Storm Point (Guides' Wall route). Other areas dedicated mostly to rock climbing—Death Canyon and Disappointment Peak—are included in the *Mountain Peaks* section above, since several incidents involved climbing to their summits.

There were 12 total incidents from 2000 to 2018, and the area experiencing the greatest number was the Exum Practice Rocks (three injuries while climbing roped, one while climbing unroped, one from stumbling on a rock, and one of unknown origin), followed by Storm Point (two injuries while climbing roped, one while rappelling), Blacktail Butte (one injury while climbing roped, one while climbing unroped), and Boulder City (a fall while bouldering).

Ten of the incidents resulted in trauma to the lower extremities, one resulted in a dislocated shoulder (Exum Practice Rocks), and the other was a fatality from multiple trauma after rappelling off the end of the rope (Storm Point).

DISCUSSION

Compared with the mountain locations, rock-climbing areas (which do not involve climbing to a summit) seem simple and straightforward; however, accidents with injuries do occur, and they are sometimes fatal. Almost all the injuries were due to falls, the lengthiest of which involved roped climbers: one 35-foot fall involved a roped climber who fell into a tree and sustained a fracture, and one fatal incident involved a lengthy fall while rappelling. On the mountain peaks, several incidents also involved rappelling mishaps, and these incidents were rarely survived.

More than a few of the rock-climbing incidents involved anchor failures. Because anchors are subject to constant wear and weathering with freeze-thaw cycles, old anchors encountered on climbing routes in the Teton Range should never be routinely trusted. Instead, before trusting an anchor, always examine the rock into which the anchor is placed, test fixed pitons with a hammer for sound placement, and replace existing webbing. Also create a rappel checklist—and use it for every rappel.

Winter Ski-Mountaineering Incidents

Winter ski-mountaineering incidents rarely happened prior to the 1970s, suggesting a limited number of backcountry excursions in the winter months during that period. Starting in the mid-1970s, winter incidents began to gradually increase to one or two incidents per year, and in the 1990s, five different years experienced three incidents. From 2000 through 2019, the number of incidents per year increased at a greater rate, to the point where it is now common to see more than three incidents per year. The most incidents occurred in 2011 (13 incidents), followed by 11 in 2018; six in 2001; four each in 2006, 2007, and 2014; and three each in 2000 and 2009. All other years had two or fewer incidents.

During the period 2000–2019, 74 winter incidents occurred, averaging about 4 incidents per year. The area with the greatest number of incidents was Granite Canyon (37), followed by the Taggart Lake area (7), Death Canyon (6), Mount Moran (3), and Cascade Canyon, Garnet Canyon, the Middle Teton, Shadow Peak, and the South Teton (2 each). Eleven additional areas had one incident each.

The most common activities corresponding to the incidents involved skiing (32) or snowboarding (4) from Jackson

Hole Mountain Resort into Granite Canyon; skiing (24), snowshoeing (7), or snowboarding (1) in the backcountry of Grand Teton National Park; and getting caught in avalanches (6) in several areas of the park, which resulted in eight fatalities.

DISCUSSION

Ski mountaineering (including snowboarding) has evolved to the point where extremely difficult ski excursions involving mountains with steep couloir descents are now common. Some of the excursions involving accidents occurred on the mountain peaks (about eight peaks over 19 years), but most occurred at lower elevations in canyons off park roads, or while descending into Granite Canyon from Jackson Hole Mountain Resort. Due to the extreme weather conditions during the winter months in the Teton Range, these mountain incidents generally occurred in late spring/early summer.

The significant increase in ski mountaineering may be explained by several factors:

- the opening of the ski area boundaries in Jackson Hole Mountain Resort in 1999;
- a significant increase in ski guiding in the park over the past 15 years, matched to a degree by an increase in ski mountaineering among the public;
- the growing popularity of ski mountaineering as a result of media and social media exposure.

Since the ski area opened its boundaries in 1999, skiers and snowboarders have commonly dropped into the steep couloirs of Granite Canyon. They are often unprepared for what may follow: a fall while skiing a steep couloir or, after exiting the couloir, a lengthy ski to exit the canyon in very deep snow on difficult terrain that is challenging to navigate. Many skiers and snowboarders who become lost or benighted lack the clothing and equipment for an overnight stay. All riders must be prepared for travel in this extremely cold environment.

Additionally, anyone engaging in winter ski trips in the Teton backcountry must have the complete avalanche skills package including, but not limited to, the following: a general sense of the season's weather and avalanche history up to the point of departure; an awareness of the daily avalanche forecast and discussion; an awareness of the current weather forecast, discussion, and outlook; good snow-stability evaluation skills; a knowledge of the terrain one is venturing into and good terrain evaluation skills; and excellent backcountry rescue skills and equipment.

Most of the 74 winter incidents from 2000 through 2019 were due to falling while skiing, getting caught in an avalanche, becoming lost while skiing, being too fatigued to continue while skiing, and being overdue. This trend is expected to continue, and perhaps increase, as expanded access and social media exposure encourage more people to undertake winter activities. There were eight fatalities attributable to avalanches, involving six different excursions.

Finally, several incidents involved parties undertaking straightforward ski or snowshoeing trips on easy terrain, such as in the Taggart Lake area, Death Canyon, and Granite Canyon. Many individuals in these parties underestimated the conditions in the Teton backcountry during winter, became lost or disoriented, or succumbed to the cold. Anyone going on treks during the winter months, as easy as such excursions may seem, needs to be prepared and knowledgeable about what they are doing. Beginners should consider staying on groomed roads or trails until gaining experience. For more advanced, off-trail outings, avalanche transceivers, probes, and shovels (and the knowledge of how to use them); GPS units; and SPOT satellite devices can all be useful, and even lifesaving. Take extra food and clothing and avoid stream channels and lake areas that are not completely frozen over.

Fatalities

Thirty-six incidents involving 41 fatalities occurred in Grand Teton National Park from 2000 to 2018, averaging about two fatalities per year. The trend over time shows a gradual increase, with most fatalities occurring during the years 2011, 2012, 2013, and 2015 (4 each), followed by 2003, 2010, and 2014 (3 each). The most recent three years (2016–2018) saw only two fatalities per year, and the remaining years saw one fatality per year, except for 2006, when there were no fatalities.

Here is a breakdown of the 41 fatalities:

- Sixteen occurred while climbing unroped.
- Eight resulted from being buried in an avalanche while skiing.
- Four resulted from falls while rappelling.
- Two fatalities each resulted from:
  - being struck by lightning while climbing roped (Grand Teton);
  - falling while climbing roped (Valhalla Traverse);
  - falling in Garnet Canyon (one while hiking, one from a slip while traveling on snow);
  - skiing in the backcountry (South Teton);
  - skiing in Granite Canyon.
- One fatality each resulted from:
  - an unroped slip while traveling on snow (Spalding Peak);
  - a fall while hiking in Glacier Gulch;
  - a fall while snowboarding (Teewinot).

The location involving the most fatalities was the Grand Teton (9), followed by Teewinot (6); Garnet Canyon (4); the Middle Teton and Mount Moran (3 each); and Granite Canyon, Ranger Peak, and the South Teton (2 each). Ten other areas experienced one fatality each. (See *Figure A-4.*)

Taking a closer look at the five locations where the most fatalities occurred:

- On the Grand Teton: four climbers died from falls while climbing unroped, two from falls while climbing roped, two from being struck by lightning, and one from a fall while rappelling.
- On Teewinot: four died from falls while climbing unroped, one from a fall while rappelling, and one from a fall while snowboarding.
- In Garnet Canyon: two died after being buried in avalanche, one from a fall while hiking, and one from a slip while traveling on snow.
- On the Middle Teton: three died from falls while climbing unroped.
- On Mount Moran: two died in an avalanche while skiing, and one died from a fall while climbing unroped.

DISCUSSION

With respect to fatal outcomes, the most high-risk activity involved climbing unroped, and the most high-risk location was the Grand Teton, especially when Garnet Canyon is included in the tally. Many incidents, including fatal ones, occurred in Garnet Canyon on the approach to or descent from the climb. (See *Figure A-5.*)

When climbing the Grand is the objective, many climbers overlook the fact that the relatively low-angle slopes of the approach have many inherent dangers as well. A minor slip while traveling on snow, with the inability to self-arrest, can land a climber in talus, a moat, or a seemingly insignificant bergschrund with no escape. A slip on a rock slab, often wet and mossy, can send a climber off a precipice. Rockfall or snow avalanches from the adjacent peaks can quickly engulf someone. Perhaps it is the beauty of the peaks on the approach, or exhaustion on the descent after a demanding ascent, that lures climbers into a false sense of security and forgetfulness of the intrinsic dangers of the mountain environment. Regardless of the reason, when something does go wrong, it happens fast, suddenly, and unexpectedly; and it takes a quick reaction, even a bit of luck, to avoid a catastrophic result. It can happen to anyone.

Slips while traveling on snow can be particularly lethal when any of the following happen:

- The snowfield is lengthy and steep, and the individual tumbles head over heels.
- There is a rock band (or several bands) over which the individual falls.
- The snowfield ends in a talus field.
- The individual sliding out of control down the snow falls into a crevasse or moat, especially one with water running into it.

When crossing snowfields, climbers must be particularly cautious when there is any potential for the above lethal circumstances to occur. It is imperative to know how to self-arrest, and to do so *immediately* if a slip while traveling on snow occurs—the golden rule of self-arrest. In one case in Garnet Canyon, a climber slipped while traveling on snow. Instead of immediately self-arresting, he slid by another group of climbers while smiling, waving, and making some comments to them, thinking nothing about his situation. When he finally attempted to self-arrest, it was too late, and his slide took him into a moat created by a waterfall. It took several days, and a significant effort by rangers, to recover his body.

So how can a disastrous situation be avoided? First and foremost, remain aware of your surroundings and anticipate what can go wrong. Also be prepared physically and mentally, and never lose focus. If you are growing tired, slow down, take a rest, and eat something. If circumstances do not feel right (or become alarming), talk to other group members and take action to correct the situation (for example, take out a rope and use it). Listen to your inner feelings: on more than one occasion this author (G. Montopoli) has listened to them, and he is here now because of it. Do not be afraid to turn around and forgo the climb if a storm is approaching. And make sure to depart early, well before sunrise, and be on the way down the mountain before noon if a storm is forecast.

Never be complacent or arrogant while undertaking a perilous ascent. Having climbed the same route 20 times without incident does not guarantee that something out of the ordinary won't happen the 21st time. Remember, the mountains are dynamic, and anyone can make a mistake. Sometimes professional guides who have climbed routes hundreds of times and have explored all the mountain ranges of the world do not come home at the end of the day because an event "that could never happen" occurred. Far too many great climbers have fallen to their deaths or been hit by rockfall or ended up buried in an avalanche. So be prepared, stay aware, and gradually gain the experience that will keep you alive.

Besides the Grand Teton and Garnet Canyon, another location where several fatal events have occurred is Teewinot. When statistically adjusted for the number of climbers that ascend its slopes, Teewinot ranks as one of the deadliest locations in the park, just behind the Grand Teton area. Most likely this is due to its accessibility (the ascent begins right at the Lupine Meadows trailhead), its reputation as being an "easy" 4th-class climb, its majestic profile, and its inherent attraction to the novice climber. Unfortunately, a misstep, a slide on snow, a thunderstorm, a routefinding error (it is easy to get off-route), a fall while scrambling unroped, etc., have all resulted in serious injuries

FIGURE A-4. Number of Fatalities by Location, 2000–2018, N = 41 (number of incidents = 36)

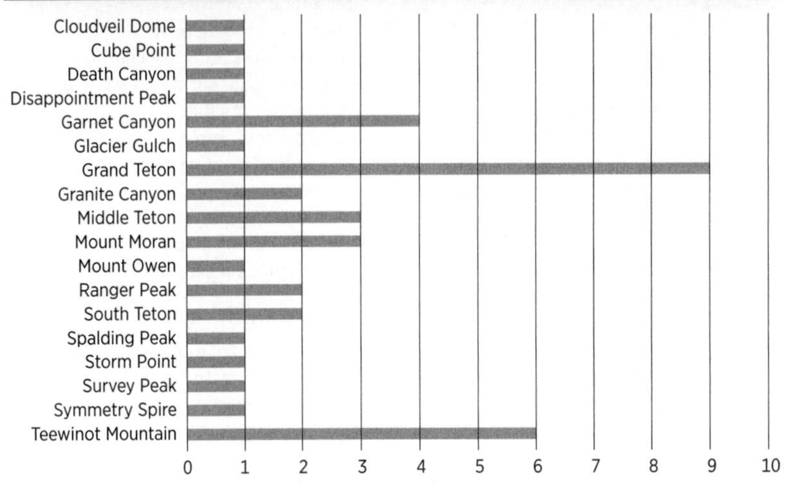

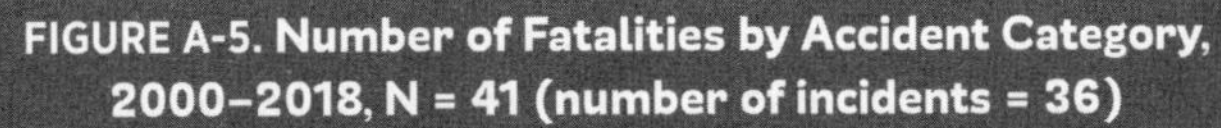

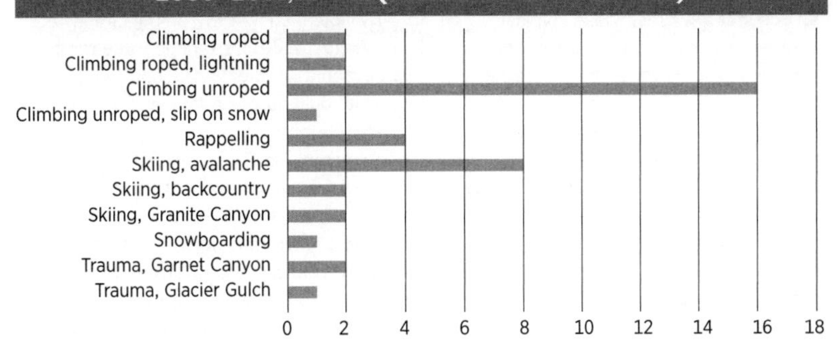

and, occasionally, death. Being aware of this fact can help, but nothing can replace being prepared, leaving early, exercising good judgment, having a rope, and turning around when events are not going according to plan.

Incident Profiles

Insight and information about incidents can help climbers be prepared for—and prevent—accidents. Knowledge can foster situational awareness, which is essential for maintaining focus on the surrounding environment and mitigating circumstances for accidents. For example, knowing when accidents tend to occur (time of day and day of week), and why, can serve as a reminder to remain vigilant.

Available data from 2000 to 2018 indicate that most incidents occur on weekends (Saturday, 71; Sunday, 57), while Wednesday sees the fewest (39). The number of incidents for the remaining days vary from 45 to 52. These numbers are perhaps a reflection of the total number of people who venture into the mountains on weekends (days off from work) versus weekdays (workdays). Weekends provide more opportunity for people in the general population to enjoy the outdoors, and the presence of more people suggests more incidents.

Of greater importance is time of day. Most accidents (68 percent) occur between 10 AM and 6 PM, with just over 20 percent occurring between 2 and 4 PM—the two-hour period with the greatest frequency of incidents. This coincides with when many parties are either beginning their descent or are well into it. Generally, significant effort is put into the ascent. Once the summit (or goal) has been attained, a sigh of relief may follow (the adrenaline rush drops off), and the climber may relax, lose focus, and become careless—an accident waiting to happen. Also, with all of one's energy and force propelled forward and downward on the descent, it becomes more difficult to catch a stumble. The bottom line: never lose focus or concentration until the trailhead is at hand. Enjoy the trip, but at only at a pace that allows you to maintain control at all times.

Do males and females present different accident profiles? From 2000 to 2018, 97 females suffered injuries while 332 males suffered injuries—a ratio of 1:3.4

FIGURE A-6. Number of Search-and-Rescue Incidents by Gender, 2000–2018, N (females) = 97 and N (males) = 332

	MALE PROFILE	FEMALE PROFILE
AVERAGE AGE	35.8	32.5
MEDIAN AGE	31	26.5
n (for age calculations)	304	84

(or roughly, for every two females who are injured, seven males are injured). This could simply result from more males undertaking mountain activities than females, but no hard data currently supports that claim. For the 84 females for whom ages were available, the average age of those suffering accidents was 32.5 years, and the median age was 26.5 years (suggesting a skew toward a few older females). For the 304 males for whom ages were available, the average age of those suffering accidents was 35.8 years, and the median age was 31 years (also suggesting a skew toward a few older males). Although the average age of males suffering injuries was slightly older than that of females, the difference was small (about three years). (See *Figure A-6.*)

Awareness of a Changing Climate

The long-term trend of climate, along with short-term, intense weather events, has resulted in unpredictable environmental changes: during the winter, average to higher-than-average snow levels may occur at higher elevations, with little to nonexistent snow levels in the valley; there are frequent rain events during late winter/early spring, layered between snow events; late spring can be dry or exceedingly wet; summers can be unusually hot; and intense, sustained wind events can occur at any time. These atypical occurrences may simply be attributable to yearly, seasonal variations in weather, but it seems likelier that they are due to widespread climatic changes. These changes—both to the climate at a regional scale and in local weather patterns—may soon become the norm. The implication is that hikers, climbers, and other outdoor adventurers will have to adapt to such shifts to prevent disastrous outcomes on their treks.

Adaptations may require new avalanche assessment strategies for spring snow conditions not previously experienced; new techniques for addressing excessively hot daily temperatures during the summer to prevent heat-related illnesses; preparation for high-wind events; and a new awareness of the power of approaching thunderstorms. The biggest rescue operation in the park's SAR history took place in 2010 after a thunderstorm hit the peaks relatively early in the morning.

Additionally, outdoor adventurers should anticipate and be prepared for other rare events that may become more frequent. For example, recent studies on the effects of a warming climate in Europe indicate that extremely warm temperatures have triggered unusual rockfall activity in the Swiss Alps. The same increase in rockfall activity may also be occurring in the Teton Range (the Stettner Couloir, Nez Perce, Cascade Canyon, etc.). These changes are most likely attributable to a warming climate, and they may be a precursor of things to come.

Climbers should be prepared for atypical, violent downpours, often interspersed with significant lightning. These storms may begin in the morning and last all day, or suddenly appear in the afternoon or evening. They may turn to snow at any moment and at any elevation. One particularly violent snowstorm on the Grand Teton on August 7, 2015, stranded three climbers between the Lower and Upper Saddles, and it could have resulted in two deaths were it not for a coordinated rescue effort among rangers, Exum guides, and a local doctor who was camped at the Lower Saddle. Unless climbers become aware of the dangers inherent in outdoor activities in an unpredictable, changing environment—and prepare for them—the frequency of such disasters is likely to increase.

Appendix B: The Best Climbs in the Tetons

Given the quantity and variety of climbing routes found in the Tetons, climbers with extensive experience in the range tend to develop preferences for certain routes. These preferences may be based on many different things such as the view from the summit or the top of the climb, the relative solidity of the rock, the position and quality of the route, or the exhilarating nature of one or more of the pitches, or of the entire climb. The climbs highlighted below are based on this author's (R. Jackson's) personal opinion and experience; an RJ indicates climbs that I have done. Note that some of the following routes were selected primarily for their historical significance. These recommended climbs are ranked further, from zero stars to ★★★★. Keep in mind that many of these routes are mountaineering objectives that require good judgment and respect.

Baxter's Pinnacle

SOUTH RIDGE TO UPPER SOUTH FACE, II, 5.9 RJ ★★★
Good climb and short approach! All of the one-pitch pinnacle climbs are excellent as well.

Buck Mountain

EAST RIDGE, II, 4.0 RJ ★★★
The final portion is a classic, exposed ridge leading directly to the summit.

NORTH CENTRAL RIDGE, III, 5.8 RJ ★
This is the ridge that is so striking during summer evenings when alpenglow lights up the north face.

Cloudveil Dome

ARMED ROBBERY, IV, 5.8R RJ ★★
Excellent climb that follows a long crack system, a rarity in the Tetons.

SILVER LINING, IV, 5.10+ RJ ★★★
A bit better and much harder than its companion to the west.

EAST RIDGE, II, 5.0 RJ ★★
Classic, short ridge climb up from col.

Cube Point

EAST RIDGE, II, 5.4 RJ ★★
Great position and scenic location.

Disappointment Peak

SOUTHEAST RIDGE, II, 4.0 RJ ★★
This has become the "regular route" up the peak and it is pretty fun.

EAST RIDGE, II, 5.6/5.7 RJ ★★★
Excellent route with great exposure, rock, and position.

CHOUINARD-FROST CHIMNEY, IV, 5.9+ RJ ★★★
This climb ascends a striking feature on a magnificent face.

OPEN BOOK, III, 5.9 RJ ★★★★
A must-do climb—one that can be done many times!

IRENE'S ARÊTE, III, 5.8 RJ ★★★★
This is one of the classic rock climbs in the entire range, another that can be returned to many times!

WHITON-WIGGINS, VARIATION: SACCO-VANZETTI MEMORIAL, III, 5.10 RJ ★★★
This is a good climb on predominantly excellent rock leading almost directly to the summit.

East Cascade Buttresses

NO PERCHES NECESSARY, I, 5.9 RJ ★★
In the never-ending search for the Teton climb with the shortest approach, this one is highly recommended—take the boat!

The Enclosure

SOUTH COULOIR, II, 3.0 RJ ★★★
This couloir is pretty grungy, but a trip to the Enclosure is worth it.

SOUTH FACE, JIM'S BIG DAY, III, 5.10- RJ ★★
The roof pitch is the main event, but there are a couple of other nice pitches.

NORTHWEST RIDGE, V, 5.7 RJ ★★★
Rarely done in its entirety, the full Northwest Ridge is a historic classic, although the upper ridge via one of the variations is probably a better option.

ENCLOSURE ICE COULOIR–UPPER NORTHWEST RIDGE, IV, 5.7, AI3 RJ ★★★★
A classic alpine tour combining a beautiful ice climb and a few pitches of excellent rock climbing.

THREE SHOTS IN THE DIZZY WIND, IV, AI5, M6 ★★
This route is perhaps the most difficult mixed climb on the Grand Teton or the Enclosure, yet it is rarely in condition.

HIGH ROUTE, IV, 5.9 RJ ★★★
An easier alternative to its two neighbors, but nevertheless an excellent alpine tour. The route has been done as an ice/mixed route, but those conditions are hard to find.

LOWE ROUTE, IV, 5.10+ RJ ★★★★
This route is perhaps the most physically demanding (chimneying!) of the three routes done thus far on this face.

NORTH FACE, EMOTIONAL RESCUE, VARIATION: DIRECT, IV, 5.10- RJ ★★★★
An outstanding rock climb in an outrageous setting with an approach that will discourage some folks.

VISIONQUEST COULOIR, IV, 5.8, AI3+ RJ ★★★★
This route is a great alternative to the regular Black Ice Couloir.

Fairshare Tower, Watchtower

CORKSCREW, II, 5.8 RJ ★★★
A good route to do on your way up Garnet Canyon.

Grand Teton

OWEN-SPALDING, II, 5.4 RJ ★★★★
The classic first-ascent route on the Grand Teton, with several variations.

POWNALL-GILKEY, II, 5.8 RJ ★★★
Quite a bit harder than the Owen-Spalding, but on really good rock.

BEAN'S SHINING WALL OF STORMS, V, 5.12B ★★★★
The hardest rock route on the Grand Teton—a proud line on excellent stone.

BEYER-HARTMAN, III, 5.10A ★★★
Located on the same wall as Bean's, this is that climb's easier neighbor.

JACKSON-RICKERT CRACK, III, 5.10R RJ ★★
The prominent crack as seen from the Lower Saddle. Try this or Burgette Arête, variation—Angel Boy OW (III, 5.10+) if up for an offwidth challenge.

EXUM RIDGE, II, 5.6 RJ ★★★★
The ultraclassic route on the Grand Teton.

DURRANCE DIRECT (LOWER EXUM RIDGE) OR PETZOLDT DIRECT TO UPPER EXUM RIDGE, III, 5.7 OR 5.7+ RJ ★★★★
The two best south side routes on the Grand Teton. For harder variations on the Durrance Direct, try Gold Face (III, 5.10-) or Wooden Ships (III, 5.10-R).

STETTNER-CHEVY-FORD COULOIRS, II, AI3, STEEP SNOW RJ ★★★
The classic south side snow/ice couloirs leading directly to the summit of the Grand Teton; also the most popular ski descent.

CRYSTAL TOWER, III, 5.10 RJ ★★★**; CRYSTAL RIGHT, III, 5.10, A0** ★★★
Crystal Tower is a classic, difficult rock route on the Underhill Ridge. It and Crystal Right, its next-door neighbor, are both on impeccable stone.

LEV, III, 5.8 RJ; EAST FACE, LEFT CENTER, III, 5.10- RJ; BEYER EAST FACE I, III, 5.9 RJ; KEITH-EDDY EAST FACE, III, 5.10- RJ ★★★
These excellent Grand Teton east face routes are all next to/near each other on exceptional rock.

EAST RIDGE WITH TRICKY TRAVERSE OF THE MOLAR TOOTH, III, 5.7 RJ ★★★
A classic, friendly alpine route—the second route done on the Grand Teton—that leads direct as an arrow to the summit.

ROUTE CANAL, IV, 5.9, WI5 ★★★
Classic, difficult ice route and fine alpine climb when linked with the upper East Ridge.

HOSSACK-MACGOWAN COULOIR, IV, 5.6, HIGH-ANGLE SNOW RJ ★★★
Analog to the Stettner-Chevy-Ford, but on the Grand's north face. Most difficult and direct ski-descent route.

GRAND NORTH COULOIR (SHEA'S CHUTE), IV, 5.8, WI5 ★★★
Rarely in condition, yet the Grand's most difficult ice line.

SIMPLETON'S PILLAR, IV, 5.9+ RJ ★★★
A more difficult alternative to the standard North Face.

NORTH FACE, IV, 5.8 RJ ★★★
The classic *nordwand* in the United States. The 1953 Direct Finish pitches—the Pendulum Pitch and the traverse into the "V"—can also be used to extend and complement the classic North Ridge or the Italian Cracks.

GOLDEN PILLAR, V, 5.12- ★★★★
The modern-day North Face and a very difficult line on golden rock, leading directly to the summit of the Grand.

NORTH RIDGE, IV, 5.8+ RJ ★★★★
The classic north side route on the Grand Teton, especially when done with the Direct Finish variation to the North Face route.

NORTH RIDGE, VARIATION: ITALIAN CRACKS, IV, 5.7/5.8 RJ ★★★
An easier alternative to the North Ridge, on good rock. Also a good one to finish with the Direct Finish of the North Face route.

LOKI'S TOWER, IV, 5.9+ RJ ★★★
Having seen very few ascents, this route is arguably a more direct, yet more difficult, North Ridge.

NORTHWEST CHIMNEY, IV, 5.9 RJ ★★★★
A dark, foreboding, and mysterious route, yet an outstanding alpine climb. Climb the Jackson-Kimbrough Contortion variation (V, 5.9, AI3) for the best of the Grand's west face routes.

WEST FACE, IV, 5.8 RJ ★★★★
The classic alpine climb on the Grand Teton. Utilize the Black Ice Couloir as the approach for the climb.

BLACK ICE COULOIR, IV, 5.7, AI3+ RJ ★★★★
The classic alpine ice couloir on the Grand Teton—and in the United States. The adjacent Alberich's Alley variation (IV, 5.9, AI4) is a more difficult and worthy alternative.

The Grand Traverse, VI, 5.8 RJ ★★★★

The must-do, classic traverse in the heart of the range.

The Jaw

EAST FACE, I, 2.0 RJ ★★★
This is a classic spring snow climb as well as an outrageous ski descent.

Matternought Peak

TAMINAH ARÊTE, III, 5.9 RJ ★★★
A full Teton adventure day awaits!

LAZY BONES, III, 5.10B; LOS HUESOS, III, 5.10+; DEM BONES, III, 5.10 RJ ★★
Pick one of these; they are apparently all pretty good. You may not want to come all the way back up for another—this author didn't!

Middle Teton

SOUTHWEST COULOIR, II, 3.0 RJ ★★
Climbs better as an early-season snow climb.

BUCKINGHAM (SOUTHEAST) RIDGE, III, 5.7 RJ ★★★★
Great climb, scenic location, excellent rock.

DIRECT EAST BUTTRESS, IV, 5.11- RJ ★★
A fun rock climb if you are in the Meadows for a few days.

MIDDLE TETON GLACIER, III, 5.4, AI2+ ★★★
A classic moderate Teton snow-and-ice climb leading to the summit of the peak.

TAYLOR, V, 5.11A ★★★
Excellent rock climb.

NORTH WALL, V, 5.10D, A2; MIDDLE FINGER, V, 5.11+/5.12A ★★
A very difficult climb in a magnificent setting.

JACKSON-WOODMENCEY DIHEDRAL, III, 5.10- RJ ★★
Fun moderate rock route.

BUFFALO GALS, III, 5.10 RJ ★★★
Another fun moderate rock route—a more difficult alternative to the regular North Ridge.

NORTH RIDGE, II, 5.6 RJ ★★
A must-do route from the Lower Saddle and a key part of the Grand Traverse.

NORTHWEST ICE COULOIR, III, 5.6, AI3 RJ ★★★★
Super-classic Teton ice moderate leading directly to the summit. A bonus AI4 pitch lies below the normal start if it's in shape.

Mount Moran

SOUTH BUTTRESS RIGHT, IV, 5.11A/B RJ ★★★★
The classic rock climb of the Teton Range!

SOUTH BUTTRESS HOUDINI, V, 5.11D ★★★
A difficult line on impeccable rock.

KELLEY-BEYER, VI, 5.12-R/X, A0 ★★★
One of the most difficult climbs in the range and definitely a Grade VI if you go all the way to the summit, as the first ascensionists did.

SOUTH BUTTRESS PROW, IV, 5.12B ★★★
A beautiful line put up in impeccable style!

DIRECT SOUTH BUTTRESS, V, 5.8, A1, OR V, 5.12A RJ ★★★★
The classic south side climb—go to the summit!

SOUTHWEST COULOIR, II, 5.4 RJ ★★
A truly spectacular place to visit in early spring or wintertime.

CMC, II, 5.5 RJ ★★
Fantastic position with spectacular views—a must-do on Moran and well worth repeating.

SKILLET GLACIER, II, 5.4, AI2+ RJ ★★★
Classic, steep snow climb and spectacular ski run!

NORTHEAST RIDGE, II, 5.4 ★
Easy and lengthy ramble up Moran, perhaps the easiest route up the peak.

TRIPLE GLACIER, II, 5.6, AI2+ ★★★
Incredible wilderness setting with spectacular views.

Mount Owen

KOVEN, II, 5.5, STEEP SNOW RJ ★★★
The best condition for the climb is early season, with hard snow, requiring an ice axe and crampons.

NORTHEAST SNOWFIELDS, III, 5.6, STEEP SNOW RJ ★★★
When in condition, this is one of the best steep snow climbs in the range.

RUN-DON'T-WALK COULOIR, IV, 5.5, WI4+/WI5 RJ ★★★
Hard to catch in the spring when both the ice is formed up and the avalanche hazard from above is low, but it is an amazing alpine route.

NORTH RIDGE, IV, 5.7, A1, OR IV, 5.9 RJ ★★
A good route and best to combine with the Italian Cracks on the Grand Teton to get home.

SERENDIPITY ARÊTE, VARIATION: JENNI'S WAY, IV, 5.10 RJ ★★★★
The original climb is a good one, and when combined with Jenni's Way it becomes a great one!

INTREPIDITY ARÊTE, IV, 5.10B ★★★★
This is reported to be a route of the highest quality.

Mount Wister

NORTHEAST COULOIR TO UPPER EAST RIDGE, II, 4.0 RJ ★★
The classic "regular route" on the peak.

DIRECT NORTH FACE, III, 5.10- RJ ★★★
Wait for late-summer dry conditions on this face and numerous high-quality pitches will be encountered.

Mount Woodring

SOUTHWEST SLOPE, I, 2.0 RJ
If you find yourself at Holly Lake with some extra time, the views of the massive south side of Mount Moran are well worth it from the top!

Nez Perce

SUNSET FACE, III, 5.8 ★★
Although the jury is still out regarding this climb, it may just be the best route on the peak!

DIRECT SOUTH RIDGE, III, 5.7+ RJ ★
If possible, climb this ridge with the Garnet Traverse variation (III, 5.8).

No Escape Buttress

DIRECT SOUTH FACE, IV, 5.9R RJ ★★★
Good-quality rock climb and relatively short approach—get a canoe!

WEST ARÊTE, IV, 5.10B RJ ★★★
Same as above!

Omega Buttresses, Central Section

GUARDIAN OF DEATH, III, 5.12+/5.13A, A0 ★★★
The route leads up and over a huge roof that awaits a first free ascent!

OMEGA TRIANGLE, III, 5.11 ★★★
Reported to be a quality climb on excellent rock.

O-MEGA CRACK, II, 5.12B ★★★★
A testpiece with two quality pitches of rock climbing.

Prospectors Mountain

SOUTHWEST RIDGE, I, 1.0 ★★
This is a nice ramble and definitely away from the crowds.

BREAKING BARRIERS, IV, 5.12- ★★★
Reportedly a good route and a guaranteed adventure climb! (See Death Canyon, South Side Rock Climbs, *Route 6*.)

Red Sentinel

RED ALERT, II, 5.11B/C; EAST FACE AND NORTH FACE, II, 5.7 RJ ★★★★
Really any of the routes on this cool little pinnacle are good; finish up with the West Face of Disappointment Peak to get back to the trailhead.

Ship's Prow (Omega Buttresses, Eastern Section/Ship's Prow)

DIHEDRAL OF HORRORS, II, 5.9 RJ ★★★
A surprisingly good climb! Approach via the lower 5.10b crack variation.

ANNALS OF TIME, II, 5.9 RJ ★★
Climb this quality pitch while in the vicinity.

Snaz Buttress

SUNSHINE DAYDREAM, IV, 5.11- RJ ★★★
This is a quality route and it sees less traffic than its western neighbors.

THE SNAZ, IV, 5.9 RJ ★★★
Same as above, perhaps a bit more of a "mountain" route.

CAVEAT EMPTOR, IV, 5.10C RJ ★★★★
A Death Canyon classic—don't miss this one!

FREEDOM FIGHTER, IV, 5.13- ★★★
A Death Canyon testpiece on a proud section of the Snaz Buttress.

THE FOUNTAINHEAD, IV, 5.12AR ★★★
Very difficult modern climb with a few runouts.

AERIAL BOUNDARIES, II, 5.10B RJ ★★★★
Great route with five high-quality and varied pitches.

South Teton

NORTHWEST COULOIR, II, 4.0 RJ ★★
Climbs better as an early-season snow climb.

Spalding Peak

SOUTH FACE RIGHT, III, 5.10C ★★
Although fairly obscure and a long way to go for a climb, this is a good one.

Static Peak

SOUTHWEST RIDGE, I, 1.0 RJ ★★
A scenic trail goes nearly to the summit!

Storm Point

GUIDES' WALL, II, 5.8 RJ ★★★★
A must-do rock climb in a spectacular setting. All the variations are good as well. (See *Cascade Canyon, North Side Rock Climbs, Storm Point Cliffs* in Section 8.)

Symmetry Spire

SOUTHWEST RIDGE, II, 5.7 RJ ★★
Probably the best of the Symmetry climbs.

DURRANCE RIDGE, II, 5.6 RJ ★★
Fun route to cruise up.

RETICENT SLABS, III, 5.8 RJ ★★
Probably has the best rock of any of the Symmetry climbs.

Table Mountain

WEST SLOPE, I, 1.0 ★★★★
Fist climbed by the members of the 1872 Hayden Survey Expedition, and photographed by William Henry Jackson, this is an enduring classic!

HEARTBREAK RIDGE, III, 5.7 ★★
Great position and fun climb.

Teewinot Mountain

EAST FACE, II, 4.0 PG-13 RJ ★★
The start to the Grand Traverse and a route that is commonly underestimated.

NORTH FACE, VARIATION: EMERSON'S CHIMNEY WITH TEEWINOT TUNNEL, III, 5.8 RJ ★★
A long way up to carry gear, but the Teewinot Tunnel is a unique feature.

Teepe Pillar

DIRECT EAST FACE, III, 5.8 RJ ★★★
A fine climb on good rock and an outstanding summit!

Thor Peak

EAST FACE, VARIATION: 1994, IV, 5.9 ★★
Wilderness setting, and the route follows the main feature of the peak as viewed from the east.

HIDDEN COULOIR, III, 5.6, AI3 RJ ★★
A guaranteed adventure climb in a wilderness setting as well as one hell of a ski adventure!

West Horn

EAST RIDGE, II, 5.6 ★★
Descend the West Ridge (II, 5.4) for a classic Teton outing!

Appendix C: General References

Alpine Journal. London: The Alpine Club.

Alpinist. Jeffersonville, VT: Height of Land Publications; Katie Ives (editor). First issue 2002.

American Alpine Journal. Golden, CO: The American Alpine Club.

Appalachia. Boston: Appalachian Mountain Club.

Bartlett, Richard A. *Great Surveys of the American West.* Norman: University of Oklahoma Press, 1962.

Betts, Robert B. *Along the Ramparts of the Tetons: The Saga of Jackson Hole, Wyoming.* Niwot: University Press of Colorado, 1978.

Brower, David R., ed. *Manual of Ski Mountaineering.* San Francisco: Sierra Club, 1962.

Canadian Alpine Journal. Toronto: Alpine Club of Canada.

Climbing Magazine. Boulder, CO: Outside (publisher); Duane Raleigh (content director). First issue 1970.

Coulter, Henry, and Merrill F. McLane. *Mountain Climbing Guide to the Grand Tetons.* Hanover, NH: Dartmouth Mountaineering Club, 1947.

Dartmouth Mountaineering Club Journal. Hanover, NH: Dartmouth College.

Daugherty, John. *A Place Called Jackson Hole: A Historic Resource Study of Grand Teton National Park.* Moose, WY: Grand Teton National Park, National Park Service, 1999.

Duffy, Katy, and Darwin Wile. *Teton Trails: A Guide to the Trails of Grand Teton National Park.* Moose, WY: Grand Teton Natural History Association, 1995.

Farquhar, Francis. "Franklin Spencer Spalding and the Ascent of the Grand Teton in 1898." *American Alpine Journal* 3, no. 3 (1939): pp. 304–9, illus.

Fryxell, Fritiof M. *The Teton Peaks and Their Ascents.* Grand Teton National Park, WY: The Crandall Studios, 1932.

———. *The Tetons: Interpretations of a Mountain Landscape.* Berkeley: University of California Press, 1938. Reprint, Moose, WY: Grand Teton Natural History Association, 1995.

Fryxell, Fritiof M., and Phil D. Smith. *Mountaineering in the Tetons: The Pioneer Period, 1898–1940.* Moose, WY: Grand Teton Natural History Association, 1995.

Gooch, Wesley. *Rock Climbing Jackson Hole and Pinedale, Wyoming.* 2nd ed. Pinedale, WY: Acroterra, 2011.

Grand Teton Natural History Association. *Campfire Tales of Jackson Hole.* Rev. ed. Moose, WY: Grand Teton Natural History Association, 1990.

Grand Teton Nature Notes. Moose, WY: Grand Teton National Park, 1935–1941.

Harvard Mountaineering Club Journal. Cambridge, MA: Harvard University.

Hayden, Elizabeth Wied. *From Trapper to Tourist in Jackson Hole.* Moose, WY: Grand Teton Natural History Association, 1992.

Hayden, Ferdinand V. *Sixth Annual Report of the United States Geological Survey of the Territories, 1872.* Washington, DC: Government Printing Office, 1873.

The Iowa Climber. Iowa City: State University of Iowa.

Jeffers, LeRoy. *The Call of the Mountains.* New York: Dodd, Mead, 1922.

Langford, Nathaniel P. "The Ascent of Mount Hayden." *Scribner's Monthly,* 6, no. 2 (June 1873): pp. 129–57, illus.

Leonard, Richard M., et al. *Belaying the Leader: An Omnibus on Climbing Safety.* San Francisco: Sierra Club, 1956.

Love, J. D., and John C. Reed. *Creation of the Teton Landscape.* Moose, WY: Grand Teton Natural History Association, 1968. Reprint, 1995.

Madsen, B. D. "History of the Upper Snake River Valley, 1807–1825." Unpublished master's thesis, University of California, Berkeley, 1940.

Mattes, Merrill J. *Behind the Legend of Colter's Hell.* Cheyenne: Wyoming State Historical Society, 1949.

———. *Colter's Hell and Jackson Hole.* Yellowstone Park, WY: Yellowstone Library and Museum Association and Grand Teton Natural History Association in cooperation with National Park Service, US Department of the Interior, 1962.

———. "Jackson Hole, Crossroads of the Western Fur Trade." *Pacific Northwest Quarterly* 37, no. 2 (April 1946): pp. 87–108; 39, no. 1 (January 1948): pp. 3–32. Reprinted with permission by Jackson Hole Historical Society, 1987.

The Mazama. Portland, OR: The Mazamas.

Minnesota Naturalist 8, no. 2 (1957); 22, no. 1 (1961).

The Mountaineer. Seattle: The Mountaineers.

Mountaineering: The Freedom of the Hills. 9th ed. Seattle: Mountaineers Books, 2017.

Murie, Olaus J. *Jackson Hole with a Naturalist.* Jackson, WY: Frontier Press, 1963.

Nielsen, Cynthia, and Elizabeth Wied Hayden. *Origins: A Guide to the Place Names of Grand Teton National Park and the Surrounding Area.* Moose, WY: Grand Teton Natural History Association, 1988.

Petzoldt, Patricia. *On Top of the World.* New York: Thomas Y. Crowell, 1953.

Raynes, Bert. *Birds of Grand Teton National Park and the Surrounding Area.* Moose, WY: Grand Teton Natural History Association, 1984.

Righter, Robert W. *Crucible for Conservation: The Creation of Grand Teton National Park.* Boulder: Colorado Associated University Press, 1982. (A newer edition, subtitled *The Struggle for Grand Teton National Park,* was published by Grand Teton Natural History Association in Moose, Wyoming, in 2008.)

Robertson, Janet. *Betsy Cowles Partridge: Mountaineer.* Niwot, CO: University Press of Colorado, 1998.

Rock & Ice Magazine. Boulder, CO. First issue March 1984; final issue January 2021 (merged with *Climbing*).

Scott, M. Douglas, and Suvi A. Scott. *Wildlife of Yellowstone and Grand Teton National Parks.* Helena, MT: Wheelwright Publishing, 2008.

Shaw, Richard J. *Wildflowers of Yellowstone and Grand Teton National Parks.* Rev. ed. Salt Lake City: Wheelwright Press, 1991.

Sierra Club Bulletin. San Francisco: Sierra Club.

Sinclair, Pete. *We Aspired: The Last Innocent Americans.* Salt Lake City: University of Utah Press, 2017.

Smith, Robert B., and Lee J. Siegel. *Windows into the Earth: The Geologic Story of Yellowstone and Grand Teton National Parks.* Oxford: Oxford University Press, 2000.

Sottile, Joe. *Jackson Hole: A Sport Climbing and Bouldering Guide.* 3rd ed. Jackson, WY: Pingora Press, 1994.

Summit. Hood River, OR: Craig Sabina (publisher); David H. Swanson (executive publisher); John Harlin III (editor). First issue 1990; final issue 1996.

Summit Magazine. Big Bear Lake, CA: Jene M. Crenshaw and H. V. J. Kilness (co-publishers and editors). First issue 1955; final issue 1989.

Trail and Timberline. Denver: Colorado Mountain Club.

Turiano, Thomas. *Teton Skiing: A History and Guide to the Teton Range.* Moose, WY: Homestead Publishing, 1995.

Turner, Jack. *Teewinot: A Year in the Teton Range.* New York: St. Martin's Press, 2000.

Watson, Walcott. "History of Jackson's Hole, Wyoming, before the Year 1907." Unpublished master's thesis, Columbia University, New York, 1935.

Woolsey, Elizabeth D. *Off the Beaten Track.* Wilson, WY: Wilson Bench Press, 1984.

Opposite: A heavily rimed North Face of the Grand Teton looms above the Crooked Thumb

Index of Peaks and Routes

A

Aeolian Arête (Webb Canyon, N Side), 496–497
Aerial Boundaries (Snaz Buttress), 114
Alberich's Alley (Grand Teton), 246
Albright Peak, 114, 114–115
Alex Lowe Memorial Route (Grand Teton), 223
Alien Wall (Prospectors Mtn), 87–88
All in a Day's Work (Webb Canyon, N Side), 496
Almost Arête (Disappointment Peak), 302
Almost Overhanging (Disappointment Peak), 302
Alone (Broken Arrow Spire), 132–133
Alpine Cow (Snaz Buttress), 108, 110
American Cracks (Grand Teton), 232
Angel Boy Ow (Grand Teton), 199
Annals of Time (Omega Buttresses, E Section/ Ship's Prow), 93
Anniversary Peak, 488
Another Trailside Attraction (Glacier Gulch), 314
Apocalypse Arête (Prospectors Mtn), 77–78
Apocalypse Couloir (Prospectors Mtn), 76–77
Armed Robbery (Cloudveil Dome), 153
Art-and-Brent Pinnacle, 348
Attritus (Storm Point Cliffs), 370
August 11th Start (Snaz Buttress), 113
Avalanche Canyon (N Fork), N side rock climbs, 133–134
Avalanche Canyon (S Fork), N side rock climbs, 126
Avocet Arête (Hanging Canyon), 407
Ayres' Crag 5, 365–366, 402–403
Ayres' Crags, 401–403

B

Banded Buttress, 365
Bannon, Mt, 79
Bat Attack Crack (Storm Point Cliffs), 371
Baxter's Pinnacle, 380–384
Bean's Shining Wall of Storms (Grand Teton), 187–188
Beckey Couloir (Grand Teton), 199
Beeline (Sentinel Turret), 101–102
Beelzebub Arête (Disappointment Peak), 305
Bee's Knees (Prospectors Mtn), 84
Berry, Mt, 499
Beyer E Face I (Grand Teton), 209–210
Beyer E Face II (Grand Teton), 211–212
Beyer S Ridge (Middle Teton), 164
Beyer-Hartman (Grand Teton), 188–189
Big Bluff (Garnet Canyon, S Side), 150
Big Guy Boulder, Good Over Evil, The (Garnet Mtn), 290
Big Guy Boulder, The (Garnet Mtn, N Side), 290
Birdbrains on Ice (Teton Canyon), 518
Bivouac Peak, 481–485
Bivouac Peak, S Shoulder, 485
Black Chimney (Sentinel Turret), 102
Black Chimney (Teewinot Mtn), 322
Black Diamond (Prospectors Mtn), 83
Black Ice Couloir (Grand Teton), 244–246
Black Ice–W Face Combination (Grand Teton), 243
Blackfin, The (Mt. Moran), 428–429
Blackhouse, The (Ayres' Crag 4), 402
Blackwelder Peak, 487
Blind Man's Bluff (Avalanche Canyon), 133–134
Blobular Oscillations (Storm Point Cliffs), 370
Bonney's Pinnacle, 177
Boy Scout Falls (Teton Canyon), 517
Braeburn's Corner (Omega Buttresses, Central Section), 94
Breaching Whale Tower, S Face (Cube Point), 387
Breaking Barriers (Prospectors Mtn), 85–87
Briggs-Higbee Pillar (Middle Teton), 172–173
Broken Arrow Spire, 132–133
Brown Wall (Fairshare Tower, Watchtower), 283
Brown-Macke (Middle Teton), 171
Bubble Fun Couloir (Buck Mtn), 122
Buchwald's Blister, 73
Buck Mtn, 117–125
Buck Mtn, W Peak, 125
Buckingham (SE) Ridge (Middle Teton), 162–163
Buckingham Buttress (Grand Teton), 201
Buckingham Palace, 360
Buffalo Gals (Middle Teton), 174
Bulge, The (Death Canyon), 513
Bum's Walls (Storm Point Cliffs), 371
Bunny Love (Fairshare Tower, Watchtower), 286
Bunton (Mt Owen), 331
Burgette Arête (Grand Teton), 199

C

Camels Head, 403–404
Canada Regional Air (Death Canyon), 513
Captain Stupid (Grand Teton), 189–190
Cardiac Arêtes (Omega Buttresses, E Section/ Ship's Prow), 92
Carson Route (Disappointment Peak), 301
Carson-Whiton (Prospectors Mtn), 88
Cascade Canyon, N side rock climbs, 365–374
Cascade Canyon to Leigh Canyon, 361–412
Cash For Less (Stewart Draw), 116
Cathy's Corner (Omega Buttresses, W Section), 97
Caveat Emptor (Snaz Buttress), 107–108
Caves Arête (Disappointment Peak), 307
Chief Joseph Buttress, Bullock-Page (Nez Perce), 149
Chief Joseph Buttress (Nez Perce), 149
Chief Joseph Left (Nez Perce), 148–149
Chimney of Death (Omega Buttresses, W Section), 98
Chockstone Bypass (Grand Teton), 236
Chockstone Chimney (Teewinot Mtn), 327
Chouinard Buttress (Glacier Gulch), 315–316
Chouinard Ridge (Middle Teton), 161–162
Chouinard-Frost Chimney (Disappointment Peak), 295–297
Cleaver Peak, 471–472
Cloudveil Dome, 151–155
CMC (Unsoeld's Needle), 453–455
Cody Peak, 70, 510–511
Collins-Coombs (Grand Teton), 186
Collins-Nume (Grand Teton), 186
Complete SE Ridge, Highway to Heaven (Storm Point), 378
Con Gusano (Cube Point), 386
Contemporary Comfort (Cloudveil Dome), 152
Corkscrew (Fairshare Tower, Watchtower), 284–285
Cottonmouth (Snaz Buttress), 111
Counterimage, 479–480
County 5 (Avalanche Canyon), 134
Cousin Leroy (Snaz Buttress), 106–107
Cousin Leroy's Uncle (Snaz Buttress), 107
Crack of Dawn (E Omega Buttresses, E of Ship's Prow), 91
Crescent Arête Direct (Mt Owen), 339
Crescent Arête (Mt Owen), 335=336
Crooked Thumb, 317–319
Crystal Right (Grand Teton), 206–207
Crystal Tower (Grand Teton), 205–206
Cube Point, 384–387
Cupa Kava (Symmetry Spire), 396
Cut Loose (Cloudveil Dome), 154

D

Darby Canyon, 518
Darkness Falls (Waterfalls Canyon), 517
Dave Adams Hill, 499
Day-of-Rest Pinnacle (Shadow Peak), 141
DCD, (see Direct Canyon Direct)
Death Canyon, N side ice climbs, 512–517
Death Canyon, N side rock climbs, 89–114
Death Canyon, S side ice climbs, 512
Death Canyon, S side rock climbs, 82–89
Delicate Arête (Disappointment Peak), 305
Deliverance (Mt Moran), 432–433
Delta Lake Tower (Glacier Gulch), 316
Dem Bones (Matternought Peak), 136–137
Destined to Become a Classic (Prospectors Mtn), 84–85
Devil's Seed (Garnet Mtn N Side), 290
Dew Drop Inn (Middle Teton), 174
Dietschy Ridge, 392–394
Dihedral of Horrors (Omega Buttresses, E Section/Ship's Prow), 93
Dike (Middle Teton), 165–166
Dike (Unsoeld's Needle), 455
Dike Pinnacle, N Face I (Middle Teton), 168–169
Dike Pinnacle, N Face II (Middle Teton), 169
Dike Pinnacle, S Ridge (Middle Teton), 164
Direct (Grand Teton), 204–205
Direct (The Enclosure), 261–262
Direct Avoidance (Leigh Canyon), 416
Direct buttress (Teewinot Mtn), 327
Direct Buttress (Veiled Peak), 126
Direct Canyon Direct (Omega Buttresses, E Section/Ship's Prow), 93

Opposite: The cherished Patriarch Tree stands watch in front of the Cathedral Group.

Direct E Buttress (Middle Teton), 167
Direct E Corner (Disappointment Peak), 305
Direct E Face (Teepe Pillar), 278–279
Direct E Ridge (Storm Point), 379
Direct E Ridge (Teewinot Mtn), 322
Direct Finish (Grand Teton), 229
Direct Finish (Leigh Canyon), 418
Direct Jensen Ridge (Symmetry Spire), 392
Direct N Face (Crooked Thumb), 318–319
Direct N Face (Disappointment Peak), 297
Direct N Face (Glencoe Spire), 275
Direct N Face (Mt Wister), 128–129
Direct N Ridge (Teewinot Mtn), 324–325
Direct S Buttress (Mt Moran), 438–446
Direct S Face (Glencoe Spire), 274
Direct S Face (Molar Tooth), 281
Direct S Face (Symmetry Spire), 390–391
Direct S Ridge (Fairshare Tower, Watchtower), 286
Direct S Ridge (Fourteen-Hour Pinnacle), 364
Direct S Ridge (Nez Perce), 144–145
Direct Start (Grand Teton), 197
Direct W Chimney (Grand Teton), 243
Direct W Face (Symmetry Spire), 389
D is for Dizzle (Teepe Pillar), 276–277
Disappointment Peak, 291–312
- E face routes, 292–294
- N routes, 294–298
- S Arêtes, couloirs, and ridges, 298–309
- W face routes, 309–312

Doane Peak, 488
Donini's Crack (E Omega Buttresses, E of Ship's Prow), 91
Doomsday Dihedral (Sentinel Turret), 101
Double Overhang (Grand Teton), 201
Doubtful Peak, 478–479
Dragon Peak, 473
Dread Falls (Death Canyon), 513
Dry Ridge Mtn, 478
Duck, The (Veiled Peak), 126
Durrance Direct (Grand Teton), 195–196
Durrance Ridge (Symmetry Spire), 391–392

E

E Buttress (Peak 11,795), 464
E Chimney (Disappointment Peak), 293
E Chimney (Ice Point), 379
E Chimney (Molar Tooth), 282
E Chimney (Unsoeld's Needle), 456
E Chimneys (Rock of Ages), 399–400
E Couloir and W Face (Sharkshead Pinnacle), 71–72
E Couloir (Bivouac Peak), 483
E Couloir (Buchwald's Blister), 73
E Couloir (Cube Point), 387
E Couloir and E Ridge (Matternought Peak), 137
E Face and N Face (Red Sentinel), 288
E Face and S Face (McCain's Pillar), 348
E Face and S Ridge (Bonney's Pinnacle), 177
E Face Approach (Buck Mtn), 122
E Face Arête (Thor Peak), 468
E Face (Ayres' Crag 2), 402
E Face (Baxter's Pinnacle), 384
E Face (Buck Mtn), 121
E Face (Camels Head), 403–404
E Face, Center (Teepe Pillar), 279
E Face, Central Buttress (Table Mtn), 353
E Face, Chouinard (Yosemite Peak), 356–357
E Face Direct (Grand Teton), 211
E Face (E Horn), 451
E Face, E Ledges (Table Mtn), 353–354
E Face (Gilkey Tower), 157
E Face (Harrington Spire), 98
E Face (Icecream Cone), 157
E Face (Jaw, The), 403
E Face, Left Center (Grand Teton), 208–209
E Face Left (Grand Teton), 208
E Face, N Buttress (Table Mtn), 354
E Face (Needles Eye Spire), 404
E Face (Nessmuk Spire), 132
E Face (Peak 10,405), 348
E Face (Pinocchio Pinnacle), 177
E Face (Rotten Thumb), 465–466
E Face, S Buttress (Table Mtn), 352–353
E Face, S Chimney (Thor Peak), 467
E Face (Teewinot Mtn), 320–321
E Face (Thor Peak), 468
E Face, Tree Surgeon, 355–356
E Face, Twenty-Four-Hour Crack (Fourteen-Hour Pinnacle), 364–365
E Face, Week's Chimney (Yosemite Peak), 357
E Gunsight Approach (Grand Teton), 234
E Horn, 450–451
E Hourglass Couloir (Nez Perce), 147
E Ledges (Sentinel Turret), 99
E Peak, E Hourglass Ridge (Nez Perce), 147–148
E Peak, N Face (Nez Perce), 147
E Prong, 327–328
E Ridge (Anniversary Peak), 488
E Ridge (Ayres' Crag 1), 401
E Ridge (Bivouac Peak), 485
E Ridge (Blackwelder Peak), 487
E Ridge (Buck Mtn), 121–122
E Ridge (Buckingham Palace), 360
E Ridge (Cloudveil Dome), 154
E Ridge Couloir (Prospectors Mtn), 76
E Ridge (Cube Point), 387
E Ridge (Disappointment Peak), 293–294
E Ridge (Eagles Rest Peak, E Peak), 487
E Ridge (Fairshare Tower), 283
E Ridge Finish (Mt Owen), 335
E Ridge (Forellen Peak), 497
E Ridge (Grand Teton), 215–217
E Ridge (Mt Hunt), 74
E Ridge (Little's Peak), 359
E Ridge (Maidenform Peak), 471
E Ridge (Marmot Point), 489
E Ridge (McClintock Peak), 360
E Ridge (Minga Spire), 404
E Ridge, N Bastion (Prospectors Mtn), 76
E Ridge (N Wigwam), 358
E Ridge (Nez Perce), 146–147
E Ridge (Mt Owen), 332–333
E Ridge (Owl Peak), 496
E Ridge (Peak 9,924), 494
E Ridge (Peak 10,245), 359
E Ridge (Peak 10,270), 494
E Ridge (Peak 10,300), 477
E Ridge (Peak 10,333), 494
E Ridge (Peak 10,422), 494
E Ridge (Peak 10,686), 490
E Ridge (Peak 10,696), 116
E Ridge (Peak 10,706), 70
E Ridge (Peak 10,716), 490
E Ridge (Peak 10,732), 490
E Ridge (Peak 10,880, Cirque Lake area), 470
E Ridge (Peak 10,880, Eagles Rest Peak), 487
E Ridge (Peak 12,000), 464–465
E Ridge (Pemmican Pillar), 283
E Ridge (Pinetop), 469
E Ridge (Point 10,000), 469
E Ridge (Raynolds Peak), 479
E Ridge (Rendezvous Peak), 71
E Ridge (Mt Robie), 490
E Ridge (Rock of Ages), 400
E Ridge (Rockchuck Peak), 409
E Ridge (S Teton), 158–159
E Ridge, SE Couloir (Storm Point), 378
E Ridge (Shadow Peak), 140–141
E Ridge (Spalding Peak), 156
E Ridge (Mt St. John), 405
E Ridge (Static Peak), 115
E Ridge, Symmetry Couloir, 378
E Ridge (Symmetry Crag 4), 397–398
E Ridge (Symmetry Crag 5), 398
E Ridge (Symmetry Spire), 395
E Ridge (Teewinot Mtn), 322
E Ridge (Traverse Peak), 480
E Ridge (Unsoeld's Needle), 452–453, 456
E Ridge (Veiled Peak), 126
E Ridge (W Horn), 452
E Ridge (Mt Woodring), 412
E Ridge (Worshipper), 316
E Side (The Outlier), 410
E Slope (Albright Peak), 115
E Slope (Mt Bannon), 79
E Slope (Mt Jedediah Smith), 79
E Slope (Peak 10,010), 493
E Slope (Peak 10,612), 78
E Slope (Peak 11,840), 327
E Slope (Ranger Peak), 490
E Summit Bypass (Nez Perce), 147
E Summit, S Face (Nez Perce), 147
E Summit, SE Face (Nez Perce), 147
E Tower (N Wigwam), 358
Eagle Scout (Teton Canyon), 518
Eagles Rest Peak, 487–488
Eagles Rest Peak, E Peak, 487
East Cascades Buttresses, 374
Eastern Omega Buttresses, E Section/Ship's Prow, 91
Edge of Horrors (Omega Buttresses, E Section/Ship's Prow), 93
Elbow Buttress, Michelle's Route (Mt Jedediah Smith), 79
Elk Mtn, 494–495
Elk Ridge, 497
Ellingwood Couloir (Middle Teton), 164
Emerson Chimney (Grand Teton), 186
Emerson's Chimney (Teewinot Mtn), 325–326
Emotional Rescue (The Enclosure), 260–261
Enclosure, The (Grand Teton), 248–264
Enclosure Ice Couloir (The Enclosure), 257–258
Escape (Mt Owen), 340
Escape from Death (Snaz Buttress), 113–114
Eudemonia (Unsoeld's Needle), 455–456
Exum Ridge (Grand Teton), 191–194

F

Fairshare Tower, 283
Fairshare Tower, Watchtower, 283–287
Fallen Angel (Snaz Buttress), 104
Faultline, 349
Fifth Column (Disappointment Peak), 299–300
Fingers (Table Mtn), 350–351
Flipping Tokens to Hoboken (Grand Teton), 195
Flying Buttress, Good for the Soul (Avalanche Canyon), 133
FNG (Fairshare Tower, Watchtower), 285
FNG (Snaz Buttress), 114
Fonda Ridge (Mt Moran), 449
Forellen Peak, 497
Forgotten Arête (Leigh Canyon), 421
Fossil Mtn, 78
Found Arrow Spire, 98
Fountainhead, The (Snaz Buttress), 111–112
Fourteen-Hour Pinnacle, 363–365
Free Wedge, The (Buck Mtn), 125
Freedom Fighter (Snaz Buttress), 111
Fryxell (Mt Owen), 330–331
Fryxell, Mt, 360

G

Gardner-Headly (Teewinot Mtn), 326
Garnet Canyon peaks, 138–177
Garnet Canyon, S side rock climbs, 150–151
Garnet Canyon to Glacier Gulch, 273–312
Garnet Mtn, N side rock climbs, 290–291
Garnet Traverse (Nez Perce), 145
Gary's Route (Second Tower), 281
Gilkey Tower, 157
Gill (Baxter's Pinnacle), 383
Gin and Tonic (Leigh Canyon), 416–417
Givler's Arête (Sharkshead Pinnacle), 72
Glacier Gulch
    N side rock climbs, 315–316
    S side rock climbs, 314
Glacier Gulch to Cascade Canyon, 313–360
Glacier Peak, 493
Glencoe Spire, 273–276
Glencoe-Teepe Gully (Glencoe Spire), 275
Glencoe-Teepe Gully (Teepe Pillar), 276
Goat Rocks, 71
Gold Face (Grand Teton), 197–198
Golden Arête (Grand Teton), 213
Golden Pillar (Grand Teton), 230
Goodrich Chimney (Middle Teton), 174
Goodro-Shane (Grand Teton), 224
Gorbachev Falls (Cascade Canyon), 516
Got to Kill (Grand Teton), 189–190
Gran (Disappointment Peak), 297–298
Grand N Couloir (Grand Teton), 222
Grand Teton, 180–244
    E Face routes, 205–214
    E ridge and N face routes, 214–236
    Exum Ridge W face, 186–191
    Italian Cracks to Owen-Spalding, 270
    S ridges, 191–205
    W face climbs, 236–246
Grand Teton and the Enclosure, 178–264
Grand Teton, Lower Glencoe-Teepe Chute (Garnet Canyon), 514–515
Grand Teton, Lower Stettner Couloir Ice (Garnet Canyon), 514
Grand Traverse, the, 265–272
Granite Canyon, S side rock climbs, 71–73
Granite Central Buttresses, 72–73
Gray Ramp (Baxter's Pinnacle), 383
Gray Slab (Disappointment Peak), 302
Great W Chimney (Disappointment Peak), 311–312
Green Lakes Mtn, 477–478
Grunt Arête (Disappointment Peak), 304
Grunt Arête, Open Book (Disappointment Peak), 303–304
Guardian of Death (Omega Buttresses, Central Section), 94
Guides' Wall (Storm Point Cliffs), 368–370

H

Habeler (Mt Moran), 433–434
Hanging Canyon, N side rock climbs, 406–408
Hangover Pinnacle, 380
Happiness (Unsoeld's Needle), 455–456
Harem Hill, 499
Harrington Spire, 98
Hawkeye (Hanging Canyon), 408
Heartbreak Ridge (Table Mtn), 352
Heather's Couloir (Peak 11,840), 466
Hell You Say, The (Granite Central Buttresses), 73
Hernando's Hideaway (Nez Perce), 147
Hidden Arête (Disappointment Peak), 298–299
Hidden Couloir (Thor Peak), 468–469
High Route (The Enclosure), 258–259
Horton E Face (Grand Teton), 212
Hossack-MacGowan Couloir (Grand Teton), 221
Hot Dogs (Storm Point Cliffs), 371
Housetop Mtn, 73–74
Howard (Baxter's Pinnacle), 384
Howe-Keith (Teepe Pillar), 277
Hummingbird Face (Disappointment Peak), 300
Hummingbird Wall (Grand Teton), 240
Hunt, Mt, 74

I

Ice Man Pinnacle, 410
Ice Point, 379–380
Icecream Cone, 157
Idol, 316–317
Image, 479
In Search Of . . . (Spearhead Peak), 74
Incognito Buttress (Symmetry Spire), 395
Inge's (Middle Teton), 170
Intrepidity Arête (Mt Owen), 346
Irene's Arête (Disappointment Peak), 305–307
Irvine Arête (Leigh Canyon), 422
It Is (Too) a Chimney (Grand Teton), 199
Italian Cracks (Grand Teton), 235–236
It's Not a Chimney (Grand Teton), 198–199

J

Jackson-Johnson (The Enclosure), 255
Jackson-Kimbrough Contortion (Grand Teton), 240
Jackson-Rickert Crack (Grand Teton), 190
Jackson-Woodmencey (Grand Teton), 207–208
Jackson-Woodmencey Dihedral (Middle Teton), 173–174
Jaw, The, 403
Jaw Crags, 403
Jedediah Smith, Mt, 79
Jenni's Way (Mt Owen), 345–346
Jensen Couloir (Symmetry Spire), 392
Jerrn-Wiggins (Disappointment Peak), 309
Jim's Big Day (The Enclosure), 249
Jones Sisters, The (Storm Point Cliffs), 372

K

Keith-Eddy E Face (Grand Teton), 210–211
Kelley (Mt Moran), 433
Kelley-Beyer (Mt Moran), 435–437
Kim Schmitz Memorial Route (Disappointment Peak), 311
Kimbrough-Olson Crack (The Enclosure), 254–255
Kimbrough-Rickert (Disappointment Peak), 297
Kimburger, Mt, 412
Kindred Spirits (Table Mtn), 354
Kligfield Arch (Fairshare Tower, Watchtower), 287–288
Knob, The (Disappointment Peak), 300
Koven (Mt Owen), 331–332

L

Lake Ledges (Disappointment Peak), 293
Lance's Arête (Disappointment Peak), 298–299
Larson Ridge (Stewart Draw), 116–117
Larson-Monopoli (The Enclosure), 255
Laughing Lions Falls (Leigh Canyon), 516
Lazy Bones (Matternought Peak), 135–136
Leaping Deer Couloir (Mt Fryxell), 360
Ledger Book (Teewinot Mtn), 323–324
Left Buttress (Glacier Gulch), 316
Left Ghost (Teton Canyon), 518
Left of Open Book (Disappointment Peak), 304
Left Pillar (Cascade Canyon), 515
Leigh Canyon, N side rock climbs, 414–422
Leigh Canyon to Moran Canyon, 413–473
Lemon Crack (Garnet Canyon, S Side), 150
Lev (Grand Teton), 206–207
Lightning Crack (Granite Central Buttresses), 72–73
Line of Fire (Table Mtn), 353
Line of Lees's Resistance (Middle Teton), 166–167
Little Wing (Grand Teton), 221–222
Little's Peak, 359
Loki's Tower (Grand Teton), 238–239
Lookin' for Trouble (The Enclosure), 262–263
Los Huesos (Matternought Peak), 136
Lost World Plateau (Point 9,840), 89
Lot's Slot (Snaz Buttress), 112
Lowe Route (The Enclosure), 259–260
Lower Chimney (Symmetry Spire), 392
Lower Exum Ridge (Grand Teton), 195–196
Lower NE Ridge (Teewinot Mtn), 323-324
Lower Ridge (Nez Perce), 145
Lower S Buttress (Symmetry Crag 4), 366–367

Lower Symmetry Couloir Ice (Cascade Canyon), 516
Lugbill-White (Avalanche Canyon), 134
Lycra (Omega Buttresses, E Section/Ship's Prow), 93

M

Magpie Acres (Garnet Mtn, N Side), 290
Maidenform Peak, 470–471
Malbec Corner (Fairshare Tower, Watchtower), 284
Manufactured Crisis (Omega Buttresses, Central Section), 94–95
Marmot Point, 489
Mas Intrepido (Mt Owen), 346
Matternought Peak, 134–137
Matthews S Face (Cloudveil Dome), 152
McCain's Pillar, 348
McClintock Peak, 360
Medrick-Ortenburger (Grand Teton), 230–231
Meek, Mt, 79
Merriam Couloir (Disappointment Peak), 304
Middle Finger (Middle Teton), 171
Middle Teton, 159–177
Middle Teton Cave Route (Garnet Canyon, S Side), 151
Middle Teton Glacier (Middle Teton), 167–168
Middle Teton, Lower N face routes, 170–171
Middle Teton, N Ridge to SW Couloir, 270
Middle Teton, Right of Dike (Garnet Canyon), 514
Middle Teton, Upper N Face routes, 172–176
Middle Teton, W side routes, 176–177
Minga Spire, 404
Minor Fourth Couloir (Unsoeld's Needle), 461
Miss Demeanor (Cloudveil Dome), 152
Molar Tooth, 281–282
Moose Mtn, 493–494
Moran, Mt, 422–450
  N Summit, 463
  NE and N aspects, 458–463
  S Buttress (S Aspect), 426, 428–446
  S Buttress (W Aspect), 446–453
  SE and E aspects, 453–458
Moran Canyon, N Side rock climbs, 485
Moran Canyon to Webb Canyon, 474–490
Morning Thunder (Storm Point Cliffs), 373
Mount Woodring Ice (Leigh Canyon), 516
Moxie Tower, 89
Murphy Peak, 75

N

N and W Faces (Glencoe Spire), 275
N Approach (Teewinot Mtn), 321
N Approach (Traverse Peak), 480
N Buttress Direct (Grand Teton), 222–223
N Buttress (Unsoeld's Needle), 462
N Buttress (Yosemite Peak), 358
N Central Ridge (Buck Mtn), 122–123
N Chimney (S Teton), 159
N Chimney (Second Tower), 281
N Chimney (Two Elk Peak), 75
N Corners (The Enclosure), 255–256
N Couloir (Buck Mtn, W Peak), 125
N Couloir (Prospectors Mtn), 78
N Couloir (Symmetry Spire), 395
N Couloir-W Ridge (Eagles Rest Peak), 487
N Couloir (Mt Woodring), 412
N Face (Art-and-Brent Pinnacle), 348
N Face (Baxter's Pinnacle), 384
N Face (Buchwald's Blister), 73
N Face, Cabot-Johnstone (Buck Mtn), 122
N Face (Cloudveil Dome), 155
N Face (Cube Point), 387
N Face, E Chimney (Spearhead Peak), 74
N Face, E Chimney (Mt Wister), 127–128
N Face, E Couloir (Buck Mtn), 122
N Face, E Couloir (Mt St. John), 406
N Face (E Horn), 451
N Face (Gilkey Tower), 157
N Face (Grand Teton), 225
N Face, Guides' Discount (Nez Perce), 149
N Face (Hangover Pinnacle), 380
N Face Ice (Disappointment Peak), 515
N Face (Ice Point), 379
N Face (Nez Perce), 149–150
N Face (Mt Owen), 340–341
N Face (Peak 11,795), 464
N Face (Pinocchio Pinnacle), 177
N Face (Red Sentinel), 288–289
N Face (S Teton), 159
N Face, Saved by the Sheep (Mt Wister), 129
N Face (Shadow Peak), 141
N Face (Static Peak), 115–116
N Face (Symmetry Spire), 396
N Face (Teepe Pillar), 279
N Face (Teewinot Mtn), 325
N Face, The Buck Sanction (Buck Mtn), 122
N Face (Unsoeld's Needle), 462–463
N Face, W Chimney (Mt Wister), 130–131
N Face, W Couloir (Buck Mtn), 123
N Face (Mt Woodring), 412
N Face (Yosemite Peak), 357–358
N Molar Tooth Couloir (Grand Teton), 220
N Peak, Annatia's (Cleaver Peak), 473
N Peak, NE Chimney (Cleaver Peak), 473
N Peak, NW Chimney (Cleaver Peak), 472
N Peak, W Chimney (Cleaver Peak), 473
N Peak, Wayne's World (Cleaver Peak), 472–473
N Prow Arête (Peak 11,795), 464
N Ridge (Albright Peak), 115
N Ridge and N Face (Mt St. John), 405–406
N Ridge (Mt Berry), 499
N Ridge (Crooked Thumb), 318
N Ridge Direct (Mt Owen), 339
N Ridge (Doane Peak), 489
N Ridge (Doubtful Peak), 479
N Ridge (Eagles Rest Peak), 488
N Ridge (Fairshare Tower, Watchtower), 287
N Ridge (Glacier Peak), 493
N Ridge (Grand Teton), 232–234
N Ridge (Image), 479
N Ridge (The Jaw), 403
N Ridge (Little's Peak), 359
N Ridge (Maidenform Peak), 471
N Ridge (McClintock Peak), 360
N Ridge (Middle Teton), 174–175
N Ridge (Mt Owen), 337–339
N Ridge (Peak 10,333), 494
N Ridge (Peak 10,345), 477
N Ridge (Peak 10,474), 478
N Ridge (Peak 10,484), 477
N Ridge (Peak 10,635), 350
N Ridge (Peak 10,640), 348
N Ridge (Peak 10,650), 358
N Ridge (Peak 10,706), 70
N Ridge (Peak 10,720), 359
N Ridge (Peak 10,753), 70
N Ridge (Peak 10,952), 470
N Ridge (Peak 11,126), 470
N Ridge (Peak 11,238), 489
N Ridge (Peak 11,840), 466
N Ridge (Peak 12,000), 465
N Ridge (Rabbit Ears), 348
N Ridge (Red Mtn), 498
N Ridge Right (Mt Owen), 340
N Ridge Start (Grand Teton), 229–230
N Ridge (Table Mtn), 354
N Ridge (Unsoeld's Needle), 461
N Ridge (Veiled Peak), 126
N Ridge (Mt Woodring), 412
N Side (Goat Rocks), 71
N Slope (Bivouac Peak), 485
N Slope (Disappointment Peak), 312
N Slope (Moose Mtn), 494
N Slope (Peak 9,970), 493
N Slope (Peak 10,080), 312
N Slope (Peak 10,612), 78
N Slope (Surprise Lake Pinnacle), 312
N Snowfield (Spalding Peak), 157
N Traverse of the Molar Tooth (Grand Teton), 218–219
N Wall (Middle Teton), 171
N Wigwam, 358
NE Buttress Couloir (Unsoeld's Needle), 459–460
NE Buttress (Grand Teton), 221
NE Chimney (Eagles Rest Peak), 488
NE Chimney (Rock of Ages), 400
NE Chimney (Teewinot Mtn), 322
NE Chute (Peak 10,245), 359
NE Couloir (Bivouac Peak), 485
NE Couloir (Buck Mtn), 122
NE Couloir (Mt Meek), 79
NE Couloir (Peak 11,094), 79
NE Couloir (Thor Peak), 469
NE Couloir (Mt Wister), 127
NE Cracks (Molar Tooth), 282
NE Face (Ayres' Crag 4), 402
NE Face Direct (Teewinot Mtn), 323
NE Face (Image), 479
NE Face (Okie's Thorn), 282
NE Face (Prospectors Mtn), 85
NE Face (Rock of Ages), 400
NE Face (Middle Teton), 169–170
NE Face (Symmetry Spire), 396
NE Face (Teewinot Mtn), 322–323
NE Face (Worshipper), 316
NE Ledges (Veiled Peak), 126
NE Ridge (Ayres' Crag 5), 402–403
NE Ridge (Baxter's Pinnacle), 384
NE Ridge (Counterimage), 480
NE Ridge (Green Lakes Mtn), 478
NE Ridge (Moxie Tower), 89
NE Ridge (Peak 9,815), 69
NE Ridge (Peak 10,308), 73
NE Ridge (Peak 10,450), 70
NE Ridge (Peak 10,484), 477
NE Ridge (Peak 10,720), 488

NE Ridge (Ranger Peak), 490
NE Ridge (Rendezvous Peak), 71
NE Ridge (Rockchuck Peak), 410
NE Ridge (Rolling Thunder Mtn), 486
NE Ridge (Spalding Peak), 157
NE Ridge (Tukuarika Peak), 75
NE Ridge (Unsoeld's Needle), 458–459
NE Slabs (Unsoeld's Needle), 458
NE Slope (Survey Peak), 499
NE Snowfield (Gilkey Tower), 157
NE Snowfields (Mt Owen), 334–335
Needles Eye Spike, 404
Needles Eye Spire, 404
Nessmuk Spire, 132
Neutron Burn (Grand Teton), 244
Nez Perce, 141–150
Nimbus (Cloudveil Dome), 154–155
N-NE Ridge (Owl Peak), 496
N-NW Ridge (Buck Mtn), 123–124
No Cumbre, No Ruta (Middle Teton), 174
No Escape Buttress, Direct S Face (Leigh Canyon), 417–418
No Escape Buttress, E Edge (Leigh Canyon), 416
No Escape Buttress, W Arête (Leigh Canyon), 419–420
No Escape Ice (Leigh Canyon), 516
No Escape Slabs (Leigh Canyon), 415–416
No Friends (Storm Point Cliffs), 371
No More Mr. Nice Guy (Storm Point Cliffs), 372–373
No Name Couloir (Disappointment Peak), 303
No Name Gully (Grand Teton), 220
No Name Peak, 70
No Perches Necessary (East Cascades Buttresses), 374
No Question (Omega Buttresses, E Section/ Ship's Prow), 93
No Survivors (Leigh Canyon), 416
Northeast Face III (Prospectors Mtn), 87
Nugget, The (Death Canyon), 512
NW Arête (Mt Wister), 131–132
NW Chimney (Grand Teton), 239–240
NW Chimney (Symmetry Spire), 396
NW Corner (Baxter's Pinnacle), 384
NW Couloir (Nez Perce), 142–143
NW Corner (Red Sentinel), 289–290
NW Corner (Rock of Ages), 401
NW Couloir (Shadow Peak), 141
NW Couloir and Ledges (Symmetry Spire), 397
NW Couloir (S Teton), 159
NW Couloir (Teewinot Mtn), 327
NW Couloir (Mt Wister), 132
NW Crack (Disappointment Peak), 297
NW Face (Idol), 317
NW Face (The Outlier), 410
NW Face (Mt Owen), 341–342
NW Face (Rock of Ages), 401
NW Face (Symmetry Spire), 397
NW Face (Teepe Pillar), 279
NW Face (Teewinot Mtn), 326
NW Face (Thor Peak), 469
NW Face (Mt Wister), 132
NW Ice Couloir (Middle Teton), 175–176
NW Ledges (Mt Kimburger), 412
NW Ridge (Anniversary Peak), 488
NW Ridge (Buck Mtn, W Peak), 125
NW Ridge (Buckingham Palace), 360
NW Ridge (Dry Ridge Mtn), 478
NW Ridge (The Enclosure), 252–254
NW Ridge (Mt Fryxell), 360
NW Ridge (Ice Point), 379–380
NW Ridge (N Wigwam), 358
NW Ridge (Mt Owen), 341
NW Ridge (Peak 10,405), 348
NW Ridge (Prospectors Mtn), 78
NW Ridge (Rendezvous Peak), 71
NW Ridge (Teewinot Mtn), 327
NW Shelf (Disappointment Peak), 298
NW Side (Rockchuck Peak), 410
NW Slope (Peak 10,277), 73
NW Slope (Peak 10,880), 360
NW Slope (Middle Teton), 176
NW Wall (Two Elk Peak), 75

O

Odette-Sherner (Grand Teton), 236
Okie's Thorn, 282
Olson-Nelson Tower (Glacier Gulch), 315
Omega Buttresses, 90–98
Omega Buttresses, Central Section, 94–97
Omega Buttresses, E Section/Ship's Prow, 91–93
Omega Buttresses, W Section, 97–98
O-Mega Crack (Omega Buttresses, Central Section), 96
Omega Tower (Omega Buttresses, E Section/ Ship's Prow), 91–92
Omega Triangle (Omega Buttresses, Central Section), 95–96
Open Heart Surgery (Sharkshead Pinnacle), 72
Opp-Hennessey (Teepe Pillar), 277–278
Opp-Van Sciver (Garnet Canyon, S Side), 150–151
Ortenburger Arête (Grand Teton), 202
Ostrich Arête (Hanging Canyon), 407
Otterbody Chimneys (Grand Teton), 214
Outlier, The, 410
Owen, Mt, 328–347
Owen, Mt, to the Grandstand, 269–270
Owen-Spalding (Grand Teton), 181–186
Owl Peak, 496

P

Peaches (Stewart Draw), 116
Peak 7,185, 497
Peak 8,582T, 499
Peak 8,602, 496
Peak 8,688T, 498
Peak 8,803T, 499
Peak 9,814, 73
Peak 9,815, 69
Peak 9,924, 494
Peak 9,925, 73
Peak 9,940, 464
Peak 9,970, 493
Peak 10,010, 493
Peak 10,080, 312
Peak 10,116, 74
Peak 10,160, 478
Peak 10,245, 359
Peak 10,270, 494
Peak 10,277, 73
Peak 10,300 (Mt Meek area), 79
Peak 10,300 (Mt Moran area), 477
Peak 10,308, 73
Peak 10,333, 494
Peak 10,345, 477
Peak 10,360, 494
Peak 10,405, 348
Peak 10,422, 494
Peak 10,450, 69–70
Peak 10,450 ice & mixed climbs, 510
Peak 10,474, 478
Peak 10,484, 477
Peak 10,612, 78
Peak 10,625, 485
Peak 10,635, 350
Peak 10,640, 348
Peak 10,650, 358
Peak 10,686, 490
Peak 10,696, 116
Peak 10,706, 70
Peak 10,716, 490
Peak 10,720 (Littles Peak area), 359
Peak 10,720 (Ranger Peak area), 488
Peak 10,732, 490
Peak 10,753 (Cody Peak), 70, 510–511
Peak 10,880 (Maidenform Peak area), 470
Peak 10,880 (Paintbrush Divide area), 360
Peak 10,880 (Ranger Peak area), 486–487
Peak 10,919, 410
Peak 10,952, 470
Peak 10,960, 132
Peak 11,094, 79
Peak 11,126, 469–470
Peak 11,200, 489
Peak 11,238, 489
Peak 11,795, 463–464
Peak 11,840 (Teewinot Mtn area), 327
Peak 11,840 (Thor Peak area), 466
Peak 12,000, 464
Pemmican Pillar, 283
Pensive (Yosemite Peak), 356
Peregrine Arête (Hanging Canyon), 407–408
Petzoldt Direct (Grand Teton), 199–200
Petzoldt Ridge (Grand Teton), 199
Petzoldt-Loomis Otterbody (Grand Teton), 213–214
Petzoldt-to-Exum Traverse (Grand Teton), 200–201
Phil's Pickle, 73
Picnic and Paranoia (Storm Point Cliffs), 371
Pika Buttress (Unsoeld's Needle), 460–461
Pilgrimage (Harrington Spire), 98
Pillar of Death (Snaz Buttress), 102–103
Pin Time (Disappointment Peak), 293–294
Pinetop and Point 10,000, 469
Pinnacle Route (Middle Teton), 174
Pinocchio Pinnacle, 177
Piss and Venom (The Enclosure), 259
Point 9,840, 89
Poop-out Pinnacle (Prospectors Mtn), 89
Pownall-Gilkey (Grand Teton), 186
Pownall-Unsold N Face (Disappointment Peak), 293–294
Predator (Prospectors Mtn), 88
Primrose Peak, 480
Prospect of an End (The Enclosure), 258

Prospectors Falls (Death Canyon), 512
Prospectors Mtn, 75–78
Pseudo Emerson (Grand Teton), 186
Putin's Pickle (Cascade Canyon), 515

R

Rabbit Ears, 348
Rags-to-Riches (Storm Point Cliffs), 371–372
Ranger Peak, 489–490
Raven Crack (Prospectors Mtn), 88
Raynolds Peak, 479
Red Alert (Red Sentinel), 288
Red and the Black, The (Grand Teton), 208
Red Arête (Glacier Gulch), 316
Red Mtn, 497–498
Red Sentinel, 287–290
Reese Arête (Teewinot Mtn), 326
Reese-Wilson (Shadow Peak), 141
Rendezvous Mtn, 69–70
Rendezvous Peak, 70–71
Renny Take the Wheel (Mt Owen), 342–343
Renny's Route (Rolling Thunder Mtn), 486
Reticent Slabs (Symmetry Spire), 394–395
Reunion Falls (Teton Canyon), 517–518
Revolutionary Crest (Mt Moran), 447
Rhinelander-Jordon (The Enclosure), 256–257
Ridge, The (Matternought Peak), 134
Ridge Edge (The Enclosure), 251
Right Buttress (Glacier Gulch), 316
Right Ghost (Teton Canyon), 518
Right of Open Book (Disappointment Peak), 304
Right Parallel Crack (Omega Buttresses, E Section/Ship's Prow), 93
Right Pillar (Cascade Canyon), 516
Rimrock Falls (Death Canyon), 512
Robbins-Fitschen (Middle Teton), 171
Robie, Mt, 490
Rock of Ages, 398–401
Rock Springs Buttress, 70
Rockchuck Peak, 408–410
Rolling Thunder Mtn, 485–486
Rotten Thumb, 465–466
Route Gully (Grand Teton), 220–221
Run-Don't-Walk Couloir (Mt Owen), 336–337

S

S and E Faces (Found Arrow Spire), 98
S and E Faces (Ice Man Pinnacle), 410
S Bowl (Storm Point), 377
S Bridge (Peak 10,308), 73
S Buttress Central (Mt Moran), 437–438
S Buttress Drifter (Mt Moran), 437
S Buttress Houdini (Mt Moran), 434–435
S Buttress (Minga Spire), 404
S Buttress (Omega Buttresses, W Section), 97
S Buttress Prow (Mt Moran), 438
S Buttress Right (Mt Moran), 430–432
S Buttress, W Face (Mt Moran), 446–447
S Buttress Wrong (Mt Moran), 446
S Central Buttress (Disappointment Peak), 304–305
S Central Buttress (Storm Point), 377
S Chimney (Mt Owen), 330
S Couloir and E Ridge (E Prong), 328
S Couloir Approach (Nez Perce), 143
S Couloir (Buck Mtn), 119
S Couloir (Buck Mtn, W Peak), 125
S Couloir E Ridge (Mt St. John), 405
S Couloir (The Enclosure), 246–249
S Couloir (Peak 10,625), 485
S Couloir (Rock of Ages), 398–399
S Couloir (Middle Teton), 162
S Couloir (Symmetry Crag 5), 398
S Couloir (Symmetry Spire), 396
S Couloir, W Ridge (Mt St. John), 405
S Couloir (Mt Wister), 127
S Edge (Disappointment Peak), 307–308
S Face (Ayres' Crag 5), 366
S Face (Banded Buttress), 365
S Face, Central Cathedral (Second Tower), 280–281
S Face Dihedral (Ayres' Crag 5), 366
S Face (Disappointment Peak), 304
S Face (E Horn), 450–451
S Face (E Prong), 328
S Face (Glencoe Spire), 273–274
S Face (Teepe Pillar), 277
S Face I (Bivouac Peak), 483
S Face (Ice Point), 379
S Face (Idol), 317
S Face II (Bivouac Peak), 482–483
S Face III (Bivouac Peak), 483
S Face IV (Bivouac Peak), 483
S Face (Nez Perce), 145–146
S Face of Guides' Wall (Storm Point Cliffs), 371
S Face (Mt Owen), 330
S Face (Teepe Pillar), 277–278
S Face Right (Spalding Peak), 156
S Face (Sentinel Turret), 99–100
S Face (Spalding Peak), 155–156
S Face Start (Symmetry Spire), 392
S Face (Symmetry Spire), 391
S Face (Teepe Pillar), 276
S Gully, W Ridge (Bivouac Peak), 482
S Molar Tooth Couloir (Grand Teton), 219
S Peak, E Face-S Ridge (Cleaver Peak), 473
S Peak, SE Shoulder (Cleaver Peak), 473
S Rib (Mt Woodring), 411–412
S Ridge, Abbey-Macke (Second Tower), 280
S Ridge (Ayres' Crag 4), 402
S Ridge (Baxter's Pinnacle), 383
S Ridge (Mt Berry), 499
S Ridge (Blackwelder Peak), 487
S Ridge, Brimstone Chimney (Second Tower), 279–280
S Ridge (Counterimage), 480
S Ridge (Cube Point), 385
S Ridge (Eagles Rest Peak), 487
S Ridge (Fairshare Tower), 283
S Ridge (Green Lakes Mtn), 478
S Ridge (Molar Tooth), 281–282
S Ridge (N Wigwam), 358
S Ridge (Peak 9,970), 493
S Ridge (Peak 10,345), 477
S Ridge (Peak 10,360), 494
S Ridge (Peak 10,405), 348
S Ridge (Peak 10,484), 477
S Ridge (Peak 10,635), 350
S Ridge (Peak 10,640), 348
S Ridge (Peak 10,650), 358
S Ridge (Peak 10,720), 359
S Ridge (Peak 10,880), 360
S Ridge (Peak 10,952), 470
S Ridge (Peak 10,960), 132
S Ridge (Peak 11,200), 489
S Ridge (Peak 11,840), 466
S Ridge (Rabbit Ears), 348
S Ridge (Ranger Peak), 489
S Ridge (Rendezvous Peak), 71
S Ridge (Mt Robie), 490
S Ridge (Rockchuck Peak), 409
S Ridge (S Teton), 158
S Ridge (S Wigwam), 358
S Ridge (Spearhead Peak), 74
S Ridge (Table Mtn), 350
S Ridge (Teepe Pillar), 278
S Ridge (Teewinot Mtn), 320
S Ridge (Veiled Peak), 125–126
S Side (Tukuarika Peak), 75
S Slope (Mt Bannon), 79
S Slope (Moose Mtn), 494
S Slope (Peak 10,612), 78
S Slope (Peak 10,880), 487
S Slope (Peak 11,238), 489
S Slope (Thor Peak), 466–467
S Slope, W Ridge (Owl Peak), 496
S Slopes (Rockchuck Peak), 410
S Teton, 158–159
S Teton, NW Couloir, 272
S Teton to Nez Perce, 270–272
S Traverse of the Molar Tooth (Grand Teton), 219
S Wigwam, 358
Sacco-Vanzetti Memorial (Disappointment Peak), 310–311
Sam's Tower Ridge (Symmetry Spire), 396
Sandinista Couloir (Mt Moran), 448–449
Satisfaction Arête (Disappointment Peak), 301
Satisfaction Buttress (Disappointment Peak), 301
Satisfaction Crack (Disappointment Peak), 302
Schmitz-Kanzler Dihedral (Snaz Buttress), 104
Schoolhouse, The (Ayres' Crag 1), 401–402
SE Approach (Teewinot Mtn), 321–322
SE Buttress (E Horn), 451
SE Chimney (Grand Teton), 209
SE Corner (Moxie Tower), 89
SE Corner (Peak 10,300), 79
SE Corner (Phil's Pickle), 73
SE Couloir and E Ridge (Eagles Rest Peak), 488
SE Couloir (Buck Mtn), 120–121
SE Couloir (Doane Peak), 489
SE Couloir (Fourteen-Hour Pinnacle), 365
SE Couloir (Middle Teton), 164–165
SE Couloir (Nez Perce), 146
SE Couloir (Peak 10,919), 410
SE Couloir (Rockchuck Peak), 409
SE Couloir (Table Mtn), 351
SE Couloir (Teewinot Mtn), 320
SE Couloir (Traverse Peak), 480
SE Couloir (Mt Wister), 127
SE Couloir (S Teton), 158
SE Face (Baxter's Pinnacle), 384
SE Face (Fourteen-Hour Pinnacle), 365
SE Face (Image), 479
SE Face (Nez Perce), 146
SE Face (Rockchuck Peak), 409–410

SE Face (Second Tower), 281
SE Face (Shadow Peak), 140
SE Face (Teewinot Mtn), 320
SE Flank (Veiled Peak), 126
SE Rib (Cloudveil Dome), 154
SE Rib (Traverse Peak), 480
SE Ridge (Buck Mtn), 119–120
SE Ridge (Disappointment Peak), 292–293
SE Ridge (Doane Peak), 489
SE Ridge (Doubtful Peak), 478–479
SE Ridge (Elk Mtn), 495
SE Ridge (Mt Fryxell), 360
SE Ridge (Housetop Mtn), 74
SE Ridge (Leigh Canyon), 421–422
SE Ridge (Okie's Thorn), 282
SE Ridge (Peak 10,625), 485
SE Ridge (Ranger Peak), 489–490
SE Ridge (Rock of Ages), 399
SE Ridge (Storm Point), 377–378
SE Ridge (Thor Peak), 467
SE Ridge (Two Elk Peak), 75
SE Side (Fossil Mtn), 78
SE Slope (Dry Ridge Mtn), 478
SE Slope (Peak 10,277), 73
SE Slope (Peak 9,925), 73
SE Slope (Prospectors Mtn), 76
SE Slope (Red Mtn), 498
SE Slope (Mt Woodring), 411
Second Tower, 279–281
Seizure Disorder (Baxter's Pinnacle), 383
Sentinel Turret, 98–102
Sentinel Winter Only (Death Canyon), 512–513
Serendipity Arête (Mt Owen), 343–345
737 Earful (Death Canyon), 513–514
Sgt. Garcia Couloir (Spalding Peak), 156–157
Shadow Peak, 139–141
Shand-Ferris (Middle Teton), 167
Sharkshead Pinnacle, 71–72
Shatter Face (Peak 10,450), 510
Shattered (Snaz Buttress), 104–105
Shea-Breashears (Middle Teton), 171
Shea's Chute (Grand Teton), 222
Sherm's Crack (E Omega Buttresses, E of Ship's Prow), 91
Ship's Prow Pillar, Man-O-War (Omega Buttresses, E Section/Ship's Prow), 92
Shoshoko Falls (Avalanche Canyon), 514
Sickle Couloir (Unsoeld's Needle), 460
Silver Lining (Cloudveil Dome), 153–154
Simpleton's Pillar (Grand Teton), 224
Skillet Buttress (Unsoeld's Needle), 457–458
Skillet Chimney (Unsoeld's Needle), 457
Skillet Glacier Headwall (Unsoeld's Needle), 458
Skillet Glacier (Unsoeld's Needle), 456–457
Skinny Dip (Storm Point Cliffs), 372
Sliver Couloir (Nez Perce), 147
Smith Otterbody (Grand Teton), 212–213
Smoke and Mirrors (Leigh Canyon), 418–419
Snake, The (Yosemite Peak), 355
Snaz, The (Snaz Buttress), 106
Snaz Buttress, 102–114
Snazette (Snaz Buttress), 106
Something Yosemite Like (Yosemite Peak), 358
Sowles (Buck Mtn), 122
Spalding Peak, 155–157
Spearhead Peak, 74
Spigolo Nero (Stewart Draw), 116
Splooge (Omega Buttresses, W Section), 97–98
Spoon Couloir (Disappointment Peak), 293
Spreadeagle (Leigh Canyon), 421
Squeeze Box (Grand Teton), 223
S-SW Ridge (Nez Perce), 144
St. John, Mt, 404–406
St. John's Wart (Hanging Canyon), 407
Staircase Arête (Leigh Canyon), 422
Staircase Ridge (Symmetry Spire), 395–396
State of Emergency (Peak 10,450), 510
Static Peak, 115–116
Stettner (Rock of Ages), 400–401
Stettner Couloir (Grand Teton), 202–203
Stewart Draw, S side rock climbs, 116–117
Storm Point, 376–379
Storm Point Cliffs, 367–373
Stuck Pig (Mt Moran), 435
Subalpinist (Garnet Canyon, S Side), 151
Sunrise Pillar (Death Canyon), 514
Sunrise Ridge (Gilkey Tower), 157
Sunset Face (Nez Perce), 143–144
Sunshine Daydream (Snaz Buttress), 105
Surprise Lake Pinnacle, 312
Survey Peak, 498–499
SW Corner (Bivouac Peak), 485
SW Couloir and SE Ridge (The Zebra), 465
SW Couloir (Buck Mtn), 118
SW Couloir (Disappointment Peak), 307
SW Couloir (Fourteen-Hour Pinnacle), 364
SW Couloir (Mt Moran), 449
SW Couloir (Rock of Ages), 398
SW Couloir (Rolling Thunder Mtn), 486
SW Couloir (Middle Teton), 160–161
SW Couloir (Storm Point), 376
SW Couloir (Symmetry Spire), 389
SW Couloirs (Teewinot Mtn), 319–320
SW Dihedral (Fairshare Tower, Watchtower), 287–288
SW Face (Ayres' Crag 4), 402
SW Face (Baxter's Pinnacle), 381
SW Ledges (Molar Tooth), 281
SW Ridge (Albright Peak), 115
SW Ridge (Crooked Thumb), 317–318
SW Ridge (Disappointment Peak), 308–309
SW Ridge (Dragon Peak), 473
SW Ridge (Elk Mtn), 495
SW Ridge (The Enclosure), 249–251
SW Ridge (Fossil Mtn), 78
SW Ridge (Fourteen-Hour Pinnacle), 365
SW Ridge (Glencoe Spire), 275–276
SW Ridge (Hangover Pinnacle), 380
SW Ridge (Ice Point), 379
SW Ridge (Maidenform Peak), 471
SW Ridge (Middle Teton), 161
SW Ridge (The Outlier), 410
SW Ridge (Mt Owen), 328–330
SW Ridge (Peak 9,815), 69
SW Ridge (Peak 9,940), 464
SW Ridge (Peak 10,450), 70
SW Ridge (Peak 10,706), 70
SW Ridge (Peak 10,720), 488
SW Ridge (Peak 10,753), 70
SW Ridge (Peak 11,126), 470
SW Ridge (Prospectors Mtn), 76
SW Ridge (Rendezvous Peak), 71
SW Ridge (Sentinel Turret), 102
SW Ridge (Static Peak), 115
SW Ridge (Storm Point), 376–377
SW Ridge (Symmetry Spire), 390
SW Ridge (Teepe Pillar), 276
SW Ridge (Window Peak), 477
SW Ridge (Mt Wister), 127
SW Ridge (Mt Woodring), 411
SW Side (Raynolds Peak), 479
SW Slope (Forellen Peak), 497
SW Slope (Mt Jedediah Smith), 79
SW Slope (Mt Meek), 79
SW Slope (Peak 10,116), 74
SW Slope (Survey Peak), 499
Swizzle Stick (Omega Buttresses, W Section), 98
Symmetry Couloir and Upper W Face (Storm Point), 379
Symmetry Crag 4, 366–367, 397–398
Symmetry Crag 5, 398
Symmetry Crags, 397
Symmetry Spire, 387–397

T

Table Mtn, 350–354
Talon, The (Avalanche Canyon), 514
Taminah Arête (Matternought Peak), 134–135
Tang-O-Max (Cascade Canyon), 516
Taylor (Middle Teton), 170–171
Technicolor Odyssey (Prospectors Mtn), 84
Teepe Pillar, 276–279
Teewinot Mtn, 319–327, 515
Teewinot Mtn to Mt Owen, 268–269
Teewinot Tunnel (Teewinot Mtn), 326
Templeton's Crack (Symmetry Spire), 392
Temporary Discomfort (Cloudveil Dome), 152
Teton Canyon, E side ice climbs, 518
Teton Canyon, S side ice climbs, 517–518
That Sushi Thing (Sentinel Turret), 100
That's Ridiculous (Ticky-Tacky Pinnacles), 89–90
Thin Man (Grand Teton), 196
Thor Peak, 466–469
Three Shots in the Dizzy Wind (The Enclosure), 258
Three Stooges, The (Death Canyon), 513
Ticky-Tacky Pinnacles, 89–90
Tilley-Nicholson Traverse (Grand Teton), 243
Tower Two Chute (Second Tower), 280
Training Wheels (The Enclosure), 264
Trapezoid Chimney (Omega Buttresses), 95
Traverse Peak, 480
Traverse to S Ridge (Symmetry Spire), 392
Traverse to Upper Saddle (Grand Teton), 243
Treeline (Hanging Canyon), 407
Tricky Traverse of the Molar Tooth (Grand Teton), 217–218
Trinity Buttress (Symmetry Crag 4), 367
Triple Glacier (Unsoeld's Needle), 463
Tukuarika Peak, 75
Two Elk Peak, 74–75

U

Underhill Ridge (Grand Teton), 203–204
Underhill-Henderson (Teepe Pillar), 278
Unsoeld's Needle, 452–463

Upper E Face (Peak 11,795), 464
Upper N Ridge (Prospectors Mtn), 78
Upper N Ridge (Teewinot Mtn), 324
Upper NE Face I (Prospectors Mtn), 76
Upper NE Face II (Prospectors Mtn), 76
Upper S Face (Baxter's Pinnacle), 381–383
Upper S Face (Symmetry Crag 4), 397
Upper S Ridge (Mt Moran), 446
Upper Saddle Start (Grand Teton), 229
Upper SE Chimney (Nez Perce), 147

V

Valhalla Approach (Grand Teton), 235
Valhalla Canyon (Grand Teton), 246–248
Vas Deferens (Snaz Buttress), 112–113
Veiled Peak, 125–126
Vieux Guide (Storm Point Cliffs), 370–371
Village Ghost (Peak 10,450), 510
Village Idiot (Peak 10,753), 510–511
Visionquest Couloir (The Enclosure), 263–264

W

W Arête (Disappointment Peak), 312
W Buttress (Disappointment Peak), 312
W Buttress (Mt Moran), 448
W Chimney (Cube Point), 384–385
W Chimney (Murphy Peak), 75
W Couloir (Buchwald's Blister), 73
W Couloir, N Face (Matternought Peak), 134
W Dihedrals (Mt Moran), 447–448
W Face and N Ridge (Mt Kimburger), 412
W Face (Ayres' Crag 1), 401
W Face (Ayres' Crag 2), 402
W Face (Ayres' Crag 4), 402
W Face (Ayres' Crag 5), 366
W Face, Chubby Bunny (Fairshare Tower, Watchtower), 286
W Face (Disappointment Peak, S), 307
W Face (Disappointment Peak, W Face), 312
W Face, Electric Corner (Middle Teton), 176
W Face (The Enclosure), 251
W Face (Faultline), 349
W Face Finish (Grand Teton), 240
W Face (Grand Teton), 240–243
W Face I (Baxter's Pinnacle), 381
W Face (Icecream Cone), 157
W Face II (Baxter's Pinnacle), 381
W Face, N Edge (Symmetry Spire), 389
W Face (Needles Eye Spike), 404
W Face of Exum Ridge (Grand Teton), 190
W Face (Peak 11,795), 464
W Face (Mt Robie), 490
W Face (Rockchuck Peak), 409
W Face (Storm Point), 376
W Face (Worshipper), 316
W Face (Yellow-Bellied Buttress), 365
W Gunsight Approach (Grand Teton), 234–235
W Horn, 452
W Hourglass Couloir (Nez Perce), 150
W Ledges (Counterimage), 480
W Ledges (Mt Owen), 346–347
W Ledges (Yosemite Peak), 355
W Peak, S Ridge (Nez Perce), 143
W Ridge (Ayres' Crag 3), 402
W Ridge (Bivouac Peak), 482
W Ridge (Broken Arrow Spire), 132
W Ridge (Buck Mtn), 118
W Ridge (Cloudveil Dome), 151
W Ridge (Crooked Thumb), 317
W Ridge (Doubtful Peak), 478
W Ridge (E Horn), 450
W Ridge (E Prong), 328
W Ridge (Eagles Rest Peak), 487
W Ridge (Fairshare Tower), 283
W Ridge (Gilkey Tower), 157
W Ridge (Mt Hunt), 74
W Ridge (The Jaw), 403
W Ridge (Little's Peak), 359
W Ridge (Minga Spire), 404
W Ridge (Mt Moran), 449–450
W Ridge (Peak 9,924), 494
W Ridge (Peak 10,245), 359
W Ridge (Peak 10,625), 485
W Ridge (Peak 10,686), 490
W Ridge (Peak 10,696), 116
W Ridge (Peak 10,716), 490
W Ridge (Peak 10,720), 488
W Ridge (Peak 10,732), 490
W Ridge (Peak 10,880, Cirque Lake area), 470
W Ridge (Peak 10,880, Eagles Rest Peak), 487
W Ridge (Peak 10,960), 132
W Ridge (Peak 11,094), 79
W Ridge (Peak 12,000), 464
W Ridge (Ranger Peak), 489
W Ridge (Raynolds Peak), 479
W Ridge (Rendezvous Peak), 71
W Ridge (Rolling Thunder Mtn), 486
W Ridge (Middle Teton), 176–177
W Ridge (S Teton), 158–159
W Ridge (Shadow Peak), 140
W Ridge (Spalding Peak), 155
W Ridge (Storm Point), 376
W Ridge (Teepe Pillar), 276
W Ridge (Traverse Peak), 480
W Ridge (Tukuarika Peak), 75
W Ridge (Two Elk Peak), 75
W Ridge (Veiled Peak), 125
W Ridge (W Horn), 452
W Ridge (Mt Wister), 127
W Ridge (Mt Woodring), 411
W Side (Pemmican Pillar), 283
W Side Story (Disappointment Peak), 311
W Side (Ticky-Tacky Pinnacles), 90
W Side (The Wall), 350
W Slope (Doane Peak), 488–489
W Slope (N Wigwam), 358
W Slope (Peak 9,814), 73
W Slope (Peak 9,925), 73
W Slope (Table Mtn), 350
W Summit, S Face (Buck Mtn), 118–119
W Summit, S Ridge (Buck Mtn), 119
W Wall (Murphy Peak), 75
Walker (Snaz Buttress), 102
Wall, The, 349–350
Wall of Leo (Cube Point), 386
Wanda Pinnacle, 132
Webb Canyon, N side rock climbs, 496
Webb Canyon, north of, 491–499
Wedge, The (Buck Mtn), 124–125
Welcome Mat (Prospectors Mtn), 84
West Arête (Fairshare Tower, Watchtower), 286–287
Western Arête (Glacier Gulch), 315
WFR (Cloudveil Dome), 154
Where in the Buckingham Are We? (Grand Teton), 201–202
Whirl of Hate (Mt Moran), 429–430
Whiton-Wiggins (Disappointment Peak), 310
Whiton-Wiggins Dihedral (Middle Teton), 172
Widowmaker, The (Snaz Buttress), 114
Wigwam Buttress (N Wigwam), 358–359
Wilderness Falls (Waterfalls Canyon), 517
Wilson Crack (Grand Teton), 204
Window Peak, 477
Windowsill, The (Ayres' Crag 1), 401–402
Wise Burgettes Go by Water (Unsoeld's Needle), 462
Wister, Mt, 126–132
Wister, Mt, N Face Ice (Avalanche Canyon), 514
Wistersheer Falls (Avalanche Canyon), 514
Wittich Crack (Grand Teton), 186
Wooden Ships (Grand Teton), 196–197
Woodring, Mt, 411–412
Worshipper, 316

Y

Y Slab (Garnet Mtn, N Side), 291
Yellow Jaundice (Prospectors Mtn), 88–89
Yellow-Bellied Buttress, 365
Yodel This (Disappointment Peak), 299
Yosemite Peak, 354–358
Yukon Jack Arête (Avalanche Canyon), 134

Z

Zebra, The, 465
Zorro Snowfield (Spalding Peak), 156

About the Authors

RENNY PHOTO CREDIT TK

A climber with over 50 years of experience, **Reynold "Renny" Jackson** has participated in seven Himalayan climbing expeditions, including two on Mount Everest and the first ascent of the North Face of Cholatse in Nepal. He has served as an instructor at the Khumbu Climbing Center in Phortse, Nepal, for the Alex Lowe Charitable Foundation on three separate occasions. The recipient of three Department of the Interior Awards for Valor, Jackson worked as a climbing ranger for 34 years at Denali and Grand Teton National Parks before retiring in 2010. Post-retirement, he guided for Exum Mountain Guides and ski patrolled at Jackson Hole Mountain Resort for several years. He lives and writes in Kelly, Wyoming.

ORTENBURGER PHOTO CREDIT TK

Leigh Ortenburger first visited the Tetons in 1948 and immediately began compiling information for the first edition of *A Climber's Guide to the Teton Range*. For the next 40 years, he followed the growth of climbing and the addition of new routes in the area and conducted research on the early exploration of the range by European Americans. Ortenburger did most of his climbing in the Tetons and the Cordillera Blanca in Peru, but he also took part in the 1961 Makalu expedition led by Sir Edmund Hillary. He passed away in 1991.

About the Photographer

Greg Winston began his photography career in the Tetons after moving to Jackson Hole, Wyoming, in 1976. His love for mountaineering and for wild places has inspired him to photograph mountain landscapes, cultures, and the natural world in remote locations, in hopes of bringing understanding and encouraging conservation. His landscape and nature images are widely published, and he has helped create natural history documentaries broadcast by NHK Japan, National Geographic, and the BBC. Winston produced *Acceptable Risk: The Story of the Jenny Lake Climbing Rangers*, a documentary about the skilled and dedicated professional mountain rescue team that operates in Grand Teton National Park.

Winston lives at the foot of the Tetons in Victor, Idaho, and travels with National Geographic Expeditions as a photography instructor. His work, as well as information about prints of images in this book, can be found at gregwinstonphoto.com.

recreation • lifestyle • conservation

MOUNTAINEERS BOOKS is a leading publisher of mountaineering literature and guides—including our flagship title, *Mountaineering: The Freedom of the Hills*—as well as adventure narratives, natural history, and general outdoor recreation. Through our two imprints, Skipstone and Braided River, we also publish titles on sustainability and conservation. We are committed to supporting the environmental and educational goals of our organization by providing expert information on human-powered adventure, sustainable practices at home and on the trail, and preservation of wilderness.

The Mountaineers, founded in 1906, is a 501(c)(3) nonprofit outdoor recreation and conservation organization whose mission is to enrich lives and communities by helping people "explore, conserve, learn about, and enjoy the lands and waters of the Pacific Northwest and beyond." One of the largest such organizations in the United States, it sponsors classes and year-round outdoor activities throughout the Pacific Northwest, including climbing, hiking, backcountry skiing, snowshoeing, camping, kayaking, sailing, and more. The Mountaineers also supports its mission through its publishing division, Mountaineers Books, and promotes environmental education and citizen engagement. For more information, visit The Mountaineers Program Center, 7700 Sand Point Way NE, Seattle, WA 98115-3996; phone 206-521-6001; www.mountaineers.org; or email info@mountaineers.org.

Our publications are made possible through the generosity of donors and through sales of 700 titles on outdoor recreation, sustainable lifestyle, and conservation. To donate, purchase books, or learn more, visit us online:

MOUNTAINEERS BOOKS

1001 SW Klickitat Way, Suite 201 • Seattle, WA 98134

800-553-4453 • mbooks@mountaineersbooks.org • mountaineersbooks.org

An independent nonprofit publisher since 1960

Mountaineers Books is proud to support the Leave No Trace Center for Outdoor Ethics, whose mission is to promote and inspire responsible outdoor recreation through education, research, and partnerships. The Leave No Trace program is focused specifically on human-powered (nonmotorized) recreation. For more information, visit www.lnt.org.